C Programmer's Guide to
Serial Communications
Second Edition

JOE CAMPBELL

C Programmer's Guide to
Serial Communications
Second Edition

SAMS
PUBLISHING

A Division of
Prentice Hall
Computer Publishing
201 West 103rd Street,
Indianapolis, Indiana
46290

COPYRIGHT © 1994 BY JOE CAMPBELL

Overview

Contents

8 The Baseline Smart Modem 247

Acknowledgments

Many people deserve thanks for their contributions to this book, but as always and for always, my wife Cynthia gets top billing.

The most important material contributor is my technical assistant William Chen. He read every word of the manuscript, built MAKE files, tested the code, wrote utilities, suggested algorithms, and drafted much of the book's artwork. Simply put, he was indispensable.

Several former colleagues from Cygnet Technologies (Everex Systems, Inc.) contributed: Mike Raven, Joe Schlessinger, Dan Anderson, Kevin Ow-Wing, and Jeff Tivel. Kevin was especially helpful in the protocol modem and facsimile chapters, and Jeff led me through the modem compatibility jungle.

My pal and former colleage from Cygnet Technologies, now of Microsoft, Joe Decuir provided moral support and kept me up-to-date on current standards. Toby Nixon, fomerly of Hayes, now of Microsoft, was unfailingly generous with his time and support. Gregory Pearson of Microcom Systems, Inc. provided useful bacground information and technical insight into the MNP protocols (of which he is the designer). Ken Kretchmer of Action Consulting (Palo Alto, California), a communications stardards expert, advised me thereof.

My friend Roger Purves gets credit for the penny-and-dime CRC simulator in Chapter 3. A tip of the hat also to Jim Lovell and Vilis Ositis.

Joe Campbell
Berkeley, California
August, 1993

About the Author

Joe Campbell is the author of several computer books, including the classic *The RS-23 Solution*. For five years he was manager of software development for Cygnet Technologies, the modem division of Everex Systems, Inc. He is the author of TIFF Class F, a standard file format for storing facsimile images. He is the creator of FaxBios, a facsimile API adopted by WordPerfect Corporation and others. He was a technical contributor to the EIA/TIA-592 standard, the "Class 2" facsimile modem. He is currently at Bristol Group in Larkspur, CA, a company specializing in network faxing.

Preface to the First Edition

Considering that every programmer must inevitably do battle with the serial port, it is odd that this book has not already been written. An obvious reason for this void is the breadth of the subject. An author writing about most topics can actually expect to cover it thoroughly; however, because of its almost limitless scope, undertaking a book on data communications is as daunting as one entitled, say, Life. In humble recognition of the demands of such an epic subject, this book is about one tiny subtopic—asynchronous serial communications as it is found on microcomputers. Other important topics—synchronous communications, networks, and so forth—will have to wait for another book.

Our chosen subject is the simplest form of digital electronic communication. Tersely put, in asynchronous serial communications, data is disassembled into bits, transmitted bit-by-bit as binary electronic pulses, then reassembled by the receiver. Little technical knowledge is required to comprehend the idea behind this form of communication because it is analogous to many things in everyday life. Take riding a ski lift, for example. While waiting for a lift chair, groups of skiers (bits) stand in parallel (bytes). Once on the lift, they are transported (transmitted) one after the other (serially). At the top of the hill, they hop off the lift (are received) and again form into groups (bytes).

Although homey, simple-minded analogies like this are usually unnecessary in books designed for a technically sophisticated audience, it is offered here to counterbalance the decidedly nontechnical and widely held opinion that serial communications is somehow inherently arcane or mysterious. Even in programmer's publications, we often read how an otherwise intelligent writer is confounded by this "black art." Evidence of this notion is everywhere, even in the names of the suppliers of hardware for serial communications: Syzygy, which evokes images of astrology and necromancy, and *The Black Box Catalog*, whose implication is clear. Even I succumbed to this attitude in *The RS-232 Solution*, which contains a chapter entitled "Elves in the Basement."

Much of what is perceived as "weird science" is a result of the technology having evolved in the essentially mechanical world of the middle and late nineteenth century. Design decisions that seem absurd by modern standards were the products of an age when AC current was essentially unknown, the DC motor was still a toy, and communications devices were powered by clockwork mechanisms. The miracle is not that this technology worked well, but that it worked at all. That this hundred-year-old technology persists—no, even thrives—in a world of high-powered computers is testimony to its vigor and reliability. One of our first undertakings, then, will be to understand today's technology in terms of how it came to be.

What You Need to Know to Read This Book

This is an intermediate-to-advanced book, leaning to the advanced. As such, it assumes that you have a grasp of fundamental computer concepts and terminology. If you are unfamiliar with terms such as "FIFO," "polling," "RAM," "vector," and so forth, you will need a good computer dictionary, a supple mind, and lots of time.

The first section of this book contains no code, so it should be of interest to all programmers. Chapters 1 and 2 might even appeal to advanced users. Chapter 3 has a certain egghead appeal, if for no other reason than that much of it is devoted to the esoteric topic of CRCs (Cyclic Redundancy Checks). But at Chapter 4, the pedal goes hard to the metal and every purely theoretical notion is juxtaposed with a practical example. Chapter 5, for example, is a theoretical look at modems, but Chapters 8 and 9 discuss the popular "smart" modem in molecular detail. Chapter 6 looks at what serial I/O hardware ideally ought to do, then Chapter 7 counters immediately by judging how well three real ICs (the NS8250, the NS16550, and the Z8SIO) measure up.

The second section is devoted entirely to programming, with examples written in C. Although the design and goal of these programming examples apply to all languages, if you do not have at least a working knowledge of C, you will soon find yourself foundering. To be completely candid, beginners in C will probably sink rather quickly. If this happens to you, do not abandon hope, but mount a new attack from time to time as your fluency increases. After all, there is no better way to learn C than to see real code doing real work in the real world.

Introduction

The first edition of this book was published in the summer of 1987. When, almost six years later, the publisher approached me about writing a second edition, I immediately began to compile a list of noteworthy technological changes since the first. The list was not long. This was no surprise—one does not expect earth-shattering changes in a technology that has been around for about a century and a half.

If the list was not long, it was very significant. When the first edition was written, 2,400 bps modems were at the leading edge of technology and pundits were predicting the extinction of modem and serial port at the hands of the much ballyhooed high-speed digital phone network, ISDN (Integrated Services Data Network). Today (mid-1993) 2,400 bps modems are a commodity and ISDN has apparently fizzled (it now stands for "I Still Don't Know"). The 14,400 bps (V.32 bis) modem has already reached commodity status, while speeds at or above 32,000 bps are already on the horizon (V.FAST). In addition to massive increased physical speed, modem channels are now error-free thanks to network-style protocols (MNP2-4, V.42). Increasing throughput even further, modems now sport on-the-fly data compression techniques (MNP-5, V.42 bis).

The net result of all this technology is an astonishing 24-fold increase in data throughput. The serial port that in 1987 was required to run at 2,400 bps, today has to run at 57,600 bps with occasional bursts much higher. Beginning in 1988, modem speeds doubled every two years. As this ramp up began, hardware manufacturers discovered that the computer's lowly serial port was barely up to the task. Software vendors were totally bewildered. Using a little technical legerdemain (flow control, discussed in Chapter 4) application software responded to the speed crisis by slowing the data-transfer rate to an acceptable level. Thus, consumers purchased jet fighters and had to fly them like crop-dusters. If the performance bottleneck was easily hidden by protocol modems, it was brought out into the open by the amazing growth of computerized facsimile. The facsimile modems (Chapter 11) that began to appear in 1987 were the first gadgets to require raw, sustained serial speeds in excess of 9,600 bps. For the first time since the IBMPC was introduced, computers were in need of a serial hardware face lift. This took the form of a new serial controller (or UART, discussed in Chapters 6 and 7).

If ever the power of communications standards needed illustration, it is facsimile. From a handful of Group 3 fax machines in 1987 to an installed base of tens of millions (including computer fax devices), the growth of fax has been breathtaking. It is interesting to note that in the era of whiz-bang Buck Rogers communication technology, the most popular communications accessory of the 90s is the lowly fax—a technology patented in 1843. Its proven robustness and simplicity, together with its recent error-correcting and file-transfer protocol, make fax an important element in the image-based paperless office of the future.

So these are the changes of the last few years addressed in this book: higher-speed modems, modem protocol modems, data compression, an improved serial controller, and the astonishing growth of facsimile. To these changes must be added the popularity of Microsoft Windows. You may be surprised to learn that this book has no chapter on this subject. The truth is, you don't need this book to write serial programs for Windows, which at present provides a crude serial programming interface—one doesn't talk to the serial hardware directly, but to the system's serial device driver. Windows serial drivers have thus far proven to be slow and buggy. It is my belief that even moderately high-speed serial I/O under Windows requires the writing of a custom serial device driver. In other words, the programmer who wishes to do serious serial I/O under Windows needs two books: one on Windows device drivers and a copy of *C Programmer's Guide to Serial Communications* to provide a model for what the device driver must do.

In summary, I am happy to report that the lowly modem and serial port are alive and well.

Let's now take a quick look at the contents of this book.

Part One: Basics

The first eight chapters present the theoretical and practical background information required to understand the objectives of the programming section. Topics in this section are of general interest to all programmers, independent of language.

- ASCII
- The mechanics of asynchronous communications viewed from an historical perspective
- Error detection, including an intelligible explanation of CRCs (Cyclic Redundancy Checks)
- Flow-control procedures such as XON/XOFF and ETX/ACK
- The XMODEM and Kermit file-transfer protocols
- Modems—why they are necessary, how they work, and their limitations
- RS-232—a practical, realistic look at this feared topic
- The UART, an IC controller for asynchronous communications
- A detailed look at three real UART chips, including the NS16550
- Detailed discussion of the industry-standard "smart" modem
- Commands and control of smart modems
- Modem protocols, including technical comparisons of MNP2-4 and V.42
- Data compression, including discussions of run-length, Huffman, and Lempel-Ziv algorithms
- Facsimile: a technical explanation of this popular (and slightly strange) form of communications

Part Two:
Asynchronous Programming in C

Using the first 11 chapters as a backdrop, the next 13 chapters develop the programming tools to accomplish everyday serial programming chores. The programming examples are in C. This section develops a library of portable functions modeled upon the standard C library's concept of "stream" I/O. By careful design, machine dependencies are wrung from high-level functions and placed in one or two hardware-specific configuration files. This design, dubbed the "virtual UART, provides a level of generality and portability not usually found in libraries for asynchronous I/O.

In particular, this section contains:

- Portable functions to set baud rate, data format, and other parameters
- Portable functions to control and monitor the RS-232 interface
- Portable functions to "open" and "close" a serial port
- Functions to perform the precise timing necessary for serial I/O
- Portable functions to perform formatting of serial input and output
- Portable functions to perform virtual flow control
- Two comprehensive chapters with complete code for high-performance interrupt I/O
- A complete library of functions to control ordinary modems as well as protocol modems
- A high-performance XMODEM file-transfer module
- CRC functions that use fast table-lookup algorithms
- Complete code for highly efficient facsimile (Group 3) data compression

A companion diskette containing complete source code and make files is available.

Appendixes

Appendixes supply important information that does not fit logically into any chapter.

- Listings for several non-serial I/O functions used but not explained in the body of the text
- Listings for three simple assembly-language functions
- Listings of all header files developed in the programming sections
- Listings of the configuration files for the IBM PC
- Listings of TERM, a demonstration terminal program

- Listings of the configuration files for the IBM PC
- Complete listings of tables and binary trees used for facsimile encoding and decoding

Basics

Although the stated purpose of this first section is to provide background information for the second (programming) section, Chapters 1 through 6 are stand-alone treatments of their respective topics. As you read through this first section, you may be puzzled by occasional references to topics not yet completely covered. For example, Chapter 4 is about flow controls and protocols; these subjects by nature overlap with the subject of modems and line usage conventions, which are not covered until Chapter 5. Similarly, the discussion of parity—an error detection scheme—belongs in Chapter 3, but the discussion of ASCII in Chapter 1 would be feloniously incomplete without pointing out the relationship between the 7-bit code and the parity bit.

This problem is brought on by the connectedness of the subtopics within the main subject of serial communications. The foundation of communications technology is so broad, encompassing so many other ideas, that it is impossible—if not intellectually dishonest—to try to treat it as a group of disassociated, solitary topics. The organization of the first section of this book may, therefore, vex you from time to time, depending upon your prior knowledge of the information covered in each chapter. While it is probably true that this problem could have been alleviated by introductory chapters on each topic, it is also true that a forklift would be required to get such a book off the shelf.

This brings up the matter of how to read this section. Paradoxically, the close interrelationship of the topics creates a book that is best read in the spirit of a novel instead of as a technical dissertation. Each chapter should be read not only for the information it contains about its declared topic, but also with an eye toward filling in a larger plot. Characters that seem sketchily drawn in one chapter inevitably appear full-blown in another. Your ultimate understanding of these characters is enriched by the earlier brief encounters. In other words, in return for your tolerance of an occasional forward reference, you are rewarded with a book of succinct, tightly structured chapters that collectively illuminate a subject that somehow is larger than the sum of its parts.

SERIAL COMMUNICATIONS

ASCII

Because the topic of this book is communications, we first need to discuss the medium in which we intend to communicate. Despite all the hi-tech glitter surrounding computers in general, the most straightforward way to analyze computer communications is with the rather old-fashioned tools of traditional morphology; that is, if we don't go overboard in doing so, we can apply the same analysis to communication between computers as we do to communication between humans. The study of human communication is, in the last couple of thousand years or so anyway, largely the study of written language.

At its most basic level, a written language can ultimately be viewed as an encoding scheme. Spelling teaches us the rules for encoding, and reading is just rapid decoding. Languages are partially identified by their coding elements (characters) and by their coding array (alphabets). For example, any valid English word can be coded into written form with only 26 unique elements, or "letters." Since there is no limitation on word length in English, it is theoretically possible to create an infinite number of words from these 26 letters, provided we are willing to tolerate words that take forever to pronounce. According to the rules of English, certain sequences of letters are prescribed (e.g., 'u' must always follow 'q'), while others are eschewed because they are phonetically unpleasant. All in all, human languages can be extremely complex.

How can we describe a computer's language? Remember, it must be a language understandable to an utter simpleton (which the computer is). By comparison to human languages, the computer's vocabulary is trivial: it possesses only two "letters" and *all* words are exactly 8 letters long. From this description, you can easily conclude that a dictionary of the computer language comprises only 2^8, or 256 words. None of these words is idiomatic or colloquial, and there are no spelling rules.

Before we examine the details of this little language, be careful not to draw a parallel between language as we are discussing it now and computer *programming* languages such as BASIC, Pascal, or C. While it is amusing to debate whether programming languages are really languages at all, this is not the sense in which the term "language" is used here.

As you doubtless already know, the two "letters" of the computer "alphabet" are 0 and 1. A computer "word"[1] is known as a byte and a computer character is a "bit."

Contextual Meaning

With such a small vocabulary, computers are hopelessly inarticulate. (Imagine the banality of your own conversations if you knew only 256 words.) The problem, then, is how to use the same 256 words to represent a much greater number of entities. The solution is *contextual meaning*.

In human languages, words generally have absolute meanings; that is, each word represents only one thing. The degree to which a word is bound to a single meaning is sometimes called its *truth value*. However, because of oddities in etymology, the meaning of many words cannot be unambiguously deduced from their spellings—for example, "bow," "row," and "sanction." These words must be interpreted according to the meaning of the sentence in which they are used. In other words, their meanings become clear only in context.

Contextual meaning is the only way to extend the expressiveness of the computer's 256 word vocabulary. This means that we can assign different meanings to the 256 words, depending upon how we intend them to be interpreted. Each contextual assignment is called a *set*.

Machine Contexts: Instruction Sets

Let's say that the byte `0100_0001` is an instruction on a hypothetical microprocessor that represents the machine-language instruction that causes the microprocessor to move the contents of the C register into the B register. Each microprocessor interprets the 256 possible words differently: a member of the 80x86 microprocessor family, for example, interprets the same `0100_0001` byte as an instruction to increment the CX register. Where compatibility between processors' *instruction sets* is desired, the instruction set of one processor includes that of another. For example, the Z80's instruction set is identical to the 8080's except that the Z80 additionally employs the unused instructions—bytes 10H, 20H, and 30H for example. When this relationship exists, the expanded character set is said to be a *superset* of the original.

---

[1]Because "word" to microcomputer users has the special meaning of "16 bits" or "2 bytes," this analogical ice is admittedly pretty thin. Here we use "word" to refer to a logical grouping of bits, whereas "word" in the other sense applies to a physical grouping of bits generally dictated by the physical architecture of the computer itself. Hence on large computers, a "word" may comprise 32, 64, or any number of bits.

Human Contexts: Character Sets

These two examples illustrate how the computer's vocabulary can be employed in non-human contexts. It is obviously possible to define contexts in which the same 256 words stand for ordinary English language letters, punctuation, digits, etc. These contexts are called *character sets*.

Sets of characters are invented as the need arises; indeed there are hundreds of character sets in use today, including those for optical code readers, paper tape, robots, and one for almost every science or academic discipline. As long as there is agreement within a field of discipline, standards evolve *ipso facto*. A slightly different situation exists among computer equipment manufacturers who wish to make their equipment broadly compatible with other equipment. Clearly, if each manufacturer invented its own set of codes, the interchange of data among different brands of equipment would be prohibitively difficult. For this reason, industry standards have been created through various standards organizations in cooperation with the computer industry itself.

By far the most important character set to the English-speaking world is the American Standard Code for Information Interchange, or ASCII for short. The ASCII code (pronounced ASS-key) is a product of the American National Standards Institute (ANSI), where it is referred to simply as *ANSI Standard X3.4, Code for Information Interchange*, or just ASCII. (It is unclear why the code is called ASCII instead of ANSCII.) There are two other, virtually identical standards from other world standards organizations: the 7-Bit Coded Character Set for Information Processing (standard number 646) of the ISO (International Standards Organization), and Alphabet No. 5 of CCITT (the International Consultative Committee for Telephone and Telegraph).[2]

Virtually every computer worldwide employs some form of these human-readable character sets. The notable exception is International Business Machines, which invented its own character set, the Extended Binary Coded Decimal Interchange Code (EBCDIC, pronounced EBB-si-dik) which, unfortunately, is incompatible with all the standards listed above. Following the clearly defined trend of the microcomputer industry, however, IBM graciously chose to employ ASCII in its microcomputer product.

A Bit About ASCII

Before we look at the details of the ASCII character set, let's first summarize some of the considerations that went into its development.

ASCII was from the start intended to be primarily a "human-readable" code. Before you get carried away with that notion, however, it should be pointed out that the distinction between human- and computer-readable codes is artificial, because humans cannot—in a physical sense, anyway—read computer codes. Computer codes are merely electronic

---

[2]See the Bibliography for information about ordering ANSI, ISO, and CCITT documents.

potentials existing across the barrier layers of semiconductors. In short, *all* computer codes are designed to interact at some primary level with other, non-human, electronic devices. The important thing to remember, though, is that the ASCII character set was designed *for use with* ordinary devices that ultimately are looked at or listened to by humans. Since a device is required for "translating" the computer code into a form that humans can read, that same code must also contain a few characters for controlling the display device itself. Hence some of the ASCII codes are explicitly designed to control other devices.

Somewhat at odds with the "human" aims of the writers of the code, was the acknowledged fact that a large fraction of the world's computers are dedicated to that vague-sounding activity, "data processing." The needs of the data processing "community" were naturally high in the minds of the creators of ASCII. As we shall see, some of the characters in the ASCII code as well as the sequence (ordering) of the characters have a distinctly data-processing flavor. Similarly, any proposed code must serve the field of data communications, which by nature relies heavily upon codes. Along these same lines, everyone realized that if ASCII were to become the standard vocabulary of computers, it had to accommodate computer programmers. ASCII therefore incorporates the character requirements of common programming languages such as FORTRAN, BASIC, and COBOL.

Also in the minds of the ASCII "fathers" was the desire to accommodate the unique alphabets of different nations, reserving certain codes for "national" usage, such as unique characters, special punctuation, and diacritical markings.

"ASCII" as an Adjective

ASCII is a 7-bit code, so the 128 positions from 128 to 255 are not defined. Character sets that employ the 8th bit (bit 7) exist, but are not, by definition, ASCII. Although the size and scope of the ASCII code are unambiguously defined in the X3.4 document, there has always been some confusion about the meaning of the term "ASCII." IBM, for example, refers to the encoding scheme for the "special" keys (such as "function" keys) on IBM PCs as "Extended ASCII," even though such keys as F1, Alt, and PgDn on the IBM keyboard clearly have nothing to do with ASCII. Many word processing programs employ the undefined "upper" (i.e., those from 80H to FF) 128 characters as end-of-line, margin, and justification markers. In the WordStar program, for example, an A0 byte (**SP** with bit 7 TRUE) represents spaces added for line justification. WordStar also sets bit 7 in the final character of every word (including Carriage Return) to simplify line reformation.

The ASCII Table

	0	1	2	3	4	5	6	7	8	9	A	B	C	D	E	F
0	00 0000 0000 NUL	01 0000 0001 SOH	02 0000 0010 STX	03 0000 0011 ETX	04 0000 0100 EOT	05 0000 0101 ENQ	06 0000 0110 ACK	07 0000 0111 BEL	08 0000 1000 BS	09 0000 1001 HT	10 0000 1010 LF	11 0000 1011 VT	12 0000 1100 FF	13 0000 1101 CR	14 0000 1110 SO	15 0000 1111 SI
1	16 0001 0000 DLE	17 0001 0001 DC1	18 0001 0010 DC2	19 0001 0011 DC3	20 0001 0100 DC4	21 0001 0101 NAK	22 0001 0110 SYN	23 0001 0111 ETB	24 0001 1000 CAN	25 0001 1001 EM	26 0001 1010 SUB	27 0001 1011 ESC	28 0001 1100 FS	29 0001 1101 GS	30 0001 1110 RS	31 0001 1111 US
2	32 0010 0000 SP	33 0010 0001 !	34 0010 0010 "	35 0010 0011 #	36 0010 0100 $	37 0010 0101 %	38 0010 0110 &	39 0010 0111 ’	40 0010 1000 (	41 0010 1001)	42 0010 1010 *	43 0010 1011 +	44 0010 1100 ,	45 0010 1101 -	46 0010 1110 .	47 0010 1111 /
3	48 0011 0000 0	49 0011 0001 1	50 0011 0010 2	51 0011 0011 3	52 0011 0100 4	53 0011 0101 5	54 0011 0110 6	55 0011 0111 7	56 0011 1000 8	57 0011 1001 9	58 0011 1010 :	59 0011 1011 ;	60 0011 1100 <	61 0011 1101 =	62 0011 1110 >	63 0011 1111 ?
4	64 0100 0000 @	65 0100 0001 A	66 0100 0010 B	67 0100 0011 C	68 0100 0100 D	69 0100 0101 E	70 0100 0110 F	71 0100 0111 G	72 0100 1000 H	73 0100 1001 I	74 0100 1010 J	75 0100 1011 K	76 0100 1100 L	77 0100 1101 M	78 0100 1110 N	79 0100 1111 O
5	80 0101 0000 P	81 0101 0001 Q	82 0101 0010 R	83 0101 0011 S	84 0101 0100 T	85 0101 0101 U	86 0101 0110 V	87 0101 0111 W	88 0101 1000 X	89 0101 1001 Y	90 0101 1010 Z	91 0101 1011 [	92 0101 1100 \	93 0101 1101]	94 0101 1110 ^	95 0101 1111 _
6	96 0110 0000 `	97 0110 0001 a	98 0110 0010 b	99 0110 0011 c	100 0110 0100 d	101 0110 0101 e	102 0110 0110 f	103 0110 0111 g	104 0110 1000 h	105 0110 1001 i	106 0110 1010 j	107 0110 1011 k	108 0110 1100 l	109 0110 1101 m	110 0110 1110 n	111 0110 1111 o
7	112 0111 0000 p	113 0111 0001 q	114 0111 0010 r	115 0111 0011 s	116 0111 0100 t	117 0111 0101 u	118 0111 0110 v	119 0111 0111 w	120 0111 1000 x	121 0111 1001 y	122 0111 1010 z	123 0111 1011 {	124 0111 1100 |	125 0111 1101 }	126 0111 1110 ~	127 0111 1111 DEL

FIGURE 1.1.
The ASCII Table.

The ASCII table is shown in Figure 1.1 and, for handy reference, is also included as a removable wall chart. When reproduced in chart form, it is all too often banished to a remote appendix where its sole purpose is to list the characters and their numerical equivalents. This is a regrettable practice—there is much to be learned about the nature of computer communications just by studying the configuration and layout of this chart.

The official chart in the ASCII document (ANSI X3.4) is in octal; that is, it is 8 units wide by 16 long. More befitting the practice among microcomputer programmers, however, our chart is laid out in hexadecimal format; that is, it is 16 units wide by 8 long. Above the graphic representation of each character are its decimal and binary values. The horizontal rows of characters are called *sticks* (a quaint sounding term) by the designers of ASCII. The *position* of any character can be expressed by its stick and its rank within the stick: 'A' is 4/1, '$' is 2/4, and so forth. The ASCII document gives row/column coordinates in decimal, but we will use hexadecimal throughout this book. Unlike ANSI's version of the chart, the consistent use of hexadecimal means that a character's coordinates on the chart are also its rank in the code. For example, official ASCII lingo refers to the letter 'k' as 6/11, whereas we would refer to it as 6B; 4/1 in ANSI notation is just plain 41 here, and 4/15 becomes 4F.

The most obvious characteristic of the ASCII code is that it defines only 128 of the 256 possible bit patterns. Specifically, the ASCII character set is a 7-bit code; this means that in systems that employ 8-bit bytes, including all microcomputers, the ASCII character set is represented in the lower 7 bits, occupying the bit positions from 0 to 127. Sometimes when we look at a byte in the range 80H to FF, we wonder what its ASCII equivalent is— that is, what its value is with a high-order bit of 1. If you are not adept at hexadecimal subtraction, the right side of the chart has indexes in hexadecimal for characters whose high-order nibble is 8 through F. Suppose, for example, that you wish to find the character that results when the high-order bit is stripped from the byte E4; quickly subtracting 8 from E yields row 6, and moving down column 4 then leads to the letter 'd'. Alternatively, you can go directly to the correct column simply by using the 'E' index on the right side of the chart.

ASCII has an organizing principle, or rather, several organizing principles, so it is easier to analyze if we regard it as several smaller groups of characters (or character *subsets*, if you will) instead of a single large one. The most general division is between the *graphics* characters and the *controls*. Control characters are those from position 0 to 1F and the DEL at 7F; the graphics characters comprise everything else.

The Graphics

Within the *graphics* are several subcategories; two of these—the *digits* and the *Latin alphabet*—are familiar to all and contain no great surprises. We shall discuss them first. The remaining category of graphics characters is known somewhat boringly as the *Specials*. These contain the more interesting characters, which we need to look at more carefully.

The Digits

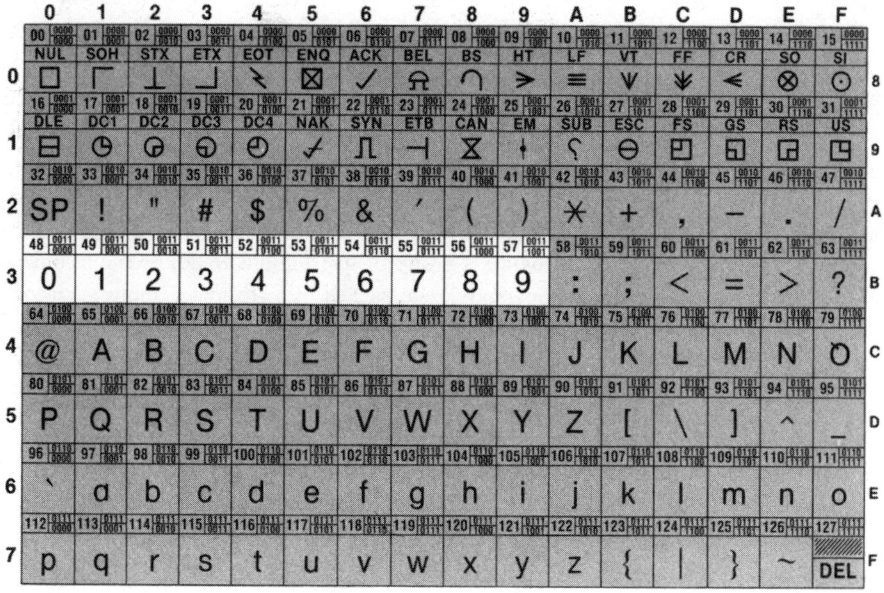

FIGURE 1.2.
The Digits.

The group highlighted in Figure 1.2 is the digits—that is, graphic representations of the ordinary cardinal decimal numbers. Note that they are specifically referred to as *digits*, not numbers, not numerals; the ASCII *number* 1 (i.e., bit pattern 0000_0001) is at position 01 in the chart, whereas the *digit* 1 is at 31. The distinction between numbers and digits is a fine one for many people and the source of much confusion. When values are used in arithmetic operations such as adding or subtracting, they are most efficiently and conveniently stored in binary form according to *value*—that is, the number 1 is stored as 0000_0001, 2 is 0000_0010, 3 is 0000_0011, and so on. On the other hand, the digits are *arbitrarily* assigned to specific graphic characters. In other words, the number 9 is stored as a "raw" binary value, 0000_1001; but the ASCII character (digit) used to display the graphic "9" is at position 39 (0011_1001) in the ASCII table.

As long as quantities in the range 0 to 9 are involved, there is no penalty for storing them as ASCII digits—a single byte suffices in either case. The ASCII storage of numbers as digits becomes increasingly expensive as the quantities become larger, because one byte of storage is required for every decade. As an example, consider the number 26,581 (67D5). It can be stored as a binary value with 2 bytes: 0110_01111101_0101. Its ASCII representation, however, requires 5 bytes:

```
0011_0010 (32H) for the "2"
0011_0110 (36H) for the "6"
0011_0101 (35H) for the "5"
0011_1000 (38H) for the "8"
0011_0001 (31H) for the "1"
```

There is a partial solution to this problem. You may have noticed that the lower nibble of the digits contains the binary value of the number they represent. This enables the use of *packed ASCII* or *binary coded decimal* (BCD) representation wherein two ASCII digits are encoded into a single byte. Using packed ASCII, 26,581 (right-justified) becomes:

```
0000_0010 for the "2"
0110_0101 for the "65"
1000_0001 for the "81"
```

Storing numbers as ASCII digits, even in BCD format results in substantial overhead—both programming and storage. Yet schemes to perform arithmetic (even floating-point arithmetic) on packed ASCII numerical data are quite common. The 80×86 microprocessor family, for example, provides a group of instructions to adjust the results of arithmetic instructions when the operands are in packed BCD format. Despite such conveniences, calculations performed in ASCII are woefully slow in comparison to the same operation performed on binary numbers.

In view of these serious disadvantages—speed, storage, and coding overhead—one might wonder why this form of representation exists at all. The answer is simple—storing data in ASCII format is, if not convenient, portable. In other words, because ASCII coding is universally recognized, virtually every computer system is equipped to handle it.

THE ARABIC ZERO

The Arabic zero is notoriously imitated by the Latin capital 'O.' Oddly, this lack of differentiation is perpetuated in ASCII. Although many display devices already display the "slashed zero," (Ø) this form is easily confused with an alphabetical character in the Scandinavian alphabet. To avoid confusion altogether, our chart uses a special uppercase 'O': ◯, or the capital 'Q' rotated 180 degrees. Lest some consider this to be too eccentric, it is the "official" method prescribed in ANSI X3.45-1982, "The Character Set for Handprinting," a facsimile of which is given in Figure 1.3.

The Latin Alphabet

Rows four through seven, highlighted in Figure 1.4, contain the ordinary characters of our alphabet. Notice that the first character in both cases is offset in its row by one; that is, **A** and **a** appear in column 1 instead of column 0. Users are often perplexed that the capital letters rank lower in the chart than the small letters. The most obvious reason for this order is historical. The lower position of the capitals creates a 5-bit ASCII subset, thus making it possible to adapt the code to the most common display device at the time, the teleprinter. (Many teleprinters, as well as early video terminals, displayed only uppercase.) For speculation about why uppercase was selected for 5-bit codes instead of the more readable lowercase, see "Why a Five-Unit Code?" in Chapter 2.

FIGURE 1.3.

The character set for handprinting from ANSI X3.45.

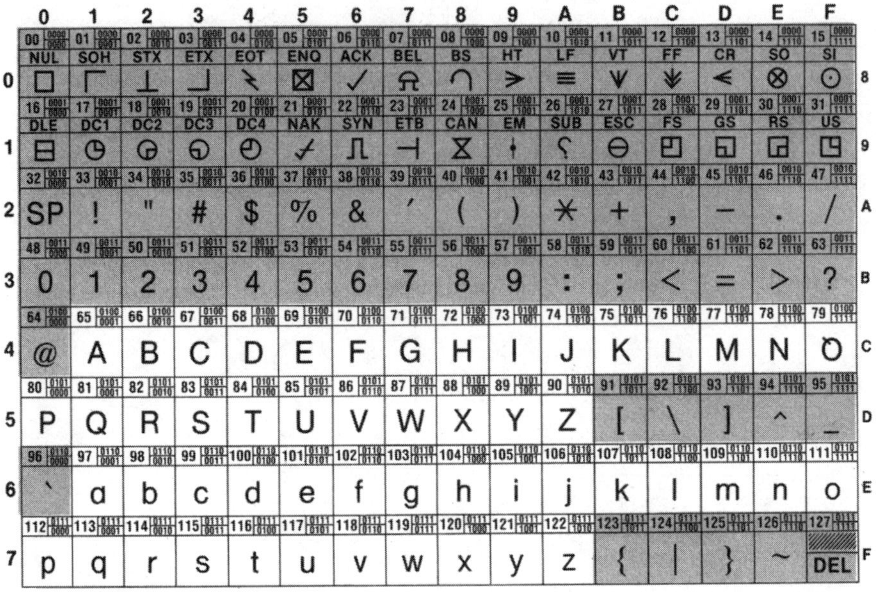

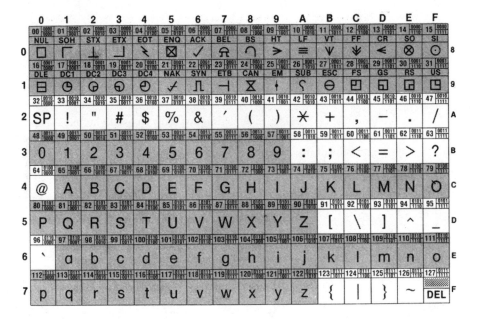

FIGURE 1.4.

The Latin alphabet.

Since the cases differ only in bit 5, uppercase can be forced by ANDing with 5F and lowercase can be forced by ORing with 20H.

The Specials

FIGURE 1.5.

The Specials.

The "Specials" that follow the digits in row 3 are familiar punctuation, **: ; ?** and the arithmetic symbols **< = >** (see Figure 1.5). The troublesome characters all reside in row 2. Let's discuss them one at a time.

■ The space (20H) is considered to be a Special, one suspects, because people tend not to think of it as a character at all; to most, a space is the same thing as a blank. In fact, some of the designers of ASCII argued for calling this character a "blank," but this name was probably rejected on the grounds it suggests a character with no graphic value—that is, a "non-printing" character. This is indeed true on "hard copy" devices such as printers and teletypes where a space is actually just a specified quantity of skipped space. This is decidedly not true, however, on video devices where an **SP** obliterates any pre-existing character that occupies the same position on the screen. The important thing to remember is that, as far as ASCII is concerned, this "blank" character is as important as any other.

Important problems arise from the use of SP. Writers of user manuals often assume that the operator is totally unfamiliar with computers. Even though writers may know that an SP is an important part of a command's syntax, there is no "nothing" character with which to represent it. For example, in the UNIX operating system, the careless use of SP in conjunction with wildcards can have cataclysmic consequences: the UNIX command rm –r *.bak would purge your file system of all backup files, but rm –r * ƀ .bak (the same command with an errant and seemingly harmless SP) would erase the entire file system!

From the preceding example, you can see the occasional extreme need for a visible character with which to represent the SP in this position. Following the suggestions given in the ANSI standard for handprinting (see Figure 1.3), many books use a "b" with a slant overstrike: ƀ . In this book, however, an explicit SP is█represented █with█a small█block█of█highlighting. (See "Format Effectors" later in this chapter for a discussion of the backspace character BS and how to create overstrike characters.)

" The Quotation Mark (22H). In ASCII, this single character must stand for both opening and closing quotation marks, whereas a typesetter has a different symbol for each. This is not really an oversight, but a simple way for a single character to serve two functions. Despite popular usage, the name of this character is "quotation mark" (a noun), not "quote" (a verb).

SPECIALS: INTERNATIONAL USAGE POSITIONS

The positions shown highlighted in Figure 1.6 are designated International Usage positions. These positions are intended to promote compatibility with other alphabets and character sets around the world. Presumably, countries with alphabets of more than 26 characters—the Scandinavian alphabet, for example, has 29—must squeeze the additional characters in these positions. Some positions, such as the "commercial at" sign (@, 40H), are part of most foreign character sets and alternative characters are seldom seen. As a general rule, though, avoid this group of characters in the textual portions of software if there is even a remote chance of international distribution.

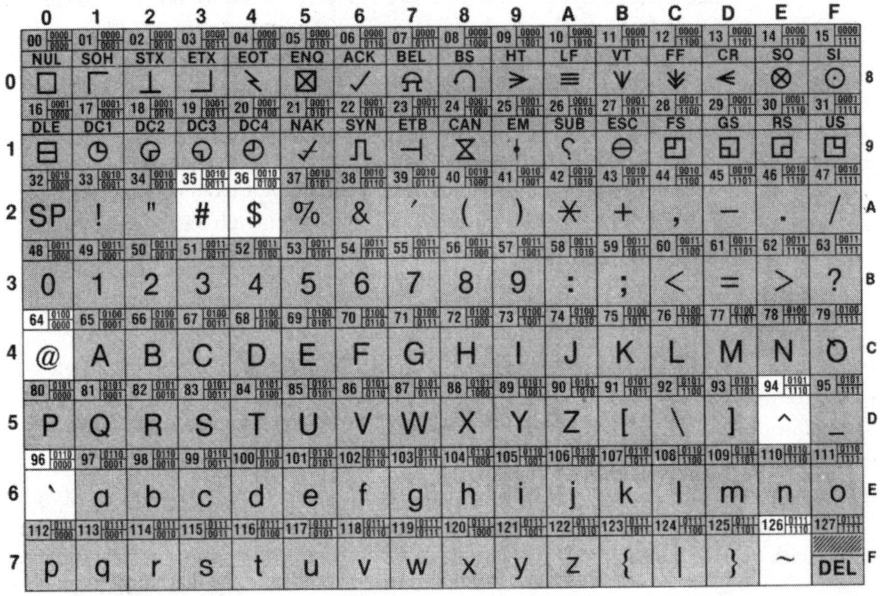

FIGURE 1.6.

International Usage positions.

	0	1	2	3	4	5	6	7	8	9	A	B	C	D	E	F	
	NUL	SOH	STX	ETX	EOT	ENQ	ACK	BEL	BS	HT	LF	VT	FF	CR	SO	SI	
0	□	⌐	⊥	⌐	↘	⊠	✓	⌂	⌐	≥	≡	∨	↓	≤	⊗	⊙	8
	DLE	DC1	DC2	DC3	DC4	NAK	SYN	ETB	CAN	EM	SUB	ESC	FS	GS	RS	US	
1	⊟	⊕	⊕	⊕	↙	⊓	⊣	⊠	↕	ς	⊖	⊡	⊡	⊡	⊡	⊡	9
2	SP	!	"	#	$	%	&	'	(	)	*	+	,	-	.	/	A
3	0	1	2	3	4	5	6	7	8	9	:	;	<	=	>	?	B
4	@	A	B	C	D	E	F	G	H	I	J	K	L	M	N	O	C
5	P	Q	R	S	T	U	V	W	X	Y	Z	[	\	]	^	_	D
6	`	a	b	c	d	e	f	g	h	i	j	k	l	m	n	o	E
7	p	q	r	s	t	u	v	w	x	y	z	{	|	}	~	DEL	F

Of the International Usage group, positions 5E, 60H, and 7E are *secondary* positions that "have been designated as supplementary use positions, which are replaceable by national characters in only those countries having an extraordinary requirement in this regard." Just what might constitute an *extraordinary* requirement is not discussed, but some countries substitute a straight overbar for the tilde at 7E and an up arrow for the circumflex at 5E. (An early version of ASCII placed an up arrow at 5E, too.)

THE CURRENCY POSITIONS

The characters at 23H and 24H are reserved for international currency symbols.

When used internationally, the character at 23H may be replaced by the national currency symbol, such as the pound sterling symbol, £.

The # is interesting because it doesn't have a name of its own, but is variously called:

1. *Sharp sign.* It is not, in fact, exactly like the "sharp" symbol in music, which is more slanty.

2. *Number sign.* True, it is occasionally used to identify ordinal measurement, as in "a #3 wash tub" or "#6/32 screw," but this quaint usage is diminishing as more precise measuring standards evolve. The current practice is to use "Nr." or "No." to stand for ordinal measurement.

3. *Pound sign.* This usage greatly confounds the British, for whom the pound sign is £ and which, in the UK, occupies this position.

4. *Tick-tack-toe sign.* This name, especially when enhanced by the gesture of overlaying the index and middle fingers of both hands, has the virtue of clarity, though its use invariably draws stares in professional circles.

$ In other countries, the dollar sign (24H) is replaced by a second national currency symbol. The ISO standard places the international currency symbol, ¤, at this position.

The Nanogram

Considering the pretense of precision in computer science, it is amazing that 1/128th of the code, #, has no name. I propose the name "nanogram" which means, roughly, "nine squares," and is easy to pronounce and remember. Other names that have been proposed include Hatch, Chiffer, Corral, Quadrux, Dunphy, Sidfrigand, Jang, and Bradgard—all submitted in a contest held by the Washington newsletter *Privacy.* The winning names in that contest were Octothorpe, judged "most authentic," and Gridlet, judged "most intriguing."

SPECIALS: PUNCTUATION AND DIACRITICAL MARKS

To represent languages other than English, several punctuation marks may, in conjunction with backspacing (see page 18), be used to form commonly used diacritical marks. These correspondences are shown in Table 1.1.

Table 1.1. Punctuation used as diacritical markings.

Position	Symbol	As punctuation	As diacritical mark
22	"	Quotation mark	Diaeresis (umlaut)
27	'	Apostrophe	Acute accent
2C	,	Comma	Cedilla
5E	^	(None)	Circumflex
60H	'	Opening single quotation mark	Grave accent
7E	~	(None)	Tilde

The ASCII Collating Sequence

The sequence achieved when items are sorted strictly and solely according to their order in the ASCII table is called the ASCII *collating sequence*. Lists "sorted" in this way are not very useful and, in fact, are usually downright counter-intuitive. That numbers (digits) collate before the alphabet is not particularly disturbing, but consider what happens when raw numbers are sorted:

Unsorted	ASCII Order
−500	+1
−10	−1
−1	−10
+1	−500
2	10
3	100
4	2
10	3
100	4

The position of **SP** at the head of graphic characters in the ASCII table is important: groups of characters containing **SP** appear at the top of any list that is sorted into ASCII order. If it seems abstractly correct that nothing (the **SP**) should come before something, consider how the following list (taken from the Oakland, CA phone book) is arranged by a purely ASCII "sort."

Phone Book Order	ASCII Order
Delabette (1)	De La Cruz (3)
Delacour (2)	de la Cruz (5)
De La Cruz (3)	De la Cruz (11)
delacruz (4)	De laCruz (8)
de la Cruz (5)	Dela Cruz (12)
Delacruz (6)	DeLa Cruz (13)
DeLaCruz (7)	Delabette (1)
De laCruz (8)	Delacour (2)
DelaCruz (9)	delacruz (4)
DeLaCruz (10)	Delacruz (6)
De la Cruz (11)	DeLaCruz (7)
Dela Cruz (12)	DelaCruz (9)
DeLa Cruz (13)	DeLaCruz (10)

Rather than belabor the point with further examples, let us just conclude that ASCII order does not a sort make.

The Controls

	0	1	2	3	4	5	6	7	8	9	A	B	C	D	E	F	
0	00 NUL	01 SOH	02 STX	03 ETX	04 EOT	05 ENQ	06 ACK	07 BEL	08 BS	09 HT	10 LF	11 VT	12 FF	13 CR	14 SO	15 SI	**8**
1	16 DLE	17 DC1	18 DC2	19 DC3	20 DC4	21 NAK	22 SYN	23 ETB	24 CAN	25 EM	26 SUB	27 ESC	28 FS	29 GS	30 RS	31 US	**9**
2	32 SP	33 !	34 "	35 #	36 $	37 %	38 &	39 '	40 (	41)	42 *	43 +	44 ,	45 -	46 .	47 /	**A**
3	48 0	49 1	50 2	51 3	52 4	53 5	54 6	55 7	56 8	57 9	58 :	59 ;	60 <	61 =	62 >	63 ?	**B**
4	64 @	65 A	66 B	67 C	68 D	69 E	70 F	71 G	72 H	73 I	74 J	75 K	76 L	77 M	78 N	79 O	**C**
5	80 P	81 Q	82 R	83 S	84 T	85 U	86 V	87 W	88 X	89 Y	90 Z	91 [	92 \	93]	94 ^	95 _	**D**
6	96 `	97 a	98 b	99 c	100 d	101 e	102 f	103 g	104 h	105 i	106 j	107 k	108 l	109 m	110 n	111 o	**E**
7	112 p	113 q	114 r	115 s	116 t	117 u	118 v	119 w	120 x	121 y	122 z	123 {	124 |	125 }	126 ~	127 DEL	**F**

FIGURE 1.7.

The control characters.

All characters discussed so far have one thing in common—they have graphic value. That is, they cause a specified graphic character to appear on a display device such as a printer or a video display terminal. By contrast, the characters in rows Ø and 1, together with **DEL** at 7F do not generate graphics characters. These are the *control characters*, thirty-three in all, shown in Figure 1.7.

As defined in X3.4, a control character, "initiates, modifies, or stops an action that affects the recording, processing, transmission, and interpretation of data." This definition hardly stirs the imagination, so it is helpful to divide the controls into several general categories for discussion:[3]

- Physical device controls
- Logical communications controls
- Physical communications controls
- Information separators
- Code extension controls

Before we consider the individual members in these categories, however, let's first clear up a few misunderstandings and establish a vocabulary for discussing control characters.

---

[3]These categories are not part of the ASCII standard.

THE CONTROL KEY

On virtually every keyboard, control characters are generated by a shift key, the *Control key*. The Control key makes it possible to generate the thirty-two contiguous control characters by subtracting 40H from the keys in rows 4 and 5. (There is no way to generate a **DEL** with the Control key.) SOH, for example, is generated by pressing the Control key and the A key. When it is necessary to describe these keystrokes, the notation is **Ctrl-A**. In practice, keyboards ignore the state of bit 5 while the Control key is depressed, thus making **Ctrl-a** and **Ctrl-A** equivalent. As shown in Table 1.2, separate ("dedicated") keys usually duplicate frequently used key combinations.

Table 1.2. How control characters are generated from the keyboard.

Control Character	Key Strokes	Dedicated Key
BEL	Ctrl-G	Bell
BS	Ctrl-H	Backspace
HT	Ctrl-I	Tab
LF	Ctrl-J	Line Feed
CR	Ctrl-M	Carriage Return
DEL	None	DEL

Because of the use of a shift key, an understandable but still regrettable confusion has arisen about control characters and the keys required to produce them. The problem is this: control characters are not popularly known by their formal names—SOH, CAN, NAK, for example—but by the keys required to create them: Control-A, Control-X, and Control-U or, worse, Ctrl-A, Ctrl-X, and Ctrl-U. We can avoid this minor form of illiteracy simply by agreeing upon a few simple rules. We will use the constuction **Ctrl-** to refer to a combination of *keystrokes*. In general, we will call the characters by their formal names, often adding (reluctantly) the popular *Control-* designation for reference.

Physical Device Controls

The eleven control characters shown in Figure 1.8 are dedicated to controlling physical computer equipment such as printers, plotters, terminals, and so forth. Within the Physical Control group, six are *Format Effectors*. These alter the layout or positioning of graphics characters on display devices and are often represented on keyboards with discrete keys.

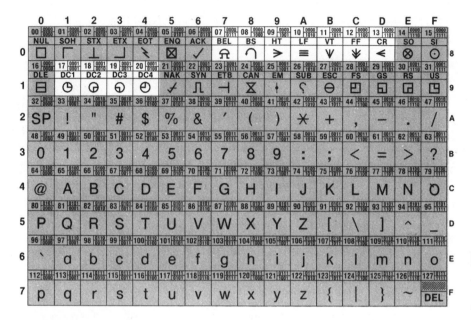

FIGURE 1.8.

Physical Device Controls—the Format Effectors.

FORMAT EFFECTORS

Today, our interaction with computers is mostly through a video terminal that may possess more computing power than some computers of just a few years ago. This power makes it easy to forget that the names of the ASCII "Format Effectors" describe the mechanical motions of the teletypewriter (TTY). Early video terminals in turn were designed to emulate the teletypewriter and were even called "glass TTYs." In short, the fancy capabilities taken for granted in modern display devices—cursor positioning, attribute (e.g, inverse video), graphics, selective screen erasure—not only are missing in ASCII, they are irrelevant to it. ASCII is a modest, very general standard not intended to embrace all needs. As we shall soon see, however, ASCII contains several trapdoors through which we can easily escape into other standards and character sets.

Instead of a cursor, ASCII refers to an "active position," where the next character will be displayed. A continuous spool of paper is the sole dimension recognized by ASCII.

> BS   (Backspace, 8, Control-G,⌒) This character is "a one-active-position Format Effector that moves the position backwards on the same line." The final phrase "on the same line," is important—BS cannot be used to move from the beginning of one line to the end of the previous one.

BS can be used to create a number of special effects: underscoring, overstriking, bold print, and inflected characters. There are three ways to create these effects in text; for example, underscoring:

1. The most "natural" way is to type your text, followed by an equal number of BS's, followed by an equal number of underscores.

2. Type a single character, followed by a single BS, followed by an underscore, followed by another single character, another BS, and so forth.

3. The same as number 2, but the underscore and BS precede the character.

   If video terminals behaved as printers, all of these methods would produce the same results on both devices. Unfortunately, the next character following a BS on a video terminal obliterates the character at that position. If method 1 or 2 is used, only the underscores remain. If method 3 is used, the special effects are lost on video terminals, but at least the text remains.

   HT   (Horizontal Tab, 9, Control-I, ≫) The behavior of this character is analogous to the Tab key on a typewriter—it "advances the active position to the next predetermined character position on that line." Predetermination of the next position is performed locally; that is, there is no corresponding ASCII code for setting the tabulation intervals.

   LF   (Line Feed, 0A, Control-J, ≡) This character "advances the active position to the same character on the next line." In other words, an LF moves the active position down one line, but does not affect its column. See "A Modest Proposal," later in this chapter for a discussion of an alternative definition of this character.

   VT   (Vertical Tab, 0B, Control-K, V) This character "advances the active position to the same character position on the next predetermined line." It is intended as a sort of super line feed—a rapid method to jump more than one line at a time. Significantly, it may also, when agreed upon in advance by all concerned, change the active position to the first character of the same line (i.e., perform a Carriage Return).

   FF   (Form Feed, 0C, Control-L, ⎍) This advances the active position to a predetermined line on the next page. The exact number of lines advanced must be predetermined locally; that is, the device receiving the FF is responsible for the actual line counting. Unbelievably, some printers do not support FF. For these devices, pagination is performed by issuing the suitable number of Line Feeds followed by Carriage Returns. On some video terminals, FF clears the screen—a logical usage.

   CR   (Carriage Return, 0D, Control-M, ≤) The purpose of this character is to advance the active position to the first column of the same line. This horizontal motion is generally used together with the vertical motion of LF to create a new line. On printers, it can be used to embolden, underscore, or overstrike entire lines. On video terminals, however, the second line obliterates the first—a serious limitation to the technique.

OTHER DEVICE CONTROLS

The remaining control characters in the Physical Control group have more general usage.

BEL (Bell, 7, Control-G, ♤) As its name implies, this control triggers some sort of attention-getting signal. Although most terminals respond to this character with an audio tone, the signal need not be an audible one. Some terminals, for example, can be configured to issue "visual bells," which might cause a portion of the screen to flash. Although it may seem a bit far-fetched, in some environments a tactile signal (a vibrator perhaps) might be required.

DC1,DC2

DC3,DC4 (Device Control, 11-14H, Control Q - T, ☉ ☉ ☉ ☉) These device controls have no assigned meaning in ASCII. They can be used for any purpose at hand, but two of them used in concert, DC1 and DC3, have become a de facto standard of flow control, a subject discussed at length in Chapter 4.

Logical Communications Control

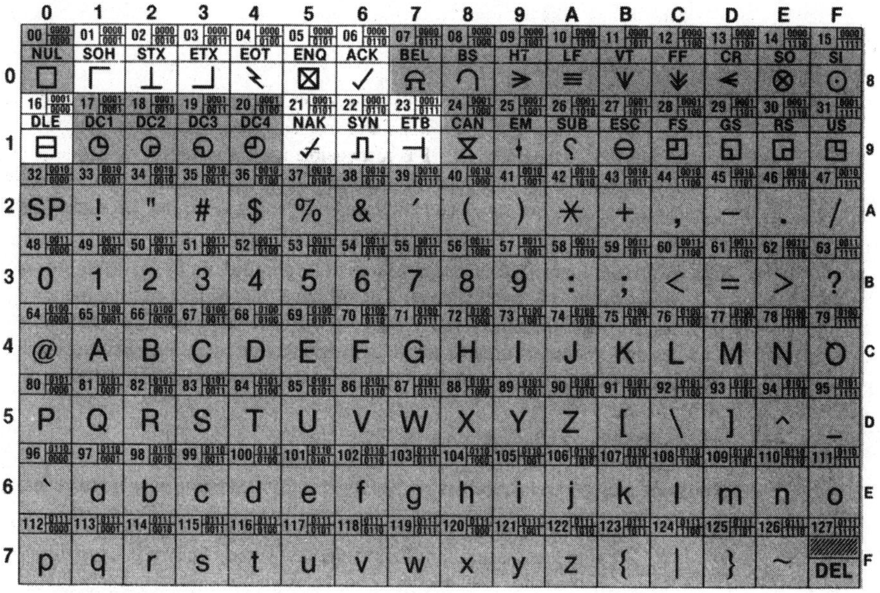

FIGURE 1.9.

Logical communications controls.

These ten control characters, highlighted in Figure 1.9, are employed to control the flow of data between two communicating devices. Although we will examine the topic of *file-transfer protocols* in detail in Chapter 4, a brief summary of the subject will help in understanding how this group of control characters is used.

A common method of transferring data is to break it into arbitrarily sized smaller blocks of data referred to as *messages*. At transmission, the message itself is "framed," or delimited with control characters. The message is preceded by a *header*, which may contain information about the length and sequence of the following message. Next comes the message block itself, followed by some sort of error-checking information.

Based on the information contained in the header, the receiver parses the data stream back into header, message, and error-checking information. Using the error-checking information, the receiver then signals that the data block is good or bad. Bad data blocks are normally retransmitted until correctly received. This process continues for each block in the message, at the end of which time the transfer is terminated.

In this kind of data transfer, the *logical* communications control characters actually mark the boundaries between header, message, and error checking. Others are used as signaling codes in the transmission itself, indicating, for example, that a data block has been correctly or incorrectly received.

SOH	(Start of Header, 1, Control-A, ⌐) This character marks the beginning of the header information. The header itself may be of any length.
STX	(Start of Text, 2, Control-B, ⊥) This character marks the beginning of the data block (referred to in ASCII as the "text") and, ipso facto, the end of the header.
ETX	(End of Text, 3, Control-C, ⏌) This character marks the end of the data (text) block.
EOT	(End of Transmission, 4, Control-D, ↘) EOT is usually transmitted where SOH would normally occur, telling the receiver that the transmission is over.
ENQ	(Enquiry, 5, Control-E, ⊠) When two computers begin to establish communications, one of them transmits ENQ to mean "Are you there?" In many cases it is a request for actual identification or status, a sort of "Who are you?"
ACK	(Acknowledge, 6, Control-F, ✓) This character is transmitted by the receiver in response to the error-free reception of a message.
DLE	(Data Link Escape, 10H, Control-P, ⊟) This character signals that a limited number of contiguous characters that follow have a special meaning. In effect, DLE is used to create *control code sequences* to supplement existing control characters.

NAK   (Negative Acknowledge, 15H, Control-U, ⊁) This character is transmitted by the receiver when an error is detected in a message.

SYN   (Synchronous Idle, 16H, Control-V, ⅄) This character is used in *synchronous* systems to establish and maintain synchronization on a communications line on which no data is flowing.

ETB   (End of Transmission Block, 17H, Control-W, ⊣) This character may be used in place of ETX, although its use suggests that the length of the preceding message may have been artificially forced by the communications apparatus (such as the end of a data volume) and is not necessarily of the size expected. For example, block size is often chosen to correspond to some logical record size in the data. If the physical volume containing the data to be transmitted is exhausted in the middle of a record, ETB might be sent instead of ETX.

Physical Communications Control

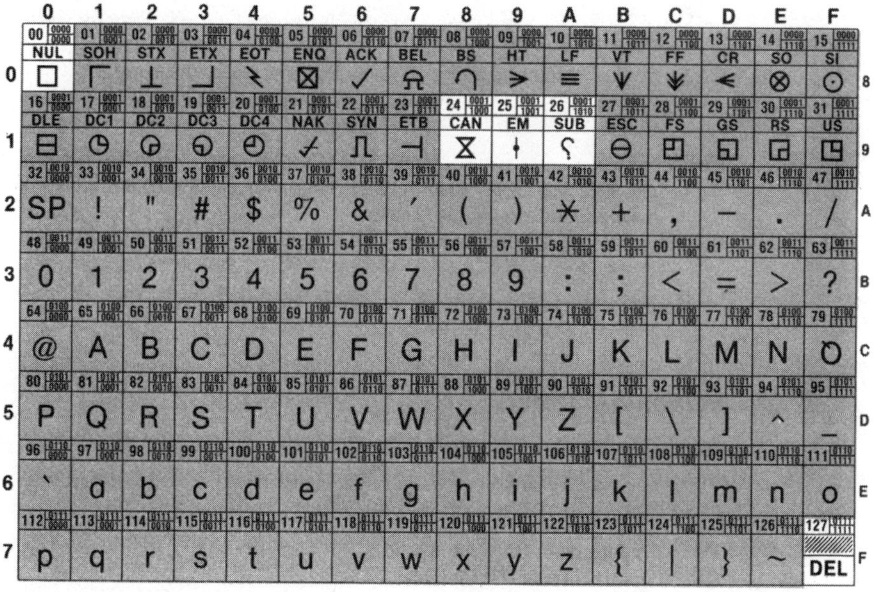

FIGURE 1.10.

Physical communications controls.

This group of controls is used for communications with physical devices such as printers, terminals, and computers.

NUL   (Nul, 0, Control-@, ☐) This character is a time-waster inserted in the data stream, usually to give a hardware device time to perform some function. When devices (such as teletypewriters and video terminals) process the incoming data stream one character at a time, the time required for mechanical operations—such as returning the print head or scrolling the screen—exceeds the time between characters. To avoid the loss of data during this time, the sending equipment inserts an agreed-upon number of NULs after each Format Effector to allow the device to complete its slow operation.

In ASCII jargon, this practice of inserting do-nothing characters into the data stream is referred to as *media fill time,* but less formally as *padding.* The standard states that NUL should not change the information content of the data stream, but "addition or removal of these characters may affect the information layout or the control of equipment." In simple terms, it means that NUL has no information value, but it *may* have special meaning to external equipment or, for that matter, may be part of a logical record structure. In other words, use it at your own risk!

Since NUL is a valid character, the amount of time it actually wastes varies with the speed of the transmission. That is, twice as many NULs are required to control the same device at 120 characters per second as at 60 characters per second.

Only in the most imprecise sense is the character NUL interchangeable with the word "null." The former is a character in the ASCII character set, the latter a synonym for zero or a "nothing." The NUL was assigned the position at 00 because that value does not punch holes in paper tape. Aside from this convenience, the function of the NUL character might have been assigned to any of the control characters.

DEL   (Delete, FF, DEL) Everything the standard ascribes to NUL, it also ascribes to DEL with two exceptions: (1) DEL is "used primarily to erase or obliterate an unwanted or erroneous character in punched tape" and, (2) it punches *all* the holes on paper tape. The choice between NUL or DEL as a padding character is usually dictated by system conventions or by hardware requirements.

CAN   (Cancel, 18H, Control-X, ☒) This character means that an agreed-upon number of preceding characters should be ignored. Some operating systems use CAN to allow a user to clear a partially typed command.

EM (End of Medium, 19H, Control-Y, ╎) This character indicates that the preceding character was the last usable character currently on the medium; it does not necessarily mean that the medium is exhausted.

SUB (Substitute, 1A, Control-Z, ⸮) If, at any point in the communications link, a character is determined to be in error, a SUB should be installed in its place. A truly "ASCII" device displays this character as a mirror-image question mark.

Information Separators

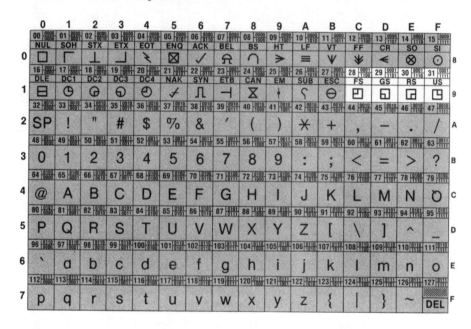

FIGURE 1.11.

Information separators.

These four control characters, highlighted in Figure 1.11, are used to impart hierarchical order to data.

FS (File Separator, 1C, Control-\, ⊟)

GS (Group Separator, 1D, Control-], ⊡)

RS (Record Separator, 1E, Control-^, ⊟)

US (Unit Separator, 1F, Control-_, ⊞) The ASCII standard states, somewhat obliquely, "These information separators may be used with data in optional fashion, except that their hierarchical relationship shall be: FS as the most inclusive, then GS, then RS, and US as least inclusive. The content and length of a file, group, record, or unit are not specified." In other words, these characters may have arbitrary meanings provided only that when they appear together, a hierarchical order is presumed. As an example of how they may be used, some computerized typesetting systems use these codes to delimit indentation levels and typeface changes associated with different headings.

Controls for Code Extension

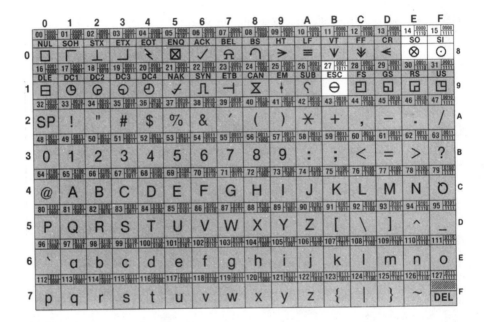

FIGURE 1.12.

Code extension controls.

Clearly, there are not enough characters in the ASCII alphabet to satisfy every need. Indeed, almost every computer user at one time or another has wished for a special character or even an entirely different character set: writers bemoan the absence of a copyright mark, businesses need the penny symbol, doctors need an "Rx," mathematicians need a host of special symbols, and so on indefinitely. The writers of ASCII were aware of this problem:

> . . .a fundamental decision had to be made as to the size of the code. In making such a decision there is usually a conscious effort to avoid the most obvious problems with a code that is either too large or too small. Should the number of characters included be too small, many users will find their needs not accommodated and will be forced to adopt "parochial" codes for their applications. Should the number of characters be too large, many users will find the code disproportionately costly to implement, or untenably inefficient in transmission or storage, and will again be driven to the use of some other code.

—ANSI Standard X3.4-1977 (Revised 1983)

ISO Standard 2375 describes the procedures for registering *alternative* character sets for international use. The actual registry is carried out by the French standards group, the Association Francaise de Normalization (AFNOR), but the listing of codes is available through ANSI.

INVOCATION OF ALTERNATIVE CHARACTER SETS

SI, **SO**, and **ESC** are used to activate extended character sets. In ASCII documents, an *Escape Sequence* is a string of characters beginning with the ESC character and is used to convey compound identifying or control information (much more on this later). An Escape sequence in conjunction with the SI and SO characters invokes alternative sets of control or graphics (i.e., non-control) characters, but not both simultaneously. First, the desired set of alternative characters is identified in an Escape sequence. The next SO in the data stream invokes the new character set, which remains in effect until an SI causes a return to the original character set. In systems that require multiple alternative character sets, the invocations may be nested; that is, other alternative sets may be invoked while in the "Shift Out" mode.

The complicated procedures for manipulating and managing character sets are beyond the scope of this book, but are exhaustively detailed in American National Standards Institute, "Code Extension Techniques with the 7-Bit Coded Character Set" (ANSI X3.41-1974).

Control Character Woes

Earlier in this chapter, we discussed how users often confuse control characters with the keys required to generate them. In fact, control characters cause a good deal of grief. Connecting a computer to a terminal or printer for which it is not configured is an almost sure-fire way to ruin a day. Even trying to transmit an "ASCII" file to a friend via modem can produce confounding and, at times, startling effects. Computer users have come to regard control characters as a kind of "X-factor" in their lives—control characters are summarily blamed for anything that goes awry in the system.[4]

Why should this be? The answer is simple: control characters are incredibly powerful, but (and here's the rub), they are *invisible*. Control characters, by definition, have no graphic value, and because they cannot be seen, their effects are mysterious. The problems began with the earliest design of ASCII keyboards when a "control" key was installed purely as a mechanical convenience. That is, the key marked "Control" simply forced uppercase and subtracted 40H from any key in rows 4 or 5. Users were then (and still are) instructed to "hit a Control-A," without receiving an explanation of what a Control-A is or what it does.

---

[4]Overheard: A computer salesman cautioning a new user against typing too many control characters because "they can burn out your screen."

What, exactly, is the conceptual relationship between the control character **SOH** and the letter A? Precisely the same intellectual relationship as, say, the asterisk has to the digit 8; namely, none at all. Calling control characters by the names of alphabetical characters is inherently misleading and uninformative. Relegated to an undefined, inferior subcategory of other keys, having no names or symbols of their own, it is no wonder that control characters have become, in the minds of the ordinary user at least, dark denizens of the keyboard.

If this sort of rhetoric seems bombastic, consider that perfectly competent touch-typists must remove their fingers from "home" to fumble for the Backspace, Tab, Line Feed, and Escape "function" keys. Once informed, however, touch-typists unanimously prefer to generate control characters with **Ctrl-H, Ctrl-I, Ctrl-J,** and **Ctrl-[.** Touch-typists are not alone here—a surprising number of computer "professionals" never make the association between the dedicated keys and their Control key equivalents.

Graphic Representation of Control Characters

Perhaps the most unusual feature of the ASCII chart in Figure 1.1 is its use of graphic figures to represent control characters. These figures are seldom seen or used, although they are a bona fide ANSI standard: ANSI X3.32-1973, "Graphic Representation of the Control Characters of ASCII." Promulgation of these graphic representations is a first step toward erasing the difficulties that users and programmers have with control characters. First, the graphic representations of the control characters shown in Figure 1.1 should be painted on the stick 4 and 5 keytops or, at the very least, on the H, I, J, and M keys. This will impart to control characters an importance at least equal to the shifted characters that now occupy other keytops. Control characters would then no longer be "functions," but legitimate characters that can be generated from the keyboard. Second, every character display device should have an optional mode that will display these symbols (or miniatures of the abbreviations for the control characters' names). Imagine how many hours of useless "debugging" would be saved by this feature. How easy it would be to solve many "communications" problems if your terminal were capable of reproducing *every* received or typed character. A fair number of terminals with this feature were once manufactured, but are now hard to find due to lack of consumer interest.

ANSI X3.64: Control Code Extension

Of rather more general interest is the subject of control codes for character-imaging devices. The meager array of control characters in sticks 0 and 1 of the ASCII code are obviously grossly inadequate to control such modern devices as video terminals, laser printers, microfiche readers, and the myriad devices as yet uninvented. In the absence of standards for device control codes, manufacturers have been forced to employ homemade codes (the "parochial" codes mentioned in ANSI X3.41). Consequently, the computer world is awash with incompatible equipment whose very uniqueness causes endless grief for professional and amateur alike.

The computer industry has responded to this disconcerting variety with ANSI X3.64-1979, "Additional Controls for Use with American National Standard Code for Information Interchange." (The equivalent ISO standard is DP6429.) This document sets forth a set of standard Escape sequences to control almost every imaginable aspect of a character display device. Table 1.3 shows some of the ANSI X3.64 video terminal control codes.

Table 1.3. Video terminal control codes in ANSI X3.64.*

Mnemonic	Action	Escape Sequence	Parameter Defaults	Function Type**
CBT	Cursor Backward Tabulation	Esc[Pn Z	1	Edit
CHA	Cursor Horizontal Absolute	Esc[Pn G	1	Edit
CHT	Cursor Horizontal Tabulation	Esc[Pn l	1	Edit
CNL	Cursor Next Line	Esc[Pn E	1	Edit
CPL	Cursor Preceding Line	Esc[Pn F	1	Edit
CPR	Cursor Position Report	Esc[Pn ; Pn R	1,1	
CSI	Control Sequence Introducer	Esc[		
CTC	Cursor Tabulation Control	Esc[Ps W	0	Edit
	0 Set HT stop at active position			
	1 Set VT stop at active line			
	2 Clear HT at active position			
	3 Clear VT at active line			
	4 Clear all HT stops in active line			
	5 Clear all HT stops in device			
	6 Clear all VT stops in device			

continues

Table 1.3. continued

Mnemonic	Action	Escape Sequence	Parameter Defaults	Function Type**
CUB	Cursor Backward	Esc[Pn D	1	Edit
CUD	Cursor Down	Esc[Pn B	1	Edit
CUF	Cursor Forward	Esc[Pn C	1	Edit
CUP	Cursor Position	Esc[Pn ; Pn H	1,1	Edit
CUU	Cursor Up	Esc[Pn A	1	Edit
CVT	Cursor Vertical Tab	Esc[Pn Y		Edit
DA	Device Attributes	Esc[Pn c	0	
DAQ	Define Area Qualification	Esc[Ps o	0	
	0 Accept all input			
	1 Accept no input (protected); do not transmit (guarded)			
	2 Accept graphics			
	3 Accept numerics			
	4 Accept alphabetics			
	5 Right justify in area			
	6 Zero-fill in area			
	7 HT at start of area (field)			
	8 Accept no input (protected); permit transmit (unguarded)			
	9 Space-fill in area			
DCH	Delete Character	Esc[Pn P	1	Edit
DL	Delete Line	Esc[Pn M	1	Edit

Mnemonic	Action	Escape Sequence	Parameter Defaults	Function Type**
DSR	Device Status Report	Esc[Ps n	0	
	0 Ready, no malfunctions detected			
	1 Busy—retry later			
	2 Busy—DSR will notify when ready			
	3 Malfunction—retry later			
	4 Malfunction—DSR will notify when ready			
	5 Please report status via DSR or DSC			
	6 Please report status active position via CPR			
EA	Erase in Area	Esc[Ps O	0	Edit
	0 From active position through end			
	1 From start through active position			
	2 All of qualified area			
ECH	Erase Character	Esc[Pn X	1	Edit
ED	Erase in Display	Esc[Ps J	0	Edit
	0 From active position through end			
	1 From start through active position			

continues

Table 1.3. continued

Mnemonic	Action	Escape Sequence	Parameter Defaults	Function Type**
	2 All of display			
EF	Erase in Field	Esc[Ps N	0	Edit
	0 From active position through end			
	1 From start through active position			
	2 All of field			
EL	Erase in Line	Esc[Ps K	0	Edit
	0 From active position through end			
	1 From start through active position			
	2 All of line			
EPA	End of Protected Area	Esc W		
ESA	End of Selected Area	Esc G		
FNT	Font Selection	Esc[Pn ; Pn■D	0,0	Format
	0;0 Primary font			
	;0 First alternative font			
	9;0 Ninth alternative font			
GSM	Graphic Size Modify	Esc[Pn ; Pn■B	100,100	Format
GSS	Graphic Size Selection	Esc[Pn■C	none	Format
HPA	Horizontal Position Absolute	Esc[Pn `	1	Format
HPR	Horizontal Position Relative	Esc[Pn a	1	Format

Mnemonic	Action	Escape Sequence	Parameter Defaults	Function Type**
HTJ	Horiz. Tab with Justification	Esc[		Format
HTS	Horizontal Tab Set	Esc H		Format
HVP	Horiz. and Vertical Position	Esc[Pn ; Pn f	1,1	Format
ICH	Insert Character	Esc[Pn @	1	Edit
IL	Insert Line	Esc[Pn L	1	Edit
IND	Index	Esc D		Format
JFY	Justify	Esc[Ps; ... ;PS■F	0	Format
	0 Terminate all justify actions			
	1 Fill action			
	2 Interword spacing			
	3 Letter spacing			
	4 Hyphenation			
	5 Flush left margin			
	6 Center text between margins			
	7 Flush right margin			
	8 Italian form (underscore last)			
MW	Message Waiting	Esc U		
NEL	Next Line	Esc E		Format
NP	Next Page	Esc[Pn U	1	Edit
PLD	Partial Line Down	Esc K		Format
PLU	Partial Line Up	Esc L		Format
PP	Preceding Page	Esc[Pn V	1	Edit
REP	Repeat Character or Control	Esc[Pn b	1	
RI	Reverse Index	Esc M		Format
RM	Reset Mode	Esc[Ps l	none	
SD	Scroll Down	Esc[Pn T	1	Edit

continues

Table 1.3. continued

Mnemonic	Action	Escape Sequence	Parameter Defaults	Function Type**
SEM	Select Extent Mode	Esc[Ps Q	O	
	0 Edit in display			
	1 Edit in active line			
	2 Edit in field			
	3 Edit in qualified area			
SGR	Select Graphics Rendition	Esc[Ps m	0	Format
	0 Primary rendition			
	1 Bold or increased intensity			
	2 Faint or decreased intensity or			
	2 secondary color			
	3 Italic			
	4 Underscore			
	5 Slow blink (# 150 per minute)			
	6 Rapid blink rate (> = 150 per minute)			
	7 Inverse negative image			
	8 Reserved			
	9 Reserved			
	10 Primary font as designated by FNT			
	11 First alternative font as designated by FNT			

Mnemonic	Action	Escape Sequence	Parameter Defaults	Function Type**
	.			
	.			
	.			
	19 Ninth alternative font as designated by FNT			
	20 Fraktur (Archaic German manuscript font)			
SL	Scroll Left	Esc[Pn■@	1	Edit
SM	Select Mode	Esc[Ps h	none	
SPA	Start of Protected Area	Esc V		
SPI	Spacing Increment	Esc[Pn; Pn■G	none	Format
SR	Scroll Right	Esc[Pn■A	1	Edit
SSA	Start of Selected Area	Esc F		
SU	Scroll Up	Esc[Pn S	1	Edit
TBC	Tab Clear	Esc[Ps g	0	Format
	0 Clear HT stop at active position			
	2 Clear VT stop at active line			
	3 Clear all HT stops in active line			
	4 Clear all HT stops			
	5 Clear all VT stops			
TSS	Thin Space Specification	Esc[Pn■E	none	Format
VPA	Vertical Position Absolute	Esc[Pn d	1	Format
VPR	Vertical Position Relative	Esc[Pn e	1	Format

**Note: Spacing is added for readability. Actual SPs are indicated by ■.

**Format—Format Effector   Edit—editing function

The ANSI X3.64 Control Code Format

The general format for ANSI X3.64 control codes is:

```
CSI   P. . .P   I. . .I   F
```

where CSI is the *Control Sequence Introducer,* P is a series of zero or more *parameter strings,* I is zero or more *Intermediate* characters, and F is a *Final* character. Let's examine these parts one at a time.

The Control Sequence Introducer

The control codes for character devices consist of Escape sequences that unambiguously identify the desired action. The first portion of the sequence is a *control sequence introducer,* or CSI. For 7-bit systems (i.e., those based upon the ASCII character set), the CSI is "**ESC** [" or 1B 5B. A few of the codes—IND, for example—are introduced by a single **ESC.**

After the CSI come the optional parameters, for which there are several formats:

- *Single numeric parameters,* indicated with Pn in Table 1.3, are expressed using the digits 30H through 39H in stick 3. For example, three digits—31H, 30H, and 30H—are required to express a numeric parameter of 100.

- *Multiple numeric parameters,* if required, are separated by semicolons indicated with "Pn;Pn. . ." in Table 1.3.

- *Selective parameters,* indicated by Ps in Table 1.3, are also expressed with digits (30H through 39H) separated by colons, but their meaning is not numeric. In this context the digits select options or modes. See "Programming for ANSI X3.64" for an illustration of selective parameters.

- *Default parameters* are assumed when parameters are omitted from functions that require them (cursor positioning, for instance).

INTERMEDIATE CHARACTERS

The Intermediate's sole purpose is to extend the number of functions beyond the 79 Final characters. Intermediates come only from the 16 characters in stick 2, yielding $16 \times 79 = 1264$ possible functions. If more than 1264 functions are ever required, additional Intermediates will be introduced. Any number of Intermediates can appear in a sequence as long as they appear between the parameters and the Final.

To understand how Intermediates work, notice that the only difference between the ICH and SL commands in Table 1.3 is the Intermediate ■ (SP) before the Final @ (40).

THE FINAL CHARACTER

The Final actually defines the function, and must come from sticks 3 through 7, excluding **DEL**. The Final character in the Select Graphics Rendition code, for example, is **m** (6D). Finals from stick 7 are reserved for private use; that is, for homemade controls.

Programming for ANSI X3.64

Let's look at a couple of examples of the ASCII extended control codes. Assume that we need to clear the screen, position the cursor to the center of the screen, and change the video mode to inverse video. First, we will decide which functions are required, then examine the formal definition of those functions, and finally put together the correct control sequences.

CLEARING THE SCREEN: ED, ERASE IN DISPLAY

This function erases some or all of the display according to the parameter supplied. The coding is

```
ESC [5-B] Ps F
```

where Ps is a selective parameter and F stands for the Final. The possible *selective* parameters are

0   (30H)—Erase from active position to end of display.

1   (31H)—Erase from beginning of display to active position.

2   (32H)—Erase entire display.

From Table 1.3, we find that the final for ED is **J** (4A). The control sequence to clear the screen is therefore

ESC [2 J   (1B,5B,32,4A)

CURSOR MOTION: CUP, CURSOR POSITION

This function moves the active position to the position specified by the parameters, which default to 1. The first parameter specifies the vertical position (row), the second parameter specifies the horizontal (column). A parameter value of 0 is converted to 1. A CUP with default parameters is therefore equivalent to a "Cursor Home" function. The format is

```
ESC [5-B] Pn;Pn F
```

The two "Pn"s are the numeric parameters for row and column screen coordinates and the Final for this function is H (48). The control code to position the cursor at row 12, column 40 is

```
ESC [ 12;40H.      (1B,5B,31,32,3B,34,30,48)
```

CHANGING TO INVERSE VIDEO:
SGR, SELECT GRAPHICS RENDITION

This function changes the next character and all subsequent characters in the data screen according to the graphics "rendition" (i.e., characteristics) described by the parameter(s). Parameters 10 through 19 invoke a font that may have been previously designated by FNT (Font Selection). The format is

```
ESC [ Ps F
```

where F is the Final character, **m** (6D). The possible parameters are shown in Table 1.3.

The code to invoke inverse video is therefore

```
ESC [ 7m      (1B,5B,37,6D)
```

Since the default for SGR is 0, if the parameter field is omitted, the display returns to normal:

```
ESC [ m       (1B,5B,6D)
```

Although manufacturers haven't exactly rushed headlong to abandon their own "parochial" codes in favor of those in ANSI X3.64, an increasing number, led by Digital Equipment Corporation, Zenith, and others, have begun to implement ANSI X3.64 in parallel with in-house codes. Thus terminals are appearing that support an "ANSI mode." The IBM PC family, which employs memory-mapped video, implements a tiny[5] subset of ANSI X3.64 via the device driver *ANSI.SYS* that is optionally loaded during power-up.

There are good reasons why ANSI X3.64 has been met with a lukewarm reception. First, certain manufacturers, especially those with an established customer base, have little or no interest in compatibility—customers are more apt to become locked into a particular brand of equipment if it is incompatible with other brands. Second, there is a decided performance disadvantage to expressing numeric parameters in ASCII instead of binary because several bytes may be required in ASCII where one would do in binary. This large coding overhead is not apparent at high data rates, but in certain applications the inefficiency is painfully apparent. Word processing over a 1200 bps modem is maddeningly slow on any terminal, but on an ANSI one it is positively an unnatural act.

---

[5]The following functions are supported by IBM PC with ANSI.SYS installed: CPR, CUB, CUD, CUF, CUP, CUU, DSR, ED, EL, HVP, RM, SGR, and SM. In addition, three "local use" functions are defined: SCP (save cursor position), RCP (restore cursor position), and keyboard reassignment.

From the programmer's point of view, writing a driver for ANSI *output* is slightly more difficult than for other kinds of terminals because ANSI expresses all numeric parameters as ASCII digits instead of binary numbers. But if ANSI output is not particularly difficult, writing code for an ANSI *input* driver is a Herculean[6] labor. Because the identifying code (the "Final") occurs last or next to last (if an Intermediate is present), there is no way to ascertain at the beginning of a control sequence how long it will be. Remember, there may be a variable number of ASCII numeric parameters *and/or* selective parameters. If necessary parameters are missing from the control string, defaults must be supplied. All input from the CSI through the Final (or Final-Intermediate combination) must therefore be buffered, then parsed into functions and parameters.

The Newline

Before we leave the subject of control characters and ASCII, we must touch upon an eternal problem—ASCII's omission of a definitive end-of-line character. The problem is this: two distinct motions are required to begin a new line on a display device—one to change the current line position and one to change the current column position. These two motions are represented by the control characters CR and LF. In another way of thinking, these two physical actions constitute a single concept—the beginning of a new line—so a single character should suffice. ASCII actually authorizes the use of a single character, calling it the "New Line option," but warns, with just a hint of disapproval, that its use "requires agreement between sender and recipient of data." ASCII assigns the LF to this role, adding that when used in this context LF should be called a New Line (NL).

Almost everyone agrees that a single end-of-line character is a good idea because it is possible to create a new line efficiently while preserving CR and LF for fancier formatting applications. But the obvious problem with ASCII's definition of the New Line is its ambiguity—its bit pattern is the same as the Line Feed. Moreover, the name "New Line" is unfortunate because it imparts the name of a logical concept, a *new line*, to a physical

---

[6]The labors of Hercules were
1. Kill Nemean Lion.
2. Slay nine-headed hydra of Lerna.
3. Capture elusive Stag of Arcadia.
4. Capture wild boar on Mt. Erymanthus.
5. Clean stables of King Augeas of Elis.
6. Shoot monstrous man-eating birds of the Stymphalian marshes.
7. Capture mad bull of Crete.
8. Kill man-eating mares of King Diomedes.
9. Steal Girdle of Hippolyta.
10. Seize cattle of Geryon of Erytheia.
11. Fetch golden apples of Hesperidies.
12. Retrieve three-headed dog Cerberus from Hell.
13. Emulate Terminal of ANSI.

entity, the ASCII character LF. When we say "output a new line," we mean "output whatever character sequence is required to return to column 1 and advance to the next line." By contrast, the phrase "output a New Line," means "output a 0A byte." In other words, the newline is a concept, only one embodiment of which is ASCII 0A. A much more general name would have been, say, EOL.

The point of a standardized character set is that each element is clearly defined independent of the environment in which it appears. At present, the single character LF simply has no standard, unambiguous meaning. In some contexts, it means LF, in others it means end-of-line. UNIX employs the New Line convention, while PC DOS and CP/M use CRLF. Apple, Tandy (Radio Shack), and Commodore use CR. The result is that text files are not portable across operating systems with different end-of-line conventions.

Conclusion: A Modest Proposal

The lack of a single end-of-line character clearly is a glaring weakness in ASCII. Although X3.4's muted approval of the "New Line Option" is an open admission of the need, the selection of an existing character may have further compounded the problem. But where would we put a new character? All positions in ASCII are in use. In fact, the problem could be solved not by adding a new *position*, but by changing the name and definition of the existing Format Effector VT, which has gone virtually unused in the industry. Few terminals and even few printers support it in its defined context. One of the authors of X3.4, R. W. Bemer, has stated,

> This is a very dangerous character to use. It cannot be used directly on any terminal I know of. Even if it could, the implementation rules are not supplied unambiguously in the ASCII standard.

One alters standards as porcupines make love—very carefully. As their name implies, standards are intended to be bulwarks against whim and frivolity. An industry creates and adopts standards to buffer itself against the caprice of fashion; if changes are effected too easily, the standard will have failed and conformity to it will quickly decrease. In a tightly packed standard like ASCII, even the most trivial change invites a visit from Chaos. Proposed alteration must therefore be scrutinized from every perspective and subjected to exhaustive public review. But if any change in ASCII can be called harmless, surely it is the changing of **VT** to **EOL**.

END-OF-LINE VOCABULARY

Because much of this book deals with programming, the discussion of end-of-line nomenclature is not a mere philosophical exercise. Even though it would be presumptuous to think we can solve all the problems raised in the issue, we must agree upon a vocabulary just to discuss it. Here is the end-of-line dictionary for this book:

CR   The ASCII Carriage Return, 0D

LF   The ASCII Line Feed, 0A

CRLF   The ASCII couplet, 0D,0A

New Line   The ASCII Line Feed, 0A

Newline   EOL, the character or sequence of characters that advances the active position to column 1 of the next row. This is the term used in the C programming language.

Fundamentals of Asynchronous Technology

In this chapter, we will examine the manner in which data is transmitted and received serially. Most computer users at some time in their careers have had to deal with serial technology when installing a peripheral such as a video terminal, mouse, modem, printer, or plotter. Unfortunately, not everyone's encounter with this technology is altogether pleasant. Its vocabulary—terms such as *baud*, *MARK*, *SPACE*, *STOP bits*, *START bits*—is so foreign-sounding that to the casual user the term *serial* has become synonymous with *incomprehensible*. Precisely because unpleasant experiences tend to be memorable, most of the topics in this chapter are probably familiar to you. In fact, you are most likely approaching this chapter with a working knowledge of the subject, seeking only to refine your ideas.

Because computer users are clearly not averse to learning technical gobbledygook, I should point out that the strangeness in the terminology comes from its being archaic, not "foreign." There is a good reason for this: it is a very old technology. Messages sent across the Transatlantic Cable in about 1886 employed essentially the same technology as the mouse in your microcomputer. Yet the outdated language associated with the subject tends to obscure an important quality: the technology's almost childlike simplicity. Students of serial technology are often taken aback to discover that the principles underlying asynchronous I/O, like most computer topics, are disarmingly easy to comprehend and can be completely mastered in only a few minutes. This is not surprising—the crude hardware in those early years demanded nothing more of a communications medium than that it be robust and uncomplicated. Frills, subtleties, and refinements made no sense in a world when the biggest problem was making the machinery work at all.

You may be a bit surprised to discover that this book contains no academic definition of the serial and parallel methods of communications (which you probably understand anyway); we will explore them in terms of the historical milieu in which they occurred.

History of Electronic Communications

On the philosophical assumption that an incomprehensible present is always clarified by an astute examination of the past, the first part of this chapter briefly (and selectively) discusses the evolution of electronic communications. Although the development of the telegraph—we can hardly say it was *invented*—proved to be a milestone in electronic communications, the technology associated with the telegraph itself—the key, the sounder, the operator with arm bands and visor—is actually incidental to our story. The telegraph, that romantic instrument fixed in our minds by countless Western movies and our how-the-West-was-won mythos, has pretty much disappeared now. More important to our story is the parallel evolution of the specialized branches of *printing telegraphy* or *teleprinting* from which the modem and the RS-232 interface are directly descended. Indeed, modern computer communications are as deeply rooted in teleprinting as the automobile design is rooted in carriage building.

Early Parallel Systems

Attempts to communicate electronically over long distances began in Europe as early as 1790. By 1810, the German von Soemmering devised a signaling device that consisted of 26 wires (one for each letter of the alphabet) attached to the bottom of an aquarium. When electrical current was passed through these wires, the electrolytic action produced bubbles. By selectively energizing the wires, Soemmering could send encoded messages with bubbles. Although Soemmering's fantastical system sounds as if it came from *Gulliver's Travels*, it is nevertheless extraordinarily important because it drew the attention of the military, who saw the tactical advantage of long-distance communications during battle.

Before long, much of the world became fascinated with the commercial and civil potential of communications. The race was on. By 1839, the two Englishmen W.F. Cooke and Charles Wheatstone had a thirteen-mile telegraph installation in commercial use by a British railroad. Their instrument consisted of five wires that powered small electromagnets, which were used to deflect low-mass needles. By selectively applying current to only two wires at a time, the corresponding needles were deflected so that they pointed at letters of the alphabet arranged in a matrix. Figure 2.1 shows this arrangement. In this *two-of-five code*, only 20 valid combinations were possible, so the letters C, J, Q, U, V, and Z were omitted.

Although the Wheatstone-Cooke five-needle telegraph was a giant advance over von Soemmering's 26-wire telebubble, the code was trinary, not binary; that is, a needle could be deflected left, right, or not at all. Code structure aside, the most crippling aspect of these designs lay in their reliance on multiple *parallel* wires carrying simultaneous signals. Indeed, one of Wheatstone and Cooke's most difficult problems was overcoming the sheer weight and bulk of the conductors (that they constructed themselves). The use of a parallel medium, at least for long-distance communication, was quickly abandoned in favor of a serial method in which the individual elements of the code were transmitted sequentially along a two-wire communications line. It should be noted that the impetus to convert from parallel to serial came not from the early inventors' belief that the serial medium was somehow theoretically superior, but because they were physically overwhelmed by the engineering problems associated with building an infrastructure for the parallel system.

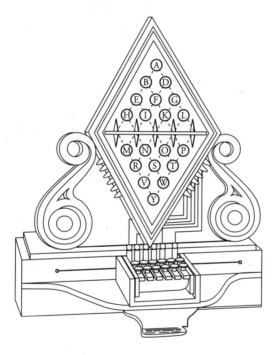

FIGURE 2.1.

The Wheatstone-Cooke five-needle telegraph.

A Serial Binary System

Although Wheatstone and Cooke eventually produced a two-wire serial device—the single-needle telegraph—they were intellectually stuck on the idea of *graphic* coding, insisting that the system yield *readable* characters (their indicator needle, for example). Indeed, this way of thinking was from the beginning embodied by the very name of the instrument: *tele-graph* (Greek for "making marks from afar").

The first practical, fully serial binary system—code and hardware—is generally credited (with protest from the British) to Samuel F.B. Morse. In the Morse code, shown in Figure 2.2, characters are represented by a series of dots and dashes (1s and 0s, if you will). Morse's first telegraph, however, was not the simple click-clacking instrument we remember from countless movies. Instead, Morse's instrument (on display at the Smithsonian Museum) was a rather complicated system in which a stylus contacted a rotating drum of paper, creating a continuous mark. Code impulses in the form of electrical current energized an electromagnet, momentarily deflecting the stylus from the paper, producing an undulating line on the paper. Here, still, the concept is one of a tele-*graph*.

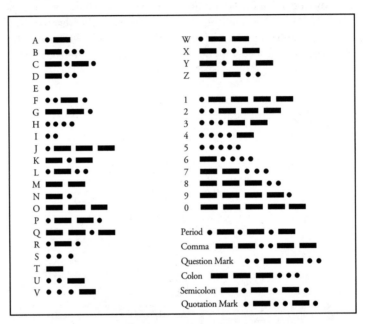

FIGURE 2.2.

The International Morse code.

Soon, telegraph operators discovered that they did not have to look at the paper created by the Morse recorder, but could interpret the code by the sound of the stylus scratching on the paper. The recorder was quickly replaced by a much simpler instrument known as a *sounder* that produced loud clicks instead of marks. It is interesting to note that at this point the "unschooled" Americans should have changed the name of the instrument from the telegraph to the *telephone* ("making sound from afar"). Would Bell have chosen the name "telepheme" ("speech from afar") for his invention?

Although the transcription of telegraphic code soon turned into the separate technology of teleprinting, for a brief period the sounder coexisted with a simplified recording device. On this device, which seems to have been known only as the "Automatic Recorder," an electronic impulse merely lifted the stylus from the rotating drum of paper. This device's practical value was an accurate graphic reproduction of the dots and dashes of the Morse code, but its greatest significance lay in its legacy of terminology. The state during idle periods when the stylus was in contact with the paper was given the no-nonsense name *MARKING*; the lifting of the stylus by a pulse was simply named the *SPACING* state. These terms, which are still in use today, are customarily written entirely in capital letters because codes of this period lacked a lowercase alphabet. This book observes this tradition.

Early Printing Telegraphs

Here, we leave the manual telegraph because its limitations (so obvious that we need not even discuss them) led inevitably to its extinction. From the outset, the commercial value of a machine that somehow produced *printed* characters was so obvious that early inventors and entrepreneurs expended much energy and money on research to develop it. Early versions of this machine consisted of a wheel with inked type uniformly spaced around its circumference. The code—a train of electrical impulses— sequentially ratcheted the type wheel to the desired character. Once the wheel was correctly positioned, a paper tape was brought into contact with it to produce the image of the character. Later methods employed a rotating type wheel at both the sender and the receiver. When the desired character rotated into position at the sender's wheel, a single "printing" pulse was sent that caused the receiver's type wheel to engage the paper tape. This machine and its complicated rotating mechanism were the progenitors of what we now refer to as asynchronous serial communications. The rotating-head system and countless others like it relied heavily on an almost unattainable factor—*synchronism* between sender and receiver. In the head-ratchet system, synchronism was required between the position of the sender's and receiver's heads. If even a single ratchet-positioning pulse in the sequence was lost during transmission, the receiver's message would be hopelessly and endlessly garbled. For this reason, frequent long "rest" periods were observed to return the heads to a null position every few characters. In the rotating-head system, strict synchronism was required between the *rate* of rotation of the sender's and receiver's type wheel.

Its oversensitivity to minor discrepancies in receiver-transmitter synchronization would probably have smothered the rotating mechanism technology, but one timely historical event breathed new life into the idea: the almost universal adoption by about 1900 of AC over DC current. Spurred, among other factors, by the inherent simplicity and superiority of Nikola Tesla's AC motor, AC power systems began to supplant DC systems. In 1896, the sheer volume of AC current produced by the new mammoth AC Niagara Falls Hydroelectric Project assured the swift adoption of AC current.

The universality of AC electrical current quickly led to the development of the *synchronous* AC motor, whose rate of rotation was dependent only on the frequency of the AC current. The new synchronous AC motor assured the future of teleprinting because it meant that once synchronized, the rotating mechanisms of distant machines would—in theory, at least—remain in synchronization indefinitely. The AC motor worked so well that speeds of up to 60 words per minute were claimed (perhaps apocryphally) for even the delicate rotating-head systems.

Amazingly, rotating-head teleprinter systems, pioneered in the early 1870s, were used extensively in the United States until the 1920s and for about ten years longer in Europe. They were ultimately brought down by the lack of precise stability between AC power sources. There was no guarantee, for example, that a power company in, say, Chicago was precisely synchronized with one several hundred miles away. As I will discuss in a moment, the maximum rate of communication depends to a large degree upon the ability of the sender and receiver to remain in synchronization. The frequency of many early power companies was given as "nominally" 60 Hz. Today, federal laws require the short-term (one minute) accuracy of the AC line frequency to be within a few tenths of a percent of 60 Hz and its long-term accuracy to be within a few thousandths of a percent. Such a high degree of stability was not only unavailable, it was not technologically practical until perhaps the late 1930s. In the absence of speed stability in the AC supply, it was inevitable that a system highly tolerant to line-frequency variations would eventually dominate telecommunications technology.

The Five-Unit Code

Neither of the teleprinting systems described in the preceding section employed a *bona fide* code. In the head-ratchet system, as many pulses as necessary were sent in order to rotate the type-head to the desired position. In the rotating head system, the "code" consisted of a single pulse. Free-form codes such as the Morse Code contain a variable number of elements: one element for an E, two for an A, six for a comma, and so on. (The length of the codes is roughly in inverse order of their frequency of use in English.) Although this sort of code is easily mastered by humans, who bring an intuitive sense of language to any code, it is very difficult to devise a machine to receive a variable-length code.

Jean Maurice Emile Baudot, an officer in the French Telegraph Service, is generally credited with the invention of the first uniform-length code in about 1874. The International Telegraph (CCITT) Alphabet #2, which is sometimes referred to as the BAUDOT[1] code, is shown in Table 2.1. Because you are probably accustomed to a binary representation of codes, the code is shown in that format as well as hexadecimal.

Table 2.1. The CCITT International Alphabet #2. The LTRS/FIGS character serves as a shift key between two sets for a total of 62 characters.

Hex	Binary	LETTERS Shift	FIGURES Shift	Hex	Binary	LETTERS Shift	FIGURES Shift
0	00000	Blank	Blank	10	10000	T	5
1	00001	E	3	11	10001	Z	+
2	00010	LF	LF	12	10010	L	)
3	00011	A	-	13	10011	W	2
4	00100	Space	Space	14	10100	H	reserved
5	00101	S	'	15	10101	Y	6
6	00110	I	8	16	10110	P	0
7	00111	U	7	17	10111	Q	1

---

[1]The attribution is incorrect. Baudot's code is The International Telegraph Alphabet #1. The International Telegraph Alphabet #2 was the invention of Donald Murray.

Hex	Binary	LETTERS Shift	FIGURES Shift	Hex	Binary	LETTERS Shift	FIGURES Shift
8	01000	CR	CR	18	11000	O	9
9	01001	D	WRU	19	11001	B	?
0A	01010	R	4	1A	11010	G	reserved
0B	01011	J	BELL	1B	11011	FIGS	FIGS
0C	01100	N	,	1C	11100	M	.
0D	01101	F	reserved	1D	11101	X	/
0E	01110	C	:	1E	11110	V	=
0F	01111	K	(	1F	11111	LTRS	LTRS

*Character 5 is an apostrophe; 0C is a comma. Shifted F, G, and H positions are reserved for national usage.

Although this is a five-unit code and therefore has only 32 primary characters, characters at positions 27 and 32 are used to shift in and out a supplementary or alternative set of characters in much the same manner as a shift key on a typewriter. The "primary" character set, shown in Table 2.1 under the column "LETTERS Shift" comprises the uppercase alphabet, CR, and LF. Under the column "Figures Shift" is the "secondary" character set, which includes the digits 0 through 9, common punctuation, and a few symbols such as BELL and the control character WRH (who are you?).

The characters in the LETTERS or FIGURES columns are selected by the control characters LTRS and FIGS, respectively. (See "Invocation of Alternative Character Sets" in Chapter 1 for a description of this technique.) Notice that some characters are present in both columns and that three positions are reserved for national usage.

Automatic Coding and Decoding by Machine

The uniform length of characters in the 5-bit[2] code greatly simplifies encoding and decoding by machine: the transmitter merely copies the character, one bit at a time, low-order bit first, onto the transmission line. By "copy," I mean that the transmitter translates the binary value of the bits—0 or 1—to a physical voltage connected to a physical piece of wire. In Chapter 5, we will examine these voltage level conventions, but for now their magnitude and polarity are unimportant. The voltage representing each bit is "impressed" on the *transmission line* for a fixed, uniform time period. Synchronous AC motors are used for accurate timing. The number of these intervals in 1 second is called

---

[2]Although it is obviously anachronistic to refer to teleprinter characters as *data* and the code units as *bits*, it is hard to resist using these terms.

the *baud rate*[3] (after Emile Baudot). Transmitting a raw 5-bit code at the rate of 40 characters per second, for example, could be expressed as 200 baud. The *bit time* is how long the bit remains on the line, in this case, 1/200th of a second, or .005 second.

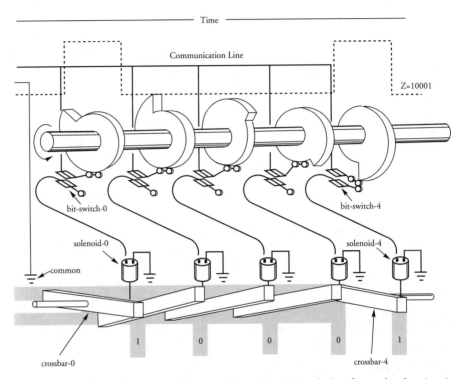

FIGURE 2.3.

The receiver mechanism of a hypothetical teleprinter.

To understand how this train of electrical impulses is decoded, refer to the drawing in Figure 2.3, which shows a hypothetical[4] teleprinter's receiving mechanism. The heart of this machine's operation is its cam shaft, which rotates in tight synchronism with the transmitter. As the receiver's shaft rotates, its cam lobes sequentially operate a bank of *bit-switches*. When closed, a bit-switch connects the transmission line to one of five electromagnetic latches, or *solenoids*. If the rotation of the cam is properly synchronized with the transmitter, the bit-switches close at precisely the instant that electrical impulses (i.e., data bits) are present on the communications line. The closure of a bit-switch connects the electrical energy represented by each bit to the corresponding solenoid. When the solenoid "fires,"

---

[3]I should acknowledge here that the term *baud rate* is incorrect usage. A baud is the unit of measurement for number of signals per second just as hertz is the measure of the number of cycles per second. In other words, **baud:hertz :: signals:cycles**. As one would never say "hertz rate," so one should not say "baud rate." Although the more general term *symbol rate* is better than baud rate and in fact is becoming more popular in the technical community, I don't wish to interrupt a century and a half of unbroken confusion. In other words, this book frequently employs the term *baud rate* where other terminology would sound unfamiliar.

[4]The mechanism depicted in Figure 2.3 is a composite of technologies used at various times in the evolution of the teleprinter. Eventually the cam system was replaced entirely by a distributor.

its plunger operates a pivoting see-saw lever called a *crossbar*. The crossbar is initially in the up position, but the plunger from an energized solenoid pushes it downward if the bit on the communications line happens to be a 1. If the bit is a 0, no energy flows through the switch to the solenoid, the plunger does not move, and the position of the crossbar does not change.

The important point here is that the crossbar's indirect connection to the communications line makes it, in effect, a mechanical memory. The cam maintains the switch in a closed position for exactly one bit time, capturing into the corresponding crossbar any voltage that appeared on the communications line during this period. As the cam continues around, it sequentially opens and closes all five switches, only one of which can be closed at any instant. After one complete rotation of the cam, the binary value of the communications line during switch closures is remembered in the up-down pattern of the array of crossbars.

Figure 2.3 shows how this mechanism would decode the bit pattern 10001, the letter *Z* in 5-bit code. If the receiver is correctly synchronized with the transmitter, the receiver's bit-0 switch closes while the transmitted bit 0 is present on the communications line; the bit-1 switch closes during bit 1, and so on. In order to see the effect of the mechanism on all bits of the character, the action in the drawing is "frozen" at the instant when the cam closes the bit-4 switch, capturing the final 1 pulse that is present on the communications line. Although the drawing depicts the capturing of a 1 pulse, it is important to realize that the absence of a pulse—that is, a 0—is just as significant, even though the position of the corresponding crossbar is not changed. For example, notice that the position of the crossbars 1, 2, and 3 are still in their 0 position because no bits (voltages) were present on the communications line while their switches were closed.

The closure of the last switch on the cam coincides with the final 1 bit on the communications line. At the end of the pulse sequence, then, the up-down pattern in the crossbars duplicates the pattern of the received pulse exactly. Now, with all the bits captured, the crossbars are jammed against a moving type-head. The up-down pattern of the crossbars causes the type-head to stop at a unique position for each encoded character (a similar mechanism is used in slot machines). A striker then drives the printing mechanism against the type-head.

Synchronization

As you can see, the decoding of a fixed-length code, though mechanically intense, is conceptually simple. Even from the oversimplified depiction in Figure 2.3, it should be apparent that such a system is completely at the mercy of precise synchronism between the cams of the sending and the receiving stations. For example, a bit-switch at the receiving station must close at almost the same instant that its corresponding pulse is transmitted. If this synchronism slips, the bits are captured into the incorrect crossbar and the wrong character is decoded. Before electrical motors—and later synchronous motors—were available, the mechanisms were powered by a large deadbeat escapement such as is found in clocks. Because of its reliance on synchronism, this form of communications is known even today as *synchronous serial communications.*

Despite the use of a fixed-length code and high-quality synchronous motors, early teleprinters were prone to drifting out of synchronism due to slight manufacturing differences between mechanical parts or, inevitably, a difference between the frequency of the power sources at the transmitter and receiver. To minimize the need of maintaining synchronism over the entire length of a message, characters on early teleprinters were not generated by human typists, but by pre-encoded perforated paper tape. Even using machine-generated codes, it was still inevitable that the mechanism would drift out of synchronism. Accordingly, early teleprinters required constant monitoring by skilled operators whose job was to make mid-message adjustments at the first sign of loss of synchronism. As you might imagine, even under the best of conditions these machines were temperamental, and at worst, maddeningly unreliable. Clearly, if the technology was to go forward, a new system had to be found.

The problem of synchronism is not as awful as it sounds. As a matter of fact, even before electrical motors were used, the combination of a deadbeat and a mechanical governor could maintain synchronism over the short term. The real problem with such a system is that once communication begins, the sender and receiver must remain in synchronism for the *entire* message. In other words, although the basic unit of encoding is the character, the unit of transmission is the message. The flaw of the system, then, is not in its use of synchronism, which is common to all forms of electronic communications, but in the period of time over which synchronism must be maintained. If the system could somehow be resynchronized for each character, a fair amount of drift in frequency between sender and receiver would be tolerable. The solution to the problem of receiver/transmitter synchronization changed the history of communications.

THE START BIT

The solution, credited to E. E. Kleinschmidt during World War I, was to transmit a *synchronizing bit* just before the first bit of each character. This additional pulse, which is identical in every way to an ordinary data bit, signals the teleprinter mechanism that the very next pulse is the first bit of a character.

Adding the sync pulse to the character, of course, required modification of the teleprinter mechanism as well. During idle periods—that is, between characters—the cam continues to rotate,[5] but the bit-switches are completely retracted from the cam lobes. Obviously, in this arrangement no switch action and no bit capture occur. Upon the arrival of a sync pulse, the entire bit-switch assembly is repositioned by means of a clutch so that the switches contact the cam lobes. After each character—that is, one complete revolution of the cam—the clutch once again disengages the cam and the bit-switches, and the system returns to rest.

---

[5]Actually, early systems simply started and stopped the cam shaft completely. This worked satisfactorily at low speeds, but inertia caused overshoot at high speeds.

Before we discuss Figure 2.4, which shows how the synchronization pulse is prepended to the code bits, notice that it employs traditional notation, which defines the *idle state* (i.e., MARK) of the communications line as logical 1 and a *negative-going pulse* (i.e., SPACE) as logical 0. The reasons for this are partly historical (Morse's telegraph), but mostly because electromechanical devices that possess contacts (relays, for example) operate much more reliably with current perpetually passing through them. For whatever reasons, though, electrical current normally flows in the communications line during idle periods.

Figure 2.4a shows a timing diagram of a communications line bearing the letter *F* (01101) preceded by its sync pulse. Because transmission of a character proceeds from least- to most-significant bit, the bit patterns given in Table 2.1 and those shown graphically in Figure 2.4 are reversed.

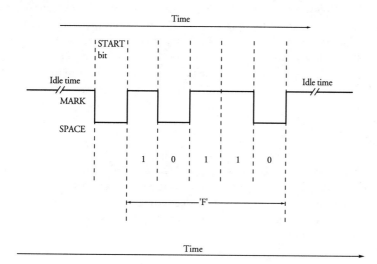

A

*The letter F (01101)
and its sync pulse.*

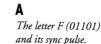

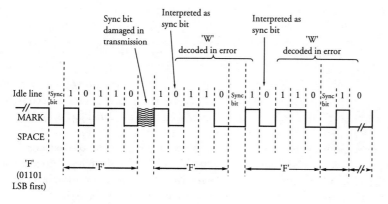

B

*Several iterations of
the letter F (01101)
and its sync pulse.*

FIGURE 2.4.

*Synchronization pulse
for code bits.*

The addition of a sync pulse alone would have advanced the art of the teleprinter enormously. Providing automatic per-character instead of per-message synchronization unconditionally cures the problems caused by discrepancies such as differences in the frequency of the AC power line. However, the sync pulse alone cannot defend against the eternal nemeses: data deformation or corruption by an imperfect communications line. To illustrate the havoc wreaked by this phenomenon, consider Figure 2.4b, which shows several iterations of the letter *F* and their sync pulses. The sync pulse on the first *F* properly engages the cam of our hypothetical teleprinter, causing 5 bits to be correctly sampled from the communications line. On the second *F*, however, the sync pulse has somehow been transformed from a SPACE into a MARK and the teleprinter mechanism does not engage. The mechanism now thinks that the next 0 bit—the first data bit of the character— is the sync bit, and subsequently copies data bit 0 into crossbar 0, data bit 1 into crossbar 1, and so forth. As shown in Figure 2.4b, when the first data bit in the *F* is interpreted as the sync bit, the next 5 bits are interpreted as 01001, the letter *D* (received as 10010). During continuous transmission, where one character follows the next with no intervening idle period, a single damaged sync bit can theoretically cause subsequent characters to be garbled indefinitely. Reestablishment of synchronization can be guaranteed only by allowing the communications line to idle for one entire character interval.

THE STOP BIT

The loss of synchronization when the sync bit is damaged is inherent in a binary system where all pulses are identical. To complement the sync bit, which identifies the first bit of the character, an additional bit is required to identify the last bit of the character. This new bit, a MARK, is simply appended to the data bits at the transmitter. The letter *F* in this new format is shown in Figure 2.5.

FIGURE 2.5.

Two iterations of the letter F with sync bit and an additional bit to mark the end of the character.

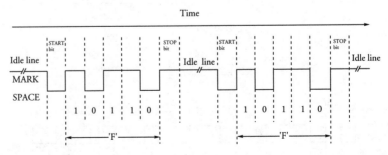

The teleprinter modifications necessary to implement this new end-of-character bit are simple. During reception, the end-of-character bit is "read" and latched into a crossbar just like the other 5 bits. After all 6 bits are received, however, a 0 in the final crossbar prevents the activation of the printing assembly. In this way, an out-of-sync character can still be received, but is discarded if its final bit is not a 1. As far as the teleprinter is concerned, a valid character must begin with a SPACE and end with a MARK.

Before we proceed, it's time we decide on some official terminology. As you probably know, the sync and end bits are traditionally referred to as *START* and *STOP* bits, respectively. Because these bits set the character off from surrounding bits, they are collectively referred to as *framing* bits, and the entire "package" of START, data, and STOP bits is given the name of *character frame* or simply *frame*. The form of serial communications we call *asynchronous*, then, is properly *START/STOP asynchronous*.

It is impossible to appreciate the robustness of this START/STOP communications method without seeing it in action. Figure 2.6 illustrates how the START and STOP bits automatically restore proper character framing following a loss of synchronization. Using the 5-bit code given in Table 2.1, the transmitted message, a ten-character portion of the familiar *HOW NOW BROWN COW* is shown in Figure 2.6a. Figure 2.6b shows the same message, but with the bit-order reversed as during transmission. Figure 2.6c marks the START and STOP bits symbolically with the letters *x* and *y*, respectively. In Figure 2.6d, the framing bits are actual 0s and 1s, which, to make them more easily discerned, are bold. Thus, Figure 2.6d shows the bit stream without errors, as it might look as it leaves the transmitter. Figure 2.6e, however, shows the message as it might look as it arrives at the receiver with an error in the START bit of the second character, *O*.

```
        H      O      W    Space   N      O      W    Space   B      R
      10100  11000  10011  00100  01100  11000  10011  00100  11001  01010
```

```
        H      O      W    Space   N      O      W    Space   B      R
      00101  00011  11001  00100  00110  00011  11001  00100  10011  01010
```

```
        H        O        W      Space    N        O        W      Space    B        R
     x00101y  x00011y  x11001y  x00100y  x00110y  x00011y  x11001y  x00100y  x10011y  x01010y
```

```
        H        O        W      Space    N        O        W      Space    B        R
     0001011  0000111  0110011  0001001  0001101  0000111  0110011  0001001  0100111  0010101
```

```
        H        O        W      Space    N        O        W      Space    B        R
     0001011  1000111  0110011  0001001  0000111  0000111  0110011  0001001  0100111  0010101
             ↑
     START bit error
```

A

Ten characters of the message HOW NOW BROWN in five-unit code.

B

Ten characters of the message with bit order reversed as in transmission.

C

Message with symbolic x for START bits and y for STOP bits.

D

Message with binary START and STOP bits installed.

E

Message with an error in the START bit of the second character.

F

Automatic resynchronization.

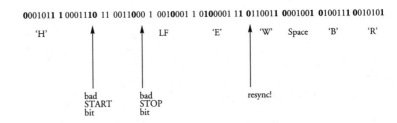

FIGURE 2.6.

Automatic resynchronization after a framing error with START and STOP bits.

Finally, Figure 2.6f shows how the teleprinter almost immediately recovers from the bad START bit. The first character *H* is received correctly. Loss of synchronization occurs, however, when the receiver interprets the damaged START bit as a period of MARK time (line idle). The next 0 bit—data bit 0 in the letter *O*—is interpreted as a START bit and the next 6 bits are decoded; because the sixth of these is not a 1 (i.e., a START bit), the character is discarded and nothing is displayed. This peg-legged stumbling continues with the receiver occasionally printing a garbage character after assembling a valid, but errone-ous, frame. The error resulting from a defective START or STOP bit is given the general name *framing error*. Framing errors occur twice, resulting in an erroneous Line Feed and the letter *E*. Eventually, though, the receiver synchronizes on one of the original START bits, and the message is back in synchronization. The teleprinter would probably display the message like this:

```
H
    EWBROWN COW
```

We have discussed the addition of a STOP bit as if it were an intellectual or theoretical invention. The truth is, however, that long before the START bit was hit upon as a fool-proof method of character framing, an equivalent resting period after each character was part of teleprinter operating procedure. The reason for its existence, however, derives not from the abstract concept of character framing but from the intensely mechanical nature of teleprinters. A period of line idle (MARK) was inserted between characters to allow time for the teleprinter mechanism to clear the previous character and reset itself for the next.[6] The duration of these "inertial" STOP bits is quite long in early models but came to be standardized at about 1-1/2 to 1 bit times for "modern" teleprinters. This amount of time, though small, is absolutely critical to correct operation of the machine.

Why a Five-Unit Code?

The absence of a lowercase alphabet and the paucity of punctuation and graphics charac-ters often lead modern users to wonder why a 5-bit code was used instead of, say, a 7-bit

---

[6]If you look closely at the drawing in Figure 2.3, you can discern a definite dead spot in the cam: a period in its rotation when no switch is closed. This is the resting period during which, among a myriad of other things, the crossbars are reset to all 0s.

one. No one seems to know for certain (or cares!) why uppercase was chosen over lower, especially because it was known at the time that lowercase is easier to read than uppercase.

There are several plausible reasons. First, because the Latin alphabet was entirely upper-case, there was a centuries-old sentiment that uppercase was somehow more "classical," somehow more dignified and formal. In fact, until well into this century, diplomatic documents such as treaties, proclamations, and accords were printed almost exclusively in uppercase. Because of these ideas, lowercase was thought to be, well, vulgar.

The second and more likely reason for the choice of uppercase has to do with the graphic ambiguity of the lowercase alphabet. A poorly printed *a* or *f*, for example, can easily be mistaken for a half-dozen other lowercase letters— depending upon which portion of the character is ill-formed or omitted. Lowercase is easier to read than uppercase only when comparing accurate and perfectly formed characters. A poorly printed *A*, on the other hand, can hardly be confused with other members of the alphabet. If the print quality of "sophisticated" modern teleprinters is any indication, early mechanisms must have produced crude output indeed. The uppercase alphabet was therefore probably selected in self defense against the early error-prone teleprinter mechanism.

The second question—why the code is limited to five units—is easier to guess. The most obvious reasons are economic—the fewer bits per character, the quicker any given message can be sent. Expressed in modern computerese, the use of a five-unit code "maximized system throughput." It is impossible to say whether such crassly commercial reasons entered into the choice of a five-unit code, but it is certain that these early engineers understood how a frame length affects reliable synchronization. To understand this, visualize a receiver detecting a START bit at precisely the middle of its bit time. If the transmitter's and receiver's bit times differ by more than one-half a bit time over the next 6 bits, the STOP bit is missed. Because this cumulative timing error is greater over a larger number of bits, codes with longer character lengths are inherently more susceptible to the effects of speed mismatches than shorter codes. Considering the variety of electrical environments around the world in which the teleprinter has been successful over the last hundred years, the five-unit code has proven to be a good choice. As a matter of fact, a considerable amount of international teleprinter communications is still encoded in the five-unit CCITT Alphabet #2.

THE BREAK SIGNAL

One special framing error is treated not as an error but as a form of communication. I mentioned earlier that teleprinters are designed so that electrical current flows in the communications line during idle periods. As we have seen, bits are electrically encoded by interrupting this quiescent line current at regular intervals. One consequence of this design—and one of the major factors in its persistence—is its capability of detecting a failure in the communications line itself. When the line is interrupted, the cessation of current is detected as a START bit. After sampling the agreed-upon number of data bits (which are all 0s), the receiver finds a SPACE where the STOP bit should be. Because this condition—an all-0 frame—cannot occur as a result of any legitimate character, it signals a "break" in the transmission line. Consistent with the no-nonsense uppercase naming conventions of the period, this condition was dubbed a *BREAK*—any SPACE condition on the communications line that lasts longer than a character and its framing bits. The term is still used today.

When generated intentionally for short, agreed-upon periods, the BREAK becomes a primary communications signal instead of just a fault indicator. In general, the BREAK is employed as a brute-force override of coded communication. A BREAK can be used to reset a mechanism, to ring a bell, to interrupt a process that would otherwise ignore coded data arriving on the communications line. Because it is often employed in this "In case of fire, break glass" fashion, BREAK detection is usually electrically separate from and parallel to the serial decoding process. The BREAK is often incorrectly called a "character," though it is manifestly just the opposite. As a matter of fact, its distinct "uncharacterness" gives it significance.

CHARACTER FRAMING IN ELECTRONIC COMMUNICATIONS

Even though we must concede that the STOP bit historically antedates the START bit, it is important to recognize that a framing STOP bit is required even in the frictionless and inertialess world of modern electronic communications. In fact, some purely electronic devices still require an inertial STOP bit in addition to the framing STOP bit. Some older terminals, for example, are notorious for losing character synchronization when scrolling a full screen at high data rates. The problem can usually be cured by using a frame with 2 STOP bits instead of 1, thus giving an extra instant for the electronics to perform the scroll.

Transmission of ASCII Code

Because most computer equipment is byte-oriented, it is natural to handle data in an eight-unit form. Although ASCII and the closely related CCITT V.3 alphabet are officially seven-unit codes, they are seldom transmitted in that format. Instead, the eighth bit is often used as a *parity bit* for error-checking (see Chapter 3), thus making ASCII in practice an eight-unit code. In addition to the format of 7 data bits and 1 parity bit, a considerable amount of computer data is binary (as opposed to textual) in nature. By binary, I mean that the meaning of the bits lies in their pattern (as in processor instructions) rather than in their representation (as in an ASCII code). In binary data, all bits are of equal value and must be included in the frame.

Serial Nomenclature

Considering that asynchronous serial technology is a century old, it is incredible that no standardized vocabulary has developed to express its concepts. In the absence of standardized terminology, the popular microcomputer press has happily responded with terms and definitions that are inaccurate, fatuous, or just plain ignorant. To avoid association with pop terminology, I will now establish a vocabulary and apply it consistently throughout the remainder of the book.

THE SERIAL DATA UNIT

First, we require a name for the entire physical "package" that is impressed upon the communications line—the START bits, data bits, parity bits (if any), and the STOP bit(s). So far, I have used the word *frame* to refer to a unit of transmitted data, but this is an ambiguous term because it incorrectly evokes the image of a "perimeter" or "framework." To avoid this connotation, I will simply use the phrase *serial data unit,* or *SDU* for short.

DATA FORMAT

With the imputation of meaning to the eighth bit of an ASCII character, we sorely need a notation that can describe the layout and contents of any SDU. Accordingly, I will refer to these variable transmission parameters—baud, number of data bits, parity bit, and number of STOP bits—as the *data format.* I will employ the following notation for the rest of this book:

```
[baud]-[data bits][parity][STOP bits]
```

For example, I would describe the data format of 1,200 baud, 7 data bits, NO parity, and 2 STOP bits in the form *1200-7N2* or, for variety, *1200-7-N-2.*

MORE ON BAUDS[7]

Because *baud* is often incorrectly used to mean *bits per second,* it is worth spending a few moments to differentiate between these two terms. Bauds are the units of the measure of the fundamental electrical *signaling rate* of a communications line. Stated another way, the signalling rate is the frequency at which electrical impulses are transferred to the communications line. Because it is an electrical unit of measure and not a units of information, baud implies no relationship between the voltages that appear on the communications line and the data represented by those voltages.

Although it sounds simple-minded to say aloud, the rate of transfer of information is the *bit transfer rate* and is expressed in *bits per second* (*bps*). The signaling rate and the bit transfer rate are therefore equal only when one data bit is encoded during one signaling period. If

---

[7]Please remember that *Baud* should be abbreviated with a capital letter in honor of Emile Baudot.

this distinction strikes you as a trifle precious, consider that 1,200 and 2,400 bps modems operate at a signaling rate of only 600 baud. In other words, these modems manage to encode 2 and 4 bits, respectively, in one baud. (I'll return to this point in Chapter 5.)

"SERIALIZATION"

We must discuss one final term before proceeding. We have seen that asynchronous transmission is essentially the translating of the individual bits of compound (parallel) data into instants of voltage. Asynchronous reception is the opposite, building compound data from periodical voltage samples taken from a wire. There is, incredibly, no perfectly apt single word to describe the idea embodied in both processes. For want of a more concise term, and in full recognition that it is only half correct, I will use the word *serialization*. As used in this book, serialization is a concept that applies both to reception and transmission. In this way of thinking, therefore, the framing error demonstrated in Figure 2.6 is a *serialization error*, even though it is literally an error of deserialization or, better perhaps, "parallelization."

Communications Line Usage

The amount of information that could be transferred over very early telegraph and teleprinter systems was amazingly small. At first, the only solution to this limitation on throughput was to erect more wires to handle the additional traffic. Because of the enormous expense and difficulty in erecting telegraph and telephone lines, researchers searched for a way to send more than one message simultaneously (or apparently so) over the same line. They used the following terminology to describe the traffic on communications lines:

Simplex:	Communication is single-direction with a receiving or a transmitting device (but not both) at either end. The classic ticker-tape is a simplex receiver.
Half-duplex:	Communication is possible in both directions, but not simultaneously. Early telegraphs worked in this manner as do many modern forms of communication (CB radio, for example). In recent years, full duplex also implies that the speed in both directions is the same.
Full-duplex:	Communication can occur simultaneously in both directions. The telegraph quickly became a full-duplex, and, thanks to Thomas Edison, a *quadruplex* (two channels in each direction) instrument. Today, most two-way communication is full-duplex.
Duplex:	Communication can occur simultaneously in both directions, but not necessarily at the same rate in both directions.

Multiplex: This form of communication, which eventually supplanted quadruplex, is used if more than a single channel of information is required. Pioneered by Baudot, multiplexing is a technique for creating several communications channels by sequentially allocating frequencies or time slices from a single channel. Modern communications increasingly relies on multiplexing.

Most of these terms are in use today, as is other jargon from this period. For example, many early telegraphs used lines that had to be oppositely polarized during transmission and reception. When changing over from transmission to reception, or vice versa, operators had to reverse the positive and negative connections on their half-duplex instruments. Their term for this, *turning the line around*, is still very much alive today in half-duplex modem operations, although, as we shall see, its use is now figurative.

Synchronous Versus Asynchronous Serial Communications

As we have seen, asynchronous communications relies heavily upon synchronism: characters arrive asynchronously, but the reception of the individual bits of each character is synchronized by the START bit. For this reason, *asynchronous* was (and still is) a poor choice to describe this technology. In fact, the fundamental differences between asynchronous and synchronous communications are ones of degree—the former requires a sync bit with every character, whereas the latter requires a sync byte much less often.

The sync/async nomenclature also tends to obscure the practical differences between the two methods of serial communications. When efficiency is of paramount importance and when data can be supplied in a carefully time-controlled, continuous bit stream, synchronous transmission is vastly superior to asynchronous START/STOP transmission. After all, adding a START and STOP bit to an 8-bit character results in a transmission overhead of one-fifth: fully 20 percent of the bits carry no data. Yet, as we saw in the discussion of early teleprinters, even if perfect synchronism were possible, the system would still have failed in many areas simply because it required data in an unbroken stream. In other words, it was transmitting characterized data with a technology that had no way to differentiate one character from another. Even in a perfect universe, therefore, purely synchronous systems are impractical for applications in which characters do not arrive according to a schedule. Without the START/STOP asynchronous serial format, all interaction between human and computer over serial lines would be impossible—we simply do not type, speak, or think synchronously. In other words, without the old-fashioned START/STOP form of communication, computer programmers would probably still be punching cards and paper tape.

Conclusion

The descriptions of teleprinters just presented are understandably oversimplified and several major questions remain unanswered. If you have a burning curiosity about teleprinter technology, consult the bibliography for sources of further information.

Do not be concerned at this point about unresolved inconsistencies in your understanding of asynchronous serial communications. Most of these topics are taken up again in later chapters where they are treated in greater detail and examined in the context of microcomputers instead of teleprinters. There, you will learn that the grimy details of asynchronous serial I/O—START bits, STOP bits, data format, and the like—are completely taken over by microcomputer hardware. Once the hardware is configured for a particular data format, sending and receiving data is almost as simple as reading and writing memory variables. In other words, the conversion from parallel to serial during transmission and back again during reception is hidden from the programmer.

Before we return to the subject of asynchronous communications technology, we will spend several chapters studying some of the larger issues in communications in general. During these discussions, you should take asynchronous I/O more or less on faith—as something that just magically happens—without undue concern for how it happens. After we have looked at some of the larger issues that face the programmer, we'll undertake a microscopic examination of the technology available to solve them.

chapter marker

Errors and Error Detection

At the end of the previous chapter, I mentioned the larger issues in communications. One such issue is certainly that of errors. In that chapter, for example, we saw that the consequences of just a single error in a single bit can result in a train of errors that persists for many characters beyond the original error. Although in this chapter we will briefly discuss the origin of such errors, our main goal will be to examine the tools available to the programmer for detecting and correcting them.

Origin of Errors

Errors are produced by two fundamentally different kinds of failures: *static* events whose behavior and existence are well-known and *transient* events that occur randomly. Signal distortion and attenuation loss are examples of static failures; atmospheric electromagnetic disturbances such as lightning or sunspots are examples of transient errors.

Errors arising from static events are much easier to handle because their effects are predictable. Because the behavior of AC signals is well-known, engineers can compensate for the problems caused by almost any environment. Equalization amplifiers can compensate for high-frequency attenuation; low-capacity or low-inductance cable can prevent bias distortion; shielding can exclude radio frequency interference—in short, given foreknowledge of an event or a phenomenon, most errors can be engineered into harmlessness. Thus by careful analysis, planning, and design, it is possible to communicate with a minuscule number of static errors.

Alas, transient causes of error are not so easily dealt with, if for no other reason than that they often involve imperfectly understood forces that occur at unpredictable times. Most transient errors, however, are caused by electrical interference (or *noise*) on the communications line. Interference may result from atmospheric events (lightning), local static (commutator noise), or dirty relay contacts in a communications device. Where the communications line is the telephone system, a whole new category of noises are possible: dropouts, crosstalk, echoes, and so forth.

The most common kind of noise, especially on telephone lines, is *impulse noise* or *burst noise*: periods of disrupting noise bounded on either side by periods of no noise. Although all forms of communication are susceptible to errors, serial is more vulnerable than parallel because the bit-by-bit nature of transmission exposes the data to the vagaries of the communications line for a longer time. Even seemingly tiny noise bursts inevitably manifest errors in several bits. For example, a noise burst of .01 second during 1200 baud communication will contaminate fully 12 bits; more bits are affected at higher data rates— 96 bits at 9600 baud. Recalling from Figure 2.6 how a single framing error can cause a ripple of errors across many characters, START/STOP asynchronous communication is particularly vulnerable to burst noise.

Error Detection

The acceptability of errors in communications depends upon the content of the data, the ultimate use to which the data is put, and the difficulty of correcting the error. Extremely high error rates are sometimes acceptable in pure text, which is still intelligible to the human eye even with 20 percent of the characters missing. At the other extreme are sensitive applications, such as the launch and guidance systems for thermonuclear weapons, where no errors can be tolerated.

Correcting errors is an entirely separate issue from detecting them. Again, the response to an error depends upon the content, importance, and uniqueness of the data. In general, if the information is still available, retransmission is the most straightforward means of correcting errors. For example, the receiver of a message containing casual text (such as newspaper copy) can simply request retransmission of the message or, more likely, that portion of the message containing errors. In some situations, however, retransmission is impossible or impractical. Raw real-time data transmitted between a remote recording instrument and its decoder cannot be repeated because the instant of time cannot be repeated. Retransmission between earth and interplanetary space vehicles, though clearly possible, is impractical because the turnaround time would be far too long. In situations that preclude retransmission, there must be not only a means to detect errors, but also a way to correct them. Since the asynchronous style of communication is not likely to become the communications medium for NASA, we will largely ignore the subject of error correction.

Redundancy

Most error detection schemes involve some degree of *redundancy*: additional bits that somehow represent the content of the message are transmitted along with the message itself. These various methods for deriving *redundancy codes* differ in the amount of the message represented and the complexity of the coding algorithm.

CHARACTER REDUNDANCY: PARITY

In Chapter 2, we noted that a *parity* bit is often appended to ASCII characters for error checking. This form of error detection is named from the mathematical idea of parity, which is the odd-even property of integers. A parity bit is formed to enforce an arbitrary rule that all characters should have either an odd (or even) number of 1 bits. When ODD parity is in effect during transmission of ASCII, for example, 0100001 becomes 01000011 because the highlighted **1** is required to create an ODD number of 1s in the byte; in an EVEN parity scheme, the byte must be 0100001**0** to *maintain* an even number of 1s. Similarly, 010001**0** under EVEN parity would become 01000100, but 1000101 under ODD parity.

During transmission, the sender calculates the parity bit, then appends it to the outgoing character. (EVEN parity is the Exclusive-OR of all data bits.) At the receiver, parity for the 7-bit data bytes is calculated and compared to the parity bit received. If the two do not agree, an error occurs.

Although in the strictest meaning of the term *parity*, only EVEN and ODD make sense. Dispensation of the eighth bit is often expressed in other ways:

NONE	The parity bit is unused and its value is unspecified.
MARK	The parity bit is always 1.
SPACE	The parity bit is always 0.

Parity is the lowest level of redundancy possible because it aims at discovering errors at the level of the individual character. Since it is a binary value reporting a binary (ODD-EVEN) relationship, it is capable of providing only minimal error detection. Specifically, parity can detect only errors that affect an odd number of bits. Table 3.1 illustrates this, in which the parity bit is the leftmost bit.

Table 3.1. Parity detects errors only in an odd number of bits (damaged bits are highlighted).

Transmitted	Received	Results for EVEN parity
01000001	01000001	Even number of 1s; parity OK.
01000001	01000011	Single-bit error: odd number of 1s; error detected.

continues

Table 3.1. continued

Transmitted	Received	Results for EVEN parity
01000001	0**0**00001**1**	Double-bit error: even number of 1s; error not detected.
01000001	01**011**101	Triple-bit error: odd number of 1s; error detected.

This insensitivity to such a wide range of bit patterns makes parity generally ineffective in asynchronous serial communications, where most errors come in bursts. Considering this fallibility, it is a wonder that parity is used at all, especially in the hostile environment of telecommunications with its relatively high probability of errors. In fact, one suspects that the use of parity in today's asynchronous applications (such as dial-up lines to mainframes) is due mainly to habit or intellectual inertia.

OVERHEAD

A few hardware devices such as video terminals indicate parity errors by somehow highlighting the offending character, but this feature is becoming rare today. Nevertheless, parity is often designed into all-ASCII text systems, then seldom used. Because modern ICs (that is, UARTs) have so simplified manipulation of data format, many programmers feel that the parity bit is somehow a freebie, or that "it's there, so why not use it?" Why not indeed? Consider that in a 10-bit SDU (1 START, 7 data, 1 parity, 1 STOP), 10 percent of the system's time is spent transmitting an error-checking bit that fails to detect errors 40 percent of the time.[1]

Block Redundancy: Parity

Its poor return upon bit investment makes character parity's overhead usuriously high. Its accuracy can be somewhat improved, however, by supplementing the parity check on individual characters with a parity check on a block of characters. With this concept, the basic unit of transmission changes from the character to the message. In the *block-check strategy*, message characters are treated as a two-dimensional array. A parity bit is appended to each character (row) of bits as usual. After an agreed-upon number of characters, a *block-check character* (BCC), which represents a parity check on the columns, is transmitted. At the receiver, the incoming characters are checked for parity as usual. After the agreed-upon number of characters has arrived, the receiver calculates the parity character and compares it against the one just received. The assumption here is that an error that is missed in one dimension may be visible in another.

---

[1]In *Telecommunications and the Computer* (Prentice Hall, 1976), author Martin shows that, based upon the statistical character of burst errors at 1200 baud on the public (switched) telephone network, the simple parity check fails to detect nearly 40 percent of the errors.

Table 3.2 illustrates this method by calculating a parity EVEN block check for the four ASCII characters CfyU: a bit is appended to each 7-bit character so that the resulting 8-bit byte contains an even number of 1 bits. An EVEN parity bit is also figured for each column.

Table 3.2. Vertical and longitudinal redundancy checks using EVEN parity (errors appear in bold).

	Transmitted	*Received*	
	Message	*Double-bit error in 1 row*	*Double-bit error in 2 rows*
C	11000011	11000011	11000011
f	01100110	01100110	01100110
y	11111001	11**00**001	11**100**001
U	01010101	01010101	010**01**101
BCC	00001001	00001001	00001001
BCC calculated by receiver	00010001 (error detected)	00001001 (error not detected)	

On the "Transmitted" side of Table 3.2 are the individual transmitted characters and BCC as they are transmitted. The parity bit is the leftmost one. On the "Received" side are the same characters as they would be received, with one and then two occurrences of 2-bit errors.

The first receive error has a single 2-bit error in the third row. The character parity bit does not reveal an error because an even number of bits are damaged. Notice, though, how in the next heading those same double-bit row errors become single-bit errors when parity is calculated on the columns. The error is detected because the BCC (parity byte) calculated (00010001) for the column does not agree with the one received (00001001).

The second example in Table 3.2 shows the same message, but with a pair of 2-bit errors: one in the third row and one in the fourth. Again, the double-bit errors are not detected by row parity. Because these double-bit errors extend across an even number of rows, no error is detected by the row-parity calculation.

Though column parity (also referred to as the *vertical redundancy check*) improves the chances of detecting an error substantially, it is blind to an even number of errors in a column in the same way character parity (also referred to as the *longitudinal redundancy check*) is susceptible to an even number of errors in the rows.

About the only virtue of parity checking in serial I/O is its simplicity: it can be implemented in hardware with just a few Exclusive-OR gates. In microcomputers, however, the asynchronous serial functions are handled completely by dedicated ICs that support single-character parity, but not a vertical/longitudinal redundancy check.

THE CHECKVALUE

Before proceeding, we must once again tackle the vocabulary surrounding the topic of error-checking and error codes, which is hopelessly inconsistent and vague. These inconsistencies are easily explained. Much of the literature on the subject has sprung from the commercial sector, where the engineer-authors (notoriously oblivious to charges of parochialism) simply adopt the jargon extant in their companies. For example, the redundant bits that bear the error-checking code in one book are referred to as the *block-check character*; another uses the simpler *check character*; while still another calls them a *frame check sequence*. For one reason or another, none of these is precise enough. Is it not misleading to refer to a single *character* when there may be more than one? For the same reason, isn't *sequence* misleading when applied to a single entity? The word *frame* is already overused in computer jargon. To avoid these ambiguities, I will henceforth use the numerical term *checkvalue* to denote the redundant bits added for error checking.

Block Redundancy: Checksum

The vertical/longitudinal redundancy check introduced an important technique: checking for errors on blocks of data instead of on individual characters. An extension of that technique is the *arithmetic checksum*, a simple sum of the numerical value of characters in the block.

Table 3.3. The arithmetic checksum (damaged bits appear in bold).

		Received		
Transmitted				
	Message	*Double-bit error in 1 row*	*Double-bit error in 2 rows*	*Single-bit error in 2 columns*
C	1000011	1000011	1000011	100001**0**
f	1100110	1100110	1100110	110011**1**
y	1111001	1**1**00001	1**1**00001	1111001
U	1010101	1010101	100**1**101	1010101
BCC	101110111	101101111	101110111	101110111
BCC calculated by receiver (detected)		101011111 (detected)	101010111 (not detected)	101110111

In Table 3.3, our familiar four-character ASCII message is shown in 7-bit format without parity. The checksum detects double-bit errors in one or two rows, but fails to detect even-numbered bit errors in columns.

Significantly, the checksum cannot detect errors of sequence: an identical checksum is produced even if the message is sent in random order. The example in Table 3.3 also reveals that the size of the arithmetic checksum varies according to the numerical value of the individual members of the message, and the size is at least n where n is the number of bits in each member. In Table 3.3, for example, the four-character message of 7-bit ASCII characters results in a 9-bit checksum. Transmitting this entire value would require two 7-bit characters or truncation of the 9-bit value to a single 7-bit one (i.e., modulo-128). The former greatly increases the accuracy, but, depending upon the length of the message, also increases the overhead. In general, however, if the size of the block to be checked is sufficiently large, the extra byte is insignificant in comparison to the additional margin of safety from the longer checkvalue.

Cyclic Redundancy Checks

An extremely powerful kind of error checking is available with the same overhead as the checksum. Consider these promises[2] for a checkvalue of only 16 bits:

Single-bit errors:	100 percent
Double-bit errors:	100 percent
Odd-numbered errors:	100 percent
Burst errors shorter than 16 bits:	100 percent
Burst errors of exactly 17 bits:	99.9969 percent
All other burst errors:	99.9984 percent

In comparison to the relatively anemic parity and checksum methods, this method, the *cyclical redundancy check* or *CRC*, seems magically powerful. The CRC is good at detecting all kinds of errors, but especially those that occur in bursts over a relatively long time.

Modulo-2 Arithmetic

You should understand from the outset that the *starting point* for designing any CRC system is the number of bits desired in the checkvalue. Because computer hardware usually manipulates in 8-bit bytes, the most common checkvalue size is 16 bits; however, 12 bits is sometimes used, and 32 bits is used for extremely critical applications. Although the examples, formulas, and discussions in this chapter center around 16-bit CRC checkvalues, keep in mind that the principles are true for CRCs of other lengths.

---

[2]Tanenbaum, Andrew S., *Computer Networks*, Prentice Hall, 1981.

Despite the efforts of various "expositors," the theory and implementation of CRCs are surprisingly simple. As a matter of fact, CRCs are best understood as a variation of the simple arithmetic checksum explained earlier. Whereas the arithmetic checksum is derived by addition, CRC-style checkvalues are derived by division. To illustrate, let's return to our earlier 4-byte message cfyU, but this time with the characters expressed in 8 bits and EVEN parity:

c	11000011
f	01100110
y	11111001
U	01010101

For simplicity's sake, assume that we wish to transmit a 16-bit checkvalue for these 4 bytes of data. Instead of considering the 4 bytes individually as before, or as a two-dimensional matrix, we will treat them as if they were one single large binary number:

11000011011001101111100101010101

or in decimal: 3,278,305,621.

The checkvalue is derived by dividing this number by another number (the divisor) chosen for its magical properties. Since we are being hypothetical, let's say the divisor is decimal 525.

$$\frac{3,278,305,621}{525} = 624,439 \text{ with } 346 \text{ remainder}$$

A problem now arises: although the 23-bit quotient is a perfectly good checkvalue, it would have to be truncated to 16 bits, compromising its accuracy. Unfortunately, we can't guarantee the number of bits in a quotient. There is no reason why we have to use the quotient of the division. Why not use the remainder, taking advantage of the fact that a remainder is by definition at least one less than the divisor? In other words, we can control the size of the remainder by our choice of divisors. In the previous example, a divisor of 17 bits guarantees a remainder no larger than 16 bits. A divisor of, say, 65,540 will produce

$$\frac{3,278,305,621}{65,540} = 50,019 \text{ with } 60,361 \text{ remainder}$$

where the remainder is clearly significant to 16 bits:

60,361 = EBC9 = 1110101111001001

Longhand Modulo-2 Division

CRC procedures, which existed long before microprocessors, were first implemented in hardware where simplicity of design and operating efficiency were important economic considerations. For reasons we will discuss later, the checkvalue remainder is not obtained by ordinary binary arithmetic, but in *modulo-2*. This technique simplifies the hardware design enormously because modulo-2 arithmetic has no carries or borrows. For example, the binary addition of

```
 01010101
 01010101
 10101010
```

is laborious because of the carries into every place. In modulo-2 addition, however, there are no carries:

```
 01010101
 01010101
 00000000
```

If the result of the modulo-2 addition operation looks familiar, it's because modulo-2 addition is identical to the Exclusive-OR. To refresh your memory, the truth table for XOR is shown below. Note that addition and subtraction are identical under these rules.

Truth table for XOR (modulo-2).

$0 \oplus 0 = 0$
$0 \oplus 1 = 1$
$1 \oplus 0 = 1$
$1 \oplus 1 = 0$

$\oplus$ is the symbol for Exclusive-OR.

Figure 3.1 shows the modulo-2 division of our 4-byte message by the divisor 69,665 (10001000000100001).

The only mechanical difference between modulo-2 division and ordinary binary division is that the intermediate results are obtained by Exclusive-OR instead of subtraction. The engine that drives binary division is the forcing of the leftmost bit in the previous remainder to 0. One by one, the message bits are brought down from the dividend and appended to the right end of the intermediate result. The brought-down bits are shown in bold. If the high-order bit of the intermediate remainder is 1, a 1 goes into the quotient and the divisor is subtracted (i.e, XORed) from the remainder; if the first bit of the intermediate answer is 0, a 0 goes into the quotient and sixteen 0 bits are subtracted. To ease the strain on the eyes, an x marks the "dead" 0s produced by each step.

Modulo-2 Division and Hardware

Students of the subject of CRCs usually assume that there is a dark, mystical mathematical reason why the division is performed in modulo-2 instead of ordinary binary arithmetic. In fact, the reason is disappointingly mundane. CRC procedures were intended from the outset for implementation in hardware communications devices, and later in disk controllers. Modulo-2 division was selected because its arithmetic can be implemented with just a few shift registers and gates; ordinary binary arithmetic, by contrast, requires additional logic to handle borrows and carries. Naturally, the simplicity of the modulo-2 design also means an increase in operating speed.

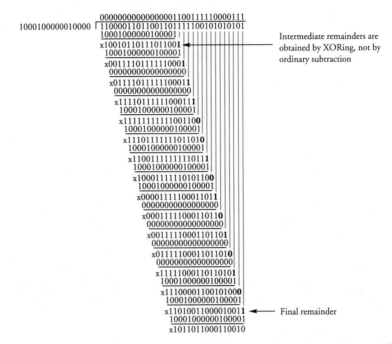

FIGURE 3.1.

Modulo-2 division of the 4-byte message CfyU by 10001000000100001.

The example of longhand division makes a good point of reference, but it does not illuminate the internal process that makes CRC such a good error-checking code. To remedy this omission, we will now study the pseudo-schematic diagram in Figure 3.2 of a hardware circuit that performs modulo-2 division, graphically illustrating the turbulent bit action that characterizes CRC checkvalues. In this figure, the boxes stand for the individual elements of a shift register, and the encircled plus symbols stand for Exclusive-OR gates.

In Figure 3.1, we saw that the procedure in longhand modulo-2 division is to bring down a bit from the dividend into the LSB of the remainder. The divisor is then XORed with the remainder to produce a new remainder; XORing forces the leftmost bit of the previous remainder to 0. This is exactly the hardware approach as well, in which the 16 elements of the shift register represent the remainder register. Message (dividend) bits are shifted (brought down) into the LSB of the remainder register, which is then shifted left. During the shift, XOR gates between the elements perform the modulo-2 subtraction. The value in the remainder register after the shift is the new remainder.

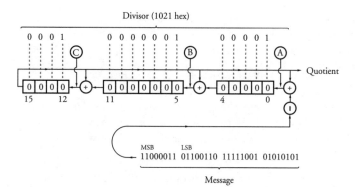

FIGURE 3.2.

Hardware simulation of longhand modulo-2 division using shift registers and Exclusive-OR gates.

Shaded lines denote the application of the divisor (1021H) to the remainder register. I will discuss the significance of the divisor later, but for now simply notice that

● It is 16, not 17 bits in length.

● For every 1 bit in the divisor, an Exclusive-OR gate corresponds immediately to the right in the remainder register.

The bit shifted out of bit 15 of the remainder register is the quotient.

A TRIAL RUN OF 2 BITS

At the beginning, the remainder register consists of all 0s. The first bit of the message, 1, is presented to the input at point I. Point I is actually one input of a two-input XOR gate whose other input comes from the high-order bit of the remainder register via the line marked QUOTIENT. Because bit 15 is 0, the output of the XOR gate at point A is also a 1. At output point B, the 0 in bit 4 is XORed with 0 in bit 15 to produce a 0. At output point C, the 0 in bit 11 is XORed with the 0 in bit 15 to yield 0. When the shifting pulse occurs, the 1 at point A is shifted into the remainder register's bit 0. All other 0s shift left one place. The remainder now contains 0000_0000000_00001.

The 1 in the first message bit produces less than startling results, but it's a good warmup for things to come. As the movement of the bits within the remainder soon becomes complex, it's a good idea to construct a visual aid. I recommend that you draw an enlarged version of Figure 3.2 and simulate the movement of the 1s and 0s with tokens of some sort—pennies and dimes work well. Physically moving these coins about and noting the contents of the remainder register after each step is an excellent way to get a feel for the process. Write the bits of the message in a column and, beside each message bit, write down the state of the remainder register before the shift. This record will help you find your place if you make mistakes or become confused.

Using the truth table in the previous shaded box, apply the next message bit, also a 1, to the point marked I. Decode the two inputs of the rightmost XOR gate. Since the message bit is 1 and bit 15 of the remainder is still 0, temporarily place the result—a dime for a 1—in the circle labeled A. Repeat the procedure for points B and C. This results in a dime in the circle at A and a penny at B and C.

Before proceeding, try to imagine the static situation just described in your mind. Now, snap your fingers (to simulate the shift pulse) and discard the dead message bit coin and the coins from bits 4, 11, and 15. Next, move all bits to the left one place, moving the penny at point C into bit 12, the penny at point B into bit 5, and the dime at point A into bit 0. This completes two steps in the division. Figure 3.3a gives the state of the remainder register.

Now, stop and reflect. Write down the contents of the remainder after the second bit: 0000_0000000_00011. Repeat the entire procedure for each message bit:

1. Use the truth table in the previous gray box to decode the inputs to the XOR gates, placing a dime or penny at the circles marked A, B, and C.

2. Snap your fingers to signify the shift.[3]

3. Discard the message bit coin and the coins from bits 4, 11, and 15.

4. Shift the remaining bits left one place.

5. Move the coins at A, B, and C into bits 0, 5, and 12 respectively.

6. Pause and record the remainder.

7. Repeat until no more message bits are left.

8. The value remaining in the register is the checkvalue.

As you process the first few bits, you will probably notice that as long as bit 15 contains 0, the XOR gates do not affect the message bits as they pass through. Because the first bit in the message is 0, bit 15 remains a 0 for the first 17 shifts, causing the circuit simply to produce *transparent shifts*. (This parallels the beginning of longhand division, where, according to convention, we do not include in the quotient the leading 0s produced by applying the divisor to the first few places of the dividend.) Regardless of the value of the first message, then, the first 16 shifts always simply copy the first 16 bits of the message into the remainder register. As soon as the first bit of the message is shifted out of the remainder, subsequent remainders correspond perfectly with the intermediate remainders in Figure 3.1.

Figure 3.3b shows the situation after 16 shifts. As predicted, the register is just a copy of bits 0 through 15 of the message. With this knowledge, you can now save yourself some work if you are using tokens to simulate the register action. Starting with the first 1 bit in the message, duplicate the next 16 message bits in the remainder register.

---

[3]Failure to snap your fingers (which produces the *Purves Effect*) may result in incorrect answers.

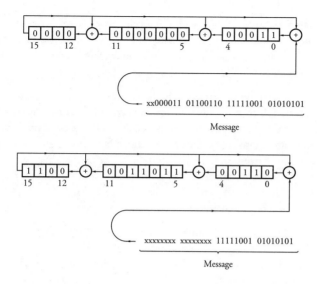

A

The remainder register after 2 shifts.

B

The remainder register after 16 shifts.

FIGURE 3.3.

The remainder register.

THE BIT HITS THE FAN

The 17th shift, however, produces a profound effect because the initial 1 bit from the message, now in bit 15 of the remainder, is applied to the Quotient line. The presence of a 1 at one input of the XOR gate means that 0 bits immediately to the right of the gate are transformed to 1 bits during the shift. Figure 3.4 shows the remainder register after the 17th step.

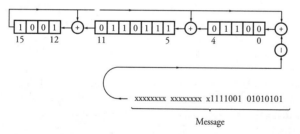

FIGURE 3.4.

The remainder register after 17 shifts: the first 1 message bit reaches the XOR gates.

The 1 of the incoming message bit and the 1 in bit 15 of the remainder are XORed to produce a 0 (penny) for circle A; the 0s at both bit 4 and 11 are XORed with bit 15 to produce 1s (dimes) in circles C and D. The very next shift, therefore, will produce the result shown in Figure 3.4. It is also the first intermediate remainder from our longhand division in Figure 3.1. This process is repeated for every bit in the message.

The important action in this simulator is that as long as a 0 appears on the gate feedback (Quotient) line, the bits shift transparently; when a 1 appears, however, the bits are XORed with 1 as they pass. Bits and ghosts of bits incestuously recirculate in the remainder long after the bit itself has died. This, together with the dramatic effect often wrought by a single bit, means that the value in the remainder register any instant depends upon a great deal of history. The remainder from modulo-2 division not only detects the bit errors missed by the arithmetic checksum discussed earlier, but it also detects errors in the order in which the message bits are sent.

Students of this method are often troubled by the location of the XOR gates to the right of their corresponding 1 bits in the divisor. Try to keep in mind that the XOR gates decode the Quotient-line feedback before the shift occurs. The earlier admonition to snap your fingers to simulate the shift was not intended as a facetious suggestion, but was intended to emphasize the correspondence between the behavior of the hardware circuit and longhand division. In short, understand fully that the action of the XOR gates on the remainder is the same as XORing the entire register with the divisor 1021 Hex; this, in turn, is equivalent to the modulo-2 subtraction in longhand division.

This brings up another frequently misunderstood point: how the hardware can get by with a 16-bit divisor (1021 Hex) when a 17-bit divisor (11021 Hex) is required in longhand division. First, recall the obvious: all divisors must contain a 1 in their high bits. Second, in longhand division, the high-order bit of the 17-bit divisor serves only to force the high-order bit of the remainder to 0, and thereafter serves no further purpose in the calculation. Because this dead bit is superfluous (it is the x in Figure 3.1), it can be altogether ignored in the design of hardware and (as we will discover in Chapter 19) software.

Purging the Remainder Register

We now encounter another vocabulary problem: there is no single, unambiguous definition of a CRC. One is tempted to dub the remainder of modulo-2 division a CRC, but one additional step is required. To understand why the remainder of modulo-2 division is not yet a CRC, recall that after 16 shifts, the remainder register contains a copy of the first 16 bits of the message. Kindly put, an error-checking method that simply duplicates the message wins no awards for cleverness.

As I noted earlier, the register does not even begin to percolate until the first 1 bit in the message reaches the Quotient line and is fed back to the XOR gates. In a real sense, then, we can complain that the very effect we seek from any given bit does not occur until that bit is actually *shifted out* of the remainder! This means that when the last bit of the message has been shifted into the remainder register, it is still fully 16 bits away from exerting an active influence on the remainder. This minor problem is easy to solve: the residual message bits are forced into the XOR feedback path by flushing the CRC remainder register with sixteen 0s. Seen another way, 16 extraneous 0 bits are appended to the message itself. (For yet another way to view the 0 bits, see the section, "Achieving a Zero Remainder".)

So important is the technique of using 0s to flush the remainder that we can, ipso facto, make the following definition: a CRC is the remainder obtained from modulo-2 division in which the number of 0 bits that are equal to the number of bits in the remainder register is appended to the message.

The Classical CRC Circuit

The need to purge the remainder register with 0 bits actually presents a design problem: who or what actually does the purging? Must the bits be manually appended to the message? Is software somehow supposed to signal the hardware when the 0s are to be added? This dilemma can be resolved by making a subtle change in the design of the circuit itself. This new circuit, shown in Figure 3.5, actually eliminates the need to purge the remainder with 0s.

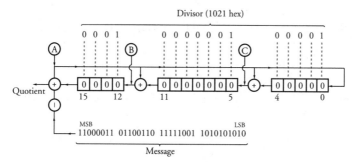

FIGURE 3.5.
Modification of division circuit eliminates flushing the remainder with 0s.

If you construct a penny-and-dime simulator for this circuit, you will discover that after the very first shift its remainder corresponds to the intermediate remainders of longhand division. As before, the incoming message bit is XORed with the high-order bit of the accumulator then shifted into the accumulator. The important difference is the manner in which the divisor is subtracted from the remainder. In the earlier circuit, bit 15 directly provided the feedback for the XOR gates; in this new circuit, however, the bit produced by XORing the data with bit 15 is actually the QUOTIENT line. Note that by placing the message bits immediately into the XOR feedback stream, their effect upon the remainder is felt immediately without the 16-bit propagation delay incurred by the simple division circuit. Processing a message through this circuit, then, produces the same remainder as the polynomial division circuit with 16 bits of 0s appended to the message.

Because the circuit in Figure 3.5 produces a CRC directly, and in order to differentiate it from the earlier circuit, which performs pure modulo-2 division, I will henceforth refer to it as the *classical* CRC prototype. (See the section entitled "The Classical CRC.")

CRC and Polynomials

So far, we have used the language of modulo-2 division to describe the various aspects of CRC calculations. In practice, though, CRCs are usually described in the language of *polynomials*. In this language, the message is expressed as a long polynomial whose bits form the coefficients of the polynomial term. The exponent for each term in the polynomial is derived from that bit's ordinal rank in the message. For example, our 4-byte message (11000011011001101111100101010101) is expressed as a polynomial like this:

$$\overset{1}{1}\overset{1}{X^{31}}+\overset{0}{1}X^{30}+\overset{0}{0}X^{29}+\overset{0}{0}X^{28}+\overset{0}{0}X^{27}+\overset{1}{0}X^{26}+\overset{1}{1}X^{25}+\overset{0}{1}X^{24}+\overset{1}{0}X^{23}+\overset{1}{1}X^{22}+\overset{0}{1}X^{21}+\overset{0}{0}X^{20}+\overset{1}{0}X^{19}+\overset{1}{1}X^{18}+1X^{17}+$$

$$\overset{0}{0}X^{16}+\overset{1}{1}X^{15}+\overset{1}{1}X^{14}+\overset{1}{1}X^{13}+\overset{1}{1}X^{12}+\overset{1}{1}X^{11}+\overset{0}{1}X^{10}+\overset{0}{0}X^{9}+\overset{1}{1}X^{8}+\overset{0}{1}X^{7}+\overset{1}{1}X^{6}+\overset{0}{1}X^{5}+\overset{1}{1}X^{4}+\overset{0}{1}X^{3}+\overset{1}{1}X^{2}+\overset{1}{1}X^{1}+\overset{1}{1}X^{0}$$

and the divisor (10001000000100001) is

$$\overset{1}{1}X^{16}+\overset{0}{0}X^{15}+\overset{0}{0}X^{14}+\overset{0}{0}X^{13}+\overset{1}{1}X^{12}+\overset{0}{0}X^{11}+\overset{0}{0}X^{10}+\overset{0}{0}X^{9}+\overset{0}{0}X^{8}+\overset{0}{0}X^{7}+\overset{0}{0}X^{6}+\overset{1}{1}X^{5}+\overset{0}{0}X^{4}+\overset{0}{0}X^{3}+\overset{0}{0}X^{2}+\overset{0}{0}X^{1}+\overset{1}{1}X^{0}$$

By convention, however, non-leading terms with a 0 coefficient are not shown. In this shorthand, the message polynomial is

$$X^{31}+X^{30}+X^{25}+X^{24}+X^{22}+X^{21}+X^{18}+X^{17}+X^{15}+X^{14}+X^{13}+X^{12}+X^{11}+X^{8}+X^{6}+X^{4}+X^{2}+X^{0}$$

and the divisor polynomial is

$$X^{16}+X^{12}+X^{5}+1$$

The convenience of this notation is clearly one of the reasons why the polynomial language is adopted. There are new names for the other parts of the process:

Message polynomial:	The message itself (i.e., the dividend), expressed as a polynomial
Generator polynomial:	The divisor, expressed as a polynomial
CRC generator:	A circuit or, by extension, software algorithm for calculating CRCs
CRC accumulator:	The CRC remainder or remainder register

Although these terms are not entirely satisfactory, for the sake of consistency with the existing literature on the subject, I will adopt them for the remainder of this chapter.

Selecting a Generator Polynomial (Divisor)

Aside from noting that all divisor polynomials must begin and end with a 1 term, a discussion of the criteria for selecting polynomials is far beyond the scope of this book. A thorough discussion of this subject requires knowledge of advanced mathematics. Additional references are provided in the bibliography for those who wish to pursue the subject further.

There are two popular 16-bit CRC polynomials. The first is specified by the CCITT in the following deadly prose:

> The…information bits, taken in conjunction, correspond to the coefficients of a message polynomial having terms from x^{n-1} (n = total number of bits in a block or sequence) down to X^{16}. This polynomial is divided, modulo-2, by the generating polynomial $x^{16} + x^{12} + x^{5} + 1$. The check bits correspond to the coefficients of the terms from x^{15} to x^{0} in the remainder polynomial found at the completion of this division.
>
> —*The CCITT Red Book*, Volume VIII, International Telecommunications Union, Geneva, 1986. Recommendation V.41, "Code-Independent Error Control System."

You may recognize this polynomial as the hypothetical in the examples of this chapter. Known simply as *CRC-CCITT*, it was used by IBM for the first floppy disk controller (Model 3770) and quickly became a standard for microcomputer disk controllers. This polynomial is also employed in IBM's popular synchronous protocols HDLC/SDLC (high-level data link control/synchronous data link control), and we will encounter it in the XMODEM file transfer protocols in Chapters 4 and 19.

Another widely used CRC polynomial is CRC-16:

$$X^{16} + X^{15} + X^2 + 1$$

This polynomial, though not quite as efficient at catching errors as CRC-CCITT, is nevertheless still popular due to its long history in IBM's binary synchronous communications protocol (BYSYNC) method of data transfer.

Achieving a Zero Remainder

After all bytes of a message have been transmitted, the 16-bit CRC checkvalue must then be transmitted. What's the easiest way to check that this received CRC value matches the CRC locally calculated by the receiver? The method that comes immediately to mind is for the receiver to fetch the two transmitted CRC bytes and perform a simple integer comparison of the two values. Although this method gives the right answer, a simpler and faster way exists, thanks to the peculiarities of modulo-2 arithmetic.

Let's assume that both receiver and transmitter are using the CRC circuit in Figure 3.5 and have successfully transferred a message without errors. It is now time for the receiver to fetch the CRC checkvalue. Instead of fetching the transmitted CRC bytes separately and comparing them to the value in its own accumulator, the receiver simply treats them as part of the message, processing them through its own CRC generator. When the message and the CRC are both error-free, the receiver's CRC accumulator is 0!

If this phenomenon seems to be magic, you can watch it happen with a penny-and-dime simulator for Figure 3.5. When the receiver's CRC calculation is complete, and before the CRC bytes are sent, the CRC in the accumulator is identical to the sender's CRC. Thus, as each message bit is applied to the accumulator, it is XORed with a copy of itself in bit 15 of the accumulator. The result (always 0) is shifted into the low-order bit of the accumulator. After 16 bits, the accumulator contains all 0s.

Another View of Accumulator Purging

Our explanation of the need to purge the modulo-2 division circuit with 0s was based upon the commonsense perception that the message bits do not participate actively in the remainder until they are shifted out onto the XOR gate feedback (QUOTIENT) line. While this observation remains valid, we now turn to a more mathematical explanation to illuminate several aspects of the subject.

Whenever programmers discuss CRCs, one point of confusion always arises. Someone complains that although their algorithm generates the correct CRC value, it does not produce a 0 remainder when the CRC is appended to the message as described above. Using the penny-and-dime CRC simulator, we can easily resolve this mystery and, along the way, arrive at a fundamental point about the relationship between CRC circuits and circuits that perform pure polynomial division. A simulator shows that although modulo-2 division produces the correct CRC remainder after purging with 0 bits, it cannot be used to produce the 0 remainder just discussed. Clearly, then, the production of a remainder of 0 is somehow related to the purging of the CRC accumulator with 0s. To understand why, let's recall some basic arithmetic. We know that

$$Message = (Quotient \times Divisor) + Remainder$$

By adding *Remainder* to both sides, we achieve

$$Message + Remainder = (Quotient \times Divisor) + Remainder + Remainder$$

This equation is seemingly useless until we remember that in modulo-2 arithmetic, addition is equivalent to Exclusive-ORing. The expression

$$Remainder + Remainder$$

is equivalent to

$$Remainder \oplus Remainder$$

From the Exclusive-OR truth table, we see that any value XORed with itself is 0. This leaves us with the more interesting equation

$$Message \oplus Remainder = Quotient \times Divisor$$

then

$$\frac{Message \oplus Remainder}{Divisor} = Quotient$$

which plainly states that in modulo-2 arithmetic, XORing the remainder of division to the orginal message creates a new message that is *evenly divisible* by the original divisor (produces a remainder of 0).

Stating it somewhat differently: when the remainder of message A is XORed with message A to form message B, division of message B by the original divisor produces a remainder of 0. Applying this principle to the longhand division in Figure 3.1 yields:

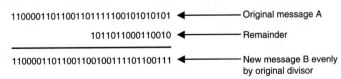

1100001101100110111110010101010101 ◄────────── Original message A

1011011000110010 ◄────────── Remainder

1100001101100110010011110110111 ◄────────── New message B evenly by original divisor

Although this procedure indeed achieves a remainder of 0, the accomplishment is, you must concede, a bit of a Pyrrhic victory: we have altered the message! Luckily, there is a simple way to preserve the original content of the message. Before performing the first division, we concatenate 16 extra 0s to the original message.

This means we need to rephrase our principle. Message A is right-padded with 0s to form message B. The remainder of message B is appended to message B to form message C. After division the remainder of message C is 0. Let's see this in action.

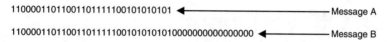

We now calculate the remainder for message B.

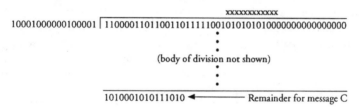

Now we create the final message by XORing the remainder with the 0-paddded message to produce the final message that is evenly divisible.

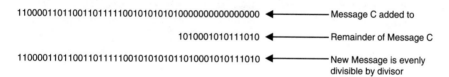

This procedure works only with the classical CRC model, which "pre-appends" the sixteen 0s, and not with simple modulo-2 division. It is therefore likely that programmers who are frustrated by the failure of their "correct" algorithms to achieve the expected 0 remainder are probably using modulo-2 division algorithms, not CRC algorithms.

In view of this discussion, it is worthwhile to examine the remainder of the CCITT specification quoted earlier:

> The complete block of message bits followed by the check bits corresponds to the coefficients of a polynomial which [are] integrally divisible in modulo 2 fashion by the generating polynomial.

> At the transmitter the...information bits are subjected to an encoding process equivalent to a division by the generator polynomial. The resulting remainder is transmitted to the line immediately after the information bits, commencing with the highest order bits.

At the receiver, the incoming block is subjected to a decoding process equivalent to a division by the generator polynomial, which in the absence of errors will result in a zero remainder. If the division results in other than a zero remainder, errors are indicated.

The important phrase here is "integrally divisible," because it means that the classic CRC (as opposed to the polynomial division) model is intended. Interestingly, the term *CRC* appears neither in this excerpt nor in the body of the specification from which it was taken.

More CRC Variations

It should come as no shock to learn that CRC procedures are not performed on one long, continuous message. Because hardware must interface to a processor, the message is usually fed into the hardware in 8-bit bytes. In serial devices that contain CRC hardware, however, the bits are sent to the CRC generator 1 bit at a time as they are transmitted or received. Because a byte is transmitted with the low-order bit first, the resulting CRC is calculated in reverse order. As long as there is a complementary CRC hardware circuit in the receiver, this process is transparent because the bits go into the receiver's generator in the same sequence as they went into the sender's.

Microcomputers seldom contain hardware for processing CRC during asynchronous I/O. In the event you are called upon to write software in support of CRC checkvalues created by hardware, you will need to perform the necessary bit reversals. Figure 3.6 shows a common reverse CRC, depicted here using the CRC-16 generator polynomial. This circuit assumes that message bits are applied low-order bit first. To compensate for bit reversal, the circuit is designed with bit flow in the opposite direction from previous models. Here, incoming message bits enter the high-order end and shift right. Notice also that even the polynomial represented by the position of the XOR gates is in inverse order as well—A001 Hex instead of 8005 Hex as expected. This circuit, which is of the auto-purge variety, produces a CRC remainder correctly reversed.

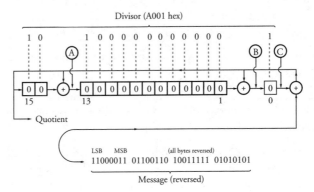

FIGURE 3.6.

A reverse circuit using the CRC-16 polynomial.

The Classical CRC

Because CRCs are so closely linked with communications hardware that processes bits in reverse order, some would argue that the circuit in Figure 3.5 should not be called the "classical" CRC model. These authors point out with some validity that because CRC error checking virtually was born in serial communications hardware, which reverses the bit order of bytes during transfer, the reverse CRC deserves the honorific "classical." In other words, the only real CRC is, a priori, the one performed by hardware.

While it is probably true that the circuit in Figure 3.5 probably never existed in real-world hardware, it is a good bet that it was built as an evolutionary step in the development of the bit-reversed CRCs that eventually were used. Besides, this book is about software—not hardware—applications of CRCs. Due to modern ICs that automate every aspect of asynchronous communications, software does not have to deal with incoming bytes bit-by-bit, but as entire bytes. Because bytes are received whole, software CRC calculations need not be concerned with the peculiarities of the processes of serialization inside the ICs. Software, therefore, can more obviously and directly parallel the CRC's theoretical roots in polynomial division. For our purposes, then, the classical CRC model continues to be that of Figure 3.5.

Leading Zeros

Like the CCITT document quoted previously, a surprising number of error-checking procedures specify that the CRC accumulator be initialized to 0. This is an odd requirement, because this makes the algorithm vulnerable to leading spurious 0s. There are two popular alternatives to initialization with 0s.

The most obvious way around susceptibility to leading extraneous 0s is to initialize the accumulator to any other value but 0. A more imaginative method is that used in IBM's popular synchronous protocol SDLC, in which the accumulator is initialized to all 1s. Upon completion of the CRC calculation, the *1s complement* of the CRC accumulator is transmitted. Through some unexplored miracle of modulo-2 arithmetic, if the receiver processes these inverted bytes as appendages to the message, the resulting remainder is 1D0F Hex instead of 0.

CRCs on Byte-Size Data

As we just noted, software implementations of CRCs feed the message into the generator one byte at a time. It is interesting to examine exactly how the 8 bits of a byte combine with the existing 16-bit accumulator to produce a new accumulator. Our goal in this section is to analyze the new accumulator in terms of the ancestry of its bits: exactly which of the original data bits combined with which of the original accumulator bits. For our example, we will use the reverse CRC-16 model shown in Figure 3.6.

Although you can duplicate this experiment with the purely manual penny-and-dime CRC simulator, be forewarned that it is an extremely tedious procedure. If you choose to do this, begin by labeling each bit in the data and the accumulator with its bit number: D0 through D7 and A0 through A15, respectively. On a separate piece of paper, maintain a cumulative chart showing each bit in the accumulator and the original bits—both data and accumulator—that were XORed to produce it. Figure 3.7 shows this chart before shifting begins. Bit numbers are represented with capital letters, while the contents of the registers use lowercase letters.

DATA BITS

	MSB							LSB
Bit number	D7	D6	D5	D4	D3	D2	D1	D0
Contents	—	d7	d6	d5	d4	d3	d2	d1

CRC ACCUMULATOR

	MSB															LSB
Bit number	A15	A14	A13	A12	A11	A10	A9	A8	A7	A6	A5	A4	A3	A2	A1	A0
Contents	a15	a14	a13	a12	a11	a10	a9	a8	a7	a6	a5	a4	a3	a2	a1	a0

FIGURE 3.7.

Reverse CRC-16 bit-combining chart before shifting.

Figure 3.8 shows the chart after only one shift. This chart now shows the ancestry of each bit: bits 15, 13, and 0 of the accumulator (C15, C13, C0) now contain the XOR of c0 and d0 (the original contents of C0 and D0).

DATA BITS

	MSB							LSB
Bit number	D7	D6	D5	D4	D3	D2	D1	D0
Contents	—	d7	d6	d5	d4	d3	d2	d1

CRC ACCUMULATOR

	MSB															LSB
Bit number	A15	A14	A13	A12	A11	A10	A9	A8	A7	A6	A5	A4	A3	A2	A1	A0
Contents	—	a15	a14	a13	a12	a11	a10	a9	a8	a7	a6	a5	a4	a3	a2	a1
	a0		a0													a0
	d0		d0													d0

FIGURE 3.8.

Reverse CRC-16 bit-combining chart after one shift.

Figure 3.9 shows the registers after the fourth shift. Notice that after only four shifts, the columns already contain many duplicate bits, making the whole chart appear hopelessly confusing. This clutter of duplicates can be greatly simplified, however, when we realize that the XOR of identical bits produces 0; these bits can therefore be eliminated from the chart. Figure 3.10 shows the chart after eight shifts with the duplicates cancelled and removed. The bits have also been rearranged to juxtapose like-numbered data and accumulator bits.

After eight shifts, the low-order byte of the new accumulator contains only bits created by XORing the data bytes with bits D7 through A15 of the original accumulator. In other words, a data byte is XORed only with the low-order byte of the existing accumulator, producing an 8-bit value we refer to as the combining value. Sparing you the tiresome mathematical proof, it is fairly apparent that the new CRC accumulator is simply the CRC of the combining value plus (XOR in modulo-2) the original high-order byte of the accumulator.

DATA BITS

	MSB							LSB
Bit number	D7	D6	D5	D4	D3	D2	D1	D0
Contents	—	—	—	—	d7	d6	d5	d4

CRC ACCUMULATOR

	MSB															LSB
Bit number	A15	A14	A13	A12	A11	A10	A9	A8	A7	A6	A5	A4	A3	A2	A1	A0
Contents	—	—	—	—	a15	a14	a13	a12	a11	a10	a9	a8	a7	a6	a5	a4
		a3	a2	a1	a0	a1	a0									a3
		a2	a1	a0	d0	a0	d0									a2
		a2	a0	d0	a2	d0										a1
		a0	d0	d1	a1	d1										a0
		d0	d1	a3	a0											d0
		d1	d2	a2	d0											d1
		d2		a1	d1											d2
		d3		a0	d3											d3
				d0												
				d1												
				d2												
				d3												

FIGURE 3.9.
Reverse CRC-16 bit-combining chart after four shifts.

DATA BITS

	MSB							LSB
Bit number	D7	D6	D5	D4	D3	D2	D1	D0
Contents	—	—	—	—	—	—	—	—

CRC ACCUMULATOR

	MSB															LSB
Bit number	A15	A14	A13	A12	A11	A10	A9	A8	A7	A6	A5	A4	A3	A2	A1	A0
Contents	—	—	—	—	—	—	—	—	a15	a14	a13	a12	a11	a10	a09	a08
		a0	a0	a6	a5	a4r	a3	a2	a1	a0	a0					a0
		d0	d0	d6	d5	d4	d3	d2	d1	d0	d0					d0
		a1	a1	a7	a6	a5	a4	a3	a2	a1						a1
		d1	d1	d7	d6	d5	d4	d3	d2	d1						d1
		a2	a2													a2
		d1	d2													d2
		a3	a3													a3
		d3	d3													d3
		a4	a4													a4
		d4	d4													d4
		a5	a5													a5
		d5	d5													d5
		a6	a6													a6
		d6	d6													d6
		a7														a7
		d7														d7

FIGURE 3.10.
CRC-16 bit-combining chart after eight shifts (duplicates cancelled).

For non-reversed CRC algorithms, the message byte combines only with the high-order bits of the existing accumulator. The new CRC accumulator is simply the CRC of the combining value XORed with the original low-order byte of the accumulator.

SO WHAT?

Although the historical relationships among the bits are interesting in themselves, it is unlikely that you can perceive their absolute worth, for they are here presented completely out of practical context. In fact, I offer them here solely as background reference to assist in writing table-driven CRC software generators in Chapter 19. I defer further discussion of the subject until then.

CHAPTER 4

Information Transfer

The previous chapters dealt with what asynchronous communication is, how it evolved, how to do it, and errors that can occur during it. This chapter looks at how the medium can be used to transfer information from one place to another intact. The first portion of this chapter deals with *flow control*: procedures to prevent overwhelming the receiver with unexpected or improperly formatted data. Here, we discuss flow-control *procedures* in which regulation of the flow of data is the responsibility of the sender and flow-control *protocols* where sender and receiver cooperatively control the flow of data. In the second portion, we turn our attention to the more complicated topic of *file-transfer protocols* where sender and receiver together not only regulate the flow of traffic, but also assure the accuracy of the data.

Flow Control

Before communications can begin, a *physical communications link* must be established. This link may take the form of a simple cable connecting a computer to its CRT, it may consist of two computers exchanging data over the telephone network with modems, or it may be a radio-telemetry conversation between two space satellites. Regardless of how simple or how complicated the physical link, there is no guarantee that the receiver is unconditionally able to accept the sender's data. Consider a few examples:

- You are sending characters to a printer. To compensate for the computer's capability of sending characters faster than they can be printed, the printer thoughtfully provides a few bytes of buffer storage where characters can wait their turn to be printed. When the buffer becomes full, the printer output becomes garbled.

- Your microcomputer is reading bytes from the communications line and storing them one-by-one onto a floppy disk file. Even though your operating system buffers the characters for you, sooner or later it must perform a physical write to the floppy. During the eternity required to write to the floppy, bytes are lost.

● You wish to transmit a file to a mainframe that treats all data as if it were created by human fingers; bytes arriving faster than humans can type are mysteriously lost.

These are all examples of a need for *flow control*: the modification of the amount or rate of transmitted data based upon the needs or responses of the receiver. The modifications may be as simple as performing the data transfer at a slower data rate or as complicated as wholesale reformatting of the outgoing data to match that of the receiver.

Software Flow-Control Procedures

As the previous examples clearly illustrate, flow control is not necessarily an aberrant situation but a fact of everyday life. Every time you press Ctrl-S (or Ctrl-NumLock on the IBM PC) to pause a screen listing, you have participated in flow control by signaling the computer that it is overwhelming a peripheral device (you) with data. Hardware devices such as printers, plotters, and (to a lesser degree) video terminals inevitably require flow control. This often takes the form of voltage changes on the pins of the serial interface connector. This is *hardware flow control*, which we examine more closely in Chapter 5. Where a physical connection between the communicating devices is impossible (such as over a modem) or when hardware flow control is not supported, *software flow control* is necessary.

Flow control between identical computers and operating systems is usually no problem, because both obey the same set of rules. But very special kinds of flow-control problems confront the programmer trying to *upload* (transmit) or *download* (receive) data between operating systems or hardware devices that possess fundamentally different concepts about I/O. We will now look at a few common types of serial I/O problems that you are likely to encounter.

The most important thing to keep in mind when dealing with foreign systems, especially large timesharing computers, is that responsibility for character I/O is usually relegated to auxiliary input hardware equipment, simply called *a communication front-end* (the IBM Model 3705, for example). These devices, which actually qualify as small computers themselves, gather input from the communications lines and package it according to the rules of the system. Incoming characters are stored in a buffer until the buffer is full or until a designated *logical terminator* character (usually a CR) is detected in the input. When the front-end signals the computer that input is ready, the computer empties the buffer as soon as it can.

During the input procedure, incoming data may be altered. The alterations may be performed by the communications front-end during receipt of the characters or by the computer itself through its device-controlling subroutines, or *device drivers*. On virtually every system, one or more of the following functions is performed on the incoming data:

- Translation of control characters to printable equivalents.
- Uppercase or lowercase translation.
- Truncation of lines that are too long.
- New line translation: converting CR to LF (or vice versa) or inserting CR before an LF (or vice versa).
- Ignoring ("swallowing") control characters. Although any given system may consider any character to be "hot," most discard NUL and DEL, which are characteristically used as *device padding*, or time-wasting characters sent to accommodate slow devices such as printers.
- Imparting special meaning to control characters, especially DC1, DC2, DC3, and DC4.
- Acting upon primitive command line editing control characters, especially NAK (Control-U), CAN (Control-X), and ESC.
- Transmitting a copy of the received character (possibly modified as just described) back to the sender. This function, known as *echoplexing*, is available only on full-duplex systems.

On some systems it may be possible to enter a raw mode to disable most of this preprocessing of the character stream, but on some systems it isn't. To complicate matters, systems often apply one set of rules to a console device but another set of rules for I/O performed by applications programs.

The method of communications-line access also varies from one system to another: half- or full-duplex, or half-duplex over full-duplex channels. Mercifully, half-duplex systems are becoming increasingly rare. Because a system's "plex" is exclusively a hardware concern, it is addressed in Chapter 5.

Character-by-Character Flow-Control Procedures

The purpose of listing these characteristics is not to provide a compendium of computer idiosyncrasies—such a list would be endless—but to emphasize how hostile one environment can be to characters originating in another. As you enter these battlefields, bear two mottos on your shield: "Assume nothing!" and "Forewarned is forearmed."

INTERCHARACTER DELAY

Before the modern video terminal was developed, interactive keyboard input was generated on teleprinters. The operator could either send characters to the computer directly from the keyboard or could punch them into paper tape for automatic uploading. Input systems designed during this stage of technology have been amazingly slow to die. Other systems, such as the DEC-system 2060, were simply designed to receive characters at a rate slightly higher than humans can type. This is not a design flaw so much as shortsightedness, but it clearly poses problems when uploading data, even at the modest rate of 60 cps. Although these problems can usually be cured by lowering the raw communications (data) rate, it is not always possible to do so, especially on dial-up lines, where only one or two modem speeds may be available. Even where it is possible to use a slower speed, the choice is not necessarily a good one. A system that can accept data at a rate of only 60 cps, for example, will certainly be overwhelmed by 120 cps (assuming a 10-bit SDU) but may perform perfectly at 55 cps. Stepping down to the next lower standard modem data rate of 30 cps would unnecessarily reduce throughput by almost 50 percent.

A fixed delay introduced between characters, often referred to as *pacing*, is a much better solution than reducing the signaling rate because it enables the sender to customize the data rate to the system in question. Using the previous example, then, how much delay would be required? Assuming a 10-bit SDU, the time required to transmit characters at 55 and 120 cps is

$$55 \text{ char/sec} = 1 \div 55 = .01818 \text{ sec/char}$$
$$120 \text{ char/sec} = 1 \div 120 = .00833 \text{ sec/char}$$

The difference between the two rates,

$$\frac{\text{Message} \oplus \text{Remainder}}{\text{Divisor}} = \text{Quotient}$$

or approximately 10 milliseconds (.01 second), is the amount of intercharacter delay that must be added to slow 120 bps to 55 bps.

Intercharacter delay is a valuable tool, but it is a successful flow-control technique only if it is individually tailored for each system. Moreover, the same delay is not always effective. On time-sharing systems, periods of heavy usage can bog down the input response of an ordinarily fast system to a few tens of characters per second; during such cases of severe loading, the system may accept no input at all for several seconds. Clearly, intercharacter delay is useless if the system remains insensitive to input for periods longer than the delay interval.

ECHO-WAIT

The problem with intercharacter delay as a flow-control method is that the sender does not interact with the receiver. The transmission of the next character is in no way related to the successful reception of the previous one. A transfer performed without feedback between sender and receiver to confirm the receipt of data is called a *one-sided* or *blind transfer* (or even "send and pray"). A two-sided transfer requires that the receiver respond in some way to the receipt of the data.

Most full-duplex systems echo input immediately back to the sender. Some systems provide echo to the user's console by default (but not always to the user's programs). When transferring data to an echoplex system, the system's echo can be used as a form of feedback between characters. After each character is transmitted, the sender enters a time-limited loop, awaiting the return echo from the receiver. If no echo arrives within a certain amount of time (the *timeout interval*), the sender retransmits the same character until an echo arrives. When the receiver fails to echo a character after several retransmissions, the software may react in several ways.

The first response is simply to send the next character anyway. Recall that many systems quietly swallow certain characters, especially control characters that are likely to be disruptive to system operations. For example, NUL and DEL traditionally are not echoed by systems that use them for device padding. Automatically transmitting the next character prevents a transmission from getting stuck if the data contains a hot character or if an error transforms an otherwise acceptable character into a hot character. After several timeout errors in succession or a large total of timeout errors indicate that the transfer may be seriously flawed, the system should give you the opportunity to terminate the transfer or simply to abandon the echo-wait and proceed with a blind transfer.

Reverting to a blind transfer may sound like a foolish response, but under certain circumstances it can be very useful. Although it is unlikely, you may learn after beginning the transfer that the receiving I/O channel is not full-duplex. Thus, the option of switching to a blind transfer is essential for dealing with systems that provide echo only to the user's console, but not to other communications channels.

Comparing the original character to the echoed character is a crude test for errors during transfer. Because a character may be damaged during the return echo portion of its voyage (when it doesn't matter), however, the number of errors reported will be about 50 percent too high under ideal circumstances. In addition, some systems do not echo an exact copy of their input (CR may be echoed as CRLF, for example).

Line Flow Control

Although character-by-character flow control is effective in the right environment and under the right circumstances, there are several conditions under which it cannot be employed at all. On half-duplex systems, for instance, the time required to reverse the communications line (see Chapter 5) between each character is prohibitively long in comparison to the time required to transmit a single character.

The success of character-by-character flow control depends upon a single, dubious assumption: the receiver's echo proves that the character has been received. This assumption is decidedly false on systems that process input as lines, or, to use a more pretentious term, *logical records*. On such a system, characters are gathered into a buffer until a delimiter (a CR or LF, for example) is encountered, at which time the system accepts the entire buffer with one gulp. Such systems differ in the details of managing the input buffer. One point of difference is the system's response to a full buffer. Some respond by playing dead: ignoring the input and turning off echo; others ignore the input but echo a BEL character to alert the sender that something is amiss. A few systems, however, have a most insidious response: they ignore the incoming character but continue to return the echo as if all were well.[1]

Transmitting data to line-oriented systems such as these can be treacherous. At the minimum, the sender must assume that the data contains end-of-line delimiting characters often enough to empty the receiver's input buffer before it becomes full. If the data does not contain delimiters at the correct intervals, the sender must insert them; if the sender's data contains delimiters of the wrong kind, the sender must translate its delimiters to those of the receiver. As you see, the list is endless.

INTERLINE DELAYS

On many systems, even inserting the correct delimiters at the correct intervals does not guarantee a successful transfer. During periods of heavy usage, some systems take an inordinately long time to empty the buffer after receiving the correct delimiter. During this period, the system loses bytes that come on the heels of the previous line. Historically, the sender solves this problem by padding every line with a few NULs (usually), thus giving the receiving system time to empty its buffer. The same effect can be achieved more efficiently by adding a slight delay after transmitting each delimiter.

Flow-Control Protocols

The flow-control measures discussed so far are just *procedures*: they assume that the sender has intimate, detailed knowledge of the receiver's ordinary response to arriving data. In each case, the sender adjusts one parameter—pace, end-of-line delimiter, and so forth—based upon prior knowledge about the receiver. Although such procedural techniques can be quite effective, they are haunted by the prospect of uncertainty—namely, is enough known about the way the receiver behaves? Flow-control procedures based upon timing are inherently unreliable due to the number of variables in the receiver's delay mechanism. For example, any of the following changes may cause a change in the receiver's timing: an increase in the number of users or jobs, installation of new device drivers, and changes in hardware (especially communications front-ends). In short, purely procedural flow-control techniques that worked perfectly yesterday may fail today.

The alternative to procedural flow control is *cooperative flow control* in which sender and receiver agree upon and observe a common set of rules to govern the exchange of data

---

[1] It is interesting how the design of an input system reflects the designer's view of human nature.

between them. The term ordinarily applied to these rules is *protocol*.[2] Echo-wait flow control is sometimes erroneously described as a protocol, presumably because the sender's behavior is dependent upon the receiver. This definition is incorrect: although the sender shows a good-natured willingness to cooperate, the receiver is oblivious. Remember, the two ingredients that transform a procedure into a protocol are *cooperation* and *agreement*, both of which are metaphorically implied in the informal name for a protocol, *hand-shaking*.

Flow-Control Protocols for Hardware Devices

So far, the transferring of data has been discussed almost as if it were exclusively the province of computers. As noted earlier, many computer systems are designed to operate without any flow control whatever on their input. Hardware devices such as printers, plotters, and, to a lesser degree, video terminals, however, inevitably require flow control. Often, this takes the form of voltage changes on the pins of the serial interface connector. We will examine this hardware flow control more closely in Chapter 5.

Where a physical connection between the communicating devices is impossible (such as over a modem) or when hardware flow control is not supported, software flow control is necessary. That is, instead of signaling by means of control wires, they make known their intentions by sending data over the communications line.

Character Protocols

The most popular (or at least the most famous) character flow-control protocol is known as *XON/XOFF*. Here, the sender and receiver assign special meaning to two characters, which are then inserted into the stream of data as flow control markers. These characters are given the functional names XON and XOFF, and their actual identity varies from system to system. By far, the most common assignment is DC3 (Control-S) for XOFF and DC1 (Control-Q) for XON.

The receiver sends the XOFF character when it wishes the sender to pause in sending data, and an XON character when it wishes the sender to resume. (XOFF is often referred to as the *holdoff* character, and XON as the *release* character.)

---

[2]Through the childish behavior of diplomats, the word now connotes "superficial etiquette," but its Greek roots refer to the table of contents affixed to a treaty. Whatever its real meaning, "protocol" is so often misapplied that it is in danger of becoming too misleading for technical use. As usual, the culprit is the trade press, which appears willing to sacrifice accuracy in the name of its war on what it calls "computerese." It is quite common, for example, to read that START, STOP, and parity bits are protocols, when in fact they are encoding parameters. Even the ASCII character set is sometimes called the "ASCII protocol." The moral is: be wary of things called protocols.

XON/XOFF HIGH JINKS

XON/XOFF is so uncomplicated that it seems foolproof so long as both sender and receiver respect the protocol. Nevertheless, many an unsuspecting computer user has been perplexed by a transfer that stopped midstream for no apparent reason. To illustrate this, let's look at a real-life example—one that occurred while sending the manuscript for Chapter 2 of this book through a UNIX electronic mail system. The sender was an IBM PC AT microcomputer using the XON/XOFF "UPLOAD" option in the TERM program developed in the programming chapters of this book. The data was in the form of an MS-DOS text file created with the WordStar word processing program. The UNIX console driver was adjusted to XON = DC1, XOFF = DC3, and echo was enabled.

The UNIX command cat > test.tmp received the incoming text into a file named test.tmp. After only a few characters, the transfer stalled and could not be restarted. On successive attempts the transfer always stalled in the same spot, so that point in the file was examined using the MS-DOS debugger DEBUG. The following box shows the printed version of the text around the failure point and the debugger's display.

Text Around the File's Failure Point and How It Appears in the Debugger

"…outdated language associated with the subject tends to obscure an important quality—the technology's almost childlike *simplicity*. Students of serial technology are often taken aback to discover that the underlying principle, like most computer topics, is…"

```
0A 6F 75 74 64 61 74 65-E4 20 6C 61 6E 67 75 61   .outdate. langua
67 E5 20 61 73 73 6F 63-69 61 74 65 E4 20 77 69   g. associate. wi
74 E8 20 74 68 E5 20 73-75 62 6A 65 63 F4 20 74   t. th. subjec. t
65 6E 64 F3 20 74 EF 20-6F 62 73 63 75 72 E5 20   end. t. obscur.
61 EE 20 8D 0A 8D 0A 69-6D 70 6F 72 74 61 6E F4   a. ....importan.
20 71 75 61 6C 69 74 F9-AD 2D 74 68 E5 20 74 65    qualit..-th. te
63 68 6E 6F 6C 6F 67 79-27 F3 20 61 6C 6D 6F 73   chnology'. almos
F4 20 63 68 69 6C 64 6C-69 6B E5 20 13 73 69 6D   . childlik. .sim
70 6C 69 63 69 74 79 13-AE 20 20 8D 0A 8D 8A 53   plicity.. ....S
74 75 64 65 6E 74 F3 20-6F E6 20 73 65 72 69 61   tudent. o. seria
EC 20 74 65 63 68 6E 6F-6C 6F 67 F9 20 61 72 E5   . technolog. ar.
20 6F 66 74 65 EE 20 74-61 6B 65 EE 20 61 62 61    ofte. take. aba
63 EB 20 74 EF 20 64 69-73 63 6F 76 65 F2 20 74   c. t. discove. t
68 61 F4 20 8D 0A 8D 0A-74 68 E5 20 75 6E 64 65   ha. ....th. unde
72 6C 79 69 6E E7 20 70-72 69 6E 63 69 70 6C 65   rlyin. principle
AC 20 6C 69 6B E5 20 6D-6F 73 F4 20 63 6F 6D 70   . lik. mos. comp
75 74 65 F2 20 74 6F 70-69 63 73 AC 20 69 F3 20   ute. topics. i.
```

Note: To simplify automatic right-column justification, WordStar marks the last character in each word by setting its high-order bit. Because there is no ASCII equivalent for the resulting bytes, DEBUG displays them as a period. These high-order bits are stripped off by some mainframe front-ends.

The failure point in the file was always within the first three characters of the word *simplicity*. Looking closely, we see that *simplicity* is bracketed by two 13H bytes. Experimentation revealed that WordStar uses DC3s (generated with the keystrokes Ctrl-P Ctrl-S) as internal markers for the beginning and end of underscoring.[3] But why do XOFFs in the outgoing data stream hang the transfer? After each byte the TERM program looks on the incoming communications line for an XOFF character. Meanwhile, UNIX busily echoes each byte it receives. When TERM sends the DC3 preceding *simplicity*, UNIX innocently echoes it. TERM, not recognizing the stream of characters on its input as its own echo, detects the echoed XOFF and promptly goes into a loop awaiting an XON. The XON, of course, never comes.[4] Disabling the console echo (with the command stty -echo) before beginning the transfer solved the problem.

There is one important variation to the XON/XOFF protocol: instead of defining XON as a single character, the receiver accepts any character as a signal to resume transmission. Used in an echoing environment, this variant, which is generally found only on video terminal drivers, enables a human user to stop and start screen output with a single key. When a nonhuman receiver uses this style of XON/XOFF, however, the sender occasionally seems to ignore an XOFF. To understand why, visualize this: the sender transmits the letter 'A', and at exactly the same instant the receiver sends an XOFF. When the sender receives the XOFF, it ceases transmission and awaits an XON. Meanwhile, after sending the XOFF, the receiver immediately receives and echoes the letter 'A', which was already in the pipe. The sender regards this echo of its own 'A' as its "any character XON" and immediately begins to transmit. Although this problem can be partially alleviated by building a delay into the code that senses the XON, the only certain remedy is turning off echo at the receiving end.

Whole-Line Protocols

Earlier we discussed how an end-of-line delay must be used when sending data to systems that accept input a line at a time. Like all flow controls that rely upon delays, this one is easily upset by minor variations in the receiving system's timing. A better solution is a protocol in which the sender appends a delimiting character to its data then waits for the receiver to request another line by sending an acknowledgment character. Because computers are so individualized in their concept of I/O, there is an almost endless variety of these *prompted upload protocols*. I will therefore discuss only the most common one, the *ETX/ACK protocol*, which has its roots in IBM's VM/370 hybrid[5] upload protocol. Reflecting their ancestry in half-duplex communications, the two protocol characters are often referred to as the *outbound* and *inbound turnaround* characters. The sender transmits an ETX after each line of data and immediately begins a wait for the receiver's ACK (acknowledgment), which is also implicitly a request for the next line.

---

[3] It is impossible to say whether this incredibly bad choice was the result of naivete or stupidity.

[4] This problem is known as the Godot Syndrome.

[5] See Chapter 5 for a discussion of half-duplex protocols over a full-duplex communications line.

FILE-TRANSFER PROTOCOLS

We have examined flow control at the level of single characters and lines. A larger, far more complicated kind of protocol governs transfer of arbitrary blocks of data. Although used for a variety of applications in synchronous communications, block protocols in asynchronous communications are usually found only in programs that transfer entire files. In this context, they are referred to as *file-transfer protocols* (FTPs).

In virtually every asynchronous file-transfer protocol used on microcomputers, the basic unit of transfer is the *packet*, a grouping of various byte-elements or *fields*. Only one of these fields contains the file data, however; the remaining fields, known as *service fields*, contain the information required for the receiver to verify that the packet is error-free. The number and purpose of the control fields vary from protocol to protocol, but in general most contain a *packet-signature field* (usually beginning with an SOH byte), a packet-sequence number, a data field, and a checkvalue. Aside from differences in the number and kinds of fields, there are also many variations in the protocols that define how the packets are exchanged.

Automatic Repeat Request (ARQ) Protocols

The most common type of packet protocol is the *automatic repeat request* (ARQ) in which an error detected in a received packet or an unacknowledged packet automatically results in the retransmission of that packet. There are several types of ARQ protocols.

Send-and-Wait ARQ

During transmission, data from the file is "packetized" by surrounding it with the service fields. An entire packet is then transmitted blindly (with no flow control), after which the sender waits for the receiver to acknowledge its receipt.

The receiver inputs the packets and, after verifying that the packet is in the correct sequence relative to the previous packet, computes a local checkvalue on the data portion of the packet. If the local checkvalue matches the one in the packet, the receiver acknowledges by sending an ACK; otherwise, the receiver negatively acknowledges with a NAK (both ACK and NAK are considered acknowledgments). The ACK and NAK may actually be in the form of entire packets instead of single characters. Upon receipt of an ACK, the sender transmits the next packet; if a NAK is received, the same packet is transmitted again. Transmission proceeds in this manner until the entire file has been transferred.

The diagram in Figure 4.1 oversimplifies the process somewhat. We tend to forget that this is a two-way conversation and that the receiver's acknowledgments are just as susceptible to damage as the packets themselves. Consider the following scene: the receiver inputs and verifies a packet, sends an ACK, then proceeds to input what it expects to be the next packet in the sequence. Somehow, though, the receiver's ACK never reaches the transmitter who, after an appropriate timeout interval, obligingly retransmits the same packet. To prevent a duplicate block of data, the receiver must recognize that it has received the same block twice. How does the receiver get back on track? Simply by ignoring the packet and sending another ACK.

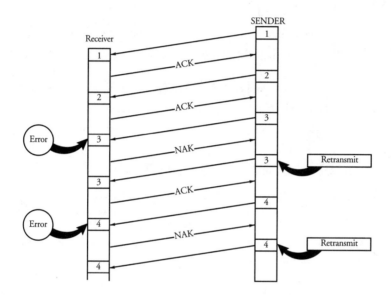

FIGURE 4.1.
Send-and-wait ARQ.

Continuous ARQ

In a continuous ARQ protocol, the transmitter does not pause after each packet but transmits several packets in a row (the packet group). The receiver examines each packet and, as in send-and-wait ARQ, sends an acknowledgment (ACK or NAK) based upon the content. In this case, however, the packet's number is included along with the acknowledgment. During transmission, the sender continually examines the stream of acknowledgments returning from the receiver and keeps track of the packets that are received in error. After the entire group of packets has been transmitted, the sender then retransmits the ones that contain errors.

There are two methods for retransmitting the erroneous packets. In *continuous ARQ with fallback*, the first packet number received in error and every subsequent packet in the group are retransmitted. In *continuous ARQ with selective repeat*, only the actual packets containing errors are retransmitted.

Despite the send-and-wait protocol's obvious inefficiency (it was originally a half-duplex protocol) it is the most common file-transfer protocol found on microcomputers, including the two discussed later in this chapter. Continuous ARQ protocols, also known as *windowing* protocols, have never become popular on microcomputers because they require substantially more computer resources and programming skill than the simpler send-and-wait protocols. For example, both continuous methods require that both sender and receiver buffer the entire packet group (window) in memory at one time.

Packets

The number of packet designs is unlimited, but their most obvious differences lie in the manner in which the DATA field is delimited within the packet. There are three basic approaches:

● Marking the beginning and end of the DATA field with control characters
● Including the length of the DATA field in the packet
● Using a fixed-length DATA field

The Control Character Delimited Packet

The simplest form of packet is that used for transferring strictly *textual data*: the file is expected to contain only ASCII plain-text—the alphanumeric characters plus the six control characters defined as Format Effectors (BS, HT, LF, VT, FF, and CR). The other control characters may not appear in the DATA field, but they may appear in other fields. Figure 4.2 shows a hypothetical version of such a packet.

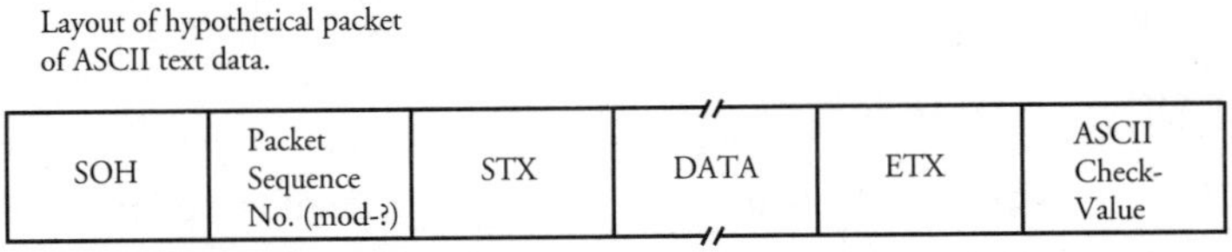

Layout of hypothetical packet of ASCII text data.

FIGURE 4.2.

The layout of a hypothetical packet for transfer of text files.

SOH	Packet Sequence No. (mod-?)	STX	DATA	ETX	ASCII Check-Value

SOH   (Start of Header) This control character marks the beginning of a packet. This is the official purpose in ASCII.

Packet Sequence Number   The next byte describes the packet's position in the current transfer. Its purpose is to enable the receiver to verify that the packet received is the one expected. To achieve this goal, it is not necessary to know the packet's absolute position in the overall transfer (which may be a huge number), but merely its relative position in a limited sequence of packets. Accordingly, this field is usually limited to a single byte and, in some cases, the sequence

	number may be confined to a few significant bits of the field. This is expressed in the label "Packet number modulo-?." In simple send-and-wait ARQ protocols, the sequence field can even be modulo-2: "this" packet or "that" packet. If all 8 bits of this field are significant, the packet number is calculated modulo-256; 6 bits are modulo-64, and so on.
STX	(Start of Text) This control character marks the beginning but is not part of the textual data.
DATA	This contains the textual data.
ETX	(End of Text) This control character marks the end but is not part of the textual data.
CHECKVALUE	The redundant byte(s) used for error checking. To preserve the ASCII character of the protocol, the checkvalue may be represented with ASCII digits.

The data in an STX/ETX-delimited packet may be of variable length, although the penalty of retransmitting a very long packet dictates that the maximum length of the packet should be short. Packet lengths for popular protocols range from 64 to 512 bytes. Regardless of its length, the receiver knows that the data begins at the byte after the STX byte in the packet and ends with the byte before the ETX byte.

Text-only protocols are necessary in some mainframe environments where the programmer cannot control the communications lines directly. These systems may use the high-order bit for parity (or may even arbitrarily toss it altogether). Despite their rigorous ACSII format, text-only protocols are not portable across operating systems because each system processes input and output differently. The STX/ETX protocol, for example, does not work on a system that swallows or translates these characters as described early in this chapter.

Size-Field Delimited Packet

When communicating between computers that have absolute control over the communications lines—and this includes microcomputers—the use of a binary packet makes more sense. Because binary files may contain any 8-bit value, the DATA field cannot—as the text packet can—be delimited with control characters. The alternative, as Figure 4.3 illustrates, is to include the size of the DATA field in the packet. The size field, labeled LEN, is the number of bytes in the DATA field. The number of bytes allotted to the length field limits the number of bytes that can be sent in one packet; a 1-byte length field, for example, limits the DATA field to 256 bytes.

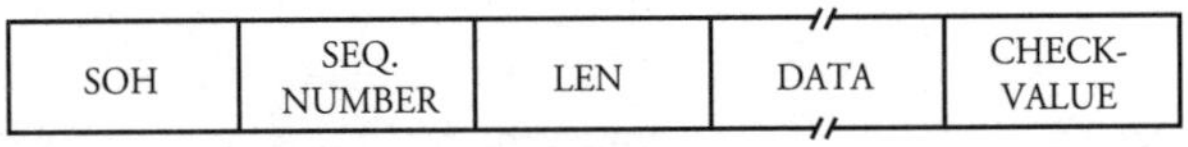

FIGURE 4.3.

The layout of a hypothetical packet for transfer of binary files.

SOH	SEQ. NUMBER	LEN	DATA	CHECK-VALUE

The Fixed-Length Data Field Packet

The third type of packet simply assumes a fixed length for the DATA field. If this seems like a reasonable approach, it has one major drawback: there is no way to send a *short packet.* A short packet is necessary whenever the original file's length is not evenly divisible by the fixed block size chosen. In other words, at the end of file transfer, there are probably not enough bytes in the file to fill an entire packet. The final packet therefore contains some non-file data: either garbage bytes or a padding byte specified in the protocol. In any case, because a file created by a fixed-length protocol likely contains one or more garbage bytes at the end, it is not an exact copy of the original. This brings up the subject of *invertibility:* if a file is transferred from one system to another, then back again, the recovered version on the first system should be identical to the original. The destination system can alter the file during its residence there, but must reverse (invert) the changes during retransmission.

Protocols with fixed-length DATA fields create inherently non-invertible files. The extra bytes at the end of the file often affect the file's utility or serviceability. Utilities that rely upon the number of bytes in a file as given in its directory entry (TYPE, for example) find the garbage bytes as well. At first thought, one would think that executable files would be unaffected by superfluous bytes appended during transfer. Suppose, though, that you write a program that relies upon indexing from the end of a file. Calculations based upon these indexes would be incorrect if the file contains extra bytes. The popular XMODEM protocol, to which we now turn our attention, is a good example of a protocol that uses fixed-length DATA fields.

The XMODEM Protocol

The XMODEM file-transfer protocol was composed in 1977 by Ward Christensen, a programmer who has contributed many useful programs to the public domain. (In honor of his effort, the protocol is frequently referred to as the Christensen Protocol.) Christensen released into the public domain his file-transfer protocol surrounded by an extremely basic terminal emulator program simply called MODEM (and later MODEM2). Public domain hackers promptly added multifile transfer capability and a multitude of smart terminal features. In this enlarged form, the program acquired the name MODEM7, which persists today in the form MODEM7*xx*, where *xx* is the current version number. The protocol is so widely known and so popular that scarcely a communications program now comes to market for microcomputers without support for XMODEM.

Technical Description of XMODEM

XMODEM is a simple send-and-wait ARQ protocol using a fixed-length data field. The checkvalue is a single-byte arithmetic checksum. Because CRC and multifile transfer were added later and are not actually part of the Christensen protocol, I will deal with them separately. Figure 4.4 shows the layout of the XMODEM packet. All fields except DATA are 1 byte in length.

SOH	Packet Sequence No.	1's Complement of Packet Sequence No.	DATA (128 bytes)	Arithmetic Checksum

FIGURE 4.4.

Layout of Christensen's XMODEM packet.

SOH	The Start-of-Header byte announcing the first byte in the packet.
Packet Sequence	The current packet number, modulo-256. The number of the first packet is 1.
1s Complement of Packet Sequence	The 1s complement of the current packet number in the previous field.
DATA	The length of the DATA field is fixed at 128 bytes. There are no restrictions upon the content: data may be binary or text.
Arithmetic Checksum	A 1-byte arithmetic sum of the content of the DATA field only, modulo-256.

XMODEM Send

As in all protocols, the sender's job under XMODEM is considerably simpler than the receiver's. Figure 4.5 shows a flow chart of the transmission portion of the protocol.

START-UP PHASE

The first task in any protocol must be the establishment of contact between sender and receiver. One side always assumes the dominant role in this phase. The XMODEM protocol is said to be *receiver-driven*: the receiver is responsible for stimulating and maintaining the flow of packets. Accordingly, the transmitter's role in the *start-up* or *synchronization* phase of the transfer consists of patiently waiting for a NAK from the receiver. When the first NAK arrives, the sender interprets it as "send the first packet." Arrival of the initial NAK ends the start-up phase.

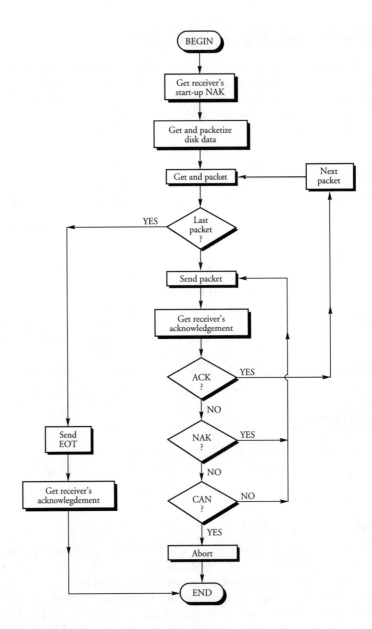

FIGURE 4.5.
XMODEM send.
Timeouts and giveups
are not shown.

MIDDLE PHASE

Once the sender receives the start-up NAK, it packetizes a 128-byte block of file data, transmits it, and waits for the receiver's acknowledgment of the just transmitted packet. An ACK from the receiver means that the packet was received without error and is interpreted as an implicit request for the next packet; a NAK requests retransmission of the same packet; a CAN unconditionally terminates the transfer.[6] When no more file data is left to send, the middle phase of the transfer is completed.

ENDING PHASE

If the middle phase ends normally, the sender transmits a solitary EOT (End-of-Transmission) to inform the receiver that no more files are forthcoming. The receiver acknowledges the sender's EOT with an ACK. An orderly shutdown follows: files are closed, memory is freed, and so forth. If the middle phase ends abnormally—with a CAN (abort) from the receiver, for example—no EOT is sent.

XMODEM Receive

It is the receiver's job not only to input the packet, but also (based upon the information contained in the service fields) to verify that the packet just received is the one expected and that it contains no errors. The XMODEM receiver therefore has much more to worry about than the transmitter. Figure 4.6 shows a flow chart of the receiver portion of the protocol.

START-UP PHASE

Aside from housekeeping chores (allocating buffers, opening files, and so on), the receiver's start-up phase consists entirely of sending a single NAK to announce its readiness to receive packets.

MIDDLE PHASE

The receiver now enters the receive loop: waiting for a packet and sending a NAK if none arrives in 10 seconds. The arrival of an SOH signals the arrival of a packet, which the receiver evaluates as follows:

1. Although a packet is formally identified as starting with an SOH, a solitary EOT byte in its place is interpreted as a sign that there are no more packets and the middle portion of the transfer ends.

2. The integrity of the packet sequence number is checked. In other words, the receiver makes certain that the second and third fields are not corrupted. Typically, this is accomplished by complementing one of the two packet-sequence fields and XORing it with the other. A result of 0 means that neither of

---

[6]Despite Christensen's protests, a CAN is used for this purpose in every known implementation.

the fields is damaged. If not identical, the receiver sends a NAK to request retransmission and loops back to await retransmission of the same packet.

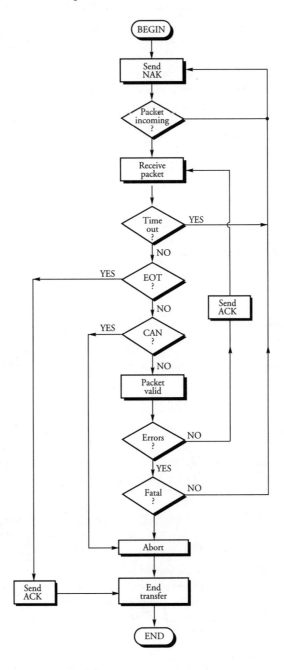

FIGURE 4.6.

XMODEM receive.
Only packet timeout
is shown.

3. Next, the receiver makes certain that the sequence number is the one expected. In general, if the packet sequence number is incorrect, something dreadful is wrong. Because there is no method for the receiver to recover from a sequence error, a CAN is sent to abort the transmission and the transfer ends. There is a single exception to this behavior. If the packet sequence number is the same as that of the previous packet, the receiver assumes that the sender never got the ACK for that packet. The receiver simply ignores the redundant packet, sends another ACK to get the transmitter back in sync, and loops back to await the next packet.
4. Finally, the receiver calculates an arithmetic sum (modulo-256) of the DATA field only and compares it to the checksum field of the packet. If the two agree, the receiver sends an ACK; if they do not agree, the receiver sends a NAK.

END PHASE

If the receiver's transfer ends normally, it performs an orderly shutdown: closing files, freeing memory, and so forth. If no errors occur during shutdown (a disk I/O error, for example), an ACK is transmitted to acknowledge the sender's EOT, and the transfer is concluded.

XMODEM-CRC

The XMODEM protocol had not been in the public domain long before a version appeared that employed a 2-byte CRC instead of Christensen's single-byte arithmetic checksum.[7] The layout of the XMODEM-CRC packet shown in Figure 4.7 is identical to that of the original XMODEM packet except for the additional byte for the enlarged value.

SOH	Packet * Sequence No.	1's Complement of Packet Sequence No.	DATA (128 bytes)	CRC**	
				high byte	low byte

* First packet is 1

** CCIT polynomial

FIGURE 4.7.
Layout of the XMODEM-CRC packet.

XMODEM uses a non-reversed CRC algorithm with the CCITT divisor polynomial $X^{16} + X^{12} + X^5 + 1$. The remainder (CRC) generated is the same as the remainder from performing polynomial division on a message with sixteen 0 bits appended. The bit-order of the bytes is not reversed before feeding them to the CRC-generating function. The high-order byte is transmitted before the low-order byte.

[7]It is unclear who is responsible for this enhancement. Although Christensen himself seems to credit John Mahr, most versions contain a note that the CRC was designed by Paul Hansknecht of Bloomfield Hills, Michigan.

START-UP UNDER XMODEM CRC

Although the CRC packet is only slightly changed, the start-up protocol is considerably altered to maintain compatibility with earlier versions that do not support CRC versions of XMODEM. Figure 4.8 provides a flow chart of the XMODEM-CRC receiver. Besides the obvious differences of a larger packet and the CRC checkvalue, the receiver's start-up protocol is also altered. A receiver desiring to use XMODEM-CRC sends the letter 'C' as an initial synchronization byte instead of the NAK used by the checksum version of XMODEM. Do not confuse the sync byte with the acknowledgment—both checksum and CRC variants always send NAK for a negative acknowledgment.

No flow chart is given for the sender under XMODEM-CRC. The sender has only to look for the 'C' at start-up instead of a NAK, to be prepared for the longer packet, and, of course, to perform the local CRC calculations on the packet's data.

CRC/CHECKSUM HYBRIDS

Most public domain derivatives of MODEM7 incorporate both CRC and checksum versions of the protocol. Under the assumption that during start-up a checksum-only sender will not respond to the CRC sync character, the receiver alternates between sync characters: a 'C' for CRC and, after 10 seconds of no response, a NAK for checksum. The transfer takes place in the mode whose sync character elicits a packet from the sender. For reasons we will explore in Chapter 18, under certain conditions these hybrid programs can establish incorrect synchronization. When this occurs, the two parties attempt transfer under different checkvalue protocols—a doomed effort.

Timeouts

Timeouts are a very important part of any protocol, where their function is to prevent the program from getting hung up if an expected event does not occur. In fact, timeouts must be built into any section of the program that waits for input from the communications line. For example, the flow chart in Figure 4.8 shows a receiver timeout after the box "Receive packet." This timeout guarantees that a NAK is sent if an expected packet does not arrive (or if only a partial packet arrives). Software usually maintains a count of timeouts, giving the user the opportunity to cancel a transfer that moves along haltingly.

Here are the timeout rules for XMODEM as published by Christensen:[8]

1. The receiver has a 10-second timeout while waiting for a packet to arrive. A NAK is sent after each timeout.

2. While receiving a packet, the timeout interval for each character is 1 second.

3. In keeping with the concept of a receiver-driven protocol, the sender should not use a timeout when waiting for a synchronization (start-up) byte. (Most XMODEM implementations have a timeout here.)

---

[8]As described in an open letter dated 1/1/82, downloaded from Christensen's bulletin board in Chicago.

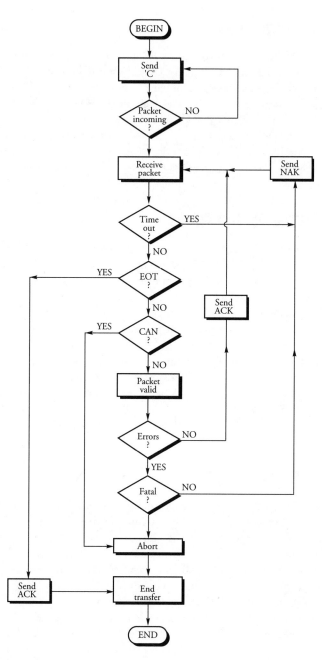

FIGURE 4.8.

Flow chart of a receiver under XMODEM-CRC.

4. Once the transfer begins, the sender should use a single 1-minute timeout. This gives the receiver ample time to perform any necessary disk I/O before sending its ACK, NAK, or CAN.

5. All timeouts (and errors) are retried at least ten times.

XMODEM Problems

Because of the XMODEM protocol's grassroots origins in the public domain, there is a tendency to wax sentimental about it. In fact, as Christensen would doubtless agree, XMODEM has all the earmarks of midnight basement hacking. Had Christensen been writing for public consumption or if he were appointed to revise it today, the XMODEM protocol would doubtless be quite different. Examining the shortcomings of the XMODEM protocol is instructive, not as an exercise in dead-horse-beating, but to gain insight into the problems that inevitably arise when a protocol is not designed with foresight or, as in this case, is pushed too far.

DUAL PACKET-SEQUENCE FIELDS

The XMODEM protocol transmits the packet sequence number in two forms: the first is the actual packet number, modulo-256; the second is the 1s complement of the first. This redundancy is difficult to justify, but it appears to stem from a desire to pinpoint the precise nature of packet-sequence errors. When the receiver finds an error in the first packet number, it must ascertain if the byte itself is bad or if a numbering error actually exists (for which there is no recovery). Comparing the packet number with an inverted copy of itself is not, in fact, a very robust method because, due to the bursty nature of errors, there is a high probability[9] that an error affecting the first byte will also affect the second. A greater degree of certainty could have been achieved with a single packet sequence field included in the checkvalue calculation. The integrity of the sequence number would then be checked as part of the ordinary checkvalue procedure; if no checkvalue error occurred, the receiver would simply test the packet-sequence field to make certain that it was the packet expected.

FIXED-LENGTH DATA FIELD

As discussed earlier, a file created by a protocol with a fixed-length DATA field contains an exact image of the original file only if the original file's length is an even multiple of the DATA field length. Otherwise, the new file will contain superfluous bytes. In general, the presence of useless bytes at the end of non-executable text files causes no problem—the system loads the file, extra bytes and all, into memory. However, on some systems, especially multitasking ones, executable files contain a block of additional data that contains detailed information used by the system to load the program into memory. In most cases, the system can calculate the size of an executable file based upon the information in this *load header*, which contains both the length of the executable portion of the file and the length of the header itself.

---

[9]At 1200 bps on the public telephone network, about one-fourth of all errors affect more than 8 bits.

If the actual size of a file (as reported by its directory entry) differs from the size given in the header, the system can justifiably decline to load or execute it. This problem, caused by applying XMODEM in an environment for which it was not designed, has produced a wealth of modified versions of XMODEM with names like "Extended XMODEM" and "Enhanced XMODEM." In most cases, these modifications consist largely of somehow including the file's actual size in the protocol.

XMODEM AMBIGUITIES

There are several ambiguities in the XMODEM protocol: its behavior is not clear under some circumstances. Here are three:

- Exactly how is a transfer terminated? In most programs, including those in Chapter 18, receiving a CAN where an ACK, NAK, SOH, or EOT is expected cancels the transfer. Yet Christensen himself (in the letter quoted earlier) recommends against this practice, warning that "a single 'abort' character makes the transmission susceptible to false termination due to an ACK, NAK, or SOH being corrupted into a CAN and canceling transmission."

- Once all records have been sent and the last packet has been acknowledged, the sender transmits an EOT. The receiver acknowledges with an ACK. What is the receiver's negative response: a NAK or a CAN? Under what circumstances would the receiver not send an ACK? Is a disk I/O error on the final disk write grounds for not sending an ACK?

- Is the sender expected to be ready to transmit immediately after receiving the start-up NAK? For example, should the transmitter perform preliminary disk I/O (file opening, reading, buffer filling, and so forth) before initiating start-up?

Multifile XMODEM

The Christensen protocol is just that: a protocol. It knows nothing about other *layers*[10] of activity involved in the file-transfer process. In a simple modem linkage, for example, there are several layers that the file-transfer protocol knows nothing about:

1. The hardware layer, RS-232 interface
2. The method of tone-signaling or modulation employed by the modem
3. The sending and receiving systems' definition of a file
4. The storage media at either end of the transfer

---

[10]The concept of layers is embodied in the International Standards Organization's (ISO) reference model for Open System Interconnect, a topic for another book.

The user, or more precisely, the system, is responsible for assigning a filename and making sure that the file is properly opened, read from or written to, and then closed at the end of the transfer. Although typing filenames does not require much effort, it quickly becomes boring when there are many files to transfer. It is not surprising, therefore, that most file-transfer protocols contain provisions for transferring more than one file at a session.

Designing a multifile layer to a protocol requires no earthshaking skill. Let's quickly concoct a multifile version of XMODEM. For unknown reasons, Christensen chose to give the first packet the number 1 instead of 0. This is actually quite handy: we will commandeer packet 0 for use in multifile transfers. How? When the receiver sees that the first packet is numbered 0, it knows not only that it is engaged in a multifile transfer but also that this *herald* (initialization) packet contains important information about the file: its name, its size, perhaps its contents, whether it is read/write, and so forth. Only the meaning of packet-sequence number and the DATA field of a herald packet differ from an ordinary packet; the functions of the other fields—SOH, 1's complement of the sequence number, and checkvalue—are unchanged. For flexibility and portability, the DATA field is pure ASCII: all numerical data is expressed as ASCII numerals, not as binary values. One field in this contains the number of files in the transfer. Of course, we will leave several fields "reserved."[11]

Our imaginations could go on, but the point here is that if the XMODEM protocol itself is a bit myopic, there is a kind of primitive elegance to it. Each part seems to fit well with the overall design. With a little thought, a multifile extension of the protocol can be designed that integrates well into the basic XMODEM way of doing things. Instead, the multifile version of XMODEM is a cluttered, amateurish kludge with which Christensen is wise to disavow any connection. Because of its poor design and its complete incompatibility with the original single-file version, it all but precludes further extension of the protocol.

Figure 4.9 shows the flow chart for the XMODEM multifile protocol. The sender waits for the receiver to send a synchronizing NAK. Once the NAK is received, the sender transmits an ACK followed immediately by the first character of an 11-character filename. The filename must be in the MS-DOS (CP/M) format: 8 characters in the base name with an optional extension of 3 characters. Both name fields are right-padded with spaces (20H, for example) with no period delimiter. All filename characters must be in uppercase and their high-order bits must be 0.

---

[11]A popular extension of XMODEM, named YMODEM, employs a herald packet much like the one described here.

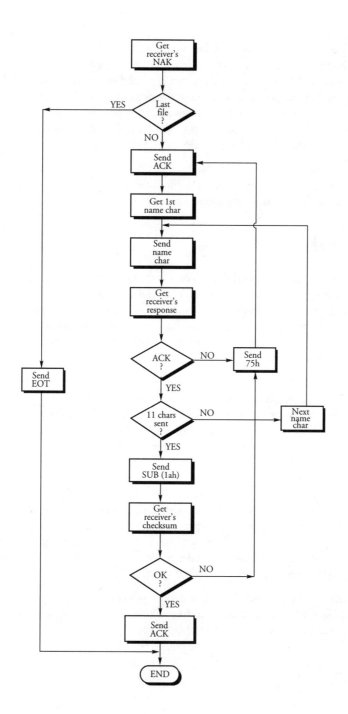

FIGURE 4.9.

Flow chart for XMODEM multifile protocol.

The receiver ACKs each character in the name. If an ACK does not arrive within the timeout period, the sender transmits a 75H (the letter 'K') and the process starts anew. After all 11 characters in the filename have been transmitted, the sender transmits a SUB (1AH) to signal the end of the filename. The receiver responds to this "EOF" by sending a 1-byte arithmetic checksum that, oddly, includes the 1A byte itself. If the receiver's checksum does not agree with the sender's, the sender sends a 75H and the process recommences. If the checksums agree, the sender transmits an ACK and the ordinary XMODEM protocol takes over.

To signal that there are no more files in the multifile transfer, the sender transmits an EOT in place of the first filename character.

Kermit

Although this book focuses on the subject of serial communications as found on microcomputers, we will now take a brief look at a protocol that makes almost no assumptions about the nature of the computer on which it runs. This study of a protocol with a more generalized design is offered as an intellectual antidote to the hopelessly parochial XMODEM protocol, whose structure is inextricably wedded to the narrow system from which it sprang.

Even if XMODEM had been designed with the utmost generality it would still have been a distinctly microcomputer protocol. That is, it would have made the one assumption that characterizes software written for microcomputers: that a single program has absolute and undeniable control over all of the system's resources. On larger computers (or on multiuser or multitasking micros) this assumption does not hold true. For example, one cannot predict whether the asynchronous I/O channel provided by the system can be adjusted to the 8-bit, no parity format required for the transmission of binary files. Also, as I have repeatedly noted, most operating systems somehow process control characters in the serial input stream. To make matters more complicated, the channel assigned to the user's terminal may have one set of characteristics whereas an auxiliary channel opened under program control may have quite different characteristics. The goal of the Kermit[12] protocol is to circumvent such hardware and system dependencies altogether, to become the Esperanto of file-transfer protocols.

Kermit comes from Columbia University where it was written by Frank Da Cruz and Bill Catchings in 1981. The protocol is in the public domain for noncommercial use. Both a technical and a user's manual are available from:

---

[12]Despite the sophomoric efforts to come up with a technical-sounding phrase from which to backform an acronym, Kermit remains just the name of the famous frog.

Columbia University Center for Computing Activities
Kermit Distribution
7th Floor, Watson Laboratory
612 West 115th Street
New York City, NY 10025

Anyone seriously contemplating composing the Great American Protocol would do well to acquire and study these Kermit manuals—they are textbook studies in software design.

In an effort to maintain portability between systems, no matter how dissimilar, Kermit is almost painfully general in its approach to file transfer. As the authors describe it:

The Kermit file-transfer protocol is intended for use in an environment where there may be a diverse mixture of computers—micros, personal computers, workstations, laboratory computers, timesharing systems—from a variety of manufacturers. All these systems need have in common is the [capability] to communicate in ASCII over ordinary serial telecommunications lines.

Kermit was originally designed at Columbia University to meet the need for file transfer between our DECSYSTEM-20/ and IBM 370/-series mainframes and various microcomputers. It turned out that the diverse characteristics of these three kinds of systems resulted in a design that was general enough to fit almost any system. The IBM mainframe, in particular, strains most common assumptions about how computers communicate.

—*Kermit Protocol Manual,* New York: Columbia University, April 1984, p. 3.

The Kermit Protocol

Although Kermit is much too complex (not to say complicated) to treat exhaustively here, we can at least look at its grand design and how it pursues its lofty goal of portability.

The "basic" Kermit is a send-and-wait ARQ packet protocol: the sender transmits a packet, then awaits the receiver's acknowledgment of the packet. The receiver can either request the next packet (ACK) or retransmission of the previous packet (NAK). At this level, Kermit is fundamentally quite similar to the XMODEM protocol. There are several important areas of difference, however:

- Kermit oversees an entire file-transfer session that may include any number of files. As we discussed earlier, XMODEM is a single-file transfer onto which is kludged an ugly and poorly designed mechanism for transferring multiple files.

- Kermit makes only minimal assumptions about the serial I/O channel over which the transfer occurs; namely that the channel is capable of sending and receiving all printable ASCII characters (characters in the range 20H – 7E). It also requires that the system be able to send and receive an SOH control character.

- Packets may be of variable length.

- Several types of packets are defined.
- The receiver's responses must consist of entire packets, although these packets may be empty. (In XMODEM, responses are single characters.) The presence of SEQ fields in the ACK and NAK packets makes possible a continuous ARQ version of Kermit.
- The sender and receiver negotiate important operating parameters such as device padding, metacharacters, and so forth. This negotiation takes place through an exchange of herald packets at the beginning of the session.
- The name of the file is included in the protocol.
- The herald packets make the protocol *extendible*: new features and capabilities can be added without affecting the behavior of earlier versions.

Figure 4.10 shows a rough block diagram (not a complete flow chart) for transfer under the Kermit protocol. Although not depicted, the receiver's response (ACK and NAK packets) must be fetched after every transmission. Start-up takes place as in XMODEM—by the receiver sending repeated NAK (packets) until the transmitter responds by sending a herald packet, which in Kermit is called a *send-initiate* (or simply *send-init*) packet. The herald packet contains the sender's preferred settings for certain important communications parameters. As shown in the chart, the receiver makes its own preference (or agreement) known by including them in its ACK packet. Next, the name of the file is transmitted in a special FILE HEADER packet; when the receiver sends its ACK, it may optionally include in the packet the name under which it is storing the file.

The transfer proceeds under the ARQ rules until the entire file is transferred. The sender then transmits a special end-of-file packet. If there are more files to transmit, it sends the file header packet for the next file. When all files have been sent, the sender transmits an end-of-transmission packet to signal the end of the session.

As you can see, there is nothing earthshaking about the design of Kermit's outer layer. The main differences lie in the details of implementation. Its most interesting characteristic stems from its minimalistic view of the transmission line. Because it expects control characters and possibly even non-ASCII characters to be somehow transformed by the transmission medium, Kermit converts such high-risk characters to a safer form.

Control Character Encoding in the Kermit Packet

The Kermit packet, shown in Figure 4.11, comprises six fields. The contents of the DATA field, which may be of variable length, vary with the packet type; in a "data" packet, this field contains a portion of the contents of the file being transferred. The Kermit manual refers to the other, non-DATA fields as "control fields." This term is dangerous because of the erroneous semantical implication that these fields contain ASCII control characters. To avoid this confusion, which would prove deadly in the discussion that follows, I will continue to use the term *service field* to describe Kermit's non-DATA fields.

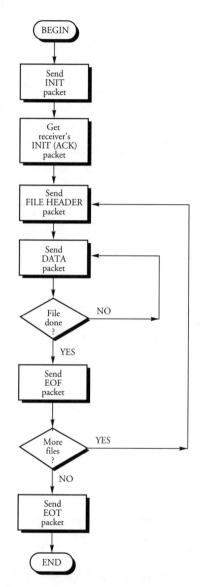

FIGURE 4.10.
A block diagram of a Kermit transmission.

Each service field consists entirely of ASCII characters (0–128) and, with the exception of the MARK field, printable ASCII characters in the range 20H–7E (i.e., SP to $NC). Although the DATA field may contain non-ASCII (i.e., 80H–FF) characters, all ASCII characters must be printable. Because the Kermit protocol so heavily relies upon printable ASCII, we must discuss the manner in which the information in the fields is encoded before we discuss the meaning of the fields themselves.

We have already noted how operating systems inevitably process, translate, or swallow control characters. Because the console is usually the most heavily processed and filtered

I/O channel in any system, Kermit's stated worst-case design goal is to effect file transfers from an ordinary user's terminal. A problem exists, though: if control characters in the I/O channel are liable to be abused by the system, how can we protect the packet? Suppose, for example, that Kermit packets were to arrive with an SEQ (packet-sequence number) of 0A. What would prevent the system from treating it as a Line Feed? (A UNIX console driver would probably expand it to a CRLF *pair*.) The solution is to convert high-risk characters to printable characters before transmission.

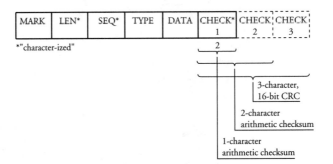

FIGURE 4.11.

The Kermit packet.

CONTROL CHARACTERS IN SERVICE FIELDS

The system doesn't know that the service fields contain numerical information. From its point of view, a byte in the range (0–20H, and 7F) is a control character and therefore fair game for processing. The solution, for which we will use the tongue-in-cheek name *character-ization*, is quite simple: control characters are promoted to printable form before transmission with the char function:

```
char(x) = x + 20H
```

and transformed back again after reception with the unchar function (*de-character-ization*):

```
unchar(x) = x - 20H
```

In this way, a byte of numerical data in the packet becomes printable by elevating it two sticks in the ASCII table. An ETX (3) byte becomes '#', an LF (0AH) becomes '*', and so on. Fields encoded in this way are noted in Figure 4.11 with an asterisk.

Unfortunately, if the char function is applied to characters greater than 5F, the resulting character is greater than FF and therefore no longer an ASCII character. The actual limit is 5E because 5F becomes a DEL, itself a control character. For this reason, the numerical data in the service fields in Kermit can be no larger than 94 (5EH).

CONTROL CHARACTERS IN DATA FIELDS

The control characters problem clearly exists in a more serious form in the DATA field. Because a file may legitimately contain any byte, we cannot limit the DATA field in the packet to 5E. Therefore, control characters cannot be encoded merely by promoting them to printing status with the char and unchar functions. Instead, a printable character (nanogram, '#', by default) is actually inserted ahead of the control character, which is then XORed with 40H.[13] This technique, dubbed *prefix encoding* in the Kermit manual, is analogous to C's use of the reverse slant (backslash \) to impart special meaning to certain characters within a string. As in C, a literal occurrence of a prefix character is "escaped" by a duplicate of itself. Thus, "#1" is encoded as "##1."

As an example of Kermit's prefix encoding of control characters, let's look at two lines created in WordStar's non-document format:

```
M   a   r   y   █   h   a   d           a   █
4D  61  72  79  20  68  61  64  0A  0D  61  20  13

l   i   t   t   l   e           l   a   m   b   .
6C  69  74  74  6C  65  13  0A  0D  6C  61  6D  62  2E  0D  0A
```

Note that WordStar uses DC3 (13H) bytes to begin and end the underlining of the word *little* and the CRLF pairs at the ends of both lines. Kermit would transmit the line like this:

```
M   a   r   y   █   h   a   d   #   M   #   J   a   █   #   S
4D  61  72  79  20  68  61  64  23  4D  23  4A  61  20  23  53

l   i   t   t   l   e   #   S   #   M   #   J   l   a   m   b   .   #   M   #   J
6C  69  74  74  6C  65  23  53  23  4D  23  4A  6C  61  6D  62  2E  23  4D  23  4A
```

This elevates control characters to ASCII rows four and five and prefixes them with nanograms.

High-Order Bit Encoding in Kermit's DATA Field

In many systems, the data format of the serial communications line is a system-wide constant. In such installations, a program often has no way to control the data format. If the system happens to be a 7-bit parity system, the transfer of 8-bit binary files is obviously impossible without some form of encoding.

---

[13]Kermit defines the ctl() function for use only where control characters are expected:

```
ctl(x) = x XOR 40H
```

XORing with 40H is preferable to adding 40H because the former preserves the high bit. As an added bonus, no unctl function is required because the XOR makes the function self-inverting:

```
ctl(ctl(x)) = x
```

The manual refers to successive calls of ctl() as *controlification*.

A byte with a TRUE high-order bit is subjected to a similar prefix encoding as control characters; namely, a printable character (a '&' is recommended) is inserted and the byte is ANDed with 7F to make it printable. Let's look at the same file created in WordStar document mode where the high-order bits denote a word or character that is marked for line reformatting. A file containing the line

> Mary had
> a little
> lamb.

literally contains

```
M   a   r           h   a
4D  61  72  F9  A0  68  61  E4  8D  0A  E1  A0  13

l   i   t   t   l   e           l   a   m           .
6C  69  74  74  6C  65  13  8D  0A  6C  61  6D  E2  2E  0D  0A
```

in which bytes with TRUE high-order bits are those greater than 7F. Kermit transmits this file like this:

```
M   a   r   &   y   &   ■   h   a   &   d   &   #   M   #   J   &   a   &   ■
4D  61  72  26  69  26  20  68  61  26  64  26  23  4D  23  4A  26  61  26  20

#   P   l   i   t   t   l   e   &   #   M   #   J   l   a   m   &   b   .   #   M   #   J
23  50  6C  69  74  74  6C  65  26  23  4D  23  4A  6C  61  6D  26  62  2E  23  4D  23  4A
```

Notice that the "soft" carriage return (as 8D is called in WordStar) must be subjected both to control character prefixing and high-order bit prefixing. A single 8D byte is thus transmitted as three ASCII characters: &#M.

Repeat-Count Encoding in Kermit's DATA Field

The expanding of control characters and bytes with high-order bits can result in a huge increase in overhead. This penalty is worst in a binary file, in which the overhead is more than 75 percent.[14] To reduce this high overhead on binary files, and to some degree on text files as well, Kermit provides a simple compression scheme called *repeat-count prefixing*. A designated character (the $NC is recommended) signals the beginning of a repeat-count sequence. Next comes a "character-ized" numerical count argument itself, followed immediately by the character to repeat.

---

[14]Assuming that all 256 possible bit combinations are distributed evenly in a file,

33 x 2 = 66	(0-20H, and 7H) control charaters expand to 2 bytes.
95 x 2 = 190	(A0-FE) high-bit bytes expand to 2 bytes.
33 x 3 = 99	(80H-9F, and FF) require both kinds and expand to 3 bytes.
95 x 1 = 4	Escapes for prefix characters.
454	

When 256 bytes expand to 454 the result is an overhead of 198 bytes, or 77 percent.

For example, the sequence below repeats the letter 'X' eleven times.

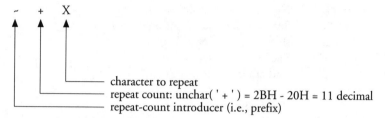

Because of the limitations on the range of the char functions, repeat counts cannot exceed 94. When repeat-count, control-character, and high-order prefixing appear in a single expansion expression, the repeat count has the highest precedence followed by the 8-bit prefix, the control-character prefix, and the data character itself. I will not pursue the topic of precedence further because copious illustrations of this hierarchy are given in the Kermit Protocol Manual.

Fields in the Kermit Packet

Now that we understand the various ways in which Kermit transforms the meanings of characters, let's quickly examine the meanings of the fields in the packet shown in Figure 4.11.

MARK   This is the start-of-packet signature byte, SOH. This is the only canonical control character permitted in the packet: its value is a 1. Why is a control character permitted in this field? Because they do not appear anywhere else in the packet, a bona fide control character makes a good packet-signature byte. The authors of Kermit chose the SOH byte because of their observation that SOH, unlike other control characters, passes through most operating systems unchanged.

LEN   This is the number of bytes in the packet following this field. In other words, the total packet length minus two. This field is character-ized, which limits total packet length to 96.

SEQ   This field contains the character-ized packet sequence number, modulo-64. Sequence numbering begins with the first packet transmitted, the 'S' packet. Its starting value is 0 and it resets to 0 after 63.

TYPE   This single, literal (unencoded) ASCII character identifies the type[15] of the packet as follows:

---

[15]Kermit also defines a server mode in which it acts as an unattended host. This feature, which will not be discussed further, uses 'C' and 'G' packets to pass commands and responses between the local and remote systems.

'D'	Data
'Y'	Acknowledge (ACK)
'N'	Negative acknowledge (NAK)
'S'	Send initiate (exchange parameters)
'B'	Break transmission (EOT)
'F'	File header
'Z'	End of file (EOF)
'E'	Error
'T'	Reserved
'X'	Display text on screen
'A'	Attribute

We will discuss some of these in more detail shortly.

DATA   The content of this field varies with the packet type. In a 'D' (data) packet, it contains data from the file being transmitted, but in an 'F' (file header) packet it contains the name of the file. In some packet types, it contains nothing.

Whatever the type, all characters must be prefix encoded. Prefix encoding of high-order bits and repeat-count encoding are optional.

CHECK   This is the packet checkvalue and includes the LEN and SEQ fields, but not the MARK. The default checkvalue is a single-character arithmetic checksum, but a 2-byte arithmetic checksum or a 3-byte, 16-bit CRC are optional. To compensate for the lost accuracy incurred by encoding with char(), bits 6 and 7 are extracted and added back to the low-order 6 bits before encoding. This odd-looking technique assures that all 8 bits participate in checkvalue calculation. If x is the arithmetic sum of the packet, then

```
check = char((x + ((x AND C0)/40H)) AND 3F)
```

Types of Kermit Packets

Before we look at the interesting way various packets are used, let's straighten out yet another linguistic ambiguity. The *Kermit Protocol Manual* speaks of empty packets and blank packets. These are never satisfactorily defined. An *empty packet* is defined as a packet whose LEN indicates that no characters are in the DATA field. An empty single-byte checksum packet, for example, contains a LEN argument of 3, or, in its character-ized format, '#'. When the Kermit manual uses the term "blank" it is referring to a *non-empty* packet whose DATA field contains one or more ASCII SP characters.[16]

---

[16]"Blank" and *space* are often used interchangeably. See the warning in Chapter 1, "The Specials."

Some types of packets always contain information in their DATA fields. A 'D' packet, for example, always contains data from the file being transmitted (otherwise, it would be a 'Z' (EOF) packet). Conversely, some packets always have an empty DATA field (the 'Z', for example). Still others may have an empty DATA field only some of the time. The ACK packet, for example, is normally empty, except when it is responding to an 'S' (Send-init) or 'F' (File Header) packet.

With these preliminary details out of the way, we will now look at some of the packet types, their contents, and uses.

THE 'S' (SEND-INIT) PACKET

This is the most interesting of all the packets. It functions to inform the receiver of the sender's preferences with regard to several important communications parameters. The SEQ number of the 'S' packet is 0. Its DATA field is structured as shown in Figure 4.12. Because sender and receiver exchange this information, personal pronouns are used to help distinguish sides.

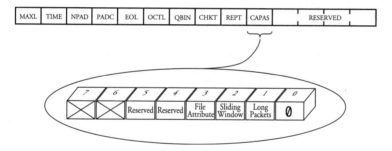

FIGURE 4.12.

The DATA field of an 'S' (Send-initiate) packet.

MAXL   The maximum packet size I can receive (character-ized). This enables the two sides to allow for small buffers, poor-quality transmission lines, and so on. Default: none.

TIME   The maximum number of seconds you should wait for a packet before timing out (character-ized). This adjusts for habitually slow systems or networks. Default: none.

NPAD   The number of padding characters you should send before each packet. This gives half-duplex systems time to switch from receive to transmit mode or vice versa (character-ized). Default: 0, no padding.

PADC   The identity of the padding character, usually a NUL or a DEL (controlified). Default: NUL. (This field is ignored if NPAD is 0.)

EOL   The character I need to terminate a packet. Line-oriented systems do not fetch the packet from their buffers unless the packet is followed by the system's line terminator. (Most systems that require a terminator accept a CR.) This character is not part of the packet (does not figure in the LEN or CHECK fields), but rather is appended to the packet at transmission. Unfortunately, no mechanism exists to state that no terminator is needed, as is the case on single-user microcomputers. This field is character-ized, not controlified. Default: CR.

QCTL The prefix character I will use in control-character encoding (literal). Default: #.

The following fields are optional: they do not have to be present on a "minimum" Kermit.

QBIN The prefix character I will use in high-bit encoding (literal). Only characters in the range 21H–3F or 60H–7F are permitted. Instead of specifying a character, a 'Y' or an 'N' can be used to indicate willingness to participate in high-bit prefixing. Default: SP—don't do high-bit prefixing.

CHKT The type of checkvalue to use: '1' for single-byte arithmetic, '2' for 2-byte arithmetic, and '3' for CRC. Default: '1', single-character arithmetic.

REPT The prefix character I will use in repeat-count encoding (literal). Only characters in the range 21H–3F or 60H–7E are permitted. An SP here indicates that no repeat-count encoding is to be done.

CAPA This is the "Advanced Capability" field: a bit mask of unspecified length organized as a linked list of bytes (character-ized). Linkage between bytes is achieved by placing a 1 in bit 0 to indicate that another bit-mask byte follows; a 0 in bit 0 therefore indicates the end of the linkage chain.

Only the first 6 bits are significant in each byte, so only 5 Capabilites can be mapped to each byte. Bits are allocated from MSB to LSB, starting at bit 5. Support for a Capability is indicated by a 1 in its assigned bit.

Bits 5 and 4 are reserved. Bit 3 marks support for Attribute packets. Bit 2 indicates the capability to use a continuous ARQ ("sliding window" in Kermitese) protocol instead of the usual send-and-wait ARQ. Bit 1 supports packets greater than 94 bytes in length. Any list of option bits is certain to become outdated almost as soon as it is published. For a complete listing, consult the current official Kermit documentation.

Because of the linkage among its bytes, the CAPAS field can expand to occupy the entire 94-character DATA field. The capability to add new Capabilities to the end of the CAPAS field enables each site to customize its own Kermit without fear of colliding with preexisting Capabilities.

THE 'Y' (ACK) PACKET

When the receiver wishes to accept a packet, it sends a 'Y' (for "yes") packet. This must be a fully constructed packet, complete with SEQ, LEN, and CHECK fields. Although the DATA field of a 'Y' packet is usually empty, it can contain the receiver's response to the sender's packet. The 'Y' packet in response to an 'S' (Send-init) packet, for example, contains the receiver's initial configuration data in the same format as the DATA field of an 'S' packet.

THE 'F' (FILE HEADER) PACKET

This contains the name of the file being transmitted. To avoid clashes with *metacharacters* (characters with special meaning or powers) on the destination system, the name should be limited to digits and upper-case alphabetical characters (30–39H, 41H–5A). A single period (2E) is also permitted. Although there are no restrictions on length, the name should contain no device or system information such as drive identifier or path.

When the receiver ACKs with a 'Y' packet, its DATA field may optionally contain the filename under which the file is stored on the destination system.

THE 'N' (NAK) PACKET

When the receiver wishes to reject a packet, it sends an 'N' (for "no") packet. This must be a fully constructed packet, complete with SEQ, LEN, and CHECK fields. Its DATA field packet is ordinarily empty.

THE 'D' (DATA) PACKET

The DATA field of this packet contains data from the file being transmitted. Like all DATA fields, control characters must be prefix encoded. If both sides agree in their initial exchange of parameters, this field may also contain high-order bit and repeat-count prefixing.

THE 'Z' (EOF) AND 'B' (EOT) PACKETS

The transmitter sends a 'Z' packet when each file has been entirely transmitted. The transmitter sends a 'B' (for "break") packet when all files have been transmitted. In both cases, the receiver responds with a 'Y' (ACK) packet.

THE 'E' (ERROR) PACKET

Both sender and receiver send error packets when either encounters a fatal error. There is currently no way to send informational or warning messages.

THE 'A' (ATTRIBUTE) PACKET

The capability to receive an 'A' packet is one of only three "advanced capabilities" currently defined in the CAPAS field of the Send-init packet. This is the medium for passing auxiliary, usually system-dependent information about the file being transmitted. These "attributes" include file size (in Kilobytes), contents (text, binary, image, etc.), date, time, path, security and access information (password, protection level, etc.), computer and operating system of origin, and type of encoding (ASCII, EBCDIC, hexadecimal, and so forth).

A Sample Kermit Session

After what must seem an eternity of explanation, let's now snoop on the communications line during a Kermit transfer session. The line numbers in the left column are for reference only and are not part of the conversation. To make the contents of the transfer completely clear, the sample uses the ASCII symbol [0-1] for SOH and ▌ for SP. A brief description of the packet traffic is at the right, and a discussion of the interesting and important points follows.

	A Kermit File Transfer[17]	
1	¬) ▌SH(▌@–#^	Send-init
2	¬) ▌YH(▌@–#%	ACK (with receiver's parameters)
3	¬ +!FMOON.DOC2	File header
4	¬ #Y?	ACK for file header
5	¬ E"D▌No▌celestial▌body▌has▌required▌J	First packet of file data
6	¬ #"Y@	ACK of first packet
7	¬ E#Das▌m%%%uch▌labor▌for▌the▌study▌of▌its#	Second packet has errors
8	¬ ##N8	NAK for second packet

---

[17]Source: Frank Da Cruz and William Catchings, "Kermit: A File-Transfer Protocol for Universities," *BYTE* (July 1984), p. 400.

```
 9  ¬ E#Das  much  labor  for  the  study  of  its#
                          Retransmission of second
                          packet
10  ¬ ##YA                ACK of second packet
11  ¬ E$D#M#Jmotion  as  the  moon.  Since  ClaA
                          Third packet of file data
12  ¬ #$YB                ACK of third packet
    .
    .
    .
13  ¬ D"Dout  300  terms  are  sufficient.#M#JU
                          Last packet in file
14  ¬ #"Y@                ACK of third packet
15  ¬ ##ZB                EOF packet
16  ¬ ##YA                ACK of EOF packet
17  ¬ #$B+                EOT packet
18  ¬ #$YB                ACK of EOT packet
```

1. Send-init

The first packet in the sample Kermit session above contains the sender's settings for the parameters given in Figure 4.12. Let's analyze this packet completely.

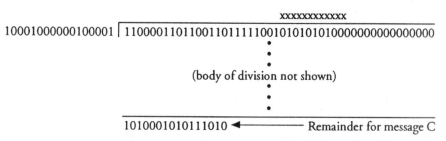

The checksum is calculated according to the formula given on page 120:

```
16C + (16C/C0) = 16C + 2 = 16E
16C + (16C/C0) = 16C + 2 = 16E
16E AND 3F = 3E
char(3E) = 5E
5E = '^'a
```

2. ACK (with Receiver's Parameters)

The receiver responds with a 'Y' packet, whose parameters agree with the sender. Notice that neither high-bit prefixing nor repeat-count prefixing is in effect. The SEQ field contains the sequence number of the packet being ACKed:

```
unchar(SP) = 0.
```

3. File Header

The filename is transmitted in the DATA field of an 'F' packet.

4. ACK for File Header

The DATA field of this packet is empty, but could contain the name under which the file was stored on the receiving system.

5. First Packet of File Data

Notice that the first packet of file data has the sequence number 2. In accordance with the MAXL field negotiated in the Send-init packets, the DATA contains only 32 (20H) characters.

7. Second Packet of Data Has Errors

An error occurred: the DATA field contains a burst of '%'.

8. NAK for Second Packet of File Data

The receiver discovers the error when the checksums don't match and sends an 'N' (NAK) packet to request retransmission.

9. Retransmission of Second Data Packet

Sender retransmits second of 'D' packets (SEQ '#').

10. ACK of Second Packet

The checksum of the retransmitted packet is valid, so receiver sends a 'Y' (ACK) packet.

15. EOF Packet

After the entire file is transmitted, sender transmits a 'Z' (EOF) packet.

17. EOT Packet

After receiver ACKs the 'Z' packet, the sender transmits a 'B' (EOT) packet to tell the receiver that the session is over.

18. ACK of EOT Packet

Receiver's ACK of the 'B' packet ends the session.

Terminating a Transfer

As we have seen, the sender manages the session and is responsible for sending 'Z' (EOF) and 'B' (EOT) packets. To terminate the current file prematurely, the sender transmits a 'Z' packet as usual but puts a 'D' (for "discard") in the data field. This instructs the receiver not to save the file. The receiver, too, may prematurely terminate the current file or the entire session by placing an 'X' or a 'Z', respectively, in the data field of a 'Y' (ACK) packet.

Kermit Extensions

Kermit is a masterly combination of imaginative conception, generalized thinking, and realistic observation. Only on the most refractory system would a Kermit implementation fail to succeed. But this portability is not without its cost. With all its encoding vestments in action, Kermit's speed resembles that of a tortoise compared with the lapin-like XMODEM protocol. Because of its inefficiency, Kermit has always been a protocol of last resort, called upon when nothing else will do.

Two extensions to the Kermit protocol, however, increase Kermit's efficiency dramatically. By relaxing many of the pessimistic assumptions about the serial I/O channel, these Capabilities, shown in the inset in Figure 4.12, are aimed directly at microcomputer users.

CONTINUOUS ARQ

As mentioned earlier, the basic Kermit protocol is a send-and-wait ARQ protocol in which the sender pauses after every packet to await the receiver's acknowledgment. Such protocols have their roots in half-duplex communications in which sending and receiving are not simultaneously possible. Kermit's "sliding window" protocol extension, on the other hand, assumes a full-duplex communications line in which a packet acknowledgment may arrive at any time, even during the transmission of another packet.

In the sliding window extension, instead of transmitting a single packet, the sender transmits a group of packets, called, for some reason, a "window." Figure 4.13 illustrates the window. As soon as the receiver acknowledges the first packet in the group (packet 'X'), the window advances (slides) and the next packet (packet X+8) is sent. The number of packets in the window is declared the first byte following the CAPAS field of the 'S' (Send-init) packets. The default window size is 8.

Within the current window, packet numbers may be acknowledged in any order. Assuming a group of 2–9, if the sender transmits packets 2–9, the receiver may ACK packets 2–6, NAK packet 7, and ACK packets 8–9. As ACKs for the first five packets arrive, the sender immediately transmits five new packets, 10–14, then retransmits packet 7. The only rule is that the sender may not advance the window beyond an outstanding ACK. If, for example, the ACKs for packets 8–9 and 10–14 arrive before the ACK for the retransmitted packet 7, the sender cannot advance the window until the ACK for packet 7 arrives. As soon as the ACK for packet 7 arrives, however, eight new packets are sent.

In normal usage, the traffic between a sliding-window sender and receiver is a constant flow of packets and acknowlededments. If the receiver is on its toes, the window never closes. Even when the window does close, the windowing procedure adds efficiency. Consider the case when a sliding window protocol is used over a packet-switching network such as Telenet. On such networks, delays between transmission and reception can amount to several seconds. During these delays, Kermit's stop-and-wait ARQ protocol would have to sit idle awaiting the acknowledgment of each packet. Under Kermit's continuous ARQ, however, the sender can transmit up to 31 packets during idle periods before pausing for an ACK.

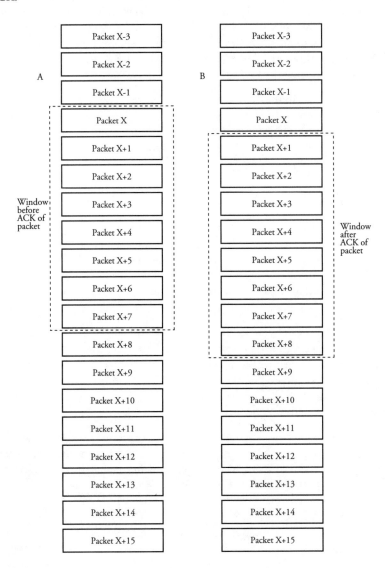

FIGURE 4.13.

Kermit's sliding window before and after receiving the ACK on packet 'X'.

LONG PACKETS

Because the number of bytes required for service fields in the Kermit protocol is independent of the length of its DATA field, the overall efficiency of the protocol is greatly improved by increasing the maximum number of bytes in a packet. As shown in Figure 4.14, 2 bytes instead of 1 are allocated to the LEN field. To make this extension easier to patch into an already existing Kermit, the original LEN field is left blank. For the same reason, the 2-byte LEN field together with a new field, HCHECK, are squeezed between the TYPE and DATA fields. To insure integrity of the enlarged header, the HCHECK ("header check") field contains a Kermit-style, single-byte checkvalue of the LEN, SEQ, TYPE, LENX1, AND LENX2 fields.

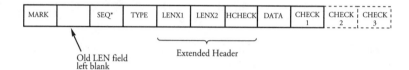

FIGURE 4.14.
Extension of Kermit's packet length.

The 2-byte maximum length of the extended data field is declared in the second and third byte following the CAPAS field of the 'S' (Send-init) packets. The 'S' packets themselves are still transferred with the basic Kermit 94-character maximum DATA fields; extended packets commence at the first 'D' packet. The maximum packet length is increased from 94 to 9,024.[18]

WHICH TO USE

Unless they are used carefully, these two extensions may turn out to be a plenitude of riches. Although both may be used simultaneously, they may work at cross-purposes. In general, the sliding window extension greatly increases Kermit's performance on full-duplex systems in which many errors or network delays are expected. The long packet extension, on the other hand, works best on half-duplex lines or when the sender and receiver are directly connected through an essentially noiseless and wait-less cable. Because of the increased time to retransmit ACKed packets, the performance of Kermit under the long packet extension is seriously affected by errors.

Although we will not create a version of Kermit in the programming section of this book, the *Kermit Protocol Manual* gives the C source code listing for a "minimum" Kermit. The *Kermit User's Guide* contains implementation and usage information for many systems.

---

[18]A further extension is proposed to extend packet length to 857,374!

Local-Link Protocols

The file-transfer protocols we've examined so far have had another name: *end-to-end protocols*. This name is significant because it suggests that the error-correction envelope is wrapped around the data from beginning to end (that is, from the sender's disk to the receiver's). This assures that errors occurring anywhere in between points are corrected.

In some applications, this womb-to-tomb guarantee is overkill. The computational resources consumed by CRC calculations and packetizing, for example, may prove onerous to background processes on heavily loaded or low-powered systems. If the vast majority of the route traveled by the data is thought to be error-free or to be susceptible only to errors of a known type, it may be architecturally more efficient to employ a simpler, less ambitious *local-link protocol* designed specifically to correct only the kinds of errors known to occur.

As an example of when such a protocol is needed, consider the case of a modem capable of delivering a very high data rate (say 57,600 bits per second) connected to a personal computer. As described in Chapter 10 on protocol modems, such modems attain such high data rates in part through data compression. They also employ their own error-correcting protocol to insure that data arrives error-free across the phone line. On the computer side, the data is quite secure once the computer's CPU has acquired it and it has been subjected to constant error checking in memory (parity) and to rigorous checking by the disk controller as it is moved to and from disk. In other words, the sole area of exposure in this connection is in the physical medium between the modem and the computer: the computer's RS-232 interface and its serial controller.

To narrow the problem down even more, we observe that only one kind of error is likely to occur in this connection. Unlike the phone line where data can be damaged by noise, cross-talk, and switching equipment, the errors that occur between the modem and computers serial ports are usually *lost data* errors caused by *input overrun*. This condition occurs when the computer's CPU cannot pluck a character out of the serial port before another arrives. When overrun occurs, the previous character is overwritten and lost, often without the high-level application software being aware that an error has occurred.

Because a serial link is not susceptible to data *corruption*, calculating a CRC or a checksum for each byte is a profligate use of CPU power. The problem, then, is to detect when bytes are lost and to ask for their retransmission.

Here are the physical assumptions for such a protocol:

- The modem's serial port is always error-free.
- The link is susceptible to data loss by input overrun.
- The link is not susceptible to data corruption.
- Regardless of the number of input overruns that occur, the most recent byte is always received correctly.

Here are the design requirements of this protocol:

● Because the modem's serial port is error-free, the protocol is needed only in the modem-to-computer direction.

● The performance of the protocol should improve if the size of the data block remains constant.

● The performance of the protocol should improve if the receiver possesses an independent means to detect overrun when it occurs.

In this protocol,[19] the sender builds the packet shown in Figure 4.15 consisting of a LEN byte containing the length of the remainder of the packet (254 or fewer data bytes) and an end-of-packet byte (EOP). To begin, the sender transmits the single LEN byte and waits for the receiver to acknowledge it. After the receiver acknowledges the LEN, the sender transmits the rest of the packet. If the receiver receives exactly the agreed-upon number of bytes and if the EOP marker is valid, the packet is acknowledged and the procedure repeats; otherwise, the receiver negatively acknowledges the packet and the transmitter retransmits the DATA and EOP fields. The flow chart for the sender is shown in Figure 4.16. The receiver's chart can be easily inferred.

LEN BYTE	DATA (0-124 bytes)	END-OF-PACKET BYTE (EOP)

FIGURE 4.15.

Local-length protocol packet.

DATA BLOCK SIZE

Using an EOP marker of ETB (ASCII 17H) indicates that the protocol will proceed as described above. To improve efficiency, however, the sender may forego the LEN-byte handshaking by using an SOH (ASCII 1) as an EOP character. This indicates that the next packet will have the same length as be the current one. This provides a mechanism for a sender to test the reliability of a link by gradually increasing the packet length, then finally enter a maximum efficiency cruise mode where packet size is highest and no handshake on the LEN byte is required.

---

[19]A protocol much like the one described here is TIA/EIA-605, Facsimile DCE-DTE Packet Protocol Standard. In that protocol, however, the LEN byte gives the number of bytes in the data field. TIA/EIA-605 was written to solve the overrun problem in facsimile modems, but it is clearly useful in other applications.

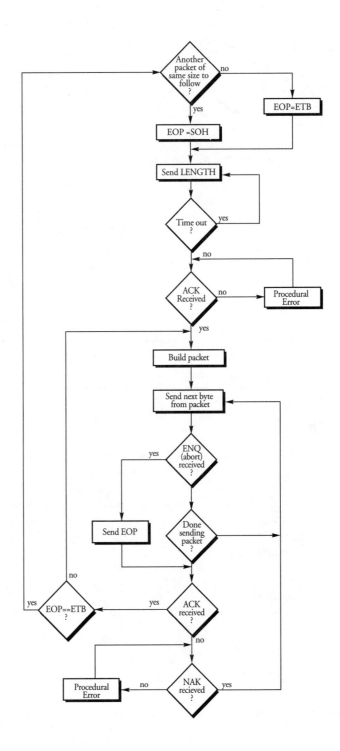

FIGURE 4.16.

Flowchart for sender side of a local link protocol.

HARDWARE OVERRUN DETECTION

This protocol discovers data loss by counting bytes. Many systems, however, can discover overruns immediately by querying the serial controller. To streamline the protocol, a receiver that detects an overrun mid-packet immediately transmits an ENQ (ASCII 5) to the sender. Upon receipt of the ENQ, the sender immediately stops transmitting and appends an EOP marker. The receiver waits for the EOP marker, then sends a NAK. The protocol proceeds normally, having been saved the overhead of completing the byte count.

Conclusion

We haven't seen the last of protocols. We return to the topic in Chapter 10, which describes how error-checking protocol are embedded directly in modems and in Chapter 11 where we examine the T.30 facsimile protocol in detail.

Modems and Modem Control

This chapter explores the fascinating topic of how computer data is transferred across ordinary telephone lines. We will examine the modem: the device that performs this technical wizardry. In the first section, we will look at some of the more technical aspects of exactly how the modem effects communications. Having arrived at a basic understanding of the principles involved, the second part of this chapter discusses how computers and related peripherals interact with modems to control their behavior. Along the way, we'll look at some of the all-too-practical problems that are likely to crop up when writing programs to control modems.

Since the first telegraph message was transmitted by Morse, telecommunications has been limited by the number of "communications lines" (wires) in existence. Due to the expense of creating and maintaining telegraph lines, even the ubiquitous telegraph found its way into only a fraction of the world's communities, and the teleprinter even fewer. Because these machines required special skills to operate, they could never be mass-marketed directly to the consumer. Consequently, the costs of these technologies were borne largely by service businesses (such as Western Union), but government at all levels provided assistance in the form of land grants, trade monopolies, and generously fixed rates.

The telephone changed this picture drastically. Here was an instrument that required no special technical skill to operate and, compared to a teleprinter, at least, was compact and physically unobtrusive. The telephone was a milestone because it was the first telecommunications product sold directly to a mass public. Driven by the consumer demand, it took only a few years for the number of telephones to exceed the combined number of telegraphs and teleprinters. In only a few more years, such a web of telephone wires was spun around the globe that today scarcely a community exists without telephone service.

While the importance of the telephone's proliferation as a cultural asset cannot be over-stated, it has another, less obvious significance. As handy as the telephone is, it does not replace printed communications. Indeed, the telephone so stimulated economic growth that the need for a telecommunications print medium was more pressing than ever. Al-most paradoxically, then, telephony resuscitated a moribund teleprinter industry, not only by increasing the demand for it, but also by providing the physical means to meet the demand. Put yourself in the place of a teleprinter mogul who, inundated with new de-mand for his product, contemplates the expense of erecting countless thousands of miles of new wires. Why invest in more wires and poles for teleprinters when the telephone company already has them?

Thus began the use of telephone lines for nonvoice communications. Today, the telephone companies rent two kinds of lines for such communications. A *public telephone line* is the ordinary voice-grade line used in residences and businesses. Because this line is routed through countless relay systems and electromechanical circuits, it is also referred to as the *public switched telephone network*, or *PSTN*. The other type of telephone line is the private line, or *leased line*. The term *private* means that the line is not subjected to the same amount of switching as the public lines and, at the lessee's option, may also accommodate a wider range of frequencies than contained in the human voice. In many, if not most cases, leased lines are actually four-wire lines consisting of two complete telephone circuits, one for traffic in each direction. Much commercial traffic is carried on leased lines, but our discussions will deal only with the public or telephone network.

Modem Fundamentals

Digital signals from devices such as teleprinters cannot be sent directly over telephone lines. Because a telephone line is intended to carry only human speech, which contains frequen-cies in the range of 200 to 8,000 Hz, its frequency response (*bandwidth*) is limited. As a matter of fact, since the goal of the telephone network is not fidelity but intelligibility, the telephone does not even reproduce voices particularly well. Figure 5.1 shows the band-width of the public telephone system.

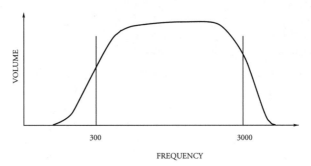

FIGURE 5.1.

The bandwidth of a public, switched telephone line.

This bandwidth limitation enormously complicates the transmission of digital pulses over the ordinary public telephone network. As I have repeatedly depicted, at some point telecommunications requires conversion of digital signals into digital electrical pulses, or bits. From the standpoint of circuit design, an instantaneous transition between the 1 and 0 states is ideal. In other words, the perfect digital signal consists of clean, sharp, square (actually, rectangular) waves with perfectly vertical sides and perfectly flat tops.

Now, a square wave can be mathematically analyzed[1] as if it were a composite of sine waves at odd multiples of its frequency. A square wave of 200 Hz, for example, can be viewed electrically as progressively smaller amounts of 600 Hz, 1,000 Hz, and 1,400 Hz, and so on. Frequencies further from that of the fundamental square wave contribute less "squareness" to the composite. To transmit an acceptably square digital signal, the communications medium must have a significantly wider bandwidth than the frequency of the square wave itself. Otherwise, the high-frequency components are stripped out and along with them the sharpness of the square waves. If the bandwidth is too narrow, then the resulting waves are not recognizably "square." At the receiver, the logic levels of the digital signal become ambiguous and communication fails. Figure 5.2 shows how a 2,000 bps signal would be deformed by progressively narrower bandwidths. Notice that the pulse becomes recognizable as a square wave only at a bandwidth of 2,500 Hz and reproduction of the wave is barely acceptable when the bandwidth is 4,000 Hz.

Modulation

The problem depicted in Figure 5.2 would occur if we attempted to transmit a computer's square waves over the voice-grade lines of the public switched telephone network. Clearly, a method is needed to convert data from square waves to a form that can pass unscathed over the telephone network. Sine waves are the best candidate because they can be easily created in a harmonically "pure" form that is less radically affected by the frequency roll-off inherent in the telephone line. The ultimate method of signaling should consist of sine waves whose frequencies are near the center of the bandwidth shown in Figure 5.1.

The process of encoding one signal with another is *modulation* and the recovery of the original signal is *demodulation*. The simplest form of modulation is *amplitude shift keying* or ASK modulation, depicted in Figure 5.3. During transmission, modulation occurs when a single sine wave tone is switched between two amplitudes (volume levels) to represent 1 and 0. In practice, one of the amplitudes is usually 0, so the modulation is attained merely by switching the tone on and off.[2] A MARK is therefore defined as the presence of a tone and a SPACE as its absence or vice versa. Because the transmission line idles at a MARK state, the continuous tone is transmitted even when no data is being encoded. The receiver demodulates the signal by outputting 1s and 0s as the tone on the communications line appears and disappears.

---

[1] This is accomplished through Fourier analysis.

[2] This is sometimes called ON/OFF keying.

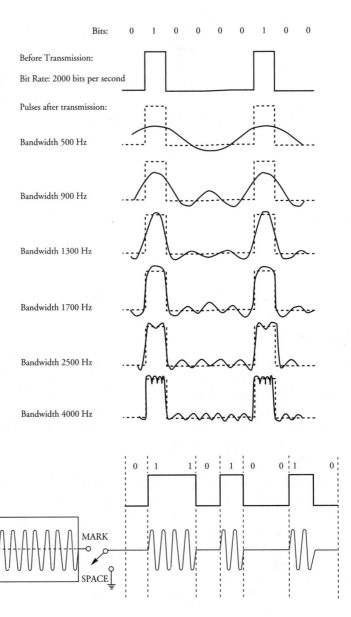

FIGURE 5.2.

The effects of bandwidth on square digital signals.

FIGURE 5.3.

Amplitude modulation.

A device that performs modulation and demodulation on a communications line is known as a *modem*.[3] Although in computerdom the term *modem* is used almost exclusively to describe devices that operate over telephone lines, modems are used on many different communications lines. A great deal of data, for example, is sent between computers at radio frequencies via *RTTY* (radio-teletype) modems. Another nontelephone modem is the *short-haul modem*, which sends modulated tones over ordinary wire. Short-haul modems are usually found where both pieces of equipment are located on the premises or where a noisy electrical environment precludes the use of ordinary cables.

"Plexes" or Bandwidth Usage

Before we examine more sophisticated modulation techniques, let's quickly review the "plex" terminology (presented briefly at the end of Chapter 2) describing the various ways of utilizing the available bandwidth of a communications line.

THE SIMPLEX CONNECTION

A transmitter (such as the simple ASK modulator just described) at one end of the telephone line and a receiver at the other end form a *simplex connection*: a connection in which data traffic moves in only one direction. This arrangement is illustrated in Figure 5.4a. Because they are inherently noninteractive, simplex installations have limited applications, but are found in one-sided applications such as stock tickers or printers at remote sites.

THE HALF-DUPLEX CONNECTION

A limited kind of two-way system can be built from two simplex connections. As illustrated in Figure 5.4b, each modem contains a transmitter and a receiver, one of which is connected to the communications line through a *talk/listen* switch. For West-to-East traffic, modem W connects its transmitter to the line and modem E connects its receiver. This arrangement is reversed for East-to-West traffic. Changing the position of the talk/listen switch is called *turning the line around*, a term from early telegraph days when operators had to reverse the physical connections on the equipment. The idea of sharing the line in this manner is known as *time division multiplexing* or TDM.

The talk/listen switch is, of course, not a physical switch but an electronic one controlled by software. The two ends convey the need to turn the line around through *half-duplex protocols* such as the ETX/ACK protocol explained in Chapter 4. In general, half-duplex

---

[3] *Modem*, as we have been told ad nauseam, is a portmanteau word formed from *modulate* and *demodulate*. One can only marvel at the heights to which the human imagination soared for this name. Equally sublime is *codec* (from *code* and *decode*), a device that encodes analog signals in a digital format. The telephone company's name for a modem is the equally imaginative *data set*.

protocols are analogous to the familiar words "over" and "over and out" used in half-duplex radio conversions. In digital communications, the software controlling the two modems agree upon a *turnaround character* to signal the need to switch from sender to receiver. If the data to be transferred is of a binary (as opposed to textual) nature, block transfer protocols like those described in Chapter 4 must be used.

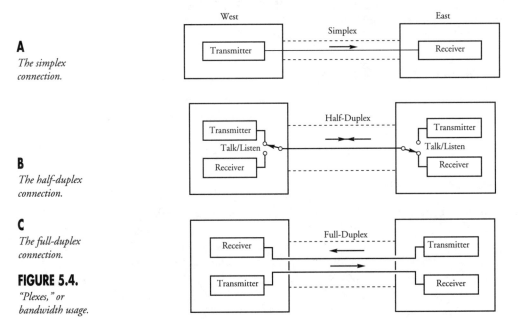

A

The simplex connection.

B

The half-duplex connection.

C

The full-duplex connection.

FIGURE 5.4.

"Plexes," or bandwidth usage.

THE FULL-DUPLEX CONNECTION

Although the half-duplex arrangement is considerably more flexible than the simplex, it is nevertheless inefficient. The time required to switch the circuitry from transmit to receive mode is commonly on the order of 200 milliseconds, but even longer delays are common in older equipment. A delay of such duration is intolerable in time-sensitive, interactive applications such as remote instrumentation monitoring and control systems. In addition, the cumulative delay incurred from repeated line reversals is responsible for the poor performance of half-duplex data transfer protocols such as the "stop-and-wait" protocol described in Chapter 4.

The shortcomings of half-duplex communications can be avoided simply by taking the idea of channel-sharing one step further. Instead of alternately sharing receiver and transmitter, in the *full-duplex* connection shown in Figure 5.4c, each end of the connection contains both a transmitter and a receiver: one pair for communicating East-to-West and another for West-to-East. To prevent interference, a separate distinct tone is assigned to traffic in each direction. The general idea of dividing a communications channel into smaller frequency bands is called *frequency division multiplexing* or FDM.

DUPLEX: ASYMMETRICAL BANDWIDTH ALLOCATION

In some applications full-duplex communications is not needed. Where a very high percentage of the traffic flows in one direction, the full-channel bandwidth may be divided asymmetrically between directions. By convention, this mode of operation, being neither half nor full, is simply referred to as *duplex*. For example, the chart of modems in Table 5.3 describes several modems as "Duplex via optional 75 bps back channel."

When the information carried in one direction is minuscule (such as the occasional XON or XOFF), the imbalance in the bandwidth of the channels is extreme as in the Bell 208 modem. Some modems monitor the traffic flow and adjust the channel bandwidth assignments dynamically.[4]

CHANNEL USAGE CONVENTIONS

Because a full-duplex connection consists of two complete channels in use simultaneously, two modems operating in full-duplex mode must agree upon how they will allocate the signals. For example, the modems might agree beforehand that the modem using the higher should be called a "Girl modem," whereas that using the lower-frequency channel be called "Boy modems." The problem with this approach is that, when the telephone rings, there is no way to know whether the caller is a Boy or Girl. Instead of using fixed definitions such as Boy and Girl, channel assignments are determined by the point of origin of the call. When new modems are designed, one channel is arbitrarily designated *originate* and the other *answer*. In use, the modem placing the call is expected to use the originate channel and the modem receiving the call is expected to use the answer channel.

Modems that both place and answer calls must contain circuitry to switch the channel assignments between originate and receive, depending upon the situation. In many applications, however, a modem either places or receives calls, but not both. Modems servicing the dial-up lines to time-sharing computers, for example, never originate calls; modems connected to dedicated terminals (such as those used in making airline reservations) never need to answer calls. Modems for such situations, known as *originate-* and *answer-only modems*, have fixed channel assignments. Because complicated switching circuitry is unnecessary, dedicated modems are considerably less complicated and therefore less expensive than full-featured originate/answer modems.

Frequency Modulation

Noise causes spurious variations in an electrical signal's amplitude. Figure 5.5 shows how small noise "spikes" may transform one amplitude logic level into the other, producing a data error. Because it uses amplitude variations to encode digital logic levels, ASK

---

[4]Microcom's trademarked term for this procedure is *Statistical Duplexing*, but a similar approach is used in many products. No public standard exists in this area.

modulation's greatest weakness is its susceptibility to noise. So profound is this limitation that ASK modulation is rapidly disappearing as low-noise environments become difficult to achieve in an increasingly electronic world.

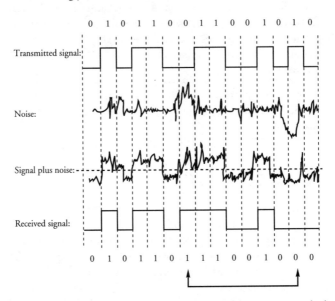

FIGURE 5.5.

Effects of noise upon a digital signal.

Whereas electrical noise changes a signal's amplitude, no known natural phenomenon changes its frequency. Much more reliable encoding can therefore be attained by *frequency modulation*. Because modems need only transmit 1s and 0s, data can be represented by switching between two tones of different frequencies. This technique, known as *frequency shift keying*, would be superior to ASK even if judged solely on its immunity to noise, but FSK is also more robust because each logic level can be decoded not only as the presence of one tone but also as the absence of the other. In other words, a 1 is decoded as 1 AND -0. Figure 5.6a depicts FSK modulation, but the frequency difference between the two tones is exaggerated for clarity. Figure 5.6b, however, shows how the dual tones are actually assigned in the Bell model 202, a half-duplex 1200 bps modem using FSK modulation. This modem uses two tones 1,000 Hz apart, centered about 1,700 Hz. The 1,200 Hz tone represents a MARK and the 2,200 Hz tone a SPACE.

FSK modulation at 1200 bps produces a wide spectrum of frequencies, indicated by the shaded area in Figure 5.6. Notice that this area occupies most of the available bandwidth of the telephone line. This modem also devotes a very small amount of bandwidth to a "backwards" (from receiver back to sender) channel. This channel consists of a continuous tone of 387 Hz and is used to inform the transmitting station that the receiver is still connected. If necessary, the tone can be modulated with *ON/OFF keying* at a maximum rate of 5 baud, thus providing very limited duplex capabilities.

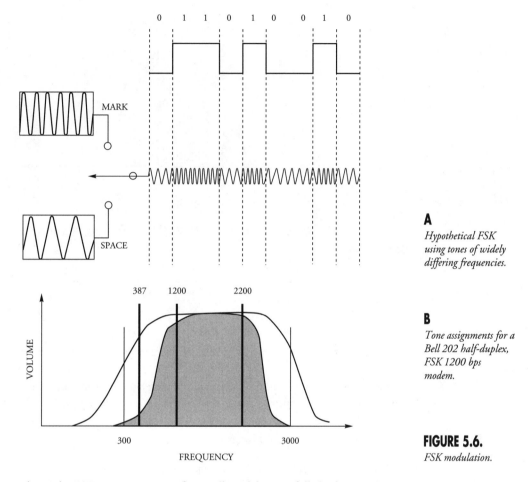

A

Hypothetical FSK using tones of widely differing frequencies.

B

Tone assignments for a Bell 202 half-duplex, FSK 1200 bps modem.

FIGURE 5.6.

FSK modulation.

Figure 5.7 shows the FSK tone assignment for a Bell model 103, a full-duplex, 110 to 300 bps FSK modem. The originate modem on the left uses two tones, 100 Hz apart, centered about the frequency 1,170; a SPACE is 1,070 and a MARK is 1,270. The answer modem tones are also 100 Hz apart, but centered about 2,125 Hz; here, a SPACE is 2,025 and a MARK is 2,225. Notice that the frequencies are chosen so that there is very little overlap between their spectra and consequently little interference between the two.

So far, our discussion of tone frequencies and their originate/answer assignments are for Bell (AT&T) modems. Table 5.1 compares the 110 to 300 bps, full-duplex modem assignments with those of its European (CCITT V.21) counterparts.

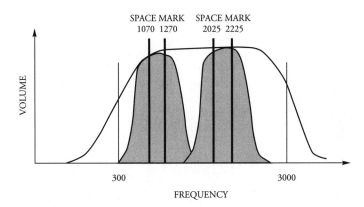

FIGURE 5.7.

Tone assignments for a Bell model 103, a full-duplex, 110 to 300 bps FSK modem.

Table 5.1. Bell 103 versus CCITT V.21 300 bps, full-duplex tone assignments.

	Originate		*Answer*	
	Mark	*Space*	*Mark*	*Space*
Bell	1270	1070	2225	2025
CCITT	980	1180	1650	1850

In both cases, the answer mode is assigned to the higher tone-pair, but CCITT modems employ different frequency pairs and the lower of the two tones produces a MARK.

Bandwidth Limitations

At first thought, modulation sounds like the ultimate solution to the telephone bandwidth problems. After all, so long as the tones lie within the bandwidth of the telephone line, they should be unaffected by the transmission speed. The temptation, then, is to think that the telephone line can bear modulation at any baud rate. The cruel fact is that in any form of modulation the communications medium must have sufficient bandwidth to pass all primary components of modulation. In half-duplex FSK, there are three primary components: the two FSK tones themselves and the baud rate of the data. In full-duplex communications, however, there are six primary components: the four FSK tones and two baud frequencies. In other words, to achieve a given data rate in full-duplex mode requires approximately the same channel bandwidth as a half-duplex connection at twice that rate.

Phase Modulation

We have seen that the total frequency spectra produced by these modems fit comfortably within the bandwidth of the telephone line, but as the baud rate increases, the modem spectra begin to flirt with bandwidth limits and reliable performance becomes problematic. Indeed, the practical limit in baud rate at the time seemed to be about 1,200 bps (half-duplex).[5] So far, we have legitimately been able to refer to modems as operating at 300, 600, or 1,200 baud because the data rate (in bps) of the modem is exactly equal to the modulation or signaling rate (in baud): every bit is encoded into a single cycle of the modulated carrier. Clearly, in order to increase the amount of data that can be put through the telephone line, a way must be devised to encode more than one bit into each modulation cycle. Let's see how this is possible.

A waveform has three properties: amplitude, frequency, and phase. We have already examined modulation techniques that encode digital data into amplitude (ASK) and frequency (FSK). We will now briefly examine *phase modulation*, in which information is encoded in the temporal relationship between two otherwise identical waveforms. In particular, we will examine the technique known as *phase shift keying* (PSK).

TWO-LEVEL PHASE SHIFT KEYING

Figure 5.8 shows three waveforms, all exactly the same amplitude and frequency, but differing in phase. One complete cycle of any period waveform is expressed as 360°. With respect to wave form A, wave form B is said to be *in phase* or, stated differently, its *phase angle* is 0°. Wave form C, however, lags behind wave form A by 180° and its phase angle is –180°.

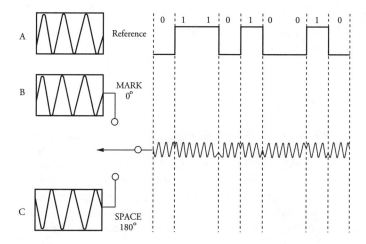

FIGURE 5.8.
Two-level phase shift keying.

---

[5]In the history of PSTN modem development, we are in the early 1980s: 600 bps full-duplex or 1,200 bps half-duplex modems. The techniques that allow for high speeds in modern modems were still at the edges of theory. Even had the theoretical notions been fully formed at the time, the processing power to implement them would have been prohibitively expensive.

Although these expressions may be foreign to you, it is fairly easy to see how this relationship can be used to encode data. Modulation consists of sending wave form C for a SPACE and wave form B for a MARK. (We assume that both sender and receiver already have local copies of wave form A, so it need not be transmitted.) To demodulate the signal, the receiver adds the incoming wave form to its local copy of wave form A. If the result of this addition is 0 (C + A = 0) a SPACE is decoded. Conversely, if the result is a nonzero number (B + A 0) a MARK is decoded.

Although phase modulation is nifty, the example just discussed does not change the basic one-to-one ratio of the data and modulation rates. Let's see how to attain this goal.

QUADRATURE (FOUR-PHASE) PSK

We all have the following phrase built in our mental ROMs: "In asynchronous I/O, a byte is broken up into bits…." To understand how a modem attains a bit rate of, say, 1,200 bps from a modulation rate of 600 baud, we have to change this phrase to: "In asynchronous I/O, a byte is broken up into dibits…." The new basic unit of data is no longer the bit, but the 2-bit pair, or *dibit*. Figure 5.9 shows how a dibit is encoded as one of four phase angles.

This encoding process, known as *quadrature*[6] *phase shift keying* (QPSK) is identical to the previous example except instead of encoding bits in two phase angles (0° and −180°), four phase angles are used: 0°, 90°, 180°, and 270°.

Demodulating the quadrature phase-encoded signal is conceptually identical to demodulating the binary phase-encoded signal. Again, the incoming wave form is added to the reference wave form, but this time both the polarity and magnitude of the sum are used to decode the dibits. Phase modulation has been around for many years: in fact, it is the technique used to modulate the RGB signal in an ordinary color television signal.

Differential Phase Shift Keying

Our earlier examples assume that both sender and receiver have local copies of the reference wave form. If this is so (you ask), what keeps the sender's and receiver's reference waveforms synchronized? (This sounds a lot like the teleprinter problem from Chapter 2, doesn't it?) In other technologies, a small *sync tone* is transmitted along with the carrier to enable the sender to reconstruct its copy of the reference wave form.[7] This is not practical on a telephone line because the energy required to transmit the sync pulse itself would consume some of the precious bandwidth.

---

[6]Quadrature just means "four-quadrant."

[7]In a color television signal, this sync pulse is called the *burst*. In a similar application in FM stereo, it is called the *pilot tone*.

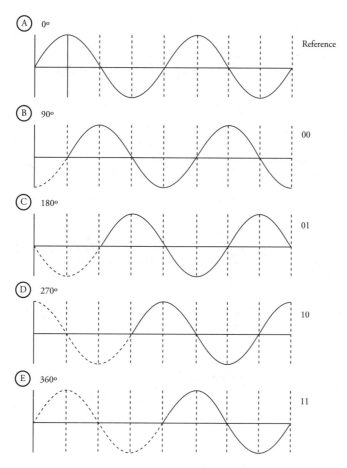

FIGURE 5.9.
Quadrature phase shift keying.

The solution, called *differential phase shift keying* (DPSK), abandons altogether the idea of deriving phase differences from a quiescent reference signal (a sync pulse). Instead, the phase angle for each cycle is calculated relative to the previous cycle. Thus, for any given modulation cycle, the dibit is encoded in the phase relationship between the current cycle and its immediate predecessor.

A modulation rate of 600 baud using four-level PSK provides a data rate of 2,400 bps. This can be used in its entirety as a single 2,400 bps half-duplex channel as in the Bell 201 modem, or divided into two full-duplex 1,200 bps channels. The latter is the configuration of the popular Bell 212A modem whose frequency assignments are shown in Table 5.2.

Table 5.2. Tone assignments for the Bell 212A.

Originate		Answer	
Transmit	Receive	Transmit	Receive
1200	2400	2400	1200

The Bell 212A modem is the 1,200 bps standard for microcomputers. The CCITT standard V.22 describes a 1,200/600 bps modem that differs mainly in minor internal details and can communicate at 1,200 bps with Bell 212A-type modems under all but the most adverse conditions.

The Ascendancy of Public Modem Standards

In the United States, modems were a natural adjunct of the phone company. In fact, before 1968 the telephone companies forbade connecting "foreign" (that is, non-Bell) equipment such as modems to the telephone line. Their argument, not without merit, was that the connection of untested circuitry to the telephone line made it impossible for them to guarantee the performance of the telephone system.

After a long legal battle, the Federal Communications Commission (FCC) in the "Carterphone" ruling declared that the telephone company's restrictions were unreasonable and ordered it to permit customers to use interconnecting devices. In the same ruling, the FCC granted the telephone company the following rights:

- To approve devices that will be connected to the telephone line

- To know when such a device is actually connected

The telephone company responded to the Carterphone decision by authorizing connection to the telephone line only through a *direct access adapter* (DAA). These devices, which had to be rented from the telephone company, were essentially transformers to isolate the telephone line from the connected equipment and a few components to suppress potentially harmful voltages. Due to subsequent FCC rulings (or the threat of them), DAAs are no longer required as long as the connected equipment meets telephone company standards and the user reports to the telephone company whenever an approved modem is connected to or disconnected from the telephone lines.[8]

It is in this atmosphere that the next important event occurred. It is therefore not surprising that the event was not technical, but political: in the United States, the

---

[8]At the same time, you may report all the mattress and pillow tags you have removed in your lifetime.

phone company gave up its patriarchal role in modem standards and turned instead to the public, worldwide telecommunications body sanctioned by the United Nations, the International Telecommunications Union, or ITU. In particular, the phone company threw its weight into the formal standards-making arm in telephony, the CCITT (International Consultative Committee for Telephone and Telegraph). The Bell 212A was the last parochial modem standard widely implemented by the American market.

In the CCITT, American companies, with AT&T taking a prominent position, joined the world community in democratic procedure for designing, approving, and publishing telecommunications standards. This move had immediate salubrious effects upon the United States modem industry. Not only did international standards make it possible to sell the US products abroad, it freed American companies from licensing fees on the one hand and worry about patent infringement on the other. Not insignificantly, public standards procedures mean fewer parochial designs, which means fewer interworking (compatibility) nightmares, which in turn leads to higher connectivity—the point of the whole endeavor.

There are now two main organizations that produce modem standards: the CCITT and EIA/TIA. As just mentioned, the CCITT is the telephony/telegraphy arm of the larger International Telecommunications Union. Its chief contribution is the internationalization of standard technology. Examples of its work are the many modem standards discussed in this chapter and the Group 3 Facsimile standards discussed in Chapter 11. At the World Telecommunications Standarization Conference in Helsinki, Finland in March 1993 a major reorganization of the ITU was approved. The CCITT section of the ITU is renamed the ITU-TSS (Telecommunications Standarization Sector). Despite the official change of name, for historical reasons the CCITT designation is expected to persist. For this reason, the remainder of this book employs the familiar name.

In 1990 the Electrical Industries Association merged its telecommunications activities with the TIA (Telecommunications Industries Association). All subsequent standards bear the label "EIA/TIA" and drop the EIA's familiar "RS-" prefix (as in RS-232). Because of its long-standing place in computer lore, this book uses the original names of EIA.

The EIA/TIA produces American standards, but lately has become more international in scope. For example, it is the State department US representative on modems to the CCITT.

Quadrature Amplitude Modulation

We have seen how data can be encoded into a signal's amplitude (ASK) and its phase (PSK). Aspects of both these forms of modulation are combined to produce yet another modulation technique known as *quadrature amplitude modulation*, or QAM. Signaling full-duplex at 600 baud, QAM results in a data rate of 2,400 bps. QAM is specified by the CCITT V.22 *bis*[9] full-duplex standard and has been adopted worldwide.

Just as the basic data unit for PSK is the dibit, QAM uses the *quadbit*, or nibble. The version of QAM employs twelve phase angles in conjunction with three amplitudes. Of the resulting 32 unique phase/amplitude combinations, only 16 are used to encode a quadbit. These are depicted in the phase "constellation" in Figure 5.10.

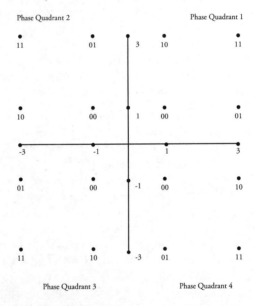

FIGURE 5.10.

The 16-point QUAM constellation from V.22 bis.

Handshaking: Establishing a Data Link

When an originate modem initiates a call, it listens patiently on the line for an answering modem to assert its carrier tone. If the originate modem recognizes the tone as belonging to one of its own species, it replies with its own carrier tone and the two are ready to communicate happily ever after. The remainder of this book refers to this phase as *handshaking*, and the resulting audio embrace is referred to variously as a *data link* or a *carrier link* or, at times, simply as a *connection*. The link is broken when either carrier is turned off or interrupted for more than a few tenths of a second.

---

[9]The suffixes *bis* and *ter* in CCITT document numbers refer to the second and third revisions, respectively.

The precise tones used to negotiate the data link depend upon the types of modems in use. For example, if the answer modem uses FSK modulation, its carrier is the answer transmitter's MARK; if a PSK modem, the carrier is just the answer modem's carrier (for example, 2,400 Hz for a Bell 212A). As soon as the FSK originate modem recognizes the MARK of the answer modem, it asserts its own transmitter's MARK; if a PSK modem, the originator asserts its carrier (1,200 Hz for a Bell 212A, for example). The handshaking procedures for QAM and high-speed modems are substantially more complicated and beyond the scope of this book.

TRAINING AND ADAPTIVE EQUALIZATION

Equalization is the electronic term for altering the shape of the receiver's frequency response to compensate for irregularities in the communications channel. The diagram in Figure 5.11 shows the frequency response of an *ideal* phone line, and the flat frequency response desired by the modem designer for best performance. To achieve this response, modem designers alter the response of the transmitting[10] modem so that frequencies at the edges (near 300 and 3,000 Hz) possess as much energy as those near the center. As depicted in Figure 5.11, when the resulting frequency response curve is superimposed on the response curve, a response curve very close to the desired one is obtained. In the non-QAM modem designs we've looked at,[11] equalization is fixed: an equalization curve based upon a statistically typical phone line. This is referred to as a *fixed compromise equalizer*.

Because QAM incorporates amplitude modulation, it is more sensitive than simpler forms of modulation to phone line response. In fact, normal line-to-line variations in response are sufficient to affect the modem's performance. The solution (optional in V.22bis) is *adaptive equalization*. During handshaking, the modems analyze the quality of the received signals and adjust their electronic equalizers accordingly. This process of adjusting equalizers is known as *training*. V.22bis also specifies a procedure whereby two already-connected modems can conduct a training session then automatically resume normal communications.

FALLBACK

In impaired environments where a DPSK modem operates flawlessly, a QAM modem may be unusable. In recognition of this problem, QAM modems generally specify an automatic *fallback* feature that senses when the signal is present and switches the modem to a

---

[10]In some modems, the receiver shares responsibility for equalization.

[11]Although V.22bis modems were the first mass-marketed modems with these features, equalization and training are not exclusive to QAM modems. PKS modems such as V.27bis and V.27ter (4800 bps) also use them.

reduced QAM speed (if available) then, if the signal is still unusable, switches to a slower and less risky mode. For example, V.22bis modems fall back to V.22 (1,200 bps DPSK).

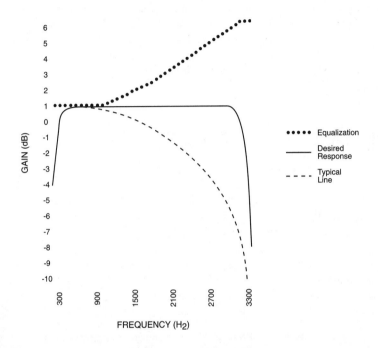

FIGURE 5.11.

Modem receiver equalization.

Table 5.3. Table of modem and related standards.

Standard	Date	Modulation	Line Usage	Max Bits/Second	Max Baud	PSTN/Leased		Comment
V.17	1991	QAM-TCM	Half	7200-14400 step 2400	2400	√		14400 fax page carrier only.
V.21	1964	FSK	Full	300	300	√		Fax HDLC carrier. Cousin to Bell 103.
V.22	1980	PSK	Full	600, 1200	600	√	√	Optional fallback to 600.
V.22bis	1984	QAM	Full	2400	600	√	√	Auto fallback to 1200.
V.23	1964	FSK	Half	75, 600, 1200	1200	√		Duplex via optional 75 bps back channel
V.26	1968	PSK	Half	2400	1200		√	Four-wire. Duplex via optional 75 bps back channel
V.26 bis	1972	PSK	Half	1200, 2400	1200	√		Duplex via optional 75 bps back channel
V.26 ter	1984	PSK	Full/Half	1200, 2400	1200	√	√	2400 Full duplex via echo cancellation.
V.27	1972	PSK	Half	4800	1600		√	Duplex via optional 75 bps back channel
V.27bis	1976	PSK	Half	2400, 4800	1600		√	Duplex via optional 75 bps back channel
V.27ter	1976	PSK	Half	2400, 4800	1600	√		4800/2400 fax page carrier. Optional 75 bps back channel
V.29	1976	QAM/PSK	Half	4800,7200, 9600	2400		√	9600/7200 fax page carrier. Fallback to 4800 (PSK)
V.32	1984	QAM,TCM	ECM	4800/9600	2400	√	√	TCM and auto fallback optional; 4800 is QAM.
V.32bis	1991	QAM,TCM	ECM	4800-14400 step 2400	2400	√	√	Two-wire. Rapid retrain. 4800 is QAM.
V.33	1988	QAM,TCM	ECM	12000, 14400	2400		√	Four-wire. Fax page carrier.
V.FAST	199?	QAM,TCM	ECM	4800-28800 step 2400	*3200	√		In development. Half-duplex fax mode. *May be 3200+.

Private	Date	Modulation	Line Usage	Max Bits/Second	Max Baud	PSTN/Leased		Comment
B103		FSK	Full	300	300	√	√	US precursor to V.21 , but incompatible.
B201		PSK	Half	2400	1200	√	√	Used for Electronic Data Interchange (EDI) in US.
B202		FSK	Half	1200	1200	√	√	Obsolete, but resurrected for caller-id in US.
B208		PSK	Half	4800	2400	√	√	5bps back channel for flow control ; used for EDI in US.
B209		QAM	Half	9600	2400	√	√	US precursor of V.29.
B212		PSK	Full	1200	600	√	√	No fallback; US cousin to V.22.
B212A		PSK	Full	600, 1200	600	√	√	Fallback to Bell 103.
PEP		PEP	Half	18K adjustable	*7	√	√	Telebit. *Multiple carriers, 7 baud per carrier.
Express 96		PSK,QAM,TCM	Half	4800, 9600	2400	√	√	Hayes.
MNP6		QAM	Half	4800, 7200, 9600	2400	√	√	Microcom.
HST		QAM,PSK	Asym	4800-16800 step 2400	*2400	√	√	US Robotics . Similar to V.32. *High speed channel

ECM	Echo Cancellation Multiplexing	**FSK**	Frequency Shift Keying	**PSK** Phase Shift Keying
QAM	Quadrature Amplitude Modulation	**TCM**	Trellis Coded Modulation	**Half** Half-duplex
Full	Full-duplex			

The modem technology in V.22bis dates to the mid-1970s. That it didn't become ratified until 1984 is testimony to the glacial pace at which the international technical community can agree upon standards. But the delay also illustrates how the implementation of theory has to wait for affordable technology. In the middle and late 1970s, modem designers used mostly analog tools to implement the critical aspects of QAM technology such as adaptive equalization, training, and its three-dimensional modulations scheme. The idea of using digital techniques of filtering, equalization, and modulation had certainly occurred to modem designers, but the supporting technology—in particular low-cost embedded micro-controllers—was unaffordable for all but the elite military and space programs.[12]

By the early 1980s, DSP (*digital signal processing*) technology began to arrive at the high-end consumer level. In the mid-1980s, it drove the price of consumer modem products far below that of comparable analog ones. While a modest implementation of DSP technology was making the V.22bis modem a commodity item, at the same time designers began to take a second look at theories that had been put aside because of the lack of affordable DSP technology. By the late 1980s and early 1990s, many of those ideas had become products. The price of a V.32bis (14,400 bps) modem is actually lower than that of a V.22bis modem at a comparable point in its life cycle.

Bandwidth Enhancement

To appreciate the impact of DSP, look at the chart in Table 5.3 and notice the differences between V.22bis, a 2,400 bps modem and V.32 a 9,600 bps modem. The most important change has been a quadrupling of the raw physical bandwidth from 600 to 2,400 baud (full-duplex). With DSP providing the computational muscle to implement sophisticated digital filters and equalizers, the bandwidth is again effectively doubled. This increase was attained by using two separate steps:

1. DSP made possible extreme equalization at the band edges without inducing massive phase distortion. Such designs are impractical with analog techniques.

2. An astonishing method of channel sharing, ECM (*echo cancellation multiplexing*), enables full-duplex communication with each end able to utilize the bandwidth of the *entire* channel.

ECM: Echo Cancellation Multiplexing

To summarize the technology employed in the modems we have discussed so far, bidirectional communications on a single phone line is achieved either by TDM, in which the two ends take turns speaking and listening on the same frequency or by FDM, in which both ends speak simultaneously by dividing the channel into two frequency bands.

---

[12]These programs actually funded much of the research in digital signal processing.

To understand how—and why—ECM works, consider the typical half-duplex (TDM) connection and ask a simple question: Why can't both ends talk and listen at the same time on the same frequency? The answer is that they can and in ECM that is exactly what happens. To try to put this in human terms, think of a two-way telephone conversation. When both parties try to speak, the conversation becomes unintelligible because each person hears his own speech scrambled with that of the person on the other end. However, you as a listener cannot differentiate the other person's words from your own words.[13] Now, suppose you could install a magical device between your ear and the telephone receiver that subtracts your words from the scrambled conversation on the phone line. What would you hear? Only the words from the other end.

If the simple subtraction of what is transmitted from what is received would have allowed for simultaneous bidirectional use of the phone line, it could have been implemented years ago with older technology. The problem, however, becomes infinitely more difficult when you realize that the transmitter hears not only its own transmission but also the echo of its own transmission.

Phone lines that run much beyond the local office have echo suppressors installed. If you've ever gotten a long-distance voice call in which the echo suppressors were not functioning correctly, you can appreciate both their purpose and how well they ordinarily work. In fact, echo suppressors are so effective at canceling energy in the reverse direction that they can prevent ordinary full-duplex modems from hearing anything from the other end. (Notice that echo is not a problem in FDM modems because transmission and reception are on different frequencies.)

To allow for full-duplex modem communications, the echo suppressors disengage from the line when startled by a large amount of energy in the high-frequency range and remain disengaged until the line is silent for a time. When an ordinary FDM modem answers the phone, it emits a burst of *2,100 Hz answer tone* that disengages the echo suppressor and enables normal full-duplex operation. ECM modems also emit an answer tone to disable echo suppressors,[14] but once disabled, they must deal with the big problem caused by the echo: they hear their own transmissions. After the training phase of handshaking, the remote modem remains silent while its partner talks and simultaneously listens to the echo. While listening, the DSP hardware in the modem adjusts its canceling logic until it hears nothing: until its own echo is totally absent. When this is completed, the remote modem performs the same operation. When both modems are satisfied with the results of the echo nulling, the handshaking operation proceeds. Due to the extreme differences between the tranmsitted and echoed signals, the echo cancellation process is at times

---

[13]Indeed this entire analogy ignores the fact that humans don't talk and listen at the same time.

[14]In addition to echo suppressors, the long-haul phone network has its own version of echo cancellation. To avoid a tug-of-war between competing echo canceling systems, the ECM modem disables the network echo cancelers by reversing the phase of the answer tone at 450 millisecond intervals. This produces the characteristic pinging in the answer tone of ECM modems.

heroic. Consider, for example, that the round-trip for an echo using two satellite hops is about 1.2 seconds.

Trellis Coding

Refer back to the signal constellation for a V.22bis modem in Figure 5.10. Notice that only 16 points out of a possible 32 were assigned. This is the same signal constellation used in V.32. Although this means that both convey the same information, V.32 modulates at 2,400 baud, whereas V.22bis uses only 600. This accounts for the difference in speed between the two: 9,600 and 2,400 bps, respectively. The higher baud rate causes V.32's error rate to increase because of increased phase errors near the edges of the pass band. In mathematical work beyond the scope of this book,[15] Ungerboeck of IBM showed that encoding a single redundant bit—that is, by encoding five bits instead of four—errors could be not only detected but also corrected. This forward-acting error correction is given the name *trellis encoding*.[16] Figure 5.12 shows the V.32 signal constellation with trellis coding applied.

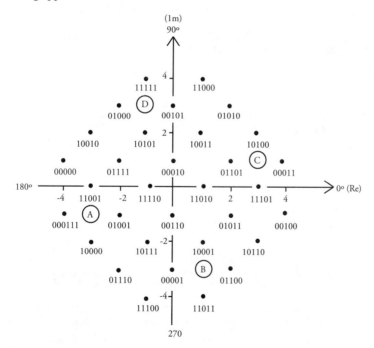

FIGURE 5.12.

The V.32 32-point constellation with trellis coding.

---

[15]See Bingham, "Theory and Practice of Modem Design."

[16]The diagrams used to illustrate how the redundant information is used to recover the correct data look like vines on a trellis.

When trellis coding was first proposed as a type of modulation, Doubting Thomases felt that it did not serve as a form of modulation, but simply as a form of error correction. In classical forward error-correcting systems, the added redundancy causes the throughput under normal conditions to decrease. In the case of trellis coding, however, performance tests demonstrate higher throughput. Whatever the nomenclature, when compared to systems that lack it, trellis-coded systems produce a higher rate of error-free data.

V.32

The CCITT standard V.32 was approved by the CCITT in 1984 but had been in the works for several years. It was not immediately implemented because it clearly required a level of DSP power whose expense priced it out of the broad consumer market. Meanwhile, in the early and middle part of the decade, the consumer industry struggled with competing proprietary schemes for high-speed modems.[17] By 1989, V.32 modems had begun to penetrate the high end of the consumer market and by 1991 they began to show up in the commodity market. In 1992, V.32bis modems effectively supplanted the proprietary modems as their manufacturers began to include V.32 compatibility.

The preceding discussions of echo cancellation multiplexing and trellis coding largely describe the technology of the V.32 modem. Here, then, are its technical high points:

- Channel separation by ECM
- Quadrature amplitude modulation (QAM)
- Optional trellis coding (TCM); V.32 modems that implemented trellis coding are required to interwork with those that don't
- Signaling rates of 9,600 (TCM) and 4,800 (QAM-optional)
- 2400 baud transmission
- Feature and speed negotiation during handshaking
- Optional speed renegotiation (fallback)
- Cleardown capabilities

V.32 RATE NEGOTIATIONS AND CLEARDOWN REQUESTS

Immediately after training, the modems exchange rate capabilities information. The answering modem sends a bitmap indicating which of the optional speeds it supports and whether it supports trellis coding. The originating modem matches these capabilities with its own and sends a bitmap describing how the connection will be conducted.[18]

---

[17]Fast retraining of half-duplex modems (such as V.29), multiple carriers, statistically allocated distributed bandwidth, just to name a few. See the chart in Table 5.3.

[18]It is worth noting that training and rate negotiation take place at 4800 bps and the modems fall forward to 9600 bps if necessary.

Once a connection has been established, both modems constantly fine-tune their echo cancelers and evaluate signal quality. If either detects a change in signal quality, it issues a *retrain request* and the two modems conduct new training, echo cancellation, and rate negotiation. The modems may shift the speed up or down based upon the results of this new round of procedures.

In other types of modems we've looked at, terminating a connection is as simple as hanging up the phone at one end. Because of the echo-canceling technology, a connection between V.32 modems cannot be terminated in this manner. When one end of the connection hangs up, the echo characteristics of the phone line changes dramatically, causing the remaining modem to hear its own echo immediately and attempt retraining. The retrain never succeeds, of course, but it can take the modem several tens of seconds before the remaining modem abandons hope and hangs up. To avoid the obvious inefficiency of needlessly tying up a line, V.32 establishes a *PSTN cleardown* signal in which the modem that intends to hang up the line sends a rate renegotiation request for a speed of zero: in other words, hang up.

V.32bis

V.32bis is the natural next step for V.32. It introduces no new technology but enhances and refines the technology presented in V.32:

- Compatibility with V.32 modems at 9,600 and 4,800 bps
- Mandatory trellis coding (except at 4,800)
- New signaling rates of 14,400, 12,000, 7,200 (all TCM)
- Fast retrain: the capability of renegotiating speeds without retraining

For completeness, Figure 5.13 shows the signal constellation for V.32bis at 14,400 bps. At a baud rate of 2,400, six bits are needed for 14,400 plus one for trellis encoding.

V.34 (V.FAST)

At the time of this writing, work is underway to specify the *last modem*: the modem predicted by modulation and bandwidth theory. In this v.34 project, nicknamed "V.FAST," baud rates of 3,200 with 9-bit trellis codes have been demonstrated, resulting in a data rate of 28,800 bps. In addition to higher rates, handshaking in V.FAST will include an unspecified interaction with the PSTN.

Modem Control

Knowing how a watch works does not teach you to tell the time. Understanding how modems work does not help you make them work. We have learned that modems, among other activities, establish data links, dial and answer the telephone, and go on-line and off-line, and that half-duplex modems must periodically turn the line around. This portion of the chapter, therefore, is an explanation of how the programmer controls and monitors such modem functions.

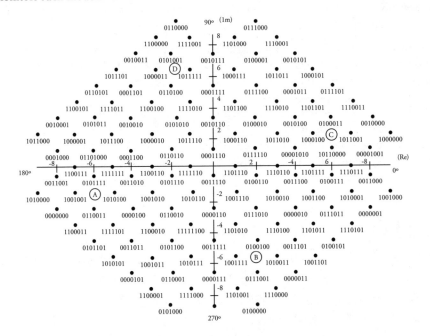

FIGURE 5.13.

The V.32bis 128-point constellation with trellis coding.

As we shall see, there are two fundamental ways to control or monitor the behavior of a modem: through hardware (wires between the computer and modem) and software (sending commands in the data stream). There are several formal standards for the first method:

- EIA/TAI-232-E is the most comprehensive: it specifies the logical, electrical, and the mechanical aspects of the 25-signal interface.
- CCITT V.24 specifies the logical interface.
- CCITT V.28 specifies the electrical interface.
- ISO 2110 specifies the mechanical interface.
- EIA/TIA 574 is a logical and electrical subset of EIA/TIA 232-E. It is a *post hoc* specification of the 9-pin connector found on IBM-compatible personal computers.
- EIA/TAI 561 is a logical and electrical subset of EIA/TIA 232-E. It specifies an 8-pin telephone-style connector and extends its operation to 38,400 baud.

There are two relevant standards, one in the making, for controlling modems via commands in the data stream:

- EIA/TIA 602 is a *post hoc* standardization of the architecture and command set developed by Hayes Microcomputer Products, Inc. This modem and its derivatives are the subject of Chapter 9.
- TIA PN-2812 (work in progress) will embed RS-232 control signals in the data.

The RS-232 Standard

Making the leap from theoretical to practical understanding, our feet unavoidably land in the great intellectual pile known as RS-232. The original standard was *Recommended Standard Number 232*, the Electronic Industries Association—better known as EIA RS-232. This standard is periodically revised: revisions A-C were editorial in nature, revision D specified the physical connector for the first time, and revision E adds new functionality for error-correcting modems.

The formal name of the document is *Interface Between Data Terminal Equipment and Data Communication Equipment Employing Serial Binary Data Interchange*. Data terminal equipment (DTE) and data communications equipment (DCE) are, for our purposes at least, the generic terms for "computer equipment" and "modem," respectively. Even though DTE and DCE are not particularly memorable terms, they are both popular and unambiguous. For these reasons, they are adopted in this chapter and throughout this book.

The most important words in the title of the EIA document are *serial interchange* and *interface*, which tell us that this document describes how to perform serial I/O in the real world of modems. The definition of the term *interface* is uncharacteristically broad for an engineering concept. The document actually describes three separate aspects of the DTE/DCE connection:

- Functional description of interchange circuits
- Electrical signal characteristics
- Mechanical description of interface circuits including connectors.

Our study will follow the same organization.

Table 5.4 is a summary of the information in this chapter. It gives:

- The standard pin assignments for EIA/TIA 232-E (25 pins), 561 (8 pins), and 574 (9 pins).
- The EIA/TIA name for the circuit: AA, BB, etc.
- The CCITT circuit number: 101, 102, etc.
- The direction of the control signal: to the DCE or DTE
- Common abbreviation for the circuits relevant to this chapter: TD, DSR, etc.
- The EIA/TIA "official" description of circuit: Transmit Data, Clear to Send, etc.

The circuits relevant to our discussion are highlighted; the remainder are either reserved or used in synchronous communications.

Table 5.4. The RS-232 circuits.

25 Pin	9 Pin	8 Pin	EIA/TIA Name	CCITT V.24	Direction of Signal	Mnemonic	Description
1	5	-	n/a	n/a	na/	n/a	Protective Ground
2	3	6	BA	103	to DCE	TD	Transmitted Data
3	2	5	BB	104	to DTE	RD	Received Data
4	7	8	CA/CJ	105/133	to DCE	RTS/RTR	Request to Send/Ready to Receive (note 1)
5	8	7	CB	106	to DTE	CTS	Clear to Send
6	6	-	CC	107	to DTE	DSR	Data Set Ready (DCE Ready)
7	-	4	AB	102	-	-	Signal Ground or Common
8	1	2	CF	109	to DTE	DCD	Data Carrier Detect (Note 2)
9	-	-	-	-	-	-	Reserved for Testing
10	-	-	-	-	-	-	Reserved for Testing
11	-	-	-	126	-	-	Reserved for Testing (Note 3)
12	-	-	SCF	122	to DTE	-	Secondary Received Line Signal Detect
13	-	-	SCB	121	to DTE	-	Secondary Clear to Send
14	-	-	SBA	118	to DCE	-	Secondary Transmitted Data
15	-	-	DB	114	to DTE	-	Transmission Signal Element Timing
16	-	-	SBB	119	to DTE	-	Secondary Received Data
17	-	-	DD	115	to DTE	-	Receiver Signal Element Timing
18	-	-	LL	141	to DCE	-	Local Loopback
19	-	-	SCA	120	to DCE	-	Secondary Request to Send
20	4	3	CD	108/1, /2	to DCE	DTR	Data Terminal Ready (DTE Ready)
21	-	-	RL/CG	140/110	to DCE	-	Remote Loopback/Signal Quality Detect
22	-	1	CE	125	to DTE	RI	Ring Indicator
23	-	-	CH/CI	111/112	either	DRI	Data Signal Rate Detector
24	-	-	DA	113	to DCE	-	Transmit Signal Element Timing
25	-	-	TM	142	to DTE	-	Test mode

Note 1: When flow control is implemented, the circuit is Ready to Recieve
Note 2: DCD is slang. EIA/TIA's official designation is Receive Line Signal Detect.
Note 3: Pin 11 is used only in V.24 where it is Select Transmit Frequency

RS-232 functions are sharply divided into *data functions* and *control functions*. The data functions are, quite simply, the transmitter on pin 2 and receiver on pin 3. These are the only two pins through which data flows. All remaining functions are control functions, so named because they carry the status or command for controlling the modem's behavior.

INPUT/OUTPUT CONVENTIONS

One of the less intuitive aspects of Table 5.4 is that the two sides of an RS-232 interface are logically complementary: an output on one side of the interface becomes an input on the other. Remembering that the functional names of the circuits reflect the point of view of the DTE helps to clarify the counterintuitive nomenclature. For example, the name "Transmitted Data" clearly denotes an output. Transmitted Data (2) is, however, an output only on a DTE output; on a DCE, it is an input. To alleviate this problem, Table 5.4 gives the direction of the intended signal.

RS-232 FROM A PROGRAMMER'S POINT OF VIEW

Control functions on the RS-232 interface are, of course, controlled through hardware. As we will see in the next chapter, commonly used asynchronous functions are built into a single controller IC known as a *UART (universal asynchronous receiver/transmitter)*. This device provides both data (transmit and receive) and many control functions. When UARTs are employed, the inner timing details of START/STOP asynchronous I/O, data format, and RS-232 interfacing are largely hidden from the programmer. In fact, transmitting or receiving a byte with a UART is simply a matter of reading or writing to a RAM location or I/O port. In a similar fashion, RS-232 inputs and outputs can be monitored and manipulated almost effortlessly.

Formal Functional Descriptions of Interchange Circuits

We will now look at the formal EIA definitions of the circuit functions in Table 5.4. Later, we will discuss many of these same functions in the light of real-world usage in "Real-World RS-232." The pin numbers given are for the EIA/TIA 25-pin connector in Figure 5.16. All quotations in the following descriptions are taken from the RS-232 standard itself.

PROTECTIVE GROUND (PIN 1)

Though not an officially defined circuit, RS-232 suggests that such a circuit exists and that it be connected internally to the chassis of the device, and therefore to the earth ground provided at the AC outlet.

SIGNAL COMMON (PIN 7)

This is the common return for all circuits and must be present on all interfaces. Connection of this pin to Protective Ground (pin 1) can prevent catastrophic destruction of equipment in the event of a transformer malfunction somewhere in the system.

TRANSMITTED DATA (TD, PIN 2, TO DCE)

The TD line carries serial data from the DTE to the modem. In conformity with long-established technology, the transmitter is held at MARK during periods of line idle. The DTE ability may be constrained by the Request to Send, Clear to Send, Data Set Ready, and Data Terminal Ready.

RECEIVED DATA (RD, PIN 3, TO DTE)

The performance of RD does not depend on any other RS-232 function. The standard requires that Received Data be held at MARK when no carrier is present or, in half-duplex modems, for a "brief" interval after switching from transmit to receive mode.

REQUEST TO SEND (RTS, PIN 4, TO DCE)
CLEAR TO SEND (CTS, PIN 5, TO DTE)

The RS-232 standard says that Request to Send conditions the modem for transmission. In fact, its only function is to switch a half-duplex modem between transmit and receive mode (to turn the line around). While a half-duplex modem is receiving, the DTE keeps Request to Send inhibited; when it's the DTE's turn to transmit, it informs the modem of its desire to transmit by asserting Request to Send. The DTE must not start sending data to the modem immediately because the modem cannot perform the switchover instantaneously. After asserting Request to Send, therefore, the DTE begins monitoring Clear to Send which is held low by the modem in receive mode. When the modem completes the switchover, it asserts Clear to Send to inform the DTE that it is now safe to send data. This RTS/CTS handshaking is performed in reverse when switching from transmit back to receive.

Because full-duplex connections are two-way channels, there is clearly no need for RTS/CTS handshaking. Accordingly, in full-duplex modems, Clear to Send is permanently asserted or tied to Data Carrier Detect.

READY FOR RECEIVING (RFR, PIN 4, TO DCE)

When modem flow control is supported, Request to Send becomes Ready to Receive. When asserted, Ready to Receive means that the DTE is ready to receive data; when inhibited, the DTE cannot accept data, so the modem must buffer it. See "Modems and Flow Control" later in this chapter.

DATA SET READY (DSR, PIN 6, TO DTE)

Data Set Ready (a.k.a. DCE ready) is asserted only when the following conditions exist simultaneously:

- The modem is "connected to a communications channel": it's off-hook, but not in test, voice, or dial mode.
- The modem has performed "any timing functions required by the switching system to complete call establishment." In originate mode, this means dialing, monitoring call progress, and anything else required to usher the call through the telephone network.
- The modem has begun "the transmission of a discrete answer tone…." In answer mode, the answer tone and Data Set Ready are asserted two seconds after the telephone goes off-hook. The originate modem does not transmit or assert its Data Set Ready until the answer tone is received from the remote modem.

● The term *Data Set* is the telephone company's name for a modem. The EIA standard calls it a DCE.

DATA CARRIER DETECT (DCD, PIN 8, TO DTE)

This pin, whose official name is Received Line Signal Detect, is asserted when the modem receives a remote carrier and is ready to exchange data with the host. DCD remains asserted for the duration of the link. On half-duplex modems Data Carrier Detect is asserted only by the receiving modem.

DATA TERMINAL READY (DTR, PIN 20, TO DCE)

This signal "prepares" modems "to be connected" to the communications line and "maintains the connection established by external means." This means that Data Terminal Ready enables (but does not cause) the modem to switch onto the line. In originate mode, Data Terminal Ready must be asserted in order to auto-dial; in answer mode, Data Terminal Ready must be asserted to auto-answer.

Once the modem is connected to the line, Data Terminal Ready must remain asserted to maintain the connection; its inhibition causes disconnection from the communications line, disrupting a data link in progress. Because an asserted Data Terminal Ready is also required for transmitting data on the Transmitted Data (pin 2) line, Data Terminal Ready is, in effect, a master control for the modem.

RING INDICATOR (RI, PIN 22, TO DTE)

This pin is asserted during a ring on the line. Ring Indicator is supposed to be asserted "approximately coincident" with the ON segment of the ringing signal and inhibited between rings. This signal appears regardless of the state of Data Terminal Ready (pin 20).

If two data rates are possible, the higher of the two is represented by asserting DSRD. This function can, by user agreement, be bidirectional: the DTE may assert DSRD (pin 23) to force the modem to use the higher of the two rates or the modem may assert DSRD to report the data rate of data link.

Electrical Signal Characteristics

Although most of the RS-232 interface's electrical characteristics are irrelevant to the programmer, some knowledge of the subject is necessary for a well-rounded understanding of the topic.

SPEED AND POWER

The RS-232 standard allows speeds from "zero to a nominal upper limit of 20,000 bits per second." In most installations, the data rate is limited to 19,200 bps. EIA 561 (the 8-pin connector) permits speeds up to 38,400 bps. The standard also cautions against cable lengths in excess of 50 feet unless the total cable capacitance is less than 2,500 picofarads. The EIA's limitation of speed is more of a warning than a prohibition. In fact, the interface on most microcomputers is driven by UARTs capable of speeds above 100,000 bps. The upper limit on speed is often imposed by cable length instead of the frequency capabilities of the ICs.

The interface must be able to sustain a short circuit of indefinite duration between any two of its pins without sustaining damage. In such cases, current must not exceed .5 ampere. These characteristics result in a safe, robust interface, which, importantly, is highly tolerant of cabling goofs.[19]

LOGIC LEVELS

The RS-232 standard specifies a *bipolar logic level.* That is, logic levels are represented not only by the magnitude of voltage levels but by the polarities as well. The maximum voltage permitted on any circuit is ±15 volts.

The RS-232 standard actually defines four logic levels. Inputs have different definitions from outputs, and the data functions—Transmitted Data (pin 2) and Received Data (pin 3)—are different from control functions. Figure 5.14 shows the logic-level definitions of RS-232 for inputs and outputs. Binary logic levels for outputs are +5 to +15 and –5 to –15; voltages between +5 and –5 are undefined. Binary logic levels for inputs are +3 to +15 and –3 to –15; voltages between +3 and –3 are undefined. The different logic level from input to output is referred to as the noise margin. It also means that the interface can tolerate 2 volts of noise (peak) or a 2-volt Ohm's Law drop between DTE and DCE.

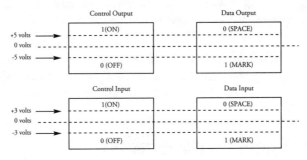

FIGURE 5.14.

Logic levels for RS-232 control functions.

[19]While the interface cannot be harmed by connection among its own pins or those of another RS-232 device, it is easily damaged by connection to a device that does not observe the same current and voltage limitations.

If this seems like an odd interface for computer equipment, remember that it was designed largely to accommodate teleprinter technology in which, by a century of tradition, the bipolar communications line idles (MARKs) at a negative voltage.

In most RS-232 interfaces, the logic level for control signal inputs is effectively monopolar, so any voltage less than +3 volts inhibits the input. As a general rule, a disconnected, or floating input behaves like an inhibited one. Although these are precisely the kind of facts that eventually lead to trouble, they can save time when troubleshooting problems on the interface.

RS-232 LEVEL CONVERSION

Because RS-232 voltages and logic levels are not normally used in computer circuitry, level conversion is necessary. This is performed by special ICs known as *EIA (RS-232) line drivers* and *line receivers*. For electronic reasons, these devices are usually inverters, which means that the inputs and outputs of an asynchronous I/O controller IC (UART) must compensate for this inversion. Figure 5.15 shows how, for instance, the RTS and the CTS inputs of a UART must actually be RTS and CTS to compensate for the level inversion caused by the interface driver ICs.

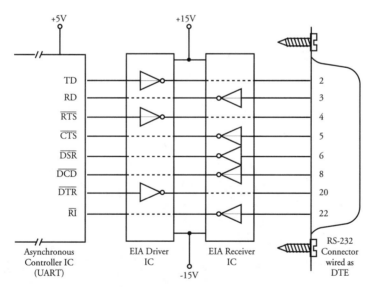

FIGURE 5.15.

Typical RS-232 logic-level conversion hardware.

Mechanical Description of Interface Circuits

The standard connector, whose specification was added to the standard in revision D, is the ever-present DB-25, which is sometimes called the *RS-232 connector*. The standard specifies a female connector for the DCE, and a male connector for the DTE. It gives some guidelines about where the connectors should be placed. While the DB-25 is likely to remain standard on large external modems, its dimensions make it impractical when size reduction is an important design.

The IBM PC AT broke with the DB-25 transition by using a 9-pin connector. This connector, shown in Figure 5.17 was standardized post hoc in EIA/TIA 572. A need for even smaller connectors produced EIA/TIA 561. Both standards are logically and electrically compatible with RS-232 except that 561 explicitly permits speeds up to 38,400 bps.

The RS-232 limitation of speed to about 19.2K is more of a warning than a prohibition. In fact, the RS-232 interface on most microcomputers is driven by UARTs capable of speeds up to 115K. The upper limit on speed is often imposed by cable length instead of the frequency capabilities of the ICs.

FIGURE 5.16.
EIA/TIA 232-E: Pin assignments on the 25-pin connector.

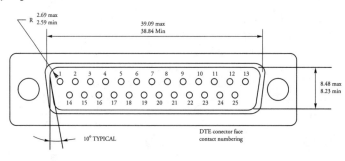

FIGURE 5.17.
EIA/TIA 574: Pin assignments on the 9-pin connector.

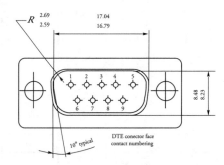

FIGURE 5.18.
EIA/TIA 561: Pin assignments on the 8-pin connector.

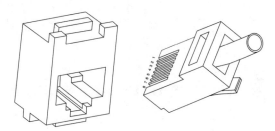

Real-World RS-232

The descriptions of the RS-232 interface presented so far are essentially recitations of the formal descriptions presented in the EIA document. We will now examine these same subjects under the harsh light of reality. In a later section, "Nonstandard Uses of RS-232," we will examine some of the unauthorized uses to which the RS-232 interface is put.

Modems and the RS-232 Interface

The control functions found on the typical microcomputer modem RS-232 interface scarcely resemble the descriptions presented earlier. Here is a brief and necessarily incomplete discussion of these control leads as you are likely to find them. The explanations assume full-duplex modems. Remember, this refers only to the modem interface; we will discuss the microcomputer side of the interface separately later.

Transmit Data	(TD, Pin 2, to DCE) The EIA standard requires that TD be held at MARK (negative voltage) when no carrier is present. Because this is always observed, it provides an almost foolproof method to classify an unknown interface.
Received Data	(RD, Pin 3, to DTE) The EIA standard requires that Received Data be held at MARK when no carrier is present. The fact that this is never observed and that the same requirement for the transmitter is always observed provides an almost foolproof method to classify an unknown interface. The transmitter can be located simply by locating the negative voltage (MARK).
Request to Send	(RTS, Pin 4, to DCE) On modems that support hardware handshaking, Request to Send is the DTE's way of flow-controlling the modem. In this role, it is called RTR, Ready to Receive. On modems without hardware handshaking, Request to Send input is unused. For a discussion of hardware handshaking, see "Modems and Flow Control" later in this chapter.
Clear to Send	(CTS, Pin 5, to DTE) On modems that support hardware handshaking, Clear to Send becomes Ready for Receiving and is the modem's way of flow controlling the DTE. On modems without hardware handshaking, the Clear to Send output is permanently asserted. For a discussion of hardware handshaking, see "Modems and Flow Control" later in this chapter.

Data Set Ready	(DSR, Pin 6,to DTE) Usually, Data Set Ready is permanently asserted on microcomputer modems. Its sole value in this role is as an indicator that the modem is powered up and ready. Occasionally, however, it is permanently wired to the Data Carrier Detect (pin 8) output.
Data Carrier Detect	(DCD, Pin 8, to DTE) Data Carrier Detect is supported on virtually every microcomputer and modem. It is asserted after the modem has completed issuing all its responses to the dialing operation.
Data Terminal Ready	(DTR, Pin 20, to DCE) Luckily, most microcomputer modems support Data Terminal Ready in a fairly standard way: as a master control for the modem. When Data Terminal Ready is inhibited, the modem does not transmit data to or receive data from the DTE, answer or dial the telephone. In short, without Data Terminal Ready, the modem goes functionally limp. Remember, though, that Ring Indicator (pin 22) operates independently of Data Terminal Ready.
Ring Indicator	(RI, Pin 22, to DTE) This signal is supported by most microcomputer modems. The voltage pulse produced does not occur at the ringer frequency, but remains asserted for the duration of the ring.
Data Signal Rate Detector	(DSRD, Pin 23, to DTE) Not all modems support this feature and where support exists, the pin designation varies. On the 212A-compatible modems, for example, DSRD is on pin 12, whereas on smart modems it is sometimes also supported on pin 23.

Of the signals on this list, it is safe to assume only that Transmitted Data (pin 2), Received Data (pin 3), Data Carrier Detect (pin 8), Data Terminal Ready (pin 20), Ring Indicator (pin 22), and perhaps Data Set Ready (pin 6) are always present and active. Request to Send (pin 4) and Clear to Send (pin 5) are usually present but may be inactive (permanently asserted) if the modem does not support hardware handshaking.

Figure 5.19 shows an illustration of the resulting connection. DSRD is also likely to be present in dual-speed modems but should be discounted because the typical microcomputer supports neither of the pins on which it is commonly found (12 and 23). Although other RS-232 inputs on the microcomputer may be available for this purpose, a special cable would be required to cross-connect DSRD on the modem to the microcomputer's input. (As we all know, there is no quicker way to deter customers than to require special cabling.)

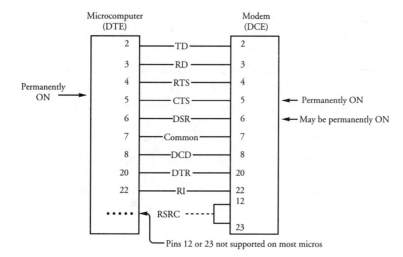

FIGURE 5.19.

The typical connection between a microcomputer and a modem.

A SAMPLE RS-232 INTERCHANGE

The interrelationship of the RS-232 signals is best understood by a step-by-step analysis of the procedure for answering an incoming call. We are assuming that the modem is full-duplex and that, uncharacteristically, Data Set Ready (pin 6) is present both as an output on the modem and as an input on the microcomputer and that it behaves in the manner prescribed by the RS-232 standard. The word ON is used to mean asserted: logic 1.

The state of the two devices just as a ring occurs is shown in Figure 5.20a.

1. The software in the microcomputer (DTE) constantly monitors the Ring Indicator (pin 22), waiting for it to be asserted (ON).

2. A ring occurs on the telephone line and the modem (DCE) asserts the Ring Indicator for the duration of the ringing pulse.

3. The software notices that the Ring Indicator is asserted and begins to count the number of rings by counting the number of ON/OFF transitions of the Ring Indicator. When the programmed ring count is reached, the software asserts the Data Terminal Ready (pin 20), which forces the modem to go off hook (answer the telephone). Figure 5.20b shows this.

4. After waiting 2 seconds (an FCC rule), the modem automatically begins to transmit its answer carrier. The modem now asserts its Data Set Ready (pin 6) to inform the microcomputer that it has performed all preliminary duties and is awaiting a carrier. (Recall that many modems permanently assert Data Set Ready.) This state is shown in Figure 5.20c.

5. While keeping Data Terminal Ready (pin 20) asserted, the microcomputer's software monitors Data Set Ready (pin 6). When Data Set Ready goes ON, the microcomputer knows that the modem is ready for a data link; the microcomputer immediately begins to monitor Data Carrier Detect (pin 8) for evidence that the data link exists.

6. When the originate modem's carrier appears on the phone line, the answer modem asserts the Data Carrier Detect (pin 8).

7. Full-duplex communication begins on Transmit Data (pin 2) and Received Data (pin 3).[20] During data link, the microcomputer monitors the Data Carrier Detect to make certain that a data link still exists. This state is shown in Figure 5.20e.

8. Communications are now complete. The microcomputer inhibits the Data Terminal Ready. The modem responds by removing its carrier tone, inhibiting the Data Carrier Detect, and inhibiting Data Set Ready. With the connection broken, the modem returns to the state shown in Figure 5.20a, ready to receive or make another call.

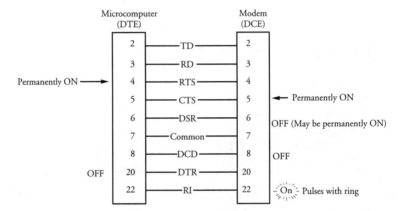

A

An incoming ring is reported on the Ring Indicator (pin 22).

B

The microcomputer tells the modem to answer the call by asserting Data Terminal Ready (pin 20).

---

[20]If this were a half-duplex connection, the modem and microcomputer would begin RTS/CTS line-turnaround handshaking on pins 4 and 5.

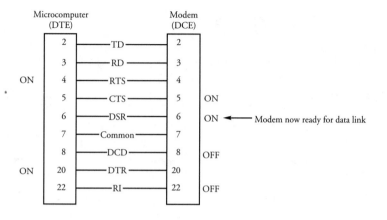

C

The modem asserts the Data Set Ready to report finishing preliminary duties.

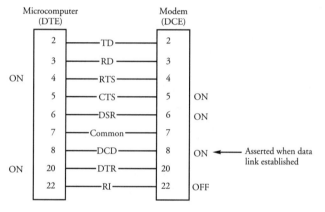

D

The modem's Data Carrier Detect reports that the data link has been established.

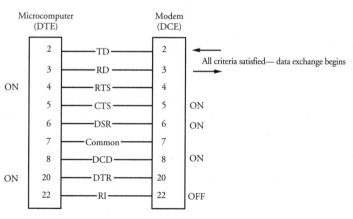

E

The modem's Data Carrier Detect reports that the data link has been established.

FIGURE 5.20.

RS-232 interchange for answering an incoming call.

The Microcomputer Interface

Because of their enormous variety, it is difficult to make general observations about the RS-232 interfaces found on microcomputers. There is a very good reason why this is so: the microcomputer lies completely outside of RS-232 considerations. As a matter of fact, microcomputers did not exist when the EIA formulated RS-232. This raises an interesting question: Is a microcomputer DTE or DCE? Should computer manufacturers configure their serial ports as DTEs to interface with modems or as DCEs to drive DTEs such as printers or terminals? Computers with two serial ports have a simple solution: configure one each way and label one "Printer" for driving a DTE and the other "Modem" for driving a DCE.

There are no ground rules in serial port configuration: manufacturers respond according to how they foresee the uses to which their equipment will be put. Two other factors shape the character of the microcomputer serial port. First, most microcomputer operating systems support modem I/O and printer I/O through the same physical port. As we shall see shortly, the needs of an operating system's printer driver are totally different from those of a modem driver. Second, the number of RS-232 control functions on current UARTs is limited. The typical UART, for example, provides two RS-232 outputs and two to four RS-232 inputs. With such a paucity of control signals, designers are understandably conservative and tend to allocate them to standard pin numbers and, where possible, standard functions.

A SYSTEM VIEW

As I just mentioned, a single microcomputer serial port usually serves several logical system functions such as modem, printer, and AUX device. Therefore, do not be surprised to discover that the system enforces arbitrary RS-232 rules on all serial I/O. The IBM PC family represents the height of folly in this regard, in which the system—DOS and ROM BIOS—does not contain simple, unadorned functions to perform character-by-character serial I/O. For every byte, the serial output function perfunctorily asserts the Request to Send (pin 4) and Data Terminal Ready (pin 20) outputs, then tests that both Clear to Send (pin 5) and Data Set Ready (pin 6) inputs are enabled before transmitting the byte. Likewise, the serial input function refuses to read data from the serial port unless Data Set Ready is asserted. If these constraints are not bad enough, the system provides no mechanism to defeat them.

There's an important lesson to be learned here. Programmers like to regard the serial port as a portable medium through which they can communicate with dissimilar (nonstandard) devices that may or may not support RS-232 control signals. Indeed, in many cases, the lowly serial port is the only way to bring down a hardware Tower of Babel. Be forewarned: as far as microcomputer operating systems are concerned, all serial I/O is to some degree RS-232 I/O. There is no such thing as "general-purpose" serial I/O. If you wish to perform I/O through the system's resources (operating system calls, ROM routines, etc.), be prepared to obey an arbitrary subset of the RS-232 modem control rules even for simple tasks that manifestly have nothing to do with modems or RS-232.

The Smart Modem

Formal RS-232 modem control, when viewed from the point of view of microcomputers, is suffocatingly medieval and certainly far more complicated than it needs to be. In this sense, the *smart* or *intelligent* modem is the microcomputer world's Enlightenment. Although Chapters 8 and 9 are devoted entirely to the study of the smart modem, the subject is worth a few paragraphs here, if for no other reason than to contrast its implicit philosophy with that of the "dumb" (RS-232-controlled) modem.

The conventional modems studied so far interact with their computer equipment at the hardware level: by sending voltages across wires and interpreting them according to a complicated set of rules. Data and control information are always separate. By contrast, the smart modem interacts with computer equipment by exchanging ASCII messages on the Transmitted Data (pin 2) and Received Data (pin 3) data leads. No RS-232 control lines are needed because all modem control functions—dialing, answering, hanging up the telephone, and so forth—are accomplished by sending the smart modem strings of ordinary ASCII characters. The smart modem, in turn, replies to each command with its own ASCII messages. These range from simple messages acknowledging receipt of a command to more complicated ones that narrate the progress of a telephone call.

Today, virtually every modem sold for use with microcomputers is a smart modem. Why? Smart modems sell because their ASCII communication invites interaction with humans who can issue commands and monitor progress in their own language instead of via invisible electronic signals with obscure names and meanings. Figure 5.21 depicts the simplicity of the connection required to control a smart modem.

Notice that the only wires between the smart modem and the computer are Transmitted Data (pin 2), Received Data (pin 3), and Signal Common (pin 7). Although the smart modem itself may not require RS-232 controls, the computer's operating system may demand them. Accordingly, Figure 5.21 shows standard output-to-input handshaking tricks. The same cable could be used to connect a modem to a computer configured DCE simply by cross-connecting Transmitted Data and Received Data.

Modems and Flow Control

We have seen how in recent years DSP technology—by increasing the baud rate and facilitating clever encoding schemes—has improved modem throughput by a factor of five or six. These schemes, however, leave one relationship unchanged: the DTE and the modem must handle data at the same rate. In other words, if a modem is rated at 14,400 bps, software need run only at that rate.

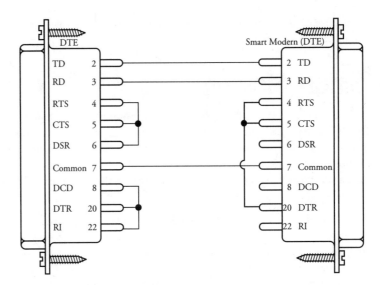

FIGURE 5.21.

A theoretical three-wire cable for a smart modem.

In rcent years, *error-correcting* and *data compression protocols*, which we will study in detail in Chapter 10, have improved the throughput of the modem by another factor of three or four. These protocols enable the modem to accept data from the DTE at rates several times that of the modulation. Because the amount of compression varies with the content of the data, maximum throughput is obtained only if the DTE's baud rate is equal to the peak bit rate of the modem. This means, however, that when the modem's bit rate drops below the baud rate of the DTE, the modem must be able to pause the DTE. Similarly, the throughput of the modem can be temporarily reduced by the retransmissions required to correct errors. In other words, bi-directional *flow control* is required between the modem and DTE.

RTS/CTS HARDWARE FLOW CONTROL

Revision E of RS-232 was the first to acknowledge the need for flow control. In the case where the modem must restrain the DTE, the traditional definition of CTS was felt to be adequate:

> *The OFF condition is an indication to the DTE that it should not transfer data across the interface on interchange Circuit BA (Transmitted Data)...*

There was no traditional circuit definition that enabled the DTE to restrain the modem. Circuit CJ (Ready for Receiving) was defined and assigned to pin 4 as a logical substitute for Request to Send:

> *This circuit is used to control the transfer of data (flow control) on Circuit BB (Received Data) when an intermediate function such as error control is being used in the DCE. The ON condition on Circuit CJ (Ready for Receiving) indicates that the DTE is capable of receiving data.*

The OFF condition indicates that the DTE is incapable of receiving data and causes the DCE, or intermediate function, to retain the data.

Flow control between one modem and one DTE is ineffective unless it is functionally extended backward through the remote modem to the ultimate source of the data, the remote DTE. Therefore in some DCEs the OFF condition also causes a signal to be transmitted to the distant DTE causing an OFF condition to be placed on Circuit CB (Clear to Send) extending the flow control to the distant DTE.

IN-BAND FLOW CONTROL

Hardware signals such as RS-232 are considered to be *out-of-band signals* because the signals are carried in a different channel from the data. There are occasions when out-of-band signaling is impossible or does not produce the desired effect when:

- Not enough control wires are present on the either the DTE or DCE interface. This is the case of the Macintosh computer, whose serial port supports but a single input and a single output.[21]
- The modem must be controlled remotely.
- The modem is controlled through a network.
- Network latency, processing delays, and buffering disrupt time-dependent commands.[22]

To solve these and other issues, TIA[23] is proposing a standard of *in-band signals* in which the control information is imbedded transparently as a character sequence in the data stream itself. This technique, known as *basic transparency*[24] requires foreknowledge and cooperation between DTE and DCE. A character, usually DLE (ASCII 10H) is chosen as the *transparency introducer* or *hot character*. The hot character is inserted into the data stream followed immediately by the control character. On the receive side, the receiver scans the data stream for the hot character and extracts the control character and the hot character from the data stream. Transparency is achieved by having the transmitter double all existing characters in the data that match the hot character. To provide symmetry, the receiver identifies pairs of hot characters as valid data and discards one of them.

---

[21]Despite the fact that the 8530 UART in the Mac has adequate inputs and outputs, Mac programmers have the choice of either RTS/CTS controlling the flow on the one hand or controlling the modem with DTR and detecting carrier with DCD on the other.

[22]For an example of a time-dependent command, see the description of the On-Line Escape procedure in Chapter 8.

[23]TIA PN-2812 in the TR-30.4 Committee.

[24]Defined in ISO 2111, "Data communication—Basic mode control procedures."

To illustrate, suppose we have a modem installed at a remote site where it operates constantly in a data link. When our local end senses some kind of trouble with the remote modem, we wish to send a signal that causes the modem to sound a buzzer indicating that it needs attention from the on-site humans. Built into the modem's design is transparency decoding using the DLE character: <DLE><BEL> makes the buzzer sound. As luck would have it, at the very moment we insert the buzz control, the unprocessed data stream looks like this:

> Mary<DLE> had <DLE><DLE>a little lamb.

Using the transparency technique of doubling natural occurrences of the hot characters, the stream is transformed to:

> Mary<DLE><DLE> had <DLE><DLE><DLE><DLE>a <DLE><BEL>little lamb.

To invert the doubling performed by our modem, the remote modem tosses one of every pair of <DLE> characters. When it encounters a single <DLE>, it extracts it and the following character from the stream. In this case, the following character is the BEL.

Using in-band transparency with hot character EM (ASCII 19H), the TIA proposes to duplicate the logical definitions of critical RS-232 circuits. Table 5.5 gives these.

Table 5.5. Proposed TIA in-band modem control.

From DTE	From DCE	Function
<EM><40><length>	<EM><60><length>	BREAK length x 10 ms
<EM><41><1ength>	<EM><61><length>	MARK length x 10 ms
<EM><42>		RTS OFF
<EM><43>		RTS ON
<EM><44>		DTR OFF
<EM><45>		DTR ON
<EM><46>		RTR OFF
<EM><47>		RTR ON
	<EM><62>	CTS OFF
	<EM><63>	CTS ON
	<EM><64>	DSR OFF
	<EM><65>	DSR ON
	<EM><66>	DCD OFF
	<EM><67>	DCD ON
	<EM><68>	RI OFF
	<EM><69>	RI ON

From DTE	From DCE	Function
	<EM><6A>	Modem off-hook
	<EM><6B>	Modem on-hook
<EM><5F>	<EM><7F>	Poll other device status

Nonstandard Uses of RS-232

A pair of modems is functionally just a wire with awful transmission characteristics. The ends of this wire ultimately connect two DTEs. This leads to the obvious observation that two devices that function properly through modems should work identically if connected directly by a cable.

The Null Modem

Attempting to cable two DTE devices directly—without going through modems—immediately gives rise to problems because the RS-232 interface in each DTE is designed for connection to a DCE (modem). The first is a hardware problem: two devices of the same sex[25] have the same connector. The second problem, illustrated in Figure 5.22, shows how an ordinary, "straight-through" cable produces an unworkable I/O arrangement by connecting inputs to inputs, outputs to outputs.

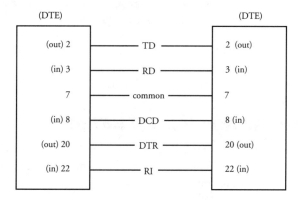

FIGURE 5.22.

Same-sex connection produces unworkable I/O connection.

---

[25]The term *gender,* which is a grammatical attribute of words, is often used to describe the physical conformation of plugs and jacks and even the concept of DTE and DCE. Null modems are even sometimes called *gender changers. Male* and *female* are sexes; *masculine* and *feminine* are genders. To say a plug is of the "male gender," therefore, is not only incorrect, it is somehow insufferably prudish.

At the time, the special cable is built to solve the connector mismatch. The two devices can also be custom-wired in such a manner that they cooperatively satisfy the handshaking requirements. This kind of connection, known as a *null modem* and shown in Figure 5.23, tricks the two interfaces by using the DTEs' own output voltages to satisfy the necessary RS-232 input logic.[26]

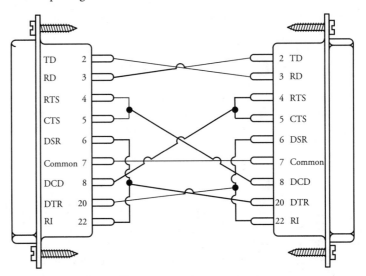

FIGURE 5.23.

The null modem cable trick.

The most important connection on the null modem is the crossing of Transmitted Data (pin 2) and Received Data (pin 3) so that the data path is correct. The remaining connections satisfy control, or handshaking, logic. For example, assertion of Request to Send (pin 4, an output) results in enabling Clear to Send (pin 5, an input) and, to simulate a data link, also enables Data Carrier Detect (pin 8) on the other interface. Similarly, assertion of Data Terminal Ready (pin 20) output simulates an incoming call by enabling its Data Set Ready (pin 6) and Ring Indicator (pin 22) inputs.

Interconnecting Non-Modem Devices

Although it is beyond the scope of this book to delve very deeply into the subject of non-RS-232 hardware interfacing,[27] we will take a look at the most common problem in this area: interfacing a computer to a serial printer.

A device that cannot use data as fast as the interface can send it requires some sort of flow control. Printers are the classic case of the need for *buffer-full handshaking*. If characters are sent to the printer at a faster rate than the printer can print them (as is usually the

---

[26]I should point out that although the null modem configuration can be used to interconnect two DCEs, such a connection is, in RS-232 terms anyway, an absurdity.

[27]A complete discussion of this subject is contained in *The RS-232 Solution*, by Joe Campbell (Sybex, 1989).

case), the printer places the incoming characters in a queue until they can be printed. The queue is in the form of an internal buffer whose size ranges from a few tens of bytes to several kilobytes in length. Because data is added to the buffer faster than it is removed, however, a buffer of any size eventually becomes full.

As explained in Chapter 4, there are two basic methods by which a peripheral and a computer can perform flow control: through software or through hardware. Software flow-control consists of a procedure such as the XON/XOFF or ETX/ACK protocols described in Chapter 4. The advantage of this method is that it can be performed over a modem link; its disadvantage is that many printers are send-only devices that cannot generate a TD data signal. The second and most common method is for the printer to use an RS-232 control signal to notify the computer of an impending full buffer.

What is the correct RS-232 pin for the printer to use? The answer is that there is no correct way because the EIA standard does not address the need for interconnecting to non-modem devices. Indeed, flow control between a DTE and a non-error-correcting modem is unnecessary because the DTE-DCE link operates at the same bit rate as the carrier. Because the standard itself is quiet on this subject, manufacturers are forced to choose handshaking pins arbitrarily. Although there is, predictably, little agreement on this topic, two broad views are discernible.

The first view, held mainly by peripheral manufacturers, uses one of the undefined pins in the EIA standard (see Table 5.4) or, failing that, a pin that is unlikely to be in use. The advantage of this method is that buffer-full handshaking, being out of the way, does not interfere with standard RS-232 modem control signals. The second view, held mainly by computer manufacturers, explicitly uses one or more RS-232 modem control pins for buffer-full handshaking. As was pointed out a few pages ago, microcomputer controller ICs (UARTs) support only a few RS-232 inputs; consequently, computer manufacturers do not wish to waste an input by devoting it exclusively to an eccentric pin. Figure 5.24, for example, shows the cable required between an IBM PC family and an NEC Spinwriter printer—once a very popular combination.

On the IBM PC side, the handshaking is performed on Data Set Ready (pin 6). Because system firmware enables the PC's transmitter only when Clear to Send (pin 5) and Data Set Ready are asserted, the positive voltage from the normally asserted Request to Send (pin 4) is jumpered to Clear to Send (pin 5) to form a trick. On the Spinwriter side, the printer refuses to print unless its Clear to Send, Data Set Ready, and Data Carrier Detect (pin 8) inputs are all enabled. These requirements are satisfied by tricks from Request to Send and Data Terminal Ready. Buffer-full handshaking is provided on pin 19[28] and connected to the IBM PC's Data Set Ready.

---

[28]**Warning:** The Spinwriter contains an internal switch which determines whether the voltage produced on pin 19 is positive or negative.

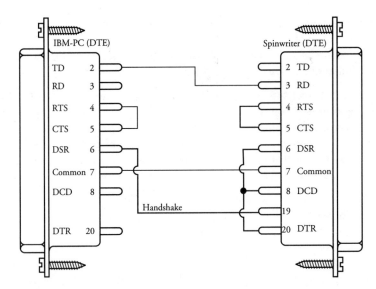

FIGURE 5.24.

Cable required between an IBM PC and an NEC Spinwriter model 3510.

In a sense, it is foolish even to talk about standards in this area; none exist. Considering the prodigious amount of pain and suffering that printer interfacing has inflicted upon computer users, it is surprising that no standard has been proposed.

Conclusion

It would be nice to report that intelligent peripherals such as smart modems have relieved the vexation associated with asynchronous serial I/O. Unfortunately, modems and the RS-232 dominate the character of serial I/O on computers in general. This is particularly true on microcomputers such as the Macintosh, which have inexplicably limited serial ports.

The lamentable conclusion to be drawn is that in order to circumvent the system's draconian enforcement of RS-232 rules, microcomputer programmers often must address the hardware directly. Yet we cannot always escape these rules by bypassing system software: RS-232 logic is actually built into some UARTs. Some, for example, refuse to transmit and receive unless the Clear to Send and Data Carrier Detect inputs are enabled. Although this *auto-handshake* mode is usually (and thankfully) under software control, its mere presence indicates how deeply intertwined serial I/O is with the RS-232 way of doing things. In summary, serial I/O and RS-232 seem, for better or for worse, inextricably wed 'til death do part.

In almost every chapter, I have mentioned the asynchronous controller IC known as the UART. Because this device seems to dominate the conversation, it is finally time to explore it in depth. In the next chapter we will construct a "conceptual UART" based upon a survey of the tasks such a device must perform. In Chapter 7, we will examine two radically different real UARTs. Chapters 8 and 9 are devoted entirely to an exhaustive analysis of the smart modem.

The UART: A Conceptual Model

In Chapter 2, we "reinvented" asynchronous I/O and in Chapter 5 we examined the workings of a modem and a typical microcomputer RS-232 interface. In this chapter, we'll see how these concepts are implemented in the real world. Luckily, today this world is more pleasant than just a few years ago when only indentured programmers could be persuaded to write asynchronous serial I/O. The rudiments of serial I/O in software, however, are deviously simple. A byte is output by writing its individual bits to a hardware latch which, in turn, drives an interface to the outside world (RS-232, for example). Conversely, input is performed by successively reading bits from a similar latch and assembling them into bytes. The difficulty in these processes arises when trying to implement the intricate timing relationships of the data and framing bits. Today, these problems are all handled almost transparently by an integrated circuit known as a Universal Asynchronous Receiver/Transmitter, or UART.[1]

Asynchronous I/O in Software

There is no better way to gain an appreciation of the UART than to see what a programmer's life would be like without it. To this end, we'll briefly study what is required to perform asynchronous serial I/O in software. Figure 6.1 shows a flow chart for a hypothetical assembly language routine to output a single byte using only the processor's clock cycle as a time reference. This chart assumes the existence of a processor instruction, SRC, that shifts all bits of the byte right and shifts the least significant bit into the carry flag. This instruction provides a rapid

---

[1]The UART has many other names: *serial controller*, ACE (Asynchronous Communications Element) and ACIA (Asynchronous Communications Interface Adaptor). All describe the same device. If the device also supports synchronous I/O, it is referred to as a USART.

method for ascertaining the value of each bit. This flow chart also assumes the existence of a data port into which data is *latched*, or written.

Software Asynchronous Output

After fetching the byte for transmission, the program immediately generates a START bit by latching the output FALSE for one bit-time. Next, the SRC instruction shifts the byte right once, placing the least significant bit into the carry flag. The value of the carry flag is then latched to the output for one bit-time. This process of shifting right and outputting the carry flag continues until all bits have been transmitted. If parity is enabled, the parity bit is calculated and latched to the output for one bit-time. The STOP bit is created by latching the output TRUE and the routine ends, leaving the output in this state (MARK-ING). The number of bits passed through the "All bits sent?" and "All STOP bits sent?" loops depends upon the data format currently in effect.

> Although most microprocessors have SRC-like instructions, the same effect can be achieved manually by successively applying AND masks to the output byte. After the AND operation, the Zero flag reflects the value of the bit to be output. This approach is slower and clumsier, however, because the value of the AND mask must correspond to the bit *number* being transmitted, 0000_0001 for the least significant bit, 1000_0000 for the most significant.

If writing the routine represented in the flow chart doesn't seem too difficult, consider the innocent-looking box labeled, "Wait one bit-time." Given the clock frequency and the number of clock cycles required for each instruction, writing a calibrated delay routine is not particularly difficult. Such a routine typically employs a register for counting the iterations of a loop of instructions of known duration. The routine depicted in Figure 6.1, however, requires a *variable* delay because the duration of a bit depends upon the current baud rate. At 300 baud, for example, a bit lasts 3.333 milliseconds (.00333 second), but at 19.2 Kbaud only 52 microseconds (.000052 second). A routine to provide an accurate variable delay over a *wide range* is rather more difficult to construct. Variable delay routines use the same principle as fixed-delay routines, but add one or more outer loops that repeatedly call a fixed-delay routine. Unfortunately, such multi-nested loop routines are not accurate over a wide range due to the time wasted in managing the loops.

An alternative to software timing loops is the use of a hardware timer, usually a crystal oscillator whose frequency is a multiple (harmonic) of the maximum baud rate desired. In this scheme, instead of counting iterations of processor instructions, software counts timer pulses, whose duration is known. We will return to the problem of timing again in Chapter 11 in another connection, so we will leave this topic for now. It is important to understand, though, that the code represented in the flow chart block "Wait one bit-time" is deceptively simple and inherently dependent on such system factors as processor type, clock frequency, and system interrupt structure.

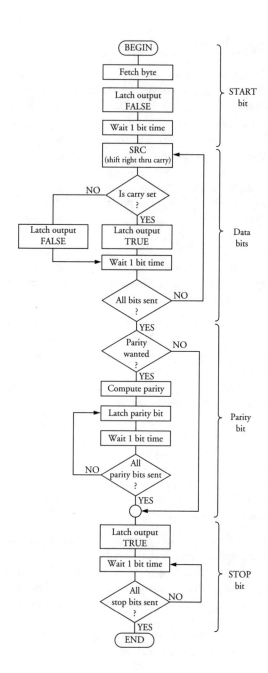

FIGURE 6.1.

A hypothetical flow chart for transmitting a single byte in software.

Software Asynchronous Input

The logic to assemble an inbound byte is, as you might expect, almost the inverse of that for transmitting a byte. The timing is similar, as is the need to deal with a variable number of data bits, the possibility of a parity bit, as well as a variable number of STOP bits. The flow chart for receiving an inbound byte is shown in Figure 6.2. Despite these similarities, however, there are important differences. The receiver continually polls the input, waiting for a START bit (FALSE) to signal the beginning of an SDU. After the START bit is detected, the specified number of data bits is successively fetched and shifted into the byte under construction. The reception of the parity bit (if needed) followed by the STOP bit complicates the receive routine, for it is at this point that serialization errors and BREAKs must be detected. The first error test occurs after the reception of the parity bit: a parity bit that differs from the one expected must be reported. Once the parity bit has been processed, the input latch is read again to verify that a valid (i.e., TRUE) STOP bit is present. If not, a serialization error must be reported. The manner in which errors are reported depends on the system: a flag may be set in memory, a system interrupt may be generated, or, as in some implementations, errors are not reported at all.

Although you can probably conceive of writing these software functions to transmit and receive data, the flow charts in Figures 6.1 and 6.2 ignore an important aspect of asynchronous serial I/O: line sharing. As shown, these functions would be suitable only for simplex or half-duplex transmission. Why? Consider the program timing problems that result from *simultaneously* transmitting and receiving data. In between the transmitted bits, the program also must monitor the incoming line for activity. Now suppose that while transmitting a byte, a valid START bit is detected on the data input line. Your software is now responsible for maintaining two separate timing sequences—one to keep the outbound bits flowing at the prescribed baud rate and another to correctly fetch bits and assembly bytes from the input line. In other words, each function—receive and send—must adjust its timing loop based upon the activity of the other. Add to this picture the possibility that the incoming and outgoing baud rates may differ and you will quickly understand why full-duplex transmission has, until recently, been the bane of system programmers.

As complicated and distasteful as software-controlled, full-duplex, polled I/O may be, it is attainable on single-user microcomputers because the processor can be devoted entirely to maintaining the interrelated timing loops. Multi-user systems, on the other hand, share processor time among many tasks. In the days when asynchronous serial I/O was still performed in software on larger computers, full-duplex I/O could be attained only through complex interrupt schemes and then only if these interrupts were given the highest priority in the system. Because of this high priority, asynchronous serial I/O jobs tended to dominate a system, usurping time from other jobs.

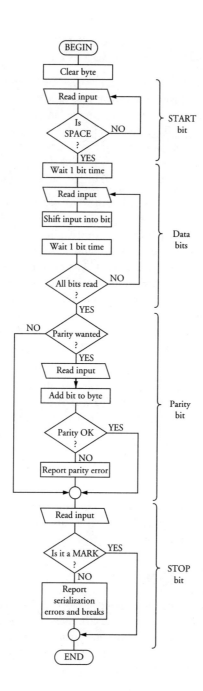

FIGURE 6.2.

Flow chart for receiving a single byte in software.

Introduction to the UART

The basic asynchronous serial I/O functions just described, plus many others we will soon describe, are built into the Universal Asynchronous Receiver/Transmitter, or UART. The idea behind a UART is to relieve both programmer and processor of the toil associated with asynchronous serial I/O. To receive and send data, the program simply reads and writes bytes to the UART, which appears to the processor as one or more ordinary memory locations or I/O ports. The UART's circuitry handles the grimy details of assembling and reassembling bytes, handles the timing, and, in general, unburdens the processor.

Appliance-level UARTs first appeared around 1973 and quickly became ubiquitous. Because of the degree of simplicity UARTs brought to the previously arcane endeavor, software asynchronous I/O faded without much protest. Because many companies had huge investments in equipment and software to perform software asynchronous serial I/O, however, one can understand that even after UARTs became permanently entrenched in new computer designs, software asynchronous serial I/O did not instantly disappear from the scene. Because the popularity of the UART coincides roughly with the inception of the microcomputer, some early micro I/O boards did not contain UARTs. Instead, these boards provided support for what was essentially software I/O: an on-board clock, local RAM, address decoding, and, in some cases, a ROM containing the actual I/O routines.[2]

A block diagram for a hypothetical full-function UART is shown in Figure 6.3. For the remainder of this chapter we will study the details of each section of a hypothetical UART, pointing out how the various sections interact with the controlling program. Try to keep in mind that the UART presented here is conceptual— *exactly* no such device exists in nature. In the real world, for instance, you may find UARTs that use *inverted logic*—a 0 bit to represent a TRUE condition. Because such inner details of internal UART design are irrelevant to a conceptual understanding of how the devices work, we will ignore them in our discussions.

In the next chapter, we'll look at three representative samples of real UARTs. Now, before we begin an examination of how the UART transmits and receives serial data, let's take a brief and preliminary look at the *serial data clock*.

The Serial Data Clock

Before we begin our discussion of the serial data clock, it should be noted that in much of the literature on serial communications, the term *baud rate* and *data clock* are used interchangeably. Although this causes no harm in casual discussion, we need the distinction here. As you will soon see, this is more than just an intellectual nicety—the correct functioning of a UART actually depends upon the existence of separate clocks for baud rate

---

[2]Historians will remember Morrow's *Keyed-up 8080* and *Speak-Easy I/O Board* as good examples of this hardware. In what must be one of the great oxymorons of all times, boards such as these later became known as software UARTs.

and internal timing. We postpone further illumination of this point until we have a better understanding of how the UART transmitter and receiver sections actually work.

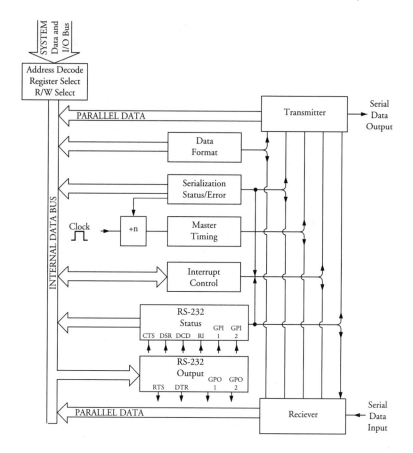

FIGURE 6.3.

A complete block diagram for our hypothetical UART.

Although our block diagram shows the serial data clock to be external to the UART, the actual circuitry for generating the clock may be part of the UART itself. If so, the frequency of the data clock is determined by the contents of a software programmable *baud rate register* (another misnomer). When the clock circuitry is external to the UART, however, the frequency of the data clock may be determined in several other ways:

- *Fixed frequency.* This, of course, occurs only in dedicated applications where the communication rate is not variable. The circuitry for these clock generators tends to be extremely simple, consisting of little more than a crystal and two or three logic gates. In some cases, the UART uses the processor's clock.

- *Variable frequency, software adjustable.* An external clock generator with adjustable frequency is programmable in much the same manner as when the generator is on the UART—by programming a specified register, memory address, or I/O port.

● *Variable frequency, hardware adjustable.* The clock generators of many early microcomputers derived their frequency from the binary value of microswitches (or jumpers) on the pc board. There are two variations to this scheme: first, the frequency of the generator can be dynamically (on the fly) altered by changing the position of the switches; second, the generator loads the value of the switches only at startup and subsequent changes in the switch positions do not affect the frequency.

There is no reason why data must be received and transmitted at the same baud rate. Indeed, in certain full-duplex modem protocols, control and handshaking information is transmitted in a secondary reverse channel at a much lower rate than in the main data channel. In many UARTs, separate clock inputs are provided for transmitter and receiver. The system designer then decides whether to provide separate clocks or to use the same clock signal for both.

The UART Transmitter

A byte to be transmitted is written to the address of the UART's transmitter where it eventually is presented to the transmission section. This section consists largely of a shift register, the control logic to load the byte into the shift register and one or more transmitter buffers. Figure 6.4 shows these functions.

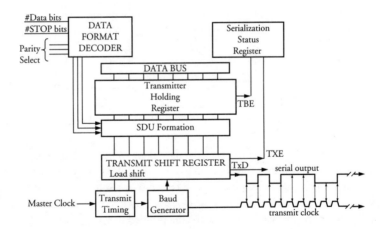

FIGURE 6.4.

Block diagram of hypothetical UART's transmitter.

The transmitter itself consists of a parallel input, serial output shift register. The bits to be transmitted are loaded into the shift register, then shifted out on the negative transition of the *transmit data clock*. When all bits have been shifted out of the transmitter's shift register, the next SDU[3] is loaded and the process repeats. Not counting the START bit, the

---

[3]To refresh your memory, SDU stands for *Serial Data Unit*, the term developed in Chapter 2 for the collective START, data, parity, and STOP bits.

shift register must be large enough to accommodate from 7 bits (5N1) to 11 bits (8P2), although the latter is rare.

The data bits may be loaded directly from the system data bus, but most UARTs contain a transmitter buffer, or *Transmitter Holding register,* which forms a small queue in which data can be temporarily stored while awaiting serialization. A byte for transmission can therefore be written into the UART's holding register while the previous byte is still being clocked out of the shift register. This buffering is not only a convenience, it makes the transmitter more efficient. Because there is an entire SDU within which the processor may replenish the buffer, it is easier to keep the shift register perpetually occupied. There may be several transmitter buffers, but most UARTs contain only one.

FRAMING

Because by definition an SDU begins with a SPACE (0) bit, a 0 can be automatically loaded into the first bit of the SDU. Three elements of the SDU, however, are variables: the number of STOP bits, parity, and the number of data bits. Interposed between the transmitter buffer and the shift register, therefore, is a section labeled *SDU Formation.* Using signals decoded from user-programmable Data Format registers, this section fabricates the actual SDU that is eventually loaded into the shift register. For example, if the UART were programmed for 7E2, the data format logic section would build an SDU for the letter 'E' like this:

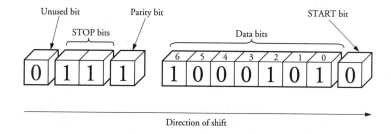

FIGURE 6.5.

Building an SDU for the letter 'E' at 7E2.

Notice that regardless of the format in effect, unused SDU bit positions are left-filled with 0s. Zeros are also shifted into the vacated left-hand positions. With unused positions guaranteed to be 0, the transmitter contains a value of 1 only when all bits except the final STOP bit have been shifted out. This condition is used to announce that the transmitter buffer will be empty after the next shift/clock cycle. If the transmitter buffer contains a byte when the next clock cycle occurs (i.e., when the transmitter becomes empty), that byte is automatically loaded into the transmitter and transmission proceeds anew.[4] If, on the other hand, the transmitter buffer is also empty, the next clock cycle sets the *transmitter empty flag (TXE),* but suppresses the final shift. The TD line, therefore, continues to

---

[4]If 1-1/2 STOP bits are selected, the format control logic arranges fractional bit timing on the last STOP bit.

assert the level of the final STOP bit and the line idles at a TRUE (MARKING) level until another byte arrives to begin the transmission process anew.

TRANSMITTER STATUS

Writing programs to transmit data requires only two items of information about the transmitter: whether both the Transmitter Buffer and the transmitter's shift registers are empty. Each of these conditions is reported through a bit in a *Serialization Status register.* When the data from the buffer is loaded into the transmitter, a *transmitter buffer empty* (TBE) flag signals that the UART can accept another byte. If TBE is clear after the final bit of the SDU is clocked from the transmitter's shift register, the TXE flag signals that the shift register is also empty.

During full-duplex communication, software need only test the value of the TBE bit (in the Serialization Status register) to make certain that the buffer is empty before writing a byte to the UART. At various points in half-duplex communication, however, the modems must reverse their roles—from transmitter to receiver and vice versa. (This action is called *turning the line around.*) Before software can instruct a transmitting modem to become a receiver, it must know not only that the transmitter buffer is empty, but also that the transmitter's shift register itself is empty. Otherwise the line may be reversed in mid-SDU, causing loss of data. (This is called *leaving one in the pipe.*)

The UART's Receiver

A received byte is acquired by reading the address of the UART's receiver section, whose job is to construct an SDU from bits fetched from the serial input line. The UART must then extract the data byte from the surrounding formatting information in the SDU and make the byte available to the data bus. A block diagram of a UART receiver is shown in Figure 6.6. The receiver perpetually monitors the incoming serial line, waiting for a START bit. Once a START bit is detected, successive bits are shifted into the receiver's shift register according to the format described in the UART's user-programmable Data Format registers. After assembly, the byte is moved into a first-in, first-out buffer. Every modern UART has a FIFO, but the size varies from 1 to 5 bytes. (Chapter 20 shows how to obtain a FIFO of essentially unlimited size.)

RECEIVER STATUS

When a byte has been moved into the receiver's FIFO, the RxRDY flag is set TRUE and remains TRUE until all elements of the FIFO are empty. For every element in the FIFO, there is a corresponding Serialization Status register.

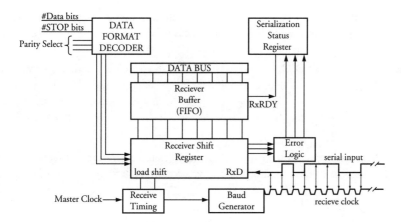

FIGURE 6.6.

A block diagram of a UART receiver.

Errors

The UART in no way forces a response to an error. Once a START bit is detected, the UART dutifully assembles a byte even in the face of cataclysmic errors. There is nothing to prevent your software from reading the resulting ersatz "byte" as it would a valid byte. Although software is under no obligation to test for errors, UARTs inevitably provide a mechanism for reporting them. The responsibility for testing for and handling errors, however, always lies entirely with the software. Throughout this discussion, please keep in mind that the term *serialization error* applies to errors in reception and transmission.

TRANSMITTER ERRORS

As might be supposed, few errors are possible in the transmission process. Writing into a nonempty transmitter buffer results in a *transmitter overwrite* error. When the tranmsitter shift register is allowed to become empty, the serial line becomes idle; this condition, known as *transmitter underrun* error, is irrelevant unless the UART is feeding a synchronous process (such as a modem). Under the assumption that transmit errors are unimportant or at least easily avoided, many UARTs do not even report them.

RECEIVER ERRORS

Unlike the transmission process, a number of problems may arise during reception.

● When bytes arrive faster than they can be read, they are placed in the receiver's FIFO buffer. When this buffer becomes full, it "wraps around" upon itself, with each new byte overwriting an older, and as yet unread, byte in the buffer. This is a *receiver overrun* error.

● If the value of the parity bit does not agree with that decoded from the user-programmable Data Format registers, a *parity error* is reported.

- If an invalid STOP bit is received, and if all data bits and the parity bit are 0, the serial line is assumed to have been FALSE for a time equal to one SDU, and a BREAK is reported.
- If an invalid STOP bit is received, the UART ascertains whether the assembled SDU contains *at least* one TRUE data bit. If so, either the START bit was invalid, or succeeding bits were damaged during transmission. Because it is not possible to ascertain the nature of the error more precisely, the catch-all *framing error* is reported.

The receiver errors just listed assume, of course, that transmitter and receiver are operating at identical baud rates and data format. A mismatch in either always generates an error.

ERROR REPORTING

Serialization errors are reported in the UART's *Serialization Status* register, which is also often used to report the TXE (transmitter's shift register empty), TBE (transmitter buffer empty), and RxRDY flags. Each error or flag is mapped to a single bit in this register. Figure 6.7a shows an example of how these bits may be mapped.

Figure 6.7b depicts how some UARTs, especially those that also support synchronous transmission (i.e., USARTs), devote an entire register to error reporting. The occurrence of an error not only sets a designated bit in this register, it also sets a bit in a general-purpose status register. In this scheme, any transmitter/receiver status and serialization error can be detected by reading a single register. To identify the exact nature of the error, however, another register must be read. In addition to serialization errors, this register also may report the change in status of the RS-232 inputs or a BREAK.

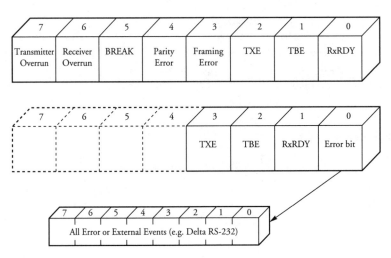

FIGURE 6.7.

Two versions of a UART's Serialization Status register.

ERROR READING

Reading the Error register usually resets all error flags, although, rarely, an explicit *error reset* operation is required. The presence of the error status bits and the transmitter/receiver empty status bits in the same register potentially gives rise to a minor programming problem. When writing receiver routines, it is somehow natural to poll the receiver until its status bit becomes TRUE, then read the byte, then test for errors. Polling in this manner resets the error bits with each poll; the error status must be held in temporary storage until time to act upon it. Of course, the same caution holds for transmitter routines.

Receiver Timing

In describing how the UART transmitter works, we have glossed over the important subject of timing. Although designers of hardware devices strive to make the device's internal timing invisible to the programmer, the UART programmer is actually expected to participate in one important area. You will remember from our discussion in Chapter 2 that the purpose of the START bit is to synchronize the receiver with the transmitter at the beginning of each SDU. Until now, we have discussed this synchronization as it occurs under ideal conditions in which the receiver and transmitter operate at identical baud rates. When the periods of the two baud rates are identical, the point at which the receiver samples the incoming data is *theoretically* unimportant. But because this never happens in practice, we need to examine how different baud rates affect operation.

Figure 6.8 shows the same relationship, but with the receiver operating at a slightly higher baud rate. To dramatize the timing relationships involved, this figure shows the data bits on the incoming line as heavy square waves. The receiver's data clock is shown as an arrow that represents the point at which the receiver actually samples the line.

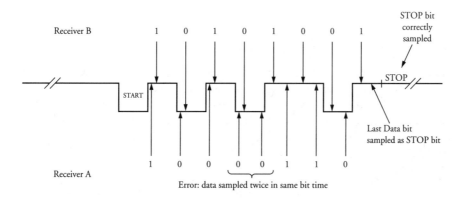

FIGURE 6.8.
Incoming data sampled by two receivers of different phases.

The byte transmitted is the binary value 1011_0101 at 8-NO-1 (remember, the low-order bit is transmitted first). As the diagram shows, receiver A detects the START bit relatively early in its period. Because receiver A's baud rate is slightly higher than the period of the incoming data, the receiver samples the first data bit yet nearer the trailing edge of the *preceding* incoming bit. So far so good. On each successive bit, however, the receiver samples the line earlier and earlier until its sampling pulse "falls over the edge" and actually occurs twice during bit 3. Sampling continues until the UART receives what it assumes is a correct STOP bit, which, due to the sampling "creep," is really just bit 7 of the data. It is important to see that receiver A assembles the wrong byte (0110_0001, the ASCII character 'e'), but *no framing error* is detected. Likewise, you should understand why this phenomenon is possible only with bytes whose low-order bit is TRUE.[5]

Now examine receiver B in Figure 6.8. Its period and bit-to-bit creep are precisely the same as receiver A. The only difference between the two receivers is the difference in the points at which they sample the incoming data (i.e., their *phase relationship*). Because receiver A begins so early in the data bit, its sampling point quickly creeps backwards into the previous data bit. Receiver B, however, begins precisely in the center of the incoming data bit. Because it has farther to creep, receiver B samples the correct incoming data bit for the entire SDU.

Because sampling earlier in the input seems to immunize against sampling creep, there is a temptation to start sampling at the earliest possible moment, say, on the leading edge. That would certainly provide the maximum protection when the receiver's baud rate is higher than the transmitter's, but would have the opposite effect when the speed relationships are reversed. ALTHOUGH there is no cure for errors caused by widely different baud rates, the UART is clearly much more tolerant when its receiver begins serialization near the center of the START bit.

Earlier in this chapter, we discussed the necessity of separate clock signals—one for the UART's internal operations and one to drive the shifting operations in the transmitter and receiver sections. The reason for these two clock signals can now be explained. The frequency of the master serial clock signal is designed to be several times higher than that of the baud rate. The ratio between the baud rate clock and the master data clock is called the *clocking factor*. A clocking factor of 16 is standard, but is programmable on some UARTs. The higher frequency of the master clock signal enables us to make a major improvement in the way START bits are detected.

Instead of sampling the input line at the baud rate frequency, the improved START bit detector samples the incoming line at the rate of the master clock. When the leading edge of a START bit is detected, the START bit detector waits for 8 data clock cycles (which together constitute one-half of a bit time), then begins reading bits from the line. Thereafter sampling of the input occurs once per bit-time (i.e., at the baud rate). By pausing to wait 8 clock cycles for the *center* of the STOP bit, the receiver is effectively "ideally" synchronized to the incoming data.

---

[5]Although the use of parity also would have caught this particular error, there is a disturbing aspect about this type of error. Indeed, one can posit a situation where virtually any single byte might be received incorrectly, but without generating an error condition. Although it is unlikely that such a condition would go undetected for more than 1 or 2 bytes, the inability to associate an error with the byte that caused it is obviously a serious problem in any form of communication.

Figure 6.9 illustrates how well the improved START bit detector works. Under the best conditions—when the line is sampled at the instant the START bit begins—the UART locates the exact center. Under worst conditions—when the line is sampled one full clock cycle into the START bit—synchronization occurs 1/16 of a bit-time past the center. This means that when the receiver's period is shorter than the transmitter's, the receiver's *cumulative* backward creep can be about 9/16 of a bit-time over the remainder of the SDU. When the receiver's period is longer than the transmitter's, the receiver's *cumulative* forward creep can be about 7/16 of a bit-time. Remember, sampling is resynchronized (recentered) with each new START bit. For a 10-bit SDU, (7E1) for example, the cumulative error is spread over all 10 bits. For a fast receiver, this means that no error occurs if the baud rate error does not exceed 9/16 × 10, or about 5.6 percent; for a slow receiver, the baud rates may differ by 7/16 × 10, or 4.3 percent.[6]

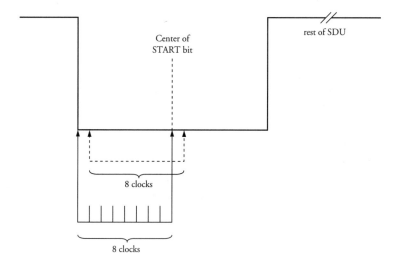

FIGURE 6.9.

Best and worst case START bit detection with a clocking factor of 16.

If a clocking factor of 16 provides good tolerance of baud rate errors, wouldn't a factor of 32 or even 64 improve performance even more? In fact, higher clocking factors force the UART and baud rate circuitry to work at higher frequencies. Considering that the performance improvement attained in this manner is insignificant (a few tenths of a percent), the trade-off hardly seems worth it. There is, however, one situation where the ability to switch clocking factors is important. As mentioned earlier, some computers do not support baud rate selection in software, but by switches or jumpers. If these switches are set to produce a reasonable baud rate with a clock factor of 32, the baud rate can be altered by reprogramming the UART's clocking factor. Suppose that the switches are adjusted to achieve 1200 baud with a clocking factor of 32. Switching to a factor of 16 produces a baud rate of 2400 while selecting a factor of 64 results in 300 baud. Although some UARTs

---

[6]This figure is theoretical because it ignores the sampling times and settling delays built into the UART. In actual practice, the range of immunity seems about +4.5 and –2.5 percent.

offer a clocking factor of 1, this is not likely to prove satisfactory because, as shown by Figure 6.8, START bit synchronization cannot be achieved.

Before we leave the subject of synchronization, we should mention another refinement in the START bit detector that makes it even more reliable. After detecting the START bit and waiting for 8 clock cycles, synchronization does not automatically begin. Instead, the UART retests the communications line to make certain that the START bit is *still* present. If not, the UART assumes that the START bit was a noise spike on the line and does not begin reception.

Data Format

Predictably, the study of how a UART assembles an SDU closely follows the asynchronous theory in Chapter 2. It is especially interesting to see how modern UARTs replace the solenoids and cross bars depicted in Figure 2.3 with silicon wizardry.

Unlike mechanical devices, where the data format is frozen in hardware, a UART obtains its definition of the SDU by decoding the bits in its user-programmable *Data Format register*. Figure 6.10 shows the bitmapping for our hypothetical UART.

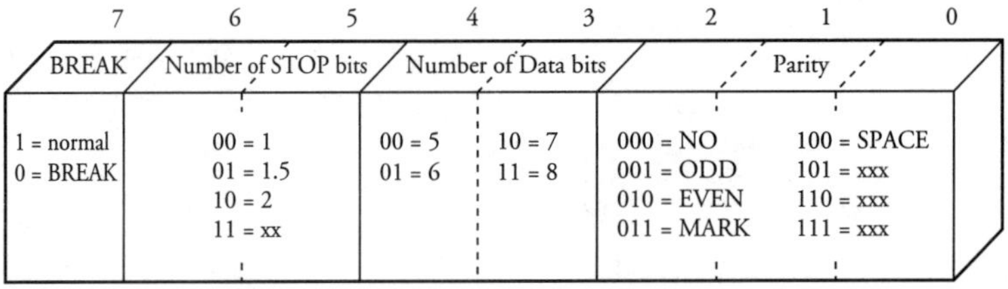

FIGURE 6.10.

Bitmap of a UART's Data Format register.

7	6	5	4	3	2	1	0
BREAK	Number of STOP bits		Number of Data bits			Parity	
1 = normal	00 = 1		00 = 5	10 = 7	000 = NO	100 = SPACE	
0 = BREAK	01 = 1.5		01 = 6	11 = 8	001 = ODD	101 = xxx	
	10 = 2				010 = EVEN	110 = xxx	
	11 = xx				011 = MARK	111 = xxx	

Parity

As described in Chapter 3, parity is a binary checkvalue. In the *ODD parity* scheme, the parity bit is added so there are an odd number of TRUE bits. Conversely, *EVEN parity* generates the parity bit necessary to make an even number of TRUE bits. ANSI X3.25-19677 designates bit [7] to be the parity bit for the ASCII code, but most UARTs support parity with any number of data bits including, although almost no one does it, 8.

If parity is enabled when a byte is received, the UART calculates the parity bit based upon the values of the data bits received. It then compares this calculated value according to the one described in the Data Format register. If the values differ, the parity error bit is set in the UART's Serialization Status register.

---

[7]The name of this two-page document is almost as long as its content: *Character Structure and Character Parity Sense for Parallel-by-bit Data Communication in the American National Standard Code for Information Exchange.*

It is interesting to note that 100 percent parity errors occur when systems attempt to communicate with mismatched parity settings (ODD/EVEN), but only 50 percent when one of the systems is set to 8-NO. Using this fact, software can ascertain the SDU of the sending system and, if desired, adjust its own. The sensing software sets its own system to 7-EVEN and emits a query that is likely to elicit a response that contains both ODD and EVEN bytes. If it is an echoplex system, for instance, you might send several consecutive ASCII characters followed by the line terminator (CR). If the response generates parity errors in about half of the bytes, the software adjusts to 8-NO; if a parity error occurs on every byte, the software adjusts to 7-ODD. After adjustment of the data format, the test is performed again until no parity errors occur.

In general, parity is falling out of favor in modern communications. There are several good reasons for this.

1. Improvement of local computer communications hardware has removed many of the causes for error. The introduction of the UART is a good example.

2. A high proportion of errors in modem communications are caused by noise, especially burst noise. Parity is almost useless in the presence of burst noise.

3. Parity's usurpation of the high-order bit precludes the transmission of binary data such as executable files (see "8-bit Parity," later in this chapter). As discussed in Chapter 4, the unavailability of a high-order bit causes enormous problems when binary data must be moved across serial data links. Such is the case in many mainframe systems which were not designed to exchange data through asynchronous serial ports. In such systems, asynchronous serial ports are designed for use with the user's terminals either connected directly or through modems; the "serious" matter of data transfer is intended to take place through synchronous data links or through interchangeable storage media.

The popularity of the microcomputer, especially as a business tool, has changed the industry's outlook on the lowly asynchronous serial port. As the need to transport data between micro and mainframe has grown, system designers are increasingly abandoning parity altogether.

MARK AND SPACE PARITY

Besides NO, ODD, and EVEN parity settings, it is possible for the parity bit to be always TRUE or always FALSE. The former is called MARK parity, the latter SPACE parity. MARK and SPACE parity are capable of detecting only errors in the parity bit itself: the receiver reports an error only if the parity bit is not TRUE or FALSE, respectively. Despite their ineffectiveness as error detection codes, MARK and SPACE parity can be found in a surprising number of applications. (Many IBM systems, for example, use MARK parity.)

Because MARK and SPACE settings are obviously not useful for error detection, when are they useful? To an 8-NO receiver, 7-SPACE parity looks exactly like an 8-NO transmission of ASCII data (i.e., bytes in the range 0–127). Because of its effect of resetting the high-order bit, 7-SPACE is occasionally useful to prevent sending non-ASCII data to an ASCII device such as a printer. MARK parity can be used to sneak in an additional STOP bit to any receiver that is not expecting a parity bit. Despite these arcane uses, however, MARK and SPACE parity have little value in modern communications.

8-BIT PARITY

It is worth noting here that virtually every UART supports 8 data bits *with parity*. For no apparent reason, most computer users find it conceptually difficult to deal with this format. In their minds, this format is somehow illegal—"it has too many bits," or it is "un-ASCII." Of course, neither of these statements is true. (Those who have qualms about its ASCII-ness do not seem to be bothered by the equally "illegal" 8-NO format.) In truth, the only valid objection to the 8-bit parity format is the additional 1-bit overhead incurred during transmission.

Number of Data Bits

Although seldom encountered by microcomputer programmers, there is still a fair number of 5- and 6-bit codes in use today. 5-bit codes can still be found in Western Union Telex (especially international) and in many teleprinters. The standard US military codes are all 6-bit codes. 6-bit codes persist in ticker output from the New York Stock Exchange and even in some more recent Teletype models. The ubiquitous Teletype US M35 is available in 5-, 6-, 7-, and 8-bit versions.

Although 5- and 6-bit codes provide a comparatively Spartan character set—usually just upper-case alphabet, numerals, and minimum graphics and punctuation—their smaller SDU allows for a higher data transmission rate than larger codes. So, despite the dwindling number of new applications for 5- and 6-bit codes, they are likely to continue where speed and efficiency are more important than subtlety of expression (in the military and in stock tickers, for example).

BIT PADDING IN CODES OF LESS THAN 8 BITS

The use of codes smaller than 8 bits brings up an interesting problem. Even though the UART receiver may assemble an SDU of only, say, 5 data bits plus a parity bit, ultimately it must construct an 8-bit byte to output on the system bus. As we might suppose, the parity bit (if present) is inserted after the most significant data bit. But with what value does the UART fill the unused data bits 6, 7, and 8? Most UART data sheets ignore this question altogether. In practice, some UARTs pad unused bits with 0s, some with 1s, and others with *random* values. In the absence of a standard, therefore, the programmer must assume that unused bits are padded randomly. Accordingly, unused bits should be masked off whenever the combination of data and parity bits is less than 8.

Number of Stop Bits

Our conceptual model of the Data Format register includes bitmapping for 1, 1-1/2, and 2 STOP bits. Most UARTs permit all three values, but there is a recent tendency to correlate the number of STOP bits to the number of data bits. Two STOP bits are seldom necessary in the 5-bit format because START bit synchronization occurs so frequently that the receiver has no time to creep. At any rate, some UARTs permit 1-1/2 STOP bits only with 5-bit data formats, but permit 1 or 2 STOP bits with any format. Some automatically switch to 1-1/2 whenever 5 data bits are selected.

The "Send BREAK" Bit

The BREAK bit does not logically fit in the Data Format register, or, for that matter, anywhere else; it is shown here for lack of a better place. The BREAK bit is implemented in a fairly standard manner in all UARTs: when TRUE, the UART's transmitter output is held at SPACE. There is one interesting variation: *programmable BREAK timing*. In this mode, the UART's transmitter is held at SPACE for exactly 1-1/2 SDUs, after which it returns to its normal MARK condition. This convenience feature, intended to free the programmer from manually timing the duration of the BREAK, is of limited usefulness because the duration of a BREAK is always defined locally.

The RS-232 Interface

Programmers new to asynchronous serial I/O are often puzzled by the presence of RS-232 input and output names on a UART. We have already discussed how asynchronous serial I/O and RS-232 are inseparably, and perhaps, unfortunately wedded. Generally speaking, a UART's so-called *modem control* inputs and outputs have nothing whatsoever to do with the basic processes of serial transmission and reception. That is, the RS-232 functions could just as well exist in a totally separate device. In fact, their presence in the same package with a transmitter, receiver, and serialization support circuitry ought to be viewed more as a programming convenience than a declaration of their participation in these processes.

On the other hand, it is naive to suppose that RS-232 devices are not a part of the serial I/O universe. Serial input and output almost presume that serial data will be transmitted to or received from a device external to the computer. After all, unless the data is bound for the outside world, why use serial (as opposed to parallel) I/O at all?[8] By convention, most serial I/O is performed through an RS-232 interface. Therefore, to program asynchronous serial I/O is, like it or not, to grapple with RS-232. Our UART model, therefore, acknowledges this close practical relationship by devoting two entire registers to RS-232 functions.

RS-232 Output Register

Only two RS-232 control outputs are commonly integrated into UARTs. These are shown in Table 6.1.

Table 6.1. RS-232 outputs supported by most UARTs.

Output	Pin #	"Official" Function (DTE)
RTS	4	(Request to Send) Classically, this line is meaningful only during half-duplex modem transmission, to instruct the modem to change from receiver to transmit or vice versa. In high-speed modems, it is also used for hardware handshaking.
DTR	20	(Data Terminal Ready) This output is the modem's master enabling signal without which the modem will not go or remain online.

Before continuing our discussion, however, it is essential to understand two important points that many programmers find confusing. First, by convention, the UART names given the RS-232 inputs and outputs assume that the UART is connected as a DTE device. This means that names such as DTR and RTS are *outputs,* while CTS and DSR are inputs. Second, all inputs and outputs, whatever their names, are really just general-purpose outputs and are not necessarily intended to perform modem-like tasks.

To illustrate the second point, there is a tale—apocryphal, no doubt—about a journeyman programmer who had worked for years doing asynchronous programming in software. Upon purchasing his first microcomputer, he discovered that its UART was defective—its receiver worked fine, but its transmitter was inoperative. Undaunted, and anxious to establish communications with the outside world, the fellow soon discovered that by writing to a specific register, he could toggle the DTR output line between MARK and SPACE. He then proceeded to write the software asynchronous serial I/O routines to transmit using, yes, the DTR pin! The moral of this story is simple: what you choose to

---

[8]This is perhaps unduly harsh. There are actually many applications in which serial communications is preferable. The use of serial technology is increasingly popular in distributed processing (where several processors must communicate), where the failure of a single parallel device will disable the entire bus. Serial I/O also sees heavy use in robots, where signals must travel long distances through noisy environments.

do with them, *if anything*, depends entirely upon your application and your imagination. Nevertheless, you should realize that most devices expect the computer to supply one or more control voltages through its RS-232 outputs.

RS-232 Inputs

Four RS-232 inputs are commonly integrated into UARTs. These are shown in Table 6.2.

Table 6.2. RS-232 inputs supported by most UARTs.

Input	Pin	"Official" Function (DTE)
CTS	5	(Clear To Send) Classically, a half-duplex modem asserts this line when it has successfully responded to the RTS (above) by turning the line around and is ready to act as a receiver. In high-speed modems, it also is used for hardware handshaking.
DSR	6	(Data Set Ready) This input announces that a modem is online and ready for communications (actually, that the modem is not doing anything else).
DCD	8	(Data Carrier Detect) This is input on which a modem announces that a data link has been established with another modem.
RI	22	(Ring Indicator) This is the input where a modem announces an incoming call.

Despite their RS-232 names, these inputs, like the outputs, are actually just general-purpose inputs whose interpretation depends upon the application. The programmer in the tale of the defective UART, instead of using an RS-232 output as a transmitter, could just as plausibly have written software to operate one of these inputs as a serial data receiver.

Handshaking

After laboring to convince you that the RS-232 inputs and outputs are *user-definable* and do not necessarily interact with basic UART transmitter and receiver functions, we must now examine the significance of the word *necessarily*.

As in most hardware appliance devices, there are two schools of thought in UART design. The flexibility school maintains that a UART should provide the basic functions required to perform asynchronous serial I/O, but should not include specialized features that favor one application at the expense of others. This is essentially the philosophy we have followed in developing our UART model.

By contrast, the convenience school holds that UARTs should take over as much drudgery as possible in their area of application. So what if the device becomes difficult to use for a few applications if it is significantly more convenient for most? This philosophy is revealed in the use of the two RS-232 inputs, CTS and DCD.

In some UARTs, the transmitter status flags (TXE and TBE) are ANDed with the CTS input. This means that unless the CTS line is asserted, the transmitter remains busy. Similarly, the receiver's RxRDY flag is ANDed with the DCD input. To understand why, in heaven's name, a designer would ever hardwire these "features" into his or her product, let's look at some of the design criteria involved in two common UART applications: a modem and serial printer.

The Serial Printer—Because printers are not capable of printing characters as fast as computers can send them, the printer must somehow signal when its input buffer is full. How convenient to have a hardware handshaking (flow-control) pin built right in the UART so when the printer needs to stop the flow of data, it merely inhibits the RS-232 CTS line, which automatically turns off the UART's transmitter.

The Modem—The official use of DCD in the RS-232 standard is to inform the computer or terminal that a modem/data link is in progress. By tying RxRDY to DCD, we effectively shut off the reception of data in the absence of a modem to send it. Similarly, by tying the UART's transmitter to the CTS input, we prohibit the transmission of data until the modem is ready to receive.

The design criteria in both cases is correct, but hopelessly optimistic. Moreover, only a very few applications require full modem control, and those that do inevitably find a UART's built-in modem support to be inadequate. In the mind of a programmer, therefore, the minor convenience of automatic handshaking is usually outweighed by the inevitable loss of software design flexibility.

There is a more practical, almost political reason not to include automatic handshaking in UARTs: applications that specifically wish *not* to utilize the automatic handshaking will require special cabling to defeat it. This necessity to trick a serial interface, perhaps more than any other quality, has led to serial I/O's bad name among users.

RS-232 Status Register

Figure 6.11a shows our hypothetical *RS-232 Status register*. Bits 0 – 3 reflect the current status of one of the RS-232 input lines. Assuming that the UART is connected to an interface, as depicted in Figure 5.12, a TRUE bit means that the input is asserted (greater than +3 volts); FALSE means that the input is inhibited (less than –3 volts). Bits 4 and 5 are general-purpose inputs whose functions are not even associated with RS-232 functions.

At times, we are not interested in the actual state of an input, but whether it has changed state. Bit 6, therefore, is labeled Delta RS-232 to suggest that this bit reports a change in any of the RS-232 inputs. This bit remains TRUE until read. The identity of the exact input that changed state can be read from another register (not shown). On UARTs that do not support general-purpose inputs, the Delta bits are usually in the same register as the status bits.

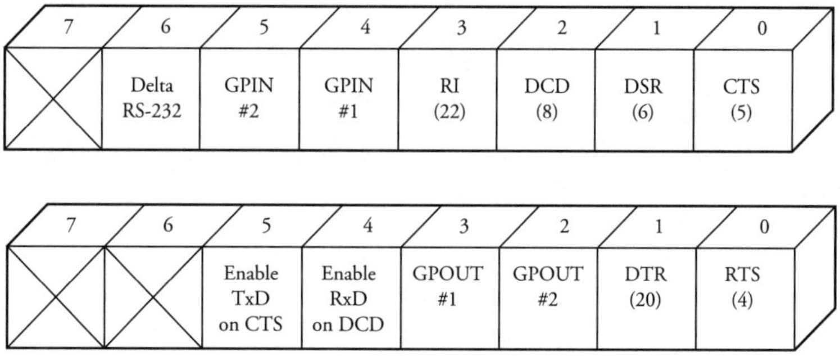

A

7	6	5	4	3	2	1	0
	Delta RS-232	GPIN #2	GPIN #1	RI (22)	DCD (8)	DSR (6)	CTS (5)

7	6	5	4	3	2	1	0
		Enable TxD on CTS	Enable RxD on DCD	GPOUT #1	GPOUT #2	DTR (20)	RTS (4)

B
FIGURE 6.11.
The modem control registers. Numbers in parentheses are DTE pin numbers.

RS-232 Output Control Register

Figure 6.11b shows an idealized *RS-232 Output Control* register. In addition to the conventional RS-232 outputs, RTS and DTR, this register also contains one or two general-purpose outputs for use as the hardware designer sees fit. For example, the designer may wish to use the additional outputs to support a more complicated form of modem control, or to interact with more than one external device.

Despite the railings against the automatic hardware handshaking built into UARTs, there are certain circumstances in which it is undeniably convenient. Therefore, we devote 2 bits in the RS-232 Output Control register to enable and disable it: *Enable TD on CTS* and *Enable RxD on DCD*. This provides the flexibility to use it when we need it, and not to have to wrestle with it when we don't.

Inverted RS-232 Logic

You will recall from our discussion of logic levels in Chapter 5 that the RS-232 standard dictates positive logic (i.e., positive voltages are TRUE) for control input and output signals, but negative logic for data signals. As you read UART data sheets (or nose around with a voltmeter), you may be puzzled to discover that the polarity of the control inputs and output voltages on the UART's pins are inverted. In other words, writing a 1 to the UART's DTR bit, for example, actually causes the UART itself to generate a negative voltage. This apparent anomaly can be explained by realizing that RS-232 line driver and receiver ICs reinvert the signals to positive logic before applying them to the output connectors (see "RS-232 Level Conversion" in Chapter 5).

UART Interrupts

If your program performs only communications duties, it may have nothing to do but poll the UART waiting for an inbound byte or wait for the opportunity to transmit a byte. But in applications where the serial I/O represents only a small fraction of the total program, there are always other things to do. While the user is entering text via the word processing section, the serial I/O section can be invisibly downloading stock quotations, transmitting the week's price lists to branch offices, or printing reports. In other words, it is impractical to tie up an entire computer while the UART pokes along at a few hundred baud.

The key to this increase in functionality lies in abandoning the concept of polling in favor of *interruption*. In contrast to polling, where I/O is supervised by the CPU by periodically checking a device's readiness, the technique of interruption transfers to the peripheral device itself the burden of notifying the CPU when an I/O operation is needed (or possible). The notification takes the form of an *interrupt request* whereby the I/O device actively solicits the CPU's attention. When the CPU finishes its current instruction, it decides if it is interested in acknowledging this request for service. If so, it issues an *interrupt acknowledgment*, then turns program control over to a section of code designed to handle the device's needs—the *interrupt service routine* (ISR), or the *interrupt handler*. Once the ISR completes, the CPU returns to the main program where execution resumes as if the interruption had never occurred.

Generating Interrupts

Because of the obvious power of interruption, our hypothetical UART must generate an interrupt under a variety of conditions:

- *Transmitter Interrupts.* An interrupt is generated when the transmitter buffer becomes empty—i.e., can accept another byte for serialization.
- *Receiver Interrupts.* An interrupt can be generated whenever an incoming byte has been assembled and placed in the receiver's FIFO. Some UARTs additionally allow interrupts on the *first* received byte only.
- *RS-232 Interrupts.* An interrupt can be generated by a change in state of any RS-232 input line—CTS, DSR, DCD, or RI.
- *Interrupt on Receiver Error or BREAK.* An interrupt can be generated by any irregular serialization condition: BREAK, parity, overrun, or framing.

The *Interrupt Enable* register shown in Figure 6.12 contains a bit to enable interrupts for each of these conditions.

It is frequently necessary to disable and re-enable UART interrupts entirely at various points in program execution. On many UARTs, this simple act requires several steps: the contents of the Interrupt Enable register must be read and stored, then all relevant bits must be reset to turn interrupts off. To turn interrupts back on, the stored bit pattern is fetched and reinstalled. To simplify this cumbersome process, our Interrupt Enable register also contains a *master interrupt enable* bit, which permits UART interrupts to be turned off entirely without disturbing the bit pattern in the rest of the register.

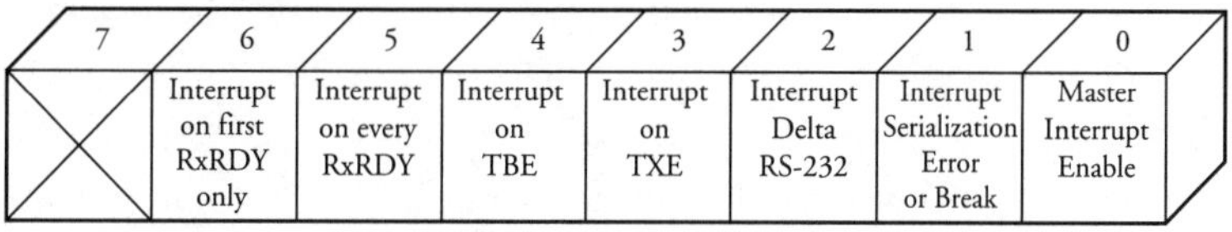

FIGURE 6.12.
The Interrupt Enable register.

7	6	5	4	3	2	1	0
	Interrupt on first RxRDY only	Interrupt on every RxRDY	Interrupt on TBE	Interrupt on TXE	Interrupt Delta RS-232	Interrupt Serialization Error or Break	Master Interrupt Enable

CLEARING PENDING INTERRUPTS

After the UART generates an interrupt, it will not generate another until the first one has been cleared. On some UARTS, clearing means resetting an *interrupt pending* bit, but the most common way to clear an interrupt is to service its cause. For example, if the interrupt was generated by RxRDY, reading the available character clears the interrupt.

NESTED INTERRUPTS

When additional interrupts occur during the on-going service of an interrupt (for example, a receiver interrupt occurs during a tramsitter interrupt service cycle), the UART should provide notification of this interrupt without having to exit the ISR.

Interrupt Vector Determination

When an interrupt occurs, the processor must somehow ascertain which of the possible interrupts has actually occurred. From this information, the processor then calculates the *interrupt vector* (i.e., the address of the interrupt handler) that must be invoked. Although the exact method of communication between the processor and the UART differs from system to system, the result must always be the address of the function that must service the condition causing the interrupt. Because there are so many possible interrupt vectoring schemes (some processors even support multiple vectoring schemes), we will not attempt to represent vectoring in our hypothetical UART. For the sake of convenience, therefore, for now we will assume that our UART somehow magically identifies itself to the processor as the source of an interrupt. In Chapter 7 and in Chapters 19 and 20, we will study in detail how interrupts on real UARTs interact with the processor.

FIFO'd UARTS

The theoretical UART we have studied so far assumes single-character transmitter and receiver buffers. Adding multi-character buffers provides considerable enhancement of performance.

Over/Underruns

In a UART with a single-character receiver buffer, a received character is immediately transferred to a holding register while the next character is assembled. If the character in the buffer is not removed (read) by the time the next one is assembled, the newer one overwrites the older one. This *overrun* condition is signaled by bit 1 in the Serialization Line Status Register.

Similarly, in a UART with a single-character transmitter buffer, a character in the transmitter buffer is immediately transferred to the transmitter's shift register as soon as the character in the transmitter shift register has been clocked onto the line. The output line goes silent if more than one character-time elapses between the transmitter buffer becoming clear and the writing of a new character into the buffer. Because this *underrun* condition results only in reduced data rate but no data loss, it is not flagged in the Serialization Status register. (As we shall see in Chapters 10 and 11, in synchronous communications, where idle time on the phone line is not permitted, transmitter underruns can in fact be more lethal than receiver overruns.)

If the software is servicing the UART by polling, the polling cycles may become delayed by external events or by the code executing some seldom-used conditional path. Whatever the reason, whenever the time between polls exceed the time required to assemble/dissassemble a character, the system becomes susceptible to over/underrun errors. Consider, for example, Table 6.3, which gives the time required to input or output a single 10-element SDU at various baud rates.

Table 6.3. Baud rate versus time.

Baud Rate	Time in Milliseconds for One 10-Element SDU
300	33
1200	8.3
2400	4.2
9600	1.04
14,400	0.69
19,200	0.52
28,800	0.35
38,400	0.26
57,600	0.17

Although we will save a through discussion of the benefits and liabilties of interrupt operation until Chapters 19 and 20 , it is worth noting here that the solving of over/underrun conditions is an area in which interrupt I/O is most useful. When the UART moves the character out of or into its receiver or transmitter buffer, it generates an interrupt signal for the host CPU. The CPU then immediately executes code that reads or writes the byte from the buffer, thus getting out of harm's way of the next character..

Interrupt Latency

The cumulative delay between the UART's physical request for interrupt service and the CPU's actually providing that service is known as *interrupt latency*.[9] The higher a system's interrupt latency is the slower its I/O capabilities are. There are several causes for interrupt latency:

1. Inefficiently written service code whose execution time exceeds one character time.

2. Serial interrupts with a very low system priority.

3. A rogue process turns off system interrupts, preventing propagation of the interrupt signal from the UART to the CPU.

Interrupt Saturation

On the other side of the coin from high overrun immunity is the condition known as *interrupt saturation*. This occurs when the baud rate is so fast that the CPU is unable to service a UART interrupt no matter how high its priority or how efficient the servicing code. As this limit approaches, the system spends more and more of its time-servicing interrupts and less and less time-servicing applications and system processes. At some critical baud rate there are not enough CPU cycles to service the UART interrupt and an overrun or underrun occurs.

When interrupt saturation occurs, either the clock speed of the CPU must be increased, or the overhead of servicing the interrupt must be reduced. A clock increase is usually out of the question, and there are hard limits on code efficiency. Often the only way to reduce the CPU overhead is to employ a UART that handles multiple characters before generating an interrupt. When an interrupt occurs, the CPU reads or writes several character on a single interrupt service cycle. This approach eliminates the considerable system overhead required to service the interrupt on a character-by-character basis. (To be fully functional, the receiver FIFO must support a parallel FIFO to hold the receiver serialization status/error for each character in the receiver FIFO.)

Upon first thought, FIFO buffers for transmitting and receiving appears to have two benefits: reduction of interrupt overhead and immunity from over- and underrun. It is obvious that interrupt overhead decreases as the size of FIFO increases. Less obvious is that

---

[9]Classically, interrupt latency describes the time between an *Interrupt Request* to the CPU and its *Interrupt Acknowledge*. Here we use the term to describe all souces of delays between an Interrupt Request and the actual execution of the CPU instructions that service that request.

while the frequency of under/overrun errors decreases with the size of the FIFO, the *susceptiblity* to it is unchanged. To understand why this is so, consider a device with an n-character FIFO where the interrupt occurs when the nth character has been received into or transmitted from the FIFO. At that instant, the CPU has only a single character-time to service the UART before under- or overrun occurs—exactly the same as the case of the UART with only a single-character buffer.

For a FIFO to provide protection from over- and underruns, some of the FIFO's storage must be held back as *headroom.* That is, the UART must generate the interrupt when the FIFO is only partly filled on reception or partly empty on transmit. Suppose that the *interrupt trigger level* is n/2—an interrupt occurs when the FIFO is only half-full. The CPU now has n/2 character-times to read or write from the UART before over- or underrun occurs.

So the FIFO presents the programmer with a happy trade-off. A trigger level near the *top* of the FIFO provides maximum relief from interrupt saturation but makes the UART proportionally more susceptible to overrun. Conversely, a trigger level near the "bottom" of the FIFO provides maximum immunity to overruns but provides proportionally less relief from interrupt saturation. Because the location of interrupt trigger point varies according to the application, it must be programmable.

The End-of-Block Problem

It may have occurred to you that the presence of both a FIFO and a trigger level lead to the possibility that the last trigger-level- minus-one characters in any data block may never be received. Assume that a UART's FIFO is set for a depth of ten and has a trigger level of five. A stream of five characters arrives, the UART generates an interrupt, and the CPU clears them from the FIFO. Now, assume that the end of the data stream occurs after the next four characters. Those four characters remain in the FIFO forever because they are below the trigger level and therefore generate no interrupt.

A similar situation would occur in serial display terminal or when using a microcomputer as a terminal emulator. Received characters would remain in the FIFO until the trigger level was reached, then squirted out at once—not exactly user friendly.

To prevent the UART from swallowing the last few characters and to smooth out its response, the FIFO must be periodically flushed. That is, if there is at least one character in the FIFO and there has been no recent receiver interrupt (say, within three or four character times), the UART generates one gratuitously. It is very important that this *time-out interrupt* be different from an interrupt generated by exceeding the FIFO's trigger level. Unlike the latter, where the number of characters that must be read from the FIF is known exactly, the code that services a time-out interrupt must be prepared to read a variable number of chararacters.

An Ideal FIFO'd UART

The ideal FIFO'd UART should be flexible. It should sport independently configurable FIFO's for transmit and receive as well as:

1. Bits for enabling and disabling the FIFO.

2. Bits for reading the maximum depth of the FIFO (say, in increments of 16 bytes), and for reading the current setting.

3. Bits for setting the FIFO trigger level (say, in increments of 16 bytes), and for reading the current setting.

Conclusion

We now have created a hypothetical UART against which we can understand and measure actual devices. As we now turn to the real world to see how these abstractions translate into nuts-and-bolts integrated ICs, you will discover an amazing variety among its members. The three UARTs we will study were selected for compelling reasons. The National 8250's use in the entire family of IBM PCs, IBM clones, and after-market PC boards ensured its posterity; the National 16550A is a high-performance (FIFO) version of the 16550. Because it was designed to support the Zilog Z80 microprocessor, the Z80SIO quickly became standard in CP/M machines; a functionally identical part, the 8530, is used in Macintosh computers. It has been estimated that one of these UARTs is contained in at least 90 percent of all microcomputers in existence. In other words, it is almost inconceivable that you could do much asynchronous programming without at some time encountering one of these devices.

Real-World UARTs

In this chapter, we will study several examples of UARTs: two from the National 8250 family the Zilog Z80SIO. Although newer and perhaps more sophisticated devices than these certainly exist, they were chosen for two reasons. First, they are enormously popular. An 8250-style UART is used in the IBM PC and the Z80SIO is generally used wherever one finds a Zilog Z80 microprocessor. Since most CPM computers were based upon the Z80, many contained the Z80SIO companion UART. Because of the millions of these machines in existence, then, there is a high likelihood that you will encounter one of them. Aside from sheer numbers, the second reason for selecting these devices is pedagogical. They illustrate, better than any other devices, fundamentally different approaches to UART architecture.

Although programmers seldom need concern themselves about the physical connections between the system and the UART, an understanding of such things is sometimes (more often than we like to admit) important to puzzling out a programming problem. We will therefore take a cursory (and very superficial) look at how our UARTs fit into a typical system.

In all the UARTs we will study in this chapter, the names of the RS-232 inputs and outputs—$\overline{RTS}$, $\overline{DTR}$, $\overline{DSR}$, $\overline{DCD}$, $\overline{CTS}$, and $\overline{RI}$—are overscored to denote inverted logic. This means, for example, that a 0 in the DTR bit of a UART's RS-232 Output register produces a 1 at the DTR output. In most designs, this inversion is not apparent to the programmer because these signals are reinverted by the EIA line-driver ICs, which are interposed between the UART and the physical interface connector. (See Chapter 5 for a discussion of RS-232 level conversion.)

To avoid the notational nightmare that comes with several layers of inversion, all our discussions are based upon the assumption that this reinversion occurs. This assumption is possible because most UARTs in microcomputers are connected to an RS-232 interface. In other words, we are assuming that writing a 1 to, say, the DTR bit in the UART's RS-232 Output register ultimately produces a *positive* voltage on the DTE RS-232 interface.

To finish this line of thought, notice that the names of the *data* inputs and outputs are not overscored to indicate inversion. As we noted in Chapter 5, the RS-232 standard specifies inverted logic for data: an idling (MARKING) transmitter must generate a *negative* voltage at the interface. Because the designers of UARTs expect the transmitter to be inverted by EIA line drivers, positive logic levels must be output at the transmitter output.

The National 8250/16450

In this section we will talk about the National Semiconductor family of UARTS. Before we look at the devices in detail, it is worth clarifying the nomenclature associated with them.

1. The 8250 is the patriarch of the National UART family under study.

2. The 16450 is a functionally identical, pin-for-pin replacement for the 8250. It is simply based on a different manufacturing technolgy and is capable of operating at faster I/O bus speeds. Everything we say about the 8250 applies to the 16450 as well, and vice versa.

3. The 16550 is a souped-up version of the 16450. It is backwardly compatible with the 16450, so everything we say about either the 8250 or the 16450 also applies to it as well. However, the 16550 has special features and capabilities that will be discussed separately in detail.

It is common industry practice to refer to the 8250 and 16450 under the name 8250s. We shall continue this practice, but you should be aware that the 16450 is actually the more popular of the two.

Because it was designed for use with a broad range of CPUs and other support hardware, in many ways the 8250 UART[1] closely resembles the conceptual UART we studied in Chapter 6. This makes it very easy to understand and to program.

8250 Hardware Basics

As shown in Figure 7.1, the 8250 requires three basic interfaces: the system I/O bus, the clock, and RS-232 I/O. The 8250 is connected to the low-order 8 bits of the CPU's data bus by means of data lines D0 through D7. This is the path of data in and out of the UART. Read and write operations are differentiated by the data input and output strobe lines $\overline{\text{DISTR}}$ and $\overline{\text{DOSTR}}$. The 8250 comprises several internal registers, all of which are individually addressable by means of three register selected inputs A0–A2. Transmitting a byte is therefore a three-step operation:

1. CPU places the outbound data byte on the 8-bit data lines D0–D7.

---

[1]National refers to the 8250 as an ACE (Asynchronous Communications Element).

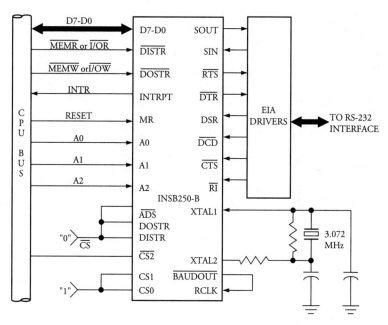

FIGURE 7.1.

A basic configuration for the National 8250.

2. The register number of the Transmitter Buffer register is placed on register select inputs A0–A2.

3. The logic on the data strobe lines DISTR and DOSTR moves the byte from D0–D7 into the transmitter's buffer. The 8250 moves the byte from the Buffer register to the transmitter's shift register when the latter is empty.

The steps in receiving a byte are similar to those for transmission. The steps summarized below assume that an incoming byte has already been received and is waiting in the Receiver Buffer register.

1. The Receiver Buffer register's number is placed on register select inputs A0–A2.

2. A read operation is performed by the logic on the data strobe lines DISTR and DOSTR.

3. The byte moves from the receive buffer to D0–D7 where it is captured by the CPU.

Although we used the transmit and receive registers in this example, reads and writes of *any* 8250 register are identical—the only difference is the register select lines A0–A2.

The final point of interface with the system I/O bus is line-marked INTRPT, or interrupt. This output becomes TRUE whenever a condition exists for which the 8250 is programmed to generate an interrupt.

8250 Clock and Timing

The 8250's reference clock signal may be externally supplied or internally generated by connecting a crystal. In either case, the reference clock is injected at the XTAL1 input, whence it passes through a user-programmable divider circuit to produce a *master data clock*. This signal is 16 times higher than the desired baud rate, thus fixing the clocking factor at 16. To understand the necessity for a master data clock at a higher frequency than the baud rate, review "Receiver Timing" in Chapter 6.

The master data clock signal is internally wired to drive the transmitter logic. So that the receiver and transmitter can be operated at different baud rates, however, the master data clock's connection to the receiver logic is external. The master data clock signal is brought out of the 8250 at $\overline{\text{BAUDOUT}}$ and the receiver's clock input is made available at RCLK. When these two are connected, the receive baud rate equals the transmit baud rate. A different baud rate for the receiver can be attained by processing the signal at $\overline{\text{BAUDOUT}}$ further before reintroducing it at RCLK.

We will return to the frequency relationships among the reference clock, the master data clock, and the baud rate when we study the Baud Rate Divisor Latch registers later in this chapter.

8250 Internal Architecture

Having ever so briefly examined the 8250's contact with the outside world, let us now undertake matters of more direct interest to programmers: the internal structure of the 8250. As you can see from the block diagram in Figure 7.2, a program exerts control over the 8250 by reading and writing ten registers.[2] Except for the Interrupt Identification register, which is read-only, data written to a register can be read back.

Register Addressing on the 8250

If you read the "8250 Hardware Basics" section carefully, you may have already spotted an anomaly: how does the 8250 address eleven registers when there are only three physical register-select lines? Actually, only ten unique register-select addresses must be decoded because the transmitter and receiver are read/write versions of the same address. But this still leaves ten registers to address with three register-select lines. A gimmick[3] is used to extend the addressing: when bit 7 of the Data Format register is 1, registers 0 and 1 become the low- and high-order bytes of the Baud Rate Divisor Latch. (Bit 7 of the Data

---

[2]An eleventh register—a scratch pad—also exists, although it is seldom mentioned. CAUTION: many manufacturers license the right to manufacture the 8250. Few of these second-sourced devices even support the scratch pad register.

[3]A gimmick is slightly ugly engineering. The difference between a gimmick and a kludge is that a gimmick is an intentional design, while a kludge is added later to correct for an oversight.

Format register is called the "Divisor Latch Access Bit," or DLAB.) Table 7.1 gives the register select codes for the eight "real" registers and illustrates the DLAB gimmick.

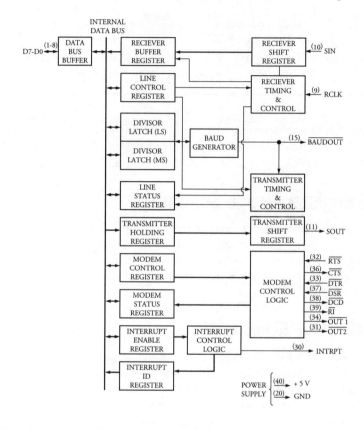

FIGURE 7.2.
A block diagram of the 8250.

Table 7.1. Register addressing and the DLAB.

DLAB*	A0	A1	A2	Read/ Write	Register
0	0	0	0	—	Receiver (read) Transmitter (write)
0	0	0	1	R/W	Interrupt Enable
X	0	1	0	READ	Interrupt Identification
X	0	1	1	R/W	Data Format (Line Control)
X	1	0	0	R/W	RS-232 Output (Modem Control)
X	1	0	1	R/W	Serialization Status (Line Status)
X	1	1	0	R/W	RS-232 Input Status (Modem Status)

*"Divisor Latch Access Bit", bit 7 of the Data Format register

continues

Table 7.1. continued

DLAB*	A0	A1	A2	Read/ Write	Register
X	1	1	1	R/W	Scratch Pad
1	0	0	0	R/W	LSB Baud Rate Divisor Latch
1	0	0	1	R/W	MSB Baud Rate Divisor Latch

In most 8250 implementations, the eight "real" registers are addressed at consecutive I/O port or memory addresses, but the exact manner of address decoding is, of course, up to the hardware designer.

8250 Register Usage Summary

We will now examine the eleven functional registers in the 8250. To maintain consistency, when necessary we retain the register names invented in Chapter 6. Where these names differ substantially from those used in the 8250 data sheet, the latter follow in parentheses. The number preceding the register name is its register-select code.

0: RECEIVER BUFFER REGISTER[4]

After a stream of bits on the 8250's SIN input has been assembled into a byte, reading this register fetches that byte. Even though the "byte" received may contain as few as 5 data bits, the CPU always fetches an 8-bit quantity. In such cases, the content of unused bits is not specified and should be masked off by software. As shown in Table 7.1, when bit 7 of the Data Format register (DLAB) is TRUE, the Receiver Buffer register becomes the read/ write LSB Baud Rate Divisor Latch. The DLAB is described in detail later.

Experimentation with several vintages of 8250s shows that it contains only one buffer— the Receiver register itself.

0: TRANSMITTER BUFFER REGISTER (HOLDING REGISTER)

Writing a byte to register 0 results in its serialization and transmission at the SOUT output in the current data format and baud rate. As shown in Table 7.1, when bit 7 of the Data Format register (DLAB) is TRUE, the 0 register becomes the read/write LSB Baud Rate Divisor Latch. The DLAB is described in detail later.

---

[4]National Semiconductor's documentation states that the 8250 contains full double buffering.

1: INTERRUPT ENABLE

The bits of this read/write register, shown in Figure 7.3, enable the four types of interrupts supported by the 8250. An interrupt is enabled by a 1 in its respective bit.

7	6	5	4	3	2	1	0
Always 0	Always 0	Always 0	Always 0	RS-232 Input	Receiver Error or BREAK	Transmitter Buffer Empty (TBE)	Receiver Data (RxRDY)

FIGURE 7.3.
The 8250's Interrupt Enable register.

Bit 0   (RxRDY) If this bit is 1, an interrupt is generated when a byte is available for reading from the Receiver Buffer register.

Bit 1   (TBE) If this bit is 1, an interrupt is generated when a byte is moved from the transmitter's Holding register to the transmitter's shift register; in other words, as soon as the 8250 can accept another byte for transmission.

Bit 2   If this bit is 1, an interrupt is generated when a parity error, overrun error, framing error, or a BREAK condition is detected by the receiver during the reception of a byte.

Bit 3   (RS-232 Input) If this bit is 1, an interrupt is generated when any of the RS-232 inputs changes states.

Bits 4–7   Always 0.

As shown in Table 7.1, when bit 7 of the Data Format register (DLAB) is true, register 1 becomes the read/write MSB Baud Rate Divisor Latch whose function is described in detail below.

2: INTERRUPT IDENTIFICATION

When an interrupt occurs, the Interrupt Identification register identifies its exact source. Figure 7.3a shows the bit mapping for this register. Note that bits 3, 6, and 7 are labeled "Reserved" and that bits 5 and 4 are "Always zero." Many a programmer has gotten into trouble by treating reserved bits the same as always-zero bits. Failure to mask off the reserved bits may cause a 8250 program to crash when run on a 16550 (more of that later in this chapter).

7	6	5	4	3	2	1	0
Reserved	Reserved	Always zero	Always zero	Reserved	See Table 7.2		Interrupt pending

FIGURE 7.3a.
The Interrupt Identification register.

A 0 in Bit 0 of this register means that an interrupt is pending; bits 1–3 identify the actual interrupt as shown in Table 7.2. Notice that each interrupt has a *priority*: while an interrupt is pending, interrupts with an equal or lower priority are not reported (i.e., locked out). This priority is not programmable.

Table 7.2. Interrupt Identification coding for the 8250.

Bit 2	Bit 1	Bit 0	Priority*	Interrupt ID
0	0	1	None	None
1	1	0	0	Serialization Error or BREAK
1	0	0	1	Received Data
0	1	0	2	Transmitter Buffer Empty
0	0	0	3	RS-232 Input

*0/ is highest.

There are two interesting details about this register. First, the interrupt is expressed with an integer, not a bitmap. Second, bit 0 (the "pending" bit) is expressed in negative logic—that is, a 0 means that an interrupt is pending. Therefore, when an interrupt occurs, the number in the Interrupt Identification register is a multiple of two. Right shifting this number one place provides a convenient index into a table of pointers to the subroutines that handle the respective interrupts.

When nested interrupts occur—a second interrupt occurs during the service of the first—the second interrupt is identified in this register as soon as the first interrupt is cleared. Therefore, the interrupt service routine must continue to read this register until bit 0 is 1. (See Table 7.4 for a list of actions that clear pending interrupts.)

3: DATA FORMAT (LINE CONTROL)

The byte map in Figure 7.4 shows the bit-mapping of the Data Format register.

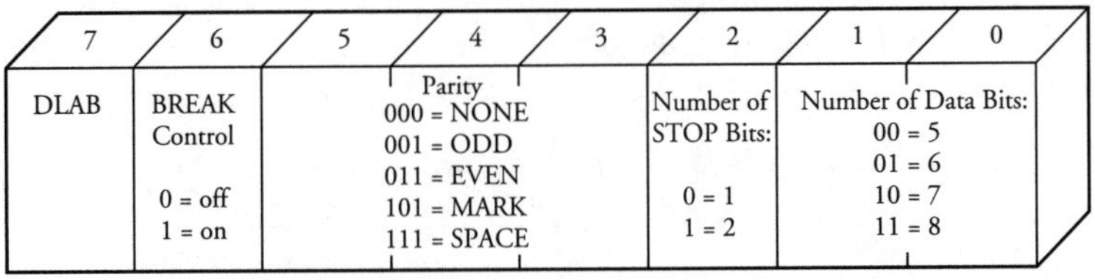

FIGURE 7.4.

The 8250's Data Format register.

Bit 2   If 5 data bits are used, 1-1/2 STOP bits are automatically selected.

Bit 3-5   Most explanations of these 3 bits, including the data sheet, call bit 3 "Parity Enable," bit 4 "Parity Select," and bit 5 by the enigmatic name "Stick Parity."

Bit 6 (The BREAK bit) When 1, this bit forces the transmitter (i.e., the SOUT output) to a logical 0 state (SPACING). The transmitter remains in this state unconditionally until a 0 is written to this bit.

Bit 7 DLAB (the Divisor Latch Access Bit) As shown in Table 7.1, this bit has nothing to do with the data format, but is a gimmick that extends the number of registers that can be addressed with three register-select control lines. When this bit is 1, registers 0 and 1 (the Transmitter/Receiver and Interrupt I/O registers) become the LSB and MSB Baud Rate Divisor Latch registers.

4: RS-232 OUTPUT CONTROL (MODEM CONTROL)

This register (Figure 7.5) controls the state of the two RS-232 outputs DTR and RTS. As previously explained, these are actually inverted signals; for example, the bit labeled DTR actually controls the "NOT" output, DTR. For the sake of clarity, however, we will use positive abbreviations and the term "assert" to suggest that these outputs are probably eventually reinverted by external circuitry.

In addition to DTR and RTS, two general-purpose outputs are provided for non-RS-232 use. Although the label "General-Purpose Output" correctly implies that these are not RS-232 outputs, the distinction is artificial; these bits affect their respective outputs in all respects like RTS and DTR.

This register also contains a bit to perform a *loopback* test in which complementary inputs and outputs are temporarily connected. In this way, the continuity of the entire system can be tested by changing an output, then testing whether the change is reflected at the complementary input.

7	6	5	4	3	2	1	0
Always 0	Always 0	Always 0	Local Loopback Test	General-Purpose Output #2 (GP02)	General-Purpose Output #1 (GP01)	RTS (4)	DTR (20)

FIGURE 7.5.

The 8250's RS-232 Output register.

Bit 0 (DTR) Writing a 1 to this bit asserts the 8250's Data Terminal Ready output.

Bit 1 (RTS) Writing a 1 to this bit asserts the 8250's Request To Send output.

Bit 2 (GP01) This is the first of two user-definable outputs. An example of its use can be found on the Hayes plug-in board Smartmodems, where GP01 unconditionally resets the Smartmodem.

Bit 3 (GP02) This is the second user-definable output. For a typical use of this bit, see "Interrupts on the 8250," below.

Bit 4   (Local Loopback) When this bit is 1, the following occur:

> **1.** The transmitter's output (SOUT) is set to the logical 1 state (MARKING).
>
> **2.** The receiver's input (SIN) is disconnected.
>
> **3.** The output of the transmitter's shift register is directly connected to the receiver's shift register.
>
> **4.** The four RS-232 control inputs are directly connected to the RS-232 outputs as follows:
>
> $\overline{\text{CTS}}$ to $\overline{\text{RTS}}$
>
> $\overline{\text{DSR}}$ to $\overline{\text{DTR}}$
>
> $\overline{\text{DCD}}$ to $\overline{\text{GP02}}$
>
> $\overline{\text{RI}}$ to $\overline{\text{GP01}}$

These connections provide a simple method for checking the major UART functions. Data written to the Transmitter register appears immediately at the Receiver register. Interrupts are fully operational and interrupts normally generated by RS-232 inputs can be generated simply by writing into the RS-232 Output Control register.[5]

5: SERIALIZATION STATUS (LINE STATUS)

This register (Figure 7.6) reports the status of the assembly and serialization process, which includes BREAK detection, receiver errors, and the readiness status of key transmitter and receiver registers.

FIGURE 7.6.

The 8250's Serialization Status register.

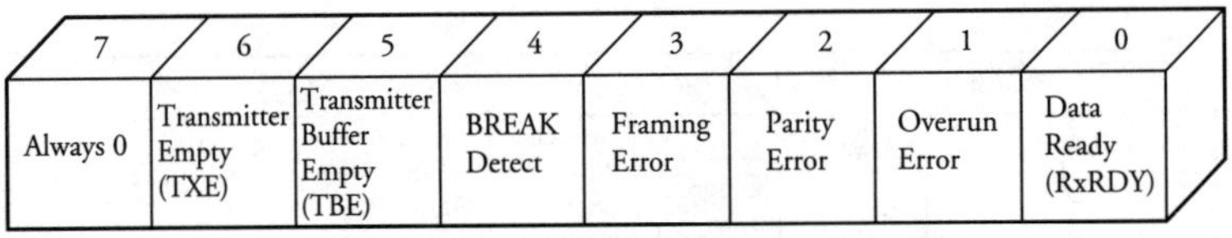

7	6	5	4	3	2	1	0
Always 0	Transmitter Empty (TXE)	Transmitter Buffer Empty (TBE)	BREAK Detect	Framing Error	Parity Error	Overrun Error	Data Ready (RxRDY)

The error conditions reported by bits 1–4 generate an interrupt when bit 2 is set in the Interrupt Enable register.

Bit 0   (RxRDY) This bit is 1 when an incoming byte has been assembled and transferred into the receiver's buffer. This bit is reset when read.

Bit 1   (Receiver Overrun) A 1 in this bit indicates that a byte in the receiver buffer has been overwritten by a newly received byte. The first byte is lost. This bit is reset by reading this register.

---

[5]For clarity, the remainder of this book will use the contraction *Z80SIO*.

Bit 2 (Parity Error) This bit is set to 1 when the parity bit of a received byte does not match the parity setting in the Data Format register. This bit is reset when read.

Bit 3 (Framing Error) A 1 in this bit means that after assembling an inbound byte, the STOP bit was incorrect (i.e., a SPACE instead of MARK). This bit is reset when read.

Bit 4 (BREAK Detect) A 1 appears in this bit whenever the receiver detects a SPACING condition lasting longer than one SDU. This bit is reset when read.

Bit 5 (Transmitter Buffer Empty) The TBE bit is set to 1 when a byte is moved from the transmitter's buffer (Holding register) into the transmitter's shift register. Failure to consult this bit before writing to the Transmitter Buffer register overwrites a byte already in the buffer awaiting transmission. It is important to understand that although TBE signals that the 8250 is ready to accept another byte for transmission, it does not mean that transmission of the previous byte is complete.

Bit 6 (Transmitter Empty) The TXE bit is set to 1 when there are no bytes in the transmitter buffer or in the transmitter's shift register. Think of this bit as an "all bytes sent" flag. Before terminating transmission, consult this bit to avoid "leaving one in the pipe."

Bit 7 Always 0.

6: RS-232 INPUT STATUS (MODEM STATUS)

Bits 0–3 of this register (Figure 7.7) report a *change* in the state of their respective RS-232 pins. A 1 in any of these bits means that its input has changed since last read. Reading this register clears bits 0–3.

Bits 4–7 report the *absolute* state of their respective RS-232 inputs. Because of the logic inversion discussed earlier, a 1 in these bits ordinarily stands for a positive voltage on the RS-232 interface.

In addition to their normal duties, bits 4–7 take on special meanings during loopback testing (see Bit 4 of the RS-232 Output Control register).

7	6	5	4	3	2	1	0
DCD	RI	DSR	CTS	Delta DCD	Delta RI	Delta DSR	Delta CTS

FIGURE 7.7.

The 8250's RS-232 Input Status register.

Bit 2   This bit is set on the *trailing* edge of the telephone ringer pulse from the modem.

Bit 4–7   During loopback testing (i.e., when bit 4 of RS-232 Output Control register is 1), these bits report the current state of the RS-232 *outputs*. The assignment is as follows:

Bit 4, CTS = RTS
Bit 5, DSR = DTR
Bit 6, RI = GP02
Bit 7, DCD = GP01

7: SCRATCH PAD

This register has no function whatsoever. You may use it as you would a byte of RAM, but be advised that it does not exist on all versions of the 8250.

0/8: LSB BAUD RATE DIVISOR LATCH
1/9: MSB BAUD RATE DIVISOR LATCH

As shown in Table 7.1, when bit 7 of the Data Format register is 1, registers 0 and 1 become the LSB and MSB Divisor Latch registers, respectively. (Their register numbers, 0/8 and 1/9, reflect this gimmick.)

The 8250's reference clock is divided by the 16-bit integer contained in the LSB and MSB Divisor Latch registers. The resulting frequency is the master data clock that drives the transmitter logic and, optionally (by means of an external connection on the 8250), the receiver logic as well. This master data clock is then again divided by 16 to produce the baud clock, which controls the speed at which data is received and transmitted. The divisor for any baud rate can therefore be calculated by the formula:

$$\text{Divisor} = \frac{\text{Reference clock frequency}}{16 \times \text{desired baud rate}}$$

Table 7.3 gives the divisors (in hexadecimal) for the most popular baud rates. Divisors are given for the two recommended clock frequencies.

Table 7.3. Hexadecimal baud rate divisor for two reference clock speeds.

Desired Baud Rate	Hex Divisor to Produce 16× Clock with Clock Crystal of:	
	1.8432 MHz	3.072 MHz
50	0900	0F00
75	0600	0A00
110	0417	06D1
134.5	0359	0594
150	0300	0500
300	0180	0280
600	00C0	0140
1,200	0060	00A0
1,800	0040	006B
2,000	003A	0060
2,400	0030	0050
3,600	0020	0035
4,800	0018	0028
7,200	0010	0016
9,600	000C	0014
12,000	—	0010
14,400	0008	—
19,200	0006	000A
28,800	0004	—
38,400	0003	0005
57,600	0002	—
115,200	0001	—

Interrupts on the 8250

The 8250's sole response to an interrupt condition is to assert its INTRPT line to inform the system (i.e., the CPU) that an interrupt occurs. The 8250 itself is not responsible for supplying the address of the associated interrupt handler. The CPU must learn the address of the 8250's interrupt handler by a combination of system hardware and software, an example of which we will study in Chapter 20.

After the CPU learns the address of the 8250's interrupt handler, it turns control over to it. When first gaining control, the handler knows only that the 8250 is the source of the interrupt; its first task, therefore, is to ascertain the precise condition that generated the interrupt. This is accomplished by reading Interrupt Identification, whose contents can easily be converted to the address of the correct subfunction to handle the pending interrupt.

RESETTING A PENDING INTERRUPT

When the 8250 generates an interrupt, all interrupts with an equal or lower priority are locked out until the current interrupt has been "cleared." The operation required to clear a pending interrupt varies according to the source of the interrupt. These relationships are given in Table 7.4.

Table 7.4. Actions required to clear pending interrupts.

Source of Interrupt	Response Required to Reset
Receiver error or BREAK	Read Serialization Status register
Received data	Read data from Receiver register
Transmit buffer empty	Write to the transmitter or read the Interrupt ID register
RS-232 input	Read the RS-232 Status register

Only one of these actions needs explanation: the response to an empty transmit buffer. This interrupt can be cleared, obviously, by writing a byte to the Transmitter Buffer register. Not so obviously, it can be cleared simply by reading the Interrupt Identification register. Suppose that 5 bytes are queued for transmission. After each byte is transmitted, a TBE interrupt is generated; writing the next byte to the Transmitter Buffer register clears the interrupt. When there are no more bytes to transmit, what will clear the interrupt generated by the fifth (and last) byte? With no more bytes to transmit, the interrupt is never cleared, locking out interrupts of lower priority. To avoid this condition, TBE interrupts can be cleared merely by reading the Interrupt Identification register.

Interrupt Service Routine

As mentioned earlier, the ISR must continue to read the Interrupt Indentification register before returning control back to the CPU. Failure to clear *all* interrupts before returning will leave an interrupt pending and prevent the UART from generating further interrupt requests to the CPU. In other words, the UART will be blocked. Figure 7.8 shows a flow chart for the proper design of an ISR.

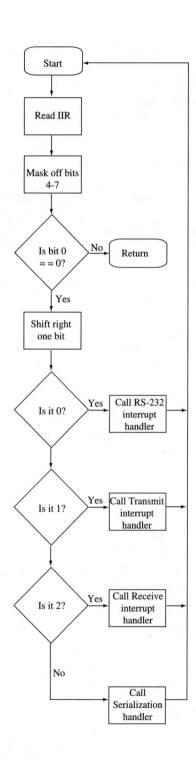

FIGURE 7.8.

Flow chart for 8250 ISR.

It is worth mentioning here the portion of the flow chart labelled *Mask off bits 3-7*. Early National documentation lists all of these bits as *Always 0*, but later came to refer to bits 3,5, and 7 as "reserved." Programmers that rely upon all bits being zero find that their software crashes when run on the supposedly compatible 16550 FIFO'ed UART discussed later in this chapter. Moral: if you don't plan to use a bit, get rid of it!

THE 8250 AND POLLED I/O

Several facts strongly suggest that the 8250 was designed explicitly for interrupt I/O and that support for polled operation is only halfhearted. First, the 8250 contains only a single buffer between the receiver's shift register and the data bus. This means that an unread byte is overwritten by the very next byte received. For a UART to work well in polled I/O, it must have *at least* two buffers, which are usually organized in a simple FIFO.

The second clue that the 8250 was designed primarily for interrupt mode is the lack of a simple interrupt enable/disable mechanism. As we discussed earlier in "The Interrupt Identification register," highly efficient polled operation is possible if the 8250 reports interrupts in its Interrupt Identification register, but does not report interrupts to the CPU via the INTRPT line. Unfortunately, there is no way to accomplish this without extra hardware. (As a matter of fact, the only way to disable interrupts entirely on the 8250 is to mask and unmask bits in the Interrupt Enable register.)

The only reasonable explanation for this "oversight" is that the designers did not anticipate the 8250 running without interrupts. Serial port designers apparently do not agree with the 8250 engineers. For example, on IBM's Asynchronous Communications Adaptor, a bus-driver IC, shown in Figure 7.9, effectively blocks the 8250's INTRPT line unless the GP02 output is asserted! With the INTRPT thus prevented from generating a processor interrupt, the 8250's internal interrupt structure can be utilized for polled operation.

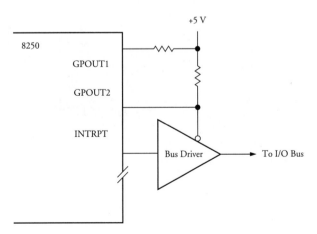

FIGURE 7.9.

The IBM PC's use of GP02 for a Master Interrupt Enable.

The National 16550 UART

The National NS16550 UART is a 16-character FIFO'ed UART that is electrically interchangeable with the 16450 UART and programmatically backwardly compatible with both the 8250 and 16450 UARTs. Software backward compatibility is achieved by assigning bits that were reserved in the 8250 and by implementing a new write-only register on top of a previously read-only register.

Unless its special features are engaged, the 16550 behaves identically to its less powerful ancestors: interrupts have the same priority and are cleared in the same manner. Best of all, an interrupt handler written properly for a 8250/16450 operates correctly on the 16550 even with its FIFO's engaged.

There are many things to love about the 16550, but there also are two things really to dislike. First, although the transmit and receive FIFO's function separately, they are not independently programmable; second, the transmit FIFO has no trigger level.

On the latter subject, National observes: "Since a lag time in servicing an asynchronous transmitter usually has no penalty, CPU latency time is of no concern to transmitter operation." The big word here is *usually*. As we shall see in our chapter on facsimile (Chapter 11), transmitter underrun is usually fatal.

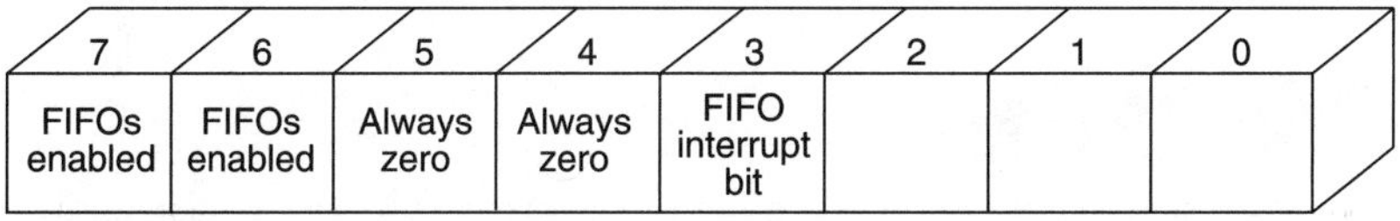

FIGURE 7.10.

Additions to the Interrupt Identification Register.

The 16550 Interrupt Identification Register

This register provides information about the interrupt.

Bit 3   When FIFOs are disabled (bit 0 of the FIFO Control register is 0), this bit is O; otherwise, this bit is set to indicate that the pending transmit or receive interrupt was generated by a timeout. Note that a FIFO timeout also sets bit 2, the FIFO trigger level interrupt.

Bits 6, 7   When FIFOs are disabled (bit 0 of the FIFO Control register is 0), these bits are 0; otherwise, they are always 1. Regrettably, they do *not* reflect the FIFO trigger level.

As shown in Table 7.5, when the FIFO reaches its programmed trigger level, it generates an interrupt that sets bit 2 only. This is the same bit set by an ordinary receiver interrupt on the 8250. However, when the receiver FIFO times out (details of which are given below), *both* bits 2 and 3 are set. As we shall see in Chapter 20, the ability to differentiate between these two kinds interrupts has profound impact on the architecture of the receiver interrupt subroutine.

Table 7.5. Interrupt identification coding for the 16550.

Bit 3	Bit 2	Bit 1	Bit 0	Priority*	Interrupt ID
0	0	0	1	None	None
0	1	1	0	0	Serialization Error or BREAK
0	1	0	0	1	FIFO Receiver Trigger level
1	1	0	0	1	FIFO Timeout
0	0	1	0	2	Transmitter Buffer Empty
0	0	0	0	3	RS-232 Input

*0/ is highest.

Line Status Register

FIGURE 7.11.

Additions to the Line Status register.

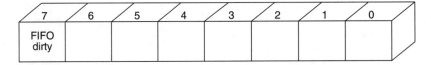

7	6	5	4	3	2	1	0
FIFO dirty							

FIFO Control Register

Recall that in the 8250, the register at offset two is a read-only register named the Interrupt Identification register. In the 16550 this location is the write-only FIFO Control register. Figure 7.12 shows the bitmapping of this new register.

FIGURE 7.12.

The 16550's FIFO Control Register.

7	6	5	4	3	2	1	0
Receive Trigger		Reserved	Reserved	DMA Mode Select	Transmit FIFO Reset	Receive FIFO Reset	FIFO Enable

Receive Trigger:

Bit 7	Bit 6	Level
0	0	1
0	1	4
1	0	8
1	1	16

Bit 0   Writing a 1 to this bit enables operation of both FIFOs . Writing a 0 to this bit clears all bytes in the FIFOs. This bit must be 1 before other bits in the register are written.

Bit 1   Writing a 1 to this bit clears all bytes from the receiver FIFO, clears the internal counters, but does not clear the shift register. The 1 written to this bit is automatically cleared.

Bit 2   Writing a 1 to this bit clears all bytes from the transmit FIFO, clears the internal counters, but does not clear the shift register. The 1 written to this bit is automatically cleared.

Bit 3   Writing a one to these bits supports DMA operations (not a very useful option with a small FIFO).

Bit 4   Reserved

Bit 5   Reserved

Bits 6-7 These bits set the receive FIFO's trigger level as follows:

Bit 7	Bit 6	Trigger Level
0	0	1
0	1	4
1	0	8
1	1	14

FIFO Interrupt Mode Operation

When the FIFO and receiver interrupts are enabled (FIFO Control register bit 0 = 1 and Interrupt Enable register 0 = 1), receive interrupts occur as follows:

1. The receive data available interrupt is issued to the CPU when the FIFO has reached its programmed trigger level; it is cleared as soon as the FIFO drops below its programmed trigger level.

2. The Interrupt Identification register receive-data-available indication also occurs when the FIFO trigger level is reached, and, like the interrupt, it is cleared when the FIFO drops below the trigger level.

3. As in polled mode, the data ready bit (Line Status register 0) is set as soon as a single character is transferred from the shift register to the receiver FIFO. It is reset when the FIFO is empty.

Receive FIFO

As explained in Chapter 6, when the count in the FIFO is below the programmed trigger level, after a certain amount of time, the UART must generate an interrupt to prevent unread characters from languishing in the FIFO. When receiver FIFO and receiver interrupts are enabled, receiver FIFO *timeout interrupts* occur as follows:

1. A FIFO timeout interrupt occurs under the following conditions:
   - At least one character is in the FIFO.
   - The most recent character was received longer than four character times ago.
   - The most recent CPU read of the FIFO occurred longer than four character times ago.

   a. Timeout interrupts are cleared and the timer reset when the CPU reads one character from the FIFO.

   b. The timeout interrupt timer is reset after each received character or when the CPU reads one character from the FIFO.

Transmit Interrupt Operation

When the transmit FIFO and transmitter interrupts are enabled interrupts occur as follows:

1. The transmitter holding register interrupt occurs when the transmit FIFO is empty; it is cleared when the transmitter holding register is written or the Interrupt Identification register is read.

2. A single spurious interrupt is often generated immediately after transmitter interrupts are enabled.

Character timeout and receiver FIFO trigger level interrupts have the same priority as the current received data interrupt. Transmit FIFO empty has the same priority as the current transmitter holding register empty interrupt.

Using the 16550 in Polled Operation

The 16550's benefit of reducing over- and under-run is available in polled applications by:

● Disabling the FIFO (FIFO Control register 0 = 1)
● Clearing Interrupt Enable register bit 0
● Clearing Interrupt Enable register bits 0 and 1

Although the trigger-level and time-out features do not operate, both FIFO's still hold characters. The status bits in the Line Status register function as expected, including bit 7, which indicates errors in the receiver FIFO.

The Zilog Z80SIO
Serial Input/Output Controller

As its name suggests, the Z80SIO is primarily intended for use with the Z80 microprocessor and associated peripheral chips. Because the Z80SIO actually contains two independent UART "channels" in a single chip, it is ideal for small microcomputers where one channel is devoted to keyboard I/O and the other channel is configured as a general-purpose RS-232 serial port. The Z80SIO not only supports START/STOP asynchronous communications but also synchronous communications, including the high-level proto-cols SDLC and HDLC. Although we will continue to refer to it as a UART, its dual ca-pability earns it the name USART—a Universal Synchronous/Asynchronous Receiver/ Transmitter.

The Z80SIO's smaller brother, the Z80 DART (Dual Asynchronous Receiver/Transmit-ter) contains only the Z80SIO's asynchronous functions. Asynchronous software that runs on the Z80SIO runs without modification on the DART, and, with a single exception,[6] vice versa. Despite very close software compatibility (the same mask is used to manufac-ture both), the less complicated DART is seldom found in programmable applications such as computers, but in stand-alone products such as printer buffers, speech synthesiz-ers, and plotters. This is not surprising, considering that the two chips have almost identical manufacturing and, consequently, selling prices. Faced with a negligible price difference, microcomputer manufacturers inevitably choose the Z80SIO's additional support for synchronous communications.

Because we are interested only in the Z80SIO as an asynchronous device, our bitmap dia-grams employ a special notation for bits related to its synchronous capabilities. Bits that govern synchronous functions are marked with the phrase "SET TO 0" in write registers, "XXXX" in read registers. The "XXXX" is a reminder to mask off these bits before evalu-ating the register.

The Z80SIO Versus the 8250

Before we look deeply into the Z80SIO, it is worth summarizing the most important dif-ferences between it and the 8250. In many areas they are similar because they are both UARTs: both predictably provide bits to monitor the readiness of the transmitter and receiver buffers to transfer data, and both provide the status and control bits for popular RS-232 lines. Beyond these generic similarities, however, the two UARTs are about as different as can be imagined.

Register Addressing

From the programmer's point of view, the most obvious difference between the 8250 and the Z80SIO is register addressing. Instead of the "flat" addressing of the 8250 where reg-isters are addressed at different locations, most Z80SIO registers are addressed at the *same* location by writing 2 bytes—the number of the register, followed by the desired read or write operation for that register. We will explore this form of addressing in detail shortly.

If register addressing is the most obvious difference between the two UARTs, the *nature* of the registers is the most significant. Alas, with one exception, the Z80SIO's writable registers cannot be read. On the superficial level, write-only registers are simply an

---

[6]The DART supports an additional RS-232 input, RI. See "Read Register 0," later in this chapter.

aggravation, forcing us to maintain a copy of each register in RAM and to update it with each write to a UART register. On a more serious level, however, the inability to query the Z80SIO about its current state makes it impossible to write programs that, upon exit, restore the interface to its original state. As we shall see in Chapter 12, this creates insurmountable impediments to good programming.

The FIFO

One of the most obvious architectural differences is that the Z80SIO's receiver and transmitter buffers are FIFOs. This means that 4 bytes can "stack up" in the receiver and 2 in the transmitter before data is lost due to receiver overrun or transmitter underrun errors. This immunity from errors accounts for the Z80SIO's legendary robustness in polled operation. The bits that report error conditions in the receiver are also held in a FIFO, assuring that errors are not reported until the offending byte is next in line to be read.

DELTA Status Bit Latching

In the 8250 we saw how several bits in the RS-232 Input register monitor changes on the RS-232 input lines. When changes occur, the new value is remembered, or latched, until the register is read by the CPU. Latching improves the efficiency of all kinds of I/O, but especially polled I/O by allowing the programmer to defer polling until it is convenient.

The idea of latching changed inputs is carried even further on the Z80SIO, where there are two categories of latched events. The first category, referred to as an "External/Status" event, comprises the just-mentioned transition of an RS-232 input as well as the BREAK. In the second category are receiver errors—parity and receiver overrun errors, but *not* framing errors (Zilog offers no explanation for this oddity).

The scope of Z80SIO's latching action is also quite different from the 8250's. When *any* of the events in a group occurs, the status bits of *all* members are latched. If a change occurs on the DCD input, for example, the DCD, CTS and BREAK status bits are all latched.

The manner in which latched events are cleared is also different. On the 8250, the RS-232 status latches are cleared merely by reading them; on the Z80SIO, however, latches must be cleared explicitly by commands—one for each category of latched event. Lamentably, this makes reading the *current* state of a status bit a two-step operation: the latch must be cleared before it is read. (Many an hour has been squandered by programmers who didn't understand this.)

Vectoring Interrupts

The way in which interrupts are handled is perhaps the most dramatic difference between the 8250 and the Z80SIO, which uses *vectored interrupts.* These differences clearly reflect the differences in the architecture of their respective CPUs. Although we will postpone exposition of this architectural topic until later in the chapter, it should be noted that only four events on the Z80SIO are capable of generating interrupts:

1. Received Data Ready (RxRDY)
2. Transmitter Buffer Empty (TBE)
3. Receiver errors: parity, framing, or receiver overrun
4. "External/Status" events: changes in RS-232 inputs or a BREAK condition

Interrupts on these conditions can be individually enabled.

Additional Z80SIO Features

Several of the features proposed for the conceptual UART in Chapter 6 are not supported by the 8250 but are found on the Z80SIO. These include the ability to enable and disable the transmitter and the receiver, hardware handshaking between the transmitter and CTS and the receiver and DCD, and a programmable clock factor. Unfortunately, the Z80SIO has no general-purpose inputs or outputs.

Z80SIO Hardware Basics

As indicated in Figure 7.13, the Z80SIO actually consists of two UARTs in the same package, referred to as "channels" A and B.

Ordinarily, six register-select lines would be used to address the Z80SIO's twenty internal registers. The constraints of fitting two full-blown UARTs in one 40-pin package, however, demands a more economic approach.[7] The solution is evident by the fact that the Z80SIO has only two address lines: (1) B/A, which selects between channels A and B, and (2) C/D, which selects between a *Data register* (the receiver and the transmitter) and the *Control/Status register* through which UART commands are issued and from which the contents of various internal registers are read. To avoid confusion between these two "master" registers and the index registers within the Control/Status register, we refer to them as the Data and Control/Status "ports." Keep in mind, though, that this in no way implies that these registers must be addressed through I/O ports instead of RAM.

The Z80SIO does not contain the circuitry to generate its own reference clock, nor the Divider registers for baud rate control. The reference clock is usually the system clock (generally 4–6 MHz on the Z80). In each channel are separate master data clock inputs for transmitter (TxCA and TxCB) and receiver (RxCA and RxCB). After division by the *programmable* clocking factor, these signals become the baud clocks for transmitter and

---

[7] The effort was not entirely successful: the Z80SIO is available in three lead-bonding options, each eliminating one signal. We are studying the Z80SIO/2, which retains full asynchronous capabilities and is the version most often used in microcomputers. A square, 44-pin package containing all leads is available as the Z80SIO/4.

receiver. In most applications, the ability to transmit and receive at different baud rates is not required and the master data clock for a given channel is applied simultaneously to both transmitter and receiver inputs.

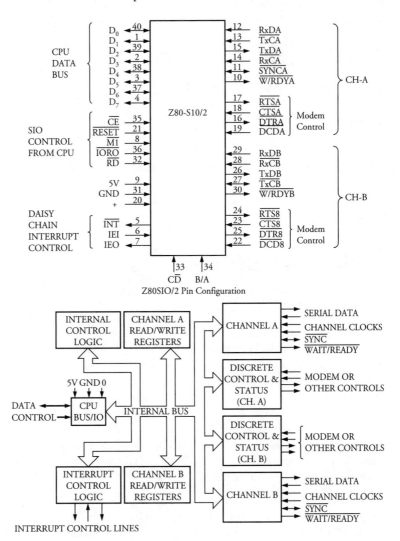

FIGURE 7.13.

Block and pin diagrams for the Z80SIO2.

The Data Register

To the programmer, each UART in the Z80SIO package appears as two memory or port addresses, one of which provides access to the Data port. The Data port is a model of simplicity: when read, it returns the contents of the UART's receiver buffer; when written, the byte on the CPU bus is written to the UART's transmitter buffer. In other words, the Data port is both the Transmitter and Receiver register.

The TBE and RxRDY bits that software must monitor for polled operation are located in Read Register 0, access to which is gained through the Control/Status port.

Control/Status Port Addressing

As we just noted, software sees a Z80SIO channel as two addresses, one each for the Data port and Control/Status port. A single data register is sufficient because it has only one function: to supervise data transfers between the buses in the CPU and Z80SIO. A single Control/Status port is obviously inadequate, however, for programming the myriad communications parameters inherent in a UART. To provide access to internal registers without increasing the number of physical address lines, the Z80SIO employs *indexed* addressing. In this scheme, a byte is written to the Control/Status port; this byte, however, does not contain data for a register, but the *number* (i.e., index) of the desired register. In a sense, the first number written into the Control/Status port "exposes" that register to the I/O bus.

It is technically more accurate to view the Control/Status port simply as two arrays of registers—three read registers and eight write registers. The value of three "index" bits in Write Register 0 (WR[0]) determines which of the other registers in the array will be addressed by the *next* read or write of the Control/Status port.

Importantly, these indexing bits automatically reset to 0 *after each register access*; thus reads and writes of the Control/Status port are steered to RR[0] and WR[0] by default. Said another way, RR[0] and WR[0] can be addressed with a *single* read or write; addressing any other register, however, is a two-step operation: (1) the index number of the desired register is first written to the Control/Status port; (2) the next access of the Control/Status port is steered to the desired register.

To illustrate the Z80SIO's addressing procedure, let's assume that you wish to read RR[1], write WR[4], and read RR[0]:

1. Show your desire to read RR[1] by writing a 1 to the Control/Status port.
2. Read the Control/Status port to fetch the contents of RR[1].
3. Show your desire to write to WR[4] by writing a 4 to the Control/Status port.
4. Writing to the Control/Status port writes into WR[4].
5. Because the index bits are returned to 0 after each access, simply reading the Control/Status port is the same as reading RR[0].

Because RR[0] and WR[0] obviously have special importance in the Z80SIO, let's examine them first.

WRITE REGISTER 0: THE BASIC Z80SIO COMMANDS

We have just seen how, by default, a write to the Control/Status port is actually a write to WR[0]. Because of the efficiency in addressing WR[0], all Z80SIO *commands* are located here along with, of course, the register indexing bits described earlier.

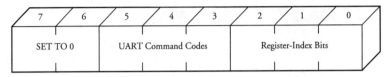

FIGURE 7.14.
The Z80SIO's WR[0] register.

As shown in Figure 7.10, when a write to the Control/Status port is performed, the Register-Index bits (the low-order 3 bits) name the register to be addressed by the *next* access of the Control/Status port. The remaining relevant bits—3, 4 and 5—are treated as data bound for WR[0] itself. Specifically, when the Register-Index bits are 0, the byte is a *command*. Commands are listed in Table 7.6.

Table 7.6. Z80SIO commands in WR[0].

Command	Bit			
Number	D5	D4	D3	Purpose of Command
0	0	0	0	Null for Register-Index operations
1	0	0	1	Used for synchronous I/O
2	0	1	0	Clear External/Status latches in RR[0]
3	0	1	1	Reset this entire channel
4	1	0	0	Enable interrupt-on-next-received-byte
5	1	0	1	Clear pending TBE (transmitter) interrupt
6	1	1	0	Reset receiver error latches in RR[0]
7	1	1	1	"Manual" return-from-interrupt instruction

Command 0 When writing to WR[0] solely to select a register for the next write, all command code bits should be 0.

Command 1 Used for synchronous I/O.

Command 2 When an RS-232 input changes state or a BREAK is detected, their bits are latched in RR[0]. All bits remain latched until Command 2 is issued.

Command 3 This command is equivalent to a hardware reset (i.e., a low on pin 21), but only affects a single channel. All registers must be reconfigured after a Command 3.

Command 4   When the number of bytes to receive is known in advance and can be easily polled for, an interrupt is necessary on the *first* byte, but not on subsequent ones. This form of interrupt is enabled in WR[1], and, having occurred, is reset with Command 4.

Command 5   If TBE (Transmit Buffer Empty) interrupts are enabled, some mechanism (besides transmitting another byte) must be provided for clearing the dangling interrupt that is pending after the *last* byte is transmitted. This is the function of command 5.

Command 6   Just as changes in RS-232 inputs or a BREAK condition are latched with a Command 2, so parity and receiver overrun errors are latched in RR[1] and must be cleared with Command 6. (Recall that framing errors are not latched.)

Command 7   The Z80SIO is designed for interface with a Z80 processor, whose RETI (return from interrupt) instruction automatically clears the "interrupt pending" flag on the interrupting device. CPUs that do not have such an instruction can issue Command 7 instead.

It is important to understand that if Command Code bits and Register-Index bits are *both* non-0, a command is issued *and* a register is indexed. For example, writing 13H (0001 0010) to Write Register 0 would simultaneously issue a Command 2 and select register 3 for the next access.

READ REGISTER 0

We have just seen that a Register Index is not required before reading RR[0]. This efficiency makes RR[0] (Figure 7.15) ideal for the bits most frequently consulted during polled operations—the RxRDY, TBE, RS-232, and BREAK status bits.

7	6	5	4	3	2	1	0
BREAK Detected	XXXXXX	CTS Status	XXXXXX (RI on Z80DART)	DCD Status	Transmitter Buffer Empty (TBE)	Interrupt Pending (Ch. A only)	Recieved Data (RxRDY)

FIGURE 7.15.
The Z80SIO's RR[0] register.

Bit 0   (Received Data) This bit is 1 when an incoming byte has been assembled and transferred into the receiver's FIFO buffer; it is 0 when the FIFO is empty.

Bit 1   This bit, which exists only in channel A, is 1 when an interrupt is pending in *either* channel. It is reset when the interrupt is serviced. This bit is mainly used in applications that do not support vectored interrupts (see "Vectored

Interrupts," later in this chapter). Without an "interrupt pending" bit, such applications would have to examine every bit in RR[0] and RR[1] in both channels to ascertain if an interrupt is pending anywhere on the chip. The corresponding bit of RR[0] in channel B is always 0.

Bit 2   (Transmitter Buffer Empty) This bit is set to 1 when a byte is moved from the transmitter FIFO buffer into the transmitter's shift register. Failure to consult this bit before writing to the Transmitter Buffer register overwrites a byte already in the FIFO awaiting transmission. This condition, transmitter underrun, is not reported by the Z80SIO.

Bit 3   (DCD)

Bit 4   (XXX or RI on Z80DART)

Bit 5   (CTS) Bits 3 and 5 show the state of the DCD and CTS inputs, respectively. On the Z80SIO, bit 4 is devoted to synchronous functions, while on the Z80DART it is the Ring Indicator input. When *any* of these bits (or the BREAK in bit 7) changes, *all* are latched. To read the *current* state of these bits, you must therefore clear the latch by preceding your read of RR[0] with a Command 2 (to WR[0]).

If External/Status Interrupts in WR[1] have been enabled, these conditions cause an interrupt. For a discussion of how CTS and DCD can influence UART I/O, see "WR[3]: Receive Parameters."

Bit 7   (BREAK detect) This bit behaves identically to the DCD and RTS RS-232 inputs in bits 3 and 5 except that it becomes 1 when a SPACING condition at the receiver input lasts longer than one SDU. Proper servicing of a BREAK condition requires issuing two Clear External/Status Latch commands—the first when the BREAK is detected, the second when it ends. Failure to issue the second command leaves the latch set.

The grouping of the BREAK bit with the RS-232 input status bits tends to make one forget that a BREAK is technically a receiver error and must be serviced as one. Specifically, when a BREAK condition is detected, the Z80SIO assembles a NULL byte and places it in the FIFO—just as with any other error. After detecting a BREAK, therefore, do not forget to read and discard the NULL from the FIFO.

Z80SIO Interrupts

Interrupts play a major role in the Z80SIO, so we must examine them early in our discussion. Interrupts in channel A have priority over interrupts in channel B. Four events can cause interrupts in the following priority:

1. Received Data Ready (RxRDY)
2. Transmitter Buffer Empty (TBE)
3. Parity, framing, or receiver overrun errors
4. "External/Status" events: changes in RS-232 inputs or a BREAK

This list is slightly different from the one given earlier because receiver error interrupts are supported only if RxRDY interrupts are enabled. Before we look at the register that enables these interrupts, we must discuss the more general topic of the Z80SIO interrupt structure.

VECTORED INTERRUPTS

When an interrupt occurs, the processor must somehow ascertain which of the possible interrupts has actually occurred. From this information, the processor then calculates the *interrupt vector* (i.e., the address of the interrupt handler) that must be invoked. In the 8250 we see the simplest of relationships between the system and an interrupting peripheral. The 8250's sole responsibility is to assert its INTRPT line; it is the exclusive province of the system to identify the interrupting device, to ascertain the address of its interrupt handler and to call that handler. The code in the handler is responsible for clearing the interrupt (i.e., inhibiting the INTRPT line).

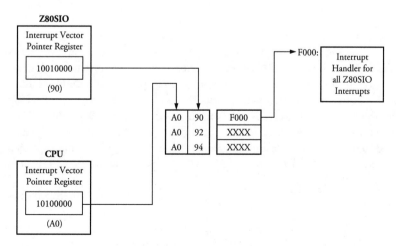

FIGURE 7.16.

Vectored interrupts on the Z80SIO.

When used in conjunction with a Z80 CPU, the Z80SIO employs a more complicated, but far more efficient approach—*Peripheral Interrupt Vectoring*, in which the peripheral itself actively participates in the calculation of the interrupt vector. Figure 7.12 illustrates this process using hypothetical addresses. Before enabling interrupts on the Z80SIO, an initialization routine stores the address of (a pointer to) the interrupt handler in RAM. The handler is at location F000 and the pointer containing its address is at A090. The interrupt cycle's mission is to recover the address of the pointer, and, *indirectly through it*, the address of the handler. The initialization routine also stores the low-order byte of the pointer's address (90H) in the Z80SIO's WR[2] and its high-order byte (A0) in the CPU's Interrupt Vector Pointer[8] register.

With the stage thus set, when an interrupt occurs, the Z80SIO places its half of the pointer's address on the system's data bus. The CPU fetches this byte, combines it with its own Pointer Vector register, thus forming the full address of the pointer.

With the interrupt vector pointer now in hand, the CPU turns control over to the interrupt handler by performing an *indirect* CALL to the pointer.

AUTOMATIC VECTOR MODIFICATION

In the approach depicted in Figure 7.16, a single interrupt handler must service the entire Z80SIO. That is, the handler must analyze registers RR[0] and RR[1] to ascertain the exact cause of the interrupt. Once the cause is known, the handler then calls the appropriate subfunction to service the interrupt. Although this is the simplest way to process interrupts for only a single source, it is inefficient when several kinds of UART interrupts are supported.

A great improvement is attained by having the Z80SIO modify its portion of the address based upon the cause of the interrupt. In this way a *unique* vector pointer is generated for each possible interrupt. Figure 7.17 illustrates modified vectoring using the hypothetical addresses from Figure 7.16. As before, the CPU's interrupt register and the Z80SIO are initialized with their respective halves of the vector pointer. This time, however, the Z80SIO outputs a different byte for each interrupt source. The portion of the address thus formed contains a pointer to the unique handler for the cause of the interrupt. If a TBE interrupt occurs, the system behaves exactly as before: the Z80SIO outputs 90H, the CPU furnishes A0, and the final address calculated is A090. In this instance, though, the address at A090 is expected to contain the address of a handler that services *only* TBE interrupts. Similarly, in response to an RxRDY interrupt, the Z80SIO outputs 94H instead of 90H. This time,

---

[8]Once again we encounter sloppy nomenclature. Zilog's documentation refers to the Interrupt registers on the Z80 and Z80SIO as "Interrupt Vector registers." Clearly, though, these registers do not produce the vector, but a pointer to the vector. (C Programmers will recognize this as a pointer to a pointer.) We use the more accurate "Vector Pointer register."

the address formed is A094, which contains the address of the code to handle RxRDY interrupts.

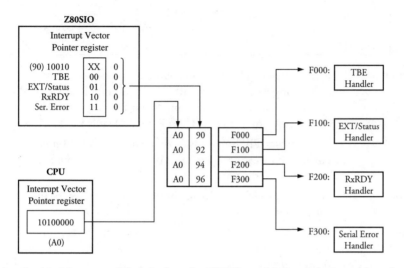

FIGURE 7.17.
Modified vector interrupts on the Z80SIO.

Notice that bit 0 is not modified. In fact, the CPU forces bit 0 to 0 during address formation to guarantee that vectors are generated in intervals of 2 bytes—the storage required for 16-bit Z80 addresses. With bit 0 always 0, only *even* addresses can be formed; it is therefore up to the programmer to begin the vector table at an *even* address.

A word of warning: do not rely upon the vector modifications shown in Figure 7.13—they are incomplete. Refer to Table 7.7 for the actual modification masks, which include a third bit for channel selection.

INTERRUPT CONTROL: WR[1], WR[2], AND RR[2]

Interrupts are controlled entirely by means of three registers. The unmodified vector is written to WR[2] (Figure 7.18) and can be read in RR[2] (the only read-write register in the Z80SIO). RR[2] and WR[2] exist only in Channel B:

7	6	5	4	3	2	1	0
V7	V6	V5	V4	V3	V2	V1	V0

FIGURE 7.18.
The Z80SIO's WR[2] register.

WR[1] (Figure 7.19) selects the sources of interrupts and whether the interrupt vector is modified.

FIGURE 7.19.

The Z80SIO's WR[1] register.

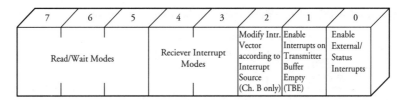

7	6	5	4	3	2	1	0
	Read/Wait Modes		Reciever Interrupt Modes		Modify Intr. Vector according to Interrupt Source (Ch. B only)	Enable Interrupts on Transmitter Buffer Empty (TBE)	Enable External/ Status Interrupts

Bit 0   This is the enabling bit for External/Status interrupts—that is, interrupts originating from the RS-232 inputs or a BREAK condition. When servicing this interrupt, do not forget to clear the interrupt with Command 2, "Clear External/Status Latches."

Bit 1   This bit enables TBE interrupts. Command 5 in WR[0] provides a mechanism for clearing a pending TBE interrupt without actually writing a byte to the transmitter.

Bit 2   If set, this bit, which is active in channel B only, causes the interrupt vector pointer to be modified as shown in Table 7.7.

Bits 3-4   These two bits select one of several variations on RxRDY interrupts as indicated in Table 7.8. If vector pointer modification is enabled in bit 1, interrupts on serialization errors are also automatically enabled. To make it possible to receive data in the presence of parity errors, code 3 does not generate an interrupt on parity errors. If you wish to override this feature entirely, simply point the serialization error vector at a function containing only a Command 6, "Clear Error Latches."

Bits 5-7   These three bits interface the Z80SIO to other hardware devices such as DMA controllers. The use of these bits is a topic for another time.

Table 7.7. Interrupt vector pointer modification.

V3	V2	V1	*Modified by Interrupt*
0	0	0	Ch.B: TBE
0	0	1	Ch.B: External/Status
0	1	0	Ch.B: RxRDY
0	1	1	Ch.B: Serialization Error
1	0	0	Ch.A: TBE
1	0	1	Ch.A: External/Status
1	1	0	Ch.A: RxRDY
1	1	1	Ch.A: Serialization Error

Table 7.8. Varieties of RxRDY interrupts.

D4	D3	RxRDY interrupt on:
0	0	No RxRDY interrupts
0	1	First byte only
1	0	Every byte, parity error modifies vector
1	1	Every byte, parity error does not modify

Summary of Remaining Registers

The remaining registers perform conventional functions similar to those proposed for the imaginary UART in Chapter 6 and found in the 8250 earlier in this chapter. We will now make a whistle-stop tour of these registers, bypassing WR[5] and WR[6], which pertain only to synchronous communications.

WR[3]: RECEIVE PARAMETERS

Most of the bits in WR[3] control some aspect of receiver operation. Of particular interest is bit 5, the "Handshaking" bit, in which control of the transmitter and receiver are tied to the CTS and DCD inputs, respectively. This feature greatly simplifies half-duplex modem control over an RS-232 interface where CTS and DCD actually control the send and receive modes. This handshaking relies upon the *current* state of these inputs, not the state of their status bits in RR[0], which might be latched.

Because half-duplex modem control has never been a popular usage for microcomputers, this feature is generally used for buffer flow control in slow peripheral devices such as printers and plotters. Flow control is achieved by connecting the printer's "Buffer Full," or BUSY output to the Z80SIO's CTS input (pin 5 on a DTE interface). When the printer has received all of the bytes it can handle, it inhibits its Buffer Full output, inhibiting the Z80SIO's CTS input and turning off the transmitter. After the character currently being assembled is sent, transmission ceases and remains in this state until CTS is asserted again.

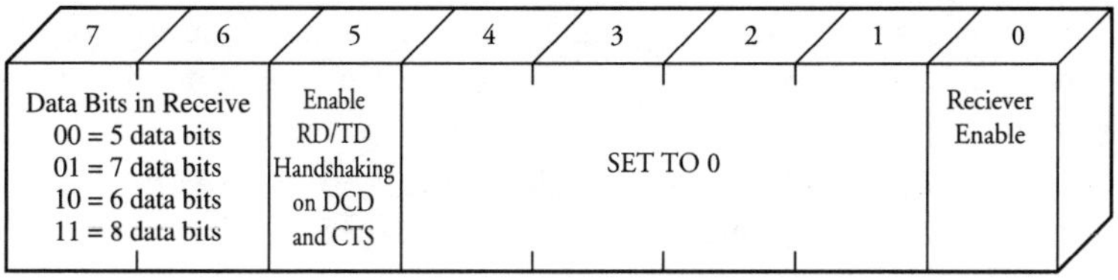

FIGURE 7.20.
The Z80SIO's WR[3] register.

7	6	5	4	3	2	1	0
Data Bits in Receive 00 = 5 data bits 01 = 7 data bits 10 = 6 data bits 11 = 8 data bits		Enable RD/TD Handshaking on DCD and CTS		SET TO 0			Reciever Enable

Bit 0   (Receiver Enable) When this bit is 0, the receiver does not function. On some UARTs the Receiver Enable simply holds the RxRDY FALSE while continuing to assemble characters from the communications line. The Z80SIO, on the other hand, completely disables the receiver by, one suspects, killing the clock pulses running its shift register. The complementary bit for the transmitter is WR[5], bit 3.

Bit 5   (Automatic Handshaking) When 1, this bit imparts special significance to the CTS and DCD status inputs, which effectively become secondary Receiver and Transmitter Enable bits, respectively. In other words, inhibiting the CTS and DCD inputs has the same effect as writing a 0 in WR[3], bit 0 (the Receiver Enable bit, just described) and in WR[5], bit 3 (the Transmitter Enable bit).

Bits 6-7   Bits 6 and 7 control the number of data bits assembled by the receiver. This number is independent of the transmitter's data bits number, which is set in WR[5], bits 5 and 6. Notice the lack of correlation between the bit patterns and the number of data bits they select.

WR[4]: MISCELLANEOUS PARAMETERS

WR[4] (Figure 7.21) controls UART functions that are common to both transmitter and receiver. Of these, only bits 6 and 7, which control the clocking factor, are interesting.

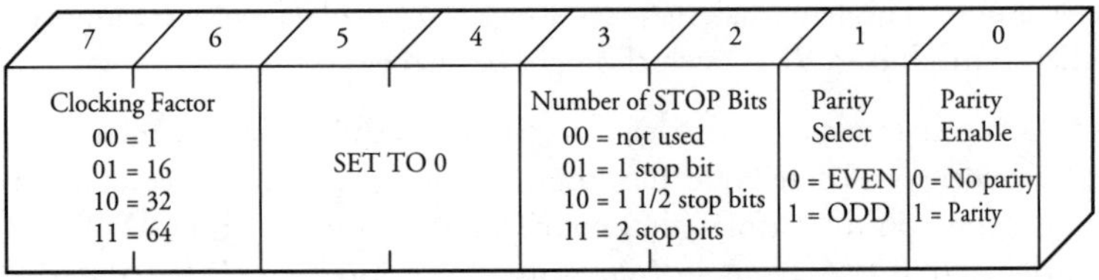

FIGURE 7.21.

The Z80SIO's WR[4] register.

7	6	5	4	3	2	1	0
Clocking Factor 00 = 1 01 = 16 10 = 32 11 = 64		SET TO 0		Number of STOP Bits 00 = not used 01 = 1 stop bit 10 = 1 1/2 stop bits 11 = 2 stop bits		Parity Select 0 = EVEN 1 = ODD	Parity Enable 0 = No parity 1 = Parity

As we noted in Chapter 6, increasing the clocking factor beyond 16 produces an insignificant improvement in synchronization (see Figure 6.8). In general, a programmable clocking factor is found on UARTs that do not contain on-board baud rate generators or baud rate divisor circuitry. On such UARTs, varying the clocking factor among 16, 32, and 64 is a simple way to change the baud rate without understanding the external baud rate circuitry. This is a handy feature when the baud rate is hardwired or set by inaccessible microswitches. For example, if the switches are adjusted to produce a baud rate of, say 1200 baud, with a clocking factor of 32, changing the clocking factor to 16 and 64 then produces baud rates of 2400 and 600 baud, respectively. Selecting a clocking factor of 1 prevents START-bit synchronization.

WR[5]: TRANSMIT AND RS-232 PARAMETERS

The bits in WR[5] (Figure 7.22) control various aspects of the transmitter, including BREAK generation. In addition, WR[5] controls the RS-232 outputs DTR and RTS.

7	6	5	4	3	2	1	0
DTR 0 = off 1 = on	Data Bits in Transmit 00 = 5 data bits 01 = 7 data bits 10 = 6 data bits 11 = 8 data bits		BREAK Control 0 = off 1 = on	Transmitter Enable	SET TO 0	RTS 0 = off 1 = on	SET TO 0

FIGURE 7.22.
The Z80SIO's WR[5] register.

Bit 1   (Request To Send) A 1 in this bit asserts the Z80SIO's RTS output.

Bit 3   (Transmitter Enable) If this bit is 0, the transmitter does not function. The transmitter goes "offline" as soon as its shift register becomes empty. The complementary bit for disabling the receiver is WR[3], bit 0.

Bit 4   (Send BREAK) As long as there is a 1 in this bit, the output of the transmitter is forced into a SPACE condition.

Bits 5-6   These bits govern the number of data bits transmitted. This number is independent of the receiver's data bits number, which is set in WR[3], bits 6 and 7. Notice the lack of correlation between the bit patterns and the number of data bits they select.

Bit 7   (Data Terminal Ready) A 1 in this bit asserts the Z80SIO's DTR output.

Conclusion

In this chapter we examined two quite different UARTs. We shall meet them again in Chapter 9 and throughout the programming chapters. In these chapters we will use these two UARTs to demonstrate that, through careful design, communications software can achieve a high degree of generality and, yes, portability. Before we begin this quest, however, let's take a close look at another familiar face in the microcomputer crowd—the Hayes Smartmodem.

The Baseline Smart Modem

Before microcomputers, modems supplied by Bell (that's the phone company) were unchallenged standards, at least in America. But in the microcomputer world and increasingly in the rest of computerdom as well, the Hayes Smartmodem[1] product family came to be a market standard in the same fashion as the IBM line of microcomputers became standard. So dominant was the Hayes influence that market analysts estimate that upwards of 90 percent of all modems manufactured for the microcomputer market now claim Hayes compatibility.

It is worth making an obvious but important distinction between the modems physical-layer characteristics (type of modulation, carrier tones, and so forth) and its user interface. Today, the CCITT is the primary source of most physical standards. These are published in the V-series recommendations (see the Bibliography). Only recently has the CCITT begun to venture into control and software interface issues. To a large extent, then, our discussion will focus on the interface used to control the physical layer characteristics.

By providing a standard software interface to which developers could write, the Hayes products caused the modem market to grow enormously. Everyone liked this. But all standards are double-edged swords: although they beneficially enlarge the market, they also stifle innovation. Market standards have the additional deleterious effect of creating an unhealthy business environment in which companies that adopt them effectively put their destiny in the hands of the competitor to whom the standard belongs. This point was resoundingly brought home

---

[1]Hayes Microcomputer Products, Inc. claims trademark on the terms Smartmodem 1200, Smartmodem 1200B, Smartmodem 2400, and Smartmodem 2400B. Although Hayes lays no claim to the neologism *smartmodem* itself, I will use the variation *smart modem* to describe a generic product that supports the features and command sets of the Hayes family of modems. To avoid confusion, I will always use Smartmodem with the first letter capitalized when referring to the Hayes product.

when Hayes began to invite smart modem manufacturers to take out licenses for certain portions of their technology and to pursue those who declined in court.

This is exactly the situation that occurred in the modem market in the middle 1980s: Hayes led, and a dozen or so manufacturers scurried to imitate. As the market matured, however, and Hayes became more aggressive in asserting its patent licensing, an increasing number of manufacturers grew weary of this master-slave relationship and sought a public standard to replace the market standard. The natural place for this was in the TIA's technical subcommittee on modem interfaces.

For reasons that are still not altogether clear, Hayes not only agreed to participate in this public standards effort, it offered to lead it. Accordingly, in August 1988, Project Number 2120 was created. Hayes made the major contribution to the committee and submitted a remarkably thorough document of its modems entitled *Hayes Smartmodem 2400 AT Command Specification.* (Document TR30.2.2/88-08006)

After many hiccups and substantial disagreement about its contents, in 1992 the TIA produced TIA 602, *Data Transmission Systems and Equipment: Serial Asynchronous Automatic Dialing and Control.* Its contents are a disappointment because the document standardizes only a small portion of what the industry and consumer considers to be a smart modem. As one participant commented, "This standard represents what we could agree on—which wasn't very much."

In this chapter, we will develop an ad hoc definition of the omnipresent commodity "baseline modem." We will draw upon the following resources:

● The early Hayes Smartmodem 300 and Smartmodem 1200

● The 1988 Hayes Smartmodem 2400 document

● The 1992 TIA 602 standard

● Common practice in the industry

Although modem technology has evolved beyond the baseline modem, the newer modems are founded on them and indeed strive to maintain backward compatibility with the baseline smart modem. I will treat this newer technology (protocols and high-speed modems) in Chapter 10. Presently, however, we must constrain ourselves to non-protocol modems whose maximum speed is 2400 bps.

What's So Smart About a Smart Modem, Anyway?

Before launching into the characteristics and attributes of the Hayes Smartmodem, we ought first to review (from Chapter 5) what we mean by the term "smart" modem and, by implication, a dumb one.

The rules for and extent of interaction between a conventional (that is, "dumb") modem and computer hardware are given by the TIA's Recommended Standard number 232 (current revision E), better known simply as RS-232. Despite the myriad other uses—mostly illicit—to which RS-232 has been put, its sole intended purpose was to standardize the interaction between *data communications equipment* (DCE, or modem) and *data terminal equipment* (DTE, or computer equipment).

As defined by RS-232, all interaction between a traditional modem and the computer equipment occurs by exchanging signal voltages across wires. For example, without DTR (pin 20) asserted, modems are disabled. Similarly, the modem announces a successful carrier linkage by asserting DCD (pin 8). Without belaboring the point, then, the RS-232 interface is the sole medium through which one device may control the other. The smart modem, by contrast, interacts with peripheral equipment by exchanging ASCII character sequences. There is no formal difference between these character sequences and ordinary data—both are in the START/STOP asynchronous format. Rather, under certain conditions, which we will explore shortly, the modem interprets these character sequences as command strings instead of data. Although it has the option of relying on RS-232 signals, properly written software can effect most modem control functions on a mere pair of RS-232 data lines and signal common.

The capability to control a modem by sending it software command strings in the data stream is enormously liberating: many of the tasks with which the programmer was previously burdened are now handled by the smart modem. On an ordinary modem, for example, answering an incoming call is a major production. The program must monitor the RS-232 RI (Ring Indicator) input for a ring signal, count the RI pulses until a predetermined number is reached, at which time the program signals via RS-232 for the modem to go off hook (that is, answer the line) and start the carrier tone. Once the modem acknowledges these instructions (via RS-232), the program begins a timing loop looking for a transition on pin 8, DCD (Data Carrier Detect) that indicates a modem carrier link has been achieved. If the timing loop expires, the program must reverse the process: turn the carrier off, reverse the phone line, and put the modem back to sleep. The same chore on a smart modem is trivial by comparison. During initialization, the smart modem is instructed via command strings not only to answer the phone automatically, but also on which ring to answer it.

The foregoing comparison is perhaps unfair because some conventional modems can automatically answer the phone. Nevertheless, the point of the comparison—that the smart modem relieves the programmer of the overwhelming minutiae of modem control—is well taken. In the remainder of this chapter, we will explore the structure and behavior of smart modems. In Chapter 21, we will develop a library of functions for programming them.

The first successful smart modem was the Hayes Smartmodem 300, followed by various iterations of the Smartmodem 1200, and the Smartmodem 2400.

A Brief History of the Hayes Smartmodem

The first Smartmodem (the Hayes Smartmodem 300, c. 1983) is a Bell 103A-type modem with data transfer rates of 110 or 300 bits per second. Under software control, it automatically answers incoming calls and, by means of an internal pulse/tone generator, automatically dials telephone numbers. The Smartmodem connects directly to the public switched telephone network through a single modular jack that accommodates standard RJ-11, RJ-12, RJ-13, RJ-41S, or RJ-45S plugs. The modem's intelligent features are controlled by sending commands in the form of ASCII character sequences to the RS-232 interface. The Smartmodem responds to commands and dialing operations with ASCII character sequences, again via its RS-232 interface. The modem has physical switches behind the front panel for configuring important features (DTR behavior, default settings for various commands, and so on).

The next development was various flavors of the Smartmodem 1200, which operated at a maximum rate of 1200 bps using the Bell 212A protocol with fallback to Bell 103A. Later models, nicknamed in this book "Smartmodem 1200+" had the capability to interpret events on the phone line such as busy signals, lack of dial tone, and so forth.

Next came the Smartmodem 2400, which operated at a maximum rate of 2400 bps using the CCITT V.22bis with fallback to V.21 (with the usual Bell 212A/103A compatibility). In addition to the higher speeds, this modem replaced the configuration switches with nonvolatile memory.

Modem States

Figure 8.1 illustrates the seven major modem states. The arrows on the figure show the directions in which state changes may occur. Two states—AL Selftest and Analog Loopback—relate to testing and are neither shown nor discussed. As shown in Figure 8.1, the modem can be in one of several states: command, dialing, handshaking, on-line, and on-line command.

Command State

In the command state, the modem is not communicating with a distant modem and is ready to accept commands. The modem is usually on hook while in the command state, but may be off hook. In command state, the modem monitors the bytes coming in from the RS-232 port in search of a particular sequence of bytes referred to as the *Command*

Sequence Introducer, or CSI.[2] The CSI is AT, supposedly an abbreviation for "attention." This sequence is not programmable.

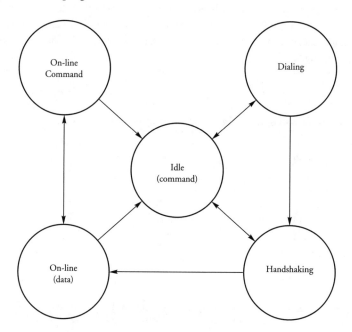

FIGURE 8.1.
Major modem states.

Dialing State

While the modem is executing a dial command, it is in the *dialing state.* In this state, the modem may be waiting for dial tone, sending dialing signals, pausing, or any other dialing operation.

Handshaking State

When the modem is sending answer tone, waiting for answer tone, or handshaking with another modem, it is in the *handshaking state.* The handshaking process can occur both in originate mode and answer mode.

On-line State

After handshaking has been completed and the modem is able to send and receive data, it is in the *on-line state.* Data from the phone line is passed to the DTE. In this state, it behaves as a simple modem and is not susceptible to commands. The modem automatically returns to the command state when the carrier is lost.

---

[2]This lingo is from ANSI 3.64. See Chapter 1 for details.

On-line Command State

In the command state, the modem is not communicating with a distant modem and, if not in dumb mode, is ready to accept commands. The modem is usually on hook while in the command state, but may be off hook. It is possible to switch the modem from the on-line to the command state and back again without breaking the carrier link. If the DTE sends the escape sequence (discussed later) while in the on-line state, the modem maintains the connection to the distant modem but treats local DTE signals as commands. This is called the on-line command state. Refer to the section entitled "Software Hang-up: On-line Command State" later in this chapter for further explanation.

Dumb Mode

Some modems have a strap, jumper, or switch to place them in the dumb mode. In this mode, the modem ignores all commands from the local DTE, even while in the command state. Escape sequences (defined later) are ignored, so the on-line command state cannot be reached. In short, command, dialing, handshaking, and on-line are the only states possible while the modem is in dumb mode. The modem does not issue result codes while in the dumb mode.

Command Syntax and Modem Responses

From the programmer's point of view, the command state is the most complicated of all the states because it is the user interface. We shall consider command state from the perspective of command syntax, command-line processing, command execution, and modems.

Command Syntax

All modem commands begin with the AT command introducer. In mode commands, the AT is followed by a single printable ASCII character, followed by an optional *numeric operand*, a single ASCII numeral in the range 0–9 (30H–39H). For example, in the string ATE1, the command E is followed by the operand 1. Note that this value must be an ASCII digit, not a binary value. In the absence of an operand, 0 is assumed: ATE is the same as ATE0. There is no mechanism for querying the modem either for the existence of a command or, if present, its range of supported values.

In addition to mode commands, the modem maintains *numeric variables* in 'S' registers, named S0, S1, and so on. These variables are addressed in the ordinary command format: *AT*, followed by the register number. Unlike other modem parameters, the ASCII digits following the register name are interpreted as true arithmetic values. An S-register assignment command is created by placing an equal sign (=, ASCII 3D) between the register name and the digit-by-digit ASCII representation of the numeric value (for example, ATS4=30). Unlike the mode commands, the current value in the S-registers can be queried by replacing the numeric value in the previous example with a question mark (?, ASCII 3F).

After the AT is encountered, the modem places subsequent characters in its internal 40-character buffer, until the buffer becomes full or it encounters the *command terminator character*. Here are the few rules governing the command buffer:

- The AT may be either upper- or lowercase.[3]
- Whether the AT itself counts toward the 40-character maximum varies across the industry.
- Space (ASCII 20H) and control characters are ignored and not counted toward the 40-character maximum.
- The backspacing character removes characters from the buffer.

When the command terminator is entered, the modem attempts to parse the buffer into individual commands. An error results if:

- More than 40 characters are entered
- On older modems, the AT contains lowercase characters
- An invalid command is encountered in the buffer
- An invalid operand is encountered in the buffer

Exactly how a command executes varies among manufacturers and sometimes among models from the same manufacturer. In general, the commands of a command line execute one at a time without regard for what may follow on the command line. If an error occurs, all subsequent commands on the command line are ignored. There are variations, however: some modems (early Hayes modems included) evaluate the entire command line prior to execution and discard the entire command line if it contains a single error. On the other hand, a few modems forge ahead even in the face of errors. In summary, because you can make no assumptions about how much or how little of the command line executed when an error results, it's important to exercise great care to assure the validity of the individual commands that constitute the command line.

Command Execution Time

The time required to execute commands consisting of manipulating memory variables generally takes about a millisecond. This time, however, is swamped by a 125-250 millisecond delay inserted by the modem between receiving the CR of a command line and beginning the response. Commands such as Dial and Answer take an indeterminate amount

---

[3]The Smartmodem 300 and early versions of the 1200 required that the AT, but not subseqent characters, be in uppercase.

of time to execute. Furthermore, a command involving nonvolatile memory may take microseconds when implemented as battery backed-up RAM, or tens of milliseconds with flash ROM, whereas the same command implemented in EEPROM can take several seconds to execute.

SOFT RESET

Because of the timing variations just described, the amount of time required to reset a modem varies widely (refer to the Z command in Chapter 9). In addition to variations in the way nonvolatile memory is implemented, modems that support the auxiliary relay typically take longer to reset than those that don't. An important detail to remember is that the modem actually issues its response to the reset command before the reset actually occurs (it says good-bye just before committing suicide). For this reason when issuing a reset command you should hard-wire a wait after the modem's response. Experience has shown that three seconds is a reasonable time.

HARD RESET

In certain confounding combinations of commands, it is not always possible to reset a modem with software commands. Because PC-card modems are directly accessible from the host's CPU, they support a hardware reset. Asserting General Purpose Output #1 resets the modem as if it had just been powered on. (See Chapter 7 for explanations of the 8250 UART's general-purpose outputs.) In modems without EEPROM, a hard reset occurs in about a second. In modems with EEPROM, hard reset may take up to three seconds.

Key Press Abort

The Dial and Answer commands initiate procedure of indefinite and unpredictable length. In such times, transmitting any character to the modem cancels the command, produces the appropriate response, and returns the modem to the command state.

Software Hang-Up: On-line Command State

While the smart modem's capability of operating without RS-232 control lines certainly simplifies its operation, it also causes a considerable problem: because the modem treats data transparently during a carrier linkage, how do we get its attention to tell it to hang up? In a conventional modem, dropping DTR forces a hang-up, and a smart modem can be configured to behave in this manner as well. But in a smart modem, there is the possibility that the modem will be configured to operate via a simple three-wire connection and therefore to ignore the RS-232 signals.

The solution to the hangup problem is a special state, the on-line command state, in which the modem returns to the command state without dropping its connection with the remote modem. When in the on-line state, the modem accepts all valid commands, including the command to hang up. The modem can be forced to on-line command state by sending it an *in-band escape signal* (as opposed to RS-232 signals, which are *out-of-band*). While in the on-line state, the modem is not entirely deaf to the data stream but listens for a string of three consecutive escape characters surrounded by a specified interval of silence known as a *guard time*. Upon hearing these conditions, the modem enters on-line command state. (The values of the escape character and the duration of the guard time are given in S-registers 2 and 12, respectively.)

Here is the procedure for performing an escape to the command state and then returning to the on-line state.

1. Send no data to the modem for the guard time (the default is 1 second).

2. Send three consecutive escape characters (the default character is '+').

3. If no data is sent during the guard time, the modem responds OK, announcing that it is now in the on-line command state.

Once in the on-line command state, the modem can be forced to command state by hanging up, or it can be returned to on-line state (with the On-line command). The mechanism for moving between modem states is straightforward, if problematical.

● To return to command state, issue the hang-up command.

● To return to the on-line state, issue the on-line command. The modem responds CONNECT XXXX to announce its return to the on-line state.

Dangers of the On-line Escape

The guard time must always be longer than the time represented by a single SDU at the current baud rate. To understand why this is so, assume that the modem is currently using a 10-bit SDU at 300 bps; here, one SDU has a duration of 33.3 milliseconds. If the guard time is set to 20 milliseconds, the guard timer expires while each character is being serialized. Because the modem's lowest data rate is 110 baud (an SDU of about 100 milliseconds), the default guard time of 1 second provides an order-of-magnitude safety margin under all circumstances. If the guard time is 0, the escape sequence is acknowledged instantaneously (without a guard band of silence).

Many early modems had a fatal flaw in their implementation of the on-line escape procedure: they acted upon the escape sequence whether it arrived over the phone line or from the DTE. To understand why this is fatal, assume that you call a remote full-duplex system with echo-back. Because the remote system happens to be using a smart modem, there is a danger inherent in the use of the on-line escape. As you send the three escape characters, the remote system also sees them and acts upon them! In other words, you not only force your modem into the command state, you force the remote system, too. You are able to return your own modem to on-line state, but you have no way to do the same for the remote modem. Your only recourse is to hang up and call again. To avoid being thus hoisted with your own petard, it's not a bad idea to change your S-register escape character from the default or make certain that the two modems are programmed with a different escape character. Fortunately, this problem exits only on very early modems.

The Great Escape

Hayes was granted a U.S. patent on the idea of programmable guard time applied to an in-band on-line escape sequence. (The patent was issued in the name of a Hayes engineer, Dale Heatherington.) In 1987 when cloning began to cut into its profits, Hayes attempted to extract royalties from the clone manufacturers. The royalty (typically four percent of revenues) was viewed by most manufacturers as punitive, unreasonable, and, importantly, based upon a patent that should never have been granted in the first place. One by one the manufacturers settled with Hayes, but Everex Systems, Inc. of Fremont, California disputed Hayes' right to the patent and allowed the issue to go to a jury trial. Everex lost and the patent was effectively upheld. The following account of this historic action is that of Joseph Schlessinger, the president of Cygnet Technologies of Berkeley California, an Everex subsidiary.

"Hayes notified Everex in 1987 that it believed Everex was infringing on Heatherington. Everex did not respond to the invitation to take out a license because Everex believed that the patent was invalid and would be so found in a trial. Everex joined an industry group to help fund the suits pending among Hayes, U.S. Robotics and Prometheus. However, both of those companies settled with Hayes. In 1989 Hayes sued Everex, Omnitel, and Ventel, all of whom chose to contest. Everex believed that the patent was worthless on the face of it. Guard times are ubiquitous in communications and were ubiquitous at the time the Heatherington patent was filed.

"Our defense in court, however, was technical. We argued that Hayes had failed to provide the proper disclosure (description) in their patent filing, for the simple reason that the patent claim itself was an afterthought. The original patent, in 1981, claimed the entire concept of an intelligent modem but didn't claim guard times. That patent was refused in 1983 because of a prior patent issued to Michael Eaton of Bizcomp. So Hayes refiled. The revised patent, filed in 1983, couldn't add new description but could and did add a new claim, for an "improved" guard time, albeit without any descriptive disclosure. The legal term for this act is 'inventing a patent.' Everex went to trial confident of having the case thrown out of court.

"Our strategy failed. Patent infringement cases are heard before lay juries, and the jury didn't understand at all what disclosure meant. That was Everex's only opportunity to prevail on the facts of the case. We appealed, but the appeal could only succeed on procedural grounds. (The facts had been established in the jury trial.) Everex had no chance to win the appeal, so Everex settled."

Subsequently, Everex and others came up with a successful workaround of Heatherington, usually called *TIES (time independent escape sequence,* my own coining). Hayes tried to bluster against TIES in a series of ads but was enjoined by a federal judge from publishing misleading ads. To my knowledge, no one has ever produced a single case of a modem inadvertly escaping due to TIES.

In the long run, both Heatherington and TIES are kludges. The real solution to mixing commands and data is a mixed data stream using <DLE>-like mechanisms, widely practiced in mainframe communications since the beginning of time. Heatherington was a hacker's solution for the days when modems were too slow and dumb to practice a protocol as subtle as <DLE>. Those days are gone.

Response to Commands

After it has evaluated and, if possible, parsed and executed the commands in its command buffer, the modem responds with its own sequence of ASCII characters. After receiving the terminating Carriage Return, the modem waits at least 125 milliseconds before beginning its response.[4] The purpose of this delay is to "duck" the Line Feed character from the DTE that often follows a carriage return. The delay between reception of a command and its execution is beneficial to programmers, too: it enables software to differentiate between characters echoed by the modem and the modem's response.

The response vocabulary of the smart modem is limited to just 11 phrases, each of which has a whole-word form and a shorter numeric form (refer to the V Command in Chapter 9). When using the word form the modem responds with multicharacter ASCII strings such as OK and ERROR; when using the short form, these strings are replaced by the single ASCII digits (numerals) 0 and 4, respectively. A complete list of modem responses is given in Table 8.1. An explanation of the circumstances producing the various dial/answer responses is found in Chapter 9.

---

[4]The dead-air time between the Carriage Return and the modem's response was given as 250 milliseconds in Hayes 300 and early 1200 modems.

Table 8.1. Smart modem responses.

Digit Code	Word Code	Description
0	OK	Non-dial command successfully executed.
1	CONNECT	Connection established at 300 baud.
2	RING	Ring signal present on phone line.
3	NO CARRIER	Carrier absent or never found.
4	ERROR	Error in command line, unrecognized command, or command buffer exceeded 40 characters.
5	CONNECT 1200	Connection established at 1200 bps.
6	NO DIALTONE	No dial tone present.
7	BUSY	Busy signal heard.
8	NO ANSWER	Returned when a call fails using the @ dial modifier (see Chapter 9).
9	CONNECT 0600	Connection established at 600 bps. This response and its corresponding digit code are reserved, but not used.
10	CONNECT 2400	Connection established at 2400 bps.

The newline punctuation included with modem responses also varies according to the modem's verbosity. In the more verbose mode, it surrounds its responses with both newline characters:

```
(nl1)(nl2)OK(nl1)(nl2)
(nl1)(nl2)ERROR(nl1)(nl2)
```

In its less verbose mode, however, the single digits are surrounded by nl1s:

```
(nl1)0(nl1)
(nl1)4(nl1)
```

INFORMATION TEXT

Some commands do not return a standard response but provide some informational or tutorial information instead. The &V command, for example, responds with a complete listing of all the stored profiles plus the active profile. *Information text*, as these responses are called, are always preceded and followed by a CRLF pair.

Hardware Considerations

Auto-bauding

The modem's serial port automatically adjusts itself to operate over a wide range of baud rates and data formats and attempts to negotiate a connection at that speed. The A and the T in command sequence introducer are used to detect speed and parity.

The binary representation of ASCII characters **a** and **A** are 1000011P and 1000001P, respectively, with the leftmost bit sent first and where P represents the parity bit. The modem estimates the duration of the start bit that precedes the leading 1 of **a** or **A** to determine the DTE speed. The bits of the **A** or **a** and **T** or **t** are checked to determine the parity used by the DTE, if any. The A and T must be in the same case, upper- or lower-case.

The speed of the most recent DTE command is called the *last DTE speed*. All responses from the modem to the DTE that occur while the modem is in command state use the last DTE speed and parity. While data is being sent, the DTE speed may differ from the last DTE speed.

After handshaking is completed and the modem leaves the handshaking state for the on-line state, the CONNECT message is sent to the DTE at the last DTE speed. If the modem goes from the on-line state to the idle or on-line command state (due to a loss of carrier or drop in DTR for example) the result code is sent at the data speed, which is the current speed at which data is being handled. It is the DTE's responsibility to adjust its speed to the data speed.

It is important to note that the modem always issues its CONNECT message before changing its internal baud rate in response to a carrier. Assume, for example, that both the computer and modem are set for 1200 baud. When a call is detected at 2400 bps, the modem issues the CONNECT message at 1200 baud, then switches immediately to 2400 baud. When the carrier is lost, the NO CARRIER response is issued at 2400 baud.[5] Afterward, if no AT command is issued to establish a new DTE speed, the baud rate at which the modem attempts to answer the next call varies throughout the industry.

Speeds and Data Format

In addition to its capability of adapting to many baud rates, the modem also adjusts itself to a wide variety of data formats. Table 8.2 shows the valid combinations.

---

[5]The Smartmodem 300's result code is issued at the data speed, then immediately changed to the last AT speed.

Table 8.2. Data formats supported.

Data Length	Parity	Stop Bits
7	MARK	1 or more
7	SPACE	1 or more
7	Even	1 or more
7	Odd	1 or more
7	None	2 or more
8	None	1 or more
8*	Even	1 or more
8*	Odd	1 or more

300 bps modems only.

Nonvolatile Memory

Starting with the Smartmodem 2400, a combination of RAM, ROM, and nonvolatile RAM replaced the hardware configuration switches. The default values for most variables (S-registers and variables) are stored in ROM and moved to RAM upon start-up or reset. The contents of the ROM are referred to as the *factory profile*. The area of modem memory that contains the modem variables is referred to as the *active profile*. By issuing commands (&F), the user makes one of the available factory profiles the active profile.

In addition to ROM, there is *NVRAM (nonvolatile RAM)* to store custom user configurations referred to as *stored profiles*. To create a custom profile, the user configures the modem as desired, then issues a write (&W) command. This command copies the active profile into NVRAM where it becomes available for recall (with the Zn command). In modems with more than one stored profile, the modem's default start-up profile is determined by the &Y command.

The Modem's RS-232 Interface

In general, smart modems employ the minimum number of RS-232 functions necessary for full-duplex modem control. Because it is a modem, it is, by definition, a DCE device (data communications equipment). RS-232 connections are made through the familiar DB-25S (female) connector. Table 8.3 shows this connector, the pins used on the modem, and a discussion of each.

Table 8.3. RS-232 functions on the DB-25 connector.

Pin	Function	Description
1	Frame Gnd	Connected to modem chassis
2	TD	Modem commands or data bound for the phone line
3	RD	Modem responses or data fetched from the phone line
4	RTS	Not implemented (except on protocol modems—see Chapter 10)
5	CTS	In 300 bps modems, permanently asserted; in 1200 bps modems, it is hardwired to RTS.
6	DSR	In 300 bps modems, hardwired to pin 8 (DCD); in 1200 bps modems, permanently asserted; in 2400 bps modems, can be conditioned by the &S1 command to assert when handshaking begins
7	Signal Gnd	Connected to circuit common
8	DCD	In 300 bps modems, asserted during carrier linkage; in 1200 bps modems, can be forced TRUE at all times by a front-panel switch; and in 2400 bps modems can be forced TRUE by &C0
12	DDSRS	Starting with 1200 bps modems, asserted when connected at the highest rate (as on Bell 212)
20	DTR	Enables modem; can be conditioned to be always asserted by front panel switches in older 300 and 1200 bps modems and by the &D1 command in 2400's; in 2400's, can be debounced by setting S25
22	RI	Asserted during each ring on the telephone line
23	DSRS	Starting with 2400 bps modems, asserted when connected at the highest rate

RS-232 CONDITIONING COMMANDS

Almost from day one in the life of the smart modem, RS-232 signals have been a nemesis. Much of the existing application software interacted with the RS-232 signals and misbehaved in ways that confounded users when these signals were not present. The single largest problem was DTR: the modems simply did not work unless the DTE asserted DTR. This meant that if the user's cable was not complete, the modem wouldn't function.

DCD has always been troublesome, too. Software that didn't understand the command state refused to communicate with the modem in the command state because the modem's

DCD was not asserted. The solution to both these problems in 300 and 1200 bps modems was front panel switches to override DTR and DCD and permanently assert them. In 2400 bps modems, the switches were replaced by the &D1 and &C1 commands.

On 300 bps modems, DSR is tied to DCD pin 8; on 1200 bps modems, it is asserted at all times. Although it is asserted by default on 2400 bps modems, the &S1 command makes DSR behave according to the RS-232 standard: DTR is asserted only when the following conditions exist simultaneously (quoted phrases are from the RS-232 standard itself):

- The modem is "connected to a communications channel": off hook and not in a self-test or "voice" mode.
- The modem has performed "any timing functions required by the switching system to complete call establishment." In originate mode, this means dialing, monitoring call progress, and anything else required to usher the call through the phone network.
- The modem has begun "the transmission of a discrete answer tone…." In answer mode, the answer tone is begun immediately after the phone goes off hook. In originate mode, however, the originate tone is not transmitted until the answer tone is received. Hence, DSR appears to track DCD.

The Front Panel

As illustrated in Figure 8.2, the front panel of a typical smart modem is an array of seven indicators. These lamps report the following conditions:

HS   (High Speed) This lamp illuminates when the modem is operating at its highest rated speed. This is not present on 300 bps modems.

CD   (Carrier Detect) A carrier link with another modem is in progress.

OH   (Off hook) The modem has seized the telephone line. This is the equivalent of manually lifting the handset from the cradle.

SD   (Send Data) This lamp flashes when the modem outputs data on pin 2 of the RS-232 interface.

RD   (Receive Data) This lamp flashes when data arrives at the modem on pin 3 of the RS-232 interface.

TR   (Terminal Ready) This lamp illuminates whenever Data Terminal Ready (pin 20) of the RS-232 interface is asserted.

MR   (Modem Ready) Power is applied to the modem.

The Rear Panel

As shown in Figure 8.2, the rear panel of a smart modem typically has two RJ-11 phone receptacles, a power switch, and a female DB-25 connector for the RS-232 interface. Early modems had a mechanical volume control mounted here, but this was done away with by the &L command, which controls the speaker volume using firmware. A smaller DB-9 connector takes the place of the DB-25 in portable or miniature units.

One phone jack, usually labeled *Line* or *Wall*, is for the incoming phone line; the second jack is for a telephone handset. On budget modems, these are usually wired in parallel, whereas on more expensive modems they are interconnected XOR so that using the handset locks out the modem and vice versa.

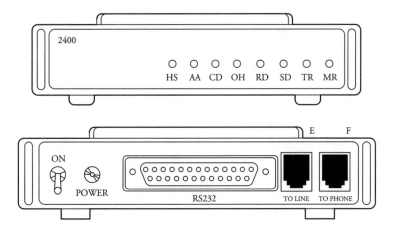

FIGURE 8.2.
Front and rear panels of a typical external modem.

Configuration Switches

One of the most popular uses of the smart modem was on dumb terminals where users could dial into a time sharing computer. Because these terminals could not be programmed to configure the modem automatically, users were required to type the configuration strings each time they sat down at the terminal. Clearly, users (and no doubt managers, too) wanted to configure the modem in one sitting, turn it off, and have it reassume that configuration at the next sitting.

The solution to the problem was *mechanical memory*: a bank of small DIP switches into which is latched the user's preference for various settings. Upon start-up, the modem reads these switches and uses their settings for defaults. The switch usage varied from model to model from the same manufacturer and wildly across the industry itself. Although configuration switches have gone the way of the buggy whip, there are several hundreds of thousands of modems that use them. For that reason, the original documentation of these switches is retained here for historical purposes (translation: as soon as you throw it away, you need it).

Table 8.4 is a cross reference between a function and its configuration switch across the entire Hayes Smartmodem family.

Table 8.4. Configuration switches cross referenced by function.

Function	300	1200	1200B	1200+	1200B+	Half-Card
DTR mode	1	1	jumper	1	4	4
Verbosity	2	2	—	2	—	—
Send codes	3	3	—	3	—	—
Echo	4	4	—	4	—	—
Auto-answer	5	5	—	5	—	—
DCD mode	6	6	3	6	3	3
Phone jack	7	7	2	7	2	2
Commands ok	x	8	—	8	—	—
Bell/CCITT	—	—	—	9	5	—
DTR resets	—	—	—	1	—	—
COMM1/COMM2	—	—	1	—	1	1
Make/Break Ratio	—	—	—	—	6	—

Table 8.5 is a cross reference between a switch number and its function across the entire Smartmodem family.

Table 8.5. Smartmodem configuration switches cross referenced by switch number.

SW	300	1200	1200B	1200+	1200B+	1200+Half-Card
1	DTR override	DTR override	COM1/COM2	DTR override	COM1/COM2	COM1/COM2
2	*V* command	*V* command	Phone type	*V* command	Phone type	Phone type
3	*Q* command	*Q* command	DCD override	*Q* command	DCD override	DCD override
4	*E* command	*E* command	—	*E* command	DTR override	DTR override
5	Auto-answer	Auto-answer	—	Auto-answer	Bell/CCITT	—
6	DCD override	DCD override	—	DCD override	Pulse ratio	—
7	Phone type	Phone type	—	Phone type	—	—
8	x	Dumb mode	—	Dumb mode	—	—
9	—	—	—	Bell/CCITT	—	—
10	—	—	—	Hardware Reset	—	—

Smart Modem Commands

The purpose of this chapter is to enumerate and examine the commands that characterize the base line smart modem. Because Hayes has traditionally been the market leader, many of the variations listed are pegged to the innovations in Smartmodem models, which the general market quickly imitated.

In this chapter, you will find a table listing these base line commands, their evolution, and whether they are supported by various standards, manufacturers, or by the market at large. There are also indexes listing the commands both alphabetically and grouped by function. Finally, Table 9.5 cross-references the command set of the modem with various models, standards, and manufacturers.

Stubs

In these command descriptions, the term *stub* describes the practice of implementing a command merely with an OK response rather than actually implementing the functions underlying the command. To understand why commands are sometimes stubbed, you must understand the power of the Hayes Smartmodem line. As new commands were added with each new model, the Hayes Smartcom software package was re-engineered to detect and take advantage of these new features. This software has become the main touchstone for "Hayes compatibility" by reviewers, buyers, and the public at large.

With each new Smartmodem, clone makers scurried to reverse-engineer the new features by observing the stream of commands between the genuine Hayes hardware and Smartcom. In many cases—the &Q command is a good example—the source of incompatibility proved to be a command controlling features that were of no interest to the clone manufacturers. Accordingly, the commands were implemented as false fronts (at one manufacturer they were called *hollywoods* instead of stubs) whose sole function was to respond "OK".

In the interest of fairness, there are more ingenuous reasons for stubbing commands. For example, a manufacturer may stub a command in order to discontinue a command that has outlived its usefulness without risking incompatibility with the installed base.[1] Hayes, for example, stubs the F and C commands, commenting that they "do not modify the modem's behavior."

Modem Commands

All modem commands begin with the AT command introducer. *Mode* commands are followed by a single printable ASCII character. An optional *numeric operand*, if present, is also a single ASCII character in the range 0–9 (30H–39H). For example, in the string *ATE1*, the command, *E*, is followed by the operand *1*. Note that this value must be an ASCII *digit*, not a binary value. If the absence of an operand 0 is assumed: *ATE* is the same as *ATE0*. Although there are manufacturer-specific mechanisms for querying the modem either for its range of valid arguments for a mode command or for its current setting, no method is widely accepted. In the absence of such a mechanism, software must resort to *probing* the modem: issuing commands and examining the response.

In addition to mode commands, the modem maintains *numeric variables* in S (for *scalar*, perhaps) registers, named S0, S1, and so on. These variables are addressed in the ordinary smart modem command format—*AT*, followed by the register number. Unlike the numerals in mode commands, the ASCII digits following the register name are interpreted as true arithmetic values. An S-register assignment command is created by placing an equal sign (=, ASCII 3D) between the register name and the digit-by-digit ASCII representation of the numeric value. Also, unlike the mode commands, S-registers can be queried by replacing the numeric value with a question mark.

Mode Commands

For purposes of discussion, mode commands fall conveniently into nine categories. These categories are:

1. User interface
2. Primary Dial and Answer
3. Dial modifiers
4. Dialing variable

---

[1] General MacArthur is rumored really to have said "Old AT commands never die, they're just stubbed away."

5. Miscellaneous
6. Profile management
7. Telephone hardware control
8. The EIA/TIA-232 Interface
9. Connectivity options

For an alphabetical listing of commands, see Table 9.4.

User Interface Group

The interface group of commands alters the way in which the modem interacts with the user, but does not affect the electrical operation of the modem.

E   COMMAND ECHO

This command controls whether the modem echoes characters when in command state. As soon as the modem enters on-line state, all input is treated as data.

COMMAND:	**En**
FUNCTION:	Command State Echo:
ARGUMENTS:	0: Command echo off
	1: Command echo on
DEFAULTS:	1
COMMENTS:	If the F1 command is in effect, the modem echoes even when in on-line state. On early modems, the power-up default of this command was controlled by a front-panel configuration switch.

Although echo is indispensable to human users, it can cause havoc when a modem is connected to a computer that also provides echo. The first character sent becomes the object of a neverending Ping-Pong match as the two devices repeatedly echo the character. Software for the modem should be carefully written so that it functions properly with or without command echo. As noted earlier, when command echo is enabled, single-digit response codes are preceded and terminated by a CR (more precisely, the nl1 character).

F   ON-LINE ECHO

This command, now largely obsolete, merely provides *local echo* while on-line. In local echo, *every* received character is transmitted back, regardless of whether a carrier link exists. This is different from the echo provided by the E command, in which input is returned only in the command state.

COMMAND: **F**
FUNCTION: Full/half-duplex
ARGUMENTS: 0: Echo all characters back to sender.
1: Do not echo.
DEFAULT: 1
VARIATIONS: Stubbed beginning in the Smartmodem 2400.
COMMENTS: This command was once called the "Full-Duplex" command, because you needed E0 to see your own typing when on a half-duplex connection.

V   VERBOSE

The modem can be made to respond to commands with whole words or with digit codes.

COMMAND: **Vn**
FUNCTION: Selects whether modem sends whole-word or digit responses.
ARGUMENTS: 0: Digit codes
1: Word codes
DEFAULT: 1
COMMENTS: On early modems, the power-up default of this command was controlled by a front-panel configuration switch.

From a programmer's point of view, the single digits are easier to detect, but they are much more likely to be misidentified. On the other hand, word codes are very difficult to process in some languages.

The newline punctuation included with modem responses also varies according to the modem's verbosity. In the more verbose mode, it surrounds its responses with both newline characters:

```
(nl1)(nl2)OK(nl1)(nl2)
(nl1)(nl2)ERROR(nl1)(nl2)
```

In its less verbose mode, however, the single digits are surrounded by nl1s:

```
(nl1)0(nl1)
(nl1)4(nl1)
```

To make matters slightly more complicated, when command echo is off (i.e., *ATE0*), single-digit response codes are terminated, but not preceded, by a CR (refer to Table 9.1). For special situations, the modem's default nl1 and nl2, CR and LF, can be reprogrammed (See S4 and S5 in "Numeric Variable Commands" later in this chapter).

Table 9.1. Newlines in modem responses. x is the modem's response assuming the default nl1, CR.

Command	Disabled	Enabled
Echo	(E0)	(E1)
V	xCR	CRxCR
V1	CRLFxCRLF	CRLFxCRLF

Information text is exempt from the punctuation effects of the Echo and Verbose commands.

Q   QUIET

In some environments—potential Ping-Pong situations, for example—it may be necessary to suppress the modem's responses entirely by using the Q command.

COMMAND: **Q**
FUNCTION: Suppress/enable modem responses
ARGUMENTS: 0: Response
               1: No response
DEFAULT: 0
COMMENTS: On early modems, the power-up default of this command was
               controlled by a front-panel configuration switch.

In general, application software depends on the ability to identify the modem's response codes. Because this ability is crippled if the user inadvertently enters the Q1 command, it is not a bad idea to include Q0 in all commands.

M   SPEAKER CONTROL

When users come to rely upon the modem's loudspeaker, doing without it seems torture. Once the progress of the call has been monitored, however, the noise of the carrier is annoying. The default setting of the M command is therefore 1—the speaker is muted as soon as a carrier link is established.

Despite the speaker's obvious utility, some environments (a hospital ward at night, or a library) require absolute quiet—or the modem user simply may not wish to announce every modem call to the rest of the world. Conversely, it may be necessary to leave the speaker on as a troubleshooting aid. ("Is that garbage on my screen caused by phone line noise or a malfunction in my modem?")

COMMAND: **Mn**
FUNCTION: Loudspeaker control
ARGUMENTS: 0: Always off
1: On until carrier link established
2: Always on
3: On except during dialing, then on until carrier
DEFAULT: 1
VARIATIONS: Introduced on the Smartmodem 2400.
COMMENTS: For compatibility reasons, modems that do not implement this command usually stub it.

Primary Answer/Dial Group

The second group of commands affects the dialing process.

A   ANSWER

This command causes the modem to go off-hook and start the answering procedure: silence, followed by an answer tone. This command is used to answer most incoming calls (i.e., calls from modems using originate tones). Sending any character to the modem while it is waiting for a carrier terminates the wait and returns the modem to command state.

COMMAND: **A**
FUNCTION: Takes the phone line off-hook and asserts the carrier using answer tones and waits S7 for an originate carrier from another modem.
COMMENTS: The length of the wait for carrier is programmable via S7 with a default of 30 seconds.

D   DIAL

Auto-dialing is actually a controlled sequence of other modem commands. The D command selects originate tones, takes the phone line off-hook, pauses S6 or waits for dial tone (see the X command for exceptions), dials the phone number, and waits for a carrier using answer tones.

COMMAND: **D**
FUNCTION: The primary dial command
VARIATIONS: Support for DTMF symbols such as * and # has evolved. The DTMF symbols A-D (that is, the fourth row) were not supported in early versions of the Smartmodem 1200.

COMMENTS: By default, the duration of the wait for carrier is 30 [S7] seconds. Sending any character to the modem while it is waiting for a carrier terminates the wait and returns the modem to command state.

The punctuation characters, ( ) and -, which may be intermixed with the digits 0–9 and spaces to improve readability, count toward the command line 40-character maximum. The characteristics of the dialing operation can be modified by including any of the dial modifiers in the command string. See "Dial Modifier Group" elsewhere.

THE ANATOMY OF DIALING

Before moving on, you should understand the sequence of events that occurs when the modem dials a call. Figure 9.1 is a flow chart of the discrete commands that constitute the dialing operation.

Dial Modifier Group

Dial modifiers affect the characteristics of the primary dial command, *D*. There are two types of dial modifiers—*dialing adverbs* and *dialing commands.*

The first kind of dial modifier, the dialing adverb, affects only the dial operation in which it appears; that is, its effect disappears as soon as the current dial operation is complete.

, CALIBRATED PAUSE (DIAL MODIFIER)

It is sometimes necessary to force the modem to pause briefly during dialing. When dialing long-distance services, for example, the modem must first dial the local access number, then pause long enough for the service's dial tone. The comma is also useful when dialing from a PBX system where considerable time may elapse between requesting and getting a secondary dial tone or "outside" line.

COMMAND: **,** (*Comma, ASCII 2C*)
FUNCTION: Introduces a calibrated pause S8 into the dial operation.
COMMENTS: The comma is an artifact from early smart modems that were incapable of detecting dial tone.[2] Where dial tone detection exists, the W dial modifier provides a more positive mechanism for waiting for dial tone.

---

[2]Inexplicably, the comma can be used as a stand-alone AT command as well as a dial modifier. Typing AT,<CR> produces a two-second [S8] delay followed by "OK".

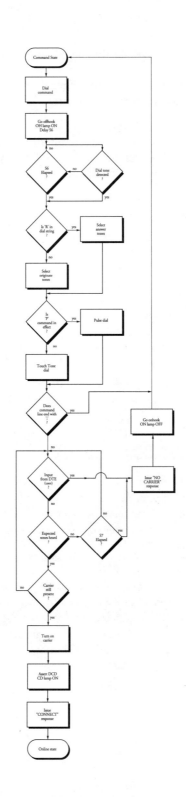

FIGURE 9.1.

Anatomy of a modem dial.

; RETURN TO COMMAND STATE (DIAL MODIFIER)

As described under the D command, the modem ordinarily dials, then immediately enters a loop awaiting an answer carrier tone from another modem. If a semicolon is present after the dial command and phone number, the modem waits for a dial tone S6 before dialing, dials the number, but then immediately returns to the command state without waiting for a carrier or hanging up.

COMMAND: ; (*Semicolon, ASCII 3B*)
FUNCTION: Returns to command state after dial.
COMMENTS: The OH (off-hook) lamp on the front panel remains illuminated and the subsequent progress of the call can be heard through the speaker as usual. The only way to terminate a successful "semicolon" call is with the *H0* hang-up command.

This feature is not used to establish a data link with another modem, but to employ the modem as an automatic tone dialer. Services such as electronic banking require the caller to enter information from a telephone's DTMF keypad. By programming the information in dial strings terminated with semicolons, such transactions can be performed entirely by modem and computer.

R REVERSE (DIAL MODIFIER)

Although *originate-only* modems are a vanishing breed, enough still exist to justify this command's existence.

COMMAND: **R**
FUNCTION: Reverse : use answer tones after dialing.
COMMENTS: After dialing, the modem supplies answer tones instead of originate tones; this enables the modem to establish a carrier link with modems that cannot configure their tones for answering. See Chapter 5, "Modems and Modem Control," for a full explanation of such situations.

! THE SWITCH HOOK FLASH (DIAL MODIFIER)

In older PBX systems, momentarily hanging up the line caused a lamp to flash on the operator's panel—a request for assistance. This verb quickly became transitive ("Flash me when you're finished") and then was backformed into a new substantive noun. Following this tradition, newer automated PBX systems use a "flash" to get the assistance of the electronic "operator."

COMMAND: ! *(ASCII 21H)*
FUNCTION: Momentarily flashes the switch hook—that is, takes the line off-hook for .5 seconds.
VARIATIONS: Duration of the flash varies from .5 to .8 seconds.

/   ONE-EIGHTH SECOND PAUSE (DIAL MODIFIER)

A slant in the dial string generates a 1/8 second pause.

COMMAND: / *(Slant, ASCII 2F)*
FUNCTION: Introduces a .125 second pause.
VARIATION: This modifier was ephemeral, existing only in the so-called Smartmodem 1200+. It was abandoned by Hayes in the Smartmodem 2400 and never used again. Apparently few noticed its absence (or its presence, for that matter), for it persists in the industry today, even in high-speed modems.

@   WAIT FOR SILENCE (DIAL MODIFIER)

This command causes the modem to wait for one or more rings followed by 5 seconds of silence before processing the next symbol in the dial string. It is used to access a system that does not provide a dial tone.

COMMAND: @ *(Commercial at, ASCII 40H)*
FUNCTION: Waits the number of seconds in S7 (30 seconds by default) for 5 seconds of silence before proceeding.
COMMENTS: If the five seconds of silence is not heard (or if a voice or other audio signal is present), the call is terminated and the response code NO ANSWER is issued. If a busy signal is heard, the modem responds BUSY.

W   WAIT FOR SECOND DIAL TONE (DIAL MODIFIER)

This modifier causes the modem to look for three seconds of dial tone for the time specified in S7. The secondary wait W is generally used to gain access to long-distance services, but it can be used on any multi-tiered system that produces recognizable dial tones. If the secondary dial tone is not forthcoming in the time allowed, the call is terminated and an ERROR results.

COMMAND: W *(ASCII 57H)*
FUNCTION: Waits for a secondary dial tone before proceeding.

DEFAULT: Wait for 30 seconds.
COMMENT: The 30-second default comes from S7.

S=   (DIAL MODIFIER): RECALL STORED NUMBER

After a dial string has been stored with the &Z command, it can be automatically redialed by appending an *S* to the primary dial command.

MODIFIER: **S**=*n*
FUNCTION: Dials stored number specified by *n*.
COMMENTS: The length of the stored phone number counts toward the maximum allowable count in the command buffer.

This dial modifier is generally appended to the primary dial command(e.g., ATDPS, ATDTS=1, or simply ATDS). Some manufacturers also allow it to be intermixed with other commands ATDTS=1P555, which tone-dials the numbers stored in S1, then pulse-dials the number 555.

Dialing Variable Commands

The second type of dial modifiers are bona fide commands that can be issued as stand-alone modem commands. Unlike dialing modifiers and regardless of the context in which they appear, these commands are identical to other modem commands—that is, they remain in effect until they are reissued with a different parameter or until the modem is reset.

P   PULSE DIALING

As out of touch with technology as it may seem, the modem defaults to pulse dialing.

COMMAND: **P**
FUNCTION: Set modem to use rotary-pulse signals for dialing.
COMMENT: Complementary to the T command. Can also be used as a dial modifier.

T   TONE DIALING

COMMAND: **T**
FUNCTION: Set modem to use tone signals for dialing.
COMMENT: Complementary to the P command. Can also be used as a dial modifier.

Some manufacturers implement the T command as *adaptive dialing* where the modem probes the phone line to ascertain if tone dialing is supported. The modem outputs the first digit in the dial string as a DTMF tone then listens for three seconds for dial tone. If the dial tone is still present, the string is pulse-dialed. The complexity of adaptive dialing schemes varies according to manufacturer.

&Z   STORE DIAL STRING

COMMAND: **&Zn=**
FUNCTION: Stores the following dial string (phone number).
COMMENTS: Up to 33 characters can be stored, not including blanks.
                Longer numbers are truncated.

X   CALL PROGRESS MONITORING

The first modem that was able to recognize dial tone and busy signals was the Smartmodem 1200+. The X command allows suppression of these capabilities and their accompanying result codes for backward compatibility.

COMMAND: **Xn**
FUNCTION: Selects level of call progress monitoring.
ARGUMENTS: 0: Result codes 0-4 enabled. Busy and dial tone detection disabled. (Smartmodem 300).
                1: Result codes 0-5,10 enabled, Busy and dial tone detection disabled (Smartmodem 1200).
                2: Result code 0-6, 10 enabled. Dial tone detection enabled, busy detection disabled.
                3: Result codes 0-5,7,10 enabled. Dial tone detection disabled, busy signal detection enabled.
                4: Result code 0-7,10 enabled. Busy and dial tone detection enabled.
DEFAULT: 4
VARIATIONS: The default setting was 0 (i.e., Smartmodem 300 mode) for most 1200 bps modems.
COMMENTS: Table 9.2 shows which response codes are valid for each X command level.

Table 9.2. Complete Smartmodem response result codes and the X command level that produces them.

Digit Code	Word Code	X Level	Description
0	OK	1,2,3,4	Non-dial command successfully executed.
1	CONNECT	1,2,3,4	Connection established at 300 bps.
2	RING	1,2,3,4	Ring signal present on phone line.
3	NO CARRIER	1,2,3,4	Carrier absent or never found.
4	ERROR	1,2,3,4	Error in command line, unrecognized command, or command buffer exceeded 40 characters.
5	CONNECT 1200	1,2,3,4	Connection established at 1200 bps.
6	NO DIALTONE	2,4	No dial tone present. Note that this response can come from either a primary dial operation or a *W* dial modifier in the dial string.
7	BUSY	3,4	Busy signal heard.
8	NO ANSWER	3,4	Returned only after the @ dial modifier to signify that the required number of seconds of silence was not heard. If the @ dial modifier encounters a busy signal, it returns a BUSY response instead of NO ANSWER.
9	CONNECT 0600		Connection established at 600 bps. This response and its corresponding digit code are reserved, but not used.
10	CONNECT 2400	2,3,4	Connection established at 600 bps.
10	CONNECT 24	2,3,4	Connection established at 2400 bps.

In addition to compatibility with older modems, in one situation the direct interconnection of two modems, the X3 setting must be employed to defeat dial tone detection (i.e. the modem must dial blindly). Although rarely done, two modems can be cabled directly together, with twisted-pair cables terminated with the appropriate RJ connectors. This interconnection is illustrated in Figure 9.2.

FIGURE 9.2.

Two modems connected as short-haul modems.

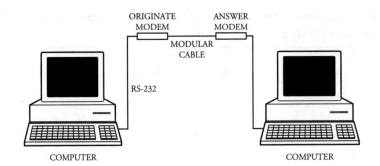

ORIGINATE MODEM   ANSWER MODEM

MODULAR CABLE

RS-232

COMPUTER   COMPUTER

Because the modems are not connected to a phone line in this arrangement, there is no dial tone to detect and, of course, no ring signal to trigger auto-answer. After issuing the command ATX3, a carrier linkage is established by one end sending

ATD, forcing one modem off-hook in originate and sending to the other modem ATA, causing it to go off-hook in the answer mode.

If dial tone detection is active, the originating modem goes off-hook, but it returns to the command state after expiration of its programmed (S6) wait for a dial tone.

One suspects the X3 setting—disable busy signal detection—exists simply because it was easy to implement. No situations come to mind where it is necessary to defeat busy signal detection, but it is just conceivable that the modem might mistake a grossly out-of-tolerance busy signal for a ring signal.

Miscellaneous Group

Most of the remaining commands deal with the technical aspects of modem communications. Although seldom required, these commands help to solve problem situations not covered by normal modem operations.

C CARRIER

During ordinary operations, the modem manages its own carrier. Normally, the modem automatically turns on its carrier signal in anticipation of and during a linkage with another modem. When the link is lost, the modem automatically turns the carrier off. The command C0 inhibits the carrier unconditionally.

> COMMAND: **C**
> FUNCTION: Carrier on/off
> ARGUMENTS: 0: Carrier always off
> 1: Carrier managed by modem

DEFAULT: 1
COMMENT: This command was dropped in the Smartmodem 2400 and is
             now considered obsolete. Nevertheless, it is still implemented
             by some manufacturers, and others stub it.

Caution should be exercised in using the C0 command. Once it has been issued, the carrier remains inhibited—even after a dial or answer command—until an explicit C1 or a
reset command is issued.

A/   LAST COMMAND REPEAT

The modem does not clear its buffer until the AT of the next command is typed. Entering
A/ (with no CR) causes the current command line to be executed again. This is useful
mainly for redialing telephone numbers.

COMMAND: **A/**
FUNCTION: Repeats last command.
COMMENTS: Neither the command prefix nor command terminator is
              necessary.

Zn   RESET

Before software configures the modem, it should issue the software reset command. A reset
returns the modem to its power-up condition, reinstalls all variables to their default values, reads the modem's configuration (either from non-volatile memory or from configuration switches), then performs a self-test.

COMMAND: **Zn**
FUNCTION: Performs a soft reset, self-test, and default configuration. In
              modems that support non-volatile memory, stored profile *n* is
              loaded.
VARIATIONS: The number of user configuration profiles supported varies.
              The original Smartmodem 2400 had one.
COMMENTS: Note that the response to the reset command occurs *before*
              executing this command. In modems without non-volatile
              memory, execution time is about .5 seconds; when non--
              volatile is present, execution can take as long as three seconds.
              The reset command clears the command buffer, so any
              commands on the same line with the reset command are lost.
              Under certain conditions the modem cannot be reset with
              software commands and must be switched on and off.

O   GO ON-LINE

When the modem has escaped from the on-line to the command state (without hanging up), this command returns it to its on-line state. The exact procedures for this feat are described in Chapter 8.

COMMAND:	**O*n***
FUNCTION:	Return to the on-line state.
ARGUMENTS:	0: Go on-line
	1: Retrain adaptive equalizers (2400 bps only)
VARIATIONS:	Some manufactures implement a 1 argument that forces the modem to retrain before connecting.

L   SPEAKER VOLUME CONTROL

When the second phone jack was added to the rear panel of the modem, the mechanical volume control was replaced by a firmware attenuator controlled by the L command. Few feel the trade was even.

COMMAND:	**L*n***
FUNCTION:	Adjusts audio output of internal speaker.
ARGUMENTS:	0: Off or low audio output
	1: Low audio output
	2: Medium audio output
	3: Highest audio output
DEFAULT:	1
VARIATIONS:	Older modems had only levels 0-2. Acoustic levels for settings 0 and 1 are often identical.
COMMENTS:	Use the M command to turn the speaker completely off. The attenuation between the high and medium settings is large and obvious. The difference between medium and the two low settings, however, is much less pronounced.

I   IDENTIFICATION

This command is inherently manufacturer-specific. Its purpose is to provide a mechanism to query the modem for model, manufacturer, checksum, feature set, and so forth. EIA 602 cautions: "The response to this command may not be reliably used to determine the manufacturer, revision level, feature set, or other information, and it should not be relied upon for software operation. In particular, expecting a specific numeric response to the I0 command to indicate which other features and commands are implemented dooms software to certain failure, because there are widespread differences in manufacturer implementation among devices that may, coincidentally, respond with identical values to this command."

COMMAND: **I***n*
FUNCTION: Provides identification information
ARGUMENTS: 0: Modem ID code
VARIATIONS: The Smartmodem 300 did not support the I command in any form. Smartmodem 2400s return 245-249. Although Hayes specifies that the modem shall respond with exactly three digits, in fact many modems respond with their highest modulation rate.
COMMENTS: Despite the warning from EIA 602, there is a very high degree of conformity in implementating the I0 command. Although the number of digits returned by the command varies, the first two identify the modem's highest modulation speed. For example, 245 and 249 represent 2400 bps modems, while 122 and 123 represent 1200 bps modems. This tradition has even been carried into the higher-speed protocol modems discussed in the next chapter.

Y LONG-SPACE DISCONNECT

Except for its duration, the "long SPACE" is identical to a BREAK condition. The BREAK, you will recall from Chapter 2, occurs when the communications line is held at SPACE for *at least* the duration of one SDU.

The long-SPACE disconnect, like the DTR-reset feature discussed elsewhere, is usually employed as a last resort to regain control of a modem at a remote, unattended location where a manual reset is impractical. In such installations, modems are usually permanently connected by leased lines. The software controlling the remote modem responds to the loss of carrier (caused by the long SPACE) by resetting the modem and attempting to reestablish a data linkage.

COMMAND: **Y***n*
FUNCTION: Long SPACE disconnect
ARGUMENTS: 0: Disabled
1: Enabled
DEFAULT: 0
COMMENTS: When enabled, the modem immediately transmits a SPACE (BREAK) for 4 seconds before going on-hook or, if &D2 is in effect, whenever DTR transitions from ON to OFF. If Y is set to 1, the modem drops the carrier and disconnects from the line upon receipt of 1.6 seconds of SPACE.

Profile Management Commands

This group of commands manages the content of the RAM work area, ROM variables, and nonvolatile memory.

&F   LOAD FACTORY DEFAULT PROFILE

COMMAND: **&F***n*
FUNCTION: Fetches factory configuration profiles specified by n.
COMMENTS: Reads selected default values from ROM into working RAM. Unlike the Z command, &F can be followed by other commands on the command line.

&W   STORE ACTIVE PROFILE

COMMAND: **&W***n*
FUNCTION: Stores current configuration in the non-volatile profile specified by *n*.
COMMENTS: Not all modems support multiple profiles.

&Y   SELECT POWER-UP PROFILE

When the modem powers up or performs soft reset (see the Z command), it loads the stored profile specified by the &Y command.

COMMAND: **&Y***n*
FUNCTION: Selects which stored user profile is used on a power-up or hardware reset.
COMMENTS: Because not all modems support more than one stored profile, not all modems support this command.

Telephone Hardware Control

H   SWITCH HOOK CONTROL

When the modem undertakes a telephone function—auto-dial, auto-answer, hang-up—it must operate the phone line. This command is the electronic equivalent of manually lifting and hanging up a telephone receiver.

COMMAND:	**H***n*
FUNCTION:	Seize and release phone line.
ARGUMENTS:	0: Hang up
	1: Off-hook
	2: Special off-hook
VARIATIONS:	In addition to the relay to operate the telephone line, the modem may contain an auxiliary relay through which external equipment may be switched. Refer to the &J command for a description of this feature.
COMMENTS:	When an auxiliary relay is present in 2400 bps modems, it is usually controlled by the &J command. In earlier modems, however, 2 is a special argument that enables operation of the hook relay independently from the auxiliary relay. In mode 1 of the H command, both the phone line and the auxiliary relay are closed; in mode 2 however, only the main relay is closed. In mode 2, the OH lamp on the front panel does not illuminate. In conformity with FCC regulations, there is a 2-second dead time after closing the switch hook, during which the modem neither responds to nor acknowledges commands.

&J   AUXILIARY RELAY CONTROL

In addition to this main telephone line relay, some modems contain an auxiliary relay through which external equipment may be switched. These relay contacts are available through pins 2 and 5 of the main phone jack on the modem. Although the auxiliary relay was originally included primarily for the benefit of radio amateurs (to key transmitters), it can be used for any external switching operation as long as the 0.5A maximum contact current is observed. A popular use for it is to operate the "in-use lamps" on key-system telephones.

COMMAND:	**&J**
FUNCTION:	Telephone jack selection
ARGUMENTS:	0: RJ-11, -41S, -45S (single line)
	1: RJ-12, -13 (multi-line)
DEFAULT:	0
VARIATIONS:	&J command was introduced on the Smartmodem 2400.
COMMENTS:	Pre-2400 modems used the O2 command to operate the auxiliary relay.

&P   MAKE/BREAK RATIO FOR PULSE DIALER

COMMAND: **&P**
FUNCTION: Makes/breaks ratio for mechanical pulse dialer.
ARGUMENTS: 0: 39 percent/61 percent (US)
             1: 33 percent/67 percent (UK, Hong Kong)
             2: 39 percent/61 percent at 20 pulses per second.
             3: 33 percent/67 percent at 20 pulses per second (Japan).
VARIATIONS: Arguments 0 and 1 are common and standard. The remaining
             arguments are widely and unpredictably implemented,
             especially in the meaning of the arguments.

&L   DIAL/LEASED-LINE OPTION

This command instructs the modem to work in a leased line environment. The modem
does not dial numbers, respond to dial tones or busy signals, or send answer tones. After
receiving a D or A command, the modem goes directly into the dialing or answering process.

COMMAND: **&Ln**
FUNCTION: Leased-line or dial-up operation
ARGUMENTS: 0: Dial-up
             1: Leased-line
DEFAULT: 0
COMMENTS: Point-to-point leased lines do not use dial tone protocols.

RS-232 Commands

This group of commands condition the behavior of the RS-232 interface.

&S   DATA SET READY CONTROL

COMMAND: **&Sn**
FUNCTION: DSR pin 6 options
ARGUMENTS: 0: DSR is always asserted.
             1: DSR is asserted at start of handshaking and inhibited when
             carrier is lost. It remains inhibited in command state.
VARIATIONS: Implemented first in 2400 modems.
DEFAULT: 0 (compatible with previous modems)

&C DATA CARRIER DETECT CONTROL

COMMAND: **&C*n***
FUNCTION: DCD pin 8 Controls
ARGUMENTS: 0: Always asserted (ON)
1: DCD asserted only during carrier linkage
DEFAULT: 0
VARIATIONS: Some manufacturers use a default of 1.
COMMENTS: On early modems, the power-up default of this command was controlled by a front-panel configuration switch.

&D DATA TERMINAL READY CONTROL

This command defines how the modem behaves when on-line. An ON-to-OFF transition occurs on DTR pin 20.

COMMAND: **&D**
FUNCTION: DTR pin 20 control
ARGUMENTS: 0: Ignores DTR.
1: Returns to command state.
2: Disables auto-answer, hangs up immediately, and returns to command state; continues responding to AT commands.
3: Performs a hard reset.
DEFAULT: 0
VARIATIONS: Some manufacturers use a default of 2.
COMMENTS: On early modems, the power-up default of this command was controlled by a front-panel configuration switch.

&R RTS/CTS CONTROL

The relationship between RTS and CTS is determined by the &R command.

COMMAND: **&R**
FUNCTION: RTS and CTS Relationship
ARGUMENTS: 0: CTS tracks RTS
COMMENTS: This command is usually stabbed.

Connectivity Options

These commands affect how the modem functions in relationship to other modems or communications standards.

B   CCITT V.21/V.22 COMPATIBILITY

This command changes the physical protocol that is used to establish a connection.

COMMAND:	**B**
FUNCTION:	Selects between Bell 103A/212A and CCITT V.21/V.22
ARGUMENTS:	0: CCITT
	1: Bell
DEFAULT:	1
VARIATIONS:	Not all modems support 300 baud operation in CCITT V.21. In these modems, attempting to dial another modem at 300 baud while in CCITT mode produces an ERROR. In some modems it is stubbed (i.e., modem will try to connect using Bell tones).

&G   GUARD TONE SELECT

COMMAND:	**&G**
FUNCTION:	Guards tone selection (not used in US)
ARGUMENTS:	0: No guard tones
	1: 550 Hz guard tone (V.22, V.22 bis only)
	2: 1800 Hz guard tone (V.22, V.22 bis only)
DEFAULT:	0

&M   COMMUNICATIONS OPTIONS

The Hayes Smartmodem 2400 introduced a number of synchronous features. Management of the "mode" (that is, whether operation was synchronous or asynchronous) was through the &M. This command was superseded by the &Q command, so its use is discouraged.

COMMAND:	**&M**
FUNCTION:	Asynchronous/Synchronous mode select
ARGUMENTS:	0: Asynchronous operation
	1–3: Synchronous operation
DEFAULT:	0
VARIATIONS:	Where it and the &Q command co-exist, use the &Q command.
COMMENTS:	If implemented at all, it is a stub.

&Q   COMMUNICATIONS MODE OPTIONS

This command replaced the &M for management of the communications "mode" (that is synchronous or asynchronous). This command would not be implemented in the asynchronous market were it not for the Hayes communication program *Smartcom*. The ability to work with Smartcom has always been a favorite test of "Hayes compatibility" among reviewers.

COMMAND:	**&Q**
FUNCTION:	Asynchronous/Synchronous mode select
ARGUMENTS:	0: Asynchronous operation
	1–3: Synchronous operation
DEFAULT:	0
VARIATIONS:	Because most manufacturers do not support synchronous operation, the Q command is often stubbed to enable the modem to pass the Smartcom compatibility test.

Numeric Variable Commands

In our earlier discussion of the modem's commands, we emphasized that parameters for "mode" commands, though ASCII digits (i.e., 0–9), are not arithmetic in nature. The modem's numeric variables are contained in a group of thirteen S (for "scalar," perhaps) registers, named S0, S1, and so on. These variables are addressed in the ordinary modem command format—*AT*, followed by the register number. Unlike other modem parameters, the ASCII digits following the register name are interpreted as true arithmetic values. An S-register assignment command is created by placing an equal sign (=, ASCII 3D) between the register name and the digit-by-digit ASCII representation of the numeric value. Thus, the ASCII sequence:

```
ATS6=125 (hex = 41 54 53 36 3D 31 32 35)
```

places value 125 into S-register 6. Conversely, the contents of an S-register can be fetched by placing a question mark (?, ASCII 3F) after the register name. Assuming the assignment command above is successful, the sequence:

```
ATS6?
```

causes the modem to reply:

```
125 (hex = 31 32 35)
```

surrounded by n11,n12 (CRLF), bracketed by n11 (CR), or just terminated by n11 (CR), depending upon the settings of the V and E commands. See Table 9.1 for details. All numeric values are reported in three digits, left-padded with 0s if necessary.

Some care is required when assigning values to S-registers. Even though several of the S-registers (S3 and S5, for example) function correctly only with a limited range of characters, the modem uncomplainingly accepts any 8-bit value. To make matters worse, the modem accepts *any* number of digits as an S-register argument. For example, the modem happily accepts the following assignment:

```
ATS6=1234567890123456
```

and, when queried for the new value of S6, replies

```
192
```

From this response, we can conclude that the modem converts the ASCII digits in its argument to an internal 8-bit variable.

Based upon how they are used, S-registers can be divided into three categories: characters, counters/timers, and bit maps.

S-Register Character Variables

Four S-register variables enable the programmer to redefine the modem's concept of important ASCII characters. All four take as an argument a digit-by-digit ASCII representation of that character's rank in the ASCII character set. Therefore, the command to set register S2 to the vertical bar (|, 124) is

```
ATS2=124
```

S2: ON-LINE ESCAPE CHARACTER

This register contains the character that forces the modem from on-line to command state without hanging up or breaking the carrier link. Refer to "Escaping from and Returning to the On-line State," in Chapter 8.

REGISTER:	S2
FUNCTION:	On-line escape character
VALID RANGE:	0–127
UNIT:	ASCII
DEFAULT:	43 (+, 2BH)
COMMENTS:	If the value in S-register 2 is greater than 127, the escape request is ignored.

S3 AND S4: NEWLINE CHARACTERS NL1 AND NL2

By default, the modem uses a CR and LF for a newline, but each of these characters is programmable.

REGISTER: S3
FUNCTION: First newline character (*nl1*) and command terminator
VALID RANGE: 0–127
UNIT: ASCII
DEFAULT: 13 (CR, 0D)
REGISTER: S4
FUNCTION: Second newline character (*nl2*)
VALID RANGE: 0–127
UNIT: ASCII
DEFAULT: 10 (LF, 0A)

Unfortunately for C programmers, there is no way to configure the modem to achieve a single-character newline.

S3 (*nl1*) is not only the first newline character, but also the command terminator. Although an S3 value greater than 127 is correctly output as part of a newline, it is not recognized as a command terminator. This register should therefore be changed only after great thought.

S5: PROGRAMMABLE BACKSPACE

This feature accommodates incomplete, eccentric, or non-ASCII keyboards. The modem accepts any character, but only ASCII control characters actually perform backspacing.

REGISTER: S5
FUNCTION: Backspace character
VALID RANGE: 0–32, 127
UNIT: ASCII
DEFAULT: 08 (BS)

S-Register Counter/Timer Variables

This category of S-register maintains count variables for fine-tuning the modem's telephone interface.

S0: RING COUNT FOR AUTO-ANSWER

This register holds the number of rings after which the modem answers the phone.

REGISTER: S0
FUNCTION: Sets ring on which to answer the phone.
VALID RANGE: 0–255
UNIT: Rings
DEFAULT: 0

When set to a value greater than 0, the AA lamp on the modem's front panel illuminates and the modem answers the phone after that many ring pulses. A ring count of 0 disables auto-answer altogether, and the AA lamp on the front panel is extinguished.

S1: NUMBER OF RINGS SO FAR

This value is automatically reset to 0 between calls or if 8 seconds elapse without a ring.

REGISTER:	S1
FUNCTION:	Counts number of rings so far.
RANGE:	0–255
UNIT:	Rings
DEFAULT:	n/a

Oddly, this is a read/write variable. A situation in which one would wish to modify this variable is barely conceivable.

S6: SECONDS TO WAIT FOR BLIND DIALING

On modems that do not detect the presence of a dial tone, S6 is the delay between taking the phone off-hook and blind-dialing the number. S6 is overridden when dial tone detection is enabled.

REGISTER:	S6
FUNCTION:	Sets number of seconds to wait before blind dialing.
VALID RANGE:	2–255
UNIT:	Seconds
DEFAULT:	2 (also the minimum value, even with dial tone detection enabled)
VARIATIONS:	300 and early 1200 bps modems were not capable of dial tone detection.
COMMENTS:	Refer to the X command for enabling and disabling dial tone detection.

S7: SECONDS TO WAIT FOR CARRIER

This register dictates how long, after dialing, the modem waits for a carrier link before returning to command mode.

REGISTER:	S7
FUNCTION:	Sets number of seconds to wait for carrier before giving up.
VALID RANGE:	1–255

UNIT: Seconds
DEFAULT: 30
COMMENTS: This time also governs the wait for:
1. Silent answer (@ dial modifier)
2. Wait for dial tone (W modifier)
3. Completion of handshaking

The modem responds CONNECT XXXX (where "XXXX" is the speed at which the connection is made) if a carrier link is established during this timing interval; otherwise it sends the NO CARRIER response and returns to the command state.

Sending any byte to the modem during this interval terminates the wait, produces the NO CARRIER response, and returns the modem to the command state.

S8: LENGTH OF PAUSE

This register holds the length of the pause produced by a comma in the dialing string.

REGISTER: S8
FUNCTION: Sets number of seconds of pause induced by comma in dial string.
VALID RANGE: 0–255
UNIT: Seconds
DEFAULT: 2

Multiple commas may be compounded for very long delays.

S9: CARRIER-RECOVERY TIME

This register determines how long a carrier, once lost, must be present before it is considered valid again. This delay guards against mistaking phone line noise for a carrier.

REGISTER: S9
FUNCTION: Sets length of time a lost carrier must be present before it is considered valid.
VALID RANGE: 1–255
UNIT: Tenths of a second (Tsecs)
DEFAULT: 6 (600 milliseconds)

The default of 600 milliseconds is actually quite conservative and works fine in ordinary environments.

S10: LOST-CARRIER DEBOUNCE

This interval determines how long a carrier must be *continually* absent before the modem acknowledges it—inhibits its own carrier, turns off the front panel CD lamp, and enters the command state.

REGISTER: S10
FUNCTION: Sets length of time the carrier must be absent before announcing it.
VALID RANGE: 1–255
UNIT: Tenths of a second (Tsec)
DEFAULT: 14 (1.4 seconds)
VARIATION: Pre-2400 modems used a default of 7 (700 milliseconds)

This register, the complement to S9, guards against periodic fluctuations in carrier level (*flutter*) or momentary total loss of carrier (*dropout*).

If register S10 is set to 255, the modem behaves as if the carrier were present at all times; that is, when the carrier linkage terminates, the modem totally ignores the loss of the receiver's carrier, continues to assert carrier, and retains control of the line. In this condition, the modem must be forced to hang up either by performing an on-line escape followed by a hang-up command or by inhibiting DTR.

S11: TOUCH TONE RATE

This S-register sets the speed of tone dialing.

REGISTER: S11
FUNCTION: DTMF (Touch Tone) signaling rate
VALID RANGE: 50–255
UNIT: Milliseconds
DEFAULT: 70
VARIATION: Oddly, this register was not supported in early Smartmodem 2400s.

The dialing rate is the reciprocal of twice the value of this register (1/2 t). The default value of 70 milliseconds therefore produces a dialing rate of about seven digits per second. A value of 255 slows the rate to about two digits per second for applications that expect to receive tones at a human's finger-rate. Although the minimum value is listed as 50 milliseconds, most modems uncomplainingly accept smaller values.

S12: ESCAPE SEQUENCE GUARD TIME

This is the amount of silence that must surround the escape sequence that forces the modem from on-line state to on-line command state.

REGISTER: S12
FUNCTION: Minimum silent interval that must surround escape sequence
VALID RANGE: 20–255
UNIT: 1/50 second
DEFAULT: 50 (i.e., 1 second)

This time must be longer than one SDU (serial data unit) at the current baud rate. If S12 is 0, the escape sequence is not checked for surrounding silence.

S25: DTR TRANSITION DEBOUNCE

REGISTER: S25
FUNCTION: Minimum time DTR must change state to be recognized.
VALID RANGE: 0–255
UNIT: Hundredths
DEFAULT: 7
VARIATION: Default values for this register vary widely in the industry.

Like S-registers 9 and 10, this register provides a delay between an RS-232 event and its recognition. This is a much-needed addition, because some UARTs momentarily change the state of RS-232 outputs ("hiccup") during writes to certain registers.

Table 9.3. Command summaries.

User Interface Group

E	Command Echo
F	Full-Duplex
V	Verbose
Q	Quiet
M	Speaker Control

Primary Answer/Dial Group

A	Answer
D	Dial

Answer/Dial Modifier Group

,	Calibrated Pause
;	Return to Command State
R	Reverse Dial Modifier

continues

Table 9.3. continued

!	The Switch Hook Flash
@	Wait for Silence
W	Wait for Second Dial Tone
S=	Recall Stored Number

Dialing Variable Commands

P	Pulse Dialing
T	Tone Dialing
&Z	Store Dial String
X	Call Progress Monitoring

Miscellaneous Group

C	Carrier
A/	Last Command Repeat
Z	Reset
O	Go On-line
L	Volume Control
I	Identification
Y	Long-SPACE Disconnect

Profile Management Commands

&F	Load Factory Default Profile
&W	Store Active Profile
&Y	Select Power-up Profile

Telephone Hardware Control

H	Switch Hook Control
&J	Auxiliary Relay Control
&P	Make/Break Ratio for Pulse Dialer
&L	Dial/Leased-Line Option

RS-232 Commands

&S	Data Set Ready Control
&C	Data Carrier Detect Control
&D	Data Terminal Ready Control
&R	RTS/CTS Control

Connectivity Options

B   CCITT V.22 Compatibility

&G   Guard Tone Select

&M   Communications Options

&Q   Communications Mode Options

Table 9.4. Base AT command set alphabetically.

CMD	*Summary*	*Page(s)*
A/	Repeat Last Command	279
A	Answer	270
B	CCITT V.21/V.22 Compatibility	286
C	Carrier	278-279
D	Primary Dial	270-271
E	Command Echo	267
F	On-line Echo	267-268
H	Hook	282-283
I	Identification	280-281
L	Speaker Volume Control	280
M	Speaker Control	269-270
O	On-line	280
P	Pulse Dialing	275
Q	Quiet	269
T	Tone Dialing	275-276
V	Verbose	268-269
X	Call Progress Monitoring	276-278
Y	Long-SPACE Disconnect	281
Z	Reset	279
&C	Data Carrier Detect Control	285
&D	Data Terminal Ready Control	285
&F	Load Factory Defaults	282
&G	Guard Tone	286
&J	Auxiliary Relay Control	283

continues

Table 9.4. continued

CMD	Summary	Page(s)
&L	Switched/Leased-Line Select	284
&M	Communications Mode Options	286
&P	Make/Break Ratio for Pulse Dialer	284
&Q	Communications Mode Options	287
&R	RTS/CTS	285
&S	Data Set Ready Control	284
&W	Store Active Profile	282
&Y	Select Power-up Profile	282
&Z	Store Dial String in EEPROM	276
S0	Number of rings so far	289-290
S1	Number of rings to answer on	290
S2	On-line escape character	288
S3	Carriage-return character	288-289
S4	Line-feed character	288-289
S5	Backspace character	289
S6	Delay before blind dialing	290
S7	Seconds to wait for carrier	290-291
S8	Length of pause (,)	291
S9	Carrier-recovery time	291
S10	Lost-Carrier debounce	292
S11	Touch Tone rate	292
S12	Escape sequence guard time	292-293
S25	DTR transition debounce	293

Table 9.5. Modem command set cross-reference.

✔ = Supported as describe in this book　　　　　　　blank = Not supported
? = Command present, but has a different function　　S = stubbed

Command	Meaning	300	1200	1200+	2400	Microcom	USR	EIA 602	2120
A	Answer	✔	✔	✔	✔	✔	✔	✔	✔
A/	Repeat previous command	✔	✔	✔	✔	✔	✔		✔
B	Bell/CCITT protocol select			✔	✔	✔	✔		✔

Command	Meaning	300	1200	1200+	2400	Microcom	USR	EIA 602	2120
C	Carrier control	✔	✔	✔	✔		✔		S
D	Dial	✔	✔	✔	✔	✔	✔	✔	✔
Dial Mod.	Characters beyond 0-9,*# ;	R	R	ABC DR! @W/	ABC DSR !@W	ABC DSR !@W	ABC DSR !@W	AB CD	ABC DS()R !@W-
E	Echo	✔	✔	✔	✔	✔	✔	✔	✔
F	Local online echo	✔	✔	✔	S	S	✔		S
H	Switch hook control	✔	✔	✔	✔	✔	✔	✔	✔
I 0	Manufacturer information		✔	✔	✔	✔	✔		✔
L	Speaker volume			✔	✔	S	✔		✔
M	Speaker control	✔	✔	✔	✔	✔	✔	✔	✔
O	Command to online state	✔	✔	✔	✔	✔	✔	✔	✔
P	Pulse dialing enable	✔	✔	✔	✔	✔	✔	✔	✔
Q	Quiet response mode	✔	✔	✔	✔	✔	✔	✔	✔
T	Tone dialing enable	✔	✔	✔	✔	✔	✔	✔	✔
V	Response format ("verbose")	✔	✔	✔	✔	✔	✔	✔	✔
X	Command response level		0-1	0-4	0-4	0-4	0-4	0-4	0-4
Y	Long SPACE disconnect			✔	✔	✔	S		✔
Z	Reset modem	✔	✔	✔	✔	✔	✔	✔	✔
&C	DCD control				✔	✔	✔		✔
&D	DTR control				✔	✔	✔		✔
&F	Restore factory profile				✔	✔	✔		✔
&G	Guard tones				✔	✔	✔		✔
&J	RJ11 select				✔	S			✔
&L	Leased line control				✔	✔	✔		✔
&P	Pulse Make/ Break ratio				✔	✔	✔		✔
&S	DSR control				✔	✔	✔		✔
&V	View profiles				✔				✔
&W	Save active profile				✔	✔	✔		✔
&Y	Default powerup preset profile				✔	✔	?		✔
&Z	Store phone strings				✔	✔	✔		✔
S0	Ring count for auto-answer	✔	✔	✔	✔	✔	✔	✔	✔

continues

Table 9.5. continued

Command	Meaning	300	1200	1200+	2400	Microcom	USR	EIA 602	2120
S1	Ring count so far	✔	✔	✔	✔	✔	✔		✔
S2	Online escape character	✔	✔	✔	✔	✔	✔		✔
S3	Carriage Return character	✔	✔	✔	✔	✔	✔		✔
S4	Line Feed character	✔	✔	✔	✔	✔	✔		✔
S5	Backspace character	✔	✔	✔	✔	✔	✔		✔
S6	Wait time for dial tone	✔	✔	✔	✔	✔	✔	✔	✔
S7	Wait time for carrier	✔	✔	✔	✔	✔	✔	✔	✔
S8	Length of dialing pause	✔	✔	✔	✔	✔	✔	✔	✔
S9	Carrier-present debounce	✔	✔	✔	✔	✔	✔		✔
S10	Carrier-absent debounce	✔	✔	✔	✔	✔	✔	✔	✔
S11	DTMF interval	✔	✔	✔	✔	✔	✔		✔
S12	Escape guard time	✔	✔	✔	✔	✔	✔		✔
S25	DTR-absent debounce				✔	?	?	✔	✔

SERIAL COMMUNICATIONS

Protocol Modems

Modem Protocols and Protocol Modems

In this chapter, we discuss modems that contain the error-correcting protocols MNP and LAPM, and the data compression procedures MNP Class 5 and V.42bis. In addition, we'll discuss the annoying subject of interworking error-correcting protocols and hi-speed (greater than 2400 bps) modems. The treatment of these subjects assumes that you understand virtually all the information contained in previous chapters, especially Chapter 4 and the treatment of the Kermit file-transfer protocol.

Modem Protocols

The vocabulary problems in this area are considerable. Much of the technology has been developed in parallel by various companies, then rephrased by the documents in international standards bodies. It is therefore worth defining a few terms:

> **DTE Speed:** The baud rate to which the DTE is set.
> **Direct Connection (Mode):** An ordinary asynchronous connection employing no protocols.
> **Data Pump:** The modem hardware that performs raw modulation and demodulation.
> **FRAME:** Used interchangeably with the term "packet." Packet is used in this book to avoid confusion with START and STOP bit framing.
> **Flow Control:** The ability to start and stop the flow of data to one's partner.
> **FCS:** Frame Check Sequence. Usually a CRC.
> **Hybrid Connection (Mode):** A combination of a protocol and a direct mode in which no protocol is active, but buffering and flow control between the modem and DTE are supported.

Line Speed: Phone line speed; that is, the modulation rate on the phone line; the carrier speed.

Modem Protocol: Any "link-layer" error-correcting protocol designed for modems; in particular, MNP or LAPM.

Protocol Connection (Mode): A connection in which a modem protocol is active.

Protocol Modem: A modem that supports a modem protocol. It may or may not include compression.

BACKGROUND

We mentioned earlier that two modems in a data link appear to the programmer as a single wire that is slow and prone to errors. In Chapter 5, we discovered how modem speed had gradually been improved by the legerdemain of digital signal processing and advanced modulation techniques. Despite these startling advances, clearly there are finite limits to the phone line's capacity. Even the most optimistic in the communications industry believes that although modem technology may not have quite reached its theoretical speed limits, those limits are clearly known and not far away.[1] Modem designers can do little about errors, most of which are inherent in the public phone network itself and therefore beyond the modem's control. In other words, with no significant speed advances on the horizon, modems have reached the end of the technological road. In markets where the technology has matured, the alternative to increased performance is increased functionality. Instead of making faster modems, the industry would build more useful modems.

With this picture in mind, the modem industry began to look for new roles for modems. If modems could be made error-free (so the thinking went), communications software could stop worrying about file-transfer protocols and get down to making the medium more friendly and useful. Also, if only they could be slightly faster[2], an error-free modem could become an inexpensive method to interconnect wide-area networks.

The idea behind modem protocols is that two modems exchange error-checked packets between themselves without the knowledge or participation of the associated DTE's computers. When viewed from the perspective of the DTE, then, a packet protocol makes the telephone line behave as if it were a *reliable link*.

---

[1]Many working on the V.FAST modem described in Chapter 5 feel it will be the "final modem."

[2]In 1987, a panel at a network trade show in San Franciso opined that a 20,000 bps modem would be an "irresistible alternative to the current expense of connecting low-traffic sites via faster leased lines."

A SHORT HISTORY OF MODEM PROTOCOLS

In the early eighties, a communications company—Microcom, Inc.—was building point-to-point electronic mailbox systems named the PCS/1000 (Personal Communication System). To provide for the error-free and orderly transfer of data between end points, Microcom designed network-like session and data-link protocols for the product. The Microcom protocol comprises several extensible hierarchical layers, referred to as *Classes*. Due to this architecture, Microcom was able to add new classes periodically.

In response to demands from customers and others interested in similar "secure" applications, Microcom began to license its protocol under the name of the *Microcom Networking Protocol* or *MNP*[3]. Microcom shipped its first modem supporting MNP Classes 2 and 3 in August, 1983, the model Microcom RX/1000. A license for the first three MNP classes was offered in August, 1983 for a one-time fee of $2500[4]. These classes were subsequently released to the public domain in August, 1985.

In March, 1986, Microcom shipped the AX/2400c modem containing two new classes of MNP, Classes 4 and 5, MNP Class 4 was an incremental improvement over Class 3, but Class 5 provided a new facility, data compression. Licenses for Class 5 were offered in March, 1987, and MNP Class 4 was released into the public domain at the same time. Additional classes of MNP have been defined up to the current level of MNP Class 10, which is designed to facilitate communications on analog cellular links. Although MNP Class 10 enjoys acceptance in its narrow market, it is fair to say that mass adoption of MNP technology ended at Class 5.

In 1985, American companies joined international companies under the aegis of the CCITT[5] to define a public modem protocol standard. Microcom, whose vice president Gregory Pearson was chairman of the effort, argued that the committee should simply adopt the MNP technology, which was proven, widely adopted[6], and now in the public domain. Objections were raised on the grounds that the new standard should be built upon already existing public standards. British Telecom, in particular, insisted upon deriving the standard from an existing ISO standard, HDLC (*High-level Data Link Control*). Hayes Microcomputer, which itself had adopted a protocol based upon HDLC (LAPB), supported British Telecom's position.

The standard that eventually emerged was CCITT V.42: *Error-Correcting Procedures for DCEs Using Asynchronous-to-Synchronous Conversion (1988)* whose error-correcting protocol is named *LAPM* (Link Access Protocol for Modems). To avoid rendering obsolete

---

[3]The former is a trademark, the latter is a registered trademark.

[4]In the world of technology licenses, this is essentially for free.

[5]This predates the certification of the TIA as U.S. representative to the CCITT, so the modem working group, named *US Working Party,* was sponsored by the U.S. Department of State.

[6]The worldwide installed base was estimated at 500,000.

the installed base of MNP users, however, Annex A of V.42 specifies MNP Classes 2-4 as an "alternate procedure." Support for MNP (which is never mentioned by name) is mandatory.

LAPM provides a general method to negotiate features. One such feature was certain to be a data compression procedure. In 1990, the CCITT approved V.42bis, a data compression method generally acknowledged to be superior to that of MNP Class 5. V.42bis does not mandate support for MNP Class 5.

THE NETWORK MODEL

While the underlying concepts of a protocol modem are quite simple, conventional thinking about them and, therefore, the terminology come from the field of computer networks. So to understand the structure of protocol modems, we need to understand the underlying architectural model on which most network technology is based.

THE OSI 7-LAYER NETWORK MODEL

Table 10.1 shows the familiar OSI[7] network model. The idea here is to build an abstract and layered approach to data movement across a network. In the ISO model, each layer can be visualized as communicating directly with its counterpart process on the remote network by means of a peer-process protocol unique to each layer. Beginning with "raw" data at the presentation layer, each layer transforms the data in accordance with its protocol (usually by packetizing it), then passes it along to the next layer. A layer is not required to understand the protocols above it or below it—just the interface to those layers.

Table 10.1. The ISO Network Seven-Layer Model.

Layer	Function	Synopsis
7	Application	Commonly needed "canned services" needed by many connections. For example, virtual-to-physical terminal conversion and data compression.
6	Presentation	Syntactical and semantics conversion of the data: e.g., ASCII to EBCDIC, newline conversion, etc.
5	Session	Establishes, manages, and maintains "connections" between cooperating applications. Responsible for orderly flow (synchronization) of data.

---

[7]"Open Systems Interconnection Reference Model," International Standards Organization Standard, ISO 7498.

Layer	Function	Synopsis
4	Transport	Provides reliable, in-sequence transfer of data regardless of reliability of lower layers.
3	Network	Attaches network address and provides suitable routing.
2	Data Link	Imposes logical order in preparation for applying data to physical layer: packets, error detection/correction, flow control, etc.
1	Physical	Mechanical aspects of interfacing to the physical medium.
0 (Implied)	"Bit-Pipe"	The physical medium itself: wire, radio, phone line, smoke signals, etc.

At the bottom of the ISO hierarchy is an *implicit but undefined* "Layer 0," the physical medium over which an unstructured bit stream is moved. In other words, the foundation of all networks is a simple *bit-pipe* which may be a shielded copper wire, a twisted pair of wires, radio, a fiber optic cable, a pair of paper cups connected by string, or, in our case, a modem. If the physical medium is a modem, the Physical layer interface is RS-232.

Modem manufacturers are fond of depicting a conventional modem's role in the ISO architecture as in Figure 10.1. In this diagram, the modem is viewed as part of the physical layer.

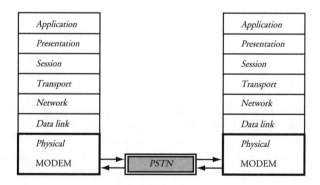

FIGURE 10.1.

Common representation of a conventional modem in the ISO model.

If one accepts this analysis[8], it is a small step to extend the modem to incorporate the data link layer as well as the physical. After all, the purpose of the data link layer is to deliver error-free, in-sequence bits to the layers above it. Thus was born the *data-link protocol modem*, or simply the *link protocol modem.*

What, Exactly, Is a Link Protocol?

The MNP and V.42 modem protocols we study later in this chapter have much in common with the file-transfer protocols emphasized in Chapter 5, especially Kermit. All employ variable length packets using a sliding-window ARQ protocol. All negotiate parameters based upon the capabilities of the remote partner. There are, however, many additional considerations.

Synchronous or Asynchronous?

Although we tend automatically to think of protocols as using synchronous communication, asynchronous protocols can and do exist. In fact, the Class 2 version of the MNP protocol discussed later specifies an async mode. If asynchronous, this means that the data on the phone line is delimited with START and STOP bits. If synchronous, bit synchronization is recovered in the form of a clock signal derived from the data.

Architecture

So far our discussion of modem protocols implies that there are undifferentiated "packets" on the phone line. In fact, there are several different kinds of packets: the interface, control, error-correction, and signaling.

INTERFACE

The RS-232 interface has the same function as it does in a normal modem—to send and receive raw data from the DTE in the asynchronous (START and STOP) format. In addition, the RTS and CTS control circuits have the responsibility of providing flow control between the modem and the DTE. We'll deal with why flow control is necessary shortly.

---

[8]Hardly anyone does. Greg Pearson, the designer of Microcom Networking Protocol, even argued against using the term "Network." The modem is *not* part of the physical layer, but is the implied bit-pipe layer mentioned earlier. If the point of a data link layer is to correct errors in the physical layer (and the bit-pipe), it makes no sense to have the data link layer under the physical. This point came up at a recent conference where one network administrator remarked while holding up a serial cable, "It may look like a data link layer to you guys, but to me it's just another error-prone serial port."

The working of the protocol is independent of the data pump (modulator/demodulator) section of the modem. Implementations exist for V.21, V.22bis, V.32, and V.32bis.

ERROR CONTROL

The error control function is the meat of the link protocol modem. It is responsible for:

1. Building and delimiting packets and transferring them in sequence.
2. Transfer of user (DTE) data as well as control signals such as BREAK.
3. Detection and recovery from transmission, format, and operational errors.
4. Flow control.

CONTROL

The control function coordinates the other functions.

1. It conducts the initial handshake to ascertain where the remote modem supports a compatible link protocol; if so, the control function conducts the negotiation (and renegotiation) of parameters; otherwise it falls back to a suitable connection.
2. Coordinates flow control between the RS-232 interface and error control functions. Both RTS/CTS and XON/XOFF are supported.
3. In synchronous implementations only: on the outbound side, it accepts data from the RS-232 interface and removes the START and STOP bits in order to convert data to a format suitable for use in synchronous transmission. Similarly, on the inbound side, it adds START and STOP bits to synchronous data for hand-off to the RS-232 interface.
4. Converts BREAK signals to and from data packets.

Data Transparency

The ability to detect the beginning and ending of packets is fundamental to any data transfer procedure. Both MNP and LAPM employ unique bit/byte sequences (*flags*) to delineate the body of the packet. In order to guarantee that these patterns appear *only* in the packet delimiters—that is, that they be transparent to the flag detectors— "naturally" occurring instances of this pattern in the body of the packet are encoded. The method of transparency encoding varies depending upon whether the protocol uses asynchronous or synchronous transmission.

ASYNCHRONOUS

The MNP Class 2 asynchronous protocol we examine later employs a byte rather than a bit sequence to delineate the packet. Each byte sequence contains the character DLE. In order to make certain that the delimiters are unique, the transmitter makes DLEs transparent; that is, the packet builder doubles all DLE characters that occur naturally in the packet body. The packet receiver is thus able to recognize single DLEs as delimiters. Once the packet boundaries have been delimited, the receiver then tosses out the redundant transparency DLEs from the body of the packet.[9] See "In-band Flow Control" in Chapter 8 for an explanation of this technique.

SYNCHRONOUS

As described in Chapter 5, bit synchronization is retained at the receiver by recovering the clock signal used by the transmitter. However, the removal of START and STOP bits raises the fundamental problem of identifying the boundary between bytes and hence the beginning and end of a packet. This problem is solved by defining a bit pattern reserved exclusively for delimiters. This pattern, 01111110, is common in byte-synchronous asynchronous protocols and is normally transmitted continually during idle periods.

Just as the DLE flag is "transparentized" in the asynchronous protocol to guarantee its uniqueness in the raw asynchronous data stream, so bit-flags must be transparent in the synchronous data stream. In this technique, known as bit-stuffing or zero-stuffing, the packet builder scans the raw data stream looking for six consecutive one-bits; if such a pattern is found, a zero-bit is inserted after the fifth one-bit. The receiver, having easily identified the opening and closing flag sequences, restores the data by removing any zero-bits that directly follow five successive one-bits. In most synchronous protocols, the closing flag of one frame may serve as the opening flag of the next.

Data Latency

Neither an MNP or an LAPM packet contains a field giving the byte count in the Information field. Understanding why this is so helps explain much about how link protocols function.

In file-transfer protocols, the input data is available as a block. Data goes from disk into a packet and is ready for transmission essentially instantaneously. Due to the serial data path inherent in a modem, however, a packet requires a non-trivial amount of time to build and, since data may arrive intermittently (asynchronously), the time required to acquire a packet's worth of data is not predictable. If a link protocol waits too long before shipping out a packet, even one containing a single byte, latent delays appear. In other words, when

---

[9]The byte count in the header does not include the bytes added for transparency.

the packet builder sees a byte at its input, it doesn't know how many bytes follow; if it waits *n* milliseconds for a "full" packet before sending the first byte, the first byte incurs a *propagation delay* of *n* milliseconds.

Much of the design of a data-link protocol centers about trade-offs between the desire for efficiency (moving the most bytes in the shortest amount of time) and immediacy (getting each byte there as soon as possible). Not surprisingly, there are only a few rules: "Keep the line busy" or "Let there be no holes between packets." To satisfy these rules, transmission of a packet must begin immediately—before its ultimate size is known. In other words, packets are opened and built on the fly. When the phone line is idle, transmission of a packet begins as soon as a single byte arrives at the input. First the packet builder transmits the opening flag and the header/control field followed by the just-arrived byte. Having sent the preliminary packet information, the packet builder buys several bytes worth of grace time during which new arrivals may be include in the departing packet. At some point the protocol's packet limit is reached or bytes stop arriving. At this time, the FCS and the closing flags are appended.

Now we see why a link packet can't contain a byte count: the length of a packet is unknown when the header is transmitted, and waiting for that knowledge would violate the desire for immediacy in the data. One's first impulse is to suggest appending byte count to the data field. In fact, knowing the count is only useful when it tells you how many bytes are coming; finding it after the data tells you what you already know.

ASYNCHRONOUS LATENCY

Propagation delays can be managed casually in asynchronous protocols because each byte carries a START and STOP bit for delineation and the packet itself is delineated by start and stop flags. The phone line may be allowed to go idle during packet transmission between bytes without corrupting the data. Therefore, the decision of when to open a packet and when to close it becomes one of perceived responsiveness to user data or other temporal requirements. For example, users connected to a remote computer expect their typing to be echoed in, at the most, one hundred milliseconds. To meet this expectation, single-character packets must be sent more than twice this often (to allow for the return trip).

SYNCHRONOUS LATENCY

During idling periods (e.g., between packets), most synchronous protocols transmit a steady stream of flags to allow the receiver to remain in byte-sync. Once a packet begins, however, the line cannot be allowed to become idle or byte-synchronism is lost and the packet is received in error. The requirement that data be tightly packed onto the line without interruption adds a sense of urgency to the practice of packetizing on the fly. A common technique is to open a new packet immediately upon receipt of the first input byte and to add additional bytes as they arrive. As long as the transmitter is busy, the packet may remain open for additional data from the input even if the input stream has temporarily ceased. However, when the transmitter begins transmitting its last byte (its transmit holding register is empty) and there is no input byte, the packet must be closed.

The requirement in synchronous communication that data bits in the packet be contiguous brings up an interesting situation when the DTE's baud rate equals the nominal modulation speed of the modem. After removal of the START and STOP bits, the DTE's effective baud rate is 20 per cent less than that of the modem speed. Although the DTE is sending 240 bytes per second, the modem's data pump will have transmitted only 196. Assuming that there are no pauses in the DTE's byte stream, this chronic "underflow" means that there are insufficient input data bytes to keep the transmitter busy. Stasis is quickly reached, however, when the packet overhead reaches 20 percent of the total packet size. On a packet with seven bytes of overhead, for example, the packet size should quickly ramp up to 35 and remain there.

Protocol Efficiency

Protocol Efficiency is the amount that the *protocol overhead*—the flags, header, and FCS—increases or decreases the throughput in the system compared to the same amount of data transmitted in a non-protocol modem. A rough estimate of protocol efficiency is

Protocol Efficiency = Amount of data in packet ÷ Packet size × Transparency cost

This formula assumes that data packets comprise 100 percent of the packet traffic and that there are no retransmissions. In fairness, however, it should be noted that in noisy environments (where retransmissions are likely), the extra time required to retransmit large packets outweighs their increased efficiency.

Asynchronous protocols always decrease data throughput, trading error correction for efficiency. The protocol overhead is significant, especially when the amount of data to be transferred is small.

The high overhead of the asynchronous protocol is more than offset by removing the START and STOP bits from the bytes. This technique is referred to as *asynchronous-to-synchronous*. Assuming that the data is arriving via the RS-232 interface as one START bit, 8 data, and one STOP bits, removal of the START and STOP bits reduces the quantity of raw data by 20 percent. Stated negatively, the use of asynchronous packets decreases throughput by 25 percent.

Break Handling

As explained in Chapter 2, a BREAK is not a character but an electrical condition when transmitting data in the START/STOP format. A BREAK occurs whenever an asynchronous line remains at logical 0 for a period longer than the time occupied by a single SDU (serial data unit). For example, in a 10-bit SDU, a BREAK occurs when the line is held at SPACE for 11-bit intervals.

Although there are no standards for the use of BREAK, its parochial use is ubiquitous. In some cases, it is employed as an in-band control signal; in other cases it is tantamount to a "cancel" command, and in still others it can be used as an emergency signal to reset a remote system. In each of these cases, the BREAK has a different temporal relationship to the data. For example, when used as an in-band end-of-data signal, the receiver must encounter the BREAK at its "real-time" location at the end of the data stream. As a contrary example, consider the use of BREAK as an emergency reset signal, where it must have priority over any data that may be already buffered.

Because BREAKs have no meaning in synchronous protocols, they must be transferred as control packets. When converted to a packet, a BREAK no longer has the special priority of hardware signaling, so it becomes susceptible to all the delays associated with a protocol—buffering, retransmission, propagation, and so forth. A BREAK packet should therefore indicate how the sender wishes the receiver to process it with respect to its priority and to how it affects other packets and processes in the system.

1. An *expedited* BREAK packet is processed immediately at both transmitter and receiver; that is, it cuts in line ahead of other packets.

2. A *destructive* BREAK packet causes an immediate bi-directional flush of all non-BREAK packets from the system.

The interpretation of a BREAK may depend upon its duration, so the BREAK packet ought also to contain this information.

The MNP Protocol

MNP protocols are defined for both asynchronous (START/STOP) and synchronous communication. The body of an MNP packet is essentially the same for both, only packet introducer/terminator sequences change. Figure 10.2 shows an MNP data packet.

	Packet Introducer Sequence	Header	Information	FCS	Packet Terminator Sequence
Field					
Number of bytes	N/A	5	Variable	2	N/A

FIGURE 10.2.
A MNP data packet.

The following MNP features and parameters are negotiated:

1. Whether synchronous or asynchronous communications shall be used.
2. The maximum allowable data field length.
3. The maximum allowable window size.

Header

The header in MNP is of variable length, depending upon the type of packet. The first field contains the length of the header, the type of packet (data, control, administrative, and so forth), and, where applicable, the packet sequence number. MNP uses eight-bit packet sequence numbers, which limits the maximum window size to 255. MNP Class 4 trims the number of the bytes in the header of data packets from 5 to 3.

Information

Information fields are variable in MNP. The maximum length of the information field varies with the Class, 64 in MNP Class 1-3, and 256 in Class 4.

Frame Check Sequence

A two-byte CRC is used employing the CRC-16 polynomial given in Chapter 3.

BREAK Handling

MNP communicates BREAKs by sending a control (Link Attention) packet whose header specifies whether the BREAK is destructive and/or expedited. There is no mechanism for expressing the duration of the BREAK.

MNP Asynchronous Protocols: Classes 1 and 2

MNP Classes 1 and 2 employ asynchronous protocols framing. (Class 1 is for operation over half-duplex modems.) This means that data moves from end to end in the system in START/STOP format. *Figure 10.3* shows an MNP Class 2 data (Link Transfer) packet.

FIGURE 10.3.

An MNP Class 2 data (Link Transfer) packet.

Field	SYN	DLE	STX	Header	Info	DLE	ETX	FCS
Number of bytes	1	1	1	5	Variable Max 64	1	1	2

Packet Introducer

The packet introducer sequence, referred to as *start flag*, comprises a SYN character (16 hex) followed by DLE and STX characters.

The Header Field

The Header field is five bytes, composed as described earlier.

The Information Field

There is no field in the header for the length of the Information field. The receiver deduces its length in relation to the opening and closing flags. DLEs are doubled for transparency.

Packet Terminator Sequence

The packet terminator sequence, referred to as the *stop flag*, comprises two bytes, DLE and ETX.[10] Notice that the FCS is located after the stop flag.

Frame Check Sequence

A two-byte CRC is used employing the CRC-16 polynomial given in Chapter 3. DLEs added for transparency are not included in the CRC calculation. Notice that the CRC lies outside the stop flag.

Protocol Efficiency

Recalling the formula for protocol's efficiency

$$\frac{\text{Amount of data in packet}}{\text{Packet size} \times \text{Transparency cost}}$$

1. Amount of data in packet = 64

2. Packet Size = 76 (12 bytes overhead)

3. Transparency cost = 256/257[11]

This is an efficiency of 84.9 percent compared to a modem without an error-correcting protocol.

---

[10]Together, the beginning and ending sequences are often referred to as *framing*. By convention, the framing bytes for asynchronous packets are referred to as start and stop flags. For synchronous packets, they are open and close flags.

[11]In random data one DLE character will have to be a inserted for transparency every 256 characters.

MNP Synchronous Protocols— Classes 3 and 4

The difference between the two Classes of MNP synchronous protocols, Class 3 and 4, is minor: Class 4 increases the maximum Information field size from 64 to 256, and reduces the header size from 5 to 3 in data-related packets. Class 4 also describes Adaptive Packet Assembly where the length of the data portion of the packet is adjusted dynamically to accommodate error conditions on the phone line.[12] For backward compatibility the link negotiations take place with asynchronous framing (that is, MNP Class 2). Figure 10.4 shows the packet for an MNP synchronous packet. Aside from the use of synchronous framing flags, the only difference between this packet and the asynchronous one is that the FCS is located inside the body of the frame.

FIGURE 10.4.

An MNP Class 3/4 data packet. The closing flag of one frame may serve as the opening frame of the next.

Field	Opening Flag 01111110	Header	INFO	FCS	Closing Flag 01111110
Number of bytes	1	3 or 5		2	1

Packet Introducer/Terminator Sequence

The open and closing flags are 01111110 with zero-bits added for transparency.

The Header Field

For non data-related packets, the header is seven bytes as in MNP Class 2. In the data (Link Transfer) packet shown, the header is five bytes.

Frame Check Sequence

A two-byte CRC is used employing the CRC-16 polynomial given in Chapter 3. Unlike MNP Class 2, however, the CRC lies inside the closing flag.

---

[12]Microcom doesn't specify an algorithm for this procedure.

Protocol Efficiency

Recalling the formula for protocol's efficiency

Protocol Efficiency = Amount of data in packet÷Packet size ×Transparency cost

1. Amount of data in packet = 256
2. Packet Size = 263 (7 bytes overhead)
3. Transparency cost = 62/63[13]

This is an efficiency of 95.8 percent compared to a modem without an error correcting protocol. Because the start and stop bits are removed, however, this improves throughput another 20 percent, or 115 percent. Keep in mind that this gain is not a function of protocol efficiency, but a side effect of synchronous communications.

LAPM (V.42)

Recommendation V.42 is the name of the public standard for error correction in modems. The name of the protocol described in V.42 is *LAPM: Link Access Procedure for Modems.* LAPM is a derivative of HDLC (and ISO standard), which in turn derives from IBM's Synchronous Data Link Control, or SDLC. The CCITT modified HDLC for use in the hugely ambitious X.25 packet protocol standard. The result was LAP (*Link Access Procedure).* When HDLC itself was revised, LAP became LAPB. Andrew Tanenbaum in *Computer Network* observes, "The nice thing about standards is that you have so many to choose from. Furthermore, if you do not like any of them, you can just wait for next year's model." While there is truth in this sarcastic remark, it is natural to base complex systems on simpler ones that are well understood.

V.42 supports MNP as an "alternative procedure." That is, if a modem is unable to establish an LAPM connection, it must attempt to establish an MNP connection. Thus implementation of MNP Classes 2,3, and 4 is mandatory for compliance with V.42.

The following features and parameters are negotiated under LAPM:

1. The ability to negatively acknowledge individual packets.
2. A remote loop-back mode to allow a modem to test itself.
3. Extended (32-bit) CRCs.
4. For each direction, the maximum allowable Information field length (no limit).
5. For each direction, the maximum allowable window size (up to 127).

Figure 10.5 shows an LAPM synchronous packet (there is no asynchronous option as in MNP).

---

[13]In random data, a zero bit is inserted on average every 62 bits.

FIGURE 10.5.

LAPM packet. The closing flag of one frame may serve as the opening flag of the next.

Field	Opening Flag 01111110	ADDRESS	Control	Information	FCS	Closing Flag 01111110
Number of bytes	1	1 or 2	1 or 2	128	2 or 4	1

Packet Introducer/Terminator Sequence

The open and closing flags are 01111110 with zero-bits added for transparency. The closing flag of one packet can be the open flag of the next.

Address Field

A body of an LAPM packet is similar to that of MNP except for the address field and the length of the CRC, which is optionally two bytes or four. The address field is a vestige of LAPM's network heritage, where the "address" might be the number of a terminal adapters on the network. Currently, the only use for this field is for single control byte and a 7-bit "data link connection identifier," for which the only currently defined value is for a V.24 (RS-232) connection. Additional uses of this field are reserved for further study, so currently the optional second byte in the field in never present.

Control Field

The first byte in the Control field identifies the type of packet. If the packet type calls for a second byte, it combines with the first byte to form a packet sequence number. LAPM uses seven-bit Packet Sequence numbers, which limits the maximum window size to 127.

The Information Field

The Information field is of variable length whose maximum is negotiation during the link establishment phase of the handshake. Although technically there is no limit on this field, a practical limit of 4096 is enforced by the desire to use a two-byte CRC. The default value is 128, which is also the maximum value negotiated by most V.42 modems.

Break Handling

LAPM communicates BREAKs by sending a control (unnumbered) packet whose Information field specifies whether the BREAK is destructive and/or expedited. The duration of the BREAK is optionally represented by a single byte whose value gives the duration of the BREAK in 10 millisecond increments. Absence of a break length means a BREAK of "default" length.

MNP Class 4 Vs V.42

For all practical purposes, the differences between MNP Class 4 and V.42 are negligible, with perhaps a tiny edge going to MNP. The table below summarizes these differences. MNP has the feel of work done in private by a small team of programmers building a modem product. It's leaner and simpler than V.42 in places where it needs to be leaner and simpler. V.42 on the other hand, has a philosophical (one might say academic) purity to it. Although it is a protocol that lives *inside a modem*, it is modeled after the more complicated computer network technology.[14] In short, MNP seems somehow better optimized for the job at hand. As we shall see shortly, however, V.42 brings to the party a demonstrably more powerful compression scheme that more than makes up for its tiny performance deficit.

		MNP 4	V.42
32-bit CRC		No	Yes*
Data Packet	Overhead (bytes)	7	7
Information	Field (bytes)		
Maximum		256	4096**
Default		256	128
Typical		256	128
Window size	(packets)		
Maximum		255	127
Default		8	15
Typical		6	6
Synchronous	Efficiency	97.3	93.3
Data Packet	Overhead (bytes)	7	7

* Never used.

** Based on maximum practical size that can be protected by a 16-bit CRC.

Compression Theory

From the standpoint of pure utility, modem protocols by themselves don't greatly improve life. Although they do a fine job of correcting errors occurring on the phone line they can do nothing about the errors that occur at the DTE's RS-232 interface due to input over-runs. That means that data arriving at the DTE is not really guaranteed to be error-free. To make it so, it is necessary to provide an end-to-end protocol located in the DTE. But wait! If there must to be a protocol on the DTE anyway, why do we need one

---

[14]This impression is reinforced by the V.42 document itself, which is poorly organized and written in almost incomprehensible English prose.

on the modem as well? Why indeed. It's a fair question and, once the modem industry grew tired of patting itself on the back, one frequently asked. The answer suggests that the tail wags the dog: a modem protocol is necessary to support data compression, which requires an absolutely error-free environment.

Data compression was added to MNP in the form of Class 5 in 1987. The CCITT specified it in V.42bis in 1990. Figure 10.6 shows how data compression fits into the architecture of a modem.

FIGURE 10.6.

The architecture of a data compression modem.

Compression	V.42bis				MNP Class 5		
Error Correction	V.42				MNP Classes 1-4		
Modulation	B103A	B212A	V. 21	V. 22	V. 22 bis	V. 32	V. 32 bis

The motivation to put compression in the modem is obvious: it increases the throughput of the modem without having to increase its modulation speed or its cost. Converting the data stream to shorthand before it reaches the error-control function in the modem makes it possible to transport a much higher volume of data per packet. On the receive side, after the data is de-packetized the shorthand is expanded again to its full size.

There are many schemes for data compression. Let's briefly examine a few.

Repetition

The idea behind data compression is *repetition*[15]: information that occurs more than once. Multiple repetitions of a byte or group of bytes are replaced with a special character (or sequence of characters), referred to as a *token* or *codeword*.

The simplest form of compression acts upon bytes that repeat immediately one after another:

```
<char1><char2><char3><...><charN>
```

The ASCII Tab character is a simple example of this form of compression: multiple contiguous repetitions of Spaces are replaced by a single byte reserved for that purpose. Our input sequence is represented in Tabs as

```
<Tab1><Tab2><Tab N/mod>
```

Where *<char>* is a Space and *<mod>* is the width of the Tab stop. Entabbing documents with large amounts of columnar information such as assembly language files produces a surprising amount of compression.

There are two drawbacks to single-character compression such as Tab substitution. First, the token must be a reserved character, which is not possible in all applications. Second,

---

[15]This attribute is usually incorrectly referred to as *redundancy*. Redundancy has the meaning of needless or superfluous repetition.

the compressed information is not *intrinsically invertible*; that is, it cannot *be* perfectly decompressed to its original form because the repetition modulus is not stored along with the data. When expanding an entabbed document, for example, there is no way to know the width of the tab stop that was in use at the time of compression.

An improvement on the single-character scheme is *run-length* compression in which the number of repetitions is part of the token:

`<char><N>`

Note, however, that this procedure causes the data to expand when applied to a repetition of one. This situation—where *every* incompressible sequence expands—clearly won't do. Suppose we wait for a two-byte repetition before applying the procedure:

`<char><char><N>`

This procedure expands a two-byte sequence to the three-byte sequence:

`<char><char><0>`

This choice—where two-byte repetitions expand to three—is still not a good choice because two-byte repetitions are common in most kinds of files. Obviously, this approach always results in the expanding of one particular repetition. The choice of a minimum repetition therefore must balance the desire not to expand ordinary data against the decreasing frequency with which longer repetitions occur.

Because it doesn't unnecessarily inflate text files, a three-byte minimum repetition, illustrated in Figure 10.7 is common:

`<char><char><char><0>`

To implement this, the compressor ignores single- and double-byte repetitions of <char>. On repetitions of three or more, however, the compressor adds the number of additional bytes required in the repetition. This expands three-byte repetitions, but doesn't affect one- or two-byte repetitions.

This	*becomes*	*This*
<char>		<char>
<char><char>		<char><char>
<char><char><char>		<char><char><char><0>
<char><char><char><char>		<char><char><char><1>
<char><char><char><char><char>		<char><char><char><2>
<char><char><char><char><char><char>		<char><char><char><3>

FIGURE 10.7.
Run-length compression with a minimum sequence of three.

In this technique a four-byte token is able to express repetitions up to 259. A two-byte byte-counter would of course extend the range, but would also increase the length of the minimum sequence, which in turn reduces the likelihood that it will appear.

Statistical Repetition: Huffman Encoding

The example of run length encoding makes no assumptions about the nature of the patterns in the byte stream, so it compresses them all equally. For example, it compresses a string of 50 FF bytes just as efficiently as a string of 50 Spaces. This broad-band approach is necessary when the compression algorithm is expected to encounter a variety of data. Suppose, however, that you knew in advance that the algorithm would be applied to data that could be ordered probabilistically. In English text, for example, we know the rough frequency of occurrence of every letter. We know for example, that the letter E accounts for 13 percent of all text, while the letter Z only .25 percent. It should be possible to construct a code that assigns a short token to E and longer token to Z. But when using text files, how can any token be smaller than a byte? It can't, so we will have to use bit patterns to stand for various byte patterns.

This technique of basing token size upon frequency of occurrence is know as Huffman Coding. Figure 10.8 shows a Huffman table based upon the 26 letters of the English alphabet.

The idea here is to start at the bottom of the table and draw lines to the right from each frequency. The lines with the two lowest frequencies are joined to produce a new line representing their composite frequencies (the two .0025 lines become a single .005 line). This process is repeated until a tree with a root node is formed. Working outward from the right, a zero is assigned to the upper branch of each decision and a one to the lower until there are no more branches. The code for each letter is formed from the binary path required to reach it. The result is a table of tokens whose length is inversely proportional to their frequency of occurrence. For example, E is a three-bit token 000 and Z is a seven-bit token 1111111.

Huffman encoding is quite fast because tokens are extracted from a simple table. Decoding is not so simple because the table is a binary tree that must be traversed. Huffman coding is ineffective unless the probability of occurrence of each character is known (or can be derived). Moreover, a Huffman encoded data stream is not intrinsically invertible because the decoder must own an exact copy of the encoder's table.

We will postpone detailed discussion of Huffman coding until Chapter 11 where we discuss its role in facsimile, and in Chapter 24 where we develop code for encoding and decoding facsimile images.

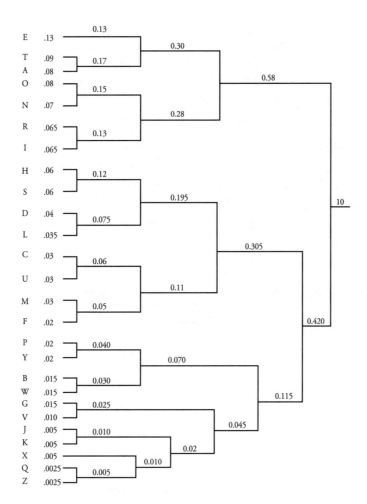

FIGURE 10.8.

A Huffman code tree for the English alphabet.

Historical Repetition: Lempel-Ziv

So far we've seen run length and statistical compression procedures, neither of which is a good general purpose algorithm. A more effective general approach is to look for *the historical repetition of strings*—to encode entire strings that have previously occurred. This is the Lempel-Ziv[16] algorithm and it is childlike in its simplicity:

1. A string is a sequence of two or more characters.

2. Remember every string you have ever seen and assign it a token.

3. The next time you see it, substitute the token for the string.

___
[16]Often referred to just as LZ. Named for the Israeli mathemeticians A. Lempel and J. Ziv. Later, refinements were added by T. Welch and the procedure is often referred to as LZW.

At the heart of the procedure is a large array for remembering strings (the "dictionary"). As bytes arrive at the input, they are collected (in the "accumulator") and compared against the existing strings in the array. If a match is not found, the unmatched string is put into the array, and its index in the array becomes its token. When an input string is matched, the token is output in place of the string.

The procedural rules are only slightly more complicated:

1. The first 256 tokens are reserved for single, unmatched bytes.
2. Attempted matching begins when the accumulator contains two characters.
3. Input characters gather in the accumulator until a dictionary match fails.
4. After the match fails, the new string accumulator is placed in the dictionary, and the token representing the partial match is output. The most recent character (the one that caused the match to fail) remains in the accumulator to begin a new match.

Table 10.2 An illustration of Lempel-Ziv compression applied to the string "!BAN!BA!BAA!BAR!BAT".

	Accumulator	*Input (8-bit)*	*Output (12-bit)*	*Dictionary*
1	-	!	-	-
2	!	B	!	100 = !B
3	B	A	B	101 = BA
4	A	N	A	102 = AN
5	N	!	N	103 = N!
6	!	B	-	-
7	!B	A	<100>	104 = !BA
8	A	!	A	105 = A!
9	!	B	-	-
10	!B	A	-	-
11	!BA	A	<104>	106 = !BAA
12	A	!	-	-
13	A!	B	<105>	107 = A!B
14	B	A	-	-
15	BA	R	<101>	108 = BAR
16	R	!	R	109 = R!

	Accumulator	Input (8-bit)	Output (12-bit)	Dictionary
17	!	B	-	-
18	!B	A	-	-
19	!BA	T	<104>	10A = !BAT
-	T	-	T	-

Table 10.2 illustrates this algorithm. The **Accumulator** column represents a buffer where in-progress matches are stored. The **Input** column shows the input character-by-character. The **Output** column shows the compressed output stream of 12-bit tokens. The **Dictionary** column contains all the remembered strings. Tokens are given in hex. A dash indicates that a match is pending and we must wait for another character. Follow the narrative for seven iterations to see how it works:

1. The first character **!** is moved into the accumulator. Neither the accumulator nor the dictionary is altered on the first character because there are not two characters in the accumulator (Rule 2). The **!** remains in the accumulator to start a new string match.

2. The second character **B** is appended to the **!** already in the accumulator. The dictionary is searched for **!B** and no match is found. This *new* string is copied into the dictionary and assigned the next available token number, 100hex (Rule 1). The **!** is output and the **B** remains in the accumulator to start a new string match.

3. The third character **A** is appended to the **B** already in the accumulator and the dictionary is searched. No match is found, so **BA** is copied into dictionary and assigned the token 101 hex. The **B** is output and the **A** remains in the accumulator to start the next string match.

4. The fourth character **N** is appended to the **A** already in the accumulator and the dictionary is searched. No match is found, so **AN** is copied into dictionary and assigned the token 102hex. The **A** is output and the **N** remains in the accumulator to start the next string match.

5. The fifth character **!** is appended to the **N** already in the accumulator and the dictionary is searched. No match is found, so the **N!** is copied into dictionary and assigned the token 103hex. The **N** is output and the **!** remains in the accumulator to start the next string match.

6. The sixth character **B** is appended to the **!** already in the accumulator and the dictionary is searched. This time a match is found. No output occurs until a match fails (Rule 3), so **!B** remains in the accumulator to continue the string matching.

7. The seventh character **A** is appended to the **!B** already in the accumulator and the dictionary is searched. No match is found, so the **!BA** is copied into dictionary and assigned the token 104hex. The token **<100>** is output in place of the **!B** (Rule 4). The unmatched **A** remains in the accumulator to start the next string match.

This procedure continues until the input is exhausted, at which time the accumulator is flushed to the output. Compression begins on the seventh byte, when a 12-bit token replaces two bytes in the output. As is evident from the example—where 157 input bits are compressed to 144 output bits—most of the time at the beginning is spent building the dictionary and very little compression takes place. As the dictionary grows, however, substitutions occur more often. To keep the table adapting to a changing input string, most implementations "age" the strings by replacing the least recently matched strings with newer ones.

Notice that every string in the output stream of Table 10.2 precedes the token that later represents it. This means that the receive can build a copy of dictionary in parallel with the transmitter, and therefore no external tables are required to recover the original data. This property of invertibility, and the elegance with which it is achieved makes the algorithm particularly well suited for modems.

The Lempel-Ziv approach is disarmingly simple. Because virtually all data contains often-repeated sequences[17], the algorithm works surprisingly well as general-purpose compression. But simplicity doesn't come without a cost. In the example shown, 12-bit tokens are used, resulting in 2^{12} or 4,096 dictionary entries, but the number is arbitrary. In data without repeated sequences, substantial expansion occurs because 8-bit bytes are replaced with 12-bit tokens. As the number of tokens increases to increase the history, so does the expansion.

The length of a dictionary entry (how long a string it can hold) is also arbitrary. Although the strings in the dictionary may themselves contain token substitutions, clearly at some combination of dictionary size and string length, both the amount of storage and the time required to search it become limiting factors. For example, a dictionary of 16-bit tokens together with 20-character strings require 1.2M of storage.

MNP Class 5 Compression

MNP Class 5 is the data compression service in MNP. It is actually a combination of Huffman and run-length encoding. The data stream is first run-length encoded with a minimum repetition of three bytes, then Huffman encoded using the table shown in Table 10.3.

---

[17]Even object and executable files have lots of repetition: uninitialized data, variable names, fix-up tables, etc. Moreover, functions generated by compilers tend to use repetitive code sequences.

Table 10.3. The Huffman encoding chart.

Data (decimal)	Token Header	Token Body
0	000	0
1	000	1
2	001	0
3	001	1
4	010	00
5	010	01
6	010	10
7	010	11
8	011	000
9	011	001
10	011	010
11	011	011
12	011	100
13	011	101
14	011	110
15	011	111
16	100	0000
17	100	0001
18	100	0010
19	100	0011
20	100	0100
21	100	0101
22	100	0110
23	100	0111
24	100	1000
25	100	1001
26	100	1010
27	100	1011

continues

Table 10.3. continued

Data (decimal)	Token Header	Token Body
28	100	1100
29	100	1101
30	100	1110
31	100	1111
32	101	00000
33	101	00001
34	101	00010
...		
247	111	1110111
248	111	1111000
249	111	1111001
250	111	1111010
251	111	1111011
252	111	1111100
253	111	1111101
254	111	1111110
255	111	1111111

Each token in the Class 5 table comprises a three-bit header that gives the number of en-coded bits[18]. For example, the header for the character 15H is 100, indicating that the rest of the token is 4 bits long; the header for the 255 token is 111 followed by 7 bits. This scheme produces a table with 32 tokens with less than 8 bits, 32 tokens with exactly eight bits, and 128 tokens greater than eight bits. The average size of a token is 9.01 bits. The entries in the table are initialized with their ordinals: entry 0 contains the token for 0, entry 1 contains the token for 1, and so on.

The operation of the compressor is simple: incoming bytes are replaced in the output by indexed tokens in the table. For example, a 15H in the input stream is replaced by the token at table location 15H, 100—a 7-bit token.

---

[18]The first and second entries are exceptions.

It has probably occurred to you that this procedure is twice as likely to expand the data instead of compressing it because tokens greater than eight bits outnumber tokens shorter than eight bits by a factor of two-to-one. This problem is compensated for by keeping statistics on how often each character appears in the data stream, then reassigning the tokens according to frequency of occurrence—*after each byte!* In this way, the most common characters are perpetually assigned the shortest tokens.

Even with the continual token sorting, the best compression attainable is for a four-bit token to replace a byte, yielding a compression ratio of 2:1. MNP Class 5 achieves maximum compression on a steady stream of the three most favored characters. A steady input stream of the letter Z, for example, would eventually produce this steady output stream:

`<0000><0000><0000><0001>`

After a few characters, both the letter Z and the run-length count of 250 (the maximum in MNP) bubble to the top because of their frequency of occurrence and are assigned the shortest tokens (four bits). Thus MNP compresses 254 bytes (2032 bits) into two bytes (16-bits) a compression ratio of 127:1. This figure, of course, seldom occurs in real life. A more reasonable[19] estimate of MNP Class 5's overall compression ratio on "average data" is nominally 2:1.

There are no negotiable MNP parameters affecting the performance of data compression. Unfortunately, MNP Class 5 is not intelligent enough to turn itself off when it becomes ineffective. Therefore, incompressible files expand by about 13 percent.

V.42bis BTLZ Compression

V.42bis employs the Lempel-Ziv compression algorithm. Its principle theory of operation is virtually identical to the explanation given earlier. The implementation defined in V.42bis is optimized for continuous real-time transmission suitable for embedded controllers. The document also specifies algorithms for pruning the dictionary tree, increasing the directory size on the fly, and so forth.

V.42's most significant enhancement to the basic Lempel-Ziv algorithm, however, is an in-band mechanism for turning compression on and off dynamically. If the transmitter discovers that data is expanding during transmission it turns off compression until the data again becomes compressible. The ability to toggle compression on the fly assures that the long-term compression ratio never drops below approximately 1:1, even with random data.

Modems supporting V.42 have a built-in mechanism (the XID packet) for negotiating V.42bis compression. The following parameters are negotiated:

---

[19]"More reasonable" only because no one will argue with it. "Nominal" figures are used because no one can agree on what "average data" is.

1. The direction of compression. All variations are possible.

2. The maximum size of the dictionary (and therefore the length of a token). The default size and minimum size are 512 bytes (9-bit tokens). There is no upper limit. A typical implementation uses a 4096-byte (12-bit) dictionary. (The size can be renegotiated on the fly.)

3. The maximum string length that can be stored. The default is 6 and the range is 6 to 250. A typical value is about 32.

Unlike V.42, where MNP Classes 2-4 were adopted as an optional procedure, V.42bis does not specifies a procedure for a V.42 connection employing MNP Class 5 compression.

V.42bis Versus MNP Class 5

For purposes of comparison, it is instructive to see how V.42bis performs with the continuous stream of repeating characters. V.42bis compresses most when using a 9-bit token and a 250-byte string length, which compresses 250 bytes to a mere 12 bits, yielding a ratio of 222:1. Moreover, the size of the dictionary can grow dynamically should the characteristics of the data suddenly change. On the other hand, it is easy to construct a realistic situation in which MNP Class 5 yields a negative compression ratio while V.42bis achieves a positive ratio of three or four.

Using the ever-elusive "average" data, the V.42bis' nominal compression ratio is given as 4:1, compared to 2:1 for MNP Class 5. These figures are endlessly debatable depending upon how the data is "rigged," but no one disputes that V.42bis is superior if for no other reason than its ability to turn itself on and off dynamically in the face of variously compressible data.

Flow Control

Recall from Chapter 4 that flow control is the ability to start and stop the flow of data to one's partner. In non-protocol modems, where the phone line is seen as an unstructured bit pipe, the DTE's baud rate need never exceed the modulation rate of the modem. Flow control is inherent in the idea of an error-correcting protocol because of the possibility that data may have to be retransmitted. The need for flow control is easiest to visualize in asynchronous procedures such as MNP Class 2 described earlier. Such a modem cannot accept data at its modulation rate because of the protocol overhead. Even if the speed of the DTE is reduced below the effective throughput of the system, the system would still be liable to "back up" due to the transmission of packets to correct errors. It is therefore necessary that the modem be able to *hold off* the DTE during these periods of reduced throughput.

In synchronous modems where the protocol efficiency is greater than 100 percent, the DTE speed must be set higher than the modem's modulation rate in order to reap the advantages of increased throughput. This slight effective "underhead" of a synchronous protocol can largely be absorbed by setting a DTE speed barely higher than the modem's modulation speed. For example, a 14,400 bps modem with V.42 error correction can be completely fulfilled by a DTE baud rate of only 17,000. The practice of placing data compression in the modem, however, requires setting the DTE to a speed *several times* higher than the modulation. As explained earlier, the compression ratio varies with the data content, under some circumstances reaching more than 200:1.

Flow Control and Compression

In order to take advantage of the increase in throughput provided by compression, the DTE speed ideally ought to be equal to the modulation speed times the compression ratio. This goal reveals a daunting prospect with a V.32bis modem (14,400 bps) with V.42bis: compression bursts of 200:1 would require the DTE to operate at 2.88 Mbps. Clearly this is impossible even on the most advanced RS-232 ports. A more reasonable upper limit to the DTE's baud rate on most systems is about 38,400 baud, yet V.42bis' promised *average* compression ratio of 4:1 requires a DTE speed 57,600 baud,[20] the upper limit at which most modems auto-baud. (See Chapter 8 for a discussion of auto-bauding.)

MNP and LAPM support bidirectional RS-2322 (RTS[21]/CTS) and software (XON/XOFF) flow control. Flow control in both protocols is local, not end-to-end: when the local DTE holds off the local modem by inhibiting RTS, the local modem need not do anything proactive. Local flow control occurs in the modem during the normal course of managing its buffers. When RTS becomes inhibited, the local modem's buffers fill quickly, which in turn causes its packet buffer to fill. Thus clogged the local modem is no longer able to acknowledge packets from the remote modem[22]. At the other end, the maximum allowable number of unacknowledged packets is reached (its window "closes"), and the modem stops trying to send additional packets. At this point, its packet buffer and DTE buffer quickly fill, causing it to inhibit CTS and the remote DTE to stop sending. XON/XOFF flow control works in the same fashion.

Error correcting and compression protocols pose an interesting problem for a DTE when controlling a protocol modem. Recall from Chapter 8 that a non-protocol modem issues a CONNECT XXXX message at the speed of the last AT command, then changes its baud rate if necessary to match the modulation rate of the connection. The DTE must be able

---

[20]Because the average compression by definition includes bursts higher than the average, setting the baud rate to achieve the average throughput guarantees that it will not be achieved.

[21]Recall from Chapter 5 that RS-232-E defined a new circuit to accommodate flow control. When flow control is implemented, Request to Send becomes Ready for Receiving.

[22]In some implementations the local modem may elect to send a "busy" packet (Receiver Not Ready in V.42; Link Acess with zero credit in MNP) to the remote modem just to keep it from worrying, but it is not necessary to do so because the remote modem must be prepared to wait forever for its packet window to reopen.

to parse the CONNECT message and immediately changes its baud rate to XXXX. (Keep in mind that in non-protocol modems the DTE never requires a baud rate higher than the line speed.)

Let's look at this procedure from the point of view of a local originating modem with V.42 and V.42bis:

1. The DTE is aware that the local modem supports these protocols, so it sets its own baud rate as high as it dare: say, to 57,600 baud. This provides a factor of times-four headroom to absorb highly compressed data should a protocol connection be established.

2. The DTE issues a dial command at 57,600 baud.

3. A 14,400 connection using V.42/V.42bis is established, producing the message CONNECT 14400.

4. The DTE reads the CONNECT message and changes its speed down to 14,400 baud.

This DTE behavior—adjusting its speed to the CONNECT message—is clearly not advisable with protocol connections because the DTE speed ought to be slightly higher in order to take advantage of error-correction and much higher still to benefit from compression. In such situations local flow control prevents the loss of data, but the added throughput from the protocols is wasted. In order to decide unambiguously what rate is required after CONNECT, the DTE must know not only the modulation rate, but also whether the connection includes error correction and/or compression. In the example above, for instance, reducing its speed to 14,400 baud is harmless on a non-protocol connection.

THE CONNECT MESSAGE FIB

Handing out advice to write more intelligence software is little help for the installed base of software that looks only at the CONNECT message. Modem manufacturers provide backward compatibility with "dumb" software by providing a command that causes the modem to report the current DTE speed (the one at which the dial or answer command was given) in the CONNECT message instead of the modulation speed.

For software that is interested in learning the true modulation speed without worrying about the veracity of the CONNECT message, most modems offer an explicit CARRIER XXXX message. In addition, optional PROTOCOL and COMPRESSION messages are offered.

HYBRID MODE

We've seen how the overspeed requirement of protocol modems can affect a DTE that changes baud rate to match the modem's CONNECT messages. The situation on the other side of the coin—where the DTE is *unable* to change its baud rate—is equally mischievous. This situation is quite common in networks environments and minicomputers where a modem device driver stands between the modem and the application software. Referring to the scenario given above, suppose the DTE was unable to change its baud rate and step three read "A 14,400 *non-protocol* connection is established, producing the message CONNECT 14400." Being unable to change its baud rate to 14,400, the local DTE would be unable to communicate with the modem.

In addition to protocol and non-protocol (direct) modes, most protocol modems provide a third *hybrid mode*. In the hybrid mode the modem does not operate under a protocol, but simulates the protocol-style DTE interface. The modem allows the current DTE speed to be reported in the CONNECT message and provides local flow control to manage the mismatch between the DTE's speed and that of the phone line.

MODEM-TO-MODEM FLOW CONTROL

It is important to remember that in hybrid modem flow control functions only *locally* in the modem-to-DTE direction. Although buffering exists in the DTE-to-modem direction, there is no end-to-end flow control because in the absence of a protocol, the remote modem cannot restrain the remote. Some modems attempt to solve this with "virtual" XON/XOFF flow control between modems during a hybrid connection. Although the scheme applies to both hardware and software handshaking, let's assume that the local modem is configured for RTS/CTS. When the local modem senses a flow-control signal on its RTS, it translates it to an XON or XOFF and sends it to the remote modem. Likewise, flow control characters received from the remote modem are translated into local RTS/CTS signals. There is of course no guarantee that the remote will honor this flow control, but, so the thinking goes, what's to lose?

Protocol Modems and Commands

As we saw in Chapters 8 and 9, there is a great deal of uniformity among manufacturers of the command set used in non-protocol 2,400 bps modems. Unfortunately, this is not the case in higher-speed modems and protocol modems. The reasons for this are largely historical. Because of its pioneering role in the protocol modem market, Microcom assumed a leadership position in the field. But Hayes was clearly the traditional overall leader in the field. Regrettably, the two command sets seldom coincide and the market is now fragmented in this area. Work is underway in the EIA/TIA to standardize these commands, but if history is any indication, the work may be too little too late. Meanwhile, the dominant vendor of modem chip sets, Rockwell International, tries to support the important commands of both.

Because of market fragmentation, it would be folly in this book to attempt to explain in detail all the different command sets for protocol modems in use today. Instead, for the sake of consistency with Chapter 9, we'll look at the Hayes command set in fair detail.

&Q: PROTOCOL ENABLE

The Hayes &Q command enables error correction, but the type of error correction is named in S46 and the terms of negotiation in S48. Automatic Speed Buffering (ASB) is Hayes' name for a hybrid connection.

Function	Communications Mode Options
Command	&Qn (S46 and S48)
	0 Direct asynchronous
	1 n/a (synchronous)
	2 n/a (synchronous)
	3 n/a (synchronous)
	4 n/a (synchronous)
	5 Enable error correction as given in S46 and S48
	6 Hybrid (Automatic Speed Buffering)

S46: PROTOCOL AND COMPRESSION SELECT

The desired type of error correction and the compression are given in S46. LAPB is the link protocol adopted by Hayes before V.42. If compression is selected, the modem first tries to negotiate V.42bis; if that fails, the modem tries to negotiate the Hayes proprietary compression.

Function	Error-Control Protocol Selection
Register	S46
	0 LAPM, fallback to LAPB
	1 LAPB only
	2 Same as 0, with compression
	3 Same as 1, with compression
	6 n/a
	134 n/a
	136 LAPM only
	138 LAPM with compression

S48: FEATURE NEGOTIATION

S48 selects how features are negotiated when making connections with a remote system. Feature negotiation enables two modems to identify the common protocols, and chooses one based on the user-configuration for the communication session.

Function	Feature Negotiation
Command	S48
	0 Disabled: the remote is known to be compatible and configured as in S46.
	3 Enabled, MNP only
	7 Full negotiation enabled
	128 Disabled. Fallback to S36 immediately

The negotiation process can be tailored to suit a particular connection, or bypassed altogether. For example, when the capabilities of the remote modem are known, negotiation is unnecessary. With feature negotiation disabled, the modem assumes that the remote is configured the same as itself, and proceeds to activate the error-correcting protocol specified by the S46 (Protocol Options) setting. Setting 128 causes the modem to skip negotiations altogether and jump right to the negotiation fallback behavior specified in S36; this is useful when calling a packet-switched network that does not support feature negotiation.

S36: NEGOTIATION FALLBACK

After an attempt to establish the protocol connection specified in S46 fails, the modem looks in S36 register for further instructions.

Function	V.42 Negotiation Failure Action
Command	S36
	0 Hang up
	1 Attempt a direct connection
	3 Attempt a hybrid connection
	5 Attempt an MNP connection, then direct
	6 Attempt an MNP connection, then hang up
	7 Attempt an MNP connection, then hybrid

&K: FLOW CONTROL

The &K command contains straightforward flow control selections. These are active only for protocol and hybrid connections. Use setting 0 at your own risk.

Function	Local Flow Control Options
Command	&Kn
	0 No flow control
	1 RTS/CTS enabled
	2 XON/XOFF
	3 Same as 1
	4 Same as 2
	5 Transparent XON/XOFF

The &K5 "transparent XON/XOFF" option requires explanation. The purpose of this scheme, which requires cooperation from the DTE software, is to accommodate systems that cannot abide XON/XOFF's in the data *and* don't support RTS/CTS flow control (or don't support the circuits).[23]

An XON or XOFF of either parity is "transparentized" by first XORing it with 21hex and then inserting a DLE character of the same parity in front of it. When the receiver locates this combination in the data, it removes the DLE and XORs the following character with 21hex to restore the original XON or XOFF.

S37: LINE SPEED CONTROL

The S37 register specifies the maximum desired modulation speed. Argument 0 allows the modem to imply the desired modulation speed from the current DTE speed. For example, if the dial or answer command is issued at 57,600 baud with S37 set to zero, the modem tries to connect at 14,400.

Function	Desired DCE Line Speed
Command	S37
	0 Attempt connection at highest line speed that does not exceed the current DTE speed (last AT)
	1 Attempt at 75bps
	2 Attempt at 110bps
	3 Attempt at 300bps
	4 reserved
	5 Attempt at 1200bps
	6 Attempt at 2400bps
	7 Attempt at 4800bps
	8 Attempt at 7200bps
	9 Attempt at 9600bps
	10 Attempt at 12000bps
	11 Attempt at 14400bps

---

[23]In other words, systems that run the modem on a three-wire cable.

WN AND S95: EXTENDED RESPONSES

Together Wn and S95 determine whether the CONNECT XXXX reports DTE or modem speed, and which of the following additional messages, if any, are reported: CARRIER, PRTOCOL, and COMPRESSION. Codes not enabled by the W command can be individually enabled by setting bits in S95. Neither Wn nor S95 affect the way in which the modem negotiates the connection.

Recall from Chapter 9 that the Xn command governs which result messages are output by the modem. If X0 is in effect, the settings Wn and S95 have no effect.

Function	Negotiation Progress Message
Command	Wn
	0 Connect XXXX reports DTE speed. If S95=0 disable extended messages.
	1 Connect XXXX reports DTE speed. If S95=0 enable CARRIER and PROTOCOL messages.
	2 Connect XXXX reports modem speed. If S95=0 disable extended messages.

Function	Negotiation Message Options
Command	S95
	0 (1) CONNECT XXXX message gives DTE speed instead of line speed
	1 (2) Append /ARQ to CONNECT message on protocol connections
	2 (4) Add CARRIER XXXX message
	3 (8) Add PROTOCOL message
	4 n/a
	5 (32) Add COMPRESSION message

Bit-mapped register S95 extends the Wn command, and providing a mechanism to select individual result codes associated with a protocol connection. The factory setting for this register is value O. To enable any combination of the bits, add the value(s) to the right of the bit number and set the register to this sum. For example, to enable the CARRIER, PROTOCOL, and COMPRESSION negotiation messages (assuming W1) select bit 2 (value of 4), bit 3 (value of 8), and bit 5 (value of 32) with the command ATS95=42.

The bits in S95 override some of the characteristics of the Wn command. Setting any of the S95 bits to "1" enables the corresponding result codes *regardless* of the Wn command in effect. However, changing the Wn command setting does not affect the bits in this register.

- W0 and S95=12 is the same as W1.

- W0 and S95=1 is the same as W2.

- S95 cannot be configured to force W2 to report DTE speed in the connect message.

- There is no setting of S95 that forces W1 to omit the CARRIER and PROTO-COL codes.

Table 10.4. Summary of Protocol Modem Commands.

PURPOSE	HAYES	ROCKWELL	USR	MICROCOM
Protocols	&Q	&Q or \N	&M	\N
Compression	S46	S46 or %C	&K	%C
Feature Negotiation	S48	S48	S27	-J
Negotiation Failure	S36	S36	&M	\N
Flow Control DTE/Modem	&K	&K	&H,&I,&R	\Q
Flow Control Modem/Modem		\G	&I	\G
DTE/Modem Speed control	&Q, S36	&Q, S36, or \J	&B	\J %U
Modulation	B	B	B, S27	B
Modulation Negotiation	N	N or F		%L
Line Speed	S37	S37	&N	%B %G
Basic Responses	Q, V, X	Q, V, X	Q, V, X	Q, V, X
Extended Responses	W, S95	W, S95	&A	\V, -M

Facsimile

The fax[1] machine is to modern telecommunications as the horse and buggy is to the supersonic fighter. Although its speeds have increased, the basic technology is essentially unchanged from the late seventies. It is old, it is slow, and it yields poor image quality. Why, then, is it one of the most popular non-entertainment electronic gadgets of all time? The answer is simple: it's easy to operate, and it works! When two-thirds of the VCRs in the world are said to be blinking 12:00, the fax machine offers old-fashioned, mode-less, one-button simplicity. In short, it presents itself as a machine instead of a computer.

The first international facsimile standard for communications across the PSTN[2], Recommendation T.2 for Group 1 facsimile, emerged from the CCITT in 1968. An American facsimile standard similar to T.2 already existed, but was just different enough to be incompatible with those in the rest of the world. A Group 1 fax machine, based on analog technology, requires about six minutes to transmit an A4 page (slightly longer and narrower than the US business letter) at a resolution of 98 lines per inch.

In 1976, the first truly international facsimile standard, T.3 for Group 2 fax was published. This time, US manufacturers—working through EIA TR.29— were the major contributors to the Group 2 standard. A Group 2 fax machine, based on analog technology, cut transmission time for a page about in half without sacrificing quality. Neither Group 1 nor Group 2 machines applied image compression.

Just as the Group 2 standard was completed, work began on Group 3. In 1980, the Group 3 standards were published. Based upon digital communications techniques (HDLC) and employing digital image compression, Group 3 provided

---

[1]Fax is often incorrectly written as FAX as if it were an acronym, which it is not. It is a neologized abbreviation for the word "facsimile."

[2]In CCITT documents it is the GSTN: *General Switched Telephone Network.*

significantly better quality and shorter transmission times than Group 2. Group 4, defined in 1984, was based upon a digital network, and was designed to provide higher resolutions, faster transmission, and more features. Because of the slower than expected growth of digital networks, Group 4 has languished in the shadow of the enormously popular Group 3 standard.

Facsimile is image transmission. Therefore, Group 3 comprises two standards: Recommendation T.30, which describes the communications protocol, and Recommendation T.4[3], which describes all aspects of the image. We will examine them in this order then take a look at the some related standards that pertain to modems and computers.

A block diagram of a typical fax machine is shown in Figure 11.1. Inside the scanner, a bright light is shined on the document. Hundreds of photosensitive cells in a very narrow line are then focused on the surface of the document. Simultaneously a snapshot is taken of the voltage output of each cell. An entire scan line is thus captured as an array of analog voltages. These voltages are then compared against a threshold voltage and declared to be either a 1 or 0. In this fashion each of the analog voltages is converted to digital *picture element (pel)*[4]. The pels are compressed, then handed to a high speed modem for transmission over the PSTN. On the other end of the phone line, the image is received by a modem of the same type, decompressed to the original pels, and sent to an output device whose printing elements are spaced similarly as the photoelectric elements in the scanner. In a computer fax device, the scanner and printer are usually replaced by a hard disk.

The Protocol: T.30

We've said that the point of fax is to transmit images of pages. We'll look at how these page images are constructed later, but for the time being let's just say that a *fax page* is bi-level (black-and-white) defined by the following *page metrics*: resolution (pel density), length, width, and compression.

The five-phase procedure for sending a page image is illustrated in the flow chart given in Figure 11.2. First, the two modems establish a telephone connection over the PSTN. Then they conduct an error-controlled T.30 "session"[5] by exchanging HDLC packets across a half-duplex 300 (optionally 2400) bps synchronous connection. In the initial part of the session, the modems agree upon acceptable parameters. The transmitter then sends a burst

---

[3]The EIA/TIA's versions of these are EIA/TIA 465 and 466. CCITT standards are revised every four years. Until 1992, T.30 and T.4 were published in the CCITT's volumes about facsimile: Volume VII, Fascicle VII.3 *Terminal Equipment and Protocols for Telematic Services.* Starting in 1992, the CCITT no longer publishes these volumes, instead publishing the individual standards.

[4]A pel is a bi-level dot; a pixel is a multi-level dot (e.g. color).

[5]Readers are cautioned that T.30 cannot be successfully shoehorned into the ISO Network model. In reality, T.30 is both a Session and a Data Link protocol.

of high-speed carrier to verify the quality of the phone line. The modems then switch up to a high speed to transfer the page image one page at a time, in half-duplex mode. At the end of each page, the modems return to the slower (usually 300 bps) session protocol to negotiate the next page, or, if necessary, to negotiate retransmission of the previous page. When there are no more pages to send, the modems disconnect.

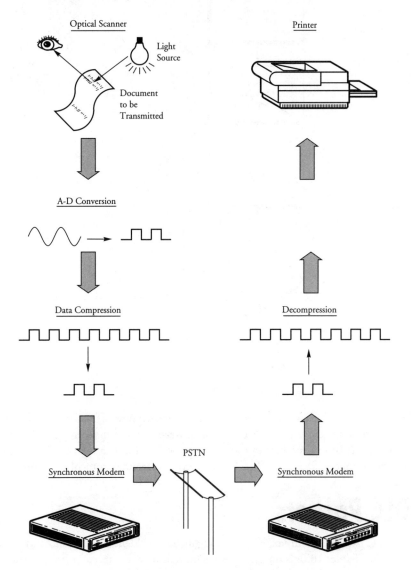

FIGURE 11.1.

Block diagram of a typical fax machine.

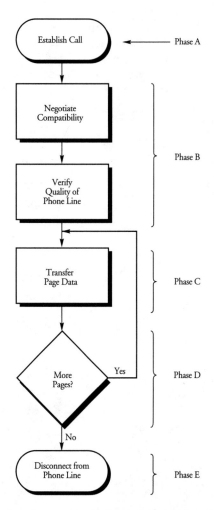

FIGURE 11.2.
The five "phases" of a T.30 session.

Before looking at each phase in more detail, first let's look at how HDLC packets are structured and how error correction is accomplished. Keep in mind that error correction applies only to the control packets in the T.30 protocol and not to the actual high-speed transfer of the image (Phase C). (The Phase C error-correcting protocol is optional.)

HDLC Packets

The HDLC packet used in fax, shown in Figure 11.3 is identical to the LAPM packet discussed in Chapter 10. It is transmitted synchronously with transparentized flag delimiters. The Address field is filled with 1s but not used. The Control field's only use is to indicate whether more packets are to come. (This assists the receiving fax in knowing when it may reverse the line and begin transmitting a response.[6]) Next follows the HDLC Information field, followed by the FCS, a 16-bit CRC.

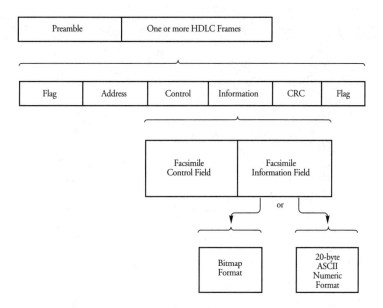

FIGURE 11.3.
A Facsimile HDLC frame.

Table 11.1. Meaning of the Facsimile Information Field (FIF) and tonal signals.

FCF	ID	Phase		Pidgin English Name	FIF Contents	Purpose
DIS	01	RX	B	Digital Id Signal	**Bitmap**	Answerer's capabilities bitmap
CSI	02	RX	B	Called Subscriber Id	**Numeric**	Answerer's phone number
NSF	04	RX	B	Non-Standard Facilities	**Bitmap**	Answerer's private capabilities bitmap
CFR	x21	RX	B	Confirmation to Recieve		G3training OK–Ready to receive
FTT	x22	RX	B	Failure to Train		G3training no good–try again
MCF	x31	RX	D	Message Confirmation		Page received OK
RTN	x32	RX	D	Retrain Negative		Page received with too many errors. Resend if possible.
RTP	x33	RX	D	Retrain Positive		Received the page acceptably, but let's G3retrain.

continues

---

[6]Don't confuse this field with the the HDLC packet's Control field.

Table 11.1. continued

DCS	x41	TX	B	Digital Command Signal	**Bitmap**	Caller's signal containing negotiated parameters
TSI	x42	TX	B	Transmitting Subscriber Id	**Numeric**	Caller's phone number.
SUB	x43	TX	B	Sub-Address	**Numeric**	A number indicating routing at the destination.
NSS	x44	RX	B	Non-Standard Set-Up	**Bitmap**	Caller's signal containing private negotiated parameters.
EOM	x71	TX	D	End of Message		Another page of different type follows.
MPS	x72	TX	D	Multi-Page Signal		Another page of same type follows.
EOP	x74	TX	D	End of Procedure		No more pages of any type follow. Procede to disconnect.
DTC	81	TX	B	Digital Transmit Command	**Bitmap**	Primary Polling Polling command: invites answerer to become transmitter. Information Field is same as DIS.
CIG	82	TX	B	Calling Subscriber Id	**Numeric**	When polling: caller's phone number or security code.
PWD	83	TX	B	Password	**Numeric**	When polling: an optional password.
NSC	84	TX	B	Non-Standard Facilities	**Bitmap**	When polling: caller's signal containing negotiated private parameters.
SEP	85	TX	B	Selective Polling	**Numeric**	When polling: specifies a document to send.
CRP	58	-		Command Repeat		Resend Packet.
DCN	5F	-		Disconnect		Hang up phone.
CED	-	A		Answer Tone		Approximately 3 seconds of a 2100 Hz tone issued by the answering fax modem shortly after going off-hook.
CNG		O		Calling Tone		Half-second beeps of 1100 Hz every three seconds. Alerts human answerer that a fax machine is calling.
TCF	-	T	Z	G3training Check		Not an HDLC packet, but 1.5 seconds of carrier at the selected speed.

Attention Readers of the CCITT T.30 Document!

Although Recommendations T.4 and T.30 are written in English, it is a perplexing English indeed. In a topic as complicated as facsimile, for example, the right choice of names and the use of acronyms can be wonderfully helpful. In fax, they're often useless. Take, for example, the names Digital Command Signal and Digital Identification Signal, arguably the two most important packets in T.30. In both cases, the words "Digital" and "Signal" are not helpful because *everything* in T.30 is a digital signal of some sort. Or take the quaint term used in T.30 for the page data: "Message," a word better applied to telegraphy, not facsimile. Although many other examples are possible, suffice it to say that a serious study of the CCITT T.30 document requires a desensitization to language, rote memorization of an unhelpful vocabulary, and an occasional emetic.

A Word About Nomenclature

The term *training* is used in the CCITT T.30 document for two entirely different procedures. The resulting confusion has confounded many a programmer. The first kind of training is the analog training explained in Chapter 10, which is a requirement of the modulation chosen in DCS. This training, which must be performed *every time* the modulation changes from the low-speed HDLC carrier to the higher-speed page carrier, is mandated by the technical specification for that modulation (V.29, for example), so there is no reason to mention it in T.30.

The second kind of "training" is a 1.5 second sample of the negotiated high-speed carrier. This signal is referred to in T.30 as TCF ("Training Check"). To avoid confusion over this issue, the analog training performed by the data pumps is not depicted in the flow charts in this book nor mentioned in the flow-chart narratives. TCF is described with the word *G3training* whose odd appearance suggests its true function.

Facsimile Fields

The length of the HDLC Information field varies, but always contains at least one byte, the *Facsimile Control Field* (FCF), which identifies the function of the packet. The packets of interest, their FCF numbers, their abbreviations, and their purpose is given in Table 11.1. (The *x*'s in front of some of the FCF numbers will be explained shortly.) Note that this list is not complete. For example, the frames necessary for optional error-correcting mode are not given.

Other packets also contain a variable-length *Facsimile Information Field* (FIF). This field contains data in one of only two formats: ASCII-numeric or bitmap. The heading

Contents of FIF in Table 11.1 indicates whether a particular packet has an FIF and, if so, its format.

THE NUMERIC FIF

The Numeric FIF consists of a 20-character string of the following characters: 0-9 (i.e., 30h-39h), and the characters + (2B) and Space (20h). These fields are optional and are primarily intended to hold phone numbers. However, during polling, the CIG, PWD, and SEP contain, respectively, a security code, a password, and the number of the desired document.

A numeric FIF is stored backwards both byte-wise and bit-wise. That is, the right-most digit is transmitted first, right to left. For example the ASCII string <35><2D><32> ("5+2")is transmitted <4C><B4><AC>.

Although the characters in the various "ID" packets are specified to contain only numerals, plus, and space, there is no mechanism to enforce this. In fact, many fax machines permit entry of any character for this packet. This explains the names, company name, or amusing messages often seen in the headers of received faxes.

THE BITMAP FIF

The primary bitmap FCFs—DIS and DCS[7]—are the key to understanding T.30. All Phase B negotiation between the fax machines is conducted by exchanging these two packets: the answering fax transmits a DIS packet containing a bitmap of all the T.30 and T.4 options it supports; the originating fax compares these options to its own capabilities and calculates the best feature match for conducting the session. The originating fax machine places these *session parameters* in a DCS packet and sends them back to the answering fax. Both machines now have copies of the parameters.

Before proceeding with a bit-by-bit explanation of the DIS/DCS bitmaps, it is worthwhile to develop a high-level view of a typical T.30 session. For the purposes of this narration, just remember that the fax machines exchange DIS and DCS to negotiate the following:

1. Species recognition: whether they both support Group 3 and they both are capable of sending and receiving.

2. Communications parameters: speed, modulation, zero-fill, etc.

3. Page metrics: compression, resolution, length, and width.

4. Optional features not covered in this chapter: error-correction, binary file transfer, character mode, and so forth.

---

[7] DTC is part of the seldom-used polling mechanism.

Synchronous Line Control

Because T.30 is a half-duplex protocol, the transmitter and the receiver have to reverse the line after each packet. Several line control rules keep the transmitter and receiver from getting hopelessly out of synchronization:

1. To aid the receiver in knowing when to reverse the line, bit 5 in the HDLC Control field is designated as the 'Final Packet' bit. If the transmitter has a single frame to send, it always sets bit 5 in its Control field to 1. If there is a group of packets to send, the 'Final Packet' bits are zeroed in all but the last one.

2. A minimum of one second of flags (referred to as the *preamble*) is required at the beginning of each packet.

3. If packets in a group are not contiguous, the transmitter sends flags during idle periods.

4. The maximum duration of any packet, not including the preamble, is 3 seconds.

5. For compatibility with future enhancements to T.30, packets with unrecognized FIF should be ignored.

6. All changes in modulation must be preceded with 75 ms (+ or - 20 ms) of silence.

Packet Groups

In most cases, a one-packet transmission elicits a one-packet response. Notice, however, the groups highlighted in Table 11.1. These are *packet groups* that may be sent in a single burst separated only by a single flag and sharing the same preamble. The 3-second limitation on packet duration is applied to each individual packet in the group, so the time required to transmit the group can be quite long; the five-frame DTC group, for example, could last up to 15 seconds. The first member of each group (DIS, DCS, DTC) is mandatory and must always be transmitted last, a rule not always followed in the real world.

Polling

Polling is the feature that allows an answering fax machine to send documents to the originator. Oddly, one has to read T.30 carefully to know that polling even exists and to read it *very* carefully to understand it. It is never mentioned by the name *polling* (nor by any other name, for that matter), and the packets used for polling are never explained. A good example of this obscurantism is the manner in which the originator discovers that the answerer "wants" to be polled (that is, has a document to send): by examining bit 9 in the answerer's DIS. This bit is humbly labeled 'Transmitter—T.4 operation' in CCITT documents. In fact, if this bit is one, it not only means that the answering device has a T.4 transmitter, but also that it has a document to send (be polled). In this chapter, bit 9 is referred to as the *polling bit*.

The X-Bit

The ambiguity between the originator/answerer roles and the roles of transmitter and receiver is resolved by the 'X-bit.' The X-bit[8] is the most significant bit of the FCF field. This is depicted in Table 11.1. The value of this bit is determined by cardinal events in the flow chart:

1. The X bit is set to one by the device that receives a valid DIS.
2. The X bit is set to zero by the device that receives a valid response to DIS. (Valid responses to DIS are: DTC, DCS, and DIS.)
3. The value of the X bit remains unchanged until the device reenters the beginning of Phase B (T or R on the flow charts in Figures 11.4 and 11.5).

The details of polling, including the use of the X-bit, are explained in a flow chart narrative later.

THE REQUEST-TO-POLL QUINTET

Notice from Table 11.1 that the request-to-poll command is actually a quintet of packets: DTC, CIG, PWD, NSC, and SEP. The DTC has exactly the same meaning as DIS. The purpose of CIG is to provide a security code for polling, although most implementations just duplicate the transmitter's phone number packet (CSI). The addition of the password packet (PWD) in 1992 adds another level of security as does the selective polling packet (SEL), which allows the transmitter to poll for specific documents.

Phases

As shown simply in Figure 11.2 and more throughly in the flow charts in Figures 11.4 and 11.5, transmision and reception of a facsimile is traditionally divided into five "Phases." We now undertake a detailed examination of each phase.

Phase A: Call Establishment

The call establishment phase consists of dialing and answering, although the details of neither is specified in T.30. Dialing may be accomplished either with an auto-dialer inside the fax unit itself or with an external telephone handset. Automatic answering is usually included in the fax machine.

---

[8]T.30 never mentions that the X-bit is a primary control mechanism in the simultaneous role reversal.

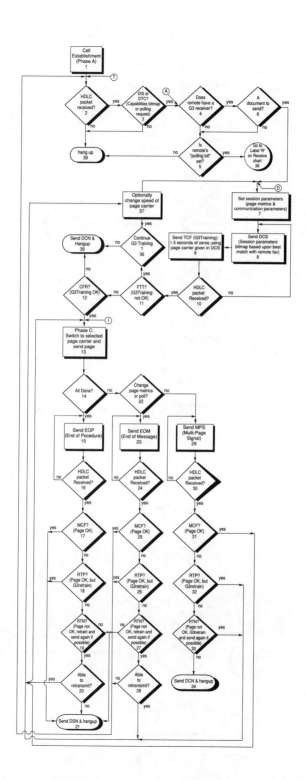

FIGURE 11.4.

The T.30 transmit flow chart.

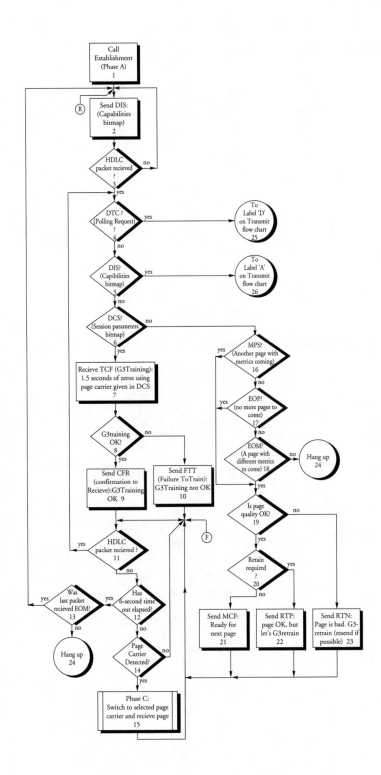

FIGURE 11.5.

The T.30 receive flow chart.

ORIGINATOR

After dialing has been accomplished, the transmitter enters a 30-40 second[9] loop listening for the distinctive fax answer tone or the preamble to an HDLC packet. If dialing was accomplished by an auto-dialer, the originating unit is *required* to emit a beeping tone known as *CNG,* a half-second burst of 1100 Hz tone every 3 seconds. The purpose of the CNG tone is to alert a human who answers the call that a fax machine is calling and to push the "start" button to receive a fax. CNG is optional when calls are originated by a human using a handset. Although CNG's original purpose was to alert human users that a fax machine is calling, it has lately been used to alert other machines (and the telephone network) that a fax is calling.

If no answer tone is heard, the originator disconnects the line after 30-40 seconds. If an answer tone or an HDLC packet is heard, however, call establishment is over, and Phase B begins.

ANSWERER

When a call is answered automatically, the fax unit takes the line off hook, waits about 2 seconds, then emits a 2100 Hz tone lasting from 2.6 to 4 seconds. This optional tone, referred to as *CED* initially identifies the answerer as a Group 3 fax machine and turns off the phone network's echo-suppressors. Alternatively, a human may answer the call. If another human has originated the fax call, the two humans synchronize the pushing of the start button on their fax machines. If, however, the characteristic beeps of CNG are audible, the answerer knows to push the start button immediately. Once the button is pushed, the machine emits CED as described above. In either case, Phase B begins.

Phase B: Identification and Negotiation

After call establishment, the two fax devices engage in an activity termed (for want of a better word) "negotiation." It works this way: the receiver sends a DIS packet containing its *capabilities bit-map,* preceded, optionally, by a CSI phone-number packet and an NSF packet containing the manufacturer's proprietary information.

The transmitter examines the DIS packet and compares the receiver's capabilities to its own. The transmitter calculates a set of parameters that provide the highest performance compatible with both machines' capabilities. These parameters are then transmitted to the receiver in a DCS packet, preceded optionally by the transmitter's own phone number in a TSI[10] packet and any manufacturer's proprietary setup information in NSS.

---

[9]This timer may be reset when the originating machine detects ringing at the remote end. If the originator is unable to detect remote ringing, a "reasonable amount" of additional time must be added for PSTN delays.

[10]The TSI identifier is now mandatory in machines sold in the United States.

If it is necessary to change parameters *during* the session, the transmitter may initiate a DIS/DCS renegotiation. For example, the transmitter may elect to renegotiate a lower speed if the receiver complains about page quality. Similarly, the ability to intermix pages of different resolutions or sizes requires renegotiation for each page.

With both fax machines now synchronized on the parameters for the session to follow, the transmitter sends a 1.5-second burst of zeros using the carrier specified in DCS. The official name of this signal is TCF, or "Training Check." For purposes of this book, we sometimes refer to it with the odd-looking term *G3training*. To understand why this term is necessary, refer to the box entitled "Attention Readers of the CCITT T.30 Documents" earlier in this chapter.

Using an unspecified algorithm, the receiver evaluates the G3training and sends a packet to accept or reject it. To accept the G3training, the receiver sends CFR (Confirmation to Receive), and both fax devices jump immediately to Phase C for page transfer. To reject the G3training, the receiver sends FTT (Failure to Train), in which case both fax devices reenter the DCS/TCF procedure. In most cases, FTT is a sign that the quality of phone line will not support the chosen speed, so the transmitter may elect to change the speed-selecting bits in the DCS. The DCS/TCF loop continues until the receiver sends CFR; if the receiver rejects G3training at the lowest supported speed, the transmitter has no recourse but to hang up.

Phase C: Data ("Message") Transmission

Phase C is governed by Recommendation T.4 (covered in detail elsewhere in this chapter), but is summarized here. Once the receiver accepts G3training, both devices are ready to transfer page data at the rate given in DCS. Immediately thereafter, the transmitter turns on its page carrier and begins to modulate it with page data. When all the data has been sent, the transmitter sends an in-band end-of-data sequence (Return to Control, RTC). It then turns off its high-speed carrier and proceeds to Phase D, the post-page phase.

The receiver accepts the page data and passes it along for decompression. When the receiver detects the end-of-data marker[11] it jumps to Phase D, the post-page phase.

Phase D: Post-Page Procedures

Immediately after shutting down its page-carrier, the transmitter sends one of three HLDC packets stating its intentions:

1. **EOP** (End of Procedure): no more pages follow.
2. **MPS** (Multi-Page Signal): another page with the same metrics follow.
3. **EOM** (End of Message): another page with different metrics follows (or that it intends to poll).

---

[11]Some devices don't look for RTC, but simply wait for the transmitter to turn off its carrier.

Now the transmitter waits for the receiver either to accept or reject the page just sent in Phase C.

Immediately after entering Phase D, the receiver receives one of the post-page HLDC packets listed above. Before acknowledging the transmitter's stated intentions, however, the receiver must first pass judgment on the quality of the page just received. It evaluates the page and replies with one of three evaluations:

1. **MCF** (Message confirmation): the page quality was acceptable—proceed.
2. **RTP** (Retrain Positive): the page quality was barely acceptable—another G3training is necessary.
3. **RTN** (Retrain Negative): the page quality was not acceptable—another G3training *and* retransmission are necessary.

If the receiver replies MCF, the flow chart proceeds according to the transmitter's stated intentions. If the receiver replies RTP or RTN, (that is, the page quality was not OK), a number of options are possible: resend G3training, return to Phase B for DCS and G3 training, or simply hang up. The possibilities are explained later in the flow chart narratives.

Phase E: Call Release

Call release is the process of disengaging from the line. If the session is at a rational place in the flow chart, it performs an *orderly* release: a DCN (Disconnect) packet is sent, followed by hanging up. If the session is in an irrational place in the flow chart—receiving an illegal response to a packet, for example—the transmitter *bails out* by simply hanging up the line.

Narratives of Sample Sessions

Mortals can learn only so much from an abstract discussion of T.30. The best learning tool is to walk through sample sessions step-by-step noting the events that take place at both fax devices. Each of the following narratives traces through a single kind of T.30 session—single-page, multi-page, and so forth—explaining what things are and why they happen. The sequential numbers in the "Step" column on the left are merely for reference; the other columns present the receiver and transmitter actions in parallel, and their numbers refer to the numbers in the flow chart in Figure 11.4 and 11.5.

Narrative: A Single Page

Table 11.2 is a narrative of the simplest session: faxing a single page with no complications. Because many subsequent narratives begin and end as this one does, it contains considerable detail.

Table 11.2. Flow-chart narrative of a single page.

STEP	Transmit Flow Chart References	Receive Flow Chart References
1	1. Call establishment (Phase A) takes place (refer to "Phase A: Call Establishment," above for details) and control passes to point T, the beginning of the negotiation and identification phase (Phase B).	1. Call establishment (Phase A) takes place (refer to "Phase A: Call Establishment," above for details) and control passes to point R, the beginning of the negotiation and identification phase (Phase B).
2	2. Originator listens for an HDLC packet. If none is received in about 40 seconds, it hangs up. In this example a packet is received.	2-3. Answerer alternately sends DIS (capabilities) packet and waits for an HDLC packet in reply. If no reply is received in about 40 seconds, it hangs up.
3	3. Originator first checks whether the packet is DIS or DTC. DIS is the "expected" capabilities bitmap packet from the answerer; DTC is a packet requesting a polling operation. In either case, optional phone number, security codes, and non-standard facilities packets might also be received. In this example, DIS is received and the originator sets its X bit to 1, designating it as the transmitter.	
4	4. Transmitter evaluates the bits in the remote's DIS and learns that its receiver is Group 3-compatible and that its poll-request bit is clear.	
5	5. In this example, the transmitter has a document to send. (Refer to the narrative "Single Page with Polling" below for a scenario where the originator doesn't have a document to send.)	

STEP	Transmit Flow Chart References	Receive Flow Chart References
6	6. Transmitter now examines the rest of the remote's capabilities, compares them to its own, and derives a group of parameters that provides the best performance.	
7	7. Transmitter now sends the DCS packet so that the receiver knows the parameters under which the session will be conducted.	6. At 3 an HDLC packet is received After checking it for polling request at 4 and 5, the receiver identifies it it as DCS containing page and session parameters. The answerer sets its X bit to 0, designating it as the receiver.
8	8. Immediately after DCS, the transmitter sends TCF— a burst of zero bits 1.5 seconds in length at the speed given in bits 11-14 of DCS.	7. Immediately after receiving DCS, the receiver receives TCF at the speed given in bits 11-14 of DCS.
9	10. Transmitter awaits an HDLC packet announcing the receiver's evaluation of TCF.	8-9. Receiver evaluates TCF according to unspecified criteria. In this example, TCF is acceptable and CFR (Confirmation to Receive) is sent.
10	12. CFR (Confirmation to Receive) is received, indicating that the receiver, based upon unspecified criteria, evaluated TCF and found the phone line to be suitable.	11-12-13-14. Receiver enters a loop with a 6-second time-out, alternately looking for an HDLC packet or high-speed page carrier.
11	13. The transmitter then turns on page carrier and transmits the page data.	14-15. Receiver detects high-speed page carrier at 14 and commences to receive page data at 15.
12	14. When the page data ends, the transmitter switches to low-speed modulation and immediately sends a post-page HDLC packet declaring its plans to send another next page. In this example there are no more pages, so it answers 'Yes' to the "All Done?" decision.	11-12-13-14. When receiver hears data and page carrier end, it enters a loop with a 6-second time-out, alternately looking for an HDLC packet or high-speed page carrier.

continues

Table 11.2. continued

STEP	Transmit Flow Chart References	Receive Flow Chart References
13	15. Transmitter sends EOP (End of Procedure) to inform the receiver that there are no more pages to come, effectively declaring an end to the current session.	11. Receiver detects an HDLC packet and evaluation of the packet number passes through 4, 5, 6, 16, and finally to 17 where it is recognized as EOP.
14	16. Transmitter awaits an HDLC packet announcing the receiver's acceptance of the page just sent.	19-20-21. Receiver evaluates the page, finds it acceptable. Retraining is deemed unnecessary at 20, and at 21 MCF (Message Confirmation) is sent.
15	17. MCF (Message Confirmation) is received, indicating that the receiver found the page acceptable.	11-12-13-14. Receiver enters a loop with a 6-second time-out, alternately looking for an HDLC packet or high-speed page carrier.
16	21. The session terminates with the transmission of DCN (Disconnect), and the phone line is hung up.	11. Receiver detects an HDLC packet and evaluation of the packet number passes through 4, 5, 6, 16, 17, and 18. The packet is unrecognized at 17, and the line is hung up at 24.

Narrative: Multiple Pages with Same Metrics

Table 11.3 is a narrative of sending several pages with identical metrics.

Table 11.3. Flow chart narrative of multiple pages with the same metrics.

STEP	Transmit Flow Chart References	Receive Flow Chart References
1-11	These steps are identical to the "Single Page Narrative" in Table 11.2.	
12	14. When the page data ends, and the transmitter switches to low-speed modulation and immediately sends a post-page HDLC packet declaring its plans for the next page. In this example there is a next page, so it answers 'No' to the "All Done?" decision.	11-12-13-14. When receiver hears data and page carrier end, it enters a loop with a 6-second time-out, alternately looking for an HDLC packet or high-speed page carrier.

STEP	Transmit Flow Chart References	Receive Flow Chart References
13	22. The transmitter determines that the next page has the same metrics as the previous page.	
14	29. The transmitter sends MPS (Multi Page Signal) to inform the receiver that an identical page will follow.	11. The receiver detects an HDLC packet and evaluation of the packet number passes through 4, 5, 6, and finally to 16 where it is recognized as MPS.
15	30. The transmitter awaits an HDLC packet announcing the receiver's acceptance of the page just sent.	19-20-21. The receiver evaluates the page, finds it acceptable. Retraining is deemed unnecessary at 20, and at 21 MCF (Message Confirmation) is sent.
16	31. MCF (Message Confirmation) is received, indicating that the receiver found the page acceptable, and control returns to 13.	11-12-13-14. Receiver enters a loop with a 6-second time-out, alternately looking for an HDLC packet or high-speed page carrier. high-speed page carrier is detected at 14 and control returns to 15.
17	After all the pages have been sent, the "All Done?" decision at 14 branches in the 'Yes' direction, and remainder of the session follows steps 12-16 in the "Single Page Narrative" in Table 11.2.	When the last page is received, an EOP instead of an MPS is received and remainder of the session follows steps 12-16 in the "Single Page Narrative" in Table 11.2.

Narrative: Multiple Pages with Different Metrics

Table 11.4 is a narrative of sending several pages with different metrics.

Table 11.4. Multiple pages with different metrics.

STEP	Transmit Flow Chart References	Receive Flow Chart References
1-11	These steps are identical to the "Multiple Pages with Same Metrics" narrative in Table 11.3.	

continues

Table 11.4. continued

STEP	Transmit Flow Chart References	Receive Flow Chart References
12	14. When the page data ends, the transmitter switches to low-speed modulation and immediately sends a post-page HDLC packet declaring its plans to send another page. In this example there are more pages, so it answers 'No' to the "All Done?" decision.	11-12-13-14. Receiver enters a loop with a 6-second time-out, alternately looking for an HDLC packet or high-speed page carrier.
13	22. The transmitter determines that the next page is different from the previous page (longer, for example).	
14	23. The transmitter sends EOM (End of Message), informing the receiver that it will be necessary to renegotiate the metrics of the new page.	11. Receiver detects an HDLC packet and evaluation of the packet number passes through 4, 5, 6, 16, and finally to 18 where it is recognized as EOM.
15	24. The transmitter awaits an HDLC packet announcing the receiver's acceptance of the page just sent.	19-20-21. Receiver evaluates the page, finds it acceptable. Retraining is deemed unnecessary at 20, and at 21 MCF (Message Confirmation) is sent.
16	25. MCF (Message Confirmation) is received, indicating that the receiver found the page acceptable. Control returns to point T.	11-12-13-14. When receiver hears data and page carrier end, it enters a loop with a 6-second time-out, alternately looking for an HDLC packet or high-speed page carrier.
17	2. Transmitter waits at the beginning of Phase B, listening for DIS.	12. The 6-second timer expires, passing control to 13. EOM was the last packet received (step 18), so receiver returns to point R and begins sending DIS.
18	After all the pages have been sent, the "All Done?" decision at 14 branches in the 'Yes' direction, and remainder of the session follows steps 12-16 in the "Single Page Narrative" in Table 11.2.	When the last page is received, an EOP instead of an MPS is received and remainder of the session follows steps 12-16 in the "Single Page Narrative" in Table 11.2.

Narrative: Single Page with Polling

Table 11.5 is a narrative of a single page followed by polling. Once the originator ascertains that the answerer has a document to send (that is, its polling bit is set), it first sends its own documents, then leaps to the beginning of Phase B of the receiver flow chart; simultaneously, the answerer leaps to the beginning of Phase B of the transmitter flow chart.

You may have already noticed that a distinction is maintained between the originator/answerer and the transmitter/receiver. For reasons that shall be apparent in a moment, this narrative retains the terms "originator" and "answerer" throughout.

Table 11.5. Flow chart narrative of a single page with polling.

STEP	Transmit Flow Chart References	Receive Flow Chart References
1-3	These steps are identical to those of the "Single Page Narrative" in Table 11.2.	
4	4. The originator evaluates the bits in the remote's DIS and learns that the answerer is Group 3-compatible and its poll-request bit is set.	
5-13	These steps are identical to those of the "Single Page Narrative" in Table 11.2.	
14	14. The originator answers 'No' to the "All Done?" decision because the answerer's poll-request bit *was* set in 4.	
15	22. Because the answerer's poll-request bit is set, the answer to the "Change page metrics or poll?" decision is 'Yes.'	
16	23. The originator sends EOM (End of Message), informing the answerer that it will be necessary to reenter Phase B to renegotiate.	11. Answerer detects an HDLC packet and evaluation of the packet number passes through 4, 5, 6, 16, and finally to 18 where it is recognized as EOM.

continues

Table 11.5. continued

STEP	Transmit Flow Chart References	Receive Flow Chart References
17	24. The originator awaits an HDLC packet announcing the answerer's acceptance of the page just sent.	19-20-21. Answerer evaluates the page, finds it acceptable. Retraining is deemed unnecessary at 20, and at 21 MCF (Message Confirmation) is sent.
18	25. MCF (Message Confirmation) is received, indicating that the answerer, found the page acceptable. Control returns to point T.	11-12-13-14. The answerer enters a loop with a 6-second time-out, alternately looking for an HDLC packet or high-speed page carrier.
19	2. Originator listens for HDLC packet. If none is received in T1 seconds, the originator hangs up the line.	12. The 6-second timer expires at 12, passing control to 13. EOM was the last packet received (step 18), so answerer returns to point R and begins sending DIS.
20	3. DIS is received and the originator sets its X bit to 1.	2-3. Answerer alternately sends DIS (capabilities) packet and waits for an HDLC packet in reply.
21	4. Originator evaluates the bits in the remote's DIS and learns that the answerer is Group 3-compatible and that its poll-request bit is *set*.	
22	6. In this example, the originator has no document to send, so the 'No' branch is taken.	
23	5. The answerer's poll-request bit is set, so the 'Yes' branch is taken.	
24	38. The originator now jumps to point R, the beginning of Phase B in the receive flow chart. *At this point both originator and answerer are receivers. This is where the X-bit comes into play.*	

STEP	Transmit Flow Chart References	Receive Flow Chart References
25	2 (on receive chart). Because the originator's X-bit is one, it sends DTC instead of DIS.	7 (on receive chart). Answerer receives DTC, control passes to 25 and answerer now jumps to point D in the transmit flow chart and sends DCS.
26	The remainder of the session follows the "Single Page Narrative" in Table 11.2.	The remainder of the session follows the "Single Page Narrative" in Table 11.2.

Narrative: Speed Step-Down During G3training

Regardless of the number of pages or their metrics, whenever G3training occurs (9 on the Transmit, 7 on the Receive the flow charts) the transmitter is liable to end up with an FTT at 11—that is, the receiver rejected the TCF. This causes control to pass through decision 36, which decides whether to continue G3training; if 'Yes,' control then passes through 37 where the speed-selecting bits in DCS can be changed.

Although repeated failure of the receiver to train is clearly grounds for stepping down the carrier speed, T.30 leaves the decision entirely to the implementers. Industry practices vary, but most machines exercise the option to reduce the speed of the page carrier at 37 after two consecutive FTTs. At some speeds, it is likely that CFR will be received at 12 and that page transfer will proceed. In cases of horrible line conditions, however, the transmitter may eventually step down to and fail at the lowest speed available. At this point, the transmitter exercises its 'No' option at 36, sends DCN, and hangs up.

Single Page, Page Rejected

Table 11.6 is a narrative of sending a single page, followed by a rejection of that page by the receiver.

Table 11.6. Flow chart narrative of single page with page rejected.

STEP	Transmit Flow Chart References	Receive Flow Chart References
1-12	These steps are identical to those of the "Single Page Narrative" in Table 11.2.	
13	16. Transmitter awaits an HDLC packet announcing the receiver's acceptance of the page just sent.	19-20-21. Receiver evaluates the page, finds it unacceptable. Receiver sends RTN (Retrain Negative) to ask for both retraining *and* retransmission.

continues

Table 11.6. continued

STEP	Transmit Flow Chart References	Receive Flow Chart References
14	19. RTN (Group 3 Retrain Negative) is received, indicating that the receiver finds the page unacceptable. *The direction of the next branch is based upon the transmitter's ability to resend the page just rejected by the receiver. Most conventional fax machines neither store an entire page in memory nor have the means of re-inserting a page in the scanner. The devices behave like this:*	
15	20. The page is unavailable for resending so the 'No' branch of the "Able to Retransmit" decision is taken.	
16	21. Transmitter sends DCN and hangs up line.	11. Receiver detects an HDLC packet and evaluation of the packet number passes through 4, 5, 6, 16, 17, and 18. The packet is unrecognized at 18, and the line is hung up at 24.
	If the device is able to retransmit— as are sophisticated fax machines and computer-based devices—it behaves like this:	
17	20. The page is available for resending so the "Yes" branch of the "Able to Retransmit" decision is taken.	
18	37-7. Control passes through 37 to 7 at point D where transmitter sends DCS and G3training. *The remainder of the narrative follows steps 8-16 of the* "Single Page Narrative" *in Table 11.2.*	11. Receiver detects an HDLC packet and evaluation of the packet number passes through 4, 5, and is recognized as DCS at 6

Note that in the case of retransmission, control passes through 37, a route that technically entitles the transmitter to reduce the speed of carrier. Most fax devices, however, do not change the speed at this point but rely on the receiver's subsequent response to TCF at 10. (Refer to the narrative "Speed Step-Down During G3training.") This sets up the potential for mischief. Occasionally fax machines are marketed that produce compression or decompression errors, usually on obscure data patterns. When such an error is triggered, an endless loop occurs: the page is repeatedly rejected with RTN or RTP because of the errors, yet the receiver always accepts the subsequent G3training. Because T.30 does not provide an escape from this loop, most machines monitor consecutive page failures and disconnect when the number seems excessive.

Narrative: Speed Step-Up During G3training

The "Speed Step-Down During G3training" narrative explains how page rejection (at 19, 27, and 33) can lead to a reduction in the speed of the page carrier. Suppose that *on the first page* of a long document an ephemeral line condition line results in a speed reduction from 14,400 bps to 4,800 bps. The transmission is stuck at 4,800 bps even though the line impairment no longer exists. Unfortunately, T.30 provides a mechanism to step-down the speed of a page carrier, but not one for stepping the speed back up.

This deficiency can be circumvented by a bit of legerdemain if the transmitter keeps track of when it is operating at a speed lower than the speed reported in the receiver's DIS. When one or more pages have been successfully transmitted at the lower speed, the transmitter answers 'Yes' at decision point 22 instead of 'No.' This forces an EOM at 29, then control passes to 37 where the speed-selecting bits in DCS can be changed to a *higher* value. The receiver, of course, is oblivious (or at least indifferent) to the fact that there is no difference between this page and the previous one. As the cost of each EOM is high (a minimum of about 10 seconds), this technique should be used sparingly.

The DIS/DCS Bitmaps

The next topic falls into the "chicken or egg" category. It would very easy for you to understand the meaning of the bits in DIS/DCS if you first had a working knowledge of the next topic, Recommendation T.4. Unfortunately, Recommendation T.4 is hopelessly opaque without at least a preview of the bits in DIS/DCS. It is probably a good idea then to read both sections superficially, then return here and begin again for a more concentrated reading.

The DIS and DCS capabilities bitmaps, shown in Table 11.7, are the heart of T.30. It is important to note that CCITT bit numbering begins with one, not zero. Before examining these packets bit-by-bit, it is worth making some general observations about them.

Backward Compatibility and Extendibility

Any popular standard faces a dilemma: how to add the features needed to grow with the times, yet simultaneously maintain compatibility with all past incarnations of the standard? In Group 3 fax, the mechanism is the *extension bit.*

Note in Table 11.7 that, beginning with bit 24, every eighth bit is labeled "Extend bit (1 = more to come)." A one in this field indicates that there are at least eight more valid bits in the information packet. This method, which we saw earlier in the Kermit protocol in Chapter 4, simultaneously provides backward compatibility and infinite extendibility, limited only by T.30's 3-second limitation on packets.

To see how this works, suppose you built a fax device based upon the 1980 specification, whose DIS/DCS field was only 24 bits long. At that time, the DIS extension bit (bit 24) would be zero for all machines, including yours. Although your machine would be designed to receive a DIS of any legal length, it need never read beyond this bit. Conversely, machines that received your machine's DIS would know immediately that it was from a previous revision of T.30 and which bits were valid.

In 1984, eight new bits were added, and bit 32 became the current extension bit. In 1988, eight more were added, with bit 40 as the extension bit. In 1992, a whopping 32 new bits were added, and bit 72 became the extension bit.

New FCFs

Although T.30 warns that packets with unrecognized FCF (packet id's) should be ignored, widespread failure to heed this stricture caused mischief when three new FCCs were added in the 1992 revision (SEL, SUB, and SEL). Apparently some manufacturers had designed their machines to terminate a session in which an unknown FCF was received. Rather than cause incompatibilities with the installed base, T.30-92 added three bits (47, 49, and 50) to the DIS to indicate explicitly the ability to receive these new frames.

Minimum Capabilities

In order to establish a baseline of functionality and to assume interoperability among all Group 3 machines, T.30 specifies a set of minimum capabilities that every machine must possess:

1. "Standard" resolution (98 pels per inch).
2. One-dimensional encoding.
3. The ability to process A4 pages.
4. Support for all zero-fill specifications.
5. Support for V.27ter (4800 bps).

A machine may elect to support sending, receiving, or both.

Table 11.7. The DIS/DCS bitmap.
Note that the bit numbers start with one.

BIT	DCS	DIS
1	T.2 transmitter	
2	T.2 Receiver	T.2 Receiver
3	T.2 IOC=176	T.2 IOC = 176
4	T.3 Transmitter	Poll request
5	T.3 Receiver	T.3 Receiver
6	Reserved for T.3	
7	Reserved for T.3	
8	Reserved for T.3	
9	T.4 Transmitter	Poll request
10	T.4 Receiver	T.4 Receiver
11-14	Phase C Signaling Rate	
0,0,0,0	V.27ter fallback (2400)	2400 bps V.27ter
0,0,0,1	Not used	14400 bps V.17
0,0,1,0	Not used	14400 bps V.33
0,0,1,1	Not used	Reserved
0,1,0,0	V.27ter (4800)	4800 bps V.27ter
0,1,0,1	Reserved	12000 bps V.17
0,1,1,0	Reserved	12000 bps V.33
0,1,1,1	Reserved	Reserved
1,0,0,0	V.29	9600 bps V.29
1,0,0,1	Not used	9600 bps V.17
1,0,1,0	Not used	Reserved
1,0,1,1	Not used	Reserved
1,1,0,0	V.27ter and V.29	7200 bps V.29
1,1,0,1	V.27ter, V.29, V.33, V.17	7200 bps V.17
1,1,1,0	V.27ter, V.29, V.33	Reserved
1,1,1,1	Reserved	Reserved
15	Vertical resolution (Vres) 0: Vres = 98 pels/inch 1: Vres = 196 pels/inch (Related to bits 41-45: see Table 11.15)	0: Vres = 98 pels/inch 1: Vres = 196 pels/inch Related to bits 41-45.

continues

Table 11.7. continued

BIT	DCS	DIS
16	Encoding (compression) 0 = 1-dimensional 1 = 2-dimensional	0 = 1-dimensional 1 = 2-dimensional
17,18	Paper widths supported	
0,0	1728 over 215 mm (A4 page)	1728 over 215 mm (A4 page)
0,1	1728 over 215 mm (A4 page) 2048 over 255 mm (B4 page) 2432 over 303 mm (A3 page)	2432 over 303 mm (A3 page)
1,0	1728 over 215 mm (A4 page) 2048 over 255 mm (B4 page)	2048 over 255 mm (B4 page)
1,1	invalid (treat as 0,1)	
19,20	Paper lengths supported	
0,0	A4 (297 mm)	A4 (297 mm)
0,1	Unlimited	Unlimited
1,0	A4 (297mm) and B4 (364mm)	B4 (364 mm)
1,1	invalid	
21-23	Time required to print one scan line	
0,0,0	20 ms at Vres = 98 or 196 ppi	20 msec
0,0,1	40 ms at Vres = 98 or 196 ppi	40 msec
0,1,0	10 ms at Vres = 98 or 196 ppi	10 msec
1,0,0	5 ms at Vres = 98 or 196 ppi	5 msec
1,0,1	40 ms at Vres = 98 or 196 ppi 0 ms at Vres = 196 ppi	
1,1,0	20 ms at Vres = 98 ppi 10 ms at Vres = 196 ppi	
1,1,1	0 ms	
24	Extend bit (1 = more to come)	Extend bit (1 = more to come)
25	2400 bps HDLC signaling	2400 bps HDLC signaling
26	Uncompressed mode	Uncompressed mode
27	Error correction mode	Error correction mode
28	(ECM packet size—sender decides. Set to 0 for DIS)	0 = packet size 256 bytes 1 = packet size 64 bytes
29	Error Limiting Mode	Error Limiting Mode
30	Reserved for G4 capabilities	Reserved for G4 capabilities

BIT	DCS	DIS
31	T.6 compression (requires error correcting mode)	T.6 compression (requires error correcting mode)
32	Extend bit (1 = more to come)	Extend bit (1 = more to come)
33	Bits 17 & 18 Valid? 0 = valid 1 = invalid A5/A6 paper sizes	Not used
34	1216 pels over 151 mm	Middle 1216 out of 1728 pels
35	864 pels over 107 mm	Middle 864 out of 1728 pels
36	1728 pels over 151 mm	
37	1728 pels over 107 mm	
38	Reserved	
39	Reserved	
40	Extend bit (1 = more to come)	Extend bit (1 = more to come)
41	4 x 4 resolution (millimeters)	4 x 4 resolution (millimeters)
42	3 x 3 resolution (inches)	3 x 3 resolution (inches)
43	4 x 4 resolution (millimeters or inches)	4 x 4 resolution (millimeters or inches)
44	Inch-based resolutions preferred	0 = millimeters 1 = inches
45	Millimeters-based resolutions preferred	Not used
46	Print time for one line when Vres > 2 0 = Same as Vres = 98 ppi 1 = Half of Vres = 196 ppi	Not used
47	Supports SEP (selective polling) packet	Set to zero
48	Extend bit (1 = more to come)	Extend bit (1 = more to come)
49	Supports the SUB (subaddress) packet	Set to zero
50	Supports the PWD (password) packet	Set to zero
51	Capability to send non-fax file	Not used
52	Facsimile service info file	Reserved
53	Binary File Transfer	Binary File Transfer

continues

Table 11.7. continued

BIT	DCS	DIS
54	Document Transfer Mode (DTM)	Document Transfer Mode (DTM)
55	Electronic Data Transfer (EDI)	Electronic Data Transfer (EDI)
56	Extend bit (1 = more to come)	Extend bit (1 = more to come)
57	Basic transfer mode (BTM)	Basic transfer mode (BTM)
58	Reserved for future file transfer modes	Reserved for future file transfer modes
59	Able to send in character mode	Send in character mode
60	Character Mode	Character Mode
61	Reserved	Reserved
62	Reserved for mixed mode (requires ECM bit 27)	Reserved for mixed mode (requires ECM bit 27)
63	Reserved	Reserved
64	Extend bit (1 = more to come)	Extend bit (1 = more to come)
65	Processable Mode 26	Processable Mode 26
66	Reserved	Reserved
67	Reserved	Reserved
68	Reserved	Reserved
69	Reserved	Reserved
70	Reserved	Reserved
71	Reserved	Reserved
72	Extend bit (0 = no more to come)	Extend bit (0 = no more to come)

DIS/DCS Bit-by-Bit

1-8   Not for Group 3 Fax

9   **T.4 Transmitter** In DIS: the receiver has a Group 3 compatible transmitter. Although not documented in T.30, this means that the receiver wishes to be polled. It is referred to in the narratives as the *polling bit*. In DCS: no meaning.

10   **T.4 Receiver** In DIS: the receiver has a Group 3 compatible receiver and therefore can receive documents. In DCS: Current session shall be Group 3.

11-14 **Phase C Signaling Rate** In DIS: the speeds at which the receiving modem is able to signal. Notice that 4800 bps is under V.27ter, not V.29. Also note that there is no way for the receiver to specify 9600 bps only. In DCS: indicates the speed at which the page(s) that follows will be transmitted, usually the highest speed supported by both devices.

15 **Vertical Resolution** In DIS: a zero in this bit indicates the ability to receive faxes at 98 lines per inch; a one bit indicates 196 lines per inch. In DCS: the resolution for the page(s) that follow. The meaning of this bit is conditioned by bits 44 and 45. See Table 11.10 for details.

16 **Compression** In DIS: a zero in this bit indicates that the receiver supports one-dimensional encoding; a one bit indicates the ability to do two-dimensional. In DCS: the encoding of the pages that follow. (See also bit 31.)

17,18 **Paper Widths** In DIS: the page-widths supported by the receiver. In DCS: the width of the pages that follow.

19,20 **Paper Lengths** In DIS: the page-lengths supported by the receiver. In DCS: the length of the pages that follow. "Unlimited" is for machines with roll paper and computerized fax devices.

21-23 **Minimum Scan Line Time** In DIS: the receiver indicates the minimum tolerable duration of a scan line (this is essentially the speed of the receiver's printer). The transmitter is responsible for "stretching" (zero-filling) each line to this value. In DCS: the scan time for the pages that follow; any values equal to or larger than the value in DIS is acceptable. A scan time of zero is usually returned by computerized fax devices. (See "The Page" later in this chapter for details.)

24 **Extend bit** At least 8 more valid bits follow.

25 **2400 bps HDLC signaling** In DIS: the receiver is able to send T.30 protocol packets at 2400 bps (V.27ter fallback). In DCS: the T.30 protocol shall be conducted at 2400 bps. Note that the initial DIS/DCS exchange must take place at 300 bps.

26 **Uncompressed mode** This bit is irrelevant unless bit 16 also indicates two-dimensional encoding capability. In DIS: the receiver is capable of the uncompressed option to two-dimensional encoding. In DCS: indicates two-dimensional encoding in the pages that follow.

27 **Error-Correcting Mode (ECM)** In DIS: the receiver supports the error-correcting protocol during data transfer (Phase C). In DCS: page transfers that follow shall use the error-correcting protocol. (Also see bits 28 and 31.)

28   **ECM packet size** This bit is irrelevant unless bit 27 indicates error-correcting mode. In DIS: this bit is set to 0—the transmitter is responsible for selecting the number of bytes in the ECM packet. In DCS: the packet size in the Phase C ECM packets that follow. Note that this value is not "negotiated" in the same sense as other capabilities because the transmitter unilaterally selects the parameter. In other words, all fax devices that support error-correcting mode must be capable of both packet sizes.

29   **Error Limiting Mode** In DIS: the receiver is capable of using the optional T.4 error-limiting encoding. (Refer to "Facsimile Encoding," elsewhere in this chapter for details.) In DCS: T.4 error-limiting encoding shall be used on the pages that follow.

30   **Reserved for G4 capabilities on PSTN** The functionality represented by this bit is currently undefined. It should be set to zero in DIS and ignored in DCS.

31   **T.6 compression** This is irrelevant unless bit 27 also indicates error-correcting mode. In DIS: the receiver is capable of using the Modified-Modified READ encoding associated with Group 4 facsimile (Recommendation T.6).

32   **Extend bit** At least 8 more valid bits follow.

33   **Bits 17,18 Valid** Bits 34-37 support note-size pages approximately 6 x 8 inches (A5: 148x210mm) and 4 x 6 inches (A6: 105x148mm). Machines that support these sizes need not support the full-size page widths defined in bits 17 and 18. In DIS: a one in bit 33 means that the receiver is capable of receiving one or more standard sizes; a zero indicates support for the widths given in pixels 34-37. In DCS: which group of page width bits is valid.

34-37 **A5/A6 page widths** In DIS: which of the page widths and densities are supported by the receiver. Note that the two 1728-pel widths essentially expect full A-4 sized pages. In DCS: the width of the page being sent.

38   **Reserved**

39   **Reserved**

40   **Extend bit** At least 8 more valid bits follow.

41   **2 x 4 resolution (millimeters)** In DIS: the receiver is capable of receiving pages at the metric equivalent of 2 x 4 resolution (see Table 11.9). In DCS: the pages that follow shall be at this resolution. This resolution is not available in inch-based measurements.

42 **3 x 3 resolution (inches)** In DIS: the receiver is capable of receiving pages at 3 x 3 resolution (see Table 11.9). Note that there is no metric equivalent to this resolution. In DCS: the pages that follow shall be at this resolution. This resolution is not available in millimeter-based measurements.

43 **4 x 4 resolution (millimeters or inches)** In DIS: the receiver is capable of receiving pages *either* of 4 x 4 resolution or their metric equivalent (see Table 11.9). The meaning of this bit is given in Table 11.11. In DCS: the pages that follow shall be at this resolution.

44 **Inch-based resolutions preferred** In DIS: the receiver prefers documents in "square" sizes and proportions. The influence of this bit is given in Table 11.11. In DCS: 0 = millimeters, 1 = inches.

45 **Millimeter-based resolutions preferred** In DIS: the receiver prefers documents in metric sizes and proportions. The influence of this bit is given in Table 11.11. In DCS: no meaning.

46 **Minimum Scan Line at higher resolutions** In DIS: whether the receiver's scan line time should be cut in half on higher resolution pages. In DCS: no meaning.

47 **Selective Polling** See "New FCFs," elsewhere in this chapter. In DIS: the receiver is prepared to handle a SUB packet. In DCS: set to zero.

48 **Extend bit** At least 8 more valid bits follow.

49 **Subaddressing capability** See "New FCFs," elsewhere in this chapter. In DIS: the receiver prepared to handle the SUB packet. In DCS: set to zero.

50 **Password capability** See "New FCFs," elsewhere in this chapter. In DIS: the receiver is prepared to handle the PWD packet. In DCS: set to zero.

The remainder of the bits select facilities, some of them still in progress or incompletely defined, that depend upon error-correcting mode. Although they are listed here for completeness, their explanations are beyond the scope of this book.

51 **Capability to send non-fax file** In DIS: the receiver supports the transfer of non-facsimile messages or documents using one or more of the procedures named in bits 51-65. All such procedures are irrelevant unless bit 27 (error-correcting mode) is one.

52 **Facsimile service info file**

53 **Binary File Transfer (BFT)** This bit is irrelevant unless bit 27 (error-correcting mode) and 51 are one. In DIS: the ability to transfer binary files encoded according to T.434 (or TIA/EIA-614). In DCS: BFT shall be used on the following file(s).

54   **Document Transfer Mode (DTM)**

55   **Electronic Data Transfer (EDI)**

56   **Extend bit** At least 8 more valid bits follow.

57   **Basic transfer mode (BTM)**

58   **Reserved for future file transfer modes**

59   **Capability to send character mode** In DIS: the receiver is capable of sending and receiving a character-mode file as in bits 60 and 61. In DCS: set to zero.

60   **Character Mode** Character mode uses the T.30 protocol to transfer ordinary character-based data (as defined in T.30-1992 Annex D). In DIS: the receiver is capable of sending and receiving a character-mode file. In DCS: character mode shall be used on the following document(s).

61   **Reserved**

62   **Mixed character/fax mode** Character mode uses the T.30 protocol to transfer ordinary character-based data (as defined in T.30-1992 Annex E). "Mixed" mode is a procedure for intermixing characters and ordinary fax image data. In DIS: the receiver is capable of sending and receiving a mixed mode file. In DCS: mixed mode shall be used on the following document(s).

63   **Reserved**

64   **Extend bit** At least 8 more valid bits follow.

65   **Processable Mode 26 (T.505)**

The Image: T.4

Recommendation T.4 contains the dimensional and coding specifications for Phase C data in Recommendation T.30. In particular, it specifies:

1. The dimensions of documents.
2. The scanner/printer resolutions.
3. The encoding algorithms for data compression.
4. The in-band line-synchronization sequence, EOL (End-of-Line).
5. The Phase C in-band escape sequence, RTC (Return to Control).
6. How fill bits are added to accommodate slow output devices.

The Group 3 image is a raster—an array of horizontal parallel scan lines. On the assumption complexity is easier to understand from an evolutionary point of view, we will look at 1988 T.4, then explain the T.4 of 1992 (the year things got complicated)[12].

Resolution

Horizontal resolution measures the pel density along the length of a scan line. Vertical resolution is usually expressed in lines per unit measure.

As shown in Table 11.8, before 1988 T.4 specified only a single horizontal resolution and two vertical resolutions. The two vertical resolutions, which differ by a factor of two, are the familiar user-selectable "low" and "high" resolutions on fax machines (the terms "normal" and "fine" are also commonly used). The vertical resolution was represented by a single bit, bit 15, in DIS/DCS.

Table 11.8. Pre-1992 facsimile resolutions.

Dimension	Millimeter	Inch
Horizontal	8.04 pels/mm	204 pels/inch
Vertical ("Low")	3.85 lines/mm	98 lines/inch
Vertical ("High")	7.70 lines/mm	196 lines/inch

All dimensions and specifications were given in millimeters. Engineers, especially American engineers, found the 1988 specification to be frustrating for three reasons.

First, American engineers were annoyed that the resolutions aren't "square"—that is, the horizontal resolution is different from the vertical, so they don't fit well with modern technologies such as laser engines, which are capable only of square resolutions.

Second, American engineers complained that the equivalent absolute values—98, 196, and 204—were an awkward fit with English/American input and output devices, which tend to be even multiples of 100. When the closest American equivalents were used—200 x 100 and 200 x 200—at either the scanner or printer device, the image is distorted by a factor of two to four percent. Although high accuracy is not necessary in consumer-grade fax products, lack of it can be fatal in specialized applications where *absolute end-to-end registration* is required.[13] In short, T.4 needed to support inch-based resolutions.

---

[12]Recall from the earlier discussion that the 1984 G3 had only 32 bits in the DIS/DCS packet. This increased to only 40 in 1988, then to 72 in 1992.

[13]This fancy term means that an object that measures one inch at the transmitter must measure exactly one inch when printed at the receiver. Architects, petroleum engineers, doctors, geologists, artists, and scores of other professions have this requirement.

Third, improved imaging technology increases made even fax's "high" (204h x 196v) resolution seem not so high. Applications employing higher-resolution input and output devices were increasingly dismayed that this quality was lost in the faxing process. In short, improved technology created a need for higher fax resolutions.

1992 T.4

Recommendation T.4-92 responded to all three criticisms with new bits in the DIS. Because of its support for both millimeter and inch-based measurements, a discussion of facsimile resolutions has the effect of making one's head swim. To simplify the discussion, we will now use the canonical notation (based upon inches) given in Table 11.9. By tradition, the horizontal dimension is given first. For example, when we refer to "2x1" we refer to a resolution of "200 horizontal by 100 vertical," you can cross reference the numbers to exact millimeters or inches. The T.4-88 inch equivalents to the millimeter resolutions are given in brackets.

Table 11.9. Canonical resolutions.

	Inches		*Millimeters*	
	Horizontal *(lines/inch)*	*Vertical* *(pels/inch)*	*Horizontal* *(pels/mm)*	*Vertical* *(lines/mm)*
1	100 [98]	n/a	n/a	3.85
2	200 [196]	200 [204]	8.04	7.70
3	300	300	none	none
4	400	400	16.08	15.4

Figures in brackets represent the pre-1992 inch equivalents.

Refer to Table 11.7 during the following discussion of the resolution bits in DIS.

- Bit 41 adds a new 2 x 4 millimeter resolution for which there is no inch equivalent.
- Bit 42 adds a new 3 x 3 inch resolution for which there is no millimeter equivalent. This is not surprising considering that 300 is not near an integer multiple of any existing millimeter resolution.
- Bit 43 adds a new 4 x 4 resolution for both millimeter and inch system.
- Bit 44 expresses the receiver's preference for inch-based resolutions.
- Bit 45 expresses the receiver's preference for millimeter-based resolutions.

Note that a zero in DIS bit 15 retains its T.4-88 meaning of 2 x 1 resolution, but its meaning can be conditioned to mean either inches or millimeters by bits 44 and 45. A one in DIS bit 15, however, is more complicated and shown in Table 11.10. Similarly, DIS bits 44 and 45 select the metrics for the new 4 x 4 resolution; these are given in Table 11.11.

Table 11.10. Hi-res/Low-res Bit 15 interaction with metric-preference bits.

Bit 15	Bit 44	Bit 45	Meaning
1	0	0	Invalid
1	0	1	2 x 2 millimeters
1	1	0	2 x 2 inches
1	1	1	Both

Table 11.11. 4 x 4 resolution's interaction with metric-preference bits.

Bit 43	Bit 44	Bit 45	Meaning
1	0	0	Invalid
1	0	1	4 x 4 millimeters
1	1	0	4 x 4 inches
1	1	1	Both

Although the introduction of new resolution and metrics bits in DIS adds powerful new capabilities, problems are foreseeable. Although a receiver may express its "preference" for either inches or millimeters, the transmitter is under no obligation to honor it. This guarantees distortion when inch-only machines communicate with millimeter-only machines.

It is also possible that the inches-only 3 x 3 resolution will be popular in the US because of the enormous popularity of desktop publishing at that resolution. Because there is no millimeter equivalent, however, it is equally possible that 3 x 3 will not be supported outside of the US and Britain. This leaves an American 3 x 3 machine with unhappy choices when talking to a 4 x 4 machine: either wastefully scale the image *up* to 4 x 4 (increasing the transmission time by 75 percent), or scaling it down to 2 x 2 (losing almost half the image detail).

Document Dimensions

Because most fax images are scanned from standard-sized documents, the dimensions expressed in DIS are related to standard ISO page sizes.

Page Sizes

Common US paper sizes are given in Table 11.12. ISO page sizes are given in Table 11.13, with those supported by Group 3 facsimile marked with an asterisk. The length and widths are reported separately. Bits 17 and 18 give the supported widths, while bits 19 and 20 give the supported lengths. Note that one of the lengths is given as "unlimited," which, of course, really means "some unspecified length" longer than the other values. As a matter of fact, most fax receivers that use roll paper limit the length of "unlimited" to some arbitrary length (usually several feet) to guard against chicanery. Oddly, no US sizes are supported. As we shall see, although an A4 page is fairly close to a US letter, the mismatch is enough to cause problems in cut-sheet feeders that use a US letter.

Table 11.12. Common US page dimensions.

	Millimeters		*Inches*	
US Paper	*Length*	*Width*	*Length*	*Width*
US Ledger	431.8	279.4	17.0	11.0
US Legal	355.6	215.9	14.0	8.5
US Letter	279.4	215.9	11.0	8.5

USABLE (IMAGEABLE) AREA

Because of the mechanics of scanning and printing—insertion loss, skew, positioning errors, slip loss, and so forth—a portion of the area of a page is not usable. T.4 specifies this loss for an A4 page at 13.4 mm horizontally and 15.5 mm vertically. Although similar specifications are not given for other paper sizes, the mechanical nature of the loss suggests that roughly the same absolute numbers can be used. The number of budget-grade machines in service makes these numbers slightly optimistic, especially in the vertical dimension where slip loss is a function of total length. In practice, subtracting 15mm x 17mm from the dimensions given in Table 11.13 is about right.

NEGOTIATING PAGE SIZES

Because not all machines are able to handle all paper sizes, fax machines must negotiate page size.

Table 11.13. ISO page dimensions.

	Mmeter		Inch	
	W	L	W	L
A0	841	1189	33.1	46.8
A1	594	841	23.4	33.1
A2	420	594	16.5	23.4
*A3	297	420	8.3	16.5
*A4	210	297	8.3	11.7
*A5	148	210	5.8	8.3
*A6	105	148	4.1	5.8
A7	74	105	2.9	5.8
A8	52	74	2.0	2.9
A9	37	52	1.5	2.0
A10	26	37	1.0	1.5
B0	1000	1414	39.4	55.7
B1	707	1000	27.8	39.4
B2	500	707	19.7	27.8
B3	353	500	13.9	19.7
*B4	250	353	9.8	13.9
B5	176	250	6.9	9.8
B6	125	176	4.9	6.9
B7	88	125	3.5	4.9
B8	62	88	2.4	3.5
B9	44	62	1.7	2.4
B10	31	44	1.2	1.7
C0	917	1297	36.1	51.0
C1	648	917	25.5	36.1
C2	458	648	18.0	25.5
C3	324	458	12.8	18.0
C4	229	324	9.0	12.8
C5	162	229	6.4	9.0
C6	114	162	4.5	6.4
C7	81	114	3.2	4.5

continues

Table 11.13. continued

	Mmeter		Inch	
	W	L	W	L
C8	57	81	2.2	3.2
C9	40	57	1.6	2.2
C10	28	40	1.1	1.6

*Supported in Group 3 facsimile

Page-size negotiation works in the usual way: the receiver reports all page sizes its supports in DIS, and the transmitter chooses the best match. Suppose, for example, the transmitter has a US Legal page to send (8.5 x 14 inches). It places the call, then learns from DIS that the receiver can accept only A4 pages (about 8.25 by 11.7). Exactly this situation arises if the receiver uses cut sheets instead of continuous-roll paper.

Now what? Remember, it is the transmitter's responsibility to transform the document so that it is compatible with the receiver's printer. In other words, it must make 14 inches appear to be 11.7 inches. Length adjustment is relatively simple: the transmitter uses T.30 to "chop" the document into A4-lengths. Starting at the top of the page, the transmitter counts the number of scan lines sent. When the count reaches about 1075 lines (A4, 98 dpi), the transmitter terminates Phase C, sends an MPS to tell the receiver that another page with the same metrics will follow, then transmits the remainder of the page. After the call, the receiver's hopper will contain a page of A4 length, as well as a page containing the last 2.3 inches of the transmitter's US Legal page.

Now let's change the example to a transmitter with a B4 page (about 10.4 x 14.3 inches)[14] to send. Again the transmitter learns from DIS that the receiver can accept only A4 pages. The extra width of the B4 page makes this a very different case from the previous example. The transmitter has only two choices: either *scale* the document horizontally by about 20 percent, or hang up. The one thing it must *not* do is to transmit the over-wide document. Most machines choose the former, using crude scaling methods (such as tossing every fifth pel) that rob the image of detail.

CUT-SHEET FAX DEVICES

Fax receivers that employ cut-sheet ("plain paper") printers containing US Letter (8.5 by 11 inch) paper have a special problem: they must routinely receive images longer than 8.5 inches. Here's why:

---

[14]The length is given here for the sake of the argument. The transmitter actually has no way of knowing the length of the paper.

1. There are no bits in DIS for US Letter dimensions. The closest size is A4, but US Letter is .23 (6mm) inches wider and .7 inches (18 mm) shorter. Therefore the transmitter is entitled to send more scan lines than will fit on the page.

2. Fax machines routinely transmit a small (.25 inches) header at the top of each page, and most don't count this toward the maximum page length.

3. Cut-sheet feeding mechanisms usually require .25 to .50-inch to use as a "grabber" for grasping the paper.

The cumulative effect of these additions can be an inch or so more scan lines than paper to print them on. What to do with the excess? If the machine is capable of buffering an entire page (for example, a laser printer), it has several options for fitting the image.

1. *Shrink*[15] *to fit.* This approach, which requires about a 9 percent reduction of the image, is the most elegant when end-to-end registration is not important. The other two choices preserve the original size of the image.

2. *Toss to fit.* Discard white (blank) lines from the top and bottom of the image. The thought of simply discarding part of the image sounds worse than it really is, for a very, very high percentage of fax pages have lots of leading and trailing all-white (blank) lines.

3. *Chop to fit.* Print the excess scan lines on a second piece of paper. This is the ugliest and most wasteful of all options.

On some sessions, none of these procedures is necessary because the received document is not too large and can be printed as is. At other times, a combination of one or more methods may make sense.

Most inexpensive cut-paper machines employ ink-jet or bubble-jet printers. Generally these machines do not buffer an entire page into memory where it can be manipulated; rather, they buffer only a few lines at a time before printing them. Because there is no way for the receiver to know in advance how many lines are coming, these machines have no choice but to shrink the image—whether it needs it or not. In other words, machines that do not buffer at least one page are inherently incapable of end-to-end registration.

ITSY-BITSY FAXES (A5 AND A6)

A5 and A6 pages are one-fourth the area of A3 and A4 pages, respectively. An A5 page is about the size of a stenographer's pad, but slightly longer. An A6 is about the size of a US 4 x 6 inch card (refer to Table 11.13 for exact dimensions). Support for these paper sizes was added in T.4-88 with the idea that a potential non-business market exists for fax

---

[15]Shrinking is the term for size reduction necessary because of a difference between the sizes of the source and destination media. The size of the image is intentionally altered. Scaling is the term for altering pixel density to accommodate differences in resolution between the source and destination media. The size of the image remains the same.

machines that sent small note-sized paper. As is clear from the logic applied to Bit 33 in DIS, the note size machines were regarded as an alternative to rather than an option for the standard A4 machine. Nevertheless, interworking between the tiny fax and the larger machines is specified. When receiving from an A4 machine, the note-size machine downscales the image (even though the results may be unreadable). Conversely, when transmitting to an A4 machine, the note-sized machine pads its smaller images with additional pels so that they print in the center on larger-format machines. So far, these gadgets have seen little success in the US.

SCAN LINE LENGTHS

If you compare the ISO A3, A4, and B4 standard paper sizes in Table 11.13 to the scan line lengths given in DIS bits 17 and 18, you'll note something odd—the scan lines are slightly longer than the width of the nearest standard paper. For example, an A4 is only 210 mm wide, yet an "A4" scan line is given as "1728 along a scan line of 215mm." Moreover, T.4 gives the actual *usable* width of an A4 page as only 196.6mm. A similar technique, known as *overscan*, is used in television receivers to make certain that the image fills the screen (a tiny part of the image is not visible). In fax, however, the overscanning is done at the input (scanner) rather than the output to allow for paper skewing on sheet-feed scanners or positioning errors on flat-bed scanners.

Table 11.14. Number of pels on a scan line for inch and millimeter resolutions.

Number of Pels on a Scan Line

Horizontal Resolution	ISO A4	ISO B4	ISO A3
204 pel/in	1728/215mm	2048/255mm	2432/303mm
8.03 pel/mm	1728/215mm	2048/255mm	2432/303mm
200 pel/in	1728/219.45mm	2048/260.10mm	2432/308.86
300 pel/in	2592/219.45mm	3072/260.10mm	3648/308.86
400 pel/in	3456/219.45mm	4096/260.10mm	4864/308.86
16.05 pel/mm	3456/215mm	4096/255 mm	4864/303mm

Table 11.14 gives the horizontal resolutions in both millimeters and inches. Notice that the conversion from 204 ppi (T.4-88) to 200 ppi is accomplished not by redefining the number of pels in a scan line, but by increasing the *overscan* by a few millimeters. If this just sounds like fudging the numbers, it is in fact vitally important that the number of pels in a scan line remain constant. Our discussion of EOLs and error detection later in the chapter will clarify this issue.

Facsimile Encoding

The raw pels from a fax scanner (or from computerized imaging) are compressed before transmission in Phase C and decompressed at the receiver before printing.

One-Dimensional (Modified Huffman) Encoding

Two compression methods are possible in facsimile, governed by DIS bit 16. The first method, one-dimensional encoding, is a modified form of the Huffman encoding technique discussed in Chapter 10. As you recall, the basic principle of Huffman encoding is to use variable length tokens to represent run lengths. The shorter tokens are assigned to the most frequently occurring bit patterns. Of course, this method requires knowledge of the statistical distribution of various run lengths in the data. The table giving the frequency of occurrence of various run lengths was derived by the CCITT by analyzing several typical[16] documents. Actually, there are two run-length tables because the probability of occurrence is significantly different for black runs versus white ones.

These scanned documents were based upon 1728 pels per line, which would require two tables of 1728 variable-length tokens. The sheer size of these tables leads to a modification of the basic Huffman encoding. Rather than defining 1728 tokens, primary tokens are defined for the 64 most frequent run lengths (including tokens for runs of zero). These are referred to as *terminating tokens*, and are given in Table 11.15.

If the run to be encoded is longer than 63 pels, a second table of *make-up tokens* comes into play. This table, reproduced in Table 11.16, contains tokens for runs from 64 through 2560 in increments of 64. Note that both black and white make-up tables define an identical EOL sequence, the end-of-line marker that must appear at the end of every encoded line.

Thus runs greater than 63 pels require more than one token: one or more make-up tokens and one terminating token. For runs longer than or equal to 2624 pels (2560 plus 64), more than one make-up code is required.

---

[16]Although these documents contained some line art, none had gray-scale art. In fact, their content is dominated by text. Work is now in progress to define new compression methods more suited to gray-scale and other complex images.

Table 11.15. The terminal tokens for black and white run lengths.

Terminal Tokens

Run	White	Black	Run	White	Black
0	00110101	0000110111	32	00011011	000001101010
1	000111	010	33	00010010	000001101011
2	0111	11	34	00010011	000011010010
3	1000	10	35	00010100	000011010011
4	1011	011	36	00010101	000011010100
5	1100	0011	37	00010110	000011010101
6	1110	0010	38	00010111	000011010110
7	1111	00011	39	00101000	000011010111
8	10011	000101	40	00101001	000001101100
9	10100	000100	41	00101010	000001101101
10	00111	0000100	42	00101011	000011011010
11	01000	0000101	43	00101100	000011011011
12	001000	0000111	44	00101101	000001010100
13	000011	00000100	45	00000100	000001010101
14	110100	00000111	46	00000101	000001010110
15	110101	000011000	47	00001010	000001010111
16	101010	0000010111	48	00001011	000001100100
17	101011	0000011000	49	01010010	000001100101
18	0100111	0000001000	50	01010011	000001010010
19	0001100	00001100111	51	01010100	000001010011
20	0001000	00001101000	52	01010101	000000100100
21	0010111	00001101100	53	00100100	000000110111
22	0000011	00000110111	54	00100101	000000111000
23	0000100	00000101000	55	01011000	000000100111
24	0101000	00000010111	56	01011001	000000101000
25	0101011	00000011000	57	01011010	000001011000
26	0010011	000011001010	58	01011011	000001011001
27	0100100	000011001011	59	01001010	000000101011
28	0011000	000011001100	60	01001011	000000101100
29	00000010	000011001101	61	00110010	000001011010
30	00000011	000001101000	62	00110011	000001100110
31	00011010	000001101001	63	00110100	000001100111

Table 11.16. The make-up tokens for black and white run lengths.

Makeup Tokens

Run	White	Black	Run	White	Black
64	11011	0000001111	**1408**	011011011	0000001010100
128	10010	000011001000	**1472**	010011000	0000001010101
192	010111	000011001001	**1536**	010011001	0000001011010
256	0110111	000001011011	**1600**	010011010	0000001011011
320	00110110	000000110011	**1664**	011000	0000001100100
384	00110111	000000110100	**1728**	010011011	0000001100101
448	01100100	000000110101	**1792**	00000001000	00000001000
512	01100101	0000001101100	**1856**	00000001100	00000001100
576	01101000	0000001101101	**1920**	00000001101	00000001101
640	01100111	0000001001010	**1984**	000000010010	000000010010
704	011001100	0000001001011	**2048**	000000010011	000000010011
768	011001101	0000001001100	**2112**	000000010100	000000010100
832	011010010	0000001001101	**2176**	000000010101	000000010101
896	011010011	0000001110010	**2240**	000000010110	000000010110
960	011010100	0000001110011	**2304**	000000010111	000000010111
1024	011010101	0000001110100	**2368**	000000011100	000000011100
1088	011010110	0000001110101	**2432**	000000011101	000000011101
1152	011010111	0000001110110	**2496**	000000011110	000000011110
1216	011011000	0000001110111	**2560**	000000011111	000000011111
1280	011011001	0000001010010	**EOL**	000000000001	000000000001
1344	011011010	0000001010011			

SINGLE PEL IN MIDDLE OF LINE

The easiest way to see how this coding works is to visualize an EOL-terminated 1728-pel line with a single black pel near the middle at position 864. This line is represented by the following notation:

```
-w863-b1-w864
```

Because the first white length is 863 long, the first token comes from the table of make-up tokens. The largest make-up token that is smaller than 863 is for 832, 011010010. The difference between the run length and the make-up token leaves 31 pels, whose token is taken from the table of white terminating tokens: 00011010. The token for the one black pel is taken directly from the table of black terminating tokens, 010. The remaining 864 white pels require a make-up token for a white run of 832, 011010010. The remaining pels require a terminating token for a white run of 32, 00011011. The coding is summarized with the following notation[17]:

```
<wm832>011010010.<wt31>00011010..<bt1>010..<wm832>011010010.<wt32>00011011:<eol>
```

Not counting the EOL, 1728 bits are replaced with 37 bits, a compression ratio of 46.

Now that you've got the idea, let's list the formal rules for *Modified Huffman* encoding.

1. White and black tokens must alternate (except on all-white lines).
2. The first token in a line must be from the white table. If the first pel in the line is black, a white zero-run-length token is used.
3. In runs less than or equal to 2623 pels, every make-up token must be followed by a terminal token. If the length of the run is evenly divisible by a makeup token, use a zero run-length terminal token.[18]
4. In runs greater than 2623 pels more than one make-up token is required. Sequential makeup tokens are *not* separated by zero run-length terminal tokens.
5. Every line must end in an EOL.

ALL-BLACK LINE

Let's look at another simple example: an EOL-terminated 1728-pel line with 1728 black pels. This line is represented by the following notation:

```
-b1728-
```

and encoded as follows:

```
<wt0>00110101..<bm1728>0000001100101.<bt0>0000110111:<eol>
```

A zero-length white token is inserted at the beginning of the line (Rule 2). Next comes the make-up token for 1728 black pels. A zero-length black token is inserted to conform to Rule 3. Not counting the EOL, 1728 bits are replaced with 31 bits, a compression ratio of 56.

---

[17]The letters *w*, *b*, *m*, and *t* in brackets are: white, black, make-up, and terminal, respectively. Double dots separate run lengths. Single dots separate makep-up from terminal tokens.

[18]It may be helpful to think of run lengths in the table in base-64.

ALL-WHITE LINE

Because the blank (all-white) line is quite common in many kinds of images, it makes sense that it should undergo maximum compression. Notation for a blank line is:

-w1728-

and is encoded as follows:

<wm1728>010011011.<wt0>00110101:<eol>

The make-up token for a run of 1728 white pels is followed by a zero run length terminal token, followed by the EOL. Not counting the EOL, 1728 bits are replaced with 17 bits, a compression ratio of 101.

HI-RESOLUTION PAGES

As shown in Table 11.14 the 3456 pels on an A4 400 ppi scan line exceeds the largest make-up code (plus 63) in the table. In this case, encoding requires more than one make-up code. Notation for this line is

-w3456-

and it is encoded as follows:

<mw2560>000000011111.<mw896>011010011<wt0>00110101:eol

The white pel run of (3456) exceeds 2560, the last entry in the make-up table. The token for 2560 used. A zero-run token of zero is *not* required. The number of uncoded pels remaining is 896, for which an exact match appears in the table. The 896 token is followed by a token for a run of zero.

A DITHERED LINE

Dithering is a technique for representing gray tones in bi-level (black-white) images by varying black pel density proportionally to the shade of gray. A 1728-pel line dithered to represent a shade of gray consists of alternating white and black pels. This produces a coded line consisting of 864 one-pel white tokens (000111) and 864 one-pel black tokens (010). Not counting the EOL, 1728 bits are replaced with 5184 + 2592 = 7776 bits, a *negative* compression ratio of 0.22. In other words, the encoded data expands by a factor of 4.5.

Two-Dimensional (READ) Encoding

A significant increase in compression (see Table 11.17a) can be achieved through the optional two-dimensional encoding method known as Modified READ[19]. This alternative is indicated by a one in bit 16 of DIS/DCS.

Modified READ takes advantage of the statistical fact that there is a high degree of *vertical correlation* between successive scan lines. That is, any given scan line usually closely resembles the one before it. The gain in compression comes from identifying pel runs with high vertical correlation and encoding them with very short tokens instead of the Modified Huffman tokens shown in Tables 11.15 and 11.16.

The procedure sounds complicated, but is quite simple. The central idea of the procedure is to identify corresponding run lengths on the *reference line* and on the *coding* line (the one to be encoded). Based upon the relationship between these corresponding runs, one of three coding techniques ("modes") is applied:

1. *Vertical Mode.* When the first pel of a run on the coding line begins within ± 3 pels of the beginning of the same run on the reference line. When the begin pels are at identical locations, the token is a single bit; if they are offset ± one bit in either direction, a larger token is used, and so forth up to an offset of ± three.

2. *Pass Mode.* When the beginning of coding run occurs after the end of the reference run.

3. *Horizontal.* When neither vertical nor horizontal mode applies—that is, when the vertical correlation is low—the next two runs are encoded with ordinary Modified Huffman tokens.

The correlation between runs is obtained by finding and comparing *transition pels*, the first pel to the left after a change in color (when scanning from left to right). As shown in Figure 11.5, place the reference line above the line to be coded and follow these simple rules:

1. All references are relative to the "current" transition pel, named C0, whose position is dictated by the coding mode just completed. At the beginning of the procedure, C0 is located at an imaginary position to the left of first pel (position -1 in Figure 11.6).

2. Locate the transition *pels* as follows:
   A. On the reference line find the first transition to the right of and opposite color from C0. Name this pel R1 and name the next transition pel R2.
   B. On the coding line, locate the first two transition pels after C0 and name them C1 and C2. Now follow this procedure until an EOL is encountered:

---

[19]Relative Element Address Designate.

3. *Pass Mode* (R2 left of C1)? Output a Pass token (0001). Set C0 under R2 on the Code line. Go back to step 2.

4. Vertical mode (R1 ± 3 positions of C1)? Send the appropriate Vertical token:

Offset	-3	-2	-1	0	+1	+2	+3
V.Token	0000010	000010	010	1	011	000011	0000011

Set C0 = C1. Go back to step 2.

5. If not Pass or Vertical, then use Horizontal mode. Send Horizontal token (001), then encode pels C0 to C1 and C1 to C2 using standard Modified Huffman coding. Set C0 = C2. Go back to 2.

Figure 11.6 depicts an example of how the first 29 pels of a reference and a coding line are encoded. The pel transitions are shown in their starting positions. Detailed intermediate positions for Vertical, Pass, and Horizontal modes are given in Figure 11.7.

	C0	C1	C2	R1	R2	Output	Description
1	-1	2	5	1	4	011	R1 - C1 = 1: Vertical, + 1 offset (Fig.11.7a)
2	2	5	7	4	7	011	R1 - C1 = 1: Vertical, + 1 offset
3	5	7	9	7	9	1	R1 - C1 = 1: Vertical, 0 offset
4	7	9	17	9	13	1	R1 - C1 = 0: Vertical, 0 offset
5	9	17	19	13	16	0001	R2 left C1 : Pass (figure 11.7b)
6	16	17	19	21	28	001..000111..11	R1 - C1 > 3: Horizontal, 1 white 2 black (fig 11.7c)
7	19	25	28	21	28	001..1110..10	R1 - C1 > 3: Horizontal, 6 white 3 black
8	28	30	30	30	30	1	R1 - C1 = 0: Vertical mode 0 offset

FIGURE 11.6.
MR encoding of first 29 pels in a line. Double dots separate tokens in Output column.

REPETITION OF MODIFIED READ-ENCODED LINES

In Chapter 10 we observed how single bit errors in compressed data have the potential to yield horrendous errors when decoded. In the case of a one-dimensional coded line, a single bit error may play havoc with the remainder of the line, but, as we shall see shortly, the effect of the error is unable to propagate for more than two lines. Suppose, however, that the 2-D reference line itself contains an error. Because of the vertical correlation, the error would propagate indefinitely. To avoid this, only a limited number of two-dimensionally encoded lines are derived from any single reference line before transmitting a one-dimensionally encoded line. The frequency of repetition of the one-dimensionally encoded lines is referred to as the *K-factor*. For low resolution, at least every other line must be one-dimensionally encoded (K = 2). In the optional higher resolution, at least every fourth line must be one-dimensionally encoded (K = 4).

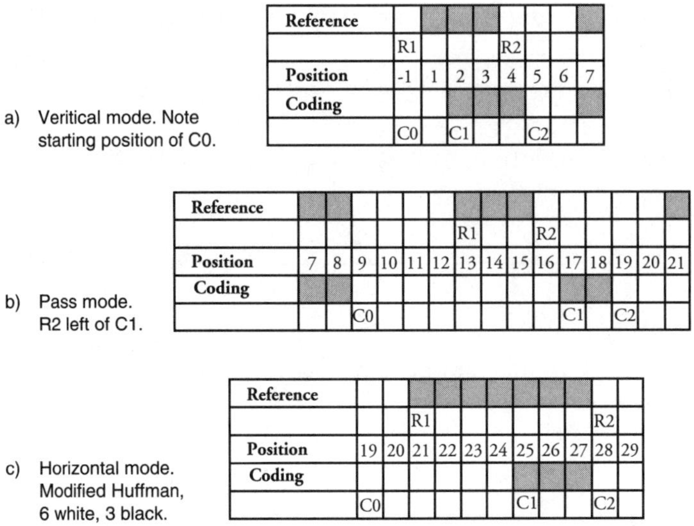

a) Veritical mode. Note starting position of C0.

b) Pass mode. R2 left of C1.

FIGURE 11.7.

Details of (a) Vertical, (b) Pass, and (c) Horizontal modes.

c) Horizontal mode. Modified Huffman, 6 white, 3 black.

Although intermixing one-dimensional and two-dimensional encoding solves the error-propagation problem, it raises the question: "How does the decoder tell the difference?" When two-dimensional encoding is in effect, a *tag bit* is appended to the EOL pattern. A 0 tag bit means that the *line to follow* is two-dimensionally encoded, and a 1 tag bit means that it is one-dimensionally encoded.

> **Note:** The K-factor presents an opportunity for deception. Several very inexpensive fax modems include software that claims to send 2-D data. Actually they just negotiate a 2-D connection, but send with K = 1: every line 1-D is encoded. Note that this technique actually causes the data to grow by one-bit per line.

ENCODING SUMMARY

It is clear that the efficiency of the various methods of encoding varies according to the image. As mentioned earlier, the Huffman tables were derived from eight images judged to be typical by the CCITT study group. Three of these documents were evaluated to judge the effectiveness of the three kinds of compression available under Group 3. Document CCITT #1 is a typical business letter; CCITT #5 is a page from a French technical journal; and CCITT #7 is a page of containing a mixture of the Japanese Kanji and Katakana symbols. Table 11.17a gives the compression ratio for the various compressions, and Table 11.17b gives the average number of bytes per line in the compressed data.

Table 11.17a. Compression ratios for three CCITT standard documents.

Compression Ratio

Method	*CCITT #1*	*CCITT #5*	*CCITT #7*
Group 3, 1-D	15.1	8.4	4.9
Group 3, 2-D	21.1	12.8	6.4
Group 4 (T.6)	30.5	17.6	7.6

Table 11.17b. Average line lengths for three CCITT standard documents.

Average Bytes/Line

Method	*CCITT #1*	*CCITT #5*	*CCITT #7*
Group 3, 1-D	14.2	25.5	44.2
Group 3, 2-D	10.1	16.8	33.6
Group 4 (T.6)	7.1	12.3	28.5

EOLs

Before lines can be sent to the fax printer, they must first be found. Fax lines are delineated by EOLs: the unique bit-pattern of eleven 0-bits followed by a one-bit. Without EOLs to mark the end of the line a single bit-error in the compressed code could cause the decompressor to lose line synchronization forever. However, with EOLs as line markers, the decoder has only to locate the next EOL to become resynchronized.

ZERO-FILLING EOLS FOR MINIMUM SCAN-LINE TIME

Due to the nature of printers, fax devices are usually able to scan lines much faster than print them. When a modern fax scanner is transmitting to an older fax printer, the mismatch can be significant. Suppose, for example, a modern fax machine whose scanner operates at 5 milliseconds per line (200 lines per second) phones a very old machine whose printer can print only one line in 20 milliseconds or (50 lines per second). At about 2200 scan lines per "high" resolution (198 ppi) A4 page, a complete page can be scanned in 11 seconds and printed every 44 seconds. For the most extreme mismatch, consider a computerized fax device that has no scanner at all, but stores pre-encoded files on disk. To prevent overwhelming the receiver with data at a rate faster than it can print, the transmitter must pace itself. The amount of pacing required by the receiver is given in DIS Bits 21-23 and expressed in the amount of time it takes the receiver to print a single line. The times vary from zero (for machines that buffer entire pages or store them on disk) to 40 milliseconds. One group of DIS scan-time parameters is absolute, but another group declares that the time required to print a line at high-resolution (198 ppi) is half the time at low-resolution. This oddity is due to the fact that some printers spend much more time moving the paper than printing. Because the paper must be moved only half as far in high resolution (198 ppi) as in low resolution, the high resolution scan time is also halved.

As we have just seen, compression applied to bit image means that line lengths vary over the length of a page. For one-dimensional encoding, the ratio between the best and worst cases—a blank line and a line of alternating pels—is 269:1. It is the transmitter's responsibility to monitor the transmission and to make certain that the time required to send a line, including the EOL, is never less than the negotiated time in DCS.

To see how this works, let's suppose we wish to send a two-dimensionally encoded A4 page of 2150 lines averaging 17 bytes in length. A speed of 14.4 bps and a minimum scan time of 40 ms are negotiated. From the transmitter's point of view, 40 milliseconds is the time required to send 576 bits, or 72 bytes. At the beginning of each line, the transmitter starts counting the bytes as they are transmitted. If the count reaches 72 bytes without encountering an EOL, no action is necessary. If, however, an EOL is encountered before transmitting all 72 bytes, the transmitter is obliged to stretch the line, out to 72 bytes. On average, then, the transmitter will have to add 72 − 17 = 55 zero bytes per line. In other words, of the total time required to send the page, three-quarters of it is spent transmitting fill.

How does one stretch a line? An approach found mostly on inexpensive machines is to insert zero-length tokens just ahead of the EOLs. Each black-white pair of tokens is 18 bits long, so four such pairs generate nine bytes. This technique cannot be used in computerized applications where data is pre-encoded for transmission at a later time to a machine whose scan-line requirements are not yet known.

By far the most popular method for stretching lines—and the method blessed by T.4—is to insert *zero-fill bits* ahead of the EOL. Notice from Table 11.16 that the EOL consists of eleven 0 bits followed by a 1 bit. Because no combination of tokens produces this many contiguous zeroes, an EOL is easy for the transmitter to identify on the fly and easy to modify with fill: once eleven contiguous zeroes are sent, the transmitter postpones the 1 bit in the EOL and adds zero bits until the scan-line time requirement has been reached. In byte-oriented computer equipment, it is usually easier to implement minimum-scan-line-time by counting the total number of bytes transmitted instead of keeping track of total time. When implemented in this manner, fill *bytes* (instead of bits) are added ahead of the EOL.

Line stretching may be used for other reasons besides avoiding receiver overrun—in fact, to avoid just the opposite condition. Recall that in synchronous communications the line must not be allowed to become idle during periods of data. For example, when a fax receiver encounters a data under-run, it usually responds by precipitously hanging up. Many computer applications have difficulty meeting this requirement because system overhead limits the speed with which data can be supplied to the modem. A clever fax modem, however, can provide a grace period for the computer by automatically adding extra zero-fill whenever the amount of data in its buffer runs low. (The maximum duration of any line, including fill bits and EOL is five seconds.[20]) Although this technique may add slightly to the transmission time, it prevents session failure.

EOL BYTE-ALIGNMENT

It is customary for fax receivers to remove the zero-fill added at the transmitter for line stretching. In computer-based fax products, however, it may be desirable to leave some of the fill in place. In computerized fax, the application software usually manipulates the image in groups of lines, which necessarily involves locating EOLs and removing them from the data. This procedure is greatly simplified if the fax receiver inserts fill at each EOL so that the final 1-bit is the last bit in the byte. The *byte-alignment* of EOLs makes it possible for any application to parse a T.4 image into lines by searching for a byte pattern rather than by decoding each line.

Page Encoding

So far we've spent a lot of time discussing what constitutes a fax line. Let's now see what constitutes a fax *page* (or "message" as the CCITT calls it). There are only five rules to page composition:

1. Every page must begin with an EOL.
2. Every line must encode the *exact* number of pels given by the page width in DCS (see Table 11.14).
3. Every line must end with an EOL.
4. The number of lines may not exceed the negotiated vertical resolution times the practical imageable page length (see "Imageable Area", elsewhere in this chapter). For example, the usable length of a high A4 page is about 280 mm. Therefore, the maximum length of an A4 page at 7.7 lines/mm is about 2155 lines.
5. The page ends with six EOLs in a row, a sequence known as Return to Control (RTC). When all the lines have been sent, the transmitter appends an RTC and turns off its page carrier and exits Phase C. When the receiver detects an RTC in the data, it stops listening for page carrier and exits Phase C.

---

[20]In practice few machines tolerate this amount of fill. A safer figure is about 3.5 seconds

ZERO FILL IN RTC

Recommendation T.4 is ambiguous on the matter of zero-filling the EOLs that constitute an RTC. Referring to Listing 11.1, say the EOL for the last line (labeled RTC/EOL-
1) clearly qualifies for filling under the T.4 definition. On the other hand, T.4 is quite
explicit that an RTC consists of the eleven-zeroes-plus-a-one pattern repeated six times.
In other words, T.4 appears to be emphasizing that an RTC/EOL must not be filled.

Listing 11.1. Zero fill in RTC.

```
<EOL-1>
...................LINE 1..........<EOL-2>
.............LINE 2..............<EOL-3>
..............LINE 3..........<EOL-4>
...................LINE 4..........<EOL-5>
.............LINE 5..........<EOL-6>
...............LINE 6..........<EOL-7>
.........LINE 7..........<EOL-8>
.............LINE 8..........<EOL-9>
.............LINE XXXX..........<EOL-XXXX+1>
.............LINE 2155....................<RTC/EOL-1>
<RTC/EOL-2>
<RTC/EOL-3>
<RTC/EOL-4>
<RTC/EOL-5>
<RTC/EOL-6>
<Exit to Phase C>
```

THE "BOL"

If you're like many people, you find EOLs to be slightly Byzantine. Take the matter of the
EOLs in an RTC: the EOL on the last line of data doubles as the first of the six EOLs that
make up the RTC. Considering that it's not wise to zero-fill an RTC, does this EOL qualify
for zero-filling? Also consider what happens when two continuous page images are *seamed*
(concatenated) onto disk. The EOL that is part of the last line (RTC/EOL-1) of page one
is adjacent to EOL-1 that begins page two. This creates a coding error because two EOLs
in a row is not a valid data pattern[21].

---

[21]Indeed, some fax machines treat more than two EOLs in a row to be an RTC; others treat 2-5 EOLs in a
row to be a fatal error.

Listing 11.2. The BOL.

```
<BOL-1>....................LINE 1
<BOL-2>...............LINE 2
<BOL-3>...............LINE 2
<BOL-4>...................LINE 3
<BOL-4>...............LINE 4
<BOL-5>................LINE 5
<BOL-6>....LINE 6
<BOL-7>...............LINE 7
<BOL-XXXX>............LINE XXXX
<BOL-2155>.................LINE 2155
<RTC/BOL-1>
<RTC/BOL-2>
<RTC/BOL-3>
<RTC/BOL-4>
<RTC/BOL-5>
<RTC/BOL-6>
<Exit to Phase C>
```

The fact is, T.4 becomes a lot more rational if one views the world not in terms of an EOL, but in terms of a *BOL—Beginning of Line*. In the BOL world-view, zero-fill occurs at the beginning of the *next* line instead at the end of the current line. Keep in mind that because there is no difference in the data, there is no functional or procedural difference between the two views.

The "to fill or not to fill" ambiguity on the last EOL also disappears because the role of each BOL in the RTC is clear. But what about fill for the last line? Recall that the purpose of fill is to buy time for the receiver's printer mechanism. After the last line, the transmitter sends RTC, then exits Phase C completely. During phase D (Post-Page negotiations), the receiver has several seconds to complete the printing, which may include page-eject procedures. In short, because there is no more data after the last line, there is simply no need for fill. The problem of seaming two EOLs in a row disappears with the BOL concept, too.

Errors

As we have noted, small errors in compressed data often become huge errors when decompressed. Because most fax machines do not support the optional T.30 error-checking protocol, the occasional streaked image, broken line, or black bar across a page are just part of daily life with facsimile. Humans are amazingly immune to errors in images; faxes with badly torn lines are nevertheless quite readable. For this reason, errors in facsimile have never been a burning issue. Nevertheless, rudimentary error-detection is required in T.30 in order to answer the question "Copy Quality OK?" at 19 in the receiver flow chart, which may lead to retransmission of the image. To answer this question, the receiver must actually decode each line and verify that the number of pels in that line is correct. (The precise number of pels in various scan lines is given in Table 11.14.) Therefore, a "bad" line is by definition a line that when decoded contains an incorrect number of pels. There are three possible ways this can happen:

1. A "hard" coding error is encountered; that is, a bit pattern is found that isn't present in the table.
2. An EOL is encountered before the correct number of pels has been decoded.
3. The correct number of pels is decoded before encountering an EOL.

In either case, once an error is detected, the decoder simply throws up its hands and discards data until the next EOL is encountered, which restores line-synchronization. It is important to note that once synchronization is lost, there is no way for a receiver to ascertain exactly how many lines were lost to damage, since an indeterminable number of EOLs may themselves have been damaged. Therefore, a single bit error affecting an EOL causes an error that persists for two lines. Neither T.4 nor T.30 specify how many bad lines are required for a negative answer to the "Copy Quality OK?" question.

DISGUISING "BAD" LINES

What does the received fax machine do with a bad line? Does it print it? Toss it? Replace it with an all-white one? Replace it with an all-black one? The most common approach is based on the same underlying principle as two-dimensional encoding—namely, that any given scan line closely resembles its immediate predecessor. In this technique, known as *charading*, the receiver replaces a bad line with a copy of the last good one. Although charading doesn't actually reconstruct lost information, it appears to do so if the bad lines are not contiguous. Several bad lines in a row, however, causes the receiver to print the same line repeatedly, producing the familiar bar-code effect.

A similar, but vastly more complicated version of charading is represented by the optional *error-limiting mode* selected by DIS Bit 29. Its intent is to limit the potential damage to a line to a small part by dividing each line into separately coded segments (12 segments for a line of 1728 pels). Each segment is classified as white or non-white, then encoded using one-dimensional encoding. A header at the beginning of each line holds each segment's classification and the number of encoded bits. When an error occurs in a segment, the corresponding segment of the previous line is substituted.

Error Correction

A full-blown optional EC (error-correcting) protocol was added to T.30 in 1988. When it was proposed in 1985 (by the United Kingdom), EC had a few opponents, but mainly the reaction to it was one of indifference. Although most felt that facsimile was good enough the way it was, they agreed not to oppose EC so long as it required no new data-link capabilities and did not impose overhead on existing error-free links. In this spirit, work on EC proceeded.

The optional error-correcting protocol, governed by DIS Bit 27, uses the HDLC packet procedures already in T.30. A sliding-window protocol have been be the natural choice for such an application, but of course fax's half-duplex communications made that impossible. The method chosen is a *selective-repeat* version of the *ARQ* protocol (described in Chapter 4).

Each page is divided into *blocks*, which are merely a concatenation of 256 ordinary HDLC frames sent at the speed negotiated in DCS Bits 11 and 12. Each page, block, and packet is numbered. All 256 packets in a block are transmitted without interruption. The line is then reversed, and the receiver sends a HDLC packet whose Information field is a 32-byte bitmap 256 bits long marking packets that contained errors. The line is again turned around and these packets are retransmitted. When all bad packets have been received and acknowledged, the same procedure is repeated for the next block. Because the number of bytes in the page may not be evenly divisible by the block size, an HLDC packet known as the *Partial-Page Signal,* gives the number of packets in the final block.

The HDLC Information field for data packets may be either 256 or 64 bytes long. This parameter is not negotiated in the ordinary T.30 sense. Support for both sizes are considered part of the error-correcting protocol itself, so both receiver and transmitter must support both packet sizes. The transmitter, however, *unilaterally* chooses the size in DCS Bit 28. This mechanism enables the transmitter to change the packet size in response to changing error rates. This field should be 64 bytes when the session is conducted over a cellular network.

MODIFIED-MODIFIED READ ENCODING

As the error-correcting protocol eliminates the possibility of bit-errors, so it eliminates the need for defenses against them. EOLs are such a counter measure, as is the K-factor in two-dimensional encoding. When the optional error-correcting mechanism is selected in DIS Bit 27 *and* Bit 31 is selected, one dimensional encoding is applied to the first line only, then two-dimensional encoding is used on every subsequent line (K=1), and EOLs are omitted. In addition, the entire session is conducted at a minimum scan-time of zero. This form of encoding is known as Modified-Modified READ.

OTHER EC-MODE FEATURES

The capabilities represented in bits 50 through 65 depend upon EC-mode. These are beyond the scope of this book.

EIA Facsimile Modems

Potential manufacturers of fax machines traditionally found the fax data pump technology to be a barrier to entering the market. For this reason, until the 1980s there were only a few vendors of fax machines, all of whom used proprietary in-house data pump technology. Consequently, the fax machine was a high-ticket item targeted at high-ticket businesses. Then in 1985, relatively inexpensive fax data pumps became widely available from Rockwell International and other vendors. These chips offered the minimum modulations, V.21 (300 bps) and V.27ter (2400, 4800), and a sensible, register-oriented programmatic interface. Shortly thereafter, enhanced data pumps were offered that added V.29 (7200 and 9600 bps). As expected, the availability of inexpensive data pumps not only brought many companies into the business, it brought them in at the consumer level, driving the cost of fax machines lower and lower over the next few years.

Computer peripheral companies bought these inexpensive chips, too, building from them fax "cards." These were little more than platforms for the data pump chips with just enough circuitry to provide a bus interface to the chip's internal registers. The first of these was shipped in 1986 by Gamma Link, Inc., of Palo Alto, California. Several other companies followed their example and produced similar hardware.

At the time, it was not generally recognized that the facsimile market would eventually be absorbed into the general modem business. Hence, none of the companies in the "computer fax" business were experienced modem companies. In December of 1987, however, Everex Systems, Inc. shipped the EverFax 12/48, the first product in which facsimile was integrated seamlessly into an ordinary data modem[22]. This product offered a 1200 bps modem in combination with a 4800 bps (V.27ter) fax modem. The fax commands, though proprietary, were in fact a simple extension of the familiar AT command set.

Feeling that standards were essential to the growth of the fax-cum-modem market, in 1988 Everex under the aegis of the EIA's began to work for on a public standard to integrate facsimile into data modems. This work was placed under the EIA TR.29 Committee (*Facsimile Systems and Control*) and became TR29.2 "Facsimile Digital Interfaces." The committee comprised makers of "fax cards" and broad representation from modem companies.

The goal of the TR29.2 committee was to specify the modem interface for a gadget that would provide facsimile services to the DTE. From the very first meeting of the committee, the membership was divided on exactly what constituted "facsimile services." The first group took the mimimalist view that "services" were essentially just a set of commands that enables the DTE to generate the modulation, and, perhaps, to participate in assembling and disassembling HDLC packets. In this model, the DTE software is responsible not only for preparing the image (T.4), but also for conducting the entire T.30 fax

---

[22]The author is privileged to have been a member of the team that accomplished this.

session. These members had a vision of very inexpensive fax/data modem chips integrated into the motherboards of every PC made.

The second group felt that the critical timing demanded by T.30 could not be guaranteed by DTE control. As proof of this limitation, they pointed to multi-tasked or multi-user systems (Macintosh, Windows, Unix, and OS/2) where heavily buffered I/O makes it extremely difficult if not impossible for the DTE to participate in timing. This group predicted the same problems for PCs as the operating systems became more sophisticated. The device seen by this group was a much more complicated and expensive device in which the modem conducted the T.30 session, and the DTE prepared the image preparation.

A much smaller third group, which had no particular product or time frame in mind, wanted to add sophisticated image-processing capabilities to the modem. In this view, the modem would take responsibility for resolving page-metrics conflicts between machines. For example, the DTE could send Modified-Modified READ data to the DCE, which would be prepared to down-convert it to one- or two-dimensional data as required by the remote. Conflicts in resolution and page dimensions would also be resolved by the modem. In view, the modem became a free-standing fax device in which DTE became little more than a file server and a data base of phone numbers.

After a couple of heated meetings, it became clear that the philosophical differences between these points of view were irreconcilable. Lest the project be abandoned, it was decided that there would be three levels of "facsimile services," Service Classes 1, 2, and 3. Members who wanted to build the simple gadget would simply have the modem identify itself as "Class 1," whereas the more complicated ones would identify themselves as "Class 2" or "Class 3." With this compromise in hand, the TR29.2 members formed two ad hoc working groups, each charged with drafting a specification for its *Service Class*. Since most of the interest in the committee focused on Class 1 or Class 2, work began to draft one standard defining both interfaces, with Class 1 mandatory and Class 2 optional. Although Class 3 was assigned a project number (PN-2725), very little work has been done on it.

In a very short time, the committee had achieved consensus on Class 1, based on a successful committee ballot. Consensus on the Class 2 specification (a vastly more complicated beast), was more elusive. After witnessing the glacial progress of the Class 2 effort, the Class 1 group became impatient and frustrated, and soon insisted[23] upon splitting their work in a separate standard. After getting an identity of its own, Class 1 breezed through the balloting procedure in August of 1990, was dubbed EIA/TIA 578, and was being shipped in quantity by several companies shortly thereafter. Class 2, on the other hand, seemed to run aground at every turn. The specification was sent out for ballot three times in the next three years, but rejected for what seemed to many as political, not technical grounds[24].

---

[23]On threat of dissolving the group.

[24]For example, the Class 1 group was accused of trying to torpedo the Class 2 effort in order to make their products the only modems that conformed to a recognized standard.

Finally, Class 2 supporters were so confident that the August, 1990, draft of the specification (known as SP-2388) would pass that many actually implemented the specification and began to sell products based upon it. This muddied the political water even more: the modem vendors who had implemented the non-standard version—some of whom were themselves committee members—suddenly seemed to have a vested interest seeing that the current (incompatible) version not pass. A compromise of sorts was reached to settle this crisis: all modems based on an illegitimate version of Class 2 identify themselves as Class 2, whereas legitimate Class 2 modems identify themselves Class 2.0. Several more squabbles threatened to torpedo Class 2, but it was finally passed in November 1992 as SP-2388-1-B and was published as EIA 592—just in time to be obsoleted by the 1992 revisions of Recommendations T.4 and T.30.

As modern operating systems seem to be moving further away from supporting real-time operations, it is almost everyone's belief that the future of facsimile modems lies in Class 2 or Class-2-like modems. If this prediction is true, the Class 1 modem will become obsolete. (TR-29.2 is studying the definition of yet another specification, with the simplicity of Class 1 and the buffering and timing support of Class 2. This is known as Class 4, PN-3130.)

Currently the market is confused by the Class 1 v. Class 2 struggle, and even more confused by the garbled Class 2 v. Class 2.0 situation. Because Class 1 modems are likely to be abundant in the short term, and because they are so much simpler as a pedagogical tool, we will ignore the Class 2 modem and look in some detail at the Class 1.

EIA 578, Class 1

For generality, EIA 578, which specifies a Service Class 1 DCE (here after referred to as *Class-1 Modem)* assumes that the specified facsimile capabilities reside in a nondescript smart modem with minimum capabilities. Because virtually all implementations of EIA 578 are found in the base-line smart modem described in Chapters 8 and 9, our discussion assumes such a gadget.

The basic notion behind a Class 1 modem is the integration of facsimile services into an "ordinary" smart modem by extending the AT command set. A '+' following the AT denotes the beginning of an extension; the next letter identifies the extension: F for fax, V for voice, and so on. EIA facsimile commands, therefore, all begin with "AT+F". Multiple commands may appear on the command line if separated by semicolons. (See TIA/EIA-615 or Section 6.1 of TIA/EIA-592 for the general syntax.)

CAPABILITIES DETERMINATION

One of the more intelligent features of the EIA modem command set standard is a standard way to query the modem for its "class," for certain commands, and its capabilities, including the range of supported arguments[25].

The "+FCLASS=?" command returns the "service classes" available from the modem. The modem returns a comma-separated list of all supported values. For example, a modem that supported data communication and Class-1 would respond: "0,1".

SERVICE CLASS INDICATION +FCLASS?

The "+FCLASS?" command returns the current "Class" setting of the modem:

0	A data modem
1	A Class-1 modem
2.0	A Class-2 modem
2	A non-standard Class-2 modem (based on an early draft, SP-2388)

SERVICE CLASS SELECTION +FCLASS=<VALUE>

The "+FCLASS=<value>" command sets the desired "service class" from the choices available. For example, to configure for Class 1, the DTE sends the command: "AT+FCLASS=1".

SERIAL OVER-SPEED

Group 3 is bit-synchronous, so the modem must delete START and STOP bits on transmit and add them on receive. This creates a data deficit in the modem of 20 percent. Therefore, in order to prevent the communications line from becoming idle, the serial port between the modem and DTE must operate at least 20 percent faster than the speed of the modulation. For example, a 9600 bps fax page carrier requires a minimum DTE-modem data rate of 12,000 bps[26].

---

[25]The general syntax for extend command syntax is ins EIA/TIA 516 /mt/ and in section 6.1 of EIA 592 (Class 2 Facsimile).

[26]Because 12,000 is not attainable on all serial ports, 14,400 or 19,200 bps should be chosen.

FLOW CONTROL

XON/XOFF flow control is mandatory, whereas RTS/CTS flow control is optional. Unfortunately, there is no Class-1 command for selecting the flow-control method, nor any way to ascertain the current setting. This ambiguity has proven to be a problem in the field.

Class-1 Services

A Class-1 modem knows nothing about either T.30 or T.4, but provides simple, low-level tools to support Group 3 facsimile signaling.

CONNECTION

After answering a call (either automatically or by command), the Class-1 modem automatically generates a 2100 CED tone. It then enters V.21 HDLC transmit state at 300 bps, then responds CONNECT. At this point the DTE is free to transmit its first HDLC packet.

After placing a call, the Class-1 modem generates the CNG tone. It then enters V.21 HDLC receive state at 300 bps, and responds CONNECT. At this point the DTE should be ready to receive the first HDLC packet.

WAITING AND SILENCE DETECTION

These commands are used to implement areas of critical timing in T.30, in particular the requirement that changes in modulation be preceded by 75 ms ± 20 ms of silence.

DATA STREAM TERMINATION

All data streams—both Phase C *and* HDLC—in both directions are terminated with the character-pair <DLE><ETX>. Both devices must participate in transparentization of these characters by doubling single DLE's that occur naturally in the data on transmission and by removing one of every pair of DLE's encountered on reception. (See "In-Band Flow Control" in Chapter 5 for a discussion of transparency.)

DATA TRANSMISSION AND RECEPTION

A Class-1 modem transfers Phase C page data using any supported signaling method, but only CCITT V.21 (300 bps) and V.27ter (4800 and 2400 bps) are mandatory.

HDLC framing is used for control signaling, and, optionally, for Phase C data if T.30 error correcting mode is implemented. Only V.21 signaling is mandatory. The modem participates in the HDLC exchange by assuming the following responsibilities:

- Transmit flags for preamble and between members of a packet group
- Delete flags from received packets
- Insert and delete zero bits used for HDLC transparency
- Generate CRCs on transmit and verify them on receive
- Recognize "final" packets

ERROR MESSAGE RESPONSE

Class-1 modems respond with the basic modem response codes OK, CONNECT, NO CARRIER, and ERROR, although they have slightly eccentric meanings for fax. Only one new response is added: +FCERROR. When the Class-1 modem is commanded to look for a particular carrier signal, but instead detects a different signal, it responds +FCERROR. This allows the DTE to implement decisions 11 and 14 (point F) in the receiver flow chart (Figure 11.5) where it must be prepared to receive either HDLC packet or page carrier.

The +FCERROR message has the following syntax:

Verbose	Numeric
+FCERROR	+F4

Command Summary

In keeping with its mandate for simplicity, Class 1 defines only a few commands, all atomic. If more than one command appears on the command line, they must be separated by semi-colons. All commands, except +FTS and +FRS, must be the last command on the command line. The commands are:

Command	Description
+FTS=<Time>	Stop transmission and pause, (10ms intervals 0-255)
+FRS=<Time>	Wait for silence, (10ms intervals 0-255)
+FTM=<MOD>	Transmit data with <MOD> carrier
+FRM=<MOD>	Receive data with <MOD> carrier
+FTH=<MOD>	Transmit HDLC data with <MOD> carrier
+FRH=<MOD>	Receive HDLC data with <MOD> carrier

The <MOD>(ulation) parameter may have any of the values give in Table 11.18.

Table 11.18. Modulation parameters.

Value	Modulation	Speed	Needed for
3	V.21 ch.2	300	HDLC
24	V.27ter	2400	Phase C, HDLC
48	V.27ter	4800	Phase C
72	V.29	7200	optional
73	V.17	7200	optional
74	V.17 quick train	7200	optional
96	V.29	9600	optional
97	V.17	14400	optional
98	V.17 quick train	14400	optional
121	V.17	12000	optional
122	V.17 quick train	12000	optional
145	V.17	14400	optional
146	V.17 quick train	14400	optional

For all commands that require a <MOD> argument, use the syntax "<COMMAND>=?" to query for the range of <MOD> values supported. The modem returns a comma-separated list of all supported values. For example, when issued "+FTH=?" a minimum Class-1 modem would report: "3" to show that it support only 300 bps for HDLC modulation. A modem that supported the optional Phase C error-correcting protocol would probably report: "3,24,48,72,96,144".

STOP TRANSMISSION AND WAIT +FTS=<TIME>

The command "+FTS=<Time>" causes the modem to cease transmitting. It then waits for the specified amount of time, then responds OK. The value of <Time> is in 10 millisecond intervals. The main purpose of this command is to enforce the 75 ± 20 milliseconds of silence required between modulation changes.

RECEIVE SILENCE +FRS=<TIME>

The command "+FRS=<Time>" causes the modem to listen for silence on the line for the amount of time specified. The value <Time> is in 10 millisecond intervals. The command terminates when the required amount of silence on the line is detected or the DTE aborts the command by sending another character (which is discarded). In either case, the modem responds OK. The main purpose of this command is to listen for carrier to disappear after a <DTL><ETX> has been received. This is the most reliable way for a receiver to ascertain when it is safe to reverse the line around and begin transmitting.

PHASE C TRANSMIT +FTM=<MOD>

The "+FTM=<MOD>" command causes the modem to transmit data using the modulation selected in <MOD>, which may have the values shown in Table 11.18. The modem responds CONNECT and performs analog training in the selected mode, followed by constant 1 bits[27] until data is received from the DTE.

Data received from the host is asssumed to be the HDLC packet body, less the CRC, and is terminated by the <DLE><ETX> stream terminator. If the modems transmit buffer becomes empty and the last transmitted character is 2 NUL byte[28], the modem continues to transmit NULs until the DTE sends more data. If the empty condition persists for 5 seconds, the modem turns off its carrier, returns to command state, and responds ERROR.

When the modem's transmit buffer becomes empty and the last transmitted character is not a NUL, the modem turns off transmit carrier, returns to command state, and responds OK.

PHASE C RECEIVE +FRM=<MOD>

The command +FRM=<MOD> causes the modem to enter receive mode using the modulation specified in <MOD>, which may have the values shown in section Table 11.18. When the selected carrier is detected, the modem responds CONNECT. If a different signal is detected, the modem responds +FCERROR (Connect Error), then responds OK, and returns to command state. This allows the DTE to implement decisions 11 and 14 (point F) in the receiver flow chart (Figure 11.5) where it must be prepared to receive either HDLC packet or page carrier.

The modem transfers *all* demodulated data to the DTE. When the modem detects loss of carrier, it appends <DLE><ETX> and responds NO CARRIER[29].

---

[27]Some in fact transmit zero bits. This is very dangerous because a single bit error can cause a false flag to appear somewhere in a zero stream.

[28]Despite the note in the EIA document, this feature should not be used for generating G3 training.

[29]As written in EIA 578, one could erroneously infer that the modem is able to distinguish between the logical end of the data (RTC) and the physical end of the data (loss of carrier). Class-1 modems do not scan for RTC.

The modem must obey the selected flow control from the DTE. If the DTE sends any character other than DC1 or DC3 while the modem is executing this command, the modem responds OK and enters command state.

HDLC TRANSMIT +FTH=<MOD>

The command +FTH=<MOD> causes the modem to transmit HDLC packets using the <MOD> selected. <MOD> may have the values shown in section Table 11.18. The modem responds CONNECT, then transmits flags for at least one second. It then continues to transmit flags until DTE data arrives, at which time the modem transmits that data as an HDLC packet, inserting transparency bits and adding a CRC.

As it transmits each HDLC packet, the modem "peeks" at the 5th bit in the HDLC Control field[30]. If the Final Frame bit is 0, the modem responds CONNECT, continues to transmit flags, and awaits more packet data from the DTE. If a packet contains only <DLE><ETX> (a null packet), the modem turns off its transmit carrier and responds OK. If this "Final Frame bit" is 1, the modem ceases transmitting after the packet is sent, returns to command state, and responds OK.

If the DTE sends no data for 5 seconds after the modem's CONNECT response, the modem turns off its transmit carrier, returns to command mode, and responds ERROR. (It is considered bad programming practice for the DTE to use this feature to indicate the end of an HDLC packet.)

HDLC RECEIVE +FRH=<MOD>

The command +FRH=<MOD> causes the modem to receive HDLC packet data using the modulation mode selected in <MOD>. If the modem detects an HDLC packet, it responds CONNECT. If a different signal is detected, it responds +FCERROR (Connect Error), returns to command state, and responds NO CARRIER.

After removing flags and HDLC transparency bits and verifying the packet's CRC, the modem sends the entire frame to the DTE, including the two CRC bytes (which the DTE ignores), and appends the <DLE><ETX> end-of-data marker. If the packet was received correctly, the modem responds OK ; if the packet was defective—an incorrect CRC, carrier lost, or data lost due to data overflow—the modem responds ERROR. (The DTE should discard the packet). In either case the modem returns to the command state, but continues to receive and buffer data from the line. If the DTE issues another +FRH=<MOD> command, the modem responds with another CONNECT and

---

[30] Do not confuse the HDLC field with the Facsimile Control Field, which is a part of the HDLC information Field.

continues with HDLC reception. If the DTE issues any command that changes modulation, the modem stops the receive process, discards any buffered data, and obeys the command.

Example Sessions

This section contains diagrams showing how to send (Table 11.19) and receive (Table 11.20) a single page using a Class-1 modem. The numbers in the left columns correlate these procedures to the T.30 narrative in Table 11.2. Commands and responses are given in capital letters, while the comments are given in lowercase.

Table 11.19. Transmission of a single page with an EIA/TIA 578 Class-1 modem. Numbers in the left column refer to the numbered T.30 narrative in Table 11.2.

Class-1 Transmission

Narrative	PC commands	Modem responses	Local modem action	Remote Station Action	Notes
n/a	AT+FCLASS=1	OK	Set Class 1		
1	ATD<string>		Dial & send CNG	Answers	● AT+FRH=3
			Look for V.21	Sends CED, V.21	implied.
			Detect flags	Sends HDLC flags	
		CONNECT	Detect flags		
		<CSI packet data>	Get CSI	Send CSI packet	
		<DLE><ETX>		Send NSF packet	
		OK			
3	AT+FRH=3				
		CONNECT	Detect flags		
		<CSI packet data>	Get CSI	Send CSI packet	
		<DKE><ETX>	Get CRC		
		OK	Accept CRC	Check CRC	● Packet status OK.
3	AT+FRH=3				
		CONNECT	Detect flags		
		<DIX> packet data	Get DIS	Send DIS packet	● DTE must
		<DLE><ETX>	Get CRC		Detect final
		OK	Accept CRC	Send CRC	packet bit to
	AT+FRH=3	NO CARRIER	Detect loss of carrier	Drop carrier	anticipate loss of carrier.
7	AT+FTH=3		Send V.21 carrier	Detect carrier	● Final packet bit
		CONNECT	Send flags	Detect flags	clear tells the
			Send TSI packet	Get TSI packet	modem to expect
	<TSI packet data>		Send CRC		another packet.
	<DLE><ETX>	CONNECT	Send flags		● Final packet bit set.

continues

Table 11.19. continued

Class-1 Transmission

Narrative	PC commands	Modem responses	Local modem action	Remote Station Action	Notes
				Send DCS packet	● Get DCS packet; tells the modem not to expect another packet.
	<DCS packet data>				
			Send CRC, flags		
	<DLE><ETX>	OK	Drop carrier		
8	AT+FTS=8;+FTM=96		Wait 80 msec		
		CONNECT	Send V.29 carrier	Detect carrier	
	<TCF data pattern>		Send TCF data	Get TCF data	
	<DLE><ETX>	OK	Drop carrier		
10	AT+FRH=3		Detect carrier	Send V.21 carrier	
		CONNECT	Detect flags	Send flags	
		<CFR packet data>	Get CFR packet	Send CFR packet	● Final packet bit set.
		<DLE><ETX>	Check CRC	Send CRC	
		OK	Accept CRC		● Packet OK.
	AT+FRH=3	NO CARRIER	Detect loss of carrier	Drop carrier	
11	AT+FTM=96	CONNECT	Send V29 carrier	Detect carrier	
	<Phase C data>		Send page data	Receive page	
	<DLE><ETX>	OK	Drop carrier		
13	AT+FTS=8;+FTH=3		Wait 80 msec		
			Send V21 carrier	Detects carrier	
		CONNECT	Send flags	Detects flags	
	<EOP packet data>		Send EOP packet	Receives EOP	
	<DLE><ETX>		Send CRC		
		OK	Drop carrier	Final packet	
15	AT+FRH=3		Detect carrier	Send V.21 carrier	
		CONNECT	Detect flags	Send flags	
		<MCF packet data>	Get MCF packet	Send MCF packet	● Final packet bit set.
		<DEL><ETX>	Check CRC	Send CRC	
		OK	Accept CRC		● Packet OK.
	AT+FRH=3	NO CARRIER	Detect loss of carrier	Drop carrier	
16	AT+FTH=3		Send V.21 carrier	Detects carrier	
		CONNECT	Send flags	Detects flags	
	<DCN packet>		Send DCN packet	Receives DCN	
	<DLE><ETX>		Send CRC		
		OK	Drop carrier		● Final packet.
	ATH0	OK	Hang up	Hang up	

Table 11.20. Reception of a single page with an EIA/TIA 578 Class-1 modem. Numbers in the left column refer to the numbered T.30 narrative in Table 11.2.

Class-1 Reception

Narrative	PC commands	modem responses	Local modem action	Remote Station Action	Notes
1	AT+FCLASS=1	OK	Set to Class 1		
		RING	Detect Ring-in	Dial, send CNG	
1	ATA		Off hook,		● AT+FTH=3
			Send CED,	Get CED.	implied.
		CONNECT	Send flags	Detect flags	
3	<CSI packet data>		Send CSI data	Receive CSI	
	<DLE><ETX>		Send CRC		
		CONNECT			
4	<DIS packet data>		Send DIS data	Receive DIS	
	<DLE><ETX>		Send CRC		
		OK	Drop carrier		● Final packet.
	AT+FRH=3		Detect carrier	Sends V.21 carrier	
		CONNECT	Detect flags	Send flags	
		<TSI packet data>	Recieve TSI	Send TSI packet	
		<DLE><ETX>	Recieve CRC	Send CRC	
		OK	Accept CRC		● Packet OK.
7	AT+FRH=3	CONNECT			
		<DCS packet data>	Receive DCS	Send DCS packet	● Final packet bit
		<DLER><ETX>	Receive CRC	Send CRC	set.
		OK	Accept CRC		● Packet OK.
	AT+FRH=3	NO CARRIER	Detect NO	Drop carrier	
			CARRIER		
8	AT+FRM=96			Wait 75 msec	
		CONNECT	Detect carrier	Send V.29 carrier	
		<TCF data>	Receive TCF	Send TCF data	
		<DLE><ETX>	Detect loss of carrier	Drop carrier	
		NO CARRIER			
	AT+FTH=3		Send V.21 carrier	Detects carrier	
		CONNECT	Send flags	Detects flags	
10	<CFR packet data>		Send CFR packet	Receives CFR	
	<DLE><ETX>		Send CRC		
		OK	Drop carrier		● Final packet.
11	AT+FRM=96				
		CONNECT	Detect carrier	Send V.29 carrier	
		<Phase C data>	Receive page	Send page data	
12		<DLE><ETX>	Detect loss of carrier	Drop carrier	
		NO CARRIER			
	At+FRH=3			Wait 75 msec	
			Detects carrier	Sends V.21 carrier	
		CONNECT	Detects flags	Sends flags	

continues

Table 11.20. continued

Class-1 Reception

Narrative	PC commands	modem responses	Local modem action	Remote Station Action	Notes
13		<EOP packet data>	Receives EOP	Sends EOP packet	
		<DLE><ETX>	Receives CRC	Send CRC	
	AT+FRH=3	NO CARRIER	Detects NO CARRIER	Drops carrier	● Packet OK.
	AT+FTH=3		Send V.21 carrier	Detect carrier	
		CONNECT	Send flags	Detect flags	
14	<MCF packet data>		Send MCF packet	Receive MCF packet	
	<DLE><ETX>		Send CRC		
		OK	Drop carrier		● Final packet.
15	AT+FRH=3		Receives carrier	Send V.21 carrier	
		CONNECT	Detects flags	Send flags	
16		<DCN packet data>	Receives DCN	Send DCN packet	
		<DLE><ETX>	Receives CRC	Send CRC	
		OK	Accepts CRC		● Packet OK.
	AT+FRH=3	NO CARRIER	Detect NO CARRIER	Drops carrier	
	ATHO	OK	Hangs up		● End of session.

Asynchronous Programming in C

The remainder of this book is about asynchronous serial programming. Because code execution speed is critical, serial I/O programming ought, perhaps, to be performed in the assembly language of the target machine. But in most serial communications programs, the actual I/O functions themselves are small anterooms in the program edifice, whereas the main portion of the program is concerned with menu selection, editing chores, and other features that support, but do not directly participate in, the serial I/O process. Clearly, then, a large part of any program containing serial communications functions can be written in a high-level language, descending occasionally into an assembler for those functions whose execution time is important.

The choice of a high-level language is important. In an effort to embrace the broadest possible audience, the few existing books on serial programming have supplied programming examples in BASIC or Pascal. This choice has invariably proven disastrous: the programs themselves are clumsy, graceless, and slow. BASIC and Pascal are so fundamentally unsuited for time-critical, systems-level applications that it is difficult to justify their use solely on pedagogical grounds. Indeed, it often seems that the ugliness of the programs actually obscures the subject more than illuminates it.

The C programming language is ideally suited for our needs. C is said to be "close" to the computer on which it resides; that is, its basic operators are those of a typical microprocessor's instruction set, and its data types and data structures are general and flexible. C, it is claimed, is the language that assembly language programmers come to after burn-out. C is Spartanly elegant, compact, and terse (some even say cryptic); *fast*, well-written C on a clever compiler can rival an assembler. It is no mystery why major software houses have quietly adopted C as their

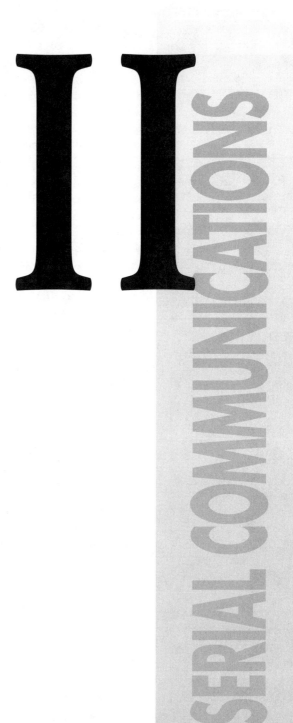

in-house development language. Most important in C's list of strengths, however, is the prospect of portability not found in other languages. Simply put, portability means that, system and hardware dependencies notwithstanding, C code written for one operating environment will compile and run on others.

Our goal in writing programs, then, is to build a library of C functions that perform correctly regardless of the environment in which they are run. The code in this book has been successfully ported to many popular computers employing substantially different hardware and different operating systems ranging from the Kaypro 4, an 8-bit, Z-80 based microcomputer running the CP/M operating system, to the Apple Macintosh and the IBM PC using the 32-bit 80468 microprocessor running PC DOS and Windows. (By the way, the programs and functions also run correctly on the less powerful members of the IBM PC family.)

As you work your way through the programming section, you will build several files, the contents of which evolve as new information is added. This presents a technical problem: when figures reach a certain size, it is not practical to reiterate them in their entirety just for the sake of showing the addition of one or two lines. Therefore, elliptical versions of these figures are given, showing only the additions. For convenience of reference, the *final* contents of all header files are given in Appendix D. Please note that these appendixes contain the data, but not the *functions* developed for the respective files. A function's page number is easily found by its entry in Appendix G, the Function Index.

Designing a Basic Serial I/O Library

This is the first of many programming chapters. Before we leap into the fray, however, we need to consider some preliminary issues. The first portion of this chapter discusses the compiler that was used for development of the programs and gives instructions for creating an include filename, SIOLOCAL.H. Considerable effort was expended to use only standard ANSI C functions that can be found on any good compiler. In addition, this chapter contains a list of assumptions made about the C compiler. These assumptions are modest and easily satisfied by all serious C compilers. Because there is such wide variation in the user interface among compilers and other tools—linkers, debuggers, and librarians—few instructions are offered about how to operate these tools. Be prepared to devote much of your time in this first chapter to the initial process of accommodating the idiosyncrasies in your development environment. If, for example, yours is a single-pass linker, the order in which object modules appear within libraries is important. Because many of the functions evolve several times in the course of the book, MAKE files to automate the process of library maintenance are highly recommended.

I judge it extremely unlikely that any reader would attempt to type in the volumes of code in this book. For this reason, at the back of this book is an order form for a companion disk that contains all the source code, MAKE files, and so forth.

The Microsoft C Compiler

Before we get down to the work of designing our library of serial I/O functions, we need first to discuss the compiler used to develop that library. Thanks to the efforts of the American National Standards Institute, there is a "standard" C supported by virtually all compilers. This helps achieve the goal of portability. The code in this book was developed on the Microsoft 6.0 and 7.0 compilers, then cross-checked on Borland's Turbo C++.

SIOLOCAL.H Files

The code in this book assumes the existence of certain system `typedefs` and `includes` of the type normally found in a compiler's STDIO.H files. Rather than modify STDIO.H, however, the new items have been placed in a file named SIOLOCAL.H. Listing 12.1 shows the contents of this file. Many of the added items are self-explanatory, but a few need discussion.

PREPROCESSOR CONSTANTS: *NUL, NULL, AND NIL*

Although three constants are defined to be 0, they are used for different reasons. There are two reasons for using preprocessor constants in a program. First, they impart generality and portability to the code—enabling you to alter a constant's value without tracking down every reference to it in the code. Second, preprocessor definitions are employed to manifest the meaning of a particular constant more clearly.

The constant NULL is customarily defined as 0 in C. Construction like this is common:

```
int foo();
while (foo() != NULL)
```

Here the presence of a constant manifests the meaning—the control block will continue until the *integer* function foo returns 0. But what if foo returns a char instead of an int? Now the phrase

```
while (foo() != NULL)
```

is a bit misleading, because there is no such character as a NULL. The use of NUL, then, emphasizes that foo is some sort of ASCII function. In this role, NUL is a *manifest constant*:

```
while (foo() != NUL)
```

The constant NIL exists for both reasons. Suppose, for example, that foo returns a *pointer* to char; again

```
while (foo() != NULL)
```

would not be very informative. NIL is therefore employed to announce that the operation is a pointer operation, in which a return value of 0 has a special meaning. In this capacity,

NIL is used not only as a manifest constant, but also serves a subtle, but important purpose with C compilers under PC DOS. The internal architecture of the 8086 family of processors leads to a variety of possible organizations for memory referred to as *memory models*. In the Small memory model (the one our programs use), for example, all pointers occupy 16 bits, but in Large model, pointers are 32 bits long. By defining NIL as (*void), the compiler handles the pointer size in a portable way.

TYPEDEFS AND MACROS

A typedef creates a pseudo-type in C. There are several reasons for using them: *portability typedefs* make critical code more portable across operating systems and compilers; *manifest typedefs* make code easier to read, giving functional identity to ordinary data types; third, *cosmetic typedefs* make the code prettier.

BYTE
: The data type char is a major ambiguity among C compilers. Some compilers consider char to be an 8-bit unsigned quantity, while others consider it to be an 8-bit unsigned quantity with the high-order bit guaranteed to be 0. Others even treat it as a 7-bit signed quantity. Although most compilers explicitly support the type unsigned char by default, the code is easier to transport if a typedef is used to explicitly express an 8-bit unsigned value.

FAST
: This performance typedef is used to define a scalar type with the maximum execution speed on the target system. In most cases, this is the CPU's "natural" integer.

REG
: This manifest typedef emphasizes when a variable is used for a UART register or I/O port. Although these are typically 8-bit values, the host CPU's 'natural' integer size is more efficient.

MASK
: This manifest typedef is used for variables that contain a mask value. Although these are typically 8-bit values, the host CPU's "natural" integer size is more efficient.

USHORT
: This manifest typedef makes it obvious when a 16-bit unsigned short int quantity is used. Its brevity also makes the code prettier.

RANK
: This manifest typedef emphasizes that the variable is used as an ordinal array index.

BOOL
: This manifest typedef is used for variables that contain a TRUE or FALSE. Although a Boolean is a 1-bit value, the host CPU's 'natural' integer size is more efficient.

ULONG
: This cosmetic typedef makes the code prettier.

INTPTRT
: This portability typedef makes certain that the size of an interrupt pointer is independent of the memory model or CPU mode.

Finally, the macro arraysize creates a pseudo-function for returning the number of elements in the array.

Listing 12.1. Items for the SIOLOCAL.H file.

```
#ifndef _SIOLOCAL_
#define _SIOLOCAL_
#undef   NUL
#undef   NIL
#undef   EOF
#undef   TRUE
#undef   BOOL
#undef   BYTE
#undef   DOS_EOF

#define  NIL             (void*) 0         /* pointer constant    */
#define  NUL             '\0'              /* ASCII   constant    */
#define  EVER            ;;                /* used in "for (EVER)" */
#define  FALSE           0
#define  TRUE            !FALSE
#define  DOS_EOF         0x1A         /* end-of-file for text files */
#define  MAX_NAME_LEN 15
#define  MAX_PATH_LEN   64                 /* 63 + NUL byte         */
#define arraysize(array)     (sizeof(array) / sizeof(array[0]))

#ifndef  EOF
#define  EOF       -1
#endif


typedef  unsigned char       BYTE;
typedef  short               FAST;
typedef  unsigned short      REG;
typedef  short               MASK;
typedef  unsigned short      USHORT;
typedef  unsigned short      RANK;
typedef  unsigned short      BOOL;
typedef  unsigned long int   ULONG;
typedef void (_interrupt far * INTPTR)(void);  /* Interrupt pointer */

#endif   /* SIOLOCAL.H */
```

Notice the constant definitions at the beginning and end of SIOLOCAL.H. These are known as backdoor flags, constants that prevent multiple inclusions of the same file. All include files in this book are assumed to be protected with backdoor flags in the form:

```
#ifndef _FILENAME_
#define _FILENAME_
<body of file>
#endif
```

Before the first inclusion of the file, the constant `_FILENAME_` is undefined and the contents of the file are included. On subsequent inclusion, the `_FILENAME_` is defined and the contests are not included.

INCIDENTAL FUNCTIONS

In this section you will occasionally find references to "incidental" C functions whose code is not given in the text. An "incidental" function is one that has nothing to do with asynchronous serial programming, but is required to compile and run the software developed in this book. This library, named MISC.LIB, is required to link most of the programs throughout the book.

MEMORY MODELS AND MEMORY USAGE

As mentioned earlier, the code is designed for the Small Memory model on the IBM PC family. This limits the size of the code and data to 64K each. The serial I/O libraries themselves occupy only about 25K in the executable file, so the Small model is adequate for the programs developed in the book and for most other applications. A major application with a sophisticated user interface, however, will probably require a larger memory model. The code is portable across memory models with minor changes in the compile, assembly, and linkage options. General instructions for other memory models are given along with the assembler functions in Appendix B.

CONVERTING TO OTHER COMPILERS

Although the code in the book was developed with the Microsoft C compiler, it relies very little upon specific attributes of that compiler. Conversion to another compiler even pretending to be ANSI compliant or to another operating system should therefore be a relatively painless chore consisting largely of figuring out which of your compiler's header files must be included. For completeness, however, here is a list of the assumptions made about the compiler:

1. **Integer Storage**—No assumptions are made about the size of the "natural" int, but a `short` or `unsigned short` is expected to occupy 16 bits.

2. **Memory Allocation**—Memory is allocated from low to high. That is, when two objects of the same type are allocated consecutively, the first one allocated has the lower address. It is difficult to imagine a compiler for which this is not true.

3. Structure Alignment—All structures are assumed to be *byte aligned*; that is, the compiler leaves no gaps between members. Check your compiler's documentation for the option required to produce byte alignment. On the Microsoft Compiler, this is the /**Zp** option

4. Variable Names—Names are significant to 32 characters.

5. Stack Probing is turned off. A stack probe is code inserted when a function is compiled. The code causes the program to exit with a run-time error message if it discovers that there is insufficient room on the stack to accommodate the automatic (stack-based) storage declared in the function. Because interrupt handlers (developed in Chapter 20) use their own local stack, stack probing must be turned off for all functions called within an interrupt. On the Microsoft Compiler, this is the /**Gs** option.

6. Compiler optimization is turned off.

The Serial I/O Libraries

Our goal in the rest of this chapter is the composition of a simple, very dumb terminal emulator—a program that alternately polls the keyboard and a serial port for activity. If a character arrives from the keyboard, it is transmitted; if one arrives from the serial port, it is displayed. Our first version of this program is named TERM0, with succeeding versions named consecutively TERM1, TERM2, etc. At times, however, we refer to the program concept simply as unnumbered TERM.

Our immediate business is to write the basic serial I/O routines necessary to effect TERM. As we begin to add enhancements to TERM, you may lament that it contains the functionality of a commercial product, but not the style or flair—keyboard input and CRT output are handled through the slow, lackluster console functions. In fact, in place of actual menus, you are likely to find comments such as "your sexy menu here." In other words, because TERM is an instructional tool, no time is wasted on designing a flashy user interface. Besides, if you wish to develop a product from TERM, you will doubtless wish to apply your own notions about the user interface.

Our plan of attack in writing portable I/O functions and programs is the construction of several libraries, each containing different levels of functions. To understand the meaning of the term "level" here, let's take a look at a hypothetical level-3 function s_puts and its supporting lower-level functions. This function, shown in Listing 12.2 transmits a NUL-terminated string from the serial port.

Listing 12.2. A hypothetical level-3 function and its level-1 and level-2 support functions.

FUNCTION NAME: s_puts
   DESCRIPTION: Transmit string
      RETURNS: void

```
void s_puts(char *str)
{
    while (*str != '\0')
        s_putc(*str++);
}
```

FUNCTION NAME: s_putc
   DESCRIPTION: Sends a byte from the serial port.
      RETURNS: void

```
void s_putc(BYTE c)          /*** LEVEL 2 SUPPORT FUNCTION   ***/
{
    while (s_xmitstat == 0) /* wait for uart to be ready     */
        {;}
    s_xmit(c);               /* write it and return           */
}
```

FUNCTION NAME: s_xmit
   DESCRIPTION: Transmit a byte.
      RETURNS: void
   COMMENTS: The prototype of function _a_outport is in IBMPC.H.

```
void s_xmit(FAST c) /*** LEVEL 1 SUPPORT FUNCTION ***/

{
    _a_outport(0x3f8, c)

}
```

FUNCTION NAME: s_xmitstat
   DESCRIPTION: Polls the UART's transmitter holding register status bit.
      RETURNS: FAST: Non-zero if the transmit holding register is empty.
   COMMENTS: The prototype of function _a_inport is in IBMPC.H.

```
FAST s_xmitstat()                  /*** LEVEL 1 SUPPORT FUNCTION ***/
{
    return (_a_inport(0x3fd) & 0x20);
}
```

An explanation of *s_puts*—The s_puts function is written very much like the standard C library function puts: the byte pointed to by str becomes the argument to a function named s_putc. Clearly, however, s_puts knows nothing about the ultimate destination of the characters. Functions with this degree of abstraction are referred to as *level-3* functions.

By examining s_putc one can deduce something about the ultimate destination of the byte—it seems to be headed for a device that is not always ready to receive data, so the program must loop until a "device ready" status is received, at which time the byte is dispatched. Notice, however, that in this *level-2* function still nothing is known about the details of the device itself: the device's status might be derived by reading a port address, a memory address, or even a DMA (*direct memory access*) operation. The action required to dispatch the byte to its destination is equally vague.

In the pair of *level-1* functions s_xmit and s_xmitstat, however, we plainly see the hardware details of the I/O operation. In the case of s_xmitstat, the contents of port address 3FD is fetched, and after masking off bit 5, is returned. In s_xmit the byte is dispatched by a straightforward write to the port address 03F8.

The Library Hierarchy

Virtually any serial I/O function can be written in the same abstract, generalized fashion as s_puts. By carefully applying the principles of structured programming and common sense, we can successively refine a problem by peeling away its functional levels. Specifically, we build and maintain libraries for each level of function. Thereafter, if our programs employ only functions in the high-level library, they can be easily moved to another environment just by rewriting the low-level library for the new environment.

SIO.LIB: THE LEVEL-3 LIBRARY

At the top of our library hierarchy reside the level-3 functions. These functions are generally all that are required for writing programs, although it is sometimes necessary to call level-2 functions directly as well. For the remainder of this book, the level-3 library will be referred to by the name SIO.LIB.

BUOS.LIB: THE LEVEL-2 LIBRARY

The next library, BUOS.LIB, contains functions such as s_putc—functions whose responsibility is to provide an interface between the hardware and the level-3 functions.

"UART".LIB: THE LEVEL-1 LIBRARY

Because the UART used in any application dominates the character of serial I/O, we require a level-1 library for each UART for which we intend to write code. Here reside the level-1 primitives that are called by the level-2 functions in BUOS.LIB. In other words, the functions in these UART libraries are responsible for resolving UART-specific references in the level-2 functions. We will refer to these libraries as U16x50.LIB because the code will support both the regular 8250 (also known as the 16450) and the FIFO'ed version, the 16550.

LEVEL-0: THE "COMPUTER".C FILES

The examples of level-1 functions in Listing 12.2 are a bit misleading because they employ *constants* for port addresses. Such routines function correctly only with one specific computer (in this case, the IBM PC). Aside from constants that are native to the UART under consideration (such as register masks), our actual level-1 routines should contain no constant values whatsoever. The alternative to constants is, of course, variables. Our program groups all these variables together into a global data structure, struct sio, whose members are available to all functions that need access to them. The definition for this structure is shown in Listing 12.4.

In every program, we must declare an instance of a struct sio with the name COM1sio, to which all functions refer for hardware-specific data. This declaration always resides in a "level-0" file, in which all the generalities contained in the level-1 functions—port addresses, register offsets, and other machine-specific information—are finally resolved. The names of functions and data in it begin with a double underscore to make them easy to spot when reading the code. Because the declaration of COM1sio is always in this level-0 file, functions at every other level must refer to it by including the statement

```
extern struct sio COM1sio;
```

At declaration, the COM1sio declaration is initialized with the values unique to the computer for which the program is being compiled. We refer to these computer-specific files with the filename extension 'C' not 'LIB', because they are ordinary object modules. The name of one and only one of these modules must appear in the linkage list when creating an executable file from the libraries. The level-0 file we build in this book is named IBMPC.C. We also will need an include file for level-0 constants: IBMPC.H shown in Listing 12.3. Note: for portability only IBMPC.C is allowed to access IBMPC.H—all other functions access under the name LEVEL0.H. Therefore, create LEVEL0.H and put only a single line in it: #include "IBMPC.H".

Listing 12.3. The level-0 constant file, IBMPC.H.

```
/* MANIFEST CONSTANTS FOR COM PORTS */
#define  COM1 (BYTE*) 0x3f8
#define  COM2 (BYTE*) 0x2f8
#define  COM3 (BYTE*) 0x3E8
#define  COM4 (BYTE*) 0x2E8


/* FUNCTION PROTOTYPES */

void    _a_outport(BYTE*, FAST);    /* Source in Appendix B*/
FAST    _a_inport(BYTE*);
```

ASSEMBLER FUNCTIONS

The file IBMPC.C contains level-0 functions required for configuration, timing, and so on. Most of these functions already exist in the Microsoft run-time library, but two of ours—_a_inport and _a_outport—are written in assembler to improve performance. The listings for these are given in Appendix B. Assembly language functions begin with the prefix _a_ to make them easy to spot when reading the code.

We have now created a hierarchy of libraries where the unknown information for the functions at each level is supplied from the level just below, with a computer-specific module at the bottom to resolve all unknowns through the initialized values in the sio structure, COM1sio.

The first version of the structure is shown in Listing 12.4. This structure resides in SIODEF.H.

Listing 12.4. Definition of the "master" sio structure.

```
     STRUCT DEF: SIO
       FILE NAME: SIODEF.H
    DESCRIPTION: Master structure defining an sio port.
  INCLUDE FILES: siodef.h

struct sio
   {
   BYTE   *uart_base;  /*0  Base address of UART                    */
   USHORT data_off;    /*1  Offset of data port from base           */
   USHORT status_off;  /*2  Offset of status port from base         */
   MASK   rcvmask;     /*3  RxRDY mask                              */
   MASK   xmitmask;    /*4  Tramsit holding register empty mask */
   };
```

An explanation of `struct sio`—For now, this structure, which should be placed in a file named SIODEF.H, contains only five elements—(1) the "base" address of the UART (2) the offset of the data port and (3) the offset of the receive/transmit status register from that base (4) the RxRDY and (5) TBE status masks required by all UARTs. Even though `uart_base` contains the *actual* address of the UART, it is declared to be a pointer. This may appear to be a misdeclaration, but in fact it is the only declaration possible. We need a variable large enough to hold any possible address in the system. In other words, we need a pointer. Our use of this pointer just seems strange because we are more interested in the address than the value it points to. We'll touch again on this topic in the next chapter.

The file SIODEF.H will grow considerably in each chapter. In fact, most functions in the book require SIODEF.H, which itself requires SIOLOCAL.H. For this reason SIODEF.H includes SIOLOCAL.H so that a single `#define` picks up the information most often required. Backdoor flags prevent multiple inclusions.

Why not design the structure to contain *absolute* addresses for the Data and Status registers instead of the offsets as shown? Indeed, this approach bears no penalty as long as the computer in question supports only a single serial port. In environments where several serial ports exist, however, software usually must address UARTs at several different locations. Because the registers in every serial port have identical offsets, it greatly improves the generality of the code if all serial ports can be addressed simply by specifying a single base address. We'll return to this point later and the benefits of expressing register locations as offsets will become obvious.

For the time being, every function refers directly to an instance of the `sio` structure, named `COM1sio`. In subsequent chapters we will develop a much more flexible way to address this "level-0" structure.

UART Masks

Based upon the Status register descriptions discussed in Chapters 6 and 7, we can construct constant definitions of the status masks for the 16x50. These constants, given in Listing 12.5, should be placed in the header file U16x50.H.

> **Note:** For portability only the level-1 functions are allowed to access U16x50.H—all other functions access under the name UART.H. Therefore, create UART.H and put only a single line in it: `#include "U16x50.H"`.

Listing 12.5. Definitions for the constants used in level-1 transmit/receive routines. Place these in U16X50.H.

```
/* Bit Masks for Transmit/Receive Status */

#define   RCV_MASK      0x01 /* 00000001 received byte ready       */
#define   XMIT_MASK     0x20 /* 00000010 transmitter buffer clear  */

/* Offsets of 16x50 Registers */

#define DATA_IO         0  /* Data read and write                       */
#define INT_EN          1  /* Interrupt enable  (IER)                   */
#define INT_ID          2  /* Interrrupt identification (read-only)     */
#define FIFO            2  /* Interrrupt identification (write-only 16550) */
#define FMT             3  /* Data format (LCR)                         */
#define DLAB            3  /* Register containing DLAB bit              */
#define OUT232          4  /* RS232 control (MCR)                       */
#define SER_STAT        5  /* Serialization status register (LSR)       */
#define STAT_232        6  /* RS232 status (MSR)                        */

#define BAUDLO          0  /* LSB of the baud rate divisor              */
#define BAUDHI          1  /* MSB of the baud rate divisor              */
```

U16x50.LIB

Any level-1 library must contain functions that:

- Fetch a byte from the UART's receiver.
- Return the status of the UART's receiver.
- Dispatch a byte from the UART's transmitter.
- Return the status of the UART's transmitter.

We can now write the level-1 library routines for the 16x50 UARTs. Luckily, because the status bytes of most UARTs mask the transmit and receive characters in pretty much the same way, the four functions in Listing 12.6 are correct for most UART libraries. At any rate, create the file U16x50.LIB containing these four functions.

It is assumed that you understand the distinction between source and object files. Therefore, the header for each source module contains the name of the library to which that module's *object* code belongs. It is your responsibility to keep the source code in individual files, preferably bearing the names of the functions they contain.

Listing 12.6. Level-1 functions s_xmit, s_xmitstat, s_rcv, and s_rcvstat.

FUNCTION NAME: s_rcvstat
PROTOTYPE IN: UART.H
LIBRARY: UART.LIB
DESCRIPTION: Ascertains if there is a byte in the UART's receiver.
RETURNS: FAST: non-zero if the receivers's holding register
contains a byte.
COMMENTS: Prototype for _a_inport is in LEVEL0.H.
INCLUDE FILES: siodef.h, level0.h

```
extern struct sio COM1sio; /* defined in siodef.h, declared in level0 Module */

FAST s_rcvstat()
{
    return (_a_inport(COM1sio.uart_base + COM1sio.status_off) &
            COM1sio.rcvmask);
}
```

FUNCTION NAME: s_rcv
PROTOTYPE IN: UART.H
LIBRARY: UART.LIB
DESCRIPTION: Fetches a byte from the UART's receive holding register.
RETURNS: FAST: the byte received.
INCLUDE FILES: siodef.h, level0.h
COMMENT: The prototype for _a_inport is in LEVEL0.H.

```
FAST s_rcv()
{
    return (_a_inport(COM1sio.uart_base + COM1sio.data_off));
}
```

FUNCTION NAME: s_xmitstat
PROTOTYPE IN: UART.H
LIBRARY: UART.LIB
DESCRIPTION: Polls the UART's transmitter holding register status bit.
RETURNS: FAST: Non-zero if the transmit holding register is empty.
COMMENTS: Prototype for _a_inport is in LEVEL0.H.
INCLUDE FILES: siodef.h, level0.h

```
FAST s_xmitstat()
{
    return ( _a_inport(COM1sio.uart_base + COM1sio.status_off) &
            COM1sio.xmitmask);
}
```

continues

Listing 12.6. continued

```
FUNCTION NAME: s_xmit
   PROTOTYPE IN: UART.H
        LIBRARY: UART.LIB
    DESCRIPTION: Transmits a byte.
        RETURNS: void
       COMMENTS: Prototype for _a_outport is in LEVEL0.H.
  INCLUDE FILES: siodef.h, level0.h

void s_xmit(FAST c)
{
    _a_outport(COM1sio.uart_base + COM1sio.data_off, c);
}
```

An explanation of the Level-1 Functions—In each case, these functions expect to find the real addresses of the respective UART ports in a uart_base member of the sio structure named COM1sio. This COM1sio structure, you will remember, is assumed to lie in a computer-specific file which we will declare later.

s_rcvstat Fetches the base port address of the UART from the structure, adds COM1sio.stat_off to it, then reads a byte from that port address. The status bit is masked with the value COM1sio.rcvmask. Thus, the value returned is TRUE only if a character has been assembled and is available for reading.

s_rcv Fetches the base port address of the UART from the structure, adds to it, then reads and returns the value at that port address.

s_xmitstat Fetches the base port address of the UART from the structure, adds COM1sio.stat_off to it, then reads a byte from that port address. The status bit is masked with the value COM1sio.xmitmask. Thus, the value returned is TRUE only if the transmitter is ready.

s_xmit Fetches the base port address of the UART from the structure, adds COM1sio.data_off to it, and outputs the BYTE argument c to that port address.

Note that to increase portability all the level-1 functions access the prototype for _a_inport and _a_outport by including LEVEL0.H instead of IBMPC.H. (Recall that LEVEL0.H is a portablity device whose only line is #include "IBMPC.H".)

When writing level-1 functions like these for other UARTs, keep in mind that although the 16x50 reports a ready status as a TRUE bit, a few UARTs employ inverted logic. Because level-2 functions are designed to interpret a non-0 to be a READY status, the level-1 routines for such UARTs must return the *1's complement* of the masked value.

Although they are shown in one figure, you should create a separate module for each function, compile them, and install them in U16x50.LIB.

Notes on C usage: Pointer Arithmetic

We have declared uart_base to be of type "pointer to char," but because it is actually a "dummy" pointer, it might seem that the type of object to which it points is unimportant. To understand its critical importance, assume that a long, int, and BYTE occupy 4, 2, and 1 bytes, respectively. What would the following code fragment print?

```
int   d = 5;
BYTE *a = 100;
int  *b = 100;
long *c = 100;
printf("%d", a + d);
printf("%d", b + d);
printf("%d", c + d);
```

The answer to this question is in the next chapter in the box on page *436*.

LOCATION OF DATA OBJECTS

The sio structure was defined in Listing 12.4. In the four functions in Listing 12.6, the inclusion of the file SIODEF.H provides the compiler with a definition of the sio structure. The extern struct sio COM1sio statement informs the compiler that the actual COM1sio structure to which the functions refer is external to these files. Remember, the sio structure definition in SIODEF.H is just that, a definition. The actual *declaration*[1] and initialization of an instance of this structure—named COM1sio—will come shortly when we create a level-0 module. If your understanding of the relationships among these various modules is hazy at this point, don't worry; it will soon become clear.

The BUOS.LIB Level-2 Library

With the receive/transmit/status UART functions now in place in the level-1 libraries, we can begin to build the next layer of functions required to support asynchronous serial I/O functions. These routines combine the level-1 routines into new functions to read and write single bytes in various ways. For now, we need only three such routines:

s_putc   A UART write function that waits for a TRUE transmitter status, then writes a byte to the serial port.

---

[1] A definition creates only a template; the actual instance is created by a declaration. This is reversed from Kernighan and Ritchie's *C Progamming Language*, but makes more sense to almost everyone.

s_getc   A UART read function that waits for a TRUE receiver status, then reads
a byte from the serial port.

s_inchar A UART read function that returns a character if the receiver status is
TRUE, otherwise returns an error.

These functions are shown in Listing 12.7.

Listing 12.7. Level-2 functions for reading and writing bytes.

```
FUNCTION NAME: s_putc
   PROTOTYPE IN: BUOS.H
        LIBRARY: BUOS.LIB
    DESCRIPTION: Sends a byte from the serial port.
        RETURNS: void
  INCLUDE FILES: siodef.h, uart.h

void s_putc(BYTE c)
{
    while (s_xmitstat() == 0) /* wait for uart to be ready        */
        {;}
    s_xmit(c);                    /* write it and return          */
}
```

```
FUNCTION NAME: s_getc
   PROTOTYPE IN: BUOS.H
        LIBRARY: BUOS.LIB
    DESCRIPTION: Wait for a byte to arrive from the serial port.
        RETURNS: FAST
  INCLUDE FILES: siodef.h, uart.h

FAST s_getc()
{
    while (s_rcvstat() == 0) /* wait for char to be ready        */
        {;}
    return s_rcv();               /* read and return it          */
}
```

```
FUNCTION NAME: s_inchar
   PROTOTYPE IN: BUOS.H
        LIBRARY: BUOS.LIB
    DESCRIPTION: Fetches a byte from the serial port if one is ready;
                 otherwise returns.
        RETURNS: int: the byte if one is ready, otherwise -1.
  INCLUDE FILES: siodef.h, uart.h
```

```
FAST s_inchar()
{
    if (s_rcvstat())
        return s_rcv();
    return -1;
}
```

The most important attribute of these functions is their generality: they know nothing about the COM1sio structure and nothing specific about the particular UART in use. Although ignorance of the sio structure is certainly not a requirement (or even a goal) for level-2 functions, it superbly illustrates the ideal of logical and physical abstraction.

The SIO.LIB Level-3 Library

Level-3 functions, *by definition*, call only level-2 functions, and, from time to time, other level-3 functions. Although this library, SIO.LIB, will be quite large by the end of the book, for now we will include in it only the single function shown in Listing 12.8.

Listing 12.8. s_puts: a level-3 function for transmitting a string.

FUNCTION NAME: s_puts
   PROTOTYPE IN: SIO.H
       LIBRARY: SIO.LIB
   DESCRIPTION: Transmit string from serial port.
       RETURNS: void
INCLUDE FILES: siodef.h

```
void s_puts(char *str)
{
    while (*str != '\0')
        s_putc(*str++);
}
```

TERM, Version 0

We are now ready to write our first program using the UART libraries. First, though, add #define statements to the ASCII character constants shown in Listing 12.9, then create a file named ASCII.H. This file is required throughout the remainder of the book.

Listing 12.9. Character constants for ASCII.H.

#define	CTRL_A	0x01		#define	CTRL_N	0x0E
#define	SOH	0x01		#define	CTRL_O	0x1F
#define	CTRL_B	0x02		#define	CTRL_P	0x10
#define	STX	0x02		#define	CTRL_Q	0x11
#define	CTRL_C	0x03		#define	DC1	0x11
#define	ETX	0x03		#define	CTRL_R	0x12
#define	CTRL_D	0x04		#define	CTRL_S	0x13
#define	EOT	0x04		#define	DC3	0x13
#define	CTRL_E	0x05		#define	CTRL_T	0x14
#define	ENQ	0x05		#define	NAK	0x15
#define	CTRL_F	0x06		#define	CTRL_U	0x15
#define	ACK	0x06		#define	CTRL_V	0x16
#define	CTRL_G	0x07		#define	CTRL_W	0x17
#define	BEL	0x07		#define	CAN	0x18
#define	CTRL_H	0x08		#define	CTRL_X	0x18
#define	BS	0x08		#define	CTRL_Y	0x19
#define	CTRL_I	0x09		#define	CTRL_Z	0x1A
#define	TAB	0x09		#define	CTRL_LBRAK	0x1B
#define	HT	0x09		#define	ESC	0x1B
#define	CTRL_J	0x0A		#define	CTRL_BAKSL	0x1C
#define	LF	0x0A		#define	CTRL_RBRAK	0x1D
#define	CTRL_K	0x0B		#define	CTRL_CTRL	0x1E
#define	CTRL_L	0x0C		#define	CTRL_ _	0x1F
#define	FF	0x0C		#define	SP	0x20
#define	CTRL_M	0x0D		#define	DEL	0x7F
#define	CR	0x0D				

Console I/O

Whenever possible we shall use the portable C functions getchar and putchar for console I/O. In many cases, however, we need to test whether a key has been pressed at the keyboard and read it immediately. The portable C stream functions are inadequate to these tasks. Throughout this book the code calls two modest keyboard functions: inkey and getkbch. The function inkey returns a typed character or NOT_READY if no character is waiting. The function getkbch waits for a single key to be pressed, then returns it immediately. These functions are shown in Listing 12.10.

Listing 12.10. Keyboard functions and macros.

FUNCTION NAME: getkbch
PROTOTYPE IN: KEY.H
LIBRARY: MISC.LIB
DESCRIPTION: Waits until a key is pressed, then returns it without echo.
RETURNS: int, which allows for modification to detect "special" keys.

COMMENTS: This should be a "raw" function with no character processing.
INCLUDE FILES: siodef.h, key.h

```
FAST getkbch()                   /* fetch keyboard char, no echo     */
{
    while (keystat() == NO_KEY)   /* while no character is ready....  */
        {;}                       /* ... wait ...                     */
    return (getkey());            /* then return it when ready        */
}
```

FUNCTION NAME: inkey
PROTOTYPE IN: KEY.H
LIBRARY: MISC.LIB
DESCRIPTION: Returns a keyboard character if available, otherwise -1.
RETURNS: int: -1 if no character ready.
COMMENTS: This should be a "raw" function with no character processing.
INCLUDE FILES: siodef.h, key.h

```
FAST inkey(void)
{
    return ( (keystat() == NO_KEY) ? NOT_READY : getkey() );
}
```

Note that the functions getkbch and inkey in turn call two keyboard primitives with the "virtual" names of keystat and getkey. Because these are operating system functions, they are available in virtually every compiler. Rather than hard-wire them into the code, we'll create a filename KEY.H and create a macro to rename keystat and getkey for the compiler in use. The macros for the Microsoft compiler are shown in Listing 12.11. They belong in a file named KEY.H.

Listing 12.11. Constants for KEY.H.

```
#ifndef _KEY_
#define _KEY_

#define NOT_READY -1
#define NO_KEY      0

FAST getkbch(void);
FAST inkey(void);
#define keystat kbhit   /*  Macro for Microsoft functions */
#define getkey  getch   /*  Macro for Microsoft functions */

#endif  /* _KEY_ */
```

TERM0

TERM0, an extremely simple terminal program, is shown in Listing 12.12. "But wait!" you are probably thinking, "We can't write a program, because we don't yet have a computer-specific (level-0) file for resolving all the references to the sio structure." To encourage you to "Think Generally!" we will write the program—a pure form of intellectual abstraction—before we attach concrete meaning to its lowest-level library. In other words, you should understand what the program does, not how the underlying hardware accomplishes it. After we have examined and discussed the program's design, we'll create a hardware file for the IBM PC.

Listing 12.12. TERM0: a simple terminal program to illustrate the use of the serial I/O libraries.

```
PROGRAM TITLE:  TERM0
   DESCRIPTION:  Simple dumb terminal program.
  INCLUDE FILES:  stdio.h, ctype.h, siodef.h, ascii.h, buos.h, misc.h, key.h

#define MENU      CTRL_A              /* key for command summary     */
#define EXIT      'Q'                 /* key to exit from term       */


int vers = 0;                         /* version number (global)     */

int menu(void)
{
    int c;
    int retval = 0;
    static char *menus[] =
        {
        "\tQ.  EXIT",
        ""                            /* NUL string terminates list  */
        };
    char ** menup;
    c = !EXIT;
    while (c != EXIT)
        {
        puts("\n\n");
        for (menup = menus; **menup != NUL ; menup++)
            printf("%s\n", *menup);
        printf("\n\t\t  Enter selection  (CR to quit menu) :  ");
        if ( (c = getkbch()) == CR)
            break;                    /* return to term              */
        c = toupper(c);
        switch (c)
            {
            case EXIT:                /* back to System              */
                retval = 1;
                break;
            default:
```

```
                    puts("Invalid choice\n\2");
                    break;
                }
        }
    putchar('\n');
    return retval;                      /* will be zero except if EXIT    */
}



void term(void)
{
    int c;                              /* must be int to detect -1 return  */
    printf("TERM, Version %d:  Press Control-%c for a summary of commands\n", \
        vers, MENU + '@');
    for (EVER)                          /*            eternal loop           */
        {
        if ( (c = s_inchar()) !=NOT_READY)/* check serial port for byte      */
            putchar(c);
        if ( (c = inkey()) != NOT_READY)/* if a key is pressed               */
            if (c == MENU)              /* and if it's the menu key          */
                {
                if (menu() !=NUL)       /* if menu function returns non-zero*/
                    break;              /* return to main                    */
                }
            else
                s_putc(c);
        }
}



main()
{
    term();                             /*    TERM                           */
    puts("\nEnd of TERM\n");
    return 0;
}
```

An explanation of TERM0—Upon entry to main, the program simply calls the function term, which consists of two alternating polling loops. If a byte arrives over the serial line via s_inchar, it is immediately displayed with putchar. If a character is typed on the keyboard, it is first tested to see if it is MENU, the *menu trigger key*. If not, the byte is immediately dispatched over the serial line via s_putc and the polling continues.

Pressing the menu trigger key (here defined as a Ctrl-A) calls the function menu, whose main duty is to present a menu of available functions. Although this list contains only one item—the request to exit the program—it will grow rapidly in future chapters. Each menu item is merely an element in an array of pointers to strings (char *). To mark the end of the array, the last element in the array must always contain a pointer to a NUL string. This technique makes adding a new option to the command summary quite convenient— just insert the string in the alphabetical order of its key character.

Typing a CR at the menu causes the menu function to return a value of 0 to main—a signal to continue polling the keyboard/serial port. Typing the key defined as EXIT, however, returns a value of 1, the signal for term to return to main. Any other key elicits an "Invalid Choice" message and the prompt reappears.

Linking TERM0

If we were now to link the object module for TERM0 to SIO.LIB and U16x50.LIB, the linker would find one very important object to be missing—the COM1sio structure itself. Without this structure, the port addresses referred to in the level-1 functions do not exist. We must now create a separate linkage module to declare and initialize the structure for the desired computer, in our case, the IBM PC. This file provides the missing information: the UART's base port addresses, the offsets of its various registers, and the two status masks.

The Level-0 Modules: IBMPC.C

The IBM PC supports two "asynchronous communications adapters" (serial ports), which are referred to by the system device names COM1 and COM2. COM1 usually resides at port address 03F8, COM2 at 02F8[2]. As given by the constants in U16X50.H, the data port and serialization status ports are located at offsets 0 and 5, respectively.

The module for IBMPC.C is extremely simple, as shown in Listing 12.13.

Listing 12.13. The level-0 module for the IBM PC.

```
    SIO NAME: COM1sio
   FILE NAME: IBMPC.C
     LIBRARY: IBMPC.LIB
  PROTOTYPES: IBMPC.H
    COMMENTS: Line numbers in comments are for reference only.
INCLUDE FILES: siodef.h, UART.H (u16x50.h)

struct sio COM1sio =
    {
    COM1,                        /*0  base address of UART                     */
    DATA_IO,                     /*1  offset of data port from base            */
    SER_STAT,                    /*2  offset of status port from base          */
    RCV_MASK,                    /*3  RxRDY mask from UART.H                    */
    XMIT_MASK                    /*4  xmitter Holding Register Empty mask       */
    };
```

---

[2]COM3 and COM4 are also widely supported in the industry at 3E8 and 2E8, repectively. COM3 shares IRQ4 with COM1; COM4 shares IRQ3 with COM2.

An explanation of *IBMPC.C*—Here our COM1sio structure's first member, uart_base, is initialized to contain the port address of the first serial port in the IBM PC, 03F8H (from IBMPC.H). The offsets of the Data and Serialization Status registers from the base address, from U16X50.H, are 0 and 5, respectively. The values required to mask off the TBE and RxRDY bits are imported from U16X50.H as are the DP_OFF and SP_OFF constants in U16x50.H.[3] During linkage, COM1sio.uart_base, COM1sio.data_off, COM1sio.xmitmask, and COM1sio.rcvmask in the level-1 functions acquire the values from this structure initialization. To create an executable file TERM0.EXE for the IBM PC, first compile IBMPC.C, then issue the following command to the Microsoft linker:

```
LINK TERM0 IBMPC,,,SIO.LIB BUOS.LIB U16x50.LIB MISC.LIB  /NOE /NOI
```

where MISC.LIB is the library containing the console functions given in Listing 12.10.

Conclusion

By careful design, we have devised a reasonably general framework within which we can write the basic code for most computer systems. By designing our libraries hierarchically downward from the general to the specific, only minor revisions are required to create workable versions for a variety of hardware configurations and operating system environments. But lest we become content with fulsome praise, the next chapter discards most of these functions in favor of others that are still more general and, therefore, more portable.

To help you while reading the remainder of this book (or if you choose to type in the code), several pertinent programming details need summarizing:

1. The include files in this book are assumed to be surrounded by backdoor flags.
2. For portability, the include files IBMPC.H and 16X50.H are accessed indirectly through the files LEVEL0.H and UART.H.
3. The names of functions in level-0 (computer-specific) files such as IBMPC.C begin with double underscores; if they are written in assembler, they begin with _a_.
4. The functions keystat and getkey are "virtual" functions. The file *KEY.H* must contain compiler-specific macro substitutions for both.
5. SIODEF.H includes SIOLOCAL.H. (Backdoor flags prevent multiple inclusions.)
6. The level-0 configuration file (IBMPC.C) is linked as an object file (IBMPC.OBJ) instead of a library file (IBMPC.OBJ). The reasons for this are stylistic, so feel free to manage it differently.

---

[3]Although it might be argued that the offsets are not inherent properties of the UART, it's hard to imagine a situation in which the registers would not be decoded sequentially.

Portability Considerations

In the previous chapter, we constructed a framework within which we can easily write serial I/O routines that run on almost any hardware. Although our level-2 and level-3 routines are general, they are not yet flexible enough to support every programming situation. With the concept of hierarchically structured libraries in mind, then, the purpose of this chapter is to revise these functions with an eye toward increasing their generality and therefore their portability. For the sake of consistency, whenever possible I will retain the function and library names begun in the previous chapter.

Level-1 Functions

Look closely at the level-1 function s_xmit in the previous chapter. Do you see anything that might limit its usefulness or that ties it to a particular computer architecture? Let's answer this question with another. Suppose you wish to write programs for a computer that does not address its UART through I/O ports but as ordinary memory locations. Wouldn't the need for *memory-mapped* serial I/O render the _a_inport and _a_outport functions in the level-1 library useless? If you're like many programmers, your first inclination might be to fix the problem by rewriting the level-0 functions _a_inport and _a_outport as memory "peek" and "poke" routines that access RAM instead of I/O ports. This would be a solution of sorts, but you would be forced to maintain separate libraries for memory- and port-mapped UARTs. Besides, how would you handle a system that contains both kinds of addressing?

If this seems farfetched, remember that a fair number of serial I/O boards exist where the user selects not only the address at which the UARTs are located but also whether they are addressed through memory or I/O ports. Although innumerable circumstances occur in which committing your library to port addressing would prove crippling, it is unnecessary to recite them. Their importance is philosophical: don't hardwire constants and other values into your code when you don't have to.

To make our level-1 functions more general, we need a UART addressing scheme that can be specified when the program is run (or linked) instead of when it is compiled. To C programmers, this means that every function in the level-1 library must employ "pointers" to as yet unknown functions that read from and write to the UART.

The almost effortless use of pointers, including the *pointers to functions* we need here, is another reason why the C language is a good choice for serial I/O programming. Before we proceed, though, let's pause for a short review of C function pointers. Listing 13.1 shows a trivial program, FPTEST1.

Listing 13.1. FPTEST1: a simple program to demonstrate C function pointers.

```
#include <stdio.h>

void function1(int a)
{
    printf("This is function 1.  The value passed is %d.\n",a);
}

void function2(int b)
{
    printf("This is function 2.  The value passed is %d.\n",b);
}

void main(void)
{
    void (*functp)(int);   /* pointer to a void function      */
    functp = function1;    /* make it point a function1       */
    (*functp)(1);          /* call the function pointed to    */
    functp = function2;    /* make it point at function2      */
    (*functp)(-1);         /* and call it again               */
}
```

Here are two simple functions named, imaginatively, function1 and function2. The declaration of the variable functp

```
void (*functp)(int);
```

is the focus of our attention. In order to understand this declaration, let's first consider it written like this:

```
void *functp(int);  /* pointer to a void function */
```

Here, the two operators in this expression—the pointer * and function call ()—compete for closest association with the variable name. Ordinarily, the function call wins because it has the highest priority (precedence); thus, functp is a function that returns a pointer to a void.

We can change this natural order of evaluation by placing *grouping parentheses* around *functp, which force the * to bind to the function name before the function call operator.[1] The declaration then says that functp is a pointer to a function that returns a void.

The pointer functp is assigned to point at function1. functp is then called, passing the value 1 as an argument:

```
(*functp)(1);
```

Although the parentheses and the pointer operator are not syntactically required in the call, I retain them to emphasize the function-pointer operation. Next, the function pointer is assigned to function2 and called with the argument −1.

Function Pointers in a Structure

Because our declared strategy in composing libraries is to maintain all relevant variables in the sio structure, we install the pointers to the read/write functions there, too. Before we examine the changes required in the sio structure definition, declaration, and initialization, let's first see how the placing of the function pointer in a structure affects the syntax in our FPTEST program. Listing 13.2 shows FPTEST2, the revised program.

Listing 13.2. The FPTEST2 program revised to demonstrate C function pointers as structure members.

```
#include <stdio.h>

void function1(int a)
{
     printf("This is function 1.  The value passed is %d.\n",a);
}

void function2(int b)
{
     printf("This is function 2.  The value passed is %d.\n",b);
}
```

continues

---

[1]Do not confuse the grouping parentheses with the parentheses that denote a function call. The former are not operators at all but punctuation directing the order of evaluation in an expression.

Listing 13.2. continued

```
struct                          /* structure with a pointer ... to  */
{                               /* ...a function                     */
    void (*functp)(int);
} x;

void main(void)
{
    x.functp = function1;  /* make it point at function1        */
    (*x.functp)(1);        /* call the function pointed to      */
    x.functp = function2;  /* make it point at function2        */
    (*x.functp)(-1);       /* and call it again                 */
}
```

As you can see, the function pointer's residing in a structure does not substantially affect the calling syntax. Because the structure member '.' operator has higher precedence than the pointer operator, parentheses are not required around the member reference.

The *sio* Structure with Pointers to UART Access Functions

The pointers to the UART access functions will reside in our sio structure. Listing 13.3 shows the sio structure with these pointers installed.

Listing 13.3. The sio structure revised to contain pointers to UART access functions.

```
struct sio
    {
    BYTE   *uart_base;                /*0  Base address of UART              */
    USHORT data_off;                  /*1  Offset of data port from base     */
    USHORT status_off;                /*2  Offset of status port from base   */
    MASK   rcvmask;                   /*3  RxRDY mask                        */
    MASK   xmitmask;                  /*4  X-mit holding register empty mask */
    MASK   tx_emptymask;              /*5  X-mit shift register empty mask   */
    FAST   (*readbyte)(BYTE *);       /*6  Pointer to RAM/port read routine  */
    void   (*writebyte)(BYTE *, FAST);/*7  Pointer to RAM/port read routine  */
    };
```

There are three new structure members here. (The tx emptymask member is not needed until Chapter 20, but belongs here for consistency.) The other two new structure members are readbyte, declared as a pointer to a function returning FAST, and writebyte, a pointer to a function returning void.

THIRTEEN ● Portability Considerations (435)

As we develop new functions throughout this book, we will modify this sio structure. When creating new versions of the structure, it's important to append new members to the previous version of the structure. Adding new members only to the end of the structure leaves the relationship between preexisting members unchanged; therefore, functions previously compiled do not have to be recompiled. The numbers at the beginning of the comments are for reference.

The Revised UART.LIB Functions

We must now revise the level-2 functions to take advantage of the function pointers in the sio structure. Listing 13.4 shows these changes. (Please do not add them to your library yet.) Notice that only one header is shown for all four functions.

Listing 13.4. Level-2 functions s_rcv, s_rcvstat, s_xmit, and s_xmitstat.

```
FUNCTION NAME:    s_rcv, s_rcvstat, s_xmit, s_xmitstat
  DESCRIPTION:    UART functions using function pointers.
     COMMENTS:    These are not the final versions, so do not add them to
                  your libraries yet.
 INCLUDE FILES:   siodef.h
```

```c
extern struct sio COM1sio;      /* master serial structure for COM1 */

FAST s_rcv()
{
    return ( (*COM1sio.readbyte)(COM1sio.uart_base + COM1sio.data_off));
}

FAST s_rcvstat()
{
  return ( (*COM1sio.readbyte)(COM1sio.uart_base + COM1sio.status_off) \
         & sio.rcvmask);
}

void s_xmit(FAST c)
{
    (*COM1sio.writebyte)(COM1sio.uart_base + COM1sio.data_off, c);
}

FAST s_xmitstat()
{
  return ( (*COM1sio.readbyte)(sio.uart_base + COM1sio.status_off) \
         & COM1sio.xmitmask);
}
```

In their previous versions, these level-2 routines relied on the sio structure only for the port addressing arguments and UART masks. The importance of the revisions in Listing 13.4 is that the reads and writes take place through pointers to functions whose exact identity need not be known at compile time. You supply the names of the actual read/write functions, initializing the sio structure in the level-0 computer specific file and freely changing them while the program executes. Listing 13.5 shows how the revised sio structure is declared and initialized.

Listing 13.5. Revised sio structure declaration and initialization.

```
struct COM1sio =
    {
    COM1,                    /*0  base address of UART                */
    DATA_IO,                 /*1  offset of data port from base       */
    SER_STAT,                /*2  offset of status port from base     */
    RCV_MASK,                /*3  RxRDY mask from UART.H               */
    XMIT_MASK,               /*4  xmitter Holding Register Empty mask  */
    TX_EMPTY_MASK,           /*5  xmitter Shift Register Empty mask    */
    _a_inport,               /*6  pointer to RAM/port read routine     */
    _a_outport               /*7  pointer to RAM/port write routine    */
    } ;
```

The structure declaration initializes the readbyte member to point at _a_inport, and the writebyte member to point at _a_outport.

Pointers in Memory-Mapped Systems

In Chapter 12, we discussed the importance of declaring the structure variable uart_base to be a pointer. We can now see why this is necessary. The alternative to declaring it as a pointer is to declare it as an arithmetic type such as an unsigned int. In most systems, you can expect that the size of an int reflects the natural size of the microprocessor registers on which the language is implemented. The natural size for ints, for example, is 16 bits on an 80286, but 32 bits on a 68000. With this in mind, it might seem safe to store addresses as ints. Such assumptions about the relationship in size between data types are notoriously treacherous and eventually cause grief. One example should illustrate. Because the 68000's registers are 32 bits wide, the natural size of an int is 32 bits, yet several 68000 C compilers offer a "16-bit integer option" in which all integer operations are truncated to 16 bits. In this mode, attempting to store a 32-bit address in an int would prove fatal: half the address would be lost in truncation.

Answer to puzzle on page *421*

The code on page *421* prints

105

110

120

In other words, if n is an integer and ptr is declared to point at an object of type x, the expression ptr + n is equivalent to ptr + (n * sizeof(x)); the compiler automatically scales pointer arithmetic to account for the size of the objects pointed to. It is therefore extremely important that uart_base point to a char; otherwise, the addresses obtained from adding an offset to the UART's base address will be incorrect. In fact, this is a good general rule: when using a pointer variable expressly for address arithmetic, make certain that it is declared as a pointer to a type that occupies a single unit of storage.

The *SIO* Object

Before we can proceed to write level-2 functions that rely upon these new level-1 functions, we must correct a severe limitation in our libraries: they are hardwired to a single sio data structure. This means that it is almost impossible to manage more than a single serial port simultaneously because all level-1 functions refer directly to a single sio structure. To appreciate how restrictive this design is, assume you wish to write a program for the IBM PC that manages two serial ports at one time: one for a modem and one, say, for displaying the incoming modem data on a serial printer. The following gymnastics would be required:

```
extern struct sio COM1sio;
struct sio printer, tmp;

s_putc(c);            /* output to the modem              */
tmp = COM1sio;        /* save current sio in a temporary  */
COM1sio = printer;    /* now copy the printer over the sio */
s_putc(c);            /* now output to the printer        */
COM1sio = tmp;        /* recover the original sio         */
        .
        .
        .
```

Pretty cumbersome isn't it? It won't set any speed records either. Clearly, this facetious example is not really a workable alternative. Ideally our code would read like this:

```
s_putc(modem, c);
s_putc(printer, c);
```

where modem and printer describe serial ports somehow associated with the printer and modem. To assist in this association, let's now make the definition shown in Listing 13.6.

Listing 13.6. The sio definition.
typedef **of master structure for defining a serial port.**

```
typedef struct sio SIO;    /* for SIOLOCAL.H */
```

Although this definition adds nothing to our code in the way of functionality, the typedef statement enables us to define our own data object: the SIO. As such, it possesses the attributes of all data types; scope, storage class, and so forth. This means that the compiler subjects it to the same type-checking rules as, say, an int. Perhaps the SIO's most important function, though, is psychological: it encourages us to think of the serial port in abstract terms, as a conceptual instead of a physical entity. For example, instead of writing

```
struct COM1sio sio;
```

which refers to a loose accumulation of data under the name sio, we can now write

```
SIO COM1sio;
```

which loudly exclaims that SIO is an important object.

MANAGING MULTIPLE *SIOS*

To manage our printer and modem simultaneously, we can now declare two SIOs for the two serial ports, COM1 and COM2:

```
SIO COM1sio =          /* declare an SIO for com1 */
     {
     COM1,
     DATA_IO,
     SER_STAT,
     RCV_MASK,
       .
       .
     };

SIO COM2sio =          /* declare an SIO for com2 */
     {
     COM2,
     DATA_IO,
     SER_STAT,
     RCV_MASK,
       .
       .
     };
```

Notice that in these declarations we refer to the physical addresses of the ports by their system names COM1 and COM2. The SIOs, that now contain all important information about their respective serial ports are named COM1sio and COM2sio. If every function's argument list contains a reference to an SIO, that function can address the serial port uniquely described by the SIO. With this idea in mind, a call to such a function looks like this:

```
s_putc(COM1sio, c);     /* to modem on com1   */
s_putc(COM2sio, c);     /* to printer on com2 */
```

which would pass the entire structure in the argument list.

This method, however, would be ludicrously inefficient because C would have to make a copy of the entire SIO for passing in the argument list. We can, however, easily and efficiently pass the SIO's address in the argument list:

```
s_putc(&COM1sio, c);          /* to modem on com1    */
s_putc(&COM2sio, c);          /* to printer on com2 */
```

Here, each call to s_putc passes the address of a different structure. The function s_putc itself can learn everything there is to learn about this SIO by examining the structure at this address. The same code can be written more eloquently using pointer variables instead of address operators:

```
SIO *modemp   = &COM1sio;
SIO *printerp = &COM2sio;
s_putc(modemp, c);          /* pass pointer to com1 SIO */
s_putc(printerp, c);        /* pass pointer to com2 SIO */
```

This looks remarkably like our ideal a few paragraphs back, doesn't it? With this technique, we can now manage an unlimited number of serial ports because we pass to our functions a description (in the form of a pointer) of the SIO describing that port. All that remains is to change our functions so that they gain access to an SIO through a pointer in the argument list instead of hard-wired references to a particular sio.

Revising the Level-1 Functions

The changes required to the four level-1 functions are trivial, although to some readers the presence of the structure pointer operator makes the functions appear more daunting. The final version of these functions is shown Listing 13.7.

Listing 13.7. Level-1 functions now address data through structure pointers.

FUNCTION NAME: s_rcv, s_rcvstat, s_xmit, s_xmitstat
          LEVEL: 1
    PROTOTYPE IN: UART.H (U16x50.H)
           LIB: U16x50.LIB
   DESCRIPTION: Uart functions using function pointers.
     COMMENTS: These versions replace those in Chapter 12.
  INCLUDE FILES: siodef.h

```
FAST s_rcv(register SIO *siop)
{
   return ( (*siop->readbyte)(siop->uart_base + siop->data_off));
}
```

continues

Listing 13.7. continued

```
FAST s_rcvstat(register SIO *siop)
{
    return ( (*siop->readbyte) (siop->uart_base + siop->status_off) \
            & siop->rcvmask);
}

void s_xmit(register SIO *siop, FAST c)
{
    (*siop->writebyte)(siop->uart_base + siop->data_off, c);
}

FAST s_xmitstat(register SIO *siop)
{
    return ( (*siop->readbyte) (siop->uart_base + siop->status_off) \
            & siop->xmitmask);
}
```

> **Warning:** Calling these functions without the SIO argument produces disastrous results.

These functions are essentially the same as those shown earlier in Listing 13.4. The sole difference is this: those in Listing 13.4 addressed their data through a fixed-named structure, sio, whereas these new functions address their data through a pointer to a structure, siop.

If you have difficulty with this notion, consider that most C programmers use an almost identical mechanism every day without really being aware of it. The stream I/O functions in C's standard library—fopen, fclose, fread, and fwrite—are designed in exactly this way. If you examine your compiler's STDIO.H file, you'll find that the data type FILE is really a typedef of a structure. The function fopen, for example, returns a pointer to a FILE, which the other stream functions must include in their argument list. The parallel between our SIO and C's FILE is, of course, intentional. In Chapter 16, I carry this parallel to fruition by composing s_open and s_close. There is, therefore, a very close parallel between:

```
fp = fopen("test.tmp","r");
    .
    .
    .
putc(c, fp);
fclose(fp);
```

and

```
siop = s_open(portnum);
    .
    .
    .
s_putc(siop, c);
s_close(siop);
```

If you know how to perform stream I/O with C's library, you will almost intuitively understand the rest of the code in this book. The main difference between the SIO and FILE functions is syntactical: the SIO functions always require the SIO pointer to be the first argument in the list.

THE *register* STORAGE CLASS

The single disadvantage to our scheme of addressing a serial port through an SIO is speed. The SIO functions perform a great deal of time-consuming indexing relative to the SIO pointer. This, together with the use of function pointers, incurs considerable overhead. Although later in this book we will solve many of the problems caused by lack of speed, we can improve performance considerably by instructing the compiler to retain, when possible, the SIO pointer in one of the microprocessor's registers for more rapid access.

Revising the Level-2 Functions

Now that we have generalized the level-1 functions, we turn our attention to the level-2 functions in BUOS.LIB. These functions suffer from the same limitation as our early versions of the level-1 functions: inflexibility. To understand where these functions may be improved, let's review the code for s_getc shown in Listing 13.8.

Listing 13.8. The current version of s_getc.

```
FAST s_getc()
{
    while (s_rcvstat() == 0) /* wait for char to be ready     */
        {;}
    return (s_rcv());        /* read and return it            */
}
```

This routine is inflexible because it assumes that bytes are received only through the level-1 functions in the UART service libraries. However, circumstances exist in which this assumption is incorrect. For example, if I/O is performed with *interrupts*, the interrupt service routine actually services the UART: the very occurrence of an interrupt signals that a byte is ready. The interrupt service routine then automatically fetches the byte from the UART, placing it in a buffer to be fetched later. Under interrupt operation, therefore, the status function must return whether the interrupt buffer is empty; similarly, the read function must know how to fetch characters from the interrupt buffer. The current version of s_putc suffers from the same limited vision as earlier versions of the level-1 functions: it assumes that bytes are dispatched only with the level-1 functions in the UART service libraries.

Without going into greater detail about interrupts right now, it should be obvious that a different set of routines than we currently use for polled I/O will be required for interrupt-driven I/O.

More Function Pointers

As you might have suspected, we will now (and for the *last* time) rewrite the level-2 routines to use pointers to functions, instead of hardwiring in the names of the functions themselves. In this way, our functions rely upon pointers instead of the level-1 UART service functions. With this technique, the exact identity of functions need not be decided until the program is actually run. As before, these new function pointers are part of the SIO, the revised version of which is shown in Listing 13.9.

Listing 13.9. The SIO definition revised to contain pointers to UART service functions.

STRUCT DEF: SIO
FILE: SIODEF.H
DESCRIPTION: Master structure defining a serial port.

```
struct sio
   {
   BYTE   *uart_base;                     /*0  Base address of UART             */
   USHORT data_off;                       /*1  Offset of data port from base    */
   USHORT status_off;                     /*2  Offset of status port from base  */
   MASK   rcvmask;                        /*3  RxRDY mask                       */
   MASK   xmitmask;                       /*4  X-mit holding register empty mask*/
   MASK   tx_emptymask;                   /*5  X-mit shift register empty mask  */
   FAST   (*readbyte)(BYTE *);            /*6  Pointer to RAM/port read routine */
   void   (*writebyte)(BYTE *, FAST);     /*7  Pointer to RAM/port read routine */
   FAST   (*s_rstat)(SIO *);              /*8  Pointer to receiver status       */
   FAST   (*s_read)(SIO *);               /*9  Pointer to fetch routine         */
   FAST   (*s_xstat)(SIO *);              /*10 Pointer to xmiter status         */
   void   (*s_send)(SIO *, FAST);         /*11 Pointer to xmit routine          */
   short  (*s_txblock)(SIO *, BYTE *, short); /*12 Pointer to block x-mit       */
   };
```

The new additions are the two receiver function pointers s_rstat and s_read and the two transmitter function pointers s_xstat and s_send. The twelfth item, s_txblock, is explained in Chapter 20.

The Revised Level-2 Functions for BUOS.LIB

With the new function pointers in the structure, we can now rewrite the level-2 functions to perform I/O through these pointers. Listing 13.10 gives the revised s_getc, s_putc, and s_inchar functions for BUOS.LIB. Don't forget to include STDIO.H.

Listing 13.10. Revised level-2 functions for reading and writing bytes via function pointers.

FUNCTION NAME: s_getc
          LEVEL: 2
   PROTOTYPE IN: BUOS.H
        LIBRARY: BUOS.LIB
    DESCRIPTION: Wait for a byte to arrive from the serial port (SIO)
                 pointed to by siop.
        RETURNS: FAST
  INCLUDE FILES: siodef.h

```
FAST s_getc(register SIO *siop)
{
    while ((*siop->s_rstat)(siop) == 0) /* wait for char to be ready   */
        {;}
    return ((*siop->s_read)(siop));      /* read and return it          */
}
```

FUNCTION NAME: s_putc
        LEVEL: 2
 PROTOTYPE IN: BUOS.H
      LIBRARY: BUOS.LIB
  DESCRIPTION: Sends a byte from the serial port (SIO) pointed to by siop.
      RETURNS: void
INCLUDE FILES: siodef.h

```
void s_putc(register SIO *siop, BYTE c)
{
    while ((*siop->s_xstat)(siop) == 0) /* wait for uart to be ready   */
        {;}
    (*siop->s_send)(siop, c);            /* write it and return         */
}
```

FUNCTION NAME: s_inchar
        LEVEL: 2
 PROTOTYPE IN: BUOS.H
      LIBRARY: BUOS.LIB

continues

Listing 13.10. continued

DESCRIPTION: Fetches a byte from the serial port (SIO) pointed to by siop
if one is ready; otherwise returns.
RETURNS: int: the byte if one is ready, otherwise -1.
INCLUDE FILES: siodef.h

```
int s_inchar(SIO *siop)
{
    if ((*siop->s_rstat)(siop))
        return ((*siop->s_read)(siop));
    return -1;
}
```

All three of these functions accomplish the same tasks as earlier versions. The important
difference here is that the new versions have absolutely no idea how a byte is fetched, or
written. The names of the functions pointed to by s_rstat, s_read, s_xstat, and s_send
are not actually assigned until the linker sees the SIO declarations and initializations in the
computer-dependent level-0 file. As we saw in Chapter 12, the pointed-to functions can
even be altered during program execution to take advantage of hardware differences.

Declaring and Initializing the *SIO*

Just as we initialized the I/O access pointers to inport and _a_outport, we will now initialize our UART service pointers to point to their corresponding level-1 routines. Listing
13.11 shows the initialization and declaration for IBMPC.C.

Listing 13.11. A revised SIO declaration and initialization for the IBM PC.

SIO NAME: COM1sio
FILE: IBMPC.C
COMMENTS: Line numbers in comments are for reference only.
INCLUDE FILES: siodef.h, u16x50.h

```
SIO COM1sio =
    {
    COM1,                /*0  base address of UART                   */
    DATA_IO,             /*1  offset of data port from base          */
    SER_STAT,            /*2  offset of status port from base        */
    RCV_MASK,            /*3  RxRDY mask from UART.H                  */
    XMIT_MASK,           /*4  xmitter Holding Register Empty mask     */
    TX_EMPTY_MASK,       /*5  xmitter Shift Register Empty mask       */
    _a_inport,           /*6  pointer to RAM/port read routine        */
    _a_outport,          /*7  pointer to RAM/port read routine        */
    s_rcvstat,           /*8  pointer to receiver status              */
    s_rcv,               /*9  pointer to fetch routine                */
```

```
    s_xmitstat,              /*10 pointer to xmiter status        */
    s_xmit,                  /*11 pointer to xmit routine         */
    NIL,                     /*12 pointer to block xmit routine   */
    };
```

In this instance of the SIO, named COM1sio, all pointers are initialized to the same functions as were employed in the original libraries. After you have correctly modified the SIO definition, declaration, and initialization, and have revised the UART libraries, you should revise the TERM program from Chapter 12 to accommodate the new SIO functions. Listing 13.12 shows these revisions.

Listing 13.12. TERM revised to use the new SIO style function calls.

PROGRAM NAME: TERM1
DESCRIPTION: Simple Dumb Terminal program.
COMMENTS: Revised to use SIO functions.
SYNTAX: TERM1
INCLUDE FILES: stdio.h, ctype.h, siodef.h, ascii.h, misc.h, buos.h

```
#define MENU      CTRL_A           /* key for command summary      */
#define EXIT      'Q'              /* key to exit from term         */

int vers = 1;                      /* version number (global)       */

int menu(SIO *siop)                /* menu now gets SIO pointer      */
{
    int c;
    int retval = 0;
    static char *menus[] =
        {
        "\tQ.  EXIT",
        ""                         /* NUL string terminates list     */
        };
    char ** menup;
    c = !EXIT;
    while (c != EXIT)
        {
        puts("\n\n");
        for (menup = menus; **menup != NUL ; menup++)
            printf("%s\n", *menup);
        printf("\n\t\t  Enter selection  (CR to quit menu) :  ");
        if ( (c = getkbch()) == CR)
            break;                 /* return to term                */
        c = toupper(c);
        switch (c)
            {
            case EXIT:             /* back to DOS                    */
```

continues

Listing 13.12. continued

```
                        retval = 1;
                        break;
                default:
                        puts("Invalid choice\n\a");
                        break;
                }
        }
    putchar('\n');
    return retval;                      /* will be zero except if EXIT     */
}

void term(SIO *siop)
{
    int c;                              /* must be int to detect -1 return  */
    printf("TERM, Version %d:  Press Control-%c for a summary of commands\n", \
        vers, MENU + '@');
    for (EVER)                          /*          eternal loop            */
        {
        if ( (c = s_inchar(siop)) !=NOT_READY)   /* check port for byte     */
            putchar(siop, c);
        if ( (c = inkey()) != NOT_READY)     /* if a key is pressed         */
            if (c == MENU)                   /* and if it's the menu key    */
                {
                if (menu(siop) !=NUL)        /* if menu returns non-zero    */
                    break;                   /* return to main              */
                }
            else
                s_putc(siop, c);
        }
}


main()
{
    extern SIO COM1sio;                 /* found in computer-specific file  */
    SIO *siop = &COM1sio;               /* pointer to an SIO                */
    term(siop);                         /*    TERM                          */
    puts("\nEnd of TERM\n");
    return 0;
}
```

A pointer to an SIO, siop is assigned the address of the COM1sio declared in the level-0 library (IBMPC.C, for example). Notice that COM1sio must be declared external here. The pointer is then passed in the call to the term functions where it is needed in the arguments to s_inchar and s_putc. Although not used in this version, the SIO pointer is also passed to menu.

While this revision doesn't increase the functionality of TERM, it lays the groundwork for enhancements that would have been impossible in the earlier version. As support

Order Form

I sell the companion disk to my book as a pedagogical accompaniment, not a commercial product. I don't maintain a programming staff and do not "support" the code. If you need a bullet-proof package complete with hand-holding and technical support, please do not order this disk.

Name_____ Company _____

Shipping Address _____

City _____ State _____ Zip _____

Phone ( )_____ Fax _____ Date _____

E-mail address _____ Disk preference   5.25 ____   3.5 ____

Number of Copies	Unit Price	US Funds
____ Companion diskette	@35.00	_____
____ ASCII Wall Chart	@ 5.00 (3 for $10)	_____

California Residents add 8.25% tax   _____
Shipping/handling, US: $1.85   _____
Shipping/handling, foreign: $4.00   _____
TOTAL   _____

- No purchase orders accepted.
- Checks must be payable in US dollars.
- Shipping/handling includes postage for US Mail. Express delivery (overnight or second-day) is billed at prevailing rates (UPS and Federal Express only).
- Because of fluctuations in exchange rates, foreign orders requesting express shipment must be paid by credit card.
- Do not request express delivery to post-office boxes.

Four ways to order:

1. Credit Card:

   Credit card number   **Expiration Date**

   ☐☐☐☐☐☐☐☐☐☐☐☐☐☐☐☐   ☐☐–☐☐

   Authorized Signature _____

   Fold over this form, then staple or tape it at the top.

2. Enclose check and mail to:

   Campbell Productions
   P.O. Box 7159
   Berkeley, CA 94707

3. Phone order by voice: (510) 526-4311

4. Fax this order form to: (510) 526-4311

_____

Check one: ____UPS   ____UPS Next Day   ____UPS 2nd Day   ____Federal Express

fold over, then tape or staple

Campbell Productions
P.O. Box 7159
Berkeley, CA 94707

(510) 526-4311

functions unfold during the remainder of this book, you will gradually gain an appreciation of the power of this design.

SIOs for Memory-Mapped UARTs

So far, I have shown how to initialize an SIO for a computer that addresses its UARTs via its port structure. One naturally expects to find memory-mapped UARTs in systems built around processors that lack port I/O instructions (the 6502 and 68000, for example). However, a surprising number of systems use memory-mapped UARTs despite the presence of port I/O instructions.

How would a memory-mapped system affect the code? Hardly at all because of the level of abstraction represented by the SIO: the readbyte and writebyte pointers in level-0 would be intialized to the memory read and write routines appropriate for that system.

Timing Functions

The subject of software portability naturally leads to the unpleasant subject of system timing. As we develop our libraries, we will frequently be faced with decisions about timing. How long should a function wait for a byte to arrive before giving up? How long after sending a smart modem command must a function wait for the smart modem's response? Before we can expect functions to deal with timing considerations such as these, we must first write a few lower-level timing functions.

Types of Timing Functions

Our subsequent high-level functions require two distinct types of timing functions, each with its own special requirements: delays and waits.

Time Delays

A delay routine is merely a calibrated time waster. Fixed delays of various durations are frequently required to provide a set-up time for another device.

INTERBYTE DELAY

In a quest for faster communications, we hope for ever faster modems and often write assembly language code to speed up time-hungry functions. As we saw in Chapter 4, however, sometimes we are required to slow down the communications rate by limiting the maximum rate at which bytes are transmitted. Many systems, especially older multiuser dial-up systems, expect a human typist to generate bytes (at the rate of a few hundred bytes per minute). If bytes arrive much faster than this finger rate, the system's input buffer may be overrun and data may be lost. Similarly, early modems often cannot process commands at their full data rate, so an *interbyte delay* must be employed whenever the modem is addressed. The most straightforward way to achieve interbyte delay is to insert a calibrated delay before each byte is transmitted.

INTERLINE DELAY

Many systems use discrete hardware input buffers to collect incoming characters. When a line terminator (a Carriage Return, for example) is entered, the buffer generates an interrupt to the computer, which then fetches the data from the hardware buffer. While this use of a separate hardware buffer certainly improves the overall efficiency of the system, there is one common problem. If the time required to empty the buffer exceeds the time between characters, the first few inbound characters immediately after the line terminator are lost and the system is said to "drop characters." This problem does not occur as long as data is entered at the finger rate, but during computerized transmission, there is (ideally) no delay between characters. When electronically uploading data at high data rates into a finger-rate buffer, however, many characters can be lost. It is the responsibility of the transmitting software to introduce a slight pause after transmitting a line terminator. An *interline delay* of one or two tenths of a second is usually sufficient to allow the host computer to service its input buffer.

Timeout Functions

The delays just described are totally passive—wasting time is the sole objective. In other situations, however, we are concerned not so much with the delay itself, but in making certain that other events happen (or don't happen) within an allotted amount of time. For example, as we discussed in Chapter 4, during a file transfer, we must deal with the possibility that an anticipated byte will never arrive. To protect against this possibility, we require a byte-fetching routine that waits only a specified time before returning. On the opposite side of this coin, we also occasionally need to know when a certain amount of time has elapsed without characters arriving.

System Timers and Timekeeping

The simplest way to measure the passage of time is by causing the processor to perform a few irrelevant instructions:

```
for (i = MAGIC_NUMBER; i > 0; --i)    /* do nothing */
    {;}
```

Although such a loop generates a more or less predictable delay, the actual time elapsed depends upon three factors:

- the assembly code generated by your compiler
- the number of system interrupts that steal processor time during the loop
- the processor speed

If any of these three factors is changed, the constant MAGIC_NUMBER has to be adjusted in order to maintain the timing interval. In other words, this sort of delay routine is inherently non-portable.

The System Metronome

This problem of portability can be solved only with an external temporal standard against which software can judge the passage of time. We refer to this standard as the *system timekeeper*, which comprises three parts:

- The *metronome*'s sole function is to generate a precise timing interval. Metronomes are implemented in a variety of ways, but a common technique employs a counter/timer IC (such as the Intel 8253 or Zilog CTC) to divide the output of a crystal oscillator by a predetermined count. At the start of a timing cycle, a register in the counter/timer is loaded with a predetermined count. Each oscillator pulse then decrements the counter register, finally setting a flag in the counter/timer when the counting register reaches 0. The counter/timer then (optionally) automatically reloads the count value and recommences the counting sequence, thus producing a pulse every F/N seconds where F is the frequency of the oscillator and N is the number loaded into the down-counter.

- The *chronometer circuitry* translates the precise timing intervals generated by the metronome into conventional time intervals of hours, minutes, seconds, and fractions of seconds. Notice that the chronometer does not necessarily keep the actual time of day—it begins counting at 0:00:00 (usually defined as midnight) when the user starts up the system.

- The *time of day clock* (or "real-time clock," as it is sometimes naively called) is a hardware device that maintains sidereal ("real") time. This device, which is powered by a battery when the computer is not turned on, is used to synchronize (set) the system chronometer during system start-up.

The Metronome's Software Interface

When a system metronome exists, software can measure the passage of time merely by polling the timer directly.[2] Assuming that the hypothetical function timerstat returns 0 if the counter has expired, a delay loop can now be written:

```
while (timerstat() )
    ;
```

---

[2]On the 8253 timer/counter, the count is monitored by actually reading the count register, but not all timer chips provide a way to examine the count in progress.

A more elegant approach to timing employs system interrupts. Here, the expiration of the timer count generates an interrupt whose service routine supports the chronographic functions. For example, each metronome interrupt increments a reserved memory cell, thus supplying to the chronometer a cumulative count of timing intervals from which can be calculated hours, minutes, and seconds. In this scheme, software can monitor the activities of the metronome simply by watching the cumulative count in memory instead of polling the timer directly.[3] The IBM PC, described below, uses this structure.

Although a system metronome makes it possible to write timing functions that are independent of both compiler and processor speed, it does little to improve portability. Even if systems contain metronomes (most do nowadays), they may use different hardware or different timing intervals. Some may be accessed through RAM, others through an I/O port. Some generate a system interrupt when the counter expires, whereas others are not integrated into the system interrupt structure at all. This absence of a standardized interval timing means that timing functions written for one system metronome probably will not operate accurately on another. This is not to say the cause is totally lost, however. By careful design, we can minimize the effect of system timing differences on our higher-level functions.

Designing a Virtual Timing System

Before we worry about solving problems that arise from inadequacies in the timing hardware, we will first make a wish list for the ideal timing function. A timing function has only two inherent attributes: *accuracy* and *resolution.* Accuracy is fairly straightforward: how well does the function measure time? The second attribute, resolution, is a bit more complicated. Here, I define timing resolution (sometimes also called *granularity*) as the native interval of the system metronome. For example, the best resolution that can be derived from a system metronome that ticks 1,000 times per second is ±1 msec (.001 second).

The ideal function is, of course, 100 percent accurate and resolves time intervals down to a single processor clock cycle. But, practically speaking, serial I/O has much more modest requirements. Since the critical aspect of timing—bit timing—is handled by UARTs and other hardware devices, our requirements are really quite modest. Although we might wish for a timing resolution of 1 millisecond, the metronomes used in the popular microcomputers are not usually that fast.

The timing interval derived from a 60 Hz metronome—17 msecs—is a logical (and historically popular) choice, but before we decide, let's see how this suits the most popular microcomputer in the market, the IBM PC.

---

[3]Direct polling of the timer chip is not reliable on systems that use timer interrupts: the interrupt service routine may reset the counter before it can be detected through polling.

Timing Routines for the IBM PC

The IBM PC/XT/AT all contain a metronome and a chronograph, but only the AT contains a built-in time-of-day clock as standard equipment. The metronome is an Intel 8253 counter/timer IC, which divides a 1,193,180 MHz crystal oscillator by 65536, yielding a timing interval of .0549255 seconds (a frequency of 18.206482 Hz). If this seems like a strange choice of intervals, consider that almost exactly 64K of these intervals occur in one hour. The expiration of the count in the 8253 generates an interrupt (Type 8) whose service routine (interrupt handler) increments a word in memory referred to as TIMER_LO. When TIMER_LO overflows every hour, another word, TIMER_HI, is incremented. At any instant, therefore, TIMER_HI contains the hours since the system was started and TIMER_LO contains the number of 18.2-second intervals, or *timer ticks*, that have occurred. TIMER_LO is located at 0000:046CH and TIMER_HI at 0000:046EH.

Now and for the foreseeable future, it's probably safe to design software around the IBM PC's 55 msec metronome. The limitation of 55 msecs is more apparent than real; as we will soon see, few situations require even this degree of resolution. Therefore, the timing arguments in our functions will be expressed in 55 msec increments which, to simplify discussion and calculation, we will treat as an even 50 msecs. We call this interval—20 to the second—a *tick-second*, or *Tsec* for short.

Having decided to design our system's timing resolution around the Tsec, have we not abandoned all hope of portability? How can we allow for generality? A fair degree of portability can be achieved if we assume that future popular computers will not employ a longer timing interval than one Tsec. (Because the IBM PC's use of 55 msecs has generated so much grumbling, this seems a safe assumption.) The existence of a shorter metronomic interval, therefore, makes it easy to compose functions that measure time in units of Tsecs. Despite our choice of the Tsec as a timing standard for our high-level functions, however, the details of reading the metronome are sufficiently different to deserve classification as level-0 functions, which must be rewritten for each computer.

Listing 13.13 gives the constants required in IBMPC.H and Listing 13.13 shows the delay for the IBMPC.C, the most basic of the three timing functions that we will compose in this chapter.

Listing 13.13. Constants for IBMPC.H required by level-0 timer functions.

```
/* FUNCTION PROTOTYPES */

unsigned  __peekw(int, int);
#define    __peekw(o,s) (*((int far*) (((long)(s) << 16) ¦ (o))))
                                        /* (offset,seg) */

/* MISCELLANEOUS MANIFEST CONSTANTS */

#define TIMER_LO 0x46C            /* Location of timer lsb of timer      */
```

A Level-0 Timing Function (__delay)

It is important to notice that this function name does not begin with the usual "s_." This means that it does not require an SIO pointer in its argument list and may, in fact, be added to your general IBM PC library. It does, however, begin with a double underscore to indicate that it is a level-0 function.

Listing 13.14. The __delay function: a calibrated time-waster for the IBM PC.

FUNCTION NAME: __delay
   PROTOTYPE IN: IBMPC.H
         LEVEL: 0
      LIBRARY: IBMPC.C
  DESCRIPTION: Does nothing for Tsecs.
       RETURNS: void
   COMMENTS: The system interval is defined as 1 Tsec (about 50 msecs). The macro function __peekw and the constant TIMER_LO are given in IBMPC.H.

```
void __delay(unsigned tsecs)
{
    unsigned volatile tickref;
    for (; tsecs > 0; --tsecs)
        {
        tickref = __peekw(TIMER_LO, 0);
        while (tickref == (unsigned) __peekw(TIMER_LO, 0))
            {;}    /* Warning: don't let compiler optimize */
        }
}
```

Only one argument is passed to __delay: the duration of the desired delay, Tsecs. The idea here is to wait for the value in TIMER_LO to change Tsecs times. At the beginning of the for loop, a call to peek captures the value of TIMER_LO in the variable tickref. Then begins a while loop that continually compares the value of TIMER_LO to the reference value in tickref. On the next metronomic pulse, the two values no longer match, the while breaks, and count in the outer for is decremented. The new value of TIMER_LO is captured in tickref and the cycle repeats until tsecs reaches 0, terminating the function.

As written, the delay function doesn't produce accurate results when Tsecs is equal to 1. Can you see why? Suppose tickref is captured an instant before TIMER_LO changes. Now the test:

```
while (tickref == __peekw(TIMER_LO,0))
```

is TRUE on the very next iteration of the loop, resulting in an unpredicatably short delay. There is no really satisfactory fix for this problem. You may be tempted to add these two lines:

```
tickref = __peekw(TIMER_LO, 0);
while (tickref == __peekw(TIMER_LO, 0))
    ;
```

at the beginning of the function to guarantee that the Tsec counting begins at the start of a metronomic interval. This fix, though, just replaces one form of inaccuracy with another—the latter produces delays too long by exactly the same amount that the former's were too short. Surprisingly, this inaccuracy causes little problem in actual use. For example, when delay is used to provide an interbyte delay (say, in transmitting a string), the average delay is, in fact, 1 Tsec because the function guarantees that at least one metronomic interval occurs between bytes. Furthermore, when called with an argument significantly larger than 1, the error on the first iteration is swamped by the additional iterations.

A Wait-for-Character Function

At the beginning of this section we noted that, in addition to a delay routine, we would need a routine that waits for the arrival of a byte but returns if none is forthcoming within a specified time limit. For the remainder of this book we will rely heavily upon this *timeout input* function, without which many of the programs cannot be reliably written. In other words, the timeout function is just a safety net intended to prevent the function from waiting forever for an event that never occurs.

We require a timeout function that returns a byte from the SIO or TIMEOUT (−1), if no byte arrives in tsecs timing intervals. A first try at this function is likely to lead to this trap:

```
#define TIMEOUT -1

int __s_waitch(siop, tsecs)
SIO *siop;
unsigned tsecs;
{
    unsigned tickref;
    int count;
    for (; count > 0; __count)
        {
        if ( (*siop->s_rstat)(siop) )
            return ( (*siop->s_read)(siop));
        tickref = __peekw(TIMER_LO, 0);
        while (tickref == __peekw(TIMER_LO, 0))
            ;
        }
    return (TIMEOUT);
}
```

This is much like __delay, but with what amounts to a call to s_inchar thrown in between metronomic intervals. Do you see the flaw with this design? Because the function samples the SIO only once per Tsec, it loses bytes that arrive at a rate faster than the metronomic interval of 50 msec. Assuming a 10-bit SDU, this design fails at speeds above about 200 baud!

There is a second design flaw with this approach. Notwithstanding the wait interval, this function should approximate a bare call to s_inchar. Notice, however, what happens if it is called with a tsecs argument of 0: the for loop is never entered and the SIO is never sampled. Thus, this design never fetches when called with a wait argument of 0.

Both of these design flaws are rectified in the final version of __s_waitch, shown in Listing 13.15.

Listing 13.15. The s_waitch function:
Wait specified Tsecs for an inbound byte before returning.

FUNCTION NAME: __s_waitch
  PROTOTYPE IN: BMPC.H
          LEVEL: 0
        LIBRARY: BMPC.C
    DESCRIPTION: Waits for a serial byte to arrive for tsecs Tsecs.
        RETURNS: int, the byte if one arrives, otherwise NOT_READY at timeout.
      COMMENTS: The system timing interval is defined as a "Tsec," or
                about 50 msec.

```
int __s_waitch(register SIO *siop, unsigned tsecs)
{
    unsigned tickref;
    tickref = _peekw(TIMER_LO, 0);              /* initialize reference count */
    while (tsecs > 0)
        {
        if ( (*siop->s_rstat)(siop) )           /* check UART for byte ready   */
            return  ((*siop->s_read)(siop)); /* return byte if ready        */
        if ((unsigned) __peekw(TIMER_LO, 0) != tickref)    /* if new == old */
            {
            tickref = __peekw(TIMER_LO, 0);  /* get new reference ....       */
            tsecs−;                          /* ...and reduce timeout        */
            }
        }
    return s_inchar(siop);                       /* timed out—no byte received */
}
```

In this design, the sampling of the SIO and the testing of TIMER_LO have equal status in the main while loop. The SIO sampling is performed by first testing the receiver status (through the SIO function pointer s_rstat). If a byte is ready, it is returned immediately by a call to the function pointer s_read; otherwise, TIMER_LO is checked. When TIMER_LO changes, a new reference value is immediately captured into tickref and the tsec is decremented. The entire process repeats until tsecs reaches 0. When the while loop expires, the result of a final call to s_inchar is returned, which guarantees correct behavior with a wait argument of 0.

Manifest Constants for Timing Arguments

Because our timing interval of 50 msecs is not expressed in even decade values (1, .1, etc.), the meaning of the arguments to delay and s_waitch is not obvious. For example, it is not readily apparent that this call produces a 1-second delay:

```
delay(18);
```

To make the code more readable, we can define constants to express the most frequently used time intervals. Place the constants shown in Listing 13.16 in the header SIODEF.H. The figures in the comments show the decimal values before they are rounded off.

Listing 13.16. Manifest decimal constants for timing arguments.

```
/* Constants for Timing */

#define  TIMEOUT    -1

#define  _0_SEC_05   1          /* 50 ms  */
#define  _0_SEC_1    2          /* 1.8    */
#define  _0_SEC_15   3          /* 150 ms */
#define  _0_SEC_2    4          /* 3.6    */
#define  _0_SEC_25   5          /* 250 ms */
#define  _0_SEC_3    6          /* 5.5    */
#define  _0_SEC_4    7          /* 7.3    */
#define  _0_SEC_5    9          /* 9.1    */
#define  _0_SEC_6    11         /* 10.9   */
#define  _0_SEC_7    13         /* 12.7   */
#define  _0_SEC_8    15         /* 14.6   */
#define  _0_SEC_9    16         /* 16.4   */
#define  _1_SEC_0    18         /* 18.2   */
```

These constant names follow a simple convention: the string _SEC_ stands for a decimal point. For example, 0_SEC_4 represents four-tenths of a second, and 1_SEC_0 is one second. Where the rounded-off error in the tenth-second constants is unacceptable, you can create more accurate hundreth-second constants—for example, 0_SEC_05 and 0_SEC_15 to represent 50 and 150 msecs, respectively.

These constants can be compounded to produce longer delays. For example, use 1_SEC_0 + 0_SEC_5 for a one and one-half second delay, or 1_SEC_0 * 5 to produce a delay of five seconds.

A UART Trash Collector

I mentioned at the beginning of this chapter that occasionally we desire to wait not for a character to arrive, but for one not to arrive. Consider the situation in which you wish to send commands to a smart modem then wait for the modem's acknowledgment (OK). Now, if the smart modem happens to be in the command-echo mode, after each command several of the characters from the commands echoed remain in your UART's receiver buffer. When you read the SIO for the modem's reply, these characters are included. In effect, you read not only the reply, but part of the command as well, making it more difficult to interpret the modem's response. To solve the problem, we require a function that continually reads bytes from the SIO until no more are received. In addition, we must be able to limit the maximum number of bytes read. This feature protects us if the function is called during a never-ending input stream. Listing 13.17 shows such a function, s_clrsio.

Listing 13.17. A function to clear trash from the UART.

FUNCTION NAME: s_clrsio
LEVEL: 3
PROTOTYPE IN: SIO.H
LIBRARY: SIO.LIB
DESCRIPTION: Clear numbytes bytes from UART's receive buffers.
RETURNS: TIMEOUT (-1) if no bytes received, or 0 after numbytes bytes are received.
COMMENTS: To avoid inaccuracies inherent in the timing functions, a minimum delay of _0_SEC_1 must be used.
INCLUDE FILES: siodef.h, level0.h

```
int s_clrsio(SIO *siop, unsigned numbytes)
{
```

```
        for (; numbytes > 0; --numbytes)
            if (__s_waitch(siop, _0_SEC_1) == TIMEOUT)
                return TIMEOUT;
        return 0;
}
```

This function simply calls `__s_waitch` the specified number of times then returns 0 to signal that the number of bytes requested were read. If, however, no bytes arrive in `_0_SEC_1` (one-tenth) seconds, the function immediately returns −1. These return values enable the calling function to ascertain the success of the operation.

In our discussion of `__delay`, we noted the inherent inaccuracy of metronome-based functions when called with a timing argument equal to one timing interval. Because the duration of the first tick is unpredictable, an argument of at least two timing intervals is necessary to guarantee a delay one timing interval in duration.

A Test Program for the Timing Functions

Listing 13.18 shows a simple program to verify that the timing functions are functioning correctly. The constant definition TIMEOUT should now be added to SIODEF.H.

Listing 13.18. A simple program to test the timing functions.

PROGRAM TITLE: TIMETEST
          SYNTAX: TIMETEST
     DESCRIPTION: Tests timing functions `__delay` and `__s_waitch`
  INCLUDE FILES: stdio.h, stdlib.h, siodef.h, sio.h

```
void main()
{
    extern SIO COM1sio;
    SIO *siop = &COM1sio;
    if (s_clrsio(siop, 10) == 0)
        exit(puts("Can't clear SIO for test.\007"));
    puts("Start byte wait.");
    if (__s_waitch(siop, 10 * _1_SEC_0) == TIMEOUT)
        puts("No byte.");
    else
        puts("Found byte.");
    puts("Start timeout.");
    __delay(10 * _1_SEC_0);
    puts("End timeout test.");
}
```

Conclusion

Although this ends our formal discussion of portability, a concern for generality should always be present during program design. In future chapters, we'll see how this philosophy pays great dividends. In particular, we'll be able to write complicated programs that know nothing about the hardware on which they run. In Chapter 22, for example, we'll add an XMODEM supervised file transfer function to the TERM program we began in Chapter 12.

It's now time to plunge into the deepest, murkiest of intellectual pools: the problem of writing portable functions to deal with baud rate and data format.

Functions for Baud Rate and Data Format

In previous programming chapters, we have discussed asynchronous serial I/O in relatively abstract terms. That is, we have always assumed that inbound and outbound bytes are correctly formed and are at the correct baud rate. In this chapter, we will develop the data structures and functions necessary to set the baud rate and to vary all elements of the SDU—data length, parity, and the number of stop bits.

There is nothing particularly glamorous about these functions. In fact, at their lowest level, such functions always consist largely of unromantic programming chores such as ORing, ANDing, and shifting. Because such chores are inherently dependent upon the system hardware, especially the UARTs, they tend to be viewed with a measure of dread by programmers, who see writing new serial "drivers" as a never-ending job. Nothing can eliminate the apprehension associated with the activity, but we can simplify it (by orders of magnitude) while simultaneously decreasing the time required and increasing the success rate.

It is only fair to warn you that this is a difficult chapter. Knowing this in advance, you should probably read it once just to gain an idea of its scope, then work, or perhaps more accurately, *hack*, your way through the code line by line. Like many of the programming chapters, this one is not designed for ingestion at a single session. As you proceed, take consolation in the knowledge that the methods and code described in this chapter have successfully tamed about 30 different UARTs on radically different systems. The great promise of this chapter, then, is that its methods will reduce from hours (or days!) to minutes the time required to "port" your software to new systems or new serial hardware. In short, by careful design and a dogged determination to "Think General!" we can bring some degree of generality and portability to an area of programming usually considered to be hopelessly hardware-dependent.

Design Goals

The primary goal of this chapter is to compose a library of functions that enable us to manipulate the UART's data format and baud rate using humane arguments and syntax such as setbaud(300) or setformat(PARITY, NONE). As always, level-3 functions such as these cannot stand alone because, by definition, they do not address the UART directly. Instead, they invoke level-2 functions, which transform the human language arguments to abstract, or logical, arguments. The level-2 functions in turn pass these logical arguments to level-1 functions where they are actually translated into reads and writes of the *physical* UART.

Level-3 functions are always simple to design—their names, arguments, and syntax are chosen for clarity and simplicity. Level-1 functions are also relatively easy to design, because the UART they address so rigidly dictates their structure. The level-2 functions present the most interesting and difficult challenge, because they must decode the "natural" syntax of the level-3 functions into abstract commands, then invoke the level-1 functions to accomplish the correct physical command.

In a real sense, level-2 functions are the interface between programmer and hardware. If this interface is correctly designed, neither side is aware of the other. To achieve generality and portability, these functions must address only the *conceptual* UART ("uartness," if you will) and make as few assumptions as possible about real UARTs.

Because of their centrality in the overall library design, and because UART functions do not lend themselves easily to abstract expression, most of our effort will go into the design of a *virtual UART*—an intellectual representation with no exact counterpart in reality. Aside from the intellectual difficulty involved in inventing a virtual device interface for the UART, there are several practical and philosophical questions to consider.

User Criteria

Users become quite annoyed when application programs disturb their primary interface with the computer. Programs that change the cursor's shape but terminate without restoring it are an obvious example. Users find the presence of an unfamiliar cursor so disturbing that they often reboot the computer to restore the "correct" one. Because the cause of and remedy for the uninvited change in cursor shape is usually obvious, such cosmetic problems are merely annoying. Unsolicited alteration of the configuration of a serial port by a program, however, is far more serious for several reasons. First, its effects are more profound, because, as far as the user is concerned, an important part of the system no longer functions correctly. Second, unlike the altered cursor shape, the victim may not associate the running of a specific program (perhaps hours earlier) with the mysterious change in behavior of the printer or modem. Finally, the remedy is not necessarily obvious.

If these considerations seem too philosophical, let's look at a real example. In Chapter 6, we pointed out that many UARTs employ automatic transmitter handshaking with one of the RS-232 control inputs. Although the Z80SIO employs this handshaking feature, it also allows the programmer to disable it. Systems designed around the Z80SIO often anticipate that it will drive a serial printer. (The Z80SIO's automatic CTS handshaking is irresistible to software designers, because it eliminates the need to code printer handshaking into the operating system itself.) After struggling to build a proper RS-232 printer cable, the user naturally takes this handshaking for granted. Now suppose that after successfully using the printer, the user calls up a favorite modem program. As we have pointed out, modem software traditionally employs software instead of hardware handshaking in order to use a simple three-wire cable. In order to use this minimalist cable, programs invariably disable the Z80SIO's CTS/transmitter and DCD/receiver handshaking. (Otherwise, a custom RS-232 cable would be necessary to trick the Z80SIO's handshaking.) Unfortunately, when the modem program terminates, it may fail to restore the Z80SIO's automatic handshaking. When next the printer is used, the Z80SIO's transmitter no longer responds to an inhibited CTS, the printer's input buffer is quickly overrun, and printer output is garbled.

If this scene were acted out frequently enough, we would expect the user to figure out the source of the printer malfunction. There is, in his mind at least, no manifest connection between running the modem software and the malfunctioning printer. The moral of this story is simple: considerable thought should go into the design of functions that manipulate important interfaces. When your software alters the interface in any way, it should, whenever possible, restore it to its original condition. In other words, always apply the maxim "Leave it as you find it." The functions in this chapter provide a mechanism to achieve this goal.

General Assumptions

Before discussing the actual design of the library functions, let's outline the characteristics of our virtual UART:

- All UART operations are byte-oriented. That is, they interface with the system data buses 8 bits at a time. No other assumptions are made about the size or architecture of the data bus.
- Registers may be write-only; that is, their contents may not be recoverable.
- The master clock generator is external to the UART.
- The clocking factor is at least 16, but may be programmable.
- 20 baud rates from 50 to 115K are available.
- The baud rate is under program control. The baud rates for both transmitter and receiver are *simultaneously* programmed by writing two 1-byte divisors to one or more registers.
- The following data format settings are supported:

```
STOP BITS        1, 1½, and 2
PARITY           NONE, ODD, EVEN, MARK, SPACE
DATA LENGTH      5 through 8
```

- Data format is manipulated by writing to bit-mapped, *write-only* registers. One set of parameters governs both transmitted and received data.

- Data format parameters are not necessarily represented in the same register. For example, the bits governing parity may be in a different register than those for governing the number of stop bits.

- The following RS-232 outputs are supported: RTS, DTR, and two general-purpose outputs, GPO1 and GPO2.

- The following RS-232 inputs are supported: CTS, DSR, DCD, RI, and two general-purpose inputs, GPI1 and GPI2.

- The transmitter can be forced into a SPACE state indefinitely for the purposes of creating a BREAK condition.

- Transmitter and receiver handshaking exists on the CTS and DCD RS-232 lines respectively.

- Transmitter and receiver sections may be separately enabled and disabled.

- Both transmitter and receiver have FIFO's whose trigger levels are programmable.

- Serialization errors and BREAK are detected by reading a bit-mapped, read-only register.

- The UART asserts its INT (interrupt) line upon the following events: transmitter holding register empty, received data ready, serialization error or BREAK, and any change in the state of an RS-232 input.

This remainder of this chapter is organized into six parts:

1. "Virtual" registers
2. Data format level-2 and -3 functions
3. Data format level-0 and -1 objects for the 16X50
4. Baud rate level-2 and -3 functions
5. Baud rate level-0 and -1 objects for the 16X50
6. Configuration and restoration of the SIO
7. Enhancements to TERM

The Virtual Register

Some of the characteristics of the virtual UART clearly influence the library design more than others. The stipulation that all registers are write-only is perhaps the most onerous. If the UART's registers were read/write, we could manipulate them as follows:

1. Fetch UART register's current bit pattern.
2. Reset selected bits with an OR.

3. Apply desired bit pattern with an AND.

4. Write new bit pattern back to the register.

Without the ability to read these registers and store their contents, however, we obviously cannot use this approach. The solution to this problem is straightforward: for each writable register in the *physical* UART, we maintain a corresponding *virtual register* in the SIO. In this way, each physical UART register has an identical counterpart in memory. In this scheme, a level-2 function manipulates the bit pattern of a virtual register, then passes the contents of the virtual register to a level-1 function, which is responsible for "updating" the corresponding registers in the physical UART:

1. Reset selected bits in the virtual register.

2. Apply new bit pattern to the virtual register.

3. Call a level-1 function to write the virtual register to the physical UART.

Let's see how this process works by examining Listing 14.1, a first-draft level-2 function to set the parity.

Listing 14.1. Hypothetical Level-2 function to set parity.

```
FUNTION NAME: changeparity
        LEVEL: 2
  DESCRIPTION: Hypothetical function to set parity.
      RETURNS: int
     COMMENTS: Experimental version—don't type this in.

BYTE vreg3 = 0x30;              /* virtual register number 3 */

int changeparity(int paritycode)
{
    int ormask = 0;

    vreg3 &= PARITYMASK;        /* clear parity bits in virtual register  */
        switch (paritycode)
            {
            case NONE:
                ormask = NONE_MASK;
                break;
            case ODD:
                ormask = ODD_MASK;
                break;
            case EVEN:
                ormask = EVEN_MASK;
                break;
            default:
                ormask = -1;
                break;
            }
```

continues

Listing 14.1. continued

```
if (ormask != -1)
    {
    vreg3 |= ormask;       /* set parity bits in virtual register   */
    _changeparity(vreg3); /* call level-1 function to write to UART */
    }
return(ormask != -1);
}
```

An explanation of *changeparity*—This function, like all the "virtual" functions in this book, expects its argument to be an *integer* code—0 for NONE, 1 for ODD, and so forth; these constants, as well as a few general constant definitions that we will need in the next few chapters, are given in Listing 14.2. These system-wide constants must reside in SIODEF.H.

Listing 14.2. System-wide constants and constant definitions. All reside in SIODEF.H.

```
/*** Parity Constants ***/
enum par { NONE = 0, ODD, EVEN, MARK, SPACE };

/*** Stop Bit Constants ***/
enum sb {STOP1 = 0, STOP1_5, STOP2 };

/*** Data Length Constants ***/
enum dl { DL5 = 0, DL6, DL7, DL8 };

/*** Constants for GET/SET FORMAT/BAUD Functions ***/
enum brfmt { BAUD = 0, STOPS, DATALEN, PARITY };

/*** Error Codes Returned by Level-3 Functions ***/
enum {
    BAD_FCN = 2,          /* Function not supported   */
    OR_ARG,               /* Argument out of range    */
    BAD_ARG,              /* Argument not supported   */
    BAD_PORT,             /* Illegal device number    */
    NO_PORT,              /* Device not installed     */
    NO_SIO,               /* No SIO declared          */
    OPEN_NOW,             /* Device already open      */
    NO_CLOSE,             /* No such device open      */
    KEY_CAN,              /* Aborted from keyboard    */
    NO_FILE,              /* File not found           */
    NO_IMEM,              /* Out of heap memory       */
    };

#define  NUMMASKS  5      /* ORDINAL number elements in "setmask" array */
#define  VIRGIN    -2     /* Dummy initializer (must be < -1)           */
#define  SUPPLIED  0      /* Dummy initializer                          */

/*** Constants for Columns in the Virtual Register Array ***/
```

```
#define  VIR       0
#define  USR       1
```

The call to this hypothetical function is

`changeparity(EVEN)`

where EVEN is one of the data format codes given in Listing 14.2. The constants PARITYMASK, NONE_MASK, ODD_MASK, and EVEN_MASK define the bit patterns required to produce the desired parity. Because these constants are unique to the UART being addressed, they must reside in the header file for the appropriate UART, in this case U16X50.H, the values for which are shown in Listing 14.3.

The bits governing parity are cleared by ANDing them with the constant PARITYMASK. The bits are then set to the desired value by ORing them with a constant (such as ODD_MASK), whose value is determined by switching on the paritycode argument. (The virtual register is arbitrarily named vreg3.) Once the desired bit pattern has been built in the virtual register, the as yet unwritten level-1 function, _changeparity, writes the virtual register to the UART.

The important thing to notice about this function is that only the virtual register vreg3, not any UART register, is manipulated; the binary value ultimately bound for the UART is first built in vreg3. In short, the level-2 function needs to know nothing about the physical UART—the act of installing the virtual register in the real UART is the responsibility of the level-1 function.

You have doubtless spotted the fatal flaw in this sample function: the mask values and virtual register may be totally different for other UARTs. In other words, it is not really a level-2 function. Because it is valid for only one UART, it would have to be recompiled for every UART supported. We can overcome this problem, however, by rewriting the function to access the masks and the virtual register as SIO members.

Data Format for the IBM PC

If all UARTs were as straightforward as the 16X50, there would be little need for virtual registers. All 16X50 write registers—Baud, Interrupt Enable, RS-232 Output, and Line Control (Data Format)—can also be read at the same address. Although it does have idiosyncrasies and one or two shortcomings, in many ways it is the ideal UART from the point of view of the programmer. Because it is such a well thought-out device, it fits quite comfortably in our virtual UART scheme.

Before installing the 16X50 functions to the libraries, add the constants shown in Listing 14.3 to U16X50.LIB. This enumeration of vir_row constants is noteworthy only because of the last constant, V_REG_SIZE, the cardinal number of entries in the virtual array. Several functions need to know the size of the divisor array, so placing it last in the enumeration automatically changes its value whenever the size of array is changed.

Listing 14.3. Masks and virtual constants for the 16X50.

```
/*** Rows in the Virtual Register Array ***/
enum vir_row {
        VBAUDLO = 0, /* lo byte of baud rate register */
        VBAUDHI,     /* hi byte of baud rate register */
        VINT_EN,     /* interrupt enable register      */
        VFIFO,       /* FIFO register                  */
        VFMT,        /* Data format register           */
        VOUT232,     /* RS-232 output register         */
        V_REG_SIZE   /* number of elements in virtual array */
        };

/*** Bit Masks for Data Length ***/
#define  DLMASK       0xFC      /* AND mask 11111100   */
#define  DL5_MASK     0x00      /* OR mask 00000000    */
#define  DL6_MASK     0x01      /* OR mask 00000001    */
#define  DL7_MASK     0x02      /* OR mask 00000010    */
#define  DL8_MASK     0x03      /* OR mask 00000011    */


/*** Bit Masks for Stop Bits ***/
#define  STOPMASK     0xFB      /* AND mask 11111011   */
#define  ONE_MASK     0x00      /* OR mask 00000000    */
#define  ONE_5_MASK   0x04      /* OR mask 00000100    */
#define  TWO_MASK     0x04      /* OR mask 00000100    */


/*** Bit Masks for Parity Bits ***/
#define  PARITYMASK   0xC7      /* AND MASK 11000111   */
#define  NONE_MASK    0x00      /* OR mask 00000000    */
#define  ODD_MASK     0x08      /* OR mask 00001000    */
#define  EVEN_MASK    0x18      /* OR mask 00011000    */
#define  MARK_MASK    0x28      /* OR mask 00101000    */
#define  SPACE_MASK   0x38      /* OR mask 00111000    */
```

The Virtual Register Array for the 16X50

Recall from Chapter 7 that there is only one significant oddity in the 16X50: the low- and high-order Baud Rate registers are addressed at the same offsets as the Transmitter and the Interrupt Enable registers. When bit 7 of the Data Format (Line Control) register is FALSE, reads and writes to these addresses are directed to the Data and the Interrupt Enable registers; conversely, when bit 7 of the Data Format register is TRUE, reads and writes to these addresses are steered to *LSB Divisor Latch* and the *MSB Divisor Latch*. The existence of these "phantom" registers precludes a one-to-one correspondence between a register's physical offset and its position in the virtual register array. Listing 14.4 shows the declaration and initialization of the array.

Listing 14.4. Virtual array for the IBM PC.

OBJECT NAME: v_regA
          TYPE: Two-dimensional array of REG.
        LEVEL: 0
     MODULE: IBMPC.C
DESCRIPTION: Used for virtual UART registers.

```
REG v_regA[V_REG_SIZE][2]=
    {
/*  VIR   USR  */
    { 0,    0 },        /* 0 = baud low byte         */
    { 0,    0 },        /* 1 = baud high byte        */
    { 0,    0 },        /* 2 = interrupt enable      */
    { 0,    0 },        /* 3 = FIFO enable           */
    { 0,    0 },        /* 4 = data format           */
    { 0,    0 },        /* 5 = RS232 output control  */
    };
```

Because computers usually contain more than one serial port, the letter A is appended to the name of this array to associate it with COM1sio, the first serial port. To support more than one SIO, a separate virtual array for each SIO must be declared—v_regB, v_regC, and so forth.

An explanation of *v_regA*—There is one small surprise in this declaration—the virtual register array is *two dimensional.* Although we will not need the second dimension of this array until later in the chapter (where it stores the "state of the UART" for later restoration), its introduction now will familiarize you with the syntax associated with its usage. The initialized values in the left column are, for tutorial convenience, assumed to be the current values of the corresponding U16X50 write registers; just how this correspondence between the virtual array and the physical UART is achieved will be explained later. In the meantime, just assume that an as yet unnamed function was called to guarantee that the U16X50's physical write registers have been initialized.

SYNTAX WITH TWO-DIMENSION ARRAY

You will notice that the two columns in v_regA are labeled VIR ("virtual") and USR ("user"). These two constants, defined in Listing 14.2 as 0 and 1 respectively, make the references to virtual registers more obvious. For example, to address cell 3,0 we write

```
v_regA[3][VIR]
```

To address the virtual Data Format register, we write

```
v_regA[VFMT][VIR]
```

A General Structure for Bit Manipulation (*vregbits_*)

With the virtual register array now declared, we could easily define a "parity" structure. But we would eventually also have to define "stopbits" and "data length" structures. In truth, we require a *general* structure that will hold the information necessary to impose selected bit patterns on *any* virtual register. To emphasize this generality, then, we will henceforth refer to struct v_regbits, shown in Listing 14.5. Our "parity" structure will merely be an instance of this structure.

Listing 14.5. *v_regbits_*: a structure for virtual register manipulation.

STRUCT NAME: vregbits_
 HEADER FILE: SIODEF.H
 DESCRIPTION: General structure for virtual register maniupulation.

```
struct vregbits_
    {
    MASK      resetmask;          /* AND mask apply to virtual register */
    MASK      setmask[NUMMASKS];   /* Array of OR masks for each setting */
    RANK      vregnum;            /* Virtual register number (row)      */
    USHORT    offset;             /* Offset of physical uart register    */
    RANK      now;                /* Code for current value             */
    RANK      start;              /* Code to use at initialization       */
    struct vregbits_ *next;       /* Next struct for this function       */
    };
```

The four highlighted structure members contain all the information needed by a level-2 function:

resetmask	This is the AND mask for clearing selected bits in the virtual register.
setmask[]	Because our virtual UART supports five parity settings— NONE, EVEN, ODD, MARK, and SPACE—we require a "five-element" array to hold the OR mask for each desired bit pattern. Because several functions need to know the size of this array, the constant NUMMASKS is used.
vregnum	This is the parity register's position (i.e., its *rank*) in the virtual register array.
offset	This is the offset (from uart_base) of the UART port controlling this function. For example, if we declare a vregbits_ to control, say, parity, offset will contain the offset of the UART register that controls parity. This value will be employed by the level-1 routine to address the correct UART register.

The remaining three members are defined now, but will be discussed later as they arise:

now
When the contents of a virtual register are changed, the code for its current rank in the setmask array is placed here for later reference. When, for example, EVEN parity is selected, 2 is stored in this member.

start
This is the setting used during initialization of the SIO (covered later in this chapter). It is expressed as a rank in the setmask array. For instance, 0 in this member tells the initialization function to set the SIO to 1 stop bit.

next
This pointer enables us to "attach" more than one vregbits_ structure to a single UART function by creating a linked list in which each structure contains a pointer to another vregbits_ structure. We will discuss this in detail later.

An instance of the vregbits_ structure for controlling parity can now be declared in IBMPC.C. This structure, given the tag parityA, is shown in Listing 14.6.

Data Format on the IBM PC

Note the declaration and initialization of the vregbits_ structures for the IBM PC in Listing 14.5. Like the virtual register array, all structure identifiers end in the letter 'A' in order to correspond with the '1' in COM1sio. If another port is supported, its declarations end in 'B', the next in 'C', and so on.

Listing 14.6. Data format structures for the IBM PC.

OBJECT NAME: parityA
TYPE: vregbits structure
LEVEL: 0
MODULE: IBMPC.C
DESCRIPTION: Control stucture for parity.

```
struct vregbits_ parityA =
    {
    PARITYMASK,                 /* AND mask to isoltate parity bits        */
    { NONE_MASK, ODD_MASK, EVEN_MASK, MARK_MASK, SPACE_MASK },  /* OR masks */
    VFMT,                       /* Virtual register--rank in v_regA        */
    FMT,                        /* Offset of physical register from uart_base */
    SUPPLIED,                   /* Rank in mask table of current setting    */
    NONE,                       /* Rank to use in initialization            */
    NIL                         /* No more structures for parity            */
    };
```

Because of the popularity of the IBM PC, one is tempted to place these structure declarations in *IBMPC.C.* If you elect to do so, keep in mind that even though the IBM method of address decoding is natural to the 16X50, its physical offsets are probably not valid for boards that are not intended for use with the IBM PC.

This declaration initializes the resetmask and setmask members from the constant values contained in *U16X50.H.* We can now explain why the setmask array is declared as the MASK (which is *signed*) each element must be able to hold a value of −1. This enables level-2 functions to detect requests for unsupported settings. We will use this technique for marking the ends of valid data for the remainder of this book.

Notice that the now member is assigned the manifest constant SUPPLIED to remind you that no initialization is necessary. The start member is set for NO parity by using the NONE rank code from *SIODEF.H.*

Because all bits required to set parity on a U16X50 are in a single register, the next pointer is initialized to NIL to show that there are no more relevant vregbits_ structures involved.

We are now ready to write a second (but still not final) draft of our level-2 function to change parity. Instead of the name chngparity, however, let's use the more general name of vsetbits to reflect that it can be used on *any* virtual register. This version merely uses a pointer to a vregbits_ structure that contains the vital information:

```
vsetbits(struct vregbits_ *p, int rank)
{
    vregA[VIR][p->vregnum] &= p->resetmask;
    vregA[VIR][p->vregnum] |= p->setmask[rank];
    _vsetbits(vregA[VIR][p->vregnum]);
}
```

The call to this function looks like this:

```
vsetbits(&parityA, ODD);
```

This call passes the address of (a pointer to) the parityA structure declared and initialized in IBMPC.C. The element of vreg (the virtual register array) containing the parity information is described by the vregnum member. In this case, vreg[VIR] [p->vregnum] refers to array element 4, 0 in the vreg array. Similarly, the rank argument is an index into the setmask array, providing the OR mask for the desired bit pattern. Finally, the level-1 function is called upon to perform the actual write to the UART.

Notice that we have changed the name of the still-unwritten level-1 function to _vsetbits. We will often employ this parallel nomenclature in the remainder of this book, deriving the name for a level-1 function by prepending an underscore to the name of a level-2 function.

Access Through an *SIO* Pointer

The passing of a regbits structure pointer greatly extends the generality of this function. We now have a level-2 function that is blissfully ignorant of the system hardware: it merely manipulates a cell in the virtual register according to the contents of a structure. The development of this function now lacks only one step: to rewrite the function in terms of the SIO. Our new function must therefore access its virtual registers and data format structures (e.g., parity) through a *pointer* to an SIO.

Before we rewrite the function, let's first see how this affects the SIO definition. We must add the following elements:

● The virtual register array. Because the size of this array varies from one UART to another, the SIO does not contain the virtual array itself, but a *pointer* to it.

● The number of elements in the virtual register array.

● A *pointer* to a vregbits_ structure devoted to parity.

● A *pointer* to a vregbits_ structure devoted to stop bits.

● A *pointer* to a vregbits_ structure devoted to data length.

● A *pointer* to a vbaud_ structure devoted to baud rate (which we shall need later in the chapter).

If your head is beginning to reel a bit from all the pointers, consider the alternative. If we had placed the actual regbit_ structures themselves in the SIO instead of pointers to them, the syntax for initializing the SIO would be incomprehensible.

Listing 14.7 highlights the new items as they appear in the SIO.

Listing 14.7. Additions to the *SIO* to support data format.

```
      STRUCT DEF: SIO
            FILE: SIODEF.H
        COMMENTS: Addition of virtual UART registers and data format structures.
     DESCRIPTION: Master structure defining a serial port.
    INCLUDE FILES: siolocal.h

struct sio
  {
  BYTE   * uart_base;              /*0  Base address of UART          */
  USHORT data_off;                 /*1  Offset of data port from base */
  .
  .
  .
  REG    (*v_regp)[2];             /*13 Pointer to a 2-dim array of BYTE */
  USHORT v_regpsize;               /*14 Length of virtual array       */
  struct vregbits_ *par;           /*15 Pointer to parity struct      */
  struct vregbits_ *sb;            /*16 Pointer to stop bit struct    */
  struct vregbits_ *dl;            /*17 Pointer to data length struct */
  struct vbaud_    *br;            /*18 Pointer to baud rate  struct  */
  };
```

The pointer to the virtual array is worthy of discussion. Pointers to multidimensional arrays are not very common, so the definition (*v_regp)[2] may seem a bit odd. First, as with pointers to functions, parentheses are required to bind the variable name to the * operator instead of to the array brackets. In other words, without the parentheses, v_regp would be a two-dimensional array of pointers to REG. Less obvious, perhaps, is that the *length* of the array (number of rows) is not required in the pointer declaration. As with single-dimension arrays, the first set of brackets may be left blank, because the compiler needs to know only the *width* of the array in order to calculate the correct *scaling factor* for arithmetic references to its members.

Structures for Stop Bits and Data Length

Let's now look at the declaration of regbit_ structures for stop bits and data length. These are shown in Listing 14.8.

Listing 14.8. The *vregbits_* structure for stop bits and data length.

OBJECT NAME: stopsA
          TYPE: vregbits structure
        LEVEL: 0
     MODULE: IBMPC.C
DESCRIPTION: Control stucture for stop bits.

```
struct vregbits_ stopsA =
     {
     STOPMASK,                    /* AND mask to isolate stop-bit bits        */
     { ONE_MASK, ONE_5_MASK, TWO_MASK, -1, -1 },
     VFMT,                        /* virtual register--rank in v_rega         */
     FMT,                         /* offset of physical register from uart_base */
     SUPPLIED,                    /* rank in mask table of current setting    */
     STOP1,                       /* rank to use in initialization            */
     NIL                          /* no more structures for parity            */
     };
```

OBJECT NAME: dlenA
           TYPE: vregbits structure
         LEVEL: 0
      MODULE: IBMPC.C
DESCRIPTION: Control stucture for data length.

```
struct vregbits_ dlenA =
     {
     DLMASK,                      /* AND mask to isolate data length bits     */
     { DL5_MASK, DL6_MASK, DL7_MASK, DL8_MASK, -1 },
     VFMT,                        /* virtual register--rank in v_rega         */
     FMT,                         /* offset of physical register from uart_base */
     SUPPLIED,                    /* rank in mask table of current setting    */
     DL8,                         /* rank to use in initialization            */
```

```
    NIL                        /* no more structures for data length        */
    };
```

The regbit_ structures stopsA and dlenA contain the relevant information for the U16X50: both are addressed through the U16X50's "control/status port" at offset FMT, and occupy virtual register VFMT.

Multiple Register Operations

How do we handle a UART operation that requires more than a single operation on a single register? As you recall from Chapter 7, data length for the transmitter and the receiver on the Z80SIO are independently adjustable. Because the bits governing these two settings reside in *different* registers, it would be impossible to describe them with a single vregbits_ structure. The next member of the vregbits_ structure provides the mechanism for describing functions that require *multiple* registers.

Because next is declared to be a pointer to another v_regbits structure, we can easily form a chain, or linked list of such structures. In Listing 14.8, its next member contains NIL, indicating that it is the *final* structure in the list and that no more v_regbits structures are required to set the data length. If this method of list linkage is a bit fuzzy now, it will become clear when we compose our final version of vsetbits, the function that actually manipulates these virtual registers.

With these new data format structures in hand, we can now declare an instance of an SIO named, as always, COM1sio. Listing 14.9 shows this declaration.

Listing 14.9. Initialization of the new *SIO* members.

```
      SIO NAME: COM1sio
          FILE: IBMPC.C
      COMMENTS: Initialization of virtual UART registers and data format structures.
                Line numbers in comments are for reference only.
SIO COM1sio =
    {
    COM1,                  /*0  base address of UART                 */
    .
    .
    .
    v_regA,                /*13 pointer to virtual register array    */
    V_REG_SIZE,            /*14 number of rows in virtual array      */
    &parityA,              /*15 parity structure                     */
    &stopsA,               /*16 stop bit structure                   */
    &dlenA,                /*17 data length structure                */
    &baudA,                /*18 baud rate structure                  */
    .
    .
    .
    };
```

Here, the pointer (v_regp) to the two-dimensional virtual register array is initialized with the address of v_regA. Similarly, the par, sb, and dl vregbits_ pointers are initialized with the address of the parityA, stopsA, and dlenA structures.

UNSUPPORTED VIRTUAL FUNCTIONS

Naturally, not all UARTs support every feature we have designed into our virtual structure. How do we initialize the SIO member if there is no structure declaration for an unsupported function? Because all these new members are pointers, we mark them as unsupported by initializing them to NIL.

LIST LINKAGE

Keep in mind these four interrelated facts:

1. The next member of *every* vregbits structure must be initialized.

2. If there is only one structure involved, its next member must be initialized to NIL; otherwise, vsetbits acts upon this uninitialized (random) value and writes garbage at the location indicated by the non-existent next "structure."

3. For the reasons just discussed in (2), the next member of the *final* structure in the list MUST be initialized with NIL.

4. The SIO must be initialized with a pointer to the *first* structure in a linked list of structures. Using later structures in the list produces incomplete (and often puzzling) results.

Vsetbits: the Final Version

Let's now look at Listing 14.10, the final version of vsetbits, the level-2 function that manipulates the bits in the virtual register. The constant definitions for return codes are from SIODEF.H and were given in Listing 14.2.

Listing 14.10. The *vsetbits* function: the final version.

```
FUNCTION NAME: vsetbits
         LEVEL: 2
   PROTOTYPE IN: BUOS.H
        LIBRARY: BUOS.LIB
    DESCRIPTION: Builds a new bit pattern in the virtual register in v_regp by
                 ANDing and ORing, then calls the level-0 _setbits, to install
                 that bit pattern in the physical UART's register.
        RETURNS: int: 0 if successful OR_ARG if argument is out of range;
```

BAD_FCN if the function is not supported (SIO pointer is NIL); BAD_ARG if the requested setting is not supported by hardware (mask initialized to –1).

COMMENTS: More than one virtual register may be attached to a function by the linked list of next pointers.

INCLUDE FILES: siodef.h, uart.h

```
int vsetbits(SIO *siop, struct vregbits_ *rbp, RANK rank)
{
    REG tmp;
    if (rbp == NIL)                  /* function not supported in hardware */
        return BAD_FCN;
    if ( rank >= NUMMASKS)           /* argument range check              */
        return OR_ARG;
    if (rbp->setmask[rank] == -1)    /* argument not supported in hardware */
        return BAD_ARG;
    do
        {
        siop->v_regp[rbp->vregnum][VIR] &= rbp->resetmask;  /* reset bits */
        tmp = siop->v_regp[rbp->vregnum][VIR] |= rbp->setmask[rank];
        rbp->now = rank;             /* update current table rank         */
        _vsetbits(siop, rbp, tmp);   /* write vreg to the UART            */
        rbp = rbp->next;             /* another structure involved?       */
        } while (rbp != NIL);        /* no, done                          */
    return 0;
}
```

An explanation of vsetbits—This function requires three arguments:

1. Like all our functions, the first argument is the SIO pointer through which all other variables are accessed.

2. A pointer to a struct vregbits_. (This may be a pointer to a parity, stop bits, or data length structure.)

3. The code for the desired setting as defined in Listing 14.2. A request for 8 data bits, for example, would require a rank argument of 3 (DL8 in *SIODEF.H*).

Error testing is performed immediately upon entry to the function. An error code of BAD_FCN is returned if the structure pointer is NIL, indicating that the function described is not supported. An error code of OR_ARG is returned if the rank argument is greater than the size of the vsetbits array. Finally, an error code of BAD_ARG is returned if the rank element of the vsetbits array is unsupported (initialized to –1).

When the arguments have been validated, a do...while loop uses the information contained in the pointed-to vregbits_ structure to modify the contents of the appropriate virtual register. First, the bits in the virtual register are cleared by applying the AND mask:

```
siop->v_regp[rbp->vregnum][VIR] &= rbp->resetmask;
```

This imposing-looking expression becomes rather more friendly with its variables evaluated for a call to set EVEN parity:

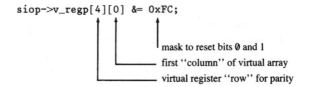

Assuming that virtual register 1 currently contains a value of 45H, the expression further evaluates to `0x45 & 0xFC`, or 44H (e.g., bit 0 is cleared).

Next, the desired bit pattern is imposed upon the virtual register and, to simplify the syntax for calling _vsetbits, the results are stored in the intermediate variable `tmp`.

```
tmp = siop->v_regp[rbp->vregnum][VIR] |= rbp->setmask[rank];
```

which evaluates to

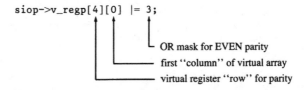

and eventually becomes `0x44 | 3`, or simply 47H. Next, the rank of the current setting effect is stored in the `now` member of the `vregbits_` parity structure. The level-1 function _vsetbits is finally called to install the value in the virtual register in the physical UART.

FOLLOWING THE LIST LINKAGE

With the information passed in the `vregbits` structure now safely installed in the physical UART, the following innocuous-looking assignment occurs:

```
rbp = rbp->next;
```

thus loading into `rbp` the address of the next `vregbits` structure in the linked list. The body of the `do...while` repeats until a NIL `next` member signals the end of the list. This design supports the use of multiple structures for a single logical operation such as would be required to support the Z80SIO and its separate settings for transmit and receive data lengths.

The Level-1 Function for the 16X50 (_vsetbits)

The final chore of implementing the data format library on the IBM PC is to write the 16X50 version of the level-1 function _vsetbits, shown in Listing 14.11.

Listing 14.11. Level-1 function to write to the physical UART.

FUNCTION NAME:	_vsetbits
LEVEL:	1
PROTOTYPE IN:	U16X50.H
LIBRARY:	U16x50.LIB
DESCRIPTION:	This is the primitive to write the format in the virtual register to the corresponding UART register.
RETURNS:	void
COMMENTS:	This function is called only by vsetbits.
INCLUDE FILES:	siodef.h

```
void _vsetbits(register SIO *siop, struct vregbits_ *brp, REG binval)
{
    (*siop->writebyte)(siop->uart_base + brp->offset, (FAST) binval);
}
```

An explanation of _vsetbits—The byte passed in binval is unceremoniously written to the offset given in the regbin_ pointer, brp. On the 16X50, the bits that govern parity, data length, and stop bits all reside in the same (Data Format) register at offset 3.

The degree to which you find this function anticlimactic is a direct measure of our success. The sole objective of our virtual UART concept is to squeeze the machine dependency out of our functions, concentrating it into innocuous droplets like _vsetbits.

The Level-3 Functions for Data Format

With the two lower-level functions in hand, the portable level-3 functions shown in Listing 14.12 can now be written to employ a simple, natural syntax.

Listing 14.12. Level-3 functions to set the data format.

FUNCTION NAME:	setformat
LEVEL:	3
PROTOTYPE IN:	SIODEF.H
LIBRARY:	SIO.LIB
DESCRIPTION:	This function sets the respective data format elements.
RETURNS:	short: the rank of the setting as defined in SIODEF.H. BAD_FCN or BAD_ARG if the function is not supported.
INCLUDE FILES:	siodef.h, buos.h

continues

Listing 14.12. continued

```
short setformat(SIO *siop, RANK whichone, RANK newval)
{
    short retval;
    switch(whichone)
        {
        case STOPS:    return vsetbits(siop, siop->sb, newval);
        case DATALEN:  return vsetbits(siop, siop->dl, newval);
        case PARITY:   return vsetbits(siop, siop->par, newval);
        default:       retval = OR_ARG;
        }
    return retval;
}
```

An explanation of the level-3 data format function—The function `setformat` receives the format elements that need to be set and simply calls the level-2 function `vsetbits`, passing it the SIO pointer, the correct `struct vregbits_` pointer, and the RANK code of the desired format. For example, these three calls are required to set the data format to 7EVEN2.

```
setformat(siop, DATALEN, DL7);
setformat(siop, PARITY, EVEN);
setformat(siop, STOPS, STOP2);
```

LEVEL-3 FUNCTIONS TO FETCH THE CURRENT DATA FORMAT

Recall that when the level-2 function has successfully written the virtual register to the physical register, it stores the rank argument in the now member of the structure for use by other functions. At any time, then, we can learn the current status of any of the data parameters by examining its structure. The level-3 function simply returns the value of the now member.

Listing 14.13. Functions to fetch the current data format rate.

FUNCTION NAME: getformat
          LEVEL: 3
    PROTOTYPE IN: SIODEF.H
        LIBRARY: SIO.LIB
    DESCRIPTION: Returns current setting of data format element
        RETURNS: int: 0 if successful. OR_ARG if argument is out of range;
                 BAD_FCN if the function is not supported (SIO pointer
                 is NIL).
   INCLUDE FILES: siodef.h

```
short getformat(SIO *siop, RANK whichone)
{
    short retval = BAD_FCN;
    switch(whichone)
        {
        case STOPS:
            if (siop->sb != NIL)
                retval = siop->sb->now;
            break;
        case DATALEN:
            if (siop->dl != NIL)
                retval = siop->dl->now;
            break;
        case PARITY:
            if (siop->par != NIL)
                retval = siop->par->now;
            break;
        default:
            retval = OR_ARG;
        }
    return retval;
}
```

An explanation of the level-3 fetch functions—The getformat function merely returns the current value in the now member of their respective structures. If the function is unsupported in the SIO—that is, initialized to NIL—getformat breaks out of the switch statement and returns BAD_FCN.

Placement of the Structure Definitions

Because the declarations and initialization for dlen, stops, and parity are all specific to the IBM PC, they belong in IBMPC.C with all level-0 functions.

Baud Rate Functions

Support for a variable baud rate is accomplished in much the same way as data format. Specifically, there are three tiers of baud rate functions, all of which refer to a structure describing the virtual and physical characteristics affecting baud rate. But there is one important difference—we are assuming that the registers holding the Baud Rate register divisors contain no other data. That is, *all* bits in a Baud Rate register constitute the baud rate divisor. Because we do not have to concern ourselves with resetting and setting selected bits in a Baud Rate register, the Baud Rate register(s) may be *write-only*. This greatly simplifies the structure of the baud rate functions. In fact, it means that the Baud Rate registers do not necessarily have to reside in the array of virtual read/write registers. Nevertheless, placing the baud registers there bundles these functions into a neat, intellectually manageable package, providing a consistency in design by anticipating a future UART that shares its Baud Rate register with other data.

The *vbaud_* Data Structure

You will remember from our virtual UART definition that we are assuming that the baud rate is programmed by writing a 2-byte divisor to two Baud Rate registers. Because we can assume nothing about the characteristic of the physical UART registers (are the registers contiguous? are they at different addresses?), the structure must contain the offset address and virtual register numbers for both the high and low byte of the divisor. The vbaud_ structure is shown in Listing 14.14.

Listing 14.14. A data structure to describe the baud rate.

STRUCT NAME: vbaud_
　　　　　　FILE: SIODEF.H
DESCRIPTION: Control structure for baud rate.

```
struct vbaud_
    {
    BYTE    vregnuml;             /* Virtual array of baud rate lo        */
    BYTE    vregnumh;             /* Virtual array of baud rate hi        */
    USHORT  offsetlo;             /* Offset of lo-order baud  rate register */
    USHORT  offsethi;             /* Offset of hi-order baud  rate register */
    short   divisor[NUMBAUDS][2]; /* Array of two-byte divisors           */
    RANK    now;                  /* Rank of current divisorin divisor array */
    RANK    start;                /* Rank of value to use at start up     */
    };
```

The functions of the members in this structure are similar to those in the vregbits_ structure. Two differences, however, are worth pointing out. First, because baud rates are not bit mapped, no "resetmasks" or "setmasks" are necessary. In place of the "set" mask are the actual divisors, represented as a two-dimensional array of short. For purposes of visualization, we refer to the divisor in the first array ("column" 0) as the high-order byte, and the other as the low-order byte. The now and start members store the rank of the baud rate codes, respectively, for the current baud rate and the baud rate to use at start-up.

The divisors array is declared to be short (signed). This enables us to mark unsupported baud rates with a –1 sentinel. The vbaud_ structure contains no next member because of our assumption that the 16-bit divisor resides in two registers.

Listing 14.15. System-wide manifest constants for baud rates. These reside in SIODEF.H.

```
/*** Manifest Constants for Baud Rate Arguments ***/

enum baudcodes
    {
    BAUD50 = 0, BAUD75, BAUD110, BAUD134_5, BAUD150, BAUD300, BAUD600,
    BAUD1200, BAUD1800, BAUD2000, BAUD2400, BAUD3600, BAUD4800, BAUD7200,
    BAUD9600, BAUD14K4, BAUD19K2, BAUD28K8, BAUD38K4, BAUD57K6, BAUD115K2,
    NUMBAUDS
    };
```

Baud Rate on the IBM PC

The 16X50 contains the circuitry for an on-board baud generator, so setting the baud rate could hardly be simpler, at least from a logical standpoint. Two 8-bit registers, referred to as *LSB and MSB Divisor Latches*, constitute a 16-bit divisor for the clock circuitry. Because the 16X50's clocking factor is *fixed* at 16 (i.e., not programmable), the frequencies actually generated by the dividing circuitry must be 16 times greater than the desired baud rate. Using the IBM PC's oscillator frequency of 1.8432 MHz, the 16-bit divisors for each baud rate can be calculated by the equation:

$$divisor = \frac{1,843,200}{(16 \times baud\ rate)}$$

Applying this equation to our 16 baud rates produces the divisor constant definitions for the IBM PC shown in Table 14.1.

Table 14.1. Baud Rate Divisor Constants for U16X50.H.

High Byte		Low Byte		High Byte		Low Byte	
BH_50	0x09	BL_50	0x00	BH_2400	0x00	BL_2400	0x30
BH_75	0x06	BL_75	0x00	BH_3600	0x00	BL_3600	0x20
BH_110	0x04	BL_110	0x17	BH_4800	0x00	BL_4800	0x18
BH_134	0x03	BL_134	0x59	BH_7200	0x00	BL_7200	0x10
BH_150	0x03	BL_150	0x00	BH_9600	0x00	BL_9600	0x0C
BH_300	0x01	BL_300	0x80	BH_14K4	0x00	BL_14K4	0X08
BH_600	0x00	BL_600	0xC0	BH_19K2	0x00	BL_19K2	0X06
BH_1200	0x00	BL_1200	0x60	BH_38K4	0x00	BL_38K4	0X04
BH_1800	0x00	BL_1800	0x40	BH_57K6	0x00	BL_57K6	0X03
BH_2000	0x00	BL_2000	0x3A	BH_115K2	0x00	BL_115K2	0X01

DECLARATION AND INITIALIZATION OF THE *vbaud_* STRUCTURE

The declaration of the vbaud_ structure uses both high-order and low-order elements of the virtual register array. Because of the peculiar fashion in which the divisor registers are addressed, their physical offsets are 0 and 1—the same as the Data and Interrupt registers.

Listing 14.16. Declaration and initialization of a *vbaud_* structure.

```
OBJECT NAME: baudA
        TYPE: struct vbaud_
       LEVEL: 0
      MODULE: IBMPC.C
 DESCRIPTION: SIO control structure for baud rate.

struct vbaud_ baudA =
    {
    VBAUDLO,   /* Virtual register for lo byte     */
    VBAUDHI,   /* Virtual register for hi byte     */
    0,         /* Offset of UART lsb baud baud reg */
    1,         /* Offset of UART msb baud reg      */
    {
{BH_50,   BL_50   }, {BH_75,   BL_75   }, {BH_110,  BL_110  },
{BH_134,  BL_134  }, {BH_150,  BL_150  }, {BH_300,  BL_300  },
{BH_600,  BL_600  }, {BH_1200, BL_1200 }, {BH_1800, BL_1800 },
{BH_2000, BL_2000 }, {BH_2400, BL_2400 }, {BH_3600, BL_3600 },
{BH_4800, BL_4800 }, {BH_7200, BL_7200 }, {BH_9600, BL_9600 },
{BH_14K4, BL_14K4 }, {BH_19K2, BL_19K2 }, {BH_38K4, BL_38K4 },
{BH_57K6, BL_57K6 }, {BH_115K2, BL_115K2 },
    },
    SUPPLIED,  /* Rank of current divisor in table */
    BAUD2400   /* Start at 2400 baud               */
    };
```

The Level-2 Function to Set the Baud Rate

The level-2 function to set the baud rate looks superficially like vsetbits. The main difference is that setbaud does not manipulate individual bits in the virtual register.

Listing 14.17. *vsetbr:* the level-2 baud rate function.

```
FUNCTION NAME: vsetbr
        LEVEL: 2
 PROTOTYPE IN: BUOS.H
      LIBRARY: BUOS.LIB
```

DESCRIPTION: Sets the baud rate to the rank element of the structure's
divisor array. Passes high- and low-order divisors to level-1
function, _vsetbr.

RETURNS: int: 0 if successful. OR_ARG if argument is out of range;
BAD_FCN if the function is not supported (SIO pointer is
NIL); BAD_ARG if the requested setting is not supported by
hardware (divisor is −1).

COMMENTS: The rank argument is an index for the array of divisors,
constants for that reside in SIODEF.H. Notice that the low
byte is passed before the high byte.

INCLUDE FILES: siodef.h, uart.h

```
int vsetbr(SIO *siop, struct vbaud_ *brp, RANK rank)
{                                       /* rank of value to install    */
    REG brlo, brhi;                     /* intermediates simplify syntax   */
    if (brp == NIL)                     /* baud rate not supported in hardware */
        return BAD_FCN;
    if ( rank >= NUMBAUDS)              /* requested rank out of range     */
        return OR_ARG;
    if (brp->divisor[rank][1] == -1 || brp->divisor[rank][0] == -1)
        return BAD_ARG;                 /* request baud rate not available */
    brlo = brp->divisor[rank][1];   /* lo byte of divisor          */
    brhi = brp->divisor[rank][0];   /* lo byte of divisor          */
    brp->now = rank;                /* update baud in effect       */
    _vsetbr(siop, brp, brlo, brhi); /* call level-1 to do it       */
    return 0;
}
```

An explanation of *vsetbr*—The fundamental task of vsetbr is to pass the individual bytes
of the baud rate divisor to the level-1 function, _vsetbr. Notice that the low byte of the
divisor is passed *before* the high byte. The use of the intermediate variables brlo and brhi
is purely stylistic, intended to clarify the expressions.

The error checking in vsetbr is identical to that in vsetbits. An error code of OR_ARG is
returned if the rank argument is out of range; an error code of BAD_FCN is returned if the
structure pointer is NIL (indicating that the baud rate is not software programmable); finally, an error code of BAD_ARG is returned if the rank element of the divisor array is unsupported (i.e., initialized to −1).

Level-1 Function Baud Rate for the 16X50 (_vsetbr)

It is the responsibility of level-1 functions to resolve the conflict arising from the 16X50's
use of coincident addresses. The function in Listing 14.18 resolves this conflict.

Listing 14.18. _vsetbr: a level-1 function for baud rate.

FUNCTION NAME:	_vsetbr
LEVEL:	1
PROTOTYPE IN:	U16X50.H
LIBRARY:	U16x50.LIB
DESCRIPTION:	Primitive for setting the baud rate.
RETURNS:	void.
COMMENTS:	The baud rate is changed by lobaud and hibaud to the 16x50's LSB and MSB baud registers. These registers can be addressed only if bit 7 in the Data Format register is TRUE. After writing to these two registers, the original contents of the Data Format register are restored.
INCLUDE FILES:	siodef.h

```
void _vsetbr(register SIO *siop, struct vbaud_ *brp, REG lobaud, REG hibaud)
{
    FAST tmpfmt;
    tmpfmt = (*siop->readbyte)(siop->uart_base + siop->par->offset) ¦ 0x80;
    (*siop->writebyte)(siop->uart_base + siop->par->offset, tmpfmt);
    (*siop->writebyte)(siop->uart_base + brp->offsetlo, (FAST)lobaud);
    (*siop->writebyte)(siop->uart_base + brp->offsethi, (FAST)hibaud);
    (*siop->writebyte)(siop->uart_base + siop->par->offset, \
            (FAST)(tmpfmt & 0x7f));
}
```

An explanation of _vsetbr—Recall from Chapter 7 that when bit 7 of the Data Format register is FALSE, the registers at offset 0 and 1 function as the Data register (i.e., transmit and receive) and the Interrupt Enable register. When bit 7 of the Data Format register is TRUE, however, these become the low- and high-order bytes of the Baud Rate Divisor registers. Because of this addressing anomaly, the first task of this function must be to reset bit 7 of the Data Format register. Because the low-order 7 bits of this register contain the data format settings (as well as the BREAK bit), they must be preserved. This is accomplished by reading the register, setting its bit 7 (ORing it with 80H), then storing it temporarily in tmp. The value in tmp is then written back to the Data Format register, "exposing" the Baud Rate Divisor registers for addressing. In the statement that accomplishes this,

```
tmpfmt = (*siop->readbyte)(siop->uart_base + siop->par->offset) ¦ 0x80;
```

the expression siop->par->offset stands for the offset of the Data Format register. Because the bits governing parity, data length, and stop bits all reside in the same register, siop->sb->offset or siop->bl->offset could also have been used. UART-dependent details such as these are permitted only in level-1 files.

Next, the low- and high-order bytes of the divisor are written to the offsets named in the vbaud_ pointer, brp. Finally, in order to restore registers 0 and 1 to their "normal" addressing modes, bit 7 of tmp is cleared, and tmp is written back to the Data Format register.

The Level-3 Function for Baud Rate

Listing 14.19 shows setbaud, the level-3 function to set the baud rate; Listing 14.20 shows the function to fetch the current baud rate.

Listing 14.19. The level-3 baud rate function.

FUNCTION NAME: setbaud
LEVEL: 3
PROTOTYPE IN: SIODEF.H
LIBRARY: SIO.LIB
DESCRIPTION: Sets the baud rate to the rank element in the divisor array.
RETURNS: int: -1 if rank is out of range or not supported by hardware, otherwise 0.
COMMENTS: The rank argument is an index into an array of divisors, constants for which reside in SIODEF.H.
INCLUDE FILES: siodef.h, buos.h

```
short setbaud(SIO *siop, RANK rank)
{
    return (vsetbr(siop, siop->br, rank));
}
```

Listing 14.20. Use of *getbaud* to fetch the current baud rate.

FUNCTION NAME: getbaud
LEVEL: 3
PROTOTYPE IN: SIODEF.H
LIBRARY: SIO.LIB
DESCRIPTION: Returns rank of current baud rate as defined in SIODEF.H.
RETURNS: short; -1 if the function is not supported (i.e., the SIO pointer is NIL).
INCLUDE FILES: siodef.h

```
short getbaud(SIO *siop)
{
    if (siop->br != NIL) /* if supported */
        return (siop->br->now);
    return -1;
}
```

An explanation of *setbaud* and *getbaud*—Very little needs to be said about these functions except to point out that the fetch function returns the error code from vsetbr. Because some hardware may not support all baud rates in our virtual UART, the return value from setbaud should always be tested, especially when the call is made in response to user input. The getbaud function returns the rank of the current baud rate setting. If the br pointer in the SIO structure is not supported, a NIL is returned[1].

Configuration and Restoration

It is nearly time to put our new libraries to work. We shall do this by enhancing *TERM* to permit changes in baud rate and data format. Before we can proceed, however, we have a bit more programming to do. It has probably occurred to you that the success of our system of virtual registers depends upon one thing: the virtual registers must start life containing the same values as the corresponding physical UART registers. Until now, we have avoided this subject merely by assuming that this initialization has already magically taken place. We must now conjure up these magical functions. To this end, we require two additional level-1 functions—s_config to save the current settings upon entry, and s_restore to restore them upon exit.

The *config* and *restore* Functions for the 16X50

All registers on the 16X50 are read/write. Therefore, the task on the 16X50 is to fetch the contents of all registers and place them in *both* dimensions of the virtual array. Storing each physical value in the VIR dimension achieves the beginning physical-to-logical correspondence assumed by our library functions. Storing a copy of the physical registers in the USR dimension also preserves the current state of the UART so that the interface can be restored upon termination of the program. Listing 14.21 shows s_config.

Listing 14.21. Use of *s_config* to load virtual registers with the UART's physical registers.

```
FUNCTION NAME: s_config
         LEVEL: 1
   PROTOTYPE IN: MODEM.H
       LIBRARY: U16x50.LIB
   DESCRIPTION: Copies the contents of the 16x50's registers into the virtual array.
       RETURNS: void
  INCLUDE FILES: siodef.h, U16x50.H
```

---

[1]On many early microcomputers, the baud rate could be set only with microswitches.

```
void s_config(SIO *siop)
{
    FAST tmp;
    short i;
    tmp = (*siop->readbyte)(siop->uart_base + FMT) | 0x80;
    (*siop->writebyte)(siop->uart_base + FMT,  tmp);
    siop->v_regp[VBAUDLO][USR] = (*siop->readbyte)(siop->uart_base + \
            siop->br->offsetlo);
    siop->v_regp[VBAUDHI][USR] = (*siop->readbyte)(siop->uart_base + \
            siop->br->offsethi);
    (*siop->writebyte)(siop->uart_base + FMT, (BYTE)(tmp & 0x7f) );
    siop->v_regp[VINT_EN][USR]   = (*siop->readbyte)(siop->uart_base + INT_EN);
    siop->v_regp[VFMT][USR]    = (*siop->readbyte)(siop->uart_base + FMT);
    siop->v_regp[VOUT232][USR] = (*siop->readbyte)(siop->uart_base + OUT232);
    for (i = 0; i < V_REG_SIZE; i++)  /* copy USR column into VIR column */
        siop->v_regp[i][VIR] = siop->v_regp[i][USR];
}
```

An explanation of s_config—The first order of business is to save the current UART values in the USR column of the virtual array. The current contents of the 16X50's two Baud Rate Divisor registers are saved first. Next, the Interrupt Enable register is saved, followed by the Data Format register, and finally the RS-232 Output (Modem Control) register. Because we have not yet developed structures for interrupts and for RS-232 control, the constants 1 and 4 are employed as addressing offsets in place of structure variables.

When every element of the USR column in the array has been initialized with its 16X50 counterpart, a for loop copies these values into the VIR column. Thus, when the function returns, both columns contain identical, *current* copies of the 16X50's write registers.

The function to restore the state of the serial port, s_restore, is shown in Listing 14.22.

Listing 14.22. UART restoration for the 16X50.

FUNCTION NAME: s_restore
LEVEL: 1
PROTOTYPE IN: U16X50.H
LIBRARY: U16x50.LIB
DESCRIPTION: Restores the SIO pointed to by siop to its original state.
RETURNS: void
INCLUDE FILES: siodef.h, U16x50.H

```
void s_restore(register SIO *siop)
{
    _vsetbr(siop,siop->br,siop->v_regp[VBAUDLO][USR],
            siop->v_regp[VBAUDHI][USR]);
```

continues

Listing 14.22. continued

```
    _vsetbits(siop,siop->par,siop->v_regp[VFMT][USR]);
    (*siop->writebyte)(siop->uart_base + INT_EN, siop->v_regp[VINT_EN][USR]);
    (*siop->writebyte)(siop->uart_base + OUT232, siop->v_regp[VOUT232][USR]);
}
```

An explanation of *s_restore*—To restore the state of the UART, this function writes the original values stored in the USR column of the virtual register to the 16X50. The level-1 primitives, _vsetbr and _vsetbits are called to restore the Baud Rate and the Data Format registers.

String Arrays for Data Format, Baud Rate, and Errors

Listing 14.2 listed a complete set of manifest constants for data format and baud rate settings as well as constants for the errors returned by the various functions. Listing 14.23 shows the string arrays that corrrespond to each group of constants. Some of the error messages will not be needed until later chapters, but they should be installed in SIO.LIB now.

Listing 14.23. Strings to support data format, baud rate, and error messages.

ARRAY NAME: sbstr, parstr, dlstr, brstr
TYPE: Array of char *
FILE: SIO.LIB
DESCRIPTION: ASCII strings for baud rate and data formats.
COMMENTS: Use the now member of each structure to index into these arrays.

```
char *sbstr[]  = { "1", "1 1/2", "2" };
char *parstr[] = { "None", "Odd", "Even", "Mark", "Space" };
char *dlstr[]  = { "5", "6", "7", "8" };
char *brstr[]  = {"50",    "75",    "110",    "134.5", "150",   "300",   "600",
                  "1200",  "1800",  "2000",   "2400",  "3600",  "4800",  "7200",
                  "9600",  "14.4K", "19.2K",  "28.8K", "38.4K", "57.6K", "115.2K"};
```

ARRAY NAME: errstr
TYPE: Array of char *
FILE: SIO.LIB
DESCRIPTION: Messages for error codes returned by data format and baud rate functions.

```
char *errstr[] =
  {
  "",
```

```
    " ",
    "Function not supported",            /* 2    BAD_FCN  */
    "Argument out of range",             /* 3    OR_ARG   */
    "Argument not supported",            /* 4    BAD_ARG  */
    "Illegal device number",             /* 5    BAD_PORT */
    "Device not installed",              /* 6    NO_PORT  */
    "Device not available",              /* 7    NO_SIO   */
    "Device already open",               /* 8    OPEN_NOW */
    "No such device or device not open", /* 9    NO_CLOSE */
    "Transfer cancelled from keyboard",  /* 10   KEY_CAN */
    "File not found",                    /* 11   NO_FIL   */
    " "                                  /* NIL array terminator */
  };
```

The first four arrays are pointers to ASCII strings whose position in the array corresponds to the data format and baud rate codes they describe. For example, using the code for MARK parity (defined as 3 in SIODEF.H), the expression

```
printf("%s", parstr[MARK]);
```

prints the word "Mark."

The second array, errstr, is an array of pointers to error messages that describe the errors resulting from calls to any of the level-3 "set" functions.

TERM2

We are now ready for the new version of our terminal program. The important change from TERM1 is the support for data format and baud rate changes. Moreover, upon exit the interface is restored to its original condition on the IBM PC, and to a reasonable state on the Kaypro. TERM2 is shown in Listing 14.24.

Listing 14.24. TERM2: terminal program with support for baud rate and data format.

PROGRAM NAME: TERM2
    DESCRIPTION: Terminal program.
       COMMENTS: New Features: Setting data format and baud rate.
    INCLUDE FILES: stdio.h, ctype.h, siodef.h, ascii.h, buos.h, key.h, term.h,
                 u16x50.h

```
#define MENU    CTRL_A      /* key for command summary      */
#define FORMAT  'A'         /* Setup serial parmeters       */
#define EXIT    'Q'         /* key to exit from term        */

int vers = 2;              /* version number (global)       */
```

continues

Listing 14.24. continued

```c
extern int s_errno;
extern char *errstr[], *brstr[], *m_codes[];

int menu(siop)                      /* menu now gets SIO pointer        */
SIO *siop;
{
    int c;
    int retval = 0;
    static char *menus[] =
            {
            "\tA. Data Format, Baud rate",
            "\tQ. EXIT",
            ""                      /* NUL  string terminates list     */
            };
    char ** menup;
    c = !EXIT;
    while (c != EXIT)
            {
            puts("\n\n");
            for (menup = menus; **menup != NUL ; menup++)
                printf("%s\n", *menup);
            printf("\n\t\t  Enter selection  (CR to quit menu) :  ");
            if ( (c = getkbch()) == CR)
                break;              /* return to term                   */
            c = toupper(c);
            switch (c)
                {
                case EXIT:      /* back to DOS                      */
                    if (m_warndcd(siop, OFF) == 0)
                        {
                        m_hup(siop);
                        retval = 1;
                        }
                    else
                        {
                        printf("Continuing in terminal\n");
                        retval = 0;
                        }
                    break;
                case FORMAT:    /* Data format, Baud rate           */
                    set_params(siop);
                    break;
                default:
                    puts("Invalid choice\n\a");
                    break;
                }
            }
    putchar('\n');
    return retval;              /* will be zero except if EXIT      */
}
```

```
void term(SIO *siop)
{
    int c;                              /* must be int to detect -1 return  */
    printf("TERM, Version %d:  Press Control-%c for a summary of commands\n", \
        vers, MENU + '@');
    for (EVER)                          /*          eternal loop            */
        {
        if ( (c = s_inchar(siop)) !=NOT_READY)   /* check port for byte     */
            putchar(siop, c);
        if ( (c = inkey()) != NOT_READY)    /* if a key is pressed          */
            if (c == MENU)              /* and if it's the menu key         */
                {
                if (menu() !=NUL)       /* if menu returns non-zero         */
                    break;              /* return to main                   */
                }
            else
                s_putc(siop, c);
        }
}

main()
{
    extern SIO COM1sio;         /* found in computer-specific file  */
    SIO *siop = &COM1sio;       /* pointer to an SIO                */
    s_config(siop);
    setbaud(siop, BAUD19K2);
    term(siop);                 /*    TERM                          */
    puts("\nEnd of TERM\n");
    return 0;
}
```

Listing 14.25. SETPARMS.C: terminal program helper function.

FUNCTION NAME: set_params
LEVEL: 3
PROTOTYPE IN: TERM.H
LIBRARY: TERMFUNC.LIB
DESCRIPTION: Function to set baud rate, parity, datalength, and stop bits.
RETURNS: void
INCLUDE FILES: stdio.h, stdlib.h, siodef.h, misc.h, key.h

```
void set_params(SIO *siop)
{
    extern char *errstr[], *sbstr[], *parstr[], *dlstr[], *brstr[];
    RANK choice, errcode;
    int whichone = 0;
    short baudnow;
    char keybuff[4];
```

continues

Listing 14.25. continued

```
while (whichone != -1)              /* loop forever, reset pointer      */
    {
    puts("\nCURRENT SETTINGS:\n");
    if ( (baudnow = getbaud(siop)) < 0)
        baudnow = BAD_FCN;
    printf("1. Baud Rate [ %-6.6s ]\n", brstr[baudnow]);
    printf("2. Parity    [ %-6.6s ]\n", parstr[getformat(siop, PARITY)]);
    printf("3. Stop bits [ %-6.6s ]\n", sbstr[getformat(siop, STOPS)]);
    printf("4. Data Bits [ %-6.6s ]\n", dlstr[getformat(siop, DATALEN)]);
    printf("5. Exit this function.\n");
    printf("Enter your choice: ");
    choice = getkbch();
    switch (choice)
        {
        case '1': whichone = BAUD;  break;
        case '2': whichone = PARITY; break;
        case '3': whichone = STOPS; break;
        case '4': whichone = DATALEN; break;
        case '5': puts("\nExiting format select");
              return;
        default: puts("\n\a- invalid entry -");
              continue;
        }
    if (whichone != -1)             /* if a valid choice was made */
        do
            {
            printf("\nEnter code for new value and press RETURN: ");
            gets(keybuff);
            choice = atoi(keybuff);
            if (whichone == BAUD)
                errcode = setbaud(siop, choice);
            else
                errcode = setformat(siop, whichone, choice);
            if (errcode != 0)
                printf("ERROR:  %s\n\007",errstr[errcode]);
            } while (errcode !=  0);
    }
}
```

An explanation of TERM2 and *set_params*—Considering the amount and density of information contained in this chapter, none of the new features of this program should be perplexing. After calling s_config to save the state of the serial port (or set it, as the case may be), the level-3 data format and baud rate functions are called to install the start-up values contained in their respective structures. Then the function term is called to enter the terminal section of the program. The function term remains unchanged from the previous versions.

As before, when Ctrl-A is typed, the menu function is called. Note that this function now makes use of the SIO pointer argument passed from term. Once in the menu, pressing "A" invokes set_params in Listing 14.25, the routine to change the data format and baud rate settings. Upon entry to this function, the current data format settings are displayed by calling the setformat and getbaud functions; the return value from these functions becomes an index into their respective string arrays. (Recall that the now member is kept current by the level-2 routines.)

Next, getkbch fetches the user's menu selection from the keyboard and places it in the variable choice to which a switch is applied. (The submenus for the four functions are left to your imagination.) The idea of this loop is to return a constant based upon the user's selection. If the function did not return a –1, then the selection was valid—the user's selection from the imaginary menu. This selection, which should be a positive integer in the range 0 to 5, is then passed as an argument to the setformat function. If the argument returned was BAUD, then the setbaud function is called. The level-2 functions vsetbits and vsetbr return 0 if the argument is reasonable, or an error code. An error code returned from the call to setformat and setbaud becomes an index into the string of error messages, errstr.

One final stylistic point: the variable whichone is set to 0 each time set_params is called. This produces an endless loop:

```
while (whichone != -1)          /* loop forever until 0, reset pointer */
```

The only way to exit the loop is to enter a '5'. That executes a return in the switch statement to exit the function.

Baud Rate Integers to Constants

Now is a good time to compose a function we will need in Chapter 21, where we will require the ability to convert integer baud rates in the modem "CONNECT" messages to the baud rate constants given earlier in Listing 14.15. Listing 14.26 gives the level-3 function br_to_bcode.

Listing 14.26. *br_to_bcode*: a function to convert integer baud rates to baud rate codes.

FUNCTION NAME: br_to_bcode
    DESCRIPTION: Converts an integer number to a baud rate code for use by
                  the setbaud function.
          LEVEL: 3
    PROTOTYPE IN: SIODEF.H
        LIBRARY: SIO.LIB
        RETURNS: int: The baud code or -1 if the integer is not in the table.

continues

Listing 14.26. continued

> COMMENTS: `br_2bc_table` is a two-element look-up table containing integers
> on the left and baud rate codes on the right.
> INCLUDE FILES: siodef.h

```c
#define WIDTH 2

USHORT br_2bc_table[][WIDTH] =
{
    {300,   BAUD300 }, {600,   BAUD600 }, {1200,  BAUD1200},{2400,  BAUD2400 },
    {4800,  BAUD4800}, {7200,  BAUD7200}, {9600,  BAUD9600}, {14400, BAUD14K4},
    {19200, BAUD19K2}, {28800, BAUD28K8}, {38400L, BAUD28K8}, {57600L, BAUD57K6},
};

int br_to_bcode(USHORT baudrate)
{
    int i;
    int numrows = WIDTH * arraysize(br_2bc_able);
    for (i = 0; i < numrows; i++)
        {
        if (baudrate == br_2bc_table[i][0])
            return br_2bc_table[i][1];
        }
    return -1;
}
```

An explanation of *br_to_bcode*—This simple look-up function declares a two-dimensional array `br_2bc_table` hold the integer baud rates in column 0 and the corresponding baud rate constants in column 1. The function merely searches for the integer baud rate passed as an argument, and, if found, returns the corresponding baud rate code; if there is no matching code, -1 is returned. Note the use of the `arraysize` defined in SIOLOCAL.H.

Conclusion

Once comprehended, the functions, structures, and data in this chapter can have an enormously liberating effect upon program design. Their most striking characteristic is their portability when complemented with the necessary level-0 and -1 files. By systematically squeezing the hardware dependencies from the two highest layers of our code, we also reap an important side benefit—a suite of functions that employ a consistent, natural calling sequence and are therefore manifestly easy to understand.

In the next chapter we will complete our virtual UART by adding RS-232 functions and one or two miscellaneous functions.

RS-232 Control

Although RS-232 subjects have a history of confounding users, programmers also have difficulty with them. As we discussed in Chapter 5, persistent and widespread confusion exists about the RS-232 interface. Programmers quickly discover that in the course of even the most mundane chore they are likely to run into this electrical Maginot Line. There is scarcely a serial application that is not in some way expected to control an external device through the RS-232 interface.

In previous chapters, I have argued that the serial interface should always be restored upon exit, yet following this advice inevitably gives rise to irresolvable conflicts. Take, for example, the case where a modem and another serial device share a single serial port (not simultaneously, of course). Good programming practice dictates that when terminating, modem software should inhibit the DTR (Data Terminal Ready) input to prevent the automatic answering of incoming calls. If a printer (or other serial device) subsequently connected to this port requires DTR to be asserted, however, it does not function properly. These two applications have fundamentally different RS-232 requirements: if DTR is asserted, the modem answers the phone; if inhibited, the printer doesn't function.

There are no pat solutions to problems of this nature because they arise from applying the RS-232 interface where it was never intended—printer handshaking, for example. Even though intelligent modems provide a partial solution to this particular problem by disabling auto-answer with software commands, other conflicts sooner or later arise that are not so easily resolved. Therefore, to enter serial I/O applications without complete control over the RS-232 interface is to enter a duel unarmed. The purpose of this chapter is to provide the armament. Continuing with the virtual UART theme from Chapter 14, we will now compose the functions required to implement the following RS-232 features:

- RS-232 outputs: RTS (Request to Send), DTR (Data Terminal Ready), and two general-purpose outputs, GPO1 and GPO2
- RS-232 inputs: CTS (Clear to Send), DSR (Data Set Ready), DCD (Data Carrier Detect), RI (Ring Indicator), and two general-purpose inputs, GPI1 and GPI2

RS-232 Output Control

Because RS-232 output control is so similar to our previous experience with data format and baud rate, we will undertake it first. For the sake of notational convenience, abbreviations for the RS-232 functions are used for the remainder of this chapter.

RS-232 UART Outputs

The goal in this section is to develop generalized functions required to assert or inhibit RTS, DTR, and the two general-purpose outputs, GPO1 and GPO2. The general-purpose outputs are not associated with any official name or pin assignment in the RS-232 standard: their use is completely at the discretion of the hardware designer. Sometimes circuit designers use these outputs to implement some of the more obscure RS-232 outputs. Other times they are used for internal functions (on the IBM PC, GPO1 is the 16X50's master interrupt enable). However they are implemented, from the programmer's point of view they behave identically to dedicated outputs.

By the way, it is worth mentioning again that the UART names for the RS-232 outputs are invariably DTE names. When UARTs are configured as DCEs, however, DTE names are misleading and, to the inexperienced programmer anyway, perplexing. Often when UARTs are configured as DCEs, you can adjust by mentally exchanging the following name pairs:

DTE Name	becomes	DCE Name
TD		RD
RD		TD
CTS		RTS
RTS		CTS
DCD		DTR
DTR		DCD
DSR		RI
RI		DSR

You are cautioned against placing too much stock in this list because the relationship between UART outputs and their RS-232 names is inherently superficial: other than the names arbitrarily given to them, there is usually no *functional* difference between, say, the DTR and RTS outputs. Because the outputs are functionally interchangeable, their names should be regarded as descriptions, not design prescriptions. Don't be surprised, for example, to discover that the output that a UART data sheet refers to as CTS is connected to pin 11 on the interface and is intended solely for hardware handshaking.

RS-232 LOGIC

In our virtual UART, each RS-232 output is governed by a single bit in the UART write registers. If you examine UART data sheets, you may be confused to find that the UART outputs often have names like $\overline{DCD}$ (i.e., NOT DCD), suggesting negative logic. As illustrated in Listing 5.12, however, UARTs do not drive the RS-232 output pins directly, but are connected to RS-232 line driver ICs that convert the UART's output voltages and currents to those dictated by the RS-232 standard. Because most RS-232 line drivers invert their signals, UARTs must generate a negative voltage in order to cause a positive voltage at the RS-232 output pins. From the programmer's point of view, then, most UARTs employ conventional positive logic: a TRUE output control bit generates a positive voltage on the corresponding interface pin. There are, of course, a few UARTs with bona fide negative logic where a TRUE bit produces a negative voltage on the interface.

RS-232 OUTPUT AND THE VIRTUAL UART

It should come as no surprise that we will implement our RS-232 output functions within the framework of the virtual register scheme. Although this chapter presents no new programming techniques or constructions, everything here depends upon your understanding the virtual concept. So be forewarned: you will find this chapter tough going without a thorough understanding of Chapter 14.

Before we begin composing the RS-232 output functions, Listing 15.1 lists the constants required for RS-232 output control. These constants should reside in SIODEF.H, and U16X50.H as indicated.

Listing 15.1. Constants to support RS-232 output functions.

These belong in SIODEF.H

```
#define  OFF   0            /* RS-232 inhibited */
#define  ON    1            /* RS-232 asserted  */

/* Constants for RS232 GET/SET RS232 Functions */

enum rs232 { DTR = 0, RTS, GPO1, GPO2, BRK };
```

These belong in U16X50.H

```
/* Bit Masks for BREAK Bits */

#define  BRK_MASK       0xBF     /* AND mask 10111111 */
#define  BRKON_MASK     0x40     /* OR mask 01000000 */
#define  BRKOFF_MASK    0x00

/* Bit Masks for RS232 Outputs */
```

continues

Listing 15.1. continued

```
#define   DTRMASK        0xFE      /* 11111110 */
#define   RTSMASK        0xFD      /* 11111101 */
#define   GPO1MASK       0xFB      /* 11111011 */
#define   GPO2MASK       0xF7      /* 11110111 */
```

THE *rs232out_* STRUCTURE

Listing 15.2 shows the structure we will use to describe an RS-232 output.

Listing 15.2. A structure to describe an RS-232 output.

STRUCT NAME: vout232_
HEADER FILE: SIODEF.H
DESCRIPTION: Control structure for an RS-232 output.
INCLUDE FILES: siolocal.h

```
struct vout232_
   {
   MASK        resetmask;      /* AND mask apply to virtual register  */
   USHORT      vregnum;        /* Virtual register number (row)       */
   USHORT      offset;         /* Offset of physical uart register    */
   BOOL        now;            /* Code for current value (ON/OFF)     */
   BOOL        start;          /* Code for initialization (ON/OFF)    */
   };
```

This structure definition is very similar to the vregbits_ structure in Chapter 14. There is, however, one very big difference: there is no array of set masks. From Boolean arithmetic, we know that a bit is reset by ANDing it with 0 and set by ORing it with 1. Stated another way, any bit can be set by ORing with the 1's complement of the mask used to reset it. This greatly simplifies the writing of our level-2 function vset232, shown in Listing 15.3.

THE *vset232* FUNCTION

The requirements of a function to control RS-232 outputs are very simple: we need only to pass it an SIO pointer and the new state we wish the output to assume. Additionally, its return code should indicate whether the action was successful or, if not, why not. This function is given in Figure 15.3.

Listing 15.3. Level-2 function to control RS-232 outputs.

FUNCTION NAME: vset232
LEVEL: 2
PROTOTYPE IN: BUOS.H
LIBRARY: BUOS.LIB
DESCRIPTION: Turns selected RS-232 output ON or OFF.
RETURNS: int: OR_ARG if state argument is other than 0 or 1;
BAD_FCN if the requested function is not supported in
hardware; otherwise 0.
COMMENTS: The test for a NIL pointer must be the first test.
OFF and ON are defined in SIODEF.H
INCLUDE FILES: siodef.h, uart.h

```
int vset232(SIO *siop, struct vout232_ *p232, BOOL state)
{
    if (p232 == NIL)
        return BAD_FCN;
    if (state != OFF && state != ON)      /* range check                  */
        return OR_ARG;
    siop->v_regp[p232->vregnum][VIR] &= p232->resetmask; /* reset bit     */
    if (state == ON)
        siop->v_regp[p232->vregnum][VIR] |= ~p232->resetmask; /* set bit */
    p232->now = state;                    /* update current state variable */
    _vset232(siop, p232, siop->v_regp[p232->vregnum][VIR]);
    return 0;                             /* no error, return 0 for success */
}
```

This function first validates both arguments: OR_ARG is returned if the state argument is not OFF or ON; BAD_FCN is returned if the pointed-to vout232_ structure is NIL (i.e., not supported). If the arguments are valid, the resetmask is applied to the virtual register, vregnum. As always, the test for a NIL pointer precedes all other tests.

First, the contents of the virtual register are ANDed with resetmask to reset the appropriate bit and turn the output OFF:

```
siop->v_regp[p232->vregnum][VIR] &= p232->resetmask;
```

If the state argument is ON, the bit is made TRUE by ORing the virtual register with the 1s complement of resetmask:

```
siop->v_regp[p232->vregnum][VIR] |= ~p232->resetmask;
```

Finally, after updating the pointed-to vout232_ structure with the state argument, the level-1 function updates the physical UART and returns.

LEVEL-1 RS-232 OUTPUT FUNCTIONS FOR THE 16X50

Listing 15.4 shows versions of the level-1 function _vset232 for the 16X50.

Listing 15.4. Level-1 functions to control RS-232 output.

FUNCTION NAME:	_vset232
LEVEL:	1
PROTOTYPE IN:	U16X50.H
LIBRARY:	U16x50.LIB
DESCRIPTION:	Writes the virtual register containing the selected RS232 output pin to the corresponding UART register.
RETURNS:	void
COMMENTS:	This function is called only by vset232.
INCLUDE FILES:	siodef.h

```
void _vset232(register SIO *siop, struct vout232_ *p232, REG binval)
{
    (*siop->writebyte)(siop->uart_base + p232->offset, (FAST) binval);
}
```

The code for the _vset232 primitive is totally uneventful. It writes a byte to the physical register whose offset is given in the p232 structure in the argument list.

THE *BREAK* SIGNAL

As discussed in Chapter 6, the BREAK signal is the source of much confusion. It is sometimes called the BREAK "character," although it is actually just the opposite of a character. Sometimes it is discussed (usually in the novice/hobbyist press) as if it were somehow part of the RS-232 standard, which it is not. To review: a BREAK is a condition in which the line is held at SPACE for longer than one SDU.

Whatever a BREAK is, a vout232_ structure can certainly describe it well. If you find the use of a vout232_ structure to describe a BREAK to be intellectually disquieting, notice that a vout232_ structure is really a general mechanism for controlling one bit or an entire group of bits as one unit. In this respect, it is a complement to vregbits_, which is a general way to control individual bits. At any rate, the structure declarations and initializations necessary to implement the BREAK signal as a vout232_ structure are included here. Just remember that including the BREAK in our discussion of RS-232 outputs does not imply that it is an RS-232 condition.

RS-232 MEMBERS IN THE *SIO*

The SIO definition in SIODEF.H requires new members to accommodate the functions that refer to vout232_ functions and defined by our virtual UART. The relevant additions are shown in Listing 15.5.

Listing 15.5. New SIO members to support RS-232 output.

STRUCT DEF:	SIO
FILE:	SIODEF.H
DESCRIPTION:	Master structure defining a serial port.
COMMENTS:	Additions to support RS-232 outputs and BREAK.
INCLUDE FILES:	siolocal.h

```
struct sio
  {
  BYTE   *uart_base;                /*0  Base address of UART        */
  .
  .
  .
  struct vout232_ *rts;             /*19 Pointer to RTS struct       */
  struct vout232_ *dtr;             /*20 Pointer to DTR struct       */
  struct vout232_ *gpo1;            /*21 Pointer to GPOUTPUT1  struct */
  struct vout232_ *gpo2;            /*22 Pointer to GPOOUTPUT2 struct */
  struct vout232_ *brkbit;          /*23 Pointer to BREAK struct      */
  };
```

The five new members—rts, dtr, gpo1, gpo2, and brkbit—are all declared to be of type "pointer to struct vout232_." Remember, these names assume that the serial port is configured as a DTE.

DECLARATION OF *vout232_* STRUCTURES

Having written the level-1 and level-2 functions, we are now ready to declare and initialize instances of the vout232_ structures. Listing 15.6 contains the structures for IBMPC.C. Listing 15.1 provided the constants required for initialization.

Listing 15.6. Declaration and initialization for vout232_ structures.

OBJECT NAME:	pin4A
TYPE:	vout232_ structure
LEVEL:	0
MODULE:	IBMPC.C
DESCRIPTION:	Control structure for RS232 RTS output.

```
struct vout232_ pin4A =
  {
  RTSMASK,                    /* AND mask to reset RTS bit      */
  VOUT232,                    /* Virtual register               */
  OUT232,                     /* Offset of UART RTS register     */
  SUPPLIED,                   /* Code for current value (ON/OFF) */
```

continues

Listing 15.6. continued

```
        ON,                            /* Initialized value              */
    };
```

OBJECT NAME: pin20A
        TYPE: vout232_ structure
        LEVEL: 0
      MODULE: IBMPC.C
DESCRIPTION: Control structure for RS232 DTR output.

```
struct vout232_ pin20A =
    {
    DTRMASK,                       /* AND mask to reset DTR bit      */
    VOUT232,                       /* Virtual register               */
    OUT232,                        /* Offset of UART DTR register    */
    SUPPLIED,                      /* Code for current value (ON/OFF) */
    OFF,                           /* Initialized value              */
    };
```

OBJECT NAME: gp1outA
        TYPE: vout232_ structure
        LEVEL: 0
      MODULE: IBMPC.C
DESCRIPTION: Control structure for RS232 GPO1 output.

```
struct vout232_ gp1outA =
    {
    GPO1MASK,                      /* AND mask to reset GPOUT1 bit   */
    VOUT232,                       /* Virtual register               */
    OUT232,                        /* Offset of GPO1 register in UART */
    SUPPLIED,                      /* Code for current value (ON/OFF) */
    OFF,                           /* Initialized value              */
    };
```

OBJECT NAME: gp2outA
        TYPE: vout232_ structure
        LEVEL: 0
      MODULE: IBMPC.C
DESCRIPTION: Control structure for RS232 GPO2 output.

```
struct vout232_ gp2outA =
    {
    GPO2MASK,                      /* AND mask to reset GPO2 bit     */
    VOUT232,                       /* Virtual register               */
    OUT232,                        /* Offset of GPO2 register in UART */
    SUPPLIED,                      /* Code for current value (ON/OFF) */
    OFF,                           /* Initialized value              */
    };
```

OBJECT NAME: breakbA
TYPE: vout232_ structure
LEVEL: 0
MODULE: IBMPC.C
DESCRIPTION: Control structure for BREAK output.

```
struct vout232_ breakbA =
    {
    BRK_MASK,                   /* AND mask to reset BREAK bit    */
    VFMT,                       /* Virtual register              */
    FMT,                        /* Offset of BREAK reg.   in UART */
    SUPPLIED,                   /* Code for current value (ON/OFF) */
    OFF,                        /* Initialized value             */
    };
```

These declarations are so straightforward they hardly merit discussion. The names of the RS-232 output structures are named after the pins defined by the RS-232 standard. Again, these pin numbers assume a DTE device. Not all UARTS support general-purpose inputs: the 16X50 supports them, but the Z80SIO, for example, does not. Finally, notice that all structures are initialized to an OFF condition except for pin4A, the RTS output. This enables flow control on devices that support it on RTS/CTS.

SIO DECLARATION

Listing 15.7 shows the relevant fragments of the SIO declaration for IBMPC.C.

Listing 15.7. Declaration and initialization of the current SIO.

SIO NAME: COM1sio
FILE: IBMPC.C
COMMENTS: Line numbers in comments are for reference only.

```
SIO COM1sio  =
    {
    COM1,                   /*0  base address of UART             */
    .
    .
    .
    &pin4A,                 /*19 RS-232 RTS output                */
    &pin20A,                /*20 RS-232 DTR output                */
    &gp1outA,               /*21 RS-232 first user-defined output */
    &gp2outA,               /*22 RS-232 first user-defined output */
    &breakbA,               /*23 BREAK bit                        */
    };
```

The addresses of the structures are used to initialize the new members of the SIO. If a UART does not support one of the general-purpose outputs its SIO must initialize these members to NIL. This value, of course, is required as a place holder in the initialization list, but it also serves another important purpose. Every level-2 function we have written so far has contained a line such as

```
if (pointer == NIL)
    return (BAD_FCN);
```

Because of this test, attempts to change the state of an unsupported bit return an error code.

LEVEL-3 FUNCTIONS FOR RS-232 OUTPUT

We have written the level-1 and level-2 functions and declared instances of vout232_ structures for the 16X50. We have added the new functions to the SIO definition and added initializers to the COM1sio declarations. We are now ready to compose the level-3 functions shown in Listing 15.8.

Listing 15.8. Level-3 RS-232 output function.

FUNCTION NAME:	set232
LEVEL:	3
PROTOTYPE IN:	SIODEF.H
LIBRARY:	SIO.LIB
DESCRIPTION:	Set RS-232 output pins.
RETURNS:	short: 0 if successful. OR_ARG if either argument is out of range; BAD_FCN if the function is not supported.
INCLUDE FILES:	siodef.h, buos.h, level0.h

```
short set232(SIO* siop, RANK whichone, BOOL state)
{
    short retval = 0;
    struct vout232_ *p232 = NIL;
    switch (whichone)
        {
        case  DTR:  p232 = siop->dtr;    break;
        case  RTS:  p232 = siop->rts;    break;
        case  GPO1: p232 = siop->gpo1;   break;
        case  GPO2: p232 = siop->gpo2;   break;
        case  BRK:  p232 = siop->brkbit; break;
        default: retval  = OR_ARG;
        }
    if ( (p232 != NIL) && (retval == 0))
        if (whichone != BRK)
            retval = vset232(siop, p232, state);
        else
```

```
        {                    /** BREAK is an exception **/
        vset232(siop, p232, ON);
        __delay(_0_SEC_3);
        retval = vset232(siop, p232, OFF);
        }
    return retval;
}
```

This function strongly resembles the functions for setting the data format and the baud rate. The case statement assigns the p232 pointer to the one of the vout232_ in the SIO. The level-2 function vset232 is then called passing that structure pointer and the desired state (i.e., on or off) for the RS-232 output. The function returns the error codes passed back from level-2 function. The BREAK is handled as an exception: the function turns the UART's BREAK bit on, pauses for about 300 milliseconds, then turns it off again. As I have mentioned several times, there is no such thing as a standard break signal; technically, UARTs interpret any SPACE condition that lasts longer than the current SDU as a BREAK. If the longest possible SDU is 12 (8E2 plus one start bit), and the baud rate is 50, any SPACE longer than 12 to 50 or roughly 250 milliseconds should be detected as a BREAK. This BREAK duration will probably suffice in most situations, but, in the absence of standardization, you must be able to adjust its duration. I leave it to you as an exercise to write the code for a BREAK function whose duration is programmable.

RS-232 OUTPUT STATUS FUNCTIONS

In addition to the function in Listing 15.8, which changes the state of an RS-232 output, it is sometimes useful—if not essential—to know the current state of an output. The simple level-3 function shown in Listing 15.9 performs that function.

Listing 15.9. Level-3 functions to return the current state of RS-232 outputs.

FUNCTION NAME:	get232
LEVEL:	3
PROTOTYPE IN:	SIODEF.H
LIBRARY:	SIO.LIB
DESCRIPTION:	Fetch current state of RS-232 outputs.
RETURNS:	int: 0 if successful. OR_ARG if argument is out of range; BAD_FCN if the function is not supported (RS-232 pointer is NIL).
INCLUDE FILES:	siodef.h

```
RANK get232(SIO *siop, RANK whichone)
{
    RANK retval = BAD_FCN;
```

continues

Listing 15.9. continued

```
    switch (whichone)
        {
        case  DTR:
            if (siop->dtr != NIL)
                    retval = (siop->dtr->now);
            break;
        case  RTS:
            if (siop->rts != NIL)
                    retval = (siop->rts->now);
            break;
        case  GPO1:
            if (siop->gpo1 != NIL)
                    retval = (siop->gpo1->now);
            break;
        case  GPO2:
            if (siop->gpo2 != NIL)
                    retval = (siop->gpo2->now);
            break;
        default:
            retval = OR_ARG;
        }
    return retval;
}
```

This function returns an error code if the requested RS-232 output function call is not supported or if the whichone argument is invalid; otherwise, it returns the now member of the relevant vout232_ structure.

TERM3

The new functions enable us to control RS-232 outputs in TERM. The capability of controlling the DTR output, which is almost universally supported by modems, is particularly important in terminal programs. DTR, you will recall, is the modem's "master enable," without which the modem ignores all data and, in the case of modems, commands.

With the wide popularity of smart modems, programmers are increasingly inclined to perform every modem function with software commands. This is unfortunate, and in most cases, degrades the performance of the software. A smart modem, for example, can be configured to assume that DTR is asserted at all times (see Chapter 8). This capability of overriding DTR makes it possible to use a simple three-wire cable instead of an eccentric RS-232 cable. DTR override is admittedly a convenience, but ultimately it is just that: a convenience. The truth is that intelligent modem control via DTR is immeasurably simpler than control via software commands.

Listing 15.10 gives the incidental changes and additions to TERM3.

Listing 15.10. TERM3: incidental changes from TERM2.

PROGRAM NAME: TERM3
DESCRIPTION: Terminal Program
COMMENTS: Features
Baud rate and data format set
Serial interface restored upon exit
RS-232 output control
Transmitted BREAK signal

```
#define FORMAT    'A'    /* Setup serial parameters       */
#define RS_232    'B'    /* RS-232 output control         */
#define BRAKE     'C'    /* send BREAK signal             */
#define EXIT      'Q'    /* key to exit from term         */

int vers = 3;            /* version number (global)       */

        .
        .
        .
        {
        "\tA.  Data Format, Baud rate",
        "\tB.  RS-232 control",
        "\tC.  Transmit BREAK signal",
        "\tQ.  EXIT",
        ""              /* NUL string terminates list     */
        };
        .
        .
        .
        case RS_232:  /* RS-232 output control            */
              setup232(siop);
              break;
        case BRAKE:   /* send BREAK                       */
              set232(siop, BRK, ON);
              break;
        .
        .
        .
```

The changes to the terminal functions are slight: two new case statements have been added to the keyboard switch in menu in order to support BREAK transmission and RS-232 output control. The BREAK case calls the level-3 function set232, while the RS_232 case calls the local function setup232, shown in Listing 15.11. The menu array has also been adjusted to reflect these changes. (The silly spelling "BRAKE" is used to avoid conflict with C-language keywords.)

Listing 15.11. Level-3 functions to control RS-232 and to transmit a BREAK.

FUNCTION NAME:	setup232
LEVEL:	3
PROTOTYPE IN:	TERM.H
DESCRIPTION:	Function to transmit BREAK and control RS-232 outputs: RTS, DTR, and two general-purpose outputs.
RETURNS:	void
COMMENTS:	The two general-purpose outputs are not necessarily mapped to RS-232 pins.
INCLUDE FILES:	stdio.h, siodef.h, misc.h, key.h

```c
void setup232(SIO *siop)
{
    extern char *errstr[];
    static char *statstr[] = {"OFF", "ON", "--"};
    short whichone, errcode, rtsstat, dtrstat, gpo1stat, gpo2stat, *statp;
    short choice = 0;
    rtsstat  = get232(siop, RTS);  dtrstat  =  get232(siop, DTR);
    gpo1stat = get232(siop, GPO1); gpo2stat =  get232(siop, GPO2);

    while (choice != -1)               /* loop forever, reinitialize pointer */
        {
        printf("\n1. Toggle RTS  [ %3s ]\n", statstr[rtsstat]  );
        printf(  "2. Toggle DTR  [ %3s ]\n", statstr[dtrstat]  );
        printf(  "3. Toggle GPO1 [ %3s ]\n", statstr[gpo1stat] );
        printf(  "4. Toggle GPO2 [ %3s ]\n", statstr[gpo2stat] );
        puts(    "5. Exit this function\n");
        printf("Enter your choice : ");
        choice = getkbch();
        switch (choice)                /* assign function & status pointer   */
            {
            case '1': whichone  = RTS; statp = &rtsstat;  break;
            case '2': whichone  = DTR; statp = &dtrstat;  break;
            case '3': whichone  = GPO1;statp = &gpo1stat; break;
            case '4': whichone  = GPO2;statp = &gpo2stat; break;
            case '5': puts("Exiting RS232 setup");
                return;
            default:puts("\a- invalid entry -");
                continue;
            }
        if (choice != -1)               /* if a valid choice was made         */
            {
            if (*statp != BAD_FCN)   /* if this function is supported      */
                *statp = !(*statp); /* toggle its status                  */
            if ( (errcode = set232(siop, whichone, *statp)) != 0)
                printf("ERROR: %s\n\a",errstr[errcode]);
            }
        }
}
```

The design of this function is similar to the data format function (setup) inherited from TERM2: a while loop polls the keyboard for a menu choice. The loop is broken only when the user chooses "Exit" from the menu.

Before entering the while loop, the status variables (dtrstatet.al) are initialized by calling the level-3 get232 function. The code assumes that they contain a value in the range 0 to 2: 0 or 1 represents the state of the respective pins; a value of BAD_FCN marks a function as being unsupported (initialized to NIL). The selection menu uses these integer status variables to index into statstr, an array of pointers describing the three possible states: OFF, ON, or "−−".

A switch is applied to the selection entered from the keyboard. Each valid case assigns a value: a constant to the variable whichone and the status pointer statp. When a valid selection is entered (i.e., if choice != -1), the pointed-to status variable is toggled between 0 and 1 with the logical NOT operator. The set232 function uses the status variable as an argument. The while loop repeats and the new setting is reflected in the menu display.

Errors are announced by using any non-0 return code from the set232 function as an index into the errstr string array given previously in Listing 14.23.

RS-232 Input Control

If control over the RS-232 outputs enables you to signal the outside world, the ability to read the RS-232 inputs enables the outside world to signal you. In many applications, including the modem library in Chapter 21, the ability to read the status of RS-232 inputs is your only contact with the hardware you are controlling. The need to monitor the status of the RS-232 inputs is not limited to modem control but is generally required for hardware flow control in which the receiving device (such as a protocol modem) can ingest data much faster than it can digest data. Despite all the efforts by manufacturers to promote software-controlled flow control, RS-232 control is still the most popular method. To complete our mastery over the RS-232 interface, then, we will compose a set of functions in support of the four RS-232 inputs in the virtual UART function described in Chapter 14:

CTS (Clear to Send) As described in Chapter 5, CTS is usually employed for hardware flow control in protocol modems.

DSR (Data Set Ready) As defined by the RS-232 standard, DSR goes high when the modem's carrier has been turned on (answer mode) or when the line is off hook waiting for a carrier (originate mode). DSR is often used less formally as an "I'm awake and ready" signal to the DTE. In these situations, it is essentially a power-on indicator.

DCD (Data Carrier Detect) When a modem achieves a data link with another modem, it asserts DCD.

RI (Ring Indicator) The modem asserts RI during phone line ringer pulses.

In addition to the preceding four RS-232 inputs, our virtual UART supports two general-purpose inputs, GPI1 and GPI2. These inputs, if present, may or may not be connected to the RS-232 interface. Listing 15.12 shows the manifest constants required to support the RS-232 input functions that follow.

THE *vin232_* STRUCTURE

By now you should be accustomed to the basic plan for new virtual features: define a structure to describe the physical attributes of that feature, write three levels of functions to relate the virtual to the physical UART, then install pointers to instances of these structures in the SIO. Listing 15.12 shows the structure definition required for RS-232 inputs.

Listing 15.12. vin232_: a structure to describe an RS-232 input.

STRUCT NAME: vin232_
  HEADER FILE: SIODEF.H
  DESCRIPTION: Control structure for an RS-232 input.

```
struct vin232_
    {
    USHORT    offset;                 /* Offset of physical register in UART */
    MASK      mask;                   /* Mask to isolate active bit          */
    BOOL      now;                    /* Current value of this input         */
    };
```

This three-member structure follows our familiar pattern of a physical description of the object, in this case an RS-232 input. Notice that the now member is defined as a BOOL. There is no member for the virtual register because RS-232 reflects transient external events, not the configuration properties of the UART itself.

CONSTANTS FOR RS-232 INPUT

Listing 15.13 gives the constants required for the remainder of this chapter. Add them to the SIODEF.H and U16X50.H include files.

Listing 15.13. RS-232 input constants for SIODEF.H and U16X50.H.

These belong in SIODEF.H

```
/* Constants for RS232 GET/SET RS232 Functions */
enum rs232 { DTR = 0, RTS, GPO1, GPO2, BRK };
```

These belong in U16X50.H

```
/* Bit Masks for RS232 Inputs */

#define  CTSMASK      0x10 /* 00010000*/
#define  DSRMASK      0x20 /* 00100000*/
#define  RIMASK       0x40 /* 01000000*/
#define  DCDMASK      0x80 /* 10000000*/
```

DECLARATIONS OF THE *vin232_* STRUCTURES

Listing 15.14 shows the declarations and initializations of the four new vin232_ structures. As always, the declarations are part of the level-0 file, in this case IBMPC.C.

Listing 15.14. The vin232_ structures for RS-232 input.

```
OBJECT NAME:    pin6A
        TYPE:   vin232_ structure
       LEVEL:   0
      MODULE:   IBMPC.C
 DESCRIPTION:   Control structure for RS232 DSR input.

struct vin232_ pin6A =
    {
    STAT_232,  /* Offset of DSR register in UART    */
    DSRMASK,   /* AND mask for isolating DSR bits   */
    SUPPLIED,  /* Current value of this input       */
    };

OBJECT NAME:    pin5A
        TYPE:   vin232_ structure
       LEVEL:   0
      MODULE:   IBMPC.C
 DESCRIPTION:   Control structure for RS232 CTS input.

struct vin232_ pin5A =
    {
    STAT_232,  /* Offset of CTS register in UART    */
    CTSMASK,   /* AND mask for isolating CTS bits   */
    SUPPLIED,  /* Current value of this input       */
    };

OBJECT NAME:    pin8A
        TYPE:   vin232_ structure
       LEVEL:   0
```

continues

Listing 15.14. continued

```
MODULE:      IBMPC.C
DESCRIPTION: Control structure for RS232 DCD input.

struct vin232_ pin8A =
    {
    STAT_232,  /* Offset of DCD register in UART    */
    DCDMASK,   /* AND mask for isolating DCD bits    */
    SUPPLIED,  /* Current value of this input        */
    };

OBJECT NAME: pin22A
       TYPE: vin232_ structure
      LEVEL: 0
     MODULE: IBMPC.C
DESCRIPTION: Control structure for RS232 RI input.

struct vin232_ pin22A =
    {
    STAT_232,  /* Offset of RI register in UART      */
    RIMASK,    /* AND mask for isolating RI bits     */
    SUPPLIED,  /* Current value of this input        */
    };
```

While 16X50 UART supports the RS-232 input functions described by our virtual UART, it does not provide general-purpose inputs. As with the RS-232 outputs, the names given these structures—"pin5," for example—are their DTE names.

THE LEVEL-2 RS-232 INPUT FUNCTION (*vstat232*)

Everything is now in place to compose the level-2 function required to handle the logical portion of RS-232 input. Listing 15.15 shows this function.

Listing 15.15. Level-2 function to fetch RS-232 status.

```
FUNCTION NAME: vstat232
        LEVEL: 2
  PROTOTYPE IN: BUOS.H
      LIBRARY: BUOS.LIB
  DESCRIPTION: Return status of RS-232 input described in p232.
      RETURNS: int: TRUE if the input is asserted, FALSE if inhibited;
               BAD_FCN if the RS-232 input requested is not supported.
     COMMENTS: The call to the level-1 function is through a function
               pointer in the vin232_ structure.
 INCLUDE FILES: siodef.h
```

```
short vstat232(SIO *siop, struct vin232_ *p232)
{
    if (p232 == NIL)
        return BAD_FCN;                          /* this input not supported    */
    if (siop->read232 != NIL)
        p232->now = (BYTE) (*siop->read232)(siop, p232) & p232->mask;
    return (p232->now  ? TRUE : FALSE);     /* return status              */

}
```

As with vsetbits and vset232 before it, this function returns an error code of BAD_FCN if the vin232_ structure in the SIO contains NIL, indicating that this particular input is not supported by the UART. The level-1 function fetches the UART register given in p232; the desired bit is masked off with an AND and stored in the now member of the structure.

NEW *SIO* MEMBERS

The level-2 function's call to the level-1 function,

```
(*siop->read232)(siop, p232)
```

is performed through a function pointer in the SIO itself. The reasons for this indirection will become apparent in Chapter 19. Now, let's look at the new SIO members, shown in Listing 15.16.

Listing 15.16. Additions to the SIO definition.

STRUCT DEF:	SIO
FILE:	SIODEF.H
DESCRIPTION:	Master structure defining a serial port.
COMMENT:	Addition of members to support RS-232 input.

```
struct sio
  {
  BYTE   * uart_base;                    /*0  Base address of UART       */
  .
  .
  .
  struct vin232_    *cts;                /*24 pointer to  CTS struct      */
  struct vin232_    *dsr;                /*25  "       to  DSR struct      */
  struct vin232_    *dcd;                /*26  "       to  DCD struct      */
  struct vin232_    *ri;                 /*27  "       to  RI struct       */
  struct vin232_    *gpi1;               /*28  "       to  GPINPUT1  struct */
  struct vin232_    *gpi2;               /*29  "       to  GPINPUT2  struct */
  FAST (*read232)(SIO *, struct vin232_*); /*30  "  to level-1 function    */
  union inbits_232 status;               /*31 RS-232 status byte          */
  union inbits_232 delta;                /*32 RS-232 deltas byte           */
  };
```

There are six routine pointers to structures, one for each input supported. The more interesting new members are the function pointer read232 and the two unions status and delta. Ordinarily, the level-2 function calls the level-1 directly. For reasons that will soon become apparent, the level-2 RS-232 input function does makes this call through a function pointer in the SIO, read232.

The two unions status and delta, given in Listing 15.17, make possible some additional functionality in the level-1 function.

Listing 15.17. The in_bits232 union in the SIO.

STRUCT NAME: inbits_232
DESCRIPTION: The map structure in the union below is a bitmap of the input
                status register that is read and stored as a REG byte.

```
union inbits_232
    {
    REG reg232;
    struct
        {
        unsigned int cts : 1;   /* <—  This is the lsb but may be msb in */
        unsigned int dsr : 1;   /*     other compilers.                  */
        unsigned int ri  : 1;
        unsigned int dcd : 1;
        unsigned int gpo1: 1;
        unsigned int gpo2: 1;
        unsigned int unused  : 10;
        }bitmap;
    };
```

The variable inbits_232 is a union between a REG and bit-field structure. If you recall, a union is an aliasing mechanism that allows a single data element to be referenced in any number of ways. In the union above, for example, when we wish to manipulate the data in the union as a REG, we simply refer to it by the name reg232. On the other hand, when we wish to refer to it as a bit-field structure, we refer to it as bitmap. Because the same data is being manipulated, a bit changed when treating it as a bit-field is reflected the next time it is treated as a REG and vice versa. The bit-field structure contains a bit for each RS-232 input as well as the general-purpose inputs.

LEVEL-1 FUNCTIONS FOR RS-232 INPUT STATUS

The unions in the SIO come into play in level-1 function. Listing 15.18 shows this function.

Listing 15.18. Level-1 functions to fetch RS-232 input status.

FUNCTION NAME:	_vstat232
LEVEL:	1
PROTOTYPE IN:	U16X50.H
LIBRARY:	U16x50.LIB
DESCRIPTION:	Reads the UART register containing the status bit for the appropriate RS-232 input; stores register in SIO. A pointer to this function resides in the SIO.
RETURNS:	FAST
INCLUDE FILES:	siodef.h
COMMENTS:	This routine is responsible for formatting the bits in the SIO's delta and status members to the following canonical defintions:

BIT	STATUS	DELTA
0	cts	cts
1	dsr	dsr
2	ri	ri
3	dcd	dcd
4	gpi1	gpi1
5	gpi2	gpi2
6-7	unused	unused

```
FAST _vstat232(register SIO *siop, struct vin232_ *p232)
{
    static FAST stat_reg;
    stat_reg = (*siop->readbyte)(siop->uart_base + p232->offset);
    siop->delta.reg232 = stat_reg &0x0F;  /* mask off status, store deltas */
    siop->status.reg232 = (stat_reg &0xF0) >> 4;   /* store status bits    */
    return stat_reg;
}
```

The 16X50 version of this function is the model of simplicity: it passes the SIO and a pointer to a vin232_ structure, stores the UART register values, and merely returns the UART register at the offset given in the structure. Before returning, it formats the RS-232 bits into canonical form—one group for input status and another for "deltas"— then stores them in the status and delta unions in the SIO.

What exactly is *canonical format?* It means that we define the order in which these bits are arranged before storing them in the REG side of the union. Functions at all levels then rely upon that bit order. The canonical order shown in the function header reflects the natural bit order of the 16X50 UART where the input status information is stored in the four most-significant bits and the deltas (that is, bit that have changed since last read) are stored in the four most significant bits. It is the responsibility of level-1 functions written for other UARTs to rearrange the bits in canonical order.

LEVEL-3 RS-232 INPUT FUNCTIONS

We have now defined, declared, and initialized the vin232_ structures to support the RS-232 input function in our virtual UART. Let's get the level-3 function, shown in Listing 15.19, out of the way.

Listing 15.19. Level-3 functions to return status of RS-232 functions.

FUNCTION NAME:	stat232
LEVEL:	3
PROTOTYPE IN:	SIODEF.H
LIBRARY:	SIO.LIB
DESCRIPTION:	Returns current state of an RS-232 input.
RETURNS:	short: the state of the input (ON or OFF);
	BAD_FCN or OR_ARG if the function is not supported or if the rank argument is out of range.
INCLUDE FILES:	siodef.h

```
short stat232(SIO *siop, RANK whichone)
{
    short retval;
    switch (whichone)
        {
        case  CTS: retval = vstat232(siop, siop->cts);  break;
        case  DCD: retval = vstat232(siop, siop->dcd);  break;
        case  DSR: retval = vstat232(siop, siop->dsr);  break;
        case   RI: retval = vstat232(siop, siop->ri);   break;
        case GPI1: retval = vstat232(siop, siop->gpi1); break;
        case GPI2: retval = vstat232(siop, siop->gpi2); break;
        default: retval = OR_ARG;
        }
    return retval;
}
```

This function proceeds in a predictable manner, returning the value of the now of the requested vin232_ structure. For the sake of consistency with the other functions, it also returns a value of BAD_FCN if the function requested is not supported.

This level-3 function is useful if you want to keep an eye on a particular RS-232 input such as waiting for a modem to assert DCD after dialing. If, however, you're interested in activity on all the inputs—such as when you're using RS-232 signals for instrumentation control, for example—you would have to call stat232 up to six times, once for each input. The following level-3 function would solve this problem:

.

```
REG delta232 (SIO *siop)
{
   (void) vstat232(siop, siop->cts);
   return(REG) siop->delta.reg232;
}
```

The bit-field side of the delta union (that is, delta.bitmap) makes it simple for a level-3 function to test for a changed condition on a specific bit.

SIO DECLARATION AND INITIALIZATION

Listing 15.20 shows the declaration and initialization of the new members in SIO for IBMPC.C. So that calls to unsupported functions will return the correct error code, all unsupported members are initialized to NIL.

Listing 15.20. Declaration and initialization of the expanded SIO.

SIO NAME:	COM1sio
FILE:	IBMPC.C
DESCRIPTION:	Unions for storing RS232 input state and delta information.
COMMENTS:	Two of the new members must be initialized to NILs because the 16x50 UART lacks support for them. Line numbers in comments are for reference only.

```
SIO COM1sio  =
   {
   COM1,                /*0  base address of UART                 */
   .
   .

   .
   &breakbA,            /*23 break bit                            */
   &pin5A,              /*24 RS-232 CTS input                     */
   &pin6A,              /*25 RS-232 DSR input                     */
   &pin8A,              /*26 RS-232 DCD input                     */
   &pin22A,             /*27 RS-232 RI  input                     */
   NIL,                 /*28 NO 1st user-defined RS-232 input     */
   NIL,                 /*29 NO 2nd user-defined RS-232 input     */
   _vstat232,           /*30 pointer to level one fetch function  */
   0,                   /*31 RS-232 status bits                   */
   0,                   /*32 RS-232 delta bits                    */
   };
```

Changes to TERM

Adding the capability to monitor the RS-232 inputs requires only minor changes to SETUP232.C. Listing 15.21 shows these modifications.

Listing 15.21. Modifications to the setup232 function to display status of the RS-232 inputs.

```
void setup232(SIO *siop)
{
    extern char *errstr[];
    static char *statstr[] = {"OFF", "ON", "--"};
    short whichone, errcode, rtsstat, dtrstat, gpo1stat, gpo2stat, *statp;
    short choice = 0;
    rtsstat  = get232(siop, RTS);  dtrstat  =  get232(siop, DTR);
    gpo1stat = get232(siop, GPO1); gpo2stat =  get232(siop, GPO2);

    while (choice != -1)                    /* loop forever, reinitialize pointer */
        {
        puts("\nCURRENT RS-232 INPUT STATUS:");
        puts("\tCTS  DSR  DCD  RI   GP1  GP2");
        printf("\t%3s  %3s  %3s  %3s  %3s  %s\n\n",
          statstr[stat232(siop, CTS  )],
          statstr[stat232(siop, DSR  )],
          statstr[stat232(siop, DCD  )],
          statstr[stat232(siop, RI   )],
          statstr[stat232(siop, GPI1 )],
          statstr[stat232(siop, GPI2 )]);
        printf("\n1. Toggle RTS  [ %3s ]\n", statstr[rtsstat]  );
        printf( "2. Toggle DTR  [ %3s ]\n", statstr[dtrstat]  );
        printf( "3. Toggle GPO1 [ %3s ]\n", statstr[gpo1stat] );
        .
        .
        .
}
```

The RS-232 inputs are displayed by calling the stat232 function and using its return value as an index into the array of pointers to strings, statstr. The status function returns a value from 0 to 2 and one of the strings is always displayed.

Conclusion

The functions required for programming support of RS-232 input/output are now complete. The most powerful use of these functions is in the degree of control they impart to your programs. There will be copious examples of this control in later chapters, where we rely heavily on RS-232 functions.

Flow Control and *SIO* Management

In the first part of this chapter, we will add functions to support *virtual flow control* in the SIO. Both XON/XOFF and RTS/CTS flow control are supported. Next, we build "open" and "close" routines to simplify managing the SIO. Finally, we complete our implementation of the virtual UART begun in Chapter 7 by adding support for five virtual functions to the SIO:

- Enable/disable the UART's transmitter
- Enable/disable the UART's receiver
- Enable/disable transmitter handshaking on RTS
- Enable/disable receiver handshaking on DCD
- Change the clocking factor

Although some common UARTs (including the 16X50) do not support these features, they are conceptually important in our UART management.

We end the chapter by applying this new functionality to the now-familiar program, TERM.

Flow Control

In Chapter 4 we discussed flow control: the capability of a device to regulate the flow of data between it and another device. For example, a printer must regulate the amount of data it receives from a computer so that it is not overwhelmed with data at a faster rate than it can print. We noted that there are two general procedures (protocols, if you will) for flow control: software and hardware. In software flow control, the device exchanges flow-control messages, usually in the form of single characters, within the data stream. Because the flow-control characters are embedded in the data, this is also referred to as *in-band* flow control. In hardware flow control, the flow messages are electronic signals exchanged via a physical connection such as an RS-232.

Virtual Flow Control

Because (from the viewpoint of an application) all flow control has the same goal, it should be a virtual process: it ought to be abstracted from hardware and system considerations. Let's look at a couple of simple examples. First, consider the needs of an application that is transmitting data. It needs to know only one fact: when to stop sending data. It doesn't need to know whether hardware or software is in effect or the internal workings of the procedure is in effect. Similarly, consider the application receiving data. It has only two requirements: the capability to turn the flow of data on and off. Again, the internal gory details of the protocol are of no interest to the application.

In both these cases, the actual flow control mechanisms are unimportant to the application—for all it knows (or cares), the flow of data is controlled by smoke signals and fairies. The application therefore needs only three functions for flow control:

- **Get Flow Request.** This function tells the transmitting application when to start or stop outputting data.
- **Turn Flow Off.** The receiver calls this function when it wants to stop the flow of input data.
- **Turn Flow On.** The receiver calls this function when it wants to start the flow of input data.

FLOW CONTROL IN THE *SIO*

You should not be surprised to learn that we will virtualize flow control through the SIO. Specifically, we will install function pointers in the SIO for each of the three functions listed above. When a level-3 or higher function requires one of these services, it merely performs the call indirectly through the SIO. Listing 16.1 shows the new constants required to support virtual flow control and the structure members required in the SIO. Notice that most of the manifest constants reside in a new include file named SIOCTL.H. Of course, the new SIO members reside in SIODEF.H.

Listing 16.1. New constants and structure members to support virtual flow control.

The following belong in SIOCTL.H

```
/* MACROS FOR CALLING FLOW CONTROL POINTERS IN SIO*/

#define flowon(p)        (*(p)->flowon)((p))
```

```
#define flowoff(p)      (*(p)->flowoff)((p))
#define getflow_req(p) (*(p)->getflow_req)((p))


/* TYPES OF FLOW CONTROL */

enum flowtypes{ NO_FLOW = 0, XON_XOFF, RTS_CTS };

/* FLOW CHARACTERS */
#define XON          0x11          /* DC1 */
#define XOFF         0x13          /* DC3 */


/* VALUES RETURNED BY GET-FLOW-REQUEST FUNCTION */

#define FLOW_OFF     0       /* this must be 0      */
#define FLOW_NONE    1
#define FLOW_ON      0xFFFF /* this must be 0xFFFF */
```

The following belongs in IBMPC.H

```
#define MAX_PORTS 4        /* number of serial ports supported */
```

The following belong in SIODEF.H

```
#define CLOSED FALSE         /* constants for s_open & s_close */
#define OPEN    TRUE


/* BAUD CLOCK CONSTANTS */

enum clk { X1 = 0, X16, X32, X64 };


/* TRANSMIT/RECEIVE ENABLE CONSTANTS */

enum enable{XMITON = 0, RCVON, RXHSON, TXHSON, SETCLK};


struct sio
   {
   BYTE   * uart_base;               /*0  Base address of UART           */
   .
   .
   .
   USHORT flow_wanted;               /*38 0 none,1 xon-xoff, 2 RTS/CTS    */
   USHORT tx_vflowstate;             /*39 State of virtual xmit flow ctrl */
   USHORT rcv_vflowstate;            /*40 State of virtual rcv    "    "  */
   USHORT tx_iflowstate;             /*41 State of interrupt xmit "    "  */
```

continues

Listing 16.1. continued

```
USHORT  rcv_iflowstate;              /*42 State of interrupt rcv  "    "   */
USHORT  (*getflow_req)(SIO *,...);   /*43 pointer to flow-status routine   */
void    (*flowon)(SIO *);            /*44 pointer to flow-off routine      */
void    (*flowoff)(SIO *);           /*45 pointer to flow-on routine       */
short   devnum;                      /*46 s_opened device number           */
};
```

Here are brief discussions of the new six members governing virtual flow control.

flow_wanted   This variable holds the type of flow control desired, if any. The enumerated values are NO_FLOW, XON_XOFF, RTS_CTS, but other values can be added as needed.

tx_flowstate   This transmit state-variable will be discussed in Chapter 21.

rcv_flowstate   This receiver state-variable will be discussed in Chapter 21.

getflow_req   This is a pointer to the Get Flow Request function described previously. The transmitting application calls this function pointer to learn if the receiver has issued a flow-off or flow-on request. The possible returned values are FLOW_OFF, FLOW_ON, and FLOW_NONE. Notice that this function accepts a variable number of arguments.

flowon   This is a pointer to the Turn Flow On function described previously. The receiver calls this function to start or restart the flow of data.

flowoff   This is a pointer to the Turn Flow Off function described previously. The receiver calls this function to stop the flow of data.

To simplify the calling syntax and to abide by our architectural rule that application-level functions never access the SIO directly, Listing 16.1 also provides a level-3 function macros for calling the three function pointers.

LEVEL-2 FUNCTIONS FOR XON/XOFF FLOW CONTROL

Exactly where the flow control function pointers point depends on how they are initialized in the SIO. The simplest case is to point the flow-on and -off routines at do-nothing dummy functions and point the flow-request function at a function that returns FLOW_NONE.

Applications that can operate without flow control are rare. Even modems, which once required a match between data rate and signaling (baud) rate, now require flow control to support protocols and compression. Listing 16.2 gives the three functions required to support XON/XOFF.

Listing 16.2. Three level-2 functions to support XON/XOFF flow control.

FUNCTIO N NAME:	flow_req_xoxo, xon, xoff
LEVEL:	2
PROTOTYPE IN:	BUOS.H
LIBRARY:	BUOS.H
DESCRIPTION:	Functions to support virtual flow control via XON/XOFF under polled I/O.
RETURNS:	USHORT/VOID
COMMENTS:	Get Flow Request: flow_req_xoxo
	Turn Flow ON: xon
	Turn Flow Off: xoff
INCLUDE FILE:	stdio.h, siodef.h, buos.h, sioctl.h

```
USHORT flow_req_xoxo(SIO *siop, ...)
{
    int i;
    i = s_inchar(siop);           /* read next char from input */
    if (i == -1)                  /* if not character ready  */
       return FLOW_NONE;
    if (i == XON)
       {
       siop->tx_vflowstate = FLOW_ON;
       return FLOW_ON;
       }
    if (i == XOFF)
       {
       siop->tx_vflowstate = FLOW_OFF;
       return FLOW_OFF;
       }
    return FLOW_NONE;
}


void xon(SIO *siop)
{
    siop->rcv_vflowstate = FLOW_ON;
    s_putc(siop, XON);            /* send DC3  (13 hex) */
}

void xoff(SIO *siop)
{
    siop->rcv_vflowstate = FLOW_OFF;
    s_putc(siop, XOFF);           /* send DC1  (11 hex) */
}
```

The two functions for turning flow on and off require little explanation: they simply transmit an XON (DC3) or XOFF (DC1). The flow request function for XON/XOFF `flow_req_xoxo` examines the return value from s_inchar. If it returns a not-ready (−1), which it will do most of the time, the function returns immediately with the `FLOW_NONE` return code. If XON or an XOFF character is received, the appropriate constant is returned. `FLOW_NONE` is also returned as a default case.

LEVEL-2 FUNCTIONS FOR RTS/CTS FLOW CONTROL

Listing 16.3 shows the triad of simple functions to support RTS/CTS hardware flow control.

Listing 16.3. Three level-2 functions to support RTS/CTS flow control.

FUNCTION NAME:	`flow_req_rcts, rtson, rtsoff`
LEVEL:	2
PROTOTYPE IN:	BUOS.H
LIBRARY:	BUOS.H
DESCRIPTION:	Functions to support virtual flow control via RTS/CTS under polled I/O.
RETURNS:	`USHORT/void`
COMMENTS:	Get Flow Request: `flow_req_rcts`
	Turn Flow ON: `rtson`
	Turn Flow OFF: `rtsoff`
INCLUDE FILES:	stdio.h, siodef.h, buos.h, sioctl.h

```
USHORT flow_req_rcts(SIO *siop, ...)
{
    USHORT i;
    i = get232(siop, CTS);
    if (i == ON)
        {
        i = FLOW_ON;
        siop->tx_vflowstate = FLOW_ON;
        }
    else
        {
        i = FLOW_OFxF;
        siop->tx_vflowstate = FLOW_OFF;
        }
    return i;
}


void rtson(SIO *siop)
{
    siop->rcv_vflowstate = FLOW_ON;
    set232(siop, RTS, ON);
}
```

```
void rtsoff(SIO *siop)
{
    siop->rcv_vflowstate = FLOW_OFF;
    set232(siop, RTS, OFF);
}
```

The two functions for turning flow on and off simply assert or inhibit the RTS output. The flow request function for flow_req_rcts converts the Boolean returned by the get232 function to the FLOW_ON and FLOW_OFF return codes; hence, this function never returns the FLOW_NONE code.

SIO INITIALIZATION FOR XON/XOFF FLOW CONTROL

All that remains is to initialize the new SIO members to the desired condition. Listing 16.3a shows the initialization for XON/XOFF flow control using the three functions from Listing 16.2. The SIO can be initialized for RTS/CTS in an identical manner simply by substituting the functions in 16.3 and by changing the value of the flow_wanted member to RTS_CTS.

Listing 16.3a. Initialization of new flow control members.

```
      SIO Name:   COM1sio
          FILE:   IBMPC.C
    COMMENTS:     Initialization of new SIO flow control members.

SIO COM1sio  =
    {
    COM1,                    /*0  Base address of UART               */
    .
    .
    .
    XON_XOFF,                /*38 Flow control wanted                */
    FLOW_ON,                 /*39 State of virtual xmit flow control */
    FLOW_ON,                 /*40 State of virtual rcv    "     "    */
    FLOW_ON,                 /*41 State of interrupt xmit  "    "    */
    FLOW_ON,                 /*42 State of interrupt rcv   "    "    */
    flow_req_xoxo,           /*43 Pointer to flow-request routine    */
    xon,                     /*44 Pointer to flow-off routine        */
    xoff,                    /*45 Pointer to flow-on routine         */
    0,                       /*46 Device number                      */
    };
```

As we shall see in Chapters 17 and 18, high-level functions can now perform flow control without any knowledge of the underlying procedures. The decision about which kinds of flow control to support and how to install the required function pointers in the SIO brings up an interesting point—and leads us naturally to our next topic, opening and closing the SIO.

Port Management

The theme of this book is flexibility, generality, and portability of serial I/O programs and functions. By careful design, we have managed to devise a system where all references to the serial port are made through a pointer to a large structure typedefed as a SIO. The SIO describes a serial port completely and contains all the data and pointers necessary to perform I/O with that port. Despite this maniacal insistence on generality, however, we have so far not put it into action by demonstrating how the same set of functions can be used to manage several serial devices. There is a good reason for this: we simply don't have the tools. Because our programs are written with foreknowledge of the system hardware, declaring the omnipresent variable siop is simple and routine:

```
SIO *siop;            /* pointer to an SIO      */
siop = &COM1sio;      /* point at "master" SIO  */
s_config(siop);       /* save/config interface  */
```

Suppose we wish to add support for a serial printer to our terminal program. We could easily manage two devices by declaring a second SIO in the level-0 file (IBMPC.C, for example) with the name, say, COM2sio, then:

```
SIO *siopA;
SIO *siopB;
siopA = &COM1sio;
siopB = &COM2sio;
s_config(siopA);
setformat(siopA, PARITY, siopA->par->start);
setformat(siopA, DATALEN, siopA->dl->start);

s_config(siopB);
setformat(siopB, PARITY, siopB->par->start);
setformat(siopB, DATALEN, siopB->dl->start);
        .
        .
        .
```

This appears simple enough, doesn't it? Suppose, however, that the serial port described by COM2sio doesn't exist. With luck, reading and writing the nonexistent device will not prove fatal. Or suppose, through some quirk of installation, that siopA and siopB point to the same device. Or that a single device is s_configed more than once. The list of possible pitfalls is almost endless.

In order to simplify the handling of multiple serial devices, we need two fundamental system-level management functions, one to open an SIO and the other to close it. Any incorrect or potentially dangerous condition—opening a nonexistent port or closing a port that is not open—can then be spotted. In keeping with the other functions in this book, I will make the syntax of these functions resemble familiar C library functions, to wit fopen and fclose. A file is managed as a stream like this:

```
typedef struct  /* From  STDIO.H */
   {
   char *ptr;
```

```
    int   cnt;
    char *base;
    char  flag;
    char  file;
    } FILE;

FILE *fopen(char *, char *);/* a function returning a pointer to a FILE */
FILE *filep;                 /* a pointer to a FILE                     */
if ( (filep = fopen("TEST", "r")) == NIL)
    {
    puts("Cannot close file");
    exit(1);
    }
    .
    .
    .
if (fclose(filep) != NUL)
    {
    puts("Cannot close file");
    exit(1);
    }
```

Just as a FILE is a typedef for the structure required for buffered device I/O, so an SIO is a typedef for the structure required for asynchronous serial I/O. Just as these C library functions require a pointer to a FILE, so our functions require a pointer to an SIO. To continue this parallel, we will now prepare an SIO for serial I/O in the same way as C prepares a FILE: by opening it. In other words, our procedure should look like this:

```
SIO *s_open(USHORT);
SIO *siop;
unsigned portnum = 0;
if ( (siop = s_open(portnum)) == NIL)
    {
    printf("Cannot open serial device # %d\n",portnum);
    exit(1);
    }

if (s_close(siop) != NUL)
    {
    puts("Cannot close file");
    exit(1);
    }
```

Opening a Serial I/O Device

Here is a summary of the tasks that s_open must perform:

- Return an error if:
  - The device requested is illegal (out of range) for this computer.
  - The device requested is legal, but the support hardware is not installed.
  - The device requested is legal, but you do not wish to support it.
  - The device is not present in the system.

- • The device is already open.
- • There is not enough memory for an SIO.
- • Mark the SIO as open in a system-wide table.
- • Install the device number in the SIO itself.
- • Configure the UART (via s_config).
- • Initialize all functions present in the virtual UART—data format, baud rate, RS-232 outputs, transmitter/receiver, clock factor, and automatic handshaking— according to the start members in their respective structures.
- • Return a pointer to the opened SIO.

All items on this list but the first are level-3 functions. Because item one obviously requires knowledge of the computer's hardware, code to implement it must reside at level-0 in the file IBMPC.C. We actually need two items. First, we need a list containing information about the devices in the system: which devices are in use (open), and how the SIOs map the physical devices. Second, we need a function for reporting whether a requested device is installed.

__siolist: LEVEL-0 DEVICE LIST

To manage the devices in the system, we first must know the total number of serial ports permitted by the system. For each possible device, we need to maintain three pieces of information: its physical mapping (that is, the address of its assigned hardware), a flag to indicate whether the SIO is open or closed, and a flag to indicate whether the device supports UART interrupts. (The interrupt flag is explained in Chapter 19.) These three items can be represented by the simple structure shown in Listing 16.4.

Listing 16.4. A level-0 structure for serial device management.

STRUCT NAME:	SIOLIST
HEADER FILE:	SIODEF.H
DESCRIPTION:	Holds status information about SIO capabilities. Used by level-0 functions.
COMMENTS:	One such structure must be declared for each serial port supported.

```
struct SIOLIST
   {
   SIO  *siop;                    /* Address of an SIO             */
   BOOL sio_openflag;             /* Whether it's already open     */
   BOOL intrpt_supp;              /* Whether it supports interrupts */
   };
```

With the SIOLIST structure in hand, let's see how to apply it to the IBMPC. We will assume that IBMPC.C file declares two SIO structures named COM1sio and COM2sio. Listing 16.5 shows_siolist for IBMPC.C.

Listing 16.5. A system list of the IBM PC's supported serial ports.

STRUCT NAME:	__siolist
HEADER FILE:	IBMPC.C
DESCRIPTION:	An array of struct _siostat, MAX_PORTS in length.
COMMENTS:	The global integer __maxsios contains the maximum number of serial devices possible in the system.

```
unsigned __maxsios = MAX_PORTS;          /* global                    */
struct SIOLIST _siolist[MAX_PORTS] = /* IBM has four serial ports */
   {
   { &COM1sio , FALSE, TRUE  },
   { &COM2sio , FALSE, TRUE  },
   { NIL      , FALSE, FALSE },
   { NIL      , FALSE, FALSE }
   };
```

The constant MAX_PORTS (from Listing 16.1) is used to initialize the global variable __maxsios and to dimension __siolist, an array of SIOLIST structures. For each element, the siop member is initialized to contain the address of the corresponding SIO. The openflag member is initialized to mark this SIO as closed. For now, ignore the intrpt_supp flag.

Notice that the portnum argument is declared to be an unsigned instead of an int. This prevents illegal indexing if a signed integer is accidentally passed.

The IBM PC is capable of supporting four serial cards or, as IBM calls them, "asynchronous communications adapters." Because a system rarely contains all four, Listing 16.6 assumes the much more common configuration of two serial cards, known in IBM parlance as COM1 and COM2. As you know, an SIO must be declared for each port. Our examples, however, have always shown only a single SIO, named COM1sio. For the remainder of this chapter, we will assume that there exists another SIO named COM2sio and the full complement of 'B' structures (i.e., parityB, baudB, etc.) and other 'B' data (i.e., v_regB) required to initialize it.[1] To save space, this second SIO is not shown in any figure, but it shouldn't be difficult to imagine.

[1]The only necessary difference between the two SIOs is their uart_base members: 3F8 for COM1sio and 2F8 for COM2sio.

__isport[2]: LEVEL-0 DEVICE VERIFICATION

When the IBM PC boots up, routines in its ROM BIOS scan configuration switches on the system board and verify the existence of various equipment by generally nosing around in the system looking for hardware. ROM BIOS builds a four-element list of serial ports pointers at memory address 0:400H. Because the port addresses on the 80x86 family of processors are 16 bits wide, each element in this list is 2 bytes wide. COM1's base address (i.e., uart_base) can therefore be learned by reading address 0:400H, COM2's at 0:402H, and so forth. To see how this works, find a system with only one serial device and set it for address 2F8. After rebooting, the device at 2F8 is becomes the logical COM1.

Although devices names such as COM 1 and COM 2 are obviously logical, the PC industry ignored this handy logical-to-physical mapping so that in virtually all software, the COM number is merely a synonym for a UART's base address. The code in __isport, alas, follows this regrettable industry practice.

Listing 16.6. The __isport function for IBM PC.

FUNCTION NAME:	__isport
PROTOTYPE IN:	IBMPC.H
LEVEL:	0
LIBRARY:	IBMPC.C
DESCRIPTION:	Verifies that a UART is present at devnum.
RETURNS:	BOOL: TRUE if the device exists.
COMMENTS:	Bits 4 and 5 of the IER are Read-only and always 0. The function writes the DLAB bit in the Data Format (Line Control Register) to uncover the MSB of the baud register, then writes 80H into it. It then flips the DLAB back to the IER register and tests its high bit. Since the IER's bits 4 and 5 are always 0, they cannot be set. Voilà.
INCLUDE FILES:	ibmpc.h, u16x50.h

```
BOOL __isport(RANK devnum)
{
    BYTE *uartp;
    BOOL retcode = 1;
    switch (devnum)
        {
        case 0: uartp = COM1; break;
        case 1: uartp = COM2; break;
        case 2: uartp = COM3; break;
        case 3: uartp = COM4; break;
        default: retcode = 0;
        }
```

---

[2]The two leading underscores on this array and the __isport function identify them as a level-0 objects.

```
    if (retcode)
        {
        FAST old_msb, old_format;
        old_format = _a_inport(uartp + DLAB);
        _a_outport(uartp + DLAB, old_format ¦ 0x80);    /* flip DLAB to baud          */
        old_msb = _a_inport(uartp + BAUDHI);            /* save old msb               */
        _a_outport(uartp + BAUDHI, 0x30);               /* bits 4&5 never 1 in IER */
        _a_outport(uartp + DLAB, old_format & 0x7f);    /* flip DLAB to IER           */
        retcode = !(_a_inport(uartp + INT_ID)  & 0x30)  /* are 4&5 now 1 in IER?     */
        _a_outport(uartp + DLAB, old_format ¦ 0x80);    /* flip DLAB to baud          */
        _a_outport(uartp + BAUDHI, old_msb);            /* ...restore msb             */
        _a_outport(uartp + DLAB, old_format & 0x7f);    /* flip DLAB to IER           */
        _a_outport(uartp + DLAB, old_format);
        }
    return retcode;
}
```

This function switches upon the device-number argument to determine a base address for the proposed UART. If the argument is within range, the next step is to test for an 8250/16x50-style UART at that base address. The test is based upon the unique manner in which baud rate registers are addressed at the same location as the Data and Interrupt Enable Register and the Data Format Register. As you recall from Chapter 7, the role of these two registers is toggled via bit 7 (the "DLAB" bit) of the Data Format Register.

First, the current contents of the IER are preserved, then the DLAB bit is set in the Data Format Register. If the device is an 8250/16x50, the two baud rate registers should be addressable at offsets 0 and 1. The function now makes use of the fact that bits 4 and 5 of the IER are always zero. The idea is to write a byte with bits 4 and 5 set into the purported Baud Rate Register, then flip the DLAB bit back and read the IER. If bits 4 and 5 are zero, it is very likely that the device is an 8250/16X50 and a nonzero code is returned. Before exit, the disturbed registers are restored.

Level-3 Open Function

With level-0 support out of the way, it is now possible to write a robust s_open function.

Listing 16.7. Using s_open to open an SIO.

FUNCTION NAME:	s_open
LEVEL:	3
PROTOTYPE IN:	SIODEF.H
LIBRARY:	SIO.LIB
DESCRIPTION:	'Opens' a serial port as if it were a system stream device.
RETURNS:	SIO*

continues

Listing 16.7. continued

```
        COMMENTS:    The s_errno variable is global.
        INCLUDE FILES:    siodef.h, buos.h

int s_errno;                                    /* global error code variable */

SIO *s_open(USHORT portnum)
{
    extern struct SIOLIST _siolist[];
    extern USHORT __maxsios;                    /* global — number of ports  */
    SIO *siop;                                  /* SIO pointer to return      */

    if (portnum >= __maxsios)                   /* is device number legal?    */
        {
        s_errno = BAD_PORT;
        return NIL;
        }
    if (__isport(portnum) == NUL)               /* is the hardware installed? */
        {
        s_errno = NO_PORT;
        return NIL;
        }
    if (__siolist[portnum].siop == NIL)         /* does an SIO exist for it?  */
        {
        s_errno = NO_PORT;
        return NIL;
        }
    if (__siolist[portnum].openflag != CLOSED)   /* is it already open?       */
        {
        s_errno = OPEN_NOW;
        return NIL;
        }
    siop = _siolist[portnum].siop;              /* SIO pointer from table     */
    __sys_disable();
    s_config(siop);                             /* set up SIO's uart          */
    __sys_enable();

    (void) setformat(siop, PARITY, siop->par->start);
    (void) setformat(siop, STOPS,  siop->sb->start);
    (void) setformat(siop, DATALEN, siop->dl->start);
    (void) setbaud(siop, siop->br->start);
    (void) set232(siop, DTR, siop->dtr->start);     /* set RS-232 and GP outputs */
    (void) set232(siop, RTS, siop->rts->start);
    (void) set232(siop, GPO1, siop->gpo1->start);
    (void) set232(siop, GPO2, siop->gpo2->start);
    (void) setuart(siop, SETCLK, siop->clkf->start);    /* set clock factor         */
    (void) setuart(siop, RXHSON, siop->dcdhs->start);   /* receiver handshaking     */
    (void) setuart(siop, TXHSON, siop->ctshs->start);   /* xmitter handshaking      */
    (void) setuart(siop, XMITON, siop->txenable->start); /* enable transmitter      */
    (void) setuart(siop, RCVON, siop->rxenable->start);  /* enable receiver         */

    _siolist[portnum].openflag = OPEN;          /* mark SIO open in list      */
    siop->devnum = portnum;                     /* put device number in SIO   */
```

```
/* install default (polled) I/O for flow control */
   if (siop->flow_wanted == XON_XOFF)
      {
      siop->flowon  = xon;
      siop->flowoff = xoff;
      siop->getflow_req = flow_req_xoxo;
      }
   else if (siop->flow_wanted == RTS_CTS)
      {
      siop->flowon  = rtson;
      siop->flowoff = rtsoff;
      siop->getflow_req = flow_req_rcts;
      }
   return siop;
}
```

Like all functions that return pointers, s_open has only a single value, NIL, available for an error code. While the calling program can test the return value for NIL to detect when an error has occurred, it has no way to ascertain the nature of the error. This is solved by placing an error code in the global variable s_errno for subsequent evaluation by the calling program. The error codes returned by s_open and s_close were presented without comment in Listing 14.2, so please refer to them now to refresh your memory.

Before opening, a phalanx of tests is performed. First, the port number[3] is checked to be sure it is legal for the system; after calling __isport to verify that the hardware is installed, the portnum argument is used to index into the __siolist array to make certain that an SIO exists for it; finally, a test is performed to see if this device is already open.

If the device number passes the foregoing tests, it is assumed to be valid. Opening consists of:

1. Copying the address of the SIO into the now-ubiquitous pointer siop.
2. Configuring the UART and/or saving its current state for subsequent restoration.
3. Calling all virtual UART functions to initialize the SIO to the values contained in the start members of its various members.

Because of the design of the level-2 functions—unsupported virtual functions that are not supported in hardware return harmlessly. Finally, with the SIO fully opened, the appropriate member in the __siolist is marked OPEN, the device number is installed in the SIO, and the address of the SIO is returned.[4]

---

[3]Notice that the portnum argument is declared to be an USHORT instead of an int; this prevents illegal indexing if a signed integer is accidentally passed.

[4]The present design of s_open opens only SIO's in memory. A much more flexible approach is to store SIO templates on disk, then read them into dynamically allocated storage when opened. The reader is encouraged to undertake this modification as an exercise.

Level-3 Close Function

An SIO opened with s_open must be closed with s_close, as shown in Listing 16.8.

Listing 16.8. Use of `s_close` to close an SIO.

FUNCTION NAME:	s_close
LEVEL:	3
PROTOTYPE IN:	SIODEF.H
LIBRARY:	SIO.LIB
DESCRIPTION:	'Closes' a serial port as if it were a system stream device.
RETURNS:	int
INCLUDES FILES:	siodef.h, buos.h

```
int s_close(SIO *siop)
{
    extern struct SIOLIST __siolist[];    /* list of available @[SIO]@s          */
    extern int __maxsios;                 /* global — maximum number of serial ports */
    int i;
    if (siop == NIL)
        return NO_CLOSE;

    for (i = 0 ;i < __maxsios; i++)
        if ( (siop == __siolist[i].siop) && (__siolist[i].openflag == OPEN))
            {
            __siolist[i].openflag = CLOSED;
            break;
            }
    if ( i == __maxsios)                  /* no match in list                    */
        return NO_CLOSE;
    s_restore(siop);                      /* restore uart as found               */
    siop->devnum  = VIRGIN;               /* install dummy device number         */
    return 0;
}
```

This function loops through __siolist, the list of available SIOs, to make certain:

- The SIO to close is actually valid
- It's already open

If both conditions obtain, the SIO is restored, the SIO is marked as CLOSED, the device number in the SIO is set to NUL, and a 0 is returned as the symbol of a successful close.

Why even bother to close an SIO? After all, it doesn't contain data in the same sense as, say, a FILE. The most important function s_close performs its restoration of the interface to its original condition. Aside from that, an SIO's failure to close is a good indication that something has gone awry in your program.

Transmitter/Receiver Functions

You may have noticed the following function calls in s_open in Listing 16.7:

```
(void) setuart (siop, SETCLK, siop->clkf->start);
(void) setuart (siop, RXHSON, siop->dcdhs->start);
(void) setuart (siop, TXHSON, siop->ctshs->start);
(void) setuart (siop, XMITON, siop->txenable->start);
(void) setuart (siop, RCVON, siop->rxenable->start);
```

The level-3 setuart function, which we will compose shortly, is merely a mechanism for making sure that the UART's configuation is to our liking. The second arguments shown configure the UART's baud-rate clock to the desired divisor, turns on or off any internal receiver and transmitter handshaking, and enables and disables the transmitter and receiver. (These features are discussed in Chapter 6.)

Although it may be argued that low-level activity such as this rightfully belongs in the s_config file, many situations exist in which these features must be manipulated under program control. For example, turning off the UART receiver is a good way to prevent garbage from collecting in the UART's receive buffer, or, as the case may be, the interrupt buffer. Similarly, software printer drivers require absolute control over the RS-232 handshaking; it is therefore important that you be able to defeat any automatic handshaking built into the UART.

Because you are now familiar with the procedure of adding support for new items by modifying the SIO definition, these new functions will be presented with much less fanfare than in previous chapters. Listing 16.9 shows the additions that SIODEF.H requires to accommodate these new functions: a few general manifest constants and the modified SIO definition. Because the SIO has grown quite long, the SIO in Listing 16.10 shows the *entire* current definition and provides reference numbers in the comments for your convenience.

Listing 16.9. Additions to SIODEF.H for supporting miscellaneous UART functions.

STRUCT DEF: SIO
      FILE: SIODEF.H
DESCRIPTION: structure defining a serial port.

```
struct sio
  {
  BYTE   * uart_base;              /*0  Base address of UART            */
  USHORT data_off;                 /*1  Offset of data port from base   */
  USHORT status_off;               /*2  Offset of status port from base */
  MASK   rcvmask;                  /*3  RxRDY mask                       */
  MASK   xmitmask;                 /*4  Xmit holding reg. empty mask     */
  MASK   tx_emptymask;             /*5  Xmit shift reg. empty mask       */
  FAST   (*readbyte)(BYTE *);      /*6  Pointer to RAM/port read routine */
  void   (*writebyte)(BYTE *, FAST); /*7  Pointer to RAM/port read routine */
  FAST   (*s_rstat)(SIO *);        /*8  Pointer to receiver status       */
```

continues

Listing 16.9. continued

```
FAST    (*s_read)(SIO *);              /*9  Pointer to fetch routine       */
FAST    (*s_xstat)(SIO *);             /*10 Pointer to xmit status         */
void    (*s_send)(SIO *, FAST);        /*11 Pointer to xmit function       */
short   (*s_txblock)(SIO *, BYTE*,short); /*12 "   block xmit function     */
REG     (*v_regp)[2];                  /*13 Virtual UART register          */
USHORT  v_regpsize;                    /*14 Length of virtual array        */
struct vregbits_ *par;                 /*15 Pointer to parity struct       */
struct vregbits_ *sb;                  /*16 Pointer to stop bit struct     */
struct vregbits_ *dl;                  /*17 Pointer to data length struct  */
struct vbaud_    *br;                  /*18 Pointer to baud rate  struct   */
struct vout232_  *rts;                 /*19 Pointer to RTS struct          */
struct vout232_  *dtr;                 /*20 Pointer to DTR struct          */
struct vout232_  *gpo1;                /*21 Pointer to GPOUTPUT1  struct   */
struct vout232_  *gpo2;                /*22 Pointer to GPOOUTPUT2 struct   */
struct vout232_  *brkbit;              /*23 Pointer to BREAK struct        */
struct vin232_   *cts;                 /*24 Pointer to  CTS struct         */
struct vin232_   *dsr;                 /*25 Pointer to  DSR struct         */
struct vin232_   *dcd;                 /*26 Pointer to  DCD struct         */
struct vin232_   *ri;                  /*27 Pointer to  RI struct          */
struct vin232_   *gpi1;                /*28 Pointer to  GPINPUT1  struct   */
struct vin232_   *gpi2;                /*29 Pointer to  GPINPUT2  struct   */
FAST  (*read232)(SIO *, struct vin232_*); /*30 * to lev-1 fetch function  */
union inbits_232 status;               /*31 See if any RS-232 inputs       */
union inbits_232 delta;                /*32 Changed since last read        */
struct vregbits_  *txenable;           /*33 "  xmitter enable struct       */
struct vregbits_  *rxenable;           /*34 "  receiver enable struct      */
struct vregbits_  *ctshs;              /*35 "  cts handshake on xmitter    */
struct vregbits_  *dcdhs;              /*36 "  dcd handshake on rcvr       */
struct vregbits_  *clkf;               /*37 "  clock factor struct         */
USHORT flow_wanted;                    /*38 0 none,1 xon-xoff, 2 RTS/CTS   */
USHORT tx_vflowstate;                  /*39 State of virtual xmit flow ctrl */
USHORT rcv_vflowstate;                 /*40 State of virtual rcv    "    "  */
USHORT tx_iflowstate;                  /*41 State of interrupt xmit "    "  */
USHORT rcv_iflowstate;                 /*42 State of interrupt rcv  "    "  */
USHORT (*getflow_req)(SIO *,...);      /*43 pointer to flow-status routine  */
void   (*flowon)(SIO *);               /*44 pointer to flow-off routine    */
void   (*flowoff)(SIO *);              /*45 pointer to flow-on routine     */
short  devnum;                         /*46 s_opened device number         */
};
```

Unlike the RS-232 input and output structures, we cannot assume that these new functions are governed by a single bit in a UART register. Why? On a few UARTs, the meaning of "transmitter on" or "receiver on" is subject to program control. In one mode, the receiver and transmitter are functional, but their respective status flags are permanently set to FALSE. In this mode, then, code that accesses the transmitter or receiver without checking the status performs as before, but code that polls the status bits does not. In another possible mode, the receiver and transmitter are unconditionally inhibited and serialization of data does not occur. Similar options exist for handshaking features. To accommodate these various modes, we therefore use a vregbits_ structure to describe the UART functions. Declarations and initializations are not given for IBMPC.C because none are required: the 16X50 UART in the IBM PC does not support these features.

Level-3 Miscellaneous Function

The simple function required to implement the new features is a mirror image of earlier functions that refer to vregbits_ structures. It calls vsetbits, passing to it the customary pointer to SIO, a pointer to the respective vregbits_ structure and a second level. These functions, given in Listing 16.10, return the customary vsetbits error codes.

Listing 16.10. Miscellaneous Level-3 functions.

FUNCTION NAME:	setuart
LEVEL:	3
PROTOTYPE IN:	SIODEF.H
LIBRARY:	SIO.LIB
DESCRIPTION:	Enable transmitter and receiver; enable transmitter handshake on CTS and receiver handshake on DCD; set clock factor.
RETURNS:	int: OR_ARG if argument is out of range; BAD_FCN if the function is not supported (SIO pointer is NIL); BAD_ARG if the requested setting is not supported by hardware; 0 if successful.
INCLUDE FILES:	siodef.j, buos.h

```
int setuart(SIO *siop, RANK whichone, USHORT state)
{
    struct vregbits_ *tr_rcv;

    switch(whichone)
        {
        case XMITON: tr_rcv = siop->txenable; break;
        case RCVON : tr_rcv = siop->rxenable; break;
        case RXHSON: tr_rcv = siop->ctshs    ; break;
        case TXHSON: tr_rcv = siop->dcdhs    ; break;
        case SETCLK: tr_rcv = siop->clkf     ; break;
        default: return OR_ARG;
        }
    return vsetbits(siop, tr_rcv, state);
}
```

Finally, Listing 16.11 shows the actual declaration and initialization for COM1sio in IBMPC.C. Again, the entire SIO is shown with line numbers in the comments.

Listing 16.11. SIO declarations and initializations for IBMPC.C.

```
SIO COM3sio  =
       {
       COM3,                   /*0   Base address of UART                */
       DATA_IO,                /*1   Offset of data port from base       */
       SER_STAT,               /*2   Offset of status port from base     */
       RCV_MASK,               /*3   RxRDY mask from UART.H               */
       XMIT_MASK,              /*4   Xmitter Holding Register Empty mask  */
       TX_EMPTY_MASK,          /*5   Xmitter Shift Register Empty mask    */
       _a_inport,              /*6   Pointer to RAM/port read routine     */
       _a_outport,             /*7   Pointer to RAM/port read routine     */
       s_rcvstat,              /*8   Pointer to receiver status           */
       s_rcv,                  /*9   Pointer to fetch routine             */
       s_xmitstat,             /*10  Pointer to xmiter status             */
       s_xmit,                 /*11  Pointer to xmit routine              */
       tx_write,               /*12  Pointer to polled block xmit routine */
       v_regC,                 /*13  Pointer to virtual register array    */
       V_REG_SIZE,             /*14  Number of rows in virtual array      */
       &parityC,               /*15  Parity structure                    */
       &stopsC,                /*16  Stop bit structure                  */
       &dlenC,                 /*17  Data length structure                */
       &baudC,                 /*18  Baud rate structure                 */
       &pin4C,                 /*19  RS-232 RTS output                   */
       &pin20C,                /*20  RS-232 DTR output                   */
       &gp1outC,               /*21  RS-232 first user-defined output    */
       &gp2outC,               /*22  RS-232 first user-defined output    */
       &breakbC,               /*23  Break bit                           */
       &pin5C,                 /*24  RS-232 CTS input                    */
       &pin6C,                 /*25  RS-232 DSR input                    */
       &pin8C,                 /*26  RS-232 DCD input                    */
       &pin22C,                /*27  RS-232 RI  input                    */
       NIL,                    /*28  NO 1st user-defined RS-232 input    */
       NIL,                    /*29  NO 2nd user-defined RS-232 input    */
       _vstat232,              /*30  * to level one fetch function       */
       0,                      /*31  RS-232 status bits                  */
       0,                      /*32  RS-232 delta bits                   */
       NIL,                    /*33  NO transmitter-on structure         */
       NIL,                    /*34  NO receiver-on structure            */
       NIL,                    /*35  NO transmitter/RTS handshake        */
       NIL,                    /*36  NO receiver/DCD handshake           */
       NIL,                    /*37  NO clock factor                     */
       FLOW_ON,                /*39  State of virtual xmit flow control  */
       FLOW_ON,                /*40  State of virtual rcv    "    "      */
       FLOW_ON,                /*41  State of interrupt xmit "    "      */
       FLOW_ON,                /*42  State of interrupt rcv  "    "      */
       flow_req_xoxo,          /*43  Pointer to flow-request routine     */
       xon,                    /*44  Pointer to flow-off routine         */
       xoff,                   /*45  Pointer to flow-on routine          */
       SUPPLIED,               /*46  Device number supplied during open  */
       };
```

TERM Revisions

The capability to open and close an SIO greatly simplifies the prologue and epilogue required to use a serial port. Listing 16.12 shows how the main portion of TERM is changed by these new functions.

Listing 16.12. The main function of TERM using s_open and s_close.

```
main (int argc, char *argv[])
{
    int portnum = 0;                /* default serial card */
    SIO *siop;                      /* pointer to an SIO   */
    if (argc > 1)
        portnum = atoi(argv[1]);
    if ( (siop = s_open(portnum)) == NIL )
        {
        printf("\aCannot open:  %s\n", errstr[s_errno]);
        return s_errno;
        }
    flowon(siop);                   /* enable flow control */
    term(siop);                     /* -- TERM -- */

    if ( (s_errno = s_close(siop)) != 0 )
        {
        printf("\aCannot close:  %s\n", errstr[s_errno]);
        return s_errno;
        }
    puts("\nEnd of TERM\n");
    return 0;
}
```

Not much commentary is required except to point out that serial port management is greatly simlified by the addition of s_open and s_close, and that the addition of the flowon function call makes flow control a level-3 procedure. By default, the device number that is opened is 0. To enable access to a different port (and to enable you to test the error-checking mechanism), a different device number may be specified on the command line. In practical use, programs probably should not automatically terminate when s_open returns an error; a more helpful approach offers the user the alternative of specifying a new device number and perhaps permanently installing it in the program.

Conclusion

We have now completed the virtual UART section of our SIO and can turn our attention to adding loftier features. In upcoming chapters, for example, we'll write a series of functions that enable you to perform formatted I/O through an SIO, to control the speed of transmission, to fix the ends of lines, to translate or remove characters, and to perform a host of other chores vital to asynchronous serial I/O.

Formatted Output

All of the functions we have written so far might fairly be called "tools"—routines that, while interesting, are of little practical value by themselves. This characterization is not intended to be pejorative, but in truth, the best of tools can sustain one's interest only so long. We now turn our attention to composing a new group of functions that perform, for want of a better term, "formatted" serial output. By formatted, we mean that our functions will perform some type of processing on ordinary or *raw* output. End-of-line handling is a good example of formatted serial output. As we discussed in Chapter 1, there is little agreement among operating systems about what character should be employed to mark the end of one line and the start of a new line. Some systems use CR *and* LF and other systems use CR *or* LF. Because many utility programs, especially those that process text, rely heavily upon a particular end-of-line character(s), files produced under one operating system are problematical under another. One of the fundamental attributes of good communication software, therefore, is its ability to translate among the various end-of-line conventions.

Formatted output means that raw data is somehow adjusted to facilitate communications with a dissimilar or at least partially incompatible environment. Since there is no way to predict whether you are on the receiving or transmitting end of such an incompatibility, you require one group of functions for formatted output and another for formatted input. Each group is governed by its own control structure, a pointer to which is located (you guessed it) in the SIO structure. Because these functions are modeled after their familiar counterparts from the C standard library, you already know how to use them.

Before we begin, place the constants shown in Listing 17.1 in a new header file named SIOCTL.H.

Listing 17.1. Constants for a new header file, SIOCTL.H.

```
/* CONSTANTS FOR FORMATTED OUTPUT */
enum ioctl
   {
   NOXLAT = 0,          /* remove nothing--i.e., "raw"    */
   LF2CR,               /* translate LF to CR             */
   CR2LF,               /* translate CR to LF             */
   EOL2SPACE,           /* rconvert CR&LF to spaces       */
   REMOVEEOL,           /* remove all CR and LF           */
   LF2CRLF,             /* convert LF to CRLF             */
   CR2CRLF,             /* convert CR to CRLF             */
   CRLF2LF,             /* convert CRLF to LF             */
   CRLF2CR,             /* convert CRLF to CR             */
   };

/* UPPER/LOWER CASE MODES */
#define  UP_LOW      0   /* upper and lower--i.e., "raw"  */
#define  UPPER       1   /* convert to upper              */
#define  LOWER       2   /* convert to lower              */

/* XON-XOFF  CONTROL */
#define  NO_XX       0   /* no XON-XOFF flow control      */
#define  XON_ONLY    1   /* accept only 'xonchar' for XON */
#define  XON_ANY     2   /* accept anything for XON       */

#define  IGNORE     -2   /* don't xmit this character     */
#define  NOECHO      1   /* don't echo                    */

#define IO_STKSIZ   10       /* Size of ioctl stack */
```

Formatted Output

At the base of our formatted output functions will be the level-2 function s_putc, whose sole function is to output "raw" bytes from the SIO. Using flags and data in an output control structure, we will build the single-byte output function s_fputc to "format" the byte stream in a variety of ways. Instead of listing the various tasks we wish s_fputc to perform, we will examine the entire structure and the individual purpose of each member. Listing 17.2 shows the output control structure soctl_.

Listing 17.2. The soctl_ control structure.

STRUCT NAME:	soctl_
HEADER NAME:	SIODEF.H
DESCRIPTION:	soctl_ structure declaration.
COMMENTS:	Declares an output control structure. The numbering in the comments are for references only.

```
struct soctl_
    {
    BOOL      rawflag;             /*0  Perform no processing at all    */
    short     eolmode;             /*1  End-of-line formatting           */
    BOOL      consflag;            /*2  Echo characters to console       */
    BOOL      wechoflag;           /*3  Interbyte wait for return echo   */
    unsigned  wecho_dly;           /*4  Tsecs to wait for return echo    */
    USHORT    casemode;            /*5  Change to upper or lower case    */
    USHORT    xxmode;              /*6  XON/XOFF control                 */
    FAST      xoffc;               /*7  XOFF character                   */
    FAST      xonc;                /*8  XON character (-1 == any char)   */
    BOOL      asciiflag;           /*9  Reset strip bit 7                */
    BOOL      cntrlflag;           /*10 Remove control characters        */
    BYTE      ok_cntrls[32];       /*11 Permitted control characters     */
    USHORT    numcc;               /*12 Number of controls  in ok_cntrls */
    BOOL      filterflag;          /*13 Filter-remove characters         */
    short     filtlist[128][2];    /*14 List of byte to remove or filter */
    USHORT    numfc;               /*15 Number of bytes in  filter list  */
    BOOL      ib_dlyflag;          /*16 Interbyte delay in  tsecs        */
    unsigned  ib_dly;              /*17 Pause between bytes              */
    BOOL      il_dlyflag;          /*18 Interline pause flag             */
    FAST      il_dlyc;             /*19 Char to begin inter-line pause   */
    unsigned  il_dly;              /*20 Inter-line     pause in tsecs    */
    FAST      kbortc;              /*21 Key to break out of loops        */
    int       lastc;               /*22 Previous byte output             */
    BOOL      flushflag;           /*23 An end of line decision pending  */
    };
```

The members of this structure have the functions shown below. The numbers in parentheses correspond to the reference numbers in the comments in Listing 17.2.

rawflg   (0)   Disables all byte processing and makes a call to s_fputc equivalent to a call to s_putc.

eolmode   (1)   Determines the end-of-line translation according to the following constants (given in Listing 17.1).

NOXLAT   No end-of-line translation is performed.

LF2CR   Line Feed is replaced with Carriage Return.

CR2LF   Carriage Return is replaced with Line Feed.

EOL2SPACE   Carriage Return and Line Feed are replaced with spaces.

REMOVEEOL   Carriage Return and Line Feed are removed.

LF2CRLF   Line Feed is replaced with Carriage Return and Line Feed.

CR2CRLF   Carriage Return is replaced with Carriage Return and Line Feed.

CRLF2LF   Carriage Return and Line Feed are replaced with Line Feed.

CRLF2CR   Carriage Return and Line Feed are replaced with Carriage Return.

consflg	(2)	Outputs the byte not only to the SIO but also to standard output.
wechoflg	(3)	Outputs the byte to the SIO then waits wecho_dly Tsecs for a byte to arrive via SIO input. In effect, this feature waits until the receiver acknowledges reception of the byte just transmitted.
casemode	(5)	Translates bytes to upper or lower case according to the following constants (given in Listing 17.1):

UP_LOW	No translation
UPPER	Convert to upper case
LOWER	Convert to lower case

asciiflg	(9)	Compensates for data format errors or "normalizes" word-processed text files by clearing bit 7 of each transmitted byte.
cntrlflg	(10)	Enables control character removal. Because in practice the controls for exclusion usually outnumber those for inclusion, the list ok_cntrls[32] contains a list of control characters *not* to be removed, and the *cardinal* number numcc contains the number of characters entered in this list.
filterflg	(13)	Enables byte translation and removal. The bytes in "column" 0 of a 128-element two-dimensional array, filtlist[128][2] are translated to the corresponding bytes in column 1. If, however, the byte in column 1 is −1, the byte in column 0 is simply not transmitted. The number of entries in the array is contained in numfc, a *cardinal* number. (This must be an integer array to accommodate the −1 values.)
ib_dlyflg	(16)	Introduces an unconditional pause of ib_dly Tsecs per *byte*.
il_dlyflg	(18)	Introduces an unconditional pause of il_dly Tsecs per *line*. The il_dlyc function defines the byte that triggers this line delay, usually CR or LF.
kbortc	(21)	Key recognized to break out of wait loops.
lastc	(22)	A 1-byte scratch pad buffer required during end-of-line conversion.
flushflg	(23)	The signal that a CRLF end-of-line translation is pending. Upon receipt of a CR in the CRLF2LF mode, the decision to translate must be postponed until the next character is known to be an LF. The primary use of this flag is to broadcast to functions that call s_fputc that an untransmitted byte remains in lastc.

Declaration and Initialization of an *soctl_* Structure

Listing 17.3 shows one possible declaration and initialization of an soctl_ structure. The numbers in comments are for refererence.

Listing 17.3. Declaration and initialization of an output control structure.

STRUCT NAME:	soctl_ octlA
FILE:	SIOCTL.H
DESCRIPTION:	Control structure for "formatted" output.
COMMENTS:	Declares and initializes an output control structure. The numbering in the comments correspond to those in the soctl_ structure definition.

```
struct soctl_ octlA =
    {
    OFF,                            /*0  "Raw" output flag                    */
    NOXLAT,                         /*1  End-of-line mode                     */
    OFF,                            /*2  Con sole output flag                 */
    OFF,                            /*3  Echowait flag                        */
    _1_SEC_0 * 5,                   /*4  Echo-wait before timeout in Tsecs    */
    UP_LOW,                         /*5  Upper/lower case conversion mode     */
    XON_ONLY,                       /*6  Flow control mode                    */
    DC3,                            /*7  XOFF character                       */
    DC1,                            /*8  XON character if mode >= 0           */
    ON,                             /*9  Strip high bits flag                 */
    ON,                             /*10 Remove unwanted controls flag        */
{NUL,BEL,BS,HT,LF,CR,FF,DC3,DC1,DOS_EOF},    /*11 permitted controls         */
    10,                             /*12 Number of controls in above list     */
    OFF,                            /*13 Translation/removal flag             */
    {0},                            /*14 Translation/removal list             */
    0,                              /*15 No entries in above array            */
    OFF,                            /*16 No interbyte delay flag              */
    _0_SEC_05,                      /*17 Delay in Tsecs                       */
    OFF,                            /*18 end-of-line pause flag               */
    LF,                             /*19 Character to pause after             */
    _0_SEC_4,                       /*20 Pause in Tsecs                       */
    ESC,                            /*21 Keyboard abort character             */
    SUPPLIED,                       /*22 'last character' buffer              */
    SUPPLIED                        /*23 Flag to flush last character         */
    };
```

An explanation of *octlA*—Most members of the structure are initialized to common-sense values. A few, however, require discussion. First, the rawflg is disabled because most applications require output processing of some sort.

Together, asciiflg, cntrlflg, and ok_cntrls, when enabled, can be used to translate outgoing text files to *plain ASCII text*. The high-order bit is cleared and only the ASCII control characters classified as Format Effectors (see Chapter 1) are transmitted. This, of course, precludes the transmission of binary files of all types as well as text files produced by most word processors.

The interbyte and interline delays are given typical values, but are *not* enabled.

As a level-3 object, oct1A could claim residence in *SIO.LIB*. It is better, however, to place it in the level-0, computer-specific file where it can be easily configured for each computer.

Additions to the *SIO* Structure

Listing 17.4 shows how the definition, declaration, and initialization of the SIO is affected by the addition of the output control structure.

Listing 17.4. Changes in definition, declaration, and initialization of the SIO.

```
STRUCT DEF:   SIO
      FILE:   SIODEF.H
DESCRIPTION:  Master structure defining a serial port.
  COMMENTS:   Members supporting formatted output.

struct sio
   {
   BYTE   *uart_base;        /*0  Base address of UART    */
   .

   .

   .
   short  devnum;            /*46 S_opened device number  */
   struct soctl_   *s_octl;  /*47 Pointer to output struct */
   };


   SIO NAME:   COM1sio
      FILE:    IBMPC.C
DESCRIPTION:   COM1sio

SIO COM1sio  =
    {
    COM1,      /*0  base address of UART                  */
    .

    .

    .
    SUPPLIED,  /*46 device number supplied during open    */
    &octlA,    /*47 pointer to output control structure   */
    };
```

Output Control Functions

With the soctl_ fully formed we can now write the output functions that refer to it. As is our custom, we will compose a single master function, s_fputc, then derive several "convenience" functions from it. The principle of s_fputc is simple: passed an SIO pointer and a *single* byte, it processes the byte based upon the flags and arrays in the SIO's s_octl member. While the code for this function is not complicated, it is, unfortunately, rather too large for explanation in a few sentences or paragraphs. Instead, the entire function is shown in Listing 17.5 and followed by a piece-by-piece discussion of its constituent parts.

Listing 17.5. The s_fputc function: a level-2 function for "formatted" output control.

FUNCTION NAME:	s_fputc
LEVEL:	2
PROTOTYPE IN:	BUOS.H
LIBRARY:	BUOS.LIB
DESCRIPTION:	Provides "formatted" character-by-character serial output according to the soctl_ structure in the structure pointed to by siop.
RETURNS:	int: NOECHO if "wait for echo" times out, KEY_CAN if a loop (e.g. XON-XOFF) is aborted from keyboard; otherwise 0.
COMMENTS:	Features:

Raw (no processing)	High bit clearing
Inter-byte and _line delay	Character filter
Flow control	Character translation
End of line conversion	Console output
Upper/lower case conversion	Wait-for-echo

INCLUDE FILES:	stdio.h, ctype.h, siodef.h, sioctl.h, ascii.h, buos.h, level0.h

```c
int s_fputc(SIO *siop, FAST c)
{
    register struct soctl_ *op;         /* saves lots of indexing time   */
    static int  i, txflag;
    txflag = TRUE;
    op = siop->s _octl;
    op->flushflag = FALSE;
    if (op->rawflag)                    /* -- RAW: XMIT --    */
        {
        s_putc(siop, c);
        return 0;
        }
    if (op->asciiflag)                  /* -- RESET BIT 7 --  */
        c = (BYTE) toascii(c);
```

continues

Listing 17.5. continued

```
if (tx_flowstat(siop) == FLOW_OFF)           /* macro */
    for (EVER)                               /* paused awaiting release or abort */
        {
        if (s_keybort(siop))
            return KEY_CAN;
        if (tx_flowstat(siop) == FLOW_ON)  /* macro */
            break;
        }

if (op->filterflag)                          /* -- TRANSLATE/REMOVE BYTE --   */
    {
    for (i = op->numfc-1; i >= 0 ; i--)
        if ((int) c == op->filtlist[i][0])
            {
            if (op->filtlist[i][1] == -1)          /* remove        */
                txflag = FALSE;
            else
                c = op->filtlist[i][1];            /* translate     */
            break;
            }
    }
if (iscntrl(c) && txflag)                /*  -- REMOVE CONTROLS --        */
    {
    if (op->cntrlflag)
        {
        txflag = FALSE;
        for (i = op->numcc-1; i >= 0 ; i--)
            if (c == (FAST)op->ok_cntrls[i]) /* loop through list */
                {
                txflag = TRUE;                     /* if on list      */
                break;
                }
        }
    if (txflag)                          /* -- END OF LINE TRANSLATION -- */
        {
        switch (op->eolmode)
            {
            case NOXLAT:                         /*    no conversion   */
                break;
            case LF2CR:                          /*      lf->cr        */
                if (c == LF)
                    {
                    s_eputc(siop, op->lastc == CR ? LF : CR);
                    txflag = FALSE;
                    }
                break;
            case CR2LF:                          /*       cr->lf       */
                if (c == CR)
                    {
                    txflag = FALSE;
                    op->flushflag = TRUE;
                    break;
```

```
                    }
            if (op->lastc == CR)
                s_eputc (siop, c == LF ? CR : LF);
        break;
    case EOL2SPACE:         /* cr and lf converted to spaces */
        if (c == CR |¦ c == LF)      /* crlf = one space    */
            {
            txflag = FALSE;
            if (c != LF && op->lastc != CR)
                s_eputc(siop, SP);
            }
        break;
    case REMOVEEOL:         /* cr and lf not transmitted    */
        if (c == CR |¦ c == LF)
            txflag = FALSE;
        break;
    case LF2CRLF:                   /* lf -> crlf            */
        if (c == LF && op->lastc != CR)
            s_eputc(siop, CR);
        break;
    case CR2CRLF:                   /*  cr->crlf            */
        if (c == CR)                /* wait for next byte   */
            {
            txflag = FALSE;
            op->flushflag = TRUE;
            }
        if (op->lastc == CR)
            {
            s_eputc(siop, CR);
            if (c != LF)
                s_eputc(siop, LF);
            }
        break;
    case CRLF2LF:                   /*      crlf -> lf       */
        if ( c == CR)
            {
            txflag = FALSE;
            op->flushflag = TRUE;
            break;
            }
        if (op->lastc == CR && c != LF)
            s_eputc(siop, CR);
        break;
    case CRLF2CR:                   /*      crlf -> cr       */
        if (op->lastc == CR && c == LF)
            txflag = FALSE;
        break;
    default:
        break;
    }                       /* end of end-of-line switch    */
}
}
```

continues

Listing 17.5. continued

```
    if (txflag)
        {                                           /* -- FLOW CONTROL --  */
        switch (op->casemode)                       /* -- CONVERT CASE --  */
            {
            case UP_LOW:
                break;
            case UPPER:
                c = toupper(c);
                break;
            case LOWER:
                c = tolower(c);
                break;
            }
        if ( op->ib_dlyflag)                 /* -- INTERBYTE, -LINE DELAYS -- */
            __delay(op->ib_dly);
        s_eputc(siop, c);              /* xmit with optional console output */
        if (op->wechoflag)                     /* -- WAIT FOR REMOTE ECHO --  */
            if (__s_waitch(siop, op->wecho_dly) == TIMEOUT)
                return NOECHO;
        if (op->il_dlyflag && (BOOL)(c == op->il_dlyc))
            __delay(op->il_dly);                     /* end of line delay   */
        }
    op->lastc = c;                               /* save this character */
    return 0;
}
```

Speed Considerations

The matter of speed is important to serial I/O. Often the speed performance of a function can be substantially improved merely by paying close attention to how data objects are represented and by anticipating how the compiler regards certain kinds of C operations.

POINTER EFFICIENCY

By now you should be convinced of the value of the general idea of accessing all data and functions through a pointer to an all-encompassing SIO. Although structures and pointers to structures provide great conceptual power, they also incur a heavy burden of CPU over-head in the form of indirect addressing and indexing. In other words, code generated from multiple layers of structures and pointers is slow and cumbersome. In s_fputc, we allevi-ate this problem somewhat by using a local pointer (op) to a s_octl structure instead of our usual siop->s_octl. Thus relieved of one index and one indirect (pointer) operation, the code runs faster and, an added bonus, is easier to read and understand.

STORAGE CLASS

Since op is addressed so frequently, a further (and marked) speed improvement can be achieved by declaring op to be a register variable, thus obviating a memory access at each mention. A similar, though less dramatic speed improvement may be obtained by declaring often-used variables to be static instead of automatic. Why? Virtually all C compilers create automatic variables on the stack, then refer to them with indirect indexed addressing. This form of addressing is more burdensome on some processors than others, but it is particularly onerous on the Intel 8086 family. Consider the following fragment of 8086 code:

```
int fnc()
{
    int x = 5;
    .
    .
    .
}
```

On the 8086, the code generated by this simple use of auto variables is:

```
fnc:
    push bp                 ; save frame pointer
    mov  bp,sp              ; move stack to frame pointer
    add  sp, 2              ; allocate stack space for variable 'a'
    mov  word ptr -2[bp],5 ; initialize 'a' with 5
```

```
Compare this to the same code but using a static variable for x:
int fn()
    {
    static int x;
    x = 5;
    .
    .
    .
```

which produces the following assembly code:

```
fnc:
mov        word ptr a_,5
```

It doesn't require a great understanding of microprocessor architecture and assembly language to guess which code runs faster. Because indexed addressing is inherently more time consuming than simple indirect addressing, this example is not intended to single out the 8086 for ridicule, rather to show how performance can often be increased dramatically simply by paying attention to details and "reading between the lines" of code. This discussion is carried even further in Chapter 18, which deals with the subject of formatted *input* where speed is relatively more critical.

An Overview of *s_fputc*

If `rawflg == TRUE` upon entry to s_fputc, the byte is transmitted immediately and the function returns. Beyond this, the basic structure of s_fputc centers around deciding whether a byte should be transmitted. The following pseudo-code illustrates how this decision is made.

```
s_fputc(siop, c)
{
        if (raw)
            transmit c;
            return(0);
        if (c is in remove/translate list)
            txflag = FALSE;
        if (c is a control character)
            if (c is not in control character list)
                txflag = FALSE;
        if (c is CR or LF and eolmode is relevant)
            txflag = FALSE;
    if (txflag == TRUE)
        various processing: flow control, delays, uppercase, etc.
        transmit c;
    lastc = c;
    return(0);
}
```

As the highlighted portion shows, a character is marked for removal by setting `txflag` to FALSE. There are three conditions under which a byte is not transmitted:

- If it is marked for removal on `filtlist`
- If it is a control character and *not* on the list `ok_cntrls`
- If it is a CR or LF and end-of-line processing is in effect

These conditions assume that the respective functions are enabled—for example, `cntrlflg == TRUE`.

If the byte is not transmitted (i.e., `txflag` is TRUE), it is immediately stored in the single-character buffer, `lastc`. If, on the other hand, the byte is OK to transmit, it undergoes additional processing—flow control management, interbyte and interline delays, case conversion, and so forth. Transmitted bytes are also stored in `lastc`.

When seen in this context, s_fputc is actually quite straightforward, submitting quite humbly to a piece-by-piece analysis.

"Raw" Mode

The first test applied is whether to perform any processing at all:

```
if (ip->rawflg)
    {
    s_putc(siop, c);
```

```
        return (0);
    }
op->flushflg = FALSE;
```

If rawflg is TRUE, the byte is immediately transmitted and a 0 is returned to signify success. In order to speed up processing, both local variables are declared to be in the regis-ter class. If raw mode is not enabled, the buffer manager flag flushflg is cleared and the test for high-byte clearing is performed immediately so that subsequent byte comparisons that differ only in bit 7 produce correct results.

```
if (op->asciiflg)
    c = toascii(c);
```

For example, word processors often use the high bits of characters for special purposes. Carriage returns in a file thus processed are 8DH (instead of 0DH) and pass unrecognized through the end-of-line processing.

Translation/Removal of Bytes

The ability to translate bytes is often a life-saving feature. It makes possible conversion of a few characters to compensate for a keyboard with a non-ASCII character set, conversion from one word processor's codes to another's, or even conversion between entire character sets (ASCII to EBCDIC, for example).

The ability to strip selected bytes during transmission can also be a boon to the receiver, removing certain characters that might disrupt the screen, printer, or operating system.

Let's assume that the soctl_ structure is initialized like this:

```
struct soctl_octlA =
    {
    FALSE,                  /*0  perform no processing at all     */
    .
    .

    .
    7,                      /*12 number of controls in ok_cntrls  */
    FALSE,                  /*13 filter-remove characters flag     */
    {                       /*14 list of bytes to remove or filter */
     {'#', '-'},            /* translation table in from-to format */
     {0x7F, -1}
    },
    2,                      /*15 number of bytes in filter list    */
    .
    .
    .

    0.5                     /*23 an end-of-line decision pending    */
    };
```

Element 0, {'#', '-'} *replaces* all occurrences of nanograms with hypens. Element 1 *removes* all occurrences of DEL (7FH). Let's see how these work:

```
if (op->filterflg)                          /* TRANSLATE/REMOVE BYTE   */
    {
    for ( i = op->numfc-1; i >=0; i--)
        if (c == op->filtlist[i][0])
            {
            if (op->filtlist[i][1] == -1)  /* remove      */
                txflag = FALSE;
            else
                c = op->filtlist[i][1];   /* translate */
            break;
            }
    }
```

If `filterflg` is TRUE, the number of elements in the two-dimensional array becomes the counter in a `for` loop that compares the byte-under-test to the byte in column 0. If a match is found, column 1 is examined. If column 1 contains a –1, the byte-under-test is marked for removal by setting `txflag` and the loop breaks. If column 1 is not –1, however, the byte in column 1 is assigned to the byte-under-test and the loop breaks.

The next two tests—for control character removal and end-of-line translation—are performed only if the byte-under-test is a control character.

Control Character Removal

The list of control characters, `ok_cntrls`, is an *inclusive* list—if the byte-under-test is *not* on this list, it is removed. If this seems backwards, or if it seems to duplicate the general ability to remove/translate bytes, consider how this function is used. In the majority of situations where control characters must be removed, the list of unwanted characters is much longer than the list of wanted ones. For example, the only control characters permitted in ASCII "plain text" are the Format Effectors BEL, BS, HT, LF, VT, FF, and CR. It is obviously simpler and much faster to search an 8-byte list for acceptable characters than to search a 24-byte list for characters to exclude.

```
if (iscntrl(c) && txflag)                   /* REMOVE CONTROLS     */
    {
    if (op->cntrlflg)
        {
        txflag = FALSE;
        for ( i = op->numcc-1; i >=0; i--)
            if (c == op->ok_cntrls[i])  /* loop through list */
                {
                txflag = TRUE;          /* if on list */
                break;
                }
        }
    if (txflag)                      /* END-OF-LINE TRANSLATION  */
```

Before entering the test, `txflag` is made FALSE, and is set to TRUE *only* if the control character-under-test is in the `ok_cntrls` array. The number of elements in the array becomes the counter in a `for` loop that compares the byte-under-test to each element in the array. If a match is found, `txflag` is made TRUE; otherwise, the loop expires with `txflag` FALSE and transmission is prevented.

End-of-Line Conversion

Still within the large `if ( c == iscntrl())`, the next test is for end-of-line conversion:

```
if (iscntrl(c) && txflag)                /* REMOVE CONTROLS     */
    {
    if (op->cntrlflg)
        {
    if (txflag)                 /* END-OF-LINE TRANSLATION      */
        {
        switch (op->eolmode)
            {
            case NOXLAT:            /*    no conversion     */
                break;
            case LF2CR:             /*      lf->cr          */
                if (c == LF)
```

Problems with end-of-line conventions are a source of endless grief and frustration. It is always desirable to solve these problems during I/O rather than leaving the job to the user, who may not understand the nature of the problem. In general, five types of conversion are necessary. Follow the discussion of each while referring to the corresponding `case` statements in Listing 17.5. To understand some of the code, you must keep in mind that each character is retained in `lastc` after it is transmitted. Discussion of the `flushflg` member is postponed until later.

LF2CR AND CR2LF: ONE EOL CHARACTER TO ANOTHER

At first thought, these two conversions appear as simple substitutions. But substitution is not what we are about here; we wish to perform intelligent end-of-line processing. We will create a special case for CRLF to CR or LF, but this case must work only on *solitary* CRs and LFs while letting CRLF pairs pass unmodified.

In LF2CR, CR must not be substituted for LF if the previous byte was a CR (i.e., the first byte of a CRLF pair). In CR2LF, the decision to convert CR to LF must be postponed until we find out if the next byte is an LF. Therefore `txflag` is made TRUE and the CR is not transmitted. If the next byte-under-test is an LF, no conversion is made: the buffered CR is output and `txflag` is not set, permitting the LF (byte-under-test) to be transmitted normally. If the byte-under-test is *not* an LF, an LF is transmitted, `txflag` is not set, and the byte-under-test is transmitted normally.

EOL2SPACE: CONVERSION OF EOL CHARACTERS TO SPACES

This is substitution of an SP (ASCII 20H) for either a CR or LF. This is a useful feature when transferring text to typesetting machines that add newlines dynamically. Spaces must be added to prevent concatenation of the word at the end of one line to the word at the beginning of the next. To prevent the converting of CRLF to two spaces, a one-character look-back controls the output of the SP.

REMOVEEOL: REMOVAL OF CR AND LF

Although it is rare, text totally devoid of EOL markings is sometimes needed—for example, in art departments during the paste-up phase of production. Here CR and LF are unconditionally removed by making `txflag` TRUE.

ONE EOL CHARACTER TO A CRLF PAIR: LF OR CR TO CRLF

These conversions use the same criteria as LF2CR and CR2LF, just explained.

Processing of Transmitted Bytes

If `txflag` has not been made FALSE by the preceding processing, the byte-under-test is output after undergoing a series of tests and manipulations, the code for most of which is obvious and requires only a little explanation.

FLOW CONTROL

The code to support flow control comes first. Recall that the `flow_wanted` variable in the SIO describes the type of flow control, if any, in effect. Before transmitting a byte, a call is made to the function `tx_flowstat`, which returns the constant `FLOW_OFF` if it is necessary to cease transmssion. The function `tx_flowstat` is a macro in *SIOCTL.H* that actually calls a function pointer of the same name in the SIO.

Detection of a flow control request causes entry into a loop awaiting the reception of a "release," or `FLOW_ON` request. If this request never arrives, there must be some means to break out of the pause loop. A timeout is impractical since the duration of a flow on/off cycle is often long and by definition unpredictable. This is provided by the `s_keybort` function shown in Listing 17.6. This function reads standard input and compares its value (–1 if no byte is ready) to the `soctl_` member, `kbortc`. The result of the comparison is returned.

**Listing 17.6. The s_keybort function
detects whether the abort key has been typed.**

FUNCTION NAME:	s_keybort
LEVEL:	3
PROTOTYPE IN:	SIODEF.H
LIBRARY:	SIO.LIB
DESCRIPTION:	Checks the keyboard to see if the designated abort key has been typed.
RETURNS:	BOOL: TRUE if the abort key was pressed otherwise FALSE.
COMMENTS:	The abort key is defined by the kbortc member of the soctl_ structure. This function can be replaced with the following macro:
	#define s_keybort(p) inkey() == (p)->s_octl->kbortc
INCLUDE FILES:	siodef.h, key.h

```
BOOL s_keybort(SIO *siop)
{
    return (BOOL) (inkey() == (int)siop->s_octl->kbortc);
}
```

CASE CONVERSION

After flow control processing, bytes are converted to upper or lower case (or neither) depending upon the value of casemode.

ECHOES, WAITS, AND DELAYS

At long last, the byte-under-test is ready to be transmitted. Because output is performed from several locations in the code and console output may also be required, all SIO output is made via the local function s_eputc, shown in Listing 17.7.

Listing 17.7. The s_eputc subfunction provides SIO and console output.

FUNCTION NAME:	s_eputc
PROTOTYPE IN:	BUOS.H
LEVEL:	2
LIBRARY:	BUOS.LIB

continues

Listing 17.7. continued

DESCRIPTION:	Output byte to the SIO and, if `consflag` set, to standard output.
RETURNS:	`void`
COMMENTS:	Declared `static`—i.e., local to this file.

```
static void s_eputc(SIO *siop, int c)
{
    s_putc(siop, c);
    if (siop->s_octl->consflag)              /* echo to standard out    */
        putchar(c);
}
```

An explanation of *s_eputc*—This function simply outputs the byte to the SIO, then, based upon the value of `consflg`, sends the byte to standard output.

If the echo-wait mode is enabled, a loop is entered waiting for any received character. No check is made to ascertain if the byte received matches the one transmitted. If no byte arrives in `wecho_dly` seconds, the function ends by returning the constant `NOECHO`, defined in *SIODEF.H*.

Finally come the two programmed delays, one for each byte and one for each line. With all processing steps now complete, the function returns a 0.

Level-3 Functions for Formatted I/O

The level-2 function `s_fputc` provides the tools to write a wealth of interesting and useful level-3 functions. Listing 17.8 shows `s_fputs`, our version of the standard library function `puts`.

Listing 17.8. Use of s_fputs for formatted string output.

FUNCTION NAME:	`s_fputs`
LEVEL:	3
PROTOTYPE IN:	SIODEF.H
LIBRARY:	SIO.LIB
DESCRIPTION:	Output string to SIO under control of the `soctl_` structure.
RETURNS:	`void`
COMMENTS:	The local function `s_fflush` clears `s_fputc`'s single-character buffer.
INCLUDE FILES:	stdio.h, siodef.h, buos.h

```
static void s_fflush(SIO *siop)
{
    if (siop->s_octl->flushflag &&  !siop->s_octl->rawflag)
        s_fputc(siop, siop->s_octl->lastc);
}

void s_fputs(SIO *siop, char *str)
{
    while (*str != '\0')
        s_fputc(siop, *str++);
    s_fflush(siop);
    if (siop->s_octl->consflag == TRUE)
        putchar('\n');
}
```

An explanation of s_fputs—The code for s_fputs is simple and predictable. Of rather more interest is the local function s_fflush. To understand why it is necessary, assume that s_fputs (with CRLF2LF processing in effect) is used to transmit a file containing CRLFs. If that file happens to end with a single CR (a not-uncommon end-of-text marker among editors), the final CR is held in the single-character buffer lastc. Return now to Listing 17.5 and notice that flushflg is always made FALSE at the beginning of s_fputc and is made TRUE *only* when a byte is placed in lastc. Therefore, flushflg serves as a kind of "dirty flag" to signal that an untransmitted byte is pending in the buffer.

Stripped-Down String Output

Despite the power and convenience of the "formatting" functions, there are some situations where speed of transmission is the sole criterion. In these cases, especially at higher baud rates, s_puts might provide a slight speed advantage over s_fputs in the rawflg mode. Listing 17.9 shows s_puts. Using s_putc, our most basic means for SIO output, this simple function outputs successive bytes from the pointed-to string until a NUL byte is reached.

Listing 17.9. The s_puts functions provides unformatted string output.

FUNCTION NAME:	s_puts
LEVEL:	3
PROTOTYPE IN:	SIODEF.H
LIBRARY:	SIO.LIB
DESCRIPTION:	Transmit string from SIO without control through the soctl_ structure.
RETURNS:	void
INCLUDE FILES:	siodef.h, buos.h

continues

Listing 17.9. continued

```
void s_puts(SIO *siop, char *str)
{
    while (*str != '\0')
        s_putc(siop, *str++);
}
```

Functions to Manipulate soctl_ Members

To take advantage of the powerful output control system we have just developed, we need a way to manipulate the soctl_ members conveniently. As it now stands, however, changing the contents of an SIO's soctl_ structure is cumbersome to say the least. The simplest approach is to create a separate function to read and write each of the structure members— setraw(siop, ON), setibdly(siop, 0_SEC_1), and so forth. As you can imagine, writing a function for every member of a structure quickly becomes tedious and is certainly inefficient. A more sensible and compact approach is to create a single general function to manipulate the structure members. When composing this function, however, you need the constants shown in Listing 17.10 in your *SIOCTL.H* file. For completeness, Listing 17.10 also shows the constant definitions required in the next chapter.

Listing 17.10. Constant definitions for use in output and input control functions.

```
/* FUNCTION ARGUMENTS FOR USE WITH I/O CONTROL FUNCTIONS */
#define   SET       0
#define   GET       1

/* CONTROL ARGUMENTS FOR USE WITH I/O CONTROL FUNCTIONS    */
enum ctlargs
      {              /**            FLAGS                 **/
      RAWFLAG = 0,   /*    Minimum processing              */
      T_OUTFLAG,     /*    Used for formatted input only    */
      EKOBAKFLAG,    /*    Used for formatted input only    */
      WECHOFLAG,     /*    Wait-for-echo flag               */
      CONSFLAG,      /*    Console   output flag            */
      ASCIIFLAG,     /*    Remove high bit flag (&0x7f)     */
      CNTRLFLAG,     /*    Remove selected controls flag    */
      FILTERFLAG,    /*    Filter unwanted charcters flag   */
      IB_DLYFLAG,    /*    Interbyte delay flag (output only) */
      IL_DLYFLAG ,   /*    Interline delay flag (output only) */
                     /**            DELAYS                 **/
      WECHO_DLY,     /*    Echo-wait delay (in tsecs)       */
      IB_DLY,        /*    Interbyte delay (in tsecs)       */
      IL_DLY,        /*    Interline delay (in tsecs)       */
      T_OUT,         /*    Timeout   on input only (in tsecs) */
                     /**              MODES                **/
```

```
        EOLMODE,      /*   End-of-line mode argument          */
        CASEMODE,     /*   Upper/lower mode argument          */
        XXMODE,       /*   Xoff mode argument                 */
                      /**        DEFINED CHARACTERS          **/
        XOFFC,        /*   Character defined as XOFF          */
        XONC,         /*   Character defined as XON           */
        IL_DLYC,      /*   Character to trigger interline delay */
        KBORTC,       /*   Keyboard abort character           */
        };
```

For ease of design, our new function, s_ocntrl, will address only the *integral* data types in the structures—the ints and chars. It will be left to the reader's imagination to develop functions for manipulating the arrays.

We will design the function to set or fetch the structure members, depending upon a "mode" (SET or GET) passed in the argument list. The complete s_ocntrl is shown in Listing 17.11.

Listing 17.11. The s_ocntrl function: a level-3 function to change the contents of an soctl_ structure.

FUNCTION NAME:	s_ocntrl
LEVEL:	3
PROTOTYPE IN:	SIODEF.H
LIBRARY:	SIO.LIB
DESCRIPTION:	Sets or fetches the value of the soctl_ output control structure.
RETURNS:	int. SET: 0 if successful, otherwise, -1; GET: -1 if unsuccessful.
COMMENTS:	Constants are in SIOCTL.H. The range of the 'code' arguments is not checked.
INCLUDE FILES:	siodef.h, sioctl.h

```
int s_ocntrl(SIO *siop, short mode, short  whichone, USHORT newval)
{
    int retval  = 0;
    if ( mode == SET)
        switch (whichone)
            {
            case RAWFLAG:   siop->s_octl->rawflag   = newval; break;
            case EOLMODE:   siop->s_octl->eolmode   = newval; break;
            case CONSFLAG:  siop->s_octl->consflag  = newval; break;
            case WECHOFLAG: siop->s_octl->wechoflag = newval; break;
            case WECHO_DLY: siop->s_octl->wecho_dly = newval; break;
            case CASEMODE:  siop->s_octl->casemode  = newval; break;
            case XOFFC:     siop->s_octl->xoffc     = newval; break;
            case XONC:      siop->s_octl->xonc      = newval; break;
            case XXMODE:    siop->s_octl->xxmode    = newval; break;
```

continues

Listing 17.11. continued

```
                case ASCIIFLAG:  siop->s_octl->asciiflag  = newval; break;
                case CNTRLFLAG:  siop->s_octl->cntrlflag  = newval; break;
                case FILTERFLAG: siop->s_octl->filterflag = newval; break;
                case IB_DLYFLAG: siop->s_octl->ib_dlyflag = newval; break;
                case IB_DLY:     siop->s_octl->ib_dly     = newval; break;
                case IL_DLYFLAG: siop->s_octl->il_dlyflag = newval; break;
                case IL_DLY:     siop->s_octl->il_dly     = newval; break;
                case IL_DLYC:    siop->s_octl->il_dlyc    = (FAST)newval; break;
                case KBORTC:     siop->s_octl->kbortc     = (FAST)newval; break;
                default:
                    retval = -1;
                    break;
            }
        else if (mode == GET)
            switch (whichone)
                {
                case RAWFLAG:    retval = (int)siop->s_octl->rawflag    ; break;
                case EOLMODE:    retval = siop->s_octl->eolmode         ; break;
                case CONSFLAG:   retval = (int)siop->s_octl->consflag   ; break;
                case WECHOFLAG:  retval = (int)siop->s_octl->wechoflag  ; break;
                case WECHO_DLY:  retval = siop->s_octl->wecho_dly       ; break;
                case CASEMODE:   retval = siop->s_octl->casemode        ; break;
                case XOFFC:      retval = siop->s_octl->xoffc           ; break;
                case XONC:       retval = siop->s_octl->xonc            ; break;
                case XXMODE:     retval = siop->s_octl->xxmode          ; break;
                case ASCIIFLAG:  retval = (int)siop->s_octl->asciiflag  ; break;
                case CNTRLFLAG:  retval = (int)siop->s_octl->cntrlflag  ; break;
                case FILTERFLAG: retval = (int)siop->s_octl->filterflag ; break;
                case IB_DLYFLAG: retval = (int)siop->s_octl->ib_dlyflag ; break;
                case IB_DLY:     retval = siop->s_octl->ib_dly          ; break;
                case IL_DLYFLAG: retval = (int)siop->s_octl->il_dlyflag ; break;
                case IL_DLY:     retval = siop->s_octl->il_dly          ; break;
                case IL_DLYC:    retval = siop->s_octl->il_dlyc         ; break;
                case KBORTC:     retval = siop->s_octl->kbortc          ; break;
                default:
                    retval = -1;
                    break;
                }
        return retval;
}
```

An explanation of s_ocntrl—There are no surprises here. It is important to note, however, that because of the if...else if expression, the function accepts only the SET or GET mode arguments. The desired member in the argument list is then applied to a switch that, based upon the SET/GET mode arguments, either sets the desired member to the new value passed in the argument list, or returns that member's current value. A single local variable, retval, serves double duty: it returns the current value of a member in the GET mode or an error code of –1 if an illegal function or member argument is accidentally passed in either mode. The constants shown in Listing 17.1 can be used in function calls to identify the soctl_ members.

The greatest virtue of this function is its simplicity and, because of liberal use of manifest constants, its clarity. Our next topic contains copious examples of how s_ocntrl is used.

Temporary Storage for Output Control Structures

Frequently we wish to alter two or three members of the SIO's output control structure upon entry to a function and to restore them to their original values upon exit. This can be accomplished by manually storing each structure member in a temporary variable for the duration of the call, then restoring them before terminating. An easier method is to save and restore a copy of the *entire* structure:

```
funct(siop)
SIO siop;
{
    struct soctl_ tmpctl;
    tmpctl = *siop->s_octl;       /* save structure */
    s_ocntrl(siop, SET, IB_DLYFLAG, OFF);
    s_ocntrl(siop, SET, IL_DLYFLAG, ON);
    s_ocntrl(siop, SET, CONSFLAG, ON);
    .
    .
    .

    *siop->s_octl = tmpctl;      /* restore structure */
}
```

Although this is quite acceptable, it is tiresome to write the same preamble repeatedly. A better solution is to write complementary functions to save and restore copies of structures automatically. These functions, s_opush and s_opop, are shown in Listing 17.12.

Listing 17.12. The s_opush and s_opop functions: temporary storage and restoration for output control structures.

FUNCTION NAME:	s_opush, s_opop
LEVEL:	3
PROTOTYPE IN:	SIODEF.H
LIBRARY:	SIO.LIB
DESCRIPTION:	Save and restore s_octl structures on local stack.
RETURNS:	int: 0 if stack operation was successful; otherwise 1.
COMMENTS:	Both functions check for balance of the local stack, so take care that every "push" is balanced with a corresponding "pop."
INCLUDE FILES:	stdio.h, stdlib.h, sioctl.h, siodef.h

```
static struct soctl_ *ostack[IO_STKSIZ] = {NIL}; /* init 1st element to NIL */
static struct soctl_ **ostackp = ostack;   /* pointer to top of stack      */
```

continues

Listing 17.12. continued

```
int s_opush(SIO *siop)
{
    if (ostackp >= &ostack[IO_STKSIZ])   /* check for end of array       */
        {
        puts("\aOstack overflow.");
        return 1;
        }
    *ostackp = (struct soctl_ *)malloc(sizeof(struct soctl_)); /* get mem */
    if (*ostackp == NIL)                 /* out of memory                */
        return 1;
    **ostackp = *siop->s_octl;           /* make copy in allocated memory */
    ++ostackp;                           /* point to next slot           */
    return 0;
}

int s_opop(SIO *siop)
{
    if (ostackp <= ostack)               /* don't let stack become unbalanced */
        {
        puts("\aIstack underflow.");
        return 1;
        }
    --ostackp;                           /* point at first active element */
    *siop->s_octl = **ostackp;           /* restore old structure from stack */
    free((VOID*) *ostackp);              /* release allocated memory     */
    return 0;
}
```

An explanation of s_opush and s_opop —These two commands work in concert like as-sembly language PUSH and POP instructions. Calling s_opush saves the SIO's output struc-ture on a local stack and s_opop restores it. The design of this system is quite simple: ostack is the stack (an array of pointers to octl_ structures), and ostackp is a pointer into the stack.

Calling s_opush results in the following:

1. A pointer to storage for an ioctl structure is malloced and saved in the stack element pointed to by ostackp.
2. The SIO's output control structure is copied into the reserved storage.
3. The stack pointer is incremented to point at the next element.

An error code is returned if the stack is already full or if the requested memory is not avail-able.

Calling s_opop results in the following:

1. The SIO's output control structure is restored from the address contained in the stack element pointed to by the stack pointer ostackp.

2. The memory allocated for temporary storage is released.

3. The stack pointer is decremented.

These functions must be used with some caution. Remember, for every s_opush, there must be a corresponding s_opop. Failure to observe this rule causes the restoration of the incorrect structures and inevitably leads to stack overflow or underflow. For example, the following code eventually leads to unexpected results when the first return is taken:

```
funct(SIO*siop, int x)
{
    s_opush(siop);
    if (x == 1)
        return (0);
    BODY OF CODE HERE
    s_opop(siop);
    return (0);
}
```

The following coding style, however, insures that the stack is automatically balanced before return:

```
funct(SIO*siop, int x)
{
    int retval = 1;
    s_opush(siop);
    if (x == 1)
        retval = 1;
    else
        retval = 0;
    if (retval)
        {
        BODY OF CODE HERE
        }
    s_opop(siop);
    return (retval);
}
```

Here the balancing s_opop is always executed.

A second caution in the use of these functions centers around the issue of speed. Although innocent-looking enough, the statements

```
*siop->s_octl = **ostackp;
**ostackp = *siop->s_octl;
```

actually copy the *entire* structure from one memory location to another. While many processors have fast block move instructions to make copying more efficient, it *does* steal processor time. Since using these functions within time-sensitive loops seriously compromises performance, s_opush and s_opop are most useful when employed as prologues and epilogues to a function.

Let's now apply our newly developed standard output library functions to an important enhancement to the terminal program, TERM.

TERM4

Data exchange between computers has always been an important province of serial I/O, because the serial port—including the RS-232 interface—is a "portable" medium. Disk and tape formats may vary but virtually every serial device manufactured recognizes and supports the START/STOP method of serial communication.

In Chapter 3 we discussed the ugly fates that can befall a byte during transmission over a serial link. We also pointed out that, because of this unreliability, an "unsupervised" transmission (i.e., without protocol or error checking) of *binary* files is exceedingly risky. With most text files, the risk is worth taking because the errors sustained during transmission are easily spotted and, at least in the cosmic scheme of things, relatively inconsequential. In situations of high incompatibility, unsupervised character-by-character transmission of text files may indeed be the only means of communication available. We will now add the ability to upload text files to TERM. We will add supervised file transfers to our terminal program in a later chapter. Listing 17.13 shows the changes in the previous version of TERM. The main module is unchanged.

Listing 17.13. Changes in TERM3 to produce TERM4. Incidental changes are highlighted.

```
PROGRAM NAME:    TERM4
 DESCRIPTION:    Terminal program.
    COMMENTS:    New Features: file upload with flow control.

#define MENU        CTRL_A              /* key for command summary     */
#define FORMAT      'A'                 /* Setup serial parmeters      */
#define RS_232      'B'                 /* RS-232 output control        */
#define BRAKE       'C'                 /* send BREAK signal           */
#define UPLOAD      'D'                 /* transmit file               */
#define EXIT        'Q'                 /* key to exit from term       */

int vers = 4;                           /* version number (global)     */


int menu(siop)                          /* menu now gets SIO pointer   */
SIO *siop;
{
    int c;
    int retval = 0;
    static char *menus[] =
        {
        "\tA.  Data Format, Baud rate",
        "\tB.  RS-232 control",
```

```
            "\tC.  Transmit BREAK signal",
            "\tD.  Upload Text File",
            "\tQ.  EXIT",
            ""                              /* NUL string terminates list    */
            };
            .
            .
            .
                case BRAKE:                 /* send BREAK                     */
                    set232(siop, BRK, ON);
                    break;
                case UPLOAD:                /* transmit a disk file           */
                    upload(siop);
                    break;
            .
            .
            .

                default:
            .
            .
            .

}

void term(siop)
SIO *siop;
{
    int c;                              /* must be int to detect -1 return */
    s_icntrl(siop, SET, CONSFLAG, ON); /* console echo on formatted input */
    s_ocntrl(siop, SET, IB_DLYFLAG, OFF);  /* interbyte delay */
    printf("TERM, Version %d:  Press Control-%c for a summary of commands\n", \
        vers, MENU + '@');
    for (EVER)                          /* eternal loop                    */
        {
        if ( (c = s_inchar(siop)) != NOT_READY)    /* check SIO for byte */
            putchar(c);
        if ( (c = inkey()) != NOT_READY)           /* if a key is pressed */
            if (c == MENU)
                {
                if (menu(siop))
                    break;              /* if menu returns non-zero        */
                }
            else
                s_fputc(siop, c);
        }
}

main(argc, argv)
int argc;
char *argv[];
{
/*      UNCHANGED FROM TERM3        */
}
```

continues

Listing 17.13. continued

FUNCTION NAME:	upload
LEVEL:	3
PROTOTYPE IN:	TERM.H
LIBRARY:	TERMFUNC.LIB
DESCRIPTION:	Function to transmit (upload) a file.
COMMENTS:	Flow control is supported.
INCLUDE FILES:	stdio.h, siodef.h, sioctl.h, misc.h, key.h, buos.h

```
void upload(SIO *siop)
{
    FILE *xmitfp;                 /* return type declarations      */
    char fnbuff[MAX_NAME_LEN];
    int c;
    int errflag = 0;
    putchar('\n');                          /* now open file, return *FILE   */
    if ( (xmitfp = rfopen("Name of file to upload", fnbuff)) == NIL)
        return;                             /* user terminated upload        */
    s_opush(siop);                          /* save output structure_        */
    s_ocntrl(siop, SET, CONSFLAG, ON); /* turn on console output        */
    while ( (c = getc(xmitfp)) != EOF) /* transmit the file             */
        {
        if (s_keybort(siop))                /* transfer aborted from keyboard? */
            break;
        s_fputc(siop, c);
        }
    putchar('\n');
    errflag = ferror(xmitfp);               /* see if getc ended with an error */
    if (errflag || fclose(xmitfp))     /* if read or close error        */
        printf("Error %s %s.\n\a", errflag ? "reading" : "closing", fnbuff);
    s_opop(siop);                           /* restore output control structure_ */
    puts("End of upload.\n\n-- Press any key to continue --");
    getkbch();
    puts("Exit upload.");
}
```

An explanation of TERM4—Aside from the miscellaneous changes to the summary menu and the version number, TERM4 contains one major change—in term itself, keyboard characters are transmitted with s_fputc instead of with s_putc. Now, the transmission of characters typed at the keyboard is governed by the SIO's soctl_ output control structure. The following lines, for example, make sure that no delays occur when keyboard characters are transmitted:

```
s_ocntrl(siop, SET, IB_DLYFLAG, OFF);
s_ocntrl(siop, SET, IL_DLYFLAG, OFF);
```

The most important addition to the term function, however, is the new UPLOAD case in the menu switch. In upload itself, a call to rfopen[1] asks the user for the name of the file for transmission; rfopen returns when the file is successfully fopened (or when the user answers the prompt by typing a solitary CR). Note that rfopen must be passed a pointer to a prompt string and a pointer to a filename buffer. Once a file is opened for reading, the SIO's output control structure is saved with

```
s_opush(siop);
```

With the "default" output control structure thus saved for later restoration, its transmission parameters can be altered by calls to s_ocntrl: console output, no interbyte delay, and a slight interline delay. The slight interline delay is necessary for some video terminals in order to give them time to perform a CRLF, which may require scrolling the entire screen up to make a blank line at the bottom of the screen. In addition, the slight interline delay gives the receiver a hiatus in which to process the contents of its input buffer. An interbyte delay can be added merely by changing the line

```
s_ocntrl(siop, SET, IB_DLYFLAG, OFF);
```

to

```
s_ocntrl(siop, SET, IB_DLYFLAG, ON);
```

Once the output file has been opened, the transmission of the file begins—bytes are fetched by getc and transmitted via s_fputc, governed by the values contained in the SIO's output control structure. Characters are echoed to the console during transmission. When end-of-file is encountered, the original output control structure is restored to the SIO, and the file is closed. If, during transmission of the file keybort discovers a termination request, the loop breaks and an orderly shutdown occurs. The test for errors in disk I/O is performed after the upload is complete instead of after each character. Flow control is totally transparent to the upload function because it is handled automatically in s_fputc.

Alternative Designs for *upload*

Two factors limit the speed with which upload can transfer data. The primary limitation is console output, which can be overcome simply by turning consflg off in the soctl_ structure. The second limitation, disk I/O, is actually not as bad as it seems. Although the code makes it look as if the disk read is performed byte-by-byte, remember that calling getc is tantamount to asking fread for a single byte. Thus, depending upon the system, C actually buffers disk I/O by several hundred bytes; the only significant delay occurs when C must actually fill the file's I/O buffer from disk. In Chapter 18, we will see how to overcome even this limitation by performing our own buffering.

---

[1]The source to this "Incidental" function is in Appendix C

Suggested Improvements

The initialization of the soctl_ is obviously overly conservative— only those control characters in the ok_cntrls_ are transmitted, and every byte is transmitted with its bit 7 reset to 0. Since most applications employ control characters and, to a lesser extent, the information in bit 7, this configuration is unlikely to prove satisfactory in the real world. TERM4, therefore, would benefit from a configuration function to customize the soctl_ structure's ok_cntrls and filtlist arrays. This is left for the reader as a programming project.

Conclusion

Control over serial output is only half the battle. In the next chapter we will apply much of the experience gained from writing s_fputc to the writing of a "formatted" input function, s_fgetc and its entourage of level-3 functions.

Formatted Input

In the previous chapter, we built a library of functions to format serial output. In this chapter, we will build a similar library for processing serial input. The plan is essentially the same: first we will compose a level-2 single-byte serial input routine, s_fgetc, whose behavior is governed by a structure pointer in the SIO. From this function, we will construct several level-3 functions to perform more complicated tasks such as string and line input. After presenting a short program to test the string input functions, we will add a remarkably simple function to our TERM program to permit the capture of incoming bytes into a RAM buffer and thence to a disk file.

A Formatted Input Function

In Chapter 17, we began a general discussion of how apparently inconsequential design decisions can greatly affect the performance of serial I/O functions. There we discussed how speed is but one of many performance parameters. In an output function, for instance, data is not jeopardized if it is transmitted slowly. In input functions, where we have no control over when bytes will arrive, speed is *the* critical performance parameter. Indeed, if an input function dawdles too long processing one inbound byte, the next byte may be missed. Due to the grave importance of speed in our input function, s_fgetc, we will apply all the design techniques discussed in the previous chapter plus a few new ones.

The *sictl_* Structure

Much can be foreseen about the design of s_fgetc simply by examining the structure that governs it. Most of the constants required for this chapter were given in the Listings in Chapter 17. Listing 18.1 shows the declaration of the sictl_ structure in SIOCTL.H

Listing 18.1. Declaration of the `sictl_` structure.

STRUCT NAME: `sictl_`
 HEADER FILE: SIOCTL.H
 DESCRIPTION: Control structure for formatted input.

```
struct sictl_
    {
    BOOL      t_outflag;       /*0  Timeout on/off flag           */
    unsigned  t_out;           /*1  Timeout period                */
    BOOL      rawflag;         /*2  Perform no processing at all  */
    BOOL      ekobakflag;      /*3  Echo all input back to sender */
    BOOL      asciiflag;       /*4  Reset strip bit 7             */
    short     eolmode;         /*5  End-of-line formatting        */
    BOOL      consflag;        /*6  Echo characters to console    */
    short     casemode;        /*7  Change to upper or lower case */
    BOOL      cntrlflag;       /*8  Remove control characters     */
    short     ok_cntrls[32];   /*9  Permitted control characters  */
    short     numcc;           /*10 Number of controls in ok_cntrls */
    BOOL      filterflag;      /*11 Filter-remove characters      */
    short     filtlist[128][2]; /*12 List of byte to remove or filter */
    short     numfc;           /*13 Number of bytes in filter list */
    FAST      lastc;           /*14 Previous byte output          */
    BOOL      rbakflag;        /*15 A pending eol decision resolved */
    FAST      rbakc;           /*16 Pending readback character    */
    };
```

Many of the structure members serve exactly the same functions as their counterparts in the `soctl_` output control structure; others have the same name but perform somewhat differently.

`t_outflg`	(0)	Enables s_fgetc's timeout input mode. When ON, s_fgetc waits t_out Tsecs for a byte to arrive; when OFF, it returns immediately if a byte is not available.
`rawflg`	(2)	Disables all byte processing and makes a call to s_fgetc equivalent to a call to s_inchar.
`ekobakflg`	(3)	When ON, a received byte is immediately retransmitted.
`asciiflg`	(4)	Compensates for parity errors or "normalizes" word-processed text files by clearing bit 7 of each transmitted byte.
`eolmode`	(5)	Determines the end-of-line translation according to the following constants (given in Listing 17.1).
`NOXLAT`		No end-of-line translation is performed.
`LF2CR`		Line Feed is replaced with Carriage Return.
`CR2LF`		Carriage Return is replaced with Line Feed.

EOL2SPACE		Carriage Return and Line Feed are replaced with spaces.
REMOVEEOL		Carriage Return and Line Feed are removed.
LF2CRLF		Line Feed is replaced with Carriage Return and Line Feed.
CR2CRLF		Carriage Return is replaced with Carriage Return and Line Feed.
CRLF2LF		Carriage Return and Line Feed are replaced with Line Feed.
CRLF2CR		Carriage Return and Line Feed are replaced with Carriage Return.
consflg	(6)	Outputs the byte not only to the SIO but also to standard output.
casemode	(7)	Translates bytes to upper or lowercase according to the following constants (given in Listing 17.1):
UP_LOW		No translation
UPPER		Convert to uppercase
LOWER		Convert to lowercase
cntrlflg	(10)	Enables control character removal. Because in practice the controls for exclusion usually outnumber those for inclusion, the list ok_cntrls contains a list of control characters *not* to be removed, and the *cardinal* number numcc contains the number of characters entered in this list.
filterflg	(13)	Enables byte translation and removal. The bytes in the first column of a 128-element two-dimensional array, filtlist, are translated to the corresponding bytes in the second column. This array is declared to be an array of int. If the byte in the second column is –1, the byte in column 1 is not transmitted. The number of bytes for translation is contained in numfc, a *cardinal* number.
lastc	(16)	A 1-byte scratch-pad buffer required during end-of-line conversion.
rbakflg	(17)	This "read-back" flag signals that the next byte is to be fetched from rbakc, below, instead of from the SIO. Used during end-of-line processing. (See "The Read-Back Mechanism," below.)
rbakc	(18)	During certain types of end-of-line processing, a CR is stored here pending receipt of the next character. (See "The Read-Back Mechanism," later in this chapter.)

Declaration and Initialization of an *sictl_* Structure

Listing 18.2 shows one possible declaration and initialization of an sictl_ structure.

Listing 18.2. Declaration and initialization of an input control structure.

OBJECT NAME:	sictl_ ictlA	
FILE:	IBMPC.C (level-0)	
COMMENTS:	Declares and initializes an input control structure. The numbering in the comments correspond to those in the sictl_ structure definition.	

```
struct sictl_  ictlA=
    {
    OFF,                            /* 0  Timeout-on-input flag         */
    _0_SEC_05,                      /* 1  Default timeout in Tsecs      */
    OFF,                            /* 2  "raw" input flag              */
    OFF,                            /* 3  Echo input back to sender flag */
    ON,                             /* 4  Reset high bit flag           */
    NOXLAT,                         /* 5  End-of-line mode              */
    OFF,                            /* 6  Console output flag           */
    UP_LOW,                         /* 7  Upper/lower case conversion mode */
    ON,                             /* 8  Remove unwanted controls flag */
{NUL,BEL,BS,HT,LF,CR,FF,DC3,DC1,DOS_EOF}, /* 9 permitted controls     */
    10,                             /*10  Number of controls in above list */
    OFF,                            /*11  Byte translation/removal mode */
    {{'a','x'},{'b', -1 }},         /*13  Translation/removal array     */
    2,                              /*14  Number of entries in above array */
    SUPPLIED,                       /*15  'last character' buffer       */
    SUPPLIED,                       /*16  Eol readback flag             */
    SUPPLIED                        /*17  Pending readback character    */
    };
```

An explanation of *sictl_ictlA*—The structure is initialized to common-sense values. First, t_outflg is OFF; that is, the function returns immediately if no byte is ready. The rawflg is disabled because most applications require some kind of input processing. The asciiflg, cntrlflg, and ok_cntrls members are enabled to convert incoming bytes to *ASCII Plain Text*. Notice that in addition to the usual Format Effectors (control characters), the DC1 and DC3 control characters are permitted. Any limitation on control characters, of course, precludes the use of "unraw" mode for reception of binary data.

Although oct1B, like ict1A in Chapter 17, is technically a level-3 object, it is probably a better idea to place it in the level-0, computer-specific file.

Additions to the *SIO* Structure

Listing 18.3 shows how the definition, declaration and initialization of the SIO is affected by the addition of the input control structure.

Listing 18.3. Changes in definition, declaration, and initialization of the SIO structure.

```
STRUCT DEF:    SIO
       FILE:   SIODEF.H
DESCRIPTION:   Master structure defining a serial port.
  COMMENTS:    Members supporting formatted input

struct sio
   {
   BYTE  * uart_base;      /*0  Base address of UART     */
   .
   .
   .
   struct soctl_    *s_octl; /*45 Pointer to output struct */
   struct sictl_    *s_ictl; /*46 Pointer to input  struct */
   };

   SIO NAME:   COM1sio
       FILE:   IBMPC.C
DESCRIPTION:   Initialization of the SIO's input control structure

SIO COM1sio  =
    {
    COM1,    /*0  base address of UART                */
    .
    .
    .
    &octlA, /*45 pointer to output control structure  */
    &ictlA, /*46 pointer input control structure      */
    };
```

An Overview of *s_fgetc*

Listing 18.4 shows s_fgetc, the level-2 function that will become the heart of all level-3 functions.

Listing 18.4. The s_fgetc function: a single-byte input function.

FUNCTION NAME:	s_fgetc
LEVEL:	2
PROTOTYPE IN:	BUOS.H
LIBRARY:	BUOS.LIB
DESCRIPTION:	Provides "formatted" character-by-character serial input according to the sictl_ structure pointed to by the SIO.
RETURNS:	int: TIMEOUT if t_outflag is TRUE and no byte arrives in t_out Tsecs; IGNORE if an EOL decision pending; otherwise the byte received.
COMMENTS:	Functions supported:

Switchable timeout mode	Raw mode
Control character filter	Character translation/filter
End of line conversion	Console output
High bit clearing	Upper/lowercase conversion
Echo-back to sender	

INCLUDE FILES:	stdio.h, ctype.h, siodef.h, sioctl.h, ascii.h, level0.h, buos.h

```c
int s_fgetc(SIO *siop)
{
    register struct sictl_ *ip;  /* registers and statics for speed */
    static int retbyte, i, c;
    static BOOL rxflag;
    if (siop->s_ictl->rawflag)   /* do raw processing asap          */
        return s_inchar(siop);
    ip = siop->s_ictl;           /* save lots of indexing time      */
    if (ip->rbakflag)            /* if byte pending                 */
        {
        ip->rbakflag = FALSE;
        if (ip->consflag)
            putchar(ip->rbakc);
        return ip->rbakc;
        }
    c = (ip->t_outflag) ? __s_waitch(siop, ip->t_out) : s_inchar(siop);
    if (c == TIMEOUT)
        return TIMEOUT;
    retbyte = -1;                /* postpone initialization         */
    rxflag  = TRUE;
    if (ip->ekobakflag)          /* -- ECHO TO SENDER --            */
        s_putc(siop, c);
    if (ip->asciiflag)           /* -- RESET BIT 7 --               */
        c = toascii(c);
    if (ip->filterflag)          /* -- TRANSLATE/REMOVE BYTE --     */
        {
        for ( i = ip->numfc-1; i >= 0 ; i--)
            if (c == ip->filtlist[i][0])
```

```
                       {
                       if (ip->filtlist[i][1] == -1)  /* remove       */
                           rxflag = FALSE;
                       else
                           c = ip->filtlist[i][1];  /* translate     */
                       break;
                       }
            }
    if (iscntrl(c) && rxflag)   /* -- REMOVE CONTROLS --        */
        {
        if (ip->cntrlflag)
            {
            rxflag = FALSE;
            for (i = ip->numcc-1; i >= 0 ; i--)
                if (c == ip->ok_cntrls[i]) /* loop through list */
                    {
                    rxflag = TRUE;  /* if on list             */
                    break;
                    }
            }
        }
    if (rxflag)                     /* -- END-OF-LINE TRANSLATION --   */
        {
        switch (ip->eolmode)
            {
            case NOXLAT:      /*     no conversion              */
                break;
            case LF2CR:       /*            lf->cr              */
                if (c == LF)
                    retbyte = CR;
                break;
            case CR2LF:       /*            cr->lf              */
                if ( c == CR)
                    retbyte = LF;
                break;
            case EOL2SPACE:   /* cr & lf converted to spaces    */
                if (c == CR || c == LF)  /*  crlf = one space  */
                    if (c != LF && ip->lastc != CR)
                        rxflag = FALSE;
                    else
                        retbyte = SP;
                break;
            case REMOVEEOL:   /*   cr and lf not transmitted     */
                if (c == CR || c == LF)
                    rxflag = FALSE;
                break;
            case LF2CRLF:     /*            lf -> crlf           */
                if (c == LF)
                    {
                    ip->rbakflag = TRUE;
                    ip->rbakc   = LF;
                    retbyte     = CR;
                    }
                break;
```

continues

Listing 18.4. continued

```
                    case CR2CRLF:      /*              cr->crlf               */
                         if (c == CR)
                             {
                             ip->rbakflag = TRUE;
                             ip->rbakc    = LF;
                             }
                         break;
                    case CRLF2LF:      /*              crlf -> lf             */
                         if ( c == CR && ip->lastc != CR)
                             rxflag = FALSE;                      else
                             retbyte = (ip->lastc == CR) ? LF : CR;
                         break;
                    case CRLF2CR:      /*              crlf -> cr             */
                         if ( c == CR && ip->lastc != CR)
                             rxflag = FALSE;
                         else
                             retbyte = CR;
                         break;
                    default:
                         break;
                    }                     /* end of end-of-line switch        */
              }
        if (rxflag)
            switch (ip->casemode)  /* -- CASE CONVERSION --              */
                {
                case UP_LOW:
                    break;
                case UPPER:
                    c = toupper(c);
                    break;
                case LOWER:
                    c = tolower(c);
                    break;
                }
        ip->lastc = c;                /*      save this character          */
        if (retbyte != -1)   /* if byte to return is not byte received */
            c = retbyte;
        if ( ip->consflag && rxflag)
            putchar(c);
        return (rxflag ? c : IGNORE);
}
```

An explanation of s_fgetc—If you understand how s_fputc in Chapter 17 works, you should have no difficulty with s_fgetc. For this reason identical sections—"raw" mode, ASCII (high-order byte) stripping, case conversion, control character inclusion, and byte translation/removal—will not be explained. If you need an explanation of these sections, please review the parallel material in Chapter 17. Instead, we will concentrate on the differences between the two functions. The explanation consists of an overview followed by a discussion of individual parts.

Chapter 17 also explained how substituting an `soctl_` pointer for the more cumbersome `SIOP` pointer together with the judicious use of `register` and `static` variables make the code more efficient. These same techniques can be found in `s_fgetc`. Why not declare all important variables to be of storage class `register`? Well, on any given processor there is clearly a limit to the number of registers available. When most compilers run out of registers for `register` variables, they convert them to `automatic`. Therefore, by greedily declaring an unreasonable number of fast variables, you may paradoxically create slow (`auto`) ones instead.

Raw Processing

So that a "raw" call to `s_fgetc` approximates the speed of an unadorned call to `s_inchar`, the test for `rawflg` is performed immediately, even before assignment of the variables. This means that `rawflg` must be addressed through the doubly indirect structure pointers, which in this case is actually faster than using the intermediate structure pointer `ip`. In other words,

```
if (siop->s_ictl->rawflg)
```

is faster than

```
ip = siop->s_ictl;
if (ip->rawflg)
```

The overhead of setting up `ip` doesn't pay unless it will be used several times later in the function. The actual read of the `SIO` is performed with a call to `s_inchar`.

Control Logic

You will recall that the organizing principle behind `s_fputc` was deciding whether to transmit a byte. The function `s_fgetc` demands a different approach: we must receive a byte before we can process it. Although `s_fgetc` cannot "read around" an incoming byte, its return value can signal that, for one reason or another, the received byte should be ignored. So, just as `txflag` in `s_fputc` serves as a transmit switch, `rxflag` in `s_fgetc` is a receive switch. If `rxflag` is `TRUE` at the end of the function, the received byte is returned; otherwise, `IGNORE` is returned (defined in Listing 17.1).

Time-Out Operation

Because we are interested in maximum speed in checking the `SIO` for a possible byte, `t_outflg` determines which function is used:

```
c = (ip->t_outflg) ? s_waitch(siop, ip->t_out) : s_inchar(siop);
if (c == TIMEOUT)
    return (TIMEOUT);
```

If t_outflg is ON, the byte is fetched by calling s_waitch, which waits t_out Tsecs for the byte to arrive. If t_outflg is OFF, however, the byte is fetched with s_inchar instead. Thus, functions built upon s_fgetc can test its return value for both negative values, IGNORE and TIMEOUT.

End-of-Line Conversion

The criteria for end-of-line formatting are no different than their counterparts in s_fputc, but the fact that s_fgetc is an input routine presents special problems. In some conversions, LF2CR for instance, s_fgetc must return a different byte than the one it actually received; that is, an LF has been received but a CR must be returned. Your first impulse here is probably to assign CR to c (the received byte variable). But remember, c must invariably be assigned to lastc; furthermore, the assignment of c may occur only after all processing has concluded. The solution to this situation is the variable retbyte, which is initialized to −1 upon entry to s_fgetc:

```
case LF2CR:
    if (c == LF)
          retbyte = CR;
    break;
```

When c has been safely tucked away in ip->lastc, and if the value of retbyte is no longer −1 (i.e., it has changed), retbyte is assigned to c:

```
ip->lastc = c;
if (retbyte != -1)
    c = retbyte;
```

Now, after optional console echo, rxflag determines whether to return a byte value or the constant IGNORE:

```
return (rxflag ? c : IGNORE);
```

The "Read-Back" Mechanism

In several of the end-of-line cases, 2 bytes must be substituted for 1. In the CR2CRLF case, for example, the reception of a CR must result in returning first a CR then an LF. But s_fgetc can return only a single value. A method can probably be devised where the extra byte is returned in the high-order byte of the returned value, but such schemes are *hopelessly* non-portable and eventually cause gargantuan troubles. A better solution is to store the second byte in a static variable, set a flag to note its presence, then return the first character as usual. When the function is next called, the flag is TRUE and the byte is immediately returned ("read back") without further processing:

```
if (ip->rbakflg)                    /* if byte pending    */
    {
    ip->rbakflg = FALSE;
```

```
    if ( ip->consflg)
        putchar(c);
    return (ip->rbakc);
    }
```

It is, of course, essential that this code appear early in the function.

Level-3 functions that call s_fgetc need to know when a character is present in the read-back buffer. The function shown in Listing 18.5 returns the look-back character or –1 if none is present.

Listing 18.5. Use of s_iflush to flush the "look-back" buffer.

FUNCTION NAME:	s_iflush
LEVEL:	2
PROTOTYPE IN:	BUOS.H
LIBRARY:	BUOS.LIB
DESCRIPTION:	Returns pending byte from s_octl's "look-back" buffer.
RETURNS:	int: byte if available, otherwise -1;
INCLUDE FILES:	siodef.h

```
int s_iflush(SIO *siop)
{
    return ((siop->s_ictl->rbakflag) ? siop->s_ictl->rbakc : -1);
}
```

More on Speed

You may have spotted that the functions of the two variables rxflag and retbyte might be combined. For example, we might initialize retbyte to –1 then change its value to –2 for IGNORE. Then, anywhere we once wrote

```
if (rxflag)
```

we could now write

```
if (retval != -1)
```

Why not? The answer is speed. Due to microprocessor logic, it is inherently faster to test for 0/not-0 (FALSE/TRUE) than to test one value against another. Because rxflag is tested frequently in s_fgetc, it is important to choose the faster method even at the expense of managing more variables.

Echo-Back

Just as s_fgetc supplies local output to standard output for communicating with equipment that does not "echo" input, s_fgetc also supplies the *echo-back* feature, which, based upon the value of the ekobakflg, simply consists of immediately retransmitting every received byte.

Level-3 Functions for Formatted Input

We now need a convenient means to change s_fgetc's behavior without worrying about its interaction with the s_ictl structure. This function, shown in Listing 18.7, allows easy configuration of the flag, mode, and delay members in the SIO's s_ictl structure. The manifest constants previously given in Listing 17.11 are used to identify the desired sictl_ member. The explanation of this function is identical to that of s_ocntrl in Listing 17.12.

Listing 18.6. Level-3 function to set/fetch integral data types from the sictl_.

FUNCTION NAME:	s_icntrl
LEVEL:	3
PROTOTYPE IN:	SIOCTL.H
LIBRARY:	SIO.LIB
DESCRIPTION:	Sets or fetches the value of the flag, delay, and mode members of an sictl_ input control structure.
RETURNS:	int. 0 if successful, otherwise, -1.
COMMENTS:	Constants are in SIOCTL.H. The range of the 'code' arguments is not checked.
INCLUDE FILES:	siodef.h, sioctl.h

```
int s_icntrl(SIO *siop, short mode, short whichone, unsigned newval)
{
    int retval = 0;
    if (mode == SET)
        switch (whichone)
            {
            case T_OUT      : siop->s_ictl->t_out     = newval;  break;
            case T_OUTFLAG  : siop->s_ictl->t_outflag = newval;  break;
            case RAWFLAG    : siop->s_ictl->rawflag   = newval;  break;
            case EKOBAKFLAG : siop->s_ictl->ekobakflag = newval; break;
            case ASCIIFLAG  : siop->s_ictl->asciiflag = newval;  break;
            case EOLMODE    : siop->s_ictl->eolmode   = newval;  break;
            case CONSFLAG   : siop->s_ictl->consflag  = newval;  break;
            case CASEMODE   : siop->s_ictl->casemode  = newval;  break;
            case CNTRLFLAG  : siop->s_ictl->cntrlflag = newval;  break;
            case FILTERFLAG : siop->s_ictl->filterflag = newval; break;
            default:
                retval = -1;
```

```
        }
    else if (mode == GET)
        switch (whichone)
            {
            case T_OUT     : retval = siop->s_ictl->t_out          ; break;
            case T_OUTFLAG : retval = (int)siop->s_ictl->t_outflag ; break;
            case RAWFLAG   : retval = (int)siop->s_ictl->rawflag    ; break;
            case EKOBAKFLAG: retval = (int)siop->s_ictl->ekobakflag; break;
            case ASCIIFLAG : retval = (int)siop->s_ictl->asciiflag ; break;
            case EOLMODE   : retval = siop->s_ictl->eolmode         ; break;
            case CONSFLAG  : retval = (int)siop->s_ictl->consflag   ; break;
            case CASEMODE  : retval = siop->s_ictl->casemode        ; break;
            case CNTRLFLAG : retval = (int)siop->s_ictl->cntrlflag  ; break;
            case FILTERFLAG: retval = (int)siop->s_ictl->filterflag; break;
            default:
                retval = -1;
            }
    return retval;
}
```

Temporary Storage for Input Control Structures

In Chapter 17, we constructed s_opush and s_opop to save and restore an entire s_octl. This provides a simple mechanism for preserving the structure across function calls that change some of its members. Listing 18.7 shows the code for the sister functions s_ipush and s_ipop to manage an input control stucture. No explanation of these functions is necessary because they exactly parallel s_opush and s_opop in Listing 17.12. The IO_STKSIZ constant was given in Listing 17.1.

Listing 18.7. The s_ipush and s_ipop functions: temporary storage for input control structures.

FUNCTION NAME:	s_ipush, s_ipop
LEVEL:	3
PROTOTYPE IN:	SIO.H
LIBRARY:	SIO.LIB
DESCRIPTION:	Save and restore s_ictl structures on local stack.
RETURNS:	int: 0 if stack operation was successful; otherwise 1.
COMMENTS:	Both funtions check for balance of the local stack, so take care that every "push" is balanced with a corresponding "pop."
INCLUDE FILES:	stdio.h, stdlib.h, siodef.h, sioctl.h

```
static struct sictl_ *istack[IO_STKSIZ] = {NIL}; /* init 1st element to NIL */
static struct sictl_ **istackp = istack;         /* pointer to top of stack */
```

continues

Listing 18.7. continued

```c
int s_ipush(SIO *siop)
{
    if (istackp >= &istack[IO_STKSIZ])
        {
        puts("\aIstack overflow.");
        return 1;
        }
    *istackp = (struct sictl_ *)malloc(sizeof(struct sictl_));
    if (*istackp == NIL)
        return 1;
    **istackp = *siop->s_ictl;
    ++istackp;
    return 0;
}

int s_ipop(SIO *siop)
{
    if (istackp <= istack)
        {
        puts("\aIstack underflow.");
        return 1;
        }
    --istackp;
    *siop->s_ictl = **istackp;
    free((VOID*)*istackp);
    return 0;
}
```

Level-3 Convenience Input Functions

In this section, we will create s_fgets and s_fgetln, a pair of level-3 "convenience" functions built upon s_fgetc. First we'll look at s_fgets.

The *s_fgets* Function

Implicit in the idea of communications is dialog. The conversation between sender and receiver in a protocol file transfer is an example of an interdevice dialog. Most serial devices are configured by transmitting to them a train of meaningful bytes (commands), then awaiting an acknowledgment. In their simplest forms, the command and reply consist of single-byte responses—XON/XOFF, ACK/NAK, etc. But as we learned in our discussion of smart modems in Chapter 8, serial devices can actually be queried for highly detailed information about their internal status. Their response to such queries is often many bytes in length and may even arrive in a variety of formats. Before we can hope to approach smart-modem programming, then, we need a function that can reliably capture these multibyte replies. The functions shown in Listing 18.8 partially satisfy this need.

Listing 18.8. Use of s_fgets to return a series of bytes—a 0/-terminated string.

FUNCTION NAME:	s_fgets
LEVEL:	3
PROTOTYPE IN:	SIO.H
LIBRARY:	SIO.LIB
DESCRIPTION:	Inputs a NUL-terminated string of numc bytes into buffer.
RETURNS:	int: number of bytes in buffer (0 if timeout occured).
COMMENTS:	Buffer must be numc+1 bytes long to accommodate the NUL terminator. Timeout mode is forced for the duration of the function. It is the responsibility of the calling function to preserve and restore the contents of the ictl_ control structure across the call.
INCLUDE FILES:	siodef.h, sioctl.h, buos.h

```
#include <sio\siodef.h>
#include <sio\sioctl.h>
#include <sio\buos.h>

int s_fgets(SIO *siop, char *buff, int numc)
{
    int count;
    int c;
    count = 0;
    while (count < numc)
        {
        if ( (c = s_fgetc(siop)) == TIMEOUT)
            return count;
        if (c == IGNORE)                /* exclude this character    */
            continue;
        *buff++ =  (char)c;             /* install byte in buffer    */
        ++count;
        }
    if ( (c =  s_iflush(siop)) != -1)  /* byte pending in s_fgetc?  */
        {
        *buff++ = (char)c;
        ++count;
        }
    *buff = NUL;                        /* terminate buffer with NUL */
    return count;
}
```

An explanation of s_fgets—Almost by definition, a function to fetch bytes that arrive asynchronously must wait some reasonable period of time before giving up. In other words, a function without a timeout is not likely to fetch bytes very successfully. Therefore, it is the responsibility of the calling function to save the structure by calling s_ipush and restore the structure by calling s_ipop.

The numc argument in s_fgets is assumed to be the number of bytes you wish to fetch. To guarantee room for the NUL terminating byte, it must be one less than the actual length of the buffer.

The body of the function is a while loop inside which bytes are fetched by s_fgetc and placed in the buffer at the location pointed to by buff. The loop breaks after numc iterations or when s_fgetc's timeout interval expires. A NUL byte is then appended to the buffer and the two previously saved sictl_ members are restored. The function s_fgets returns the number of bytes in the buffer, *not* including the NUL terminator.

Keep in mind that many systems, especially those that accommodate slow TTY devices, often pad their output with NUL bytes. It is not unusual, for example, for such a system to transmit ten or more NUL bytes after a newline to give the device an opportunity to return its literal or figurative carriage. Although s_fgets itself does not exclude received NUL bytes from the buffer, this is easily accomplished by either the ok_cntrls inclusion array or the filtlist conversion/removal array.

The s_fgets function is extremely useful for retrieving a string of indefinite length. That is, s_fgets unconditionally gathers bytes until the buffer is full or until a timeout occurs.

TERM5

We are now ready to add an important feature to our terminal program— the ability to capture incoming bytes into a disk file. Before we design that feature, however, Listing 18.9 shows the incidental additions to TERM4 required to produce TERM5 —version number, function menu, and so forth.

Listing 18.9. Changes in TERM4 required to produce TERM5.

```
PROGRAM NAME:    TERM5
 DESCRIPTION:    Terminal program.
    COMMENTS:    New Feature:  file download with flow control.
INCLUDE FILES:   stdio.h, ctype.h, siodef.h, ascii.h, buos.h,
                 misc.h key.h, sioctl.h, term.h, u16x50.h


#define MENU      CTRL_A          /* key for command summary   */
#define FORMAT    'A'             /* Setup serial parmeters    */
#define RS_232    'B'             /* RS-232 output control      */
#define BRAKE     'C'             /* send BREAK signal          */
#define UPLOAD    'D'             /* transmit file              */
```

```
#define DNLOAD1   'E'             /* Download with C's buffer    */
#define DNLOAD2   'F'             /* Download with local buffer  */
#define EXIT      'Q'             /* key to exit from term       */

int vers = 4;                     /* version number (global)     */

int menu(siop)                    /* menu now gets SIO pointer    */
SIO *siop;
{
    int c;
    int retval = 0;
    static char *menus[] =
        {
        "\tA.  Data Format, Baud rate",
        "\tB.  RS-232 control",
        "\tC.  Transmit BREAK signal",
        "\tD.  Upload Text File",
        "\tE.  Download Text File (small buffer)",
        "\tF.  Download Text File (large buffer)",
        "\tQ.  EXIT",
        ""                        /* NUL string terminates list  */
        };
        .
        .
        .
            case UPLOAD:          /* transmit a disk file         */
                upload(siop);
                break;
            case DNLOAD1:         /* receive a file: use C's file buffer   */
                dnload(siop, cbuff);
                break;
            case DNLOAD2:         /* receive a file: use local file buffer */
                dnload(siop, locbuff);
                break;
            default:
                puts("Invalid choice\n\a");
                break;
            }
    }
        .
        .
        .
}

void term(siop)
SIO *siop;
{
    int c;                        /* must be int to detect -1 return      */
    s_ipush(siop);                /* save both control structures         */
    s_opush(siop);
    s_icntrl(siop, SET, CONSFLAG, ON); /* console echo on formatted input */
    s_ocntrl(siop, SET, IB_DLYFLAG, OFF);  /* interbyte delay              */
```

continues

Listing 18.9. continued

```
    printf("TERM, Version %d:  Press Control-%c for a summary of commands\n", \
        vers, MENU + '@');
    for (EVER)                          /* eternal loop                       */
        {
        s_fgetc(siop);                  /* s_fgetc will echo                  */
        if ( (c = inkey()) != NOT_READY)  /* if a key is pressed              */
            if (c == MENU)
                {
                if (menu(siop))
                    break;    /* if menu returns non-zero                     */
                }
            else
                s_fputc(siop, c);
        }
    s_opop(siop);
    s_ipop(siop);
}

main(argc, argv)
int argc;
char *argv[];
{
/*    UNCHANGED FROM TERM4       */
}
```

In earlier versions of this function, serial I/O was performed with the "raw" functions s_getc and s_putc. The use of s_fgetc and s_fputc in this version enables us to apply the entire battery of formatted control to every byte that is received or sent. As shown, we disable delays on output, and enable console echo on input. Notice that incoming bytes are no longer sent to the console by putchar, but by turning on console echo for s_fgetc. Turning on console echo for output (for half-duplex use, for example), requires only a single additional line:

```
s_ocntrl(siop, SET, CONSFLAG, ON);
```

Design Considerations for *dnload*

There are two distinct ways we can choose to capture data into a disk file. Because each of these methods has strengths and weaknesses, we will write both: cbuff, which captures incoming data into C's file buffer, and locbuff, which captures data into a large local buffer. In addition, we will compose a single "administrative" module named dnload to handle the common chores such as file opening, closing, error detection, and so on.

As shown in the menu function in Listing 18.9, selecting either 'E' or 'F' from the menu produces a call to dnload, passing to it the address of the chosen function. The dnload module itself must:

1. Open a file to capture inbound data.
2. Save the existing s_ictl structure and then configure it for downloading.
3. Call the selected capture function via a function pointer passed in its argument list.
4. Upon return, add the appropriate end-of-file byte to the captured file. This step is not necessary in all systems.
5. Close the file.
6. Differentiate between write errors and file-closing errors.
7. If no errors occur, display the total number of bytes in the new file.
8. Restore the s_ictl structure saved in step 2.

Listing 18.10 shows the function to accomplish this.

Listing 18.10. The `dnload` function: an administrative function for downloading serial data.

FUNCTION NAME:	dnload
LEVEL:	3
PROTOTYPE IN:	TERM.H
LIBRARY:	TERMFUNC.LIB
DESCRIPTION:	Adminstrative function for downloading captured serial data into a disk file.
RETURNS:	void
COMMENTS:	This module calls the actual capture function by passing its address.
INCLUDE FILES:	stdio.h, siodef.h, sioctl.h, buos.h, misc.h, key.h

```
ULONG bytetot;                          /* total number of bytes captured    */

void dnload(SIO *siop, int (*captfp)(SIO *, FILE *) )
{
    FILE   *rcvfp;
    char   fnbuff[MAX_NAME_LEN];      /* filename buffer                      */
    int    errflag;                  /* inbound byte, counter, I/O error    */
    bytetot = 0;
    if ( (rcvfp = wfopen("File name for downloaded file", fnbuff)) == NIL)
        {
        puts("Input file not opened.");
        return;
        }
    s_ipush(siop);                          /* save control structure        */
    s_icntrl(siop, SET, CONSFLAG, ON);  /* console echo on              */
    s_icntrl(siop, SET, T_OUTFLAG, OFF);  /* no timeout on input function */
    s_icntrl(siop, SET, T_OUT, _0_SEC_05); /* but set the interval for later */
    printf("\n%s is now ready for capture. Press Esc key to end.\n", fnbuff);
```

continues

Listing 18.10. continued

```
    printf("Terminal output is %s.\n",\
    s_icntrl(siop, GET, CONSFLAG) ? "on": "off");
    xon(siop);                              /* send XON to get started      */
    errflag = (*captfp)(siop, rcvfp);   /* return code from disk write      */
    if (!errflag && bytetot)
        {
        fputc(DOS_EOF, rcvfp);              /* tack on end-of-file          */
        ++bytetot;
        errflag = fflush(rcvfp);            /* error on flush == disk prob. full */
        }
    putchar('\n');
    if (errflag ¦¦ fclose(rcvfp))           /* don't show stats if error    */
        printf("Error %s %s.\n\a", errflag ? "writing" : "closing", fnbuff);
    else
        printf("%lu bytes written to %s.\n", bytetot, fnbuff);
    puts("\n-- Press any key to continue --\a");
    getkbch();                              /* ask user to acknowledge error */
    s_ipop(siop);                           /* restore control structure    */
    puts("Exiting download");
}
```

An explanation of *dnload*—Upon entry to dnload the function wfopen[1] is called to fetch a file pointer. As given in Appendix B, wfopen prompts the user for a file name and asks permission before overwriting an existing file. It returns NIL if unsuccessful; otherwise, it returns the file pointer open for writing.

After saving the contents of the SIO's input control structure with s_ipush, the input console flag, timeout flag, and timeout delay are all set to their default values. Although to achieve maximum speed we wish s_fgetc to run with the timeout feature off during most of the file capture, it will be on from time to time; the desired timeout interval is therefore installed in advance. After displaying an announcement verifying the name of the open file and the state of the console output flag, a flow-on request is made to wake up the sender. Finally, the capture function is invoked:

```
errflag = (*captfp)(siop,rcvfp);
```

This calls the capture function selected from the menu, passing to it the ever-present siop and the FILE pointer for the disk file.

ERROR HANDLING IN *dnload*

We will design the capture functions to return a 0 if no write errors occur and non-0 otherwise. To understand the rather odd-looking error checking that follows, a quick review

---

[1]The source to this "Incidental Function" is in Appendix A.

is in order of C's "f," or stream I/O file functions— fopen, fread, fwrite, fclose, and so forth. Recall that fwrite caches data in an internal buffer BUFSIZ bytes in length. A pointer to this buffer is contained in the FILE structure pointer returned by fopen. (The definitions for FILE and BUFSIZ are given in STDIO.H.) Because of the buffering, fwrites do not produce physical disk writes until the FILE buffer fills. At that time, C hands responsibility for the disk write to the operating system which, depending upon its own buffering scheme, still may not generate an immediate disk write. When the file is closed, any bytes in the buffer are written to disk before the file is closed.

That C may postpone the physical disk write creates a potential problem. To understand the problem, suppose that your C compiler employs a 512-byte FILE buffer and you fopen a file on a disk that has no free remaining space. Suppose further that you "f" write (putc or fwrite) 511 bytes to this file. This produces no physical disk write because C's buffer is only partially full; Because there is no physical write, the operating system cannot inform C that there is no space remaining on the disk. In other words, you cannot trust an "f" write's "no error" return code. In the absence of a reliable positive error return from the write function, then, we can only hope that fclose will inform us of the disk-space error when it flushes the buffer to disk. But, and here's the problem, a number of popular C compilers fail to report the write error at fclose! It therefore seems worthwhile to write a little extra code to promote reliable, compiler-independent error operation.

Because the whole idea of the stream I/O functions is to free the programmer from such concerns as the nature or frequency of physical disk writes, we need another way to test for errors. The most reliable method is to write the contents of the buffer to disk *explicitly* with a call to fflush, which always correctly reports I/O errors. If upon return from the capture function, errflag is 0, an end-of-file is written and the buffer is fflushed. The return code from the flush operation becomes the new value for errcode, which is then logically OR'ed with the return code from fclose. Thus, we are able to detect whether an error occurred during any of the three phases—write, flush, or close. Notice, as an added bonus, this method enables us to uniquely identify a genuine close error, such as might result from a damaged disk directory.

Design Considerations for Data Capture Functions

When a byte is received from the SIO, we have our choice of how to capture it to disk. The first capture method, employed in our cbuff capture function, simply putcs each byte as it is received, letting C graciously and transparently buffer several hundred (i.e., BUFSIZ from STDIO.H) bytes in its FILE buffer for us, eventually ferrying the accumulated bytes to disk. The second method, used in the locbuff function, squirrels away the incoming bytes in a large RAM buffer, performing a disk write only when the buffer is full. In this scheme, the programmer is responsible not only for ushering the bytes into the correct buffer location, but for deciding when the buffer is full and must be written to disk.

Each method clearly has its strengths and weaknesses. The automatic buffering of cbuff is convenient, but the code overhead incurred by byte-to-byte I/O (via putc) inevitably renders cbuff unsuitable as the data rate increases. Because locbuff stores incoming bytes in RAM instead of putcing them to disk immediately, it performs dramatically better at higher speeds; the penalty for locbuff's higher performance is the increased complexity of managing a large RAM buffer. There are other practical reasons for choosing one method over the other. When capturing large files onto a floppy, cbuff's frequent pauses while C writes its buffer to disk may be intolerable. The local buffer gives you the option to manipulate the data—to view and edit it, for example—before writing it to disk. On the other hand, cbuff's frequent disk writes safely tuck data away in small increments, thus limiting the amount of data that a disk or other system error can destroy.

FLOW CONTROL

As just discussed, locbuff's use of a very large buffer solves many problems by postponing time-consuming disk writes. Remember, though, that the physical disk access is just *postponed* and, as in cbuff, must sooner or later occur. Meanwhile, as the operating system is preoccupied with the physical disk access, incoming SIO bytes are lost. The classic way to prevent this sort of data loss is *flow control* (see Chapter 4). Because our flow control is virtual, the level-3 applications are ignorant of the protocol or procedures involved. Immediately before a disk write is scheduled, we make a flow-off request to inform the sender to pause; then, after completing the disk write, we make a flow-on request to restart the sender. Because the details of flow control vary slightly from cbuff to locbuff, a complete explanation will be offered along with the general discussion of each function.

Capture Function One: *cbuff*

Acknowledging the need for flow control, mindful of the relative merits of each capture method, and within the overall framework of upload, let us now look at cbuff, shown in Listing 18.11.

Listing 18.11. The cbuff function: employing C's internal FILE buffer to capture serial data into a disk file.

FUNCTION NAME:	cbuff
LEVEL:	3
PROTOTYPE IN:	TERM.H
DESCRIPTION:	Subfunction for capturing serial data into a disk file using C's internal FILE buffer.
RETURNS:	int: 1 if a disk write error occurred, otherwise 0.
COMMENTS:	Flow control supported. Size of buffer is given by the constant BUFSIZ in STDIO.H.
INCLUDE FILES:	stdio.h, siodef.h, sioctl.h, buos.h, key.h

```c
#define BYTESLEFT  25                    /* buffer remaining after XPAUSE */
#define XPAUSE     BUFSIZ - BYTESLEFT    /* bytes before sending flow-off */

int cbuff(SIO *siop, FILE *rcvfp)
{
    extern ULONG bytetot;
    int    buffcnt = 0, error = 0;    /* bytes in C's I/O buffer         */
    int c;                            /* must be int for negative returns */
    long  i;     printf("C's %d buffer in use.\n",BUFSIZ);
    s_ipush(siop);
    for (EVER)
        {
        if ( (c = inkey()) == (int) siop->s_octl->kbortc) /* get key byte */
            break;                    /* end download if abort            */
        if (c != -1)
            s_fputc(siop, c);         /* transmit keyboard byte           */
        if ( (c = s_fgetc(siop)) < 0) /* now check SIO for byte           */
            continue;
        putc(c, rcvfp);
        ++bytetot;
        if (++buffcnt == XPAUSE )      /* C's I/O buffer almost full?      */
            {
            flowoff(siop);                   /* flow off sender           */
            s_icntrl(siop, SET, T_OUTFLAG, ON); /*1 tsec for late comers  */
            for (i = BYTESLEFT; i > 0; i--) /* wait for sender to stop    */
                {
                if ( (c = s_fgetc(siop)) == TIMEOUT)
                    break;            /* timeout, so sender is paused      */
                else if (c == IGNORE)
                    continue;
                else
                    {
                    putc(c, rcvfp); /* catch slow pokes, too              */
                    ++buffcnt; ++bytetot;
                    }
                }
            if (c != TIMEOUT)         /* sender didn't respond            */
              puts("\nRemote ignored flow-off request.\007");
            error = fflush(rcvfp) != 0;
            s_icntrl(siop, T_OUTFLAG, OFF); /* restore zero wait on input */
            if (s_icntrl(siop, GET, CONSFLAG) == OFF)
                printf("%lu total bytes written.\r", bytetot);
            buffcnt = 0;
            flowon(siop);                             /* release sender */
            if (error)                         /* disk error ends capture */
                break;
            }
        }
    puts("\nExit Menu");
    s_ipop(siop);
    return error;                     /* return 0 if no error, 1 if error */
}
```

An explanation of *cbuff*—The idea behind cbuff is to write bytes into C's FILE buffer, then, when the buffer is almost full, to call fflush to write the buffer to disk. The question is this: how do we gain insight into C's internal workings—i.e. how do we know when C's internal disk buffer is nearing capacity? Luckily (and for just such purposes as this), the size of C's buffer, BUFSIZ, is published in STDIO.H. By counting how many bytes are putc ed into C's buffer, we can easily ascertain when to flush the buffer. In a sense, then, we are piggybacking flow control onto C's buffered I/0 functions. Here, in pidgin C, is the simplified version of our plan of attack:

```
#define XPAUSE      BUFSIZ - (some constant)
     int buffcnt = 0;
     while (keybort() == FALSE)
          {
          read c;
          putc(c);
          if (buffcnt++ == XPAUSE)
               {
               flowoff();
               flush I/O buffer
               buffcnt = 0;
               flowon();
               }
          }
```

The number of bytes written is counted by the variable buffcnt. When buffcnt reaches some percentage of the buffer's capacity, XPAUSE, a flow-off request is made to the sender. C's I/O buffer is then flushed, buffcnt is reset, and a flow-on request finally restarts the sender. The loop continues until terminated from the keyboard. It is worth observing again that virtual flow control is used as decribed in Chapter 16. The functions flowon and flowoff are merely macros in SIOCTL.H that actually call functions pointers with the same names in the SIO.

The use of a constant instead of a variable for XPAUSE is counter to conventional explanations of flow control procedures, which usually conceive the flow-off point as a percentage of the total buffer size. It is difficult to understand why this concept prevails—is the celerity of the sender's response governed by the size of the receiver's buffer? Problems of scale are also produced by allocating the flow-off point based upon buffer size. Five percent of a 1K buffer is about 51 bytes, which should be plenty for almost every occasion; five percent of a megabyte, however, is a whopping 50K. If you cannot realistically expect your sender to respond in at *most* a few tens of bytes, you should seriously consider another means of transfer. The value given for use in both cbuff and locbuff has proven universally satisfactory on a wide variety of senders over several years.

This uncomplicated approach is tantalizingly close to complete. Only one interesting detail must be resolved. The transfer obviously fails if the sender totally ignores the flow-off request, but what happens if the sender merely is slow to respond to it? As we have seen, the transmitter's UART probably has at least one transmit buffer. Let's assume that at the instant the flow-off request is dispatched, the sending UART has just written a byte into its Transmitter Holding register and is currently outputting a byte from its transmitter. Even under perfect conditions—if the sender reacts to the flow-off request *instantaneously*—the 2 bytes already in the pipeline will still be transmitted. Clearly, if the receiver proceeds with a disk write immediately after sending the flow-off request, these two stragglers will be lost. This potential data loss can be avoided if, after sending the flow-off request but before flushing the buffer, we first pause briefly to recover any bytes in the pipe:

```
flowoff(siop);
s_icntrl(siop, SET, T_OUTFLAG, ON);
for (i = BYTESLEFT; i > 0 ; i--)
    {
    if ( (c = s_fgetc(siop)) == TIMEOUT)
        break;
    else if (c == IGNORE)
        continue;
    else
        {
        putc(c, rcvfp);
        ++buffcnt; ++bytetot;
        }
    }
if (c != TIMEOUT)          /* sender didn't respond          */
    puts("\nRemote ignored flow-off request.\a");
```

Here, we transmit a flow-off request followed immediately by a call to s_icntrl to enable timeout input operation. Then a for loop is entered to catch any late-arriving bytes and place them in the buffer. If s_fgetc times out, we know that the sender has honored the flow-off request and it is now safe to fflush the buffer. If, on the other hand, the loop ends without s_fgetc's timeout ever expiring (i.e., c != TIMEOUT), a warning message is displayed and the flush is made anyway. The timeout flag in s_fgetc must be switched on at the beginning of the loop and back on again at the end. Because a "raw" s_fgetc can be called dozens of times before even the first straggler arrives, a nominal amount of timeout is required to prevent s_fgetc from quickly buzzing through the for loop.

With the slowpokes now safe in the buffer, the disk buffer is flushed. The error code returned by fflush is assigned to the error variable. If the flush is successful, the loop repeats. If error is TRUE, however, the loop breaks after switching off s_fgetc's timeout and transmitting a flow-on request to the sender.

Upon return to upload, an end-of-file (DOS_EOF from STDIO.H) is appended, the final flush is performed, and write/close errors are handled.

Something *not* present in the slowpoke for loop is worthy of mention. You may be thinking to yourself, "Each time a slowpoke arrives, let's send another flow-off request in case the sender missed the first one." This is good thinking but produces perplexing results in many cases, depending on the sender's definition of flow control. For example, in XON/XOFF if the sender is programmed to interpret *only* a specific byte—DC1, for example—as XON, the additional XOFF's are simply ignored. But if, as is often the case, the sender is programmed to interpret *any* byte as XON, the first redundant XOFF is paradoxically treated as an XON! It is therefore not a good idea to send multiple flow-off requests unless you know the receiver's mind on the subject.

Capture Function Two: *locbuff*

Despite its need for more complicated buffer management, the design of locbuff is remarkably similar to that of cbuff. The basic ideas are the same—just before a buffer is full, write it to disk, making sure to catch the Johnny-come-latelies. The most interesting part of locbuff is not its *handling* of the buffer so much as its *declaring* the buffer. The complete locbuff is shown in Listing 18.12.

Listing 18.12. The `locbuff` function: a capture function with a large local buffer.

FUNCTION NAME: locbuff
LEVEL: 3
PROTOTYPE IN: TERM.H
LIBRARY: TERMFUNC.LIB
DESCRIPTION: Subfunction for capturing serial data into a disk file using an externally declared RAM buffer.
RETURNS: int: 1 if a disk error occurred, -1 if buffer allocation failed, otherwise 0.
COMMENTS: Flow control supported.
INCLUDE FILES: stdio.h, stdlib.h, siodef.h, sioctl.h, buos.h, misc.h, key.h

```
#define BYTESLEFT       25
#define HEADROOM         5              /* blocks to save for locals      */
#define BLKSIZE        128

int locbuff(SIO *siop, FILE *rcvfp)
{
    extern ULONG bytetot;
    BYTE    *buff, *p, *pausep;      /* buffer, buffer pointer, pause marker */
    FAST    c, i;
    int     error = 0;
    unsigned numblks;                  /* number of BLKSIZE blocks allocated   */
    ULONG bufflen = 1;
    p = buff = bigbuff(BLKSIZE, HEADROOM, &numblks);
    if (buff == NIL ¦¦ numblks == 0)
        {
        puts("Insufficient memory for buffer.");
        return -1;                     /* not tested upon return              */
        }
    s_ipush(siop);
    bufflen = numblks * BLKSIZE;       /* now convert from blocks to bytes    */
    pausep = (char *)(buff + (bufflen - BYTESLEFT)); /* flow-off point       */
    printf("%lu byte local buffer in use.\n",bufflen);
    for (EVER)
        {
        if ( (c = inkey()) == siop->s_octl->kbortc)  /* get keyboard byte   */
            break;                     /* end download                        */
        if (c != -1)
            s_fputc(siop, c);          /* transmit keyboard byte              */
```

```
            if ( (c = s_fgetc(siop)) < 0) /* now check SIO for byte         */
                continue;
            *p++ = (BYTE)c;              /*byte to buffer                    */
            if (p == pausep)
                {
                flowoff(siop);              /* flow-off request to sender    */
                s_icntrl(siop, SET, T_OUTFLAG, ON); /* 1 sec for late arrivers */
                for (i = BYTESLEFT; i > 0; --i) /* wait for sender to pause   */
                    {
                    if ( (c = s_fgetc(siop)) != TIMEOUT) /* catch slow pokes  */
                        (FAST) *p++ = c;
                    else
                        break;          /* timeout = sender acknowledged     */
                    }
                if (c != TIMEOUT)       /* sender didn't respond             */
                    puts("\nRemote ignored flow-off request.\a");
                error = fwrite(buff, sizeof(BYTE), p - buff, rcvfp) \
                        != (unsigned)(p - buff);
                bytetot += p - buff;   /* running byte total                 */
                if (s_icntrl(siop, GET, CONSFLAG) == OFF  && !error)
                    printf("%lu total bytes written.\r", bytetot);
                p = buff;               /* reset buffer                      */
                s_icntrl(siop, T_OUTFLAG, OFF); /* restore zero wait on input */
                flowon(siop);               /* now release sender            */
                if (error == TRUE)
                    break;
                }
        }
    if(!error)
        {
        bytetot += p - buff;            /* running byte total                */
        error = fwrite(buff, sizeof(BYTE), p - buff, rcvfp) \
                != (unsigned)(p - buff);
        }
    free((VOID*)buff);
    s_ipop(siop);
    return error;
}
```

An explanation of *locbuff* —Because we are committed to declaring a local buffer, we might as well allocate *all* memory available, reserving a few hundred bytes of heap space for subsequent function calls. This is accomplished by the function bigbuff[2], which returns a pointer to the allocated memory:

```
p = buff = bigbuff(BLKSIZE, HEADROOM, &numblks);
```

The constant BLKSIZE is the block size for allocation and, though arbitrarily chosen, should be a power of 2. The constant HEADROOM is the number of these blocks to *reserve* from

[2]The source to this "Incidental Function" is in Append A. Most compilers provide a function that returns the amount of heap space remaining. For example, in the Microsoft compiler its name is _memaval.

allocation. The values shown in Listing 18.12 result in an allocation of all memory except BLKSIZE * HEADROOM bytes—more than enough for current needs. Note that we pass a pointer to numblks, through which bigbuff informs us how many blocks were actually allocated.

Now the number of allocation blocks in bufflen is converted to bytes where it can be used to calculate the pointer to the flow-control pause-point in the buffer:

```
bufflen *= BLKSIZ;
pausep = (char*)(buff + (bufflen - BYTESLEFT));
```

BUFFER MANAGEMENT IN *locbuff*

The buffer is managed by three pointers: buff, the address of the beginning of the buffer; p, the location in the buffer where the next byte is to be stored; and pausep, the address where the flow control is to be engaged. In overall design, locbuff is no different from cbuff. The actual buffer writes are accomplished with

```
error = fwrite(buff, sizeof(BYTE), p - buff, rcvfp) != p - buff;
```

Because fwrite returns the number of bytes actually written, error is TRUE when the return value does not equal the number of bytes in the buffer (i.e., buff - p).

Conclusion

We now have a complete set of basic tools for performing asynchronous serial I/O. We can control data format, baud rate, RS-232 input, time-sensitive operations, and can meter the input and output of data in almost every conceivable fashion. From these tools, we have already built an edifice of considerable utility—TERM. With a few more tools, we can add the much-needed support for smart modems, the subject of the next chapter.

An Introduction to Interrupt I/O

Interrupt Basics

Interrupt I/O is often touted over polled I/O because it is faster. Even if this were true—and usually it is not—it misses the point horribly. It is the kind of reasoning that says jets are preferable to horses because jets use less hay; or that clocks are better than sundials because clocks can be read at night. In fact, interrupt I/O is preferable to polled I/O because it pushes the whole question of speed into the background where it belongs. In the face of the constant pressure of polling for newly arrived data, software can undertake no task longer than the time required for the UART receiver's FIFO buffer to fill. This is an intolerable constraint on any software and essentially precludes functional elegance. To the programmer, an interrupt buffer is a temporal safety net, offering freedom to imagine, experiment, and create.

So far we have only muttered about interrupts. In fact, we haven't even bothered to define interrupt I/O, or, for that matter, its counterpart, polled I/O. Our only significant foray into the subject was our discussion of the 16X50 and Z80SIO UARTs in Chapter 7. At various times throughout the book, however, we have also made certain software design decisions based upon the prospect of interrupts. There are several reasons for this obliqueness, not the least of which is the anxiety—largely unspoken—that many programmers feel about interrupts.

There is another, more philosophical reason to wait until the eleventh hour to add interrupts to the SIO. If you have plowed through the previous eighteen chapters, by now you probably have a fairly good idea about the ideology of this book: *Generality is the soul of good program design.* The major tenet of this philosophy is that hardware should not unduly influence the design of the software. To introduce inter-rupts—the *ultimate* hardware dependence—early in the book would have posed a temp-tation to optimize the design for speed and efficiency rather than generality.

This chapter and the next one together constitute the full course on serial interrupts. This chapter provides all the background information and code necessary to understand the design of the interrupt code in the next chapter. Specifically, this chapter contains:

1. A discussion of the concept of interrupts.
2. A discussion of system interrupts as found on the IBM PC and the code to manage them.
3. A discussion of 16x50 UART interrupts and the code to manage them.
4. Modifications to the s_open and s_close functions.

The next chapter contains the four interrupt handlers themselves and their intimate sup-port routines.

Interrupts

An interrupt is one example of a class of events known as exceptions, which are charac-terized by the involuntary passing of CPU control from the normal path of program execution to code especially designed to "service" the event. Exceptions are not necessarily benevolent[1]; CPUs, for example, may generate exceptions under these unhealthy condi-tions:

- Addressing errors
- Bus errors
- Privilege violations
- Illegal or non-existent opcodes
- Illogical operations (division by 0, for example)

Interrupts and Asynchronous I/O

In asynchronous serial I/O, bytes arrive at unpredictable intervals— that is, asynchronously. Software must continually monitor the UART's receiver status in order to snatch up each just-arrived byte before the next one arrives. Similarly, during transmission the software must monitor the transmitter's status to ascertain when the next byte may be sent. As long as the software has nothing else to do—as is the case in our TERM program—this per-petual *polling* imposes no hardship. But when polling is impossible or inconvenient, such as during periods of disk I/O, incoming characters are lost or transmission ceases, or both.

---

[1]In fact, the term "exception" is often used to describe only *fault* detection, but is increasingly used in the more general sense described here.

Interrupts offer a more efficient alternative to continual polling because the UART receives attention *only* when it needs it. That is, the occurrence of an event *automatically* and more-or-less instantaneously causes execution of code that is similar to the code executed as a result of polling. This code itself is classically known as the *interrupt service routine* (ISR), but for architectural clarity in this chapter, we shall refer to it as the "main ISR." The address of the main ISR code is referred to as its *vector*.

VECTORING

In any given system, several interrupts may be active at any time. When an interrupt occurs, the CPU must somehow ascertain which of the possible interrupts has actually occurred. From this information, the CPU then calculates the vector associated with the interrupt. Although the exact method of communication between the CPU and the UART differs from system to system, the result must always be the vector that services the condition causing the interrupt. Since our concern in this chapter is the IBM PC, we'll have to deal in detail with its system architecture which, of course, is dominated by the 80x86 CPU.

TYPES OF UART INTERRUPTS

Generally, only four UART events generate interrupts:

1. The arrival of a byte
2. The transmitter's holding register (buffer) becoming empty
3. A serialization error or BREAK
4. Changes on external inputs such as RS-232 status inputs

Although abstractly all such events are of equal importance, in practice the nature of the software application gives one event precedence over the others. In practice, however, the arrival of a byte (RXRDY) is granted fairly high priority because of the potential for data loss if another byte arrives and overruns it. (Interrupt priorities are given in Table 7.5)

The IBM PC's Interrupt Architecture

Before we compose the functions to support interrupts for the IBM PC, we must understand its interrupt structure. As explained in Chapter 7, the 16X50 UART's participation in the host computer's interrupt system is limited to asserting its INTRPT signal on the system's I/O bus. It is the system's responsibility to produce the proper vector for each interrupt.

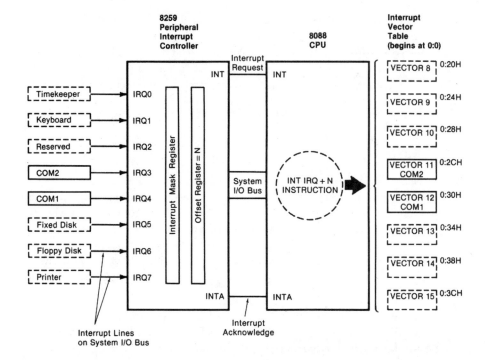

FIGURE 19.1.

The interrupt structure of the IBM PC.

The 8259 Peripheral Interrupt Controller (PIC)

Figure 19.1 illustrates the interrupt structure of the IBM PC. The first piece in the puzzle is the 8259 Peripheral Interrupt Controller (PIC), which administrates the relationship between the CPU and as many as six peripherals plugged into the mother board. (Actually, the PIC supports eight peripherals, but two—the keyboard and the system timekeeper—are permanently wired to the I/O bus). Each peripheral's interrupt line is connected via the plug-in connector to a discrete wire, referred to as an IRQ line. The IRQs are inputs to the PIC—the timekeeper gets IRQ0, the keyboard gets IRQ1, the system printer (PRN) gets IRQ7, and so forth. The two serial ports, COM1 and COM2, are assigned interrupt lines IRQ4 and IRQ3, respectively[2].

When a peripheral generates an interrupt, the interrupt signal travels (via its IRQ) to the PIC, which relays it to the CPU. The PIC is a formidably complicated device with many responsibilities besides relaying interrupts. Only two of these features are of concern to us: the Interrupt Mask register (IMR) and the Offset register. The IMR, a read/write register located at port address 21H, is refreshingly simple. Each bit in the IMR corresponds to a

---

[2]Notice that no IRQ's are assigned to COM3 and COM4 and must share IRQ4 and IRQ3 with COM1 and COM2, respectively. This means that both devices sharing an IRQ cannot be used simultaneously.

peripheral interrupt input line—the timekeeper's is bit 0, COM2 is bit 3, COM1 is bit 4, and so forth. When a bit is TRUE in the IMR, the PIC does *not* relay interrupts on that IRQ; in other words, that peripheral's interrupt is masked. Before we look at the purpose of the Offset register, let's look at the other hardware participants in the interrupt scheme.

THE 80X86 INT INSTRUCTION

The most distinguishing characteristic of the 80x86 instruction set is the INT instruction, which takes the form *INT nn*, where *nn* is an 8-bit argument. The CPU treats this argument as an index into a table of vectors, then calls the vector at the indexed location. When an *INT nn* occurs, for example, the CPU calls the address located in element *nn* of the vector table. A call generated in this way is identical to an ordinary 80x86 FAR call except that the CPU's Flag register is pushed onto the stack ahead of the FAR return address. For this reason a special instruction exists for returning from an INT instruction: IRET.

With the INT mechanism in mind, let's now see how the hardware behaves when a device at COM1 generates an interrupt on IRQ4. If bit 4 in the IMR mask is clear, the PIC passes an interrupt request to the CPU on its INT line. When the CPU finishes its current instruction, it acknowledges the PIC via its INTA line. The PIC then blurts the IRQ number of the interrupting peripheral onto the system I/O bus. The CPU fetches this number and uses it as the argument for an INT instruction.

But wait! There is a problem: the first eight vectors in the table are usurped by the system—the divide-by-zero vector is in element 0, the print screen vector is in element 5, and so on (elements 6 and 7 are reserved). This is where the PIC's Offset register comes into play—instead of outputting the IRQ number of the peripheral directly onto the I/O bus, the PIC first adds the value in its Offset register. The PIC's Offset register is configured with a value of 8 during power-up, so the INT arguments provided to the CPU begin at eight. An interrupt from the timekeeper has the same effect as an INT 8: the 0 of IRQ0 plus the 8 in the Offset register.

There is one difference between an INT instruction generated by software and one generated by an interrupt peripheral—the PIC must be informed when it is safe to "clear" the current interrupt. Accordingly, at the end of every peripheral's interrupt service routine must appear a *non-specific End-of-Interrupt* command. This is accomplished by writing the value 20H to one of the PIC's port addressees, 20H.

System Interrupt Functions

In this section we construct the code necessary to support interrupts at the system (hardware) level. In a later section we'll do the same for UART interrupts.

New *SIO* members and Constants

Listing 19.1 gives the new constants required for the code in this chapter. Most are explained as we proceed, but take special note of the two functions __sys_enable and __sys_disable, which merely enable and disable CPU interrupts[3]. These are simply macros assignments for the Microsoft run-time library (the prototypes are in the Microsoft DOS.H. include file).

Listing 19.2 gives the new members required in the SIO, while Listing 19.3 shows their level-0 initialization.

Listing 19.1. New constants required for general interrupt support.

The following belongs in SIODEF.H

```
    /* Manifest constants for UART Interrupts */
enum intrp                      /* Manifest constant names for interrupts */
{
    RS232 =   0,                        /* Changes on RS232 inputs   */
    THRE,                               /* Transmitter buffer emtpy  */
    RXRDY,                              /* Receive data ready        */
    SERERR                              /* Serialization errors      */
}
```

The following belong in U16X50.H

```
        /* Bit mask constants for Interrupt Enable Register   */
#define I_RXRDY  0x01
#define I_THRE   0x02                /* Values may be compounded..*/
#define I_SERERR 0x04                /* e.g., I_RXRDY + I_THRE    */
#define I_RS232  0x08

    /* Index number for interrupts */
enum
    {
    INDEX_RS232 =  0,
    INDEX_THRE,          /* Transmitter holding register empty   */
    INDEX_RXRDY,         /* Receiver data read                   */
    INDEX_SERERR,        /* Serialization error                  */
    INDEX_UNUSED1,
    INDEX_UNUSED2,
    INDEX_RXTIMEOUT,     /* Recevier FIFO timed out unfull       */
    NUM_INTRPT           /* Dimensions the isr array in SIODEF.H */
    };
```

---

[3]On an 80x86, these macros should evaluate to STI (on) and CLI (off) instructions.

```
    /* MASK FOR  Interrupt ID Register */
#define INT_ID_MASK    7               /* only bits 1,2&3 relevant  */
```

The following belong in IBMPC.H

```
#define   __sys_disable  _disable    /* MACRO for Microsoft      */
#define   __sys_enable   _enable     /* MACRO for Microsoft      */
```

Listing 19.2. New SIO members to support interrupts.

```
struct sio
    {
    BYTE   * uart_base;                 /*0  Base address of UART          */
    USHORT data_off;                    /*1  Offset of data port from base */
    USHORT status_off;                  /*2  Offset of status port from base */
    .
    .
    .
    struct                              /*47 Interrupt status bitfield     */
       {
       unsigned int rcv_wanted    :1;  /*  Are interrupts desired?        */
       unsigned int tx_wanted     :1;
       unsigned int rs232_wanted  :1;
       unsigned int serr_wanted   :1;
       unsigned int rcv_on        :1;  /*  Are interrupts on?             */
       unsigned int tx_on         :1;
       unsigned int rs232_on      :1;
       unsigned int serr_on       :1;
       unsigned int reserved      :8;
       } intrpt_status;
    void (*isr[NUM_INTRPT])(SIO * siop);/*48 Array of interrupt vectors   */
    void (*old_isr_232)(SIO *);         /*49 Pointer to saved: rs232 ISR  */
    void (*old_isr_serr)(SIO *);        /*50 : serial error ISR           */
    void (*old_isr_rcv)(SIO *);         /*51 : rcv ISR                    */
    void (*old_isr_tx)(SIO *);          /*52 : xmit ISR                   */
    }
```

Listing 19.3. Level-0 initialization of the new SIO members.

```
SIO COM1sio =
{
COM3,                    /*0  Base address of UART               */
DATA_IO,                 /*1  Offset of data port from base      */
SER_STAT,                /*2  Offset of status port from base    */
```

continues

Listing 19.3. continued

```
.
.
.
{TRUE,FALSE,TRUE,TRUE,0,0,0,0},/*47 Interrupt status bitfield           */
    {                          /*48 UART Interrupt vectors (s_iadmin)    */
        isr_stat232_dummy,     /*--  index 0 = RS232 input status        */
        isr_tx_dummy,          /*--  index 1 = transmit hold reg empty   */
        isr_rcv_dummy,         /*--  index 2 = received data ready        */
        isr_serr_dummy         /*--  index 3 = serialization error        */
    },
    NIL,                       /*49 Pointer to old rs232 isr             */
    NIL,                       /*50 Pointer to old ser-error isr         */
    NIL,                       /*51 Pointer to old rcv interrupt handler */
    NIL,                       /*52 Pointer to old xmit interrupt handler*/
};
```

The Main Interrupt Handler

You may be pleasantly surprised to discover in Chapter 20 that the code that actually processes the interrupts is written in C instead of assembler. That is the good news; the bad news is that because it is written in C it is not suitable to be a main ISR (that is, directly callable with an INT instruction). Why? By definition, an interrupt always occurs when the CPU is doing something else. Before servicing the interrupt, therefore, the CPU's first responsibility is to preserve the state of its own registers. In other words, a main ISR must make certain that no registers are changed during interrupt servicing. To prevent this, we need the simple assembly language main ISR shown in Listing 19.4 whose primary objective is to preserve the CPU registers across its call to s_iadmin, the C interrupt administrator (composed later in this chapter).

Listing 19.4. A Main ISR.

```
 5  procdef __a_com1isr
10          push  ax                 ; this on system's stack
15          mov   oldss, ss          ; save SS
20          mov   oldsp, sp          ; save SP
25          push  cs                 ; set SS:SP ...
30          pop   ss                 ; ...to address ...
35          mov   sp, OFFSET newstack ; ... our local stack
40                ;; -- remaining stack operations use local stack --
45          push  bp
50          push  bx
55          push  cx
60          push  dx
65          push  si
70          push  di
75          push  es
```

```
 80          push   ds
 85          mov    ax, SEG DGROUP:_COM1sio     ; address C's data
 90          mov    ds, ax
 95          push   ax                          ; push segment add on stack first
100          mov    ax, OFFSET DGROUP:_COM1sio  ; pass the address of COM1sio on stack
105          push   ax
110          call   _s_iadmin          ; call C interrupt administrator
115          add    sp, NUMARGS        ; remove siop argument from stack
120          pop    ds                 ; restore registers from local stack
125          pop    es
130          pop    di
135          pop    si
140          pop    dx
145          pop    cx
150          pop    bx
155          pop    bp
160          mov    ss, oldss          ; restore the caller's stack (SS:SP)
165          mov    sp, oldsp
170          mov    al, 20H            ; bid adieu to the 8259 PIC
175          out    20H, al
180          pop    ax
185          iret                      ; allons!
190      __a_com1isr ENDP
```

An explanation of the __a_com1isr—For each SIO that supports interrupts, a simple assembler function is required to handle the interrupts generated for that SIO. The handler for COM1, __a_com1isr, is given in Listing 19.5. The substantive code for all four handlers is identical; only their names and the names of the SIO's whose address is passed as an argument are different. The remainder of this book assumes that the other three SIOs exist: COM2sio, COM3sio, and COM4sio; and that main ISRs exist for each: __a_com2isr, __a_com3isr, and __a_com4isr.

The mission of __a_com1isr is simple—to protect the CPU registers during execution of the administrative function s_iadmin at line 110. The caller's stack must also be protected because when an interrupt occurs there may not be enough room on the caller's stack to save the CPU's registers. DOS's internal stack is guaranteed to be just large enough to hold the PUSH of all the registers. In addition to storing the CPU registers, the stack must be large enough to accommodate the stack space required by C for passing arguments and for automatic storage[4]. In other words, a local stack is required.(See details in Appendix B). In lines 15 and 20, the caller's SS and SP registers are saved in local variables, and the address of the local 128-byte stack is loaded into them in lines 25 to 35. With the new stack in effect, the remaining CPU registers can be safely PUSHed. Lines 85 and 90 guarantee that the DS register points to C's data.

---

[4]In Microsoft C, the _interrupt far keywords in a function declaration generate code that preserves the registers and terminates with an IRET, but there is no similar mechanism to generate a local stack.

The s_iadmin interrupt administrator for the 16x50 UART expects an siop argument, so line 95 pushes the address of COM1sio onto the stack prior to calling it. (The s_iadmin function itself is developed later in the chapter.) After return from s_iadmin, the protection process is reversed: the saved registers are POPed off the local stack and the caller's stack is restored. Just before the IRET instruction, line 175 sends an End-of-Interrupt command to the Peripheral Interrupt Controller. Upon exit at line 185, the caller's environment is restored.

The code in Listing 19.5 is written for the Microsoft assembler and for interfacing to the Small Model library. Only small changes are required to accommodate other memory models. Please consult Appendix B for instructions. (The underscores prepended to assembler variables accommodate the Microsoft compiler.)

Global System Structures

Two level-0 global data structures are used to manage interrupts. The first, SIOLIST, already discussed in Chapter 16, provides system-level logical support for the s_open and s_close functions. Referring to Listing 16.5 in that chapter, the intrpt_supp member indicates whether that serial port and/or the system supports interrupts for that port.

THE *sys_ilist* STRUCTURE

The contents of this structure, like the SYS_ILIST structure, contain variables to support functions that enable and restore system interrupts. It contains information highly specific to the system hardware and its implementation. Listing 19.5 shows the structure itself and the declaration of an array of them—one array element for each possible SIO.

Listing 19.5. The SYS_ILIST structure and array.

STRUCT:	SYS_ILIST
HEADER FILE:	SIODEF.H
DESCRIPTION:	Holds pertinent system information about the SIO. Used by level-1 functions.

```
struct SYS_ILIST
    {
    RANK    inum;               /* Rank in system interrupt vector table      */
    MASK    imask;              /* Mask for Interrupt Mask Register of 8259    */
    INTPTR  isr;                /* Pointer to interrupt handler function       */
    INTPTR  oldivect;           /* Save existing vector here                   */
    FAST    oldimr;             /* Save existing Interrupt Mask Register here */
    struct vout232_ *oldgpo2;   /* Save address of gpo2 structure              */
    };
```

STRUCT NAME: `__sys_ilist`
FILE: IBMPC.C
DESCRIPTION: An array, MAX_PORTS in length, of structures describing
interrupt information for each serial port.
COMMENTS: "Supplied" members are installed during s_open. All four ports are
initialized.

```c
struct SYS_ILIST __sys_ilist[MAX_PORTS] =
    {
        {
        I_COM1,        /* Number in vector table */
        IMR_IRQ4,      /* IMR Mask for the PIC   */
        _a_com1isr,    /* Interrupt handler      */
        SUPPLIED,      /* Old interrupt vector   */
        SUPPLIED,      /* Old IMR of PIC         */
        SUPPLIED       /* Save GPO2 structure    */
        },
        { I_COM2, IMR_IRQ3, _a_com2isr, SUPPLIED, SUPPLIED, SUPPLIED },
        { I_COM3, IMR_IRQ4, _a_com3isr, SUPPLIED, SUPPLIED, SUPPLIED },
        { I_COM4, IMR_IRQ3, _a_com4isr, SUPPLIED, SUPPLIED, SUPPLIED },
    };
```

The members of the SYS_ILIST structure are:

`inum`	This is the rank in the system vector table assigned to this peripheral card.
`imask`	This is the AND mask that must be applied to the PIC's Interrupt Mask register to activate interrupts for this port.
`(*isr)()`	This is a pointer to the main ISR such as that shown in Listing 19.5.
`oldivect`	Before installing the vector of our interrupt handler in the system's vector table, the existing vector is saved here for restoration.
`oldimr`	Before changing the new value in the PIC's Interrupt Mask register, its current value is saved here for restoration.
`oldgpo2`	Since GPO2 enables and disables UART interrupts, we must remove it from user control. Before installing a NIL pointer in the SIO, however, its current pointer is saved here for restoration.

Interrupt Vectors and Pointers

An annoying problem arises on 80x86 compilers around the declaration of a pointer variable for vectors. In the Small memory model, for example, data and code are expected to fit entirely in 64K bytes each—that is, within the same *physical* address segment of the CPU. Since the segment portions of all data addresses are the same in Small model, pointers consist only of the 16-bit offset portion of the address. In other words, Small model pointers do not supply the absolute address of an object, just its *offset* within its 64K segment.

This method of pointer representation poses a problem when dealing with system vectors (FAR pointers) that, by definition, specify the complete, 32-bit segment:offset address. This problem is solved by creating a model-independent data type for the 32-bit system pointer. Recall from Chapter 12 that the following line occurs in the file SIOLOCAL.H:

```
typedef void (_interrupt far  *INTPTR)();
```

This data type uses the modifiers[5] _interrupt and far to define a pointer data type that is the 32 bits for *all* models.

THE __sys_intron FUNCTION

In our survey of the components in the IBM PC's interrupt system vis-a-vis the 16X50 UART, we noted that the following steps are required to activate interrupts:

1. Replace the current entry in the vector table with the address of the ISR for that port. The table number for COM1 is 12, for COM2 is 11.
2. Unmask the corresponding bit in the PIC's IMR: bit 3 for IRQ4, bit 4 for IRQ3.
3. Unblock the 16X50's INTRP line by asserting GPO2.

Let's now translate this checklist into __sys_intron for the IBM PC. The complete function is shown in Listing 19.6.

Listing 19.6. The __sys_intron function for the IBM PC.

FUNCTION NAME:	__sys_intron
PROTOTYPE IN:	IBMPC.H
LEVEL:	0
LIBRARY:	IBMPC.C

---

[5]These are the modifiers for the Microsoft compiler; other 80x86 compilers have similar keywords.

DESCRIPTION: Deactivates system interrupts for the port specified. (UART's
GPO2 output is considered a system function.)
RETURNS: void
COMMENTS: The assembly-language functions a_inport and a_outport
reside in INTRP.ASM.
INCLUDE FILES: siodef.h, uart.h, ibmpc.h, dos.h

```
void __sys_intron(SIO *siop, RANK portnum)
{
    REG tmp;
    FAST imr;

        /** STEP 1: change the interrupt vector, save current value **/
    __sys_ilist[portnum].oldivect =   _dos_getvect(__sys_ilist[portnum].inum);
    _dos_setvect( __sys_ilist[portnum].inum, __sys_ilist[portnum].isr);

        /** STEP 2: unmask bit in 16x50's Interrupt Mask register **/
    __sys_disable();
    __sys_ilist[portnum].oldimr =  imr = _a_inport ((BYTE*)IMR);
    imr = (BYTE) (imr &  __sys_ilist[portnum].imask);
    _a_outport((BYTE*) IMR, imr);
    __sys_enable();

        /** STEP 3: Unblock 16x50's INTR line **/
    set232(siop, GPO2, ON);                        /* Unblock interrupts */
    __sys_ilist[portnum].oldgpo2 = siop->gpo2;     /* Save gpo2 structure */
    siop->gpo2 = NIL;                              /* Remove gpo2 control */
    s_iadmin(siop);
    return;
}
```

An explanation of __sys_intron—The structure of this function is dictated by two requirements: (1) to support *every* SIO in the system and (2) to preserve the existing configuration for later restoration by __sys_introff.

STEP ONE: INSTALLING THE INTERRUPT
HANDLER IN THE VECTOR TABLE

Now that we have a storage type for vector address, we're now able to manipulate entries
in the system vector table. Luckily, the Microsoft compiler provides such functions:
_dos_getvect and _dos_setvect. The function _dos_getvect simply returns the specified
element of the system vector table. When opening COM1 (i.e., portnum 0), for example,
the call

```
_ilist[portnum].oldivec =  _dos_getvect(_ilist[portnum].inum);
```

evaluates to

```
_ilist[0].oldivec =  _dos_getvect(12);
```

which fetches the 4-byte contents of element 12 of the vector table and stores it in our local structure array for later recall.

With the current vector for our device safely tucked away, we call the function _dos_setvect to install the address of the main ISR function.

STEP TWO: UNMASKING THE PIC

This section is considerably more straightforward than dealing with system vectors. The PIC's Interrupt Mask register is fetched from port 21H and stored in the structure array for later restoration. It is also assigned to a local variable imr, which is ANDed with the mask in the imask member of the structure, then written back to port 21H.

Assuming that the IMR currently contains FA hex, when opening COM1 (i.e., port 0), for example, the lines

```
imr = (BYTE) (imr &  __sys_ilist[portnum].imask);
_a_outport((BYTE*) IMR, imr);
```

evaluate to

```
imr = ( 0xFA &  0xEF);
_a_outport(0x21,  0xEA );
```

STEP THREE: UNBLOCKING UART INTERRUPTS

The final piece of the interrupt puzzle involves the 16X50, but it is unique to the IBM PC and *not* part of the 16X50 itself. Recall from Figure 7.9 that the IBM PC uses its General-Purpose Output 2 (GPO2) to block and unblock its INTRPT output. In effect, then, GPO2 is used on the IBM PC as a Master Interrupt Enable, allowing its interrupt to reach the Peripheral Interrupt Controller.

After issuing the command to assert GPO2, we must "un-support" it to prevent the user or an application program from disabling it and turning off the interrupts. After saving the SIO's current gpo2 pointer, a NIL is stored there. To verify that this is effective, the RS-232 control menu in TERM should show

    4. Toggle GPO2 [---]

and selecting item four from the menu should produce the message, "Function not supported."

The __*sys_introff* Function

The __sys_introff function for turning off system interrupts, shown in Listing 19.7, consists of reversing the effects of __sys_intron by restoring the values saved in the sys_ilist structure array.

Listing 19.7. The `__sys_introff` function restores system interrupts.

FUNCTION NAME:	`__sys_introff`
PROTOTYPE IN:	IBMPC.H
LEVEL:	0
LIBRARY:	IBMPC.C
DESCRIPTION:	Deactivates system interrupts for the port specified. (UART's GPO2 output is considered a system function.)
RETURNS:	`void`
COMMENTS:	Values are restored from the `__sys_ilist` structure array. The assembly-language functions `a_inport` and `a_outport` reside in INTRP.ASM.
INCLUDE FILES:	siodef.h, ibmpc.h, dos.h

```
void __sysintroff(SIO *siop, RANK portnum)
{
    __sys_disable();
/* restore Interrupt Mask Register */
    _a_outport( (BYTE*)IMR, __sys_ilist[portnum].oldimr);
    __sys_enable();
    _dos_setvect(__sys_ilist[portnum].inum, __sys_ilist[portnum].oldivect);
    siop->gpo2 = __sys_ilist[portnum].oldgpo2 ;  /* Restore gpo2 */
    set232(siop, GPO2, OFF);
}
```

UART Interrupt Functions

In the first part of the chapter, we studied how to enable and manage serial interrupts at the system level. We now must do the same for interrupts at the UART level. It is likely that the descriptions of the interrupt structures of the 16X50 have quietly slipped from your memory, so you are encouraged to review the relevant information in Chapters 6 and 7.

The UART Interrupt Manager

The 16X50 UART supports 80x86 system interrupts via two registers—the Interrupt Enable register (Listing 7.3) and the Interrupt Identification register (Table 19.1, below). The Interrupt Enable register contains a bit for each of the four kinds of 16X50 interrupts: receive data, transmitter holding register empty, RS-232 input, and serialization errors. The first function we require is one to selectively turn these individual interrupts on and off dynamically. The function to accomplish this, `u_int_mgr` is given in Listing 19.8.

Listing 19.8. The `u_intrpt_mgr` **function enables and disables interrupt control bits on the UART.**

FUNCTION NAME: `u_intrpt_mgr`
LEVEL: 1
PROTOTYPE IN: U16X50.H
LIBRARY: U16X50.LIB
RETURNS : `void`
DESCRIPTION: Activates and deactivates 16x50 UART interrupts.
COMMENTS: These routines work by reading the Interrupt Enable register, flipping the appropriate bits, then writing the register back out.
INCLUDE FILES: siodef.h, u16x50.h, level0.h

```c
void u_intrpt_mgr(SIO * siop, short int_wanted, BOOL state)
{
    REG  reg;
    MASK mask;
    switch (int_wanted)
        {
        case RXRDY :  mask = I_RXRDY;  break;
        case THRE  :  mask = I_TBE;    break;
        case SERERR:  mask = I_SERERR; break;
        case RS232 :  mask = I_RS232;  break;
            default:  break;
        }
    reg = (*siop->readbyte)(siop->uart_base + INT_EN);
    if (state == ON)
        reg |= mask;      /* set bit  */
    else
        reg &= ~mask;     /* clear bit */
    __sys_disable();
    (*siop->writebyte)(siop->uart_base + INT_EN, reg);
    __sys_enable();
}
```

An explanation of *u_intrpt_mgr*—The purpose of this function is to manage the individual bits in the Interrupt Identification register. The bit to manipulate is passed in the `int_wanted` variable. It is important to understand that because this is a level-1 function, the `int_wanted` argument contains a manifest constant (not a register mask) which must be converted to the bit mask specific to the 16x50 UART. Whether the interrupt should be turned on or off is passed in the Boolean `state` variable.

The current value of the Interrupt Identification register is read into a temporary variable, which is then either ORed or ANDed with the derived mask value, depending upon whether the bit is being set or cleared. Finally, the new value of the Interrupt Identification register is written back.

An SIO Interrupt Administrator: *s_iadmin*

As discussed earlier in this chapter, when an interrupt occurs, the CPU turns control over to a main ISR such as _a_com1sio given in Listing 19.4. This in turn calls an interrupt administrator function whose responsibility it is to ascertain which of the four possible interrupts has just occurred. It is the duty of the administrator to call the appropriate C-language *interrupt sub-handler* to service the interrupt. Listing 19.9 shows the s_iadmin function.

Listing 19.9. The s_iadmin function: the 16X50 interrupt administrator.

FUNCTION NAME: s_iadmin
          LEVEL: 1
 PROTOTYPE IN: U16X50.H
       LIBRARY: U16x50.LIB
  DESCRIPTION: 16x50 interrupt administrator. When called by the assembly interrupt handler, it reads the Interrupt Identification register to identify the event that requires service, then calls the correct interrupt service routine.
      RETURNS: void
   COMMENTS: Bits 4-7 of the Interrupt Identification register are not relevent, and Bit 0 is 0 when an event needs service. After right-shifting one place, this value becomes an index into an array of function pointers.
INCLUDE FILES: siodef.h, u16x50.h buos.h

```
void s_iadmin(SIO *siop)
{
    FAST index;
    for (EVER)                        /* loop while there are interrupts   */
        {
        index = (*siop->readbyte)(siop->uart_base + INT_ID) & INT_ID_MASK;
        if (index & 01)               /* bit 1 indicates interrupt pending */
            break;
        index >>= 1;                  /* adjust index                      */
        (*siop->isr[index])(siop);    /* call the correct handler          */
        }
}
```

An explanation of *s_iadmin*—The design of this function is based upon the 16X50's Interrupt Identification register shown in Table 19.1.

Table 19.1. The Interrupt Identification register.

Bit 2	Bit 1	Bit 0	Priority	Interrupt Pending
0	0	1	None	None
1	1	0	0	Serialization Error or BREAK
1	0	0	1	Received Data
0	1	0	2	Transmitter Holding Register Empty
0	0	0	3	RS-232 Input

A 0 in bit 0 signifies a pending interrupt whose identity is encoded in bits 1–2. When right-shifted one place and unwanted six high order bits masked off, this register becomes a handy two-bit *integer* index into an array containing pointers to four interrupt sub-handlers. This array, simply called isr, is item number 48 in the SIO given in Listing 19.3:

```
void (*isr[4])(SIO * siop);
```

THE INTERRUPT SUB-HANDLERS

In Chapter 20, we shall compose bona fide, functional interrupt sub-handlers for all four types of interrupts, but for now we need dummy interrupt sub-handlers with which to initialize the isr array in the SIO. This is necessary because when certain interrupts on the 16x50 are enabled, a spurious interrupt is sometimes[6] generated and the three low-order bits of Interrupt Identification register hold garbage. The entire system dutifully treats the spurious interrupt as a real one, with s_iadmin finally calling the function(s) identified by the garbage in the index variable. Unless there is a dummy interrupt sub-handler in place, the CPU begins executing code in outer space. A safety net costs very little: four dummy functions are given in Listing 19.10. These dummy functions, which are used to initialize the isr array in the SIO in Listing 19.2, perform the minimum necessary actions required to clear the spurious interrupt (see Table 7.5).

Listing 19.10. Four dummy interrupt sub-handlers.

```
/* Dummy ISRs to handle spurious interrupts */

void isr_tx_dummy(SIO *siop)
{ /* No code: reading INT_ID clears a the interrupt */  }
```

---

[6]The exact behavior depends upon the brand of the part. On the genuine National part, enabling the transmit interrupt occasionally generates a spurious interrupt, and the IIR usually indicates both a transmit and an RS-232 interrupt.

```
void isr_serr_dummy(SIO *siop)
{      (*siop->readbyte)(siop->uart_base + SER_STAT);     }

void isr_stat232_dummy(SIO *siop)
{      (*siop->readbyte)(siop->uart_base + STAT_232);     }

void isr_rcv_dummy(SIO *siop)
{      (*siop->readbyte)(siop->uart_base + DATA_IO);     }
```

Revectoring UART Interrupts

Successful management of interrupts requires the ability to change interrupt sub-handlers dynamically. For example, you may need a different transmit sub-handler when a modem is in data mode than when in fax mode. Changes in the flow control method may require changing both transmit and receiver interrupt sub-handlers. The s_revector function in Listing 19.11 simplifies swapping UART interrupt sub-handlers.

Listing 19.11. The s_revector function swaps interrupt sub-handlers on the fly.

FUNCTION NAME: s_revector
LEVEL: 1
PROTOTYPE IN: U16X50.H
LIBRARY: U16X50.LIB
DESCRIPT: Installs new UART interrupt sub-handlers.
RETURNS: A pointer to the previous handler.
COMMENTS: Declaration is "function returning a pointer to a function returning void."
INCLUDE FILES: siodef.h, level0.h

```
void (*s_revector(SIO *siop, short int_wanted, void (*newisr)(SIO*))) ()
{
    void (*oldisr)(SIO *);        /* temporary storage for current isr */
    short index;   /* index into the interrupt vector array in s_iadmin */
    short error = 0;
    switch (int_wanted)
        {
        case RS232     :  index = INDEX_RS232; break;
        case THRE      :  index = INDEX_THRE; break;
        case RXRDY     :  index = INDEX_RXRDY; break;
        case SERERR    :  index = INDEX_SERERR; break;
        case RXTIMEOUT:  index = INDEX_RXTIMEOUT; break;
        default:  error = 1; break;
        }
    if (!error)        /* don't revector an undefined interrupt */
        {
```

continues

Listing 19.11. continued

```
        __sys_disable();
        oldisr     = siop->isr[index];    /* save current isr */
        siop->isr[index] = newisr;        /* install new isr  */
        __sys_enable();
        }
    else
        oldisr = NIL;
    return oldisr;                         /* return old isr   */
}
```

An explanation of *s_revector*—The arguments to this function are the address of the new interrupt sub-handler and the number of the interrupt it replaces. Like the int_wanted argument in the u_intrpt_mgr function, the value passed in is a high-level manifest constant and must be converted into an index into the interrupt vector array in the SIO. After the new value is installed, the function returns the replaced vector.

Summary

It is worth drawing the big picture of the management of interrupts in the SIO. Listing 19.13 shows a block diagram of how a receiver interrupt on the UART at COM1 propagates through the system.

The received character arrives at the UART from the modem. The UART sets its Interrupt Identification register to 4, and asserts its INT line. The Peripheral Interrupt Controller (PIC) prioritizes this interrupt and eventually interrupts the CPU. When the CPU completes its current instruction, it asserts its INTA (Interrupt Acknowledge) back to the PIC. The PIC then adds the number of the interrupting IRQ (four for COM1) to its offset register (eight) and outputs the number twelve to the CPU via the I/O bus.

The CPU performs an INT 12 instruction, which has the effect of performing a FAR CALL to vector twelve in the system interrupt vector table. This vector was previously configured by s_open to contain the address of the a_com1isr, the main ISR handler for COM1. Upon being called, a_com1isr switches stacks, protects the registers, then calls the interrupt administrator s_iadmin, passing the address of the SIO structure associated with COM1.

The s_iadmin function reads the 4 from the UART's Interrupt Identification register and converts it to an index of two. It then calls the sub-handler at index number two in the isr table in the SIO—the routine that fetches the byte from the UART. Control now returns to the main ISR which restores the stack and saved registers, then outputs an EOI instruction to the PIC. After the IRET instruction, the CPU begins executing at the point where it was interrupted.

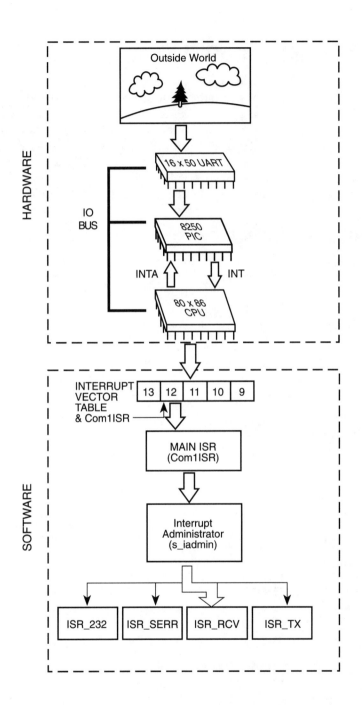

FIGURE 19.2.

Hardware and software components of an interrupt.

Level-Three Modifications

We now need to incorporate the support functions and structures in this chapter into the
s_open and s_close functions so that the nature of the I/O—that is, whether interrupt or
polled I/O—is not apparent to the level-three functions. Before we look at those functions, however, we need a data structure that tells them what kind of I/O to install. This
is the intrpt_status bit-field structure, new item number 47 in the SIO. For each type of
interrupt, there are two semaphore bits: a "wanted" and an "on" bit. The caller of s_open
indicates whether each kind of interrupt is desired by setting its associated "wanted" bit.
Later, the state of each interrupt can then be read from in the "on" bit.

Changes to *s_open*

The logical place to perform the switch-over from polled to interrupt I/O is when the SIO
is s_open'ed. Of course, the interrupts have to be turned off again when the file is s_close'd.
In modifying s_open and s_close, we must keep in mind that they are level-3 functions
and must remain ignorant of the system hardware. Listings 19.12 and 19.13 show the
modifications required to these two functions.

Listing 19.12. Revisions to s_open.

```
FUNCTION NAME:  s_open
         LEVEL:  3
  PROTOTYPE IN:  SIODEF.H
       LIBRARY:  SIO.LIB
   DESCRIPTION:  Modifications support interrupt I/O.
       RETURNS:  SIO*
 INCLUDE FILES:  siodef.h, malloc.h, buos.h, sioctl.h, uart.h, level0.h

int s_errno;

SIO *s_open(USHORT portnum)
{
    extern struct SIOLIST __siolist[];
    extern struct SYS_ILIST __sys_ilist[];
    extern USHORT _maxsios;                  /* global -- number of ports */
    .
    .
    .
        if ( __siolist[siop->devnum].intrpt_supp == TRUE)
        {
        if (siop->intrpt_status.rs232_wanted)
            siop->intrpt_status.rs232_on   = rs232_ion(siop);

        if (siop->intrpt_status.serr_wanted)
            siop->intrpt_status.serr_on = serr_ion(siop);
```

```
        if (siop->intrpt_status.rcv_wanted)
            siop->intrpt_status.rcv_on = rcv_ion(siop);

        if (siop->intrpt_status.tx_wanted)
            siop->intrpt_status.tx_on  = tx_ion(siop, TX_NUMBUFFS, TX_BUFSIZ);
        __sys_intron(siop, portnum);    /* enable system and uart interrupts */
        }
    else if (siop->flow_wanted == RTS_CTS)
        {
        siop->flowon  = rtson;
        siop->flowoff = rtsoff;
        siop->getflow_req = flow_req_rcts;
        }

    __siolist[portnum].sio_openflag = OPEN;     /* mark SIO open in list  */
    return siop;
}
```

An explanation of s_open—Whether interrupts can be enabled at all is determined by the intrpt_supp in the level-0 system capabilities array __siolist. This flag indicates whether interrupts are supported on this SIO (see Listing 19.5). If the flag is FALSE, the code makes no attempt to evaluate the individual interrupts. If the flag is TRUE, however, the semaphore bits in the intrpt_status structure are evaluated one-by one. For example:

```
    if (siop->intrpt_status.rs232_wanted)
siop->intrpt_status.rs232_on = rs232_ion(siop);
```

Here, if the RS-232 semaphore bit is TRUE, a call is made to the rs232_ion function (as yet unwritten) whose sole responsibility is to take whatever steps are necessary to enable RS-232 input interrupts and return its success (ON) or failure (OFF). The return value from rs232_ion is assigned into the RS-232 status semaphore bit intrpt_status.rs232_on. (The "interrupt on" function for each type of interrupt is composed in Chapter 20 along with its actual interrupt sub-handler.) Once each type of interrupt has been processed, system interrupts are enabled by calling __sys_intron.

Changes to s_close

Disabling interrupts in s_close exactly parallels enabling them in s_open.

Listing 19.13. Revisions to s_close.

FUNCTION NAME: s_close
           LEVEL: 3
    PROTOTYPE IN: SIODEF.H
        LIBRARY: SIO.LIB
    DESCRIPTION: Modifications in support of interrupt I/O.

continues

Listing 19.13. continued

```
            RETURNS: SIO*
      INCLUDE FILES:  stdlib.h, siodef.h, buos.h, uart.h level0.h

int s_close(SIO *siop)
{
    extern struct SIOLIST __siolist[];           /* list of available SIO */
    extern struct SYS_ILIST __sys_ilist[];            /* info on each SIO */
    extern int _maxsios;        /* global -- maximum number of serial ports */
    int i;
    if (siop == NIL)
        return NO_CLOSE;
    for (i = 0 ;i < _maxsios; i++)
        if ( (siop == __siolist[i].siop)
            && (__siolist[i].sio_openflag == OPEN))
            {
            __siolist[i].sio_openflag = CLOSED;
            break;
            }
    if ( i == _maxsios)                                 /* no match in list */
        return NO_CLOSE;

    if ( __siolist[siop->devnum].intrpt_supp == ON)
        {
        if (siop->intrpt_status.rs232_on == ON)
            siop->intrpt_status.rs232_on = rs232_ioff(siop);

        if (siop->intrpt_status.serr_on == ON)
            siop->intrpt_status.serr_on = serr_ioff(siop);

        if (siop->intrpt_status.rcv_on == ON)
            siop->intrpt_status.rcv_on  = rcv_ioff(siop);

        if (siop->intrpt_status.tx_on == ON)
            siop->intrpt_status.tx_on       = tx_ioff(siop, WAIT_TIL_FINISH);
        }
    __sys_introff(siop, siop->devnum); /* shut down entire interrupt system */
    s_restore(siop);                              /* restore uart as found  */
    siop->devnum  = VIRGIN;              /* install dummy device number   */
    return 0;
}
```

An explanation of s_close—Whether or not any interrupts need to be disabled is determined by examining the "on" semaphore bits in the intrpt_status structure one-by-one. For example:

```
if (siop->intrpt_status.rs232_on == ON)
    siop->intrpt_status.rs232_on   = rs232_ioff(siop);
```

Here, if the RS-232 semaphore bit is TRUE, a call is made to the `rs232_ioff` function (as yet unwritten) whose sole responsibility is to take whatever steps are necessary to disable RS-232 input interrupts and return a success (OFF) or failure (ON). This return value from `rs232_off` is assigned into the RS-232 status semaphore bit `intrpt_status.rs232_on`. (The "interrupt off" function for each type of interrupt is composed in Chapter 20 along with its actual interrupt sub-handler.)

Once each type of interrupt has been processed, system interrupts are disabled by calling `__sys_introff`.

Conclusion

We have now completed all the ancillary functions to support serial interrupts. The task for the next chapter is to compose for each kind of interrupt a trio of functions: interrupt-on, interrupt-off, and a sub-handler.

Interrupt Sub-Handlers

In the previous chapter we developed the level-0 and -1 functions to support interrupt serial I/O on the IBM PC. This chapter completes the implementation by writing for *each* interrupt:

1. A design for integrating the interrupt into the SIO.

2. An interrupt sub-handler function (called by s_iadmin through the isr array in the SIO) to implement that design.

3. A function that performs whatever tasks are necessary to enable the interrupt: initialization, memory allocation, etc.

4. A function that performs whatever tasks are necessary to disable the interrupt and return the SIO to polled operation.

Since the hardware and system dependencies are resolved in the level-0 and -1 functions, the code written in this chapter is highly portable. That is, it should run properly on any system, any processor, and any UART with little modification. In general, the interrupts are implemented in order of increasing complexity: serialization, RS-232, receiver, and transmitter.

Before we begin composing the actual code, let's first get the bureaucratic overhead out of the way by looking at the constants required for this chapter (Listing 20.1) as well as the new SIO members (Listing 20.2) and their initialization (Listing 20.3). As always, individual items are explained as needed. You may notice that some of the SIO members—numbers 8-12 and 30-32—were introduced in earlier chapters. The reasons for their repetition will become apparent shortly.

New *SIO* Members and Constants

Listing 20.1. New constants required by interrupt sub-handlers.

The following belong in SIODEF.H

```
/* CONSTANTS FOR INTERRUPT ROUTINES */

#define RCV_BUFSIZ  2000        /* Size of receiver ring buffer  */
#define TX_BUFSIZ   BUFSIZ      /* Size of transmit each buffer  */
#define TX_NUMBUFFS 10          /* Number of buffers in tx_queue */

/* Transmit shutdown mode arguments for tx_ioff */

#define WAIT_TIL_FINISH  0
#define SHUTDOWN_NOW     1


/* Return Codes from tx_write */

#define Q_OK        0
#define Q_FULL      1
#define Q_BUF2BIG   2


/* Manifest constants for tx_queue in_useflag member */

#define TX_INUSE    1
#define TX_FREE     0

/* Manifest constants for serial_status function arguments */

enum serstat
    {
    ANY_ERRORS = 0,
    PARITY_ERR, OVERRUN_ERR,
    FRAME_ERR,  BREAK_ON
    };
```

The following belong in U16X50.H

```
/* Receiver's FIFO Trigger Depth */

#define TRIG_1  0x01
#define TRIG_4  0x41
#define TRIG_8  0x81
#define TRIG_16 0xC1


/* Macro to return whether UART's shift register is clear */

#define s_txempty(x) (*(x)->readbyte)((x)->uart_base\
                     (x)->status_off)&(x)->tx_emptymask
```

Listing 20.2. New SIO members required by interrupt sub-handlers.

```
            STRUCT TAG: SIO
                  FILE: SIODEF.H
            DESCRIPTION: Master structure defining a serial port.

struct sio
   {
   .
   .
   .
   FAST    (*s_rstat)(struct sio *);     /*8  Pointer to receiver status    */
   FAST    (*s_read)(struct sio *);      /*9  Pointer to fetch routine      */
   FAST    (*s_xstat)(struct sio *);     /*10 Pointer to xmit status        */
   void    (*s_send)(struct sio *, FAST); /*11 Pointer to xmit function      */
   short   (*s_txblock)(SIO *, BYTE*,short); /*12 "     block xmit function  */
   .
   .
   .
   FAST    (*read232)(SIO *, struct vin232_*); /*30 * to lev-1 fetch function */
   union inbits_232 status;              /*31 See if any RS-232 inputs      */
   union inbits_232 delta;               /*32 Changed since last read       */
   .
   .
   .
   union                                 /*55 SERIALIZATION ERRORS          */
        {
        REG       s_errors;              /* The raw bit-map                 */
        struct                           /* Individual bits                 */
           {
           unsigned  overrun : 1;        /* Overrun error flag              */
           unsigned  parity  : 1;        /* Parity error flag               */
           unsigned  frame   : 1;        /* Framing error flag              */
           unsigned  Break   : 1;        /* Break error flag                */
           unsigned  reserved: 12;
           } bitmap;
        } serr;
   short  rcv_buffsize;                  /*56 Size of the rxrdy buffer      */
   short  rcv_fifo_depth;                /*57 Size UART's receive FIFO      */
   short  rcv_fifo_trigger;              /*58 Receive FIFO Trigger Level    */
   FAST  *rcv_buff;                      /*59 Pointer to receive buffer     */
   FAST  *rcv_buffend;                   /*60 Pointer to end of  "          */
   FAST  *rcv_headp;                     /*61 Where to put next byte        */
   FAST  *rcv_tailp;                     /*62 Where to fetch next byte      */
   short  tx_fifo_depth;                 /*63 Size of UART's xmit FIFO      */
   short  tx_fifo_trigger;               /*64 Transmit FIFO Trigger Level   */
   short  tx_numbuffs;                   /*65 Number of xmit buffers        */
   short  tx_buffsize;                   /*66 Size of each xmit buffer      */
   struct tx_queue *tx_list;             /*67 The circular queue            */
   struct tx_queue *tx_headp;            /*68 Input to tx queue             */
   struct tx_queue *tx_tailp;            /*69 Output to tx queue            */
   struct tx_queue *tx_queue_end;        /*70 Pointer to last member   "    */
   FAST   tx_idle;                       /*71 Transmitter needs kickstart   */
   };
```

Listing 20.3. Initializaton of new SIO members.

SIO NAME:	COM1sio
FILE:	IBMPC.C
LEVEL:	0
DEFINED IN:	SIODEF.H
DECLARED IN:	IBMPC.C
COMMENTS:	Initialization of members for interrupt sub-handlers.

```
SIO COM1sio  =
    {
    .
    .
    .
    s_xmitstat,              /*10 Pointer to xmiter status               */
    s_xmit,                  /*11 Pointer to xmit routine                */
    tx_write,                /*12 Pointer to polled block xmit routine   */
    .
    .
    .
    _vstat232,               /*30 * to level one fetch function          */
    0,                       /*31 RS-232 status bits                     */
    0,                       /*32 RS-232 delta bits                      */
    .
    .
    .
    0,                       /*55 Serialization errors                   */
    RCV_BUFSIZ,              /*56 Size of receive interrupt buffer       */
    SUPPLIED,                /*57 Size of UART's Receive FIFO            */
    SUPPLIED,                /*58 Receive FIFO Trigger Level             */
    NIL,                     /*59 Pointer to receive buffer              */
    NIL,                     /*60 Pointer to end of   "          "       */
    NIL,                     /*61 Where in buff to put next byte         */
    NIL,                     /*62 Where in buff to fetch next byte       */
    SUPPLIED,                /*63 Size of UART's Transmit FIFO           */
    SUPPLIED,                /*64 Transmit FIFO Trigger Level            */
    SUPPLIED,                /*65 Number of trasmit buffers              */
    SUPPLIED,                /*66 Transmit buffer size                   */
    NIL,                     /*67 Pointer to transmit interrrupt queue   */
    NIL,                     /*68 Pointer to tx queue headp              */
    NIL,                     /*69 Pointer to tx queue tailp              */
    NIL,                     /*70 Pointer to last element in tx queue    */
    FALSE,                   /*71 Transmit queue empty                   */
    };
```

Serialization-Error Interrupts

We shall implement serialization error interrupts first. Unlike the other three kinds of interrupts, there is no preexisting *polled* support in the SIO for serialization errors. This makes it possible for us to implement serialization-error interrupts in the simplest possible fashion—that is, without having to integrate it into an existing multi-level infrastructure.

Serialization Errors in the *SIO*

Refer to Chapter 7 to refresh your memory on the subject of serialization errors. Then notice the new union (item 53) in the SIO in Listing 20.2. Declaring this union inside the SIO itself is a departure from our usual style of using only *pointers* to aggregate structures. In truth, the main purpose of the pointer-only style is notation convenience—it makes the SIO appear neater and therefore less daunting.

The Serialization-Error Sub-Handler

Similar to the union that supports RS-232 inputs (Listing 15.17), the serr (serial-error) structure is a union of scalar member s_errors and bit-field structure bitmap[1]. That is, a value written to s_errors can be read as individual bits in bitmap (and vice versa). This simplifies the design of the interrupt sub-handler routine whose sole responsibility is to read the serialization-error register from the UART, make certain that its bits are correctly organized, then write the entire register to the s_errors member. Higher-level functions, however, are free to examine the individual bits. The interrupt sub-handler for serialization errors is shown in Listing 20.4.

Listing 20.4. The isr_serr interrupt sub-handler.

```
FUNCTION NAME: isr_serr
         LEVEL: 1
  PROTOTYPE IN: U16X50.H
       LIBRARY: U16x50.LIB
   DESCRIPTION: Serial error interrupt handler.
       RETURNS: void
      COMMENTS: When an interrupt occurs, this function reads Line Status
                register, then one-by-one masks and copies the next four bits
                into the SIO variables. For portability, this routine is also
                responsible for setting the bits in the SIO's s_errors member
                as follows:
                Error   Overrun   Parity   Framing   BREAK
                Bit     0         1        2         3
 INCLUDE FILES: siodef.h, u16x50.h

void isr_serr(register SIO* siop)
{
    static short err_reg;
    err_reg = (*siop->readbyte)(siop->uart_base + SER_STAT);
    siop->serr.s_errors |= ((err_reg >> 1) & 0x0F);  /* store as bit map */
}
```

[1]The bit-field Break uses an initial capital letter to avoid conflict with the C keyword of the same name.

An explanation *isr_serr*—The actual code for the interrupt sub-handler is disarmingly simple. The serialization status register is read into a temporary variable. To provide for portability to the higher-level functions, the value ultimately placed in the s_errors must follow the canonical bit order:

Error	Over run	Parity	Framing	BREAK	Reserved
Bit	0	1	2	3	4-7

The relevant bits in the 16x50's serialization register (Figure 7.6) are already in canonical order but not in canonical position. The temporary register is therefore right-shifted one place before moving it into the s_errors member of the union. The reserved four upper bits (bits 4-7) are also masked off. Note that the adjusted register is ORed into the s_errors, thus preserving any existing one-bits.

Serialization-Error High-Level Interface

Now that the serialization-error sub-handler is in place, let's take a look at the level-3 function that interfaces to it. (Remember, the level-2 function is omitted here for simplicity.)

Listing 20.5. The `serial_status` function.

FUNCTION NAME: `serial_status`

            LEVEL: 3

    PROTOTYPE IN: SIODEF.H

          LIBRARY: SIO.LIB

    DESCRIPTION: Reports serialization errors.

          RETURNS: short: 1 if the requested error has occured, 0 if it hasn't, and -1 if the error argument is out of range.

     COMMENTS: Errors are cleared upon exit.

               Array index constants are in UART.H. The value returned when the ANY_ERRORS can be treated as a BOOL, but it is actually a bit-map of the errors as follows:

                      Overrun = bit 0   Framing = bit 2

                      Parity = bit 1   BREAK = bit 3

  INCLUDE FILES: siodef.h, levelo,h

```
short serial_status(SIO *siop, RANK whichone)
{
    short errtmp;
    switch (whichone)
        {
        case ANY_ERRORS: errtmp = siop->serr.s_errors;
            siop->serr.s_errors = 0;
            break;
        case  PARITY_ERR: errtmp = siop->serr.bitmap.parity;
            siop->serr.bitmap.parity = FALSE;
            break;
```

```
        case OVERRUN_ERR: errtmp = siop->serr.bitmap.overrun;
            siop->serr.bitmap.overrun = FALSE;
            break;
        case   FRAME_ERR: errtmp = siop->serr.bitmap.frame;
            siop->serr.bitmap.frame = FALSE;
            break;
        case    BREAK_ON: errtmp = siop->serr.bitmap.Break;
            siop->serr.bitmap.Break = FALSE;
            break;
        default: errtmp = -1;
        }
    return errtmp;
}
```

An explanation of `serial_status`—The `whichone` in this function is a manifest (level-3) constant naming the desired serialization status. This constant is applied to a case statement, which copies the named member from the `bitmap` field into a temporary variable. The just-read bit is then cleared. The constant `ANY_ERRORS` returns the entire `s_errors`, thus providing a convenient manner of clearing all the bits in the bit-field as well as indicating whether any errors have occurred in the SIO since it was last read. In this design, the `ANY_ERRORS` argument causes a *destructive read;* that is, it clears all bits in the bit-field. Whether this read is destructive is a matter of taste, so you may wish to omit it and write a separate function to clear the entire bit-field explicitly.

Serialization-Error Interrupt Control

Recall from Chapter 19 that for each interrupt desired, s_open calls a function whose responsibility is to perform whatever configuration is necessary to activate that interrupt. This function for the serialization-error interrupt is given in Listing 20.6.

SERIALIZATION-ERROR INTERRUPTS ON

Listing 20.6. The `serr_ion` function.

FUNCTION NAME:	`serr_ion`
LEVEL:	2
PROTOTYPE IN:	BUOS.H
LIBRARY:	SIO.LIB
DESCRIPTION:	Enables UART serialization interrupts.
RETURNS:	`short`: Always returns ON.
INCLUDE FILES:	siodef.h, buos.h, uart.h

continues

Listing 20.6. continued

```
short serr_ion(SIO *siop)
{
    if (siop->intrpt_status.serr_on == ON)
        return ON;
    siop->old_isr_serr = s_revector(siop, SERERR, isr_serr); /* isr handler */
    u_intrpt_mgr(siop, SERERR, ON);                          /* UART interrupt on */
    return ON;
}
```

An explanation of *serr_ion*—If the serr_on flag in the SIO indicates that serialization-error interrupts are already on, no action is taken and the function returns the constant ON. Otherwise, s_revector is called to install isr_serr (Listing 20.4) in the sub-handler vector table in the SIO. The value returned from s_revector is the current vector at that location, which is stored in the SIO for later restoration. Finally, the u_intrpt_mgr function enables serialization interrupts at the UART.

SERIALIZATION-ERROR INTERRUPTS OFF

Recall from Chapter 19 that for each interrupt desired, s_close calls a function whose responsibility is to perform whatever "un-configuration" is necessary to deactivate that interrupt. This function for the serialization-error interrupt is given in Listing 20.7.

Listing 20.7. The serr_ioff function.

FUNCTION NAME: serr_ioff
          LEVEL: 2
   PROTOTYPE IN: BUOS.H
        LIBRARY: BUOS.LIB
    DESCRIPTION: Disables UART transmitter interrupts.
        RETURNS: short: Always returns OFF.
   INCLUDE FILES: siodef.h, buos.h, uart.h

```
short serr_ioff(SIO *siop)
{
    s_revector(siop, SERERR, siop->old_isr_serr );  /* restore old handler */
    u_intrpt_mgr(siop, SERERR, OFF);                /* UART interrupt on   */
    return OFF;
}
```

An explanation of *serr_ioff*—The s_revector function is called to restore the sub-handler vector saved in the SIO by the serr_ion function (Listing 20.6), then u_intrpt_mgr disables the serialization interrupts in the UART.

RS-232 Status Interrupts

Implementing serialization-error interrupts is easy because it bypasses the virtualization architecture applied to other SIO objects. For example, the high-level function `serial_status` addresses the SIO structure members directly as opposed to calling an intermediate level-2 function.

The situation is different with RS-232 status interrupts where there is a preexisting multi-level virtual structure. For instance, the level-3 function, `stat232`, calls the level-2 function, `vstat232`, to read the status of an RS-232 input. In `vstat232`, a level-1 SIO *function pointer* is called to fetch the appropriate UART register, mask off the necessary bits, and store the results in the *now* member of the RS-232 control structure for that input. Afterward, the user gains access to the *now* function for DTR like this:

```
if (siop->dtr != NIL)
    retval = (siop->dtr->now);
    break;
```

Because polled I/O is employed, before requesting the state of an input, the status function must first be called to update the *now* member of the structure. Let's see how to fit the interrupt sub-handler into this architecture.

RS-232 Interrupt Sub-Handler

The strategy for implementing RS-232 interrupts is to integrate them into the existing structure. In other words, applications calling only level-3 functions are shielded from the internal workings of the underlying implementation. To understand how this strategy is applied, let's look at Listing 20.8, the RS-232 interrupt sub-handler itself.

Listing 20.8. The RS-232 interrupt sub-handler.

FUNCTION NAME: `isr_stat232`
           LEVEL: 1
   PROTOTYPE IN: U16X50.H
        LIBRARY: U16x50.LIB
    DESCRIPTION: RS232 status interrupt handler.
      RETURNS : `void`
     COMMENTS: When an interrupt occurs, this function reads RS232 Status register (aka Modem Status Register), then stores bits 0-3 as deltas, bits 4-7 as status bits, then one-by-one masks and copies 4-7 into individual SIO variables. This routine is also responsible for setting the bits in the SIO's `delta` and `status` member as follows:

continues

Listing 20.8. continued

bit	status	delta
0	cts	cts
1	dsr	dsr
2	ri	ri
3	dcd	dcd
4	gpi1	gpi1
5	gpi2	gpi2

INCLUDE FILES: siodef.h, U16x50.H

```
void isr_stat232(register SIO* siop)
{
    static short stat_reg;
    stat_reg = (*siop->readbyte)(siop->uart_base + STAT_232);
    siop->delta.reg232 = stat_reg &0x0F;  /* mask off status, store deltas */
    siop->status.reg232 = (stat_reg &0xF0) >> 4;   /* store status bits */

    siop->cts->now = (stat_reg >> 4) &1;    /* bit 4 */
    siop->dsr->now = (stat_reg >> 5) &1;
    siop->ri ->now =  (stat_reg >> 6) &1;
    siop->dcd->now = (stat_reg >> 7) &1;    /* bit 7 */
}
```

An explanation *of* `isr_stat232`—Like the sub-handler for serialization errors, this function reads the relevant UART register, formats the bits into canonical order, and stores the scalar members of the two RS-232 unions in the SIO. Now comes the interesting part: the individual status bits are then shifted into the now members of the RS-232 input control structure where the high-level functions will find them.

Have you spotted the problem with this approach? If the polling function is allowed to remain active simultaneous with RS-232 status interrupts, a *race condition* is created and the value of the now member becomes insensitive to short-term events. Consider the following chain of events:

1. The low-level polling function has just read the UART register while DTR is not asserted.

2. At the next instant, a very short-duration pulse (shorter than the polling cycle) occurs on the DTR RS-232 input. This generates an interrupt.

3. Control is vectored to the `isr_stat232` sub-handler, which correctly places a 1 in the now member of the SIO's DTR control structure.

4. The polling routine reads the UART. Since the short DTR pulse is no longer present, the polling routine correctly installs a zero in the now member.

5. The level-3 function `get232` never sees the short duration pulse.

RS-232 Interrupt Control

To understand how the race condition between the polling and the interrupt functions is avoided, let's look at rs232_ion in Listing 20.9, the function called by s_open to perform whatever configuration of the RS-232 interrupt.

RS-232 STATUS INTERRUPTS ON

Listing 20.9. The 232_ion function.

```
FUNCTION NAME:  rs232_ion
        LEVEL:  2
  PROTOTYPE IN:  BUOS.H
      LIBRARY:  SIO.LIB
  DESCRIPTION:  Enables UART transmitter interrupts.
      RETURNS:  short: 1 if successful; otherwise 0;
 INCLUDE FILES:  siodef.h, buos.h, uart.h
```

```c
short rs232_ion(SIO *siop)
{
    if (siop->intrpt_status.rs232_on == ON)          /* already on */
        return ON;
    siop->read232 = NIL;                      /* disable polling funtion */
    siop->old_isr_232 = s_revector(siop, RS232, isr_stat232);
    u_intrpt_mgr(siop, RS232, ON);                   /* UART interrupt on */
    return ON;
}
```

An explanation of 232_ion—If the rs232_on flag in the SIO indicates that interrupts are already on, no action is taken and the function returns the constant ON. Otherwise, s_revector is called to install the isr_stat232 function (Listing 20.8) in the sub-handler vector table in the SIO. The value returned from s_revector is the current vector at that location, which is stored in the SIO for later restoration. Finally, the u_intrpt_mgr function enables the RS-232 status interrupts at the UART.

This function is almost identical to the parallel function for serialization errors. There is, however, one important addition:

```c
siop->read232 = NIL;    /* Disable the polling function */
```

The variable siop->read232 is a pointer to a level-1 status-fetching function. This line prevents the race condition between the interrupt sub-handler and the polling routine. The following line in vstat232 (the level-2 RS-232 status function, Listing 15.15) explains it:

```
if (siop->read232 != NIL)
    p232->now = (BYTE) (*siop->read232)(siop, p232) & p232->mask;
```

In other words, if the level-1 pointer is NIL, the value in the now structure member is untouched.

RS-232 STATUS INTERRUPTS OFF

Recall from Chapter 19 that for each interrupt desired, s_close calls a function whose responsibility is to perform whatever "un-configuration" is necessary to deactivate that interrupt. This function for the RS-232 interrupt is given in Listing 20.10.

Listing 20.10. The rs232_ioff function.

```
FUNCTION NAME:  rs232_ioff
         LEVEL:  2
   PROTOTYPE IN:  BUOS.H
       LIBRARY:  SIO.LIB
   DESCRIPTION:  Disables UART RS232 input interrupts.
       RETURNS:  short: Alwayws returns OFF.
  INCLUDE FILES:  siodef.h, buos.h, uart.h
```

```
short rs232_ioff(SIO *siop)
{
    s_revector(siop, RS232, siop->old_isr_232 );    /* restore old handler */
    u_intrpt_mgr(siop, RS232, OFF);                 /* UART interrupt off */
    siop->read232 = _vstat232;                      /* restore polling funtion */
    return OFF;
}
```

An explanation of *rs232_ioff*—The s_revector function is called to restore the sub-handler vector saved in the SIO by the rs232_ion function (Listing 20.9), then u_intrpt_mgr disables the serialization interrupts in the UART. In addition, the level-1 pointer NIL'ed out in rs232_ion is restored.

Detecting the 16550

As explained in Chapter 7, the 16550 FIFO'ed UART's performance is superior to that of its wimpier cousins, the 8250 and the 16450. Wherever the 16550 is present, therefore, its capabilities ought to be utilized. Recall also from Chapter 7 that the 16550's FIFO trigger-level mechanism applies only to receiver interrupts. That is, transmitter interrupts *always* occur when the last byte has been moved from the holding register into the shift register[2]. The new members in the SIO include four new members dealing with the UART FIFO:

rcv_fifo_depth	The size of the UART's receiver FIFO.
rcv_fifo_trigger	The number of bytes in the UART receiver FIFO required to generate a receiver interrupt.
tx_fifo_depth	The size of the UART's transmitter FIFO. The maximum number of bytes that can be written to the UART in response to a transmitter interrupt.
tx_fifo_trigger	The number of bytes in the UART transmitter FIFO at which a transmitter interrupt occurs.

Modification of the *s_config* Function

As given in Chapter 14, the physical UART is configured by the s_config function (given in Listing 14.21). Listing 20.11 gives the modificatons that enable s_config to detect the presence of a 16550 and configure it to sensible values.

Listing 20.11. The s_config function.

```
FUNCTION NAME: s_config
         LEVEL: 1
   PROTOTYPE IN: MODEM.H
       LIBRARY: U16x50.LIB
   DESCRIPTION: Copies the contents of the 16x50's write registers into the
                virtual array for siop.  Detects the presence of a 16550 and
                configures its FIFO, then stores its state in the virtual array.
       RETURNS: void
  INCLUDE FILES: siodef.h, U16x50.H

/* copy physical UART regs into virtual regs */
void s_config(SIO *siop)
{
.
.
.

    for (i = 0; i < V_REG_SIZE; i++)       /* copy USR column into VIR column */
        siop->v_regp[i][VIR] = siop->v_regp[i][USR];
```

continues

---

[2]This unfortunate design was based on the observation that delays in servicing an interrupt are unimportant in asynchronous applications. As synchronous modems driven by an asynchronous interface (fax modems, for example) become more popular, some industrious manufacturer will doubtless add the trigger level feature. The SIO supports a variable transmitter FIFO trigger level in anticipation of this future development.

Listing 20.11. continued

```
.
.
.
    if ( (*siop->readbyte)(siop->uart_base + FIFO) & 0xC0 )
        /* if FIFO already on */
        siop->v_regp[VFIFO][USR] = 0x81;
    else
        siop->v_regp[VFIFO][USR] = 0;
    (*siop->writebyte)(siop->uart_base + FIFO, 1);   /* turn Bit 1 of IIR on */
    if ( (*siop->readbyte)(siop->uart_base + FIFO) & 0xC0 )
        {
        (*siop->writebyte)(siop->uart_base + FIFO, TRIG_8); /* turn FIFO on */
        siop->tx_fifo_depth    = 16;  siop->tx_fifo_trigger  = 0;
        siop->rcv_fifo_depth   = 16;  siop->rcv_fifo_trigger = TRIG_8;
        }
    else
        {
        siop->tx_fifo_depth    = 1;   siop->tx_fifo_trigger  = 0;
        siop->rcv_fifo_depth   = 1;   siop->rcv_fifo_trigger = 0;
        }
}
```

An explanation of *s_config*—Recall from Chapter 7 that bits 6 and 7 of the Interrupt Identification register are always zero on a 16450/8250 and on a 16550 with its FIFOs disabled. A 16550 is assumed to be present if these bits change after enabling FIFO operation (writing a 1 to bit 1 of the FIFO Control register). The state of the FIFO control register is stored in the virtual UART for later restoration by s_restore.

If a FIFO is detected, the FIFO Control register is then configured to the desired receiver FIFO trigger level. Setting a 16550's 16-byte receiver FIFO to a trigger level of eight is a good compromise between immunity from receiver overrun on the one hand and reducing the per-interrupt overhead of the CPU on the other. As shown in Figure 7.12, the two most significant bits in this register set the FIFO trigger level, and the value 81 hex selects a trigger level of 8. If a 16550 is present, the four FIFO members in the SIO are configured with the selected values; otherwise, they are configured for a 16450/8250-style UART. Although the transmitter FIFO's trigger level is not programmable, it is maintained in the SIO for the benefit of the level-1 functions. For the same reason, the depth of both FIFOs—fixed at 16 in a 16550—are also maintained in the SIO.

Receiver Interrupts

It is possible to conceive of software that obtained its information about serialization errors or RS-232 status via polling. It is hard to grant the same license for receiver interrupts. Its advantages so outweigh its drawbacks that the decision should be automatic— just do it.

Receiver Interrupt Buffer Design

In Chapter 7, we noted that most UART's receivers are actually small FIFO buffers into which incoming bytes are moved as they are assembled from the communications line. Though typically only a few bytes in length, a FIFO of almost any length frees the programmer from writing the frantic catch-it-or-lose-it routines necessary when no FIFO exists. In Chapter 7 we also noted that if the UART's FIFO could somehow be greatly enlarged, much of the pressure placed on software by polling would disappear; that is, without fear of overrunning the receiver's buffer, software could safely extend its polling interval. This, then, is the design goal for our implementation of receiver interrupts: to extend the size of the UART's buffer. We will approach this goal in a characteristically abstract fashion.

The type of buffer we will use to extend the receiver FIFO is called a ring buffer, so named because the action within it is circular. The movement of bytes in and out of this buffer is managed via two pointers, known by convention as the head and tail pointers. Both pointers are initialized to the beginning of the buffer. When a receiver interrupt occurs, the interrupt sub-service routine reads the byte, places it at the location pointed to by the head pointer, then increments the head pointer. Bytes are fetched from the buffer by reading the byte pointed to by the tail pointer, then incrementing the tail pointer. To protect the data following the buffer, if a pointer's value after incrementation points beyond the buffer, the pointer is reset to the beginning of the buffer.

The buffer is "empty" whenever the head and tail pointers are equal. Similarly, the buffer is "full" when the *next* incrementation of the head pointer will make it equal to the tail pointer. This brings up a crucial point in ring buffer design: how should the Receiver handler behave when it encounters a full buffer? There are only two choices: (1) to protect existing data in the buffer by discarding new bytes or (2) to allow new bytes to overwrite existing ones. Since there is no "right" way, we will choose the simpler design of ignoring the overlap of the pointers and allowing new data to overwrite old.

Referring to Listing 20.2, let's look at the SIO variables related to receiver interrupts:

s_rstat	(8)	The SIO's pointer to a function that ascertains whether a byte is available for reading.
s_read	(9)	The SIO's pointer to a function that fetches a byte.
rcv_buffsiz	(56)	The size of the ring buffer in bytes.
rcv_buff	(57)	A pointer to the beginning of the ring buffer.
rcv_headp	(58)	A pointer to the location where the next received byte is stored. The interrupt sub-handler increments this pointer after each byte is safely tucked away.
rcv_tailp	(59)	A pointer to the location from where the next stored byte will be read. The byte-fetch routine increments this pointer after each byte is read.

The Receiver Interrupt Sub-Handlers

The strategy here is to develop receiver interrupt support for a 16550 style (FIFO'd) UART while keeping an eye on compatibility with the 8250/16450 style. As discussed in Chapter 7, a 16550 has two distinct kinds of receiver interrupts: *trigger* and *time-out*. The trigger interrupt occurs when the number of bytes in the receive FIFO equals the programmed trigger level. The interrupt sub-handler for this kind of interrupt can therefore blindly read the UART's receive *trigger-level* times. A FIFO time-out interrupt occurs when there are not enough bytes in the buffer to generate a trigger interrupt, thus guaranteeing that stale bytes are automatically flushed. Specifically, a time-out occurs when the following conditions exist:

1. There is at least one byte in the FIFO.

2. The most recent byte received was longer ago than four continuous byte-times (SDU's).

3. The last read of the receiver register occurred longer ago than four continuous byte-times (SDU's).

To simplify things, let's first compose the sub-handler that will be employed for 16450 interrupts and for 16550 FIFO time-out interrupts. This function, isr_rcv450, is given in Listing 20.12.

Listing 20.12. The isr_rcv450 receiver interrupt sub-handler.

FUNCTION NAME:	isr_rcv450
PROTOTYPE IN:	U16X50.H
LEVEL:	1
LIBRARY:	SIO.LIB
DESCRIPTION:	Byte-read interrupt sub-handler for 16450/8250 (index 2) interrupts. Also used for 16550 FIFO timeout interrupt (index 6).
RETURNS:	void
COMMENTS:	Reads a byte from the UART's FIFO, places it in the interrupt buffer at _rcv_headp. If, after incrementation, rcv_headp points past the end of the buffer, it is reset to point to the beginning of the buffer.
INCLUDE FILES:	siodef.h, buos.h

```
void isr_rcv450(register SIO *siop)
{
    *siop->rcv_headp = s_rcv(siop);                      /* read receiver */
    if ( ++siop->rcv_headp == siop->rcv_buffend)    /* if at end of buffer */
        siop->rcv_headp = siop->rcv_buff;                /* reset pointer end */
}
```

An explanation of `isr_rcv450`—This is a classic ring buffer manager. First, the byte is acquired by calling the receiver function pointer in the SIO, then placed in the ring buffer at the location pointed to by `rcv_headp`. After incrementation, `rcv_headp` is boundary-checked against the end of the buffer, whose address is given in `rcv_buffend`. When `rcv_headp` points outside the allocated buffer, it is "wrapped" back to the beginning.

In addition to fetching single bytes from a 16450 UART receiver interrupt, this sub-handler will also service a 16550 time-out interrupt where an unknown number of bytes must be read. If you are wondering where the support for the 16550 is located, the answer is: there is none. Let's see how this could be so.

Look again at the `s_iadmin` function in Listing 19.9. Notice that it continues to call interrupt sub-handlers as long as interrupts are reported in the Interrupt Identification register. This means when a FIFO time-out occurs, an interrupt is generated. The `s_iadmin` function identifies the interrupt (its index[3] is 6) and calls `isr_rcv450` via the `isr` array in the SIO. As we have seen, this function reads only a single byte into the interrupt buffer. Upon return, `s_iadmin` does not exit, but again reads the Interrupt Identification register, which reports another FIFO time-out interrupt. In this, `s_rcv450` is called repeatedly— once for every byte in the FIFO—until every byte in the receiver FIFO is empty.

Let's now look at the interrupt sub-handler designed especially to service FIFO interrupts.

Listing 20.13. The `isr_rcv550` receiver interrupt sub-handler.

FUNCTION NAME:	`isr_rcv550`
PROTOTYPE IN:	U16X50.H
LEVEL:	1
LIBRARY:	SIO.LIB
DESCRIPTION:	Multiple byte-read interrupt subhandler for 16550 level-trigger (index 2) interrupt.
RETURNS:	`void`
COMMENTS:	Reads a byte from the UART's FIFO, places it in the interrupt buffer at `rcv_headp`. If, after incrementation, `rcv_headp` points past the end of the buffer, it is reset to point to the beginning of the buffer.
CAUTION:	Do not use as a 16450/8250 sub-handler.
INCLUDE FILES:	siodef.h, buos.h

continues

---

[3]The term index is used to describe the contents of the Interrupt Indentification register after it has been right-shifted one place.

Listing 20.13. continued

```
void isr_rcv550(register SIO *siop)
{
    short fifo_bytes = siop->rcv_fifo_trigger;          /* num bytes in FIFO */
    while (fifo_bytes—)                         /* while there's a byte in the FIFO */
    {
    *siop->rcv_headp = s_rcv(siop);                         /* read receiver */
    if ( ++siop->rcv_headp == siop->rcv_buffend)    /* if at end of buffer */
        siop->rcv_headp = siop->rcv_buff;                    /* reset pointer */
    }
}
```

An explanation of *isr_rcv550*—This handler is called when the FIFO in a 16550 reaches it programmed trigger level. There is only one difference between this function and the isr_rcv450 interrupt handler: this one reads the receiver register a fixed number of times, depending upon the setting of rcv_fifo_trigger in the SIO. This approach is *vastly* more efficient than isr rcv450 in Listing 20.13 because the bytes are read from the FIFO in one gulp—that is, without incurring the considerable overhead of multiple trips through the outer loop of s_iadmin.

Interfacing Receiver Interrupts to the *SIO*

In the SIO scheme developed in this book, a function at one level "translates" its arguments for the function below it, which in turn translates its arguments, and so on. Only at the very lowest levels in this hierarchy—in our case, levels 0 and 1—is the raw hardware addressed. In this fashion, we are able to move from the abstract to the concrete in a series of gradually descending steps.

Recall that the level-2 data receive routines in the SIO library call function pointers in the SIO. Here's the function s_getc, for example:

```
FAST s_getc(register SIO *siop)
{
    while ((*siop->s_rstat)(siop) == 0)      /* wait for char to be ready    */
        {;}
    return ((*siop->s_read)(siop));          /* read and return it           */
}
```

In other words, this function knows nothing about the mechanics of fetching a byte, but it does know what is *abstractly* required—it must first wait for the receiver's "status" to become TRUE, then it "reads" and returns the just-arrived byte. The anatomical details of actually fetching the status and reading the byte are performed through the functions pointed to by the s_rstat and s_read variables in the SIO. These two pointers begin life pointing to the level-1 UART functions s_rcvstat and s_rcv. In other words, the SIO is initialized to perform *polled* I/O using the UART's status bits.

To implement receiver interrupts—or, for that matter, any alternative method of I/O—we need only substitute two new pointers for s_rstat and s_read: pointers that return the status and data from the ring buffer instead of from UART registers. These new level-1 functions—for consistency we shall call them s_ircvstat and s_ircv—are given in Listing 20.14 and 20.15.

INTERRUPT RECEIVE AND RECEIVE-STATUS

Listing 20.14. The s_ircvstat function.

```
FUNCTION NAME:  s_ircvstat
         LEVEL:  2
  PROTOTYPE IN:  BUOS.H
       LIBRARY:  BUOS.LIB
   DESCRIPTION:  Interrupt equivalent to s_rcvstat. Ascertains whether a byte is
                 available in the interrupt buffer.
       RETURNS:  FAST: Non-zero if a byte is avaialable.
      COMMENTS:  The interrupt buffer is empty when the two pointers are equal.
 INCLUDE FILES:  siodef.h, level0.h


FAST s_ircvstat(SIO *siop)
{
    return siop->rcv_headp != siop->rcv_tailp;
}
```

An explanation of *s_ircvstat*—This function is spectacularly unspectacular: it simply returns the answer to the question, "Is there a character in the buffer?" Only if the head and tail pointers are equal is the buffer empty. (Quiz: why would return (rcv_headp–rcv_tailp) not work?)

Listing 20.15. The s_ircv function.

```
FUNCTION NAME:  s_ircv
         LEVEL:  2
  PROTOTYPE IN:  BUOS.H
       LIBRARY:  BUOS.LIB
   DESCRIPTION:  Interrupt function to read a character.
       RETURNS:  FAST
      COMMENTS:  Returns the byte in the interrupt buffer pointed to by the SIO
                 member rcv_tailp. If, after incrementation, rcv_tailp points
                 past the end of the buffer, it is reset to the beginning.
 INCLUDE FILES:  siodef.h, level0.h
```

continues

Listing 20.15. continued

```
FAST s_ircv(register SIO *siop)
{
    static FAST c;                              /* static for speed      */
    __sys_disable();
    c = *siop->rcv_tailp;                       /* put in buffer at pointer */
    if ( ++siop->rcv_tailp == siop->rcv_buffend)
        siop->rcv_tailp = siop->rcv_buff;  /* wrap back to beginning   */
    __sys_enable();
    return c;
}
```

An explanation of s_ircv—The byte-read function is essentially the obverse of the interrupt sub-handler shown in Listing 20.12. Here, however, the byte at rcv_tailp is read before its boundary is tested and adjusted.

Receiver Interrupt Control

With the two SIO function pointers for servicing the receiver interrupt buffer in hand, let's now look at the functions required to enable receiver interrupt operation.

RECEIVER INTERRUPTS ON

Recall from Chapter 19 that for each interrupt desired, s_open calls a function whose responsibility is to perform whatever configuration is necessary to activate that interrupt. This function for the receiver interrupt is given in Listing 20.16.

Listing 20.16. The rcv_ion function.

```
FUNCTION NAME: rcv_ion
         LEVEL: 2
   PROTOTYPE IN: BUOS.H
       LIBRARY: SIO.LIB
   DESCRIPTION: Enables UART receiver interrupts.
       RETURNS: short: ON if successful; otherwise OFF.
  INCLUDE FILES: malloc.h, siodef.h, buos.h, uart.h
```

```
short rcv_ion(SIO *siop)
{
    if (siop->intrpt_status.rcv_on == ON)                  /* Already on */
        return ON;
    siop->rcv_buff  = (FAST*)malloc(siop->rcv_buffsize * sizeof(FAST));
    if (siop->rcv_buff == NIL)                             /* If malloc fails */
        return OFF;
    /* initialize pointers */
```

```
    siop->rcv_headp  = siop->rcv_tailp = siop->rcv_buff;
    siop->rcv_buffend = siop->rcv_buff + siop->rcv_buffsize;
    /* swap pointers in SIO */
    siop->s_rstat = s_ircvstat;
    siop->s_read  = s_ircv;
    if (siop->rcv_fifo_depth > 1)
        {                          /* if 16550, install two sub handlers */
        s_revector(siop, RXTIMEOUT, isr_rcv450);
        siop->old_isr_rcv = s_revector(siop, RXRDY, isr_rcv550);
        }
    else                           /* if 16450, install one sub handler */
        siop->old_isr_rcv = s_revector(siop, RXRDY, isr_rcv450);
    s_clearerr(siop);                          /* clear garbage */
    u_intrpt_mgr(siop, RXRDY, ON);             /* UART interrupt on */
    return ON;
}
```

An explanation of `rcv_ion`—Like previous interrupt-enabling functions, this one returns immediately if the receiver interrupts are already enabled. Otherwise, it attempts to allocate `rcv_buffsize` bytes of memory for the ring buffer. If the `malloc` fails, the function returns immediately, otherwise the `rcv_headp` and `rcv_tailp` members are pointed at the allocated memory and the `rcv_buffend` marker is pointed at the first byte beyond the buffer. The interrupt function pointers are installed in the SIO in place of the polled ones. Note also that if a 16450 is present, `isr_rcv450` is the sole receiver sub-handler (index 2); if a 16550 is present, however, `isr_rcv450` becomes the timeout interrupt (index 6) sub-handler and `isr_rcv550` services the trigger-level (index 2) interrupts.

Finally, the `u_intrpt_mgr` function enables the receiver interrupts at the UART.

RECEIVER INTERRUPTS OFF

Recall from Chapter 19 that for each interrupt desired, `s_close` calls a function whose responsibility is to perform whatever "un-configuration" is necessary to deactivate that interrupt. This function for the receiver interrupt is given in Listing 20.17.

Listing 20.17. The `rcv_ioff` function.

FUNCTION NAME: `rcv_ioff`
          LEVEL: 2
  PROTOTYPE IN: BUOS.H
        LIBRARY: SIO.LIB
  DESCRIPTION: Disables UART receiver interrupts.
       RETURNS: `short`: Always returns `OFF`.
  INCLUDE FILES: malloc.h, siodef.h, buos.h, uart.h

continues

Listing 20.17. continued

```
short rcv_ioff(SIO *siop)
{
    s_revector(siop, RXRDY, siop->old_isr_rcv );    /* restore old handler */
    free((VOID*)siop->rcv_buff);                    /* free ring buffer    */
    siop->s_rstat = s_rcvstat;              /* restore poll status funct   */
    siop->s_read  = s_rcv;                  /* restore poll read funct     */
    siop->intrpt_status.rcv_on  = FALSE;
    u_intrpt_mgr(siop, RXRDY, OFF);                 /* UART interrupt OFF  */
    return OFF;
}
```

An explanation of *rcv_ioff*—As expected, this function reverses the effects of the rcv_ion function. The s_revector function is called to restore the sub-handler vector saved in the SIO by the rcv_ion function (Listing 20.16). Next the memory occupied by the ring buffer is freed. The two polled function pointers are reinstalled in the SIO in place of the interrupt ones. Finally the u_intrpt_mgr disables the receiver interrupts in the UART.

Transmitter Interrupts

The design for implementing transmitter interrupts is an extension of the one used for receiver interrupts. A buffer of data is submitted to the transmitter interrupt sub-handler, which stuffs one or more bytes into the UART's FIFO. When all the bytes in the UART's FIFO have been transmitted, another interrupt is generated, and the process repeats until all the bytes in the buffer are transmitted.

Transmitter Interrupt Buffer Design

The buffer itself is not passed to the interrupt sub-handler, but rather a structure that describes the buffer. The tx_queue structure is given in Listing 20.18. Let's review its members:

locbuff	A pointer to the beginning of the ring buffer.
buffp	A pointer to the location in locbuff to the next byte for transmission.
buffcnt	The size of the buffer in bytes.
inuseflag	An indicator that this buffer is currently being transmitted by the interrupt sub-handler.

One of the primary concerns in designing a transmitter interrupt architecture is keeping the UART supplied with enough data to keep it busy. Ideally, when transmitting large amounts of data the serial output should never be idle, even for so little as a single bit-time. For synchronous modems employing a asynchronous interface, this is an absolute requirement. This goal would be difficult to attain when employing only a single buffer:

after the last byte of a buffer has been sent, the line goes idle in only a single byte-time[4]—
scarcely enough time to obtain more data, refill the empty buffer, then resubmit it. Indeed, such an architecture is scarcely better than polling—scrambling to assemble an entire buffer of data is hardly easier easier than scrambling to fetch a single character.

Listing 20.18. The `tx_queue` structure.

```
struct tx_queue
   {
   char *locbuff;          /* pointer to local buffer       */
   char *buffp;            /* pointer to next char in buffer */
   short buffcnt;          /* size of this buffer            */
   char  inuseflag;        /* buffer status flag             */
   };
```

To avoid the time pressure wrought of a single transmit buffer, we will build an architecture based upon many buffers. This takes a form of an array of tx_queue structures—the
tx_list. After submission for transmission, a buffer is encapsulated in one of the tx_queue
structures in this array. The management of the array is similar in principle to the ring
buffer used in the receiver sub-handler: a structure (instead of a byte) is queued for transmission at a head pointer, while the transmitter sub-handler transmits the buffer in the
structure at a tail pointer. This architecture is illustrated in Listing 20.1. Notice that the
storage pointed to by locbuff in each tx_queue is dynamically allocated.

Referring to Listing 20.2 let's examine the SIO variables that implement the tx_list:

tx_numbuffs	(63)	The number of tx_queue structures in the tx_list array.
tx_buffsize	(64)	The number of bytes in the structure's buffer (locbuff).
tx_list	(65)	A pointer to an array of tx_queue structures.
tx_headp	(66)	A pointer to the next available array member where a tx_queue structure can be inserted.
tx_tailp	(67)	A pointer to the tx_queue structure whose buffer is currently being transmitted.
tx_queue_end	(68)	The lower boundary marker of the tx_list array. (The upper boundary is always the first element of the tx_list array.)
tx_idle	(69)	A semaphore to indicate that the UART's transmitter is idle.

Notice that tx_list is not an array of tx_queue structures, but a pointer to such an array.
This arrangement is necessary in order to support a variable number of buffers of a variable size. While looking at the transmitter interrupt sub-handler itself, also look at Figure
20.1, which illustrates how the transmitter queue is managed.

---

[4]Assuming a non-FIFO'ed UART.

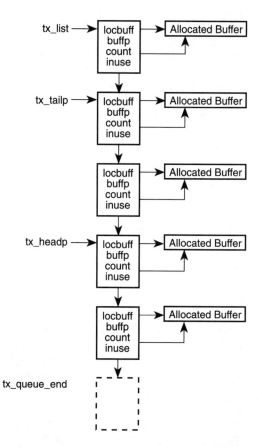

FIGURE 20.1.

Illustration of the `tx_list` *array of* `tx_queue` *structure.*

The Transmitter Interrupt Sub-Handler

The code for the transmitter interrupt sub-handler is an uneventful exercise in queue management—with one exception. In Chapter 19 we discussed how some UARTs (and the 16x50 in particular) can generate spurious interrupts when interrupts are enabled[5]. In a single-buffer interrupt handler such as that employed for the receiver interrupt handler, a spurious interrupt is relatively harmless since it simply delivers an ersatz character. Suprious interrupts are much more dangerous in a multi-buffer sub-handler because they can actually unbalance the entire queue. Note how this problem is solved in Listing 20.19.

---

[5]It is informative to ignore this trap and trace a spurious transmitter interrupt and note how quickly the equilibrim of the `tx_list` is upset.

Listing 20.19. The `isr_tx` function.

FUNCTION NAME: isr_tx
   PROTOTYPE IN: U16X50.H
         LEVEL: 1
      LIBRARY: U16X50.LIB
  DESCRIPTION: Transmit interrupt subroutine. Transmits data from buffer at
                 tx_tailp.
     RETURNS: void
   COMMENTS: A circular buffer of queues. Queues are allocated by the tx_ion
                 function.
 INCLUDE FILES: siodef.h, buos.h

```
     void isr_tx(SIO *siop)
     {
05   short tx_cnt; /* handle spurious interrupts */
10   if (siop->tx_tailp->inuseflag == TX_FREE)
15       return;
20   tx_cnt = siop->tx_fifo_depth - siop->tx_fifo_trigger; /* Bytes to xmit */
25   if (siop->tx_tailp->buffcnt > tx_cnt)   /* Try to pipeline */
30       {
35       short pipecnt = tx_cnt;
40       register char *buffp = siop->tx_tailp->buffp;
45       while (pipecnt--)
50           {
55           s_xmit(siop, *buffp);
60           ++buffp;
65           }
70       siop->tx_tailp->buffcnt -= tx_cnt;
75       return;
80       }
85   while (tx_cnt-- > 0)                            /* fill UART fifo    */
90       {
95       if (siop->tx_tailp->buffcnt == 0 )      /* current buffer is empty? */
100          {
110          siop->tx_tailp->inuseflag = TX_FREE;      /* else mark it free */
115          if (++siop->tx_tailp == siop->tx_queue_end) /* Q-pointer wrap? */
120              siop->tx_tailp = &siop->tx_list[0];
125          if (siop->tx_tailp->inuseflag == TX_FREE)      /* all done ? */
130              {
135              siop->tx_idle = TRUE;              /* mark data underflow    */
140              return;
145              }
150          }
155      s_xmit(siop, *siop->tx_tailp->buffp);     /* send next char in buff */
160      --siop->tx_tailp->buffcnt;                /* adjust counter         */
165      ++siop->tx_tailp->buffp;
170      }
175  return;
180  }
```

An explanation of *isr_tx*—To detect spurious interrupts, the first question upon entering the transmitter interrupt sub-handler is "How did I get here?" Therefore line 10 checks to see if the structure pointed to by tx_tailp is actually being transmitted by checking its inuseflag marker for the value TX_FREE.

Line 20 calculates the number of bytes that can be written to the UART during one interrupt cycle. This number is always the difference between the size of the UART's transmit FIFO and its interrupt trigger level. In the case of a 16450/8250-style UART, the value is one. For a 16550 the value is sixteen (recall that it doesn't support *transmitter* interrupt trigger levels).

Skip for a moment to line 85. The variable tx_cnt controls the while loop that follows. At line 95, the structure's buffer counter is tested to ascertain if the buffer is empty; if so, its pointer (buffp) is reset to the beginning, and the structure is marked free for reuse at line 110. After marking the structure free, the tail pointer is incremented and boundary-tested at line 115. If tx_tailp after incrementation points beyond the end of the array, it is reset to the beginning. The inuseflag of the new structure is then tested at line 125. The value TX_FREE means there are no more structures to transmit, so the SIO semaphore tx_idle is made TRUE. If the code makes it past the gamut of boundary testing and pointer adjustment, the character pointed to by buffp is written to the UART at line 100, followed by housekeeping arithmetic. This loop is repeated for for every character (i.e., tx_cnt times).

The loop from lines 85 to 150 performs extensive pointer dereferencing on *each* byte. To avoid this inefficiency, we employ a technique known as *pipelining*. At 25 we ascertain if there are currently enough bytes in the buffer to fill the UART's FIFO. If not, the code proceeds to line 85 as described above. If there is enough room, however, the bytes are jammed into the UART with a minimum of fanfare, the counter is adjusted, and the function returns. To increase efficiency, the buffer variable is dereferenced into a local register variable for ever faster operation.

Notice how the sub-handler automatically keeps the UART busy: as soon as a buffer in one tx_queue is exhausted, the next tx_queue is undertaken. But the astute reader will have asked: "What happens when there is no more data?" Since the next interrupt depends on the *previous* byte, interrupts cease. How, then, is the initial UART interrupt generated when a buffer of data is submitted to an "idle" sub-handler? The answer lies in the tx_idle semaphore, which broadcasts the idle state. We will return to this point when we examine the tx_iwrite function a bit later.

Transmitter Interrupt Control

We now need to compose the two functions that configure and unconfigure transmitter interrupts. Because of the transmitter interrupt architecture, these functions are more complicated than their earlier counterparts. The configuration function is given in Listing 20.20 and the unconfiguration function in Listing 20.21.

TRANSMITTER INTERRUPTS ON

By now the basics here should be familiar: turn on the UART's transmitter interrupt, revector the transmitter interrupt, and so forth. In the case of transmitter interrupts, however, there is much more work to be done.

Listing 20.20. The `tx_ion` function.

FUNCTION NAME: `tx_ion`
           LEVEL: 2
   PROTOTYPE IN: BUOS.H
       LIBRARY: BUOS.LIB
   DESCRIPTION: Enables UART transmitter interrupts, allocates, and initializes buffers.
        RETURNS: short: ON if successful; otherwise OFF.
  INCLUDE FILES: siodef.h, malloc.h, buos.h, uart.h, level0.h

```
#define Q_SIZE (numbuffs * sizeof(struct tx_queue))

short tx_ion(SIO *siop, short numbuffs, short bufflen)
{
10      int i;
15      char *guinea_pig;
20      unsigned q_size, local_size;
25      if (siop->intrpt_status.tx_on == ON)       /* already on        */
30          return ON;
    /* Before beginning, test that there's enough heap */
35      q_size = numbuffs * sizeof(struct tx_queue);
40      local_size = bufflen * sizeof(char) * numbuffs;
45      guinea_pig = (char*)malloc(qsize + localsize);
50      if (guinea_pig == NIL)                     /* if malloc fails   */
55          return OFF;
60      free (guinea_pig);                         /* ok, release it    */
    /* Yep, enough heap */
65      siop-> tx_numbuffs = numbuffs;             /* publish           */
70      siop->tx_buffsize  = bufflen;
    /* allocate memory for queue and buffers */
75      siop->tx_list = (struct tx_queue *)malloc(Q_SIZE);
80      for (i = 0; i < numbuffs; ++i)             /* initialize queue  */
85          {
90          siop->tx_list[i].locbuff   = (char *) malloc(siop->tx_buffsize);
95          siop->tx_list[i].buffp     = siop->tx_list[i].locbuff;
100         siop->tx_list[i].inuseflag = TX_FREE;
105         siop->tx_list[i].buffcnt   = 0;
110         }
115     siop->tx_headp = siop->tx_tailp
                       = siop->tx_queue_start
                       = &siop->tx_list[0];
120     siop->tx_queue_end = &siop->tx_list[numbuffs];    /* Mark end */
    /* Install interrupt function pointers */
```

continues

Listing 20.20. continued

```
125     siop->s_xstat   = s_ixmitstat;
130     siop->s_send    = s_ixmit;
135     siop->s_txblock = tx_iwrite;
140     siop->old_isr_tx = s_revector(siop, THRE, isr_tx);
145     u_intrpt_mgr(siop, THRE, ON);              /* UART interrupts on */
150     siop->intrpt_status.tx_on = TRUE;
155     __sys_disable();
160     siop->tx_idle = TRUE;
165     __sys_enable();
170     return ON;
      }
```

An explanation of *tx_ion*—The storage for the tx_list array is allocated as well as the buffers contained in each tx_queue structure. In lines 35 to 60 the total memory require-ment is calculated in the guinea_pig variable, then a trial malloc is performed to make certain that there is sufficient storage available. If not, the function returns OFF. If malloc succeeds, however, guinea_pig is immediately freed and the tx_list array is allocated at line 75. Next, each tx_queue structure is initialized by mallocing its buffer storage, install-ing its count, setting pointers, and marking each in_useflag open for business. At line 115 the head, tail, and pointers boundary pointers are initialized.

As in rcv_ion several function pointers are swapped to provide a transparent interface between the high-level transmit functions and the transmit interrupt I/O. (We discuss these in detail shortly.) Finally, the transmitter interrupt is revectored and enabled, and the en-tire transmitter interrupt mechanism is declared ready to go by installing TRUE in the tx_idle semaphore.

It is important to notice that the size of the buffers in each tx_queue structure are the same *fixed* size. The tx_ion call in s_open, for example, specifies a length of TX_BUFSIZ, which is in turn defined as BUFSIZ, the size of C's stream I/O buffer given in STDIO.H.

TRANSMITTER INTERRUPTS ON

It is obvious that the function to unconfigure transmitter interrupts, tx_ioff, shown in Listing 20.21, must be composed with care so that valid data already in the queue is not discarded. But there lurks a more sinister way to lose data. In fact, one of the classic gotchas in UART programming is a transmit interrupt handler that intermittently and inexplica-bly fails to transmit the last character in the last buffer.

Listing 20.21. The `tx_ioff` function.

FUNCTION NAME: `tx_ioff`
LEVEL: 2
PROTOTYPE IN: BUOS.H
LIBRARY: BUOS.LIB
DESCRIPTION: Disables UART transmit interrupts and restores pointers, vectors, and frees memory.
RETURNS: `short`: Always returns `OFF`.
COMMENTS: Mode argument causes either an immediate shutdown or causes a wait for the queue to empty and the last byte to clear the UART. (`s_txempty` is a macro in `uart.h`)
INCLUDE FILES: malloc.h, siodef.h, buos.h, uart.h

```
short tx_ioff(SIO *siop, short mode)
{
    short i;
    if (mode == WAIT_TIL_FINISH)  /* Gentle shutdown */
        while(!siop->tx_idle || !s_txempty(siop) )
            {;}            /* CAUTION: compiler optimizer may toss this! */

    u_intrpt_mgr(siop, THRE, OFF);              /* UART interrupt off */
    (void*) s_revector(siop, THRE, siop->old_isr_tx); /* ... restore old handler */
    /* clean up heap */
    for (i = 0; i < siop->tx_numbuffs; ++i)
        free(siop->tx_list[i].locbuff);         /* Release buffers ... */
    free(siop->tx_list);                        /* ...release queue ...*/
    siop->tx_queue_end = siop->tx_headp = NIL;  /*... nil out ...      */
    siop->tx_tailp     = NIL;                   /*... pointers....     */
    siop->s_xstat      = s_xmitstat;            /* restore the ...     */
    siop->s_send       = s_xmit;                /* ... polling pointers*/
    siop->s_txblock    = tx_write;
    siop->tx_idle      = FALSE;                 /* mark ready to go    */
    return OFF;
}
```

An explanation of `tx_ioff`—Notice that `tx_ioff` requires a mode parameter. To understand why, pretend that several seconds' worth of structures have just been queued up in `tx_list` for transmission. The `s_close` function is then immediately called. What shall become of the untransmitted buffers of data? If `tx_ioff` is called with the SHUTDOWN_NOW parameter, the entire transmitter interrupt structure is destructively dismantled: transmitter interrupts are disabled, its sub-handler is revectored, and `tx_list` and all buffers are released back to the heap.

If, however, `tx_ioff` is called with the WAIT_TIL_FINISH parameter, two events come to pass before shutdown occurs. The obvious case is the wait for the `tx_idle` semaphore signal that the sub-handler has completed sending all the buffers in `tx_list`. Less obvious is the wait for the transmitter's shift register to become empty. Recall that transmitter interrupts occur when the last byte in the FIFO moves into the UART's shift register for serialization. In other words, when the interrupt occurs on which the tx_idle semaphore is set, the last byte written is at that instant still being clocked out of the UART. The s_txempty function (a macro in Listing 20.1) therefore waits until the UART's shift-register-empty bit becomes TRUE.

Interfacing Transmitter Interrupts to the *SIO*

We have seen how the transmitter interrupt sub-handler in Listing 20.19 walks through the tx_list array emptying its buffers. It is now time to build an interface between the high-level functions and this array. The philosophy is exactly as that developed for the receiver interrupt interface—transparency. That is, the details of the underlying I/O—polled or interrupts—are invisible to the higher-level functions.

Referring to Listing 20.2 let's examine the SIO variables that implement the interface to the tx_list array:

s_xstat	(10)	A pointer to a transmit status function. It is initialized to the polling function s_xmitstat.
s_send	(11)	A pointer to a single-byte transmit function. It is initialized to the polling function s_xmit.
s_txblock	(12)	A pointer to a function to transmit a buffer of characters. It is initialized to the polling function s_write (disussed later).

The Block-Write Interface

The value of transmitter interrupts is the ability to submit entire buffers of data for transmission by adding them to the tx_list array. This brings up two interesting problems: (1) how to provide a level-3 function for transmitting a buffer of data even when polled I/O is employed; and (2) how to transmit characters one at a time when the entire system is optimized for transmitting blocks of characters.

INTERRUPT BLOCK-TRANSMIT

Because the cornerstone of the transmitter interrupt architecture is the ability to submit entire buffers for transmission, our first chore is to compose tx_iwrite, the function that adds structures (buffers) to the tx_list array. This function, given in Listing 20.22, is called by all high-level functions that wish to submit buffers for interrupt transmission.

Listing 20.22. The tx_iwrite function.

FUNCTION NAME: tx_iwrite
    DESCRIPTION: Submits a block of data for interrupt-driven transmission.
          LEVEL: 3
    PROTOTYPE IN: SIODEF.H
        LIBRARY: SIO.H
        RETURNS: Q_OK if there was room in the queue, Q_FULL if not, or Q_BUF2BIG if
                 the buffer passed is larger than the local buffer.
     COMMENTS: Used as an initializer, so it cannot be a macro.
  INCLUDE FILES: siodef.h, uart.h, memory.h

```
short tx_iwrite(SIO *siop, BYTE *newbuff, short count)
{
05    if (siop->tx_headp->inuseflag == TX_INUSE)  /* queue was full, try again */
10        return Q_FULL;
15    if (count > siop->tx_buffsize)
20        return Q_BUF2BIG;
25    siop->tx_headp->buffp = siop->tx_headp->locbuff;        /* reset pointer */
30    memcpy(siop->tx_headp->buffp, newbuff, count);/* copy into local storage */
35    siop->tx_headp->buffcnt = count;
40    siop->tx_headp->inuseflag = TX_INUSE;        /* mark queue element busy */
45    if (++siop->tx_headp == siop->tx_queue_end)   /* test boundary        */
50        siop->tx_headp = siop->tx_queue_start;   /* wrap pointer         */
55    if (siop->tx_idle == TRUE)            /* if transmitter is off, kickstart */
60        {
65        siop->tx_idle = FALSE;
70        (*siop->isr[INDEX_THRE])(siop);   /* call the transmit interrupt */
75        }
80    return Q_OK;
}
```

An explanation of tx_iwrite—If no tx_queue structures are free in tx_list, Q_FULL is returned, signifying that the calling function should try again later. As noted earlier, the buffer in the tx_queue structure is a fixed size; therefore, the error Q_BUFF2BIG is returned if count exceeds this size[6].

If there is a free structure, the caller's buffer (newbuff) is copied into the locbuff member in the tx_queue pointed to by tx_headp. The count is also copied, and the inuseflag is set to TX_INUSE so that the interrupt sub-handler will know to transmit it. After queuing up this structure, if the incrementation of the head pointer exceeds the boundary of tx_list, tx_headp is reset to the beginning of the array.

---

[6]Applications wishing to call any block-transmitter function must first learn the size of the buffers from the SIO variable tx_buffsize. This limitation may easily be circumvented by installing a dynamic cache in tx_iwrite.

After queuing a structure and attending to housekeeping, the semaphore `tx_idle` is examined. If TRUE, this means that the transmitter sub-handler had previously exhausted the data in `tx_list` and the transmitter is now "asleep." Therefore, the transmitter sub-handler itself is called to kick-start the UART's interrupt mechanism again. Afterward, the `tx_idle` semaphore is made FALSE.

s_write

Now that there is a function for submitting entire blocks (buffers) of data for transmission, we require a high-level interface to it. As always the details (polled or interrupt) of the underlying I/O must remain invisible to the high-level functions. Let's see how the SIO function pointer s_txblock (Listing 20.23) provides this interface.

Listing 20.23. The s_write function.

```
FUNCTION NAME:  s_write
         LEVEL:  3
  PROTOTYPE IN:  SIODEF.H
       LIBRARY:  SIO.H
   DESCRIPTION:  Transmit a block of data
       RETURNS:  short: 0 if successful, non-zero otherwize.
      COMMENTS:  Can be written as a macro.
 INCLUDE FILES:  siodef.h
```

```c
short s_write(SIO *siop, BYTE *newbuff, short count)
{
    return (*siop->s_txblock)(siop, newbuff, count);
}
```

An explanation of s_write—This function consists merely of a call to the block-transmit function pointer in the SIO, s_txblock. In tx_ion this pointer is changed to tx_iwrite, the function just discussed. The SIO initialization in Listing 20.3 shows it initialized to point at the polled function tx_write, discussed next.

POLLED BLOCK-TRANSMIT

The function for submitting buffers for transmission under polled I/O, shown in Listing 20.24, contains no surpises.

Listing 20.24. The `tx_write` function simulates block transmission.

FUNCTION NAME: `tx_write`
    DESCRIPTION: Transmit a block of data using polled I/O.
          LEVEL: 3
  PROTOTYPE IN: SIODEF.H
       LIBRARY: SIO.H
       RETURNS: `0` (always successful)
    COMMENTS: Used as an initializer, so it cannot be a macro.
INCLUDE FILES: siodef.h, buos.h

```
short tx_write(SIO *siop, BYTE *newbuff, short count)
{
    while (count > 0)
        {
        s_putc(siop, *newbuff);
        --count;
        ++newbuff;
        }
    return 0;
}
```

An explanation of *tx_write* — This trivial function, which is the initializer for `tx_block` function pointer in the SIO, accomplishes block transmission by transmitting the buffer character by character.

Figure 20.2 illustrates the relationship between `s_write`, the `s_txblock` function pointer, and the two functions `tx_write` and `tx_iwrite`.

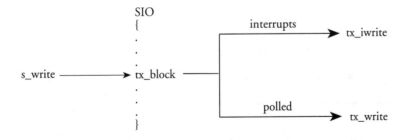

FIGURE 20.2.

Illustration of the indirection in the block-transmit interface.

THE CHARACTER INTERFACE

Because the block-write functions are the most efficient, they are instinctively employed where speed is important. It is therefore tempting to skip the writing of a single-character interface on the grounds that polled I/O is just fine where efficiency is unimportant. But as we have seen in the case of RS-232 interrupts, intermixing polled and interrupt driven I/O can produce subtly unpredictable results. In short, interrupt-driven, single-character I/O functions are necessary to harmonize the SIO interface even though their relatively high procedural overhead makes them much less efficient[7].

INTERRUPT TRANSMIT AND TRANSMIT STATUS

Paralleling the character interface for receiver interrupts, the two SIO function pointers s_xstat and s_send provide the interface between the tx_list and other high-level functions. These are shown in Listings 20.25 and 20.26.

Listing 20.25. The s_ixmitstat function simulates a transmitter status-bit.

FUNCTION NAME: s_ixmitstat
LEVEL: 2
PROTOTYPE IN: BUOS.H
LIBRARY: BUOS.LIB
DESCRIPTION: Interrupt equivalent of s_xmitstat. Returns whether there is a room in the transmit queue.
RETURNS : FAST: Non-zero if there is room in the queue.
COMMENTS: Used as an initializer, so it cannot be a macro.
INCLUDE FILES: siodef.h

```
FAST s_ixmitstat(register SIO *siop)
{
    return (siop->tx_headp->inuseflag == TX_FREE);
}
```

An explanation of *s_ixmitstat*—This status function simply peeks into the tx_list array to see if the buffer at the head pointer is free. The code is written so that TRUE is returned if the buffer is free, otherwise FALSE.

---

[7]Efficiency is often not an issue in single-character I/O applications such as typing or even file-filtering. In such cases, it probably makes more sense to leave polled I/O in place (set the intrpt_status.tx_wanted bit in the SIO to FALSE before calling s_open). You are then free to manage the transmitter interrupts on your own by calling tx_ion and tx_ioff only when economies of scale make interrupt transmission desirable.

Listing 20.26. The s_ixmit function: polled character I/O.

```
FUNCTION NAME: s_ixmit
        LEVEL: 2
 PROTOTYPE IN: BUOS.H
      LIBRARY: BUOS.LIB
  DESCRIPTION: The interrupt equivalent of s_xmit. Adds a byte to the transmit
               interrupt queue via a call to tx_iwrite. This function is never
               called directly, but through a function pointer in the SIO.
      RETURNS: void
     COMMENTS: Used as an initializer, so it cannot be a macro.
INCLUDE FILES: siodef.h
```

```c
void s_ixmit(register SIO *siop, FAST c)
{
    while (tx_iwrite(siop, (BYTE*)&c, 1) != Q_OK)
    {;}
}
```

An explanation of *s_ixmit*—The interrupt-driven, single character transmit routine is nothing more than a call to tx_iwrite with a buffer of one. The per-character overhead incurred—queuing the buffer and kick-starting the UART—makes this function a poor performer when high throughput is required.

TERM6

The introduction of interrupt I/O doesn't change a single line of code in the TERM program. All functions—transmit, receiver, and RS-232—work as before. For good measure, however, TERM6 in Listing 20.27 adds a menu item to give statistics on the I/O structure. No attempt is made to make serious use of the serialization-error functions, but to demonstrate that they are functioning, a BREAK detecting function is installed in the main polling loop in the term function.

Listing 20.27. Changes to TERM.

```
PROGRAM NAME: TERM6
 DESCRIPTION: Terminal program.
    COMMENTS: New Features: A menu item displaying statistics of the I/O
              system.
INCLUDE FILES: stdio.h, stdlib.h, ctype.h, siodef.h, ascii.h, misc.h, sioctl.h, buos.h,
               key.h, term.h, xmod.h, modem.h
```

continues

Listing 20.27. continued

```
#define UART_ID        'G'                    /* 16450 (8250) or 16550        */

int vers = 6;                                 /* version number (global)      */

int menu(siop)                                /* menu gets SIO pointer        */
SIO *siop;
{
.

.

        "\tG.  Identify the UART",
.

.       UART_ID:
            printf("\nUART on device %d is a %s :\n", siop->devnum,
                siop->rcv_fifo_trigger == 0 ? "16450/8250" : "16550");
            printf("\t      TX FIFO depth is: %2d\n"
                    "\t   TX Trigger level is: %2d\n"
                    "\t    RCV FIFO depth is: %2d\n"
                    x"\tRCV Trigger level is: %2d\n",
                        siop->tx_fifo_depth,
                        siop->tx_fifo_trigger,
                        siop->rcv_fifo_depth,
                        siop->rcv_fifo_trigger);
            printf("\nInterrupts Active:\n"
                    "\t        Serial Errors: %s\n"
                    "\t               RS232: %s\n"
                    "\t             Receiver: %s (%d-byte buffer)\n"
                    "\t          Transmitter: %s  (%d %d-byte buffers)\n",
                        siop->intrpt_status.serr_on ?  "Yes" : "No",
                        siop->intrpt_status.rs232_on ? "Yes" : "No",
                        siop->intrpt_status.rcv_on?    "Yes" : "No",
                        siop->rcv_buffsize,
                        siop->intrpt_status.tx_on ?    "Yes" : "No",
                        siop->tx_numbuffs,
                        siop->tx_buffsize);
            haktc();
            break;
.

.
}


void term(siop)
{
.

.

    for (EVER)                                /*  eternal loop        */
        {
        s_fgetc(siop);                        /* s_fgetc will echo    */
        if ( (c = inkey()) != NOT_READY)
            if (c == MENU)
                {
```

```
            if (menu(siop))
                break;              /* if menu returns non-zero */
        }
    else
        s_fputc(siop, c);
if(serial_status(siop, BREAK_ON)) /* was BREAK detected?    */
    puts("Break Detected");
}
.
.
.
}
```

Smart Modem Programming

By combining the tools from preceding chapters, we are now able to compose a library of functions for controlling modems such as those discussed in Chapters 8, 9, and 10. The term *ordinary modem* is employed throughout this chapter to mean any non-protocol modem that implements the commands summarized in Table 9.5 in the General Market column. Although no official public standard incorporates all these commands, they are in fact almost universally implemented.

Basic Design Criteria

Because several of the modem's variables profoundly affect its behavior, our *first* and most important goal is to design library functions that are independent of these variables. Although perhaps unrealistically lofty, we can come surprisingly near to this goal. Before we begin to compose the library, then, we will consider the design problems and formulate an approach to them.

The User Interface

No matter how carefully we plan our library, how clever our design, or how ingenious our coding techniques—none of these matter unless we restrict user access to the modem. In other words, if our software is to exert absolute control over a modem, we must have the *exclusive* right to send it commands. Our software, therefore, assumes an environment where the user issues modem commands by making menu selections instead of by sending commands from the keyboard while in terminal mode. In older smart modems (such as the Hayes 1200 and early 2400 modems) it is possible to enforce this restriction by keeping the modem's Data Terminal Ready (DTR) inhibited, thus keeping the modem in the comatose state where it ignores all commands. Although the baseline modem described in Chapter 8 does not support this use of DTR, to be on the safe side of compatibility, the library functions should still manipulate DTR in this traditional manner.

USER INTERFACE COMMANDS

The interface commands having the greatest effect upon modem behavior are

Q0   Forces the modem to respond to commands.

E1   Disables the modem's local echo. The sole purpose of command echo is to enable human users to see the commands they are typing. Since we are assuming a programming environment where the user *never* issues commands directly to the modem, command echo is of no value. In fact, it is a headache. Why? Some of our functions send commands to the modem, then await a response. If command echo is enabled, these functions are unable to distinguish between an echo of a command and the modem's actual response. Command echo, therefore, must be disabled.

V1   In the function for interpreting modem responses we will compare the modem's response to a list of valid responses. We obviously stand a greater chance of misidentifying a single-digit code than a longer word-code string. The V1 command causes the modem to use full-word responses.

So critical are these codes to the basic design of the library, they shall be included in *every* command sent to the modem.

RS-232 Control

We noted in Chapter 8 that the smart modem's "smartness" liberates programmers from the drudgery of managing the minutiae of RS-232 control. We learned that most functions can be accomplished either with RS-232 signals or by sending command strings to the modem. What we didn't mention at the time is that only a masochist would choose the latter.

In fact, there is no reason to choose one method exclusively—the best form of control is a combination of modem command strings and RS-232 hardware signals. Accordingly, we assume that DTR and DCD (Data Carrier Detect) behave in the following manner:

● **DTR (pin 20)**, when inhibited, unconditionally forces the modem into its command state: if the modem is on-line, it immediately drops the connection, hangs up the phone, and returns to command state. (This is behavior conditioned by the &D2 command.)

● **DCD (pin 8)** is asserted only during a connection. DCD remains inhibited until all handshaking has been accomplished and all modem responses and messages have been issued. In other words, the assertion of DCD after dialing means that the modem is in on-line state, connected and ready to transfer data. (This is behavior conditioned by the &C1 command.)

RS-232 CABLING

One of the most rigid requirements is that the modem can be controlled with an off-the-shelf straight-through RS-232 cable. The cable *may* contain connections for all 25 pins, but only pins 2 (TD), 3 (RD), 4 (RTS), 5 (CTS), 7 (common), 8 (DCD), and 20 (DTR) are required.

Compatibility

Most modems claim to be compatible with the industry-standard AT command set. Many features must be present to support that claim. These commands are specified in Table 9.5 under the General Market heading. Although this standard is derived from a 2400 baseline product, the non-protocol behavior of higher speed modems implements the specification.

Generality

Now that we have made some important decisions about the environment in which our modem library will operate—no echo, word codes, RS-232, and so forth—we can set forth the number one design goal of all: independence from the environment we just specified. Complicated software built on a myriad of niggling environment specifications is like a house of cards. Sooner or later (usually sooner), an insignificant deviation from specification brings the whole construct down around the programmer's ears. For example, although it is much easier to write code for a modem if we make the assumption that command echo is off, we must defend against the user turning it on behind our backs.

The Modem Structure and Constants

By now, you have come to expect that however we may elect to compose the modem functions, they will be implemented by means of a new structure pointer in the SIO. The name of this new member is sm (short for smart modem) and is a pointer to an instance of the modem structure we will define in a moment. Listing 21.1 shows the new addition to the SIO.

Listing 21.1. The new modem member for the SIO.

STRUCT DEF:	SIO
FILE:	SIODEF.H
DESCRIPTION:	Master structure defining a serial port.
COMMENTS:	New member supporting baseline modem

```
struct sio
  {
  BYTE   * uart_base;        /*0  Base address of UART    */
  .
  .
  .
  struct modem     *sm;      /*70 Pointer to modem struct */
  };
```

The modem structure itself contains the information required to control a smart modem. For the sake of completeness, the entire modem structure is shown in Listing 21.3a and its initialization in Listing 21.3b, but it will be explained piecemeal during development of the modem functions. The definition of the modem structure and most of the constant definitions are assumed to be in a new file named MODEM.H. As with all structures, the initialization of the modem structure occurs in the level-0 file, IBMPC.C.

Listing 21.2. Constants for this chapter. All but two of the constants reside in MODEM.H.

These belong in SIODEF.H

```
/****** General Modem Constants  ******/
#define CMDBUFSIZ   50        /* Capacity of modem's command buffer */
#define CMDSIZ      7         /* Max storage needed for modem command */
```

These belong in MODEM.H

```
/****** Buffer Size Constants ******/
#define  MAX_MSG_LEN 30    /* max length of a modem message     */
#define  COMPRESSSIZE 20   /* max length of compression message */
#define  LPSIZE       20   /* max length of protocol message    */


/****** Constants for message validation ******/
#define MSG_INVALID        -1
#define MSG_NON_TERMINAL   -2

/****** How to configure Baud Rate ******/
enum baudcnfg {BAUD_MAX = 0, BAUD_FOUND};
```

```
/****** Manifest Constants for Modem Functions ******/
enum results
    {
    M_OK = 0,       /*0  Successful command                        */
    M_CONN,         /*1  Connect                                   */
    M_RING,         /*2  Call incoming                             */
    M_NODCD,        /*3  No carrier detected                       */
    M_CMDERR,       /*4  Error in modem command                    */
    M_NOTONE,       /*5  No dial tone heard                        */
    M_BUSY,         /*6  Busy signal heard                         */
    M_NOANSW,       /*7  Silence not heard after @                 */
    M_BADMSG,       /*8  Invalid modem response                    */
    M_NORING,       /*9  Looked for and didn't hear incoming'RING' */
    M_ONLINE,       /*10 Can't dial into a high dcd                */
    M_NILNUM,       /*11 Blank dial string                         */
    M_USRCAN,       /*12 Call cancelled from keyboard              */
    M_NORESET,      /*13 Reset Failed                              */
    M_NOID,         /*14 ID function failed                        */
    M_CONFIG_MEM,   /*15 Configuration memeory alloc error         */
    M_CONFIG_NOK,   /*16 Modem didn't configure as requested       */
    M_DCD_HIGH,     /*17 DCD went high (not a message)             */
    M_PROTOCOL,     /*18 Protocol message detected during connect  */
    M_CARRIER,      /*19 Carrier message detected during connect   */
    M_COMPRESS,     /*20 Compression message detected during connect */
    };
```

Listing 21.3a. The modem structure declaration. This belongs in the MODEM.H.

```
struct modem
    {
    unsigned ibdelay;               /*0  Interbyte delay                           */
    BOOL     cmdechoflag;           /*1  Modem commands to console                 */
    char     cmdbuff[CMDBUFSIZ];    /*2  Build all commands here                   */
    int      cmdt_out;              /*3  Tsecs to wait after a modem cmd           */
    int      cmdretry;              /*4  Number of times to try a command          */
    unsigned guardtime;             /*5  Escape guard time                         */
    short    escape_arg;            /*6  (S2)on-line to command mode escape        */
    int      baudtry[7];            /*7  Baud rates to try reset                   */
    unsigned max_DTE_baud;          /*8  Maximum baud rate of modem                */
    short    modtype;               /*9  Our code for modem                        */
    short    max_carrier_speed;     /*10 Maximum baud rate of modem                */
    short    autoans_arg;           /*11 (S0)# of rings before autoanswer          */
    short    dtwait_arg;            /*12 (S6)dialtone wait (secs)                  */
    short    dcdwait_arg;           /*13 (S7)# secs to wait for carrier            */
    short    speaker_arg;           /*14 Speaker mode                              */
    short    xcmd_arg;              /*15 Result code set                           */
    short    speakvol_arg;          /*16 Speaker volume (0,  1, or 2)              */
    short    firmdcd_arg;           /*17 DCD configuration                         */
```

continues

Listing 21.3a. continued

```
short     firmdtr_arg;          /*18 DTR configuration                  */
short     baudmode;             /*19 Baud rate initialization mode      */
BOOL      configokflag;         /*20 Modem successfully configured      */
short     connect_XXXX_code;    /*21 Code for baud rate of local link   */
short     carrier_baud_code;    /*22 Code for baud rate of carrier      */
BOOL      linkprot_wanted;      /*23 Want link protocol if available?   */
BOOL      linkprot_supported;   /*24 Is a link protocol supported?      */
char      linkname [LPSIZE];    /*25 ID from the CONNECT message        */
BOOL      compress_wanted;      /*26 Want compression if available?     */
BOOL      compress_supported;   /*27 Is compression supported? (at init)*/
char compressname[COMPRESSSIZE]; /*28 ID from COMPRESSION message       */
BOOL      autobrflag;           /*29 Switch baud rate to incoming call  */
char      dialbuff[CMDBUFSIZ];  /*30 Build numeric dial string here     */
char      okalpha[18];          /*31 Alpha chars ok in dial string      */
char      dialmode;             /*32 (T)one or (P)ulse dialing          */
char      enddial;              /*33 Dial suffix—e.g., ';' or 'R'       */
char      unconfig[CMDBUFSIZ];  /*34 String to send to smodem at exit   */
};
```

Listing 21.3b. The modem structure initialization.
This belongs in the computer-specific file (LEVEL0.H).

```
struct modem baselineA =
     {
     0,                              /*0  Interbyte delay                    */
     OFF,                            /*1  Console echo off                   */
     "",                             /*2  Build all commands here            */
     _0_SEC_3,                       /*3  Tsecs to wait after a modem cmd    */
     2,                              /*4  Number of times to try a command   */
     _1_SEC_0  + _0_SEC_5,           /*5  Escape guard time (Tsecs)          */
     '|',                            /*6  (S2) online escape char            */
     {BAUD57K6, BAUD38K4, BAUD14K4,  /*7  Baud rates to try reset            */
     BAUD9600, BAUD2400,BAUD1200,-1},
     SUPPLIED,                       /*8  Baud rate at which reset occured   */
     VIRGIN,                         /*9  Our own code for modem type        */
     SUPPLIED,                       /*10 Maximum baud rate of modem         */
     0,                              /*11 (S0) 0 = "Don't answer"            */
     2,                              /*12 (S6)dialtone wait  (secs)          */
     30,                             /*13 (S7) timeout wait for connect (secs)*/
     1,                              /*14 speaker mode arg: on till connect  */
     4,                              /*15 Result codes: highest level        */
     1,                              /*16 Speaker volume (1, 2, or 3)        */
     1,                              /*17 Enable DCD                         */
     2,                              /*18 Enable DTR                         */
     BAUD_FOUND,                     /*19 How to leave baud rate after reset */
     FALSE,                          /*20 Modem sucessfully configured       */
     SUPPLIED,                       /*21 DTE baud rate (parsed from CONNECT) */
     SUPPLIED,                       /*22 Carrier rate (parsed from CARRIER) */
```

```
    TRUE,                        /*23 Yes, link protocol wanted        */
    SUPPLIED,                    /*24 Link protocol supported?         */
    "",                          /*25 Name of link protocol            */
    TRUE,                        /*26 Yes, compression wanted           */
    SUPPLIED,                    /*27 Compression protocol supported?   */
    "",                          /*28 Name of compression protocol      */
    TRUE,                        /*29 Switch baud rate to incoming call */
    ""  ,                        /*30 Build numeric dial string here    */
    "",                          /*31 Valid chars in dial string        */
    'T',                         /*32 Tone dialing                      */
    ' ',                         /*33 No dial suffix                    */
    "Z",                         /*34 Unconfiguration string            */
    };
```

Modem Commands

In this section, we will compose several low-level modem functions. Because they deal with the primary actions of reading from and writing to the modem, these functions are analogous to the level-2 SIO functions in BUOS.LIB. Nevertheless, it is a good idea to segregate them into a separate library, MODEM.LIB.

Structure Members for Commands and Responses

For your convenience, the structure members and their initialized values that support the modem command functions are repeated in Listing 21.4. Initialization is shown in the right column. (The complete structure and its initialization are given in Listings 21.3a and 21.3b.)

Listing 21.4. The modem structure members required for modem command functions.

```
unsigned ibdelay;             /* 0 */   0,
BOOL     cmdechoflag;         /* 1 */   OFF,
char     cmdbuff[CMDBUFSIZ];  /* 2 */   "",
int      cmdt_out;            /* 3 */   _0_SEC_3,
int      cmdretry;            /* 4 */   2,
unsigned guardtime;           /* 5 */   _1_SEC_0  + _0_SEC_5,
```

ibdelay	The inter-byte delay that is used during output to the modem. A nominal inter-byte delay of 1 Tsec (_0_SEC_05) is introduced.
cmdechoflag	Whether commands should be sent to the console as well as the SIO.
cmdbuff[]	This is where all modem commands are built and retained.
cmdt_out	This is the time-out interval in Tsecs while awaiting the modem's response to a command.

cmdretry   When an expected modem response is not forthcoming, this is the number of times to retry the command before giving up.

guardtime   When forcing the modem from on-line to command state, this is the quiet time in Tsecs that must surround the escape sequence.

Send a Modem Command: *m_cmd*

From the structure members just discussed we can compose our first modem function. The code for m_cmd, a function to build and send a command to the modem, is shown in Listing 21.5.

Listing 21.5. The m_cmd function sends a single command to the modem.

FUNCTION NAME:	m_cmd
LEVEL:	3
PROTOTYPE IN:	MODEM.H
LIBRARY:	MODEM.LIB
DESCRIPTION:	Builds a modem command in the modem structure's command buffer, then outputs it to the SIO.
RETURNS:	void
COMMENTS:	The following modem characteristics are forced: no command echo, word responses, and a fixed inter-byte delay and uppercase ASCII output. Commands are echoed to the console based upon the cmdechoflag structure member.
INCLUDE FILES:	stdio.h, string.h, siodef.h, modem.h, sioctl.h

```
void m_cmd(SIO *siop, char *cmdstr)
{
    struct modem *smp = siop->sm;                   /* for notational convenience*/
    RANK dtr_stat;                                  /* save state of dtr         */
    if ((dtr_stat = get232(siop, DTR)) == OFF)  /* if dtr inhibited now...   */
        set232(siop, DTR, ON);                      /* assert it                 */
    s_opush(siop);                                  /* preserve output structure */
    s_ocntrl(siop, SET, CASEMODE, UPPER);           /* convert to upper case     */
    s_ocntrl(siop, SET, ASCIIFLAG, ON);             /* strip high bits           */
    s_ocntrl(siop, SET, IB_DLYFLAG, ON);            /* interbyte delay           */
    s_ocntrl(siop, SET, IB_DLY, smp->ibdelay);
    s_ocntrl(siop, SET, CONSFLAG, (USHORT)smp->cmdechoflag); /* echo         */
    sprintf(smp->cmdbuff,"ATQ0E1V1%s\r", cmdstr);
    s_fputs(siop, smp->cmdbuff);                    /* output buffer to SIO      */
    if (dtr_stat == OFF)                            /* restore DTR               */
        set232(siop, DTR, OFF);
    s_opop(siop);                                   /* restore output structure  */
}
```

An explanation of *m_cmd*—Our strategy here is to build a valid modem command based upon the command string passed in the argument list. Commands are built in the structure member cmdbuff instead of in automatic local storage; in this way, subsequent functions can, if necessary, scrutinize the preceding command.

Since we have already vowed to use RS-232 control wherever possible, it is important to assert DTR. Remember, many older modems *completely ignore* commands when DTR is inhibited. At the beginning of the function, then, we test the state of DTR and assert it if it is currently inhibited. DTR is restored upon exit *only* if it was changed upon entry, thus avoiding unnecessary and potentially disruptive perturbations of DTR.

Before the command is built, the SIO is configured to strip the high bits from all output and to convert all output to uppercase. Optionally, based upon the ibdelay and cmdechoflag members in the modem structure, an inter-byte delay is introduced and output is echoed to the console.[1]

With the output characteristics set, the command is assembled in the cmdbuff member of the modem structure. The strategy is to build a C format string containing the Q(quiet), E(echo), and V(verbose) commands with fixed arguments. The transitory command passed in the argument list is the last element in the format string, followed by a Carriage Return for a command terminator.

The C-formatted string is then output into the modem structure's command buffer by the sprintf function and sent to the modem with the s_fputs. After transmission, the state of DTR and the SIO's output configuration are restored.

Capturing Modem Responses

It is dangerous to send a command without confirming both that the modem has received it and the outcome of the command. Luckily, the modem acknowledges every command with a response. In this section, we will write the functions required to capture modem responses reliably, after which we can write the functions to evaluate that response.

Fetch a Response: *s_fgetln*

Our function to fetch responses can take advantage of the fact that when in verbose mode (that is, when the V1 command is in effect), modem responses begin and end with CRLF pairs. For example, the response OK is actually <CRLF>OK<CRLF>. Because we are designing code that will also have to support protocol modems, which can produce a *stream* of responses, this function has to be able to fish individual responses from that stream. Listing 21.6 shows the function s_fgetln, which is a level-3 function for SIO.LIB.

---

[1]Console echo can be very useful as a debugging tool.

Listing 21.6. The `s_fgetln` function captures a single modem response.

FUNCTION NAME:	`s_fgetln`
LEVEL:	2
PROTOTYPE IN:	SIODEF.H
LIBRARY:	BUOS.LIB
DESCRIPTION:	Converts a carriage-return-delimited string into a NUL-terminated string of bytes. Leading and trailing carriage returns are removed.
RETURNS:	`int`: number of bytes in the buffer (0 if timeout occurs).
COMMENTS:	Buffer must be `numc+1` bytes long to accommodate the NUL terminator. The calling function is responsible for calling `s_iocntrl` to enable and set the timeout interval.
INCLUDE FILES:	siodef.h, sioctl.h, buos.h, ascii.h

```c
enum {LEADING_CR = 0, LEADING_LF, IN_MSG, TRAILING_CR, TRAILING_LF, EXIT};

int s_fgetln(SIO *siop, char *buff, short numc)
{
    int c;
    int  count;
    int state = LEADING_CR;
    count = 0;
    while (state != EXIT && count < numc)
        {
        c = s_fgetc(siop);
            {
            if (c == TIMEOUT)
                {
                count = TIMEOUT;
                state = EXIT;
                }
            }
        switch (state)
            {
            case LEADING_CR:
                if (c == CR)
                    state = LEADING_LF;
                break;
            case LEADING_LF:
                if (c == LF)
                    state = IN_MSG;
                break;
            case IN_MSG:
                if (c == CR)
                    state = TRAILING_LF;
```

```
                else
                        {
                        ++count;
                        *buff++ = (char)c;
                        }
                break;
            case TRAILING_LF:
                if (c == LF)
                        state = EXIT;
                break;
            }                           /* end of switch          */
        }                               /* end of while           */
    if ( (c = s_iflush(siop)) != -1)    /* byte pending in s_fgetc?   */
        {
        *buff++ = (char)c;
        ++count;
        }
    *buff = NUL;
    return count;
}
```

An explanation of s_fgetln—The code is designed as a simple finite-state machine, driven by the value of each byte received. At start up, the state is initialized to wait for a Carriage Return, which it assumes is the leading CR of a CRLF pair that precedes a modem response. Receipt of a Carriage Return causes a switch to the state of waiting for a *leading* Line Feed, which it assumes is the LF following the CR just received. Receipt of a Line Feed causes a change to the *in-message* state, where data is placed in the buffer. This state ends upon receipt of a Carriage Return, which is assumed to be the CR of the *trailing* CRLF pair; after inputting the LF, the state is set to EXIT, the loop is broken, the buffer terminated with a NUL, and the function returns the number of characters actually input. If a time-out occurred before receiving the leading Carriage Return, the count variable contains -1.

Fetch a Response: *m_getstr*

The s_fgetln gets its input from the formatted input s_fgetc. As documented in Chapter 18, "Formatted Input," the behavior of s_fgetc is conditioned by a myriad of variables in the s_octl structure in the SIO. If critical variables are not correctly set before calling s_fgetc, it is likely to fail. For example, if s_fgetc's time-out mechanism is not configured, s_fgetln returns immediately with a time-out value. In short, it requires a supervisor function to configure it. The function m_getstr, shown in Listing 21.7, serves this purpose.

Listing 21.7. The `m_getstr` function fetches a response string from the modem.

FUNCTION NAME:	m_getstr
LEVEL:	3
PROTOTYPE IN:	MODEM.H
LIBRARY:	MODEM.LIB
DESCRIPTION:	Fetches bytes from the modem. The maximum number of bytes to be fetched is specified in numc.
RETURNS:	The number of bytes actually fetched.
COMMENTS:	The timeout interval is derived from the modem structure.
INCLUDE FILES:	siodef.h, modem.h, sioctl.h

```
short m_getstr(SIO *siop, char * replybuff, short numc)
{
    s_ipush(siop);
    s_icntrl(siop, SET, T_OUTFLAG, ON);
    s_icntrl(siop, SET, T_OUT, siop->sm->cmdt_out);
    numc = s_fgetln(siop, replybuff, numc);          /* get response buffer */
    s_ipop(siop);
    return numc;
}
```

An explanation of *m_getstr*—The zero-terminated buffer containing the command to send is passed in the argument list. There are two other requirements: first, the function must protect against buffer overwrite if accidentally asked to fetch bytes from a continuous stream; second, it must not wait endlessly when there are no bytes in the data stream. This protection takes two forms:

1. The maximum number of bytes to be fetched is passed in numc in the argument list.

2. The formatted-input function s_fgetln enables us to specify a time-out beyond which m_getstr will not wait.

The length of the time-out interval must reside in the modem structure because many modems do not observe the specification that guarantees 250 milliseconds between receipt of a command and issuing a response. Oddly, most modems that don't observe this specification err on the short side—that is, they send the response too quickly. The default value of 0_SEC_3 may therefore have to be adjusted for some modems.

Once the SIO is configured, s_fgetln attempts to fetch the requested number of bytes into replybuff. The function m_getstr returns the number of bytes actually received or zero if there is no response.

Evaluating Modem Responses

After every command, a non-protocol modem issues a *single* response delimited by CRLF: OK, CONNECT, and so forth. It is necessary to know exactly what that response is so that program flow can be based upon it. After dialing, for example, the software must know whether the modem responded CONNECT or NO CARRIER in order to know how to proceed. The simple handshake between issuing a single command and receiving a single reply makes it fairly simple to parse the response:

1. Capture the response (with, say, m_getstr).

2. Compare the response against a list of valid responses.

3. If the response is valid, map it to an integer return code.

4. If the response is invalid, return an error.

Protocol modems respond in the same way, with one very important exception: their response to a successful dial or answer command may contain not only a CONNECT message, but a stream of *several additional* CRLF-delimited responses. Since these responses may contain information upon which important decisions are based, it is necessary to parse the response stream into individual messages. Rather than writing a special function to interpret the modem response to a dial or answer command, let's build a general function to handle the responses of *any* modem, whether it supports protocols or not.

We begin by listing the information we need in order to characterize a modem response:

1. The text itself: BUSY, NO CARRIER, and so forth.

2. An arbitrary integer ID code for the response.

3. Whether the response is *terminal*—that is, whether another message follows. For example, in protocol modems several additional messages may follow the CONNECT XXXX response. (Recall from Chapter 8 that 'XXXX' actually contains the speed of the connection.)

4. Instructions for parsing the response, if required. For example, extracting the "9600" numeric portion of the CONNECT 9600 response and converting it to an integer.

These characteristics are embodied in the parse_info structure shown in Listing 21.8.

Listing 21.8. The parse_info structure for modem messages and return constants.

STRUCT NAME:	parse_info
HEADER FILE:	MODEM.H
DESCRIPTION:	Control structure used by modem message parser.

continues

Listing 21.8. continued

```
struct parse_info
    {
    char *message;          /* pointer to the modem response */
    BOOL terminal;          /* is it "terminal"              */
    short id;               /* id code for this message      */
    void (*fn)(SIO *, struct parse_info *, char *);  /* parse function */
    };
```

Validating a Response: *m_ismessage*

We can now build an array of these parse_info structures—one structure for every possible modem response. This enables us to write a function that validates modem responses by looking them up in this array. If valid, the integer equivalent of the response is returned. The function that performs this function, m_ismessage, is given in Listing 21.9.

Listing 21.9. m_ismessage: validates modem responses and calls a parsing function parser.

FUNCTION NAME:	m_ismessage
LEVEL:	3
PROTOTYPE IN:	MODEM.H
LIBRARY:	MODEM.LIB
DESCRIPTION:	Converts modem message to an integer code.
RETURNS:	int: an integer result code or -1 if the code is not valid or is not a terminal. Calls parser function if indicated.
INCLUDE FILES:	stdlib.h, string.h, siodef.h, modem.h

```
static struct parse_info m_result[] =
    {
        /* String        Terminal  Code        Parser */
        { "OK",           TRUE,   M_OK,          NIL },
        { "NO CARRIER",   TRUE,   M_NODCD ,      NIL },
        { "ERROR",        TRUE,   M_CMDERR,      NIL },
        { "NO DIAL",      TRUE,   M_NOTONE,      NIL },
        { "BUSY",         TRUE,   M_BUSY  ,      NIL },
        { "NO ANSWER",    TRUE,   M_NOANSW,      NIL },
        { "RING",         TRUE,   M_RING,        NIL },
        { "CONNECT",      FALSE,  M_CONN,        m_parsemsg },
        { "PROTOCOL:",    FALSE,  M_PROTOCOL,    m_parsemsg },
        { "COMPRESSION:", FALSE,  M_COMPRESS,    m_parsemsg },
        { "CARRIER",      FALSE,  M_CARRIER,     m_parsemsg },
    };
```

```
int m_ismessage(SIO* siop, char *str)
{
    int row;
    int numrows = arraysize(m_result);              /* macro             */
    for (row = 0; row < numrows; row++)             /* for every row     */
        {
        if (strstr(str, m_result[row].message))     /* string submatch?  */
            {
            if (m_result[row].fn != NIL)            /* if processing needed */
                m_result[row].fn(siop, &m_result[row], str);
            if (m_result[row].terminal)
                return m_result[row].id;
            else
                return MSG_NON_TERMINAL;            /* continue          */
            }
        }
    return MSG_INVALID;                             /* -1 if not a substring */
}
```

An explanation of *m_ismessage* —This function contains a local array of parse_info structures—one for each possible modem response. The message member of each structure contains (a pointer to) the actual text of the message. Whether the message is terminal is initialized to TRUE or FALSE. The id member is initialized with one of the manifest constants given in Listing 21.2. The final member contains a pointer to the function required to parse that message. If no parsing is required, the function pointer is initialized to NIL.

The body of the function is remarkably simple. A modem's response is passed in the argument list. For each row in the array, the function searches linearly for a submatch between the strings in the structure array and the modem response.[2] If no match is found, the function returns the MSG_INVALID constant, given in Listing 21.2. If a match is found, however, it is time to call the parsing function given in the function pointer fn. If this fn is initialized to NIL, no parsing is necessary; otherwise, the pointed-to parser is called. If the message is a terminal (for example, BUSY), the integer code in the array is returned. If the message is not a terminal, the constant MSG_NOT_TERMINAL is returned, thus signaling the calling function to be on the lookout for additional responses from the modem.

It is worth observing that if an application has no need to parse the modem's responses, m_ismessage could be made to serve as is by initializing all the parse function pointers to NIL. We can therefore postpone composing the parsing function m_parsemsg until the larger discussion of protocol modems that appears later in this chapter.

---

[2]The modem's response is considered to be the major string, and the array entry is the substring. This means that the strings in the array can be abbreviated substantially from those shown; for example, the string COMPRESSION could be shortened to COMP.

High-Level Modem Functions

Now that we have the basic functions to send a command to the modem and fetch its reply, we will compose three more functions:

- m_cmd_str, which sends a command then fetches the modem's response.
- m_cmd_OK, which sends a command and waits for an OK response.
- m_gocmd, which forces the modem from on-line state into the command state.

Send Command, Fetch Response: *m_cmd_str*

The m_cmd_str function, shown in Listing 21.10, issues a command, fetches the modem's response, and returns it to the caller. It is essentially a composite of the previous two functions, m_cmd and m_getstr.

Listing 21.10. The m_cmd_str function sends a command and fetches a response.

FUNCTION NAME:	m_cmd_str
LEVEL:	3
PROTOTYPE IN:	MODEM.H
LIBRARY:	MODEM.LIB
DESCRIPTION:	Outputs a command, then fetches the modem's response. The maximum number of bytes to be fetched is specified in numc.
RETURNS:	short: the number of characters in the modem's response, zero if no response.
COMMENTS:	Any echoed bytes are cleared from the SIO between issuing the command and fetching the response.
INCLUDE FILES:	stdio.h, siodef.h, string.h, modem.h

```
short m_cmd_str(SIO *siop, char* cmdstr, char* replybuff, USHORT numc)
{
    if (s_clrsio(siop, CMDBUFSIZ) == NUL)    /* clear SIO              */
        {
        puts("SIO won't clear");
        return 0;
        }
    m_cmd(siop, cmdstr);                      /* send desired command */
    s_clrsio(siop, strlen(cmdstr));           /* clear echo           */
    numc = m_getstr(siop, replybuff, numc); /* get response         */
    return numc;
}
```

An explanation of *m_cmd_str*—Two calls to s_clrsio make the function interesting. In the first portion of this chapter, we decided that we would base our functions on *word* result codes with *no* command echo. While establishing such parameters is an important part of software design, it is equally important to ensure that the code behaves reasonably if these parameters somehow do not obtain. Fortunately, this is not difficult.

If for some reason the modem is echoing commands, some of the echoed bytes of the previous command may still be in the SIO. Since we don't want them to be included in the modem's response, the SIO must be cleared. How many bytes to clear? To be on the safe side, we assume that CMDBUFSIZ bytes are in the SIO buffer. If there are more, we can assume that the SIO is still receiving bytes from a source other than a modem echo:

```
if (s_clrsio(siop, CMDBUFSIZ) == NUL)
    return 0;
```

Once the SIO is clear, the command is sent to the modem. Immediately, s_clrsio is called again to clear the number of bytes equal to the length of the command just transmitted. Next, m_getstr is immediately called to fetch the reply. The timing between these two calls is important. As you will recall, the time-out interval for s_clrsio is only 1 Tsec and the specification guarantees a minimum of 250 milliseconds between the receipt of a command and the response. This leaves an ample safety margin between the last character of the echo and the modem's response.

Send a Command, Check Its Validity: *m_cmd_OK*

Because most modem commands respond with either OK or ERROR, we need a function that issues a command, waits for the reply, validates the reply, then returns a code indicating success or failure. We now have all the tools to compose this extremely useful function, shown in Listing 21.11.

Listing 21.11. The m_cmd_OK function issues a command, then returns SUCCEED/FAIL.

FUNCTION NAME:	m_cmd_OK
LEVEL:	3
PROTOTYPE IN:	MODEM.H
LIBRARY:	MODEM.LIB
DESCRIPTION:	Outputs the modem command, then waits for a response of "OK."
RETURNS:	int: M_SUCCEED if command is successful, otherwise M_FAIL.
COMMENTS:	Not intended to fetch result codes from dial/answer operations.
INCLUDE FILES:	siodef.h, modem.h

continues

Listing 21.11. continued

```
int m_cmd_OK(SIO *siop, char *cmdstr)
{
    int retries;
    char message[MAX_MSG_LEN + 1];
    retries = siop->sm->cmdretry;    /* from structure        */
    do                               /* do at least once       */
        {
        m_cmd_str(siop, cmdstr, message, MAX_MSG_LEN);
        if ( m_ismessage(siop, message) == M_OK)
            return M_SUCCEED;
        } while (--retries > 0);
    return M_FAIL;
}
```

An explanation of *m_cmd_OK*—Here m_cmd_str is called to execute the modem command in cmdstr. If a non-NIL pointer is returned, it is immediately passed to m_ismessage for validation against the strings contained in the array m_result. If the response is valid, the constant M_SUCCEED is returned. If m_cmd_str returns a NIL pointer indicating no response, or if a response is invalid, the loop repeats until the loop-controlling variable retries expires, at which time the constant M_FAIL is returned.

The constant MAX_MSG_LEN determines the maximum number of characters that m_cmd_str can fetch. Even though the longest valid reply is only 16 bytes long, MAX_MSG_LEN is set slightly larger to tolerate gratuitous newlines and white space characters that modems place before and after an otherwise valid response.

The variable retries is a copy of the modem structure member cmdretry, which is initialized in the structure. In practice, a value of 2 is usually adequate.

Force Modem to Command State: *m_gocmd*

Our final command function, shown in Listing 21.12, makes it possible to issue a command while the modem is on-line—that is, during a connection. As you will recall from Chapter 8, "The Baseline Smart Modem," the modem can be forced from its on-line state to the command state *without hanging up* by sending it three escape characters (defined in S2) surrounded by a quiet period (defined in S12). The modem acknowledges its transition to the command state by issuing the OK response. Sending *ATO0* (that's "oh zero") returns it to the on-line state.

Listing 21.12. The m_gocmd function forces to the on-line command state and issues a command.

FUNCTION NAME:	m_gocmd
LEVEL:	3
PROTOTYPE IN:	MODEM.H
LIBRARY:	MODEM.LIB
DESCRIPTION:	Forces modem from on-line to command state.
RETURNS:	int: M_SUCCEED if modem exits to on-line command state.
COMMENTS:	Three "escape" characters are sent, surrounded by the quiet interval given by the modem structure member guardtime.
INCLUDE FILES:	stdio.h, siodef.h, sioctl.h, buos.h, level0.h, modem.h

```
int m_gocmd(SIO *siop, int escchar)
{
    char msgbuff[MAX_MSG_LEN+1];
    int time_tmp, errcode = M_FAIL;
    s_ipush(siop);
    --delay(siop->sm->guardtime);        /* silence on front end   */
    s_fputc(siop, escchar);              /* send three escape chars */
    s_fputc(siop, escchar);
    s_fputc(siop, escchar);
    time_tmp = siop->sm->cmdt_out;       /* save time out          */
    siop->sm->cmdt_out = _1_SEC_0 * 5;   /* extend wait for OK     */
     if (m_getstr(siop, msgbuff, MAX_MSG_LEN))
         errcode = m_ismessage(siop, msgbuff);
    siop->sm->cmdt_out = time_tmp;       /* restore normal timeout */
    s_ipop(siop);
    return (errcode == M_SUCCEED) ? M_SUCCEED : M_FAIL;
}
```

An explanation of *m_gocmd*—For reasons that will become clear when we compose the reset function, the escape character is passed in the argument list. The timer function delay produces the quiet interval that must precede the escape sequence. The trailing quiet interval, however, is supplied by m_getstr, which also fetches the modem's response to the escape sequence. Because some modems are tardy about issuing the OK message, the time-out interval for s_fgets is made aggressively long.

If the modem does not respond to the escape sequence or if its response is invalid, errcode still contains M_FAIL. Otherwise errcode contains M_SUCCEED.

Reset Functions

In this section, we will write the high-level functions that must be called before using the modem. The first function, m_reset returns the modem to its default state so that it responds in a predictable fashion to commands. The second function, m_whoru, attempts to identify the modem and ascertain its maximum baud rate.

Modem Structure Members Required for Reset

The structure members required for the reset function are highlighted in Listing 21.13, followed by a brief discussion of each. (The complete structure and its initialization are given in Listings 21.3a and 21.3b.)

Listing 21.13. The modem structure members required for the reset function. Initialization is shown in the right column.

```
short    escape_arg;        /* 9 */    '¦',
int      baudtry[7];        /*10 */    {BAUD57K6, BAUD38K4,
                                        BAUD14K4,  BAUD9600,
                                        BAUD2400, BAUD1200,-1},
unsigned max_DTE_baud;      /*11 */    SUPPLIED,
```

baudtry[]   This array contains a list of the baud rates at which the software reset commands are sent. The first element should be the highest feasible baud rate expected from the target modem. The list of baud rates *must* be terminated by a –1.

escape_arg   This is the modem's escape character. It is initialized to ¦, and installed in S-register 2 during modem configuration. If the modem fails to respond to software reset commands, it is possible that it is in the on-line state and must be forced to the command state using this character in the escape sequence (see "Escape from and Return to On-line State," in Chapter 8 for a discusssion).

max_DTE_baud If reset is successful, the baud rate at which the modem responded to the reset command.

A Function to Reset the Modem: *m_reset*

Oddly enough, one of the most difficult functions to design is the one to reset the modem. As we noted in Chapter 8, in certain circumstances the modem cannot be reset at all. For example:

1. The command terminator (*nl1*) S3 has been changed to a value greater than 127. Here, the modem simply ignores all commands.

2. A connection exists and the escape character S2 has been changed to a value greater than 127. Here, there is no way to force the modem from on-line to command state so that the reset command can be issued.

3. DTR control has been overridden and cannot be used to force the modem to the command state where a reset command can be issued.

Now, there are two philosophies with respect to resetting a modem. In the first approach, you make *no assumptions* whatsoever about the modem's current state or configuration. Beginning with a simple reset command, and proceeding to ever more heroic measures, you try every conceivable technique to reset the modem. If, after this exhaustive testing, the modem still does not respond, you give up and sheepishly resort to asking the user to reset the modem by switching it off and back on.

The second philosophy is less energetic. Here you make only *one assumption* about the current state of the modem: that it was last used by your own software or, at least, is in a fathomable state. This implies that it has been correctly installed—the cable is correct, the power-up configuration produces sensible settings for your software, and so on.

If the normal reset does not occur, it can take several more minutes to work through every possibility for resetting the modem. Is it worth it? From a statistical standpoint, once correctly installed, the modem should reset normally every time. Of the tiny fraction of cases where normal reset fails, most are hopeless—that is, no amount of effort on your part will reset it. Therefore, it makes sense to consult the user before attempting heroic treatment of a rare and almost certainly fatal malady. A simple reset—wiggling DTR and sending the Z command—requires only 2-3 seconds. Only 10-20 seconds are required even if it is necessary to attempt this at all the listed baud rates. Once this simple reset procedure has failed all baud rates, the user decides whether to proceed.

Listing 21.14. The m_reset function for MODEM.H: a function to reset the modem.

FUNCTION NAME:	m_reset
LEVEL:	3
PROTOTYPE IN:	MODEM.H
LIBRARY:	MODEM.LIB
DESCRIPTION:	Attempts to reset the modem to default condition.
RETURNS:	int: M_SUCCEED if reset is successful; M_FAIL if user aborts.
COMMENTS:	Resetting when on-line takes up to a minute, depending upon AT speed of modem.
INCLUDE FILES:	stdio.h, stdlib.h, siodef.h, ascii.h, misc.h, key.h, level0.h, modem.h

continues

Listing 21.14. continued

```c
int m_reset(SIO *siop)
{
    extern char *brstr[];
    struct modem *smp = siop->sm;
    int  i, j, errcode, user_redo;
    int  tmptries, tmptime;            /* temporary storage                */
    s_clrsio(siop, CMDBUFSIZ);         /* clear SIO of garbage             */
    tmptime  = smp->cmdt_out;          /* save command response time out   */
    set232(siop, DTR, OFF);            /* inhibit DTR to force command state */
    --delay(_0_SEC_3);                 /* a bit of DTR delay               */
    set232(siop, DTR, ON);             /* assert DTR to enable command mode */
    tmptries = smp->cmdretry;          /* save number of retries           */
    smp->cmdretry = 1;                 /* make m_cmd_OK retry only once     */
    user_redo = FALSE;                 /* TRUE = try online escape ('+++') */
    for(EVER)                          /* only reset or user can end loop   */
        {
        for (i = 0; smp->baudtry[i] != -1; ++i) /* at every baud rate listed */
            {
            setbaud(siop, smp->baudtry[i]);
            printf("Trying Reset at %s\n", brstr[smp->baudtry[i]]);
            for (j = tmptries; j > 0; --j)--/* issue reset command          */
                {
                if (user_redo && j <= 2)   /* 2nd time through; modem...    */
                    {
                    m_gocmd(siop, '+');              /* default escape character */
                    m_cmd_OK(siop, "H0");            /* issue hangup command   */
                    if (smp->escape_arg != '+')
                        m_gocmd(siop,smp->escape_arg);       /* ditto local    */
                    m_cmd_OK(siop, "H0");            /* hangup command again   */
                    set232(siop, GPO1, ON);          /* GPO1 resets card modems */
                    --delay(_0_SEC_05);              /* leave on a while       */
                    set232(siop, GPO1, OFF);
                    }
                if ( (errcode = m_cmd_OK(siop, "")) == M_SUCCEED)
                    {                                /* If modem responds OK to AT */
                    smp->max_DTE_baud = smp->baudtry[i];  /* save rate        */
                    goto EXIT;
                    }
                }
            }
        puts("\a\nModem won't reset. Press any key to retry, ESC to quit");
        if (getkbch() == ESC)
            {
            errcode = M_USRCAN;
            goto EXIT;
            }
        if (user_redo == FALSE)        /* next time through, try on-line escape */
            user_redo = !user_redo;
        }
EXIT:
    if (errcode == M_SUCCEED)
        {
        smp->cmdt_out = _1_SEC_0 * 3; /* allow at least 3 secs for reset    */
```

```
        errcode = m_cmd_OK(siop, "Z");
        }
    set232(siop, DTR, OFF);
    smp->cmdt_out = tmptime;           /* restore from temporaries        */
    smp->cmdretry = tmptries;
    return errcode;
}
```

An explanation of _m_reset_—Immediately after declaring variables, the following strategy is undertaken:

```
inhibit dtr;
wait;
assert dtr;
for (EVER)
    {
    for (every baud rate listed)
        {
        for (several tries)
            {
            send reset command;
            if (reset successful)
                if (return (M_SUCCEED);
            }
        if (user chose to retry)
            {
            send on-line escape;
            send hangup command;
            }
        }
'Won't reset' message;
user decides to redo or terminate;
if (user redo)
    if (continue;
return (M_FAIL);
}
```

The function is essentially an eternal loop that can be broken in only two ways: through a successful reset or a user abort.[3] One by one, the SIO is set to the baud rates listed in the structure's baudtry array, and the reset command is issued. If the modem responds to this command with OK, M_SUCCEED is returned. By temporarily changing the cmd_retry and cmdt_out members, the reset command is issued twice with a 2-second timeout interval to allow for the long reset time of some modems. If the modem doesn't respond OK, the next baud rate is selected and the reset command is sent again.

After all baud rates have been tried (about 20 seconds), the user is informed that the modem will not reset and is given the alternative to try again or terminate. If he elects to retry, the whole process repeats, beginning again with the first baud rate in the list. This time through

[3]Those who feel that the goto statement should be banished from the C language should try writing a _reasonable_ version of m_reset without it.

the loop, two new commands are issued in addition to the reset command: the on-line escape command followed by the hangup command. If the modem is in the on-line state (i.e., in a carrier linkage), these commands force it back to the command mode, where it then responds to the reset command. Note that the escape command is issued twice, once with the default setting of S2 and once (for good measure) with the setting contained in the modem structure. In case the modem is a PC-card modem, the UART's general-purpose output #1 is toggled.[4] The loop continues as before until reset is successful or the user elects to quit trying. Upon exit under any circumstances, the modem structure members that were changed upon entry are restored to their original values.

This reset function is designed to be quite strict in that it does not allow the user to ignore the modem's failure to reset. In practice, however, there are many circumstances under which one might elect to proceed despite the failure of the modem to respond; the proper modem cable may not be available, for example, or the user may not be trying to communicate with a modem at all but with some other kind of device. An intelligently designed communications program should provide a convenient method—perhaps in the form of an installation variable—to enable the user[a] to ignore the modem altogether.

Identifying the Modem: *m_whoru*

Because various vintages and models differ so widely in their capabilities, once the modem has been reset, we must learn as much about it as we can. The information gained here will be used to determine the manner in which we later configure the modem.

MODEM TYPES

We will employ the constants shown in Listing 21.15 to describe a modem. These values have absolutely no meaning to the modem itself, but are codes created privately by us to simplify references to the various types of modems.

Listing 21.15. Constants defining the various types of modems.

```
enum m_types{
    ID_UNKNOWN= 0,    /* Unable to identify modem */
    ID_12,            /* Likely 1200 bps modem    */
    ID_12PLUS,        /* 1200 bps modem           */
    ID_24,            /* 2400 bps modem           */
    ID_96 ,           /* 9600 bps modem           */
    ID_14K4           /* 14,400 bps modem         */
    };
```

---

[4]Writing to this output is harmless when it is not a card modem.

Structure Members Required for Identification

Listing 21.16 shows the modem structure members and their initialized values that are required by m_whoru. (The complete structure and its initialization are given in Listings 21.3a and 21.3b.)

Listing 21.16. The modem structure members required for the modem identification function. Initialization is shown in the right column.

```
    short   modtype;              /* 9  */    VIRGIN,
    short   max_carrier_speed;    /* 10 */    SUPPLIED,
```

modtype   This is our own code for the modem based upon analysis of the modem's product identification code. It is normally initialized to VIRGIN, but it may be initialized to any of the valid modem types listed in Listing 21.17.

max_carrier_speed   This is the value contained in the first two digits of the I0 command, normalized to a library baud rate value. For instance, a 9600 bps modem would be represented by the constant BAUD9600 constant in SIODEF.H.

The actual code for m_whoru is shown in Listing 21.17.

Listing 21.17. The m_whoru function identifies the type of modem in use.

```
FUNCTION NAME: m_whoru
         LEVEL: 3
   PROTOTYPE IN: MODEM.H
       LIBRARY: MODEM.LIB
   DESCRIPTION: Queries modem to ascertain its identity. The results
                are stored in the modem structure.
       RETURNS: int:  M_FAIL if the response is unidentifiable;
                otherwise M_SUCCEED.
      COMMENTS: Only the first two digits in the product ID are used.
  INCLUDE FILES: stdio.h, stdlib.h, string.h, siodef.h, modem.h, misc.h
```

```c
int m_whoru(SIO *siop)
{
    struct modem *smp = siop->sm;
    int errcode = M_SUCCEED;
    char id_string[MAX_MSG_LEN+1];
    set232(siop, DTR, ON);
    m_cmd_str(siop, "I0", id_string, MAX_MSG_LEN);  /* get ID */
    if (id_string == NIL)
```

continues

Listing 21.17. continued

```
        return M_FAIL;
    id_string[2] = NUL;                     /* First two characters    */
    switch (str_atoi(id_string))            /* Convert string to integer */
        {
        case 12: smp->modtype  = ID_12;
             smp->max_carrier_speed = BAUD1200;
             break;
        case 13: smp->modtype = ID_12PLUS;
             smp->max_carrier_speed = BAUD1200;
             break;
        case 14: smp->modtype = ID_14K4;
             smp->max_carrier_speed = BAUD14K4;
             break;
        case 24: smp->modtype = ID_24;
             smp->max_carrier_speed = BAUD2400;
             break;
        case 96: smp->modtype = ID_96;
             smp->max_carrier_speed = BAUD9600;
             break;
        default: smp->modtype = ID_UNKNOWN;
             smp->max_carrier_speed = BAUD300;
             errcode = M_FAIL;
             break;
        }
    return errcode;
}
```

An explanation of *m_whoru*—The first effort is to fetch the modem's product identification by sending the I0 command. The first two digits of the return string, which act as an indicator of the modem speed and, in some cases, other capabilities, are then converted to an integer value and analyzed (source code for the "incidental" str_atoi function is in Appendix A). A switch statement analyzes the two-digit number and installs one of the modem codes listed in Listing 21.15 in the structure member modtype. Because 300 bps modems do not support the I command, no case is present for them. When the identification code does not match any of the case statements, the modem under test is simply identified as "unknown."

Configuring a Baseline Modem

If we are to take advantage of the spiffy features of modems, we must include their commands in the configuration string. But what happens when this configuration string is sent to one of the older modems that does not support all the features? Recall from Chapter 8 that if a command string contains a single invalid command, *none* of the commands is executed. Clearly, we must make certain that commands are not sent to modems that cannot understand them.

Before we look at the m_config function, let's discuss the structure members that will be needed. These are shown in Listing 21.18.

Listing 21.18. The modem structure members required for configuring the modem. Initialization is shown in the right column.

```
short    autoans_arg;      /* 11 */    0,
short    dtwait_arg;       /* 12 */    2,
short    dcdwait_arg;      /* 13 */    30,
short    speaker_arg;      /* 14 */    1,
short    xcmd_arg;         /* 15 */    4,
short    speakvol_arg;     /* 16 */    1,
short    firmdcd_arg;      /* 17 */    1,
short    firmdtr_arg;      /* 18 */    2,
short    baudmode;         /* 19 */    BAUD_FOUND,
BOOL     configokflag;     /* 20 */    FALSE,
```

The strategy for configuration is uncomplicated, though perhaps unintuitive. We will build two separate configuration strings—pri_config for those commands that are supported by all modems and sec_config for evolutionary commands. The commands to be included in each string are shown below as subheadings of these configuration buffers.

configokflag	A flag to broadcast that the modem has been successfully configured.
baudmode	How to initialize the SIO's baud rate relative to the type of modem in use. The choices are given in the baud_cnfg enumeration in Listing 21.2.
max_line_speed	The maximum data rate for modems of this type.
autoans_arg	S-register 0: number of rings before auto-answer. Initialized for 0 rings, that is, don't answer.
dtwait_arg	S-register 6: the delay between taking the phone off hook and dialing the call. Initialized to 2 seconds.
dcdwait_arg	S-register 7: how long after dialing to wait for a carrier before giving up. Initialized to 30 seconds.
speaker_arg	M command that controls the speaker. Initialized to 1, speaker on until carrier is detected.
xcmd_arg	Selects the command set in use based upon the modtype structure member. Initialized to 4, but must be changed to 1 for the vanilla 1200.
okalpha	A list of characters that are valid in a dial string.
speakvol_arg	The firmware volume control, the L command. Initialized to 1—medium volume.
firmdcd_arg	DCD is configured in software. It is initialized to &C2—that is, DCD reflects the carrier.
firmdtr_arg	DTR is configured in software. It is initialized to &D2—that is, if on-line, forces the modem to command state.

Configuration: *m_config* and *m_unconfig*

The challenge of this function is to ascertain which commands to place in the secondary configuration buffer. Listing 21.19 shows the code for m_config.

Listing 21.19. Configuring and Unconfiguring.

FUNCTION NAME: m_config
LEVEL: 3
PROTOTYPE IN: MODEM.H
LIBRARY: MODEM.LIB
DESCRIPTION: Configures the modem as described in the modem structure.
RETURNS: int: M_SUCCEED or M_FAIL
COMMENTS: Builds two configuration strings: pri_config containing commands that are recognized by all modems, and sec_config containing commands that are supported by only some. Note that sec_config must be sent first.
INCLUDE FILES: stdlib.h, siodef.h, string.h, modem.h, sioctl.h

```c
int m_config(SIO *siop)
{
    struct modem *smp = siop->sm;
    int errcode = M_SUCCEED;
    char *pri_config, *sec_config;
    strcpy(smp->okalpha, ",*#()-R");          /* chars common to all      */
    if ( (pri_config = (char *)malloc(CMDBUFSIZ)) == NIL)
        return M_CONFIG_MEM;
    if ( (sec_config = (char *)malloc(CMDBUFSIZ)) == NIL)
        return M_CONFIG_MEM;

    s_opush(siop);
    s_ocntrl(siop, SET, IL_DLYFLAG, OFF);
    set232(siop, DTR, ON);
/* Build modem-indepent primary string first */
    sprintf(pri_config,"M%dS0=%dS2=%dS6=%dS7=%d",
            smp->speaker_arg, smp->autoans_arg,
            smp->escape_arg, smp->dtwait_arg,  smp->dcdwait_arg
            );

/* Now build modem-dependent secondary string */
    switch (smp->modtype)
        {
        case ID_12:
            smp->xcmd_arg = 1;                /* only X1 supported        */
            sprintf(sec_config,"X%d", smp->xcmd_arg);
            break;
        case ID_12PLUS: strcat(smp->okalpha, "/!@W");
            sprintf(sec_config,"X%dL%d",
            smp->xcmd_arg,
```

```
                smp->speakvol_arg);
                break;
        case ID_14K4:
        case ID_24:
        case ID_96:
        strcat(smp->okalpha, "/!@WABCD");
                sprintf(sec_config,"&FX%dL%d&D%d&C%d", smp->xcmd_arg,
                    smp->speakvol_arg,smp->firmdtr_arg, smp->firmdcd_arg);
                break;
        }
    errcode |= m_cmd_OK(siop, sec_config);   /* send secondary first!    */
    free(sec_config);
    errcode |= m_cmd_OK(siop, pri_config);
    free(pri_config);
    switch (smp->baudmode)                    /* set baud rate            */
        {
        case BAUD_MAX:                        /* to modem's highest speed */
                setbaud(siop, smp->max_carrier_speed);
                break;
        case BAUD_FOUND:                      /* where modem reset        */
                setbaud(siop, smp->max_DTE_baud);
                break;
        }
    set232(siop, DTR, ON);
    errcode |= m_cmd_OK(siop, "");            /* Send AT at current baud rate */
    if (errcode == M_SUCCEED)
        smp->configokflag = TRUE;             /* broadcast init           */
    set232(siop, DTR, OFF);                   /* inhibit DTR              */
    s_opop(siop);
    if (errcode != M_SUCCEED)
        errcode = M_CONFIG_NOK;
    return errcode;                           /* return 0 if "OK"         */
}
```

FUNCTION NAME: m_unconfig
LEVEL: 3
PROTOTYPE IN: MODEM.H
LIBRARY: MODEM.LIB
DESCRIPTION: Sends "unconfiguration" string to modem as described in the modem structure.
RETURNS: int:M_SUCCEED or M_FAIL
INCLUDE FILES: siodef.h, modem.h

```
short m_unconfig(SIO *siop)
{
    short retval = M_SUCCEED;
    if (siop->sm->configokflag == TRUE)
```

continues

Listing 21.19. continued

```
            {
            siop->sm->configokflag = FALSE;
            retval = m_cmd_OK(siop, siop->sm->unconfig);
            }
        return retval;
}
```

An explanation of *m_config* **and** *m_unconfig*—Once the basic strategy of the configuration function is understood, the code becomes quite routine. The *primary* configuration string is built by concatenating only those commands that are universally palatable to all modems. The *secondary* configuration string, however, is unique for each vintage of modem, so its contents must be built dynamically, based upon the value of the modtype structure member supplied by m_whoru.

First, the primary configuration string is built by sprintf in the primary buffer. Then a switch is applied to the modtype structure variable with each case represents a type of modem. For the early 1200 bps modems, the X command for extending the call progress response codes is added to the secondary buffer. The X command is initialized to 4 in the structure, but because the 1200 does not support this parameter, its value is changed later to 1. The code for the later 1200 bps modems places not only the X command in the secondary buffer but also appends four characters to the list of characters permitted in dialing commands and adds the L command for controlling speaker volume.

The secondary configuration buffer for 2400 bps modems begins with the &F command that recalls the factory configuration. This command must appear first in the format string because the reset performed by m_reset installs the *user's* configuration profile, which may contain bizarre settings. Next appear the speaker volume control and commands to control the RS-232 configuration. These RS-232 commands, &C and &D, enable the DCD and DTR RS-232 inputs as described in "RS-232 Control" earlier in this chapter.

Upon exit from the switch, the primary and secondary buffers contain the commands appropriate for the modem whose code is in the modtype structure member.

Despite the "secondary" in its name, sec_config must be transmitted *first*. This guarantees that the modem sees the &F command before it sees subsequent commands. In other words, an &F embedded later in the string would overwrite the effects of the previous commands. (The &F command, unlike the Z command, does not cancel the effect of subsequent commands in the string.)

After sending the configuration strings, one decision remains: at what baud rate shall the SIO begin life? The answer to this question is embodied in the modem structure member baudmode. The choices are represented by the constant BAUD_MAX and BAUD_FOUND definitions given in Listing 21.3. The former sets the SIO's baud rate to maxbaud, the modem's highest data rate, while the latter sets the SIO to the baud rate at which the modem responded to the reset command in m_reset.

The m_unconfig function sends the un-configuration string of commands contained in the modem structure.

The Protocol Modem

The section on programming protocol modems is in some ways almost impossible to write. The reasons for this? First, unlike baseline modems, there are no standards—ad hoc, de jure, or otherwise—specifying the functionality, command set, and syntax for protocol modems. Hayes was unable to force its way of doing things on others because leadership in this area clearly belonged to Microcom. Second, the need to maintain backward compatibility with simpler modems has produced several thickets to ensnare careless programmers (extended messages, for example). Finally, the topic of layered protocols is inherently complex, far beyond the abilities of even "power" users, and, if one is to judge from commercial software, beyond the abilities of many programmers.

Rather than throw up our hands in frustration over the difficulty of the task, let's make a few simplifying assumptions about the hardware. Although Microcom may have been leading the technology in protocol modems, Hayes' time-tested way of doing things was culturally ingrained in the technical community. By contrast, many programmers find Microcom's command set to be haphazard, incoherent, and overly complicated. This is reflected by the two most popular vendors of integrated[5] modem chip vendors, Rockwell and AT&T, who invariably support the Hayes command set more thoroughly than others. So shall we.

Since the ordinary workings of a protocol modem are based upon the baseline command set given in Chapter 9, "Smart Modem Command," their differences can be isolated to two areas: configuration and interpretation of response codes when a connection is established. As noted several times before, once the modem is successfully configured and connected, it becomes a low-bandwidth, error-free bit-pipe. Indeed, there are only a few areas where an application may take advantage of an error-free connection. For example, if an application knows that its bit-pipe is error-free, it can employ file-transfer protocols with huge data packets because the risk of an error is low.[6] But aside from such high-level decisions, the details of the bit-pipe should be transparent to application software. For instance, in what way might software behave differently under an MNP4/MNP5 connection versus a V.42/V.42bis connection?

Baud Rate Switching

The most difficult aspect of dealing with protocol modems is managing the baud rate on the serial port. Recall that in ordinary, non-protocol connections the DTE speed must

---

[5]That is, chip sets that contain both command interpreter and data pumps.

[6]The risk is not as low as one might imagine, due to the high error rate on typical DTE serial ports at high baud rates.

match the speed of the carrier. If a modem says CONNECT 9600, the DTE's baud rate must be 9600; that is, the 9600 is assumed to refer to the speed of the carrier. If, however, a protocol connection is established, the DTE is able to send data at a higher baud rate than that given in the CONNECT message.

Let's consider several possibilities:

1. In the case of an ordinary (non-protocol) modem, the DTE sets its baud rate to 2400 bps, the modem's highest carrier speed. A 300 bps connection is established and the modem issues the message CONNECT 300 at 2400 bps, then changes its baud rate to 300 to match the speed of the carrier. The DTE must examine the speed in the CONNECT message and change its baud rate to 300 bps.

2. In the case of a protocol modem, the DTE, in expectation of a protocol connection, sets its baud rate to 38,000 bps, twice as high as the modem's highest carrier speed. A protocol connection occurs, and flow control between the modem and the DTE prevent overwhelming each other with data.

3. In the case of a protocol modem, the DTE, in expectation of a protocol connection, sets its baud rate to 38,000 bps, twice as high as the modem's highest carrier speed. But instead of making a protocol connect as expected, a non-protocol connection occurs. The DTE must examine the speed in the CONNECT message and change its baud rate.

Fallback to Non-Protocol

In two of the three examples just cited, the DTE is required to change its baud rate when it is different from the carrier speed. Making the baud rate change is avoidable by using *hybrid mode* (refer to "Hybrid Mode" in Chapter 10), also referred to as *normal* or *buffered asynchronous mode*. Hybrid mode simulates the protocol-style interface, allowing a mismatch between DTE baud rate and carrier speeds governed by flow control—even on non-protocol connections. Thus hybrid mode enables the DTE to employ the same modem interface for all connections, protocol or otherwise. Unfortunately, hybrid mode, tempting though it may be, is not general enough: DTE software written to take advantage of it doesn't work on non-protocol modems. For this reason we shall bite the bullet, and deal with the necessity of changing baud rates after a connection is established. This means that we must configure protocol modems to fall back to non-protocol instead of hybrid mode.

The CONNECT Message

As explained in "The CONNECT Message Fib" in Chapter 10, it is possible to configure the modem so that the modem's CONNECT message protocol connections reports the DTE (serial port) baud rate instead of the speed of the carrier. On non-protocol connections, the CONNECT message reports the speed of the carrier. In both cases the speed of the carrier is always correctly reported in the optional CARRIER message.

Let's summarize this feature succinctly. When so configured, the modem's CONNECT message reports the DTE speed *except for non-protocol connections.* This behavior provides a simple tool for deciding when to change the DTE baud rate. We always dial at the maximum DTE speed (supplied by m_reset), then examine the speed reported in the CONNECT message. If the speed reported is equal to the maximum DTE speed, a protocol connection exists. On the other hand, if the speed reported is different, a non-protocol connection exists and it is necessary to change the DTE baud rate to equal the reported speed. Listing 21.1 shows a program flow chart for this procedure.

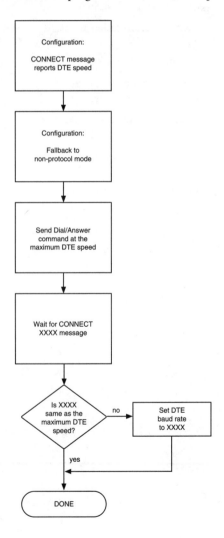

FIGURE 21.1.

Flow chart for deciding when to change the baud rate in response to a connection.

Configuration

We have already established two configuration criteria (fallback and CONNECT messages). Let's now look at a complete list of configuration criteria.

- Choose the error-correcting protocol. We select LAPM (from V.42) because it subsumes the MNP protocol.

- Enable the selected error-correcting protocol.

- Enable compression (in this case, V.42bis).

- Enable full-feature negotiation. In other words, don't get fancy—let the two modems arrive at the best connection.

- Attempt to connect at the speed of the DIAL or answer command.

- Select fallback strategy. As already discussed, we elect to fall back to an ordinary, non-protocol connection instead of a hybrid one.

- Set flow control method. This must be extracted from the `flow_wanted` member in the `SIO`.

- Select full messaging: CONNECT, CARRIER, PROTOCOL, and COMPRESSION.

- Configure the CONNECT message to report the speed of the serial port, not the speed of the carrier.

These criteria are summarized in Table 21.1, which also shows the Hayes-type commands required to implement them. Please refer to the command section of Chapter 10 for a complete explanation of the commands.

Table 21.1. Protocol configuration criteria and Hayes-style commands.

Command Name	Command	Action
Protocol Enable	Q5	Enable error correction
Protocol Select	S46=136	Select LAPM (V.42)
Compression Enable	S46=138	Enable data compression (V.42bis)
Feature Negotiation	S48=7	Full negotiation
Carrier Fallback Strategy #1	S37=0	Attempt to connect at the speed of last AT command
Carrier Fallback Strategy #2	N1	Negotiate the highest speed common to both modems
V.42 Fallback strategy	S36=5	If LAPM fails, try for MNP, then settle for an ordinary connection
Flow Control Select	&Kx	Enable flow control as given in SIO

Command Name	Command	Action
Enable Extended Message	W1	Enable extended messages. DTE rate appears in CONNECT message
Select Extended Message	S95=44	Select all messages

Structure Members for Protocol Configuration

For your convenience, the structure members and their initialized values that support the protocol configuration function are repeated in Listing 21.20. Initialization is shown in the right column. The complete structure and its initialization are given in Listings 21.3a and 21.3b.

Listing 21.20. Modem structure members required for protocol operation. Initialization is shown in the right column.

```
short      connect_XXXX_code;       /* 21 */    SUPPLIED,
short      carrier_baud_code;       /* 22 */    SUPPLIED,
BOOL       linkprot_wanted;         /* 23 */    TRUE,
BOOL       linkprot_supported;      /* 24 */    SUPPLIED,
char       linkname [LPSIZE];       /* 25 */    "",
BOOL       compress_wanted;         /* 26 */    TRUE,
BOOL       compress_supported;      /* 27 */    SUPPLIED,
char compressname[COMPRESSSIZE];    /* 28 */    "",
```

carrier_baud_code   This is the virtual baud-rate code[7] representing the numeric portion of the CARRIER XXXX message. It is supplied when the m_parsemsg function parses a CARRIER message.

linkprot_wanted   This user-supplied variable tells the protocol configuration function to try to configure the modem for error-correcting link protocol operation.

linkprot_supported   This variable is set to TRUE when the protocol configuration function successfully enables error-correcting link protocol operation.

linkname[]   This is the name of the error-correcting link protocol in use, if any. This field is supplied when the m_parsemsg function parses a PROTOCOL message.

---

[7]That is, suitable for use with the getbaud and setbaud functions.

compress_wanted	This user-supplied variable causes the protocol configuration function to try to configure the modem for data compression.
compress_supported	This variable is set to TRUE when the protocol configuration function successfully enables data compression.
compressname[]	This is the name of the compression protocol in use, if any. This field is supplied when the m_parsemsg function parses a COMPRESSION message.

Configuring the Protocol Modem: *m_protoconfig*

The wide differences in support for protocol commands, as well as in their implementation, produces an unambitious design goal for a configuration function. It is no doubt impossible to write a single function that will unambiguously configure all protocol modems, although it is possible to succeed most of the time. Therefore the m_protoconfig function given in Listing 21.21 ought not to be regarded as a code appliance, but as a guideline and as an example of the kinds of configuration decisions that must be made.

Listing 21.21. The m_protoconfig function configures a protocol modem.

FUNCTION NAME: m_protoconfig
LEVEL: 3
PROTOTYPE IN: MODEM.H
LIBRARY: MODEM.LIB
DESCRIPTION: Configures a modem for protocol operation.
RETURNS: int—M_SUCCEED or M_FAIL
INCLUDE FILES: stdlib.h, siodef.h, string.h, modem.h, sioctl.h

```
#define PROTO_ENABLE         "&Q5"
#define SPEED_SELECT         "N1S37=0"
#define PROTO_SEL            "S46=136"
#define NEGOTIATION          "S48=7"
#define FALLBACK             "S36=5"
#define COMPRESSION          "S46=138"
#define EXTEND_MSG           "W1S95=44"

int m_protoconfig(SIO *siop)
{
    struct modem *smp = siop->sm;
    int errcode = M_SUCCEED;
    char *flowcmd, *proto_config;
    if (smp->linkprot_wanted == FALSE)
      return M_SUCCEED;
    if (smp->max_carrier_speed < BAUD2400)
        return M_SUCCEED;
    if ( (proto_config = (char *)malloc(CMDBUFSIZ)) == NIL)
        return M_CONFIG_MEM;
    s_opush(siop);
```

```
        s_ocntrl(siop, SET, IL_DLYFLAG, OFF);
        set232(siop, DTR, ON);
        smp->linkprot_supported = smp->compress_supported = FALSE;

/* Probe for Link-Layer Protocol Services */
    if ( (errcode ¦= m_cmd_OK(siop, PROTO_ENABLE)) == M_SUCCEED)
            {
            smp->linkprot_supported = TRUE;
            strcpy(proto_config, PROTO_ENABLE);
            if ( (errcode ¦= m_cmd_OK(siop, NEGOTIATION)) == M_SUCCEED)
                strcat(proto_config, NEGOTIATION);
            if ( (errcode ¦= m_cmd_OK(siop, FALLBACK)) == M_SUCCEED)
                strcat(proto_config, FALLBACK);
    }
    if (errcode == M_FAIL)
            goto EXIT;

/* Probe for Compression */
    if (smp->compress_wanted)
            {
            if ( (errcode ¦= m_cmd_OK(siop, COMPRESSION)) == M_SUCCEED)
                {
                smp->compress_supported = TRUE;
                strcat(proto_config, COMPRESSION);
                }
            }
/* Probe for Flow Control */
    switch (siop->flow_wanted)
            {
            case NO_FLOW : flowcmd = "&K0";  break;
            case XON_XOFF: flowcmd = "&K4";  break;
            case RTS_CTS : flowcmd = "&K3";  break;
            default:       flowcmd = "&K0";  break;
            }
    if ( (errcode ¦= m_cmd_OK(siop, flowcmd)) == M_SUCCEED)
        strcat(proto_config, flowcmd);

/* Probe for Physical-Layer Conditioning */
    if ( (errcode ¦= m_cmd_OK(siop, SPEED_SELECT)) == M_SUCCEED)
        strcat(proto_config, SPEED_SELECT);
    if ( ( errcode ¦= m_cmd_OK(siop, EXTEND_MSG)) == M_SUCCEED)
        strcat(proto_config, EXTEND_MSG);
    errcode ¦= m_cmd_OK(siop, proto_config);    /* send primary to modem  */
EXIT:
    free(proto_config);
    s_opop(siop);
    return (errcode ? M_CONFIG_NOK : M_SUCCEED);
}
```

An explanation of *m_protoconfig*—As with m_config for non-protocol modems, the strategy here is to build a configuration string based upon the capabilities of the modem. Unlike baseline modems, however, there is no portable and convenient method (such as evaluating the I0 command) for deducing a protocol modem's capabilities. This means that m_protoconfig must *probe* the modem, discovering if a command is supported by evaluating the modem's response to it. The failure of a command causes an M_FAIL error code to be returned.[8] All functionality associated with protocol modems is dependent upon the presence of an error-correcting link protocol such as MNP or V.42. If protocol operation simply isn't desired (smp->linkprot_wanted), it makes little sense to proceed with the remainder of the configuration.

Assuming that protocol operation is desired, however, we must find out if it is supported; again, if it is not supported, it makes little sense to proceed. The first task, then, is to provide a value for the structure member linkprot_supported, which is initialized to FALSE at the beginning of the function. To answer this question, we probe with the &Q5 command, the most basic and widely supported of the protocol enabling commands. If the modem answers ERROR, we assume that the modem does not support protocols; the variable linkprot_supported remains FALSE and the code unceremoniously jumps to the EXIT label. If the &Q5 command succeeds, however, linkprot_supported is set TRUE and several critical commands are probed and their results OR'ed with the variable errcode. If *any* of the commands in this critical block fail, errcode will be non-zero and the code will jump to the EXIT label.

Assuming that none of the commands in the critical block failed, we now proceed to configure compression where the variable compress_wanted is configured. Next is flow control, whose value is taken from the SIO variable flow_wanted. The other features are then probed and configured: speed selection and extended messaging (these commands are composites of two separate commands.) If all configuration commands were successful, errcode contains M_SUCCESS upon return.

Parsing Modem Responses: *m_parsemsg*

As discussed earlier in this chapter ("Evaluating Modem Responses"), protocol modems respond to commands in the same way as ordinary modems except that their response to a successful dial or answer command may contain not only a CONNECT message, but also *several additional* CRLF-delimited responses. For example, a protocol modem may be configured to respond many ways to the same call:

---

[8]Sending individual commands, then resending them as a string of successful commands, is a stylistic quirk of the author.

```
CONNECT 2400
```

or

```
   CONNECT 2400
   CARRIER 9600
```

or

```
   CONNECT 2400
   CARRIER 9600
   PROTOCOL: LAP-M
```

or

```
   CONNECT 2400
   CARRIER 9600
   COMPRESSION: V42BIS
```

or

```
   CONNECT 2400
   CARRIER 9600
   PROTOCOL: LAP-M
   COMPRESSION: V42BIS
```

If you recall to handle this insanity we wrote m_ismessage, a general function to evaluate and validate modem responses where, a function is called for messages that require parsing into constituent parts. Although the code makes it possible to specify a different parsing function for each message, only a single function is actually required. That function, m_parsemsg is shown in Listing 21.22.

Listing 21.22. The m_parsemsg function: a general-purpose modem response parser.

FUNCTION NAME: m_parsemsg
          LEVEL: 3
  PROTOTYPE IN: MODEM.H
       LIBRARY: MODEM.LIB
   DESCRIPTION: Parses CONNECT, CARRIER, PROTOCOL, and
                COMPRESSION messages into constituent parts.
       RETURNS: void
  INCLUDE FILES: stdio.h, stdlib.h, ctype.h, string.h, siodef.h, modem.h, misc.h

```
void m_parsemsg(SIO *siop, struct parse_info *msgp, char * modemstr)
{
    short baudcode;
    struct modem *smp = siop->sm;
    char *parsep, *destp;
    switch (msgp->id)
        {
```

continues

Listing 21.22. continued

```
        case M_CONN:
        case M_CARRIER:
            baudcode = br_to_bcode(str_atoi(modemstr));
            if(baudcode == -1 )
                printf("M_parsemsg: baudrate not in table\n");
            else
                {
                if (msgp->id == M_CONN)
                    smp->connect_XXXX_code = baudcode;
                else
                    smp->carrier_baud_code = baudcode;
                }
            break;
        case M_PROTOCOL:
        case M_COMPRESS:
            parsep = strchr(modemstr,':');
            if (parsep == NIL)
                break;
            if (msgp->id == M_PROTOCOL)
                destp = &smp->linkname[0];
            else
                destp = &smp->compressname[0];
            while (*++parsep != '\0')
                {
                if (*parsep == ' ' || iscntrl(*parsep))
                    continue;
                *destp++ = *parsep;
                }
            *destp = '\0';
            break;
        }
    }
```

An Explanation of *m_parsemsg*

This function is called (through a function pointer) by m_ismessage whenever the modem message must for some reason be parsed. It is passed pointers to the SIO and to a parse_info structure (see Listing 21.9). There are four messages that bear variable information for parsing:

1. The CONNECT message is followed by a string of ASCII numerals that, depending upon configuration, reflect either the speed of the DTE (serial port) or the carrier.

2. The CARRIER message is followed by a string of ASCII numerals that report the speed of the carrier.

3. The PROTOCOL: message (note the colon) is followed by an ASCII string describing the link-layer protocol, if any. Examples are NONE, V.42, and ALT.[9] These are spelled various ways, depending upon the manufacturer.

4. The COMPRESSION: message (note the colon) is followed by an ASCII string describing the data-compression protocol, if any. Examples are NONE, Class 5, and V42BIS. These are spelled various ways, depending upon the manufacturer.

The code switches on the id member of the structure describing the type of message. In the case of CONNECT and CARRIER messages, str_atoi[10] converts the string of ASCII numerals into an integer. This value is then passed to br_to_bcode (Listing 14.26) for conversion to a code acceptable to the baud rate functions in the library. This baud rate code is then stored in the modem structure variables smp->connect_XXXX_code or carrier_baud_code for inspection by other functions.[11]

In the case of the PROTOCOL: and COMPRESSION: messages, the text appearing to the right of the colon is copied in the modem structure arrays linkname and compressname, respectively.

Dial and Answer Functions

We now turn to the modem functions for dialing and answering the phone. We will compose functions to perform the most common operations: dialing, redialing, answering, and hanging up. The modem structure members in Listing 21.23 are required in these operations.

Listing 21.23. The modem structure members required for dial/answer functions.

```
BOOL    autobrflag;             /*29 */      TRUE,
char    dialbuff[CMDBUFSIZ];    /*30 */      "" ,
char    okalpha[18];            /*31 */      "",
char    dialmode;               /*32 */      'T',
char    enddial;                /*33 */      ' ',
```

autobrflag   When the modem answers a call, this flag determines whether the baud rate of the SIO is automatically changed to match the data rate of the connection. This is initialized to TRUE.

---

[9]ALT is an abbreviation for "alternative procedure;" in other words, MNP Class 3 or MNP Class 4.

[10]The listing for this Incidental function is given in Appendix A.

[11]Please note that the CONNECT and CARRIER messages containing "12000" will not function correctly because this baud rate is not attainable on IBM PC hardware.

`dialbuff[]`	The dial string is assembled in this buffer, where it will be available for subsequent redialing.
`okalpha[]`	A list of characters that are valid in the dial command.
`dialmode[]`	This is the dial command itself, initialized to *D*.
`enddial[]`	This buffer is for command modifiers that result in an error if they appear anywhere but at the end of a dial string. At present, only the ; (semicolon) command (return to command mode) currently meets this description.

Return Call-Progress Response: *m_wait4dcd*

The final kind of modem responses we must address are those generated by making or receiving a call. These messages occur during or after a telephone operation. BUSY, NO DIAL TONE, and NO ANSWER are returned as a result of a failure in the dialing operation (see Chapter 8). CONNECT, CONNECT XXXX, and CARRIER XXXX occur after a successful dial or answer command. Depending upon whether the modem supports error-correcting and compression protocols, additional messages may be generated.

Listing 21.24 shows the function m_wait4dcd, which is designed to be called after a modem dial or answer command.

Listing 21.24. The `m_wait4dcd` function waits for modem response to dial answer.

FUNCTION NAME: `m_wait4dcd`
                LEVEL: 3
        PROTOTYPE IN: MODEM.H
             LIBRARY: MODEM.LIB
         DESCRIPTION: Evaluates stream of modem messages until a 'terminal' message is received, DCD is asserted, or the command is terminated from the keyboard.
             RETURNS: `int`: an integer code to describing the result of dialing.
            COMMENTS: The duration of the wait for carrier is determined by the modem's S7 register (set by m_config).
       INCLUDE FILES: siodef.h, sioctl.h, modem.h

```
int m_wait4dcd(SIO *siop)
{
    extern char *brstr[];                    /* baud codes to strings    */
    short retcode;
    char waitbuff[MAX_MSG_LEN + 1];
    struct modem *smp = siop->sm;
```

```
        s_clrsio(siop, CMDBUFSIZ);
        s_ipush(siop);
        s_icntrl(siop, SET, T_OUTFLAG, ON);    /* turn on timeout mode    */
        s_icntrl(siop, SET, T_OUT, _0_SEC_2);  /* timeout for s_fgets     */
/* bait baud/link protocol/compression variables */
        smp->connect_XXXX_code = getbaud(siop);
        smp->carrier_baud_code = getbaud(siop);
        strcpy (smp->compressname, "NONE");
        strcpy(smp->linkname, "NONE");
        retcode = MSG_NON_TERMINAL ;            /* initialize like this!   */

        while (retcode == MSG_NON_TERMINAL)     /* timeout or non-terminal */
            {
            if (s_fgetln(siop, waitbuff, MAX_MSG_LEN) != TIMEOUT)
                retcode = m_ismessage(siop, waitbuff);
            else if (stat232(siop, DCD))        /* if timeout and DCD is high */
                retcode = M_DCD_HIGH;           /* connect phase is over      */
            else if (retcode == MSG_INVALID)
                retcode = M_BADMSG;
            if (s_keybort(siop))
                retcode = M_USRCAN;             /* canceled call from keyboard*/
            }
        s_ipop(siop);

    if (stat232(siop, DCD) == TRUE)
        printf("CONNECT: Carrier: %s Local: %s  LLP: %s  COMP: %s\n",
                brstr[smp->carrier_baud_code],
                brstr[smp->connect_XXXX_code],
                smp->linkname,
                smp->compressname);

    if (smp->autobrflag == TRUE
        && smp->connect_XXXX_code != getbaud(siop)
        && stat232(siop, DCD)== TRUE)
        {
        printf("Changing DTE baud rate to %s\n",
                brstr[smp->connect_XXXX_code]);
        setbaud(siop, smp->connect_XXXX_code);
        }
    return retcode;
}
```

An explanation of _m_wait4dcd_—The substance of the function is a `while` loop that alternately polls the keyboard, checks for DCD on the RS-232 interface to become asserted, and calls s_fgetln to test for a modem response. When s_fgetln returns a response, it is sent to m_ismessage for validation and parsing, if necessary. The loop is broken if m_ismessage returns either MSG_INVALID or TIMEOUT, or if the user presses an abort key.

However, the loop sustains as long as m_ismessage returns a MSG_NON_TERMINAL, which means that the just-submitted message is likely to be followed by other messages.

Because of implementation differences[12] between manufacturers, the order of the multiple messages is not predictable. How, then, do we know when all the messages are complete? As mentioned earlier, the modem asserts its DCD output when it is ready to send and receive data. In other words, when DCD is asserted, we know that the last message has been received.

Before entering the s_fgetln loop, the protocol variables subject to parsing are initialized. The baud rate variables are given the current baud rate and the string variables are set to "NONE."

After the loop breaks, the code tests the modem structure variable autobrflag to ascertain if the DTE (computer) baud rate should be set to the speed of the carrier. Why is this decision necessary? In Figure 21.1 we saw that dialing occurs at the highest possible DTE speed in anticipation of a protocol connection. Variations in data throughput are then regulated between the local and remote DTEs by the modem flow-control method selected during configuration.

What happens when a connection is established with a non-protocol modem? Because the remote modem has no link protocol, it therefore has no concept of flow control. In the absence of flow control, the local DTE will quickly overwhelm the local modem with data it cannot send. Therefore, when the speed reported in the CARRIER message differs from the DTE baud rate (to which it is initialized at the top of the function), a DTE baud rate reduction is required.

Auto-Dial Telephone: *m_dial*

A modem dialing command is actually a series of operations (see Listing 9.1). Thanks here to the internal design of the modem and our modem library, this relatively complicated procedure is reduced to a single function, m_dial, shown in Listing 21.25.

Listing 21.25. The m_dial function: a modem auto-dial function.

FUNCTION NAME:	m_dial
LEVEL:	3
PROTOTYPE IN:	MODEM.H
LIBRARY:	MODEM.LIB
DESCRIPTION:	Dials the number specified and waits for return a result code.
RETURNS:	int: result code returned from dial operation.
COMMENTS:	The duration of the wait for the response is given in the dcdwait structure member. The filtered dial string is built into the modem structure for use by redial.
INCLUDE FILES:	stdio.h, ctype.h, siodef.h, ascii.h, string.h, buos.h, modem.h

---

[12]In one manufacturer's protocol modems, for example, the order of the messages seems to depend on the setting of the X command.

```
int m_dial(SIO *siop, char  phonenum[])
{
    struct modem *smp = siop->sm;
    int  resultcode;
    char dialstr[CMDBUFSIZ];           /* build dial command here       */
    char *dbp = smp->dialbuff;
    do                                 /* filter string for illegal bytes  */
        {
        if (isdigit(*phonenum) ¦¦ strchr(smp->okalpha, *phonenum))
            *dbp++ = *phonenum;        /* copy valid characters to dialbuff */
        } while( *++phonenum != NUL );
    *dbp = '\0';                       /* terminate  buffer             */
    sprintf(dialstr,"D%c%s%c",smp->dialmode, smp->dialbuff, smp->enddial);
    if (strlen(smp->dialbuff) == 0)    /* exit if string is NIL         */
        return M_NILNUM;
    set232(siop, DTR, ON);
    m_cmd(siop, dialstr);              /* output command to SIO         */
    resultcode = m_wait4dcd(siop);     /* go wait for carrier           */
    switch (resultcode)
        {
        case M_NODCD:                  /* no carrier (or timeout)       */
        case M_NOTONE:                 /* no dial tone heard            */
        case M_BUSY:                   /* busy signal heard             */
        case M_NOANSW:                 /* silence not heard after @     */
            set232(siop, DTR, OFF);    /* return to command state       */
            break;
        case M_USRCAN:                 /* call cancelled from keyboard   */
            set232(siop, DTR, OFF);    /* return to command state       */
            s_putc(siop, SP);          /* cancel call                   */
            break;
        default: break;
        }
    return resultcode;                 /* exit with DTR still high      */
}
```

An explanation of `m_dial`—The string containing the phone number is passed to `m_dial` as an argument. Our plan is to copy the phone number argument into `dialbuff` in the `modem` structure so it will be available for a subsequent redialing operation. During copying, the phone number argument is filtered; that is, only numerals and those characters listed in the array `okalpha` are placed in `dialbuff`. (Recall that `okalpha` may be modified during modem configuration.)

Once the `phonenum` argument has been filtered and tucked safely away in the `modem` structure, `sprintf` builds the actual dial string that will be sent to the modem in the local buffer `dialstr`. The first argument in the format string is the dial command (i.e., D or T), followed by the appended filtered `phonenum` argument, followed by the `enddial` buffer of commands that may appear only at the end of the dial string.

Before sending the compound `dialstr` to the modem, `dialstr` is tested for NIL. If no dial string is present, the function immediately returns the error code M_NILNUM. Otherwise, DTR is asserted and `dialstr` is passed along to `m_cmd`, which outputs the command to the SIO. Next, m_wait4dcd is called to await the modem's response to the dial command. The time-out interval for m_wait4dcd is the value in S-register 9, which is set during configuration.

The return code from m_wait4dcd is then subjected to a switch. If the call is successful, DTR remains asserted; if resultcode indicates that no connection has been established, DTR is inhibited. If the user aborts from the keyboard, a character (here a SPACE) is sent to the modem to terminate the wait. The function ends by returning resultcode.

SPECIAL DIAL STRINGS

Communicating with a receive-only modem requires the modem to go off hook and respond to a carrier with originate tones. This is accomplished with a blank dial string, *ATD*, but m_dial's refusal to dial a blank string apparently prevents it. To overcome this problem, simply place a single dummy comma in the dial string.

Redial Last Number: *m_redial*

As just described, when a call is dialed with m_dial the filtered phone number is stored in the modem structure for later redialing. With no string processing required, m_redial (shown in Listing 21.24) merely consists of a single call to m_dial itself.

Listing 21.26. The m_redial function: a function to redial a previously dialed number.

FUNCTION NAME:	m_redial
LEVEL:	3
PROTOTYPE IN:	MODEM.H
LIBRARY:	MODEM.LIB
DESCRIPTION:	Redial previously dialed number.
RETURNS:	int: response code as described in SIODEF.H.
COMMENTS:	The previously dialed number was left in the modem structure by m_dial.
INCLUDE FILES:	siodef.h, modem.h

```
int m_redial(SIO *siop)
{
    return (m_dial(siop, siop->sm->dialbuff));
}
```

An explanation of `m_redial`—Remember that `m_dial` stores the alphanumeric portion of the dial string in the `modem` structure. The previously dialed number is therefore present in the `modem` structure—we need only pass the string in `dialbuff` to `m_dial` itself.

Answer the Telephone: *m_answer*

When the answer command (*A*) is issued, the modem performs three operations: it (1) takes the line off hook, (2) asserts its carrier tone using receive tones, and (3) issues a response code. Since these operations are performed automatically by the modem, the answer function need only send the answer command and wait for the modem's response. The code for `m_answer` is shown in Listing 21.27.

Listing 21.27. The `m_answer` function: a function to answer an incoming call.

FUNCTION NAME: `m_answer`
            LEVEL: 3
    PROTOTYPE IN: MODEM.H
          LIBRARY: MODEM.LIB
      DESCRIPTION: Answers incoming call.
          RETURNS: `int`: integer response code from `m_wait4dcd`.
        COMMENTS: The duration of the wait for carrier is given in
                  the `dcdwait` structure member. Waits for a `RING` message
                  from the modem before sending answer command.
    INCLUDE FILES: stdio.h, siodef.h, buos.h, level0.h, modem.h

```c
int m_answer(SIO *siop)
{
    int anscode, tmptime;
    char ringmsg[MAX_MSG_LEN + 1];
    siop->sm->cmdt_out = _1_SEC_0 * 10;          /* long time between rings */
    s_clrsio(siop, CMDBUFSIZ);
    set232(siop, DTR, ON);
    printf("\nWaiting for RING.....\n");
    m_getstr(siop, ringmsg, MAX_MSG_LEN);        /* fetch reply            */
    siop->sm->cmdt_out = tmptime;                /* restore command time out */
    if (m_ismessage(siop, ringmsg) != M_RING)    /* wrong response         */
        return M_NORING;
    --delay (_0_SEC_3);                          /* superstitious wait     */
    printf("Ring Detected: Answering...\n");
    m_cmd(siop,"A");                             /* ok to send answer cmd  */
    anscode = m_wait4dcd(siop);
    switch (anscode)
        {
        case M_USRCAN:
            s_putc(siop, SPACE);
```

continues

Listing 21.27. continued

```
        case M_NODCD:
                set232(siop, DTR, OFF);
        }
    return anscode;
}
```

An explanation of _m_answer_—While sending a response to a command, some modems are unable to process incoming commands. It is therefore prudent to make certain that the answer command is not sent when the modem is sending a RING message. Before issuing the answer command, therefore, the SIO is cleared and the modem is queried for a RING message. If RING is not detected, the function exits with the error code M_NORING; otherwise the answer command from the modem structure is sent to the modem, then wait4dcd is called to await the modem's response, which is assigned to the variable anscode.

If no connection is established, DTR is inhibited. If the user aborts from the keyboard, a character (here a SPACE) is sent to the modem to terminate the wait. The function ends by returning anscode.

The requirement that an answer command follow a RING message prevents using this function when two modems are connected directly through a cable instead of through the phone line. A mode argument may easily be added, however, to instruct the function to skip the check for an incoming ring signal.

Terminate a Connection: _m_hup_

Because terminating a connection in progress is essentially the same as hanging up the phone, the function is called _hup_. Hanging up the phone should be as simple as inhibiting DTR, but the function must also deal with the possibility that DTR is not properly configured. The code for m_hup is shown in Listing 21.28.

Listing 21.28. The _m_hup_ function: a function to terminate a connection.

FUNCTION NAME:	m_hup
LEVEL:	3
PROTOTYPE IN:	MODEM.H
LIBRARY:	MODEM.LIB
DESCRIPTION:	Hangs up phone.
RETURNS:	int: M_SUCCEED or M_FAIL
COMMENTS:	If DCD indicates that a connection is in progress, an on-line escape command is issued to force the modem to command mode where an explicit hangup command can be issued. If this operation fails, DTR is inhibited to force hangup.
INCLUDE FILES:	stdlib.h, siodef.h, level0.h, modem.h

```
int m_hup(SIO *siop)
{
    int time_tmp, errcode = 0;              /* initialize this !      */
    if (stat232(siop, DCD))                 /* if DTR is asserted     */
        {
        time_tmp = siop->sm->cmdt_out;      /*save time out           */
        siop->sm->cmdt_out = _1_SEC_0 * 5;  /* extend wait for OK     */
        errcode = m_gocmd(siop, siop->sm->escape_arg);  /* onlinecmd state */
        errcode ¦= m_cmd_OK(siop, "H0");    /* send hangup  cmd       */
        siop->sm->cmdt_out = time_tmp;      /* restore normal timeout */
        }
    set232(siop, DTR, OFF);
    --delay(_0_SEC_3);
    return errcode;
}
```

An explanation of *m_hup*—Inhibiting DTR immediately would force an immediate hangup, but it would cause problems at higher-speed protocols such as V.32, where the two modems actually negotiate line disengagement. A better strategy is to force the modem into on-line command state and issue the explicit hangup command, H0. If the modem does not respond OK to this command, DTR is inhibited.

Consult Data Carrier Detect: *m_warndcd*

Our final function in this section is designed to prevent accidentally calling a modem function when DCD is not in the required state. It is pointless, for example, to attempt to dial a number when a connection already exists or to hang up the phone when there is no connection. This function, m_warndcd, shown in Listing 21.29, is passed the expected state of the DCD input, and issues a warning if that state is not present.

Listing 21.29. The m_warndcd **function:
a function to alert the user to an incorrect carrier state.**

FUNCTION NAME: m_warndcd
LEVEL: 3
PROTOTYPE IN: MODEM.H
LIBRARY: MODEM.LIB
DESCRIPTION: Issues a warning and overrides the prompt if the current DCD state does not match the argument.
RETURNS: int: M_SUCCEED if DCD state is OK, if the user elects to ignore the DCD state; otherwise M_FAIL.
INCLUDE FILES: stdio.h, siodef.h, modem.h, misc.h, key.h, ctype.h

continues

Listing 21.29. continued

```
short m_warndcd(SIO *siop, BOOL warnmode)
{
    int   c = -1;
    char *warnp;
    if (siop->sm == NIL)                  /* modem structure not present */
        return M_SUCCEED;
    warnp = (warnmode) ? "no" : "a";
    if ( (BOOL)stat232(siop, DCD) != warnmode)
        {
        for (EVER)
            {
            printf("\nTests indicate %s carrier present. OK to ignore?\a (Y/N):",\
                        warnp);
            c = getkbch();
            c = toupper(c);
            putchar('\n');
            if (c == 'N')
                return M_FAIL;
            if (c == 'Y')
                return M_SUCCEED;
            }
        }
    return M_SUCCEED;
}
```

An explanation of *m_warndcd*—The argument warnmode is the *required* state of the carrier. If the SIO's DCD input doesn't match warnmode, a message (which the user may wish to ignore) is printed explaining the discrepancy. The function returns M_SUCCEED if DCD is in the expected state or if the user elects to proceed in the face of an error. M_FAIL is returned only if the user decides not to proceed.

Before the state of DCD is even tested, we see this test:

```
if (siop->sm == NIL)
    return (M_SUCCEED);
```

This tests for the presence of a modem structure. If no modem structure is present in the SIO, the carrier test is pointless.

String Arrays for Modem Functions

Before we modify TERM to include modem functions, let's take a look at some handy strings. Listing 21.30 shows the string arrays m_codes, which correspond to the first eighteen modem response constants given in Listing 21.2.

Listing 21.30. The m_codes strings identify modem types.

```
ARRAY NAME:  m-codes
    LIBRARY:  MODEM.LIB
DESCRIPTION:  Strings for modem functions.
  COMMENTS:  Corresponding constants are shown in comments.
```

```c
char *m_codes[] =
    {
    "Successful",                           /*0  M_OK        */
    "Connection Established",               /*1  M_CONN      */
    "Call incoming",                        /*2  M_RING      */
    "No connection Established",            /*3  M_NODCD     */
    "Command Error",                        /*4  M_CMDERR    */
    "No Dialtone",                          /*5  M_NOTONE    */
    "Number Dialed is Busy",                /*6  M_BUSY      */
    "No answer",                            /*7  M_NOANSW    */
    "Unknown Modem Response",               /*8  M_BADMSG    */
    "Didn't hear RING report from modem",   /*9  M_NORING    */
    "Call Already in Progress",             /*10 M_ONLINE    */
    "Blank Dial String",                    /*11 M_NILNUM    */
    "Operation cancelled by user",          /*12 M_USRCAN    */
    "Modem Reset Failed",                   /*13 M_NORESET   */
    "Modem Fails ID request",               /*14 M_NOID,     */
    "Config. error: Out of memory",         /*15 M_CONFIG_MEM */
    "Modem failed to configure",            /*16 M_CONFIG_NOK */
    "Connection Established",               /*17 M_DCD_HIGH  */
    };
```

TERM6

Now that we have a full complement of modem control functions, we can add several new features to our terminal program. Listing 21.31 shows these enhancements. As usual, only the functional additions are shown.

Listing 21.31. TERM6: modem enhancements to the terminal program.

```
PROGRAM NAME:  TERM6
  DESCRIPTION:  Terminal program.
     COMMENTS:  New Features:  Modem control.  The main and term functions
                are unchanged from previous version.
 INCLUDE FILES:  stdio.h, stdlib.h, ctype.h, siodef.h, ascii.h, misc.h,
                sioctl.h, buos.h, key.h, term.h, modem.h
                .
                .
                .
```

continues

Listing 21.31. continued

```c
#define DIAL            'H'      /* Dial phone number        */
#define REDIAL          'I'      /* Redial previous number   */
#define ANSWER          'J'      /* Answer phone phone       */
#define HUP             'K'      /* Hang up phone            */
#define BASELINE_CFG    'L'      /* Configure base line modem */
#define PROTO_CFG       'M'      /* Configure protocol modem */
                .
                .
                .
#define EXIT            'Q'      /* Exit from term           */

int vers = 6;                    /* version number (global)  */
extern char *m_codes[];          /* modem id strings         */

void baseline_cfg(SIO* siop)
{
    struct modem *smp;
    short errcode;
    smp = siop->sm;
    s_ipush(siop);                          /* save both control structures */
    s_icntrl(siop, SET, CONSFLAG, OFF); /* console echo off         */
    putchar('\n');
    if ( ( errcode = m_reset(siop)) != M_SUCCEED)
        printf("%s.   (%d)\n",m_codes[errcode], errcode);
    else if ( (errcode = m_whoru(siop)) != M_SUCCEED)
        printf("%s.   (%d)\n",m_codes[errcode], errcode);
    else if ( (errcode = m_config(siop)) != M_SUCCEED)
        printf("%s.   (%d)\n",m_codes[errcode], errcode);
    else
        {
         printf("\nFound %s bps modem (id = %d) at %s baud. " \
            "Baud rate now set to %s\n", brstr[smp->max_carrier_speed], \
            smp->modtype, brstr[smp->max_DTE_baud], brstr[getbaud(siop)]);
        }
    s_ipop(siop);                           /* restore control structure    */
}

void proto_cfg(SIO* siop)
{
    short errcode;
    struct modem *smp = siop->sm;
    s_ipush(siop);
    s_icntrl(siop, SET, CONSFLAG, OFF);                 /* console echo off   */
    s_ipop(siop);
    putchar('\n');
    if ( (errcode = m_protoconfig(siop)) != M_SUCCEED)
        printf("%s.   (%d)\n",m_codes[errcode], errcode);
}

int dial(SIO *siop)             /* Manage DIAL and REDIAL menu items*/
{
    extern char *m_codes[];
    int result;
```

```
        char numbuff[CMDBUFSIZ +1];
        printf("\nEnter phone number:   ");
        gets(numbuff);
        result = m_dial(siop, numbuff);
        return result;
}

int redial(SIO *siop)
{
        printf("\nRedialing previous number:   %s\n",siop->sm->dialbuff);
        return (m_redial(siop));
}


int menu(siop)                          /* menu gets SIO pointer */
SIO *siop;
{
    int c;
    int retval = 0;
    static char *menus[] =
        {
        .

        .

        .
        "\tH.  Dial a phone number",
        "\tI.  Redial last phone number",
        "\tJ.  Answer incoming call",
        "\tK.  Hang up phone",
        "\tL.  Attempt to configure baseline modem",
        "\tM.  Attempt to configure protocol modem",
        .

        .

        .
        "\tQ.  EXIT",
        ""                              /* NIL string terminates list    */
        };

    char ** menup;
    c = !EXIT;
    while (c != EXIT)
        {
        puts("\n\n");
        for (menup = menus; **menup != NUL ; menup++)
            printf("%s\n", *menup);
        printf("\n\t\t  Enter selection  (CR to quit menu) :   ");
        if ( (c = getkbch()) == CR)
            break;                      /* return to term                 */
        c = toupper(c);
        switch (c)
            {
            case EXIT:              /* all done */
            if (m_warndcd(siop, OFF) == 0)
                {
```

continues

Listing 21.31. continued

```c
            m_hup(siop);    /* hang up */
            if (siop->sm->configokflag == TRUE)
                {    /* "unconfig" modem */
                siop->sm->configokflag = FALSE;
                m_cmd_OK(siop, siop->sm->unconfig);
                }
            retval = 1;
            }
        else
            {
            printf("Continuing in terminal\n");
            retval = 0;
            }
        break;
        .
        .

        .
        case DIAL:
            s_icntrl(siop, SET, CONSFLAG, OFF);    /* console echo off */
            if (m_warndcd(siop, OFF) == 0)
                printf("\n%s. \n",m_codes[dial(siop)]);
            s_icntrl(siop, SET, CONSFLAG, ON);  /* console echo on formatted
                                                    input */
            c = EXIT;                    /* leave menu after dial       */
            break;
        case REDIAL:
            s_icntrl(siop, SET, CONSFLAG, OFF);    /* console echo off */
            if (m_warndcd(siop, OFF) == 0)
                printf("\n%s. \n",m_codes[redial(siop)]);
            s_icntrl(siop, SET, CONSFLAG, ON);    /* console echo off */
            c = EXIT;                /* leave menu after redial     */
            break;
        case ANSWER:
            s_icntrl(siop, SET, CONSFLAG, OFF);    /* console echo off */
            if (m_warndcd(siop, OFF) == 0)
                printf("\n%s. \n",m_codes[m_answer(siop)]);
            s_icntrl(siop, SET, CONSFLAG, ON);  /* console echo on    */
            c = EXIT;                /* leave menu after answer     */
            break;
        case HUP:
            puts("\nHanging up...");
            if (m_warndcd(siop, ON) == 0)
                printf("\nHangup %s.\n",\
                    m_hup(siop) == 0 ? "OK" : "error");
            c = EXIT;                /* leave menu after hangup      */
            break;
        case BASELINE_CFG:
            (void)baseline_cfg(siop);
            haktc();
            break;
        case PROTO_CFG:
            if (siop->sm->configokflag != TRUE)
```

```
            puts("\nBaseline Configuration Required.");
          else
            proto_cfg(siop);
          haktc();
          break;

      default:
          puts("Invalid choice\n\a");
          break;
      }
   }
  putchar('\n');
  siop->sm->cmdechoflag = FALSE;
  s_icntrl(siop, SET, CONSFLAG, OFF); /* console echo off           */
  m_echo(siop, ON);
  s_icntrl(siop, SET, CONSFLAG, ON);  /* console echo off           */
  return retval;      /* will be zero except if EXIT */
}
```

An Explanation of TERM6

The library of modem functions makes these new functions seem trivially easy. The menu includes new choices for configuration, dialing, redialing, configuring, hanging up, and exiting the program.

Inside the menu function, strings are installed in the menus array to represent the new modem functions. As before, menu choices are applied to the switch, turning control over to the local functions which, in turn, call the indicated function from the modem library. In all cases, the value returned from each function contains the result code of the requested operation. This code is then displayed by using it to index into the string pointer array m_codes.

Configuration is divided into two parts: one for the identification and configuration of the baseline functions, and one for configuration of the protocol functions.

If DCD does not match the ON/OFF argument, the user is given the opportunity to proceed or to terminate the function. The user's choice, in the form of M_SUCCEED or M_FAIL, determines whether the operation eventually occurs. Although not shown here, protective calls to m_warndcd should now also be retrofitted to the upload and dnload cases.

Flow Control Revisited

Before we move on, the subject of protocol high-speed modems brings up an important subject: flow control under interrupt operation. The remainder of this chapter is devoted to modifying our existing interrupt functions to support XON/XOFF flow control. After you understand the underlying principles, you should find it straightforward to make the adjustments necessary to support RTS/CTS or any other protocol.

The assumption underlying the flow control functions in Chapter 8 is that their effect occurs more or less instantly. So, when in Chapter 18 dnload calls the flowoff function, it assumes direct, real-time coupling to the controlled device; that is, it assumes that the XOFF or RTS signal is sent immediately. Under polled I/O, this is a sensible assumption: after sending the XOFF, dnload hovers in a loop for a "reasonable" period, waiting for the incoming data flow to cease. Under polled operation, a reasonable period might be a dozen bytes. But what happens when hundreds—perhaps thousands—of bytes are already stored in the receiver's interrupt buffer? In this case dnload would fail because, although sending an XOFF may successfully pause the remote device, it does nothing to staunch the flow of data from the local receiver interrupt buffer.

The preceding example illustrates that flow control is not synchronized between the application and interrupt levels. The dnload function's need to stop the flow of data is unrelated to the number of characters in the receiver's interrupt buffer. When characters arrive into the interrupt buffer faster than an application removes them, the buffer may be in danger of overflowing even though the application's internal buffers are not. Conversely, a receiver's interrupt buffer may very well have plenty of room when the application makes its flow-off request. Because flow-control between the two levels is asynchronous, the only practical way to implement flow control is to implement it independently on both levels.

Level-3 Virtual Flow Control

We have just seen that when flow control is in effect at the interrupt level, it is neither necessary nor desirable for the virtual flow functions to perform physical I/O. Because the virtual flow control functions in Listings 16.2 and 16.3 do just that, we shall need new ones for interrupt operation. These functions, given in Listing 21.32, still manipulate the rcv_vflowstate semaphore in the SIO, but perform no physical I/O.

Listing 21.32. New virtual flow control functions for interrupt I/O.

FUNCTION NAME:	iflow_req_xoxo, ixon, ixoff
LEVEL:	2
PROTOTYPE IN:	BUOS.H
LIBRARY:	BUOS.H
DESCRIPTION:	Functions to support virtual flow control via XON/XOFF under interrupt I/O.
RETURNS:	USHORT/VOID
COMMENTS:	Get Flow Request: iflow_req_xoxo
	Turn Flow ON: ixon
	Turn Flow OFF: ixoff
INCLUDE FILES:	stdio.h, siodef.h, buos.h, sioctl.h

```
USHORT iflow_req_xoxo(SIO *siop, ...)
{
    return siop->rcv_iflowstate;
}

void ixon(SIO *siop)
{
    siop->rcv_vflowstate = FLOW_ON;
}

void ixoff(SIO *siop)
{
    siop->rcv_vflowstate = FLOW_OFF;
}
```

With that new virtual function out of the way, let's now turn our attention to modifying the level-2 and level-1 functions.

Level-2 Interrupt Flow Control

Although a virtual flow request under interrupt operation does not result in issuing a flow request to the controlled device, the level-2 functions must behave as if it did. That is, for architectural reasons, the details of the flow control scheme in effect must remain hidden from level-3 functions such as s_putc and s_getc. How? Recall how dnload ascertains whether the device has honored the request: after making a flow-off request, it loops until s_fgetc returns TIMEOUT. The trick, then, is somehow to make s_fgetc's return value dependent upon the state of the virtual flow control variables. The mechanism for this bit of chicanery already exists: the rcv_flowstate variable in the SIO.

Recall that s_fgetc's TIMEOUT actually comes from calling __s_waitch (Listing 13.15), which in turn calls s_inchar (Listing 13.10). These two functions (as well as __s_getc in Listing 13.10) contain the following couplet:

```
if ((*siop->s_rstat)(siop))
    return ((*siop->s_read)(siop));
```

Change these lines to:

```
if ((*siop->s_rstat)(siop) & siop->rcv_vflowstate)
    return ((*siop->s_read)(siop));
```

The values returned by these level-2 functions are now effectively controlled by the rcv_vflowstate variable. They behave normally when the rcv_vflowstate variable contains FLOW_ON (defined as 0xFFFF), but return zero when rcv_vflowstate contains FLOW_OFF (defined as zero). The result is that the level-2 status functions return "not ready," causing the level three functions to behave as if the controlled device has responded to the flow-off request, when in fact no physical request was sent.

Level-1 Flow Control

Clearly at some point the remote device must be physically controlled. The interrupt sub-handlers themselves are responsible for providing the physical flow control—totally independent from the flow control provided for the level-2 and -3 functions. For instance, whenever the receiver interrupt sub-handler isr_rcv detects that its buffer is near overflow, it must take direct unilateral action without knowledge of or concern for the needs of the application.

RECEIVER FLOW CONTROL

Two new receiver interrupt functions are required for each method of flow control supported: a receiver interrupt handler itself, and the receiver function. The new functions for XON/XOFF are derived from isr_rcv and s_ircv, respectively. These are shown in Listings 21.33 and 21.34. Notice that these functions manipulate physical (as opposed to virtual) flow-control semaphores, rcv_iflowstate and tx_iflowstate, items 41 and 42 in the SIO.

Listing 21.33. The interrupt sub-handler for XON/XOFF flow control.

FUNCTION NAME:	isr_rcv450_xoxo
PROTOTYPE IN:	U16X50.H
LEVEL:	1
LIBRARY:	SIO.LIB
DESCRIPTION:	XON/XOFF, byte-read Interrupt subhandler for 16450/8250 interrupts. Also used for 16550 FIFO timeout interrupt (index 6). For XON/XOFF flow control.
RETURNS:	void
COMMENTS:	Reads a byte from the UART's FIFO, places it in the interrupt buffer at rcv_headp. If, after incrementation, rcv_headp points past the end of the buffer, it is reset to point to the beginning of the buffer.
INCLUDE FILES:	stdlib.h, siodef.h, buos.h, sioctl.h, level0.h

```
#define FLOW_HEADROOM 10                        /* for SIOCTL.H */

void isr_rcv450_xoxo(register SIO *siop)
   {
10   int diff;
20   static int bytes_left = FLOW_HEADROOM +1 ;
```

```
 30    *siop->rcv_headp = s_rcv(siop);                        /* read char into buff*/
 40    if (*siop->rcv_headp  == XOFF  || *siop->rcv_headp  == XON)
 50        {
 60        if (*siop->rcv_headp == XOFF )
 70            siop->tx_iflowstate = FLOW_OFF;        /* semaphore for transmit isr */
 80        else
 90            {
100            siop->tx_iflowstate = FLOW_ON;
110            siop->tx_idle = FALSE;                 /* set kickstart flag      */
120            (*siop->isr[index_thre])(siop);        /* call the xmit interrupt */
130            }
140        return;                                    /* xon/xoff's not saved    */
150        }
160
170    diff = siop->rcv_headp - siop->rcv_tailp;
180    bytes_left = (diff >= 0) ? siop->rcv_buffsize - diff : abs(diff);
190    if (bytes_left > 1)                            /* don't let head wrap tail */
200        {
210        if ( ++siop->rcv_headp == siop->rcv_buffend) /* if at end of buffer */
220                siop->rcv_headp = siop->rcv_buff;    /* reset pointer       */
230        diff = siop->rcv_headp - siop->rcv_tailp;   /* compute space       */
240        bytes_left = (diff >= 0) ? siop->rcv_buffsize - diff : abs(diff);
250        }
260    if (bytes_left <= FLOW_HEADROOM)              /* if at highwater      */
270        {
280        siop->rcv_iflowstate = OFF;                /* publish this         */
290        s_xmit(siop, XOFF);                        /* send flow-off char   */
300        }
310 }
```

An explanation of `isr_rcv450_xoxo`—Ignoring lines 0-160 for the moment, the core strategy for the interrupt subhandler is simple: read each byte as usual, but make certain there is room for it before putting it in the buffer. If there isn't room, don't adjust the head pointer. Specifically, whenever there is less than FLOW_HEADROOM bytes of free space remaining, transmit an XOFF to the controlled device and set the rcv_iflowstate semaphore to OFF. Note that once the buffer reaches FLOW_HEADROOM, an XOFF is sent for every character received.

The only noteworthy portion of this function is the code that calculates the amount of room left in the circular buffer. The calculation becomes simple pointer subtraction if we assume that the head (input) pointer is never allowed to wrap beyond the tail (output) pointer:

```
diff = siop->rcv_headp - siop->rcv_tailp;
```

The amount of room remaining in the buffer is based solely on the sign of this difference. A positive difference represents the amount of space used; therefore, the amount of room remaining is this value subtracted from the size of the buffer. If the difference is negative, the amount of room remaining is simply the absolute (no sign) value of the difference:

```
bytes_left = (diff >= 0) ? siop->rcv_buffsize - diff : abs(diff);
```

Notice that the logic to prevent the head from exceeding the tail is based upon the variable `bytes_left`, whose value is not derived until later in the function. The `bytes_left` variable must be an ititialized static varaiable.

Now look at lines 40-150. Functionally, this code is not receiver flow control at all, but is transmitter flow control. It just so happens that when using in-band flow control the receiver is responsible for processing the special characters and posting them for use by the transmitter. In this case, at line 40 the byte fetched from the UART is filtered for XON and XOFF. If the byte is an XON or XOFF, the appropriate value is posted in transmitter semaphore variable `tx_iflowstate`. If the byte is XOFF, the semaphore is set. If the byte is XON and transmitter is currently in a shutdown-state, the semaphore is cleared. If XON is received, it is assumed that the transmitter is currently in a shutdown state and must be restarted:

```
100   siop->tx_iflowstate = FLOW_ON;     /* kickstart transmitter  */
110   siop->tx_idle = FALSE;             /* set kickstart flag      */
120   (*siop->isr[index_thre])(siop);    /* call the xmit interrupt */
```

For a discussion of how and why the transmitter must be restarted, refer to the explanations of `tx_isr` and `tx_iwrite`, Listings 20.19 and 20.22, respectively.

Just as the transmit interrupt subhandler (isr_rcv_xoxo) is responsible for sending the XOFF when the receiver buffer is near overflow, the receiver function s_ircv_xoxo in Listing 21.34 sends XON when the buffer is almost empty.

Listing 21.34. The character status function for XON/XOFF flow control.

FUNCTION NAME:	s_ircv_xoxo
LEVEL:	2
PROTOTYPE IN:	BUOS.H
LIBRARY:	BUOS.LIB
DESCRIPTION:	Interrupt function to read a character from the buffer. Supports XON/XOFF flow control.
RETURNS:	FAST
COMMENTS:	Returns the byte in the interrupt buffer pointed to by the SIO member rcv_tailp. If, after incrementation, rcv_tailp points past the end of the buffer, it is reset to the beginning. XON/XOFF flow control is implemented based upon the amount of room remaining in the buffer.
INCLUDE FILES:	stdlib.h, siodef.h, buos.h, sioctl.h, level0.h

```
#define FLOW_TAILROOM 10                    /* Place in SIOCTL.H */

FAST s_ircv_xoxo(register SIO *siop)
{
    static FAST c;
    int diff;                                    /* pointer difference    */
    int bytes_left;                  /* room left in buffer      */
    c = *siop->rcv_tailp;            /* put in buffer at pointer*/
    if ( ++siop->rcv_tailp == siop->rcv_buffend)
        siop->rcv_tailp = siop->rcv_buff;    /* pointer wrap */
    diff = siop->rcv_headp - siop->rcv_tailp;
    bytes_left = (diff >= 0) ? siop->rcv_buffsize - diff : abs(diff);
    if ((bytes_left > siop->rcv_buffsize - FLOW_TAILROOM)
        && siop->rcv_iflowstate == OFF)
      {
      siop->rcv_iflowstate = ON;
      s_xmit(siop, XON);
      }
    return c;
}
```

An explanation of *s_ircv_xoxo*—This function complements the interrupt subhandler. As each character is removed from the buffer, the number of bytes remaining is calculated using the same algorithm as the subhandler in Listing 21.33. When this number reaches `FLOW_TAILROOM` bytes, an XON is transmitted to the controlled device. Once the buffer reaches `FLOW_TAILROOM`, a single XON is sent.

TRANSMITTER FLOW CONTROL

Strictly speaking, while operating under interrupts, no special effort is necessary to pass flow-off requests to the level-2 and -3 transmitter functions. Because of the architecture of the transmitter interrupt structure, when there are no free transmit buffers available, the s_ixmitstat (Listing 20.25) automatically returns FALSE, causing level-3 functions such as s_putc to loop waiting for a buffer to become available. For symmetry, however, we will convey to the level-3 transmit functions that a flow-off request has been received. This is accomplished by the iflow_req_xoxo function in Listing 21.32, which returns the state of the transmitter via the tx_iflowstate semaphore in the SIO.

This leaves us with a single detail: how to shut down the transmitter when a flow-off request occurs. Recall that when the isr_rcv_xoxo function just discussed receives an XON or XOFF character, it posts the fact in the tx_iflowstat semaphore in the SIO. This semaphore is used to shut down the transmitter in the most obvious way: at the top of the transmitter interrupt isr_tx, we place the following couplet:

```
if (rcv_iflowstate == FLOW_OFF)
    return;
```

Don't forget, however, that the function responsible for detecting flow-on requests is responsible not only for changing the state of rcv_iflowstate, but also for restarting transmitter interrupts. In our case, that function is isr_rcv_xoxo in Listing 21.34, which accomplishes transmitter restart with lines 100-120.

Although we have not addressed the 16550 UART in this discussion, it is worth noting in passing that FIFO'ed UARTS can cause flow-control problems. In general, flow control mechanisms are incapable of quenching the outbound flow of bytes once they have be placed in the UART. This means that the buffer in the receiving device's has fewer bytes of headroom than the trigger level of the UART, data is lost. In such cases, the trigger level of the FIFO'ed UART must be adjusted downward so as not to overwhelm the receive.

Opening the SIO

As you doubtless have imagined, the grimy details of interrupt flow control are hidden in the pointer initializations. For brevity, Listing 21.35 shows how the configuration changes can be embedded in the s_open function, but in truth the changes logically belong in the rcv_ion and tx_ion functions.

Listing 21.35. Revising s_open to support interrupt flow control.

FUNCTION NAME:	s_open
LEVEL:	3
PROTOTYPE IN:	SIODEF.H
LIBRARY:	SIO.LIB
DESCRIPTION:	Device-style open for serial port.
RETURNS:	SIO*
INCLUDE FILES:	malloc.h, siodef.h, buos.h, sioctl.h, uart.h, level0.h

```
int s_errno;

SIO *s_open(USHORT portnum)
{
    .
    .
    .
    switch (siop->flow_wanted)
        {
        case NO_FLOW:
            siop->flowon      = flowon_none;     /* always returns FLOW_ON */
            siop->flowoff     = flowoff_none;    /* dummy function  */
            siop->getflow_req = flow_req_none;   /* dummy function  */
            break;
        case XON_XOFF:
            if (siop->intrpt_status.rcv_on = ON)
```

```
            {
            siop->flowon  = ixon;
            siop->flowoff = ixoff;
            (void) s_revector(siop, RXRDY, isr_rcv450_xoxo); /* or rcv550 */
            siop->s_read = s_ircv_xoxo;    /* reader for XON/XOFF */
            }
        else
            {
            siop->flowon  = xon;
            siop->flowoff = xoff;
            }
        if (siop->intrpt_status.tx_on = ON)
            siop->getflow_req = flow_req_xoxo;
        else
            siop->getflow_req = flow_req_xoxo;
        break;
    case RTS_CTS:
        if (siop->intrpt_status.rcv_on = ON)
            {
            siop->flowon      = irtson;
            siop->flowoff     = irtsoff;
            (void) s_revector(siop, RXRDY, isr_rcv450_rcts); /* or rcv550 */
            siop->s_read = s_ircv_rcts;   /* reader for RTS/CTS */
            }
        else
            {
            siop->flowon      = rtson;
            siop->flowoff     = rtsoff;
            }
        if (siop->intrpt_status.tx_on = ON)
            siop->getflow_req = iflow_req_rcts;
        else
            siop->getflow_req = flow_req_rcts;
        break;
    default:
            break;
    }
    __siolist[portnum].sio_openflag = OPEN;     /* mark SIO open in list */
    return siop;
}
```

When interrupt operation is discovered, the SIO pointers for virtual flow control flowon, flowoff, and getflow_req are set to the functions that support the interrupt versions.

Conclusion

Using the techniques given in this chapter, it is possible to support virtually any modem claiming even remote compatibility with the baseline modem described in Chapter 8. In fact, the clever software developer can supply a *modem profile* for every popular brand of modem supported. Such a profile consists merely of an image of the modem structure for that modem, to be overlaid during installation.

XMODEM File Transfers

In the first part of this chapter, we will compose the functions x_snd and x_rcv to transfer files using the popular XMODEM protocol explained in Chapter 3. Later in the chapter we will write the code to implement the checksum error-checking method used in XMODEM protocol. The functions for CRC error checking will be composed in Chapter 23.

Please note that we will develop functions only for XMODEM *single-file* transfers. The specifications for multi-file transfer, along with other technical details of the XMODEM protocol, are given in Chapter 3. The present chapter assumes you are familiar with the material in Chapter 3, so if you have not read it, please do so now.

Design Considerations in File Transfers

If our file-transfer modules had to send and receive files only at typical modem speeds—300 to 2400—we would not need to worry about speed performance. But such software is often called upon to transfer files between two directly connected computers in order to transport files between incompatible disk formats or operating systems. In such nose-to-nose configurations, the transfer speed limits the ultimate usefulness of the software. We will therefore design these functions with particular attention to speed. Unfortunately, the programming practices that lead to good speed performance often conflict with the qualities normally associated with good C programming. Let's see how.

In earlier programs, we stressed a top-down, highly structured approach to program design, relegating logical procedures to functions. We have unhesitatingly passed as many arguments to these functions as necessary to achieve our goals. We have also used temporary auto variables liberally to manifest meaning and make the code easier to understand.

Although the copious use of functions is considered to be a mark of good program design, we do pay a price for it. Even with the cleverest of compilers running on a microprocessor with highly efficient addressing modes, a function call *inherently* takes longer to execute than the equivalent in-line code. Furthermore, due to the architecture of many popular microprocessors, *direct* memory addressing associated with static C variables can be substantially faster than the *indexed-indirect* addressing associated with auto variables and function-call arguments. As microprocessors become more sophisticated in their memory management capabilities, this discrepancy has decreased, but for now we must take such factors into consideration. In general, we will observe the following design principles:

- Each packet should be input and output without interruption between fields.

- In time-sensitive sections, we will place as much code as possible in-line; where function calls are unavoidable, we will employ the least complicated ones available. For example, we will fetch bytes with s_waitch instead of s_fgetc.

- To take advantage of the speed advantage of direct memory addressing, we will declare critical data *global* instead of passing it in function argument lists or declaring it as local auto variables.

- When inputting and outputting packets, we will be stingy with assignments, conditionals, and other expressions.

The remainder of this chapter comprises three sections. First, we will formulate a strategy for processing *exceptions*—errors, messages, and so on. Second, we will compose the module to transmit a file using the XMODEM protocol. Third, we will compose the complementary module to receive a file. In these two modules, we will show only the code for performing error checking with the *arithmetic checksum* method. Chapter 23 is dedicated to a more comprehensive presentation of the code for the CRC error-checking method.

To make the functions easier to understand and the explanation of them easier to follow, flow charts preceding the code line numbers are used in the main modules.

CONSTANT DEFINITIONS

Before plunging in, the general constants required by the code in this chapter are given in Listing 22.1. These constants, the significance of which will be explained as we proceed, should be placed in a new file named XMOD.H. All functions and modules created in this chapter are assumed to reside in a single module named XMODEM.LIB.

Listing 22.1. General XMODEM constant definitions for XMOD.H.

```
#define DBLKSIZ    128       /* size of data field in packet       */
#define HEADROOM   10        /* amount of memory to save from buffer */

#define SOH_TIMOUT _1_SEC_0 /* timeout interval for SOH            */
#define ACK_RETRY  30        /* used in loop to wait for ACK        */

#define CRCPAKSIZ  133       /* number of bytes in CRC packet       */
#define CKSPAKSIZ  132       /* number of bytes in checksum packet  */
```

Exception Processing

A great many interruptions—both momentary or long-lasting—can occur during a transfer. Some of these are errors from which the transfer will recover, some are normal pauses, and still others are fatal errors that require the transfer to be terminated. We use the term *exception* to cover all the reasons why a transfer is derailed.

It may strike you as odd to begin this chapter with a discussion of exception handling, but from practical as well as pedagogical points of view, strong exception processing lies at the heart of any well-made program. Moreover, the nature of the programming task at hand—file transfer under a protocol—adds new importance to the topic. Exceptions in data communications, being the black art it is, arise from unexpected sources and present themselves in unfamiliar guises. The most important aspect of file-transfer software—more important even than speed—is the robustness with which exceptions are handled. Other kinds of programs may respond to an exception simply by announcing that one has occurred and issuing a description of it. In communications governed by a protocol, however, every identifiable exception must result not only in sending a message to the user, but in a unique response directed at the other participant in the transfer. The inclusion of these responses (which are sometimes complicated) and the accompanying messages in the *body* of the send and receive modules would make the code impenetrably difficult to understand. This congestion would be particularly deadly in the functions where, in an effort to increase speed, we have decided to place in-line much of the code that would ordinarily be placed in functions. In the XMODEM modules we are about to compose, then, the matter of exception handling cannot be parenthetical "user-friendliness," but must be central to the structure of the code itself.

THE ERRCODE VARIABLE

The structure of both the transmit and the receive function centers about a main while loop within which are managed the details of the transfers. The *single* condition for sustaining this loop is the local variable errcode, which contains an exception code. Whereas the *detection* of exceptions occurs within the main while loop, the *response* to them is relegated to a central exception-processing function named x_except. The following snipit of code illustrates the relationship of x_except to the two modules x_snd and x_rcv:

```c
#define CONTINUE   0
#define BREAK      1
#define X_COUNT   10
#define Y_COUNT    5

#define EXCEPT_X 0
#define EXCEPT_Y 1

char *msg[] =      /* messages corresponding to exception codes */
    {
    "Timeout waiting for X",
    "Sorry, Fatal Error Y"
    };

int x_except(SIO *siop, int exceptnum, int *ex_cntp, int maxexcepts);
{
    int errval = CONTINUE;
    switch (exceptnum)
        {
        case EXCEPT_X:
            puts(msg[EXCEPT_X]);
            ++*ex_cntp;
            break;
        case EXCEPT_Y:
            puts(msg[EXCEPT_Y]);
            errval = BREAK;
            break;
        }
    if (*ex_cntp > maxexcepts)
        if (ask_user_2_cancel() == TRUE)
            errval = BREAK;
    return errval;
}

x_snd()
{
    int errcnt = 0, errcode = 0, x;
    while(errcode == CONTINUE)
        {
        x = s_getc();
        if (x == 0)
            {
            errcode = x_except(EXCEPT_X, &errcnt, X_COUNT);
            continue;
            }
        }
}
```

```
x_rcv()
{
    int errcnt = 0, errcode = 0, y;
    while (errcode == CONTINUE)
        {
        y = s_getc();
        if (y == 1)
            {
            errcode = x_except(EXCEPT_Y, &errcnt, Y_COUNT);
            continue;
            }
        }
}
```

When an exception occurs in the transmission module x_snd, a code, EXCEPT_X, is passed to x_except. A *pointer* to the local count variable errcnt and the maximum number of exceptions permitted are also passed. Inside x_except, the exception number in the argument list is applied to a switch. When the EXCEPT_X case is detected, the exception number also selects the corresponding message by indexing into msg an array of pointers to exception messages. Because the exception is not fatal in this case, the only action taken is the incrementation of the pointed-to exception counter (that is, ++*ex_cntp).

Importantly, the value of errval is unchanged from its initialized value of CONTINUE. Before returning the value in errval, *ex_cntp is tested to ascertain whether the pointed-to counter has reached its maximum permitted value as passed in maxexcept. When the limit is reached, the user decides whether to proceed or terminate; if the latter, errval is assigned the value BREAK. We'll assume here that the limit has not been reached and CONTINUE is returned.

Back in x_snd, the x_except's return value is assigned to the local variable errcode and a continue statement forces execution to the top of the while loop. Because EXCEPT_X was not fatal, errcode still contains CONTINUE and the transfer proceeds.

The module x_rcv proceeds like x_snd except this time EXCEPT_Y is a fatal error. In addition to displaying the error message, the EXCEPT_Y case sets errval to BREAK. Upon return to x_rcv the continue statement is executed as before, but this time errcode contains BREAK, causing the main while loop to terminate.

CONSTANT DEFINITIONS AND STRING ARRAYS FOR EXCEPTIONS

Before examining the actual code for x_except, let's first look at the constants to support it in Listing 22.2. These constants should reside in XMOD.H along with the general constants in Listing 22.1. As always, the significance of these constants will be explained as we go along.

Listing 22.2. Exception code constant definitions for XMOD.H.

```
/* EXCEPTION CODES */

#define X_ESNDMAX   10   /* max exceptions during transmission     */
#define X_ERCVMAX   10   /* max exceptions during receiving        */
#define X_NOSOHMAX 100   /* max SOH timeout exceptions             */

#define CONTINUE     0   /* errcode value that sustains snd/rcv loop */
#define BREAK        1   /* one of the errcode value that breaks same */

/* EXCEPTION CODE USED IN BOTH XMIT AND RECEIVE */
#define E_USRCAN     0   /* user cancelled transfer     */

enum xsndcodes    /* CODES USED ONLY IN X_SND */
    {
    E_FILEMTY = 1,  /* file to transmit is empty     */
    E_NOACK,        /* time out waiting on ACK       */
    E_RCVCAN,       /* receiver canceled             */
    E_BADPAK,       /* NAK instead of ACK            */
    E_EOF,          /* End of file read              */
    E_LASTACK,      /* final ack not acknowledged    */
    E_SNDOK,        /* successful transmission       */
    E_DSKREAD,      /* disk read error               */
    };

enum xrcvcodes   /* CODES USED ONLY IN X_RCV */
    {
    E_NOSOH = E_DSKREAD+1, /* timeout receiving SOH    */
    E_BADCKV,       /* invalid checkvalue received    */
    E_SNDCAN,       /* transmitter cancelled transfer */
    E_BADSOH,       /* invalid SOH received           */
    E_NODATA,       /* timeout receiving data in block*/
    E_PAKNUM,       /* invalid block number received  */
    E_SNDACK,       /* sender missed last ack         */
    E_PAKSEQ,       /* FATAL: packet out of sequence  */
    E_DSKWRITE,     /* disk write error               */
    E_RCVOK         /* successful reception           */
    };
```

Listing 22.3 gives the array of string pointers whose elements correspond to the exception code constants in Listing 22.2. For example, the expression msgs[E_BADCKV] refers to the message "Data error detected. Requesting retransmission." This array should appear at the beginning of XMODEM.LIB.

Listing 22.3. Strings corresponding to the constants in Listing 22.2.

```
    ARRAY NAME: x_msg
          TYPE: char *
 PROTOTYPE IN: XMOD.H
      LIBRARY: XMODEM.LIB
```

DESCRIPTION: Array of pointers to message strings used in XMODEM file transfer modules.
COMMENTS: The rank-equivalent constants are shown in comments.

```
char *x_msg[] =
    {
    "\nTransfer cancelled from keyboard.\a",            /* E_USRCAN    0   */
    "Input file is empty.\a",                           /* E_FILEMTY   1   */
    "Timeout waiting for ACK.",                         /* E_NOACK     2   */
    "Receiver cancelled transfer.\a",                   /* E_RCVCAN    3   */
    "Resending last packet.",                           /* E_BADPAK    4   */
    "End of file read.",                                /* E_EOF       5   */
    "\nWarning: receiver did not acknowledge EOT.\a",   /* E_LASTACK   6   */
    "Successful transmission.",                         /* E_SNDOK     7   */
    "Fatal error reading disk.",                        /* E_DSKREAD   8   */
    "Timeout waiting for SOH.",                         /* E_NOSOH     9   */
    "\nData error detected. Requesting retransmission.", /* E_BADCKV   10  */
    "Transfer cancelled by sender.\a",                  /* E_SNDCAN    11  */
    "\nByte received, but not SOH.",                    /* E_BADSOH    12  */
    "\nTimeout waiting for packet data.",               /* E_NODATA    13  */
    "\nBad packet number.",                             /* E_PAKNUM    14  */
    "\nSender missed ACK.",                             /* E_SNDACK    15  */
    "Fatal packet sequence error.\a",                   /* E_PAKSEQ    16  */
    "Fatal error writing disk.",                        /* E_DSKWRITE  17  */
    "Successful reception."                             /* E_RCVOK     18  */
    };
```

GLOBAL VARIABLES

All variables shown in Listing 22.4 are declared global—some in order to increase access speed, and some to avoid cluttering up the argument lists of function calls. We will discuss the use of these variables as the need arises.

Listing 22.4. Global variables for XMODEM.LIB.

OBJECT: Global variables for XMOD.LIB
LIBRARY: XMOD.LIB
COMMENTS: Compile these and add them to the XMOD library
INCLUDE FILES: stdio.h, siodef.h, xmod.h

```
struct rcvpacket *rcvbuffp = NIL; /* pointer to receive packet buffer */
int     paksize  = 0;             /* number of bytes to xmit or rcv   */
char    *ckvname = 0;             /* string indicating CRC or cksum    */
BYTE    csync    = 0;             /* "NAK" for checksum, 'C' for crc   */
USHORT  (*r_errckp)()= NIL;       /* pointer to the error check funct  */
USHORT  *crctblp     = NIL;       /* pointer to the CRC lookup table   */
```

A FUNCTION TO PROCESS XMODEM EXCEPTIONS: X_EXCEPT

Listing 22.5 shows the actual code for x_except, the function to handle exceptions for both the send and receive modules.

Listing 22.5. The x_except function: an XMODEM exception handler.

FUNCTION NAME: x_except
LEVEL: 3
PROTOTYPE IN: XMOD.H
LIBRARY: XMODEM.LIB
DESCRIPTION: Handles execptions (e.g., errors) that occur during XMODEM ransfers.
RETURNS: USHORT: one of the error codes given in XMOD.H
COMMENTS: A pointer to an exception counter variable and its maximum permitted value are passed as arguments.
INCLUDE FILES: stdio.h, ctype.h, siodef.h, misc.h, ascii.h, xmod.h, level0.h, buos.h, key.h

```
  5  USHORT x_except(SIO *siop, USHORT exceptnum, USHORT *ex_cntp, USHORT maxexcept)
 10  {
 15     extern struct rcvpacket *rcvbuffp; /* pointer to receive packet buffer */
 20     extern int   paksize;         /* number of bytes to xmit or rcv   */
 25     extern USHORT (*r_errckp)();   /* pointer to the error check funct */
 30     extern char  *ckvname;         /* string indicating CRC or cksum   */
 35     extern BYTE  csync;            /* "NAK" for checksum, 'C' for crc  */
 40     extern char *x_msg[];
 45     extern struct rcvpacket *rcvbuffp; /* pointer to receive packet buffer */
 50     int errval = CONTINUE;
 55     switch (exceptnum)
 60         {
 65         case E_USRCAN:                 /* user aborts from keyboard     */
 70             puts(x_msg[E_USRCAN]) ;
 75             errval = BREAK;
 80             __delay(_0_SEC_5);
 85             s_putc(siop, CAN);
 90             break;
        /* errors in transmission */
 95         case E_FILEMTY:
100             puts(x_msg[E_FILEMTY]);
105             break;
110         case E_RCVCAN:                 /* transmitter aborted           */
115             puts(x_msg[E_RCVCAN]);
120             errval = BREAK;            /*          FATAL                */
125             break;
130         case E_NOACK:                  /* timeout waiting for ACK       */
135             puts(x_msg[E_NOACK]);
140             ++*ex_cntp;
145             break;
150         case E_BADPAK:                 /* resending previous packet     */
155             puts(x_msg[E_BADPAK]);
```

```
160             ++*ex_cntp;
165             s_clrsio(siop, CRCPAKSIZ);  /* clear buffer              */
170             break;
175         case E_EOF:                     /* end of disk file read     */
180             puts(x_msg[E_EOF]);
185             errval  = E_EOF;
190             *ex_cntp = X_ESNDMAX;
195             break;
200         case E_DSKREAD:                 /* disk read error           */
205             puts(x_msg[E_DSKREAD]);
210             errval = BREAK;             /*             FATAL          */
215             break;
220         case E_LASTACK:                 /* no ACK response to EOT     */
225             puts(x_msg[E_LASTACK]);
230             s_putc(siop, CAN);
235             break;
240         case E_SNDOK:                   /* good transfer             */
245             errval = E_EOF;
250             printf("%s",x_msg[E_SNDOK]);  /* use printf--no newline  */
255             break;
        /* errors in reception */
260         case E_NOSOH:                   /* timeout waiting for SOH    */
265             ++*ex_cntp;                 /* bump caller's error count  */
270             puts(x_msg[E_NOSOH]);
275             if (rcvbuffp->pnum1 == VIRGIN) /* negotiate startup mode */
280                 {
285                 r_errckp = (r_errckp == x_rcvcrc) ? x_rcvcksum : x_rcvcrc;
290                 paksize = (r_errckp == x_rcvcrc) ? CRCPAKSIZ-1: CKSPAKSIZ-1;
295                 csync   = (BYTE) ((r_errckp == x_rcvcrc) ? 'C': NAK);
300                 ckvname = (r_errckp == x_rcvcrc) ? "CRC"      : "CHECKSUM";
305                 s_putc(siop, csync);
310                 printf("\nAttempting to synchronize in %s mode.\n", ckvname);
315                 }
320             else
325                 s_putc(siop, NAK);
330             break;
335         case E_BADCKV:                  /* bad checksum or CRC        */
340             puts(x_msg[E_BADCKV]);
345             ++*ex_cntp;
350             s_putc(siop, NAK);
355             break;
360         case E_SNDCAN:                  /* transmitter aborted        */
365             puts(x_msg[E_SNDCAN]);
370             errval = BREAK;             /*             FATAL          */
375             break;
380         case E_BADSOH:                  /* invalid SOH received       */
385             puts(x_msg[E_BADSOH]);
390             s_clrsio(siop, CRCPAKSIZ);  /* ignore rest of packet      */
395             s_putc(siop, NAK);          /* tell sender to retry       */
400             ++*ex_cntp;
405             break;
410         case E_NODATA:                  /* timeout in packet          */
415             puts(x_msg[E_NODATA]);
420             ++*ex_cntp;
```

continues

Listing 22.5. continued

```
425              s_putc(siop, NAK);
430              break;
435         case E_PAKNUM:                     /* packet numbers don't agree   */
440              puts(x_msg[E_PAKNUM]) ;
445              s_clrsio(siop, CRCPAKSIZ);
450              ++*ex_cntp;
455              s_putc(siop, NAK);        /* ask for retransmission       */
460              break;
465         case E_SNDACK:                     /* duplicate of previous packet */
470              puts(x_msg[E_SNDACK]) ;
475              ++*ex_cntp;
480              s_putc(siop, ACK);
485              break;
490         case E_PAKSEQ:                     /* packets out of order --FATAL */
495              puts(x_msg[E_PAKSEQ]);
500              errval = BREAK;          /*            FATAL             */
505              break;
510         case E_DSKWRITE:                   /* disk write error             */
515              puts(x_msg[E_DSKWRITE]);
520              errval = BREAK;          /*            FATAL             */
525              s_putc(siop, CAN);
530              break;
535         case E_RCVOK:                      /* good transfer                */
540              errval = BREAK;
545              printf("%s",x_msg[E_RCVOK]);  /* use printf--no newline  */
550              __delay(_0_SEC_5);       /* let receiver get ready       */
555              s_putc(siop, ACK);       /* send final ACK               */
560              break;
565         default:
570              break;
575         }
580    if (errval == CONTINUE && *ex_cntp > maxexcept)
585         {
590         errval = BREAK;
595         printf("%d errors or waits have occured: Keep trying?\
600              (y/n):\a", maxexcept);
605         if (toupper(getkbch()) == 'Y')
610             {
615             errval   = CONTINUE;
620             *ex_cntp = 0;                  /* reset caller's error counter */
625             }
630         putchar('\n');
635         }
640    return errval;
645 }
```

An explanation of *x_except*—Several of the cases in this giant switch need no elabora-
tion because they do nothing more than display a message and test the limits of the counter.
The remaining cases will be discussed with the send and receive modules to which they
apply. Notice that only one case is common to both send and receive modules:

E_USRCAN   Executed when the user presses the *Escape* key during a transfer. The message is displayed and, after a half-second wait to allow the other end to finish its current packet operation, a CAN character is sent. The value BREAK is returned, terminating the caller's main packet loop.

For now, ignore the rather complicated-looking E_NOSOH case—we will discuss this along with the receive module. Instead of a global variable to count exceptions, x_except addresses the counter through a pointer passed in its argument list. The maximum value permitted for that counter is also passed. This design enables us to manage any number of counter variables, all with different limits.

If *ex_cntp has reached its limit of maxexcept at line 580, the user is asked to decide whether the transfer should proceed in the face of so many exceptions. If he chooses to abort, the pointed-to exception counter is reset and errval is set to BREAK in order to force termination of the transfer within the calling module.

XMODEM Transmission

With a basic understanding of x_except, we can now study the flow chart for the XMODEM transmission module, shown in Figure 22.1. After a general discussion of this chart, we will compose the corresponding code.

THE TRANSMITTER FLOW CHART

The flow chart in Figure 22.1 can be divided into four distinct phases:

1. Variable declaration and initialization
2. Start-up
3. Packet transmission
4. Terminating transmission

VARIABLE DECLARATION AND INITIALIZATION

The first three blocks of the flow chart are devoted to general housekeeping chores such as setting the SIO's data format to 8-N-1, opening the file, allocating a data buffer, building the CRC table (explained in Chapter 23), and initializing variables. Please notice the emphasis on initializing the exception code variable errcode.

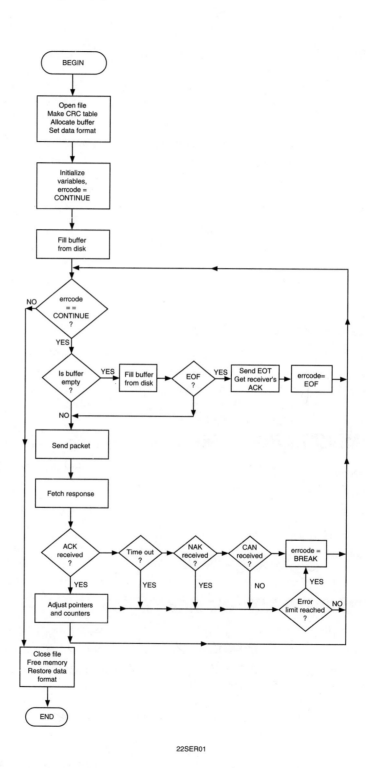

FIGURE 22.1.

*Flow chart of
XMODEM transmit
module.*

22SER01

START-UP

In the next block, the buffer is filled from the disk *before* entering the *start-up* (synchronization) loop. Most XMODEM programs postpone this step until start-up has been established. The authors of these programs must have been thinking, "Why bother to fill the buffer until the transfer is underway?" Most of the time this is sound thinking; as a matter of fact, this is exactly how the original versions of XMODEM were designed. To understand why the buffer must be filled *before* attempting to establish communications, we need to review the start-up process.

As discussed in Chapter 3, the XMODEM protocol is *receiver-driven*—that is, the receiver is responsible for initiating the transfer and for dictating the type of error checking that is used. Once the receiver is ready to begin the transfer, it commences sending a synchronization byte at 10-second intervals. When a receiver wishes to use an arithmetic checksum, it sends a NAK (15H) for the sync byte; when CRC error is desired, a 'C' (43H) is sent.

In most current programs, the receiver actually "hunts" between checksum and CRC modes. By convention, the receiver first tries to establish CRC synchronization by sending the 'C' sync. If the transmitter does not respond (by sending its first packet) within the 10-second interval, the receiver automatically switches to a NAK sync byte in an attempt to establish a transfer using checksum error checking. If there is no response to the checksum sync byte, however, the receiver switches back to the CRC sync byte at the next 10-second timeout. This alternation of sync bytes repeats until synchronization is established or a timeout limit is reached.

Early XMODEM users complained that the 10-second timeout interval was too long: when the sender missed the sync byte (even by an instant), the transfer could not commence for another 10 seconds. Ever anxious to oblige, the public-domain hackers quickly modified the start-up procedure. Instead of sending 1 sync byte every 10 seconds, the new procedure sent 1 sync byte per second for 10 seconds. A timeout—and hence the change in the value of the sync byte—is still defined as 10 seconds. This new timing causes no problems for checksum-only versions of the protocol, but can cause fatal errors in checksum/CRC versions. Let's see why.

Suppose that a receiver transmits its first 'C' sync byte at 1-second intervals. Now, and here's the fatal part, suppose the sender comes online after the eighth 'C' (out of ten) has just been sent. The sender sees this request for a CRC transfer, adjusts itself accordingly, then begins to fill its buffer from a *very* slow floppy. If 3 seconds are required to fill the buffer and send the first packet, a full 11 seconds have now elapsed since the sync byte was transmitted.

Now let's go back and see what the receiver has been up to during this 3-second hiatus. After sending two more 'C' sync bytes with no response from the transmitter, the receiver dutifully switches to checksum mode. After all, it has no way to know that the sender is being detained by the glacial response time of the floppy. "What we have here is a failure to communicate." The receiver is now looking for a 132-byte checksum packet while the slowpoke transmitter is busily sending a 133-byte CRC packet.

There is only one practical way for the sender to avoid this false sychronization: reduce the delay between receiving a sync byte and responding with the first packet. In other words, the sender must be poised, ready to send the first packet *immediately* upon receiving an acceptable sync byte. This, of course, means the sender must fill its local buffer from disk and be prepared to transmit the first packet even *before* inviting start-up.

PACKET TRANSMISSION

Once synchronization has been established, program flow pivots about the answer to a single question: does the variable errcode still contain its initial value CONTINUE? As long as it does, the next packet is transmitted. The receiver's response to that packet is then evaluated: if the receiver responds with ACK, the next packet is transmitted and the process repeats; if the receiver responds with a NAK or a timeout, the same packet is transmitted and the process repeats; if the receiver responds with a CAN, x_except returns the value BREAK, terminating the main transmission loop.

Receiving a CAN is only one of the ways in which errcode can acquire a non-CONTINUE value: the user can cancel the transfer from the keyboard, a disk read error can occur, or there can be an excessive number of exceptions during transmission. The loop "normally" breaks, however, after the successful transmission of all the data in the file. When an attempt to fill the buffer from disk returns an EOF, errcode acquires the value E_EOF.

TERMINATING TRANSMISSION

When the main transmission loop breaks, the exact value of errcode determines how the module terminates. If errcode contains E_EOF, the transfer is assumed to have been successful and an EOT character is sent to inform the receiver that no more packets are forthcoming. The receiver acknowledges this EOT by sending a final ACK. If errcode contains *any* value other than E_EOF, no EOT is sent and, of course, no attempt is made to fetch the receiver's final ACK. Regardless of the success of the transmission, however, shutdown is orderly: the disk file is closed, memory is freed, the data format of the SIO is restored. The function returns a zero if successful or errcode if not.

THE XMODEM TRANSMISSION MODULE: x_snd

The flow chart does not reveal the details of how packets are transmitted. In the introduction to this chapter, we set out a list of design principles, one of which declares that "each packet should be input and output without interruption between fields." This may sound like a common-sense objective, but a surprising number of implementations do not follow it. Instead, it is common practice to transmit a start-of-header byte, pause to calculate the two packet-number bytes, then transmit the 128-byte data field, pause to process the checkvalue, then finally, transmit the checkvalue. These pauses, which inevitably contain time-consuming calculations, measurably reduce the effective rate of data transmission.

The solution to such jerky transmission is to build the entire packet in memory *before* transmission begins. As a matter of fact we will fill memory with as many packets as possible. To accomplish this, we must think of memory as an array of packets or, more specifically, an array of sndpacket *structures*, whose definition is given in Listing 22.6.

Listing 22.6. Structure definition of an XMODEM transmission packet.

```
STRUCT NAME:   sndpacket
INCLUDE FILE:  XMOD.H
DESCRIPTION:   Description of an XMODEM packet for transmission.
```

```
struct sndpacket
     {
     BYTE soh;                /* start of header         */
     BYTE pnum1;              /* packet number           */
     BYTE pnum2;              /* 1's comp packet number */
     BYTE data[DBLKSIZ];      /* data block              */
     USHORT ckval;            /* block-check character   */
     };
```

Our transmit buffer can now be declared like this:

```
struct sndpacket *sndbuff;
```

As you see, the buffer is really just a pointer. The actual storage is allocated by bigbuff, given in Appendix A. Carefully phrasing the arguments to bigbuff, we can allocate the buffer in units of sndpackets:

```
struct sndpacket *sndbuff;
sndbuff = (struct sndpacket *)bigbuff(sizeof(struct sndpacket), HEADROOM,
          &numpax);
```

This instructs bigbuff to allocate all of memory in 133-byte blocks, leaving HEADROOM of these blocks free for local use. It also returns, via a pointer to numpax, the *number* of elements allocated. (The cast is necessary because bigbuff returns a pointer to char.)

Because we know the address of the first packet in the buffer array and that there are numpax packets in the array, we can write the function makepacket, shown in Listing 22.7, to fill the packets.

Listing 22.7. The makepacket function: a function to build transmission packets in memory.

FUNCTION NAME: makepacket
LEVEL: 3
PROTOTYPE IN: XMOD.H
LIBRARY: XMODEM.LIB
DESCRIPTION: Makes sndpackets in buffer. Checkvalue character is not installed.
RETURNS: USHORT: the number of packets made.
COMMENTS: The checkvalues are installed after start-up.
INCLUDE FILES: stdio.h, ascii.h, siodef.h, xmod.h

```
USHORT makepacket(struct sndpacket *pbp, USHORT pakcnt, ULONG paknum, FILE *fp)
{
    USHORT  paksread = 0;                          /* first read in data from disk */
    while (fread(pbp->data, sizeof(BYTE), sizeof(pbp->data), fp) != 0)
        {
        pbp->soh   = SOH;                           /* install SOH                  */
        pbp->pnum1 = (BYTE)(paknum++ & 0x00FF); /* install packet number and    */
        pbp->pnum2 = (BYTE)(~(pbp->pnum1));    /* its one's complement         */
        if (++paksread == pakcnt)
            break;
        ++pbp;                                      /* next packet, please          */
        }
    return paksread;
}
```

An explanation of *makepacket*—Four arguments are passed:

*pbp   A pointer to the array of packets.

pakcnt   The number of packets in the buffer array (i.e., numpax).

paknum   The total number of packets already sent. The XMODEM packet sequence number is this number MOD 256.

fp   The file pointer from which to load the data portion of each packet.

One-by-one, using pbp as a buffer pointer, each packet in the buffer is loaded. First, the 128-byte data block is filled from the file indicated by fp, then the SOH and packet sequence numbers are added. When the entire buffer has been filled or an end-of-file is read, makepacket returns the number of packets actually made.

Our treatment of the buffer as an array of sndpackets relies on two important assumptions:

1. Your compiler builds structures from low to high memory. In a sndpacket structure, therefore, soh must have a lower address than ckval.

> **2.** Structure members must be contiguous in memory. In other words, your compiler must produce byte-aligned structures with *no* gaps between members for alignment. Most compilers for microcomputers use byte alignment by default, and provide an option for other types of alignment. The sndpacket definition has to be adjusted to accommodate the rare compiler that does not support byte alignment, or compilers for computers that address memory only on even boundaries.

ADDING CHECKVALUES TO THE PACKETS

You may have noticed that makepacket does not install checkvalues in the memory packets. This is because the error-checking method is not known before start-up. This presents no problem: with the time-consuming disk I/O portion of packet construction out of the way *before* start-up, we can call a separate function to add the checkvalues to the packets *afterward*. This function is shown in Listing 22.8.

Listing 22.8. Use of ckvinstall to add checkvalues to the transmission packets in RAM.

FUNCTION NAME: ckvinstall
LEVEL: 3
PROTOTYPE IN: XMOD.H
LIBRARY: XMODEM.LIB
DESCRIPTION: Installs checkvalue(s) in the array of packet structures.
RETURNS: void
COMMENTS: numpaks is the cardinal size of the packet array. The error-checking function is responsibile for returning the checkvalue in the correct byte-order.
INCLUDE FILES: stdio.h, siodef.h, xmod.h

```
void ckvinstall (struct sndpacket *pbp, USHORT numpaks,
                 USHORT (*ckvfn)(BYTE*))
{
    for (; numpaks > 0; --numpaks, ++pbp)
        pbp->ckval = (*ckvfn)(pbp->data);
}
```

An Explanation of *ckvinstall*—The identity of the error-checking method is established at start-up then passed to ckvinstall as a function pointer, (*ckvfn)(). The call to the error-checking function passes the address of the data field packet and returns the checkvalue of that field, which, in turn, is assigned to the ckval member of the current sndpacket structure. Note that because ckval is an unsigned short, it is large enough to hold either a 1-byte checksum value or a 2-byte CRC.

THE XMODEM TRANSMISSION MODULE: X_SND

With preliminary design considerations out of the way and with the two important functions makepacket and ckvinstall in hand, we are now ready to tackle the code for x_snd, shown in Listing 22.9. For the sake of consistency, our explanation of x_snd follows the flow chart discussed earlier.

Listing 22.9. The XMODEM transmission module, x_snd.

FUNCTION NAME: x_snd
LEVEL: 3
PROTOTYPE IN: XMOD.H
LIBRARY: XMODEM.LIB
DESCRIPTION: Transmit a file using XMODEM file-transfer protocol.
RETURNS: int: 0 if successful; otherwise, the terminating error code.
COMMENTS: mk_crctbl and crchware and the constant CRCCCITT will not
be composed until Chapter 23. In the meantime, create dummies.
INCLUDE FILES: stdio.h, stdlib.h, siodef.h, ascii.h, xmod.h,
misc.h, level0.h, buos.h, key.h, crc.h

```
  5 int x_snd(SIO *siop)
 10 {
 15    extern USHORT paksize;              /* number of bytes to xmit or rcv    */
 20    extern USHORT *crctblp;             /* pointer to the CRC lookup table   */

/* ---- static locals for speed of access ----- */
 25    static struct sndpacket *sndbuff, *sndbuffp;  /* buff & pointer        */
 30    static BYTE     *bytep;             /* for addressing structure as array */
 35    static USHORT ack, i;
 40    static USHORT numpax;               /* buffer size in packets            */
 45    static USHORT paxmade;              /* number of packets received so far */
 50    static USHORT (*s_errckp)();        /* pointer to checkval funct         */
 55    static ULONG paktot;                /* running total of packets sent     */
/* -- */
 60    FILE *sfp;
 65    char fnbuff[MAX_NAME_LEN];          /* file name buffer                  */
 70    int  errcode;
 75    int  errcnt;
 80    RANK paritytmp, stoptmp, dltmp;  /* to store current data format         */
 85    if ( (sfp = rfopen("Name for file to transmit", fnbuff)) == NIL)
 90       {
 95       printf("Cannot open %s.\n", fnbuff);  /* input file                  */
100       return 1;
105       }
110    if ( (crctblp = mk_crctbl(CRCCCITT, crchware)) == NIL) /* CRC table     */
```

```
115     {
120         puts("Insufficient memory for CRC table.");
125         return 1;
130     }
135     sndbuff = (struct sndpacket *)bigbuff(sizeof(struct sndpacket),
                    HEADROOM, &numpax);
140     if (sndbuff == NIL ¦¦ numpax == 0)
145     {
150         puts("Insufficient memory for packet buffer.");
155         return 1;
160     }
165     printf("Buffer size = %u packets (%lu bytes).\n", numpax,
                (long)numpax * CRCPAKSIZ );
170     paritytmp = getformat(siop, PARITY);  /* save current data format    */
175     stoptmp   = getformat(siop, STOPS);
180     dltmp     = getformat(siop, DATALEN);
185     setformat(siop, PARITY, NONE);   /* now set for 8-N-1               */
190     setformat(siop, DATALEN, DL8);
195     setformat(siop, STOPS, STOP1);
/* ------------------------------------------------------------ */
/* -- the following variables MUST be explicitly initialized -- */
/* ------------------------------------------------------------ */
200     errcnt  = 0;                    /* maintained by x_except          */
205     paktot  = 1;                    /* running total of packets sent   */
210     paxmade = 0;                    /* number of packets read from disk */
215     sndbuffp = sndbuff;             /* pointer to main buffer          */
220     errcode = CONTINUE;             /* this value sustains the main loop */
225     s_errckp = NIL;                 /* use as a marker in loop below   */
/* ------------------------------------------*/
230     if ( (paxmade = makepacket(sndbuff, numpax, paktot, sfp)) == 0)
235         errcode = x_except(siop, E_FILEMTY, &errcnt, X_ESNDMAX);
240     if ferror(sfp)
245         errcode = x_except(siop, E_DSKREAD, &errcnt, X_ESNDMAX);
250     s_clrsio(siop, CRCPAKSIZ * numpax); /* clear entire buffer          */
255     puts("Awaiting startup");
260     while (errcode == CONTINUE && s_errckp == NIL)
265     {
270         if (inkey() == ESC)         /* user kills from keyboard        */
275         {
280             errcode = x_except(siop, E_USRCAN, &errcnt, X_ESNDMAX);
285             break;
290         }
295         switch (__s_waitch(siop, _0_SEC_1))
300         {
305         case 'C':                   /* receiver wants crc              */
310             s_errckp = x_sndcrc;
315             paksize = CRCPAKSIZ;
320             puts("\nCRC startup received");  /* now put ckvals..       */
325             ckvinstall(sndbuff, paxmade, s_errckp); /*in struct         */
330             break;
335         case NAK:                   /* receiver wants checksum         */
340             s_errckp = x_sndcksum;
345             paksize = CKSPAKSIZ;
350             puts("\nChecksum startup received");  /* put ckvals        */
```

continues

Listing 22.9. continued

```
355              ckvinstall(sndbuff, paxmade, s_errckp);  /*in struct    */
360              break;
365          case CAN:                    /* receiver quit             */
370              errcode = x_except(siop, E_RCVCAN, &errcnt, X_ESNDMAX);
375              break;
380          case TIMEOUT:                /* no timeout limit          */
385              break;
390          default:
395              putchar('?');            /* not meaningful            */
400          }
405      }
410  while (errcode == CONTINUE)      /* BEGIN MAIN TRANSMIT LOOP      */
415      {
420      if (paxmade == 0)                /* all packets in buffer sent ?  */
425          {
430          printf("\nDisk Read:  ");
435          sndbuffp = sndbuff;
440          paxmade = makepacket(sndbuff, numpax, paktot, sfp);
445          if (paxmade != 0)            /* no more packets           */
450              {
455              ckvinstall(sndbuff, paxmade, s_errckp);
460              printf("%d packets.\n", paxmade);
465              }
470          else
475              {
480              errcode = x_except(siop, E_EOF, &errcnt, X_ESNDMAX);
485              --paktot;
490              continue;
495              }
500          if ferror(sfp)
505              {
510              errcode = x_except(siop, E_DSKREAD, &errcnt, X_ESNDMAX);
515              continue;
520              }
525          }
530      s_write(siop, (BYTE *) sndbuffp, paksize);

535      for (i = ACK_RETRY; i > 0; i--)  /* get ACK or NAK            */
540          {
545          if (inkey() == ESC)          /* user kills from keyboard  */
550              {
555              errcode = x_except(siop, E_USRCAN, &errcnt, X_ESNDMAX);
560              break;
565              }
570          if ( (ack = __s_waitch(siop, _1_SEC_0 )) == ACK)
575              {
580              printf("%lu\r", paktot);
585              ++paktot;
590              --paxmade;
595              errcnt = 0;              /* this is optional          */
600              ++sndbuffp;              /* next packet structure     */
605              break;
```

```
610                 }
615             if (ack == NAK)            /* receiver wants last packet again  */
620                 {
625                 errcode = x_except(siop, E_BADPAK, &errcnt, X_ESNDMAX);
630                 break;
635                 }
640             if (ack == CAN)            /* receiver wants last packet again  */
645                 {
650                 errcode = x_except(siop, E_RCVCAN, &errcnt, X_ESNDMAX);
655                 break;
660                 }
665             }
670         if (i == 0)                    /* no ack received                   */
675             {
680             errcode = x_except(siop, E_NOACK, &errcnt, X_ESNDMAX);
685             s_clrsio(siop, CRCPAKSIZ); /* clear buffer                      */
690             }
695         }                              /* END OF MAIN TRANSMIT LOOP         */
/* control comes here when receive loop breaks */
700     if (errcode == E_EOF)              /* normal transfer                   */
705         {
710         errcode = 0;                   /* for final return                  */
715         printf("%lu packets sent.\nAwaiting receiver's ACK: ", paktot);
720         for (i = ACK_RETRY; i > 0; i--)
725             {
730             s_putc(siop, EOT);
735             if ( (ack = __s_waitch(siop, _1_SEC_0 * 2)) == ACK)
740                 {
745                 putchar('\n');
750                 x_except(siop, E_SNDOK, &errcnt, X_ESNDMAX);
755                 printf(" of %s: %lu bytes.\n", fnbuff, paktot * 128);
760                 break;
765                 }
770             if (ack == CAN)            /* receiver cancelled                */
775                 {
780                 x_except(siop, E_RCVCAN, &errcnt, X_ESNDMAX);
785                 break;
790                 }
795             if (inkey() == ESC)        /* user killed from keyboard         */
800                 {
805                 errcode = x_except(siop, E_USRCAN, &errcnt, X_ESNDMAX);
810                 ack = !ACK;            /* for the test below                */
815                 break;
820                 }
825             putchar('.');              /* for each timeout                  */
830             }
835         if (ack != ACK)                /* final ACK never came              */
840             x_except(siop, E_LASTACK, &errcnt, X_ESNDMAX);
845         }
850     if (fclose(sfp) != 0)
855         printf("\nFatal error closing %s\n", fnbuff);
860     free((VOID*) sndbuff);             /* release memory                    */
865     free((VOID*) crctblp);
870     setformat(siop, PARITY, paritytmp);  /* restore data format             */
```

continues

Listing 22.9. continued

```
875     setformat(siop, STOPS, stoptmp);
880     setformat(siop, DATALEN, dltmp);
885     printf("\nEnd of X-Send\n");
890     return (errcode != E_EOF);         /* return success or fail         */
895 }
```

Before we begin the examination of this x_snd, notice that several items dealing with CRC error checking—notably the functions mk_crctbl and crchware and the constant CRCCCITT in line110—do not yet exist. If you wish to test this function now using only its checksum mode, install dummies for the missing items.

VARIABLE DECLARATION AND INITIALIZATION

For the reasons discussed earlier in the chapter, several variables are declared static. This does not affect their scope; that is, they are still local to this function. Depending upon the mode defined at start-up, the function pointer s_errckp is pointed at either a checksum or CRC error-checking function.

Following variable declarations, a file and two buffers are allocated. First, rfopen opens the file to send (the code for rfopen is given in Appendix B); after rfopen, the name of the file entered by the user is in fnbuff. The as yet unwritten function mk_crctbl builds the CRC lookup table used by the as yet unwritten CRC routines. As described earlier, bigbuff returns a pointer to the largest available buffer, which is then cast into a pointer to an array of sndpacket structures. After the call to bigbuff, the variable numpax contains the number of sndpackets actually allocated. A failure of any of the three operations just described results in an immediate return. If successful, however, the current data format of the SIO is stored in temporary variables, then changed to 8-N-1.

Before entering the actual transmission portion of the code, several variables are initialized in lines 200–225. The comments insist that they must be explicitly initialized instead of initialized at declaration. This is not exactly true—hyperbolic comments are just a cheap way to draw your attention to the importance of initializing them at all.

errcnt
: A *local* exception counter maintained by x_except through a pointer. It is initialized to zero at line 200.

paktot
: An unsigned long int containing the running total of the number of packets sent. This is initialized to 1 at line 205 so that the transmitted packet number can be derived from it. (Recall that the first packet sent in XMODEM is numbered 1, not 0.)

paxmade
: The number of packets read into the buffer by makepacket. It is decremented as packets are successfully transmitted, thus indicating when another disk read is required. It begins life at zero at line 210.

sndbuffp   Within the main transmission loop, this variable always points at the current sndpacket in the buffer. It begins life at line 215 by pointing to sndbuff and must be reset to this value after every disk read.

errcode   The presence of CONTINUE in this variable is the sole sustaining condition for the main transmission loop. Failure to initialize it as in line 220 therefore leads to precipitous failure.

s_errckp   A pointer to the error-checking function. During start-up, it is pointed at either x_sndcrc or x_sndcksum. It must be initialized to NIL (line 225) because the start-up loop tests for that value.

START-UP

For reasons explained earlier, the buffer is filled with fully constructed sndpacket structures before start-up synchronization is attempted. Notice that if the disk file is empty (i.e., numpax == 0), the transfer is *not* aborted; x_except's only action is to display an informative message. In all other respects, an empty file is treated as any other.

Lines 260–405 constitute the actual synchronization polling loop. The purpose of this loop is not only to detect an incoming sync byte, but also to point s_errckp at the correct error-checking function and to add checkvalues to the packets already in memory. The arrival of a valid sync character also assigns a value to the global variable paksize, which contains the number of bytes to transmit. (Such a variable is necessary because a CRC packet is 1 byte longer than a checksum packet.)

There are two sustaining conditions for the start-up loop: errcode must be CONTINUE *and* s_errckp must contain its original, initialized value. The pointer s_errckp is pointed at x_sndcrc if a 'C' sync byte is received, or at x_sndcksum if a NAK is received. Any other character causes a question mark to be displayed.

The reception of a valid sync byte breaks the loop, but importantly, errcode still contains CONTINUE. The value of errcode is changed only if the user aborts the transfer by pressing the *Escape* key or if the number of invalid sync bytes exceeds the limit in x_except.

Although the start-up loop never times out, a dummy TIMEOUT case is provided in the event you wish to hook the module to an unattended, noninteractive application where a human is not available to press the Escape key.

PACKET TRANSMISSION

Lines 410–695 are the body of the transmit loop, which continues as long as errcode contains CONTINUE. If synchronization is not successful, errcode already contains a non CONTINUE value, and control passes immediately to line 700 for orderly shutdown.

The first order of business inside the loop proper is to test for an empty buffer; if (numpax == 0), makepacket fills an empty buffer with sndpacket structures. If makepacket returns a 0, x_except sets errcode to E_EOF, and a continue statement forces control back to the conditional evaluation at line 410. Because errcode no longer contains CONTINUE, the main loop breaks and control passes to line 700.

"But," you are probably thinking, "didn't we fill the buffer just before beginning synchronization? Why test again so soon?" This seeming redundancy is necessary to process zero-byte files properly. Recall that if the pre-start-up disk read returns zero blocks, the start-up *and* the transfer is allowed to continue normally. Upon entry to the main transmit loop we therefore cannot assume that the previous disk read actually placed data in the buffer. If this second disk read yields zero blocks, the call to x_except now sets errcode to EOF and the loop breaks. For non-zero length files, however, numpax is not yet zero, no disk read is required, and the transmission of the buffer begins immediately. With the number of packets in memory in the variable paxmade, transmission of the packet begins at line 530.

If you have been less than enthusiastic about the advantages of building the packets in memory, now consider that the transmission of the entire packet is accomplished with just one line of code:

```
530        s_write(siop, (BYTE *) sndbuffp, paksize);
```

Recall that the pointer sndbuffp points at the current packet in the buffer. The number of bytes in the packet was assigned to paksize during start-up. In hacker's argot, this form of packet output really screams.

FETCHING THE RECEIVER'S REPLY

Once the packet has been sent, line 535 enters a for loop to await the receiver's response to the packet just transmitted. This "ACK" loop consists of a series of if statements instead of a switch because a break statement in the latter would not force an exit from the loop.

This loop checks the SIO for the receiver's response several (ACK_RETRY) times before giving up. Remember, the total wait must allow the receiver enough time to write its data to disk. As written, the wait is about 30 seconds—ample time for even the slowest of floppies. Using a single 30-second timeout interval for s_waitch in 535, however, would be unacceptable. Do you see why? Such a large interval would introduce an unacceptably long delay between a user's pressing the *Escape* key and the program's response. Calling a 1-second timeout 30 times guarantees that the check for keyboard input at line 535 occurs more frequently.

Upon exit from this loop, a value of zero in the loop counter i indicates that timeout occurred. A message is issued, and control returns to the top of the main while at line 410 where the same packet is retransmitted.

Besides timing out, the reply loop can be broken by reception of any of three bytes:

CAN   If a CAN byte is received (or if the user types *Escape*), a terminating message is displayed, control returns to line 410 with a non-CONTINUE value in errcode, and the transfer ends.[1]

ACK   Reception of an ACK advances pointer and counter variables, displays the packet number, and selects the next sndpacket with the simple statement, ++sndbuffp. Now the loop breaks, and control returns to line 410, ready for the next block.

NAK   A received NAK displays a retry message and returns control to line 410 ready to retransmit.

TERMINATING THE TRANSMISSION

At some point, makepacket finds no more data on the disk. The resulting call to x_except places EOF in errcode, breaking the main transmission loop. Control passes then to line 700, yet another timed loop. This loop "finishes off" the transmission by sending an EOT to inform the receiver that no more packets are coming. If all goes well, the receiver answers with a final ACK. The transmitter then displays a summary of packets and bytes, and performs an orderly shutdown: the input file is quietly closed, allocated memory is freed, the original data format is restored from the temporaries, and the function returns a zero. Inside the loop, the SIO is polled for 2 seconds for the final ACK. For each 2-second interval that none arrives, a period is displayed, and another EOT is sent. If the loop times out ACK_RETRY times, or if a CAN is received, or if the user presses *Escape*, x_snd terminates unsuccessfully by returning a non-zero. If the main transmission loop is broken by any errcode besides E_EOF, no attempt is made to "finish off" the transmission, but the shutdown is still orderly and a non-zero result is returned.

XMODEM Reception

The design of a receiver module poses two design problems not present in the transmitter module. The first is our old nemesis, speed. Because the transmitter sets the rate of data transfer, it has no *inherent* speed requirements—a slow transmitter is just as robust as a fast one. But a slow receiver that cannot keep up with the transmitter drags *all* transfers down to its speed. In our receiver module, then, we will pay special attention to details that affect speed. As in the transmission module, one major principle will especially guide us: once the reception of a packet has begun, it should proceed *uninterrupted* until completion. That is, absolutely no testing, verification, or other operation should be performed on *any* byte until the *entire* packet is safely in memory.

---

[1]This use of CAN is ambiguous in XMODEM, but most implementations use it.

Our approach will be much the same as in the transmission module where a packet for transmission is ultimately treated as a simple array. But our design of an rcvpacket structure must deal immediately with a second problem—data representation. When receiving a packet, we must be able to detect when s_waitch times out and returns a −1. But if each member is an 8-bit unsigned BYTE variable, it cannot store the 16-bit signed value −1 returned by s_waitch at timeout. The only workable solution to this problem is to create a new structure definition, the rcvpacket, comprising integer members instead of BYTE members. The definition for this structure is given in Listing 22.10. Note that because the SOH byte is just a precursor to a packet, a rcvpacket has no soh member.

Listing 22.10. A structure for XMODEM received packets.

STRUCT NAME: rcvpacket
INCLUDE FILE: XMOD.H
DESCRIPTION: Structure to describe a packet during reception.
COMMENTS: The SOH is discarded upon reception so is not stored structure.

```
struct rcvpacket
    {
    short pnum1;                /* packet number         */
    short pnum2;                /* 1's comp packet number */
    short int data[DBLKSIZ];    /* data block            */
    short int ckvhi;            /* high byte of checkval  */
    short int ckvlo;            /* low byte of checkval   */
    };
```

THE RECEIVER FLOW CHART

Continuing with our method of analysis begun in Chapter 4, we can now study the flow chart for the XMODEM reception module shown in Figure 22.2 before examining the corresponding code.

The flow chart for receiving an XMODEM file, like the one for transmission, naturally divides into four distinct phases:

1. Variable declaration and initialization
2. Start-up
3. Packet transmission
4. Terminating transmission

In addition to these phases, the manner in which the receiver module "hunts" between CRC and checksum mode will be discussed as a separate topic.

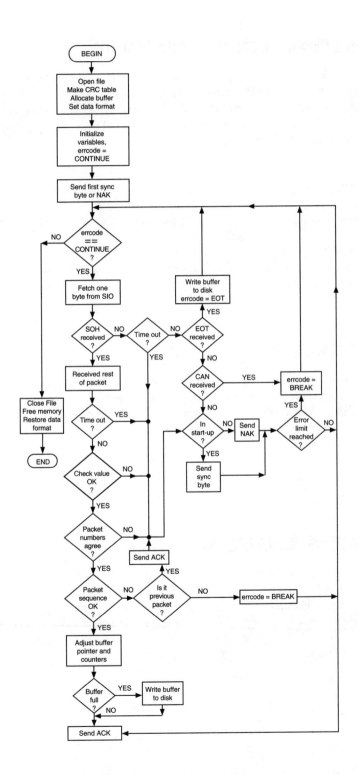

FIGURE 22.2.

Flow chart for the XMODEM receiver.

VARIABLE DECLARATION AND INITIALIZATION

The first few blocks in the receiver's flow chart are devoted to general housekeeping chores such as setting the SIO's data format to 8-N-1, opening a file to receive the incoming data, allocating the data buffer, and building the CRC table (discussed in Chapter 23). This phase also initializes several variables, the most important of which is errcode, which governs the main receiving loop.

START-UP

The receiver has no start-up sequence in the same sense as the transmitter. In the XMODEM protocol, the receiver initiates the transmission by sending a synchronization byte. The identity of the synchronization byte—either a 'C' or a NAK—tells the sender whether to use CRC or checksum, respectively. By convention, the receiver first attempts to establish a CRC transfer. With every timeout, the receiver alternates sync bytes until the transmitter acknowledges by sending its first packet.

PACKET TRANSMISSION

A solitary sync byte is transmitted immediately before entering the familiar main receiving loop. If the transmitter is already waiting, it responds by sending its first packet. Inside the loop, the receiver polls the SIO waiting for the arrival of an SOH, the packet-signature byte. If none arrives, the receiver sends sync bytes in 10-second intervals until it reaches the timeout limit. If an SOH byte is detected, the rest of the packet is stored in RAM and evaluated later for errors. If errors are found, a NAK is sent to the receiver to request retransmission of the packet. If no errors are discovered, the receiver writes its buffer (if full) to disk, then sends an ACK to request the next packet.

TERMINATING TRANSMISSION

As in the transmission module, all paths lead back to the main while loop. In a successful transmission, an EOT eventually arrives instead of an SOH, indicating that no more packets are forthcoming. The receiver then writes to disk the data portions of the packets currently in the buffer, acknowledges the EOT by sending a final ACK, then breaks the main transmission loop. An orderly shutdown follows: closing the file, freeing memory, restoring the data format, and returning a zero to the calling function.

At various points in the packet loop, the transfer may be prematurely ended by an EOT byte, a packet-sequence error, exceeding the exception limit, or by the user pressing the *Escape* key. The transmitter can end the transfer by sending a CAN byte instead of an SOH or an EOT. When a transfer is prematurely terminated, the shutdown is orderly but the buffer is not written to disk and no final ACK is sent. Notice that a prematurely terminated transfer leaves a partial file on the disk.

THE XMODEM RECEIVER MODULE: X_RCV

Our discussion of the receiver module shown in Listing 22.11 follows the flow chart explanation just completed. As in x_snd, the functions mk_crctbl and crchware and the constant CRCCCITT (line 140) do not yet exist. If you wish to test this function now using only its checksum mode, install dummies for the missing items.

Listing 22.11. The x_rcv function: the XMODEM receiver module.

FUNCTION NAME: x_rcv
LEVEL: 3
PROTOTYPE IN: XMOD.H
LIBRARY: XMODEM.LIB
DESCRIPTION: Receive a file using the XMODEM protocol.
RETURNS: int: 0 if transfer is successful, otherwise, the terminating error code.
COMMENT: mk_crctbl and crchware and the constant CRCCCITT will not be composed until Chapter 23. In the meantime, create dummies.
INCLUDE FILES: stdio.h, stdlib.h, siodef.h, ascii.h, xmod.h, crc.h, buos.h, misc.h, key.h, level0.h

```
 5 int x_rcv(SIO *siop)
10 {
15     extern USHORT (*r_errckp)(USHORT*);  /* pointer to err-check funct  */
20     extern struct rcvpacket *rcvbuffp; /* buffer pointer is global     */
25     extern USHORT paksize;           /* number of bytes to xmit or rcv */
30     extern char  *ckvname;           /* string indicating CRC or cksum */
35     extern BYTE csync;               /* "NAK" for checksum, 'C' for crc */
40     extern USHORT *crctblp;          /* pointer to the CRC lookup table */

/* ----- static locals for speed of access ----- */

45     static USHORT        i, j;
50     static USHORT        *intp;      /* for addressing struct as array  */
55     static unsigned long paktot;     /* running packet total            */
60     static USHORT        numpax;     /* number of packets in buffer     */
```

continues

Listing 22.11. continued

```
 65    static USHORT         buffpax;    /* number of packets received so far */
 70    static int            soh;        /* received start of header byte     */
/*  ----- automatic locals ----- */
 75    struct rcvpacket *rcvbuff;
 80    FILE *rfp;                         /* file pointer                      */
 85    char fnbuff[MAX_NAME_LEN];         /* file name buffer                  */
 90    int errcode;                       /* sustains main receive loop        */
 95    int errcnt;                        /* main exception counter            */
100    int nosohtot;                      /* special counter for soh timeouts  */
105    RANK paritytmp, stoptmp, dltmp;    /* to save current data format       */
110    if ( (rfp = wfopen("Name of file to receive", fnbuff)) == NIL)
115        {
120        if (*fnbuff)
125            printf("Cannot open %s.\n",fnbuff);  /* input file           */
130        return 1;
135        }
140    if ( (crctblp = mk_crctbl(CRCCCITT, crchware)) == NIL) /* CRC table */
145        {
150        puts("Insufficient memory for CRC table.");
155        return 1;
160        }
165    rcvbuff = (struct rcvpacket*)bigbuff(sizeof(struct rcvpacket),
                  HEADROOM, &numpax);
170    if (rcvbuff == NIL || numpax == 0)
175        {
180        puts("Insufficient memory for packet buffer.");
185        return 1;
190        }
195    printf("Buffer = %u packets (%lu bytes).\n", numpax,
                (long)numpax * DBLKSIZ);
200    paritytmp = getformat(siop, PARITY);     /* save current data format */
205    stoptmp   = getformat(siop, STOPS);
210    dltmp     = getformat(siop, DATALEN);
215    setformat(siop, PARITY, NONE);           /* now set for 8-N-1        */
220    setformat(siop, DATALEN, DL8);
225    setformat(siop, STOPS, STOP1);
/* ------------------------------------------------------------ */
/* -- the following variables MUST be explicitly initialized -- */
/* ------------------------------------------------------------ */
230    errcnt   = 0;
235    buffpax  = 0;                     /* packets received so far          */
240    paktot   = 1;                     /* running packet total             */
245    errcode  = CONTINUE;
250    nosohtot = 0;                     /* SOH timeout counter              */
255    rcvbuffp = rcvbuff;              /* pointer to main rcvbuffer         */
260    rcvbuffp->pnum1 = VIRGIN;        /* used for startup routine          */
265    r_errckp = x_rcvcrc;            /* starting check value routine       */
270    csync    = (BYTE) ((r_errckp == x_rcvcrc) ? 'C': NAK);
275    ckvname  = (r_errckp == x_rcvcrc) ? "CRC": "CHECKSUM";
280    paksize  = (r_errckp == x_rcvcrc) ? CRCPAKSIZ-1 : CKSPAKSIZ-1;
/* --------------------------------- */
285    s_clrsio(siop, CRCPAKSIZ * numpax); /* clear buffer */
290    printf("\nAttempting to synchronize in %s mode.\n", ckvname);
```

```
295    s_putc(siop, csync);                    /* send start-up sync character    */
300    while (errcode == CONTINUE)
305        {
310        if ( (soh = __s_waitch(siop, SOH_TIMEOUT)) != SOH)      /* bad SOH */
315            {
320            switch (soh)
325                {
330                case TIMEOUT:
335                    if (!(++nosohtot % 10))             /* every 10th time    */
340                        errcode = x_except(siop, E_NOSOH, &nosohtot, X_NOSOHMAX);
345                    break;
350                case EOT:                       /* no more packets */
355                    for (rcvbuffp = rcvbuff, i = buffpax; i > 0; --i, ++rcvbuffp)
360                        for (j = 0; j < DBLKSIZ; j ++)
365                            putc(rcvbuffp->data[j], rfp);
370                    if (fflush(rfp) == 0)
375                        {
380                        --paktot;
385                        errcode = x_except(siop, E_RCVOK, &errcnt, X_ERCVMAX);
390                        printf(" of %s:  %lu bytes (%lu blocks).\
395                            \n", fnbuff, paktot * 128, paktot);
400                        }
405                    else
410                        errcode = x_except(siop, E_DSKWRITE, &errcnt, X_ERCVMAX);
415                    break;
420                case CAN:                       /* sender canceled transfer  */
425                    errcode = x_except(siop, E_SNDCAN, &errcnt, X_ERCVMAX);
430                    break;
435                default:                        /* unmeaningful char received*/
440                    printf("rcvbuffp->pnum1 = %d\n",rcvbuffp->pnum1);
445                    errcode = x_except(siop, E_BADSOH, &errcnt, X_ERCVMAX);
450                }
455            if (inkey() == ESC)   /* user kills from keyboard */
460                errcode = x_except(siop, E_USRCAN, &errcnt, X_ERCVMAX);
465            continue;
470            }
475        for (i = 0, intp = (short *)rcvbuffp; i < paksize; i++)
480            *intp++ = __s_waitch(siop, _0_SEC_1);   /* rest of packet */
485        if (rcvbuffp->ckvhi == TIMEOUT)
490            {
495            errcode = x_except(siop, E_NODATA, &errcnt, X_ERCVMAX);
500            continue;
505            }
510        if ( (*r_errckp)(rcvbuffp->data) != 0) /* bad checkvalue */
515            {
520            errcode = x_except(siop, E_BADCKV, &errcnt, X_ERCVMAX);
525            continue;
530            }
535        if (rcvbuffp->pnum1 ^ (~rcvbuffp->pnum2 & 0x00ff)) /* integrity */
540            {
545            errcode = x_except(siop, E_PAKNUM, &errcnt, X_ERCVMAX);
550            continue;
555            }
560        if (rcvbuffp->pnum1 != (short)(paktot & 0x00FF)) /* wrong sequence */
```

continues

Listing 22.11. continued

```
565         {
570             if (rcvbuffp->pnum1 == (short)((paktot & 0x00FF)) -1)
575                 errcode = x_except(siop, E_SNDACK, &errcnt, X_ERCVMAX);
580             else                    /* FATAL ERROR */
585                 errcode = x_except(siop, E_PAKSEQ, &errcnt, X_ERCVMAX);
590             continue;
595         }
600         printf("%lu\r", paktot); /* running total on screen  */
605         ++rcvbuffp;                 /* next packet in array      */
610         ++paktot;
615         errcnt = 0;
620         if (++buffpax == numpax)                 /* buffer full */
625             {
630             printf("\nDisk write\n");
635             for (rcvbuffp = rcvbuff, i = buffpax ; i > 0; --i, ++rcvbuffp)
640                 for (j = 0; j < DBLKSIZ; j ++)
645                     putc(rcvbuffp->data[j], rfp);
650             if (ferror(rfp))
655                 {
660                 errcode = x_except(siop, E_DSKWRITE, &errcnt, X_ERCVMAX);
665                 break;
670                 }
675             buffpax  = 0;               /* reset counter and ...   */
680             rcvbuffp = rcvbuff;         /* buffer pointer          */
685             s_clrsio(siop, CRCPAKSIZ * numpax); /* clear buffer    */
690             }
695         s_putc(siop, ACK);              /* ACK is your final act   */
700         }                               /* end of receive loop     */
705     if (fclose(rfp) != 0)               /* here when rcv loop breaks */
710         printf("Fatal error closing %s\n", fnbuff);
715     free((VOID*)rcvbuff);               /* release buffer          */
720     free((VOID*)crctblp);               /* release crc table       */
725     setformat(siop, PARITY, paritytmp); /* restore data format     */
730     setformat(siop, STOPS, stoptmp);
735     setformat(siop, DATALEN, dltmp);
740     puts("\nEnd of X-Receive");
745     return (errcode == E_RCVOK ? 0 : 1);  /* success or fail       */
750 }
```

VARIABLE DECLARATION AND INITIALIZATION

For reasons discussed earlier in the chapter, several variables are declared static. All variables declared here are local. Much of the code prior to start-up closely parallels that of x_snd. Following the declaration of variables, wfopen opens a file to capture the incoming data (the code for wfopen is given in Appendix B), and mk_crctbl builds the CRC lookup table. The receive buffer is rcvbuff, which was declared to be global in Listing 22.4. In line 165, we call bigbuff to allocate the largest buffer available and simultaneously cast its return value into an array of rcvpacket. If the three operations just described are successful, the current data format of the SIO is stored in three temporary variables, then changed to 8-N-1.

Before entering the receive loop, several variables are initialized in lines 230 to 280. Some of these have similar functions to their counterparts in x_snd:

errcnt
: A *local* exception variable maintained by x_except through a pointer.

buffpax
: The amount of free space remaining in the buffer, expressed as the number of rcvpackets. When this reaches zero, the buffer is written to disk.

paktot
: Contains a running total of the number (unsigned long) of packets received. The current packet number is paktot (modulus 256). It must be initialized to 1 so that the first packet sent in XMODEM is number 1, not zero.

errcode
: The presence of CONTINUE in this variable is the sole sustaining condition for the main reception loop. Failure to initialize it leads to precipitous failure.

nosohtot
: A special counter for SOH timeout errors. The reasons for its existence are explained later in "Packet Reception."

rcvbuffp
: A pointer to the location in the buffer where the next incoming packet will be stored. This pointer must begin life pointing to the beginning of the buffer (i.e., rcvbuff) and must be reset after every disk write.

The remaining explicitly initialized variables—r_errckp, csync, ckvname, and paksize—all participate in the start-up process described in our discussion of the start-up procedure:

r_errckp
: This is a function pointer to the error-checking method. Its initialized value dictates whether CRC or checksum error checking is tried first. According to convention, we initialize it at line 265 to x_rcvcrc.

csync
: The synchronization byte used during start-up. Because its value must always correspond to the error-checking method currently being used, its initialization at line 270 depends upon the function pointer r_errckp.

ckvname
: A pointer to a string used to announce the start-up mode. Its initialization at line 275 depends upon the function pointer r_errckp.

paksize
: The number of bytes in the current packet. Because checksum packets and CRC packets are different sizes, paksize's initialization at line 280 depends upon the function pointer r_errckp.

START-UP

Aside from transmitting a sync byte before entering the main while loop, x_rcv itself contains no start-up procedure *per se.* That is, the first packet is treated no differently than subsequent packets.

To simplify design of x_rcv, x_except contains the start-up procedure, which "hunts" between CRC and checksum modes. Before we begin a discussion of hunting, it is important to understand that the NAK that is used as sync byte is conceptually different from the NAK that is used to negatively acknowledge a packet. A NAK byte is *always* used to negatively acknowledge a packet, even in CRC mode. Stated another way, during start-up the SOH timeout routine responds with the byte contained in a *variable*—either a NAK or a 'C'; after start-up, the *constant* NAK is used.

If, after sending a sync byte, a packet is not forthcoming from the transmitter, the receiver times out at line 330, resulting in a call x_except at line 340. In x_except, the desire is to switch "modes" from checksum to CRC (or vice versa) and begin sending the alternative sync byte. If start-up is still in progress, the sync byte must be sent; if the transfer has begun, a NAK must be sent.

Differentiating between the start-up and packet-transfer phases is not difficult to do heavy-handedly. We might, for example, simply create a global flag named, say, inxfer. Whenever a valid SOH is detected (remember, the SOH portion of an incoming packet is not saved), we set the flag:

```
inxfer = soh;
```

Inside x_except, the state of inxfer can determine whether to send a sync byte or a NAK:

```
s_putc(siop, (inxfer == 0) ? csync : NAK );
```

This concept is sound, but suffers from a familiar fatal flaw: it adds an extra assignment to the receive loop. This resulting minor degradation in receiver performance can be avoided by letting the pnum1 *packet member* inform us when start-up has occurred. We'll use a technique known as *baiting*—that is, initializing a variable to a value it can never acquire during normal operation. The assignment of this variable should reside in a unique branch of the program flow. If we later discover that this variable has acquired a different value, we know that the program flow must have taken that branch. In our case, the pnum1 member of the first buffer packet is perfectly suited to our needs. Its contents can change *only* through normal reception of a packet; that is, *after* start-up. Because the pointer rcvbuff never changes, we can use rcvbuff->pnum1 as our test variable.

Which values are illegal for pnum1? Although pnum1 is declared to be an int, XMODEM itself limits packet numbers to 8 bits. Thus the reception of a packet number can assign into pnum1 only the numbers 0–255. It may also contain –1 if s_waitch times out. This leaves us with numbers –2 to –32,768 to use as bait. Once initialized to one of these values, any other value in pnum1 signals that start-up has occurred. We will use the constant VIRGIN (defined in SIODEF.H as –2) as our initializer.

If the main receive loop times out while waiting for an SOH, x_except (refer back to Listing 22.5) looks at rcvbuff->pnum1 for guidance, at line 275:

```
275    if (rcvbuff->pnum1 == VIRGIN)  /* negotiate error-checking mode */
280        {
285        r_errckp = (r_errckp == x_rcvcrc) ? x_rcvcksum : x_rcvcrc;
290        paksize  = (r_errckp == x_rcvcrc) ? CRCPAKSIZ-1: CKSPAKSIZ-1;
295        csync    = (r_errckp == x_rcvcrc) ? 'C'        : NAK;
300        ckvname  = (r_errckp == x_rcvcrc) ? "CRC"      : "CHECKSUM";
305        s_putc(siop, csync);
310        printf("\nAttempting to synchronize in %s mode.\n", ckvname);
315        }
320    else
325        s_putc(siop, NAK);
330    break;
```

If startp->pnum1 no longer contains VIRGIN, the packet transfer must be underway and a NAK is sent. However, if startp->pnum1 still contains VIRGIN, start-up must still be underway, all start-up variables are switched to their alternative values, and the appropriate sync byte is transmitted.

(Notice that the variable paksize must be 1 byte smaller than the number of bytes in the packets because there is no SOH member in a rcvpacket. The definitions for the size constants are in Listing 22.1.)

PACKET RECEPTION

We have already seen how important it is to send a sync byte only every 10 seconds. Like the "ACK" loop in x_snd (lines 535-665), a single timeout interval of 10 seconds in s_waitch at line 310 is unacceptable because of the long delay before responding to the keyboard. Using a timeout of 1 second (SOH_TIMEOUT) increases the frequency of keyboard polling, but creates another problem: when fishing for an SOH, x_rcv times out every second, exceeding the exception/timeout limit very rapidly. The obvious solution to the problem is also the best one—the number of SOH timeouts is maintained in the local variable nosohtot, and x_except is called only after every *tenth* SOH timeout:

```
335    if (!(++nosohtot % 10))
340        errcode = x_except(siop, E_NOSOH, &nosohtot, X_NOSOHMAX);
```

Upon reception of a valid SOH byte, the rest of the packet must be received. Because the receiver's buffer is declared as unsigned int, we must treat each incoming packet as a simple array of int. To accomplish this, the buffer pointer—a pointer to type struct rcvpacket—is cast to a simple integer pointer and assigned to intp. Incoming bytes are then stored at successive locations by incrementing intp:

```
475    for (i = 0, intp = (int *)rcvbuffp; i < paksize; i++)
480        *intp++ = s_waitch(siop, _0_SEC_1);
```

Once the entire packet is on board, it is scrutinized in lines 485–595 for exceptions or inconsistencies. Four exceptions are possible:

1. *Timeout receiving data* (line 485). If a timeout occurs during reception of the data portion in the packet, the loop is nevertheless completed, filling the remaining buffer elements with –1 (i.e., TIMEOUT). The ability to detect this negative value is why the packet elements must be an array of int, not BYTE. A value of –1 in the ckvhi structure member therefore indicates that a timeout occurred. (Question: Why can't ckvlo be used?)

2. *Checkvalue error* (line 510). The received checkvalue does not agree with the checkvalue calculated on the data buffer. In x_except, a NAK is sent to request retransmission.

3. *Packet number integrity error* (line 535). The first packet number is not the same as the 1s complement of the second. This error occurs if one of these bytes is deformed during transmission, or if a "1" byte in random SIO data is mistaken for the SOH of a packet. Because neither risks data corruption, retransmission is requested in x_except.

4. *Packet sequence error* (line 560). The packet number received is not the one expected. There are two variations on this error. A packet with the same number as the *previous* packet suggests that the transmitter somehow missed the ACK for the last packet. The condition is easily corrected (in x_except) by sending another ACK and ignoring the duplicate packet. A packet sequence in any other incorrect order (line 585) indicates a systemic problem in the transmitter and x_except aborts the transfer by returning an error code of BREAK.

Assuming that no errors are discovered in the packet, when the number of packets received (buffpax) equals the capacity of the buffer numpax (line 620) the buffer is written to disk and the buffer pointer and buffpax are reset. If there are still "unfilled" packets in the buffer, however, the relevant counters are adjusted and the buffer pointer is incremented to the next packet. Only now—with all the housekeeping out of the way—is the ACK sent at line 695. The program returns to the top of the receive loop at line 325 to await the SOH of the next packet.

TERMINATING RECEPTION

The receive loop continues until an EOT (line 350) or a CAN (line 420) is received instead of an SOH. In either case, the return code from x_except terminates the receive loop. A CAN begins shutdown immediately; an EOT, however, first writes the partial buffer to disk, then acknowledges to the EOT by sending (in x_except) a final ACK. Orderly shutdown follows.

Checksum Error-Checking Functions

Both x_snd and x_rcv perform error checking through the function pointers s_errckp and r_errckp, respectively. Employing function pointers for error checking means that the send/ receive loops themselves remain totally ignorant of the error-checking process. During start-up, the sender and receiver negotiate the error-checking method, pointing these two pointers at either the checksum or the CRC function. In this section, we'll compose only the two checksum functions, x_sndcksum and x_rcvcksum. In Chapter 23, we will compose the CRC functions x_sndcrc and x_rcvcrc.

CHECKSUM FUNCTIONS: *x_sndcksum* AND *x_rcvcksum*

If the sender and receiver agree to use the checksum method during the transfer, their error-checking function pointers are aimed at x_sndcksum, shown in Listing 22.12, and x_rcvcksum, shown in Listing 22.13. Because arithmetic checksums are themselves fundamentally easy to comprehend, we need to spend little time discussing this pair of functions.

Listing 22.12. Use of x_sndcksum to calculate and return an arithmetic checksum.

FUNCTION NAME: x_sndcksum
LEVEL: 3
PROTOTYPE IN: XMOD.H
LIBRARY: XMOD.LIB
DESCRIPTION: Calculates and returns an arithmetic checksum on the buffer indicated.
RETURNS: USHORT
INCLUDE FILES: stdio.h, siodef.h, xmod.h

```
USHORT x_sndcksum(BYTE *buff)
{
    static int cksum, i;
    for (cksum = i = 0; i < 128; ++i)       /* round 'em up     */
        cksum += *buff++;                   /* add 'em up       */
    return (cksum & 0x00FF);                /* take 'em back    */
}
```

An explanation of *x_sndcksum*—This function is called only by makepacket, which installs its return value in the ckval member of a sndpacket. Based upon the assumption that static variables can be accessed faster than auto variables, both local variables are declared static. Passed a pointer to the beginning of data block, this function simply adds together the next 128 bytes, then returns their sum. Because the sum is kept in an integer,

ANDing with 0x00FF (i.e., modulo-256) converts it to the 8-bit format required by the XMODEM protocol.

Listing 22.13. The `x_rcvcksum` function validates the receiver's arithmetic checksum.

FUNCTION NAME: x_rcvcksum
LEVEL: 0
PROTOTYPE IN: XMOD.H
LIBRARY: See "Portability Considerations" in text.
DESCRIPTION: Verifies 8-bit arithmetic checksum on indicated buffer.
RETURNS: USHORT: 0 if checksums agree.
COMMENTS: The checksum byte is assumed to be contiguous with the last byte of the data field.
INCLUDE FILES: stdio.h, siodef.h, xmod.h

```
USHORT x_rcvcksum(USHORT *data)
{
    static int i;
    static USHORT cksum;
    cksum = data[128];
    for (i = 0; i < DBLKSIZ ; ++i)
        cksum -= *data++; /* subtract data bytes from checksum */
    return (cksum & 0x00FF);
}
```

An explanation of *x_rcvcksum*—This function's purpose is to verify that the sum of the data portion of a received packet agrees with its checksum. It must return zero if the sums agree, or non-zero if they disagree. Accordingly, this function assumes that the pointer in the argument list points to the 128-*integer* data array of rcvpacket. In such a structure, the 129th element is the checksum, which is captured in the local variable cksum.[2] The preceding 128 array elements are then subtracted from cksum. Because cksum is zero only if the two checksums agree, its value ANDed with 0x00FF (i.e., modulo-256) is returned directly.

PORTABILITY CONSIDERATIONS

Earlier in this chapter we admitted the assumption that a compiler builds structures from low to high memory, and that the compiler leaves no "alignment" gaps between structure members. These are safe, although not failsafe, assumptions.

---

[2]Even including the assignment, decrementing a static intermediate variable is faster than directly decrementing the byte in ckvhi.

The function x_sndcksum contains another assumption about the internal representation of integers that is *inherently* non-portable. To understand this, you must be aware that some microprocessors — the Intel family, for example — store words with the low-order byte lowest in memory; other processors store them in just the opposite order. The consequences of this representation are important, because in a sndpacket structure, the byte lowest in memory is transmitted first. The function x_sndcksum assumes that the 8-bit checksum occupies the low-order byte of the integer. The version of x_rcvcksum in Listing 22.13, therefore, functions correctly only if the checksum is assigned to the integer's low-order byte and that low-order byte ultimately occupies a lower memory address than the high-order byte. Because this function is inherently machine and compiler dependent, its header classifies it as a "level-0" function and as you might wish to place it in the computer file and not in the XMODEM.LIB library.

Conclusion

Although we will not compose a library of CRC functions until Chapter 23, Listing 22.14 shows the trivial changes required to add XMODEM file transfer modules to TERM6, producing TERM7. Neither the main nor the term module is affected.

Listing 22.14. XMODEM support; incidental changes required to convert TERM6 to TERM7.

```
PROGRAM NAME: TERM7
 DESCRIPTION: Terminal program.
    COMMENTS: New Features: XMODEM file transfers.


         .
         .
         .
#define XSEND     'N'               /* Send file with XMODEM protocol   */
#define XRECV     'O'               /* Receive file with XMODEM protocol */

int vers = 7;                       /* version number (global)          */


int menu(siop)                      /* menu now gets SIO pointer         */
SIO *siop;
{
    int c;
    int retval = 0;
    static char *menus[] =
        {
        "\tA.  Data Format, Baud rate",
        .
        .
        .
```

continues

Listing 22.14. continued

```
            "\tN.  Send a file using XMODEM protocol",
            "\tO.  Receive a file using XMODEM protocol",
            "\tQ.  EXIT",
            ""                          /* NUL string terminates list    */
            };
            .
            .
            .
    case XSEND:
        if (m_warndcd(siop, ON) == 0)
            x_snd(siop);
        haktc();
        break;
    case XRECV:
        if (m_warndcd(siop, ON) == 0)
            x_rcv(siop);
        haktc();
        break;
        .
        .
        .
```

CRC Calculations

The purpose of this chapter is twofold: first, to fulfill the promise in Chapter 22 to compose the CRC functions x_sndrcrc and x_rcvcrc for use in the XMODEM protocol, and second, to provide the code to implement the CRC procedures presented in Chapter 3. This chapter contains only a summary of polynomial division and its relation to the Cyclical Redundancy Check. The rather terse treatment of these subjects here therefore assumes that you have a thorough understanding of Chapter 3, where the topic is covered in depth.

Polynomials and CRC Functions

You will recall that CRC calculations are closely linked to polynomial division. In CRC parlance, a message is thought of as a long polynomial in which each 0 or 1 bit is expressed as the coefficient of a polynomial term. The exponent of each polynomial term is derived from that bit's ordinal rank in the message. For example, in a message polynomial the message 01011010 is expressed as

```
0X⁷ + 1X⁶ + 0X⁵ + 1X⁴ + 1X³ + 0X² + 1X¹ + 0X⁰
0      1      0      1      1      0      1      0
```

By convention, however, terms with a 0 coefficient are omitted from the expression:

```
1X⁶ + 1X⁴ + 1X³ + 1X¹
```

A second polynomial, the *generator polynomial*, is divided into the message polynomial producing a quotient and a remainder. The division is performed in modulo-2 arithmetic; that is, an XOR operation is used in place of ordinary subtraction and there are no borrows. The remainder of this division does not become a CRC until the remainder is "flushed" by appending a 0 bit to the message polynomial for every term in the remainder. For 16-bit CRCs, therefore, the dividend must be padded with sixteen 0 bits. The remainder from the modulo-2 division of the padded message polynomial is the CRC checkvalue. The quotient is discarded. All routines in this book assume a 16-bit CRC.

CRCs are employed to detect errors that occur during communication. During data transfer, the sender calculates the CRC on each block of data. After each block is transmitted, the CRC is also transmitted. The receiver divides the incoming message by the same polynomial. If the data block is received without errors, the receiver's CRC matches the CRC appended to the message. The two most commonly used 16-bit polynomials are the CCITT polynomial

$$X^{16} + X^{12} + X^5 + 1$$

and CRC-16

$$X^{16} + X^{15} + X^2 + 1$$

Polynomial Division in Hardware and Software

Polynomial division is easily simulated in hardware using flip-flops and exclusive-OR gates. The classical hardware circuit to perform polynomial division using the CCITT polynomial is shown in Figure 23.1. Here, the high-order data bit is fed into the low-order byte of the remainder register. The remainder register shifts *left* after every step. After the division, the value in the remainder register is exactly the remainder attained by long division.

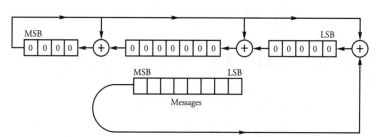

FIGURE 23.1.

Polynomial division hardware using CRC-CCITT divisor (1021 Hex).

This circuit divides a byte-oriented message polynomial of any length by the specified 17-bit polynomial as follows:

1. The high-order data bit is applied to the remainder register.
2. The data bit is shifted into the remainder register's low-order bit; the remainder's high-order bit is shifted out and lost. (Actually, these high-order bits constitute the *quotient*, which is of no interest to us.)
3. If the bit shifted out of the remainder is TRUE, the entire divisor polynomial is subtracted (XORed) from the remainder.
4. The data byte is shifted left one place; the bit shifted out is of no further use.
5. Repeat steps 1–4 until all bits have been applied to the remainder register.
6. The remainder contains the remainder of polynomial division.

SIMULATION OF POLYNOMIAL DIVISION: *polydiv*

Although we have no need for a function that performs this polynomial division *per se*, it is included here to enable you to verify the theoretical procedure presented in Chapter 3. The function shown in Listing 23.1 is an engine that duplicates longhand polynomial division, using the global variable remainder to hold the remainder.

Listing 23.1. A function to simulate polynomial division.

FUNCTION NAME:	polydiv
LEVEL:	3
PROTOTYPE IN:	CRC.H
LIBRARY:	CRC.LIB
DESCRIPTION:	Simulates longhand polynomial division.
RETURNS:	USHORT
COMMENTS:	This function produces a remainder, not a CRC.
INCLUDE FILES:	siodef.h

```
USHORT polydiv(USHORT data, USHORT divisor, USHORT remainder)
{
    static  USHORT quotient, i;
    for (i = 8; i > 0; i--)
        {
        quotient = remainder & 0x8000; /* remember if bit 15 is set    */
        remainder <<= 1;               /* shift remainder; bit 0 = 0   */
        if ( (data <<= 1) & 0x0100)    /* shift data; if old bit 7 was 1 */
            remainder |= 1;            /* put into bit 0 of remainder  */
        if (quotient)                  /* if divisible                 */
            remainder ^= divisor;      /* subtract polynomial          */
        }
    return remainder;
}
```

An explanation of *polydiv* — This function follows the preceding description almost line for line. The variable and constant names have been selected to emphasize the parallel with longhand division. As you study this function, keep four facts in mind:

1. Subtraction in modulo-2 arithmetic is the same as XORing.

2. The sole criterion for subtracting the divisor from the remainder is whether the high-order bit is TRUE *before* the shift.

3. The data is a 16-bit unsigned integer instead of an 8-bit BYTE.

4. Although the polynomial is assumed to contain 17 bits, it can be expressed in 16 bits because the division process always forces the high-order bit to 0.

Since it will be lost after every shift, the remainder's high-order bit must be stashed in the variable `quotient`. Inside the loop, both the remainder and the data are shifted left. With each shift, a data bit (high-order bit first), is copied into the low-order bit of the remainder register with the following couplet:

```
if ( (data <<= 1) & 0x100)
    remainder |= 1;
```

It is not necessary to copy 0 bits because the left-shifting of the remainder automatically fills the vacated bits with 0s. After the shift, the divisor is subtracted from the remainder only if a TRUE bit is shifted out of the remainder register:

```
if (quotient)
    remainder ^= divisor;
```

This process is repeated for each data bit. At the end of the message, `remainder` contains the remainder resulting from the division of the message (i.e., the dividend polynomial) by the polynomial specified in `divisor`. The low-order bits shifted out constitute the quotient of that division.

To confirm that this actually simulates longhand polynomial division, Listing 23.3 shows *PDIVTEST*, a program to duplicate the example in Figure 3.1, Chapter 3.

Listing 23.2. PDIVTEST: a simulation of the longhand polynomial division in Figure 3.1.

FUNCTION NAME:	`p_div`
DESCRIPTION:	Simulates longhand polynomial division on a 4-byte message.
COMMENTS:	For comparison with the longhand division, polydiv has been modified to show the intermediate remainder stages. Source for the putbin function is in Appendix B.
INCLUDE FILES:	siodef.h

```c
USHORT p_div(USHORT data, USHORT divisor, USHORT remainder)
{
    static  USHORT quotient, i;
    for (i = 8; i > 0; i--)
        {
        quotient = remainder & 0x8000; /* remember if bit 15 is set    */
        remainder <<= 1;               /* shift remainder; bit 0 = 0   */
        if ( (data <<= 1) & 0x0100)    /* shift data; if old bit 7 was 1 */
            remainder |= 1;            /* put into bit 0 of remainder  */
        if (quotient)                  /* if divisible                 */
            remainder ^=  divisor;     /* subtract polynomial          */
        printf("        ");
        putbin(remainder);             /* display binary for each step */
        }
    return remainder;
}
```

```
main()                                  /* perform polynomial divisions   */
{
    static char message[4] = {'C', 'f', 'y', 'U'};   /* from Chapter Three */
    int i;
    unsigned short remainder = 0;         /* must initialize to zero        */
    for (i = 0; i < 4; ++i)
        {
        remainder = p_div(message[i], 0x1021, remainder);  /* CCITT poly */
        putbin(remainder);
        }
}
```

An explanation of *PDIVTEST*—Because this program shows all the intermediate steps of the division, it is easy to compare its output with the intermediate ("below the line") steps of longhand division in Chapter 3. Notice that 16 shifts are required to arrive at the initial step of longhand division. In other words, after the first 16 steps, the register simply contains a copy of the data. Two of the data bytes are ORed with 80H to simulate a 1 in their parity bits.

Short Integer Representation

Some mention should be made of the extensive use of the data type unsigned short. K & R (page 36) states that the data type int has the *natural* size suggested by the host machine architecture, and that "the other sizes (of integers) are provided to meet special needs." On microprocessor implementations of C for the 80x86 family of processors, the size of an int is traditionally 16 bits; an int and a short int are therefore identical and may be used interchangeably. But this picture is rapidly changing as the 32-bit microprocessors become commonplace. On C compilers for 68000-based computers, where the natural size is 32 bits, a plain int therefore consists of 32 bits, with the short int reserved for 16-bit quantities. On the assumption that the short int will be 16 bits for the foreseeable future of micros, our functions employ it to simulate the 16-bit CRCs in this chapter. (Recall that unsigned short int is typedefed to USHORT in SIOLOCAL.H.)

Simulation of CRC Hardware: *crchware*

The remainder from "pure" polynomial division is not the same as a CRC. In order to apply every term of the generator polynomial to every bit of the message, sixteen 0 bits must be put into the circuit to "flush" the remainder. The value in the remainder afterward is, *by definition*, the CRC. The necessity of flushing the remainder with 0s effectively adds 2 bytes of overhead to every message. This inefficiency is cured by modifying the basic polynomial division circuit. This new circuit, which does not require the appending of 0 bytes to the message, is shown in Figure 23.2.

FIGURE 23.2.

The "classical" CRC hardware circuit shown with the CRC-CCITT polynomial (1021 Hex).

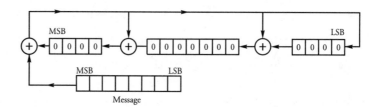

Unlike the polynomial division circuit, here the incoming data bit is XORed with the high-order bit of the accumulator, and the result is shifted into the accumulator. The important difference is the manner in which the XOR feedback is derived (i.e., how the polynomial is subtracted). Here, the result of XORing the data with the high bit of the accumulator actually becomes the feedback to the XOR gates. Using this scheme, the data bits immediately affect the feedback instead of waiting until they have propagated through the register. This circuit, then, produces the same results as the polynomial division circuit in Listing 23.1 with two 0 bytes appended to the message.

The function shown in Listing 23.3 duplicates the action of the CRC hardware. To emphasize that we are no longer simulating the longhand division technique, this function abandons the remainder/divisor terminology in favor of the accumulator/generator polynomial nomenclature. In general, the generator polynomial and the current contents of the accumulator are passed as arguments.

Listing 23.3. The crchware function: simulation of CRC hardware.

FUNCTION NAME:	crchware
LEVEL:	3
PROTOTYPE IN:	CRC.H
LIBRARY:	CRC.LIB
DESCRIPTION:	Simulates CRC hardware circuit.
RETURNS:	USHORT: the new CRC.
COMMENTS:	Generates a CRC directly—produces the same remainder as polynomial division with two 0 bytes appended to the message.
INCLUDE FILES:	siodef.h

```
USHORT crchware(USHORT data,  USHORT genpoly,  USHORT accum)
{
    static int i;
    data <<= 8;                         /* data to high byte            */
    for (i = 8; i > 0; i--)
        {
        if ((data ^ accum) & 0x8000) /* if msb of (data XOR accum) is TRUE */
            accum = (accum << 1) ^ genpoly; /* shift and subtract poly   */
        else
            accum <<= 1;                /* otherwise, transparent shift  */
```

```
        data <<= 1;                    /* move up next bit for XOR        */
    }
    return accum;
}
```

An explanation of crchware—Here the sole criterion for subtracting the polynomial is the value of the bit shifted out of the accumulator XORed with the data bit. This means that the first 1 data bit immediately produces feedback to the other XOR gates, producing the characteristic CRC "bit action." Due to this immediate feedback, there is no need to flush the accumulator with 0 bits.

CRC Calculation by Table Lookup

The function crchware is more efficient than polydiv in Listing 23.2 for two reasons: first, no NULL bytes are appended to the message; second, the code is simpler—there is no need to copy each data bit into the accumulator, and no intermediate variable is required to remember the state of the "quotient" bit. Indeed, crchware is functionally suitable for calculating the CRC in our XMODEM modules. But the CRC method is only slightly more efficient than the polynomial division method. In truth, both methods (with their repeated shifts, ANDs, and XORs) are woefully slow. Considering the care we have taken in designing the XMODEM modules for speed, using *either* of these CRC methods creates a palpable bottleneck in data transfer. The consequences of such a bottleneck can readily be seen in many commercial programs, where transfers using the checksum method are four to ten times faster than their CRC counterparts. But is such a speed sacrifice necessary to gain the benefits of the more rigorous CRC error checking? Luckily, no—a better way is available.

In Chapter 3, we discovered that when an 8-bit message byte is added to the 16-bit accumulator, only the high-order *or* the low-order 8 bits of the accumulator interact with the data bits. We referred to the 8-bit result of this interaction (i.e, XORing) as the *combining value*. This leads to the observation that the new accumulator is equal to the *CRC of the combining value* plus (XOR in modulo-2) the unchanged half of the accumulator. This relationship can easily be expressed in C using an intermediate variable for clarity:[1]

```
unsigned short tmp;
tmp = crchware((accum >> 8) ^ data, poly, 0);
accum = ((accum << 8)   ^ tmp);
```

Here, crchware is called to calculate the CRC of the combining value and the result is stored in tmp. The final CRC is derived by XORing the low-order byte of the accumulator with tmp.

---

[1]The high- or low-order bytes used in the steps of this procedure are reversed, depending upon the CRC model used. In this example, the high-order byte of the accumlator is XORed with the data to form the combining value, and the final step uses the low-order byte. The opposite bytes would be used for models that assume bit reversals, such as the CRC-16 shown in Listing 23.6.

BUILDING A CRC TABLE

Although the relationship of the *combining value* to the CRC is interesting, a function derived from it obviously performs more *slowly* than crchware. Pushing our thinking just a bit further, however, we discover a startlingly simple shortcut. Since there are only 256 possible combining values, why not calculate their CRCs in advance and store them in a table? Each element of this surprisingly simple table (shown in Listing 23.7) contains the CRC of its rank in the table; for example, element 1 contains the CRC for 1, element 50 contains the CRC for 50, and so on. The function to build this table automatically is given in Listing 23.4.

Listing 23.4. Use of the *mk_crctbl* function to build a CRC lookup table.

FUNCTION NAME:	mk_crctbl
LEVEL:	3
PROTOTYPE IN:	CRC.H
LIBRARY:	CRC.LIB
DESCRIPTION:	Builds a CRC lookup table based upon specified polynomial and CRC function.
RETURNS:	USHORT*: a pointer to the table.
COMMENTS:	Each table element contains the CRC of its rank in the table. For example, element 50 contains the CRC of 50.
INCLUDE FILES:	stdlib.h, siodef.h

```
USHORT *mk_crctbl( USHORT poly, USHORT (*crcfn)(USHORT, USHORT, USHORT) )
{
    USHORT *crctp;                      /* pointer to the table          */
    int i;
    if ( (crctp = (USHORT *)malloc(256 * sizeof(unsigned))) == NIL)
        return NIL;
    for (i = 0; i < 256; i++ )      /* fill table with CRCs of values... */
        crctp[i] = (*crcfn)(i, poly, 0); /* ... 0 -255                    */
    return crctp;                       /* return a table to the pointer */
}
```

An explanation of *mk_crctbl*—The two arguments passed to this are the generator polynomial and a pointer to a CRC function (crchware, for example). It not only builds the table of CRC values, it also allocates the memory for the table and returns its address. The for loop calculates and stores the CRC of the counter variable i in the ith element of the table. In cases where space is not critical, the table can be stored in the static array listed in Listing 23.5.

Listing 23.5. Lookup table for the CRC-CCITT for a classic hardware model.

ARRAY NAME:	crctab
TYPE:	USHORT
LIBRARY:	CRC.LIB
DESCRIPTION:	Lookup table for CCITT (XMODEM) polynomial.
COMMENTS:	Use this in place of `mk_crctbl` or just to verify that `mk_ctctbl` generates the correct table.
INCLUDE FILES:	siodef.h

```
USHORT crctab[256] =
  {
  0x0000,  0x1021,  0x2042,  0x3063,  0x4084,  0x50A5,  0x60C6,  0x70E7,
  0x8108,  0x9129,  0xA14A,  0xB16B,  0xC18C,  0xD1AD,  0xE1CE,  0xF1EF,
  0x1231,  0x0210,  0x3273,  0x2252,  0x52B5,  0x4294,  0x72F7,  0x62D6,
  0x9339,  0x8318,  0xB37B,  0xA35A,  0xD3BD,  0xC39C,  0xF3FF,  0xE3DE,
  0x2462,  0x3443,  0x420,   0x1401,  0x64E6,  0x74C7,  0x44A4,  0x5485,
  0xA56A,  0xB54B,  0x8528,  0x9509,  0xE5EE,  0xF5CF,  0xC5AC,  0xD58D,
  0x3653,  0x2672,  0x1611,  0x0630,  0x76D7,  0x66F6,  0x5695,  0x46B4,
  0xB75B,  0xA77A,  0x9719,  0x8738,  0xF7DF,  0xE7FE,  0xD79D,  0xC7BC,
  0x48C4,  0x58E5,  0x6886,  0x78A7,  0x0840,  0x1861,  0x2802,  0x3823,
  0xC9CC,  0xD9ED,  0xE98E,  0xF9AF,  0x8948,  0x9969,  0xA90A,  0xB92B,
  0x5AF5,  0x4AD4,  0x7AB7,  0x6A96,  0x1A71,  0x0A50,  0x3A33,  0x2A12,
  0xDBFD,  0xCBDC,  0xFBBF,  0xEB9E,  0x9B79,  0x8B58,  0xBB3B,  0xAB1A,
  0x6CA6,  0x7C87,  0x4CE4,  0x5CC5,  0x2C22,  0x3C03,  0x0C60,  0x1C41,
  0xEDAE,  0xFD8F,  0xCDEC,  0xDDCD,  0xAD2A,  0xBD0B,  0x8D68,  0x9D49,
  0x7E97,  0x6EB6,  0x5ED5,  0x4EF4,  0x3E13,  0x2E32,  0x1E51,  0x0E70,
  0xFF9F,  0xEFBE,  0xDFDD,  0xCFFC,  0xBF1B,  0xAF3A,  0x9F59,  0x8F78,
  0x9188,  0x81A9,  0xB1CA,  0xA1EB,  0xD10C,  0xC12D,  0xF14E,  0xE16F,
  0x1080,  0x00A1,  0x30C2,  0x20E3,  0x5004,  0x4025,  0x7046,  0x6067,
  0x83B9,  0x9398,  0xA3FB,  0xB3DA,  0xC33D,  0xD31C,  0xE37F,  0xF35E,
  0x02B1,  0x1290,  0x22F3,  0x32D2,  0x4235,  0x5214,  0x6277,  0x7256,
  0xB5EA,  0xA5CB,  0x95A8,  0x8589,  0xF56E,  0xE54F,  0xD52C,  0xC50D,
  0x34E2,  0x24C3,  0x14A0,  0x0481,  0x7466,  0x6447,  0x5424,  0x4405,
  0xA7DB,  0xB7FA,  0x8799,  0x97B8,  0xE75F,  0xF77E,  0xC71D,  0xD73C,
  0x26D3,  0x36F2,  0x0691,  0x16B0,  0x6657,  0x7676,  0x4615,  0x5634,
  0xD94C,  0xC96D,  0xF90E,  0xE92F,  0x99C8,  0x89E9,  0xB98A,  0xA9AB,
  0x5844,  0x4865,  0x7806,  0x6827,  0x18C0,  0x08E1,  0x3882,  0x28A3,
  0xCB7D,  0xDB5C,  0xEB3F,  0xFB1E,  0x8BF9,  0x9BD8,  0xABBB,  0xBB9A,
  0x4A75,  0x5A54,  0x6A37,  0x7A16,  0x0AF1,  0x1AD0,  0x2AB3,  0x3A92,
  0xFD2E,  0xED0F,  0xDD6C,  0xCD4D,  0xBDAA,  0xAD8B,  0x9DE8,  0x8DC9,
  0x7C26,  0x6C07,  0x5C64,  0x4C45,  0x3CA2,  0x2C83,  0x1CE0,  0x0CC1,
  0xEF1F,  0xFF3E,  0xCF5D,  0xDF7C,  0xAF9B,  0xBFBA,  0x8FD9,  0x9FF8,
  0x6E17,  0x7E36,  0x4E55,  0x5E74,  0x2E93,  0x3EB2,  0x0ED1,  0x1EF0
  };
```

THE CRC TABLE LOOKUP FUNCTION: *crcupdate*

Precalculating the CRCs of combining values and storing them in a table greatly simplifies and speeds up calculation of the CRC. Listing 23.6 shows the function to add a byte to the CRC accumulator.

Listing 23.6. The crcupdate function: CRC calculation with a lookup table.

FUNCTION NAME:	crcupdate
LEVEL:	3
PROTOTYPE IN:	CRC.H
LIBRARY:	CRC.LIB
DESCRIPTION:	Calculates CRC using table-lookup method.
RETURNS:	void
COMMENTS:	Looks up the CRC of combining value in the table pointed to by crctab.
INCLUDE FILES:	siodef.h

```
void crcupdate(USHORT data, USHORT *accum, USHORT *crctab)
{
    static short comb_val;
    comb_val  = (*accum >> 8) ^ data;
    *accum = (*accum << 8) ^ crctab[comb_val];
}
```

An explanation of *crcupdate*—The combining value is formed by XORing the data byte with the high-order byte of the accumulator (here expressed as a pointer). The CRC of the combining value—stored in the table previously built by mk_crctbl—is then XORed with the low-order byte of the accumulator. Freed from much of the overhead of bit shifting, this function is four to ten times faster than the crchware function. Importantly, because it contains no mention of a polynomial, it can be used to calculate the classical CRC using *any* generator polynomial. Actually, crcupdate is shown in this form only for clarity; in practice, it would be replaced with a single, more efficient statement:

```
*accum = (*accum << 8)  ^ crctab[(*accum >> 8) ^ data];
```

or, better yet, by the macro shown in Listing 23.9.

CRC Functions for *x_snd* and *x_rcv*

The CRC calculation in XMODEM uses the classical hardware *zero-purge* model: bytes are presented MSB first and then shifted left. The CRC is identical to the remainder produced by dividing the message longhand (with two 0 bytes appended) by the CCITT generator polynomial. The high-order byte of the CRC is transmitted first.

Before we compose the CRC functions to complete the XMODEM file transfer modules begun in Chapter 22, create a new header file named CRC.H and install in it the constants shown in Listing 23.7. Notice that CRC.H contains macro expressions for two CRC lookup functions.

Listing 23.7. Constants for CRC.H.

```
#define  CRCCCITT    0x1021    /* CCITT polynomial                */
#define  CCITT_REV   0x8408    /* Reverse CCITT polynomial        */
#define  CRC16       0x8005    /* CRC16 polynomial                */
#define  CRC16_REV   0xA001    /* Reverse CRC16 polynomial 0x8005 */

/* Remove comments if you wish to use macros */
/*
#define  crcupdate(d,a,t)    *(a) = (*(a) << 8) ^ (t)[(*(a) >> 8) ^ (d)];
#define  crcupdate16(d,a,t) *(a)=((*(a)>>8) ^ (t)[(*(a) ^ (d)) &0x00ff])
*/
```

Reviewing the details of x_snd and x_rcv in Chapter 22, recall that the CRC functions x_sndcrc and x_rcvcrc are called via function pointers. Since their argument lists contain only a pointer to the data member of a packet structure, both functions share the variable *crctblp, a global pointer to the CRC lookup table that was built during the initialization phases of x_snd and x_rcv:

```
if ( (crctblp = mk_crctbl(CRCCCITT, crchware)) == NIL)
    {
    puts("Insufficient memory for CRC lookup table.");
    return (1);
    }
```

Transmit CRC: x_sndcrc

The function x_sndcrc, shown in Listing 23.8, is called only by ckvinstall (through the function pointer r_errckp). Its purpose is to calculate and return the CRC of the data field of an sndpacket; the CRC is then installed in the ckval member of each packet.

Listing 23.8. The x_sndcrc function: the XMODEM sender's CRC function.

FUNCTION NAME:	x_sndcrc
LEVEL:	3
PROTOTYPE IN:	XMOD.H
LIBRARY:	IBMPC.C
DESCRIPTION:	Calulates CRC for indicated data block.

continues

Listing 23.8. continued

RETURNS:	USHORT
COMMENTS:	This function is inherently nonportable because there is no way to know how the processor stores words. As shown, we assume that the processor stores the LSB lower in memory than the MSB.
INCLUDE FILES:	stdio.h, siodef.h, xmod.h, crc.h

```
USHORT x_sndcrc(BYTE *buff)
{
    extern USHORT *crctblp;               /* pointer to lookup table  */
    static USHORT accum;                  /* CRC accumulator          */
    static int i;
    for (accum = i = 0; i < DBLKSIZ; ++buff, ++i)
        crcupdate(*buff, &accum, crctblp);  /* macro in CRC.H is better */
    return ( (accum >> 8) + (accum << 8) ); /* non-portable:  see text */
}
```

An explanation of *x_sndcrc*—For speed of access, the CRC is calculated in a static local variable, accum. The single variable in the argument list is a pointer to the data array in an XMODEM send packet. A simple for loop calls crcupdate 128 times, on each call passing the next byte in the array. Since crcupdate requires a *pointer* to the accumulator variable, the *address* of accum is passed. The address of the CRC lookup table—the global pointer crctblp—is also passed to crcupdate.

Notice that the header for this function lists it as a "level-0" file; that is, it should reside in the computer-specific configuration file. Because the XMODEM protocol specifies that the high-order byte of the CRC is transmitted first, the high-order byte must reside at a lower memory address in the sndpacket structure. As discussed in Chapter 22, the manner in which data is stored in memory varies from microprocessor to microprocessor. Therefore, x_sndcrc is inherently nonportable. Since the microprocessor in both machines for which we are developing code stores the low-order byte lower in memory, x_sndcrc byte-swaps the CRC before returning it. External variables are declared explicitly here so that this function can reside in the level-0 module.

Receive CRC: x_rcvcrc

Listing 23.9 shows x_rcvcrc, the XMODEM receive CRC function. It calculates the CRC for a receive packet's data field and compares it to the CRC in the ckval field. It returns a 0 if the CRCs agree, otherwise a non-0.

Listing 23.9. The *x_rcvcrc* function: the XMODEM receiver's CRC function.

FUNCTION NAME:	x_rcvcrc
LEVEL:	3
PROTOTYPE IN:	XMOD.H
LIBRARY:	XMODEM.C
DESCRIPTION:	Calulate CRC for a rcvpacket.
RETURNS:	USHORT
COMMENTS:	The CRC bytes in the rcvpacket are assumed to be contiguous with data bytes. The CRC (in accum) is zero if no errors occurred.
INCLUDE FILES:	stdio.h, siodef.h, crc.h, xmod.h

```
USHORT x_rcvcrc(USHORT *data)
{
    extern USHORT *crctblp;              /* pointer to the CRC lookup table */
    static USHORT i, accum;
    for (accum = i = 0; i < DBLKSIZ+2; i++)    /* include CRC bytes as data */
        crcupdate(*data++, &accum, crctblp);
    return accum;                        /* zero if no errors              */
}
```

An explanation of *x_rcvcrc*—The data passed in the argument list is, of course, a pointer to the 128-byte data array of the current rcvpacket structure. Immediately following this array are the CRC members ckvhi and ckvlo. In Chapter 3, we discovered that when the remainder of *MessageA* is concatenated to *MessageA*, the remainder of the resulting message is 0. The function x_rcvcrc takes advantage of this happy phenomenon by treating the data as an array of 130 instead of 128 bytes, thus including in the calculation the two CRC bytes that immediately follow the data. The value in accum can be returned directly because it is 0 only if no errors occur.

CRC-16 Calculation

When most programmers think of CRCs, they think of the CRC-16 hardware circuit shown in Listing 23.12. In reality, though, the CRC-16 hardware is a specialized version of CRC-type polynomial arithmetic that compensates for peculiarities in serial I/O. Recall from our discussion of CRC-16 in Chapter 3 that the CRC-16 hardware circuit actually performs an inverse division to compensate for the convention of transmitting data low-order bit first. To compensate for this bit reversal, the reverse CRC-16 polynomial is applied (i.e., A001 instead of 8005 Hex), data bits are shifted into the high-order bit of the CRC accumulator, and the quotient bit is shifted out of the low-order bit.

FIGURE 23.3.

The CRC-16 reverse hardware circuit. Note reversed divisor (reverse CRC-16 polynomial used).

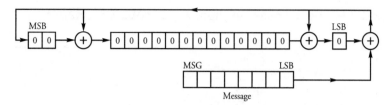

Neither of the CRC methods—classic or inverse—is superior. They are merely two versions of the same procedure, the latter designed to accommodate the peculiarities of hardware. On the rare occasion when you need to communicate with a CRC calculated in hardware, a reverse CRC algorithm comes in handy. It is certainly possible to calculate a reverse CRC using just the classic CRC functions we have already composed. However, the code overhead required to peform the reversals (the order of bits in each data integer would have to be reversed and shifted right eight places) would render CRC calculations absurdly slow. Considering the importance of speed in CRC calculations, it makes more sense to compose two special functions designed to simulate the reverse CRC. Listing 23.10 gives the new function crcrevhware to calculate the reverse CRC, and Listing 23.11 shows the matching table lookup function crcrevupdate. The existing mk_crctbl may be used because the CRC function is passed as a function pointer in its argument list.

Listing 23.10. Use of the *crcrevhware* function to simulate reverse CRC hardware.

FUNCTION NAME:	crcrevhware
LEVEL:	3
PROTOTYPE IN:	CRC.H
LIBRARY:	CRC.LIB
DESCRIPTION:	Simulates a "reverse" CRC hardware circuit.
RETURNS:	USHORT.
COMMENTS:	The generator polynomial in the argument list must already be reversed.
INCLUDE FILES:	siodef.h

```
USHORT crcrevhware(USHORT data, USHORT genpoly, USHORT accum)
{
   static int i;
   data <<= 1;                       /* in preparation for loop below    */
   for (i = 8; i > 0; i--)
      {
      data >>= 1;
      if ((data ^ accum) & 0x0001)   /* if msb of (data XOR accum) is TRUE */
         accum = (accum >> 1) ^ genpoly;  /* shift and subtract poly      */
      else
         accum >>= 1;                /* otherwise, transparent shift     */
      }
   return accum;
}
```

An explanation of *crcrevhware*—This function is structurally identical to the plain crchware function given earlier in Listing 23.5. The difference is that the *low-order* (& 0x0001) data bit is *right* shifted into the *high-order* accumulator bit and the quotient bit is shifted out of the low-order bit of the accumulator. It is important to notice that this function does not invert the generator polynomial; that is, it is the calling function's responsibility to pass the *exact* bit pattern.

Listing 23.11. The *crcrevupdate* function: the CRC-16 table-lookup function.

FUNCTION NAME:	crcrevupdate
LEVEL:	3
PROTOTYPE IN:	CRC.H
LIBRARY:	CRC.LIB
DESCRIPTION:	Calculates "reverse" CRC-16 on data byte passed using the lookup table.
RETURNS:	void
COMMENTS:	The genpoly is applied in the form it is passed. For CRC-16, therefore, A001 (inverse CRC-16) must be passed.
INCLUDE FILES:	siodef.h

```
void crcrevupdate(USHORT data, USHORT *accum, USHORT *crcrevtab)
{
    static int comb_val;
    comb_val  = *accum ^ data;
    *accum = (*accum >> 8) ^ crcrevtab[comb_val & 0x00ff];
}
```

An explanation of *crcrevupdate*—This function is identical to its sister function crcupdate in Listing 23.7, except the combining value is calculated by XORing the *high-order* byte of the accumulator with the data byte. This function can be simplified to

```
*accum = (*accum >> 8) ^  crcrevtab[(*accum  ^ data) &0x00ff];
```

or, for even faster performance, the macro from Listing 23.8. Listing 23.12 gives the table of combining values for the reverse CRC algorithm using CRC-16. This is the table generated by the following call:

```
mk_crctbl(CRC16_REV, crcrevhware);
```

Listing 23.12. Lookup table for reverse CRC-16 hardware model.

ARRAY NAME:	crc16tab
TYPE:	USHORT

continues

Listing 23.12. continued

LIBRARY:	CRC.LIB
DESCRIPTION:	Combining–value lookup table for CRC–16 reverse polynomial.
COMMENTS:	Use this in place of `mk_crctbl` or just to verify that the correct table is generated.
INCLUDE FILES:	siodef.h

```
USHORT crc16tab[256] =
    {
    0x0000,  0xC0C1,  0xC181,  0x0140,  0xC301,  0x03C0,  0x0280,  0xC241,
    0xC601,  0x06C0,  0x0780,  0xC741,  0x0500,  0xC5C1,  0xC481,  0x0440,
    0xCC01,  0x0CC0,  0x0D80,  0xCD41,  0x0F00,  0xCFC1,  0xCE81,  0x0E40,
    0x0A00,  0xCAC1,  0xCB81,  0x0B40,  0xC901,  0x09C0,  0x0880,  0xC841,
    0xD801,  0x18C0,  0x1980,  0xD941,  0x1B00,  0xDBC1,  0xDA81,  0x1A40,
    0x1E00,  0xDEC1,  0xDF81,  0x1F40,  0xDD01,  0x1DC0,  0x1C80,  0xDC41,
    0x1400,  0xD4C1,  0xD581,  0x1540,  0xD701,  0x17C0,  0x1680,  0xD641,
    0xD201,  0x12C0,  0x1380,  0xD341,  0x1100,  0xD1C1,  0xD081,  0x1040,
    0xF001,  0x30C0,  0x3180,  0xF141,  0x3300,  0xF3C1,  0xF281,  0x3240,
    0x3600,  0xF6C1,  0xF781,  0x3740,  0xF501,  0x35C0,  0x3480,  0xF441,
    0x3C00,  0xFCC1,  0xFD81,  0x3D40,  0xFF01,  0x3FC0,  0x3E80,  0xFE41,
    0xFA01,  0x3AC0,  0x3B80,  0xFB41,  0x3900,  0xF9C1,  0xF881,  0x3840,
    0x2800,  0xE8C1,  0xE981,  0x2940,  0xEB01,  0x2BC0,  0x2A80,  0xEA41,
    0xEE01,  0x2EC0,  0x2F80,  0xEF41,  0x2D00,  0xEDC1,  0xEC81,  0x2C40,
    0xE401,  0x24C0,  0x2580,  0xE541,  0x2700,  0xE7C1,  0xE681,  0x2640,
    0x2200,  0xE2C1,  0xE381,  0x2340,  0xE101,  0x21C0,  0x2080,  0xE041,
    0xA001,  0x60C0,  0x6180,  0xA141,  0x6300,  0xA3C1,  0xA281,  0x6240,
    0x6600,  0xA6C1,  0xA781,  0x6740,  0xA501,  0x65C0,  0x6480,  0xA441,
    0x6C00,  0xACC1,  0xAD81,  0x6D40,  0xAF01,  0x6FC0,  0x6E80,  0xAE41,
    0xAA01,  0x6AC0,  0x6B80,  0xAB41,  0x6900,  0xA9C1,  0xA881,  0x6840,
    0x7800,  0xB8C1,  0xB981,  0x7940,  0xBB01,  0x7BC0,  0x7A80,  0xBA41,
    0xBE01,  0x7EC0,  0x7F80,  0xBF41,  0x7D00,  0xBDC1,  0xBC81,  0x7C40,
    0xB401,  0x74C0,  0x7580,  0xB541,  0x7700,  0xB7C1,  0xB681,  0x7640,
    0x7200,  0xB2C1,  0xB381,  0x7340,  0xB101,  0x71C0,  0x7080,  0xB041,
    0x5000,  0x90C1,  0x9181,  0x5140,  0x9301,  0x53C0,  0x5280,  0x9241,
    0x9601,  0x56C0,  0x5780,  0x9741,  0x5500,  0x95C1,  0x9481,  0x5440,
    0x9C01,  0x5CC0,  0x5D80,  0x9D41,  0x5F00,  0x9FC1,  0x9E81,  0x5E40,
    0x5A00,  0x9AC1,  0x9B81,  0x5B40,  0x9901,  0x59C0,  0x5880,  0x9841,
    0x8801,  0x48C0,  0x4980,  0x8941,  0x4B00,  0x8BC1,  0x8A81,  0x4A40,
    0x4E00,  0x8EC1,  0x8F81,  0x4F40,  0x8D01,  0x4DC0,  0x4C80,  0x8C41,
    0x4400,  0x84C1,  0x8581,  0x4540,  0x8701,  0x47C0,  0x4680,  0x8641,
    0x8201,  0x42C0,  0x4380,  0x8341,  0x4100,  0x81C1,  0x8081,  0x4040
    };
```

So that these functions and their uses are not total abstractions to you, we will now compose a simple function to calculate both a classical CRC (using the CCITT polynomial) and a reverse CRC (using the CRC-16 polynomial on the contents of a disk file).

A CRC Test Program for the CRC Functions: CRC.C

The number of ways in which disk files can be quietly damaged is too long to list here, but the most common ways are changing floppy disks during file I/O, and (as RAM disks become more popular) unauthorized overwriting of RAM by errant software. A program for calculating the CRC for a disk file is therefore an extremely handy utility. More software publishers should follow the lead of Manx Software, which includes such a program in its Aztec C package along with a file listing and the correct CRC for each file in the package. A user of Manx software is thus able to verify a file's integrity in just a few moments. Listing 23.16 uses our CRC library to create CRC.C, a quick-and-dirty program to perform two kinds of CRC checks on the specified file.

Listing 23.13. CRC.C: a simple program to calculate the CRCs for a file's data.

PROGRAM NAME: CRC
DESCRIPTION: Calculates both CRCCCITT and CRC-16 on specified file.
SYNTAX: CRC FILENAME
INCLUDE FILES: stdio.h, stdlib.h, siodef.h, crc.h

```
main(int argc, char *argv[])
{
    FILE *fp;
    USHORT *tablep, accum;
    USHORT *table16p, accum16;
    int c;
    if (argc < 2)
        exit(puts("Need filename."));
    if ( (fp = fopen(argv[1], "rb")) == NIL)
        exit(printf("Cannot open %s.", argv[1]));
    if ( (tablep = mk_crctbl(CRCCCITT, crchware)) == NIL)
        exit(puts("No space for CCITT table."));
    if ( (table16p = mk_crctbl(CRC16_REV, crcrevhware)) == NIL)
        exit(puts("No space for CRC-16 table."));
    accum = accum16 = 0;                    /* clear both CRC accumulators */
    while ( (c = getc(fp)) != EOF)
        {
        crcupdate(c, &accum, tablep);
        crcrevupdate(c, &accum16, table16p);
        }
    printf("CCITT for %s  = %4.4X\n",argv[1], accum);
    accum16 = (accum16 >> 8) + (accum16 << 8);        /* byte-swap CRC-16 */
    printf("CRC-16 for %s = %4.4X\n ",argv[1], accum16);
    free((VOID*)tablep);
    free((VOID*)table16p);
    return 0;
}
```

An explanation of CRC.C—The earlier contents of this chapter should obviate an explanation of this program. One interesting semantic point arises, however: how do we display the CRCs? This is not merely a rhetorical question, but one that exposes the ambiguity implicit in the term *CRC*. For the classical CRC, we display the exact contents of the accumulator; that is, the high-order byte first. For the reverse CRC-16, however, we display the accumulator in the same order in which it is naturally transmitted—low-order byte first.

Conclusion

Do not be surprised if, having worked your way through this chapter, you feel a bit benumbed by CRCs or that your grasp of the topic is ephemeral. There is a cure for this: reread Chapter 3, where it is suggested that you construct a physical model of a CRC register and physically move the 1s and 0s (pennies and dimes) about. Although you may have scoffed at such a blue-collar approach on the first reading, you are probably now much more receptive to the notion. Why not give it another try?

Group 3 Facsimile Image Encoding and Decoding

First, a caution: the explanations that accompany the code in this chapter make no attempt to explain the concepts behind T.4 encoding. Therefore, you will find this chapter to be incomprehensible unless you are familiar with the general concepts of data compression explained in Chapter 10 and the detailed explanation of T.4 encoding in Chapter 11.

When programmers begin work on a facsimile project they quickly see that there are really two quite different jobs: real-time control (T.30) and digital image compression (T.4). Because of the scope of this book, supplying code for the former—say driving an EIA-567 Class 1 modem—is out of the question. This is not necessarily bad, for some programmers are far more at home programming a physical device than crunching bits. After all, hardware devices are usually accompanied by reasonably comprehensible documentation; in many cases, the manufacturer provides support and even education for developers. However, none of these perquisites exist when writing the function for encoding and decoding T.4 data. The documentation is dense and gnarled, and the CCITT doesn't have a technical telephone support department.

Obviously the time required to transmit a fax is determined by immutable physical constants such as baud rate and data size. Although the programmer can do nothing to shorten the time to send an image, he can certainly have a major impact upon the time required to *prepare* it. This is an important consideration,

SERIAL COMMUNICATIONS

considering that fax products usually transmit and receive faxes in the background, but perform image encoding and decoding in the foreground.[1] This means that users must twiddle their thumbs as the foreground application transforms the image from its native format into T.4 data. By employing sound procedures and algorithms for T.4 encoding and decoding the programmer is able to enhance the performance in a palpable, demonstrable manner. To this end, in this chapter we undertake to develop a suite of complementary functions for one-dimensional facsimile encoding and decoding.[2] The goal in this chapter is to present a suite of tools general enough to be dropped into any architecture with a minimum of effort.

During encoding, one begins with a raw bitmap of the right width (pels per line); the bitmap is converted into run lengths; the run lengths are then compressed using Huffman encoding. The inverse happens for decoding: the Huffman codes are converted to run lengths, and the run lengths are converted to a bitmap. Because each procedure depends upon the accuracy of the process that precedes it, a single mistake at any step produces errors (sometimes spectacular) in every downstream procedure. This can make development frustrating because of the difficulty of pinpointing the source of errors appearing in the final data. To ease this frustration, we will construct from scratch a completely invertible test suite to verify every step. The suite consists of the following programs:

1. **MAKEBMAP** constructs a bitmap file containing all possible run lengths.
2. **BMAP2RUN** converts the bitmap file to run lengths.
3. **RUN2T4** converts the run-length file to a file of T.4 Huffman codes.
4. **T4TORUN** converts the file of T.4 Huffman codes to a run-length file.
5. **RUN2BMP** converts the run-length file to a bitmap file.

This is a round-trip (invertible) procedure: if every step is correct, the bitmap file produced by RUN2BMP is identical to the one created in step 1.

The code is algorithmically quite robust, but little effort is made to defend against I/O errors and boundary data conditions. The goal is to produce code modules that can be easily integrated in any architecture. Adding the layers of code require for bullet-proofing would obscure the design of the underlying algorithm and coding procedures and make the code less flexible. For example, a real-life T.4 decoder would be expected to return an error if the number of pels per line disagreed with the expected value. Our decoder, however, uncomplainingly decodes a line of *any* width. After you've understood the code, you may add complexity to taste.

Before undertaking the program to create a test bitmap, please look at Listing 24.1, which contains the constants required for this chapter. These belong in a new include file named T4.H.

---

[1] This is due largely to architectural flaws in PC operating systems.

[2] Code for two-dimensional encoding is not presented, but is a relatively small step beyond the one-dimensional.

Listing 24.1. T4.H constants for T.4 encoding and decoding.

```
STRUCTURE: MHcode (typedef)
   FUNCTION: Contains a description of a Huffman code.
     LIBRARY: T4.H

typedef struct
    {
    USHORT t4token;             /* The Huffman code      */
    USHORT t4token_len;         /* Number of bits in same */
    } MHcode;

STRUCTURE: T4NODE (typedef)
   FUNCTION: Contains a note for the Huffman code binary tree.
     LIBRARY: T4.H

typedef struct t4node
    {
    struct t4node near *zero;   /* pointer to the next zero branch */
    struct t4node near *one;    /* pointer to the next one branch  */
    short  run_len;
    } near T4NODE;

#define NOTTERMINAL    12000                  /* Arbitrary number */
#define WHITE          0x0000
#define BLACK          0xFFFF
#define EOL_MARKER     32512                  /* Arbitrary number */
#define EOL_INDEX        104     /* Index into the encoding tables */
#define BYTES_PER_LINE   216
#define LINES_PER_PAGE 1728
```

Creating a Test Bitmap

Before we can build encoding and decoding tools, we must have a bitmap to operate on. Since bitmap files of the dimensions required by facsimile are not always easy to come by, we'll create our own. While we're at it, we'll make certain that the bitmap contains every run length possible on an A4 page (1,728 pels wide). Graphically, this is a line one pel in width that runs from the upper-left corner to the lower-right corner. To cover all possible run lengths, two such pages are required: one with a white line on a black page and one with a black line on a white page. Listing 24.2 shows the MAKEBMP program that creates this bitmap.

Listing 24.2. The MAKEBMP program creates an A4 test image containing all possible run lengths.

PROGRAM NAME: MAKEBMP

DESCRIPTION: Makes a bitmap image suitable for one-dimensional facsmile encoding. Beginning at pel 0 line 0, a single pel moves one bit to the right on successive lines. This produces a left-to-right diagonal, one pel wide.

COMMENTS: The output file is BITMAP0.A4: 746,496, CRC = 7160.

INCLUDE FILES: stdio.h, stdlib.h, memory.h, siolocal.h, t4.h

```
#define ALL_BLACK      0xFF
#define ALL_WHITE      0x00

void main(void)
{
    char * outfilename = "BITMAP0.A4";
    FILE *outfile;
    USHORT i, j;                     /* general counters          */
    USHORT page_num;                 /* page number in progress   */
    USHORT maskbyte;                 /* masked byte in each line  */
    USHORT prebits;                  /* number bytes before maskbyte */
    USHORT postbits;                 /* number bytes after maskbyte  */
    BYTE   color;                    /* color of current diagonal line */
    BYTE   line_of_bits[BYTES_PER_LINE -1]; /* array of bytes     */

    BYTE   mask[8][2] =              /* black & white maskbyte table */
        {
        {0x80, 0x7F}, {0x40, 0xBF}, {0x20, 0xDF}, {0x10, 0xEF},
        {0x08, 0xF7}, {0x04, 0xFB}, {0x02, 0xFD}, {0x01, 0xFE}
        };

    if ( (outfile = fopen(outfilename, "wb")) == NIL)
        exit(puts("Cannot open output file."));
/* for each page */
    for (color = ALL_BLACK, page_num = 1; page_num < 2; --page_num)
        {
        maskbyte = prebits = 0;
        postbits = BYTES_PER_LINE -1;
        memset(line_of_bits, color, BYTES_PER_LINE -1);
/* for each line */
        for (i = 0; i < LINES_PER_PAGE ; ++i)
            {
            printf("%s: %d\r", color == ALL_BLACK ? "Black" : "White", i+1);
            fwrite(line_of_bits, 1, prebits, outfile);
            fwrite(&mask[maskbyte][page_num], 1, 1, outfile);
            fwrite(line_of_bits, 1, postbits, outfile);
            if (++maskbyte == 8)     /* if all bits have been used ... */
                {                    /* ... scoot the mask byte right  */
                maskbyte = 0;
```

```
            ++prebits;
            --postbits;
            }
        }
    color = (BYTE) ~color;        /* flip the color              */
    putchar('\n');
    }
  fclose(outfile);
}
```

An explanation of MAKEBMP—Any line of the desired image is treated as two partial lines of the background color separated by a single dot (pel) of the foreground color. In the first line of the test bitmap, the partial line that precedes the dot is zero pels long; the dot is one pel; and the partial line following is 1,727 pels long. On the next line, the partial line that precedes the dot is 1 pel long; the dot is one pel; and the partial line following is 1,726 pels long. This process continues until the dot is the right-most pel.

To avoid a myriad of annoying loops to print the preceding and following lines, we construct a dummy line of 1,726 pels:

```
BYTE  line_of_bits[BYTES_PER_LINE -1];
```

This line is initialized to the background color using the `memset` function.

The partial lines are output by using `fwrite` to two partial lines of complementarily changing lengths on either side of a single byte containing a single dot. Each triad of two partial lines and a center byte is written eight times while the center byte changes. The center byte is taken from a table containing bytes with a single 1-bit. The table stores bytes for both background colors. On the second pass through the loop, the `page` variable is decremented, which changes the background color, and the center byte is taken from the other column of the table.

The program produces a file containing a single large image with a color inversion at the midway point. This is 3,456 lines of 216 bytes each, or 746,496 bytes. Its CRC-16[3] is 7160.

T.4 Encoding

As discussed in Chapter 11, T.4 encoding is a modified form of Huffman encoding, which uses variable-length codes to stand for run lengths. Therefore, before we can Huffman-encode the bitmap file produced by the MAKEBMP program, we must first convert the bitmap to run lengths. This is accomplished by the BMAP2RUN program given in Listing 24.3.

---

[3]As generated by the CRC.C program in Chapter 23.

Listing 24.3. BMAP2RUN converts a bitmap file to a run-length file.

```
       PROGRAM:  BMAP2RUN
   DESCRIPTION:  Converts 216-bytes per line bitmap to runlength file.
      COMMENTS:  Input file is BITMAP0.A4: 746,496 bytes CRC = 7160. Output
                 file is RUNLEN0.A4:  31,096 bytes CRC = 26D0
 INCLUDE FILES:  stdio.h, stdlib.h, siolocal.h, t4.h
```

```c
void main(void)
{
    char    *infilename =  "BITMAP0.A4";
    char    *outfilename = "RUNLEN0.A4";
    FILE    *outfilep, *infilep;
    BYTE    *bitbuffp;                          /* buffer for bits       */
    USHORT  *runbuffp;                          /* buffer for run lengths */
    USHORT  count, lines, bytes_per_line;

    if ( (bitbuffp = (BYTE*) malloc(BYTES_PER_LINE)) == NIL)
        exit(puts("Error allocating bit buffer."));
    if ( (runbuffp = (USHORT *) malloc(BYTES_PER_LINE * 8)) == NIL)
        exit(puts("Error allocating run-length buffer."));

    if ( (infilep = fopen(infilename, "rb")) == NIL)
            exit(printf("Error opening %s\n", infilename));
    if ( (outfilep = fopen(outfilename, "wb")) == NIL)
            exit(printf("Error opening %s\n", outfilename));

    printf("Input file = %s  Output file = %s \n", infilename, outfilename);

/* Read bits, make run lengths, write run lengths */
    bytes_per_line = BYTES_PER_LINE;
    for(lines = 1; count = bytes_per_line; lines++)
        {
        if (!fread(bitbuffp, sizeof(BYTE), bytes_per_line, infilep))
            {
            if (ferror(infilep))
                    printf("Error reading %s\n", infilename);
              break;
              }
        count = bit2run(bitbuffp, count, runbuffp);    /* encode */
        if (!fwrite(runbuffp, sizeof(short), count, outfilep))
            {
                printf("Error writing %s\n", outfilename);
                break;
                }
        printf("Writing line: %d\r",lines);
        }
    free(bitbuffp);                             /* clean up  */
    free(runbuffp);
    fclose(infilep);
    fclose(outfilep);
}
```

An explanation of BMAP2RUN—This program takes the line-by-line approach. That is, an input buffer is created to hold one line of the bitmap, and an output buffer is created to hold the run lengths produced. The input buffer is filled from the bitmap file BITMAP0.A4 and the output buffer is emptied to disk into the new run length file, RUNLEN0.A4. In between, the function bit2run performs the transformation. Any 8-bit random bitmap potentially expands to seven 16-bit run lengths. Although this relationship does not obtain in the highly repetitive bitmap used here, to be on the safe size, the size of the run-length buffer is made a conservative eight times larger.

The interesting work occurs in the calls to the bit2run function given in Listing 24.4.

Listing 24.4. The bit2run function converts a buffer of bits into a buffer of run lengths.

FUNCTION NAME: bit2run
LEVEL: 3
PROTOTYPE IN: T4.H
LIBRARY: FAX.LIB
DESCRIPTION: Converts a line of 1728 bits to a buffer of run lengths. An EOL starts each line.
RETURNS: USHORT
COMMENTS: The bit buffer is BYTE, the run length buffer is USHORT. A zero run length is generated if the first bit on a line is black.
INCLUDE FILES: stdio.h, siolocal.h, t4.h

```
USHORT bit2run(BYTE bitbuff[], USHORT numbytes, USHORT runbuff[] )
{
    USHORT  *runbuffp = runbuff;
    BYTE    *bitbuffp = bitbuff;
    register USHORT accumulator;    /* length of the current run          */
    short   color;                  /* color of the current run length    */

    *runbuffp++   = EOL_MARKER;     /* Start each line with BOL           */
    for (accumulator = 0, color = WHITE; numbytes; --numbytes)
        {
        register int bits;          /* The current bits to encode         */
        register int mask;          /* Used to mask off the bits          */
        bits = *bitbuffp++;
        if (bits ^= color)          /* if entire byte is not current color */
            {
            mask = 0x80;
            do
                {
                if (bits & mask)                /* if the bit is set      */
                    {
                    bits  ^= 0xFFFF;            /* invert bits            */
```

continues

Listing 24.4. continued

```
                    color ^= 0xFFFF;            /* toggle color         */
                    *runbuffp++ = accumulator; /* add run to buffer     */
                    accumulator = 0;
                    }
                accumulator++;
                } while (mask >>= 1);
        }
            else
                accumulator += 8;
        }
    *runbuffp++ = accumulator;
    return runbuffp - runbuff;           /* number of bytes in runbuffp      */
}
```

An explanation of *bit2run*—The strategy of this function is simple: each byte in bitbuffer is examined, one bit at a time, by masking and shifting. As long as the current bit is the same "color" as the previous bit, the count in the accumulator variable is incremented. Whole bytes that match the current color are pipelined; that is, the time-consuming masking-shifting is bypassed and the accumulator is incremented by eight.

When a bit doesn't match the current color, the accumulator is placed into the run-length buffer, the accumulator is reset to zero, and the current color is changed. So that the logical sense of the and-mask remains constant irrespective of the color, the bits-under-test must also be inverted. For reasons of efficiency, both inversion and color-flipping are accomplished by XORing with all-ones.

The bit operations that drive this procedure depend heavily upon the fact that the colors BLACK and WHITE are defined as all-ones and all-zeros, respectively. You may be puzzled to see that the bits-under-test are XOR'ed with the current color at the beginning of the loop: if (bits ^= color). Since color is initialized to WHITE (0x0000) and the accumulator is zero, this operation produces a zero run length when the first pel in the line is BLACK. Thus, as specified by T.4, each line begins with a white pel.

When all the bits have been converted to run lengths, the function returns the number of run lengths (not bytes) in the output buffer. Note that the first byte in the output buffer is always EOL_MARKER, a constant whose value is arbitrary, but must be greater than the largest legal run length in Group 3 facsimile (4,864).

RUN2T4: Run Lengths to Modified Huffman

With the run-length file RUNLEN0.A4 in hand, we now need a program to convert it to Huffman codes. Listing 24.5 shows RUN2T4.

Listing 24.5. The RUN2T4 function converts a run-length file to a file of T.4 codes.

```
PROGRAM NAME: RUN2T4
   DESCRIPTION: Reads runlength file, outputs 1-D T.4 file.
     COMMENTS: Input file RUNLEN0.A4: 31,096 bytes, CRC = 26D0.
                Output file  T4_1D.A4: 26,486 bytes, CRC = 07BC.
 INCLUDE FILES: stdio.h, stdlib.h, siolocal.h, t4.h
```

```c
#define RUNBUFFSIZE  2048
#define T4BUFFSIZE   RUNBUFFSIZE

void main(void)
{
    char  *infilename  = "RUNLEN0.A4"; /* File of run-lengths       */
    char  *outfilename = "T4_1D.A4";   /* File of 1-D T.4 codes      */
    FILE  *outfilep, *infilep;
    FAST  *runbuff;                    /* Input buffer for run lengths */
    FAST  *t4buff;                     /* Output buffer for T.4 codes  */
    USHORT num_t4codes;                /* Number of T.4 codes in buffer */
    USHORT rl_read;                    /* Run lengths read from disk   */
    USHORT t4_written;                 /* Number of T.4 codes in written*/
    USHORT read_total, write_total;    /* Statistics                   */

    if ((t4buff  = (FAST*) malloc(T4BUFFSIZE * sizeof(FAST))) == NIL)
        exit(puts("Error allocating T.4 buffer."));
    if ( (runbuff = (FAST *) malloc(RUNBUFFSIZE * sizeof(FAST))) == NIL)
        exit(puts("Error allocating run-length buffer."));

    if ( (infilep = fopen(infilename, "rb")) == NIL)
        exit(printf("Error opening %s\n", infilename));
    if ( (outfilep = fopen(outfilename, "wb")) == NIL)
        exit(printf("Error opening %s\n", outfilename));
    printf("Input file = %s  Output file = %s \n", infilename, outfilename);

/* Read run lengths, encode T.4, write T.4 codes */
    read_total = write_total = 0;
    do
        {
        rl_read = fread(runbuff, sizeof(FAST), RUNBUFFSIZE, infilep);
        if ( (rl_read != RUNBUFFSIZE)  && ferror(outfilep) )
            {
            printf("Error reading %s\n", infilename);
            break;
            }
        num_t4codes = t4encode(runbuff, rl_read, t4buff); /* encode    */
        t4_written = fwrite(t4buff, sizeof(short), num_t4codes, outfilep);
        if ( (t4_written != num_t4codes)  && ferror(outfilep) )
            {
            printf("Error writing %s\n", outfilename);
            break;
            }
```

continues

Listing 24.5. continued

```
            read_total += rl_read;
            write_total += t4_written;
        } while (t4_written);
    printf("\n%d Runlength bytes read\n", read_total * 2);
    printf("%d T4 bytes written\n", write_total * 2);
    fclose(infilep);                        /* clean up            */
    fclose(outfilep);
    free(t4buff);
    free(runbuff);
}
```

An explanation of RUN2T4—The BMAP2RUN program presented earlier is line-oriented—it reads and writes one line at a time. RUN2T4 takes a different approach. Buffers of arbitrary size are malloc'ed and run lengths from the RUNLEN0.A4 file are read without regard for line boundaries. Run lengths are encoded into t4buff by the t4encode function, which returns the number of Huffman codes in the buffer. After the data is exhausted, a final call to the encoding function with a count of zero flushes its accumulator. The program ends when all the run lengths have been read, encoded, and the Huffman codes written to the file T4_1D.A4.

T.4 ENCODING TABLES

Before looking at the t4encode function called by RUN2T4, a preliminary explanation is in order. Our general strategy for T.4 encoding is to create two tables, black and white, containing Huffman codes. Element n of this table contains the Huffman code for a run length of n. Since the longest assigned Huffman code is thirteen bits, sixteen bits of storage are sufficient. However, because Huffman codes by definition vary in length, the table must also contain how many bits of the sixteen bits comprise the code. The table, then, is actually an array of MHcode structures that were given in Listing 24.1. Listing 24.6 shows a partial listing of these arrays. The complete listings are given in Appendix F.

Listing 24.6. Snippets of the T.4 encoding tables. Complete listings appear in Appendix F.

ARRAY NAMES:	encwhite, encblack
TYPE:	Array of MHcode
FUNCTION:	Each element contains the Huffman variable-length code and the number of bits in that code.
LIBRARY:	FAX.LIB
INCLUDE FILES:	stdio.h, siolocal.h, t4.h

```
MHcode encwhite[] = {
    {0x00ac, 8},  {0x0038, 6},  {0x000e, 4},  {0x0001, 4},    /*  0*/
    {0x000d, 4},  {0x0003, 4},  {0x0007, 4},  {0x000f, 4},    /*  4*/
    {0x0019, 5},  {0x0005, 5},  {0x001c, 5},  {0x0002, 5},    /*  8*/
    {0x0004, 6},  {0x0030, 6},  {0x000b, 6},  {0x002b, 6},    /* 12*/
    {0x0015, 6},  {0x0035, 6},  {0x0072, 7},  {0x0018, 7},    /* 16*/
        .
        .

        .
    {0x00b2, 9},  {0x0006, 6},  {0x01b2, 9},  {0x0080, 11},   /* 88*/
    {0x0180, 11}, {0x0580, 11}, {0x0480, 12}, {0x0c80, 12},   /* 92*/
    {0x0280, 12}, {0x0a80, 12}, {0x0680, 12}, {0x0e80, 12},   /* 96*/
    {0x0380, 12}, {0x0b80, 12}, {0x0780, 12}, {0x0f80, 12},   /*100*/
    {0x0800, 12}                              /*EOL*/         /*104*/
};

MHcode encblack[] = {
    {0x03b0, 10}, {0x0002, 3},  {0x0003, 2},  {0x0001, 2},    /*  0*/
    {0x0006, 3},  {0x000c, 4},  {0x0004, 4},  {0x0018, 5},    /*  4*/
    {0x0028, 6},  {0x0008, 6},  {0x0010, 7},  {0x0050, 7},    /*  8*/
    {0x0070, 7},  {0x0020, 8},  {0x00e0, 8},  {0x0030, 9},    /* 12*/
    {0x03a0, 10}, {0x0060, 10}, {0x0040, 10}, {0x0730, 11},   /* 16*/
        .
        .

        .
    {0x1b40, 13}, {0x04c0, 13}, {0x14c0, 13}, {0x0080, 11},   /* 88*/
    {0x0180, 11}, {0x0580, 11}, {0x0480, 12}, {0x0c80, 12},   /* 92*/
    {0x0280, 12}, {0x0a80, 12}, {0x0680, 12}, {0x0e80, 12},   /* 96*/
    {0x0380, 12}, {0x0b80, 12}, {0x0780, 12}, {0x0f80, 12},   /*100*/
    {0x0800, 12}                              /*EOL*/         /*104*/
};
```

An explanation of T.4 encode tables—To find the entry for any run length, simply use that run length to index into the appropriate table below. Referring to Table 11.15, note for example that the Huffman code for a white run of 0 is the eight-bit code 00110101. Element zero four in the encwhite table in Listing 24.6 contains the code 0000000010101100 (0x00AC), which has a length of 8. This means that only the Huffman code comprises only the eight least significant bits, or 10101100. This is indeed the correct code, but reversed least-to-most bit.

Why are the codes in our table backward? Recall from Chapter 11, T.30 specifies that the least significant bit in the data be transmitted first. Stated another way, our table entries contain the Huffman codes as they appear *on the phone line*, not how they appear in the CCITT documentation. This is the most useful way to store the codes, since fax pumps are oblivious to bit order. In other words, our arrays contain data that is ready for transmission. If stored in "book" order, the bits must be reversed upon transmission.

Run lengths in the range 0 to 63 are all *terminating* codes and their values can be read directly from the array. However, recall from Table 11.16 that runs from 64-2560 in steps of 64 are *makeup* codes. To avoid an array 2,561 elements long, index numbers greater than 63 are in effect considered to be expressed in base-64 (sexihexidecimal). For example, to find the index for a makeup run of 1,856, divide by 64 and add 63, or 92. Index 92 in the table produces the code 0x0180, 0000000110000000. Since this is an 11-bit code, only the 11 least significant bits are valid: 00110000000. Bit-reversing this value yields 00000001100, the value from Table 11.16. Makeup codes are identical for black-and-white runs, so they appear in both tables. The last entry in the table is the 12-bit code for an EOL.

"?ENOYNA ,LASREVER TIB"

The need to bit-reverse Phase C data has caused an ongoing clown show in the fax modem industry. Accepting technical followship from inept attempts at early fax application software developers, some early EIA 592 (Class 2) modems required data inversion in one direction, but not in the other. As it turned out, almost no one understood the issues, and silly arguments abounded in committees. This latest manifestation of the big/little-endian debate was eventually settled by the *Data Bit Order Command* (+FB0), which selects between "modes": *Direct* (as our in our arrays) or *Reversed* (as in CCITT documentation).

THE *t4encode* FUNCTION

The T.4 encoding function shown in Listing 24.7 converts the run-length file RUNLEN0.A4 to a one-dimensionally encoded Modified Huffman file T4_1D.A4.

Listing 24.7. The t4encode function converts run lengths to Huffman codes.

FUNCTION NAME:	t4encode
PROTOTYPE IN:	T4.H
LIBRARY:	FAX.LIB
DESCRIPTION:	Converts a buffer of run lengths to a buffer of 1-dimensional Group 3 (T.4) facsimile Modified Huffman codes.
RETURNS:	int: the number of Huffman codes in the output buffer.
COMMENTS:	EOLs are byte-aligned. Calling with a run-length count of zero flushes the buffer.
CAUTION:	The T.4 buffer must be large enough to hold all the codes generated from the run-length buffer.
INCLUDE FILES:	stdio.h, siolocal.h, t4.h

```
#define START_TABLE encblack
#define TERMINATING 63
#define MAKEUP_CODE runlen>63

short t4encode(FAST *runbuffp, short run_count, FAST *t4buffp)
{
         extern MHcode encwhite[], encblack[];/* The Huffman tables      */
50       FAST t4token;                      /* Huffman code for current run len */
55       FAST t4token_len;                  /* Number of bits in Huffman code   */
60       FAST runlen;                       /* Run length to be encoded         */
65       FAST bits_lost;                    /* Used in bit-smooshing            */
70       FAST index;                        /* Converts make-up to base-64 index */

75       FAST *t4startbuffp = t4buffp;      /* Remember buffer address    */
80       static MHcode *t4tblp = START_TABLE; /* Initialize like this!    */
85       static FAST accum     = 0;         /* The T4 bit-smoosher         */
90       static FAST accum_len = 0;         /* Number of bits in the accum */

95       if (run_count == 0)               /* Zero flushes accum         */
100          {
105          short num_codes = 0;
110          if (accum_len)
115              {
120              *t4buffp = accum;          /* Put accumulator in buffer   */
125              num_codes = 1;
130              accum = accum_len = 0;     /* Re-initialize all statics ..*/
135              t4tblp = START_TABLE;      /* ... for next user.          */
140              }
145          return num_codes;
150          }

155      ++run_count;                      /* Use pre-increment          */
160      while (--run_count)
165          {
170          runlen  = *runbuffp++;        /* Fetch run length           */
175          t4tblp = (t4tblp == encwhite) ? encblack : encwhite; /* flip */
180          if (runlen == EOL_MARKER)     /* Special run length          */
185              {
190              runlen = EOL_INDEX;        /* Change it to an index       */
195              t4tblp = START_TABLE;      /* Use white table after EOL   */
200              if (accum_len <= 4)        /* Byte align EOL: make sure ... */
205                  accum_len = 4;         /* .. accum is 4 or 12 bits long */
210              else if (accum_len <= 12)
215                  accum_len = 12;
220              else
225                  {
230                  *t4buffp++ = accum;    /* Output to accumulator      */
235                  accum      = 0;        /* Clear accum, then claim..*/
240                  accum_len  = 4;        /* ..4 bits ...                */
245                  }
250              }
255          else
260              {
265              if (MAKEUP_CODE)                        /* If runlen > 63 */
```

continues

Listing 24.7. continued

```
270                        {
275                        index = (runlen >> 6) + 63;
280                        t4token = t4tblp[index].t4token;
285                        t4token_len = t4tblp[index].t4token_len;
290                        accum |= t4token << accum_len;
295                        if (accum_len + t4token_len >= 16)
300                            {
305                            *t4buffp++ = accum;
310                            bits_lost = 16 - accum_len;
315                            accum     = t4token >> bits_lost;
320                            accum_len = t4token_len - bits_lost;
325                            }
330                        else
335                            accum_len += t4token_len;
340                        runlen &= 63;          /* remainder = terminating code */
345                        }
350                    }

355        t4token     = t4tblp[runlen].t4token;     /* from table        */
360        t4token_len = t4tblp[runlen].t4token_len; /* from table        */
365        accum     |= t4token << accum_len;         /* drop it in        */
370        if (accum_len + t4token_len >= 16)        /* if it didn't fit.. */
375            {
380            *t4buffp++ = accum;                   /* ..output to buffer */
385            bits_lost = 16 - accum_len;           /* .. then install .. */
390            accum     = t4token >> bits_lost;     /* .. what didn't fit */
395            accum_len = t4token_len - bits_lost;
400            }
405        else
410            accum_len += t4token_len;
415        }
420    return t4buffp - t4startbuffp;       /* number of t4 codes in buffer */
425 }
```

An explanation of *t4encode*—Although the amount of code in this function suggests complexity, most of it is rather obvious pre-processing for the core algorithm found in the ten lines of code 355-410.

Because Huffman codes are variable-length, the output code must be assembled in an accumulator. Two variables manage the accumulator: accum and accum_len; the latter keeps track of the number of T.4 bits in the accumulator or, by subtraction, the number of unused bits. Because these variables must persist across function calls, they are declared static. Bits in the accumulator are packed toward the LSB and new bits are OR'ed in at the MSB end. When the accumulator is full, it is installed in the output buffer. Let's see how this works, line-by-line. (It is illustrated graphically in Figure 24.1.)

160 For every run length in the buffer, do the following:

170 Fetch the run length for encoding.

175 Switch the current table to the other color.

355 Use the run length to index into the Huffman table pointed to by t4tblp. The variable-length Huffman code t4token and its length t4token_len are copied from the table into local variables to eliminate the overhead of repeatedly de-referencing them through the pointer.

365 Visualize the token positioned above the accumulator. The token is left-shifted by the number of bits in the accumulator; this has the effect of positioning the token's least-significant bits "above" the accumulator's free space most-significant bits. The left-shifted token is then OR'ed into the accumulator.

370 If this operation caused an overflow in the accumulator, the accumulator is flushed:

380 The accumulator is put in the output buffer.

390 The token bits that were lost (wouldn't fit) at line 365 are now right-shifted and OR'ed into the LSB end of the accumulator.

395 The accum_len is adjusted to reflect the "lost" bits just added.

410 If the accumulator was not full after the token was OR'ed, the length of the accumulator is adjusted upward by the length of the token.

Once this algorithm is understood, the rest of the code becomes a handmaiden. For example, EOL processing:

180 Recognize special EOL run-length marker.

190 Assign it the index for an EOL, 104 (in both black and white tables).

195 Set the table pointer to its startup-value. (It must be set opposite to the desired state because it is complemented at 175.)

200 Make certain the EOL is byte-aligned by fudging zeros into the accumulator.

The core algorithm is repeated (for efficiency) in lines 265-340 in order to handle makeup codes.

265 Recognize makeup code.

275 As described a few paragraphs earlier, convert the makeup code to a base-64 index. Proceed according to the core algorithm.

340 The makeup code is converted to a terminal code and "falls through" to the core algorithm for processing.

The final unexplained block of code is the accumulator flushing mechanism at lines 95-145. After the calling program has encoded all its run lengths, the accumulator may contain data. To flush the accumulator to disk, the calling program passes a run_count of zero. If the accumulator contains data, it is moved into the output buffer, the static accumulator variables are reset, and the function returns with a count of one.

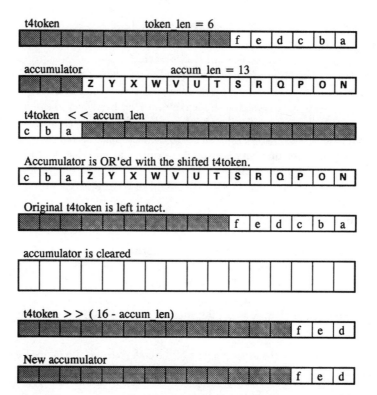

FIGURE 24.1.

Illustration of accumlator packing during T.4 encoding.

One odd-looking couplet occurs repeatedly in the rest of the code in this chapter:

```
155     ++run_count;           /* so pre-incrementation can be used below */
160     while (--run_count)
```

This coding is employed for efficiency reasons. In many compilers, post-decrementation requires the compiler to generate several more memory accesses than pre-decrementation.

T.4 Decoding

At this point we're halfway to the goal of a round trip from bitmap to run lengths to T.4 encoding and back. The trip back promises to be longer than the trip out. There is one major reason for this. The T.4 encoding process is at heart a table-lookup operation wherein a run length indexes into a simple table of values. Hence, an equal effort is required for encoding all run lengths. In the decoding process, by comparison, the effort required to render a Huffman code to a run length varies directly as the number of bits in the code. Although by definition longer codes occur less frequently, on average substantially more effort is required to decode even the shortest codes than to encode them. In one popular approach to decoding, the Huffman code is accumulated bit-by-bit and compared against a list of valid codes equal to the accumulated length. For example, when four bits have been accumulated, a table containing the valid four-bit values is searched. If a match is found in the four-bit table, the corresponding run length is extracted in much the same manner as employed in the t4encode function developed earlier. If a match is not found, however, another bit is added to the accumulator, and a table of five-bit values is searched. Obviously, as the length of the accumulated bits increases, so does the length of the list of valid codes and, since T.4 codes may be up to 13 bits long, 26 tables of ever increasing size are required for lookup. For this reason, the effort required to decode a run length with this method is not a linear function of the number of bits in the Huffman code.

T4DECODE: Decoding Modified Huffman Codes

The approach we shall take linearizes the decoding—exactly twice as long is required to decode an eight-bit code as a four-bit one. The method is based on the process used to create the Huffman table in the first place—the binary tree. Reviewing Listing 10.8, a Huffman table is a binary tree in which each node leads to the next code. A node "terminates" at the code represented. In Listing 10.8, for example, the path 000 terminates at the letter 'E', the most frequently occurring letter in the alphabet. Since T.4 codes are based upon the probability of occurrence of various run lengths, we should be able to construct an array of structures in which each node (structure) contains two pointers: a pointer to the next node on the zero-bit path and a pointer to the next node on the one-bit path. At each node we shall install a marker indicating whether there are more nodes to pursue; if not, the marker contains the run length represented by that branch. The definition of this node, previously shown in Listing 24.1, is disarmingly simple[4]:

```
typedef struct t4node
    {
    struct t4node near *zero;    /* pointer to the next zero branch */
    struct t4node near *one;     /* pointer to the next one branch */
    short  run_len;
    } near T4NODE;
```

Listing 24.8 shows a partial listing of the binary-tree array for the black run lengths. The complete listing for this array and for the white tree are given in Appendix F. Listing 24.9 also shows a binary-tree array eoltree whose function is explained later.

---

[4]The modifier near is a Microsoft reserved word that forces 16-bit bit pointers, regardless of the 80x86 memory model.

Listing 24.8. Binary-tree arrays for black run lengths and EOL synchronization.

```
T4NODE blacktree[] = {
/* 000 */    {&blacktree[1],   &blacktree[2],    NOTTERMINAL},
/* 001 */    {&blacktree[3],   &blacktree[4],    NOTTERMINAL},
/* 002 */    {&blacktree[5],   &blacktree[6],    NOTTERMINAL},
/* 003 */    {&blacktree[7],   &blacktree[8],    NOTTERMINAL},
/* 004 */    {&blacktree[9],   &blacktree[10],   NOTTERMINAL},
/* 005 */    {&whitetree[1],   &whitetree[2],    3},
/* 006 */    {&whitetree[1],   &whitetree[2],    2},
/* 007 */    {&blacktree[11],  &blacktree[12],   NOTTERMINAL},
/* 008 */    {&blacktree[13],  &blacktree[14],   NOTTERMINAL},
/* 009 */    {&whitetree[1],   &whitetree[2],    1},
/* 010 */    {&whitetree[1],   &whitetree[2],    4},
                 .
                 .
                 .
/* 209 */    {&blacktree[1],   &blacktree[2],    1024},
/* 210 */    {&blacktree[1],   &blacktree[2],    1088},
/* 211 */    {&blacktree[1],   &blacktree[2],    1152},
/* 212 */    {&blacktree[1],   &blacktree[2],    1216},
};

T4NODE eoltree[] = {
/* 000 */    {&eoltree[1],    &eoltree[0],      NOTTERMINAL},
/* 001 */    {&eoltree[2],    &eoltree[0],      NOTTERMINAL},
/* 002 */    {&eoltree[3],    &eoltree[0],      NOTTERMINAL},
/* 003 */    {&eoltree[4],    &eoltree[0],      NOTTERMINAL},
/* 004 */    {&eoltree[5],    &eoltree[0],      NOTTERMINAL},
/* 005 */    {&eoltree[6],    &eoltree[0],      NOTTERMINAL},
/* 006 */    {&eoltree[7],    &eoltree[0],      NOTTERMINAL},
/* 007 */    {&eoltree[8],    &eoltree[0],      NOTTERMINAL},
/* 008 */    {&eoltree[9],    &eoltree[0],      NOTTERMINAL},
/* 009 */    {&eoltree[10],   &eoltree[0],      NOTTERMINAL},
/* 010 */    {&eoltree[11],   &eoltree[0],      NOTTERMINAL},
/* 011 */    {&eoltree[11],   &eoltree[12],     NOTTERMINAL},
/* 012 */    {&whitetree[1],  &whitetree[2],    EOL_MARKER }
};
```

An explanation of `blacktree`—The black tree was chosen because it illustrates the structure of the table with a minimum of elements. In each array element, the pointer elements of the T4NODE structure—`zero` and `one`—contain the address of the next element in the tree.

Let's see how to climb this tree. Suppose that we are decoding in the black tree and the decode is 01111001. Looking at the bits from left to right, and starting at element zero (`blacktree[0]`), decoding proceeds like this:

1. The first bit is 0. The `run_len` member of element zero is NOTTERMINAL, so we examine the `zero` member and discover that the next element in the table is `blacktree[1]`. Jump to that element.

2. The second bit is 1. The `run_len` member of the current element is NOTTERMINAL, so we examine the `one` member and discover that the next element in the table is `blacktree[4]`. Jump to that element.

3. The third bit is 1. The `run_len` member of the current element is NOTTERMINAL, so we examine the `one` member and discover that the next element in the table is `blacktree[10]`. Jump to that element.

4. This time, however, the `run_len` member of the current element contains the run length four instead of the value NOTTERMINAL. We extract this run length. This is the end of the path in black path, so the pointers lead back to `whitetree`. Since the fourth bit is 1, we jump to `whitetree[2]`.

5. And so on.

After only three bits, 011, we reached a "terminal" value: a run length of four. The T.4 table in Listing 24.8 confirms this. Listing 24.9 shows `t4decode`, the function that climbs the trees.

Listing 24.9. The T.4 decoding function decodes by climbing binary trees.

FUNCTION NAME: `t4decode`
PROTOTYPE IN: T4.H
LIBRARY: FAX.LIB
RETURNS: `int`: 0 if file I/O successful; otherwise 1.
DESCRIPTION: Binary-tree T.4 decoder. The 1-D T.4 data is read from input file handle, decoded, and written as run lengths to output handle.
INCLUDE FILES: stdio.h, memory.h, siolocal.h, t4.h

```
int t4decode(FILE *t4file, FILE *runfile, short *runbufp,
             USHORT runbuff_len, FAST *t4bufp, USHORT t4_len)
   {
 5   extern   T4NODE eoltree[];            /* Start in EOL tree    */
10   register FAST t4_code;                /* The current T.4 byte */
15   register T4NODE *curr_node;           /* Current node in tree */
20   register FAST numbits;                /* Bit counter          */
25   FAST    *t4buff_start = t4bufp;
30   short   *runlen_startp = runbufp;
35   short    t4_read;                     /* Num codes in T.4 buff*/
40   int      errcode = 0;
45   USHORT   numruns   = 0;
50   memset(runbufp, 0, runbuff_len * sizeof(short));
55   curr_node = eoltree;
```

continues

Listing 24.9. continued

```
60    while (t4_read = fread(t4bufp, sizeof(FAST), t4_len, t4file))
65        {
70        ++t4_read;
75        while (--t4_read)
80            {
85            t4_code = *t4bufp++;                         /* Fetch byte    */
90            numbits = sizeof(FAST) * 8;
95            ++numbits;
100           while (--numbits)                           /* For every bit */
105               {
110               curr_node = t4_code & 1 ? curr_node->one :  curr_node->zero;
115               if (curr_node->runbuff_len != NOTTERMINAL)
120                   {
125                   *runbufp += curr_node->runbuff_len;
130                   if ( (curr_node->runbuff_len < 64) ¦¦
                          (*runbufp == EOL_MARKER))
135                       {
140                       ++numruns;
145                       ++runbufp;
150                       }
155                   if (numruns == runbuff_len)          /* Buffer full? */
160                       {
165                       if (fwrite(runlen_startp, sizeof(short),
170                           runbuff_len, runfile) != runbuff_len)
175                           {
180                           errcode = 1;                 /* Write error   */
185                           goto EXIT;
190                           }
195                       numruns = 0;                     /* Reset         */
200                       runbufp = runlen_startp;
205                       memset(runbufp, 0, runbuff_len * sizeof(short));
210                       }
215                   }
220               t4_code >>= 1 ;                          /* Next bit, please */
225               }
230           }
235       t4bufp = t4buff_start;                          /* Reset   */
240       }
245   if (fwrite(runlen_startp, sizeof(short), numruns, runfile) != numruns)
250       errcode = 1;                                    /* If flush causes an error */
255 EXIT:
260     return errcode;
265 }
```

An explanation of *t4decode*—After all the crepe hanging about the amount of "effort" required to decode Huffman codes, you are probably astonished at the elegence and simplicity of this function. The core algorithm consists of just five lines:

```
100     while (--numbits)
105         {
110         curr_node = t4_code & 1  ?  curr_node->one :  curr_node->zero;
115         if (curr_node->runlen != NOTTERMINAL)
125             *runbufp += curr_node->run_len;
130         ....
```

The variable curr_node points at the current node. If the bit-under-test is one, the current node is switched to the node pointed to by the one member of the T4NODE structure; if the bit-under-test is zero, the current node is switched to the node pointed to by the zero member of the T4NODE structure.[5] If the run_len structure member indicates that this node is at the end of the path, the run length is plucked from the node and added to the run-length buffer. Notice (line 130) that the run-length buffer pointer runbufp is not incremented when makeup codes are found, thus consolidating any number of makeup codes into a single run length. Because the run lengths are placed directly into the buffer without going through an intermediate variable, the buffer is initialized to zeros each time it is flushed to disk.

Notice that at start-up curr_node points to eoltree. Recall from Chapter 10 that each T.4 page begins with an EOL (or BOL, if you will[6]). The nodes of eoltree build a path of at least eleven zeros followed by a one—the definition of an EOL. Remember, though, that an EOL may contain extra zeros inserted as fill bits during transmission. Therefore, at node eleven, the zero path points at itself; thus the tree loops at node eleven indefinitely waiting on a one bit. When the one-bit arrives, the tree points into whitetree.

Subsequent EOLs are handled by the black and white trees. For example, starting at the first node in the black tree in Appendix F, follow the zero path through the following nodes: 1, 3, 7, 11, 15, 19, 25, 33, 43, 58, 85. The white path at node 85 loops back to itself until it hits a one-bit, then jumps to node 128, which identifies itself as EOL_MARKER, then jumps into the white table.

You may have noticed several nodes in the two main trees that jump into eoltree. These are *dead-end* (or pruned) nodes. These nodes end in illegal codes or reserved codes (such as the vertical codes used in two-dimensional encoding). When such a code appears, a jump into eoltree will essentially discard all bits until an EOL announces the beginning of the next line. The decoder is thus able to recover from bit errors in the Huffman codes such as might be received on a noisy phone line.

T4TORUN: Modified Huffman to Run Lengths

The t4decode makes the program that calls it a bit anticlimactic. The code for T4TORUN is given in Listing 24.10.

---

[5]Tree climbing can be speeded up somewhat by dereferencing curr_node:
curr_node = *((T4NODE **)curr_node + (t4_code & 1));

[6]If you don't wish to think of EOLs as BOLs, you'll need to use a start-up tree that doesn't generate a run length, but jumps immediately into the white treee.

Listing 24.10. The T4TORUN program converts a file of T.4 Huffman codes to run lengths.

PROGRAM: T4TORUN

DESCRIPTION: Converts a T.4 encode (1-Dimensional) input file to an output of run lengths.

COMMENTS: Input file is T4_1D.A4: 26,496 bytes, CRC = 07BC.
Output file is RUNLEN1.A4: 44,406 bytes, CRC = 26D0.

INCLUDE FILES: stdio.h, stdlib.h, malloc.h, siolocal.h, t4.h

```
#define RUNBUFFSIZE  2048
#define T4BUFFSIZE   RUNBUFFSIZE

void main(void)
{
    char *infilename = "T4_1D.A4";
    char *outfilename = "RUNLEN1.A4";
    FILE *outfilep, *infilep;
    FAST *t4buffp;
    short *runbuffp;
    short t4_len, run_len, errcode;
    run_len = t4_len = 100;

    if ((t4buffp  = (FAST*) malloc(T4BUFFSIZE * sizeof(FAST))) == NIL)
        exit(puts("Error allocating T.4 buffer."));
    if ( (runbuffp = (short *) malloc(RUNBUFFSIZE * sizeof(short))) == NIL)
        exit(puts("Error allocating run-length buffer."));

    if ( (outfilep = fopen(outfilename, "wb")) == NIL)
        exit(printf("Error opening output %s\n", outfilename));
    if ((infilep = fopen(infilename, "rb"))  == NIL)
        exit(printf("Error opening input %s\n", infilename));

    printf("Input file = %s  Output file = %s \n", infilename, outfilename);

    errcode = t4decode(infilep, outfilep, runbuffp, run_len, t4buffp, t4_len);

    if (errcode)
        puts("I/O error during decoding.");
    fclose(outfilep);
    fclose(infilep);
    free(runbuffp);              /* clean up */
    free(t4buffp);
}
```

An explanation of T4TORUN—The only remarkable characteristic of this executable is that unlike previous programs in this chapter, the decoder function is responsible for disk I/O. This design was chosen because the T.4 data expands when converted to run lengths and the decoder must be free to flush the output buffer independent of the number of bytes left in the input buffer. The value returned by the decoder gives the status of the disk I/O.

Run Lengths to Bitmaps

This is the final leg on the round-trip from bitmap to bitmap. We now need a program to render the run lengths generated by T4TORUN into a bitmap file identical to the one we started with. Let's first look at the function that does the work, then we'll examine the inconsequential program to drive it. Listing 24.11 shows run2bits.

Listing 24.11. The `run2bits` function converts a run length to a bitmap.

FUNCTION NAME: run2bits
LEVEL: 3
PROTOTYPE IN: T4.H
LIBRARY: FAX.LIB
DESCRIPTION: Converts a buffer of run lengths to a line of 1728 bits. An EOL starts each line.
RETURNS: int
COMMENTS: The bit buffer is BYTE, the run length buffer is short.
INCLUDE FILES: stdio.h, stdlib.h, siolocal.h, t4.h

```
#define NUMBITS  8
#define WIDTH    NUMBITS/8
#define BUFF_LEN (bitbufp-bitbuff_start)*WIDTH

 int run2bits(FILE *infilep, FILE *outfilep, BYTE *bitbufp,
                short bitbuf_len, short *runbufp, short runbuffp)
 {
 5    int num_read = 0;
10    FAST   accum;
15    USHORT accum_len;
20    BYTE  *bitbuff_start = bitbufp;
25    short *runbuff_start = runbufp;
30    FAST whole_bytes, space_left;       /* For pipelining               */
35    BYTE color;                         /* The color of the current run */
40    register short runlen = 0;          /* The length of the current run */
45    register short mask = 0x01;
50    space_left = bitbuf_len;
55    accum = accum_len = 0;
60    while(num_read = fread(runbufp, sizeof(short), runbuffp, infilep))
65       {
70       ++num_read;
75        while (--num_read)
80          {
85          runlen = *runbufp++;
90          if (runlen > space_left * NUMBITS)
95             {
100             if ((int)fwrite(bitbuff_start, 1, BUFF_LEN, outfilep) !=
                          BUFF_LEN)
105                return 1;
110             space_left = bitbuf_len;
115             bitbufp = bitbuff_start;
```

continues

Listing 24.11. continued

```
120                        }
125                   if(runlen == EOL_MARKER)          /* Toss EOL codes */
130                        {
135                        mask = 0x01;
140                        color = (BYTE)BLACK;
145                        continue;
150                        }
155                   color = (BYTE) ~color;            /* Invert color   */
160                   mask ^= 0x1;                      /* Invert mask    */
165                   while(runlen)
170                        {
175                        if ((runlen >= NUMBITS) && (accum_len == 0))
180                             {                        /* Pipeline whole bytes */
185                             whole_bytes = runlen/NUMBITS;
190                             memset(bitbufp, color, whole_bytes);
195                             bitbufp += whole_bytes;
200                             space_left -= whole_bytes;
205                             runlen = runlen % NUMBITS;
210                             }
215                        while (runlen)     /* Stay in tight loop here */
220                             {
225                             accum <<= 1;
230                             accum ¦= mask;
235                             ++accum_len;
240                             --runlen;
245                             if (accum_len == NUMBITS)
250                                  {
255                                  *bitbufp++ = (BYTE)accum;
260                                  accum = accum_len = 0;
265                                  --space_left;
270                                  break;      /* for possible pipeline  */
275                                  }
280                             }
285                        }
290                   }
295              runbufp = runbuff_start;
300              }
305         if ((int)fwrite(bitbuff_start, 1, BUFF_LEN, outfilep) != BUFF_LEN)
310              return 1;
315         return 0;
320 }
325
```

An explanation of *run2bits*—This function converts run lengths to bits through uninteresting proletariat bit-crunching in an accumulator at lines 215-280. EOL codes are discarded at line 125. The rest of this function is obvious, but two areas of optimization merit discussion: output buffer management and the pipelining of large single-color run lengths.

Buffer management can be quite restricting in decompression operations because of the potentially great expansion undergone by the data from input to output. For example, a single run length of two bytes can potentially expand to sixteen kilobytes. A common way to avoid buffer management is to write the accumulator to disk each time it is full, thereby letting C's internal I/O perform the buffering. In images where there are few long run lengths, this approach is acceptable because the time spent bit-crunching swamps the time cost of the byte-by-byte stream I/O. But in text-oriented facsimile images, many blank lines and generous margins almost guarantee a high percentage of long run lengths.

A great performance improvement is attained, therefore, by retaining a bit buffer. The bit buffer's management is greatly simplified by imposing one simple specification: the output buffer must be large enough to hold the bits generated by the longest possible run length. Once this is granted, a single decision effectively manages the buffer. Before beginning to decode each run length, the buffer is written to disk if the buffer won't hold the *entire* expanded run length. This technique means that the buffer will seldom be completely full, but, on the other hand, there is almost no code overhead involved so performance improves. This decision occurs at line 90.

It would be easy to let the core algorithm at lines 215-280 grind away bit-by-bit. But with buffer management worries out of the way, it becomes possible to pipeline long run lengths by writing large blocks into the buffer at one time. At line 175, a test is made to see it the runlen remaining to be decoded is greater than size of the accumulator; that is, is this run length long enough for pipelining? If so, and if the accumulator is empty, the entire run length is expanded into the buffer using the memset function. At the end of the pipelining code at line 205, the modulus operator assigns to runlen the odd bits that were not pipelined.

After pipelining, the code then drops into the core algorithm at 215 for crunching. Once inside this code, another optimization is possible. To understand it, consider the seemingly redundant while at line 215. Without this loop, execution would return to line 165 after every bit. The tight inner loop at 215 keeps the processor grinding away until the accumulator is full, at which time the loop breaks; then control passes to 165. This has the effect of always looking for a chance to pipeline. For example, consider what happens when the first bit in a file is white, followed by a run of 1,727 (exactly the case in our test file). First, the one in runlen is put into the accumulator. Next runlen gets a value of 1,727 at line 75. The test at 175 fails because the accumulator is not empty and the run of 1,727 drops into the bit grinder for processing. When the accumulator is full, it is put in the bit buffer and the code breaks, returning control to 165. Now this time the test at 175 succeeds because the accumulator is empty and 1,720 bits (215 bytes) are moved into the bit buffer in a single operation.

It is worth noting that the code shown uses an 8-bit accumulator because 16-bit quantities are generally stored byte-reversed on disk on Intel-based machines. The widths of various quantities are defined as constants to facilitate this change for other processors or if you wish to embed an assembly language byte-swapping instruction (XCHG ah, al) in the C code.

RUN2BMP: RUN LENGTHS TO BITMAPS

We are now ready to compose the program to call run2bits. Listing 24.12 shows RUN2BMP.

Listing 24.12. The RUN2BMP program converts a run-length file to a bitmap file.

PROGRAM: RUN2BMP
DESCRIPTION: Converts runlength file to 216-bytes-per-line bitmap.
COMMENTS: Input file is RUNLEN1.A4: 31,096 bytes, CRC = 26D0
Output file is BITMAP1.A4: 746,496 bytes, CRC = 7160
INCLUDE FILES: stdio.h, stdlib.h, siolocal.h, t4.h

```
#define NUMBITS   8
#define WIDTH     NUMBITS/8

void main(void)
{
    FILE *infilep, *outfilep;
    char *infilename = "RUNLEN1.A4";
    char *outfilename = "BITMAP1.A4";
    int   errcode = 0;
    BYTE *bitbufp;                    /* Points to the buffer filled with data */
    short *runbufp;
    short bitbuf_len = 608;
    short run_len = BYTES_PER_LINE;
    if ((bitbufp  = (BYTE*)malloc(WIDTH * bitbuf_len)) == NIL)
        exit(puts("Error allocating bitmap buffer."));
    if ((runbufp = (short*)malloc(sizeof(short) * run_len)) == NIL)
        exit(puts("Error allocating runlength buffer."));

    if ( (outfilep = fopen(outfilename, "wb")) == NIL)
        exit(printf("Error opening %s\n", outfilename));
    if ( (infilep = fopen(infilename, "rb")) == NIL)
        exit(printf("Error opening %s\n", infilename));
    printf("Input file = %s  Output file = %s \n", infilename, outfilename);

    errcode = run2bits(infilep, outfilep, bitbufp, bitbuf_len, runbufp, run_len);

    if (errcode)
        puts("I/O error");
    fclose(infilep);
    fclose(outfilep);
    free(runbufp);
    free(bitbufp);
}
```

An explanation of RUN2BMP—This program is all ceremony and housekeeping. After allocating buffers and opening the input and output files, run2bits is called to do the work. Because 4864 is the longest run length possible in facsimile, the output buffer is declared to be 608 (4864÷8) bytes long.

Bibliography

Periodicals

Bremer, R.W. "All about ASCII." *The Best of Interface Age*. Forest Grove Oregon: dilithium Press, 1978. This series of articles, by one of the authors of ASCII, contains a wealth of information unavailable elsewhere. Unfortunately, neither the magazine nor the publisher is still in business.

da Cruz, Frank, and Catchings, Bill. "Kermit: A File-Transfer Protocol for Universities. Part 1: Design Considerations and Specifications." *BYTE*. (June, 1984): 255. "Part 2: States and Transitions, Heuristic Rules, and Examples." *BYTE*. (July, 1984): 143. A highly condensed explanation of the Kermit protocol by its authors.

Morse, Greg. "Calculating CRCs by Bits and Bytes." *BYTE*. (September, 1986): 115-124.

Perez, A. "Byte-wise CRC Calculations." *IEEE Micro*. (June 1983): 4-5. This article explains how byte-sized CRCs combine with the existing 16-bit accumulator. It contains a chart giving all 16 intermediate combining values for CRC-16. The author builds the combining lookup table through a tortuous mathematical procedure unique for each CRC divisor. The programming examples are in Fortran and 88 Assembler.

Ritter, Terry. "The Great CRC Mystery." *Dr. Dobb's Journal of Software Tools*. (February, 1986): 26. This is the best of the CRC articles and the only one to perceive the simple way of building the combining value lookup table explained in Chapter 19. Programming examples are in Pascal.

Segal, Mark L. "Toward Standardized Video Terminals." *BYTE*. (April 1984): 365. An overview of how ANSI 3.64 relates to video terminals.

Schwaderer, W. David. "CRC Calculations." *PC Tech Journal.* (April 1985): 118-32. Similar in scope to the Perez article, including the method of building the lookup table. The programming examples are in C.

Urban, Stephen. "Review of standards for electronic imaging for facsimile systems." *Journal of Electronic Imaging* 1, 5-21 (January, 1992).

Ziv, J., and Lempel, A. "A universal algorithm for sequential data compression." *IEEE Transactions on Information Theory*, Volume 23, Number 3, May 1977, pp. 337-343.

Ziv, J., and Lempel, A. "Compression of individual sequences via variable-rate coding." *IEEE Transactions on Information Theory*, Volume 24, Number 5, September 1978, pp. 530-536.

Books

Bingham, John. *The Theory and Practice of Modem Design.* John Wiley & Sons, 1988. Although this is an electrical engineering book written for modem designers, it contains interesting general material about modems.

Brooks, John. *Telephone: The First Hundred Years.* New York: Harper and Row, 1976. Although a puff piece on the history of AT&T, it is nonetheless worthwhile because, unlike most accounts, it stresses the business aspects of the company.

Campbell, Joe. *Crafting C Tools for the IBM PCs.* Englewood Cliffs, N.J.: Prentice-Hall, Inc., 1986. A book on systems programming in C, stressing the interface between C and the PC DOS operating system. It contains important background information about the IBM PC's interrupt system as well as an alternative serial interrupt handler.

Campbell, Joe. *The RS-232 Solution.* Berkeley: SYBEX, Inc., Second Edition, 1989. A book on the distressing realities of interfacing non-standard RS-232 hardware. Case studies are given for major deviations.

da Cruz, Frank. *Kermit: A File Transfer Protocol.* Bedford, Mass.: Digital Press, 1987. This book is delightful. It is one of those rare books that speaks with equal clarity to novice and expert alike. It is also a treasure chest of practical information about the problems involved in adapting Kermit to a variety of hardware environments.

Halsall, Fred. *Data Communications, Computer Networks, and Open Systems.* Addison-Wesley, 1992. Although its delcared subject is computer networks, it contains a surprising amount of information of general interested.

Harrison, H. H. *Printing Telegraph Systems and Mechanisms.* London: Longmans, Green, and Co., 1923. Like the Pendry book, a look at the design and functioning of the teleprinter.

Hayes Microcomputer. *Technical Reference fo Hayes Modem Users*. Atlanta: 1990. Despite its name, this is a detailed description of Hayes modems and probably the best reference for "Hayes Compatiblity."

Held, Gilbert. *Data Compression*. John Wiley & Sons, Second Edition. 1987. This volume is a good introduction to the subject of data compression, but not as through as the Nelson book. Its programming examples are in BASIC.

Marland, E.A. *Early Electrical Communication*. New York: Abelard-Schuman, 1964. Early history of telecommunications with emphasis on Wheatstone and Cooke.

Martin, James. *Telecommunications and the Computer*. Englewood Cliffs, N.J.: Prentice-Hall, Inc., 1976. A good text for a college-survey course.

McConnell, Kenneth; Brodson, Dennis; Schaphorst, Richard. *Fax: Digital Facsimile Technology and Applications*. Artech House, Inc, Second Edition, 1992. This is a book for people who already know *a lot* about fax.

McNamara, John E. *Technical Aspects of Data Communication*. Bedford, Mass.: Digital Press, 1977. An indispensable volume of practical information plainly written.

Nelson, Mark. *The Data Compression Book*. M&T Books, 1992. The title says it all for this impressive volume.

Nelson, Mark. *Serial Communications: A C++ Developer's Guide*. M&T Books, 1992. This book contains lots of useful information and techniques for serial programming. It is long on programming (C++ code, obviously) and short on overview and theory. Contains a good description of the ZMODEM protocol.

Pendry, H. W. *The Baudot Printing Telegraph*. London: Whittaker & Co., 1913. A wonderful book of explanations and incredible drawings of the Baudot teleprinter.

Peterson, W. W., and Weldon, Jr., E.J. *Error-Correcting Codes*. Cambridge: MIT Press, 1972. Considering the subject matter, this book is amazingly readable to non-mathematicians.

Pierce, John R. *Signals*. San Francisco: W.H. Freeman and Company, 1981. An interesting, if somewhat dilettantish, survey of the history of electronic communications in general, with emphasis on and much praise for the accomplishments of Bell Labs.

Pless, Vera. *Introduction to the Theory of Error-Correcting Codes*. New York: John Wiley & Sons, 1982. Its title says it all. If you want to know why one CRC divisor polynomial is better than another, this is your book.

Schwaderer, W. David. *Digital Communications Programming on the IBM PC*. New York: John Wiley & Sons, Inc., 1984. This book is full of good, useful information written in an entertaining style. Unfortunately, its programming examples are in BASIC. This book was re-released in 1987 under the title *Modems and Communications on the IBM PC*.

Shiers, George. *The Electric Telegraph: An Historical Analogy.* Salem, N.H.: The Arno Press, 1977. This is a collection of articles by and about those involved in the early years of telegraphy. The book is worth looking at if only for the drawings of early equipment.

Stallings, William. *Data and Computer Communications.* New York: Macmillan Publishing Co., Third Edition, 1991. This is a good college-level text with more of an engineering flavor than the Martin book.

Stevens, David. *A Programmer's Guide to Video Display Terminals.* Dallas: Atlantis Publishing Corp., 1985. This book contains control codes for dozens of video terminals.

Tanenbaum, Andrew. *Computer Networks.* Prentice-Hall, Second Edition, 1989. An excellent description of all kinds of networks. Contains loads of useful parenthetical information.

Thompson, R.L. *Wiring A Continent.* Princeton, N.J.: Princeton Univ. Press, 1947. This book documents the spread of the telegraph.

Standards and Reference

Documentation American National Standards Institute

ANSI X3.15

For Bit Sequencing of American Standard Code for Information Interchange.

ANSI X3.25

Character Structure and Character Parity Sense for Parallel-by-bit Data Communications in American Standard Code for Information Interchange.

ANSI X3.28

Procedures for the Use of the Communication Control Characters of American Standard Code for Information Interchange in Specified Data Communications Links.

Graphic Representation of the Control Characters of American Standard Code for Information Interchange.

Code for Information Exchange.

ANSI X3.41

Code Extension Techniques for use with the 7-bit Character Set of American Standard Code for Information Interchange.

ANSI X3.45

Character Set for Handprinting.

ANSI X3.64

Additional Controls for use with American Standard Code for Information Interchange.

Documents of the American National Standards Institute may be purchased from:

American National Standards Institute
1430 Broadway
New York, NY 10018

Electrical/Telecommunications Industries Associations

EIA/TIA-602

Serial Asynchronous Automatic Dialing and Control

EIA/TIA-578

Asynchronous Facsmile Control (Service Class 1)

EIA/TIA-466

Group 3 Facsimile Apparatus for Document Transmission (Equivalent of CCITT T.30)

EIA/TIA-592

Asynchronous Facsmile Control (Service Class 2)

EIA/TIA-605

Facsimile DCE-DTE Packet Protocol Standard

EIA/TIA-465

Group 3 Facsimile Apparatus for Document Transmission (Equivalent to CCITT Recommendation T.4)

EIA/TIA-466

Procedures for Document Facsimile Transmission (Equivalent to CCITT Recommendation T.30)

EIA/TIA-614

Binary File Transfer Format for Group 3 Facsimile

The EIA/TIA (Electrical/Telecommunications Industries Associations) recommendations mentioned in the book may be obtained from:

> EIA/TIA
> Engineering Department
> 2001 Pennsylvania Ave. N.W.
> Washington, DC 20006
> Voice: (202) 457-4966

CCITT

CCITT T.4

Standardization of Group 3 Facsimile Apparatus for Document Transmission

CCITT T.30

Procedures for Document Facsimile Transmission in the General Switched Telephone Network

CCITT (The International Consultative Committee for Telephone and Telegraph) documents were formerly published every four years in many volumes. A volume is not a single book, but many books; individual books are referred to as "fascicles" and contain the individual recommendations (standards) relevant to a specific area of communications. Volume VIII.1 about modems, for example, is entitled "Data Communication over the Telephone Network" and is referred to as the "Series V. Recommendations." Volume VII.3 containing the facsimile specifications is entitled "Terminal Equipment and Protocols for Telematic Services."

The volumes for a given year were all printed in the same color and in the industry were referred to by that color (Yellow: 1980 Red: 1984, Blue: 1988, and so forth). Rumor has it that sometime in the mid 1990's the volumes will not be printed; instead, recommendations will be sold individually. The supplier in the United States is:

> OMNICOM
> 115 Park St., S.E.
> Vienna, VA 22180
> Voice: (800)-OMNICOM Fax: (703) 281-1505

Those wishing to montitor the proceedings of the CCITT, may purchase draft documents and meeting reports of Study Group 8 (facsimile), Study Group 14 (telephone modems), and Study Group 15 WP1 (conferencing, H series) from:

Communications Standards Review
(415) 856-9018.

Incidental Functions

This appendix contains C functions that, though necessary to compile and run the software developed in this book, have nothing to do with serial programming. If your C compiler supplies similar functions, and many do, you will be able to utilize them by modifying the calling syntax for the functions presented here. In any case, these functions are all useful in their own right, and you will doubtless find use for them in many areas. The functions are:

bigbuff—Allocates very large buffer.

haktc—Waits for the user to hit a key to continue.

putbin—Prints integer in binary.

rfopen—Opens a stream for reading—gets name from user.

stratoi—Scans a string for an integer and then calls atoi to convert it.

wfopen—Opens a stream for writing—gets name from user.

BIGBUFF

Listing A.1. The bigbuff function.

FUNCTION NAME:	bigbuff
PROTOTYPE IN:	MISC.H
LEVEL:	3
LIBRARY:	MISC.LIB
DESCRIPTION:	Allocate large buffer.
RETURNS:	char *: the address of the allocated buffer or NIL if no memory available.

continues

Listing A.1. continued

COMMENTS: Allocates nblks of memory, in `blksize` chunks. The headroom argument is the number of `blksize` chunks to return to the system for local use. The actual number of blocks allocated is returned to the caller with the pointer `numblkp`.

INCLUDE FILES: stdlib.h, siodef.h

```c
char *bigbuff(USHORT blksize, USHORT headroom, USHORT *numblkp)
{
    char *p;
    unsigned nblks = 1;
    while ( (p = malloc(nblks * blksize)) != NIL) /* call until failure */
        {
        free((VOID*)p);                 /* release it                 */
        ++nblks;                        /* ask for more next time     */
        }
    if (headroom >= --nblks)            /* not enough memory          */
        {
        nblks = 0;
        return NIL;
        }
    nblks -= headroom;                  /* adjust for headroom        */
    *numblkp = nblks;                   /* pass back to caller        */
    return (malloc(nblks * blksize));   /* allocate & return the pointer */
}
```

An explanation of *bigbuff*—Situations frequently arise when you need all the heap available. Some systems have functions with names like `heapleft` or `corenow` to let you know how much to allocate. On the Microsoft compiler, for example, the name of the function is `_memaval`. Other systems maintain global pointers that can be subtracted to ascertain the amount of heap space remaining.

The `bigbuff` function is for systems where none of these methods is available. It returns a pointer to the allocated heap space requested or NIL if the request cannot be fulfilled. Its arguments provide great flexibility in the way in which the storage is allocated:

blksize   This enables allocation of storage in multiples of aggregate data objects.

headroom   Exhausting the heap is often dangerous because there is no storage left for subsequent function calls. Usually, then, we need to leave some storage for the system. This is the number of `blksize` units to leave on the heap; that is, the number of units *not* to allocate.

numblkp   Since the function must return a pointer to the storage actually allocated, it returns the *number of blocks* successfully allocated in the variables whose address is supplied in the argument list.

Here is an example of how to allocate a buffer for an array of structures named xyz:

```
struct xyz
    {
    long a;
    char b;
    int  c[25];
    };

unsigned numstructs;
struct xyz *buffp;
buffp = bigbuff(sizeof(struct xyz),  10,  &numstructs);
if (buffp == NIL)
      exit();
```

This call asks for storage to hold the maximum number of xyz structures, minus 10. After the call, buffp contains a pointer to the storage (or NIL) and numstructs contains how many xyz structures the storage will hold.

HAKTC

Listing A.2. The haktc function.

```
#include <stdio.h>
#include <sio\key.h>

void haktc(void)
{
    puts("\n\t\t\tHit Any Key To Continue");
    getkbch();
    putchar('\n');
}
```

PUTBIN

Listing A.3. The putbin function.

FUNCTION NAME: putbin
PROTOTYPE IN: MISC.H
LEVEL: 3
LIBRARY: MISC.LIB
DESCRIPTION: Displays 16-bit integer in binary.
RETURNS: void
INCLUDE FILES: stdio.h, siodef.h

continues

Listing A.3. continued

```
void putbin(USHORT data)
{
    USHORT shifter = 0x8000;
    for (; shifter > 0; shifter >>= 1)
        putchar((data & shifter) ? '1' : '0');
    putchar('\n');
}
```

RFOPEN

Listing A.4. The rfopen function.

FUNCTION NAME: rfopen
PROTOTYPE IN: MISC.H
LEVEL: 3
LIBRARY: MISC.LIB
DESCRIPTION: Continually prompts for filename until file is opened for reading or the user aborts.
RETURNS: FILE *
COMMENTS: The filename buffer passed must be long enough to hold the largest valid system name.
INCLUDE FILES: stdio.h, siodef.h, errno.h, string.h

```
FILE *rfopen(char *promptstr, char *fnbuff)
{
    FILE *rfp;
    do
        {
        printf("\n%s: ",promptstr);
        gets(fnbuff);
        if (strcmp(fnbuff,"") == 0)              /* user typed CR to exit    */
            return NIL;
        if ( (rfp = fopen(fnbuff, "rb")) == NIL) /* open failure             */
            if (errno == ENOENT)
                printf("%s not found.", fnbuff);
            else
                printf("\nOpen error on %s.", fnbuff); /* error message  */
        } while (rfp == NIL);                    /* repeat until open succeeds */
    return rfp;
}
```

An explanation of *rfopen*—This function prompts for a filename, opens it, and returns a pointer to it. The prompt to issue to the user is passed in the argument list. Also passed is the location of a filename buffer into which the filename should be placed. It is the caller's responsibility to make certain that this buffer is large enough to accommodate the maximum filename possible on the system. For more protection, the length of the buffer should be passed in the argument list and enforced in rfopen.

The design of rfopen is fairly straightforward. The prompt is issued and the user's response is captured by gets into the filename buffer. An "empty" filename buffer is taken as a signal to terminate the function; otherwise fopen is called repeatedly until the file is successfully opened.

STR_ATOI

Listing A.5. The str_atoi function.

FUNCTION NAME: str_atoi
LEVEL: 3
PROTOTYPE IN: MISC.H
LIBRARY: MISC.LIB
DESCRIPTION: Scans a string looking for a numeral, then calls atoi.
RETURNS: int: the integer or -1 if the string contains no numerals.
INCLUDE FILES: stdlib.h, ctype.h, siodef.h

```
int str_atoi(char *buffp)
{
    if ( buffp!= 0)
        for (; *buffp != NUL; buffp++)
            if (isdigit(*buffp))
                return (atoi(buffp));
    return -1;
}
```

WFOPEN

Listing A.6. The wfopen function.

FUNCTION NAME: wfopen
PROTOTYPE IN: MISC.H
LEVEL: 3
LIBRARY: MISC.LIB

continues

Listing A.6. continued

DESCRIPTION: Continually prompts for name of output file until file is successfully opened or the user aborts.

RETURNS: FILE *: the FILE pointer or NIL if open unsuccessful.

COMMENTS: Asks permission before overwriting a pre-existing file. The filename buffer passed must be long enough to hold the largest valid system name.

INCLUDE FILES: stdio.h, siodef.h, ctype.h, string.h

```c
FILE *wfopen(char *promptstr, char *fnbuff)
{
    FILE *wfp;
    char locbuff[10];
    for (EVER)
        {
        printf("\n%s: ",promptstr);
        gets(fnbuff);
        if (strcmp(fnbuff,"") == 0)
            return NIL;
        fclose(wfp = fopen(fnbuff, "rb"));  /* open it for reading    */
        if (wfp == NIL)                     /* doesn't already exist  */
            return (fopen(fnbuff, "wb"));
        printf("\n%s already exists. Overwrite\007?  ", fnbuff);
        gets(locbuff);
        if (toupper(locbuff[0]) == 'Y')
            return (fopen(fnbuff, "wb"));
        }
}
```

An explanation of *wfopen*—This function serves the same function as rfopen, except that it opens a file for writing, and asks permission before overwriting an existing file.

APPENDIX

Assembler Interface and Memory Models

B

SERIAL COMMUNICATIONS

It is a widely and mistakenly held opinion that "you can do anything in C that you can do in assembler." Sorry, but there are times when nothing but assembler will do. Consider for example, the main ISR given in Listing B.2. If the keywords _interrupt far are placed in front of a function definition, the Microsoft C compiler produces a file that is usable as a vector for a *software* INT instruction. Our main ISR, however, is called as a result of a *hardware* interrupt which requires a non-specific EIO instruction be sent to the system PIC. Our ISR also requires a local stack. Although it is possible to use C in conjunction with in-line assembler to switch stacks, there is no way to get the compiler to insert code for the EOI. In other words, the alternative to typing in the assembler code in this chapter is to (1)add in-line assembler code to a C function, (2)compile the function with the /Fa option to obtain an assembler listing, (3)manually edit the listing file to modify the order of the PUSH and POP instructions, (4)manually add the EOI code, then (5)assemble and link the hand-tweaked code.

In other words, it just ain't worth it! Just type it in...it is not necessary that you understand it.[1] If entered and assembled exactly as shown here, you need never deal with it again.

The "MASM-compatible" *Microsoft Macro Assembler Version 6.0* was used for the examples in this book, but it also assembles on 5-year-old versions of the Microsoft MASM product. The exact assembler command line required is shown in the comments in Listing B.1.

---

[1]If you don't understand the raw assembler, you certainly won't understand the issues surrounding in-line assembler.

The Assembler Code

The assembler code itself consists of three modules. All three are required for assembly.

1. The assembler body, Listing B.1.
2. One or more main ISRs, Listing B.2.
3. The assembler macros, Listing B.3 contains macros for model-specific functions.

The Assembler Body: CPGSC.ASM

The assembler body in Listing B.1 contains the local stack for the main ISRs, the INCLUDE statements to read in the selected main ISR functions, and the I/O functions a_outport and a_inport. The latter can be replaced by code macros that substitute the Microsoft C functions _inp and _outp:

```
#define _a_outport(x,y) outp((unsigned)(x), (char)(y))
#define _a_inport(x) inp((unsigned)(x))
```

Although this approach works, it regrettably requires a cast for each argument, a procedure that generates unnecessary code (and warning messages) with 32-bit pointers. Again, it's far simpler just to type in the 15 lines of assembler.

The command line syntax for invoking the assembler appears at the top of the file.

LARGE OR SMALL MEMORY MODEL?

The most annoying thing about the 80x86 is its segmented architecture, which produces several possible memory models: Tiny, Small, Large, and so forth. The C source can be recompiled for any model supported by the compiler, but the assembler code supports only the Small and Large models. The model desired is selected by passing in a constant on the assembler command line as shown at the top of Listing B.2.

HOW MANY SIOS?

Constant names for the SIOs you wish to support must be passed in on the assembler command line as shown at the top of Listing B.1.

Listing B.1. CPGSC.ASM: The assembler body.

```
INCLUDE CPGSC.MAC        ; contains model-dependent macros
;.................................................
;MASM COMMAND LINE:
;MASM CPGSC,, /Ml XXXX YYYY;
;Where XXXX is
```

```
;       For LARGE Model: /DLARGEMODEL
;       For SMALL Model: /DSMALLMODEL
;Where YYYY is
;       For 1 SIO, /DCOM1SIO
;       For 2 SIOs /DCOM1SIO  /DCOM2SIO
;       For 3 SIOs /DCOM1SIO  /DCOM2SIO   /DCOM3SIO
;       For 4 SIOs /DCOM1SIO  /DCOM2SIO   /DCOM3SIO   /DCOM4SIO
;....................................................
;Global/external functions in this file:        ;
; one or more of the comXisr's will be public also  ;
PUBLIC      __a_inport, __a_outport                 ;
externfunct _s_iadmin           ;macro              ;
;..................................................;
CODESEG                         ; macro declaring code segment
DATAGROUP                       ; macro declaring DGROUP


STACKSIZ   EQU 128
           ;; new stack and storage for SS/SP during interrupt
           DB   STACKSIZ-2 dup (?)       ; stack size
newstack   DW   0
oldss      DW   0
oldsp      DW   0
ASSUME DS:NOTHING, ES:NOTHING, SS:NOTHING
;;..............................................................;
; FUNCTION NAME:  __a_com1isr, __a_com2isr, __a_com3isr, __a_com4isr  ;
;      LIBRARY:  PCDOS.LIB                                    ;
;  DESCRIPTION:  Main ISR's for devices 0-3 (COM1-4).        ;
;     COMMENTS:  All four handlers share the same stack--this is fine.;
;..............................................................;
IFDEF COM1SIO     ;                                          ;
INCLUDE COM1ISR.ASM;                                         ;
ENDIF             ;                                          ;
;.................;                                          ;
IFDEF COM2SIO     ;                                          ;
INCLUDE COM2ISR.ASM;                                         ;
ENDIF             ;                                          ;
;.................;                                          ;
IFDEF COM3SIO     ;                                          ;
INCLUDE COM3ISR.ASM;                                         ;
ENDIF             ;                                          ;
;.................;                                          ;
IFDEF COM4SIO     ;                                          ;
INCLUDE COM4ISR.ASM;                                         ;
ENDIF             ;                                          ;
;.................;                                          ;
;;..............................................................;
;....................................................;
; FUNCTION NAME:  __a_outport                       ;
;      LIBRARY: ASM.LIB                              ;
;  DESCRIPTION: Port output routine for the IBM PC.  ;
;      RETURNS: void                                 ;
; SYNTAX FROM C: __a_outport(BYTE * port, FAST data) ;
;....................................................;
```

continues

Listing B.1. continued

```
procdef __a_outport
        push bp
        mov  bp,sp
        mov  dx, [bp + ARG1]      ; low order byte of pointer
        LOAD_DATA                 ; macro to get data off stack
        out  dx, al               ; null out high byte
        pop  bp
        ret
__a_outport ENDP
;.....................................................;
; FUNCTION NAME:  __a_inport                          ;
;       LIBRARY:  ASM.LIB                              ;
;   DESCRIPTION:  Port input routine for the IBM PC.  ;
;       RETURNS:  FAST                                 ;
; SYNTAX FROM C:  c = __a_inport(BYTE *port)          ;
;.....................................................;
procdef __a_inport
        push bp
        mov  bp,sp
        mov  dx, [bp + ARG1]      ; low order byte of pointer
        in   al, dx               ; data returned in ax (al)
        and  ax, 00FFh            ; reset hi bitso can be used as an int
        pop  bp
        ret
__a_inport ENDP
endpseg          ;macro
END
```

Main ISR: COM1ISR.ASM

Listing B.2 shows one of the main ISRs previously discussed in Listing 19.5, but this time with all its assembler directives in place. As indicated in Listing B.2, *for each serial port you wish to support there must be a corresponding COMxISR.ASM file.* The four files are exact duplicates except as shown in the following table:

Table B.1. How to reproduce _a_com1isr for other serial ports.

File Name	ISR Name	SIO Address
COM1SIO.ASM	a_com1isr	COM1sio
COM2SIO.ASM	a_com2isr	COM2sio
COM3SIO.ASM	a_com3isr	COM3sio
COM4SIO.ASM	a_com4isr	COM4sio

Listing B.2. COM1ISR: The Main Interrupt Sub-Routine (ISR). (Four are needed.)

```
externdata _COM1sio        ;macro
PUBLIC  __a_com1isr
procdef __a_com1isr
        push  ax                   ; this on system's stack
        mov   oldss, ss            ; save SS
        mov   oldsp, sp            ; save SP
        push  cs                   ; set SS:SP ...
        pop   ss                   ; ...to address ...
        mov   sp, OFFSET newstack  ; ... our local stack
              ;; -- remaining stack operations use local stack --
        push  bp
        push  bx
        push  cx
        push  dx
        push  si
        push  di
        push  es
        push  ds
        mov   ax, SEG DGROUP:_COM1sio    ; address C's data
        mov   ds, ax
        PUSH_SEG                         ; macro to push seg address on stack
        mov   ax, OFFSET DGROUP:_COM1sio ; pass the address of COM1sio  on stack
        push  ax
        call  _s_iadmin            ; call C interrupt administrator
        add   sp, NUMARGS          ; remove siop argument from stack
        pop   ds                   ; restore registers from local stack
        pop   es
        pop   di
        pop   si
        pop   dx
        pop   cx
        pop   bx
        pop   bp
        mov   ss, oldss            ; restore the caller's stack (SS:SP)
        mov   sp, oldsp
        mov   al, 20H              ; bid adieu to the 8259 PIC
        out   20H, al
        pop   ax
        iret                       ; allons!
__a_com1isr ENDP
```

Macros: CPGSC.MAC

This file contains simple macros for model-dependent assembler directives. For aesthetic reasons, it also contains as much as possible of the hocus-pocus needed to accommodate the 80x86's segmented linker. Only Small and Large models are supported.

Listing B.3. CPGSC.MAC: Memory-model independent macros.

```
;-----------------------------------
;Macro for BP-relative stack indexing
;-----------------------------------
    IFDEF SMALLMODEL
ARG1        EQU 4                    ; offset of first stack argument
ARG2        EQU 6                    ;         2nd
ARG3        EQU 8                    ;         3rd
NUMARGS     EQU 2
    ENDIF   ;SMALLMODEL
    IFDEF LARGEMODEL
ARG1        EQU 6
ARG2        EQU 8
ARG3        EQU 10
NUMARGS     EQU 4
    ENDIF   ;LARGEMODEL
;-----------------------------------------
;Declaration of DGROUP (not model-dependent)
;-----------------------------------------
DATAGROUP MACRO
   CONST    SEGMENT  WORD PUBLIC 'CONST'
   CONST    ENDS
   _BSS     SEGMENT  WORD PUBLIC 'BSS'
   _BSS     ENDS
   _DATA    SEGMENT  WORD PUBLIC 'DATA'
   _DATA ENDS
   DGROUP   GROUP    CONST, _BSS,  _DATA
ENDM


;------------------------------
;Macro to declare code segment
;------------------------------
CODESEG  MACRO
    IFDEF SMALLMODEL
_TEXT           SEGMENT  BYTE PUBLIC 'CODE'        ; CSEG macro
ASSUME CS: _TEXT
    ENDIF
    IFDEF LARGEMODEL
CPGSC_TEXT          SEGMENT  BYTE PUBLIC 'CODE'        ; CSEG macro
ASSUME CS: CPGSC_TEXT
    ENDIF
    ENDM
;------------------
;Procedural Macros
;------------------
procdef   MACRO procname
    IFDEF SMALLMODEL
procname PROC NEAR
    ENDIF
    IFDEF LARGEMODEL
procname PROC FAR
    ENDIF
    ENDM
;----------
```

```
endpseg  MACRO
    IFDEF SMALLMODEL
_TEXT ENDS
    ENDIF
    IFDEF LARGEMODEL
CPGSC_TEXT ENDS
    ENDIF
    ENDM
;----------
externfunct MACRO functname
    IFDEF SMALLMODEL
EXTRN functname:NEAR
    ENDIF
    IFDEF LARGEMODEL
EXTRN functname:FAR
    ENDIF
    ENDM
;----------
externdata MACRO dataname
    IFDEF SMALLMODEL
EXTRN dataname:WORD
    ENDIF
    IFDEF LARGEMODEL
EXTRN dataname: DWORD
    ENDIF
    ENDM
;------------------------------------------
;Macro for getting second argument off stack
;------------------------------------------
LOAD_DATA MACRO
    IFDEF SMALLMODEL
mov ax, [bp + ARG2]
    ENDIF
    IFDEF LARGEMODEL
mov ax, [bp + ARG3]
    ENDIF
    ENDM
;----------
PUSH_SEG  MACRO
    IFDEF SMALLMODEL
;                       null in small model
    ENDIF
    IFDEF LARGEMODEL
push ax
    ENDIF
    ENDM
```

IBMPC.C

All machine (level-0) dependencies for the SIO are encapusulated in the file IBMPC.C. All the C code in IBMPC.C is model-independent—just recompile for the desired memory model. The following reside in IBMPC.C:

Table C.1. Code and data residing in IBMPC.C.

Includes	Functions	Code Macros	Data
stdio.h (C)	__delay	__peekw	__siolist (array)
conio.h (C)	__sysintron	__sys_disable	__sys_ilist (array)
siodef.h	__sysintroff	__sys_enable	__maxsios (unsigned)
ascii.h	__isport		
uart.h	__s_waitch		
sioctl.h			
ibmpc.h			
buos.h			
modem.h			

Listing C.1 shows the conditional inclusions in IBMPC.C; these appear at the top of the file after the defines and before any of the code or data listed in Table C.1.

Listing C.1. IBMPC: Conditional includes.

```
#define COM1SIO      /* These must either be defined here or    */
#define COM2SIO      /* passed in on the compiler command line. */
#define COM3SIO      /* If defined here they must be at the top */
#define COM4SIO      /* of this file, before all #includes      */


         #ifdef COM1SIO
#include "COM1SIO.C"
         #endif
         #ifdef COM2SIO
#include "COM2SIO.C"
         #endif
         #ifdef COM3SIO
#include "COM3SIO.C"
         #endif
         #ifdef COM4SIO
#include "COM4SIO.C"
         #endif
```

HOW MANY SIOS?

The number of SIOs present depends entirely upon the number of #defines at the top of IBMPC.C (Listing C.1), which conditionally includes one or more files containing the initialized SIO structures. Recall that the __siolist and __sys_ilist arrays (Listings 16.5 and 19.6) are used by s_open and s_close to ascertain which SIOs are present and their capabilities. The two arrays are shown again in Listing C.2, but with their conditional code.

Listing C.2. IMBPC.C: Conditional inclusions for system arrays.

```
/* STRUCT NAME:  __siolist */

struct SIOLIST __siolist[MAX_PORTS] =
    {
                    #ifdef COM1SIO
        { &COM1sio , FALSE, TRUE },
                    #else
        { NIL, FALSE, FALSE },
                    #endif
                    #ifdef COM2SIO
        { &COM2sio , FALSE, TRUE },
                    #else
        { NIL, FALSE, FALSE},
                    #endif
                    #ifdef COM3SIO
```

```
            { &COM3sio , FALSE, TRUE },
                        #else
            { NIL, FALSE, FALSE },
                        #endif
                        #ifdef COM4SIO
            { &COM4sio , FALSE, TRUE}
                        #else
            { NIL, FALSE, FALSE,}
                        #endif
    };

/* STRUCT NAME:  __sys_ilist */

struct SYS_ILIST __sys_ilist[MAX_PORTS] =
    {
                        #ifdef COM1SIO
      _ I_COM1, IMR_IRQ4, _a_com1isr, SUPPLIED, SUPPLIED,SUPPLIED },
                        #else
            { 0, 0, NIL, 0, 0, 0},
                        #endif
                        #ifdef COM2SIO
            {  I_COM2, IMR_IRQ3, _a_com2isr, SUPPLIED, SUPPLIED, SUPPLIED },
                        #else
            { 0, 0, NIL, 0, 0, 0},
                        #endif

            {  I_COM3, IMR_IRQ4, _a_com3isr, SUPPLIED, SUPPLIED, SUPPLIED },
                        #else
            { 0, 0, NIL, 0, 0, 0},
                        #endif
                        #ifdef COM4SIO
            {  I_COM4, IMR_IRQ3, _a_com4isr, SUPPLIED, SUPPLIED, SUPPLIED },
                        #else
            { 0, 0, NIL, 0, 0, 0},
                        #endif
    };
```

SIO Inititalization: COM1SIO.C

It is illuminating to see an entire SIO initialized in one place. Listing C.3 shows a complete listing of COM1SIO.C, one of the files included in the body of IBMPC.C. The objects need not be in any particular order save for the SIO structure itself, which must appear last to avoid forward references.

For each serial port you wish to support there must be a corresponding COMxSIO.ASM file. The four files are exact duplicates except as shown in Table C.2. The "Object Suffix" mentioned in the table refers to the naming conventions used for the structures and arrays in the SIO. For example, the name of the baud rate structure for COM1 is baudA, for COM2 is baudB, and so on.

Table C.2. Naming conventions for SIOs.

SIO File Name	SIO Name	Object Suffix
COM1SIO.C	COM1sio	A
COM2SIO.C	COM2sio	B
COM3SIO.C	COM3sio	C
COM4SIO.C	COM4sio	D

Listing C.3. COM1SIO.C: Initialization of an SIO. (Four are needed.)

```
/*** SERIAL PORT A    (COM1) ***/

/*
OBJECT NAME:  baselineA
 DEFINED IN:  MODEM.H
DESCRIPTION:  SIO control structure for baseline modem.
*/
struct modem baselineA =
    {
    0,                              /*0  Interbyte delay              */
    OFF,                            /*1  Console echo off             */
    "",                             /*2  Build all commands here      */
    _0_SEC_3,                       /*3  Tsecs to wait after a modem cmd */
    2,                              /*4  Number of times to try a command */
    _1_SEC_0 + _0_SEC_5,            /*5  Escape guard time (Tsecs)    */
    '|',                            /*6  (S2) online escape char      */
    {BAUD57K6, BAUD38K4, BAUD14K4,  /*7  Baud rates to try reset      */
    BAUD9600, BAUD2400,BAUD1200,-1},
    SUPPLIED,                       /*8  Baud rate at which reset occurred */
    VIRGIN,                         /*9  Our own code for modem type  */
    SUPPLIED,                       /*10 Maximum baud rate of modem    */
    0,                              /*11 (S0) 0 = "Don't answer"       */
    2,                              /*12 (S6)dialtone wait  (secs)     */
    30,                             /*13 (S7) timeout wait for connect (secs)*/
    1,                              /*14 speaker mode arg: on till connect */
    4,                              /*15 Result codes: highest level   */
    1,                              /*16 Speaker volume (1, 2, or 3)   */
    1,                              /*17 Enable DCD                    */
    2,                              /*18 Enable DTR                    */
    BAUD_FOUND,                     /*19 How to leave baud rate after reset */
    FALSE,                          /*20 Modem sucessfully configured  */
    SUPPLIED,                       /*21 DTE baud rate (parsed from CONNECT) */
    SUPPLIED,                       /*22 Carrier rate (parsed from CARRIER) */
    TRUE,                           /*23 Yes, link protocol wanted     */
    SUPPLIED,                       /*24 Link protocol supported?      */
    "",                             /*25 Name of link protocol         */
    TRUE,                           /*26 Yes, compression wanted       */
    SUPPLIED,                       /*27 Compression protocol supported? */
    "",                             /*28 Name of compression protocol  */
    TRUE,                           /*29 Switch baud rate to incoming call */
    "",                             /*30 Build numeric dial string here */
```

```
        "",                     /*31 Valid chars in dial string     */
        'T',                    /*32 Tone dialing                   */
        ' ',                    /*33 No dial suffix                 */
        "Z",                    /*34 Unconfiguration string         */
        };

/*
OBJECT NAME:  baudA
 DEFINED IN:  SIODEF.H
DESCRIPTION:  SIO control structure for baud rate.
*/
struct vbaud_ baudA =
    {
    VBAUDLO,                        /* Virtual register for lo byte    */
    VBAUDHI,                        /* Virtual register for hi byte    */
    0,                              /* Offset of UART lsb baud reg     */
    1,                              /* Offset of UART msb baud reg     */
    {
{BH_50,    BL_50   }, {BH_75,    BL_75   }, {BH_110,   BL_110  },
{BH_134,   BL_134  }, {BH_150,   BL_150  }, {BH_300,   BL_300  },
{BH_600,   BL_600  }, {BH_1200,  BL_1200 }, {BH_1800,  BL_1800 },
{BH_2000,  BL_2000 }, {BH_2400,  BL_2400 }, {BH_3600,  BL_3600 },
{BH_4800,  BL_4800 }, {BH_7200,  BL_7200 }, {BH_9600,  BL_9600 },
{BH_14K4,  BL_14K4 }, {BH_19K2,  BL_19K2 }, {BH_28K8,  BL_28K8 },
{BH_38K4,  BL_38K4 }, {BH_57K6,  BL_57K6 },  {BH_115K2, BL_115K2 },
    },
    SUPPLIED,                       /* Rank of current divisor in table */
    BAUD2400                        /* Start at 1200 baud               */
    };

/*
OBJECT NAME:  ictlA
      LEVEL:  0
 DEFINED IN:  SIODEF.H
DESCRIPTION:  Declares and initializes an input control structure.
*/
struct sictl_  ictlA=
    {
    OFF,                            /* 0  Timeout-on-input flag          */
    _0_SEC_05,                      /* 1  Default timeout in Tsecs       */
    OFF,                            /* 2  "raw" input flag               */
    OFF,                            /* 3  Echo input back to sender flag */
    ON,                             /* 4  Reset high bit flag            */
    NOXLAT,                         /* 5  End-of-line mode               */
    OFF,                            /* 6  Console output flag            */
    UP_LOW,                         /* 7  Upper/lower case conversion mode */
    ON,                             /* 10 Remove unwanted controls flag  */
{NUL,BEL,BS,HT,LF,CR,FF,DC3,DC1,DOS_EOF}, /* 11 permitted controls      */
    10,                             /* 12 Number of controls in above list */
    OFF,                            /* 13 Byte translation/removal mode  */
    {{'a','x'},{'b', -1 }},         /* 14 Translation/removal array      */
    2,                              /* 15 Number of entries in above array */
    SUPPLIED,                       /* 16 'last character' buffer        */
    SUPPLIED,                       /* 17 Eol readback flag              */
```

continues

Listing C.3. continued

```
    SUPPLIED                          /* 18 Pending readback character    */
    };

/*
OBJECT NAME:   struct soctl_ octlA
 DEFINED IN:   SIODEF.H
DESCRIPTION:   Declares and initializes an output control structure.
*/
struct soctl_ octlA=
    {
    OFF,                              /*0  "Raw" output flag              */
    NOXLAT,                           /*1  End -of-line mode              */
    OFF,                              /*2  Con sole output flag           */
    OFF,                              /*3  Echowait flag                  */
    _1_SEC_0 * 5,                     /*4  Echo-wait before timeout in Tsecs */
    UP_LOW,                           /*5  Upper/lower case conversion mode */
    ON,                               /*9  Strip high bits flag           */
    ON,                               /*10 Remove unwanted controls flag  */
{NUL,BEL,BS,HT,LF,CR,FF,DC3,DC1,DOS_EOF},  /*11 permitted controls        */
    10,                               /*12 Number of controls in above list */
    OFF,                              /*13 Translation/removal flag       */
    {0},                              /*14 Translation/removal list       */
    0,                                /*15 No entries in above array      */
    OFF,                              /*16 No interbyte delay flag        */
    _0_SEC_05,                        /*17 Delay in Tsecs                 */
    OFF,                              /*18 end-of-line pause flag         */
    LF,                               /*19 Character to pause after       */
    _0_SEC_4,                         /*20 Pause in Tsecs                 */
    ESC,                              /*21 Keyboard abort character       */
    SUPPLIED,                         /*22 'last character' buffer        */
    SUPPLIED                          /*23 Flag to flush last character   */
    };


/*
OBJECT NAME:   v_regA
DECLARED IN:   IBMPC.C
DESCRIPTION:   Used for virtual UART registers
*/
REG v_regA[V_REG_SIZE][2]=
    {
/*  VIR   USR  */
    { 0,    0 },                      /* 0 = baud low byte                */
    { 0,    0 },                      /* 1 = baud high byte               */
    { 0,    0 },                      /* 2 = interrupt enable             */
    { 0,    0 },                      /* 3 = FIFO enable                  */
    { 0,    0 },                      /* 4 = data format                  */
    { 0,    0 },                      /* 5 = RS232 output control         */
    };
```

```
/*
OBJECT NAME:  pin4A
 DEFINED IN:  SIODEF.H
DESCRIPTION:  Control stucture for RS232 RTS output.
*/
struct vout232_ pin4A =
     {
     RTSMASK,                         /* AND mask to reset RTS bit         */
     VOUT232,                         /* Virtual register                  */
     OUT232,                          /* Offset of UART RTS register        */
     SUPPLIED,                        /* Code for current value (ON/OFF)    */
     OFF,                             /* Initialized value                 */
     };

/*
OBJECT NAME:  pin20A
 DEFINED IN:  SIODEF.H
DECLARED IN:  IBMPC.C
DESCRIPTION:  Control stucture for RS232 DTR output.
*/
struct vout232_ pin20A =
     {
     DTRMASK,                         /* AND mask to reset DTR bit         */
     VOUT232,                         /* Virtual register                  */
     OUT232,                          /* Offset of DTR register in UART     */
     SUPPLIED,                        /* Code for current value (ON/OFF)    */
     OFF,                             /* Initialized value                 */
     };

/*
OBJECT NAME:  gp1outA
 DEFINED IN:  SIODEF.H
DESCRIPTION:  Control stucture for RS232 GPO1 output.
*/
struct vout232_ gp1outA =
     {
     GPO1MASK,                        /* AND mask to reset GPOUT1 bit       */
     VOUT232,                         /* Virtual register                  */
     OUT232,                          /* Offset of GPO1 register in UART    */
     SUPPLIED,                        /* Code for current value (ON/OFF)    */
     OFF,                             /* Initialized value                 */
     };

/*
OBJECT NAME:  gp2outA
 DEFINED IN:  SIODEF.H
DESCRIPTION:  Control stucture for RS232 GPO2 output.
*/
struct vout232_ gp2outA =
     {
     GPO2MASK,                        /* AND mask to reset GPO2 bit         */
     VOUT232,                         /* Virtual register                  */
     OUT232,                          /* Offset of GPO2 register in UART    */
     SUPPLIED,                        /* Code for current value (ON/OFF)    */
```

continues

Listing C.3. continued

```
    OFF,                                /* Initialized value           */
    };

/*
OBJECT NAME:  break
 DEFINED IN:  SIODEF.H
DESCRIPTION:  Control stucture for BREAK output.
*/
struct vout232_ break =
    {
    BRK_MASK,                           /* AND mask to reset BREAK bit  */
    VFMT,                               /* Virtual register             */
    FMT,                                /* Offset of GPO1 register in UART */
    SUPPLIED,                           /* Code for current value (ON/OFF) */
    OFF,                                /* Initialized value           */
    };

/*
OBJECT NAME:  pin6A
 DEFINED IN:  SIODEF.H
DESCRIPTION:  Control structure for RS232 DSR input.
*/
struct vin232_ pin6A =
    {
    STAT_232,                           /* Offset of DSR register in UART */
    DSRMASK,                            /* AND mask for isolating DSR bits */
    SUPPLIED,                           /* Current value of this input  */
    };

/*
OBJECT NAME:  pin5A
 DEFINED IN:  SIODEF.H
DESCRIPTION:  Control structure for RS232 CTS input.
*/
struct vin232_ pin5A =
    {
    STAT_232,                           /* Offset of CTS register in UART */
    CTSMASK,                            /* AND mask for isolating CTS bits */
    SUPPLIED,                           /* Current value of this input  */
    };

/*
OBJECT NAME:  pin8A
 DEFINED IN:  SIODEF.H
DESCRIPTION:  Control structure for RS232 DCD input.
*/
struct vin232_ pin8A =
    {
    STAT_232,                           /* Offset of DCD register in UART */
    DCDMASK,                            /* AND mask for isolating DCD bits */
    SUPPLIED,                           /* Current value of this input  */
    };
```

```
/*
OBJECT NAME:  pin22A
 DEFINED IN:  SIODEF.H
DESCRIPTION:  Control structure for RS232 RI input.
*/
struct vin232_ pin22A =
     {
     STAT_232,                        /* Offset of RI register in UART    */
     RIMASK,                          /* AND mask for isolating RI bits    */
     SUPPLIED,                        /* Current value of this input       */
     };


/*
OBJECT NAME:  parityA
 DEFINED IN:  SIODEF.H
DESCRIPTION:  Control stucture for parity.
*/
struct vregbits_ parityA =
     {
     PARITYMASK,                 /* AND mask to isolate parity bits        */
     { NONE_MASK, ODD_MASK, EVEN_MASK, MARK_MASK, SPACE_MASK },  /* OR masks */
     VFMT,                       /* Virtual register--rank in v_rega       */
     FMT,                        /* Offset of physical register from uart_base */
     SUPPLIED,                   /* Rank in mask table of current setting  */
     NONE,                       /* Rank to use in initialization          */
     NIL                         /* No more structures for parity          */
     };


/*
OBJECT NAME:  stopsA
 DEFINED IN:  SIODEF.H
DESCRIPTION:  Control stucture for stop bits.
*/
struct vregbits_ stopsA =              /* for 16x50 UART */
       {
       STOPMASK,               /* AND mask to isolate stop-bit bits          */
       { ONE_MASK, ONE_5_MASK, TWO_MASK, -1, -1 },
       VFMT,                   /* virtual register--rank in v_rega           */
       FMT,                    /* offset of physical register from uart_base */
       SUPPLIED,               /* rank in mask table of current setting      */
       STOP1,                  /* rank to use in initialization              */
       NIL                     /* no more structures for stop bits           */
       };


/*
OBJECT NAME:  dlenA
 DEFINED IN:  SIODEF.H
DESCRIPTION:  Control stucture for data length.
*/
struct vregbits_ dlenA =              /* for 16x50 UART */
     {
     DLMASK,                      /* AND mask to isolate data length bits     */
     { DL5_MASK, DL6_MASK, DL7_MASK, DL8_MASK, -1 },
     VFMT,                        /* virtual register--rank in v_rega         */
```

continues

Listing C.3. continued

```
        FMT,                           /* offset of physical register from uart_base */
        SUPPLIED,                      /* rank in mask table of current setting    */
        DL8,                           /* rank to use in initialization            */
        NIL                            /* no more structures for parity            */
        };

/*
    SIO NAME:   COM3sio
        FILE:   IBMPC.C
       LEVEL:   0
  DEFINED IN:   SIODEF.H
 DECLARED IN:   IBMPC.C
    COMMENTS:   The main SIO structure for COM 1 (device 0).
                Line numbers in comments are for reference only.
*/

SIO COM3sio  =
        {
        COM3,                          /*0  Base address of UART                   */
        DATA_IO,                       /*1  Offset of data port from base          */
        SER_STAT,                      /*2  Offset of status port from base        */
        RCV_MASK,                      /*3  RxRDY mask from UART.H                  */
        XMIT_MASK,                     /*4  Xmitter Holding Register Empty mask     */
        TX_EMPTY_MASK,                 /*5  Xmitter Shift Register Empty mask       */
        _a_inport,                     /*6  Pointer to RAM/port read routine        */
        _a_outport,                    /*7  Pointer to RAM/port read routine        */
        s_rcvstat,                     /*8  Pointer to receiver status              */
        s_rcv,                         /*9  Pointer to fetch routine                */
        s_xmitstat,                    /*10 Pointer to xmiter status                */
        s_xmit,                        /*11 Pointer to xmit routine                 */
        tx_write,                      /*12 Pointer to polled block xmit routine    */
        v_regC,                        /*13 Pointer to virtual register array       */
        V_REG_SIZE,                    /*14 Number of rows in virtual array         */
        &parityC,                      /*15 Parity structure                        */
        &stopsC,                       /*16 Stop bit structure                      */
        &dlenC,                        /*17 Data length structure                   */
        &baudC,                        /*18 Baud rate structure                     */
        &pin4C,                        /*19 RS-232 RTS output                       */
        &pin20C,                       /*20 RS-232 DTR output                       */
        &gp1outC,                      /*21 RS-232 first user-defined output        */
        &gp2outC,                      /*22 RS-232 first user-defined output        */
        &breakbC,                      /*23 Break bit                               */
        &pin5C,                        /*24 RS-232 CTS input                        */
        &pin6C,                        /*25 RS-232 DSR input                        */
        &pin8C,                        /*26 RS-232 DCD input                        */
        &pin22C,                       /*27 RS-232 RI  input                        */
        NIL,                           /*28 NO 1st user-defined RS-232 input        */
        NIL,                           /*29 NO 2nd user-defined RS-232 input        */
        _vstat232,                     /*30 * to level one fetch function           */
        0,                             /*31 RS-232 status bits                      */
        0,                             /*32 RS-232 delta bits                       */
        NIL,                           /*33 NO transmitter-on structure             */
        NIL,                           /*34 NO receiver-on structure                */
```

```
    NIL,                          /*35 NO transmitter/RTS handshake       */
    NIL,                          /*36 NO receiver/DCD handshake          */
    NIL,                          /*37 NO clock factor                    */
    FLOW_ON,                      /*39 State of virtual xmit flow control */
    FLOW_ON,                      /*40 State of virtual rcv    "    "     */
    FLOW_ON,                      /*41 State of interrupt xmit "    "     */
    FLOW_ON,                      /*42 State of interrupt rcv  "    "     */
    flow_req_xoxo,                /*43 Pointer to flow-request routine    */
    xon,                          /*44 Pointer to flow-off routine        */
    xoff,                         /*45 Pointer to flow-on routine         */
    SUPPLIED,                     /*46 Device number supplied during open */
    &octlC,                       /*47 Pointer to output control structure*/
    &ictlC,                       /*48 Pointer input control structure    */
    {TRUE,TRUE,FALSE,FALSE,0,0,0,0},/*49 Interrupts wanted/on bitfield     */
    {                             /*50 UART Interrupt vectors (s_iadmin)  */
        isr_stat232_dummy,        /*--   index 0 = RS232 input status     */
        isr_tx_dummy,             /*--   index 1 = transmit hold reg empty*/
        isr_rcv_dummy,            /*--   index 2 = received data ready     */
        isr_serr_dummy,           /*--   index 3 = serialization error     */
        isr_rcv_dummy,            /*--   index 4 = unused                  */
        isr_rcv_dummy,            /*--   index 5 = unused                  */
        isr_rcv_dummy             /*--   index 6 = receiver FIFO timeout   */
    },
    NIL,                          /*51 Pointer to old rs232 isr           */
    NIL,                          /*52 Pointer to old ser  error isr      */
    NIL,                          /*53 Pointer to old rcv interrupt handler */
    NIL,                          /*54 Pointer to old xmit interrupt handler*/
    0,                            /*55 Serialization union                */
    RCV_BUFSIZ,                   /*56 Size of receive interrupt buffer   */
    SUPPLIED,                     /*57 Size of UART's Receive FIFO        */
    SUPPLIED,                     /*58 Receive FIFO Trigger Level         */
    NIL,                          /*59 Pointer to receive buffer          */
    NIL,                          /*60 Pointer to end of  "        "      */
    NIL,                          /*61 Where in buff to put next byte     */
    NIL,                          /*62 Where in buff to fetch next byte   */
    SUPPLIED,                     /*63 Size of UART's Transmit FIFO       */
    SUPPLIED,                     /*64 Transmit FIFO Trigger Level        */
    SUPPLIED,                     /*65 Number of transmit buffers         */
    SUPPLIED,                     /*66 Transmit buffer size               */
    NIL,                          /*67 Pointer to transmit interrupt queue*/
    NIL,                          /*68 Pointer to tx queue headp          */
    NIL,                          /*69 Pointer to tx queue tailp          */
    NIL,                          /*70 Pointer to last element in tx queue*/
    FALSE,                        /*71 Transmit queue empty               */
    &baselineC,                   /*72 Modem control structure            */
    };
```

Include Files

ASCII.H

```
#ifndef  _ASCII_
#define  _ASCII_

#define  CTRL_A      0x01
#define  SOH         0x01
#define  CTRL_B      0x02
#define  STX         0x02
#define  CTRL_C      0x03
#define  ETX         0x03
#define  CTRL_D      0x04
#define  EOT         0x04
#define  CTRL_E      0x05
#define  ENQ         0x05
#define  CTRL_F      0x06
#define  ACK         0x06
#define  CTRL_G      0x07
#define  BEL         0x07
#define  CTRL_H      0x08
#define  BS          0x08
#define  CTRL_I      0x09
#define  TAB         0x09
#define  HT          0x09
#define  CTRL_J      0x0A
#define  LF          0x0A
#define  CTRL_K      0x0B
#define  CTRL_L      0x0C
#define  FF          0x0C
#define  CTRL_M      0x0D
#define  CR          0x0D
#define  CTRL_N      0x0E
#define  CTRL_O      0x1F
#define  CTRL_P      0x10
#define  CTRL_Q      0x11
```

continues

```
#define   DC1         0x11
#define   CTRL_R      0x12
#define   CTRL_S      0x13
#define   DC3         0x13
#define   CTRL_T      0x14
#define   NAK         0x15
#define   CTRL_U      0x15
#define   CTRL_V      0x16
#define   CTRL_W      0x17
#define   CAN         0x18
#define   CTRL_X      0x18
#define   CTRL_Y      0x19
#define   CTRL_Z      0x1A
#define   CTRL_LBRAK  0x1B
#define   ESC         0x1B
#define   CTRL_BAKSL  0x1C
#define   CTRL_RBRAK  0x1D
#define   CTRL_CTRL   0x1E
#define   CTRL__      0x1F
#define   SP          0x20
#define   DEL         0x7f

#endif   /* _ASCII_ */
```

BUOS.H

```
#ifndef  _BUOS_
#define  _BUOS_

/*** FUNCTION PROTOTYPES ***/
int    s_fgetc(SIO*);
int    s_fputc(SIO*, FAST);
BYTE   s_getc(SIO *);
int    s_iflush(SIO *);
int    s_inchar(SIO *);
int    s_ircv(SIO *);
int    s_ircvstat(SIO *);
void   s_putc(SIO *, int);
FAST   s_rcv(SIO *);
FAST   s_rcvstat(SIO *);
void   s_xmit(SIO *, FAST);
FAST   s_xmitstat(SIO *);
void   s_ixmit(SIO *, FAST);
FAST   s_ixmitstat(SIO *);
int    vset232(SIO*, struct vout232_ *, BOOL);
int    vsetbits(SIO* , struct vregbits_ *, RANK);
int    vsetbr(SIO*, struct vbaud_ *, RANK );
short  vstat232(SIO*, struct vin232_ *);
void   xon(SIO * );
void   xoff(SIO *);
USHORT flow_req_xoxo(SIO *, ... );
USHORT flow_req_rcts(SIO *siop, ...);
```

```
void    rtson(SIO *siop);
void    rtsoff(SIO *siop);

short   rs232_ion(SIO *);
short   rs232_ioff(SIO *);
short   serr_ion(SIO *);
short   serr_ioff(SIO *);
short   tx_ion(SIO *, short, short);
short   tx_ioff(SIO *, short);
short   rcv_ion(SIO *);
short   rcv_ioff(SIO *);

#endif   /*_BUOS_*/
```

CRC.H

```
#ifndef   _CRC_
#define   _CRC_

/*** FUNCTION PROTOTYPES ***/
USHORT   crchware(USHORT ,USHORT ,USHORT );
USHORT   crcrevhware(USHORT ,USHORT ,USHORT );
void     crcrevupdate(USHORT ,USHORT *,USHORT *);
void     crcupdate(USHORT, USHORT*, USHORT *);
USHORT *mk_crctbl(USHORT ,USHORT (*)(USHORT, USHORT, USHORT));
USHORT   polydiv(USHORT, USHORT, USHORT);


#define   CRCCCITT  0x1021       /* CCITT polynomial            */
#define   CCCITT_REV 0x8408      /* reverse CCITT polynomial    */
#define   CRC16     0x8005       /* CRC16 polynomial            */
#define   CRC16_REV 0xA001       /* reverse CRC16 polynomial 0x8005 */

/*#define  crcupdate(d,a,t)    *(a) = (*(a) << 8) ^ (t)[(*(a) >> 8) ^ (d)];
#define   crcupdate16(d,a,t) *(a)=((*(a)>>8) ^ (t)[(*(a) ^ (d)) &0x00ff])*/

#endif            /* _CRC_ */
```

IBMPC.H

```
#ifndef   _IBMPC_
#define   _IBMPC_

#include <dos.h>          /* for _enable/_disable */
#include <conio.h>


/* NOTICE:
*    One or more of the following must either be defined here or passed in
*    on the compiler's command line:
*       #define COM1SIO       (Com1)
*       #define COM2SIO       (Com2)
```

continues

```
*         #define COM3SIO        (Com3)
*         #define COM4SIO        (Com4)
*/

/* FUNCTION PROTOTYPES */
unsigned  __peekw(int, int);
#define   __peekw(o,s) (*((int far*) (((long)(s) << 16) ¦ (o)))) /* (offset,seg)
*/
#define   __sys_disable   _disable      /* Use Microsoft runtime */
#define   __sys_enable    _enable       /* Use Microsoft runtime */
void      __delay(unsigned);
void      __sysintroff(SIO *,RANK);
void      __sysintron(SIO *, RANK);
BOOL      __isport(RANK);
int       __s_waitch(SIO *, unsigned);

/* C prototypes for assembler functions */
void      _a_outport(BYTE*, FAST);
FAST      _a_inport(BYTE*);


#ifdef COM1SIO
void _interrupt far _a_com1isr(void);     /* Declaration of ISR    */
#endif

#ifdef COM2SIO
void _interrupt far _a_com2isr(void);
#endif

#ifdef COM3SIO
void _interrupt far _a_com3isr(void);
#endif

#ifdef COM4SIO
void _interrupt far _a_com4isr(void);
#endif

/**** MISCELLANEOUS MANIFEST CONSTANTS ****/
#define MAX_PORTS 4              /* Maximum ports Supported in the System */
#define TIMER_LO 0x46C           /* Location of timer                    */

/**** MANIFEST CONSTANTS FOR COM PORTS ****/
#define  COM1 (BYTE*) 0x3f8
#define  COM2 (BYTE*) 0x2f8
#define  COM3 (BYTE*) 0x3E8
#define  COM4 (BYTE*) 0x2E8

/**** INTERRUPTS USED WITH COM PORTS ****/
#define I_COM1    0x0C
#define I_COM2    0x0B
#define I_COM3    I_COM1
#define I_COM4    I_COM2

/**** Constants 8259 PIC ****/
#define IMR       0x21   /* Port addresss of the IMR   */
```

```
#define IMR_IRQ4  0xEF    /* Mask to reset bit 4 in IMR */
#define IMR_IRQ3  0xF7    /* Mask to reset bit 3 in IMR */


#endif   /* _IBMPC_*/
```

KEY.H

```
#ifndef  _KEY_
#define  _KEY_


#include <sio\siolocal.h>
#include <conio.h>

/*** FUNCTION PROTOTYPES ***/
FAST getkbch(void);
FAST inkey(void);

/*** CODE MACROS ***/
#define keystat kbhit          /* For Microsoft's run-time*/
#define getkey  getch          /* For Microsoft's run-time*/

#define NOT_READY -1
#define NO_KEY     0

#endif /* _KEY_     */
```

LEVEL0.H

```
#ifndef  _LEVEL0_
#define  _LEVEL0_

#include <sio\ibmpc.h>

#endif /* _LEVEL0_ */
```

MISC.H

```
#ifndef  _MISC_
#define  _MISC_

/**** FUNCTION PROTOTYPES ****/
BYTE *bigbuff(USHORT ,USHORT ,USHORT *);
void  putbin(USHORT);
FILE *rfopen(char *,char *);
FILE *wfopen(char *,char *);
int  str_atoi(char *);
void haktc(void);

#endif /* _MISC_ */
```

MODEM.H

```c
#ifndef  _MODEM_
#define  _MODEM_

/*** FUNCTION PROTOTYPES ***/
int   m_answer(SIO *);
void  m_cmd(SIO *, char *);
int   m_config(SIO *);
int   m_protoconfig(SIO *siop);
void  m_echo(SIO *, BOOL);
int   m_dial(SIO *,char *);
int   m_hup(SIO *);
int   m_ismessage(SIO*, char *);
void  m_parsemsg(SIO *, struct parse_info *, char *);
int   m_cmd_OK(SIO *,char *);
short m_cmd_str(SIO *, char *, char *, USHORT);
short m_getstr(SIO *, char *, short);
int   m_redial(SIO *);
int   m_reset(SIO *);
short m_unconfig(SIO *);
int   m_wait4dcd(SIO *);
short m_warndcd(SIO *, BOOL);
int   m_whoru(SIO *);
int   m_gocmd(SIO *, int);

/****** Modem "types" ******/
enum m_types{
                ID_UNKNOWN= 0,    /* Unable to identify modem    */
                ID_12,            /* Likely 1200 bps modem       */
                ID_12PLUS,        /* 1200 bps modem              */
                ID_24,            /* 2400 bps modem              */
                ID_96 ,           /* 9600 bps modem              */
                ID_14K4           /* 14,400 bps modem            */
                };

/****** Function Return Codes ******/
#define  M_SUCCEED     0          /* all modem functions return 0 if successful */
#define  M_FAIL        1          /* most return 1 if unsuccessful              */

/****** Constants for message validation ******/
#define MSG_INVALID        -1
#define MSG_NON_TERMINAL   -2


/****** Buffer Size Constants ******/
#define  MAX_MSG_LEN 30          /* max length of a modem message         */
#define  COMPRESSSIZE 20         /* max length of compression message     */
#define  LPSIZE      20          /* max length of protocol message        */

/****** Manifest Constants for Modem Functions ******/

enum results
{
```

```
    M_OK = 0,              /*0  Successful command                     */
    M_CONN,                /*1  Connect                                */
    M_RING,                /*2  Call incoming                          */
    M_NODCD,               /*3  No carrier detected                    */
    M_CMDERR,              /*4  Error in modem command                 */
    M_NOTONE,              /*5  No dial tone heard                     */
    M_BUSY,                /*6  Busy signal heard                      */
    M_NOANSW,              /*7  Silence not heard after @              */
    M_BADMSG,              /*8  Invalid modem response                 */
    M_NORING,              /*9  Looked for and didn't hear incoming'RING'  */
    M_ONLINE,              /*10 Can't dial into a high dcd             */
    M_NILNUM,              /*11 Blank dial string                      */
    M_USRCAN,              /*12 Call cancelled from keyboard           */
    M_NORESET,             /*13 Reset Failed                           */
    M_NOID,                /*14 ID function failed                     */
    M_CONFIG_MEM,          /*15 Configuration memeory alloc error      */
    M_CONFIG_NOK,          /*16 Modem didn't configure as requested    */
    M_DCD_HIGH,            /*17 DCD went high (not a message)          */
    M_PROTOCOL,            /*18 Protocol message detected during connect   */
    M_CARRIER,             /*19 Carrier message detected during connect    */
    M_COMPRESS,            /*20 Compression message detected during connect */
    };

/****** How to configure Baud Rate ******/

enum baudcnfg {  BAUD_MAX = 0, BAUD_FOUND};

struct modem
    {
    unsigned ibdelay;                   /*0  Interbyte delay                       */
    BOOL     cmdechoflag;               /*1  Modem commands to console             */
    char     cmdbuff[CMDBUFSIZ];        /*2  Build all commands here               */
    int      cmdt_out;                  /*3  Tsecs to wait after a modem cmd       */
    int      cmdretry;                  /*4  Number of times to try a command      */
    unsigned guardtime;                 /*5  Escape guard time                     */
    short    escape_arg;                /*6  (S2)on-line to command mode escape    */
    int      baudtry[7];                /*7  Baud rates to try reset               */
    unsigned max_DTE_baud;              /*8  Maximum baud rate of modem            */
    short    modtype;                   /*9  Our code for modem                    */
    short    max_carrier_speed;         /*10 Maximum baud rate of modem            */
    short    autoans_arg;               /*11 (S0)# of rings before autoanswer      */
    short    dtwait_arg;                /*12 (S6)dialtone wait (secs)              */
    short    dcdwait_arg;               /*13 (S7)# secs to wait for carrier        */
    short    speaker_arg;               /*14 Speaker mode                          */
    short    xcmd_arg;                  /*15 Result code set                       */
    short    speakvol_arg;              /*16 Speaker volume (0,  1, or 2)          */
    short    firmdcd_arg;               /*17 DCD configuration                     */
    short    firmdtr_arg;               /*18 DTR configuration                     */
    short    baudmode;                  /*19 Baud rate initialization mode         */
    BOOL     configokflag;              /*20 Modem successfully configured         */
    short    connect_XXXX_code;         /*21 Code for baud rate of local link      */
    short    carrier_baud_code;         /*22 Code for baud rate of carrier         */
    BOOL     linkprot_wanted;           /*23 Want link protocol if available?      */
    BOOL     linkprot_supported;        /*24 Is a link protocol supported?         */
```

continues

```
    char      linkname [LPSIZE];       /*25 ID from the CONNECT message        */
    BOOL      compress_wanted;         /*26 Want compression if available?     */
    BOOL      compress_supported;      /*27 Is compression supported? (at init) */
    char      compressname[COMPRESSSIZE];
                                       /*28 ID from COMPRESSION message        */
    BOOL      autobrflag;              /*29 Switch baud rate to incoming call  */
    char      dialbuff[CMDBUFSIZ];     /*30 Build numeric dial string here     */
    char      okalpha[18];             /*31 Alpha chars ok in dial string      */
    char      dialmode;                /*32 (T)one or (P)ulse dialling         */
    char      enddial;                 /*33 Dial suffix—e.g.,  ';' or 'R'      */
    char      unconfig[CMDBUFSIZ];     /*34 String to send to smodem at exit   */
};


/*
STRUCT NAME:  parse_info
HEADER FILE:  MODEM.H
DESCRIPTION:  Control structure used by modem message parser.
   COMMENTS:
*/
struct parse_info
    {
    char *message;                     /* pointer to the modem response */
    BOOL terminal;                     /* is it "terminal"              */
    short id;                          /* id code for this message      */
    void (*fn)(SIO *, struct parse_info *, char *);
                                       /* function to process reply     */

    };
#endif     /*_MODEM_ */
```

SIOCTL.H

```
#ifndef _SIOCTL_
#define _SIOCTL_

/* CODE MACROS FOR CALLING FLOW CONTROL POINTERS IN SIO */
#define flowon(p)       (*(p)->flowon)((p))
#define flowoff(p)      (*(p)->flowoff)((p))
#define getflow_req(p)  (*(p)->getflow_req)((p))


/* TYPES OF FLOW CONTROL */

enum flowtypes{ NO_FLOW = 0, XON_XOFF, RTS_CTS };

#define XON        0x11     /* DC1                                      */
#define XOFF       0x13     /* DC3                                      */

/* VALUES RETURNED BY GET-FLOW-REQUEST FUNCTION */
#define FLOW_OFF     0
#define FLOW_NONE    1
#define FLOW_ON      0xFFFF    /* this must be 0xFFFF                   */

#define FLOW HEADROOM 10
#define FLOW TAILROOM FLOW HEADROOM
```

```
#define FLOW_HEADROOM 50

#define IO_STKSIZ  10          /* Size of I/O push/pop stack      */
int    s_ocntrl(SIO *,short, short, USHORT);
int    s_icntrl(SIO *, short, short,...);
#define NOT_READY -1
#define IGNORE    -2
#define NOECHO     1

/* Constants for formatted output */
enum ioctl
    {
    NOXLAT = 0,          /* remove nothing—i.e., "raw"         */
    LF2CR,               /* translate LF to CR                 */
    CR2LF,               /* translate CR to LF                 */
    EOL2SPACE,           /* rconvert CR&LF to spaces           */
    REMOVEEOL,           /* remove all CR and LF               */
    LF2CRLF,             /* convert LF to CRLF                 */
    CR2CRLF,             /* convert CR to CRLF                 */
    CRLF2LF,             /* convert CRLF to LF                 */
    CRLF2CR,             /* convert CRLF to CR                 */
    };

             /* UPPER/LOWER CASE MODES */
#define  UP_LOW   0    /* upper and lower—i.e., "raw",        */
#define  UPPER    1    /* convert to upper                    */
#define  LOWER    2    /* convert to lower                    */

             /* "function" codes */

/* "FUNCTION" ARGUMENTS FOR USE WITH I/O CONTROL FUNCTIONS  */
#define   SET       0
#define   GET       1

/* CONTROL ARGUMENTS FOR USE WITH I/O CONTROL FUNCTIONS     */

             /** FLAGS **/
enum ctlargs
    {
    RAWFLAG = 0,         /*  Minimum processing               */
    T_OUTFLAG,           /*  Used for formatted input only     */
    EKOBAKFLAG,          /*  Used for formatted input only     */
    WECHOFLAG,           /*  Wait-for-echo flag               */
    CONSFLAG,            /*  Console output flag              */
    ASCIIFLAG,           /*  Remove high bit flag (&0x7f)     */
    CNTRLFLAG,           /*  Remove selected controls flag    */
    FILTERFLAG,          /*  Filter unwanted charcters flag   */
    IB_DLYFLAG,          /*  Interbyte delay flag (output only) */
    IL_DLYFLAG ,         /*  Interline delay flag (output only) */
                         /**            DELAYS               **/
    WECHO_DLY,           /*  Echo-wait delay (in tsecs)       */
    IB_DLY,              /*  Interbyte delay (in tsecs)       */
    IL_DLY,              /*  Interline delay (in tsecs)       */
    T_OUT,               /*  Timeout on input only (in tsecs) */
```

continues

```
                            /**              MODES              **/
          EOLMODE,          /*  End-of-line mode argument        */
          CASEMODE,         /*  Upper/lower mode argument        */
          XXMODE,           /*  Xoff mode argument               */
                            /**         DEFINED CHARACTERS       **/
          XOFFC,            /*  Character defined as XOFF         */
          XONC,             /*  Character defined as XON          */
          IL_DLYC,          /*  Character to trigger interline delay */
          KBORTC,           /*  Keyboard abort character          */
          };

#endif            /* _SIOCTL_ */
```

SIODEF.H

```
#ifndef  _SIODEF_
#define  _SIODEF_

#include <sio\siolocal.h>
#include <sio\uart.h>

/**** FUNCTION PROTOTYPES ****/
int    br_to_bcode(USHORT);
RANK   get232(SIO*, RANK);
short  getbaud(SIO *);
short  getformat(SIO*, RANK);
int    s_close(SIO*);
void   s_clearerr(SIO *);
int    s_clrsio(SIO *,USHORT);
int    s_fgetln(SIO *, char *, short);
int    s_fgets(SIO *, char *, int );
void   s_fputs(SIO *,char *);
int    s_ipop(SIO *);
int    s_ipush(SIO *);
USHORT s_keybort(SIO *);
SIO    *s_open(USHORT);
int    s_opop(SIO *);
int    s_opush(SIO *);
void   s_puts(SIO *,char *);
short  s_write(SIO *, BYTE *, short);
short  serial_status(SIO *, RANK);
short  set232(SIO*, RANK, BOOL);
short  setbaud(SIO *, RANK);
short  setformat(SIO *, RANK, RANK);
short  stat232(SIO *, RANK);
int    setuart(SIO *, RANK, USHORT);
short  tx_iwrite(SIO *, BYTE *, short);
short  tx_write(SIO *, BYTE *, short);

#define  OFF  0
#define  ON   1
#define  CLOSED FALSE
#define  OPEN   TRUE

#define NOT_READY  -1
```

```
#define CMDBUFSIZ    50          /* Capacity of modem's command buffer   */
#define CMDSIZ       7           /* Max storage needed for modem command */

#define TX_BUFSIZ    BUFSIZ      /* From stdio.h                         */
#define TX_NUMBUFFS  10          /* Number of buffers in tx queue        */
#define RCV_BUFSIZ   2000        /* Size of rxrdy interrupt buffer       */


/**** Manifest contants for UART Interrupts ****/

enum intrp                      /* Manifest constant names for interrupts */
  {
    RS232 =   0,                /* Changes on RS232 inputs              */
    THRE,                       /* Transmitter buffer emtpy             */
    RXRDY,                      /* Receive data ready                   */
    SERERR,                     /* Serialization errors                 */
    RXTIMEOUT                   /* For receiver FIFO                    */
  };

/**** CONSTANTS FOR INTERRUPT TRANSMIT ROUTINES ****/

/* Transmit shut down modes*/
#define WAIT_TIL_FINISH  0
#define SHUTDOWN_NOW     1

/* Return Codes from tx_write */
#define Q_OK             0
#define Q_FULL           1
#define Q_BUF2BIG        2

#define TX_INUSE         1
#define TX_FREE          0

/**** Constants for Baud Clock Functions ****/
enum clk { X1 = 0, X16, X32, X64 };

/**** Constants for Transmit/Recieve enable Arguments ****/
enum enable{XMITON = 0, RCVON, RXHSON, TXHSON, SETCLK};

/**** Constants for S_OPEN/S_CLOSE ****/
#define  CLOSED FALSE
#define  OPEN   TRUE

/**** Constants for GET/SET FORMAT/BAUD Functions ****/
enum brfmt { BAUD = 0, STOPS, DATALEN, PARITY };

/**** Constants for RS232 GET/SET RS232 Functions ****/
enum rs232 { DTR = 0, RTS, GPO1, GPO2, BRK };

/**** Constants for STAT232 Function ****/
enum st232 { CTS = 0, DCD, DSR, RI, GPI1, GPI2 };

/**** Arguments for serial_status function ****/
enum serstat { ANY_ERRORS = 0, PARITY_ERR, OVERRUN_ERR, FRAME_ERR, BREAK_ON };
```

continues

```
/**** Constants for Parity Arguments ****/
enum par { NONE = 0, ODD, EVEN, MARK, SPACE };

/**** Constants for Stop Bit Arguments ****/
enum sb {STOP1 = 0, STOP1_5, STOP2 };


/**** Constants for Receive Data Length Arguments ****/
enum rcvdl { DL5 = 0, DL6, DL7, DL8 };


/**** Constants for Transmit Arguments ****/
enum txdl { TxDL5 = 0, TxDL6, TxDL7, TxDL8 };

/**** Manifest Constants for Baud Rate Arguments ****/
enum baudcodes
    {
    BAUD50 = 0, BAUD75, BAUD110,  BAUD134_5, BAUD150,  BAUD300,  BAUD600,
    BAUD1200, BAUD1800, BAUD2000, BAUD2400,  BAUD3600, BAUD4800, BAUD7200,
    BAUD9600, BAUD14K4, BAUD19K2, BAUD28K8,  BAUD38K4, BAUD57K6, BAUD115K2,
    NUMBAUDS
    };


/*
 STRUCTURE sictl_
HEADER FILE: SIODEF.H
DESCRIPTION: Control structure for formatted input.
*/
struct sictl_
    {
    BOOL      t_outflag;        /*0  Timeout on/off flag            */
    unsigned  t_out;            /*1  Timeout period                 */
    BOOL      rawflag;          /*2  Perform no processing at all   */
    BOOL      ekobakflag;       /*3  Echo all input back to sender  */
    BOOL      asciiflag;        /*4  Reset strip bit 7              */
    short     eolmode;          /*5  End-of-line formatting         */
    BOOL      consflag;         /*6  Echo characters to console     */
    short     casemode;         /*7  Change to upper or lower case  */
    BOOL      cntrlflag;        /*10 Remove control characters      */
    short     ok_cntrls[32];    /*11 Permitted control characters   */
    short     numcc;            /*12 Number of controls in ok_cntrls */
    BOOL      filterflag;       /*13 Filter-remove characters       */
    short     filtlist[128][2]; /*14 List of byte to remove or filter */
    short     numfc;            /*15 Number of bytes in filter list */
    FAST      lastc;            /*16 Previous byte output           */
    BOOL      rbakflag;         /*17 A pending eol decision resolved */
    FAST      rbakc;            /*18 Pending readback character     */
    };

/*
 STRUCTURE soctl_
```

```
HEADER FILE: SIODEF.H
DESCRIPTION: Control Structure for formatted output.
*/
struct soctl_
    {
    BOOL      rawflag;              /*0  Perform no processing at all    */
    short     eolmode;             /*1  End-of-line formatting           */
    BOOL      consflag;            /*2  Echo characters to console       */
    BOOL      wechoflag;           /*3  Interbyte wait for return echo   */
    unsigned  wecho_dly;           /*4  Tsecs to wait for return echo    */
    USHORT    casemode;            /*5  Change to upper or lower case    */
    BOOL      asciiflag;           /*9  Reset strip bit 7                */
    BOOL      cntrlflag;           /*10 Remove control characters        */
    BYTE      ok_cntrls[32];       /*11 Permitted control characters     */
    USHORT    numcc;               /*12 Number of controls  in ok_cntrls */
    BOOL      filterflag;          /*13 Filter-remove characters         */
    short     filtlist[128][2];    /*14 List of byte to remove or filter */
    USHORT    numfc;               /*15 Number of bytes in filter list   */
    BOOL      ib_dlyflag;          /*16 Interbyte delay in tsecs         */
    unsigned  ib_dly;              /*17 Pause between bytes              */
    BOOL      il_dlyflag;          /*18 Interline pause flag             */
    FAST      il_dlyc;             /*19 Char to begin inter-line pause   */
    unsigned  il_dly;              /*20 Inter-line pause in tsecs        */
    FAST      kbortc;              /*21 Key to break out of loops        */
    int       lastc;               /*22 Previous byte output             */
    BOOL      flushflag;           /*23 An end of line decision pending  */
    };

/**** Constants for Timing ****/

#define  TIMEOUT     -1
#define  _0_SEC_05    1            /* 50 ms  */
#define  _0_SEC_1     2            /* 1.8    */
#define  _ 0_SEC_15   3            /* 150 ms */
#define  _0_SEC_2     4            /* 3.6    */
#define  _ 0_SEC_25   5            /* 250 ms */
#define  _0_SEC_3     6            /* 5.5    */
#define  _0_SEC_4     7            /* 7.3    */
#define  _0_SEC_5     9            /* 9.1    */
#define  _0_SEC_6     11           /* 10.9   */
#define  _0_SEC_7     13           /* 12.7   */
#define  _0_SEC_8     15           /* 14.6   */
#define  _0_SEC_9     16           /* 16.4   */
#define  _1_SEC_0     18           /* 18.2   */

/**** Error Codes Returned by SIO Functions ****/

enum {
    BAD_FCN = 2,    /* Function not supported */
    OR_ARG,         /* Argument out of range  */
    BAD_ARG,        /* Argument not supported */
    BAD_PORT,       /* Illegal device number  */
    NO_PORT,        /* Device not installed   */
```

continues

```
        NO_SIO,        /* No SIO declared        */
        OPEN_NOW,      /* Device already open    */
        NO_CLOSE,      /* No such device open    */
        KEY_CAN,       /* Aborted from keyboard  */
        NO_FILE,       /* File not found         */
        NO_IMEM,       /* Out of heap memory     */
        };

#define  NUMMASKS   5           /* ORDINAL elements in "setmask" array  */
#define  VIRGIN    -2           /* Dummy initializer (must be < -1)     */
#define  SUPPLIED   0           /* Dummy initializer                    */

/****Manifest Constants for Columns in the Virtual Register Array ****/
#define  VIR        0
#define  USR        1


/*
 STRUCTURE :  vregbits_
HEADER FILE:  SIODEF.H
DESCRIPTION:  General structure for virtual register maniupulation.
   COMMENTS:
*/
struct vregbits_
    {
    MASK      resetmask;          /* AND mask apply to virtual register */
    MASK      setmask[NUMMASKS];  /* Array of OR masks for each setting */
    BYTE      vregnum;            /* Virtual register number (row)      */
    USHORT    offset;             /* Offset of physical uart register   */
    RANK      now;                /* Code for current value             */
    USHORT    start;              /* Code to use at initialization      */
    struct vregbits_ *next;       /* Next struct for this function       */
    };


/*
 STRUCTURE :  vout232_
HEADER FILE:  SIODEF.H
DESCRIPTION:  Control structure for an RS-232 output.
   COMMENTS:  The next member enables constuction of a linked list.
*/
struct vout232_
    {
    MASK      resetmask;          /* AND mask apply to virtual register */
    USHORT    vregnum;            /* Virtual register number (row)      */
    USHORT    offset;             /* Offset of physical uart register   */
    BOOL      now;                /* Code for current value             */
    BOOL      start;              /* Code to use at initialization      */
    };


/*
 STRUCTURE :  vin232_
HEADER FILE:  SIODEF.H
DESCRIPTION:  Control structure for an RS-232 input.
*/
struct vin232_
    {
```

```
    USHORT    offset;            /* Offset of physical register in UART */
    MASK      mask;              /* Mask to isolate active bit          */
    BOOL      now;               /* Current value of this input         */
    };

/*
 STRUCTURE :  ser_err_
HEADER FILE: SIODEF.H
DESCRIPTION: Control structure for serialization errors.
*/
struct ser_err_
    {
    USHORT    offset;            /* Offset of physical register in UART */
    MASK      mask;              /* Mask to isolate active bit          */
    BOOL      now;               /* Current value of this input         */
    };

/*
 STRUCTURE :  vbaud_
HEADER FILE: SIODEF.H
DESCRIPTION: Control structure for baud rate.
*/
struct vbaud_
    {
    BYTE      vregnuml;       /* Virtual array of baud rate lo         */
    BYTE      vregnumh;       /* Virtual array of baud rate hi         */
    USHORT    offsetlo;       /* Offset of lo-order baud  rate register */
    USHORT    offsethi;       /* Offset of hi-order baud  rate register */
    short     divisor[NUMBAUDS][2]; /* Array of two-byte divisors      */
    RANK      now;            /* Rank of current divisorin divisor array */
    RANK      start;          /* Rank of value to use at start up       */
    };

union inbits_232
    {
    REG reg232;
    struct
        {
        unsigned int cts : 1;    /* <—  This is the lsb but may be msb in */
        unsigned int dsr : 1;    /*     other compilers.                  */
        unsigned int ri  : 1;
        unsigned int dcd : 1;
        unsigned int gpi1: 1;
        unsigned int gpi2: 1;
        unsigned int unused : 10;
        }bitmap;
    };

/*
 STRUCTURE :  SIOLIST
HEADER FILE: SIODEF.H
DESCRIPTION: Holds status information about SIO capabilities.  Used by
             level-1 functions.
    COMMENTS:
*/
```

continues

```
struct SIOLIST
    {
    SIO  *siop;                         /* Address of an SIO           */
    BOOL sio_openflag;                  /* Whether it's already open   */
    BOOL intrpt_supp;                   /* Whether it supports interrupts */
    };

/*
  STRUCTURE:  SYS_ILIST
HEADER FILE:  SIODEF.H
DESCRIPTION:  Holds pertinent system information about the SIO.  Used by
              level-1 functions.
   COMMENTS:
*/
struct SYS_ILIST
    {
    RANK    inum;           /* Rank in system interrupt vector table   */
    MASK    imask;          /* Mask for Interrupt Mask Register of 8259 */
    INTPTR isr;             /* Pointer to interrupt handler function    */
    INTPTR oldivect;        /* Save existing vector here                */
    FAST  oldimr;           /* Save existing Interrupt Mask Register here */
    struct vout232_ *oldgpo2;  /* Save address of gpo2 structure        */
    };

/*
  STRUCTURE: tx_queue
DESCRIPTION: Ring buffer for transmitter interrupts.
   COMMENTS: tx_list is used only for high speed data transmission
*/
struct tx_queue
    {
    char *locbuff;          /* pointer to local buffer                 */
    char *buffp;            /* pointer to next charater to be transmitted */
    short buffcnt;          /* actual size of this buffer              */
    char  inuseflag;        /* 'buffer empty or ready to be xmitted' flag */
    short id;               /*debug*/
    };

/*
/*
    STRUCTURE:  SIO
         FILE:  SIODEF.H
  DESCRIPTION:  Master structure defining a serial port.
*/

struct sio
    {
    BYTE  * uart_base;                  /*0  Base address of UART          */
    USHORT data_off;                    /*1  Offset of data port from base */
    USHORT status_off;                  /*2  Offset of status port from base */
    MASK   rcvmask;                     /*3  RxRDY mask                    */
    MASK   xmitmask;                    /*4  Xmit holding reg. empty mask  */
    MASK   tx_emptymask;                /*5  Xmit shift reg. empty mask    */
    FAST   (*readbyte)(BYTE *);         /*6  Pointer to RAM/port read routine */
    void   (*writebyte)(BYTE *, FAST);  /*7  Pointer to RAM/port read routine */
```

```
FAST    (*s_rstat)(SIO *);          /*8  Pointer to receiver status      */
FAST    (*s_read)(SIO *);           /*9  Pointer to fetch routine        */
FAST    (*s_xstat)(SIO *);          /*10 Pointer to xmit status          */
void    (*s_send)(SIO *, FAST);     /*11 Pointer to xmit function        */
short   (*s_txblock)(SIO *, BYTE*,short); /*12 "   block xmit function    */
REG     (*v_regp)[2];               /*13 Virtual UART register           */
USHORT  v_regpsize;                 /*14 Length of virtual array         */
struct vregbits_ *par;              /*15 Pointer to parity struct        */
struct vregbits_ *sb;               /*16 Pointer to stop bit struct      */
struct vregbits_ *dl;               /*17 Pointer to data length struct   */
struct vbaud_    *br;               /*18 Pointer to baud rate  struct    */
struct vout232_  *rts;              /*19 Pointer to RTS struct           */
struct vout232_  *dtr;              /*20 Pointer to DTR struct           */
struct vout232_  *gpo1;             /*21 Pointer to GPOUTPUT1  struct    */
struct vout232_  *gpo2;             /*22 Pointer to GPOOUTPUT2 struct    */
struct vout232_  *brkbit;           /*23 Pointer to BREAK struct         */
struct vin232_   *cts;              /*24 Pointer to  CTS struct          */
struct vin232_   *dsr;              /*25 Pointer to  DSR struct          */
struct vin232_   *dcd;              /*26 Pointer to  DCD struct          */
struct vin232_   *ri;               /*27 Pointer to  RI struct           */
struct vin232_   *gpi1;             /*28 Pointer to  GPINPUT1  struct    */
struct vin232_   *gpi2;             /*29 Pointer to  GPINPUT2  struct    */
FAST (*read232)(SIO *, struct vin232_*); /*30 * to lev-1 fetch function  */
union inbits_232 status;            /*31 See if any RS-232 inputs        */
union inbits_232 delta;             /*32 Changed since last read         */
struct vregbits_  *txenable;        /*33 "  xmitter enable struct         */
struct vregbits_  *rxenable;        /*34 "  receiver enable struct        */
struct vregbits_  *ctshs;           /*35 "  cts handshake on xmitter      */
struct vregbits_  *dcdhs;           /*36 "  dcd handshake on rcvr         */
struct vregbits_  *clkf;            /*37 "  clock factor struct           */
USHORT flow_wanted;                 /*38 0 none,1 xon-xoff, 2 RTS/CTS    */
USHORT tx_vflowstate;               /*39 State of virtual xmit flow ctrl */
USHORT rcv_vflowstate;              /*40 State of virtual rcv   "     "  */
USHORT tx_iflowstate;               /*41 State of interrupt xmit "    "  */
USHORT rcv_iflowstate;              /*42 State of interrupt rcv  "    "  */
USHORT (*getflow_req)(SIO *,...);   /*43 pointer to flow-status routine  */
void    (*flowon)(SIO *);           /*44 pointer to flow-off routine     */
void    (*flowoff)(SIO *);          /*45 pointer to flow-on routine      */
short   devnum;                     /*46 s_opened device number          */
struct soctl_   *s_octl;            /*47 Pointer to output struct        */
struct sictl_   *s_ictl;            /*48 Pointer to input  struct        */
struct                              /*49 Interrupt status bitfield       */
  {
  unsigned int rcv_wanted    :1;    /* Are interrupts desired?           */
  unsigned int tx_wanted     :1;
  unsigned int rs232_wanted  :1;
  unsigned int serr_wanted   :1;
  unsigned int rcv_on        :1;    /* Are interrupts on?                */
  unsigned int tx_on         :1;
  unsigned int rs232_on      :1;
  unsigned int serr_on       :1;
  unsigned int reserved      :8;
  } intrpt_status;
void (*isr[NUM_INTRPT])(SIO * siop);/*50 Array of sub-handlers vectors   */
```

continues

```
void    (*old_isr_232)(SIO *);           /*51 Pointer to saved: rs232 ISR    */
void    (*old_isr_serr)(SIO *);          /*52 : serial error ISR             */
void    (*old_isr_rcv)(SIO *);           /*53 : rcv ISR                      */
void    (*old_isr_tx)(SIO *);            /*54 : xmit ISR                     */
union                                    /*55 : serialization errors         */
        {
        REG       s_errors;              /* The raw bit-map                  */
        struct                           /* Individual bits                  */
           {
           unsigned  overrun : 1;        /* overrun error flag               */
           unsigned  parity  : 1;        /* parity error flag                */
           unsigned  frame   : 1;        /* framing error flag               */
           unsigned  Break   : 1;        /* break error flag                 */
           unsigned  reserved: 12;
           } bitmap;
        } serr;
short   rcv_buffsize;                    /*56 Size of the rxrdy buffer       */
short   rcv_fifo_depth;                  /*57 Size UART's receive FIFO       */
short   rcv_fifo_trigger;                /*58 Receive FIFO Trigger Level     */
FAST    *rcv_buff;                       /*59 Pointer to receive buffer      */
FAST    *rcv_buffend;                    /*60 Pointer to end of  "           */
FAST    *rcv_headp;                      /*61 Where to put next byte         */
FAST    *rcv_tailp;                      /*62 Where to fetch next byte       */
short   tx_fifo_depth;                   /*63 Size of UART's xmit FIFO       */
short   tx_fifo_trigger;                 /*64 Trasmit FIFO Trigger Level     */
short   tx_numbuffs;                     /*65 Number of xmit buffers         */
short   tx_buffsize;                     /*66 Size of each xmit buffer       */
struct tx_queue *tx_list;                /*67 The circular queue             */
struct tx_queue *tx_headp;               /*68 Input to tx queue              */
struct tx_queue *tx_tailp;               /*69 Output to tx queue             */
struct tx_queue *tx_queue_end;           /*70 Pointer to last member   "     */
FAST    tx_idle;                         /*71 Transmitter needs kickstart    */
struct modem    *sm;                     /*72 Pointer to modem struct        */
};
```

SIOLOCAL.H

```
#ifndef _SIOLOCAL_
#define _SIOLOCAL_

#undef   NUL
#undef   NIL
#undef   EOF
#undef   TRUE
#undef   BOOL
#undef   BYTE
#undef   DOS_EOF

#define  NIL          (void*) 0     /* pointer constant            */
#define  NUL          '\0'          /* ASCII  constant             */
#define  EVER         ;;            /* used in "for (EVER)"        */
#define  FALSE        0
#define  TRUE         !FALSE
#define  DOS_EOF      0x1A          /* end-of-file for text files  */
```

```
#define  MAX_NAME_LEN 15
#define  MAX_PATH_LEN  64                   /* 63 + NUL byte                    */
#define arraysize(array)     (sizeof(array) / sizeof(array[0]))

#ifndef  EOF
#define  EOF        -1
#endif

typedef  unsigned char       BYTE;
typedef  short               FAST;
typedef  unsigned short      REG;
typedef  short               MASK;
typedef  unsigned short      USHORT;
typedef  unsigned short      RANK;
typedef  unsigned short      BOOL;
typedef  unsigned long int   ULONG;
typedef  void                VOID;
typedef  struct sio          SIO;
typedef  void (_interrupt far  *INTPTR)();

#endif    /* _SIOLOCAL_ */
```

T4.H

```
#ifndef   _T4_
#define   _T4_

/**** FUNCTION PROTOTYPES ****/
USHORT bit2run(BYTE *, USHORT, USHORT *);
int    run2bits(FILE *, FILE *, BYTE *, short, short *, short);
short  t4encode(FAST *, short, FAST *);
int    t4decode(FILE *, FILE *, short *, USHORT, FAST *, USHORT);

/*
STRUCTURE:  MHcode (typedef)
 FUNCTION:  Contains a description of a Huffman code.
*/
typedef struct
    {
    USHORT t4token;         /* The Huffman code              */
    USHORT t4token_len;     /* Number of bits in same        */
    } MHcode;

/*
STRUCTURE:  T4NODE (typedef)
 FUNCTION:  Contains a node for the Huffman code binary tree.
*/
typedef struct t4node
    {
    struct t4node near *zero; /* pointer to the next zero branch  */
    struct t4node near *one;  /* pointer to the next one branch   */
    short  run_len;
    } near T4NODE;
```

continues

```
#define NOTTERMINAL   12000
#define WHITE         0x0000
#define BLACK         0xFFFF
#define EOL_MARKER    32512
#define EOL_INDEX       104    /* Index into the encoding tables   */
#define BYTES_PER_LINE  216
#define LINES_PER_PAGE 1728

#endif    /* _T4_ */
```

TERM.H

```
#ifndef   _TERM_
#define   _TERM_
/**** FUNCTION PROTOTYPES ****/
int  cbuff(SIO *,FILE *);
int  dial(SIO *);
void dnload(SIO*, int (*)(SIO*, FILE*));
int  locbuff(SIO*, FILE *);
int  menu(SIO *);
int  redial(SIO *);
void set_params(SIO*);
void setup232(SIO *);
void upload(SIO*);
void term(SIO *);

#endif       /* _TERM_ */
```

UART.H

```
#ifndef   _16x50_
#define   _16x50_

#include <sio\u16x50.h>

#endif    /* _16x50_ */
```

U16X50.H

```
#ifndef _U16x50_
#define _U16x50_

/**** FUNCTION PROTOTYPES ****/
void isr_tx(SIO *);              /* transmit interrupt handler      */
void isr_stat232(SIO *);         /* RS232 interrupt handler         */
void isr_serr(SIO *);            /* Serialization interrupt handler */
void isr_rcv450(SIO *);          /* Receive data interrupt handler  */
void isr_rcv550(SIO *);          /* Receive data interrupt handler  */
void isr_tx_dummy(SIO *);        /* transmit interrupt handler      */
void isr_stat232_dummy(SIO *);   /* RS232 interrupt handler         */
```

```
void isr_serr_dummy(SIO *);        /* Serialization interrupt handler */
void isr_rcv_dummy(SIO *);         /* Receive data interrupt handler  */
void s_iadmin(SIO *);
void s_config(SIO *);
void s_restore(SIO *);
void u_intrpt_mgr(SIO*, short, BOOL);
void _vset232(SIO *,struct vout232_ *, REG);
void _vsetbr(SIO *,struct vbaud_ *, REG, REG);
FAST _vstat232(SIO *,struct vin232_ *);
void _vsetbits(SIO *,struct vregbits_ *, REG);
void (*s_revector(SIO *, USHORT, void (*)(SIO *) )) (SIO*);

/*** Offsets of 16x50 Registers ***/
#define DATA_IO       0   /* Data read and write                       */
#define INT_EN        1   /* Interrupt enable  (IER)                   */
#define INT_ID        2   /* Interrupt identification (read-only)      */
#define FIFO          2   /* Interrupt identification (write-only 16550) */
#define FMT           3   /* Data format (LCR)                         */
#define DLAB          3   /* Register containing DLAB bit              */
#define OUT232        4   /* RS232 control (MCR)                       */
#define SER_STAT      5   /* Serialization status register (LSR)       */
#define STAT_232      6   /* RS232 status (MSR)                        */

#define BAUDLO        0   /* LSB of the baud rate divisor              */
#define BAUDHI        1   /* MSB of the baud rate divisor              */

/*** Rows in the Virtual Register Array ***/
enum vir_row {
    VBAUDLO = 0,          /* lo byte of baud rate register        */
    VBAUDHI,              /* hi byte of baud rate register        */
    VINT_EN,              /* interrupt enable register            */
    VFIFO,                /* FIFO register                        */
    VFMT,                 /* Data format register                 */
    VOUT232,              /* RS-232 outpu register                */
    V_REG_SIZE            /* number of elements in virtual array  */
    };

/***************************
* Constants for Interrupts *
***************************/

/* Bit masks for Interrupt Enable register */

#define I_RXRDY    0x1
#define I_THRE     0x2      /* Values may be compounded....      */
#define I_SERERR   0x4      /* e.g., I_RXRDY + I_THRE            */
#define I_RS232    0x8

#define INT_ID_MASK   0x0F   /* Only bits 1,2,&3 needed after shift  */

/* Index number for interrupts */
enum {
```

continues

```
            INDEX_RS232 =  0,
            INDEX_THRE,
            INDEX_RXRDY,
            INDEX_SERERR,
            INDEX_UNUSED1,
            INDEX_UNUSED2,
            INDEX_RXTIMEOUT,              /* when recevier FIFO times out unfull */
            NUM_INTRPT                /* This is dimensions isr array in SIODEF.H */
            };

/* Receiver's FIFO Trigger Depth */

#define TRIG_1  0x01
#define TRIG_4  0x41
#define TRIG_8  0x81
#define TRIG_16 0xC1


/*** Bit Masks for Transmit/Receive Status ***/
#define   RCV_MASK        0x01     /* 00000001 received byte ready      */
#define   XMIT_MASK       0x20     /* 00000010 transmitter buffer clear */
#define   TX_EMPTY_MASK   0x40     /* 00000100 shift register clear     */

#define s_txempty(x) (*(x)->readbyte)((x)->uart_base+(x)->status_off)
                     &(x)->tx_emptymask

/*** Bit Masks for Data Length ***/
#define   DLMASK          0xFC     /* AND mask 11111100 */
#define   DL5_MASK        0x00     /* OR mask 00000000  */
#define   DL6_MASK        0x01     /* OR mask 00000001  */
#define   DL7_MASK        0x02     /* OR mask 00000010  */
#define   DL8_MASK        0x03     /* OR mask 00000011  */

/*** Bit Masks for Stop Bits ***/
#define   STOPMASK        0xFB     /* AND mask 11111011 */
#define   ONE_MASK        0x00     /* OR mask 00000000  */
#define   ONE_5_MASK      0x04     /* OR mask 00000100  */
#define   TWO_MASK        0x04     /* OR mask 00000100  */

/***Bit Masks for Parity Bits ***/
#define   PARITYMASK      0xC7     /* AND MASK 11000111 */
#define   NONE_MASK       0x00     /* OR mask 00000000  */
#define   ODD_MASK        0x08     /* OR mask 00001000  */
#define   EVEN_MASK       0x18     /* OR mask 00011000  */
#define   MARK_MASK       0x28     /* OR mask 00101000  */
#define   SPACE_MASK      0x38     /* OR mask 00111000  */

/*** Bit Masks for BREAK Bits ***/
#define   BRK_MASK        0xBF     /* AND mask 10111111 */
#define   BRKON_MASK      0x40     /* OR mask  01000000 */
#define   BRKOFF_MASK     0x00

/*** Bit Masks for RS232 Inputs ***/
#define   CTSMASK         0x10     /* 00010000 */
#define   DSRMASK         0x20     /* 00100000 */
```

```
#define  RIMASK          0x40       /* 01000000 */
#define  DCDMASK         0x80       /* 10000000 */

/*** Bit Masks for RS232 Outputs ***/
#define  DTRMASK         0xFE       /* 11111110 */
#define  RTSMASK         0xFD       /* 11111101 */
#define  GPO1MASK        0xFB       /* 11111011 */
#define  GPO2MASK        0xF7       /* 11110111 */

/*** Masks for Baud Rate Divisior Registers ***/
#define  BH_50           0x09
#define  BL_50           0x00
#define  BH_75           0x06
#define  BL_75           0x00
#define  BH_110          0x04
#define  BL_110          0x17
#define  BH_134          0x03
#define  BL_134          0x59
#define  BH_150          0x03
#define  BL_150          0x00
#define  BH_300          0x01
#define  BL_300          0x80
#define  BH_600          0x00
#define  BL_600          0xC0
#define  BH_1200         0x00
#define  BL_1200         0x60
#define  BH_1800         0x00
#define  BL_1800         0x40
#define  BH_2000         0x00
#define  BL_2000         0x3A
#define  BH_2400         0x00
#define  BL_2400         0x30
#define  BH_3600         0x00
#define  BL_3600         0x20
#define  BH_4800         0x00
#define  BL_4800         0x18
#define  BH_7200         0x00
#define  BL_7200         0x10
#define  BH_9600         0x00
#define  BL_9600         0x0C
#define  BH_14K4         0x00
#define  BL_14K4         0x08
#define  BH_19K2         0x00
#define  BL_19K2         0x06
#define  BH_28K8         0x00
#define  BL_28K8         0x04
#define  BH_38K4         0x00
#define  BL_38K4         0x03
#define  BH_57K6         0x00
#define  BL_57K6         0x02
#define  BH_115K2        0x00
#define  BL_115K2        0x01

#endif  /* _U16x50_*/
```

XMOD.H

```c
#ifndef _XMOD_
#define _XMOD_

/**** FUNCTION PROTOTYPES ****/
int x_snd(SIO *);
int x_rcv(SIO *);
USHORT x_except(SIO *, USHORT , USHORT *, USHORT);
USHORT x_rcvcrc(USHORT *);
USHORT x_rcvcksum(USHORT *);
USHORT x_sndcrc(BYTE *);
USHORT x_sndcksum(BYTE *);
USHORT makepacket(struct sndpacket *,USHORT ,ULONG , FILE *);
void ckvinstall(struct sndpacket *,USHORT , USHORT(*)(BYTE*));


#define DBLKSIZ    128          /* size of data field in packet          */
#define HEADROOM   10           /* amount of memory to save from buffer  */
#define SOH_TIMOUT _1_SEC_0     /* timeout interval for SOH              */
#define ACK_RETRY  30           /* used in loop to wait for ACK          */
#define CRCPAKSIZ  133          /* number of bytes in CRC packet         */
#define CKSPAKSIZ  132          /* number of bytes in checksum packet    */

/*
   STRUCT NAME:  rcvpacket
   HEADER FILE:  XMOD.H
   DESCRIPTION:  Structure to describe a packet during reception.
      COMMENTS:  The SOH is discarded upon reception so is not stored
                 structure.
*/
struct rcvpacket
      {
      short pnum1;             /* packet number                 */
      short pnum2;             /* 1's comp packet number        */
      short int data[DBLKSIZ]; /* data block                    */
      short int ckvhi;         /* high byte of checkval         */
      short int ckvlo;         /* low byte of checkval          */
      };


/*
   STRUCT NAME:  sndpacket
   HEADER FILE:  XMOD.H
   DESCRIPTION:  Description of an XMODEM packet for transmission.
*/
struct sndpacket
      {
      BYTE soh;               /* start of header               */
      BYTE pnum1;             /* packet number                 */
      BYTE pnum2;             /* 1's comp packet number        */
      BYTE data[DBLKSIZ];     /* data block                    */
      USHORT ckval;           /* block-check character         */
      };

/* EXCEPTION CODES */
```

```c
#define X_ESNDMAX    10          /* max exceptions during transmission    */
#define X_ERCVMAX    10          /* max exceptions during receiving       */
#define X_NOSOHMAX 100           /* max SOH timeout exceptions            */

#define CONTINUE     0           /* errcode value that sustains snd/rcv loop */
#define BREAK        1           /* one of the errcode value that breaks same */

/* EXCEPTION CODE USED IN BOTH XMIT AND RECEIVE */
#define E_USRCAN     0           /* user cancelled transfer               */
enum xsndcodes               /* CODES USED ONLY IN X_SND               */
    {
    E_FILEMTY = 1,           /* file to transmit is empty              */
    E_NOACK,                 /* time out waiting on ACK                */
    E_RCVCAN,                /* receiver canceled                      */
    E_BADPAK,                /* NAK instead of ACK                     */
    E_EOF,                   /* End of file read                       */
    E_LASTACK,               /* final ack not acknowledged             */
    E_SNDOK,                 /* successful transmission                */
    E_DSKREAD                /* disk read error                        */
    };
enum xrcvcodes               /* CODES USED ONLY IN X_RCV               */
    {
    E_NOSOH = E_DSKREAD+1,    /* timeout receiving SOH                  */
    E_BADCKV,                /* invalid checkvalue received            */
    E_SNDCAN,                /* transmitter cancelled transfer         */
    E_BADSOH,                /* invalid SOH received                   */
    E_NODATA,                /* timeout receiving data in block        */
    E_PAKNUM,                /* invalid block number received          */
    E_SNDACK,                /* sender missed last ack                 */
    E_PAKSEQ,                /* FATAL: packet out of sequence          */
    E_DSKWRITE,              /* disk write error                       */
    E_RCVOK                  /* successful reception                   */
    };
#endif       /* _XMOD_ */
```

TERM7

```c
#include <malloc.h>
#include <stdio.h>
#include <stdlib.h>
#include <ctype.h>
#include <sio\siodef.h>
#include <sio\ascii.h>
#include <sio\misc.h>
#include <sio\sioctl.h>
#include <sio\buos.h>
#include <sio\key.h>
#include <sio\term.h>
#include <sio\xmod.h>
#include <sio\modem.h>

#define MENU          CTRL_A       /* Command summary              */
#define FORMAT        'A'          /* Setup serial parmeters       */
#define RS_232        'B'          /* RS-232 output control        */
#define BRAKE         'C'          /* Send BREAK signal            */
#define UPLOAD        'D'          /* Transmit file                */
#define DNLOAD1       'E'          /* Download with C's buffer     */
#define DNLOAD2       'F'          /* Download with local buffer   */
#define UART_ID       'G'          /* 16450 (8250) or 16550        */
#define DIAL          'H'          /* Dial phone number            */
#define REDIAL        'I'          /* Redial previous number       */
#define ANSWER        'J'          /* Answer phone                 */
#define HUP           'K'          /* Hang up phone                */
#define BASELINE_CFG  'L'          /* Configure base line modem    */
#define PROTO_CFG     'M'          /* Configure protocol modem     */
#define XSEND         'N'          /* Send file with XMODEM protocol */
#define XRECV         'O'          /* Xmit file with XMODEM protocol */
#define EXIT          'Q'          /* Exit from term               */
```

continues

```
int vers = 7;                              /* version number (global)     */

extern int s_errno;
extern char *errstr[],  *brstr[];
extern char *m_codes[];                    /* modem id strings            */


int menu(siop)           /* menu now gets SIO pointer       */
SIO *siop;
{
    int c;
    int retval = 0;
    static char *menus[] =
        {
        "\tA.  Data Format, Baud rate",
        "\tB.  RS-232 control",
        "\tC.  Transmit BREAK signal",
        "\tD.  Upload Text File",
        "\tE.  Download Text File (small buffer)",
        "\tF.  Download Text File (large buffer)",
        "\tG.  Identify the UART",
        "\tH.  Dial a phone number",
        "\tI.  Redial last phone number",
        "\tJ.  Answer incoming call",
        "\tK.  Hang up phone",
        "\tL.  Attempt to configure baseline modem",
        "\tM.  Attempt to configure protocol modem",
        "\tN.  Send a file using XMODEM protocol",
        "\tO.  Receive a file using XMODEM protocol",
        "\tQ.  EXIT",
        ""                                 /* null string terminates list   */
        };

    char ** menup;
    c = !EXIT;
    while (c != EXIT)
        {
        puts("\n\n");
        for (menup = menus; **menup != NUL ; menup++)
            printf("%s\n", *menup);
        printf("\n\t\t  Enter selection  (CR to quit menu) :  ");
        if ( (c = getkbch()) == CR)
            break;                         /* return to term */
        c = toupper(c);
        switch (c)
            {
            case EXIT:
                if (m_warndcd(siop, OFF) == 0)
                    {
                    m_hup(siop);                   /* hang up */
                    if (siop->sm->configokflag == TRUE)
                        {   /* "unconfig" modem */
                        siop->sm->configokflag = FALSE;
                        m_cmd_OK(siop, siop->sm->unconfig);
                        }
```

```
            retval = 1;
              }
          else
              {
              printf("Continuing in terminal\n");
              retval = 0;
              }
        break;
    case FORMAT:              /* Data format, Baud rate        */
        set_params(siop);
        break;
    case RS_232:                  /* RS-232 output control     */
        setup232(siop);
        break;
    case BRAKE:                       /* send BREAK             */
        set232(siop, BRK, ON);
        break;
    case UPLOAD:                      /* transmit a disk file       */
        upload(siop);
        haktc();
        break;
    case DNLOAD1:             /* receive a file: use C's buffer */
        dnload(siop, cbuff);
        break;
    case DNLOAD2:            /* receive a file: use local buffer */
        dnload(siop, locbuff);
        break;
    case DIAL:
        s_icntrl(siop, SET, CONSFLAG, OFF); /* console echo off */
        if (m_warndcd(siop, OFF) == 0)
            printf("\n%s. \n",m_codes[dial(siop)]);
        s_icntrl(siop, SET, CONSFLAG, ON);  /* console echo on  */
        c = EXIT;                     /* leave menu after dial */
        break;
    case REDIAL:
        s_icntrl(siop, SET, CONSFLAG, OFF); /* console echo off */
        if (m_warndcd(siop, OFF) == 0)
            printf("\n%s. \n",m_codes[redial(siop)]);
        s_icntrl(siop, SET, CONSFLAG, ON);  /* console echo off */
        c = EXIT;                     /* leave menu after redial */
        break;
    case ANSWER:
        s_icntrl(siop, SET, CONSFLAG, OFF); /* console echo off */
        if (m_warndcd(siop, OFF) == 0)
            printf("\n%s. \n",m_codes[m_answer(siop)]);
        s_icntrl(siop, SET, CONSFLAG, ON);   /* console echo on */
        c = EXIT;                     /* leave menu after answer */
        break;
    case HUP:
        puts("\nHanging up...");
        if (m_warndcd(siop, ON) == 0)
            printf("\nHangup %s.\n",\
                m_hup(siop) == 0 ? "OK" : "error");
```

continues

```
                        c = EXIT;                           /* leave menu after hangup   */
                        break;
                case XSEND:
                        if (m_warndcd(siop, ON) == 0)
                            x_snd(siop);
                        haktc();
                        break;
                case XRECV:
                        if (m_warndcd(siop, ON) == 0)
                            x_rcv(siop);
                        haktc();
                        break;
                case BASELINE_CFG:
                        (void)baseline_cfg(siop);
                        haktc();
                        break;
                case PROTO_CFG:
                            if (siop->sm->configokflag != TRUE)
                                    puts("\nBaseline Configuration Required.");
                        else
                            proto_cfg(siop);
                        haktc();
                        break;
                case UART_ID:
                        printf("\nUART on device %d is a %s :\n", siop->devnum,
                            siop->rcv_fifo_trigger == 0 ? "16450/8250" : "16550");
                        printf("\t    TX FIFO depth is: %2d\n"
                              "\t TX Trigger level is: %2d\n"
                              "\t   RCV FIFO depth is: %2d\n"
                              "\tRCV Trigger level is: %2d\n",
                                  siop->tx_fifo_depth,
                                  siop->tx_fifo_trigger,
                                  siop->rcv_fifo_depth,
                                  siop->rcv_fifo_trigger);
                        printf("\nInterrupts Active:\n"
                              "\t        Serial Errors: %s\n"
                              "\t                RS232: %s\n"
                              "\t             Receiver: %s (%d-byte buffer)\n"
                              "\t          Transmitter: %s  (%d %d-byte buffers)\n",
                                  siop->intrpt_status.serr_on ? "Yes" : "No",
                                  siop->intrpt_status.rs232_on ? "Yes" : "No",
                                  siop->intrpt_status.rcv_on? "Yes" : "No",
                                  siop->rcv_buffsize,
                                  siop->intrpt_status.tx_on ? "Yes" : "No",
                                  siop->tx_numbuffs,
                                  siop->tx_buffsize);
                        haktc();
                        break;
                default:
                        puts("Invalid choice\n\a");
                        break;
            }
        }
    putchar('\n');
    siop->sm->cmdechoflag = FALSE;
```

```
        s_icntrl(siop, SET, CONSFLAG, OFF);  /* console echo off */
        m_echo(siop, ON);
        s_icntrl(siop, SET, CONSFLAG, ON);  /* console echo off */
        return retval;      /* will be zero except if EXIT */
}



void term(siop)
SIO *siop;
{
        int c;                               /* must be int to detect -1 return   */

        s_ipush(siop);                       /* save both control structures      */
        s_opush(siop);
        m_echo(siop, ON);
        s_icntrl(siop, SET, CONSFLAG, ON); /* console echo on formatted input  */
        s_ocntrl(siop, SET, IB_DLYFLAG, OFF);  /* interbyte delay              */
        printf("TERM, Version %d:  Press Control-%c for a summary of commands\n", \
            vers, MENU + '@');

    flowon(siop);
    for (EVER)                           /*          eternal loop        */
        {
        s_fgetc(siop);                      /* s_fgetc will echo          */
        if ( (c = inkey()) != NOT_READY)
            if (c == MENU)
                {
                if (menu(siop))
                    break;          /* if menu returns non-zero         */
                }
            else
                s_fputc(siop, c);
        if(serial_status(siop, BREAK_ON))
            puts("Break Detected");
        }
    s_opop(siop);                        /* restore both control structures   */
    s_ipop(siop);
    m_unconfig(siop);
}



main(argc, argv)
int argc;
char *argv[];
{
    short portnum;
    SIO *siop;                               /* pointer to an SIO */
    portnum = 2;
    if (argc > 1)
        portnum = atoi(argv[1]);
    if ( (siop = s_open(portnum)) == NIL)
        {
        printf("\aCannot open:  %s\n",errstr[s_errno]);
```

continues

```
        return s_errno;
        }
setbaud(siop, BAUD19K2);
term(siop);                           /*   TERM */
if ( (s_errno = s_close(siop)) != 0 )
    {
    printf("\aCannot close:%s\n",errstr[s_errno]);
    return s_errno;
    }
puts("\nEnd of TERM\n");
return 0;
}
```

Facsimile Encoding and Decoding Tables

Listing F.1. T.4 Huffman Encoding tables.

ARRAY NAMES: encwhite, encblack
TYPE: Array of MHcode
FUNCTION: Each element contains the Huffman variable-length code and the number of bits in that code.
LIBRARY: FAX.LIB
INCLUDE FILES: T4.h

```
MHcode encwhite[] = {
    {0x00ac, 8},   {0x0038, 6},   {0x000e, 4},   {0x0001, 4},    /*  0*/
    {0x000d, 4},   {0x0003, 4},   {0x0007, 4},   {0x000f, 4},    /*  4*/
    {0x0019, 5},   {0x0005, 5},   {0x001c, 5},   {0x0002, 5},    /*  8*/
    {0x0004, 6},   {0x0030, 6},   {0x000b, 6},   {0x002b, 6},    /* 12*/
    {0x0015, 6},   {0x0035, 6},   {0x0072, 7},   {0x0018, 7},    /* 16*/
    {0x0008, 7},   {0x0074, 7},   {0x0060, 7},   {0x0010, 7},    /* 20*/
    {0x000a, 7},   {0x006a, 7},   {0x0064, 7},   {0x0012, 7},    /* 24*/
    {0x000c, 7},   {0x0040, 8},   {0x00c0, 8},   {0x0058, 8},    /* 28*/
    {0x00d8, 8},   {0x0048, 8},   {0x00c8, 8},   {0x0028, 8},    /* 32*/
    {0x00a8, 8},   {0x0068, 8},   {0x00e8, 8},   {0x0014, 8},    /* 36*/
    {0x0094, 8},   {0x0054, 8},   {0x00d4, 8},   {0x0034, 8},    /* 40*/
    {0x00b4, 8},   {0x0020, 8},   {0x00a0, 8},   {0x0050, 8},    /* 44*/
    {0x00d0, 8},   {0x004a, 8},   {0x00ca, 8},   {0x002a, 8},    /* 48*/
    {0x00aa, 8},   {0x0024, 8},   {0x00a4, 8},   {0x001a, 8},    /* 52*/
    {0x009a, 8},   {0x005a, 8},   {0x00da, 8},   {0x0052, 8},    /* 56*/
    {0x00d2, 8},   {0x004c, 8},   {0x00cc, 8},   {0x002c, 8},    /* 60*/
    {0x001b, 5},   {0x0009, 5},   {0x003a, 6},   {0x0076, 7},    /* 64*/
    {0x006c, 8},   {0x00ec, 8},   {0x0026, 8},   {0x00a6, 8},    /* 68*/
    {0x0016, 8},   {0x00e6, 8},   {0x0066, 9},   {0x0166, 9},    /* 72*/
```

continues

Listing F.1. continued

```
      {0x0096, 9},   {0x0196, 9},   {0x0056, 9},   {0x0156, 9},    /* 76*/
      {0x00d6, 9},   {0x01d6, 9},   {0x0036, 9},   {0x0136, 9},    /* 80*/
      {0x00b6, 9},   {0x01b6, 9},   {0x0032, 9},   {0x0132, 9},    /* 84*/
      {0x00b2, 9},   {0x0006, 6},   {0x01b2, 9},   {0x0080, 11},   /* 88*/
      {0x0180, 11},  {0x0580, 11},  {0x0480, 12},  {0x0c80, 12},   /* 92*/
      {0x0280, 12},  {0x0a80, 12},  {0x0680, 12},  {0x0e80, 12},   /* 96*/
      {0x0380, 12},  {0x0b80, 12},  {0x0780, 12},  {0x0f80, 12},   /*100*/
      {0x0800, 12}                                 /*EOL*/         /*104*/
};

MHcode encblack[] = {
      {0x03b0, 10},  {0x0002, 3},   {0x0003, 2},   {0x0001, 2},    /*  0*/
      {0x0006, 3},   {0x000c, 4},   {0x0004, 4},   {0x0018, 5},    /*  4*/
      {0x0028, 6},   {0x0008, 6},   {0x0010, 7},   {0x0050, 7},    /*  8*/
      {0x0070, 7},   {0x0020, 8},   {0x00e0, 8},   {0x0030, 9},    /* 12*/
      {0x03a0, 10},  {0x0060, 10},  {0x0040, 10},  {0x0730, 11},   /* 16*/
      {0x00b0, 11},  {0x01b0, 11},  {0x0760, 11},  {0x00a0, 11},   /* 20*/
      {0x0740, 11},  {0x00c0, 11},  {0x0530, 12},  {0x0d30, 12},   /* 24*/
      {0x0330, 12},  {0x0b30, 12},  {0x0160, 12},  {0x0960, 12},   /* 28*/
      {0x0560, 12},  {0x0d60, 12},  {0x04b0, 12},  {0x0cb0, 12},   /* 32*/
      {0x02b0, 12},  {0x0ab0, 12},  {0x06b0, 12},  {0x0eb0, 12},   /* 36*/
      {0x0360, 12},  {0x0b60, 12},  {0x05b0, 12},  {0x0db0, 12},   /* 40*/
      {0x02a0, 12},  {0x0aa0, 12},  {0x06a0, 12},  {0x0ea0, 12},   /* 44*/
      {0x0260, 12},  {0x0a60, 12},  {0x04a0, 12},  {0x0ca0, 12},   /* 48*/
      {0x0240, 12},  {0x0ec0, 12},  {0x01c0, 12},  {0x0e40, 12},   /* 52*/
      {0x0140, 12},  {0x01a0, 12},  {0x09a0, 12},  {0x0d40, 12},   /* 56*/
      {0x0340, 12},  {0x05a0, 12},  {0x0660, 12},  {0x0e60, 12},   /* 60*/
      {0x03c0, 10},  {0x0130, 12},  {0x0930, 12},  {0x0da0, 12},   /* 64*/
      {0x0cc0, 12},  {0x02c0, 12},  {0x0ac0, 12},  {0x06c0, 13},   /* 68*/
      {0x16c0, 13},  {0x0a40, 13},  {0x1a40, 13},  {0x0640, 13},   /* 72*/
      {0x1640, 13},  {0x09c0, 13},  {0x19c0, 13},  {0x05c0, 13},   /* 76*/
      {0x15c0, 13},  {0x0dc0, 13},  {0x1dc0, 13},  {0x0940, 13},   /* 80*/
      {0x1940, 13},  {0x0540, 13},  {0x1540, 13},  {0x0b40, 13},   /* 84*/
      {0x1b40, 13},  {0x04c0, 13},  {0x14c0, 13},  {0x0080, 11},   /* 88*/
      {0x0180, 11},  {0x0580, 11},  {0x0480, 12},  {0x0c80, 12},   /* 92*/
      {0x0280, 12},  {0x0a80, 12},  {0x0680, 12},  {0x0e80, 12},   /* 96*/
      {0x0380, 12},  {0x0b80, 12},  {0x0780, 12},  {0x0f80, 12},   /*100*/
      {0x0800, 12}                                 /*EOL*/         /*104*/
};
```

Listing F.2. The T.4 binary decoder tree.

ARRAY NAMES:	whitetree, blacktree, eoltree
TYPE:	Array of T4NODE (typedef)
FUNCTION:	Each element contains a binary tree node to the T.4 Huffman variable-length. The eoltree provides indefinite looping through zero-fill bits.
LIBRARY:	FAX.LIB
INCLUDE FILES:	T4.h

```
T4NODE whitetree[], blacktree[], eoltree[];

T4NODE whitetree[] = {
/* 000 */    {&whitetree[1],    &whitetree[2],    NOTTERMINAL},
/* 001 */    {&whitetree[3],    &whitetree[4],    NOTTERMINAL},
/* 002 */    {&whitetree[5],    &whitetree[6],    NOTTERMINAL},
/* 003 */    {&whitetree[7],    &whitetree[8],    NOTTERMINAL},
/* 004 */    {&whitetree[9],    &whitetree[10],   NOTTERMINAL},
/* 005 */    {&whitetree[11],   &whitetree[12],   NOTTERMINAL},
/* 006 */    {&whitetree[13],   &whitetree[14],   NOTTERMINAL},
/* 007 */    {&whitetree[15],   &whitetree[16],   NOTTERMINAL},
/* 008 */    {&whitetree[17],   &whitetree[18],   NOTTERMINAL},
/* 009 */    {&whitetree[19],   &whitetree[20],   NOTTERMINAL},
/* 010 */    {&whitetree[21],   &whitetree[22],   NOTTERMINAL},
/* 011 */    {&whitetree[23],   &whitetree[24],   NOTTERMINAL},
/* 012 */    {&whitetree[25],   &whitetree[26],   NOTTERMINAL},
/* 013 */    {&whitetree[27],   &whitetree[28],   NOTTERMINAL},
/* 014 */    {&whitetree[29],   &whitetree[30],   NOTTERMINAL},
/* 015 */    {&whitetree[31],   &whitetree[32],   NOTTERMINAL},
/* 016 */    {&whitetree[33],   &whitetree[34],   NOTTERMINAL},
/* 017 */    {&whitetree[35],   &whitetree[36],   NOTTERMINAL},
/* 018 */    {&whitetree[37],   &whitetree[38],   NOTTERMINAL},
/* 019 */    {&whitetree[39],   &whitetree[40],   NOTTERMINAL},
/* 020 */    {&whitetree[41],   &whitetree[42],   NOTTERMINAL},
/* 021 */    {&whitetree[43],   &whitetree[44],   NOTTERMINAL},
/* 022 */    {&blacktree[1],    &blacktree[2],    2},
/* 023 */    {&blacktree[1],    &blacktree[2],    3},
/* 024 */    {&whitetree[45],   &whitetree[46],   NOTTERMINAL},
/* 025 */    {&whitetree[47],   &whitetree[48],   NOTTERMINAL},
/* 026 */    {&blacktree[1],    &blacktree[2],    4},
/* 027 */    {&blacktree[1],    &blacktree[2],    5},
/* 028 */    {&whitetree[49],   &whitetree[50],   NOTTERMINAL},
/* 029 */    {&blacktree[1],    &blacktree[2],    6},
/* 030 */    {&blacktree[1],    &blacktree[2],    7},
/* 031 */    {&whitetree[51],   &whitetree[52],   NOTTERMINAL},
/* 032 */    {&whitetree[53],   &whitetree[54],   NOTTERMINAL},
/* 033 */    {&whitetree[55],   &whitetree[56],   NOTTERMINAL},
/* 034 */    {&whitetree[57],   &whitetree[58],   NOTTERMINAL},
/* 035 */    {&whitetree[59],   &whitetree[60],   NOTTERMINAL},
/* 036 */    {&whitetree[61],   &whitetree[62],   NOTTERMINAL},
/* 037 */    {&whitetree[63],   &whitetree[64],   NOTTERMINAL},
/* 038 */    {&blacktree[1],    &blacktree[2],    10},
/* 039 */    {&blacktree[1],    &blacktree[2],    11},
/* 040 */    {&whitetree[65],   &whitetree[66],   NOTTERMINAL},
/* 041 */    {&whitetree[67],   &whitetree[68],   NOTTERMINAL},
/* 042 */    {&whitetree[69],   &whitetree[70],   NOTTERMINAL},
/* 043 */    {&whitetree[71],   &whitetree[72],   NOTTERMINAL},
/* 044 */    {&whitetree[73],   &whitetree[74],   NOTTERMINAL},
/* 045 */    {&whitetree[1],    &whitetree[2],    128},
/* 046 */    {&blacktree[1],    &blacktree[2],    8},
/* 047 */    {&blacktree[1],    &blacktree[2],    9},
/* 048 */    {&whitetree[75],   &whitetree[76],   NOTTERMINAL},
/* 049 */    {&whitetree[77],   &whitetree[78],   NOTTERMINAL},
/* 050 */    {&whitetree[1],    &whitetree[2],    64},
```

continues

Listing F.2. continued

```
/* 051 */     {&whitetree[79],  &whitetree[80],  NOTTERMINAL},
/* 052 */     {&whitetree[81],  &whitetree[82],  NOTTERMINAL},
/* 053 */     {&whitetree[83],  &whitetree[84],  NOTTERMINAL},
/* 054 */     {&blacktree[1],   &blacktree[2],   13},
/* 055 */     {&whitetree[85],  &whitetree[86],  NOTTERMINAL},
/* 056 */     {&whitetree[87],  &whitetree[88],  NOTTERMINAL},
/* 057 */     {&whitetree[89],  &whitetree[90],  NOTTERMINAL},
/* 058 */     {&blacktree[1],   &blacktree[2],   1},
/* 059 */     {&blacktree[1],   &blacktree[2],   12},
/* 060 */     {&whitetree[91],  &whitetree[92],  NOTTERMINAL},
/* 061 */     {&whitetree[93],  &whitetree[94],  NOTTERMINAL},
/* 062 */     {&whitetree[95],  &whitetree[96],  NOTTERMINAL},
/* 063 */     {&whitetree[97],  &whitetree[98],  NOTTERMINAL},
/* 064 */     {&whitetree[99],  &whitetree[100], NOTTERMINAL},
/* 065 */     {&whitetree[101], &whitetree[102], NOTTERMINAL},
/* 066 */     {&whitetree[103], &whitetree[104], NOTTERMINAL},
/* 067 */     {&whitetree[105], &whitetree[106], NOTTERMINAL},
/* 068 */     {&whitetree[107], &whitetree[108], NOTTERMINAL},
/* 069 */     {&whitetree[109], &whitetree[110], NOTTERMINAL},
/* 070 */     {&whitetree[1],   &whitetree[2],   192},
/* 071 */     {&whitetree[1],   &whitetree[2],   1664},
/* 072 */     {&whitetree[111], &whitetree[112], NOTTERMINAL},
/* 073 */     {&whitetree[113], &whitetree[114], NOTTERMINAL},
/* 074 */     {&whitetree[115], &whitetree[116], NOTTERMINAL},
/* 075 */     {&blacktree[1],   &blacktree[2],   16},
/* 076 */     {&blacktree[1],   &blacktree[2],   17},
/* 077 */     {&blacktree[1],   &blacktree[2],   14},
/* 078 */     {&blacktree[1],   &blacktree[2],   15},
/* 079 */     {&whitetree[117], &whitetree[118], NOTTERMINAL},
/* 080 */     {&whitetree[119], &whitetree[120], NOTTERMINAL},
/* 081 */     {&whitetree[121], &whitetree[122], NOTTERMINAL},
/* 082 */     {&blacktree[1],   &blacktree[2],   22},
/* 083 */     {&blacktree[1],   &blacktree[2],   23},
/* 084 */     {&whitetree[123], &whitetree[124], NOTTERMINAL},
/* 085 */     {&blacktree[1],   &blacktree[2],   20},
/* 086 */     {&whitetree[125], &whitetree[126], NOTTERMINAL},
/* 087 */     {&whitetree[127], &whitetree[128], NOTTERMINAL},
/* 088 */     {&whitetree[129], &whitetree[130], NOTTERMINAL},
/* 089 */     {&blacktree[1],   &blacktree[2],   19},
/* 090 */     {&whitetree[131], &whitetree[132], NOTTERMINAL},
/* 091 */     {&whitetree[133], &whitetree[134], NOTTERMINAL},
/* 092 */     {&blacktree[1],   &blacktree[2],   26},
/* 093 */     {&whitetree[135], &whitetree[136], NOTTERMINAL},
/* 094 */     {&whitetree[137], &whitetree[138], NOTTERMINAL},
/* 095 */     {&whitetree[139], &whitetree[140], NOTTERMINAL},
/* 096 */     {&blacktree[1],   &blacktree[2],   21},
/* 097 */     {&blacktree[1],   &blacktree[2],   28},
/* 098 */     {&whitetree[141], &whitetree[142], NOTTERMINAL},
/* 099 */     {&whitetree[143], &whitetree[144], NOTTERMINAL},
/* 100 */     {&whitetree[145], &whitetree[146], NOTTERMINAL},
/* 101 */     {&blacktree[1],   &blacktree[2],   27},
/* 102 */     {&whitetree[147], &whitetree[148], NOTTERMINAL},
/* 103 */     {&whitetree[149], &whitetree[150], NOTTERMINAL},
```

```
/* 104 */    {&blacktree[1],   &blacktree[2],   18},
/* 105 */    {&blacktree[1],   &blacktree[2],   24},
/* 106 */    {&whitetree[151], &whitetree[152], NOTTERMINAL},
/* 107 */    {&whitetree[153], &whitetree[154], NOTTERMINAL},
/* 108 */    {&blacktree[1],   &blacktree[2],   25},
/* 109 */    {&whitetree[155], &whitetree[156], NOTTERMINAL},
/* 110 */    {&whitetree[157], &whitetree[158], NOTTERMINAL},
/* 111 */    {&whitetree[159], &whitetree[160], NOTTERMINAL},
/* 112 */    {&whitetree[161], &whitetree[162], NOTTERMINAL},
/* 113 */    {&whitetree[163], &whitetree[164], NOTTERMINAL},
/* 114 */    {&whitetree[165], &whitetree[166], NOTTERMINAL},
/* 115 */    {&whitetree[167], &whitetree[168], NOTTERMINAL},
/* 116 */    {&whitetree[1],   &whitetree[2],   256},
/* 117 */    {&whitetree[169], &eoltree[0],     NOTTERMINAL},
/* 118 */    {&whitetree[170], &whitetree[171], NOTTERMINAL},
/* 119 */    {&blacktree[1],   &blacktree[2],   29},
/* 120 */    {&blacktree[1],   &blacktree[2],   30},
/* 121 */    {&blacktree[1],   &blacktree[2],   45},
/* 122 */    {&blacktree[1],   &blacktree[2],   46},
/* 123 */    {&blacktree[1],   &blacktree[2],   47},
/* 124 */    {&blacktree[1],   &blacktree[2],   48},
/* 125 */    {&blacktree[1],   &blacktree[2],   33},
/* 126 */    {&blacktree[1],   &blacktree[2],   34},
/* 127 */    {&blacktree[1],   &blacktree[2],   35},
/* 128 */    {&blacktree[1],   &blacktree[2],   36},
/* 129 */    {&blacktree[1],   &blacktree[2],   37},
/* 130 */    {&blacktree[1],   &blacktree[2],   38},
/* 131 */    {&blacktree[1],   &blacktree[2],   31},
/* 132 */    {&blacktree[1],   &blacktree[2],   32},
/* 133 */    {&blacktree[1],   &blacktree[2],   53},
/* 134 */    {&blacktree[1],   &blacktree[2],   54},
/* 135 */    {&blacktree[1],   &blacktree[2],   39},
/* 136 */    {&blacktree[1],   &blacktree[2],   40},
/* 137 */    {&blacktree[1],   &blacktree[2],   41},
/* 138 */    {&blacktree[1],   &blacktree[2],   42},
/* 139 */    {&blacktree[1],   &blacktree[2],   43},
/* 140 */    {&blacktree[1],   &blacktree[2],   44},
/* 141 */    {&blacktree[1],   &blacktree[2],   61},
/* 142 */    {&blacktree[1],   &blacktree[2],   62},
/* 143 */    {&blacktree[1],   &blacktree[2],   63},
/* 144 */    {&blacktree[1],   &blacktree[2],   0},
/* 145 */    {&whitetree[1],   &whitetree[2],   320},
/* 146 */    {&whitetree[1],   &whitetree[2],   384},
/* 147 */    {&blacktree[1],   &blacktree[2],   59},
/* 148 */    {&blacktree[1],   &blacktree[2],   60},
/* 149 */    {&whitetree[172], &whitetree[173], NOTTERMINAL},
/* 150 */    {&whitetree[174], &whitetree[175], NOTTERMINAL},
/* 151 */    {&blacktree[1],   &blacktree[2],   49},
/* 152 */    {&blacktree[1],   &blacktree[2],   50},
/* 153 */    {&blacktree[1],   &blacktree[2],   51},
/* 154 */    {&blacktree[1],   &blacktree[2],   52},
/* 155 */    {&blacktree[1],   &blacktree[2],   55},
/* 156 */    {&blacktree[1],   &blacktree[2],   56},
/* 157 */    {&blacktree[1],   &blacktree[2],   57},
```

continues

Listing F.2. continued

```
/* 158 */    {&blacktree[1],   &blacktree[2],   58},
/* 159 */    {&whitetree[1],   &whitetree[2],   448},
/* 160 */    {&whitetree[1],   &whitetree[2],   512},
/* 161 */    {&whitetree[176], &whitetree[177], NOTTERMINAL},
/* 162 */    {&whitetree[1],   &whitetree[2],   640},
/* 163 */    {&whitetree[1],   &whitetree[2],   576},
/* 164 */    {&whitetree[178], &whitetree[179], NOTTERMINAL},
/* 165 */    {&whitetree[180], &whitetree[181], NOTTERMINAL},
/* 166 */    {&whitetree[182], &whitetree[183], NOTTERMINAL},
/* 167 */    {&whitetree[184], &whitetree[185], NOTTERMINAL},
/* 168 */    {&whitetree[186], &whitetree[187], NOTTERMINAL},
/* 169 */    {&whitetree[188], &eoltree[0],     NOTTERMINAL},
/* 170 */    {&whitetree[189], &whitetree[190], NOTTERMINAL},
/* 171 */    {&whitetree[191], &whitetree[192], NOTTERMINAL},
/* 172 */    {&whitetree[1],   &whitetree[2],   1472},
/* 173 */    {&whitetree[1],   &whitetree[2],   1536},
/* 174 */    {&whitetree[1],   &whitetree[2],   1600},
/* 175 */    {&whitetree[1],   &whitetree[2],   1728},
/* 176 */    {&whitetree[1],   &whitetree[2],   704},
/* 177 */    {&whitetree[1],   &whitetree[2],   768},
/* 178 */    {&whitetree[1],   &whitetree[2],   832},
/* 179 */    {&whitetree[1],   &whitetree[2],   896},
/* 180 */    {&whitetree[1],   &whitetree[2],   960},
/* 181 */    {&whitetree[1],   &whitetree[2],   1024},
/* 182 */    {&whitetree[1],   &whitetree[2],   1088},
/* 183 */    {&whitetree[1],   &whitetree[2],   1152},
/* 184 */    {&whitetree[1],   &whitetree[2],   1216},
/* 185 */    {&whitetree[1],   &whitetree[2],   1280},
/* 186 */    {&whitetree[1],   &whitetree[2],   1344},
/* 187 */    {&whitetree[1],   &whitetree[2],   1408},
/* 188 */    {&whitetree[193], &eoltree[0],     NOTTERMINAL},
/* 189 */    {&whitetree[194], &whitetree[195], NOTTERMINAL},
/* 190 */    {&whitetree[196], &whitetree[197], NOTTERMINAL},
/* 191 */    {&whitetree[198], &whitetree[199], NOTTERMINAL},
/* 192 */    {&whitetree[200], &whitetree[201], NOTTERMINAL},
/* 193 */    {&whitetree[193], &whitetree[202], NOTTERMINAL},
/* 194 */    {&whitetree[1],   &whitetree[2],   1792},
/* 195 */    {&whitetree[203], &whitetree[204], NOTTERMINAL},
/* 196 */    {&whitetree[205], &whitetree[206], NOTTERMINAL},
/* 197 */    {&whitetree[207], &whitetree[208], NOTTERMINAL},
/* 198 */    {&whitetree[1],   &whitetree[2],   1856},
/* 199 */    {&whitetree[1],   &whitetree[2],   1920},
/* 200 */    {&whitetree[209], &whitetree[210], NOTTERMINAL},
/* 201 */    {&whitetree[211], &whitetree[212], NOTTERMINAL},
/* 202 */    {&whitetree[1],   &whitetree[2],   EOL_MARKER },
/* 203 */    {&whitetree[1],   &whitetree[2],   1984},
/* 204 */    {&whitetree[1],   &whitetree[2],   2048},
/* 205 */    {&whitetree[1],   &whitetree[2],   2112},
/* 206 */    {&whitetree[1],   &whitetree[2],   2176},
/* 207 */    {&whitetree[1],   &whitetree[2],   2240},
/* 208 */    {&whitetree[1],   &whitetree[2],   2304},
/* 209 */    {&whitetree[1],   &whitetree[2],   2368},
/* 210 */    {&whitetree[1],   &whitetree[2],   2432},
```

```
/* 211 */      {&whitetree[1],   &whitetree[2],   2496},
/* 212 */      {&whitetree[1],   &whitetree[2],   2560},
};

T4NODE blacktree[] = {
/* 000 */      {&blacktree[1],   &blacktree[2],   NOTTERMINAL},
/* 001 */      {&blacktree[3],   &blacktree[4],   NOTTERMINAL},
/* 002 */      {&blacktree[5],   &blacktree[6],   NOTTERMINAL},
/* 003 */      {&blacktree[7],   &blacktree[8],   NOTTERMINAL},
/* 004 */      {&blacktree[9],   &blacktree[10],  NOTTERMINAL},
/* 005 */      {&whitetree[1],   &whitetree[2],   3},
/* 006 */      {&whitetree[1],   &whitetree[2],   2},
/* 007 */      {&blacktree[11],  &blacktree[12],  NOTTERMINAL},
/* 008 */      {&blacktree[13],  &blacktree[14],  NOTTERMINAL},
/* 009 */      {&whitetree[1],   &whitetree[2],   1},
/* 010 */      {&whitetree[1],   &whitetree[2],   4},
/* 011 */      {&blacktree[15],  &blacktree[16],  NOTTERMINAL},
/* 012 */      {&blacktree[17],  &blacktree[18],  NOTTERMINAL},
/* 013 */      {&whitetree[1],   &whitetree[2],   6},
/* 014 */      {&whitetree[1],   &whitetree[2],   5},
/* 015 */      {&blacktree[19],  &blacktree[20],  NOTTERMINAL},
/* 016 */      {&blacktree[21],  &blacktree[22],  NOTTERMINAL},
/* 017 */      {&blacktree[23],  &blacktree[24],  NOTTERMINAL},
/* 018 */      {&whitetree[1],   &whitetree[2],   7},
/* 019 */      {&blacktree[25],  &blacktree[26],  NOTTERMINAL},
/* 020 */      {&blacktree[27],  &blacktree[28],  NOTTERMINAL},
/* 021 */      {&blacktree[29],  &blacktree[30],  NOTTERMINAL},
/* 022 */      {&blacktree[31],  &blacktree[32],  NOTTERMINAL},
/* 023 */      {&whitetree[1],   &whitetree[2],   9},
/* 024 */      {&whitetree[1],   &whitetree[2],   8},
/* 025 */      {&blacktree[33],  &blacktree[34],  NOTTERMINAL},
/* 026 */      {&blacktree[35],  &blacktree[36],  NOTTERMINAL},
/* 027 */      {&blacktree[37],  &blacktree[38],  NOTTERMINAL},
/* 028 */      {&blacktree[39],  &blacktree[40],  NOTTERMINAL},
/* 029 */      {&whitetree[1],   &whitetree[2],   10},
/* 030 */      {&whitetree[1],   &whitetree[2],   11},
/* 031 */      {&blacktree[41],  &blacktree[42],  NOTTERMINAL},
/* 032 */      {&whitetree[1],   &whitetree[2],   12},
/* 033 */      {&blacktree[43],  &eoltree[0],     NOTTERMINAL},
/* 034 */      {&blacktree[44],  &blacktree[45],  NOTTERMINAL},
/* 035 */      {&blacktree[46],  &blacktree[47],  NOTTERMINAL},
/* 036 */      {&blacktree[48],  &blacktree[49],  NOTTERMINAL},
/* 037 */      {&whitetree[1],   &whitetree[2],   13},
/* 038 */      {&blacktree[50],  &blacktree[51],  NOTTERMINAL},
/* 039 */      {&blacktree[52],  &blacktree[53],  NOTTERMINAL},
/* 040 */      {&whitetree[1],   &whitetree[2],   14},
/* 041 */      {&blacktree[54],  &blacktree[55],  NOTTERMINAL},
/* 042 */      {&blacktree[56],  &blacktree[57],  NOTTERMINAL},
/* 043 */      {&blacktree[58],  &eoltree[0],     NOTTERMINAL},
/* 044 */      {&blacktree[59],  &blacktree[60],  NOTTERMINAL},
/* 045 */      {&blacktree[61],  &blacktree[62],  NOTTERMINAL},
/* 046 */      {&blacktree[63],  &blacktree[64],  NOTTERMINAL},
/* 047 */      {&blacktree[65],  &blacktree[66],  NOTTERMINAL},
/* 048 */      {&blacktree[67],  &blacktree[68],  NOTTERMINAL},
```

continues

Listing F.2. continued

```
/* 049 */    {&blacktree[69],   &blacktree[70],   NOTTERMINAL},
/* 050 */    {&blacktree[71],   &blacktree[72],   NOTTERMINAL},
/* 051 */    {&blacktree[73],   &blacktree[74],   NOTTERMINAL},
/* 052 */    {&blacktree[75],   &blacktree[76],   NOTTERMINAL},
/* 053 */    {&blacktree[77],   &blacktree[78],   NOTTERMINAL},
/* 054 */    {&whitetree[1],    &whitetree[2],    15},
/* 055 */    {&blacktree[79],   &blacktree[80],   NOTTERMINAL},
/* 056 */    {&blacktree[81],   &blacktree[82],   NOTTERMINAL},
/* 057 */    {&blacktree[83],   &blacktree[84],   NOTTERMINAL},
/* 058 */    {&blacktree[85],   &eoltree[0],      NOTTERMINAL},
/* 059 */    {&blacktree[86],   &blacktree[87],   NOTTERMINAL},
/* 060 */    {&blacktree[88],   &blacktree[89],   NOTTERMINAL},
/* 061 */    {&blacktree[90],   &blacktree[91],   NOTTERMINAL},
/* 062 */    {&blacktree[92],   &blacktree[93],   NOTTERMINAL},
/* 063 */    {&whitetree[1],    &whitetree[2],    18},
/* 064 */    {&blacktree[94],   &blacktree[95],   NOTTERMINAL},
/* 065 */    {&blacktree[96],   &blacktree[97],   NOTTERMINAL},
/* 066 */    {&blacktree[98],   &blacktree[99],   NOTTERMINAL},
/* 067 */    {&blacktree[100],  &blacktree[101],  NOTTERMINAL},
/* 068 */    {&blacktree[102],  &blacktree[103],  NOTTERMINAL},
/* 069 */    {&blacktree[104],  &blacktree[105],  NOTTERMINAL},
/* 070 */    {&blacktree[1],    &blacktree[2],    64},
/* 071 */    {&blacktree[106],  &blacktree[107],  NOTTERMINAL},
/* 072 */    {&blacktree[108],  &blacktree[109],  NOTTERMINAL},
/* 073 */    {&blacktree[110],  &blacktree[111],  NOTTERMINAL},
/* 074 */    {&whitetree[1],    &whitetree[2],    16},
/* 075 */    {&whitetree[1],    &whitetree[2],    17},
/* 076 */    {&blacktree[112],  &blacktree[113],  NOTTERMINAL},
/* 077 */    {&blacktree[114],  &blacktree[115],  NOTTERMINAL},
/* 078 */    {&blacktree[116],  &blacktree[117],  NOTTERMINAL},
/* 079 */    {&blacktree[118],  &blacktree[119],  NOTTERMINAL},
/* 080 */    {&blacktree[120],  &blacktree[121],  NOTTERMINAL},
/* 081 */    {&blacktree[122],  &blacktree[123],  NOTTERMINAL},
/* 082 */    {&blacktree[124],  &blacktree[125],  NOTTERMINAL},
/* 083 */    {&blacktree[126],  &blacktree[127],  NOTTERMINAL},
/* 084 */    {&whitetree[1],    &whitetree[2],    0},
/* 085 */    {&blacktree[85],   &blacktree[128],  NOTTERMINAL},
/* 086 */    {&blacktree[1],    &blacktree[2],    1792},
/* 087 */    {&blacktree[129],  &blacktree[130],  NOTTERMINAL},
/* 088 */    {&blacktree[131],  &blacktree[132],  NOTTERMINAL},
/* 089 */    {&blacktree[133],  &blacktree[134],  NOTTERMINAL},
/* 090 */    {&blacktree[1],    &blacktree[2],    1856},
/* 091 */    {&blacktree[1],    &blacktree[2],    1920},
/* 092 */    {&blacktree[135],  &blacktree[136],  NOTTERMINAL},
/* 093 */    {&blacktree[137],  &blacktree[138],  NOTTERMINAL},
/* 094 */    {&blacktree[139],  &blacktree[140],  NOTTERMINAL},
/* 095 */    {&blacktree[141],  &blacktree[142],  NOTTERMINAL},
/* 096 */    {&blacktree[143],  &blacktree[144],  NOTTERMINAL},
/* 097 */    {&blacktree[145],  &blacktree[146],  NOTTERMINAL},
/* 098 */    {&blacktree[147],  &blacktree[148],  NOTTERMINAL},
/* 099 */    {&whitetree[1],    &whitetree[2],    24},
/* 100 */    {&whitetree[1],    &whitetree[2],    25},
/* 101 */    {&blacktree[149],  &blacktree[150],  NOTTERMINAL},
```

```
/* 102 */        {&blacktree[151], &blacktree[152], NOTTERMINAL},
/* 103 */        {&blacktree[153], &blacktree[154], NOTTERMINAL},
/* 104 */        {&blacktree[155], &blacktree[156], NOTTERMINAL},
/* 105 */        {&blacktree[157], &blacktree[158], NOTTERMINAL},
/* 106 */        {&whitetree[1],   &whitetree[2],    23},
/* 107 */        {&blacktree[159], &blacktree[160], NOTTERMINAL},
/* 108 */        {&blacktree[161], &blacktree[162], NOTTERMINAL},
/* 109 */        {&blacktree[163], &blacktree[164], NOTTERMINAL},
/* 110 */        {&blacktree[165], &blacktree[166], NOTTERMINAL},
/* 111 */        {&blacktree[167], &blacktree[168], NOTTERMINAL},
/* 112 */        {&blacktree[169], &blacktree[170], NOTTERMINAL},
/* 113 */        {&blacktree[171], &blacktree[172], NOTTERMINAL},
/* 114 */        {&blacktree[173], &blacktree[174], NOTTERMINAL},
/* 115 */        {&blacktree[175], &blacktree[176], NOTTERMINAL},
/* 116 */        {&blacktree[177], &blacktree[178], NOTTERMINAL},
/* 117 */        {&whitetree[1],   &whitetree[2],    22},
/* 118 */        {&blacktree[179], &blacktree[180], NOTTERMINAL},
/* 119 */        {&blacktree[181], &blacktree[182], NOTTERMINAL},
/* 120 */        {&blacktree[183], &blacktree[184], NOTTERMINAL},
/* 121 */        {&whitetree[1],   &whitetree[2],    19},
/* 122 */        {&whitetree[1],   &whitetree[2],    20},
/* 123 */        {&blacktree[185], &blacktree[186], NOTTERMINAL},
/* 124 */        {&blacktree[187], &blacktree[188], NOTTERMINAL},
/* 125 */        {&blacktree[189], &blacktree[190], NOTTERMINAL},
/* 126 */        {&whitetree[1],   &whitetree[2],    21},
/* 127 */        {&blacktree[191], &blacktree[192], NOTTERMINAL},
/* 128 */        {&whitetree[1],   &whitetree[2],    EOL_MARKER},
/* 129 */        {&blacktree[1],   &blacktree[2],    1984},
/* 130 */        {&blacktree[1],   &blacktree[2],    2048},
/* 131 */        {&blacktree[1],   &blacktree[2],    2112},
/* 132 */        {&blacktree[1],   &blacktree[2],    2176},
/* 133 */        {&blacktree[1],   &blacktree[2],    2240},
/* 134 */        {&blacktree[1],   &blacktree[2],    2304},
/* 135 */        {&blacktree[1],   &blacktree[2],    2368},
/* 136 */        {&blacktree[1],   &blacktree[2],    2432},
/* 137 */        {&blacktree[1],   &blacktree[2],    2496},
/* 138 */        {&blacktree[1],   &blacktree[2],    2560},
/* 139 */        {&whitetree[1],   &whitetree[2],    52},
/* 140 */        {&blacktree[193], &blacktree[194], NOTTERMINAL},
/* 141 */        {&blacktree[195], &blacktree[196], NOTTERMINAL},
/* 142 */        {&whitetree[1],   &whitetree[2],    55},
/* 143 */        {&whitetree[1],   &whitetree[2],    56},
/* 144 */        {&blacktree[197], &blacktree[198], NOTTERMINAL},
/* 145 */        {&blacktree[199], &blacktree[200], NOTTERMINAL},
/* 146 */        {&whitetree[1],   &whitetree[2],    59},
/* 147 */        {&whitetree[1],   &whitetree[2],    60},
/* 148 */        {&blacktree[201], &blacktree[202], NOTTERMINAL},
/* 149 */        {&blacktree[203], &blacktree[204], NOTTERMINAL},
/* 150 */        {&blacktree[1],   &blacktree[2],    320},
/* 151 */        {&blacktree[1],   &blacktree[2],    384},
/* 152 */        {&blacktree[1],   &blacktree[2],    448},
/* 153 */        {&blacktree[205], &blacktree[206], NOTTERMINAL},
/* 154 */        {&whitetree[1],   &whitetree[2],    53},
/* 155 */        {&whitetree[1],   &whitetree[2],    54},
```

continues

Listing F.2. continued

```
/* 156 */    {&blacktree[207], &blacktree[208], NOTTERMINAL},
/* 157 */    {&blacktree[209], &blacktree[210], NOTTERMINAL},
/* 158 */    {&blacktree[211], &blacktree[212], NOTTERMINAL},
/* 159 */    {&whitetree[1],   &whitetree[2],    50},
/* 160 */    {&whitetree[1],   &whitetree[2],    51},
/* 161 */    {&whitetree[1],   &whitetree[2],    44},
/* 162 */    {&whitetree[1],   &whitetree[2],    45},
/* 163 */    {&whitetree[1],   &whitetree[2],    46},
/* 164 */    {&whitetree[1],   &whitetree[2],    47},
/* 165 */    {&whitetree[1],   &whitetree[2],    57},
/* 166 */    {&whitetree[1],   &whitetree[2],    58},
/* 167 */    {&whitetree[1],   &whitetree[2],    61},
/* 168 */    {&blacktree[1],   &blacktree[2],   256},
/* 169 */    {&whitetree[1],   &whitetree[2],    48},
/* 170 */    {&whitetree[1],   &whitetree[2],    49},
/* 171 */    {&whitetree[1],   &whitetree[2],    62},
/* 172 */    {&whitetree[1],   &whitetree[2],    63},
/* 173 */    {&whitetree[1],   &whitetree[2],    30},
/* 174 */    {&whitetree[1],   &whitetree[2],    31},
/* 175 */    {&whitetree[1],   &whitetree[2],    32},
/* 176 */    {&whitetree[1],   &whitetree[2],    33},
/* 177 */    {&whitetree[1],   &whitetree[2],    40},
/* 178 */    {&whitetree[1],   &whitetree[2],    41},
/* 179 */    {&blacktree[1],   &blacktree[2],   128},
/* 180 */    {&blacktree[1],   &blacktree[2],   192},
/* 181 */    {&whitetree[1],   &whitetree[2],    26},
/* 182 */    {&whitetree[1],   &whitetree[2],    27},
/* 183 */    {&whitetree[1],   &whitetree[2],    28},
/* 184 */    {&whitetree[1],   &whitetree[2],    29},
/* 185 */    {&whitetree[1],   &whitetree[2],    34},
/* 186 */    {&whitetree[1],   &whitetree[2],    35},
/* 187 */    {&whitetree[1],   &whitetree[2],    36},
/* 188 */    {&whitetree[1],   &whitetree[2],    37},
/* 189 */    {&whitetree[1],   &whitetree[2],    38},
/* 190 */    {&whitetree[1],   &whitetree[2],    39},
/* 191 */    {&whitetree[1],   &whitetree[2],    42},
/* 192 */    {&whitetree[1],   &whitetree[2],    43},
/* 193 */    {&blacktree[1],   &blacktree[2],   640},
/* 194 */    {&blacktree[1],   &blacktree[2],   704},
/* 195 */    {&blacktree[1],   &blacktree[2],   768},
/* 196 */    {&blacktree[1],   &blacktree[2],   832},
/* 197 */    {&blacktree[1],   &blacktree[2],  1280},
/* 198 */    {&blacktree[1],   &blacktree[2],  1344},
/* 199 */    {&blacktree[1],   &blacktree[2],  1408},
/* 200 */    {&blacktree[1],   &blacktree[2],  1472},
/* 201 */    {&blacktree[1],   &blacktree[2],  1536},
/* 202 */    {&blacktree[1],   &blacktree[2],  1600},
/* 203 */    {&blacktree[1],   &blacktree[2],  1664},
/* 204 */    {&blacktree[1],   &blacktree[2],  1728},
/* 205 */    {&blacktree[1],   &blacktree[2],   512},
/* 206 */    {&blacktree[1],   &blacktree[2],   576},
/* 207 */    {&blacktree[1],   &blacktree[2],   896},
/* 208 */    {&blacktree[1],   &blacktree[2],   960},
```

```
/* 209 */       {&blacktree[1],   &blacktree[2],   1024},
/* 210 */       {&blacktree[1],   &blacktree[2],   1088},
/* 211 */       {&blacktree[1],   &blacktree[2],   1152},
/* 212 */       {&blacktree[1],   &blacktree[2],   1216},
};


T4NODE eoltree[] = {
/* 000 */       {&eoltree[1],     &eoltree[0],     NOTTERMINAL},
/* 001 */       {&eoltree[2],     &eoltree[0],     NOTTERMINAL},
/* 002 */       {&eoltree[3],     &eoltree[0],     NOTTERMINAL},
/* 003 */       {&eoltree[4],     &eoltree[0],     NOTTERMINAL},
/* 004 */       {&eoltree[5],     &eoltree[0],     NOTTERMINAL},
/* 005 */       {&eoltree[6],     &eoltree[0],     NOTTERMINAL},
/* 006 */       {&eoltree[7],     &eoltree[0],     NOTTERMINAL},
/* 007 */       {&eoltree[8],     &eoltree[0],     NOTTERMINAL},
/* 008 */       {&eoltree[9],     &eoltree[0],     NOTTERMINAL},
/* 009 */       {&eoltree[10],    &eoltree[0],     NOTTERMINAL},
/* 010 */       {&eoltree[11],    &eoltree[0],     NOTTERMINAL},
/* 011 */       {&eoltree[11],    &eoltree[12],    NOTTERMINAL},
/* 012 */       {&whitetree[1],   &whitetree[2],   EOL_MARKER}
};

#ifdef NO_EOL_OUTPUT

T4NODE _eoltree[] = {
/* 000 */       {&_eoltree[1],    &_eoltree[0],    NOTTERMINAL},
/* 001 */       {&_eoltree[2],    &_eoltree[0],    NOTTERMINAL},
/* 002 */       {&_eoltree[3],    &_eoltree[0],    NOTTERMINAL},
/* 003 */       {&_eoltree[4],    &_eoltree[0],    NOTTERMINAL},
/* 004 */       {&_eoltree[5],    &_eoltree[0],    NOTTERMINAL},
/* 005 */       {&_eoltree[6],    &_eoltree[0],    NOTTERMINAL},
/* 006 */       {&_eoltree[7],    &_eoltree[0],    NOTTERMINAL},
/* 007 */       {&_eoltree[8],    &_eoltree[0],    NOTTERMINAL},
/* 008 */       {&_eoltree[9],    &_eoltree[0],    NOTTERMINAL},
/* 009 */       {&_eoltree[10],   &_eoltree[0],    NOTTERMINAL},
/* 010 */       {&_eoltree[11],   &_eoltree[0],    NOTTERMINAL},
/* 011 */       {&_eoltree[11],   &_eoltree[12],   NOTTERMINAL},
/* 012 */       {&whitetree[1],   &whitetree[2],   NOTTERMINAL}
};

#endif
```

Function Cross-Reference

continues

continues

TIFF Class F File Format

TIFF stands for *Tag Image File format*. The TIFF specification, now maintained by Aldus Corporation, describes a file format specifically for images. The file is organized into a linked list of pointers to images. Associated with each image is a group of *tags*, descriptors that define the image.

Readers unfamilar with the TIFF specification may obtain a copy of the base TIFF Specification from:

Developer's Desk
Aldus Corporation
411 First Avenue South
Seattle, WA 98104
(206) 622-5500

TIFF Class F:
Version March 1, 1992

TIFF Class F was defined in late 1989 by Joe Campbell (then of Everex Systems, Inc.) from the results of a poll of the facsimile industry. The goal was to define a file format that is simultaneously suitable for native use in Group 3 computer facsimile products and as a file interchange medium with the outside world. Since that time, there have been only three minor revisions, mostly editorial in nature.

TIFF Class F defines a subset (a "Class") of existing TIFF tags, necessary to support Group 3 facsimile data. In many cases, the values and sizes of these tags are also defined. Three new optional tags are also defined.

TIFF Classes reduce the information burden on TIFF readers and writers that wish to support narrow applications. For example, Appendix G-1 of TIFF 5.0 states that classes enable TIFF readers "to know when they can stop adding TIFF features." In other words, defining a Class enables applications interested only in reading that Class to give up if the characteristic tags and values are not present. Therefore, TIFF Class F insists on a rather narrow definition of tags. In a general TIFF file, for example, the writer would be free to create single-page documents without the NewSubFileType and PageNumber tags. Not so for a Class F file, where the multi-page tag is required even for a single page.

TIFF Class B (Bilevel) is a sub-class of TIFF. That is, all tags that are required in TIFF are also required in Class B. TIFF Class F (Facsimile) is a sub-class of Class B (Bilevel). That is, all tags that are required in Class B are also required in Class F. For some common tags, however, Class F limits the range of acceptable values. The YResolution tag, for example, is a Class B tag, but its Class F value is limited to either 98 or 196 dpi. Such tags are listed here under the heading, "Required Class F Tags."

Other Class B tags have a slightly eccentric meaning when applied to facsimile images. These are discussed in the section, "Bilevel Required." There are also tags that may be helpful but are not required. These are listed in the "Recommended Tags" section. A brief list of all the tags required by TIFF Class F, grouped by class, is in the section, "Required Facsimile Tags Grouped by Class." Finally, technical topics are discussed in the "Technical Points" and "Warnings" sections.

References

A machine-readable copy of this document can be downloaded from the Aldus Forum on CompuServe. Type **GO ALDUS** and look through the "Libraries" menu. (Make certain that you download the most recent revision.) Substantive questions about TIFF Class F can be faxed to its author: Joe Campbell (510) 526-4311, or via CompuServe Mail 71331,1237. Internet users can contact the author through the CompuServe gateway at **71331.1237@compuserve.com**.

Group 3 facsimile is described in the "Blue Book," Volume VII, Fascicle VII.3, Terminal Equipment and Protocols for Telematic Services, The International Telegraph and Telephone Consultative Committee (CCITT), Melbourne, 1988. (The 1992 revision of the Group 3 specification—due sometime in 1993—has already been incorporated into this revision of TIFF Class F.)

Class F Required

Compression = 3 or 4. *SHORT.* Group 3, one-dimensional encoding with "byte-aligned" EOLs. An EOL is said to be byte-aligned when fill bits have been added as necessary before EOL codes such that EOL always ends on a byte boundary, thus ensuring an EOL-sequence of a one-byte preceded by a zero-nibble: xxxx0000 00000001. The data in a

Class F image is not terminated with an RTC. Please see items 4 and 5 in the "Warnings" section. For Group 3 two-dimensional encoding, set bit 1 in Group3Options. Please see item 2 in the "Warnings" section.

4 Group 4 two-dimensional encoding. MMR (*Modified-Modified READ*) compression, formerly found only in Group 4 facsimile, are now available in Group 3 devices. When this option is used, bits zero and one in the Group3Options tag are ignored.

FillOrder = 1, 2. *SHORT.* TIFF Class F readers must be able to read data in both bit orders, but the vast majority of facsimile products store data LSB first, exactly as it appears on the telephone line.

1. Most Significant Bit first.

2. Least Significant Bit first.

Group3Options = 4,5. *LONG.* Data may be one- or two-dimensional, but EOLs must be byte-aligned. Uncompressed data is not allowed. When Group 4 compression is used, bits zero and one in the Group3Options tag should be ignored.

> bit 0   0 for 1-Dimensional, 1 for 2-Dimensional
> bit 1   Must be 0 (uncompressed data not allowed)
> bit 2   1 for byte-aligned EOLs

ImageWidth = 864, 1216, 1728, 2048, 2432. *SHORT or LONG.* LONG recommended. These are the fixed page widths in pixels defined in CCITT Group 3.

NewSubFileType = 2. *LONG.* The value 2 identifies a single page of a multi-page image, even if the document contains only one page.

PageNumber. *SHORT/SHORT.* This tag specifies the page numbers in the fax document. The tag comprises two SHORT values: the first value is the page number, the second is the total number of pages. The number of the first page is zero. Single-page documents therefore use 00000001 hex. The total number of pages is required only in the PageNumber tag associated with the first IFD, and is optional in subsequent IFDs. Writers utilizing this option should set the page count portion of the subsequent PageNumber tags to zero. (Please remember that the first IFD is not necessarily page one.)

ResolutionUnit = 2,3. *SHORT.* The units of measure for resolution:

> 2 = Inch
> 3 = Centimeter

XResolution = 204, 300, 400 (inches). *RATIONAL.* The horizontal resolution of the image expressed in pixels per resolution unit. See the section "Technical Points," number 6, later in this appendix.

YResolution = 98, 196, 300, 400 (inches). *RATIONAL.* The vertical resolution of the image expressed in pixels per resolution unit. See the section, "Technical Points," number 6, later in this appendix.

Bi-level Required

Although these tags are already required in Class B (bi-level) files, an explanation of their usage for facsimile images may be helpful.

BitsPerSample = 1. *SHORT.* Because facsimile is a black-and-white medium, this must be 1 (the default) for all files.

ImageLength. *SHORT or LONG. LONG* Recommended. The total number of scan lines in the image.

PhotometricInterp = 0,1. *SHORT.* This tag allows notation of an inverted ("negative") image:

> 0 = Normal
> 1 = Inverted

RowsPerStrip. *SHORT or LONG. LONG* Recommended. The number of scan lines per strip. When a page is expressed as one large strip, this is the same as the `ImageLength` tag.

SamplesPerPixel = 1. *SHORT.* The value of 1 denotes a bi-level, gray scale, or palette color image.

StripByteCounts. *SHORT or LONG. SHORT* Recommended. For each strip, the number of bytes in that strip. If a page is expressed as one large strip, this is the total number of bytes in the page after compression.

StripOffsets. *SHORT or LONG.* For each strip, the offset of that strip. The offset is measured from the beginning of the file. If a page is expressed as one large strip, there is one such entry per page.

New Tags

There are only three new tags for Class F. All three tags describe page quality. The information contained in these tags is usually obtained from the receiving facsimile hardware, but because not all devices are capable of reporting this information, the tags are optional.

Some applications need to understand exactly the error content of the data. For example, a CAD program may wish to verify that a file has a low error level before importing it into a high-accuracy document. Because Group 3 facsimile devices do not necessarily perform error correction on the image data, the quality of a received page must be inferred from the pixel count of decoded scan lines. A "good" scan line is defined as a line that, when decoded, contains the correct number of pixels. Conversely, a "bad" scan line is defined as a line that, when decoded, comprises an incorrect number of pixels.

BADFAXLINES

Tag = 326 (146 hex)

Type = SHORT or LONG

This tag reports the number of scan lines with an incorrect number of pixels encountered by the facsimile during reception (but not necessarily in the file).

Note: `PercentBad = (BadFaxLines/ImageLength) * 100`

CLEANFAXDATA

Tag = 327 (147 hex)

Type = SHORT

> 0 = The data is "pure": it contains no lines with incorrect pixel counts and no substituted lines. Computer-generated files should always have a value of 0.
> 1 = The receiving device substituted good lines for lines having an incorrect pixel count.
> 2 = Lines with an incorrect pixel count exist in the data.

Many facsimile receiving devices do not actually output bad lines. Instead, when a bad line is encountered, the receiver substitutes a good line. A variety of methods are employed to derive the pixel content of the substituted line. The most common are:

1. Fixed-pattern substitution (for example, an all-white or all-black line).

2. Substitution of a previous good line.

3. Artificial intelligence may be employed to reconstruct the line based upon context.

Although line substitution usually results in a visual improvement in the image, the image data is nevertheless corrupted. The `CleanFaxData` tag describes the error content of the data. That is, when the `BadFaxLines` and `ImageLength` tags indicate that the facsimile device encountered lines with an incorrect number of pixels during reception, the `CleanFaxData` tag indicates whether these lines are actually in the data or if the receiving facsimile device replaced them with substitute lines.

CONSECUTIVEBADFAXLINES

Tag = 328 (148 hex)

Type = LONG or SHORT

This tag reports the maximum number of consecutive lines containing an incorrect number of pixels encountered by the facsimile device during reception (but not necessarily in the file).

The BadFaxLines and ImageLength data indicate only the quantity of such lines. The ConsecutiveBadFaxLines tag is an indicator of their distribution and may therefore be a better general indicator of perceived image quality.

Recommended Tags

BadFaxLines. *LONG.*   The number of "bad" scan lines encountered by the facsimile during reception.

ConsecutiveBadFaxLines. *LONG or SHORT.*   The maximum number of consecutive scan lines with incorrect pixel count encountered by the facsimile device reception.

DateTime. *ASCII.*   Date and time in the format YYYY:MM:DD HH:MM:SS, in 24-hour format. String length including NUL byte is 20 bytes. Space between DD and HH.

DocumentName. *ASCII.*   This is the name of the document from which the document was scanned.

ImageDescription. *ASCII.*   This is an ASCII string describing the contents of the image.

Orientation. *SHORT.*   This tag might be useful for displayers that always want to show the same orientation, regardless of the image. The default value of 1 is "0th row is visual top of image, and 0th column is the visual left." A 180-degree rotation is 3. See TIFF 5.0 for an explanation of other values.

Software. *ASCII.*   The optional name and release number of the software package that created the image.

Required Tags Grouped Class

Required Tags, all TIFF: NewSubFileType, ImageWidth, ImageLength, StripOffsets, RowsPerStrip, StripByteCounts, XResolution, YResolution, NewSubFileType, ImageWidth, ImageLength, StripOffsets, RowsPerStrip, StripByteCounts, XResolution, YResolution, ResolutionUnit.

Required Tags, Class B: BitsPerSample, Compression, PhotometricInterp, SamplesPerPixel.

Required Tags, Class F: FillOrder, Group3Options, PageNumber.

File Interchangeability

File portability among various TIFF F applications, regardless of platform or operating system, is a primary goal of TIFF Class F. The following tag values should be used to assure maximum portability:

1. FillOrder is 2 (least-significant bit first).

2. Group3Options = 4 (one-dimensional encoding).

3. ImageWidth is 1728 (that is, an A4 page).

4. ImageLength must not exceed 1084 for 98 dpi documents and 2167 for 196 dpi documents (that is, an A4 page). See Note 2, below.

5. PhotometricInterp is 0 (normal).

6. ResolutionUnit = 2 (inches).

7. XResolution is 204.

8. YResolution tag is 98 or 196.

Technical Points

1. Strips

Those new to TIFF may not be familiar with the concept of *strips* embodied in the three tags RowsPerStrip, StripByteCount, StripOffsets.

In general, third-party applications that read and write TIFF files expect the image to be divided into horizontal strips, also known as *bands*. Each strip contains a few lines of the image. By using strips, a TIFF reader need not load the entire image into memory, thus enabling it to fetch and decompress small random portions of the image as necessary.

The dimensions of a strip are described by the RowsPerStrip and StripByteCount tags. The location in the TIFF file of each strip is contained in the StripOffsets tag. It is perfectly acceptable for a Class F file to store an entire page in a single strip.

In addition to strips, TIFF also permits image data to be divided into rectangular tiles. Class F images may not be organized as tiles.

2. EOL Placement in Strips

As illustrated in FIGURE 1/T.4 in Recommendation T.4 (the "Blue Book"), facsimile documents begin with an EOL (End-of-Line) code. The last line of the image is not terminated by an EOL. Expressed differently, EOLs are actually BOLs (Beginning-of-Line).

When a page is stored as a multi-strip image, one must consider where to divide scanline data. With the RTC not included, treating EOL codes like BOL codes permits all strips to have a consistent format: RowsPerStrip EOL-prefixed lines of data. Consequently, multi-strip Class F images must break data such that each strip begins with an EOL code. This is easily done if these codes are treated like BOL codes.

3. Bit Order

Although the TIFF 5.0 documentation lists the `FillOrder` tag in the category "No Longer Recommended," Class F resurrects it. Facsimile data appears on the phone line in bit-reversed order relative to its description in CCITT Recommendation T.4. Therefore, a wide majority of facsimile applications choose this natural order for storage. Nevertheless, TIFF Class F readers must be able to read data in both bit orders.

4. Multi-Page

Many existing applications already read Class F-like files, but do not support the multi-page tag. Because a multi-page format greatly simplifies file management in fax application software, Class F specifies multi-page documents (`NewSubfileType = 2`). A "multi-page document" may contain only one page.

5. Two-dimensional Encoding

PC Fax applications that wish to support two-dimensional encoding may do so by setting `Bit 0` in the `Group3Options` tag.

6. Two-Dimensional Encoding EOL Tag Bits

When two-dimensional encoding is used, the tag bit that specifies whether the next line is one- or two-dimensionally encoded is part of the byte that follows the byte-aligned EOL code. That is, the tag bit is logically considered to be part of the scan line that it describes.

7. Example Use of Page-quality Tags

Here are examples for writing the `CleanFaxData`, `BadFaxLines`, and `ConsecutiveBadFaxLines` tags:

- Facsimile hardware does not provide page quality information: write no tags.
- Facsimile hardware provides page quality information, but reports no bad lines. Write only `BadFaxLines = 0`.
- Facsimile hardware provides page quality information, and reports bad lines. Write both `BadFaxLines` and `ConsecutiveBadFaxLines`. Also write `CleanFaxData = 1 or 2` if you know whether the hardware can replace bad lines.
- Computer generated file: write `CleanFaxData = 0`.

8. High Resolution

Although 300 and 400 dpi are, strictly speaking, Group 4 resolutions, it is virtually certain that they will soon be added to Group 3 and, more important, are already in common use today through Group 3's NSF mechanism. Only the following resolutions are valid (horizontal x vertical): 204 x 98, 204 x 196, 300 x 300, 400 x 400. Those who choose to store images at the "Group 4" resolutions risk incompatibility with other fax applications.

9. Plain Paper Fax

Many plain-paper printing mechanisms such as those found on laser printers are unable to print on the entire surface of the paper. The amount of unusable space (referred to as the "grabber") varies from device to device, but as a general rule, allow about six-tenths of an inch. Failure to reduce the image accordingly may cause the receiving fax machine to shrink the image to make it fit on one page (thus changing its scale), or to print it on two sheets of paper.

The standard paper size for America (8.5 inches by 11.0 inches), is still not supported by CCITT specifications. Therefore, if you wish your images to print at scale on American plain paper fax machines, you must limit the number of lines per page to 2050 in high resolution and 1025 in low resolution.

10. Minimum TIFF Class F Support

Fax applications that do not wish to embrace TIFF Class F as a native format may elect to support it as import/export medium:

- Export   The simplest form of support is a Class F writer that produces individual single-page Class F files with the proper `NewSubFile` and `PageNumber` tags.

- Import   A Class F reader must be able to handle a Class F file containing multiple pages.

Warnings

1. Class F requires the ability to read and write at least one-dimensional T.4 Huffman ("compressed") data. Due to the disruptive effect to application software of line-length errors and because such errors are likely in everyday facsimile transmissions, uncompressed data is not allowed. In other words, "Uncompressed" bit in `Group3Options` must be 0.

2. Because two-dimensional encoding is not required for Group 3 compatibility, Class F readers may decline to read such files. Therefore, for maximum portability write only one-dimensional files. Although the same argument technically holds for "fine" (196 dpi) vertical resolution, only a tiny fraction of facsimile products support only 98 dpi. Therefore, 196-dpi files are quite portable in the real world.

3. In the spirit of TIFF, all EOLs in data must be byte-aligned. An EOL is said to be byte-aligned when Fill bits have been added as necessary before EOL codes such that EOL always ends on a byte boundary, thus ensuring an EOL-sequence of a one-byte preceded by a zero-nibble: xxxx0000 00000001.

Recall that Huffman encoding compresses bits, not bytes. This means that the end-of-line token may end in the middle of a byte. In byte alignment, extra zero bits (Fill) are added so that the first bit of data following an EOL begins on a byte boundary. In effect, byte alignment relieves application software of the burden of bit-shifting every byte while parsing scan lines for line-oriented image manipulation (such as writing a TIFF file).

4. Aside from EOLs, TIFF Class F files contain only image data. This means that the Return-to-Control sequence (RTC) is specifically prohibited. Exclusion of RTCs not only makes possible the simple concatenation of images, it eliminates the mischief of failed communications and unreadable images that their mistreatment inevitably produces.

Index

PROGRAMMING

C

G

H

I

M

N

O

V

Add to Your Sams Library Today with the Best Books for Programming, Operating Systems, and New Technologies

The easiest way to order is to pick up the phone and call

1-800-428-5331

between 9:00 a.m. and 5:00 p.m. EST.

For faster service please have your credit card available.

ISBN	Quantity	Description of Item	Unit Cost	Total Cost
0-672-30168-7		Advanced C	$39.95	
0-672-30158-X		Advanced C++	$39.95	
0-672-48470-6		Assembly Language: For Real Programmers Only!	$44.95	
0-672-30050-8		C Programmer's Guide to NetBIOS, IPX, and SPX	$49.95	
0-672-30291-8		DOS 6 Developer's Guide	$39.95	
0-672-30300-0		Real World Programming for OS/2	$39.95	
0-672-22753-3		Reference Data for Engineers: Radio, Electronics, Computers, and Communications	$99.95	
0-672-30287-X		Tom Swan's Code Secrets	$39.95	
0-672-30370-1		Visual C++ Developer's Guide	$49.95	
0-672-30150-4		Visual C++ Object-Oriented Programming	$39.95	
0-672-30030-3		Windows Programmer's Guide to Serial Communications	$39.95	
0-672-30363-9		Your Borland C++ Consultant	$29.95	
❏ 3 ½" Disk		Shipping and Handling: See information below.		
❏ 5 ¼" Disk		TOTAL		

Shipping and Handling: $4.00 for the first book, and $1.75 for each additional book. Floppy disk: add $1.75 for shipping and handling. If you need to have it NOW, we can ship product to you in 24 hours for an additional charge of approximately $18.00, and you will receive your item overnight or in two days. Overseas shipping and handling adds $2.00 per book and $8.00 for up to three disks. Prices subject to change. Call for availability and pricing information on latest editions.

201 West 103rd Street, Indianapolis, Indiana 46290

1-800-428-5331 — Orders   1-800-835-3202 — FAX   1-800-858-7674 — Customer Service

GO AHEAD. PLUG YOURSELF INTO
PRENTICE HALL COMPUTER PUBLISHING.

Introducing the PHCP Forum on CompuServe®

Yes, it's true. Now, you can have CompuServe access to the same professional, friendly folks who have made computers easier for years. On the PHCP Forum, you'll find additional information on the topics covered by every PHCP imprint—including Que, Sams Publishing, New Riders Publishing, Alpha Books, Brady Books, Hayden Books, and Adobe Press. In addition, you'll be able to receive technical support and disk updates for the software produced by Que Software and Paramount Interactive, a division of the Paramount Technology Group. It's a great way to supplement the best information in the business.

WHAT CAN YOU DO ON THE PHCP FORUM?

Play an important role in the publishing process—and make our books better while you make your work easier:

- Leave messages and ask questions about PHCP books and software—you're guaranteed a response within 24 hours

- Download helpful tips and software to help you get the most out of your computer

- Contact authors of your favorite PHCP books through electronic mail

- Present your own book ideas

- Keep up to date on all the latest books available from each of PHCP's exciting imprints

JOIN NOW AND GET A FREE COMPUSERVE STARTER KIT!

To receive your free CompuServe Introductory Membership, call toll-free, **1-800-848-8199** and ask for representative **#597**. The Starter Kit Includes:

- Personal ID number and password

- $15 credit on the system

- Subscription to CompuServe Magazine

HERE'S HOW TO PLUG INTO PHCP:

Once on the CompuServe System, type any of these phrases to access the PHCP Forum:

GO PHCP   **GO BRADY**
GO QUEBOOKS   **GO HAYDEN**
GO SAMS   **GO QUESOFT**
GO NEWRIDERS   **GO PARAMOUNTINTER**
GO ALPHA

Once you're on the CompuServe Information Service, be sure to take advantage of all of CompuServe's resources. CompuServe is home to more than 1,700 products and services—plus it has over 1.5 million members worldwide. You'll find valuable online reference materials, travel and investor services, electronic mail, weather updates, leisure-time games and hassle-free shopping (no jam-packed parking lots or crowded stores).

Seek out the hundreds of other forums that populate CompuServe. Covering diverse topics such as pet care, rock music, cooking, and political issues, you're sure to find others with the sames concerns as you—and expand your knowledge at the same time.